ROGET'S
UNIVERSITY
THESAURUS

ROGET'S UNIVERSITY THESAURUS

EDITED BY

C. O. Sylvester Mawson, Litt.D., Ph.D.

BARNES & NOBLE BOOKS
A DIVISION OF HARPER & ROW, PUBLISHERS
New York, Cambridge, Hagerstown,
Philadelphia, San Francisco, London,
Mexico City, São Paulo, Sydney

PREFACE
TO THE FIRST EDITION
(1852)

IT IS now nearly fifty years since I first projected a system of verbal classification similar to that on which the present work is founded. Conceiving that such a compilation might help to supply my own deficiencies, I had, in the year 1805, completed a classed catalogue of words on a small scale, but on the same principle, and nearly in the same form, as the Thesaurus now published. I had often during that long interval found this little collection, scanty and imperfect as it was, of much use to me in literary composition, and often contemplated its extension and improvement; but a sense of the magnitude of the task, amidst a multitude of other avocations, deterred me from the attempt. Since my retirement from the duties of Secretary of the Royal Society, however, finding myself possessed of more leisure, and believing that a repertory of which I had myself experienced the advantage might, when amplified, prove useful to others, I resolved to embark in an undertaking which, for the last three or four years, has given me incessant occupation, and has, indeed, imposed upon me an amount of labour very much greater than I had anticipated. Notwithstanding all the pains I have bestowed on its execution, I am fully aware of its numerous deficiencies and imperfections, and of its falling far short of the degree of excellence that might be attained. But, in a work of this nature, where perfection is placed at so great a distance, I have thought it best to limit my ambition to that moderate share of merit which it may claim in its present form; trusting to the indulgence of those for whose benefit it is intended, and to the candour of critics who, while they find it easy to detect faults, can at the same time duly appreciate difficulties.

P. M. ROGET

April 29, 1852.

PETER MARK ROGET

(*1779–1869*)

PETER MARK ROGET was the only son of John Roget, who hailed from Geneva and later had oversight of the French Protestant Church in Threadneedle Street, London, where Peter was born in 1779. His father died a few years later, and his mother removed to Edinburgh, where the son entered the university at the age of fourteen. He graduated M.D. from the medical school at the early age of nineteen and distinguished himself by valuable research work on such subjects as consumption and the effects of laughing gas. In 1802 he went to Geneva, his father's home, in company with the sons of a wealthy merchant of Manchester, to whom he acted as tutor. The disturbances caused by the breach of the Peace of Amiens interrupted their tour and Roget was for a time held a prisoner at Geneva. He succeeded in getting away, however, at the end of 1803 and became private physician to the Marquis of Lansdowne.

In 1805 he became physician to the Manchester Infirmary and made a name for himself there by giving courses of lectures on scientific subjects. He combined in an unusual degree exact knowledge with a power of apt and vivid presentation, and this work he continued for well-nigh fifty years after his removal to London in 1808. He became physician to the Northern Dispensary in 1810 and lectured assiduously on medical and other subjects in various parts of the metropolis. A testimony to his versatility is afforded by the fact that he was asked by the Government to make an inquiry into the water supply of London, and in 1828 he published a report on the subject. For three years he held the post of Fullerian Professor of Physiology at the London Institution.

Dr. Roget was made a Fellow of the Royal Society in 1815, and served as secretary of the organization for over twenty years. He was appointed Examiner in Physiology in the University of London. He wrote various papers on physiology and health, among them *On Animal and Vegetable Physiology*, a Bridgewater treatise, 1834; a work on phrenology in two volumes, 1838; and *Electricity, Galvanism*, 1848.

These activities would be more than enough for most men, but Roget's insatiable thirst for knowledge and his appetite for work led him into yet other fields. He was no high-and-dry scientist who thought that learning was the prerogative of the elect; his aim was to broadcast it as widely as possible. He was a founder of the Society for the Diffusion of Knowledge and wrote for it a series of popular manuals. He devised a slide rule and spent much time in attempting to perfect a calculating machine. He showed remarkable ingenuity in inventing and solving chess problems and designed a pocket chessboard called the "Economic Chessboard."

However, the work which extended and perpetuated his fame on two continents was one which he probably regarded as a mere avocation. In the year 1852 he brought out his *Thesaurus of English Words and Phrases Classified and Arranged so as to Facilitate the Expression of Ideas and Assist in Literary Composition*. A second edition followed the next year, a third two years later, and still others in the next few years. The work was extended and corrected by his son. In the present "University" edition, edited by C. O. Sylvester Mawson, this treasury of ideas has had an ever widening distribution.

Peter Mark Roget died in West Malvern, on September 12, 1869, at the advanced age of ninety.

PREFACE

In devising a book of synonyms two different methods are open to us: one is the so-called dictionary method, in which the synonymized words are given in alphabetical order; the other is the plan adopted by Roget, which today still stands preëminent. What the dictionary plan gains in facility of reference it loses in suggestiveness and comprehensiveness. It appeals to the novice rather than to the practiced writer.

ROGET'S UNIVERSITY THESAURUS, by means of its Index Guide and its prominent key words, combines the advantages of the dictionary plan with the masterly scheme conceived by Roget. In short, it is not an accretion but an organism, each word being related to its neighbors and each part to the whole.

The dictionary is the birthplace of the synonym: almost every definition supplies an affinitive term for the word defined. The making of dictionaries thus affords a rare training for the preparation of a book of synonyms and antonyms. The editors have always applied such experience in its revisions of Roget.

Lexicography is not a prophetic science: it merely records the past and the present and plays an important part in the standardization of speech. It follows therefore that the dictionary and the thesaurus must constantly be kept abreast of present-day requirements. Not only is the language actually growing, but old words take on new senses, while others drift into desuetude. The scientist and the inventor are constantly adding to the linguistic store.

ROGET'S UNIVERSITY THESAURUS has been modernized and systematized and brought into line with the latest lexicographical science. Just as Noah Webster's epoch-making work has been merged in its vigorous descendants, so has the pioneer achievement of Roget been embodied in the UNIVERSITY THESAURUS.

The UNIVERSITY edition offers the user (1) a greatly enlarged list of synonyms and antonyms; (2) a special grouping of comparisons and associated terms; (3) the systematization of scientific and technical terminology; (4) a regrouping of synonyms, so that each paragraph consists of words more or less related and interchangeable; (5) characterization of all obsolete, obsolescent, rare, archaic, colloquial, dialectal, and slang words, as well as all British, foreign, and special terms, as is done in the best dictionaries; (6) plural forms, in all cases of unusual difficulty; (7) numerous phrases and idioms; (8) many citations from modern authors, felicitous and keen in phrase and thought.

The new words run well into the thousands and embrace every department of knowledge. Particular attention has been given to scientific and technical terms and the newer words of the schools and the street. The special needs of the student, the speaker, and the writer have been kept in view, and the aim has been not merely to supply a selection of synonyms but to suggest ideas and new turns of

PREFACE

thought. The parallel arrangement of synonyms and antonyms, peculiar to Roget's scheme, adds further to the usefulness of the book and gives a completeness to every page. Books on the dictionary plan usually cover the antonyms (if they give them at all) by cross-references to other groups of synonyms in the main vocabulary. Thus, under *goodness* they refer to *badness* as an antonym. Roget gives *goodness* and *badness* side by side.

Apart from the scientific and logical arrangement, the distinguishing feature of Roget is the inclusion of phrases. Not only does the use of phrases enlarge the group of synonyms for any particular word, but in many instances the phrase furnishes the only possible synonym. The improvement of this unique feature has received the most painstaking attention. The plays of modern dramatists have been searched for the pithy phrase, the apt expression, the well-turned aphorism — in short, for spoken English at its best. Scores of other modern writers have also been laid under contribution, while, as the quotations themselves will show, new and old alike have given of their choicest in thought and form.

The international character of the book is evidenced by the variant spellings and by the scope of the vocabulary. All Briticisms and Americanisms are labeled, and where the usage differs in the two countries such difference is pointed out. The English language marches with no frontiers; it is a world possession. Every race and country is reflected in its vocabulary. The UNIVERSITY THESAURUS is alive to this universality, and, to assist writers in giving local color, the home of every imported word is duly recorded.

C. O. SYLVESTER MAWSON

CONTENTS

INTRODUCTION

THE present work is intended to supply, with respect to the English language, a desideratum hitherto unsupplied in any language; namely, a collection of the words it contains and of the idiomatic combinations peculiar to it, arranged, not in alphabetical order as they are in a dictionary, but according to the *ideas* which they express.[1] The purpose of an ordinary dictionary is simply to explain the meaning of words; and the problem of which it professes to furnish the solution may be stated thus:— The word being given, to find its signification, or the idea it is intended to convey. The object aimed at in the present undertaking is exactly the converse of this: namely, — The idea being given, to find the word, or words, by which that idea may be most fitly and aptly expressed. For this purpose, the words and phrases of the language are here classed, not according to their sound or their orthography, but strictly according to their *signification*.

The communication of our thoughts by means of language, whether spoken or written, like every other object of mental exertion, constitutes a peculiar art, which, like other arts, cannot be acquired in any perfection but by long-continued practice. Some, indeed, there are more highly gifted than others with a facility of expression, and naturally endowed with the power of eloquence; but to none is it at all times an easy process to embody, in exact and appropriate language, the various trains of ideas that are passing through the mind, or to depict in their true colors and proportions, the diversified and nicer shades of feeling which accompany them. To those who are unpracticed in the art of composition, or unused to extempore speaking, these difficulties present themselves in their most formidable aspect. However distinct may be our views, however vivid our conceptions, or however fervent our emotions, we cannot but be often conscious that the phraseology we have at our command is inadequate to do them justice. We seek in vain the words we need, and strive ineffectually to devise forms of expression which shall faithfully portray our thoughts and sentiments. The appropriate terms, notwithstanding our utmost efforts, cannot be conjured up at will. Like "spirits from the vasty deep," they come not when we call; and we are driven to the employment of a set of words and phrases either too general or too limited, too strong or too feeble, which suit not the occasion, which hit not the mark we aim at; and the result of our prolonged exertion is a style at once labored and obscure, vapid and redundant, or vitiated by the still graver faults of affectation or ambiguity.

It is to those who are thus painfully groping their way and struggling with the difficulties of composition, that this work professes to hold out a helping hand. The assistance it gives is that of furnishing on every topic a copious store of words and phrases, adapted to express all the recognizable shades and modifications of the general idea under which those words and phrases are arranged. The inquirer can readily select, out of the ample collection spread out before his eyes in the following pages, those expressions which are best suited to his purpose, and which might not have occurred to him without such assistance. In order to make this selection, he scarcely ever need engage in any critical or elaborate study of the subtle distinctions existing between synonymous terms; for if the materials set before him be sufficiently abundant, an instinctive tact will rarely fail to lead him to the proper choice. Even while glancing over the columns of this work, his eye may chance to light upon a particular term which may save the cost of a clumsy paraphrase, or spare the labor of a tortuous circumlocution. Some felicitous turn

[1] See note on p. xx.

of expression thus introduced will frequently open to the mind of the reader a whole vista of collateral ideas, which could not, without an extended and obtrusive episode, have been unfolded to his view; and often will the judicious insertion of a happy epithet, like a beam of sunshine in a landscape, illumine and adorn the subject which it touches, imparting new grace and giving life and spirit to the picture.

Every workman in the exercise of his art should be provided with proper implements. For the fabrication of complicated and curious pieces of mechanism, the artisan requires a corresponding assortment of various tools and instruments. For giving proper effect to the fictions of the drama, the actor should have at his disposal a well-furnished wardrobe, supplying the costumes best suited to the personages he is to represent. For the perfect delineation of the beauties of nature, the painter should have within reach of his pencil every variety and combination of hues and tints. Now, the writer, as well as the orator, employs for the accomplishment of his purposes the instrumentality of words; it is in words that he clothes his thoughts; it is by means of words that he depicts his feelings. It is therefore essential to his success that he be provided with a copious vocabulary, and that he possess an entire command of all the resources and appliances of his language. To the acquisition of this power no procedure appears more directly conducive than the study of a methodized system such as that now offered to his use.

The utility of the present work will be appreciated more especially by those who are engaged in the arduous process of translating into English a work written in another language. Simple as the operation may appear, on a superficial view, of rendering into English each of its sentences, the task of transfusing, with perfect exactness, the sense of the original, preserving at the same time the style and character of its composition, and reflecting with fidelity the mind and the spirit of the author, is a task of extreme difficulty. The cultivation of this useful department of literature was in ancient times strongly recommended both by Cicero and by Quintilian, as essential to the formation of a good writer and accomplished orator. Regarded simply as a mental exercise, the practice of translation is the best training for the attainment of that mastery of language and felicity of diction which are the sources of the highest oratory, and are requisite for the possession of a graceful and persuasive eloquence. By rendering ourselves the faithful interpreters of the thoughts and feelings of others, we are rewarded with the acquisition of greater readiness and facility in correctly expressing our own; as he who has best learned to execute the orders of a commander, becomes himself best qualified to command.

In the earliest periods of civilization, translators have been the agents for propagating knowledge from nation to nation, and the value of their labors has been inestimable; but, in the present age, when so many different languages have become the depositories of the vast treasures of literature and of science which have been accumulating for centuries, the utility of accurate translations has greatly increased and it has become a more important object to attain perfection in the art.

The use of language is not confined to its being the medium through which we communicate our ideas to one another; it fulfills a no less important function as an *instrument of thought;* not being merely its vehicle but giving it wings for flight. Metaphysicians are agreed that scarcely any of our intellectual operations could be carried on, to any considerable extent, without the agency of words. None but those who are conversant with the philosophy of mental phenomena can be aware of the immense influence that is exercised by language in promoting the development of our ideas, in fixing them in the mind, and in detaining them for steady contemplation. Into every process of reasoning, language enters as an essential element. Words are the instruments by which we form all our abstractions, by which we fashion and embody our ideas, and by which we are enabled to glide along a series of premises and conclusions with a rapidity so great as to leave in the memory no trace of the successive steps of the process; and we remain unconscious how much we owe to this potent auxiliary of the reasoning faculty. It is on this ground, also, that the present work founds a claim to utility. The review of a catalogue of words of analogous signification, will often suggest by association other trains of thought, which, presenting the subject under new and varied aspects, will vastly expand the sphere of our mental vision. Amidst the many objects thus brought within the range of our contemplation, some striking similitude or appropriate image, some excursive flight or brilliant conception, may flash on the mind, giving point and force to our arguments, awakening a responsive chord in the imagination or sensibility of the reader, and procuring for our reasonings a more ready access both to his understanding and to his heart.

It is of the utmost consequence that strict accuracy should regulate our use of language, and that every one should acquire the power and the habit of expressing his thoughts with perspicuity and correctness. Few, indeed, can appreciate the real extent and importance of that influence which language has always exercised on human affairs, or can be aware how often these are determined by causes much slighter than are apparent to a superficial observer. False logic, disguised under specious phraseology, too often gains the assent of the unthinking multitude, disseminating far and wide the seeds of prejudice and error. Truisms pass current, and wear the semblance of profound wisdom, when dressed up in the tinsel garb of antithetical phrases, or set off by an imposing pomp of paradox. By a confused jargon of involved and mystical sentences, the imagination is easily inveigled into a transcendental region of clouds, and the understanding beguiled into the belief that it is acquiring knowledge and approaching truth. A misapplied or misapprehended term is sufficient to give rise to fierce and interminable disputes; a misnomer has turned the tide of popular opinion; a verbal sophism has decided a party question; an artful watchword, thrown among combustible materials, has kindled the flame of deadly warfare, and changed the destiny of an empire.

In constructing the following system of classification of the ideas which are expressible by language, my chief aim has been to obtain the greatest amount of practical utility. I have accordingly adopted such principles of arrangement as appeared to me to be the simplest and most natural, and which would not require, either for their comprehension or application, any disciplined acumen, or depth of metaphysical or antiquarian lore. Eschewing all needless refinements and subtleties, I have taken as my guide the more obvious characters of the ideas for which expressions were to be tabulated, arranging them under such classes and categories as reflection and experience had taught me would conduct the inquirer most readily and quickly to the object of his search. Commencing with the ideas expressing abstract relations, I proceed to those which relate to space and to the phenomena of the material world, and lastly to those in which the mind is concerned, and which comprehend intellect, volition, and feeling; thus establishing six primary Classes of Categories.

1. The first of these classes comprehends ideas derived from the more general and ABSTRACT RELATIONS among things, such as *Existence, Resemblance, Quantity, Order, Number, Time, Power.*

2. The second class refers to SPACE and its various relations, including *Motion,* or change of place.

3. The third class includes all ideas that relate to the MATERIAL WORLD; namely, the *Properties of Matter,* such as *Solidity, Fluidity, Heat, Sound, Light,* and the *Phenomena* they present, as well as the simple *Perceptions* to which they give rise.

4. The fourth class embraces all ideas of phenomena relating to the INTELLECT and its operations; comprising the *Acquisition,* the *Retention,* and the *Communication of Ideas.*

5. The fifth class includes the ideas derived from the exercise of VOLITION; embracing the phenomena and results of our *Voluntary and Active Powers;* such as *Choice, Intention. Utility, Action, Antagonism, Authority, Compact, Property,* &c.

6. The sixth and last class comprehends all ideas derived from the operation of our SENTIENT AND MORAL POWERS; including our *Feelings, Emotions, Passions,* and *Moral and Religious Sentiments.*[1]

The further subdivisions and minuter details will be best understood from an inspection of the Tabular Synopsis of Categories prefixed to the Work, in which are specified the several *topics* or *heads of signification,* under which the words have been arranged. By the aid of this table, the reader will, with a little practice, readily discover the place which the particular topic he is in search of occupies in the series; and on turning to the page in the body of the work which contains it, he will find the group of expressions he requires, out of which he may cull those that are most appropriate to his purpose. For the convenience of reference, I have designated each separate group or heading by a particular number; so that if, during the search, any doubt or difficulty should occur, recourse may be had to the copious alphabetical Index of words at the end of the volume, which will at once indicate the number of the required group.[2]

The object I have proposed to myself in this work would have been but imperfectly attained if I had confined myself to a mere catalogue of words, and had omitted the numerous phrases and forms of expression composed of several words, which are of such frequent use as to entitle them to rank among the constituent parts of the language.[3] Very few of these verbal combinations, so essential to the knowledge of our native tongue, and so profusely abounding in its daily use, are to be met with in ordinary dictionaries. These phrases and forms of expression I have endeavored diligently to collect and to insert in their proper places, under the general ideas that they are designed to convey. Some of these conventional forms, indeed, partake of the nature of proverbial expressions; but actual proverbs, as such, being wholly of a didactic character, do not come within the scope of the present work; and the reader must therefore not expect to find them inserted.[4]

For the purpose of exhibiting with greater distinctness the relations between words expressing opposite and correlative ideas, I have, whenever the subject admitted of such an arrangement, placed them in two parallel columns in the same page, so that each group of expressions may be readily contrasted with those which occupy the adjacent column, and constitute their antithesis. By carrying the eye from the one to the other, the inquirer may often discover forms of expression, of which he may avail himself advantageously, to diversify and infuse vigor into his phraseology. Rhetoricians, indeed, are well aware of the power derived from the skillful introduction of antitheses in giving point to an argument, and imparting force and brilliancy to the diction. A too frequent and indiscreet employment of this figure of rhetoric may, it is true, give rise to a vicious and affected style; but

---

[1] It must necessarily happen in every system of classification framed with this view, that ideas and expressions arranged under one class must include also ideas relating to another class; for the operations of the *Intellect* generally involve also those of the *Will,* and *vice versâ;* and our *Affections* and *Emotions,* in like manner, generally imply the agency both of the *Intellect* and of the *Will.* All that can be effected, therefore, is to arrange the words according to the principal or dominant idea they convey. *Teaching,* for example, although a Voluntary act, relates primarily to the Communication of Ideas, and is accordingly placed at No. **537,** under Class IV, Division (II). On the other hand, *Choice, Conduct, Skill,* &c., although implying the coöperation of Voluntary with Intellectual acts, relate principally to the former, and are therefore arranged under Class V.

[2] If often happens that the same word admits of various applications, or may be used in different senses. In consulting the Index the reader will be guided to the number of the heading under which that word, in each particular acceptation, will be found, by means of *supplementary words* printed in Italics; which words, however, are not to be understood as explaining the meaning of the word to which they are annexed, but only as assisting in the required reference. I have also, for shortness' sake, generally omitted words immediately derived from the primary one inserted, which sufficiently represents the whole group of correlative words referable to the same heading. Thus the number affixed to *Beauty* applies to all its derivatives, such as *Beautiful, Beauteous, Beautifulness, Beautifully,* &c., the insertion of which was therefore needless.

[3] For example: — To take time by the forelock; — to turn over a new leaf; — to show the white feather; — to have a finger in the pie; — to let the cat out of the bag; — to take care of number one; — to kill two birds with one stone, &c., &c.

[4] See Trench, *On the Lessons in Proverbs.*

INTRODUCTION

it is unreasonable to condemn indiscriminately the occasional and moderate use of a practice on account of its possible abuse.

The study of correlative terms existing in a particular language may often throw valuable light on the manners and customs of the nations using it. Thus, Hume has drawn important inferences with regard to the state of society among the ancient Romans from certain deficiencies which he remarked in the Latin language.[1]

In many cases, two ideas which are completely opposed to each other admit of an intermediate or neutral idea, equidistant from both; all these being expressible by corresponding definite terms. Thus, in the following examples, the words in the first and third columns, which express opposite ideas, admit of the intermediate terms contained in the middle column, having a neutral sense with reference to the former.

Identity,	Difference,	Contrariety.
Beginning,	Middle,	End.
Past,	Present,	Future.

In other cases, the intermediate word is simply the negative to each of two opposite positions; as, for example, —

| Convexity, | Flatness, | Concavity. |
| Desire, | Indifference, | Aversion. |

Sometimes the intermediate word is properly the standard with which each of the extremes is compared; as in the case of

| Insufficiency, | Sufficiency, | Redundance; |

for here the middle term, *Sufficiency*, is equally opposed, on the one hand, to *Insufficiency*, and on the other to *Redundance*.

These forms of correlative expressions would suggest the use of triple, instead of double, columns, for tabulating this threefold order of words; but the practical inconvenience attending such an arrangement would probably overbalance its advantages.

It often happens that the same word has several correlative terms, according to the different relations in which it is considered. Thus, to the word *Giving* are opposed both *Receiving* and *Taking;* the former correlation having reference to the *persons* concerned in the transfer, while the latter relates to the *mode* of transfer. *Old* has for opposite both *New* and *Young*, according as it is applied to *things* or to *living beings*. *Attack* and *Defense* are correlative terms; as are also *Attack* and *Resistance*. *Resistance*, again, has for its other correlative *Submission*. *Truth in the abstract* is opposed to *Error;* but the opposite of *Truth communicated* is *Falsehood*. *Acquisition* is contrasted both with *Deprivation* and with *Loss*. *Refusal* is the counterpart both of *Offer* and of *Consent*. *Disuse* and *Misuse* may either of them be considered as the correlative of *Use*. *Teaching*, with reference to what is taught,

[1] "It is an universal observation," he remarks, "which we may form upon language, that where two related parts of a whole bear any proportion to each other, in numbers, rank, or consideration, there are always correlative terms invented which answer to both the parts, and express their mutual relation. If they bear no proportion to each other, the term is only invented for the less, and marks its distinction from the whole. Thus, man and woman, master and servant, father and son, prince and subject, stranger and citizen, are correlative terms. But the words seaman, carpenter, smith, tailor, &c., have no correspondent terms, which express those who are no seamen, no carpenters, &c. Languages differ very much with regard to the particular words where this distinction obtains; and may thence afford very strong inferences concerning the manners and customs of different nations. The military government of the Roman emperors had exalted the soldiery so high that they balanced all the other orders of the state: hence *miles* and *paganus* became relative terms; a thing, till then, unknown to ancient, and still so to modern languages." — "The term for a slave, born and bred in the family was *verna*. As *servus* was the name of the genus, and *verna* of the species without any correlative, this forms a strong presumption that the latter were by far the least numerous: and from the same principles I infer that if the number of slaves brought by the Romans from foreign countries had not extremely exceeded those which were bred at home, *verna* would have had a correlative, which would have expressed the former species of slaves. But these, it would seem, composed the main body of the ancient slaves, and the latter were but a few exceptions." — HUME, *Essay on the Populousness of Ancient Nations.*

The warlike propensity of the same nation may, in like manner, be inferred from the use of the word *hostis* to denote both *a foreigner* and *an enemy*.

is opposed to *Misteaching;* but with reference to the act itself, its proper reciprocal is *Learning.*

Words contrasted in form do not always bear the same contrast in their meaning. The word *Malefactor,* for example, would, from its derivation, appear to be xactly the opposite of *Benefactor:* but the ideas attached to these two words are far from being directly opposed; for while the latter expresses one who confers a benefit, the former denotes one who has violated the laws.

Independently of the immediate practical uses derivable from the arrangement of words in double columns, many considerations, interesting in a philosophical point of view, are presented by the study of correlative expressions. It will be found, on strict examination, that there seldom exists an exact opposition between two words which may at first sight appear to be the counterparts of one another; for, in general, the one will be found to possess in reality more force or extent of meaning than the other with which it is contrasted. The correlative term sometimes assumes the form of a mere negative, although it is really endowed with a considerable positive force. Thus *Disrespect* is not merely the absence of *Respect;* its signification trenches on the opposite idea, namely, *Contempt.* In like manner, *Untruth* is not merely the negative of *Truth;* it involves a degree of *Falsehood.* *Irreligion,* which is properly *the want of Religion,* is understood as being nearly synonymous with *Impiety.* For these reasons, the reader must not expect that all the words which stand side by side in the two columns shall be the precise correlatives of each other; for the nature of the subject, as well as the imperfections of language, renders it impossible always to preserve such an exactness of correlation.

There exist comparatively few words of a general character to which no correlative term, either of negation or of opposition, can be assigned, and which therefore require no corresponding second column. The correlative idea, especially that which constitutes a sense negative to the primary one, may, indeed, be formed or conceived; but, from its occurring rarely, no word has been framed to represent it; for, in language, as in other matters, the supply fails when there is no probability of a demand. Occasionally we find this deficiency provided for by the contrivance of prefixing the syllable *non;* as, for instance, the negatives of *existence, performance, payment,* &c., are expressed by the compound words, *nonexistence, nonperformance, nonpayment,* &c. Functions of a similar kind are performed by the prefixes *dis-,*[1] *anti-, contra-, mis-, in-,* and *un-.*[2] With respect to all these, and especially the last, great latitude is allowed according to the necessities of the case; a latitude which is limited only by the taste and discretion of the writer.

On the other hand, it is hardly possible to find two words having in all respects the same meaning, and being therefore interchangeable; that is, admitting of being employed indiscriminately, the one or the other, in all their applications. The investigation of the distinctions to be drawn between words apparently synonymous forms a separate branch of inquiry, which I have not presumed here to enter upon; for the subject has already occupied the attention of much abler critics than myself, and its complete exhaustion would require the devotion of a whole life. The purpose of this work, it must be borne in mind, is, not to explain the signification of words, but simply to classify and arrange them according to the sense in which they are now used, and which I presume to be already known to the reader. I enter into no inquiry into the changes of meaning they may have undergone in the course of time.[3] I am content to accept them at the value of their present

[1] The words *disannul* and *dissever,* however, have the same meaning as *annul* and *sever; to unloose* is the same as *to loose,* and *inebriety* is synonymous with *ebriety.*

[2] In case of adjectives, the addition to a substantive of the terminal syllable *less,* gives it a negative meaning: as *taste, tasteless; care, careless; hope, hopeless; friend, friendless; fault, faultless;* &c.

[3] Such changes are innumerable: for instance, the words *tyrant, parasite, sophist, churl, knave, villain,* anciently conveyed no opprobrious meaning. *Impertinent* merely expressed *irrelative;* and implied neither *rudeness* nor *intrusion,* as it does at present. *Indifferent* originally meant *impartial; extravagant* was simple *digressive;* and *to prevent* was properly *to precede* and *assist.* The old translations of the Scriptures furnish many striking examples of the alterations which time has brought in the signification of words. Much curious information on this subject is contained in Trench's *Lectures on the Study of Words.*

currency, and have no concern with their etymologies, or with the history of their transformations; far less do I venture to thread the mazes of the vast labyrinth into which I should be led by any attempt at a general discrimination of synonyms. The difficulties I have had to contend with have already been sufficiently great, without this addition to my labors.

The most cursory glance over the pages of a dictionary will show that a great number of words are used in various senses, sometimes distinguished by slight shades of difference, but often diverging widely from their primary signification, and even, in some cases, bearing to it no perceptible relation. It may even happen that the very same word has two significations quite opposite to one another. This is the case with the verb *to cleave*, which means *to adhere tenaciously*, and also *to separate by a blow*. *To propugn* sometimes expresses *to attack;* at other times *to defend*. *To let* is *to hinder*, as well as *to permit*. *To ravel* means both *to entangle* and *to disentangle*. *Shameful* and *shameless* are nearly synonymous. *Priceless* may either mean *invaluable* or *of no value*. *Nervous* is used sometimes for *strong*, at other times for *weak*. The alphabetical Index at the end of this work sufficiently shows the multiplicity of uses to which, by the elasticity of language, the meaning of words has been stretched, so as to adapt them to a great variety of modified significations in subservience to the nicer shades of thought, which, under peculiarity of circumstances, require corresponding expression. Words thus admitting of different meanings have therefore to be arranged under each of the respective heads corresponding to these various acceptations. There are many words, again, which express ideas compounded of two elementary ideas belonging to different classes. It is therefore necessary to place these words respectively under each of the generic heads to which they relate. The necessity of these repetitions is increased by the circumstance, that ideas included under one class are often connected by relations of the same kind as the ideas which belong to another class. Thus we find the same relations of *order* and of *quantity* existing among the ideas of *Time* as well as those of *Space*. Sequence in the one is denoted by the same terms as sequence in the other; and the measures of time also express the measures of space. The cause and the effect are often designated by the same word. The word *Sound*, for instance, denotes both the impression made upon the ear by sonorous vibrations, and also the vibrations themselves, which are the cause or source of that impression. *Mixture* is used for the act of mixing, as well as for the product of that operation. *Taste* and *Smell* express both the sensations and the qualities of material bodies giving rise to them. *Thought* is the act of thinking; but the same word denotes also the idea resulting from that act. *Judgment* is the act of deciding, and also the decision come to. *Purchase* is the acquisition of a thing by payment, as well as the thing itself so acquired. *Speech* is both the act of speaking and the words spoken; and so on with regard to an endless multiplicity of words. Mind is essentially distinct from Matter; and yet, in all languages, the attributes of the one are metaphorically transferred to those of the other. Matter, in all its forms, is endowed by the figurative genius of every language with the functions which pertain to intellect; and we perpetually talk of its phenomena and of its powers, as if they resulted from the voluntary influence of one body on another, acting and reacting, impelling and being impelled, controlling and being controlled, as if animated by spontaneous energies and guided by specific intentions. On the other hand, expressions, of which the primary signification refers exclusively to the properties and actions of matter, are metaphorically applied to the phenomena of thought and volition, and even to the feelings and passions of the soul; and speaking of a *ray of hope*, a *shade of doubt*, a *flight of fancy*, a *flash of wit*, the *warmth of emotion*, or the *ebullitions of anger*, we are scarcely conscious that we are employing metaphors which have this material origin.

As a general rule, I have deemed it incumbent on me to place words and phrases which appertain more especially to one head, also under the other heads to which they have a relation, whenever it appeared to me that this repetition would suit the convenience of the inquirer, and spare him the trouble of turning to other parts of the work; for I have always preferred to subject myself to the imputation of redundance, rather than incur the reproach of insufficiency.[1] When, however, the divergence of the associated from the primary idea is sufficiently marked, I have contented myself with making a reference to the place where the modified signification will be found. But in order to prevent needless extension, I have, in general, omitted *conjugate words*[2] which are so obviously derivable from those that are given in the same place, that the reader may safely be left to form them for himself. This is the case with adverbs derived from adjectives by the simple addition of the terminal syllable -*ly;* such as *closely, carefully, safely,* &c., from *close, careful, safe,* &c., and also with adjectives or participles immediately derived from the verbs which are already given. In all such cases, an "&c." indicates that reference is understood to be made to these roots. I have observed the same rule in compiling the Index; retaining only the primary or more simple word, and omitting the conjugate words obviously derived from them. Thus I assume the word *short* as the representative of its immediate derivatives *shortness, shorten, shortening, shortened, shorter, shortly,* which would have had the same references, and which the reader can readily supply.

The same verb is frequently used indiscriminately either in the active or transitive, or in the neuter or intransitive sense. In these cases, I have generally not thought it worth while to increase the bulk of the work by the needless repetition of that word; for the reader, whom I suppose to understand the use of the words, must also be presumed to be competent to apply them correctly.

There are a multitude of words of a specific character which, although they properly occupy places in the columns of a dictionary, yet, having no relation to general ideas, do not come within the scope of this compilation, and are consequently omitted.[3] The names of objects in Natural History, and technical terms belonging exclusively to Science or to Art, or relating to particular operations, and of which the signification is restricted to those specific objects, come under this category. Exceptions must, however, be made in favor of such words as admit of metaphorical application to general subjects, with which custom has associated them, and of which they may be cited as being typical or illustrative. Thus, the word *Lion* will find a place under the head of *Courage,* of which it is regarded as the type. *Anchor,* being emblematic of *Hope,* is introduced among the words expressing that emotion; and in like manner, *butterfly* and *weathercock,* which are suggestive of fickleness, are included in the category of *Irresolution.*

With regard to the admission of many words and expressions, which the classical reader might be disposed to condemn as vulgarisms, or which he, perhaps, might stigmatize as pertaining rather to the slang than to the legitimate language of the day, I would beg to observe, that, having due regard to the uses to which this work was to be adapted, I did not feel myself justified in excluding them solely on that ground, if they possessed an acknowledged currency in general intercourse. It is obvious that, with respect to degrees of conventionality, I could not have attempted to draw any strict lines of demarcation; and far less could I have presumed to erect any absolute standard of purity. My object, be it remembered, is

---

[1] Frequent repetitions of the same series of expressions, accordingly, will be met with under various headings. For example, the word *Relinquishment,* with its synonyms, occurs as a heading at No. **624,** where it applies to *intention,* and also at No. **782,** where it refers to *property.* The word *Chance* has two significations, distinct from one another: the one implying the *absence of an assignable cause;* in which case it comes under the category of the relation of Causation, and occupies the No. **156:** the other, the *absence of design,* in which latter sense it ranks under the operations of the Will, and has assigned to it the place No. **621.** I have, in like manner, distinguished *Sensibility, Pleasure, Plain, Taste,* &c., according as they relate to *Physical,* or to *Moral Affections;* the former being found at Nos. **375, 377, 378, 390,** &c., and the latter at Nos. **822, 827, 828, 850,** &c.

[2] By "*conjugate* or *paronymous* words" is meant, correctly speaking, different parts of speech from the same root, which exactly correspond in point of meaning." — *A Selection of English Synonyms,* edited by Archbishop Whately.

[3] [This rule was not in all cases rigorously observed by the author; and the present editor has used his discretion in including such words in the interest of the general writer. C. O. S. M.]

INTRODUCTION

not to regulate the use of words, but simply to supply and to suggest such as may be wanted on occasion, leaving the proper selection entirely to the discretion and taste of the employer. If a novelist or a dramatist, for example, proposed to delineate some vulgar personage, he would wish to have the power of putting into the mouth of the speaker expressions that would accord with his character; just as the actor, to revert to a former comparison, who had to personate a peasant, would choose for his attire the most homely garb, and would have just reason to complain if the theatrical wardrobe furnished him with no suitable costume.

Words which have, in process of time, become obsolete, are of course rejected from this collection.[1] On the other hand, I have admitted a considerable number of words and phrases borrowed from other languages, chiefly the French and Latin, some of which may be considered as already naturalized; while others, though avowedly foreign, are frequently employed in English composition, particularly in familiar style, on account of their being peculiarly expressive, and because we have no corresponding words of equal force in our own language.[2] The rapid advances which are being made in scientific knowledge, and consequent improvement in all the arts of life, and the extension of those arts and sciences to so many new purposes and objects, create a continual demand for the formation of new terms to express new agencies, new wants, and new combinations. Such terms, from being at first merely technical, are rendered, by more general use, familiar to the multitude, and having a well-defined acceptation, are eventually incorporated into the language, which they contribute to enlarge and to enrich. *Neologies* of this kind are perfectly legitimate, and highly advantageous; and they necessarily introduce those gradual and progressive changes which every language is destined to undergo.[3] Some modern writers, however, have indulged in a habit of arbitrarily fabricating new words and a newfangled phraseology, without any necessity, and with manifest injury to the purity of the language. This vicious practice, the offspring of indolence or conceit, implies an ignorance or neglect of the riches in which the English language already abounds, and which would have supplied them with words of recognized legitimacy, conveying precisely the same meaning as those they so recklessly coin in the illegal mint of their own fancy.

A work constructed on the plan of classification I have proposed might, if ably executed, be of great value, in tending to limit the fluctuations to which language has always been subject, by establishing an authoritative standard for its regulation. Future historians, philologists, and lexicographers, when investigating the period when new words were introduced, or discussing the import given at the present time to the old, might find their labors lightened by being enabled to appeal to such a standard, instead of having to search for data among the scattered writings of the age. Nor would its utility be confined to a single language; for the principles of its construction are universally applicable to all languages, whether living or dead. On the same plan of classification there might be formed a French, a German, a Latin, or a Greek Thesaurus, possessing, in their respective spheres, the same advantages as those of the English model.[4] Still more useful would be a conjunction of these methodized compilations in two languages, the French and

---

[1] [An appreciable number of obsolete terms have nevertheless found their way into the *Thesaurus*, but these in the present edition have been specially characterized, thus rendering the book of enhanced value to the dramatist and *littérateur*. C. O. S. M.]

[2] All these words and phrases are printed in Italics.

[3] Thus, in framing the present classification, I have frequently felt the want of substantive terms corresponding to abstract qualities or ideas denoted by certain adjectives; and have been often tempted to invent words that might express these abstractions: but I have yielded to this temptation only in the four following instances; having framed from the adjectives *irrelative, amorphous, sinistral,* and *gaseous,* the abstract nouns *irrelation, amorphism, sinistrality,* and *gaseity.* I have ventured also to introduce the adjective *intersocial,* to express the active voluntary relations between man and man.

[4] [Similar works in other languages have since appeared, notably *Dictionnaire Idéologique* by T. Robertson (Paris, 1859); *Deutcher Sprachschatz* by D. Sanders (Hamburg, 1878), and *Deutscher Wortschatz, oder Der passende Ausdruck* by A. Schelling (Stuttgart, 1892). C. O. S. M.]

English, for instance; the columns of each being placed in parallel juxtaposition. No means yet devised would so greatly facilitate the acquisition of the one language, by those who are acquainted with the other: none would afford such ample assistance to the translator in either language; and none would supply such ready and effectual means of instituting an accurate comparison between them, and of fairly appreciating their respective merits and defects. In a still higher degree would all those advantages be combined and multiplied in a *Polyglot Lexicon* constructed on this system.

Metaphysicians engaged in the more profound investigation of the Philosophy of Language will be materially assisted by having the ground thus prepared for them, in a previous analysis and classification of our ideas; for such classification of ideas is the true basis on which words, which are their symbols, should be classified.[1] It is by such analysis alone that we can arrive at a clear perception of the relation which these symbols bear to their corresponding ideas, or can obtain a correct knowledge of the elements which enter into the formation of compound ideas, and of the exclusions by which we arrive at the abstractions so perpetually resorted to in the process of reasoning, and in the communication of our thoughts.

Lastly, such analyses alone can determine the principles on which a strictly *Philosophical Language* might be constructed. The probable result of the construction of such a language would be its eventual adoption by every civilized nation; thus realizing that splendid aspiration of philanthropists, — the establishment of a Universal Language. However utopian such a project may appear to the present generation, and however abortive may have been the former endeavors of Bishop Wilkins and others to realize it,[2] its accomplishment is surely not beset with greater difficulties than have impeded the progress to many other beneficial objects, which in former times appeared to be no less visionary, and which yet were successfully achieved, in later ages, by the continued and persevering exertions of the human intellect. Is there at the present day, then, any ground for despair, that at some future stage of that higher civilization to which we trust the world is gradually

---

[1]The principle by which I have been guided in framing my verbal classification is the same as that which is employed in the various departments of Natural History. Thus the sectional divisions I have formed, correspond to Natural Families in Botany and Zoölogy, and the filiation of words presents a network analogous to the natural filiation of plants or animals.

The following are the only publications that have come to my knowledge in which any attempt has been made to construct a systematic arrangement of ideas with a view to their expression. The earliest of these, supposed to be at least nine hundred years old, is the AMERA CÓSHA, or *Vocabulary of the Sanscrit Language*, by Amera Sanha, of which an English translation, by the late Henry T. Colebrooke, was printed at Serampoor, in the year 1808. The classification of words is there, as might be expected, exceedingly imperfect and confused, especially in all that relates to abstract ideas or mental operations. This will be apparent from the very title of the first section, which comprehends "*Heaven, Gods, Demons, Fire, Air, Velocity, Eternity, Much;*" while *Sin, Virtue, Happiness, Destiny, Cause, Nature, Intellect, Reasoning, Knowledge, Senses, Tastes, Odors, Colors,* are all included and jumbled together in the fourth section. A more logical order, however, pervades the sections relating to natural objects, such as *Seas, Earth, Towns, Plants,* and *Animals,* which form separate classes; exhibiting a remarkable effort at analysis at so remote a period of Indian literature.

The well-known work of Bishop Wilkins, entitled, *An Essay towards a Real Character and a Philosophical Language,* published in 1668, had for its object the formation of a system of symbols which might serve as a universal language. It professed to be founded on a "scheme of analysis of the things or notions to which names were to be assigned;" but notwithstanding the immense labor and ingenuity expended in the construction of this system, it was soon found to be far too abstruse and recondite for practical application.

In the year 1797, there appeared in Paris an anonymous work, entitled "PASIGRAPHIE ou *Premiers Eléments du nouvel Art-Science d'écrire et d'imprimer une langue de manière à être lu et entendu dans toute autre langue sans traduction,*" of which an edition in German was also published. It contains a great number of tabular schemes of categories; all of which appear to be excessively arbitrary and artificial, and extremely difficult of application, as well as of apprehension.

[2] "The Languages," observes Horne Tooke "which are commonly used throughout the world, are much more simple and easy, convenient and philosophical, than Wilkins's scheme for a *real character;* or than any other scheme that has been at any other time imagined or proposed for the purpose." —ᴱπεα Πτερόεντα, p. 125.

INTRODUCTION

tending, some new and bolder effort of genius towards the solution of this great problem may be crowned with success, and compass an object of such vast and paramount utility? Nothing, indeed, would conduce more directly to bring about a golden age of union and harmony among the several nations and races of mankind than the removal of that barrier to the interchange of thought and mutual good understanding between man and man, which is now interposed by the diversity of their respective languages.

P. M. ROGET.

ABBREVIATIONS USED IN THIS BOOK

abbr. abbreviated, abbreviation
adj. adjective, adjectival expression
adv. adverb, adverbial expression
Afr. Africa
Am. *or* **Amer.** America, American
Am. hist. American history
anat. anatomy
anc. ancient
Anglo-Ind. Anglo-Indian
anon. anonymous
antiq. antiquities
Ar. Arabic
arch. architecture
archæol. archæology
arith. arithmetic
A.-S. Anglo-Saxon
astrol. astrology
astron. astronomy
Austral. Australian
Bib. Biblical
biol. biology
bot. botany
Brit. British
Can. Canada, Canadian
Can. F. Canadian French
Celt. Celtic
chem. chemistry
Chin. Chinese
Ch. of Eng. Church of England
Cic. Cicero
class. classical
colloq. colloquial
com. commerce, commercial
conj. conjunction
Du. Dutch
Dan. Danish
derog. derogatory
dial. dialect, dialectal
dim. diminutive
E. East
eccl. ecclesiastical
econ. economics
elec. electricity
Eng. English, England
erron. erroneous, -ly
esp. especially
exc. except
fem. feminine
fig. figurative, -ly
G. *or* **Ger.** German
Gr. Greek
gram. grammar
Gr. Brit. Great Britain
Heb. Hebrew
her. heraldry
Hind. Hindustani
hist. history, historical
Hor. Horace
Icel. Icelandic
Ind. Indian
Ir. Irish, Ireland

int. interjection
It. Italian
Jap. Japanese
Jew. Jewish
joc. jocular
Juv. Juvenal
l.c. lower case
L. L. L. *Love's Labor's Lost*
Luc. Lucretius
Mar. Martial
masc. masculine
math. mathematics
Meth. Methodist
Mex. Mexico, Mexican
M. for M. *Measure for Measure*
mil. military
M. N. D. *Midsummer Night's Dream*
M. of V. *Merchant of Venice*
Moham. Mohammedan
myth. mythology
N. North
n. noun
N. Am. North American
naut. nautical
N. E. *or* **New Eng.** New England
neut. neuter
Nfld. Newfoundland
NL. New Latin
Norw. Norwegian
N. W. Northwest, -ern
N. Z. New Zealand
obs. obsolete
obsoles. obsolescent
OE. Old English
opp. opposed
orig. original, -ly
parl. parliamentary
path. pathology
Per. Persian
Pg. Portuguese
pharm. pharmacy
philos. philosophy
physiol. physiology
P. I. Philippine Islands
pl. plural
P. L. *Paradise Lost*
Plut. Plutarch
pol. *or* **polit.** political
pop. popular, -ly
prep. preposition
Prot. Epis. Protestant Episcopal
prov. proverb, provincial
psychol. psychology
Quin. Quintilian
R. C. Ch. Roman Catholic Church
relig. religion
rhet. rhetoric, rhetorical
Russ. Russian
S. *or* **So.** South
S. Afr. South African
Sal. Sallust

S. Am. South American
Scand. Scandinavian
Scot. Scottish, Scotland
Sen. Seneca
sing. singular
Skr. Sanskrit
surg. surgery
Sw. Swedish
S. W. Southwest, -ern
S. W. U. S. Southwest United States
Tac. Tacitus
tech. technical
Ter. Terence

Tertul. Tertullian
theat. theatrical
theol. theology
theos. theosophy
Turk. Turkish
typog. typography
Univ. University
U. S. United States
v. verb
Ver. Vergil
W. West
W. Ind. West Indies
zoöl. zoölogy

Dashes and hyphens are used to avoid the repetition of some term common to each word or phrase in the same group. For example: —

"over –, above– the mark;" = { "over the mark," "above the mark" }

"on the -verge, – brink, – skirts- of;" = { "on the verge of," "on the brink of," "on the skirts of" }

"brush –, whisk –, turn –, send- -off, – away;" = { "brush off," "brush away," "whisk off," "whisk away," "turn off," "turn away," "send off," "send away" }

"quick-, keen,- clear-, sharp- -eyed, -sighted, -witted;" = { "quick-eyed," "quick-sighted," "quick-witted," "keen-eyed," "keen-sighted," "keen-witted," "clear-eyed," "clear-sighted," "clear-witted," "sharp-eyed," "sharp-sighted," "sharp-witted" }

"away from –, foreign to –, beside- the -purpose, – question, – transaction, – point;" = { "away from the purpose," "away from the question," "away from the transaction," "away from the point," "foreign to the purpose," &c., "beside the purpose," &c. }

"fall, – to the ground;" = { "fall," "fall to the gound" }

"shortness &c. *adj.*;" "shortly &c. *adj.*;" "shortening &c. *v.*;" = { in a similar manner form other words from the groups of *adjectives* or *verbs* in the same category }

[See also "*How to Use the Book*," p. xxiv.]

HOW TO USE THE BOOK

I. To find a synonym or antonym for any given WORD:

Turn to the Index Guide and find the particular word or any term of kindred meaning; then refer to the category indicated. Under the part of speech sought for [N., V., Adj., Adv.] will be found a wide choice of synonymous and correlative terms, with their antonyms in the adjoining column. For example, suppose a synonym is wanted for the word "rare" in the sense of "choice." Turn to the Index Guide, where the following references will be found:—

> **rare** *unique* 20
> *exceptional* 83
> *few* 103
> *infrequent* 137
> *underdone* 298
> *tenuous* 322
> *neologic* 563
> *choice* 648

The italicized words denote the general sense of the affinitive terms in the respective categories. Turning to No. **648** (the sense required) we select the most appropriate expression from the comprehensive list presented. To widen the selection, suggested references are given to allied lists; while in the parallel column, viz., **649**, are grouped the corresponding antonyms. The groups are arranged, not merely to supply synonyms for some special word, but to suggest new lines of thought and to stimulate the imagination.

The story-writer at a loss for some archaism, colloquialism, or even slang, will find the *University Thesaurus* a veritable mine, such terms being clearly indicated in the text.

II. To find suitable words to express a given IDEA:

Find in the Index Guide some word relating to the idea, and the categories referred to will supply the need. Thus, suppose a writer wishes to use some less hackneyed phrase than "shuffle off this mortal coil," let him look up "die" or even the phrase itself, and reference to No. **360** will immediately furnish a generous list of synonymous phrases.

III. To find appropriate words or new ideas on any given SUBJECT:

Turn up the subject or any branch of it. The Index Guide itself will frequently suggest various lines of thought, while reference to the indicated groups will provide many words and phrases that should prove helpful.

Thus, suppose " philosophy " is the theme, No. **451** will be found most suggestive. Or again, the subject may be "the drama" (**599**), "music" (**415**), "zoölogy" (**368**), "psychical research" (**992a**), or " mythology " (**979**). The writer may perhaps be hazy about the titles of the ruling chiefs of India. The Thesaurus (**875**) will prevent his applying a Hindu title to a Mohammedan prince. The subject may be such an everyday one as " food " (**298**), " automobiles " (**272**), "aviation" (**267** and **269a**), or various kinds of "amusements" (**840**); whatever it is, the Thesaurus will not prove altogether unprofitable as regards ideas. Writers and speakers who have acquired the " Roget habit " do not need to be reminded of this valuable aid.

N.B. To grasp the underlying principle of the classification, study the *Tabular Synopsis of Categories* (pp. 889–899). Reference may be made direct from this Synopsis to the body of the work; but it is usually found more convenient to consult the Index Guide first.

[See also "*Abbreviations Used in This Book*," pp. xxii and xxiii.]

The Guide numbers always refer to the *section numbers* in the text and *not to* pages.

THESAURUS OF
ENGLISH WORDS
AND PHRASES

CLASS I

Words expressing ABSTRACT RELATIONS

Section I. EXISTENCE

1. Being, in the Abstract

1. Existence.— N. EXISTENCE, being, entity, *ens* [*L.*], *esse* [*L.*], subsistence; quid, hypaxis [*rare*], automaton.

REALITY, actuality; positiveness &c. *adj.;* fact, matter of fact, sober reality; truth &c. 494; actual existence.

PRESENCE &c. (*existence in space*) 186; coexistence &c. 120.

STUBBORN FACT; not a dream &c. 515; no joke.

ESSENCE, inmost nature, center of life, inner reality, vital principle.

[SCIENCE OF EXISTENCE] ontology.

V. EXIST, be; have being &c. *n.;* subsist, live, breathe, stand, obtain, be the case; occur &c. (*event*) 151; have place, rank, prevail; find oneself, pass the time, vegetate.

come into existence &c. *n.;* arise &c. (*begin*) 66; come forth &c. (*appear*) 446.

BECOME &c. (*be converted*) 144; bring into existence &c. 161; coexist, postexist [*rare*], preëxist [*rare*].

CONSIST IN, lie in; be comprised in, be contained in, be constituted by.

ABIDE, continue, endure, last, remain.

Adj. EXISTING &c. *v.;* existent, subsistent, under the sun; in existence &c. *n.;* extant; afloat, on foot, current, prevalent; undestroyed.

REAL, actual, positive, absolute; factual, veritable, true &c. 494; substan-

2. Nonexistence. — N. NONEXISTENCE, nonsubsistence; inexistence; nonentity, *nil* [*L.*]; negativeness &c. *adj.;* nullity; nihility, nihilism; *tabula rasa* [*L.*], blank; abeyance; absence &c. 187; no such thing &c. 4; nonbeing, nothingness, oblivion, *non esse* [*L.*].

ANNIHILATION; extinction &c. (*destruction*) 162; extinguishment, extirpation, Nirvana, obliteration.

V. NOT EXIST &c. 1; have no existence &c. 1; be null and void; cease to exist &c. 1; pass away, perish; be *or* become extinct &c. *adj.;* die out; disappear &c. 449; melt away, dissolve, leave not a rack behind; go, be no more; die &c. 360.

ANNIHILATE, render null, nullify; abrogate &c. 756; destroy &c. 162; take away; remove &c. (*displace*) 185; obliterate, extirpate, deracinate [*rare*].

Adj. INEXISTENT, nonexistent &c. 1; negative, blank; null, minus, missing, omitted; absent &c. 187; insubstantial, shadowy, spectral, visionary.

UNREAL, potential, virtual; baseless, *in nubibus* [*L.*]; unsubstantial &c. 4; vain.

UNBORN, uncreated, unbegotten, unconceived, unproduced, unmade.

PERISHED, annihilated &c. *v.;* extinct, exhausted, gone, lost, departed; defunct &c. (*dead*) 360.

tial, substantive; self-existing, self-exist-
ent; essential, beënt.

WELL-FOUNDED, well-grounded; unideal, unimagined; not potential &c. 2;
authentic.

Adv. ACTUALLY &c. *adj.*; in fact, in
point of fact, in reality; indeed; *de facto* [L.], *ipso facto* [L.].

. *ens rationis; cogito ergo sum;* "think'st thou existence doth depend on time?" [Byron];
"all is concenter'd in a life intense" [Byron]; "to live is not merely to breathe, it is to act"
[Rousseau]; "the mainspring of life is in the heart" [Amiel]; "I came like Water, and like
Wind I go" [Omar Khayyám — Fitzgerald].

FABULOUS, ideal &c. (*imaginary*) 515;
supposititious &c. 514.

Adv. negatively, virtually &c. *adj.*

. *non ens;* "and what's her history? A
blank, my Lord" [*Twelfth Night*].

2. BEING, IN THE CONCRETE

3. Substantiality.— N. SUBSTANTIAL-
ITY, hypostasis; person, thing, object,
article; something, a being, an existence;
creature, body, substance, flesh and
blood, stuff, substratum; matter &c.
316; corporeity, element, essential nature, groundwork, materiality, substantialness, vital part.

[TOTALITY OF EXISTENCES] world &c.
318; *plenum* [L.].

Adj. SUBSTANTIVE, substantial; hypostatic *or* hypostatical; personal, bodily, practical, effective; tangible &c.
(*material*) 316; corporeal; right, sober.

Adv. SUBSTANTIALLY &c. *adj.;* bodily,
essentially.

. "The heavy and the weary weight Of
all this unintelligible world" [Wordsworth].

4. Unsubstantiality. — N. UNSUB-
STANTIALITY, insubstantiality; nothingness, nihility; no degree, no part, no
quantity, no thing.

NOTHING, naught, *nil* [L.], nullity,
zero, cipher, no one, nobody; never a
one, ne'er a one; no such thing, none in
the world; nothing whatever, nothing at
all, nothing on earth; not a particle &c.
(*smallness*) 32; all talk, all moonshine,
all stuff and nonsense; matter of no
importance, matter of no consequence.

THING OF NAUGHT, man of straw,
John Doe and Richard Roe, fagot (*or*
faggot) voter [*polit. cant, Eng.*]; *nominis
umbra* [L.], nonentity, cipher, nought,
nothing, obscurity, lay figure; flash in
the pan, *vox et præterea nihil* [L.].

PHANTOM &c. (*fallacy of vision*) 443;
shadow; dream &c. (*imagination*) 515; *ignis fatuus* [L.] &c. (*luminary*) 423; "such
stuff as dreams are made on" [*Tempest*]; air, thin air; bubble &c. 353; mockery.

BLANK; void &c. (*absence*) 187; hollowness.

INANITY, fatuity, fool's paradise.

V. VANISH, evaporate, fade, fleet, sink, fly, dissolve, melt away; die, die away,
die out; disappear &c. 449.

Adj. UNSUBSTANTIAL; baseless, groundless; ungrounded; without foundation,
having no foundation.

VISIONARY &c. (*imaginary*) 515; immaterial &c. 317; spectral &c. 980;
dreamy; shadowy; ethereal, airy, gaseous, imponderable, tenuous, vague,
vaporous, dreamlike, mushroom; cloud-built, cloud-formed; gossamery, illusory,
insubstantial, unreal, unsolid [*rare*], slight, bodiless.

VACANT, vacuous; empty &c. 187; eviscerated; blank, hollow; nominal; null;
inane [*rare*].

. there's nothing in it; "an ocean of dreams without a sound" [Shelley]; "the baseless
fabric of this vision" [*Tempest*]; "this bodiless creation ecstasy Is very cunning in" [*Hamlet*]

3. FORMAL EXISTENCE

Internal conditions

5. Intrinsicality. — N. INTRINSICAL-
ITY, intrinsicalness, inbeing, inherence,
inhesion, immanence, indwelling; sub-
jectiveness; ego; egohood; essence, quin-

External conditions

6. Extrinsicality. — N. EXTRINSICAL-
ITY, objectiveness, *non ego* [L.]; extraneousness &c. 57; accident.

Adj. EXTRINSIC, extrinsical; derived

2

tessence, elixir; essentialness &c. *adj.;* essential part, incarnation, quiddity, gist, pith, core, kernel, marrow, sap, lifeblood, backbone, heart, soul, life, substance, flower; important part &c. (*importance*) 642.

PRINCIPLE, nature, constitution, character, type, quality, crasis, diathesis.

TEMPER, temperament; spirit, humor, grain, nature, vein, mood, frame, cue; disposition; habit.

CAPACITY, endowment; capability &c. (*power*) 157.

ASPECTS, moods, declensions, features; peculiarities &c. (*speciality*) 79; idiosyncrasy; idiocrasy &c. (*tendency*) 176; diagnostics.

V. be in the blood, run in the blood; be born so; be intrinsic &c. *adj.*

Adj. INTRINSIC, intrinsical; derived from within, subjective; idiocratic *or* idiocratical, idiosyncratic *or* idiosyncratical; fundamental, normal; implanted, inherent, essential, natural; innate, inborn, inbred, ingrained, indwelling, inwrought; coeval with birth, genetic, genetous, hæmatobious, syngenic; radical, incarnate, thoroughbred, hereditary, inherited, immanent; congenital, congenite [*obs.*]; connate, running in the blood; ingenerate, ingenit *or* ingenite [*obs.*], ingenita [*obs.*], indigenous; in the grain &c. *n.;* bred in the bone, instinctive; inward, internal &c. 221; to the manner born; virtual.

CHARACTERISTIC &c. (*special*) 79, (*indicative*) 550; invariable, incurable, ineradicable, fixed.

Adv. INTRINSICALLY &c. *adj.;* at bottom, in the main, in effect, practically, virtually, substantially, *au fond* [*F.*]; fairly.

. "character is higher than intellect" [Emerson]; "the head is not more native to the heart" [*Hamlet*]; "come give us a taste of your quality" [*Hamlet*]; *magnos homines virtute metimur non fortunâ* [Nepos]; *non numero hæc judicantur sed pondere* [Cicero]; "vital spark of heavenly flame" [Pope]; "the all-important factor in national greatness is national character" [Roosevelt].

4. MODAL EXISTENCE

Absolute

7. State.—N. STATE, condition, category, estate, lot, case, trim, mood, temper; aspect &c. (*appearance*) 448.

DILEMMA, pass, predicament, quandary, corner, hole, *impasse* [*F.*], fix, pickle, plight.

FRAME, fabric &c. 329; stamp, set, fit, mold *or* mould; constitution, habitude, diathesis.

FORM, fettle, shape, kilter *or* kelter; tone, tenor, turn; trim, guise, fashion, light, complexion, style, character; build &c. 240; mode, modality, schesis [*obs.*]

V. be in–, possess–, enjoy– a state &c. *n.;* be on a footing, do, fare; come to pass.

Adj. CONDITIONAL, modal, formal; structural, organic.

Adv. CONDITIONALLY &c. *adj.;* as the matter stands, as things are; such being

Relative

8. Circumstance. — N. CIRCUMSTANCE, situation, phase, position, posture, attitude, place, point; terms; *régime* [*F.*]; footing, standing, status.

OCCASION, juncture, conjuncture; contingency &c. (*event*) 151.

PREDICAMENT; emergency; exigency, crisis, pinch, pass, plight, push; occurrence; turning point.

BEARINGS, how the land lies.

Adj. CIRCUMSTANTIAL; given, conditional, provisional; critical; modal; contingent, incidental; adventitious &c. (*extrinsic*) 6; limitative.

DETAILED, minute, full, fussy.

Adv. THUS, in such wise; in *or* under the circumstances &c. *n.;* in *or* under the conditions &c. 7.

ACCORDINGLY; that being the case; such being the case; that being so;

from without; objective; extraneous &c. (*foreign*) 57; modal, adventitious; ascititious, adscititious; incidental, accidental, nonessential, unessential, accessory; contingent, fortuitous, casual, subsidiary.

IMPLANTED, ingrafted; inculcated, infused.

OUTWARD &c. (*external*) 220.

Adv. EXTRINSICALLY &c. *adj.*

. "these but the trappings and the suits of woe" [*Hamlet*]; "the accident of an accident" [Thurlow] .

the case &c. 8; *quæ cum ita sint* [*L.*].

. "it is a condition which confronts us — not a theory" [Grover Cleveland].

sith [*obs. or archaic*], sithen [*obs.*], since, seeing that.

as matters stand; as things go, as times go.

CONDITIONALLY, provided, if, in case; if so, if so be, if it be so; if it so happen, if it so turn out; in the event of; in such a contingency, in such a case, in such an event; provisionally, unless, without.

according to circumstances, according to the occasion; as it may happen, as it may turn out, as it may be; as the case may be, as the wind blows; *pro re natâ* [*L.*].

. "yet are my sins not those of circumstance" [Lytton]; "the happy combination of fortuitous circumstances" [Scott]; "fearful concatenation of circumstance" [Daniel Webster]; "circumstances alter cases" [Haliburton].

Section II. RELATION

1. Absolute Relation

9. Relation. — N. RELATION, bearing, reference, connection, concern, cognation, applicability, apposition, appositeness; correlation &c. 12; analogy; similarity &c. 17; affinity, homology, alliance, nearness, rapport, homogeneity, association; approximation &c. (*nearness*) 197; filiation &c. (*consanguinity*) 11; interest; relevancy &c. 23; dependency, relationship, relative position; correlation, interrelation, interconnection.

RATIO, proportion; comparison &c. 464.

LINK, tie, bond of union, privity [*law*].

V. BE RELATED &c. *adj.;* have a relation &c. *n.;* relate to, refer to; bear upon, regard, concern, touch, affect, have to do with; pertain to, belong to, appertain to; answer to; interest.

ASSOCIATE, connect; bring into relation with, bring to bear upon; draw a parallel; link &c. 43.

Adj. RELATIVE; correlative &c. 12; relating to &c. *v.;* relative to, in relation with, referable *or* referrible to; belonging to &c. *v.;* appurtenant to, in common with.

RELATED, connected; implicated, associated, affiliated; allied, allied to; collateral, connate [*rare*], cognate, congenerous, connatural, affinitive, paronymous; *en rapport* [*F.*], in touch with.

APPROXIMATIVE, approximating; proportional, proportionate, proportionable; allusive, comparable, equiparable [*obs. or rare*].

RELEVANT &c. (*apt*) 23; applicable,

10. [WANT OR ABSENCE OF RELATION.] **Irrelation. — N.** IRRELATION, dissociation; misrelation; inapplicability; inconnection; multifariousness; disconnection &c (*disjunction*) 44; inconsequence, independence; incommensurability; irreconcilableness &c. (*disagreement*) 24; heterogeneity; unconformity &c. 83; irrelevancy, impertinence, *nihil ad rem* [*L.*]; intrusion &c. 24; nonpertinence.

V. NOT CONCERN &c. 9; have no relation to &c. 9; have no bearing upon, have no concern with &c. 9; have no business with; have nothing to do with, have no business there; intrude &c. 24.

bring—, drag—, lug— in by the head and shoulders.

Adj. IRRELATIVE, irrespective, unrelated, disrelated, irrelate [*rare*]; arbitrary; independent, unallied; disconnected, unconnected, adrift, isolated, insular; extraneous, strange, alien, foreign, outlandish, exotic.

not comparable, incommensurable, heterogeneous; unconformable &c. 83.

IRRELEVANT, inapplicable; not pertinent, not to the purpose; impertinent [*legal*], unessential, inessential, accidental, inapposite, beside the mark, *à propos de bottes* [*F.*]; aside from—, away from—, foreign to—, beside— the —purpose, —question, — transaction, — point; misplaced &c. (*intrusive*) 24; traveling out of the record.

REMOTE, far-fetched, out-of-the-way, forced, neither here nor there, quite another thing; detached, apart, segre-

equiparant; in the same category &c. 75; like &c. 17.

Adv. RELATIVELY &c. *adj.;* pertinently &c. 23.

THEREOF; as to, as for, as respects, as regards; about; concerning &c. *v.;* anent; relating to, as relates to; with relation to, with reference to, with respect to, with regard to; in respect of; speaking of, *à propos* [*F.*] of; in connection with; by the way, by the by; whereas; for as much as, in as much as; in point of, as far as; on the part of, on the score of; *quoad hoc* [*L.*]; *pro re natâ* [*L.*]; under the head of &c. (*class*) 75; in the matter of, *in re* [*L.*].

gated, segregate; disquiparant.

MULTIFARIOUS; discordant &c. 24.

INCIDENTAL, parenthetical, *obiter dictum* [*L.*], episodic.

Adv. PARENTHETICALLY &c. *adj.;* by the way, by the by; *en passant* [*F.*], incidentally, *obiter* [*L.*]; irrespectively &c. *adj.;* without reference to, without regard to; in the abstract &c. 87; *a se* [*L.*].

** "remote, unfriended, melancholy, slow" [Goldsmith]; "she stood in tears amid the alien corn" [Keats]; "so she went into the garden to cut a cabbage-leaf to make an apple pie" [S. Foote].

** "thereby hangs a tale" [*Taming of the Shrew*]; "but that's another story" [Kipling]; "a man is a bundle of relations, a knot of roots" [Emerson].

11. [RELATIONS OF KINDRED.] **Consanguinity. — N.** CONSANGUINITY, relationship, kindred, blood; parentage &c. (*paternity*) 166; filiation, affiliation; lineage, agnation, connation [*obs.*], cognation, connection, alliance; people [as, my *people*], family, family connection, family tie; ties of blood, blood relation; nepotism.

KINSMAN, kinsfolk; kith and kin; relation, relative; connection; sib [*rare*]; next of kin; uncle, aunt, nephew, niece; cousin, cousin-german; first cousin, second cousin; cousin once removed, cousin twice removed &c.; near relation, distant relation; brother, sister, one's own flesh and blood.

FAMILY, fraternity; brotherhood, sisterhood, cousinhood.

RACE, stock, generation; sept &c. 166; stirps, side; strain; breed, clan, tribe.

V. BE RELATED TO &c. *adj.;* claim relationship with &c. *n.*

Adj. RELATED, akin, sib [*Scot. or archaic*], consanguineous, of the blood, family, allied, collateral; cognate, agnate, connate [*rare*]; kindred; affiliated; fraternal.

intimately related, nearly related, closely related, remotely related, distantly related; intimately allied, nearly allied, closely allied, remotely allied, distantly allied; affinal, german.

** "A little more than kin and less than kind" [*Hamlet*]; "I'm all o'er sib to Adam's breed that I should bid him go" [Kipling]; "and so do his sisters and his cousins and his aunts" [Gilbert].

12. [DOUBLE OR RECIPROCAL RELATION.] **Correlation. — N.** RECIPROCALNESS &c. *adj.;* reciprocity, reciprocality, reciprocation; mutuality, correspondence, correlation, interrelation, interconnection, interdependence; interchange &c. 148; exchange, barter, *quid pro quo* [*L.*].

ALTERNATION, seesaw, shuttle [*rare*], to-and-fro.

reciprocitist.

V. RECIPROCATE, alternate, interact; interchange &c. 148; exchange; counterchange.

Adj. RECIPROCAL, mutual, commutual [*rare*], correlative; correspondent, corresponding; alternate; interchangeable; international; complemental, complementary; equivalent.

Adv. *mutatis mutandis* [*L.*]; *vice versâ* [*L.*]; each other; by turns &c. 148; reciprocally &c. *adj.*

** "happy in our mutual help" [Milton]; "my true love hath my heart and I have his" [Sidney].

13. Identity. — N. IDENTITY, sameness, identicalness, unity, selfsameness, coincidence, coalescence; convertibility;

14. [NONCOINCIDENCE.] **Contrariety. — N.** CONTRARIETY, contrast, foil, antithesis, antipode, counterpole, counter-

equality &c. 27; selfness, self, oneself; identification.

CONNATURALITY, connature, connaturalness, homogeneity.

MONOTONY; tautology &c. (*repetition*) 104.

FACSIMILE &c. (*copy*) 21; homoousia; *alter ego* [*L.*] &c. (*similar*) 17; *ipsissima verba* [*L.*] &c. (*exactness*) 494; same; selfsame, very same, one and the same; counterpart; very thing, actual thing; no other.

V. BE IDENTICAL &c. *adj.;* coincide, coalesce.

treat as the same, render the same; treat as identical; render identical; identify; recognize the identity of.

Adj. IDENTICAL; self, ilk [*archaic*]; the identical same &c. *n.;* selfsame, homoousian, one and the same; ditto.

COINCIDENT, coinciding, coalescing, coalescent, indistinguishable; one; equivalent &c. (*equal*) 27; much the same, much of a muchness; unaltered.

Adv. IDENTICALLY &c. *adj.;* on all fours with; *ibidem* [*L.*], *ibid.*

*** "Liberty and Union, now and forever, one and inseparable" [Webster]; "All one body we, One in hope, in doctrine, One in charity" [Baring-Gould]; "the selfsame flight, the selfsame way" [*Merchant of Venice*]; "another, yet the same" [Pope].

point; counterpart; complement; *vis-à-vis* [*F.*], oppositeness; contradiction; antagonism &c. (*opposition*) 708; clashing, repugnance, antipathy.

INVERSION &c. 218; the opposite, the reverse, the inverse, the converse, the antipodes, the other extreme.

V. BE CONTRARY &c. *adj.;* contrast with, oppose, antithesize [*rare*]; differ *toto cœlo* [*L.*].

INVERT, reverse, turn the tables; turn topsy-turvy, turn end for end, turn upside down; retrograde, transpose, invaginate, intussuscept.

CONTRADICT, contravene; antagonize &c. 708.

Adj. CONTRARY, contrarious [*archaic*], contrariant [*rare*], opposite, counter, dead against; adverse, averse, converse, reverse; opposed, antithetical, contrasted, antipodean, antagonistic, opposing; conflicting, inconsistent, contradictory, at cross purposes; negative; hostile, inimical &c. 703.

differing *toto cœlo* [*L.*]; diametrically opposite; as opposite as black and white, as opposite as light and darkness, as opposite as fire and water, as opposite as the poles; "Hyperion to a satyr" [*Hamlet*]; quite the contrary, quite the reverse; no such thing, just the other way, *tout au contraire* [*F.*].

Adv. CONTRARILY &c. *adj.;* contra, contrariwise, *per contra* [*L.*], on the contrary, nay rather; *vice versâ* [*L.*]; on the other hand &c. (*in compensation*) 30.

*** "all concord's born of contraries" [B. Jonson]; "our antagonist is our helper" [Burke]; "woman's| at best a contradiction still" [Pope]; "the innate perversity of inanimate objects" [Gail Hamilton]; "opposition is the surest persuasion" [*Cynic's Calendar*].

15. Difference. — N. DIFFERENCE;

variance, variation, variety; diversity, divergence, heterogeneity, discongruity, contrast, inconformity, incompatibility, antithesis, antitheticalness, discrepation [*rare*], dissimilarity &c. 18; disagreement &c. 24; disparity &c. (*inequality*) 28; distinction, dissimilitude [*rare*], distinctness, contradiction, contradictoriness, contrariety, contradistinction; alteration.

nice distinction, fine distinction, delicate distinction, subtle distinction; shade of difference, *nuance* [*F.*]; discrimination &c. 465; differentia.

DIFFERENT THING, something else, apple off another tree, another pair of shoes; this, that, or the other.

MODIFICATION, commutation [*rare*], moods and tenses.

V. BE DIFFERENT &c. *adj.;* differ, vary, ablude [*obs.*], mismatch, contrast; diverge from, depart from, deviate from, disaccord with, discrepate [*rare*]; divaricate; differ *toto cœlo* [*L.*], differ *longo intervallo* [*L.*].

VARY, modify &c. (*change*) 140.

DISCRIMINATE &c. 465.

Adj. DIFFERING &c. *v.;* different, diverse, heterogeneous; distinguishable; varied, variant, divergent, contrastive, incongruous, discrepant, dissonant, inharmonious, disparate, inconformable, differential, modified; diversified, various, divers [*archaic*], all manner of; variform &c. 81; dædal.

OTHER, another, not the same; unequal &c. 28; unmatched; widely apart.

DISTINCTIVE, characteristic; discriminative, differentiative, distinguishing; diacritic, diacritical; diagnostic.

Adv. DIFFERENTLY &c. *adj.*

** *il y a fagots et fagots; tot homines tot sententiæ;* "a distinction without a difference" [Fielding]; "you must wear your rue with a difference" [*Hamlet*]; "But she is in her grave, and oh, The difference to me" [Wordsworth]; "not Lancelot, nor another" [Tennyson].

2. CONTINUOUS RELATION

16. Uniformity. — N. UNIFORMITY; homogeneity, homogeneousness; stability, continuity, permanence, consistency; connature [*rare*], connaturality [*rare*], connaturalness; homology; accordance; conformity &c. 82; agreement &c. 23; consonance, uniformness.

REGULARITY, constancy, evenness, sameness, unity, even tenor, routine; monotony.

V. BE UNIFORM &c. *adj.;* accord with &c. 23; run through.

BECOME UNIFORM &c. *adj.;* conform to &c. 82.

RENDER UNIFORM &c. *adj.;* assimilate, level, smooth, dress.

Adj. UNIFORM; homogeneous, homologous; of a piece, consistent, connatural; singsong, drear [*rare*], drearisome, dreary, monotonous, even, equable, constant, level; invariable; regular, unchanged, undeviating, unvaried, undiversified, unvarying; jog-trot.

Adv. UNIFORMLY &c. *adj.;* uniformly with &c. (*conformably*) 82; in harmony with &c. (*agreeing*) 23; in a rut.

ALWAYS, ever, evermore, perpetually, forever, everlastingly, invariably, without exception, never otherwise; by clockwork.

** *ab uno disce omnes;* "Consistence, thou art a jewel!" [*Anon.*]; "a foolish consistency is the hobgoblin of little minds" [Emerson]; "Young Obadias, David, Josias, — All were pious" [*New England Primer*].

16a. [ABSENCE OR WANT OF UNIFORMITY.**] Nonuniformity. — N.** DIVERSITY, irregularity, unevenness; multiformity &c. 81; unconformity &c. 83; roughness &c. 256; dissimilarity, dissimilitude, divarication, divergence, heteromorphism, heterogeneity.

Adj. DIVERSIFIED, varied, irregular, checkered, dædal, uneven, rough &c. 256; multifarious; multiform &c. 81; of various kinds; all manner of, all sorts of, all kinds of.

Adv. in all manner of ways; here, there, and everywhere.

** "I do desire we may be better strangers" [*As You Like It*]; "of every shape that was not uniform" [Lowell].

3. PARTIAL RELATION

17. Similarity. — N. SIMILARITY, resemblance, likeness, similitude [*rare*], semblance, consimilarity [*rare*]; affinity, approximation, parallelism; agreement &c. 23; analogy, analogicalness; correspondence, homoiousia, parity.

CONNATURALNESS, connature [*rare*], connaturality [*rare*]; brotherhood, family likeness.

ALLITERATION, rime *or* rhyme, pun.

REPETITION &c. 104; sameness &c. (*identity*) 13; uniformity &c. 16; isogamy.

ANALOGUE; the like; match, pendant, fellow, companion, pair, mate, twin, double, congener, counterpart, brother,

18. Dissimilarity. — N. DISSIMILARITY, dissimilitude; unlikeness, diversity, disparity, dissemblance; divergence, variation; difference &c. 15; novelty, originality; creativeness; oögamy.

V. BE UNLIKE &c. *adj.;* vary &c. (*differ*) 15; bear no resemblance to, differ *toto cælo* [*L.*].

RENDER UNLIKE &c. *adj.;* vary &c. (*diversify*) 140.

Adj. DISSIMILAR, unlike, disparate; divergent, nonidentical, unidentical; of a different kind &c. (*class*) 75; unmatched, unique; new, novel; unprecedented &c. 83; original.

nothing of the kind; no such thing,

sister; one's second self, *alter ego* [*L.*], chip of the old block, *par nobile fratrum* [*L.*], *Arcades ambo* [*L.*], birds of a feather, *et hoc genus omne* [*L.*]; *gens de même famille* [*F.*].

SIMILE; parallel; type &c. (*metaphor*) 521; image &c. (*representation*) 554; photograph; close-, striking-, speaking-, faithful &c. *adj.* - -likeness, – resemblance.

V. BE SIMILAR &c. *adj.*; look like, resemble, favor [*colloq.*], follow, echo, reproduce, bear resemblance; savor of, smack of; approximate; parallel, match, rime *or* rhyme with; take after; imitate &c. 19; span [*U. S.*]; hunt in couples, run in couples.

RENDER SIMILAR &c. *adj.*; assimilate, approximate, bring near; connaturalize, make alike; rime *or* rhyme, pun.

Adj. SIMILAR; resembling &c. *v.*; like, alike; twin.

ANALOGOUS, analogical; parallel, of a piece; such as, so; homoiousian.

CONNATURAL, correlative, corresponding, cognate, congeneric, congenerous, allied to; akin to &c. (*consanguineous*) 11.

APPROXIMATE, much the same, near, close, something like, near- [as *near*-silk, *colloq.*, *U.S.*], such like; a show of; mock, pseudo, simulating, representing.

EXACT &c. (*true*) 494; lifelike, faithful; true to nature, true to life; the very image of, the very picture of; for all the world like, *comme deux gouttes d'eau* [*F.*], as like as two peas, as like as it can stare; *instar omnium* [*L.*], cast in the same mold, ridiculously like.

Adv. AS IF, so to speak; as it were, as if it were; *quasi* [*L.*], just as, *veluti in speculum* [*L.*].

⁎ *et sic de similibus; tel maître tel valet; tel père tel fils*, like father like son; "as lyke as one pease is to another" [Lyly]; "they say we are Almost as like as eggs" [*Winter's Tale*]; "Fair Portia's counterfeit" [*M.of V.*]; "so and no otherwise hill-men desire their hills" [Kipling].

quite another thing; far from it, other than, cast in a different mold, *tertium quid* [*L.*], as like a dock as a daisy, "very like a whale" [*Hamlet*]; as different as chalk from cheese, as different as Macedon and Monmouth; *lucus a non lucendo* [*L.*].

diversified &c. 16*a*.

Adv. OTHERWISE, elsewise; alias.

⁎ *dis aliter visum;* "no more like my father Than I to Hercules" [*Hamlet*]; "it is a custom More honoured in the breach than in the observance" [*Hamlet*]; "agreed to differ" [Southey].

19. Imitation. — N. IMITATION; copying &c. *v.*; transcription; repetition, duplication, reduplication; quotation; reproduction; mimeography.

MOCKERY, apery, mimicking, mimicry.

SIMULATION, personation; parrotism, parrotry; representation &c. 554; semblance, pretense; copy &c. 21; assimilation.

paraphrase, parody &c. 21.

PLAGIARISM; forgery &c. (*falsehood*) 544.

IMITATOR, echo, cuckoo, parrot, ape, monkey, mocking bird, mimic; copyist.

V. IMITATE, copy, mirror, reflect, reproduce, repeat; do like, echo, reëcho, catch; transcribe; match, parallel.

MOCK, take off, borrow, mimic, ape, simulate, personate; act &c. (*drama*) 599; represent &c. 554; counterfeit, forge, parody, travesty, caricature, burlesque.

FOLLOW in the steps of, follow in the footsteps of; follow in the wake of; tread in the steps of, tread in the footsteps of; take pattern by; follow suit [*colloq.*], follow the example of; walk in the shoes of, take a leaf out of another's book, strike in with; take after, model after; emulate.

20. Nonimitation. — N. NONIMITATION, no imitation; originality; creativeness.

Adj. UNIMITATED, uncopied; unmatched, unparalleled; inimitable &c. 33; unique, original, archetypal, prototypal, prototypical, primordial, creative, untranslated; exceptional, rare, *sui generis* [*L.*], uncommon, unexampled, out-of-the-way, insusitate [*rare*], unwonted, *recherché* [*F.*], unordinary [*rare*], supernormal.

⁎ "wrapped in the solitude of his own originality" [Charles Phillips —*of Napoleon*].

Adj. IMITATED &c. *v.;* mock, mimic; modeled after, molded on.

PARAPHRASTIC; literal; imitative; secondhand; imitable; aping, apish, mimicking, borrowed, counterfeit, imitation, false, pseudo, near- [as, *near*-silk, *colloq., U. S.*].

Adv. LITERALLY, to the letter, verbatim, *literatim* [*L.*], *sic* [*L.*], *totidem verbis* [*L.*], word for word, *mot à mot* [*F.*], *verbatim et literatim* [*L.*]; exactly, precisely.

** like master like man; "like — but oh! how different!" [Wordsworth]; "genius borrows nobly" [Emerson]; "pursuing echoes calling 'mong the rocks" [A. Coles]; "quotation confesses inferiority" [Emerson]; "the little actor cons another part" [Wordsworth]; "play the sedulous ape to men of letters" [Stevenson].

20a. Variation. — N. VARIATION; alteration &c. (*change*) 140.

MODIFICATION, moods and tenses; discrepance, discrepancy.

DIVERGENCY &c. 291; deviation &c. 279; aberration; innovation.

V. VARY &c. (*change*) 140; deviate &c. 279; diverge &c. 291; alternate, swerve.

Adj. VARIED &c. *v.;* modified; diversified &c. 16a; dissimilar &c. 18.

** "variety is the very spice of life" [Cowper]; "age cannot wither her, nor custom stale Her infinite variety" [*Antony and Cleopatra*].

21. [RESULT OF IMITATION.] **Copy.—**
N. COPY, facsimile, counterpart, *effigies* [*L.*], effigy, form, likeness, similitude, semblance, cast, tracing, ectype, electrotype; imitation &c. 19; model, representation, adumbration, study; "counterfeit presentment" [*Hamlet*]; portrait &c. (*representment*) 554; resemblance.

duplicate; transcript, transcription; counterscript; reflex, reflexion; shadow, echo; chip of the old block; reprint, replica, offprint, transfer, reproduction; second edition &c. (*repetition*) 104; *réchauffé* [*F.*]; apograph, fair copy, revise, rewriting.

MATTER; manuscript, typescript *or* typoscript, flimsy [*cant*].

22. [THING COPIED.] **Prototype. —**
N. PROTOTYPE, original, model, pattern, precedent, standard, scantling [*rare*], type; archetype, antitype; protoplast, protoplasm, plasm [*obs.*], proplasm [*rare*], module, exemplar, example, ensample [*archaic*], paradigm; lay-figure; fugleman, guide.

COPY, text, design; keynote.

DIE, mold; matrix, last, mint, seal, punch, intaglio, negative; stamp.

V. be an example, set an example; set a copy.

** "a precedent embalms a principle" [Disraeli]; *exempla sunt odiosa;* "I do not give you to posterity as a pattern to imitate, but as an example to deter" [*Letters of Junius*].

PARODY, caricature, burlesque, travesty, *travestie* [*F.*], paraphrase; cartoon. servile copy, servile imitation; counterfeit &c. (*deception*) 545; *pasticcio* [*It.*].

Adj. FAITHFUL; lifelike &c. (*similar*) 17; close, exact, strict, conscientious.

** "nature's copy's not eterne" [*Macbeth*]; "follow the copy though it fly out of the window" [*Printers' Saying*]; "parody might indeed be defined as the worshipper's half-holiday" [Chesterton].

4. GENERAL RELATION

23. Agreement. — N. AGREEMENT, accord, accordance; unison, harmony; concord &c. 714; concordance, concert; understanding, mutual understanding; gentleman's agreement, *entente cordiale* [*F.*], consortium; unanimity, consension [*rare*], concentus, consentaneity.

CONFORMITY &c. 82; conformance; uniformity &c. 16; assonance, consonance, consentaneousness, consistency; congruity, congruence *or* congruency; keeping; congeniality; correspondence, concinnity, parallelism, apposition, union.

24. Disagreement. — N. DISAGREEMENT; discord, discordance, discordancy; dissonance, dissidence, disunity, disunion, discrepancy; unconformity &c. 83; incongruity, incongruence; discongruity, *mésalliance* [*F.*]; jarring &c. *v.;* dissension &c. 713; conflict &c. (*opposition*) 708; bickering, clashing, misunderstanding, wrangle.

DISPARITY, mismatch, disproportion; dissimilitude, inequality; disproportionateness &c. *adj.;* variance, divergence, repugnance.

UNFITNESS &c. *adj.;* inaptitude, im-

FITNESS, aptness &c. *adj.;* relevancy; pertinence *or* pertinency; sortance [*obs.*]; case in point; aptitude, coaptation, propriety, applicability, admissibility, commensurability, compatibility; cognation &c. (*relation*) 9.

ADAPTATION, adaption, adjustment, graduation, accommodation; reconciliation, reconcilement; assimilation.

CONSENT &c. (*assent*) 488; concurrence &c. 178; consensus, *rapport* [*F.*], meeting of minds, coöperation &c. 709.

right man in the right place, very thing; quite the thing, just the thing.

V. BE ACCORDANT &c. *adj.;* agree, accord, harmonize; correspond, tally, respond; meet, suit, fit, befit, do, adapt itself to; fall in with, chime in with, square with, quadrate with, consort with, comport with; dovetail, assimilate; fit like a glove; fit to a tittle, fit to a T; match &c. 17; become one; homologate.

consent &c. (*assent*) 488.

RENDER ACCORDANT &c. *adj.;* fit, suit, adapt, accommodate; graduate; adjust &c. (*render equal*) 27; dress, regulate, readjust; accord, harmonize, reconcile; fadge, dovetail, square.

Adj. AGREEING, suiting &c. *v.;* in accord, accordant, concordant, consonant, congruous, consentaneous [*archaic*], answerable, correspondent, congenial; coherent; becoming; harmonious, reconcilable, conformable; in accordance with, in harmony with, in keeping with, in unison with &c. *n.;* at one with, of one mind, of a piece; consistent, compatible, proportionate; commensurate; on all fours with.

APT, apposite, pertinent, pat; to the point, to the purpose; happy, felicitous, germane, *ad rem* [*L.*], in point, bearing upon, applicable, relevant, admissible.

FIT, adapted, *in loco* [*L.*], *à propos* [*F.*], appropriate, seasonable, sortable, suitable, idoneous [*rare*], deft; meet &c. (*expedient*) 646.

at home, in one's proper element.

Adv. *à propos* of; pertinently &c. *adj.*

propriety; inapplicability &c. *adj.;* inconsistency, inconcinnity; irrelevancy &c. (*irrelation*) 10.

MISJOINING, misjoinder; syncretism, intrusion, interference.

fish out of water.

V. DISAGREE; clash, conflict, dispute, quarrel, jar &c. (*discord*) 713; interfere, intrude, come amiss; not concern &c. 10; mismatch; *humano capiti cervicem jungere equinam* [*L.*]

Adj. DISAGREEING &c. *v.;* discordant, discrepant; at variance, at war; hostile, antagonistic, repugnant, inaccordant, clashing, jarring, factious, dissentient, dissentious, dissident, inacquiescent, incompatible, irreconcilable, inconsistent with; unconformable, exceptional &c. 83; intrusive, incongruent, incongruous; disproportionate, disproportioned; unharmonious; unconsonant; divergent, repugnant to.

INAPT, unapt, inappropriate, malappropriate [*rare*], improper; unsuited, unsuitable; inapplicable; unfit, unfitting, unbefitting; unbecoming; ill-timed, ill-adapted, dissuitable [*rare*], infelicitous, unseasonable, *mal à propos* [*F.*], inadmissible; inapposite &c. (*irrelevant*) 10.

UNCONGENIAL; ill-assorted, ill-sorted; mismatched, misjoined, misplaced; unaccommodating, irreducible, uncommensurable; unsympathetic.

out of character, out of keeping, out of proportion, out of joint, out of tune, out of place, out of season, out of its element; at odds, at variance with.

Adv. in defiance of, in contempt of, in spite of; discordantly &c. *adj.;* *à tort et à travers* [*F.*].

⁎ *asinus ad lyram;* "fill'd the air with barbarous dissonance" [Milton]; "all discord, harmony not understood" [Pope]; "I heard him speak disrespectfully of the equator" [Sydney Smith]; "the dissidence of dissent" [Burke].

⁎ *rem acu tetigisti;* the cap fits; *auxilia humilia firma consensus facit* [Syrus]; *concordia discors* [Hor.]; "Be not the first by whom the new is tried, Nor yet the last to lay the old aside" [Pope].

Section III.   QUANTITY

1. Simple Quantity

25. [Absolute quantity.] **Quantity.**
— N. quantity, magnitude; size &c.
(*dimensions*) 192; amplitude, mass,
amount, quantum, measure, measurement, substance, strength.

[Science of quantity] mathematics,
mathesis [*rare*].

[Logic] category, general conception, universal predicament.

[Definite or finite quantity] armful, handful, mouthful, spoonful, capful;
stock, batch, lot, dose; quota, quotiety
[*rare*], quotum, pittance, driblet, grist
[*U. S.*]; yaffle [*dial.*].

V. quantify, rate.

Adj. quantitative, some, any, more
or less.

Adv. to the tune of.

* "I waive the quantum o' the sin"
[Burns].

26. [Relative quantity.] **Degree.**—
N. degree, grade, step, extent, measure,
amount, ratio, stint *or* stent, standard,
height, pitch; reach, amplitude, range,
scope, caliber; gradation, shade; tenor,
compass; sphere, station, rank, standing; rate, way, sort.

point, mark, stage &c. (*term*) 71;
interval, line [*music*], space [*music*];
intensity, strength &c. (*greatness*) 31.

V. graduate, calibrate, measure; rectify.

Adj. comparative; gradual, grada-
tional, gradatory [*rare*], shading off;
within the bounds &c. (*limit*) 233.

Adv. by degrees, gradually, inasmuch, *pro tanto* [*L.*]; however, howso-
ever; step by step, bit by bit, little by
little, inch by inch, drop by drop; by
inches, by slow degrees, by little and
little; in some degree, in some measure;
to some extent; *di grado in grado* [*It.*].

* "the rank is but the guinea's stamp"
[Burns].

2. Comparative Quantity

27. [Sameness of quantity or degree.] **Equality.** — N. equality, parity, coextension, symmetry, balance,
poise; evenness, monotony, level.

equivalence; equipollence, equipoise, equilibrium, equiponderance; par,
quits; not a pin to choose; distinction
without a difference, six of one and
half a dozen of the other; identity &c.
13; similarity &c. 17; coequality, co-
evality [*rare*], isonomy, isopolity, isotropy, parallelism, owelty [*law*].

equalization, equation; equilibration,
coördination, adjustment, readjustment.

tie, dead heat; drawn game, drawn
battle; neck-and-neck race.

match, peer, compeer, equal, mate,
fellow, brother; equivalent.

V. be equal &c. *adj.*; equal, match,
reach, keep pace with, run abreast; come
to, amount to, come up to; be on a level
with, lie on a level with; balance; cope
with; come to the same thing, even off.

render equal &c. *adj.*; equalize,
level, dress, balance, equate, handicap,

28. [Difference of quantity or
degree.] **Inequality.**— N. inequality,
inequalness [*rare*]; disparity, imparity
[*rare*]; odds; difference &c. 15; unevenness; inclination of the balance,
partiality; shortcoming; casting weight,
makeweight; superiority &c. 33; inferiority &c. 34; inequation, inadequation
[*archaic*], inadequacy.

V. be unequal &c. *adj.*; countervail;
have the advantage, give the advantage;
turn the scale; kick the beam; topple,
topple over; overmatch &c. 33; not come
up to &c. 34.

Adj. unequal, inequal [*rare*], uneven,
disparate, partial, inadequate; over-
balanced, unbalanced; top-heavy, lop-
sided; disquiparant; unequaled, unparalleled, fellowless [*rare*], unmatched
[*rare*], unrivaled, unique, unapproached,
matchless, inimitable, transcendent,
peerless, nonpareil, unexampled, unpatterned [*rare*], unpeered [*rare*].

Adv. unequally &c. *adj.*; *haud passibus æquis* [Vergil].

give points, trim, adjust, poise; fit, accommodate; adapt &c. (*render accordant*) 23; strike a balance; establish equality, restore equality, establish equilibrium, restore equilibrium; readjust; stretch on the bed of Procrustes.

Adj. EQUAL, even, level, monotonous, coequal, symmetrical, coördinate; on a par with, on a level with, on a footing with; up to the mark; equiparant, equiparate [*rare*].

EQUIVALENT, tantamount; quits; homologous; synonymous &c. 522; resolvable into, convertible, much at one, as broad as long, neither more nor less; much the same as, the same thing as, as good as; all one, all the same; equipollent, equiponderant, equiponderous, equibalanced; equalized &c. *v.*; drawn; half and half; isochronal, isochronous; isoperimetric *or* isoperimetrical; isobath, isobathic.

Adv. EQUALLY &c. *adj.*; *pari passu* [*L.*], *ad eundem* [*L.*], *cœteris paribus* [*L.*], *in equilibrio* [*L.*]; to all intents and purposes.

*** it comes to the same thing, it amounts to the same thing; what is sauce for the goose is sauce for the gander; "the modern zeal for equality makes a counterpoise for Darwinism" [Amiel].

29. Mean. — **N.** MEAN, medium, intermedium [*obsoles.*], average, balance, normal, rule, run; mediocrity, generality; golden mean &c. (*mid-course*) 628; middle &c. 68; compromise &c. 774; middle course, middle state; neutrality.

V. AVERAGE, split the difference; take the average &c. *n.*; reduce to a mean &c. *n.*; strike a balance, pair off.

Adj. MEAN, intermediate; medial, middle &c. 68; average, normal, standard; neutral.

MEDIOCRE, middle-class, *bourgeois* [*F.*], commonplace &c. (*unimportant*) 643.

Adv. ON AN AVERAGE, in the long run; taking one with another, taking all things together, taking it for all in all; *communibus annis* [*L.*], in round numbers.

IN THE MIDDLE, *in medias res* [*L.*], *meden agan* [*Gr.* μηδὲν ἄγαν].

*** *medium tenuere beati;* "keep the golden mean" [Publius Syrus]; *est modus in rebus* [Horace]; "give me neither poverty nor riches" [*Bible*].

30. Compensation. — **N.** COMPENSATION, equation; commutation; indemnification; compromise &c. 774; neutralization, nullification; counteraction &c. 179; reaction; measure for measure; retaliation &c. 718; equalization &c. 27; redemption, recoupment.

SET-OFF, offset; makeweight, casting weight; counterpoise, ballast; indemnity, equivalent, *quid pro quo* [*L.*]; bribe, hush money; gift, donation &c. 784; amends &c. (*atonement*) 952; counterbalance, counterclaim, countervailing; cross debt, cross demand.

PAY, payment, reward &c. 973.

V. COMPENSATE, compense [*obs.*], make compensation, indemnify; counteract, countervail, counterpoise; balance; counterbalance, offset, outbalance, overbalance, set off; hedge, square, give and take; make up for, make leeway; cover, fill up, neutralize, nullify; equalize &c. 27; make good; recoup, redeem &c. (*atone*) 952; pay, reward &c. 973.

Adj. COMPENSATING, compensatory, compensative, amendatory, indemnificatory, reparative; countervailing &c. *v.*; in the opposite scale; equivalent &c. (*equal*) 27.

Adv. FOR A CONSIDERATION, in return, in consideration.

NOTWITHSTANDING, but, however, yet, still, nevertheless, natheless *or* nathless [*archaic*]; although, though; howbeit, albeit; mauger *or* maugre, at all events, in spite of, in despite of, despite, at any rate; be that as it may, for all that, even so, on the other hand, at the same time, *quoad minus* [*L.*], *quand même* [*F.*], however that may be; after all, after all is said and done; taking one thing with another &c. (*average*) 29.

*** robbing Peter to pay Paul; "light is mingled with the gloom" [Whittier]; *primo avulso non deficit alter* [Vergil]; *saepe creat molles aspera spina rosas* [Ovid].

QUANTITY BY COMPARISON WITH A STANDARD

31. Greatness. — N. GREATNESS &c. *adj.*; magnitude; size &c. (*dimensions*) 192; multitude &c. (*number*) 102; immensity, enormity, muchness; infinity &c. 105; might, strength, intensity, fullness.

GREAT QUANTITY, quantity, deal [*colloq.*], power [*colloq.*], sight [*colloq.*], pot [*colloq.*], volume, world; mass, heap &c. (*assemblage*) 72; stock &c. (*store*) 636; peck, bushel, load, cargo; cartload, wagonload, shipload; flood, spring tide; abundance &c. (*sufficiency*) 639.

principal part, chief part, main part, greater part, better part, major part, best part, essential part; bulk, mass &c. (*whole*) 50.

FAME, distinction, grandeur, dignity; importance &c. 642; generosity.

V. BE GREAT &c. *adj.*; run high, soar, tower, loom, tower above, rise above, transcend; rise to a great height, carry to a great height; bulk, bulk large; know no bounds; ascend, mount.

ENLARGE &c. (*increase*) 35, (*expand*) 194.

Adj. GREAT; greater &c. 33; large, considerable, fair, above par; big, bulky, huge &c. (*large in size*) 192; titanic, Atlantean, Herculean, cyclopean, voluminous; ample; abundant &c. (*enough*) 639; wholesale; many &c. 102; full, intense, strong, sound, passing [*archaic*], heavy, plenary, deep, high; signal, at its height, in the zenith.

WORLD-WIDE, widespread, far-famed, extensive.

GOODLY, noble, precious, mighty; sad, grave, serious; far gone, arrant, downright; uttermost; crass, gross, tall [*slang, U. S.*], mickle [*archaic*], arch, profound, intense, consummate; rank, unmitigated, red-hot desperate; glaring, flagrant, stark staring; thorough-paced, thoroughgoing; roaring, whacking [*colloq.*], magnitudinous [*rare*], thumping; extraordinary; important &c. 642; unsurpassed &c. (*supreme*) 33; complete &c. 52.

AUGUST, grand dignified, sublime, majestic &c. (*repute*) 873.

VAST, immense, enormous, extreme; inordinate, excessive, extravagant, exorbitant, outrageous, preposterous, unconscionable, swinging, monstrous, overgrown; towering, stupendous, prodigious,

32. Smallness. — N. SMALLNESS &c. *adj.*; littleness &c. (*small size*) 193; tenuity; paucity; fewness &c. (*small number*) 103; meanness, insignificance &c. (*unimportance*) 643; mediocrity, moderation.

SMALL QUANTITY, modicum, minimum; vanishing point; material point, atom, particle, electron, molecule, corpuscle, point, speck, dot, mote, jot, iota, ace; minutiæ, details; look, thought, idea, *soupçon* [*F.*], dab, dight [*dial.*], whit, tittle, shade, shadow; spark, scintilla, gleam; touch, cast; grain, scruple, granule, globule, minim, sup, sip, sop, spice, drop, droplet, sprinkling, dash, *morceau* [*F.*], screed [*Scot.*], smack, tinge, tincture; inch, patch, scantling, tatter, cantle, cantlet, flitter, gobbet, dole, mite, bit, morsel, crumb; scrap, shred, tag, splinter, rag; seed, fritter, shive; snip, snippet; snick, snack [*dial.*], snatch, slip; chip, chipping; shiver, sliver, driblet, clipping, paring, shaving, hair.

nutshell; thimbleful, spoonful, handful, capful, mouthful; fragment; fraction &c. (*part*) 51; drop in the ocean.

animalcule &c. 193.

TRIFLE &c. (*unimportant thing*) 643; mere nothing, next to nothing; hardly anything; just enough to swear by; the shadow of a shade.

FINITENESS, finite quantity.

V. BE SMALL &c. *adj.*; lie in a nutshell.

DIMINISH &c. (*decrease*) 36, (*contract*) 195.

Adj. SMALL, little; diminutive &c. (*small in size*) 193; minute, miniature, minikin; fine; inconsiderable, dribbling, paltry &c. (*unimportant*) 643; faint &c. (*weak*) 160; slender, light, slight, scanty, scant, limited; meager &c. (*insufficient*) 640; sparing; few &c. 103; low; soso *or* so-so *or* so so [*colloq.*], middling, tolerable, no great shakes [*slang*]; below par, under par, below the mark, under the mark; at a low ebb; halfway; moderate, modest; tender, subtle.

INAPPRECIABLE, evanescent, infinitesimal, homeopathic *or* homœopathic, very small; atomic, corpuscular, microscopic, molecular; skin-deep.

MERE, simple, sheer, stark, bare; near run.

astonishing, incredible, pronounced, fearful [*colloq.*], thundering [*slang*], terrible [*colloq.*], dreadful [*colloq.*], terrific [*colloq.*]; marvelous &c. (*wonder*) 870.

UNLIMITED &c. (*infinite*) 105; unapproachable, unutterable, indescribable, ineffable, unspeakable, inexpressible, beyond expression, fabulous.

UNDIMINISHED, unabated, unreduced, unrestricted.

ABSOLUTE, positive, stark, decided, unequivocal, essential, perfect, finished.

REMARKABLE, of mark, marked, pointed, veriest; notable, noticeable, noteworthy; renowned.

Adv. [IN A POSITIVE DEGREE] truly &c. (*truth*) 494; decidedly, unequivocally, purely, absolutely, seriously, essentially, fundamentally, radically, downright, in all conscience; for the most part, in the main.

[IN A COMPLETE DEGREE] entirely &c. (*completely*) 52; abundantly &c. (*sufficiently*) 639; widely, far and wide.

[IN A GREAT OR HIGH DEGREE] greatly &c. *adj.*; much, muckle [*archaic*], well, indeed, very, very much, a deal, no end of, most, not a little; pretty, pretty well; enough, in a great measure, no end [*colloq., U. S.*], passing, richly; to a large extent, to a great extent, to a gigantic extent; on a large scale; so; never so, ever so; ever so much; by wholesale, mighty [*colloq.*], mightily, powerfully; with a witness [*colloq.*], ultra, in the extreme, extremely, exceedingly, intensely, exquisitely, acutely, indefinitely, immeasurably; beyond compare, beyond comparison, beyond measure, beyond all bounds; out of sight [*colloq.*]; incalculably, infinitely.

[IN A SUPREME DEGREE] preëminently, superlatively &c. (*superiority*) 33.

DULL, petty, shallow, stolid, phlegmatic, unintelligent; Bœotian, ungifted &c. 499.

Adv. [IN A SMALL DEGREE] to a small extent, on a small scale; a little, a wee bit; slightly &c. *adj.*; imperceptibly; miserably, wretchedly; insufficiently &c. 640; imperfectly; faintly &c. 160; passably, pretty well, well enough.

[IN A CERTAIN OR LIMITED DEGREE] partially, in part; in a certain degree, to a certain degree; to a certain extent; comparatively; some, rather, middling [*colloq.*]; in some degree, in some measure; something, somewhat; simply, only, purely, merely; at least, at the least, at most, at the most; ever so little, as little as may be, *tant soit peu* [*F.*], in ever so small a degree; thus far, *pro tanto* [*L.*], within bounds, in a manner, after a fashion.

ALMOST, nearly, well-nigh, short of, not quite, all but; near upon, close upon; *peu s'en faut* [*F.*], near the mark; within an ace of, within an inch of; on the brink of; scarcely, hardly, barely, only just, no more than.

[IN AN UNCERTAIN DEGREE] about, thereabouts, somewhere about; nearly, say; be the same more or less, be the same little more or less.

[IN NO DEGREE] noway *or* noways, nowise, not at all, not in the least, not a bit, not a bit of it, not a whit, not a jot, not a shadow; in no wise, in no respect; by no means, by no manner of means; on no account, at no hand.

⁎⁎ *dare pondus idonea fumo* [Persius]; *magno conatu magnas nugas* [Terence]; "small sands the mountain, moments make the year" [Young].

[IN A TOO GREAT DEGREE] immoderately, monstrously, preposterously, inordinately, exorbitantly, excessively, enormously, out of all proportion, with a vengeance.

[IN A MARKED DEGREE] particularly, remarkably, singularly, curiously, uncommonly, unusually, peculiarly, notably, signally, strikingly, pointedly, mainly, chiefly; famously, egregiously, prominently, glaringly, emphatically, strangely, wonderfully, amazingly, surprisingly, astonishingly, incredibly, marvelously, awfully, stupendously.

[IN AN EXCEPTIONAL DEGREE] peculiarly &c. (*unconformity*) 83.

[IN A VIOLENT DEGREE] furiously &c. (*violence*) 173; severely, desperately, tremendously, extravagantly, confoundedly, deucedly [*slang*], devilishly [*colloq.*], with a vengeance, *à outrance* [*F.*], *à toute outrance* [*F.*].

[IN A PAINFUL DEGREE] painfully, sadly, grossly, sorely, bitterly, piteously, grievously, miserably, cruelly, woefully, lamentably, shockingly, frightfully;

dreadfully, fearfully, terribly, horribly, distressingly, balefully, dolorously.

₊ *a maximis ad minima;* "greatness knows itself" [*Henry IV*]; "mightiest powers by deepest calms are fed" [B. Cornwall]; *minimum decet libere cui multum licet* [Seneca]; "some are born great, some achieve greatness, and some have greatness thrust upon them" [*Twelfth Night*]; "with Atlantean shoulders, fit to bear" [Milton].

QUANTITY BY COMPARISON WITH A SIMILAR OBJECT

33. Superiority. [SUPREMACY.] — N. SUPERIORITY, majority, plurality; greatness &c. 31; advantage; pull [*slang*]; preponderance, preponderation; vantage ground, prevalence, partiality; personal superiority; scepter, sovereignty, sovranty [*poetic*]; nobility &c. (*rank*) 875; Triton among the minnows, *primus inter pares* [*L.*], *nulli secundus* [*L.*]; superman, overman; captain; crackajack [*slang, U. S.*].

SUPREMACY, supremeness, supremity [*rare*], primacy, paramountcy, preëminence; lead; maximum, record; crest, climax; culmination &c. (*summit*) 210; transcendence; *ne plus ultra* [*L.*]; lion's share, Benjamin's mess; excess, surplus &c. (*remainder*) 40; redundance &c. 641.

V. BE SUPERIOR &c. *adj.;* exceed, excel, transcend; outdo. outbalance, outweigh, outrank, outrival, out-Herod Herod; pass, surpass, get ahead of; overtop, override, overpass, overbalance, overweigh, overmatch; top, o'ertop, cap, beat, cut out [*colloq.*]; beat hollow [*colloq.*]; outstrip &c. 303; eclipse, throw into the shade, take the shine out of [*colloq.*], put one's nose out of joint [*colloq.*]; have the upper hand, have the whip hand of, have the advantage; turn the scale; play first fiddle &c. (*importance*) 642; preponderate, predominate, prevail; precede, take precedence, come first; come to a head, culminate; beat &c. all others, bear the palm; break the record; take the cake [*slang, U. S.*].

34. Inferiority. — N. INFERIORITY, minority, subordinacy [*obs.*], subordinance [*obs.*]; shortcoming, deficiency; minimum; smallness &c. 32; imperfection; subjacency [*rare*]; lower quality, lower worth; meanness, poorness, baseness, shabbiness.

[PERSONAL INFERIORITY] commonalty &c. 876; juniority, subordinacy; subaltern, sub [*colloq.*].

V. BE INFERIOR &c. *adj.;* fall short of, come short of; not pass, not come up to; want.

become smaller, render smaller &c. (*decrease*), 36, (*contract*) 195; hide its diminished head, retire into the shade, yield the palm, play second fiddle, take a back seat [*colloq.*], kick the beam.

Adj. INFERIOR, deterior [*rare*], smaller; small &c. 32; minor, less, lesser, deficient, minus, lower, subordinate, secondary, junior, humble; second-rate &c. (*imperfect*) 651; sub-, subaltern.

LEAST, smallest &c. (*see little, small* &c. 193); lowest.

DIMINISHED &c. (*decreased*) 36; reduced &c. (*contracted*) 195; unimportant &c. 643.

Adv. LESS; under the mark, below the mark, under par, below par; at the bottom of the scale, at a low ebb, at a disadvantage; short of, under.

₊ weighed in the balance and found wanting; not fit to hold a candle to; thrown into the shade.

become *or* render larger &c. (*increase*) 35, (*expand*) 194.

Adj. SUPERIOR, greater, major, higher; exceeding &c. *v.;* great &c. 31; distinguished, ultra; vaulting; more than a match for.

SUPREME, greatest, maximal, maximum, utmost, paramount, preëminent, foremost, crowning, hegemonic [*rare*]; first-rate &c. (*important*) 642, (*excellent*) 648; unrivaled; peerless, matchless; second to none, *sans pareil* [*F.*]; unparagoned, unparalleled, unequaled, unapproached, unsurpassed; superlative, inimitable, *facile princeps* [*L.*], incomparable, sovereign, without parallel, *nulli secundus* [*L.*], *ne plus ultra* [*L.*]; beyond compare, beyond comparison; culminating &c (*topmost*) 210; transcendent, transcendental; *plus royaliste que le Roi* [*F.*].

INCREASED &c. (*added to*) 35; enlarged &c. (*expanded*) 194.

Adv. BEYOND, more, over; over the mark, above the mark; above par; upwards of, in advance of; over and above; at the top of the scale, at its height.

[IN A SUPERIOR OR SUPREME DEGREE] eminently, egregiously, preëminently, surpassing, prominently, superlatively, supremely, above all, of all things, the most, to crown all, *par excellence* [F.], principally, especially, particularly, peculiarly, *a fortiori* [L.], even, yea, still more.

. "I shall not look upon his like again" [*Hamlet*]; *deos fortioribus adesse* [Tacitus]; "the doors of opportunity are marked 'push' and 'pull' " [*Cynic's Calendar*]; "Eclipse first and the rest nowhere" [*Annals of Sporting*]; "great men are the true men, the men in whom Nature has succeeded" [Amiel].

CHANGES IN QUANTITY

35. Increase. — N. INCREASE, augmentation, increasement [*rare*], addition, enlargement, extension; dilatation &c. (*expansion*) 194; increment, accretion; accession &c. 37; development, growth; aggrandizement, accumulation, reënforcement, redoubling, intensification, inflation, enhancement, aggravation; rise; ascent &c. 305; exaggeration, exacerbation; spread &c. (*dispersion*) 73; flood tide, spring tide.

GAIN, produce, product, profit, gettings [*archaic*], advantage, booty, plunder, superlucration [*rare*], clean-up [*U. S.*].

V. INCREASE, augment, add to, enlarge; dilate &c. (*expand*) 194; grow, wax, get ahead, gain strength; advance; run up, shoot up; rise; swell, mount, ascend &c. 305; sprout &c. 194.

AGGRANDIZE; raise, exalt; deepen, heighten, lengthen, greaten [*archaic*], thicken; eke [*archaic*], inflate; strengthen, intensify, enhance, magnify, redouble, double, triple, &c.; aggravate, exaggerate; exasperate, exacerbate; add fuel to the flame, *oleum addere camino* [L.]; superadd &c. (*add*) 37; spread &c. (*disperse*) 73.

Adj. INCREASED &c. *v.;* on the increase, undiminished; additional &c. (*added*) 37.

INCREASING, growing, crescent, crescive [*rare*], lengthening, multiplying, intensifying, intensive, intensitive [*rare*], incretionary [*rare*]; crescendo.

Adv. crescendo, increasingly.

. *vires acquirit eundo* [Vergil]; "they go from strength to strength" [*Bible*].

36. Nonincrease, Decrease. — N. DECREASE, diminution, decrescence, decrement, diminishment, lessening &c. *v.;* subtraction &c. 38, reduction, rebatement [*rare*], abatement, declension; shrinkage &c. (*contraction*) 195; coarctation [*obs.*]; curtailment, abridgment &c. (*shortening*) 201; extenuation.

SUBSIDENCE, wane, ebb, decline; ebb tide, neap tide, ebbing; descent &c. 306; reflux, depreciation, wear and tear, erosion, consumption; deterioration &c. 659; anticlimax; mitigation &c. (*moderation*) 174; catabasis [*med.*].

V. DECREASE, diminish, lessen; abridge &c. (*shorten*) 201; shrink &c. (*contract*) 195; drop off, fall off, tail off; fall away, waste, wear; wane, ebb, decline; descend &c. 306; subside; melt away, die away; retire into the shade, hide its diminished head, fall to a low ebb, run low, languish, decay, crumble, erode, consume away.

BATE, abate [*archaic*], dequantitate [*obs.*]; discount, belittle, minify [*rare*], minimize, minish [*rare*], depreciate; extenuate, lower, weaken, attenuate, fritter away; mitigate &c. (*moderate*) 174; dwarf, throw into the shade; reduce &c. 195; shorten &c. 201; subtract &c. 38; deliquesce, ease, remit [*rare*].

Adj. UNINCREASED &c. (*see* increase &c. 35); decreased, decreasing &c. *v.;* decrescent, reductive; deliquescent, contractive; decrescendo; on the wane &c. *n.*

Adv. decrescendo, decreasingly.

. "a gilded halo hovering round decay" [Byron]; "fine by degrees and beautifully less" [Prior].

3. Conjunctive Quantity

37. Addition. — N. ADDITION, annexation, adjection [*rare*], junction &c. 43; superposition, superaddition, superjunction, superfetation; accession, reënforcement; increase &c. 35; increment.

AFFIX, codicil, subscript, tag, rider, appendage, continuation, equation, postscript, adjunct, &c. 39; supplement; accompaniment &c. 88; interlineation, interposition &c. 228; insertion &c. 300.

COMPUTATION, footing, totaling, casting, summation.

V. ADD, annex, affix, superadd, subjoin, superpose; clap on, saddle on; tack to, append, tag, adject [*rare*], attach, postfix, adjoin [*rare*], ingraft; saddle with; sprinkle; introduce &c. (*interpose*) 228; insert &c. 300.

COMPUTE, foot up, total, cast, sum, count up.

BECOME ADDED, accrue; supervene, advene.

REËNFORCE or reinforce, restrengthen; strengthen, swell the ranks of; augment &c. 35.

Adj. ADDED &c. *v.*; additional; supplement, supplemental, supplementary; suppletive [*rare*], supervenient [*rare*], suppletory, subjunctive; adjectitious, adscititious, ascititious; additive, extra, further, fresh, more, new, ulterior, other, remanent [*rare*]; auxiliary, contributory, accessory; spare.

38. Nonaddition. Deduction. — N. DEDUCTION, subtraction, subduction; retrenchment; removal; sublation [*rare*], ablation; abstraction &c. (*taking*) 789; garbling &c. *v.*; mutilation, detruncation; amputation; recision, abscision, excision; abrasion; curtailment &c. 201.

REBATE &c. (*decrement*) 40a; minuend, subtrahend; decrease &c. 36.

V. SUBDUCT, subtract, deduct, deduce; bate, retrench; remove, withdraw; take from, take away; detract; garble.

MUTILATE, amputate, detruncate; cut off, cut away, cut out; abscind, excise.

PARE, thin, prune, decimate, eliminate, rebate; bant [*colloq.*], reduce; abrade, scrape, file.

GELD, castrate, envirate [*rare*], cut, spay (*female*), capon or caponize (*a cock*), eunuchize [*rare*], unman, emasculate.

DIMINISH &c. 36; curtail &c. (*shorten*) 201; deprive of &c. (*take*) 789; weaken.

Adj. SUBTRACTED &c. *v.*; subtractive.

TAILLESS, acaudal, acaudate.

Adv. IN DEDUCTION &c. *n.*; less; short of; minus, without, except, excepting, with the exception of, barring, bar, save, exclusive of, save and except, with a reservation, ablatitious [*rare*].

Adv. *au reste* [*F.*]; in addition, more, plus, extra; and, also, likewise, too, furthermore, further, item; and also, and eke [*archaic*]; else, besides, to boot; et cætera, &c.; and so on, and so forth; into the bargain, *cum multis aliis* [*L.*], over and above, moreover.

with, withal; including, inclusive, as well as, not to mention, let alone; together with, along with, coupled with, in conjunction with; conjointly; jointly &c. 43.

₊ *adde parvum parvo magnus acervus erit.*

39. [THING ADDED.] Adjunct. — N. ADJUNCT; addition, additament; *additum* [*L.*], affix, appendage, annex or annexe; augment, augmentation; increment, reënforcement, supernumerary, accessory, item; garnish, sauce; accompaniment &c. 88; adjective, addendum (*pl.* addenda); complement, supplement; continuation.

rider, offshoot, episode, side issue, corollary, codicil &c. (*addition*) 37.

FLAP, lug, lapel, apron, tab, fly, tuck, lap, piece, lappet, skirt, embroidery,

40. [THING REMAINING.] Remainder. — N. REMAINDER, residue; remains, remanet [*rare*], relict [*rare*], remanence [*rare*], remnant, rest, relic; leavings, heeltap, odds and ends, cheeseparings, candle ends, orts; residuum; dregs &c. (*dirt*) 653; refuse &c. (*useless*) 645; stubble, result, educt; fag-end; ruins, wreck, skeleton, stump, rump; alluvium.

SURPLUS, overplus, excess; balance [*commercial slang*], complement; superplus [*obs.* or *Scot.*], surplusage; superfluity &c. (*redundance*) 641; survival,

trappings, cortege or cortège [F.]; tail, suffix &c. (sequel) 65; wing.

V. ADD, annex &c. 37.

Adj. ADDITIONAL &c. 37.

WINGED, alate or alated.

Adv. in addition &c. 37.

survivance [rare]; fossil, shadow, caput mortuum [L.].

V. REMAIN; be left &c. adj.; exceed, survive; leave.

Adj. REMAINING, left; left behind, left over; residual, residuary; over, odd; unconsumed, sedimentary; surviving; net; exceeding, over and above; outlying, outstanding; cast off &c. 782; superfluous &c. (redundant) 641.

₊ "it is strange that men should see sublime inspiration in the ruins of an old church and see none in the ruins of a man" [Chesterton].

40a. [THING DEDUCTED.] **Decrement.** — **N.** DECREMENT, discount, rebate, rebatement, tare, offtake, drawback, draft, reprise; defect, loss, deduction; afterglow; eduction; waste.

41. [FORMING A WHOLE WITHOUT COHERENCE.] **Mixture.** — **N.** MIXTURE, admixture, mixtion [obs.], admixtion, commixture, commixtion or commixion [obs.], intermixture, immixture, minglement, eucrasy [med.], interfusion, intertanglement, interlacement, interlacery, intertexture, levigation, alloyage; matrimony; junction &c. 43; combination &c. 48; miscegenation.

IMPREGNATION; infusion, diffusion, suffusion, transfusion; infiltration; seasoning, sprinkling, interlarding; interpolation &c. 228; adulteration, sophistication.

[THING MIXED] tinge, tincture, touch, dash, smack, sprinkling, spice, seasoning, infusion, soupçon [F.].

[COMPOUND RESULTING FROM MIXTURE] alloy, amalgam; brass, chowchow, pewter; magma, half-and-half, mélange

42. [FREEDOM FROM MIXTURE.] **Simpleness.** — **N.** SIMPLENESS &c. adj.; purity, homogeneity.

ELIMINATION; sifting &c. v.; purification &c. (cleanness) 652.

V. RENDER SIMPLE &c. adj.; simplify.

SIFT, winnow, bolt, eliminate; exclude, get rid of; clear; purify &c. (clean) 652; disentangle &c. (disjoin, 44).

Adj. SIMPLE, uniform, of a piece, homogeneous, Attic, homespun, single, pure, clear, sheer, neat.

UNMIXED, unmingled, unblended, uncombined, uncompounded; elemental, elementary, undecomposed; unadulterated, unsophisticated, unalloyed, untinged, unfortified; pur et simple [F.]; incomplex, incomposite [rare].

free from, exempt from; exclusive.

Adv. SIMPLY &c. adj.; only.

[F.], tertium quid [L.], miscellany, ambigu [obs.], medley, mess, hash, hodgepodge, hotchpotch, hotchpot, pasticcio [It.], patchwork, odds and ends, all sorts; jumble &c. (disorder) 59; salad, sauce, mash, omnium-gatherum [colloq.], gallimaufry, olla-podrida, olio, salmagundi, potpourri, Noah's ark; texture; mingled yarn; mosaic &c. (variegation) 440.

HALF-BLOOD, half-breed, half-caste; mulatto; quarteron or quarteroon [rare], quintroon or quinteron, quadroon, octoroon, sambo or zambo; cafuzo; Eurasian; fustee or fustie [W. Ind.], mestee [W. Ind.], mestizo (fem. mestiza), griffe, ladino, marabou, sacatra [U.S.]; zebrule; catalo; mule; cross, hybrid, mongrel; cross-breed &c. (unconformity) 83.

V. MIX; join &c. 43; combine &c. 48; commix, immix, intermix; levigate, mix up with, mingle; commingle, intermingle, bemingle; shuffle &c. (derange) 61; pound together; hash up, stir up; knead, brew; impregnate with; interlard &c. (interpolate) 228; intertwine, interweave &c. 219; associate with; miscegenate.

BE MIXED &c.; get among, be entangled with.

IMBUE; infuse, suffuse, transfuse, instill or instil, infiltrate, dash, tinge, tincture, season, sprinkle, besprinkle, attemper, medicate, blend, cross; alloy, amalgamate, compound, adulterate, sophisticate, infect.

Adj. MIXED &c. v.; implex [rare], composite, half-and-half, linsey-woolsey, medley, chowchow, hybrid, mongrel, heterogeneous; motley &c. (*variegated*) 440; miscellaneous, promiscuous, indiscriminate; miscible.

Adv. AMONG, amongst, amid, amidst; with; in the midst of, in the crowd.

43. Junction. — N. JUNCTION; joining &c. *v.*; joinder, union; connection; conjunction, conjugation; annexion, annexation, annexment [*rare*]; astriction, attachment, compagination [*rare*], subjunction, vincture [*obs.*], ligation, alligation; accouplement; marriage &c. (*wedlock*) 903; infibulation, inosculation, symphysis, anastomosis, confluence, communication, concatenation; meeting, reunion; assemblage &c. 72.

COITION, copulation; sexual congress, sexual conjunction, sexual intercourse.

JOINT, joining, juncture, chiasm, osculature, pivot, hinge, articulation, commissure, seam, gore, gusset, suture, stitch; link &c. 45; miter, mortise.

CONTINGENCY, emergency, predicament, crisis, concurrence.

CLOSENESS, tightness &c. *adj.*; coherence &c. 46; combination &c. 48.

annexationist.

V. JOIN, unite; conjoin, connect; associate; put together, lay together, clap together, hang together, lump together, hold together, piece together, tack together, fix together, bind up together; embody, reëmbody; roll into one.

ATTACH, fix, affix, immobilize [*rare*], saddle on, fasten, bind, secure, clinch, twist, make fast &c. *adj.*; tie, pinion, string, strap, sew, lace, stitch, tack, knit, button, buckle, hitch, lash, truss, bandage, braid, splice, swathe, gird, tether, moor, picket, harness, chain; fetter &c. (*restrain*) 751; lock, latch, belay, brace, hook, grapple, leash, couple, accouple, link, yoke, bracket; marry &c. (*wed*) 903; bridge over, span.

pin, nail, bolt, hasp, clasp, clamp, screw, rivet; impact, solder, braze; cement, set; weld together, fuse together; tighten, trice up, screw up; wedge, rabbet, mortise, miter, jam, dovetail, enchase; graft, ingraft, inosculate.

ENTWINE *or* intwine; interlink, interlace, intertwine, intertwist, interweave; entangle; twine round, belay.

BE JOINED &c.; hang together, hold together; cohere &c. 46.

Adj. JOINED &c. *v.*; joint; conjoint, conjunct; corporate, compact; hand in hand.

44. Disjunction. — N. DISJUNCTION, disconnection, disunity, disunion, disassociation, disengagement, dissociation, disjointure; discontinuity &c. 70; abjunction [*obs.*]; cataclasm; inconnection [*obs.*]; abstraction, abstractedness; isolation; insularity, insulation; oasis; island; separateness &c. *adj.*; severalty; *disjecta membra* [*L.*]; dispersion &c. 73; apportionment &c. 786.

SEPARATION; parting &c. *v.*; circumcision, detachment, segregation; divorce, sejunction [*obs.*], seposition [*obs.*], diduction [*rare*], diremption [*rare*], discerption; elision; cæsura, division, subdivision, break, fracture, rupture; compartition [*obs.*]; dismemberment, disintegration, dislocation; luxation; severance, disseverance; scission; rescission, abscission; laceration, dilaceration; disruption, abruption; avulsion, divulsion; section, resection, cleavage; fission; partibility, separability, separatism.

FISSURE, breach, rent, split, rift, crack, slit, incision.

DISSECTION, anatomy; decomposition &c. 49; cutting instrument &c. (*sharpness*) 253; buzz saw, circular saw.

separatist.

V. BE DISJOINED &c.; come off, come to pieces, fall off, fall to pieces; peel off; get loose.

DISJOIN, disconnect, disengage, disunite, dissociate, dispair [*obs.*]; divorce, part, dispart, detach, separate, cut off, rescind, segregate; set apart, keep apart; insulate, isolate; throw out of gear; cut adrift; loose; unloose, undo, unbind, unchain, unlock &c. (*fix*) 43, unpack, unravel; disentangle; set free &c. (*liberate*) 750.

SUNDER, divide, subdivide, sever, section, sectionize [*rare*], segment, dissever, abscind; circumcise; cut; incide [*obs.*], incise; saw, snip, nib [*obs.*], nip, cleave, rive, rend, slit, split, splinter, chip, crack, snap, break, tear, burst; rend &c., asunder, rend in twain; wrench, rupture, shatter, shiver, crunch, craunch *or* cranch, chop; cut up, rip up; hack, hew, slash; whittle; haggle, hackle, discind [*obs.*], lacerate, scamble [*obs.*], mangle, gash, hash, slice; cut up, carve,

FIRM, fast, close, tight, taut *or* taught, secure, set, intervolved [*obs.*]; inseparable, indissoluble, insecable [*obs.*], inseverable.

Adv. JOINTLY &c. *adj.;* in conjunction with &c. (*in addition to*) 37; fast, firmly, &c. *adj.;* intimately.

** *tria juncta in uno;* "in every union there is a mystery — a certain invisible bond which must not be disturbed" [Amiel].

quarter, dissect, anatomize; dislimb; take to pieces, pull to pieces, pick to pieces, tear to pieces; tear to tatters, tear piecemeal; divellicate; skin &c. 226.

DISINTEGRATE, dismember, disbranch, disband; disperse &c. 73; dislocate, disjoint; break up; mince; comminute &c. (*pulverize*) 330; apportion &c. 786.

PARTITION, parcel, demarcate [*rare*], graduate, district, chapter, canton.

PART, part company; separate, leave; alienate, estrange.

Adj. DISJOINED &c. *v.;* discontinuous &c. 70; bipartite, biparted [*rare*], multipartite, abstract; disjunctive; secant; isolated &c. *v.;* insular, separate, disparate, discrete, apart, asunder, far between, loose, free; lobate, lobulate, lobulated, lobulose, digitate; unattached, unannexed, unassociated, unconnected; distinct; adrift; straggling; rift [*obs.*], reft, cleft.

[CAPABLE OF BEING CUT] scissile, divisible, discerptible [*rare*], partible, separable, severable, dividuous [*rare*].

Adv. SEPARATELY &c. *adj.;* one by one, severally, apart; adrift, asunder, in twain; in the abstract, abstractedly.

** "separatism . . . is the abstraction of a negation, the shadow of a shadow" [Amiel].

45. [CONNECTING MEDIUM.] **Vinculum. — N.** VINCULUM, link; connective, connection; junction &c. 43; bond of union, copula, intermedium, hyphen; bracket; bridge, stepping-stone, isthmus.

bond, tendon, tendril; fiber; cord, cordage; ribband, ribbon, rope, guy, cable, line, halser [*obs.*], hawser, painter, moorings, wire, chain; string &c. (*filament*) 205.

FASTENING, tie; ligament, ligature; strap; tackle, rigging; standing rigging; running rigging; traces, harness; yoke; band, bandage; brace, roller, fillet; inkle; with, withe, withy; thong, braid; girder, tiebeam; girth, girdle, cestus, garter, halter, noose, lasso, surcingle, knot, running knot; *cabestro* [*Sp. Amer.*], cinch [*U. S.*], lariat, *legadero* [*Sp. Amer.*], oxreim [*S. Africa*]; suspenders.

PIN, corking pin, nail, brad, tack, skewer, staple, clamp; cramp, cramp iron, detent, *larigo* [*Sp. Amer.*], pawl, terret, screw, button, buckle, clasp, hasp, bar, hinge, hank, catch, latch, bolt, latchet, tag; tooth; hook, hook and eye; lock, holdfast, padlock, rivet, couple, coupler, ring; anchor, grappling iron, treenail *or* trennel, stake, post; prop &c. (*support*) 215.

CEMENT, glue, gum, paste, size, wafer, solder, lute, putty, birdlime, mortar, stucco, plaster, grout; viscum.

SHACKLE, rein &c. (*means of restraint*) 752.

V. BRIDGE OVER, span; connect &c. 43; hang &c. 214.

46. Coherence. — N. COHERENCE, cohesion, cohesiveness, adherence, adhesion, adhesiveness; concretion, accretion; conglutination, conglomeration, agglutination, agglomeration; aggregation; consolidation, set, cementation; sticking, soldering &c. *v.;* connection; dependence.

TENACITY, toughness; stickiness &c. 352; inseparability, inseparableness; bur *or* burr, remora.

CONGLOMERATE, concrete &c. (*density*) 321.

V. COHERE, adhere, coagulate, stick, cling, cleave, hold, take hold of, hold

47. [NONADHESION, IMMISCIBILITY.] **Incoherence. — N.** INCOHERENCE, nonadhesion; immiscibility; looseness &c. *adj.;* laxity; relaxation; loosening &c. *v.;* freedom; disjunction &c. 44; rope of sand.

V. MAKE LOOSE &c. *adj.;* loosen, slacken, relax; unglue &c. 46; detach &c. (*disjoin*) 44.

Adj. NONADHESIVE, immiscible; incoherent, detached, loose, baggy, slack, lax, relaxed, flapping, streaming; disheveled; segregated, like grains of sand; unconsolidated &c. 231; uncombined &c. 48; noncohesive.

fast, close with, clasp, hug; grow together, hang together; twine round &c. (*join*) 43.

stick like a leech, stick like wax, stick like the paper on the wall; stick closer than a brother; stick close; cling like ivy, cling like a bur; adhere like a remora, adhere like Dejanira's shirt.

glue; agglutinate, conglutinate; cement, lute, belute [*rare*], paste, gum; solder; weld; ferruminate [*archaic*]; cake, consolidate &c. (*solidify*) 321; agglomerate.

Adj. ADHESIVE, cohesive, adhering, cohering &c. *v.*; tenacious, tough; sticky &c. 352.

united, unseparated, sessile, inseparable, inextricable, infrangible; compact &c. (*dense*) 321.

∗ "Closer is He than breathing, Nearer than hands or feet" [Tennyson].

48. Combination. — N. COMBINATION; mixture &c. 41; junction &c. 43; union, unification, synthesis, synizesis, synæresis *or* syneresis, incorporation, amalgamation, embodiment, coalescence, crasis, fusion, coalescing, blend, blendure [*rare*], blending, absorption, centralization.

ALLOY, compound, amalgam, composition, *tertium quid* [*L.*]; resultant, impregnation.

V. COMBINE, unite, incorporate, inosculate, consubstantiate, alloy, intermix, interfuse, interlard, syncretize, interlace, agglutinate, amalgamate, embody, absorb, reëmbody, blend, merge, fuse, melt into one, consolidate, coalesce, solidify, commix [*archaic*], contemper, centralize, impregnate; put together, lump together.

LEAGUE, interleague [*rare*], federate, confederate, fraternize, club, associate, amalgamate, cement a union, marry, couple, pair, ally.

Adj. COMBINED &c. *v.*; wedded; indiscrete, conjunctive, conjugate, conjoint; inoculated.

ALLIED, amalgamated, federate, confederate, corporate, leagued.

∗ "and our spirits rushed together at the touching of the lips" [Tennyson].

49. Decomposition. — N. DECOMPOSITION, analysis, diæresis *or* dieresis, dissection, resolution, catalysis, dissolution, break-up; dispersion &c. 73; disjunction &c. 44; disintegration.

DECAY, rot, putrefaction, putrescence, putridity, caries; corruption &c. (*uncleanness*) 653.

ELECTROLYSIS, electrolyzation, hydrolysis, proteolysis, thermolysis, catalysis.

V. DECOMPOSE, decompound [*rare*]; analyze, disembody, dissolve; resolve into its elements, separate into its elements; dissect, decentralize, break up; disintegrate, disperse &c. 73; unravel &c. (*unroll*) 313; crumble into dust.

CORRUPT [*archaic*], rot, decay, consume; putrefy, putresce.

ELECTROLYZE, hydrolyze, thermolyze, catalyze.

Adj. DECOMPOSED &c. *v.*; catalytic, analytical; resolvent, separative, solvent.

impregnated with, ingrained; imbued,

4. CONCRETE QUANTITY

50. Whole. [PRINCIPAL PART.] — N. WHOLE, totality, integrity; totalness &c. *adj.*; entirety, entire [*rare*], ensemble [*F.*], collectiveness; unity &c. 87; completeness &c. 52; indivisibility, indiscerptibility; integration, embodiment; integer, integral.

ALL, general [*archaic*], the whole, total, aggregate, one and all, gross amount, sum, sum total, the altogether [*humorous*], *tout ensemble* [*F.*], length and breadth of, Alpha and Omega, "be all

51. Part. — N. PART, portion; dose, item, particular; aught, any; division; ward, parcel [*law or archaic*], count; sector, segment; fraction, fragment; cantle, cantlet; frustum [*rare*]; detachment, subdivision.

section, chapter, verse; article, clause, phrase, paragraph, passage, number, book, fascicle, fascicule *or* fasciculus, *livraison* [*F.*].

PIECE, lump, bit, snatch; cut, cutting; chip, chunk, collop, slice, scrap, crumb,

and end all"; complex, *complexus* [*L.*]; lock, stock, and barrel.

BULK, mass, lump, tissue, staple, body, compages; trunk, torso, bole, hull, hulk, skeleton; greater part, major part, best part, principal part, main part; essential part &c. (*importance*) 642; lion's share, Benjamin's mess; the long and the short; nearly all, almost all.

V. FORM A WHOLE, constitute a whole; integrate, embody, amass; aggregate &c. (*assemble*) 72; amount to, come to.

Adj. WHOLE, total, integral [*rare*], integrate [*rare*], entire; complete &c. 52; one, individual.

UNBROKEN, uncut, undivided, unsevered, unclipped, uncropped, unshorn; seamless; undiminished; undemolished, undissolved, undestroyed, unbruised.

INDIVISIBLE, indissoluble, indissolvable, indiscerptible.

WHOLESALE, sweeping; comprehensive.

Adv. WHOLLY, altogether; as a whole, one and indivisible; totally &c. (*completely*) 52; entirely, all, all in all, wholesale, in a body, collectively, all put together; in the aggregate, in the lump, in the mass, in the gross, in the main, in the long run; *en masse* [*F.*], on the whole, bodily, *en bloc* [*F.*], *in extenso* [*L.*], throughout, every inch; substantially.

⁂ *tout bien ou rien*: "I am the Vine, ye are the branches" [*Bible*].

52. Completeness. — N. COMPLETENESS &c. *adj.*; completion &c. 729; integration; allness [*rare*], totality, integralness, totalness, integrality [*rare*], integrity.

ENTIRETY; perfection &c. 650; solidity, solidarity; unity; all; *ne plus ultra* [*L.*], ideal, limit; undividedness, intactness, universality.

COMPLEMENT, supplement, makeweight; filling up &c. *v.*

FILL; impletion; saturation, saturity [*obs.*]; high water; high tide, flood tide, springtide; load, bumper, bellyful; brimmer; sufficiency &c. 639.

V. BE COMPLETE &c. *adj.*; come to a head.

RENDER COMPLETE &c. *adj.*; complete &c. (*accomplish*) 729; fill, charge, load, stevedore, replenish; make up, make good; piece out, eke out; supply deficien-

scale; lamina &c. 204; small part; morsel, moiety, particle &c. (*smallness*) 32; installment, dividend; share &c. (*allotment*) 786.

ODDMENTS, *débris* [*F.*], odds and ends, detritus; *excerpta* [*L.*], excerpt.

MEMBER, limb, lobe, lobule, arm, wing, scion, branch, bough, joint, link, offshoot, ramification, twig, bush, spray, sprig; runner, tendril; leaf, leaflet; stump; component part &c. 56; sarmentum.

CUE, rôle, cast; lines, pageant [*archaic*].

COMPARTMENT; department &c. (*class*) 75; county &c. (*region*) 181.

V. PART, divide, break &c. (*disjoin*) 44; partition &c. (*apportion*) 786.

Adj. FRACTIONAL, fragmentary, portional [*rare*]; sectional, aliquot; divided &c. *v.*; in compartments, multifid; disconnected; incomplete, partial.

DIVIDED, broken, cut, severed, clipped, cropped, shorn; seamed.

DIVISIBLE, dissoluble, dissolvable, discerptible.

Adv. PARTLY, in part, partially; piecemeal, part by part; by installments, by snatches, by inches, by driblets; bit by bit, inch by inch, foot by foot, drop by drop; in detail, in lots.

⁂ "a snapper-up of unconsidered trifles" [*Winter's Tale*].

53. Incompleteness. — N. INCOMPLETENESS &c. *adj.*; deficience [*rare*], deficiency, short weight, short measure; shortcoming &c. 304; want, lack, insufficiency &c. 640; imperfection &c. 651; immaturity &c. (*nonpreparation*) 674; half measures.

[PART WANTING] defect, deficit, defalcation, omission; caret; wantage [*rare*], ullage, shortage; interval &c. 198; break &c. (*discontinuity*) 70; noncompletion &c. 730; missing link.

V. BE INCOMPLETE &c. *adj.*; fall short of &c. 304; lack &c. (*be insufficient*) 640; neglect &c. 460.

Adj. INCOMPLETE; imperfect &c. 651; unfinished; uncompleted &c. (*see complete* &c. 729); defective, deficient, wanting, failing; bobtailed; in default, in arrear; short, short of; hollow, meager, jejune, poor, scarce, lame, half-and-half,

cies; fill up, fill in, fill to the brim, fill the measure of; satiate; saturate.

go the whole hog [colloq.], go the whole length; go all lengths; go the limit [colloq.].

Adj. COMPLETE, entire; whole &c. 50; perfect &c. 650; full, good, absolute, thorough, plenary; solid, undivided; with all its parts; all-sided.

EXHAUSTIVE, radical, sweeping, thorough-going; dead.

REGULAR, consummate, unmitigated, sheer, unqualified, unconditional, free; abundant &c. (sufficient) 639.

BRIMMING; brimful, topful; chock-full, choke-full; as full as an egg is of meat, as full as a vetch; saturated, crammed; replete &c. (redundant) 641; fraught, laden; full-laden, full-fraught, full-charged; heavy laden.

COMPLETING &c. v.; supplemental, supplementary; ascititious.

Adv. COMPLETELY &c. adj.; altogether, outright, wholly, totally, in toto [L.], quite; all out; over head and ears; effectually, for good and all, nicely, fully; through thick and thin, head and shoulders, out of sight [slang, U. S.]; neck and heel, neck and crop; in all respects, in every respect; at all points, out and out, to all intents and purposes; toto cœlo [L.]; utterly; clean, clean as a whistle; to the full, to the utmost, to the limit, to the backbone; hollow, stark; heart and soul, root and branch, down to the ground.

to the top of one's bent, as far as possible, à outrance [F.].

THROUGHOUT; from first to last, from beginning to end, from end to end, from one end to the other, from Dan to Beersheba, from head to foot, from top to toe, from top to bottom; de fond en comble [F.]; à fond [F.]; a capite ad calcem [L.]; ab ovo usque ad mala [L.]; fore and aft; every whit, every inch; cap-à-pie [F.], to the end of the chapter; up to the brim, up to the ears, up to the eyes; as . . . as can be.

on all accounts; sous tous les rapports [F.]; with a vengeance, with a witness [colloq.].

⁎ falsus in uno falsus in omnibus; omnem movere lapidem; una scopa nuova spazza bene.

perfunctory, sketchy; crude &c. (unprepared) 674.

MUTILATED, garbled, hashed, mangled, butchered, docked, lopped, truncated.

IN PROGRESS, in hand; going on; proceeding.

Adv. INCOMPLETELY &c. adj.; by halves.

⁎ cætera desunt; caret; "And I smiled to think God's greatness Flowed around our incompleteness" [E. B. Browning].

---

54. Composition. — N. COMPOSITION, constitution; crasis, synizesis, synæresis or syneresis; confection [rare], synthesis, compaction [rare], make, make-up; combination &c. 48; inclusion, admission, comprehension, reception; embodiment; formation.

AUTHORSHIP, compilation, composition, recueil [F.], production, inditing or inditement, conflation, invention; writing &c. 590.

HYMNODY, hymnology, instrumentation; opus, aria &c. (music) 415.

PAINTING, scenography, etching, design &c. (painting) 556; relief, relievo &c. (sculpture) 557.

TYPESETTING, typography &c. (printing) 591.

V. BE COMPOSED OF, be made of, be formed of, be made up of; consist of, be resolved into.

INCLUDE &c. (in a class) 76; contain,

55. Exclusion. — N. EXCLUSION, nonadmission, omission, exception, rejection, repudiation; exile &c. (seclusion) 893; noninclusion, preclusion, debarrance [rare], debarment, lock-out, disfellowship [rare], ostracism, prohibition.

SEPARATION, segregation, seposition [obs.], elimination, expulsion; cofferdam.

V. be excluded from &c.

EXCLUDE, bar; leave out, shut out, bar out; reject, repudiate, blackball, ostracize; lay apart, lay aside, put apart, put aside, set apart, set aside; relegate, segregate; throw overboard; strike off, strike out; neglect &c. 460; banish &c. (seclude) 893; separate &c. (disjoin) 44.

pass over, omit; garble; eliminate, weed, winnow.

Adj. EXCLUDING &c. v.; exclusive, exclusory; excluded &c. v.; unrecounted, not included in; inadmissible, preclusive, preventive, prohibitive.

hold, comprehend take in, admit, embrace, embody; involve, implicate; drag into; synthesize.

COMPOSE, constitute, form, make; make up, fill up, build up; fabricate, weave, construct; compile, redact, collate, dash off, address, indite, score, scribble, draw, write; set (*in printing*); enter into the composition of &c. (*be a component*) 56.

Adj. containing, constituting &c. *v.*

Adv. exclusive of, barring; except; with the exception of; save; bating.

56. Component. — N.

COMPONENT, integrant; component part, integral part, integrant part; element, constituent, ingredient, leaven; part and parcel; contents; appurtenance; feature; member &c. (*part*) 51; personnel.

V. ENTER INTO, enter into the composition of; be a component &c. *n.*; be *or* form part of &c. 51; merge in, be merged in; be implicated in; share in &c. (*participate*) 778; belong to, appertain to; combine, inhere in, unite.

FORM, make, constitute, compose, precompose, recompose; sonnetize [*rare*]; fabricate &c. 54.

Adj. FORMING &c. *v.*; inherent, intrinsic, essential.

INCLUSIVE, all-embracing, compendious, comprehensive, inclusory.

57. Extraneousness. — N.

EXTRANEOUSNESS &c. *adj.*; extrinsicality &c. 6; exteriority &c. 220; alienage, alienism.

foreign body, foreign substance, foreign element.

ALIEN, stranger, intruder, interloper, foreigner, *novus homo* [L.], newcomer, new chum [*colloq., Australia*], jackaroo [*Australia*], griffin [*Anglo-Ind.*]; recruit, immigrant, emigrant; creole, Africander; outsider, outlander [*archaic*], barbarian, extern [*rare*], tramontane [*rare*], ultramontane; Guinea [*slang, U. S.*], Wop [*slang, U. S.*], Dago [*slang*], Chink [*slang*], kike [*slang*], sheeny [*slang*], mick [*slang*], nigger [*colloq.*], Easterner [*U. S.*], Dutchman, tenderfoot [*slang*].

Adj. EXTRANEOUS, foreign, alien, ulterior, exterior, external, outlandish, outside, outland [*archaic*]; barbaric, barbarian, metic, oversea, tramontane [*rare*], ultramontane.

EXCLUDED &c. 55; inadmissible; exceptional.

Adv. ABROAD, in foreign parts, in foreign lands; beyond seas; oversea, overseas; on one's travels.

SECTION IV. ORDER

1. ORDER IN GENERAL

58. Order. — N.

ORDER, regularity, uniformity, symmetry, *lucidus ordo* [L.]; harmony, music of the spheres.

GRADATION, progression; series &c. (*continuity*) 69.

COURSE, even tenor, routine; method, disposition, arrangement, array, system, economy, discipline; orderliness &c. *adj.*; subordination.

RANK, place &c. (*term*) 71.

V. FORM; be *or* become in order &c. *adj.*; fall in, draw up; arrange itself, range itself, place itself; fall into one's place, fall into rank, take one's place, take rank; rally round.

ADJUST, methodize, regulate, systematize, standardize, normalize; time, police.

Adj. ORDERLY, regular; in order, in

59. [ABSENCE OR WANT OF ORDER, &c.] Disorder. — N.

DISORDER; derangement &c. 61; irregularity; deray [*archaic*], deordination [*rare*]; anomaly &c. (*unconformity*) 83; anarchy, anarchism; want of method; untidiness &c. *adj.*; disunion; discord &c. 24.

CONFUSION; confusedness &c. *adj.*; mishmash, mix; disarray, jumble, topsyturvy, botch, huddle, litter, lumber; *cahotage* [*F.*]; farrago; mess, mash, muddle, muss [*colloq., U. S.*], hash, hodgepodge, hotchpotch, hotchpot; what the cat brought in [*colloq., U. S.*]; imbroglio, chaos, omnium-gatherum [*colloq.*], medley; mere mixture &c. 41; fortuitous concourse of atoms, *disjecta membra* [L.], *rudis indigestaque moles* [Ovid].

trim, in apple-pie order, in its proper place; neat, tidy, *en règle* [*F.*], well regulated, correct, methodical, uniform, symmetrical, shipshape, businesslike, systematic, systematical, normal, habitual; unconfused &c. (*see* confuse &c. 61); arranged &c. 60.

Adv. IN ORDER; methodically &c. *adj.;* in turn, in its turn; step by step; by regular steps, by regular gradations, by regular stages, by regular intervals; *seriatim* [*NL.*], systematically, by clockwork, gradatim; at stated periods &c. (*periodically*) 138.

** natura non facit saltum; "order is heaven's first law" [Pope]; "order from disorder sprung" [*Paradise Lost*]; *ordo est parium dispariumque rerum sua loca tribuens dispositio* [St. Augustine].

COMPLEXITY; complexness &c. *adj.;* complexus, complication, implication; intricacy, intrication [*rare*]; perplexity; network, maze, labyrinth; wilderness, jungle; involution, raveling, entanglement, dishevelment; coil &c. (*convolution*) 248; sleave, tangled skein, knot, Gordian knot, wheels within wheels; kink, gnarl *or* knarl [*obs.*]; webwork.

TURMOIL; ferment &c. (*agitation*) 315; to-do [*colloq.*], trouble, pudder [*obs. or dial.*], pother, row [*colloq.*], disturbance, convulsion, tumult, uproar, riot, rumpus [*colloq.*], stour [*archaic*], scramble, fracas, embroilment, *mêlée* [*F.*], spill and pelt, rough and tumble; whirlwind &c. 349; bear garden, pandemonium, Babel, Saturnalia, Donnybrook Fair, confusion worse confounded, most admired disorder, *concordia discors* [*L.*]; Bedlam broke loose, hell broke loose; bull in a china shop; all the fat in the fire, *diable à quatre* [*F.*], Devil to pay; pretty kettle of fish; pretty piece of work, pretty piece of business.

SLATTERN, slut, drab, dowdy, trollop, sloven, draggle-tail [*colloq.*].

V. BE DISORDERLY &c. *adj.;* ferment, play at cross-purposes.

PUT OUT OF ORDER; botch, derange &c. 61; drag from under the bed [*colloq., U. S.*]; ravel &c. 219; ruffle, rumple.

Adj. DISORDERLY, orderless; out of order, out of place, out of gear, out of kilter [*colloq.*]; irregular, desultory; anomalous &c. (*unconformable*) 83; acephalous; aimless; disorganized; straggling; unmethodical, immethodical; unsymmetric, unsystematic; untidy, slovenly, messy [*colloq.*], hugger-mugger, dislocated; out of sorts; promiscuous, indiscriminate; chaotic, anarchic, anarchical; unarranged &c. (*see* arrange &c. 60); confused; deranged &c. 61; topsy-turvy &c. (*inverted*) 218; shapeless &c. 241; disjointed, out of joint; gnarled *or* knarled [*obs.*].

COMPLEX, complexed; intricate, complicated, perplexed, involved, raveled, entangled, knotted, tangled, inextricable; irreducible.

TROUBLOUS, tumultuous, turbulent; riotous &c. (*violent*) 173.

Adv. IRREGULARLY &c. *adj.;* by fits, by fits and snatches, by fits and starts; pellmell; higgledy-piggledy; helter-skelter [*colloq.*], harum-scarum [*colloq.*]; in a ferment; at sixes and sevens, at cross-purposes; upside down &c. 218.

** the cart before the horse; chaos is come again; "the earth was without form and void" [*Bible*]; "the wrecks of matter and the crush of worlds" [Addison].

60. [REDUCTION TO ORDER.] **Arrangement. — N.** ARRANGEMENT; plan &c. 626; preparation &c. 673; disposal, disposition, disposure; collocation, allocation; distribution; sorting &c. *v.;* assortment, allotment, apportionment, taxis, taxonomy, syntaxis, graduation, organization, ordination, grouping, groupage.

ANALYSIS, classification, division, systematization, categorization, codification, digestion.

[RESULT OF ARRANGEMENT] orderliness, form, lay, array, digest; synopsis &c. (*compendium*) 596, syntagma, table,

61. [SUBVERSION OF ORDER; BRINGING INTO DISORDER.] **Derangement.— N.** DERANGEMENT &c. *v.;* muss [*colloq.*] *U. S.*], mess, touse [*colloq.*], disorder &c. 59; evection, discomposure, disturbance; disorganization, deorganization; dislocation; perturbation [*rare*], interruption; shuffling &c. *v.;* inversion &c. 218; corrugation &c. (*fold*) 258; involvement; insanity &c. 503.

V. DERANGE; misarrange, disarrange, displace, misplace; mislay, discompose, disorder; disorganize; embroil, unsettle, disturb, confuse, trouble, perturb, jumble, tumble; huddle, shuffle, mud-

atlas; register &c. (*record*) 551; cosmos, schematism, organism, architecture; instrumentation, orchestration, score &c. (*music*) 415; stipulation, settlement, *bandobast* or *bundobust* [*Anglo-Ind*.].

[INSTRUMENT FOR SORTING] sieve, riddle, screen, bolter, colander, grate, grating.

FILE, card index.

V. REDUCE TO ORDER, bring into order; introduce order into; rally.

ARRANGE, dispose, place, form; put in order, set in order, place in order; set out, collocate, allocate, compose, space, range, pack, marshal, array, size, rank, group, parcel out, allot, distribute, deal; cast the parts, assign the parts; dispose of, assign places to; assort, sort; sift, riddle; put to rights, put into shape, put in trim, put in array, set to rights, set into shape, set in trim, set in array; tidy [*colloq*.]; apportion.

CLASS, classify; divide; file, list, string together, thread; register &c. (*record*) 551; catalogue, tabulate, index, alphabetize, graduate, digest, grade, codify; orchestrate, score, harmonize.

METHODIZE, regulate, systematize, coördinate, organize, brigade, echelon, seriate [*rare*], settle, fix.

UNRAVEL, disentangle, unweave, ravel, card; disembroil; feaze.

Adj. ARRANGE &c. *v.*; embattled, in battle array; cut and dried; methodical, orderly, regular, systematic, on file; tabular, tabulate.

dle, toss, hustle, fumble, riot; bring into disorder, put into disorder, throw into disorder &c. 59; muss [*colloq*., *U. S*.], mess, touse [*obs. or dial*.]; break the ranks, disconcert, convulse; break in upon.

UNHINGE, dislocate, put out of joint, throw out of gear.

TURN TOPSY-TURVY &c. (*invert*) 218; bedevil; complicate, involve, perplex, confound; embrangle *or* imbrangle, tangle, entangle, ravel, tousle [*colloq*.], dishevel, ruffle; rumple &c. (*fold*) 258; dement, become insane &c. 503.

LITTER, scatter; mix &c. 41.

Adj. DERANGED &c. *v.*; syncretic, syncretistic; mussy [*colloq*., *U. S*.].

. "a nice derangement of epitaphs" [Sheridan].

2. CONSECUTIVE ORDER

62. Precedence. — N. PRECEDENCE; predecession [*rare*]; coming before &c. *v.*; the lead, *le pas* [*F*.]; superiority &c. 33; importance &c. 642; premise *or* premiss; antecedence *or* antecedency; anteriority &c. (*front*) 234; precursor &c. 64; priority &c. 116; precession [*rare*] &c. 280; anteposition; epacme; preference.

PREFIX, prefixture [*rare*], prelude, affix, preamble, overture, ritornel, *ritornello* [*It*.], voluntary.

V. PRECEDE, forerun, forego [*archaic*], prevene [*rare*]; come before, come first; head, lead, take the lead; lead the way, lead the dance; introduce, prologize [*rare*], usher in; have the *pas* [*F*.]; set the fashion &c. (*influence*) 175; open the ball, lead the cotillion [*U. S*.], lead the german [*U. S*.]; rank, outrank; take precedence, have precedence; have the start &c. (*get before*) 280.

PLACE BEFORE; prefix; premise, prelude, preface; affix.

Adj. PRECEDING &c. *v.*; precedent, antecedent; anterior; prior &c. 116;

63. Sequence. — N. SEQUENCE, train, coming after; pursuance, going after &c. (*following*) 281; consecution, succession; posteriority &c. 117.

CONTINUATION, prolongation; mantle of Elijah; order of succession; successiveness; paracme.

SECONDARINESS; subordinancy [*obs*.], subordinacy &c. (*inferiority*) 34.

AFTERBIRTH, afterburden, afterclap, aftercrop, afterglow, aftergrass, aftermath, afterpain, afterpiece, aftertaste; placenta, secundines; sequelæ.

V. SUCCEED; come after, come on, come next; follow, ensue, step into the shoes of; alternate.

FOLLOW, tag [*colloq*.], heel, dog, dodge, shadow, hound, bedog, hunt; trace, retrace.

PLACE AFTER, suffix, append, subjoin.

Adj. SUCCEEDING &c. *v.*; sequent; subsequent, consequent; sequacious, proximate, next; consecutive &c. (*continuity*) 69; alternate, amœbean.

before; former, foregoing; before mentioned, above mentioned, aforementioned; aforesaid, said; precursory, precursive; prevenient, preliminary, prefatory, introductory; prelusive, prelusory; proemial, preparatory.

LATTER; posterior &c. 117.

Adv. AFTER, subsequently; behind &c. (*rear*) 235.

Adv. BEFORE; in advance &c. (*precession*) 280.

** *seniores priores; prior tempore prior jure.*

---

64. Precursor. — **N.** PRECURSOR, antecedent, precedent, predecessor; forerunner, apparitor, vancourier [*obs.*]; pioneer, prodrome [*obs.*], *prodromos* [Gr. πρόδρομος], prodromus [*rare*], outrider; leader, bellwether; herald, harbinger; dawn; bellmare, *avant-coureur* [*F.*], avantcourier, *avant-courrier* [*F.*], forelooper *or* foreloper *or* forelouper [*S. Afr.*], *voorlooper* [Dutch], *voortrekker* [Dutch].

PRELUDE, preamble, preface, prologue, foreword, *avant-propos* [*F.*], protasis, proemium, prolusion [*rare*], proem, prolepsis, prolegomena, prefix, exordium, introduction; heading, frontispiece, groundwork; preparation &c. 673; overture, voluntary, ritornel, *ritornello* [*It.*], descant, symphony; premises.

PREFIGUREMENT &c. 511; omen &c. 512.

Adj. PRECURSORY; prelusive, prelusory, preludious; proemial [*rare*], introductory, preludial, prefatory, prodromous [*rare*], inaugural, preliminary; precedent &c. (*prior*) 116.

** "a precedent embalms a principle" [Disraeli].

---

65. Sequel. — **N.** SEQUEL, suffix, successor; tail, queue, train, wake, trail, rear; retinue, suite; appendix, postscript, subscript, postlude, conclusion, epilogue; peroration; codicil; continuation, sequela [*pl.* sequelæ]; appendage; tailpiece, heelpiece; tag, more last words; colophon.

FOLLOWER, successor, sectary, heeler [*slang*], pursuer, adherent, partisan, disciple, client; sycophant, parasite.

AFTERCOME [*Scot.*], aftergrowth, afterpart, afterpiece, after course, aftergame, afterthought; *arrière pensée* [*F.*], second thoughts; outgrowth.

---

66. Beginning. — **N.** BEGINNING, incunabula [*pl.*], commencement, opening, outset, incipience, incipiency, inception, inchoation, inchoacy [*rare*]; introduction &c. (*precursor*) 64; alpha, initial; inauguration, ingress [*archaic*], *début* [*F.*], *le premier pas* [*F.*], embarkation, rising of tne curtain; curtainraiser, maiden speech; exordium; outbreak, onset, brunt; initiative, move, first move; prelude, prime, proem, gambit; narrow *or* thin end of the wedge, fresh start, new departure.

first stage, first blush, first glance, first impression, first sight.

ORIGIN &c. (*cause*) 153; source, rise; bud, germ &c. 153; egg, embryo, rudiment; genesis, birth, nativity, cradle, infancy; forefront, outstart, start, starting point &c. 293; dawn &c. (*morning*) 125.

HEAD, heading; title-page; van &c. (*front*) 234; caption, *fatihah* [*Ar.*].

ENTRANCE, entry; inlet, orifice, mouth, chops, lips, porch, portal, portico, propy-

---

67. End. — **N.** END, close, termination; desinence [*rare*], conclusion, finis, finale, period, term, terminus, last, omega; extreme, extremity; gable end, butt end, fag-end; tip, nib, point; tail &c. (*rear*) 235; verge &c. (*edge*) 231; tag, peroration, appendix, epilogue; bottom dollar [*colloq.*], bitter end, tail end [*colloq.*], terminal, apodosis.

CONSUMMATION, *dénouement* [*F.*]; finish &c. (*completion*) 729; fate; doom, doomsday; crack of doom, day of Judgment, fall of the curtain; goal, destination; limit, stoppage, end-all, wind-up [*colloq.*]; determination; expiration, expiry; dissolution, death &c. 360; end of all things; finality; eschatology.

BREAK UP, *commencement de la fin* [*F.*], last stage, evening (*of life*); turning point; *coup de grâce* [*F.*], deathblow; knock-out, knock-out blow; sockdolager [*slang, U. S.*], K. O. [*slang*].

V. END, close, finish, terminate, conclude, be all over; expire; die &c. 360; come to a close, draw to a close &c. *n.*;

lon, door; gate, gateway; postern, wicket, threshold, vestibule; propylæum; skirts, border &c. (*edge*) 231; tee.

RUDIMENTS, elements, principia, outlines, grammar, protasis, alphabet, ABC.

V. BEGIN, commence, inchoate, rise, arise, originate, conceive, initiate, open, start, gin [*archaic*], dawn, set in, take its rise, enter upon, enter; set out &c. (*depart*) 293; embark in; incept [*rare*], institute.

USHER IN; lead off, lead the way, take the lead, take the initiative; inaugurate, auspicate, head; stand at the head, stand first, stand for; lay the foundations &c. (*prepare*) 673; found &c. (*cause*) 153; set up, set on foot, set agoing, set abroach, set the ball in motion; apply the match to a train; launch, broach; open up, open the door to; set about, set to work; make a beginning, make a start; handsel; take the first step, lay the first stone, cut the first turf; break ground, break the ice, break cover; pass the Rubicon, cross the Rubicon; open fire, open the ball; ventilate, air; undertake &c. 676.

perorate; have run its course; run out, pass away.

BRING TO AN END &c. *n.*; put an end to, make an end of; determine; get through; achieve &c. (*complete*) 729; stop &c. (*make to cease*) 142; shut up shop; hang up the fiddle [*colloq.*].

Adj. ENDING &c. *v.*; final, terminal, terminative [*rare*], conclusive, conclusory, determinative, definitive; crowning &c. (*completing*) 729; last, ultimate; hindermost; rear &c. 235; caudal; vergent [*rare*].

conterminate [*obs.*], conterminous, conterminable [*rare*].

ENDED &c. *v.*; at an end; settled, decided, over, played out, set at rest; conclusive.

penultimate; last but one, last but two, &c.

Adv. FINALLY &c. *adj.*; in fine; at the last; once for all.

*** "as high as Heaven and as deep as hell" [Beaumont and Fletcher]; *deficit omne quod nascitur* [Quintilian]; *en toute chose il faut considérer la fin; finem respice; ultimus Romanorum.*

come into existence, come into the world; make one's *début* [*F.*], take birth; burst forth, break out; spring up, crop up.

RECOMMENCE; begin at the beginning, begin *ab ovo* [*L.*], begin again, begin *de novo* [*L.*]; start afresh, make a fresh start, shuffle the cards, resume.

Adj. BEGINNING &c. *v.*; initial, initiatory, initiative; inceptive, introductory, incipient; proemial [*rare*], inaugural, inauguratory; inchoate, inchoative [*rare*]; embryonic, rudimentary, rudimental; primal, primary, prime, premier [*rare*], primigenial, primigenious *or* primigenous, primogenial; primeval &c. (*old*) 124; aboriginal; natal, nascent.

FIRST, foremost, front, head, leading; maiden.

BEGUN &c. *v.*; just begun &c. *v.*

Adv. at *or* in the beginning &c. *n.*; first, in the first place, *imprimis* [*L.*], first and foremost; *in limine* [*L.*]; in the bud, in embryo, in its infancy; from the beginning, from its birth; *ab initio* [*L.*], *ab ovo* [*L.*], *ab incunabilis* [*L.*], *ab origine* [*L.*]; formerly, erst [*archaic*].

*** *aller Anfang ist schwer; dimidium facti qui cœpit habet* [Cicero]; *omnium rerum principia parva sunt* [Cicero]; *il n'y a que le premier pas qui coûte.*

68. Middle.— N. MIDDLE, midst, mid [*rare*], thick, midmost, middlemost, [*rare*], mediety [*obs.*]; mean &c. 29; medium, middle term; center &c. 222, mid-course &c. 628; *mezzo termine* [*It.*], *mezzo cammin* [*It.*]; *juste milieu* [*F.*] &c. 628; halfway house, nave, navel, omphalos; nucleus, nucleolus.

EQUIDISTANCE- bisection, half distance; equator, diaphragm, midriff; interjacence &c. 228.

Adj. MIDDLE, medial, mesial, mesian, mean, mid, middlemost, midmost, midway [*rare*], midship, mediate [*rare*]; intermediate &c. (*interjacent*) 228; equidistant; central &c. 222; mediterranean, equatorial; homocentric.

Adv. MIDWAY, halfway; in the middle; midships, amidships, *in medias res* [*L.*] *meden agan* [*Gr.* μηδὲν ἄγαν.]

69. [Uninterrupted sequence.] **Continuity.** — **N.** continuity, continuousness, unbrokenness; consecution, consecutiveness &c. *adj.;* succession, round, suite, progression, series, train, catena, chain; catenation, concatenation; scale; gradation, course; ceaselessness, constant flow, unbroken extent; perpetuity.

procession, column; retinue, *cortège* [F.], cavalcade, parade; funeral, ovation, triumph; rank and file, line of battle, array.

pedigree, genealogy, lineage, history, tree, race; ancestry, descent, family, house; line, line of ancestors; strain.

rank, file, line, row, range, tier, string, thread, team; suit; colonnade.

V. form a series &c. *n.;* fall in; follow in a series &c. *n.*

arrange in a series &c. *n.;* string together, file, list, thread, graduate, tabulate.

Adj. continuous, continued; consecutive; progressive, gradual; serial, successive; immediate, unbroken, entire; linear; in a line, in a row &c. *n.;* uninterrupted, unintermitting; unremitting; perennial, evergreen; constant.

Adv. continuously &c. *adj.; seriatim* [NL.]; in a line &c. *n.;* in succession, in turn; running, gradually, step by step, gradatim, at a stretch; in file, in column, in single file, in Indian file.

⁎⁎⁎ "what! will the line stretch out to th' crack of doom?" [*Macbeth.*]

70. [Interrupted sequence.] **Discontinuity.** — **N.** discontinuity, discontinuousness, discreteness, disconnectedness; disjunction [*rare*] &c. 44; anacoluthon; interruption, break, fracture, flaw, fault, crack, cut; gap &c. (*interval*) 198; solution of continuity, cæsura; broken thread; parenthesis, episode, rhapsody, crazy quilt [*colloq.*], patchwork; intermission; alternation &c. (*periodicity*) 138; dropping fire.

V. be discontinuous &c. *adj.;* alternate, intermit.

discontinue, pause, interrupt; intervene; break, break in upon, break off; interpose &c. 228; break the thread, snap the thread; disconnect &c. (*disjoin*) 44; dissever.

Adj. discontinuous, unsuccessive, disconnected, broken, interrupted, *décousu* [F.]; disconnected, unconnected; discrete, disjunct [*rare*], disjunctive; fitful &c. (*irregular*) 139; spasmodic, desultory; intermitting &c. *v.*, intermittent; alternate; recurrent &c. (*periodic*) 138.

Adv. at intervals; by snatches, by jerks, by skips, by catches, by fits and starts; skippingly, *per saltum* [L.]; *longo intervallo* [L.].

⁎⁎⁎ like "angel visits, few and far between" [Campbell]; "it struggles and howls at fits" [Shelley].

71. Term. — **N.** term, rank, station, stage, step; degree &c. 26; scale, remove, grade, link, peg, round of the ladder, status, state, position, place, point, mark, *pas* [F.], period, pitch; stand, standing; footing, range.

V. hold a place, occupy a place, find a place, fall into a place &c. *n.;* rank.

3. Collective Order

72. Assemblage. — **N.** assemblage; collection, collocation, colligation; compilation, levy, gathering, ingathering, mobilization, meet, forgathering, muster, *attroupement* [F.]; team; concourse, conflux, congregation, contesseration [*obs.*], convergence &c. 290.

meeting, levee, reunion, drawing room, at home; *conversazione* [It.] &c. (*social gathering*) 892; assembly, congress, house, senate, legislature, convocation; caucus, séance, eisteddfod, gemot *or* gemote; convention, conventicle; con-

73. Nonassemblage. Dispersion. — **N.** dispersion; disjunction &c. 44; divergence &c. 291; aspersion; scattering &c. *v.;* dissemination, diffusion, dissipation, distribution; apportionment &c. 786; spread, respersion [*obs.*], circumfusion, interspersion, spargefaction [*obs.*], affusion.

waifs and estrays, flotsam and jetsam, *disjecta membra* [Hor.]; waveson.

V. disperse, scatter, sow, disseminate, diffuse, radiate, shed, spread, bestrew, overspread, dispense, disband,

clave &c. (*council*) 696; Noah's ark.

company, platoon, faction, caravan, claque, posse, *posse comitatus* [*L.*]; watch, squad, corps, troop, troupe; army, regiment &c. (*combatants*) 726; host &c. (*multitude*) 102; populousness.

miscellany, *collectanea* [*L.*]; museum, menagerie &c. (*store*) 636; museology.

crowd, throng; flood, rush, deluge; rabble, mob, rout, press, crush, *cohue* [*F.*], horde, body, tribe; crew, gang, knot, squad, band, party; swarm, shoal, school, covey, flock, herd, drove; kennel; *atajo* [*Sp. Amer.*]; bunch, drive, force, *mulada* [*U. S.*]; *remuda* [*Sp.*]; round-up [*U. S.*]; array, bevy, galaxy.

clan, brotherhood, association &c. (*party*) 712.

group, cluster, Pleiades, clump, pencil; set, batch, lot, pack; budget, assortment, bunch; parcel; packet, package; bundle, fascine, bale, *seron* [*Sp.*], fagot,

disembody, dismember, distribute; apportion &c. 786; blow off, let out, dispel, cast forth, draft (*or* draught) off; strew, straw [*obs.*], strow [*archaic*]; ted; spurtle *or* spirtle [*obs.*], cast, sprinkle; issue, deal out, retail, utter; intersperse, resperse [*obs.*]; set abroach, circumfuse.

spread like wildfire, disperse themselves.

turn adrift, cast adrift; scatter to the winds; sow broadcast.

Adj. unassembled &c. (*see* assemble &c. 72); diffuse, disseminated scattered, strown, strewn, dispersed &c *v.*, dispersive, dissipative, diffusive, dispellent [*rare*]; sparse, dispread, broadcast, sporadic, widespread; epidemic &c. (*general*) 78; adrift, stray; disheveled, streaming resolvent, discutient [*med.*].

Adv. *sparsim* [*L.*], here and there, *passim* [*L.*].

wisp, truss, tuft; grove, thicket, plump [*archaic*]; shock, rick, fardel, stack, sheaf, haycock, swath; fascicle, fascicule, fasciculus, gavel, hattock [*dial. Eng.*], stook [*dial.*].

volley, shower, storm, cloud.

accumulation &c. (*store*) 636; congeries, heap, lump, pile, rouleau, tissue, mass, pyramid; bing [*obs.*]; drift; snowball, snowdrift; acervation [*rare*], cumulation, amassment; glomeration, agglomeration; conglobation; conglomeration, conglomerate; coacervation [*rare*], coagmentation [*obs.*], aggregation, concentration, congestion, omnium-gatherum [*colloq.*], spicilegium [*L.*], Black Hole of Calcutta; quantity &c. (*greatness*) 31.

collector, gatherer; whip, whipper-in.

V. [Be or come together] assemble, collect, muster; meet, unite, join, rejoin; cluster, flock, swarm, surge, stream, herd, crowd, throng, associate; congregate, conglomerate, concentrate; center round, rendezvous, resort; come together, flock together, get together, pig together; forgather *or* foregather; huddle; reassemble.

[Get or bring together] assemble, muster; bring together, get together, put together, draw together, scrape together, lump together; collect, collocate, colligate; get in, whip in; gather; hold a meeting; convene, convoke, convocate; rake up, dredge, heap, mass, pile; pack, put up, truss, cram; acervate [*rare*]; agglomerate, aggregate; compile; group, aggroup, concentrate, unite; collect into a focus, bring into a focus; amass, accumulate &c. (*store*) 636; collect in a dragnet; heap Ossa upon Pelion.

Adj. assembled &c. *v.*, closely packed, dense, serried, crowded to suffocation, teeming, swarming, populous; as thick as hops; swarming like maggots; all of a heap, fasciculated; cumulative.

. the plot thickens; *acervatim; tibi seris tibi metis;* "in narrow room throng numberless" [Milton].

74. [Place of meeting.] Focus. — N. focus; point of convergence &c. 290; corradiation [*rare*]; center &c. 222; gathering place, resort; haunt; retreat; venue; rendezvous; rallying point, headquarters, home, club; depot &c. (*store*) 636; tryst, trysting place; place of meeting, place of resort, place of assignation; *point de réunion* [*F.*] issue

V. bring to a point, bring to a focus, bring to an issue, focus, corradiate [*rare*].

. all friends round St. Paul's; "I have a rendezvous with Death" [Seeger].

4. DISTRIBUTIVE ORDER

75. Class. — N. CLASS, division, subdivision, category, head, order, section; department, province, domain, sphere.

KIND, sort, estate, genus, species, variety, family, race, tribe, caste, sept, phylum, clan, breed; clique, coterie; type, kit, sect, set; assortment; feather [*rare*], kidney; suit; range; gender, sex, kin.

MANNER, description, denomination, persuasion, connection, designation, character, stamp; predicament; indication, particularization, selection, specification.

SIMILARITY &c. 17.

76. Inclusion. [COMPREHENSION UNDER, OR REFERENCE TO, A CLASS.] — **N.** INCLUSION, admission, incorporation, comprisal, comprehension, reception.

COMPOSITION &c. (*inclusion in a compound*) 54.

V. BE INCLUDED in &c.; come under, fall under, range under; belong to, pertain to; range with; merge in.

INCLUDE, comprise, comprehend, contain, admit, embrace, subsume, receive, inclose &c. (*circumscribe*) 229; incorporate, cover, embody, encircle.

reckon among, enumerate among, number among; refer to; place under, place with, arrange under, arrange with; take into account.

Adj. INCLUSIVE, inclusory; included, including &c. *v.;* congener [*rare*], congenerous; of the same class &c. 75; comprehensive, sweeping, all-embracing, liberal, unexclusive [*rare*].

⁎⁎* *a maximis ad minima, et hoc genus omne; et cætera,* &c., etc.

77. Exclusion.[1] — **N.** EXCLUSION &c. 55.

78. Generality. — N. GENERALITY, generalization; universality; catholicity, catholicism; miscellany, miscellaneousness; dragnet; common run; worldwideness.

Pan-Americanism, Pan-Anglicanism, Pan-Hellenism, Pan-Germanism, Panslavism *or* Pansclavism.

EVERYONE, everybody, *tout le monde* [*F.*]; all hands [*colloq.*], all the world and his wife [*humorous*]; anybody, N or M, all sorts.

PREVALENCE, rifeness, run.

V. BE GENERAL &c. *adj.;* prevail, be going about, stalk abroad.

RENDER GENERAL &c. *adj.;* spread, broaden, universalize, generalize.

Adj. GENERAL, generic, collective; current, wide, broad, comprehensive, sweeping; encyclopedic *or* encyclopedical, panoramic; widespread &c. (*dispersed*) 73.

UNIVERSAL; catholic, catholical; common, worldwide, nationwide, statewide, heavenwide, ecumenical *or* œcumenical; prevalent, prevailing, rife, epidemic, besetting; all over [*colloq.*], covered with.

79. Speciality. — N. SPECIALITY, *spécialité* [*F.*]; individuality, individuity [*obs.*]; particularity, peculiarity; *je ne sais quoi* [*F.*], *nescio quid* [*L.*]; idiocrasy &c. (*tendency*) 176; personality, characteristic, mannerism, idiosyncrasy, physiognomic [*rare*], diagnostic; specificness &c. *adj.;* singularity &c. (*unconformity*) 83; reading, version, lection; state; trait; distinctive feature; technicality; differentia.

PARTICULARS, details, items, counts; minutiæ.

I, self, I myself; myself, himself, herself, itself.

V. SPECIFY, particularize, individualize, realize, specialize, designate, determine; denote, indicate, point out, select, differentiate, specificize [*rare*], come to the point.

ITEMIZE, detail, descend to particulars, enter into detail.

Adj. SPECIAL, particular, individual, specific, proper, personal, original, private, respective, definite, determinate, minute, especial, certain, esoteric, endemic, partial, party, peculiar, marked,

---

[1] The same set of words are used to express *Exclusion from a class* and *Exclusion from a compound.* Reference is therefore made to the former at 55. This identity does not occur with regard to *Inclusion,* which therefore constitutes a separate category.

Pan-American, Pan-Anglican, Pan-Hellenic, Pan-Germanic, Panslavic *or* Pansclavic, Panslavonic, Panslavonian; panharmonic.

EVERY, all; unspecified, impersonal, indefinite.

CUSTOMARY &c. (*habitual*) 613.

Adv. whatever, whatsoever; to a man, one and all.

GENERALLY &c. *adj.;* always, for better for worse; in general, generally speaking; speaking generally; for the most part; in the long run &c. (*on an average*) 29; by and large, roughly speaking.

intimate, appropriate, several, characteristic, diagnostic, exclusive, restricted; singular &c. (*exceptional*) 83; idiomatic; typical, representative.

this, that; yon, yonder.

Adv. SPECIALLY &c. *adj.;* in particular, *in propriâ personâ* [L.]; *ad hominem* [L.]; for my part.

EACH, apiece, one by one; severally, respectively, each to each; *seriatim* [NL.], in detail, bit by bit; *pro hac vice* [L.], *pro re natâ* [L.].

NAMELY, that is to say, *videlicet* [L.], viz.; to wit.

** *le style est l'homme même.*

5. ORDER AS REGARDS CATEGORIES

80. Rule. — **N.** REGULARITY, uniformity, constancy, clockwork precision; punctuality &c. (*exactness*) 494; even tenor, rut; system; routine &c. (*custom*) 613; formula; canon, convention, maxim, rule &c. (*form, regulation*) 697; keynote, standard, model; precedent &c. (*prototype*) 22; conformity &c. 82.

LAW, capitular *or* capitulary, gnomology [*rare*], *règlement* [F.], order of things; normality, normalcy; normal state, normal condition, natural state, natural condition, ordinary state, ordinary condition, model state, model condition; standing dish, standing order; Procrustean law; law of the Medes and Persians; hard and fast rule; nature, principle.

Adj. REGULAR, uniform, symmetrical, constant, steady; according to rule &c. (*conformable*) 82; normal, habitual, customary &c. 613; methodical, orderly, systematic, systematical.

** "Order is heav'n's first law " [Pope].

82. Conformity. — **N.** CONFORMITY, conformance; observance; habituation; naturalization; conventionality &c. (*custom*) 613; agreement &c. 23.

EXAMPLE, instance, specimen, sample, quotation; exemplification, illustration, case in point; object lesson; elucidation.

PATTERN &c. (*prototype*) 22.

CONVENTIONALIST, formalist, bromide [*slang*], Philistine.

V. CONFORM TO, conform to rule; accommodate oneself to, adapt oneself to; rub off corners.

BE REGULAR &c. *adj.;* move in a

81. Multiformity. — **N.** MULTIFORMITY, omniformity; variety, diversity; multifariousness &c. *adj.;* varied assortment.

Adj. MULTIFORM, multifold, multifarious, multigenerous, multiplex; variform [*rare*], diversiform, amœbiform, manifold, many-sided; omniform, omnigenous, omnifarious; polymorphic, polymorphous, multiphase, metamorphotic, protean, proteiform, heterogeneous, motley, mosaic; epicene.

indiscriminate, desultory, irregular, diversified, different, divers; all manner of; of every description, of all sorts and kinds; *et hoc genus omne* [L.]; and what not?

** *de omnibus rebus et quibusdam aliis;* "harmoniously confused" [Pope]; "variety's the very spice of life" [Cowper].

83. Unconformity. — **N.** NONCONFORMITY &c. 82; unconformity, disconformity; unconventionality, informality, abnormity, anomaly; anomalousness &c. *adj.;* exception, peculiarity; infraction-, breach-, violation-, infringement- of -law, -custom, -usage; teratism, eccentricity, *bizarrerie* [F.], oddity, *je ne sais quoi* [F.], monstrosity, rarity; freak of nature; rouser [*colloq.*], snorter [*slang, U. S.*].

INDIVIDUALITY, idiosyncrasy, singularity, selfness [*rare*], originality, mannerism.

groove, move in a rut, travel in a rut; follow –, observe –, go by –, bend to –, obey- -rules, – precedents; agree with, comply with, tally with, chime in with, fall in with; be guided by, be regulated by; fall into a custom, fall into a usage; follow the fashion, follow the multitude; assimilate to, shape, harmonize, conventionalize, pass muster, do as others do, *hurler avec les loups* [F.]; do at Rome as the Romans do; go with the -stream,– current,– tide; swim with the -stream,– current,– tide; pass current; tread the beaten track &c. (*habit*) 613; keep one in countenance.

EXEMPLIFY, illustrate, example, sample, type [*rare*], cite, quote, put a case; produce an instance &c. *n.;* elucidate, explain.

Adj. CONFORMABLE TO RULE; adaptable, consistent, agreeable, compliant; regular &c. 80; according to regulation, according to rule, according to Cocker, according to Gunter, according to Hoyle [*all colloq.*]; *en règle* [F.|, *selon les règles* [F.], well regulated, orderly; symmetric &c. 242.

CONVENTIONAL &c. (*customary*) 613; of daily occurrence, of everyday occurrence; in the natural order of things; ordinary, common, habitual, usual, commonplace, prosaic, bromidic [*slang*], Philistine.

in the order of the day; naturalized.

TYPICAL, normal, formal; canonical, orthodox, sound, strict, rigid, positive, uncompromising, Procrustean.

secundum artem [L.], shipshape, point-device [*archaic*], technical.

EXEMPLARY, illustrative, in point.

Adv. CONFORMABLY &c. *adj.;* by rule; agreeably to; in conformity with, in accordance with, in keeping with; according to; consistently with; as usual, *ad instar* [L.], *instar omnium* [L.]; *more solito* [L.], *more majorum* [L.].

for the sake of conformity; of course, as a matter of course; *pro formâ* [L.], for form's sake, by the card.

invariably &c. (*uniformly*) 16.

FOR EXAMPLE, for instance; *exempli gratiâ* [L.]; *e. g.; inter alia* [L.].

** cela va sans dire; ex pede Herculem; noscitur a sociis; ne e quovis ligno Mercurius fiat [Erasmus]; "they are happy men whose natures sort with their vocations" [Bacon].

ABERRATION; irregularity; variety; singularity; exemption; salvo [*rare*] &c. (*qualification*) 469.

NONCONFORMIST, bohemian, sulphite [*slang*], nondescript, character [*colloq.*], original, nonesuch *or* nonsuch [*rare*], freak, crank [*colloq.*], prodigy, wonder, miracle, curiosity, missing link, flying fish, black swan, monster, white blackbird, basilisk, salamander, *lusus naturæ* [L.], *rara avis* [L.], queer fish [*slang*].

MONGREL; half-caste, half-blood, half-breed &c. 41; metis, crossbreed, hybrid, mule, mulatto; *tertium quid* [L.], hermaphrodite.

MONSTER, phœnix, chimera, hydra, sphinx, minotaur; griffin *or* griffon; centaur; xiphopagus; hippogriff, hippocentaur; sagittary; kraken, cockatrice, wivern *or* wyvern [*obs.*], roc, dragon, sea serpent; mermaid; unicorn; Cyclops, "men whose heads do grow beneath their shoulders" [*Othello*]; teratology.

fish out of water; neither one thing nor another; neither fish, flesh, fowl, nor good red herring; one in a way, one in a thousand.

OUTCAST, outlaw, Ishmael, pariah.

V. BE UNCOMFORTABLE &c. *adj.;* abnormalize; leave the beaten track, leave the beaten path; infringe –, break –, violate – a -law,– habit,– usage,– custom; drive a coach and six through; stretch a point; have no business there; baffle all description, beggar all description.

Adj. UNCOMFORTABLE, exceptional; abnormal, abnormous; anomalous, anomalistic; out of order, out of place, out of keeping, out of tune, out of one's element; irregular, arbitrary; teratogenic, teratogenetic; lawless, informal, aberrant, stray, wandering, wanton; peculiar, exclusive, unnatural, eccentric, egregious; out of the beaten track, out of the common, out of the common run, out of the pale of; misplaced; funny [*colloq.*].

UNUSUAL, unaccustomed, uncustomary, unordinary, unwonted, uncommon; rare, singular, unique, curious, odd, extraordinary, strange, monstrous; wonderful &c. 870; unexpected, unaccountable; *outré* [F.], out of the way, remarkable, noteworthy, *recherché* [F.], queer, quaint, nondescript, *sui generis* [L.]; original, unconventional, supernormal [*rare*], bohemian, sulphitic [*slang*], unfashionable; undescribed, unprecedented, unparalleled, unexampled, unheard of, unfamiliar; fantastic, newfangled, grotesque, bizarre; outlandish, exotic, *tombé des nues* [*F*.], preternatural; denaturalized.

HETEROGENEOUS, heteroclite, amorphous, mongrel, amphibious, epicene, half blood, hybrid; androgynous, androgynal; unsymmetric &c. 243; adelomorphic *or* adelomorphous, gynandrous, bisexual, hermaphrodite, androgynic, androgynous, monoclinous.

Adv. UNCONFORMABLY &c. *adj.;* except, unless, save, barring, beside, without, save and except, let alone.

HOWEVER, yet, but.

Int. what on earth! what in the world!

. never was seen the like, never was heard the like, never was known the like; "not conventionally unconventional" [Shaw].

SECTION V. NUMBER

1. NUMBER, IN THE ABSTRACT

84. Number. — **N.** NUMBER, symbol, numeral, figure, cipher, digit, integer; counter; round number; formula; function; series.

sum, difference, complement, subtrahend; product, total, aggregate; multiplicand, multiplier, multiplicator; coefficient, multiple; dividend, divisor, factor, quotient, submultiple, fraction; mixed number; numerator, denominator; decimal, circulating decimal, repetend; common measure, aliquot part; reciprocal; prime number; totient; quota, quotum [*rare*].

figurate numbers, pyramidal numbers, polygonal numbers.

permutation, combination, variation; election.

RATIO, proportion; progression; arithmetical progression, geometrical progression, harmonical progression; percentage.

POWER, root, radix, exponent, index, logarithm, antilogarithm; modulus.

differential, integral, fluxion, fluent.

Adj. NUMERAL, complementary, divisible, aliquot, reciprocal, prime, fractional, decimal, figurate, incommensurable.

proportional, exponential, logarithmic, logometric, differential, fluxional, integral, totitive.

positive, negative; rational, irrational; surd, radical, real, imaginary, impossible.

85. Numeration. — **N.** NUMERATION; numbering &c. *v.;* pagination; tale, tally, telling [*archaic*], recension, enumeration, summation, reckoning, computation, supputation [*obs.*]; calculation, calculus; algorithm [*obs.*], algorism, rhabdology, dactylonomy; measurement &c. 466; statistics, logistics.

arithmetic, analysis, algebra, fluxions; differential calculus, integral calculus, infinitesimal calculus; calculus of differences.

[STATISTICS] dead reckoning, muster, poll, census, capitation, roll call, recapitulation; account &c. (*list*) 86.

[OPERATIONS] notation, addition, subtraction, multiplication, division, proportion, rule of three, practice, equations, extraction of roots, reduction, involution, evolution, approximation, interpolation, differentiation, integration, indigitation [*rare*].

[INSTRUMENTS] abacus, suan pan, logometer, sliding rule, tallies, Napier's bones, calculating machine, difference engine; adding machine; cash register.

ARITHMETICIAN, calculator, geodesist, abacist; algebraist, geometrician, trigonometrician, mathematician, actuary, statistician.

V. NUMBER, count, tell; call over, run over; take an account of, enumerate, call the roll, muster, poll, recite, recapitulate; sum; sum up, cast up; tell off, score, cipher, reckon, reckon up, estimate, make an estimate, furnish an estimate, make up accounts, compute, calculate, suppute [*obs.*], add, subtract, multiply, divide, extract roots, algebraize, "tell his tale" [Milton].

CHECK, prove, demonstrate, balance, audit, overhaul, take stock.

PAGE, affix numbers to, foliate, paginate.

AMOUNT TO, come to, total.

Adj. NUMERAL, numerical; arithmetical, analytic, algebraic, statistical, countable, reckonable, numberable, computable, calculable, rhabdological; commensurable, commensurate; incommensurable, incommensurate.

86. List. — **N.** LIST, catalogue *or* catalog, inventory, schedule, calends [*rare*]; register &c. (*record*) 551; account; bill, bill of costs; syllabus; terrier, tally, file; calendar, index, table, atlas, contents; book, ledger; synopsis, *catalogue raisonné* [*F.*]; scroll, brief [*obs.*], screed, manifest, invoice, bill of lading; prospectus, program *or* programme; bill of fare, menu, carte; score, bulletin, *tableau* [*F.*], census, statistics, returns; Red Book, Blue Book, Domesday Book; directory, gazetteer.

almanac; army list, clergy list, civil service list, navy list; Statesman's Year-Book, Whitaker's Almanack, *Almanach de Gotha*, cadastre *or* cadaster, *cadre* [*F.*], card index; Lloyd's Register, Nautical Almanac, Who's Who.

DICTIONARY, lexicon, glossary, word-book, thesaurus, gloss [*rare*], gradus.

ROLL; check roll, checker roll, bead roll; muster roll, muster book; roll of honor; roster, slate, rota, poll, panel; chartulary *or* cartulary, diptych.

V. LIST, enroll, schedule, inventorize [*rare*], inventory, register, catalogue *or* catalog, invoice, bill, book, indent, slate, post, manifest, docket; matriculate, empanel, calendar, tally, file, index, tabulate, enter, score, keep score; census.

Adj. inventorial, cadastral; listed &c.*v.*

** "How index-learning turns no student pale, Yet holds the eel of science by the tail" [Pope].

2. DETERMINATE NUMBER

87. Unity. — **N.** UNITY; oneness &c. *adj.*; individuality; solitude &c. (*seclusion*) 893; isolation &c. (*disjunction*) 44; unification &c. 48; completeness &c. 52.

ONE, unit, ace, monad; individual; none else, no other, nought beside.

INTEGER, item, point, module.

V. BE ONE, be alone &c. *adj.*

ISOLATE &c. (*disjoin*) 44.

RENDER ONE; unite &c. (*join*) 43, (*combine*) 48.

Adj. ONE, sole, only-begotten, single, solitary, companionless; individual, apart, alone; kithless.

UNACCOMPANIED, unattended; *solus* (*fem.*, *sola*) [*L.*], single-handed; singular, odd, unique, unrepeated, azygous, first and last; isolated &c. (*disjoined*); insular.

MONADIC, monadical; unific, uniflorous, unilobed, uniglobular, unifoliolate, unigenital, uniliteral, unilocular, unimodular, unitary; monospermous.

insecable [*obs.*], inseverable, indiscerptible; compact, irresolvable.

LONE, lonely, lonesome; desolate, dreary.

88. Accompaniment. — **N.** ACCOMPANIMENT; adjunct &c. 39; context; appendage, appurtenance.

COMPANY, association, companionship; coexistence, concomitance; partnership, copartnership; coefficiency.

CONCOMITANT, accessory, coefficient; companion, attendant, fellow, associate, *fidus Achates* [*L.*], consort, spouse, colleague; partner, copartner; satellite, hanger-on, shadow; escort, *cortège* [*F.*], suite, train, convoy, follower &c. 65; attribute.

V. ACCOMPANY, coexist, attend, company [*archaic*], convoy, chaperon; hang on, wait on; go hand in hand with; synchronize &c. 120; bear company, keep company; row in the same boat; bring in its train; associate with, couple with.

Adj. ACCOMPANYING &c. *v.*; concomitant, fellow, twin, joint; associated with, coupled with; accessory, attendant, comitant [*rare*], obbligato.

Adv. WITH, withal; together with, along with, in company with; hand in hand, side by side; cheek by jowl (*or*

Adv. SINGLY &c. *adj.*; alone, by itself, *per se* [*L.*], only [*rare*], apart, in the singular number, in the abstract; one by one, one at a time; simply; one and a half, *sesqui-*.

⁎ *natura il fece, e poi roppe la stampa; du fort au faible;* "two souls with but a single thought, two hearts that beat as one."

jole); arm in arm; therewith, herewith; and &c. (*addition*) 37.

TOGETHER, in a body, collectively, in conjunction.

⁎ *noscitur a sociis; virtutis fortuna comes;* "into their inmost bower. Handed they went" [Milton].

89. Duality — N. DUALITY, dualism; duplicity; biplicity [*rare*], biformity; polarity.

two, deuce, couple, couplet, both, twain, brace, pair, cheeks, twins, Castor and Pollux, gemini, Siamese twins; fellows; yoke, conjugation; dispermy, doublets, dyad, duad, twosome [*rare*], distich, span.

V. [UNITE IN PAIRS] pair, couple, bracket, yoke; conduplicate; mate, span [*U.S.*]

Adj. TWO, twain; dual, dualistic; binary, binomial; twin, biparous; dyadic; conduplicate; duplex &c. 90; biduous, binate, binary, binal [*rare*], diphyletic, dispermic, paired, unijugate; *tête-à-tête* [*F.*].

COUPLED &c. *v.;* conjugate.

BOTH, both the one and the other.

90. Duplication. — N. DUPLICATION; doubling &c. *v.*; gemination, ingemination; reduplication; iteration &c. (*repetition*) 104; renewal.

DUPLICATE, facsimile, copy, replica, counterpart &c. (*copy*) 21.

V. DOUBLE; redouble, reduplicate; geminate [*rare*]; repeat &c. 104; renew &c. 660.

Adj. DOUBLE; doubled &c. *v.*; bicipital, bicephalous, bidental, bilabiate, bivalve, bivalvular, bifold, biform, bilateral, bifarious, bifacial; twofold, two-sided; disomatous; duple [*rare*], duplex; double-faced, double-headed; twin, duplicate, geminous [*rare*], geminate, ingeminate; second: dual &c. 89.

Adv. TWICE, once more; over again &c. (*repeatedly*) 104; as much again, twofold.

secondly, in the second place, again.

91. [DIVISION INTO TWO PARTS.] Bisection. — N. BISECTION, bipartition; dichotomy, subdichotomy [*rare*]; halving &c. *v.*; dimidiation.

BIFURCATION, furcation, forking, branching, ramification, divarication; fork, crotch, furculum, prong; fold.

HALF, moiety.

V. BISECT, halve, hemisect [*rare*], divide, split, cut in two, cleave, dimidiate, dichotomize.

GO HALVES, divide with.

SEPARATE, fork, bifurcate, furcate, divaricate; branch off *or* out; ramify.

Adj. BISECTED &c. *v.*; cloven, cleft; bipartite, dimidiate, divaricate, biconjugate, bicuspid, bifid; bifurcous [*rare*], bifurcate, bifurcated; bigeminate, distichous, distichal, dichotomous, furcular, furcate, lituate [*rare*]; semi-, demi-, hemi-.

92. Triality. — N. TRIALITY [*rare*], trinity,[1] triunity, Trimurti [*Hindu*], triplicity, trialism [*rare*].

THREE, triad, triplet, ternion, ternary, trine [*rare*], trey, trio, leash; shamrock, tierce, delta, spike-team [*U. S.*], trefoil; triangle, trident, triennium, trigon [*rare*], trinomial, trionym, triplopia *or* triplopy, tripod, trireme, triseme, triskelion *or* triskele, trisul *or* trisula, triumvirate.

third power, cube.

Adj. THREE; triform, trinal, trinomial; tertiary; triune; triarch, triadic.

⁎ *tria juncta in uno.*

93. Triplication. — N. TRIPLICATION; triplicity; trebleness, terza, trine; trilogy.

94. [DIVISION INTO THREE PARTS.] Trisection. — N. TRISECTION, tripartition, trichotomy; third, third part.

[1] *Trinity* is hardly ever used except in a theological sense; *see* Deity 976.

V. TREBLE, triple, triplicate, cube.

Adj. TREBLE, triple; tern, ternary, ternate, tertiary; triplicate, threefold, trilogistic; triplasic; third; trinal, trine [*rare*].

Adv. THREE TIMES, thrice, in the third place, thirdly, threefold, triply, trebly &c. *adj.*

V. TRISECT, divide into three parts, third.

Adj. TRIFID; trisected &c. *v.;* tripartite, trichotomous, trisulcate; ternal, trident, tridental.

triadelphous, triangular, trichotomic, tricuspid, tricapsular, tridental, tridentate *or* tridentated, tridentiferous, trifoliolate, trifurcate *or* trifurcated, trigonoid, trigonous, trigonal, trigrammic *or* trigrammatic, tripedal, trilateral, tripetalous, tripodal, tripodic, triquetral, triquetrous.

95. Quaternity. — **N.** QUATERNITY [*rare*], four, tetrad, quartet *or* quartette, quatre [*rare*], quadruplet, quaternion, square, quadrilateral, quadrinomial, biquadrate, quarter, quarto, tetract, tetragon.

quadrangle, quadrature, quadruplet; quatrefoil; tetragram, tetragrammaton; tetrahedron, tetrapody, tetrology, quatrefoil *or* quadrefoil.

V. SQUARE, biquadrate, reduce to a square.

Adj. FOUR; quaternary, quaternal; quadratic; quartile, quartic, quadrifid, quadriform, quadric, biquadratic; tetract, tetractine, tetractinal [*zoöl.*], four-rayed; tetrad, quadrivalent; quadrangular, tetragonal, quadrilateral, tetrahedral.

96. Quadruplication. — **N.** QUADRUPLICATION.

V. QUADRUPLICATE, biquadrate, multiply by four.

Adj. FOURFOLD; quadrable, quadruple, quadruplex, quadruplicate, quadrible; fourth.

Adv. FOUR TIMES; in the fourth place, fourthly.

97. [DIVISION INTO FOUR PARTS.] **Quadrisection.** — **N.** QUADRISECTION, quadripartition; quartering &c. *v.;* fourth; quart, quarter, quartern; farthing (*i. e.*, fourthing).

V. QUARTER, divide into four parts, quadrisect.

Adj. QUARTERED &c. *v.;* quadrifid, quadripartite [*rare*]; quadrifoliolate *or* quadrifoliate, quadrigeminal, quadrigeminous, quadrigeminate, quadripennate, quadriplanar, quadriserial, quadrivial, quadrifurcate, quadrumanal, quadrumane, quadrumous.

98. Five, &c. — **N.** FIVE, cinque, quint, quincunx, quintet *or* quintette, quintuple [*rare*], quintuplet, quinary [*rare*], pentad; pentagon, pentagram, pentameter, pentapody, pentarchy, pentastich, Pentateuch.

SIX, sise *or* size [*rare*], hexad, sextuplet, hexagon, hexahedron, hexagram, hexameter, hexapod, hexapody, hexastich, Hexateuch, sextet, half-a-dozen.

SEVEN, heptad, septenary [*rare*], heptagon, heptahedron, heptameter, heptarchy, Heptateuch.

99. Quinquesection. &c. — **N.** QUINQUESECTION &c.; division by five &c. 98; decimation; fifth &c.

V. DECIMATE; quinquesect; decimalize.

Adj. QUINQUEFID, quinqueliteral, quinquepartite.

sexpartite; octofid; decimal, tenth, tithe; duodecimal, twelfth; sexagesimal, sexagenary; hundredth, centesimal; millesimal &c.

EIGHT, octave, octonary, octad, ogdoad, octagon, octahedron, octameter, octastyle, octavo, octet.

NINE, novenary [*rare*], ennead, nonary [*rare*]; nonagon, three times three; *novena* [*R. C. Ch.*]

TEN, decad [*rare*], decade, dicker; decagon, decagram *or* decagramme, decahedron, decapod, decare, decastere, decastyle, decasyllable, decemvir, decemvirate, decennium.

eleven; twelve, dozen; thirteen; long dozen, baker's dozen; twenty, score; twenty-four, four and twenty, two dozen; twenty-five, five and twenty, quarter of a hundred; forty, twoscore; fifty, half a hundred; sixty, sexagenary, threescore; seventy, threescore and ten; eighty, fourscore; ninety, fourscore and ten.

HUNDRED, centenary, hecatomb, century, bicentenary, tercentenary; hundred-weight, cwt.; one hundred and forty-four, gross.

THOUSAND, chiliad, milliad [*rare*], millenary [*rare*], millennium; myriad, ten thousand; one hundred thousand, lac *or* lakh [*India*], plum [*obs.*], million; ten million, crore [*India*]; thousand million, billion, milliard.

billion, trillion &c.

V. quintuplicate, sextuple, centuplicate, centuriate [*obs.*].

Adj. FIVE, fifth, quinary, quintuple; quintuplicate, pentangular, pentagonal, pentastyle.

SIXTH, senary [*rare*], sextuple, hexagonal, hexangular, hexastyle, hexahedral, sextan.

SEVENTH, septuple, septenary, septimal [*rare*]; heptagonal, heptahedral, heptamerous, heptangular.

EIGHTH, octuple, octonary; octagonal, octahedral, octan, octangular, octastyle.

NINTH, ninefold, novenary [*rare*], nonary [*rare*], enneahedral, enneastyle.

TENTH, tenfold, decimal, denary, decuple, decagonal, decahedral, decasyllabic.

ELEVENTH, undecennial, undecennary.

TWELFTH, duodenary, duodenal.

in one's teens, thirteenth, &c.

TWENTIETH, vicenary, vicennial, vigesimal, vicesimal.

SIXTIETH, sexagesimal, sexagenary.

SEVENTIETH, septuagesimal, septuagenary.

CENTUPLE, centuplicate, centennial, centenary, centurial; secular, hundredth; thousandth, millenary, millennial &c.

3. INDETERMINATE NUMBER

100. [MORE THAN ONE.] **Plurality.**
— **N.** PLURALITY; a number, a certain number; one or two, two or three &c.; a few, several; multitude &c. 102; majority.

Adj. PLURAL, more than one, upwards of, some, certain; not, not alone &c. 87.

Adv. et cetera, &c., etc.

*** *non deficit alter.*

100a. [LESS THAN ONE.] **Fraction.**—
N. FRACTION, fractional part; part &c. 51.

Adj. FRACTIONAL, fragmentary, inconsiderable, partial, portional.

101. Zero. — **N.** ZERO, nothing; naught, nought; cipher, none, nobody; *nichts* [*Ger.*], goose egg [*U. S.*], duck [*slang*], nixie [*slang*], nix [*slang*]; not a soul; absence &c. 187; unsubstantiality &c. 4.

Adj. NO, not one, not any.

102. Multitude. — **N.** MULTITUDE; multitudinousness, numerousness &c. *adj.*; numerosity, numerality [*obs.*]; multiplicity; profusion &c. (*plenty*) 639; legion, host; great number, large number, round number, enormous number; a quantity, numbers, array, sight, army, sea, galaxy; scores, peck, bushel, shoal, oodles [*slang*], pile [*colloq.*], heap [*colloq.*], power [*colloq.*], sight [*colloq.*], lot [*colloq.*], lots [*colloq.*], swarm, bevy, cloud, flock, herd, drove, flight, covey, hive, brood, litter, farrow, fry, nest; mob, crowd &c. (*assemblage*) 72; all the world and his wife [*humorous*].

[INCREASE OF NUMBER] greater number, majority; multiplication, multiple.

V. BE NUMEROUS &c. *adj.*; swarm with, teem with, be alive with, creep with; crowd, swarm, come thick upon;

103. Fewness. — **N.** FEWNESS &c. *adj.*; paucity, scarcity, sparseness, sparsity, small number; only a few; small quantity &c. 32; rarity; infrequency &c. 137; handful; minority; exiguity.

[DIMINUTION OF NUMBER] reduction; weeding &c. *v.*; elimination, sarculation [*obs.*], decimation; eradication.

V. BE FEW &c. *adj.*

RENDER FEW &c. *adj.*; reduce, diminish, diminish the number, weed, eliminate, thin, decimate.

Adj. FEW; scant, scanty; thin, rare, scarce, sparse, thinly scattered, few and far between; exiguous; infrequent &c. 137; *rari nantes* [*L.*]; hardly any, scarcely any; to be counted on one's fingers, to be counted on the fingers of one hand; reduced &c. *v.*; unrepeated.

Adv. here and there.

outnumber, multiply; people; swarm like locusts, swarm like bees.

Adj. MANY, several, sundry, divers, various, not a few; Briarean; a hundred, a thousand, a myriad, a million, a billion, a quadrillion, a nonillion, a thousand and one; some ten or a dozen, some forty or fifty &c.; half a dozen, half a hundred &c.; alive with; very many, full many, ever so many; numerous; profuse, in profusion; manifold, multifold, multiplied, multitudinous, multiple, multinomial, teeming, populous, peopled, outnumbering, crowded, thick, studded; galore [*colloq.*].

thick coming, many more, more than one can tell, a world of; no end of, no end to; *cum multis aliis* [*L.*], thick as hops, thick as hail; plenty as black-berries; numerous as the stars in the firmament, numerous as the sands on the seashore, numerous as the hairs on the head; and what not, and heaven knows what; endless &c. (*infinite*) 105.

. their name is "Legion"; *acervatim; en foule;* "many-headed multitude" [Sidney]; "Thick as autumnal leaves that strow the brooks In Vallombrosa" [Milton]; "numerous as glittering gems of morning dew" [Young]; *vel prece vel pretio.*

104. Repetition. — N. REPETITION, iteration, reiteration, iterance [*rare*], reiterance [*rare*], alliteration, duplication, reduplication, ding-dong [*colloq.*], monotone, harping, recurrence, succession, run; battology, tautology; monotony, tautophony; rhythm &c. 138; diffuseness, pleonasm, redundancy.

chimes, repetend, echo, reëcho, encore, dilogy [*rare*], *ritornello* [*It.*], burden of a song, refrain, undersong; rehearsal; *réchauffé* [*F.*], *rifacimento* [*It.*], recapitulation.

cuckoo &c. (*imitation*) 19; reverberation &c. 408; drumming &c. (*roll*) 407; renewal &c. (*restoration*) 660.

TWICE-TOLD TALE, chestnut [*slang*], old stuff [*slang*], old story, old song; second edition, new edition; reappearance, reproduction; periodicity &c. 138.

V. REPEAT, iterate, reiterate, reproduce, echo, reëcho, drum, harp upon, battologize, tautologize, hammer, redouble.

RECUR, revert, return, reappear; renew &c. (*restore*) 660.

REHEARSE; do over again, say over again; ring the changes on; harp on the same string; din in the ear, drum in the ear; conjugate in all its moods, tenses and inflexions; begin again, go over the same ground, go the same round, duplicate, reduplicate, never hear the last of; resume, return to, recapitulate, reword.

Adj. REPEATED &c. *v.;* warmed up, warmed over, repetitional, repetitionary, repetitive, repetitious, reduplicatory [*rare*], reduplicative, recurrent, recurring; ever recurring, thick coming; frequent, incessant; redundant, pleonastic, tautological, tautologous, tautophonical; inexhaustible, unplumbed.

MONOTONOUS, ding-dong [*colloq.*], harping, iterative, unvaried; mocking, chiming; retold; habitual &c. 613; another.

AFORESAID, aforenamed; above-mentioned, said.

Adv. REPEATEDLY, often, again, anew, over again, afresh, once more; ditto, encore, *de novo* [*L.*], bis, *da capo* [*It.*].

again and again; over and over, over and over again; many times over; time and again, time after time; times without number; year after year; day by day &c.; many times, several times, a number of times; many a time, full many a time; frequently &c. 136; inexhaustibly, depth beyond depth.

. *ecce iterum Crispinus; toujours perdrix;* "cut and come again" [Crabbe]; "to-morrow and to-morrow and to-morrow" [*Macbeth*]; *cantilenam eandem canis* [Terence]; *nullum est jam dictum quod non dictum sit prius* [Terence].

105. Infinity. — N. INFINITY, infinitude, infiniteness &c. *adj.;* perpetuity &c. 112; inexhaustibility, immensity, boundlessness.

V. BE INFINITE &c. *adj.;* know no limits, know no bounds, have no limits, have no bounds; go on forever.

Adj. INFINITE; immense; numberless, countless, sumless, measureless, innumerable, immeasurable, incalculable, illimitable, interminable, unfathomable, unapproachable; exhaustless, indefinite; without number, without measure, without limit, without end; incomprehensible; limitless, endless, boundless, termless; untold, unnumbered, unmeasured, unbounded, unlimited, illimited; perpetual &c. 112.

Adv. INFINITELY &c. *adj.; ad infinitum* [*L.*].

*** "as boundless as the sea" [*Romeo and Juliet*]; "a dark Illimitable ocean, without bound, Without dimension, where length, breadth, and height, And time, and place are lost" [Milton].

Section VI. TIME

1. Absolute Time

106. Time. — **N.** TIME, duration; period, term, stage, space, tide [*archaic*], span, spell, season; the whole time, the whole period; course &c. 109; snap.

INTERMEDIATE TIME, while, bit, breathing, interim, interval, pendency; intervention, intermission, intermittence, interregnum, interlude; respite.

ERA, epoch, Kalpa, eon, cycle; time of life, age, year, date; decade &c. (*period*) 108; point, bell, moment &c. (*instant*) 113; reign &c. 737.

glass of time, ravages of time, whirligig of time, noiseless foot of Time; scythe of Time.

107. Neverness.[1] — **N.** "NEVERNESS"; absence of time, no time; *dies non* [*L.*]; St. Tib's eve; Greek Calends (*or* Kalends).

Adv. NEVER, ne'er; at no time, at no period; on *or* at the Greek Calends (*or* Kalends); on no occasion, never in all one's born days [*colloq.*], *jamais de ma vie* [*F.*], nevermore, *sine die* [*L.*], in no degree.

*** "Quoth the raven, 'Nevermore.'" [Poe].

V. CONTINUE, last, endure, stay, go on, remain, persist, subsist, abide, run, stand, dure [*archaic*], perdure [*rare*], perennate [*rare*], stick [*colloq.*]; intervene; elapse &c. 109; hold out.

take time, take up time, fill time, occupy time.

PASS TIME; pass away time, spend time, while away time, consume time, talk against time; tide over; use time, employ time; seize an opportunity &c. 134; linger on, drag on, drag along, tarry &c. 110; waste time &c. (*be inactive*) 683; procrastinate &c. 133.

Adj. CONTINUING &c. *v.*; on foot; permanent &c. (*durable*) 110; timely &c. (*opportune*) 134.

Adv. WHILE, whilst, during, pending; during the time, during the interval; in the course of; for the time being, day by day; in the time of, in the consulship of [*humorous*], when; meantime, meanwhile; in the meantime, in the interim; *ad interim* [*L.*], *pendente lite* [*L.*]; *de die in diem* [*L.*]; from day to day, from hour to hour &c.; hourly, always; for a time, for a season; till, until, up to, yet; the whole time, all the time; all along; throughout &c. (*completely*) 52; for good &c. (*diuturnity*) 110.

THEN, hereupon, thereupon, whereupon; *anno Domini* [*L.*], A.D.; *ante Christum* [*L.*], A.C.; before Christ, B.C.; *anno urbis conditæ* [*L.*], A.U.C.; *anno regni* [*L.*], A.R.; once upon a time, one fine morning.

*** time runs, time runs against; *tempus fugit.*
ad calendas Græcas; "panting Time toileth after him in vain" [Johnson]; "'gainst the tooth of time and razure of oblivion" [*Measure for Measure*]; "rich with the spoils of time" [Gray]; *tempus edax rerum* [Horace]; "the long hours come and go" [C. G. Rossetti]; "the time is out of joint" [*Hamlet*]; "Time rolls his ceaseless course" [Scott]; "Time the foe of man's dominion" [Peacock]; "time wasted is existence, used is life" [Young]; *truditur dies die* [Horace]; *volat hora per orbem* [Lucretius].

<hr>

[1] A term introduced by Bishop Wilkins.

108. [DEFINITE DURATION, OR POR-
TION OF TIME.] **Period.** — **N.** PERIOD;
second, minute, hour, day, week, month,
octave, *novena* [*L.*], semester, quarter,
year, decade, decennium, luster *or*
lustrum, indiction; cycle-, era- of indiction (*or* indictions); quinquennium, lifetime, generation; epoch, era, epact,
ghurry *or* ghari [*India*], lunation, moon.

century, age, millennium; *annus magnus* [*L.*], *annus mirabilis* [*L.*].

Adj. horary; hourly, annual, epochal
&c. (*periodical*) 13 ; *ante bellum* [*L.*].

108a. Contingent Duration. — **Adv.**
during pleasure, during good behavior;
quandiu se bene gesserit [*L.*].

Adv. IN TIME; in due time, in due season, in due course; in course of time, in
process of time, in the fullness of time.

.*. *labitur et labetur* [Horace]; *truditur dies die* [Horace]; *fugaces labuntur anni* [Horace]; "to-
morrow and to-morrow and to-morrow Creeps in this petty pace from day to day" [*Macbeth*].

---

109. [INDEFINITE DURATION.] **Course.**
— **N.** corridors of time, sweep of time,
vista of time, halls of time, course of
time, progress of time, process of time,
succession of time, lapse of time, flow
of time, flux of time, stream of time,
tract of time, current of time, tide of
time, march of time, step of time, flight
of time; duration &c. 106.

[INDEFINITE TIME] æon *or* eon, age,
Kalpa; aorist.

V. ELAPSE, lapse, flow, run, proceed,
advance, pass; roll on, wear on, press on;
flit, fly, slip, slide, glide; crawl, drag;
run its course, run out; expire; go by,
pass by; be past &c. 122.

Adj. ELAPSING &c. *v.*; aoristic; transient &c. 111; progressive.

---

110. [LONG DURATION.] **Diuturnity.**
— **N.** DIUTURNITY [*rare*]; a long time,
length of time; an age, æon *or* eon, a
century, an eternity; slowness &c. 275;
coeternity, sempiternity, perpetuity &c.
112; blue moon [*colloq.*], coon's age
[*U. S.*], dog's age [*colloq.*].

DURABLENESS, durability; persistence,
eternalness, lastingness &c. *adj.*; continuance, standing; permanence &c.
(*stability*) 150; survival, survivance;
longevity &c. (*age*) 128; distance of
time.

PROTRACTION of time, prolongation
of time, extension of time; delay &c.
(*lateness*) 133.

V. LAST, endure, stand, remain, abide,
continue &c. 106; brave a thousand
years.

TARRY &c. (*be late*) 133; drag on, drag
its slow length along, drag a lengthening
chain; protract, prolong; spin out, eke
out, draw out, lengthen out; temporize;
gain time, make time, talk against time.

OUTLAST, outlive; survive; live to
fight again.

Adj. DURABLE, endurable [*rare*]; lasting &c. *v.*; of long duration, of long
standing; permanent, chronic, long-
standing; diuturnal [*rare*]; intransient,
intransitive; intransmutable, persistent;
lifelong, livelong; longeval [*rare*], longevous, endless, fixed, immortal, per-
durant [*rare*], perdurable, long-lived,

---

111. [SHORT DURATION.] **Transience.**
— **N.** TRANSIENCE, transiency, ephem-
erality, transientness [*rare*] &c. *adj.*;
evanescence, impermanence *or* imper-
manency, preterience [*rare*], volatility,
fugacity, caducity [*rare*], mortality,
span; nine days' wonder, bubble, May-
fly; spurt; temporary arrangement, interregnum, interim.

VELOCITY &c. 274; suddenness &c.
113; changeableness &c. 149.

EPHEMERON; transient, transient
boarder, transient guest, transient rates
[*all colloq., U. S.*].

V. BE TRANSIENT &c. *adj.*; flit, pass
away, fly, gallop, vanish, fleet, sink,
melt, fade, evaporate; pass away like
a -cloud, - summer cloud, - shadow,
- dream.

Adj. TRANSIENT, transitory, transitive; passing, evanescent, fleeting; flying
&c. *v.*; fugacious, fugitive; transeunt,
interim, shifting, slippery; spasmodic.

TEMPORAL, temporary; provisional,
provisory; cursory, short-lived, ephem-
eral, ephemerous [*rare*], preterient [*rare*],
caducous [*rare*], deciduous; perishable,
mortal, precarious; impermanent.

BRIEF, quick, brisk, fleet, cometary,
meteoric, volatile, extemporaneous, summary; pressed for time &c. (*haste*) 684;
sudden, momentary &c. (*instantaneous*)
113.

Adv. TEMPORARILY &c. *adj.*; *pro tem-*

macrobiotic, evergreen, perennial; sempervirent [*rare*], sempervirid; unintermitting, unremitting; perpetual &c. 112.

LINGERING, protracted, prolonged, spun out &c. *v.*; long-pending, longwinded; slow &c. 275.

Adv. LONG; for a long time, for an age, for ages, for ever so long, for many a long day; long ago &c. (*in a past time*) 122; *longo intervallo* [*L.*].

all the day long, all the year round; the livelong day, as the day is long, morning, noon and night; hour after hour, day after day &c.; for good, for good and all; permanently &c. *adj.*; *semper eadem* (Queen Elizabeth's motto) [*L.*], *semper et ubique* [*L.*].

pore [*L.*]; for the moment, for a time; awhile, *en passant* [*F.*], *in transitu* [*L.*]; in a short time; soon &c. (*early*) 132; briefly &c. *adj.*; at short notice; on the point of, on the eve of; *in articulo* [*L.*]; between cup and lip.

*** one's days are numbered; the time is up; here to-day and gone to-morrow; *non semper erit æstas; eheu! fugaces labuntur anni; sic transit gloria mundi;* "a schoolboy's tale, the wonder of the hour!" [Byron]; *dum loquimur fugerit invidia ætas; fugit hora.*

---

112. [ENDLESS DURATION.] Perpetuity.
— **N.** PERPETUITY, eternity, everness,[1] aye, sempiternity, perenniality [*rare*], coeternity, immortality, athanasy, athanasia; everlastingness &c. *adj.*; perpetuation; continued existence, uninterrupted existence; perennity [*obs.*].

V. HAVE NO END; last forever, endure forever, go on forever.

ETERNIZE, immortalize, eternalize, monumentalize, perpetuate.

Adj. PERPETUAL, eternal; everduring, everlasting, everliving, everflowing; continual, sempiternal, sempiternous [*rare*], eviternal [*rare*]; coeternal; endless, unending; ceaseless, incessant, uninterrupted, indesinent [*obs.*], unceasing; interminable, eterne [*poetic*], having no end; unfading, evergreen, amaranthine; never-ending, never-dying, never-fading; deathless, immortal, undying, imperishable.

Adv. PERPETUALLY &c. *adj.*; always, ever, evermore [*archaic*], aye; forever, for aye, forevermore, forever and a day, forever and ever; forever and aye, in all ages, from age to age; without end; world without end, time without end; *in secula seculorum* [*L.*]; to the end of time, to the crack of doom, to the "last syllable of recorded time" [*Macbeth*]; till doomsday; constantly &c. (*very frequently*) 136.

*** *esto perpetuum; labitur et labetur in omne volubilis ævum* [Horace]; "but thou shall flourish in immortal youth" [Addison]; "Eternity! thou pleasing, dreadful thought" [Addison]; "her immortal part with angels lives" [*Romeo and Juliet*]; *ohne Hast aber ohne Rast* [Goethe's motto]; *ora e sempre.*

113. [POINT OF TIME.] Instantaneity.
— **N.** INSTANTANEITY, instantaneousness; suddenness, abruptness.

MOMENT, instant, second, minute; twinkling, flash, breath, crack, jiffy [*colloq.*], coup [*F.*], burst, flash of lightning, stroke of time.

TIME; epoch, time of day, time of night; hour, minute; very minute &c., very time, very hour; present time, right time, true time, exact time, correct time.

V. BE INSTANTANEOUS &c. *adj.*; twinkle, flash.

Adj. INSTANTANEOUS, momentary, extempore, sudden, instant, abrupt; subitaneous [*obs.*], hasty; quick as thought,[2] quick as lightning; rapid as electricity.

Adv. INSTANTANEOUSLY &c. *adj.*; in no time, in less than no time; presto, *subito* [*It. and L.*], instanter, forthright [*archaic*], eftsoon *or* eftsoons [*archaic*], in a trice, in a jiffy [*colloq.*], suddenly, at a stroke, like a shot; in a moment &c. *n.*; in the twinkling of an eye, in the twinkling of a bedpost [*humorous*]; in one's tracks; right away; *toute à l'heure* [*F.*]; at one jump, in the same breath, *per saltum* [*L.*], *uno saltu* [*L.*]; at once, all at once; plump, slap [*colloq.*]; "at one fell swoop" [*Macbeth*]; at the same instant &c. *n.*; immediately &c. (*early*) 132; extempore, on the moment, on the spot, on the dot [*colloq.*], on the spur of the moment; just then; slapdash &c. (*haste*) 684.

*** touch and go; no sooner said than done; "we shall all be changed, in a moment, in the twinkling of an eye" [*Bible*].

---

[1] Bishop Wilkins.

[2] See note on 264.

114. [ESTIMATION, MEASUREMENT, AND RECORD OF TIME.] **Chronometry.** — N. CHRONOMETRY, horometry, chronology, horology; date, epoch; style, era, age.

almanac, calendar, ephemeris; standard time, daylight-saving time; register, registry; chronicle, annals, journal, diary, chronogram, isochronon.

[INSTRUMENTS FOR THE MEASUREMENT OF TIME] clock, watch; chronometer, chronoscope, chronograph; repeater; timekeeper, timepiece; dial, sundial, gnomon, horologe, horologium [rare], hydroscope, *pendule* [F.], hourglass, clepsydra; ghurry or ghari [Hind.].

CHRONOGRAPHER, chronologer, chronologist, horologer; annalist.

V. FIX THE TIME, mark the time; date, register, chronicle, chronologize; measure time, beat time, mark time; bear date.

Adj. CHRONOLOGIC or chronological, chronometric or chronometrical, chronogrammatical; datal [rare], temporal, isochronous, isochronal, cinquecento, quattrocento, trecento.

Adv. o'clock.

. "we were none of us musical, though Miss Jenkins beat time, out of time, by way of appearing so" [Gaskell].

115. [FALSE ESTIMATE OF TIME.] **Anachronism.** — N. ANACHRONISM, metachronism, parachronism, prochronism; prolepsis, misdate; anticipation, antichronism [rare].

disregard of time, neglect of time, oblivion of time.

intempestivity [rare] &c. 135.

V. MISDATE, antedate, postdate, overdate; anticipate; take no note of time; anachronize [rare].

Adj. MISDATED &c. v.; undated; overdue; out of date, anachronous, anachronistic, intempestive, behind time.

2. RELATIVE TIME

1. *Time with reference to Succession*

116. Priority. — N. PRIORITY, antecedence, anteriority, precedence, preëxistence; precession &c. 280; precursor &c. 64; the past &c. 122; premises.

V. PRECEDE, come before; forerun; prevene [rare], antecede; go before &c. (lead) 280; preëxist; dawn; presage &c. 511; herald, usher in, announce.

be beforehand &c. (be early) 132; steal a march upon, anticipate, forestall; have the start, gain the start.

Adj. PRIOR, previous; preceding, precedent [rare]; anterior, antecedent; preëxistent; former, aforegoing, aforesighted, aforementioned, aforethought, fore [obs.], foregoing; before-mentioned, above-mentioned; aforesaid, said; introductory &c. (precursory) 64; prodromal.

Adv. BEFORE, prior to; earlier; previously &c. adj.; afore [obs.], aforehand [archaic], ere, theretofore, erewhile; ere then, ere now, before then, before now; already, yet, beforehand; or ever, aforetime; on the eve of.

. *prior tempore prior jure;* "When I was a king in Babylon And you were a Christian slave" [Henley].

117. Posteriority. — N. POSTERIORITY; succession, sequence; following &c. 281; subsequence, subsequency, supervention; continuance, prolongation; futurity &c. 121; successor; sequel &c. 65; remainder, reversion.

V. FOLLOW AFTER &c. 281, come after, go after; succeed, supervene; ensue, attend, emanate [rare], occur, result; step into the shoes of.

Adj. SUBSEQUENT, posterior, following, after, later, succeeding, sequacious [rare], successive, sequential [rare], ensuing, consecutive, attendant, sequent. postliminary [rare], postnate [obs.]; postdiluvial, postdiluvian; posthumous; future &c. 121; after-dinner, postprandial.

Adv. SUBSEQUENTLY, after, afterwards, since, later; at a subsequent period, at a later period; next, in the sequel, close upon, thereafter, thereupon, upon which, eftsoon or eftsoons [archaic]; from that time, from that moment; after a while, after a time; in process of time.

. "He smiled a sickly smile and he curled up on the floor, And the subsequent proceedings interested him no more" [Bret Harte].

118. Present Time. — **N.** THE PRESENT TIME, the present day, the present moment, the present juncture, the present occasion; the times, existing time, time being; twentieth century; crisis, epoch, day, hour.

age, time of life.

Adj. PRESENT, actual, instant, current, nonce, latest, existing, that is.

Adv. AT THIS TIME, at this moment &c. 113; at the present time &c. *n.*; now, at present; at hand.

at this time of day, to-day, now-a-days; already; even now, but now, just now; on the present occasion; for the time being, for the nonce; *pro hâc vice* [*L.*]; on the nail, on the spot; on the spur of the moment, on the spur of the occasion.

119. [TIME DIFFERENT FROM THE PRESENT.] **Different time.** — **N.** different time, other time.

[INDEFINITE TIME] aorist.

Adj. aoristic; indefinite.

Adv. THEN, at that time, at that moment, at that instant; at which time, at which moment, at which instant; on that occasion, upon.

WHEN; whenever, whensoever; whereupon, upon which, on which occasion; at another time, at a different time, at some other time, at any time; at various times; some of these days, one of these days, some fine morning, one fine morning; some fine day, on divers occasions, sooner or later; some time or other.

ONCE, formerly, once upon a time.

UNTIL NOW; to this day, to the present day.

⁎⁎ "upon this bank and shoal of time" [*Macbeth*]; "unborn To-morrow and dead Yesterday" [Omar Khayyám — Fitzgerald]; "the present hour alone is man's" [Johnson].

120. Synchronism. — **N.** SYNCHRONISM; coexistence, coincidence; simultaneousness &c. *adj.*; concurrence, concomitance, unity of time, interim.

[HAVING EQUAL TIMES] isochronism.

CONTEMPORARY, coeval, coetanian [*obs.*].

V. COEXIST, concur, accompany, go hand in hand, keep pace with; synchronize, isochronize.

Adj. SYNCHRONOUS, synchronal, synchronic *or* synchronical, synchronistic *or* synchronistical, simultaneous, coexisting, coincident, concomitant, concurrent; coeval, coevous [*obs.*]; contemporary, contemporaneous; coetaneous [*rare*], coinstantaneous, coterminous, collateral, coeternal; isochronous.

Adv. AT THE SAME TIME; simultaneously &c. *adj.*; together, in concert, during the same time; in the same breath; *pari passu* [*L.*]; in the interim.

at the very moment &c. 113; just as, as soon as; meanwhile &c. (*while*) 106.

121. [PROSPECTIVE TIME.] **Futurity.** — **N.** FUTURITY, futurition [*rare*]; future, hereafter, time to come; approaching -, coming -, subsequent -, after- -time, -age, -days, -hours, -years, -ages, -life; morrow, to-morrow, by and by, the yet [*rare*]; millennium, chiliad [*rare*], millenary, doomsday, day of judgment, crack of doom, remote future.

APPROACH OF TIME, advent, time drawing on, womb of time; destiny &c. 152; eventuality.

HERITAGE, heirs, posterity, descendants.

PROSPECT, anticipation &c. (*expectation*) 507; foresight &c. 510.

V. LOOK FORWARDS; anticipate &c. (*expect*) 507, (*foresee*) 510; forestall &c. (*be early*) 132.

122. [RETROSPECTIVE TIME.] **Preterition.** — **N.** PRETERITION; priority &c. 116; the past, past time; heretofore [*rare*]; days of yore, days of old, days past, days gone by; times of yore, times of old, times past, times gone by; bygone days; old **times**, ancient times, former times; foretime [*rare*]; yesterday, the olden time, good old time; langsyne; eld [*obs. or poetic*].

ANTIQUITY, antiqueness, ancientness, *status quo* [*L.*]; time immemorial, distance of time; history, remote age, remote time; remote past; rust of antiquity.

paleontology, paleography, paleology; palætiology, archæology; archaism, antiquarianism, medievalism, Pre-Raphaelitism.

RETROSPECTION, looking back; memory &c. 505.

APPROACH, await, threaten; impend &c. (be destined) 152; come on, draw on; draw near.

Adj. FUTURE, to come; coming &c. (impending) 152; next, near; near at hand, close at hand; eventual, ulterior; anticipant, expectant, prospective, in prospect &c. (expectation) 507; millenary, millennial.

Adv. PROSPECTIVELY, hereafter, in future; on the knees of the gods; kal [Hind.], to-morrow, the day after to-morrow; in course of time, in process of time, in the fullness of time; eventually, ultimately, sooner or later; proximo; paulo post futurum [L.]; in after time; one of these days; after a time, after a while.

FROM THIS TIME; henceforth, henceforwards; thence; thenceforth, thenceforward; whereupon, upon which.

SOON &c. (early) 132; on the eve of, on the point of, on the brink of; about to; close upon.

. quid sit futurum cras fuge quærere [Horace]; "The Bird of Time has but a little way To flutter — and the Bird is on the Wing" [Omar Khayyám — Fitzgerald].

ANTIQUARY, antiquarian; paleologist, archæologist &c.; Oldbuck, Dryasdust; laudator temporis acti [L.]; medievalist, Pre-Raphaelite.

ANCESTRY &c. (paternity) 166.

V. BE PAST &c. adj.; have expired &c. adj., have run its course, have had its day; pass; pass by, pass away, pass off; go by, go away, go off; lapse, blow over.

LOOK BACK, trace back, cast the eyes back; exhume.

Adj. PAST, gone, gone by, over, passed away, bygone, foregone [archaic]; elapsed, lapsed, preterlapsed [rare], expired, no more, run out, blown over, that has been, bypast, agone [archaic], whilom [archaic], extinct, never to return, exploded, forgotten, irrecoverable; obsolete &c. (old) 124.

FORMER, pristine, quondam, ci-devant [F.], late; ancestral.

FOREGOING; last, latter; recent, overnight, preterit or preterite, past, pluperfect, past perfect.

LOOKING BACK &c. v.; retrospective, retroactive; archæological &c. n.

Adv. FORMERLY; of old, of yore; erst [archaic or poetic], erstwhile [archaic], whilom [archaic], erewhile [archaic], time was, ago, over; in the olden time &c. n.; anciently, long ago, long since; a long while ago, a long time ago; years ago, ages ago; some time ago, some time since, some time back.

yesterday, the day before yesterday; last year, last season, last month &c.; ultimo [L.]; lately &c. (newly) 123.

RETROSPECTIVELY; ere now, before now, till now; hitherto, heretofore; no longer; once, once upon a time; from time immemorial; in the memory of man; time out of mind; already, yet, up to this time; ex post facto [L.].

. time was; the time has been, the time hath been; fuimus Troës [Vergil]; fuit Ilium [Vergil]; hoc erat in more majorum; "O call back yesterday, bid time return" [Richard II]; tempi passati; "the eternal landscape of the past" [Tennyson]; ultimus Romanorum; "what's past is prologue" [Tempest]; "whose yesterdays look backward with a smile" [Young]; "the old days were great because the men who lived in them had mighty qualities" [Roosevelt].

2. Time with reference to a particular Period

123. Newness. — **N.** NEWNESS &c. adj.; novelty, recency; neology, neologism; immaturity; youth &c. 127; gloss of novelty.

INNOVATION; renovation &c. (restoration) 660.

MODERNIST, neoteric; neologist.

UPSTART, narikin [Jap.], start-up [rare], nouveau riche [F.], parvenu.

MODERNISM, modernness, modernity; modernization; dernier cri [F.]; latest fashion; mushroom.

V. RENEW &c. (restore) 660; modernize.

124. Oldness. — **N.** OLDNESS &c. adj.; age, antiquity, eld [obs. or poetic]; cobwebs of antiquity.

MATURITY, matureness, ripeness.

DECLINE, decay; senility &c. 128.

SENIORITY, eldership, primogeniture.

ARCHAISM &c. (the past) 122; thing of the past, relic of the past; megatherium; Babylonian, Assyrian, Sanskrit.

TRADITION, prescription, custom, immemorial usage, common law; folklore.

V. BE OLD &c. adj.; have had its day, have seen its day.

Adj. NEW, novel, recent, fresh, green; young &c. 127; evergreen; raw, immature; virgin; untried, unhandseled, unheard-of, untrodden, unbeaten; fire-new, span-new.

MODERN, late, neoteric, neoterical; new-born, new-fashioned, newfangled, newfledged; of yesterday; just out [colloq.], brand-new, up-to-date [colloq.]; fin-de-siècle [F.], vernal, renovated; sempervirent [rare], sempervirid [rare].

fresh as a rose, fresh as a daisy, fresh as paint [colloq.]; spick-and-span, spick-and-span-new, unhandled.

Adv. NEWLY &c. adj.; afresh, anew, lately, just now, only yesterday, the other day; latterly, of late.

not long ago, a short time ago.

₊ di novello tutto par bello; nullum est jam dictum quod non dictum est prius; una scopa nuova spazza bene; "an upstart crow decked in our feathers" [Peele — of Shakespeare].

BECOME OLD &c. adj.; age, fade.

Adj. OLD, ancient, olden [archaic], eldern [archaic], antique; of long standing, time-honored, venerable, hoary, vetust [obs.]; elder, eldest; firstborn.

PRIMITIVE, prime, primeval, primigenous, primigenial, primigenious; paleoanthropic; primordial, primordiate [rare]; aboriginal &c. (beginning) 66; diluvian, antediluvian, protohistoric, prehistoric, dateless, patriarchal, preadamite; palæocrystic; fossil, paleozoic, preglacial, antemundane; archaic, Vedic, classic, medieval, Pre-Raphaelite, ancestral; black-letter.

IMMEMORIAL, traditional, traditive, traditionary [rare], prescriptive, customary, unwritten, whereof the memory of man runneth not to the contrary; inveterate, rooted.

ANTIQUATED, of other times, old as the hills, of the old school, after-age, obsolete; out-of-date, out-of-fashion; fusty, outworn, moth-eaten [humorous], gone out, gone by, passé [F.], extinct, dead, disused, past, run out; senile &c. 128; time-worn; crumbling &c. (deteriorated) 659; secondhand.

stale, old-fashioned, old-fangled [rare], behind the age; old-world; exploded; dead, disused, past, run out; senile &c. 128; time-worn; crumbling &c. (deteriorated) 659; secondhand.

old as the hills, old as Methuselah, old as Adam, old as history.

Adv. since the world was made, since the year one, since the days of Methuselah.

₊ vetera extollimus recentium incuriosi [Tacitus]; "How weary, stale, flat, and unprofitable Seem to me all the uses of this world" [Hamlet.]

125. Morning. [NOON.] — N. MORNING, morn, matins [eccl.], morningtide [rare or poetic], forenoon, a.m., prime, dawn, daybreak; dayspring, foreday [chiefly Scot.], sun-up [U. S.], peep of day, break of day; aurora; first blush of the morning, first flush of the morning, prime of the morning; twilight, crepuscle or crepuscule, sunrise; daylight, daypeep, cockcrow, cockcrowing; the small hours, the wee sma' hours [Scot.].

NOON, midday, noonday, noontide, meridian, prime; nooning, noontime.

SPRING, springtide, springtime, seed-time; vernal equinox.

SUMMER, summertide, summertime, midsummer.

Adj. MATIN, matutinal, matinal, matutinary [rare]; crepuscular.

NOON, noonday, midday, meridional [rare in this sense].

SPRING, vernal, vernant [obs.].

SUMMER, æstival or estival.

126. Evening. [MIDNIGHT.] — N. EVENING, eve; decline of day, fall of day, close of day; candlelight, candlelighting; eventide, evensong [eccl. or archaic], vespers [eccl.], nighttide [archaic], nightfall, curfew, dusk, twilight, eleventh hour; sunset, sundown; going down of the sun, cockshut [obs.], dewy eve, gloaming, bedtime.

AFTERNOON, post meridiem [L.], p.m.

MIDNIGHT; dead of night, witching hour of night, witching time of night, killing-time.

AUTUMN; fall, fall of the leaf; harvest, autumnal equinox; Indian summer, St. Luke's summer, St. Martin's summer.

WINTER, hiems [L.].

Adj. VESPER, vespertine, nocturnal; autumnal.

WINTRY, winterly, brumous, brumal.

₊ "midnight, the outpost of advancing day" [Longfellow]; "sable-vested Night" [Milton]; "this gorgeous arch with golden worlds inlay'd" [Young]; "the gradual dusky veil" [Collins].

Adv. AT SUNRISE &c. *n.;* with the lark, when the morning dawns.

*** "at shut of evening flowers" [*Paradise Lost*]; *entre chien et loup;* "flames in the forehead of the morning sky" [Milton]; "the breezy call of incense-breathing morn" [Gray].

---

127. Youth. — N. YOUTH; juvenility, juvenescence [*rare*]; juniority; infancy; babyhood, childhood, boyhood, girlhood, youthhood [*archaic*]; incunabula; minority, boyage [*rare*], immaturity, nonage, teens, tender age, bloom.

CRADLE, nursery, leading strings, pupilage [*rare*], puberty, pucelage.

FLOWER of life, springtide of life, seedtime of life, prime of life, golden season of life; heyday of youth, school days; rising generation.

Adj. YOUNG, youthful, juvenile, juvenescent, green, callow, budding, sappy, puisne [*law*], beardless, under age, in one's teens, *in statu pupillari* [*L.*]; younger, junior; hebetic, unfledged, unripe.

*** "youth on the prow and pleasure at the helm" [Gray]; "youth . . . the glad season of life" [Carlyle]; *"si jeunesse savait! si vieillesse pouvait!"* [*F. prov.*].

128. Age. — N. AGE; oldness &c. *adj.* old age, advanced age; senility, senescence; years, anility, gray hairs, climacteric, grand climacteric, declining years, decrepitude, hoary age, caducity [*rare*], eld [*archaic*], superannuation; second childhood, childishness; dotage; vale of years, decline of life, senectitude [*rare*], "sear and yellow leaf" [*Macbeth*]; threescore years and ten; green old age, ripe age; longevity; time of life.

SENIORITY, eldership; elders &c. (*veteran*) 130; firstling; *doyen* [*F.*], dean, father; primogeniture.

[SCIENCE OF OLD AGE.] nostology; gerocomy [*med.*].

V. BE AGED &c. *adj.;* grow old, get old &c. *adj.;* age; decline, wane; senesce [*rare*].

Adj. AGED; old &c. 124; elderly, eldern [*archaic*], senile; matronly, anile; in years; ripe, mellow, run to seed, declining, waning, past one's prime; gray, grayheaded; hoar, hoary; venerable, time-worn, antiquated, *passé* [*F.*], effete, decrepit, superannuated; advanced in life, advanced in years; stricken in years; wrinkled, marked with the crow's foot; having one foot in the grave; doting &c. (*imbecile*) 499; like the last of pea time.

years old; of a certain age, no chicken [*colloq.*], old as Methuselah; ancestral; patriarchal &c. (*ancient*) 124; gerontic.

OLDER, elder, oldest, eldest; senior; firstborn.

*** "give me a staff of honor for my age" [Titus Andronicus]; *bis pueri senes; peu de gens savent être vieux; plenus annis abiit plenus honoribus* [Pliny the Younger]; "old age is creeping on apace" [Byron]; "slow-consuming age" [Gray]; "the hoary head is a crown of glory" [*Proverbs xvi*, 31]; "the silver livery of advised age" [*II Henry VI*]; to grow old gracefully; "to vanish in the chinks that Time has made" [Rogers].

129. Infant. — N. INFANT, babe, baby; nursling, suckling, yearling, weanling; papoose, *bambino* [*It.*]; vagitus.

CHILD, bairn [*Scot.*], tot, mite, scrap, chick, kid [*slang*], butcha or bacha [*Hind.*]; little one, brat, chit, pickaninny [*U. S.*], urchin; bantling, bratling elf.

YOUTH, boy, lad, laddie, slip, sprig, stripling, youngster, younker [*colloq.*], whipster [*rare*], youngling [*rare*], damoiseau [*archaic*], cub, callant [*Scot.*], whippersnapper [*colloq.*], whiffet [*U. S.*], schoolboy, hobbledehoy, hopeful, cadet, minor, master.

SCION, sapling, seedling; tendril, olive-branch, nestling, chicken, duckling,

130. Veteran. — N. VETERAN, old man, reverend sir, seer, patriarch, graybeard; grandfather, grandsire [*archaic*], grisard [*rare*], oldster [*colloq.*], pantaloon [*obs.*]; gaffer, sexagenarian, octogenarian, nonagenarian, centenarian; *doyen* [*F.*], old stager; dotard &c. 501.

GRANNY, grandam *or* grandame [*archaic*], gammer [*dial. Eng.*], crone, hag, oldwife, beldam *or* beldame.

preadamite, Methuselah, Nestor, old Parr; elders; forefathers &c. (*paternity*) 166; Darby and Joan, Philemon and Baucis, "John Anderson, my jo" [Burns].

Adj. VETERAN; aged &c. 128.

*** "superfluous lags the veteran on the stage" [Johnson].

larva, chrysalis, tadpole, whelp, cub, pullet, fry, callow [*obs.*], codling *or* codlin; fœtus, calf, colt, pup, puppy, foal, kitten; lamb, lambkin; aurelia, caterpillar, cocoon, nymph, nympha, pupa, staddle.

GIRL, lass, lassie; wench [*dial.*], miss, damsel; damoiselle, damosel *or* damozel [*archaic*]; demoiselle; maid, maiden; virgin; nymph, colleen, girleen, flapper [*slang*], girly [*colloq.*], minx, missy, baggage, hussy; schoolgirl; hoyden, tomboy, romp.

Adj. INFANTINE, infantile; puerile; boyish, girlish, childish, babyish, kittenish; childly [*rare*], boylike, girllike, kiddish [*colloq.*], dollish [*colloq.*]; youngling, infant, baby; newborn, unfledged, newfledged, callow.

in the cradle, in swaddling clothes, in long clothes, in arms, in leading strings; at the breast; in one's teens; young &c. 127.

*** "first the infant Mewling and puking in the nurse's arms" [*As You Like It*].

131. Adolescence.— N. ADOLESCENCE, pubescence, majority; adultism; adulthood, adultness &c. *adj.*; manhood, virility; flower of age; full bloom; spring of life.

man &c. 373; woman &c. 374; adult, pubescent, no chicken [*colloq.*].

MIDDLE AGE, *mezzo cammin* [*It.*], maturity, full age, ripe age, prime of life, meridian of life.

V. COME OF AGE, come to man's estate, come to years of discretion; attain majority, put on long trousers, assume the *toga virilis* [*L.*]; have cut one's eyeteeth [*colloq.*], settle down, have sown one's wild oats.

Adj. ADOLESCENT, pubescent, of age; of full age, of ripe age; out of one's teens; grown up, full-blown, in full bloom, full-grown, manly, manlike, virile, adult; womanly, matronly; marriageable, marriable, nubile.

MIDDLE-AGED, mature, in one's prime; matronly.

*** "Yet ah, that Spring should vanish with the Rose! That Youth's sweet-scented manuscript should close!" [Omar Khayyám — Fitzgerald].

3. Time with reference to an Effect or Purpose

132. Earliness. — N. EARLINESS &c. *adj.*; morning &c. 125.

PUNCTUALITY; promptitude &c. (*activity*) 682; haste &c (*velocity*) 274; suddenness &c. (*instantaneity*) 113.

PREMATURITY, precocity, precipitation, anticipation, prevenience; a stitch in time.

V. BE EARLY &c. *adj.*; be beforehand &c. *adv.*; keep time, take time by the forelock, anticipate, forestall; have the start, gain the start; steal a march upon; gain time, draw on futurity; bespeak, secure, engage, preëngage.

ACCELERATE; expedite &c. (*quicken*) 274; make haste &c. (*hurry*) 684.

Adj. EARLY, prime, timely, seasonable, in time, punctual, forward; prompt &c. (*active*) 682; summary.

PREMATURE, precipitate, precocious; prevenient, anticipatory; rath *or* rathe [*obs. or poetic*].

SUDDEN &c. (*instantaneous*) 113; unexpected &c. 508; imminent, impending, near, near at hand; immediate.

Adv. EARLY, soon, anon, betimes,

133. Lateness. — N. LATENESS &c. *adj.*; tardiness &c. (*slowness*) 275.

DELAY, cunctation [*rare*] tarriance, moration [*rare*], delation [*archaic*], procrastination; deferring &c. *v.*; postponement, adjournment, prorogation, retardation, respite; protraction, prolongation; after-time; circumlocution office [*ridicule*], "circumlocution court" [Dickens], chancery suit, Fabian policy, *médecine expectante* [*F.*], moratorium; leeway; high time; truce, reprieve, demurrage; stop, stay, suspension, remand.

V. BE LATE &c. *adj.*; tarry, wait, stay, bide, take time; dawdle &c. (*be inactive*) 683; linger, loiter; bide one's time, take one's time; gain time; hang fire; stand over, lie over; hang, hang around *or* about [*colloq.*], hang back [*colloq.*], hang in the balance, hang in the hedge, hang up [*colloq.*], sit up for, stay up for.

PUT OFF, defer, delay, lay over, suspend; shift off, stave off; waive, retard,

rath *or* rathe [*poetic*]; eftsoon *or* eftsoons [*archaic*]; ere long, before long; punctually &c. *adj.;* to the minute; in time; in good time, in military time, in pudding time [*obs.*], in due time; time enough, on time, on the dot [*slang*].

BEFOREHAND; prematurely &c. *adj.;* precipitately &c. (*hastily*) 684; too soon; before its time, before one's time; in anticipation; unexpectedly &c. 508.

SUDDENLY &c. (*instantaneously*) 113; before one can say "Jack Robinson," at short notice, extempore; on the spur of the moment, on the spur of the occasion [Bacon]; at once; on the spot, on the instant; at sight; off hand, out of hand; *à vue d'œil* [*F.*]; straight, straightway, straightforth; forthwith, incontinently, summarily, instanter, forthright [*archaic*], immediately, briefly, shortly, erewhile [*archaic*], quickly, speedily, apace, before the ink is dry, almost immediately, presently, at the first opportunity, in no long time, by and by, in a while, directly.

*** touch and go, no sooner said than done; *tout vient à point à qui sait attendre;* "misers get up early in the morning; and burglars . . . get up the night before" [Chesterton].

remand, postpone, adjourn; procrastinate; dally; prolong, protract; spin out, draw out, lengthen out; prorogue; keep back; tide over; push to the last, drive to the last; let the matter stand over; table, lay on the table, shelve; respite [*rare*], perendinate [*rare*]; reserve &c. (*store*) 636; temporize, filibuster [*U. S.*], stall [*slang*]; consult one's pillow, sleep upon it.

BE KEPT WAITING, dance attendance; kick one's heels [*colloq.*], cool one's heels [*colloq.*]; *faire antichambre* [*F.*]; wait impatiently; await &c. (*expect*) 507; sit up, sit up at night; lose an opportunity &c. 135.

Adj. LATE, tardy, slow, cunctatious *or* cunctative [*rare*], behindhand, serotine [*rare*], belated, postliminary [*rare*], posthumous, backward, unpunctual, impunctual [*rare*], overdue, moratory; dilatory &c. (*slow*) 275; delayed &c. *v.;* in abeyance.

Adv. LATE; backward, lateward [*obs.*], late in the day; at sunset, at the eleventh hour, at length, at last; ultimately; after time, behind time; too late; too late for &c. 135.

SLOWLY, leisurely, deliberately, at one's leisure; *ex post facto* [*L.*]; *sine die* [*L.*].

*** *nonum prematur in annum* [Horace]; "against the sunbeams serotine and lucent" [Longfellow]; *è meglio tardi che mai; deliberando sæpe perit occasio* [Syrus]; "seven years, my lord, have now passed since I waited in your outward rooms, or was repulsed from your door" [Johnson].

134. Occasion. — N. OCCASION, opportunity, opening, room, scope, space, place, liberty, show [*colloq., U. S.*]; suitable time, suitable season, proper time, proper season; high time; opportuneness &c. *adj.;* tempestivity [*obs.*].

nick of time; golden opportunity, well-timed opportunity, fine opportunity, favorable opportunity; clear stage, fair field; *mollia tempora* [*L.*]; spare time &c. (*leisure*) 685.

CRISIS, turn, emergency, juncture, conjuncture; turning point, given time.

V. IMPROVE THE OCCASION; seize &c. (789) an opportunity *or* an occasion; use &c. (677) an opportunity *or* an occasion; give &c. (784) an opportunity *or* an occasion.

suit the occasion &c. (*be expedient*) 646.

strike the iron while it is hot, *battre le fer sur l'enclume* [*F.*], make hay while

135. Intempestivity. — N. INTEMPESTIVITY [*rare*]; unsuitable time, improper time; unreasonableness &c. *adj.;* evil hour; *contretemps* [*F.*], misventure [*archaic*], misadventure; intrusion; anachronism &c. 115.

V. BE ILL-TIMED &c. *adj.;* mistime, intrude, come amiss, break in upon; have other fish to fry; be busy, be occupied, be engaged.

LOSE AN OPPORTUNITY; throw away an opportunity, waste an opportunity, neglect &c. (460) an opportunity; allow *or* suffer the opportunity *or* occasion to -pass, – slip, – go by, – escape, – lapse; waste time &c. (*be inactive*) 683; let slip through the fingers, lock the stable door when the steed is stolen.

Adj. ILL-TIMED, mistimed; ill-fated, ill-omened, ill-starred; untimely, intrusive, unseasonable; out of date, out of season; inopportune, timeless [*archaic*],

the sun shines, seize the present hour, take time by the forelock, *prendre la balle au bond* [*F.*].

Adj. OPPORTUNE, timely, well-timed, timeful [*obs.*], seasonable, tempestive [*archaic*], timeous [*rare*].

lucky, providential, fortunate, happy, favorable, propitious, auspicious, critical; suitable &c. 23; *obiter dicta* [*L.*].

OCCASIONAL, accidental, extemporaneous, extemporary; contingent &c. (*uncertain*) 475.

Adv. OPPORTUNELY &c. *adj.;* in proper time, in proper course, in proper season; in due time, in due course, in due season; for the nonce; in the nick of time, in the fullness of time; all in good time; just in time, at the eleventh hour, now or never.

BY THE WAY, by the by; *en passant* [*F.*], *à propos* [*F.*]; *pro re natâ* [*L.*], *pro hac vice* [*L.*]; *par parenthèse* [*F.*], parenthetically, by way of parenthesis; while on this subject, speaking of; *par exemple* [*F.*]; extempore; on the spur of the moment, on the spur of the occasion; on the spot &c. (*early*) 132.

* *carpe diem* [Horace]; *occasionem cognosce;* one's hour is come, the time is up; that reminds me; *bien perdu bien connu; è sempre l'ora; ex quovis ligno non fit Mercurius; nosce tempus; nunc aut nunquam;* "there is a tide in the affairs of men Which taken at the flood, leads on to fortune" [*Julius Caesar*]; "The Moving Finger writes; and, having writ, Moves on" [Omar Khayyám — Fitzgerald].

inconvenient, intempestive [*rare*], untoward, *mal à propos* [*F.*], unlucky, inauspicious, unpropitious, unfortunate, unfavorable; unsuited &c. 24; inexpedient &c. 647.

unpunctual &c. (*late*) 133; too late for; premature &c. (*early*) 132; too soon for; wise after the event.

Adv. INOPPORTUNELY &c. *adj.;* as ill luck would have it, in an evil hour, the time having gone by, a day after the fair.

* After meat mustard, after death the doctor.

3. RECURRENT TIME

136. Frequency. — N. FREQUENCY, frequence, oftness [*rare*], oftenness [*rare*], quotiety [*rare*]; repetition &c. 104.

V. KEEP, keep on; recur &c. 104; do nothing but.

Adj. FREQUENT, often [*archaic*], many, many times, not rare, thickcoming, incessant, perpetual, continual, constant, repeated &c. 104; habitual &c. 613; hourly &c. 138.

Adv. OFTEN, oft, ofttime [*archaic*], ofttimes, oftentimes; oftentime [*rare*], oftentide [*obs.*], not seldom, frequently; repeatedly &c. 104; unseldom, not unfrequently; in quick succession, in rapid succession; many a time and oft; oftly [*rare*], daily, hourly &c.; every day, every hour, every moment &c.

PERPETUALLY, continually, constantly, incessantly, unchangingly, steadfastly, without ceasing, at all times, daily and hourly, night and day, day and night, day after day, morning noon and night, ever and anon.

COMMONLY &c. (*habitually*) 613; most often.

SOMETIMES, occasionally, at times, now and then, from time to time, there being times when, *toties quoties* [*L.*], often enough, again and again.

* "I'll do and I'll do and I'll do!" [*Macbeth*].

137. Infrequency. — N. INFREQUENCY, infrequence, unfrequency [*rare*], rareness, rarity; sparseness, fewness &c. 103; seldomness; uncommonness.

V. BE RARE &c. *adj.*

Adj. INFREQUENT, unfrequent [*rare*], seldseen [*archaic*], uncommon, sporadic; rare, rare as a blue diamond; few &c. 103; scarce; almost unheard of, scarce as hen's teeth [*colloq.*], unprecedented, which has not occurred within the memory of the oldest inhabitant, not within one's previous experience.

Adv. SELDOM, rarely, scarcely, hardly; not often, unfrequently, infrequently, uncommonly, sparsely, unoften; scarcely ever, hardly ever; once in a blue moon [*colloq.*].

once; once for all, once in a way; *pro hac vice* [*L.*].

* *einmal keinmal;* "like angel visits, few and far between" [Campbell].

138. Regularity of recurrence. **Periodicity. — N.** PERIODICITY, intermittence; beat; oscillation &c. 314; pulse, pulsation; systole and diastole; rhythm; alternation, alternateness, alternacy [*rare*], alternativeness, alternity [*rare*].

ROUND, revolution, rotation, bout, turn, say.

ANNIVERSARY, biennial, triennial, quadrennial, quinquennial, sextennial, septennial, octennial, decennial; tricennial, jubilee, centennial, centenary, bicentennial, bicentenary, tercentenary; birthday, birthright, natal day, fête day, saint's day.

CATAMENIA, courses, menses, menstrual flux.

[REGULARITY OF RETURN] rota, cycle, period, stated time, routine; days of the week; Sunday, Monday &c.; months of the year; January &c.; feast, festival, fast &c.; Christmas, Yuletide, New Year's day, Ash Wednesday, Maundy Thursday, Good Friday, Easter; Allhallows, Allhallowmas, All Saints' Day; All Souls' Day; Candlemas, Dewali [*Hindu*], Holi *or* Hoolee [*Hindu*], Memorial *or* Decoration Day [*U. S.*], Independence Day [*U. S.*], Labor Day [*U. S.*], Thanksgiving [*U. S.*], ground-hog day [*U. S.*], woodchuck day [*U. S.*], Halloween, Hallowmas, Lady Day; leap year, bissextile; Bairam, Ramadan, Muharram [*Mohammedan*]; St. Swithin's Day; Midsummer Day; May Day &c. (*holiday*) 840; yearbook.

PUNCTUALITY, regularity, steadiness.

V. RETURN, revolve; recur in regular -order, - succession; come again, come in its turn; come round, - again; beat, pulsate; alternate; intermit.

Adj. PERIODIC, periodical; serial, recurrent, cyclic, cyclical, rhythmic *or* rhythmical; recurring &c. v.; intermittent, remittent; alternate, every other; every.

hourly; diurnal, daily, quotidian [*rare*]; tertian, weekly; hebdomadal, hebdomadary; biweekly, fortnightly; bimonthly; monthly, catamenial, menstrual; yearly, annual; biennial, triennial &c.; centennial, secular; paschal, lenten &c.

REGULAR, steady, constant, methodical, punctual, regular as clockwork.

Adv. PERIODICALLY &c. *adj.;* at regular intervals, at stated times; at fixed periods, at established periods; punctually &c. *adj.; de die in diem* [*L.*]; from day to day, day by day.

BY TURNS; in turn, in rotation; alternately, every other day, off and on, ride and tie, round and round.

139. Irregularity of recurrence. — **N.** IRREGULARITY, uncertainty, unpunctuality; fitfulness &c. *adj.;* capriciousness, ecrhythmus; acatastasia [*med.*].

Adj. IRREGULAR, uncertain, unpunctual, capricious, erratic, heteroclite, ecrhythmic, ecrhythmous, desultory, fitful, flickering; rambling, rhapsodical; spasmodic; immethodical, unsystematic, unequal, uneven, variable.

Adv. IRREGULARLY &c. *adj.;* by fits and starts &c. (*discontinuously*) 70.

SECTION VII. CHANGE

1. SIMPLE CHANGE

140. [DIFFERENCE AT DIFFERENT TIMES.] **Change. — N.** CHANGE, alteration, mutation, permutation, variation, novation [*rare*], modification, modulation, inflection *or* inflexion, mood, qualification, innovation, eversion, deviation, shift, turn; diversion; break.

TRANSFORMATION, transfiguration, transfigurement; metamorphosis; metabola *or* metabole [*med.*], transmorphism [*rare*], transmutation; deoxidization, deoxidation; transubstantiation; metagenesis, transanimation, transmigration,

141. [ABSENCE OF CHANGE.] **Permanence. — N.** PERMANENCE, permanency, fixity, persistence, endurance; durableness, durability, lastingness; standing, *status quo* [*L.*]; maintenance, preservation, conservation; conservatism; *laisser faire* [*F.*], *laisser aller* [*F.*]; law of the Medes and Persians; standing dish.

stability &c. 150; quiescence &c. 265; obstinacy &c. 606.

V. LET ALONE, let be; persist, remain, stay, tarry, rest; hold, hold on; last,

metempsychosis, version [*rare*]; metasomatism *or* metasomatosis, metathesis; metabolism, metastasis; transmogrification [*colloq.*]; avatar; alterative.

resolution, conversion &c. (*gradual change*) 144; revolution &c. (*sudden or radical change*) 146; inversion &c. (*reversal*) 218; displacement &c. 185; transference &c. 270.

CHANGEABLENESS &c. 149; tergiversation &c. (*change of mind*) 607.

V. CHANGE, alter, vary, wax and wane; modulate, diversify, qualify, tamper with; turn, shift, veer, gybe *or* jibe, jib, tack, chop, shuffle, swerve, warp, deviate, dodge, tergiversate, turn aside, evert, intervert [*obs.*]; pass to, take a turn, turn the corner, resume.

WORK A CHANGE, modify, vamp, patch, piece, vamp up, superinduce; transform, transfigure, transmute, transmogrify [*colloq.*], transume [*rare*], transverse [*rare*], transshape [*rare*], metabolize, convert, transubstantiate, resolve, revolutionize; chop and change; metamorphose, ring the changes.

innovate, introduce new blood, shuffle the cards; give a turn to, give a color to; influence, turn the scale; shift the scene, turn over a new leaf.

recast &c. 146; reverse &c. 218; disturb &c. 61; convert into &c. 144.

Adj. CHANGED &c. *v.;* newfangled; eversible; changeable &c. 149; transitional; modifiable; metagenetic; alterative.

Adv. *mutatis mutandis* [*L.*].

Int. *quantum mutatus!* [*L.*].

** "a change came o'er the spirit of my dream" [Byron]; *nous avons changé tout cela* [Molière]; *tempora mutantur nos et mutamur in illis; non sum qualis eram* [Horace]; *casaque tourner; corpora lente augescent cito extinguuntur* [Tacitus]; *in statu quo ante bellum;* "still ending and beginning still" [Cowper]; *vox audita perit littera scripta manet;* "all things are in perpetual flux and fleeting" [*Proverb*].

endure, bide, abide, aby *or* abye[*archaic*], dwell, maintain, keep; stand, – still, – fast, – pat [*colloq.*]; subsist, live, outlive, survive; hold – , keep- one's -ground, – footing; hold good.

Adj. PERMANENT; stable &c. 150; persisting &c. *v.;* established; fixed, irremovable, durable; pucka *or* pakka [*Hind.*]; unchanged &c. (change &c. 140); renewed; intact, inviolate; persistent; monotonous, uncheckered; unfailing, unfading.

UNDESTROYED, unrepealed, unsuppressed; conservative, *qualis ab incepto* [*L.*]; prescriptive &c. (*old*) 124; stationary &c. 265.

Adv. FINALLY; *in statu quo* [*L.*]; for good, at a stand, at a standstill, *uti possidetis* [*L.*]; without a shadow of turning; as you were!

** *esto perpetua; notumus leges Angliæ mutari; j'y suis et j'y reste.*

142. [CHANGE FROM ACTION TO REST.] **Cessation. — N.** CESSATION, discontinuance, desistance, desinence.

intermission, remission; suspense, suspension; interruption; stop; hitch [*colloq.*]; stopping &c. *v.;* stoppage, halt; arrival &c. 292.

PAUSE, rest, lull, respite, truce, truce of God, armistice, stay, drop; interregnum, abeyance.

[IN DEBATE] closure, cloture, *clôture* [*F.*].

DEADLOCK, checkmate, backwater, dead water, dead stand, dead stop; end &c. 67; death &c. 360.

PUNCTUATION, comma, semicolon, colon, period, full stop, cæsura.

V. CEASE, discontinue, desist, stay; break off, leave off; hold, stop, pull up,

143. Continuance in action. — **N.** CONTINUANCE, continuation; run, pursuance, maintenance, extension, perpetuation, prolongation; persistence &c. (*perseverance*) 604a; repetition &c. 104.

V. CONTINUE, persist; go on, jog on, keep on, run on, hold on; abide, keep, pursue, stick to; take -, maintain- its course; carry on, keep up, drag on, stick [*colloq.*], persevere, endure, carry on.

SUSTAIN, uphold, hold up, keep on foot; follow up, perpetuate, prolong, maintain; preserve &c. 604a; harp upon &c. (*repeat*) 104.

KEEP GOING, keep alive, keep the pot boiling [*colloq.*], keep up the ball [*colloq.*]; die in harness; plug at it *or* along [*slang*]; keep the field, keep the ball rolling,

stop short; check, check in full career, deadlock; stick, hang fire; halt; pause, rest.

come to a -stand, – standstill, – deadlock, – full stop; arrive &c. 292; go out, die away; wear away, wear off; pass away &c. (be past) 122; be at an end.

HAVE DONE WITH, give over, surcease, shut up shop; give up &c. (relinquish) 624.

hold –, stay- one's hand; rest on one's oars, repose on one's laurels.

INTERRUPT, suspend, interpel [obs.]; intermit, remit; put an end to, put a stop to, put a period to; derail; bring to a -stand,- standstill; stop, stall, cut short, arrest, stem the -tide, – torrent; pull the check-string.

Int. STOP! hold! enough! avast! [naut.], have done! a truce to! soft! leave off! tenez! [F.], fade away! [slang], let up! [slang], cut it out! [slang].

***** "I pause for a reply" [Julius Caesar].

keep at it, keep up; hold on –, pursue -the even tenor of one's way.

LET BE; stare super antiquas vias [L.]; quieta non movere [L.]; let things take their course.

Adj. CONTINUING &c. v.; uninterrupted, unintermitting, unvarying, persistent, unceasing, unremitting, unshifting; unreversed, unstopped, unrevoked, unvaried; sustained; chronic; undying &c. (perpetual) 112; inconvertible.

Int. carry on! stand fast!

***** nolumus leges Angliæ mutari; vestigia nulla retrorsum [Horace]; labitur et labetur [Horace].

144. [GRADUAL CHANGE TO SOMETHING DIFFERENT.] **Conversion. — N.** CONVERSION, reduction, transmutation, resolution, assimilation; chemistry, alchemy; lapse, assumption, growth, progress; naturalization; transportation.

PROSELYTIZATION, regeneration, Catholicization, Protestantization.

PASSAGE, transit, transition, transmigration; shifting &c. v.; flux; phase; conjugation; convertibility.

LABORATORY &c. 691; crucible, alembic, caldron, retort, mortar; potter's wheel, anvil, lathe, blowpipe.

CONVERT, neophyte, catechumen, proselyte; pervert, renegade, apostate, turncoat.

V. BE CONVERTED INTO; become, get, wax; come –, turn- -to, –into; turn out, lapse, shift; run –, fall –, pass –, slide –, glide –, grow –, ripen –, open –, resolve itself –, settle –, merge- into; melt, grow, come round to, mature, mellow; assume the - form, – shape, – state, – nature, character- of; illapse [rare]; assume a new phase, undergo a change.

CONVERT INTO, resolve into; make, render; mold, form &c. 240; remodel, newmodel, refound, reform, reorganize; assimilate to, bring to, reduce to.

Adj. CONVERTED INTO &c. v.; convertible, resolvable into; conversible [rare], chemical, transitional; naturalized.

Adv. gradually &c. (slowly) 275; in transitu [L.] &c. (transference) 270.

***** "But doth suffer a sea-change Into something rich and strange" [Tempest].

145. Reversion. — N. REVERSION, return; revulsion.

TURNING POINT, turn of the tide; status quo ante bellum [L.]; calm before a storm.

alternation &c. (periodicity) 138; inversion &c. 219; recoil &c. 277; retrocession, retrospection, regression &c. 283; restoration &c. 660; relapse &c. 661; atavism, throwback; vicinism; escheat.

V. REVERT, reverse, return, turn back; relapse &c. 661; invert &c. 219; recoil &c. 277; retreat &c. 283; restore &c. 660; undo, unmake; turn the tide, turn the scale; escheat.

Adj. REVERTING &c. v.; revulsive, reactionary; retrorse.

Adv. REVULSIVELY, retrorsely, on the rebound, à rebours [F.].

146. [SUDDEN OR VIOLENT CHANGE.] **Revolution. — N.** REVOLUTION, revolt, bouleversement [F.], subversion, breakup; destruction &c. 162; sudden –, radical –, sweeping –, organic- change; clean sweep, debacle, débâcle [F.], overturn, overthrow, *coup d'état* [*F*.], rebellion, rising, uprising, mutiny, sansculottism, bolshevism, counter-revolution.

SPASM, convulsion, throe, revulsion; storm, earthquake, eruption, upheaval, cataclysm, transilience *or* transiliency [*rare*], jump, leap, plunge, jerk, start, dash; explosion.

LEGERDEMAIN &c. (*trick*) 545.

V. REVOLUTIONIZE, revolt, rebel, insurrect, rise; new-model, remodel, recast; strike out something new, break with the past; change the face of, unsex.

Adj. UNRECOGNIZABLE; transilient.

REVOLUTIONARY, catastrophic, cataclysmic, cataclysmal, convulsionary, insurgent, Red, insurrectional, insurrectionary, mutinous, rebellious, sansculottic, bolshevist *or* bolshevik.

---

147. [CHANGE OF ONE THING FOR ANOTHER.] **Substitution. — N.** SUBSTITUTION, commutation, subrogation [*law*], surrogation [*rare*]; supplanting &c. *v.*, supersession, supersedence, supersedure; metonymy &c. (*figure of speech*) 521.

[THING SUBSTITUTED] substitute, succedaneum, makeshift, temporary expedient; shift, apology, *pis aller* [*F*.], stopgap, jury mast, *locum tenens* [*L*.], alternate, warming pan [*colloq*.], dummy, scapegoat; double; changeling; *quid pro quo* [*L*.], alternative; representative &c. (*deputy*) 759; palimpsest.

PRICE, purchase money, consideration, equivalent.

V. SUBSTITUTE, put in the place of, change for; make way for, give place to; supply –, take- the place of; surrogate [*rare*], subrogate [*law*], supplant, supersede, replace, cut out [*colloq*.], serve as a substitute; step into the shoes of, stand in the shoes of; make a shift with, put up with; borrow of Peter to pay Paul; commute, redeem, compound for.

Adj. SUBSTITUTED &c. *v.*; vicarious, vicarial, substitutional, subdititious [*r. re*].

Adv. INSTEAD; by proxy; in place of, in lieu of, in the stead of, in the room of; *faute de mieux* [*F*.].

*** "Compound for sins they are inclined to By damning those they have no mind to" [Butler].

148. [DOUBLE OR MUTUAL CHANGE.] **Interchange. — N.** INTERCHANGE, exchange; commutation, permutation, intermutation; reciprocation, transposition, transposal, shuffle, shuffling; alternation, reciprocity; castling [at chess]; hocus-pocus; swap [*colloq*.].

barter &c. 794; a Roland for his Oliver; tit for tat &c. (*retaliation*) 718; cross fire, battledore and shuttlecock; *quid pro quo* [*L*.].

INTERCHANGEABLENESS, interchangeability.

V. INTERCHANGE, exchange, counterchange; bandy, barter, transpose, shuffle, change hands, swap [*colloq*.], permute, reciprocate, commute; interwork, give and take, return the compliment; play at -puss in the corner, – battledore and shuttlecock; take in one another's washing; retaliate &c. 718; requite.

Adj. RECIPROCAL, interactive, mutual, commutative, interchangeable; interchanged &c. *v.*; intercurrent [*rare*].

international, interstate, interurban, intercollegiate, intertribal, interdenominational, interscholastic.

Adv. IN EXCHANGE, *vice versa* [*L*.], conversely, *mutatis mutandis* [*L*.], backwards and forwards, forward and back, to and fro, back and forth, by turns, turn about, contrariwise, commutatively, turn and turn about; each in his turn, every one in his turn.

---

2. COMPLEX CHANGE

149. Changeableness. — N. CHANGEABLENESS &c. *adj.*; mutability, inconstancy; versatility, mobility; instability, unstable equilibrium; vacillation &c. (*irresolution*) 605; fluctuation, vicissitude; dysphoria; alternation &c. (*oscillation*) 314; transientness &c. 111.

150. Stability. — N. STABILITY; immutability &c. *adj.*; unchangeableness &c. *adj.*; constancy; stable equilibrium, immobility, soundness, vitality, stability ment [*rare*], stabilization; stiffness, ankylosis, solidity, *aplomb* [*F*.]; coherence.

permanence &c. 141; obstinacy &c. 606.

[Comparisons] moon, Proteus, kaleidoscope, chameleon, quicksilver, shifting sands, weathercock, vane, weathervane, harlequin, turncoat, Vicar of Bray, Cynthia of the minute, April showers; wheel of Fortune.

restlessness &c. adj.; fidgets, disquiet; disquietude, inquietude; unrest; agitation &c. 315.

V. fluctuate, vary, waver, flounder, flicker, flitter [archaic], flit, flutter, shift, shuffle, shake, totter, tremble, vacillate, wamble [dial.], turn and turn about, ring the changes; sway –, shift- to and fro; change and change about; oscillate &c. 314; vibrate –, oscillate- between two extremes; alternate; have as many phases as the moon.

Adj. changeable, changeful; changing &c. 140; mutable, variable, checkered, ever changing, kaleidoscopic; protean, proteiform; versatile.

inconstant, unstaid, unsteady, unstable, unfixed, unsettled; fluctuating &c. v.; restless, uneasy; agitated &c. 315; erratic, fickle; mercurial, irresolute &c. 605; capricious &c. 608; touch and go; inconsonant, fitful, spasmodic; vibratory; vagrant, feathery [rare], lightheaded, wayward; desultory; afloat; alternating; alterable, plastic, mobile; transient &c. 111; wavering.

Adv. seesaw &c. (oscillation) 314; off and on.

. "a rolling stone gathers no moss"; *pietra mossa non fa muschis; honores mutant mores; varium et mutabile semper femina* [Vergil].

fixture, establishment; rock, pillar, tower, foundation, leopard's spots, Ethiopian's skin; law of the Medes and Persians.

standpatter [U. S. politics].

V. be firm &c. adj.; stick fast; stand firm, keep firm, remain firm; stand pat; weather the storm.

establish, settle, stablish [archaic], ascertain, fix, set, stabilitate [obs.], stabilize; stet [printing], retain, keep hold; make good, make sure; fasten &c. (join) 43; set on its legs [colloq.], set on its feet; float; perpetuate.

settle down; strike root, take root; take up one's abode &c. 184; build one's house on a rock.

Adj. unchangeable, immutable; unaltered, unalterable; not to be changed; constant; permanent &c. 141; invariable, unyielding, undeviating; stable, durable; perennial &c. (diuturnal) 110.

fixed, steadfast, firm, firm as Gibraltar, firm as a rock, on a rock; tethered, anchored, moored, at anchor, firmly -seated, – established &c. v.; deep-rooted, ineradicable; fast, steady, balanced; confirmed, inveterate, valid; fiducial; immovable, irremovable, riveted, rooted; stated, settled, stereotyped, established &c. v.; obstinate &c. 606; vested; incontrovertible, indeclinable.

stuck fast, transfixed, aground, high and dry, stranded.

incommutable, indefeasible, irretrievable, intransmutable, irresoluble, irrevocable, irreversible, reverseless, inextinguishable, irreducible; indissoluble, indissolvable; indestructible, undying, imperishable, indelible, indeciduous; insusceptible, – of change.

Int. stet [L., printing].

. *littera scripta manet;* "Come one, come all! this rock shall fly From its firm base a' soon as I" [Scott]; *cælum non animum mutant qui trans mare currunt* [Horace].

Present Events

151. Eventuality. — N. eventuality, eventuation, event, occurrence, supervention, incident, affair, transaction, proceeding, fact; matter of fact, naked fact; phenomenon: advent.

circumstance, particular, casualty, accident, happening, adventure, passage, crisis, pass, emergency, contingency; concern, business.

consequence, issue, result, termination, conclusion.

Future Events

152. Destiny. — N. destiny &c. (necessity) 601; future existence, postexistence; hereafter; foredoom, future state, next world, world to come, after life; futurity &c. 121; everlasting life, everlasting death; life beyond the grave, life to come, world beyond the grave; prospect &c. (expectation) 507.

V. impend; hang over, lie over; threaten, loom, await, hover, come on, approach, stare one in the face; fore-

AFFAIRS, matters; the world, life, things, doings; things –, affairs- in general; the times, state of affairs, order of the day; course –, tide –, stream –, current –, run –, march- of -things, – events; ups and downs of life; chapter of accidents &c. (*chance*) 156; situation &c. (*circumstances*) 8; memorabilia.

V. HAPPEN, occur; take place, take effect; come, become of; come -off, – about, – round, – into existence, – forth, – to pass, – on; pass, present itself; fall; fall out, turn out; run, be on foot, fall in; befall, betide, bechance; prove, eventuate, draw on; turn up, crop up, spring up, cast up; supervene, survene, |*obs.*] issue, arrive, ensue, result, eventuate, arise, start, hold, take its course; pass off &c. (*be past*) 122.

EXPERIENCE; meet with; fall to the lot of; be one's -chance, – fortune, – lot; find; encounter, undergo; pass through, go through; endure &c. (*feel*) 821.

Adj. HAPPENING &c. *v.*; going on, doing, current; in the wind, afloat; on foot, on the carpet, on the tapis; at issue, in question; incidental.

EVENTFUL, stirring, bustling, full of incident; memorable, momentous, signal.

Adv. EVENTUALLY, ultimately, finally; in the event of, in case; in the course of things; in the natural *or* ordinary course of things; as things go, as times go; as the world -goes, – wags; as the tree falls, as the cat jumps [*colloq.*]; as it may -turn out, – happen.

⁎⁎* the plot thickens; "breasts the blows of circumstance" [Tennyson]; "so runs the round of life from hour to hour" [Tennyson]; "sprinkled along the waste of years" [Keble]; "Life is our dictionary" [Emerson]; "A Moment's Halt — a momentary taste Of Being from the Well amid the Waste" [Omar Khayyám — Fitzgerald].

ordain, preordain; predestine, doom, foredoom, have in store for.

Adj. IMPENDING &c. *v.*; destined; about to be, about to happen; coming, in store, to come, going to happen, instant, at hand, near; near at hand, close at hand; overhanging, hanging over one's head, imminent; brewing, preparing, forthcoming; in the wind, on the cards [*colloq.*], in reserve; that will be, that is to be; in prospect &c. (*expected*) 507; looming in the -distance, – horizon, – future; postexistent, unborn, in embryo; in the womb of -time, futurity; on the knees of the gods, in the future; pregnant &c. (*producing*) 161.

Adv. IN TIME, in the long run; all in good time; eventually &c. 151; whatever may happen &c. (*certainly*) 474; as chance &c. (156) would have it.

⁎⁎* "see future sons and daughters yet unborn" [Pope].

SECTION VIII.   CAUSATION

1. CONSTANCY OF SEQUENCE IN EVENTS

153. [CONSTANT ANTECEDENT.] **Cause.** — **N.** CAUSE, origin, source, principle, element; prime mover, *primum mobile* [*L.*], primordium [*rare*]; *vera causa* [*L.*], ultimate cause, Great First Cause; author &c. (*producer*) 164; mainspring, agent; leaven; groundwork, foundation &c. (*support*) 215.

SPRING, fountain, well, font; fountainhead, springhead, reservoir, headspring, wellspring, wellhead; *fons et origo* [*L.*], genesis; descent &c. (*paternity*) 166; remote cause; influence.

PIVOT, hinge, turning point, lever; key; heart, nucleus, hub, focus; proximate cause, *causa causans* [*L.*]; last straw that breaks the camel's back.

154. [CONSTANT SEQUENT.] **Effect.** — **N.** EFFECT, consequence; aftercome [*Scot.*], aftergrowth, afterclap, aftermath, aftercrop, derivative, derivation; result; resultant; upshot, issue, outcome, resultance [*rare*], *dénouement* [*F.*], conclusion; falling action, catastrophe, end &c. 67; impress, impression; development, outgrowth; blossom, bud, ear, fruit, crop, harvest, product.

PRODUCTION, produce, work, handiwork, fabric, performance; creature, creation; offspring, offshoot; first fruits, firstlings; heredity, telegony; premices [*obs.*], primices [*obs.*].

V. BE THE EFFECT OF &c. *n.*; be due to, be owing to; originate in *or* from;

REASON, reason why; ground; why and wherefore [colloq.], rationale, occasion, derivation; final cause &c. (intention) 620; les dessous des cartes [F.]; undercurrents.

RUDIMENT, egg, germ, embryo, fetus or fœtus, bud, root, radix, radical, radication [rare], etymon, nucleus, seed, stem, stock, stirps, trunk, taproot, gemma, gemmule, radicle, semen, sperm.

NEST, cradle, nursery, womb, nidus, birthplace, breeding-place, hotbed.;

CAUSALITY, causation; origination; causative; production &c. 161.

V. BE THE CAUSE OF &c. n.; originate; give origin to, give rise to, give occasion to; cause, occasion, sow the seeds of, kindle, suscitate [obs.]; bring on, bring to pass, bring about; produce; create &c. 161; set up, set afloat, set on foot; found, broach, institute, lay the foundation of; lie at the root of.

PROCURE, induce, draw down, open the door to, superinduce, evoke, entail, operate; elicit, provoke.

rise from, arise from, take its rise from, spring from, proceed from, emanate from, come from, grow from, bud from, sprout from, germinate from, issue from, flow from, result from, follow from, derive its origin from, accrue from; come to, come of, come out of; depend upon, hang upon, hinge upon, turn upon.

TAKE THE CONSEQUENCES, reap where one has sown, make one's bed and lie on it, sow the wind and reap the whirl-wind.

Adj. OWING TO; resulting from &c. v.; resultant, firstling; derivable from; due to; caused by &c. 153; dependent upon; derived from, evolved from; derivative; hereditary; telegonous.

Adv. CONSEQUENTLY, of course, it follows that, naturally; as a consequence, in consequence; through, all along of [dial.], necessarily, eventually.

⁎ cela va sans dire, "thereby hangs a tale" [Taming of the Shrew].

CONTRIBUTE; conduce to &c. (tend to) 176; have a hand in; have a finger in the pie [colloq.]; determine, decide, turn the scale, have the deciding vote, have the final word; have a common origin; derive its origin &c. (effect) 154.

Adj. CAUSED &c. v.; causal, ætiological or etiological, original; primary, primitive, primordial; aboriginal; originative, generative, inceptive, productive, creative, constitutive, procreative, formative, demiurgic, protogenic, protogenal; radical; in embryo, embryonic, embryotic; in ovo [L.]; seminal, germinal; at the bottom of; connate, having a common origin.

Adv. FROM THE BEGINNING, in the first place, before everything; because &c. 155; behind the scenes.

⁎ causa latet vis est notissima [Ovid]; felix qui potuit rerum cognoscere causas [Vergil]; "gentlemen, who made all that?" [Bonaparte].

155. [ASSIGNMENT OF CAUSE.] **Attribution.** — **N.** ATTRIBUTION, theory, ascription, assignment, reference to, rationale; accounting for &c. v.; ætiology or etiology, palætiology, imputation, derivation from.

FILIATION, affiliation; filiality; pedigree &c. (paternity) 166.

EXPLANATION &c. (interpretation) 522; reason why &c. (cause) 153.

V. ATTRIBUTE TO, ascribe to, impute to, refer to, lay to, point to, trace to, bring home to; put down to, set down to; blame; blame upon [colloq.]; charge on, ground on; invest with, assign as cause, lay at the door of, father upon, saddle; filiate, affiliate; account for,

156. [ABSENCE OF ASSIGNABLE CAUSE.] **Chance.**[1] — **N.** CHANCE, indetermination, accident, fortune, hazard, hap [rare], haphazard, chance-medley, random, luck, raccroc [F.], fluke [cant], casualty, fortuity, contingence, adventure, hit; fate &c. (necessity) 601; equal chance; lottery; tombola; lotto; toss-up [colloq.] &c. 621; turn of the -table, - cards; hazard of the die, chapter of accidents; cast -, throw- of the dice; heads or tails, wheel of Fortune; sortes [L.], sortes Virgilianæ [L.].

PROBABILITY, possibility, contingency, odds, long odds, run of luck; accidentalness, accidentalism, accidentality; main chance.

[1] The word Chance has two distinct meanings: the first, the absence of assignable cause, as above; and the second, the absence of design — for the latter see 621.

derive from, point out the reason &c. 153; theorize; tell how it comes; put the saddle on the right horse; find the real culprit.

Adj. ATTRIBUTED &c. *v.*; attributable &c. *v.*; referable *or* referrible; due to, derivable from; affiliate, derivate [*rare*]; owing to &c. (*effect*) 154; putative; ecbatic.

Adv. HENCE, thence, therefore, for, since, on account of, because, owing to; on that account; from this cause, from that cause; thanks to, forasmuch as; whence, *propter hoc* [*L.*].

WHY? wherefore? whence? how comes it? how is it? how happens it? how come? [*colloq., esp. negro*], how does it happen? how so?

IN SOME WAY, in some such way; somehow, somehow or other.

. that is why; *hinc illæ lachrymæ* [Terence]; *cherchez la femme.*

theory of -Probabilities, – Chances; bookmaking; assurance; gamble, speculation, gaming &c. 621.

V. CHANCE, hap, turn up; fall to one's lot; be one's fate &c. 601; stumble on, light upon; blunder upon, hit, hit upon; take one's chance &c. 621.

Adj. CASUAL, fortuitous, accidental, chance, chanceable [*archaic*], chanceful [*archaic*], haphazard, random, casual, adventive, adventitious, causeless, incidental, contingent, uncaused, undetermined, indeterminate; possible &c. 470; unintentional &c. 621.

Adv. BY CHANCE, by accident; at random, casually; perchance &c. (*possibly*), 470; for aught one knows; as -good, – bad, – ill-luck &c. *n.*- would have it; as it may -be, – chance, – turn up, – happen; as the case may be.

. "grasps the skirts of happy chance" [Tennyson]; "the accident of an accident" [Lord Thurlow].

2. CONNECTION BETWEEN CAUSE AND EFFECT

157. Power. — N. POWER; potency, potentiality; *jiva* [*theos.*]; puissance, might, force; energy &c. 171; dint; right hand, right arm; ascendancy, sway, control; prepotency, prepollence *or* prepollency [*rare*]; almightiness, omnipotence; *carte blanche* [*F.*], authority &c. 737; strength &c. 159; predominance.

ABILITY; ableness &c. *adj.*; competency; efficiency, efficacy; validity, cogency; enablement; vantage ground; influence &c. 175.

PRESSURE, electromotive force, high pressure; conductivity; elasticity; gravity, electricity, magnetism, magneto-electricity, galvanism, voltaic electricity, voltaism, electromagnetism, electrostatics, electrokinetics, electrodynamics; electromotion, electrification; magnetization, galvanization; attraction, pull; *vis inertiæ* [*L.*], *vis mortua* [*L.*], *vis viva* [*L.*]; potential –, dynamic- energy; friction, suction; live- circuit, – rail, – wire; volt, voltage.

[INSTRUMENTS] galvanometer, rheometer; variometer, magnetometer, magnetoscope, electrometer, electroscope, galvanoscope, electrophorus, electro-dynamometer, voltameter, ammeter, voltammeter, voltmeter, wattmeter.

CAPABILITY, capacity; *quid valeant hu-*

158. Impotence. — N. IMPOTENCE; inability, disability; disablement, impuissance [*rare*], caducity, imbecility; incapacity, incapability; inaptitude, ineptitude; indocility; invalidity, inefficiency, incompetence, disqualification.

telum imbelle [*L.*], *brutum fulmen* [*L.*], blank cartridge, flash in the pan, *vox et præterea nihil* [*L.*], dead letter, bit of waste paper, dummy; Quaker gun; cripple.

INEFFICACY &c. (*inutility*) 645; failure &c. 732.

HELPLESSNESS &c. *adj.*; prostration, paralysis, palsy, apoplexy, syncope, sideration [*obs.*], vincibility, vincibleness, deliquium, collapse, exhaustion, softening of the brain, senility, superannuation, atony, decrepitude, imbecility, neurasthenia, invertebracy, inanition; emasculation, orchotomy; eunuch.

MOLLYCODDLE, old woman, muff [*colloq.*], tenderling [*rare*], milksop, molly [*colloq.*], sissy [*colloq.*], mother's darling.

V. BE IMPOTENT &c. *adj.*; not have a leg to stand on.

vouloir rompre l'anguille au genou [*F.*], *vouloir prendre la lune avec les dents* [*F.*].

COLLAPSE, faint, swoon, fall into a swoon, drop; go by the board; end in smoke &c. (*fail*) 732.

meri quid ferre recusent [*L.*]; faculty, quality, attribute, endowment, virtue, gift, property, qualification, susceptibility.

V. BE POWERFUL &c. *adj.;* gain power &c. *n.*

BELONG TO, pertain to; lie –, be– in one's power; can.

EMPOWER; give –, confer –, exercise-power &c. *n.;* enable, invest; indue, endue; endow, arm; strengthen &c. 159; compel &c. 744.

ELECTRIFY, magnetize, energize, galvanize, attract.

Adj. POWERFUL, puissant; potent, potential [*rare*]; capable, able; equal to, up to; cogent, valid; effective, effectual; efficient, efficacious, adequate, competent; multipotent [*rare*], plenipotent [*rare*], prepollent [*rare*], predominant; mighty, ascendent, prepotent, omnipotent, armipotent, mightful [*archaic*]; almighty.

forcible &c. *adj.* (*energetic*) 171; influential &c. 175; productive &c. 168.

ELECTRIC, electrodynamic, electrokinetic, electromagnetic, electrometric, electrometrical, electromotive, electronegative, electropositive, electroscopic; magnetic, magneto-electric *or* magneto-electrical, magnetomotive; voltametric, voltaic; galvanic, galvanometric, galvanoscopic, dynamo-electric *or* dynamo-electrical; dynamic, static, potential.

Adv. POWERFULLY &c. *adj.;* by virtue of, by dint of.

** à toute force; δός μοι ποῦ στῶ καὶ κινῶ τὴν γῆν; *eripuit cœlo fulmen sceptrumque tyrannis; fortis cadere cedere non potest.*

RENDER POWERLESS &c. *adj.;* depotentiate [*rare*], deprive of power; disable, disenable; disarm, incapacitate, disqualify, unfit, invalidate, disinvigorate [*rare*], undermine, deaden, cramp, tie the hands; double up, prostrate, paralyze, muzzle, cripple, becripple, maim, lame, hamstring, unsinew [*rare*], draw the teeth of; throttle, strangle, garrote *or* garrotte, ratten [*trade-union cant*], silence, sprain, clip the wings of, put *hors de combat* [*F.*], spike the guns; take the wind out of one's sails, scotch the snake, put a spoke in one's wheel; break the -neck, – back; unhinge, unfit; put out of gear.

UNMAN, unnerve, devitalize, effeminize, attenuate, enervate; emasculate, evirate [*rare*], spay, eunuchize [*rare*], caponize, castrate, geld, alter.

SHATTER, exhaust; weaken &c. 160.

Adj. POWERLESS, impotent, unable, incapable, incompetent; inefficient, ineffective; inept; unfit, unfitted; unqualified, disqualified; unendowed; doddering [*colloq.*], wambly [*Scot. and dial. Eng.*], inapt, unapt; crippled, disabled &c. *v.;* armless; senile, decrepit, superannuated.

harmless, unarmed, weaponless, defenseless, *sine ictu* [*L.*], unfortified, mightless [*archaic*], indefensible, vincible, pregnable, untenable.

paralytic, paralyzed; palsied, imbecile; nerveless, sinewless, marrowless, pithless, lustless; emasculate, disjointed; out of joint, out of gear; unnerved, unhinged; water-logged, on one's beam ends, rudderless; laid on one's back; done up [*colloq.*], done for [*colloq.*], done brown [*colloq.*], done [*colloq.*], dead-beat [*colloq.*], exhausted, shattered, atonic, demoralized; graveled [*colloq.*] &c. (*in difficulty*) 704; helpless, unfriended, fatherless; without a leg to stand on, *hors de combat* [*F.*], laid on the shelf.

NUGATORY, null and void, inoperative, good for nothing, invertebrate, ineffectual &c. (*failing*) 732; inadequate &c. 640; inefficacious &c. (*useless*) 645.

** der kranke Mann; "desirous still but impotent to rise" [Shenstone]; "it has been well said that there is no surer way of courting national disaster than to be 'opulent, aggressive, and unarmed' " [Roosevelt].

---

159. [DEGREE OF POWER.] **Strength.** — **N.** STRENGTH; power &c. 157; energy &c. 171; vigor, force; main –, physical –, brute- force; spring, elasticity, tone, tension, tonicity.

[COMPARISONS] adamant, steel, iron, oak, heart of oak; iron grip; bone.

VIRILITY, vitality; stoutness &c. *adj.;*

160. Weakness. — **N.** WEAKNESS &c. *adj.;* debility, atony, relaxation, languor, enervation; impotence &c. 158; infirmity, effeminacy, feminality; fragility, flaccidity; inactivity &c. 683.

[COMPARISONS] reed, thread, rope of sand, house of cards, house built on sand.

59

lustihood, stamina, nerve, muscle, sinew *or* sinews, thews and sinews, physique; grit, pith, pithiness.

ATHLETICS, athleticism; gymnastics, acrobatism, agonistics, feats of strength.

ATHLETE, gymnast, pancratiast, acrobat; Atlas, Hercules, Antæus, Samson, Cyclops, Briareus, Colossus, Polyphemus, Titan, Brobdingnagian, Goliath; tower of strength; giant refreshed

STRENGTHENING &c. *v.;* invigoration, refreshment, refocillation [*obs.*].

[SCIENCE OF FORCES] dynamics, statics.

V. BE STRONG &c. *adj.,* be stronger; overmatch.

RENDER STRONG &c. *adj.;* give strength &c. *n.;* strengthen, invigorate, potentiate [*rare*], brace, nerve, fortify, buttress, sustain, harden, caseharden, steel, gird; screw up, wind up, set up; gird –, brace-up one's loins; recruit, set on one's legs [*colloq.*]; vivify; refresh &c. 689; refect [*archaic*], reinforce *or* reënforce &c. (*restore*) 660.

Adj. STRONG, mighty, vigorous, forcible, hard, adamantine, stout, robust, sturdy, husky [*colloq., U. S.*], doughty, hardy, powerful, potent, puissant, valid.

RESISTLESS, irresistible, invincible, proof against, impregnable, unconquerable, indomitable, inextinguishable, unquenchable; incontestable; more than a match for; overpowering, overwhelming; all-powerful, all-sufficient; sovereign.

ABLE-BODIED; athletic, gymnastic, carobatic, agonistic, palæstral [*rare*]; Herculean, Briarean, Brobdingnagian, Titanic, Cyclopean, Atlantean; muscular, brawny, wiry, well-knit, broad-shouldered, sinewy, sinewous [*rare*], strapping, stalwart, gigantic.

MANLY, manlike, manful; masculine, male, virile, in the prime of manhood.

UNWEAKENED, unallayed, unwithered, unshaken, unworn, unexhausted; in full force, in full swing; in the plentitude of power.

SOUND; stubborn, thick-ribbed, made of iron, deep-rooted; strong as -a lion, – an ox, – a horse – brandy; sound as a roach; in fine feather, in high feather [*both colloq.*]; like a giant refreshed.

ANÆMIA, bloodlessness, deficiency of blood, poverty of blood.

INVALIDATION; declension –, loss –, failure– of strength; delicacy, decrepitude, asthenia, adynamy [*rare*], cachexia *or* cachexy, sprain, strain.

WEAKLING; softling [*obs.*]; infant &c. 129; youth &c. 127.

V. BE WEAK &c. *adj.;* drop, crumble, give way, totter, dodder, tremble, shake, halt, limp, fade, languish, decline, flag, fail, have one foot in the grave.

RENDER WEAK &c. *adj.;* weaken, enfeeble, debilitate, invalidate, shake, deprive of strength, relax, enervate; unbrace, unnerve; cripple, unman &c. (*render powerless*) 158; cramp, reduce, sprain, strain, blunt the edge of; dilute, impoverish; decimate; extenuate; reduce in strength, reduce the strength of; *mettre de l'eau dans son vin* [*F.*].

Adj. WEAK, feeble, debile [*obs.*]; impotent &c. 158; relaxed, unnerved &c. *v.;* sapless, strengthless, powerless; weakly, unstrung, flaccid, adynamic, asthenic; nervous.

SOFT, effeminate, feminate [*obs.*], womanish.

FRAIL, fragile, shattery; flimsy, sleazy, gossamery, papery, unsubstantial, gimcrack, gingerbread; rickety, jerry-built, *kucha* or *kachcha* [*Hind.*], cranky; craichy [*dial. Eng.*], drooping, tottering, doddering [*colloq.*] &c. *v.;* broken, lame, withered, shattered, shaken, crazy, shaky, tumbledown; palsied &c. 158; decrepit.

UNSOUND, poor, infirm; faint, faintish; sickly &c. (*disease*) 655; dull, slack, evanid [*obs.*], languid; spent, short-winded, effete; weather-beaten; decayed, rotten, forworn [*archaic*], worn, seedy, languishing, wasted, washy, wishy-washy [*colloq.*], laid low, pulled down, the worse for wear.

UNSTRENGTHENED &c. 159, unsupported, unaided, unassisted; aidless, defenseless &c. 158.

on its last legs; weak as a -child, – baby, – chicken, – cat, – rat, – rag; weak as -water, – water gruel, – gingerbread, –milk and water; colorless &c. 429.

⁂ *non sum qualis eram;* "at the hour when sick men mostly die and sentries on lonely ramparts stand to their arms" [Dunsany]; "to be weak is miserable, Doing or suffering" [Milton].

Adv. STRONGLY &c. *adj.;* by force &c. *n.;* by main force &c. (*by compulsion*) 744.

*** "our withers are unwrung" [*Hamlet*]. *Blut und Eisen; cœlitus mihi vires; du fort au diable; en habiles gens; ex vi termini; flecti non frangi;* "he that wrestles with us strengthens our nerves and sharpens our skill" [Burke]; "inflexible in faith, invincible in arms" [Beattie].

3. POWER IN OPERATION

161. Production. — N. PRODUCTION, creation, construction, formation, fabrication, manufacture; building, architecture, erection, edification; coinage; diaster; organization; *nisus formativus* [*L.*]; putting together &c. *v.;* establishment; workmanship, performance; achievement &c. (*completion*) 729.

FLOWERING, fructification, fruition; inflorescence.

BRINGING FORTH &c. *v.;* parturition, birth, birth throe, childbirth, delivery, confinement, *accouchement* [*F.*], travail, labor, midwifery, obstetrics; geniture [*obs.*]; gestation &c. (*maturation*) 673; assimilation; evolution, development, growth; entelechy; fertilization, gemination, germination, heterogamy, genesis, generation, histogenesis, breeding, begetting, isogamy, epigenesis, procreation, progeneration, propagation; fecundation, impregnation; albumen &c. 357.

spontaneous generation; archigenesis, archebiosis, abiogenesis, biogenesis, biogeny, dysmerogenesis, eumerogenesis, heterogenesis, oögenesis, merogenesis, metogenesis, monogenesis, parthenogenesis, homogenesis, xenogenesis.[1]

dissogeny, digenesis, physiogeny, phylogeny, ontogeny, ontogenesis, mitosis, xenogeny; theogony, tocogony, tocology, vacuolation, vacuolization.

PUBLICATION; works, *œuvres* [*F.*], opus (*pl.* opera) [*L.*]; authorship.

STRUCTURE, building, edifice, fabric, erection, pile, tower; flower, fruit, blossom.

V. PRODUCE, perform, operate, do, make, gar [*obs.*], form, construct, fabricate, frame, contrive, manufacture; weave, forge, coin, carve, chisel; build, raise, edify, rear, erect, put together; set up, run up; establish, constitute, compose, organize, institute; achieve, accomplish &c. (*complete*) 729.

flower, burgeon *or* bourgeon, blossom, bear fruit, fructify, teem, ean [*obs.*], yean, farrow, drop, pup, whelp, kitten, kindle [*obs.*], spawn, spat; bear, lay, bring forth, give birth to, lie in, be

162. [NONPRODUCTION.] Destruction — N. DESTRUCTION; waste, dissolution, breaking up; disruption; diruption [*obs.*], consumption; disorganization.

FALL, downfall, ruin, perdition, debacle, *débâcle* [*F.*], crash, *éboulement* [*F.*], smash [*colloq.*], havoc, *délabrement* [*F.*], breakdown, break-up; prostration, cave-in [*colloq.*]; desolation, *bouleversement* [*F.*], wreck, wrack [*archaic*], shipwreck, cataclysm; washout.

EXTINCTION, annihilation; destruction of life &c. 361; knock-out, K. O. [*slang*], knock-out blow, knock-down blow; doom, crack of doom.

DESTROYING &c. *v.;* demolition, demolishment [*rare*], overthrow, subversion, suppression; abolition &c. (*abrogation*) 756; biblioclasm; sacrifice; ravage, devastation, razzia; incendiarism; revolution &c. 146; extirpation &c. (*extraction*) 301; *commencement de la fin* [*F.*], road to ruin; dilapidation &c. (*deterioration*) 659; *sabotage* [*F.*].

V. BE DESTROYED &c.; perish; fall, fall to the ground; tumble, topple; go –, fall- to pieces; break up; crumble, – to dust; go to -the dogs, – the wall, – smash, – shivers, – wreck, – pot [*colloq.*], – wrack and ruin; go by the board, go all to smash [*colloq.*]; be all over with, be all up with [*colloq.*], go to glory [*colloq. or slang*], go to pieces, go under, go up the spout [*colloq.*], go bung [*slang*], totter to its fall.

DESTROY; do –, make- away with; nullify; annul &c. 756; sacrifice, demolish; tear up; overturn, overthrow, overwhelm; upset, subvert, put an end to, seal the doom of, do for [*colloq.*], dish [*slang*], undo; break up, cut up; break down, cut down, pull down, mow down, blow down, beat down; suppress, quash, put down; cut short, take off, blot out; efface, obliterate, cancel, erase, strike out, expunge, delete, dele; dispel, dissipate, dissolve; consume.

smash, crash, quell, squash [*colloq.*], squelch [*colloq.*], crumple up, shatter, shiver; batter; tear –, crush –, cut –,

[1]Huxley.

brought to bed of, evolve, pullulate, usher into the world.

MAKE PRODUCTIVE &c. 168; create; beget, get, generate, fecundate, impregnate; procreate, progenerate, propagate; engender; bring –, call– into –being, – existence; breed, hatch, develop, bring up.

INDUCE, superinduce; suscitate [*obs.*]; cause &c. 153; acquire &c. 775.

Adj. PRODUCED, PRODUCING &c. *v.*, productive of; prolific &c. 168; creative; formative; procreant, generative, genitive, genetic, genial [*rare*], genital; pregnant; *enceinte* [*F.*], big with, fraught with; in the family way [*colloq.*], teeming, parturient, in the straw [*colloq.*], brought to bed of; lying-in; puerperal, puerperous [*rare*].

digenetic, heterogenetic, oögenetic, xenogenetic; ectogenous, gamic, hæmatobious, sporogenous, sporophorous.

ARCHITECTONIC *or* architectonical, constructive.

*** *ex nihilo nihil; fiat lux; materiam superabat opus* [Ovid]; "he who hath put forth his total strength in fit actions has the richest return of wisdom" [Emerson].

shake –, pull –, pick –to pieces; laniate [*rare*]; nip; tear to –rags, – tatters; crush –, knock– to atoms; ruin; strike out; throw down, throw over, knock down, knock over, lay out [*slang*], lay by the heels, fell, sink, swamp, scuttle, wreck, shipwreck, engulf *or* ingulf, submerge; lay in ashes, lay in ruins; sweep away, raze; level, – with the –ground, – dust.

deal destruction, lay waste, ravage, gut; disorganize; dismantle &c. (*render useless*) 645; devour, swallow up, desolate, devastate, sap, mine, blast, confound; exterminate, extinguish, quench, annihilate; snuff out, put out, stamp out, trample out; lay –, trample– in the dust; prostrate; tread –, crush –, trample– under foot; lay the ax to the root of; make short work of, make a clean sweep of, make mincemeat of; cut up root and branch; fling –, scatter– to the winds; throw overboard; strike at the root of, sap the foundations of, spring a mine, blow up; ravage with fire and sword; cast to the dogs; eradicate &c. 301.

Adj. DESTROYED &c. *v.*; perishing &c. *v.*; trembling –, nodding –, tottering– *n.*; extinct; all-destroying, all-devouring, all-engulfing.

to its fall; in course of destruction &c. all-engulfing.

DESTRUCTIVE, subversive, ruinous, incendiary, deletory [*obs.*]; destroying &c. *n.*; suicidal; deadly &c. (*killing*) 361.

Adv. with crushing effect, with a sledge hammer.

*** *delenda est Carthago; dum Roma deliberat Saguntum perit; écrasez l'infâme* [Voltaire]; "I would fain die a dry death" [*Tempest*].

163. Reproduction. — **N.** REPRODUCTION, renovation; restoration &c. 660; renewal; new edition, reprint &c. (*copy*) 21; revival, regeneration, palingenesis, revivification; apotheosis; resuscitation, reanimation, resurrection, resurgence, reappearance; regrowth; Phœnix.

generation &c. (*production*) 161; multiplication.

V. REPRODUCE; restore &c. 660; revive, renovate, renew, regenerate, revivify, resuscitate, reanimate, refashion, stir the embers, put into the crucible; multiply, repeat; resurge.

CROP UP, crop out, spring up like mushrooms.

Adj. REPRODUCED &c. *v.*; renascent, resurgent, reappearing; reproductive, proligerous [*rare*], progenitive, proliferous, gametal; hydra-headed; suigenetic.

164. Producer. — **N.** PRODUCER, originator, inventor, author, founder, generator, mover, architect, grower, raiser, introducer, deviser, constructor, begetter; creator; maker &c. (*agent*) 690; prime mover.

165. Destroyer. — **N.** DESTROYER &c. (*destroy* &c. 162); cankerworm &c. (*bane*) 663; assassin &c. (*killer*) 361; executioner &c. (*punish*) 975; biblioclast; eidoloclast, iconoclast, idoloclast; vandal, destructor [*rare*], Hun, nihilist.

166. Paternity. — N. PATERNITY; parentage; consanguinity &c. 11.

PARENT, father, sire, dad, papa, governor [*slang*], pater [*colloq*.], daddy [*colloq*.], paterfamilias, abba; genitor [*rare*], progenitor, procreator, begetter; ancestor; grandsire, grandfather; great-grandfather; fathership, fatherhood; *mabap* [*Hind*.].

MOTHERHOOD, maternity, motherhead [*rare*], mothership; mother, dam, mamma *or* mama, mammy, mam [*colloq*.], motherkin, matriarch, materfamilias; grandmother.

STEM, trunk, tree, stock, stirps, pedigree, house, lineage, line, family, tribe, sept, race, clan; genealogy, family tree, descent, extraction, birth, ancestry; forefathers, forbears, patriarchs.

Adj. PARENTAL; paternal; maternal; family, ancestral, linear, patriarchal; racial, phyletic.

⁎ *avi numerantur avorum;* "happy he with such a mother" [Tennyson]; *philosophia stemma non inspicit* [Seneca]; "thank God for the iron in the blood of our fathers" [Roosevelt].

167. Posterity. — N. POSTERITY, progeny, breed, issue, offspring, brood, litter, seed, farrow, spawn, spat; family, children, grandchildren, heirs; great-grandchildren.

CHILD, son, daughter, bairn, baby, kid [*colloq*.], papoose [*Am. Ind*.], imp, brat, moppet [*archaic*], lambkin, cub, cherub, nestling, tot, innocent, urchin, chit [*colloq*.]; infant &c. 129; *butcha* or *bacha* [*Hind*.]; bantling, scion; acrospire, plumule, shoot, sprout, olive-branch, sprit, branch; offshoot, offset; ramification; descendant; heir, heiress; heir-apparent, heir-presumptive; chip of the old block; heredity; rising generation.

LINEAGE, straight descent, sonship, line, filiation, primogeniture.

Adj. FILIAL; diphyletic.

⁎ "the child is father of the man" [Wordsworth].

168. Productiveness. — N. PRODUCTIVENESS &c. *adj.;* fecundity, fertilization, fertility, luxuriance, uberty [*obs*.].

[COMPARISONS] milch cow, rabbit, hydra, warren, seed plot, land flowing with milk and honey.

AFTERMATH, second crop, aftercrop, aftergrowth, arrish [*dial. Eng*.], eddish [*dial. Eng*.], rowen.

MULTIPLICATION, multiparity, propagation, procreation; superfetation, pregnancy, pullulation [*rare*], fructification.

V. MAKE PRODUCTIVE &c. *adj.;* fructify; procreate, pullulate, generate, fertilize, spermatize, impregnate; fecundate, fecundify; teem, spawn, multiply; produce &c. 161; conceive.

Adj. PRODUCTIVE, prolific, copious; teeming, teemful [*dial*.]; fertile, fruitful, frugiferous [*obs*.], fructuous [*rare*], plenteous, proliferous, fructiferous, fruitbearing; fecund, luxuriant; pregnant, uberous.

PROCREANT, procreative; generative, life-giving, spermatic, inceptive, originative; multiparous; omnific; propagable.

parturient &c. (*producing*) 161; profitable &c. (*useful*) 644.

169. Unproductiveness. — N. UNPRODUCTIVENESS &c. *adj.;* infertility, sterility, infecundity; impotence &c. 158; unprofitableness &c. (*inutility*) 645.

WASTE, desert, Sahara, wild, karoo, wilderness, howling wilderness.

V. BE UNPRODUCTIVE &c. *adj.;* hang fire, flash in the pan, come to nothing.

Adj. UNPRODUCTIVE, acarpous, inoperative, barren, addle, unfertile, unprolific, arid, sterile, unfruitful, infecund, [*rare*], jejune, infertile; useless, otiose; *sine prole* [*L*.]; fallow; teemless, issueless, fruitless, infructuose [*rare*]; unprofitable &c. (*useless*) 645; null and void, of no effect.

⁎ "no one can dam the Mississippi" [Roosevelt].

170. Agency. — N. AGENCY, operation, force, working, strain, function, office, maintenance, exercise, work, swing, play; interworking, interaction; procuration procurement.

CAUSATION &c. 153; mediation, intermediation, instrumentality &c. 631; conation, influence &c. 175; action &c. (*voluntary*) 680; *modus operandi* [*L*.] &c. 627.

quickening –, maintaining –, sustaining- power; home stroke.

V. BE IN ACTION &c. *adj.;* operate, work; act, act upon; perform, play, support, sustain, strain, maintain, take effect, quicken, strike.

come –, bring- into -operation, – play; have play, have free play; bring to bear upon.

Adj. OPERATIVE, operant [*rare*], efficient, efficacious, practical, exertive, conative, effectual.

at work, on foot; acting &c. (*doing*) 680; in operation, in force, in action, in play, in exercise; acted upon, wrought upon.

Adv. BY THE AGENCY OF &c. *n.;* through &c. (*instrumentality*) 631; by means of &c. 632.

*** "I myself must mix with action lest I wither by despair" [Tennyson]; "the day is always his who works in it with serenity and great aims" [Emerson].

171. Energy. — N. ENERGY, physical energy, force; keenness &c. *adj.;* intensity, vigor, backbone [*colloq.*], vim [*colloq.*], mettle, *vis viva* [*L.*], *vis vitæ* [*L.*], pep [*slang*], ginger [*slang*], go [*colloq.*]; strength, elasticity; high pressure; fire; rush; human dynamo.

ACTIVITY, agitation, effervescence; ferment, fermentation; ebullition, splutter, perturbation, stir, bustle; voluntary energy &c. 682; quicksilver.

EXERTION &c. (*effort*) 686; excitation &c. (*mental*) 824; resolution &c. (*mental energy*) 604.

ACRIMONY, acridity, acritude [*obs.*]; causticity, virulence, poignancy; harshness &c. *adj.;* severity, edge, point; pungency &c. 392.

EXCITANT, stimulant; Spanish fly, cantharides; seasoning &c. (*condiment*) 393.

172. Inertness. — N. INERTNESS, physical inertness, inertia, *vis inertiæ* [*L.*], inertion, inactivity, torpor, languor; dormancy, *fainéance* [*F.*], quiescence &c. 265; latency, inaction; passivity; stagnation; dullness &c. *adj.*

mental inertness; sloth &c. (*inactivity*) 683; inexcitability &c. 826; irresolution &c. 605; obstinacy &c. 606; permanence &c. 141.

V. BE INERT &c. *adj.;* hang fire, smolder *or* smoulder.

Adj. INERT, inactive, passive; torpid &c. 683; sluggish, stagnant, *fainéant* [*F.*], dull, heavy, flat, slack, tame, slow, blunt; lifeless, dead, uninfluential.

LATENT, dormant, smoldering *or* smouldering, unexerted.

Adv. INACTIVELY &c. *adj.;* in suspense, in abeyance.

V. GIVE ENERGY &c. *n.;* energize, stimulate, kindle, excite, exert; activate, potentialize [*rare*], dynamize, doubleshot; sharpen, intensify; inflame &c. (*render violent*) 173; wind up &c. (*strengthen*) 159.

strike – into, – hard, – home; make an impression.

Adj. ENERGETIC, strong, forcible, active, strenuous, forceful, mettlesome, enterprising; go-ahead [*colloq.*]; intense, deep-dyed, severe, keen, vivid, sharp, acute, incisive, trenchant, brisk.

rousing, irritating; poignant; virulent, caustic, corrosive, mordant, harsh, stringent; double-edged, double-shotted, double-distilled; drastic, escharotic; racy &c. (*pungent*) 392; excitant, excitative, excitatory.

potent &c. (*powerful*) 157; radio-active.

Adv. STRONGLY &c. *adj.;* *fortiter in re* [*L.*]; with telling effect.

*** the steam is up; *vires acquirit eundo;* "the race by vigor not by vaunts is won" [Pope]; "like a steam-engine in trousers" [Sydney Smith — *of Daniel Webster*].

173. Violence. — N. VIOLENCE, inclemency, vehemence, might, impetuosity, furiosity [*rare*]; boisterousness &c. *adj.;* effervescence, ebullition; turbulence, bluster; uproar, callithump [*U. S.*], riot, row [*colloq.*], rumpus [*colloq.*], *le diable à quatre* [*F.*], devil to pay [*colloq.*], all the fat in the fire [*colloq.*].

FEROCITY, rage, fury; exacerbation,

174. Moderation. — N. MODERATION; lenity &c. 740; temperateness, temperance, passability, passableness, gentleness &c. *adj.;* sobriety; quiet; mental calmness &c. (*inexcitability*) 826.

MODERATING &c. *v.;* anaphrodisia; relaxation, remission, mitigation, tranquilization, assuagement, alleviation, contemporation [*obs.*], pacification.

exasperation, malignity; severity &c. 739.

FORCE, brute force; outrage; *coup de main* [*F.*]; strain, shock, shog [*rare*].

FIT, paroxysm, spasm, convulsion, throe; hysterics, passion &c. (*state of excitability*) 825; orgasm, aphrodisia.

OUTBREAK, outburst; debacle; burst, bounce, dissilience [*rare*], discharge, volley, explosion, blow-up, blast, detonation, rush, eruption, displosion [*obs.*], torrent.

TURMOIL &c. (*disorder*) 59; ferment &c. (*agitation*) 315; storm, tempest, rough weather; squall &c. (*wind*) 349; earthquake, volcano, thunderstorm.

FURY, berserk *or* berserker, dragon, demon, tiger, beldam *or* beldame, madcap, wild beast; fire eater [*colloq.*] &c. (*blusterer*) 887; Erinys (*pl.* Erinyes), Eumenides, Tisiphone, Megæra, Alecto.

V. BE VIOLENT &c. *adj.;* run high; ferment, effervesce; romp, rampage; run wild, run riot; break the peace; rush, tear; rush headlong, rush headforemost; run amuck, raise a storm, make a riot; make –, kick up- a row [*colloq.*]; rough-house [*slang*]; bluster, rage, roar, riot, storm; boil, boil over; fume, foam, come in like a lion, wreak, bear down, ride roughshod, out-Herod Herod; spread like wildfire.

EXPLODE, go off, displode [*obs.*], detonate, detonize, fulminate, let off, let fly, discharge, thunder, blow up, flash, flare, burst; shock, strain.

BREAK OPEN, force open, prize open, pry open; break out, fly out, burst out.

RENDER VIOLENT &c. *adj.;* sharpen, stir up, quicken, excite, incite, urge, lash, stimulate; irritate, inflame, kindle, suscitate [*obs.*], foment; accelerate, aggravate, exasperate, exacerbate, convulse, infuriate, madden, lash into fury; fan the flame, add fuel to the flame; *oleum addere camino* [*L.*].

Adj. VIOLENT, vehement; warm; acute, sharp; rough, tough [*colloq.*], vicious [*colloq.*], rude, ungentle, bluff, boisterous, wild; brusque, abrupt, waspish; impetuous; rampant.

TURBULENT; disorderly; blustering, towering, raging &c. *v.;* troublous, riotous; tumultuary, tumultuous; obstreperous, uproarious; extravagant; unmitigated, immitigable; ravening, tameless;

MEAN, measure, *juste milieu* [*F.*], golden mean, *meden agan* [*Gr.* μηδὲν ἄγαν]. *ariston metron* [*Gr.* ἄριστον μέτρον].

MODERATOR; lullaby, sedative, calmative, lenitive, palliative, demulcent, antispasmodic, carminative; laudanum; rose water, balm, poppy, chloroform, opium: soothing sirup, opiate, anodyne, milk.

V. BE MODERATE &c. *adj.;* keep within -bounds, – compass; sober down, settle down; keep the peace, remit, relent; take in sail.

MODERATE, soften, mitigate, temper, accoy [*obs.*]; attemper, contemper [*obs.*], mollify, lenify [*rare*], dulcify, dull, take off the edge, blunt, obtund, sheathe, subdue, chasten; sober down, tone down, smooth down, slow down; weaken &c. 160; lessen &c. (*decrease*) 36; check; palliate.

TRANQUILLIZE, assuage, appease, suage *or* swage [*dial.*], lull, soothe, compose, still, calm, cool, quiet, hush, quell, sober, pacify, tame, damp, lay, allay, rebate [*archaic*], slacken, smooth, alleviate, rock to sleep, deaden, smother; throw cold water on, throw a wet blanket over; slake; curb &c. (*restrain*) 751; tame &c. (*subjugate*) 749; smooth over; pour oil on the -waves, – troubled waters; pour balm into; *mettre de l'eau dans son vin* [*F.*].

go out like a lamb, "roar you as gently as any sucking dove" [*M. N. D.*].

Adj. MODERATE; lenient &c. 740; gentle, mild; cool, sober, temperate, reasonable, measured; tempered &c. *v.;* calm, unruffled, quiet, tranquil, still; slow, smooth, untroubled; tame; peaceful, peaceable; pacific, halcyon.

UNEXCITING, unirritating; soft, bland, oily, demulcent, lenitive, anodyne; hypnotic &c. 683; sedative, calmative, assuaging, assuasive, calmant; antiorgastic, anaphrodisiac.

mild as mother's milk, mild as milk, milk and water, gentle as a lamb.

Adv. MODERATELY &c. *adj.;* gingerly; piano; under easy sail, at half speed, in moderation; within bounds, within compass; in reason.

⁎⁎⁎ est modus in rebus [Horace]; "not poppy nor mandragora, Nor all the drowsy syrups of the world "[*Othello*].

frenzied &c. (*insane*) 503; desperate &c. (*rash*) 863; infuriate, furious, outrageous, frantic, hysteric, in hysterics.

FIERY, flaming, scorching, hot, red-hot, ebullient.

SAVAGE, fierce, ferocious, fierce as a tiger.

EXCITED &c. *v.;* unquelled, unquenched, unextinguished, unrepressed, unbridled, unruly; headstrong; ungovernable, unappeasable, unmitigable; uncontrollable, incontrollable; insuppressible, irrepressible; orgastic.

SPASMODIC, convulsive, explosive; detonating &c. *v.;* volcanic, meteoric; stormy &c. (*wind*) 349.

Adv. VIOLENTLY &c. *adj.;* amain; by storm, by force, by main force; with might and main; tooth and nail, *vi et armis* [*L.*], at the point of the -sword; - bayonet; at one fell swoop; with a high hand, through thick and thin; in desperation, with a vengeance; *à outrance* [*F.*], *à toute outrance* [*F.*]; headlong, headfirst, headforemost.

APHRODISIAC, aphrodisiacal, aphroditous.

** furor arma ministrat; "blown with restless violence round about the pendent world" [*Measure for Measure*]; "*hysterica passio!* down, thou climbing sorrow!" [*King Lear*].

4. INDIRECT POWER

175. Influence. — N. INFLUENCE; importance &c. 642; weight, pressure, preponderance, prevalence, sway; predominance, predominancy; ascendancy; dominance, reign; control, domination, pull [*colloq. or slang*]; authority &c. 737; power, potency, capability &c. (*power*) 157; interest; spell, magic, magnetism.

FOOTING; purchase &c. (*support*) 215; play, leverage, vantage ground, advantage.

175a. Absence of Influence. — N. IMPOTENCE &c. 158; powerlessness; inertness &c. 172; irrelevancy &c. 10.

V. have no influence &c. 175.

Adj. UNINFLUENTIAL; unconducing [*rare*], nonconductive, unconductive; forceless, powerless &c. 158; irrelevant &c. 10.

TOWER OF STRENGTH, host in himself; protection, patronage, auspices; patron &c. (*auxiliary*) 711.

V. HAVE INFLUENCE &c. *n.;* be influential &c. *adj.;* carry weight, sway, bias, actuate, weigh, tell; have a hold upon, magnetize, bear upon, gain a footing, work upon; take root, take hold; strike root in.

PERVADE, run through; spread like wildfire, be rife &c. *adj.;* rage, gain head.

DOMINATE, subject, predominate; outweigh, overweigh; override, overbear; have -, get -, gain- -the upper hand, -full play; prevail.

BE RECOGNIZED, be listened to; make one's voice heard, gain a hearing; play a -part, - leading part- in; lead, control, rule, manage, master, get the mastery of, get control of, make one's influence felt; take the lead, pull the strings; wind round one's finger; turn -, throw one's weight into- the scale; set the fashion, lead the dance.

Adj. INFLUENTIAL, effective, effectual [*rare*], potent; important &c. 642; weighty; prevailing &c. *v.;* prevalent, rife, rampant, dominant, regnant, predominant, in the ascendant, hegemonical; authoritative, recognized, telling.

Adv. with telling effect, with authority.

** tel maître tel valet.

176. Tendency. — N. TENDENCY; aptness, aptitude; proneness, proclivity, bent, turn, tone, bias, set, warp, leaning (*with* to *or* towards), predisposition, inclination, tendence [*rare*], propensity, susceptibility; conatus, conation [*obs.*], nisus; liability &c. 177; quality, nature, temperament; idiocrasy, idiosyncrasy; cast, vein, grain; humor, mood; trend; drift &c. (*direction*) 278; conduciveness, conducement; applicability &c. (*utility*) 644; subservience &c. (*instrumentality*) 631.

V. TEND, contribute, conduce, lead, influence, dispose, incline, verge, bend to, warp, turn, work towards, trend, affect, carry, redound to, bid fair to, gravitate towards; promote &c. (*aid*) 707.

Adj. TENDING &c. *v.;* conative, conducent [*obs.*], conducive, working towards, in a fair way to, likely to, calculated to; liable &c. 177; subservient&c. (*instrumental*) 631; useful &c. 644; subsidiary &c. (*helping*) 707; idiocratic, indiosyncratic, idiosyncratical.

Adv. for, whither; for the purpose of.

** "all men that are ruined are ruined on the side of their natural propensities" [Burke].

177. Liability. — N. LIABILITY, liableness; possibility, contingency; susceptivity, susceptiveness, susceptibility.

V. BE LIABLE &c. *adj.;* incur, lay oneself open to, be subjected to, run the chance, stand a chance; lie under, expose oneself to, open a door to.

Adj. LIABLE, subject, susceptive; in danger &c. 665; open to, exposed to, obnoxious to; answerable, responsible, accountable, amenable; unexempt from; apt to; dependent on; incident to.

CONTINGENT, incidental, possible, on the cards, within range of, at the mercy of.

5. COMBINATIONS OF CAUSES

178. Concurrence. — N. CONCURRENCE, coöperation, coagency; union; coadunation, coaction [*rare*], coworking [*rare*], synergy [*rare*], collaboration, conformity, conformableness, agreement &c. 23; consilience; consent &c. (*assent*) 488; alliance; concert &c. 709; partnership &c. 712.

V. CONCUR, conduce, conspire, contribute; agree, unite, harmonize, hitch [*colloq.*], jibe [*colloq., U. S.*], coadunate, combine; hang –, pull– together &c. (*coöperate*) 709; help to &c. (*aid*) 707.

keep pace with, run parallel; go with, go along with, go hand in hand with.

Adj. CONCURRING &c. *v.;* concurrent, conformable, corresponsive [*rare*], joint, coöperative, concomitant, coincident, concordant, harmonious, consentaneous [*archaic*]; coadunate, coadunative, consilient, in alliance with, banded together, of one mind, at one with.

Adv. with one consent.

179. Counteraction. — N. COUNTERACTION, opposition; contrariety &c. 14; antagonism, polarity; clashing &c. *v.;* collision, interference, resistance, renitency, friction; reaction; retroaction &c. (*recoil*) 277; counterblast; neutralization &c. (*compensation*) 30; *vis inertiæ* [*L.*]; check &c. (*hindrance*) 706.

voluntary opposition &c. 708; voluntary resistance &c. 719; repression &c. (*restraint*) 751.

V. COUNTERACT; run counter, clash, cross; interfere with, conflict with; contravene; jostle; go –, run –, beat –, militate– against; stultify; antagonize, frustrate, oppose &c. 708; traverse; overcome, overpower, withstand &c. (*resist*) 719; impede, hinder &c. 706; repress &c. (*restrain*) 751; react &c. (*recoil*) 277.

UNDO, neutralize, offset, cancel; counterpoise &c. (*compensate*) 30; overpoise.

Adj. COUNTERACTING &c. *v.;* antagonistic, conflicting, retroactive, renitent, reactionary; contrary &c. 14.

Adv. ALTHOUGH &c. 30; against; mauger *or* maugre, malgre *or* maulgre [*obs.*], malgrado [*obs.*], notwithstanding; in spite of &c. 708.

CLASS II

Words relating to SPACE

Section I. SPACE IN GENERAL

1. Abstract Space

180. [Indefinite space.] **Space. —
N.** space, extension, extent, superficial
extent, expanse, stretch; room, accommodation, capacity, scope, range, latitude, field, way, expansion, compass,
sweep, play, swing, spread.

spare room, elbowroom, houseroom;
leeway, seaway, headway, stowage,
roomage [obs.], tankage, margin; opening, sphere, arena.

OPEN SPACE, free space; void &c.
(absence) 187; waste, desert, wild; wildness [obs.], wilderness; moor, down,
downs, upland, moorland; prairie,
steppe, llano [Sp. Amer.], campagna.

UNLIMITED SPACE; heavens, ether,
plenum, infinity &c. 105; world, wide
world; ubiquity &c. (presence) 186;
length and breadth of the land; abyss
&c. (interval) 198.

PROPORTIONS, acreage; acres, – roods
and perches; square -inches, – yards
&c.; ares, arpents.

Adj. SPACIOUS, roomy, extensive, expansive, capacious, ample; widespread,
vast, world-wide, wide, far-flung, vasty
[rare], uncircumscribed; boundless &c.
(infinite) 105; shoreless, trackless, pathless; extended; beyond the verge, far
as the eye can see.

Adv. EXTENSIVELY &c. adj.; wherever;
everywhere; far and -near, – wide; right
and left, all over, all the world over;
throughout the -world, - length and
breadth of the land; under the sun, in
every quarter; in all -quarters, – lands;
here, there, and everywhere; from pole
to pole, from China to Peru [Johnson],
from Indus to the pole [Pope], from Dan
to Beersheba, from end to end; on the
face of the earth, in the wide world, on
the face of the waters, "from the four

180a. Inextension. — N. INEXTEN-
SION, nonextension, point, dot, speck,
spot, pinprick, tittle; atom &c. (smallness) 32.

181. [Definite space.] **Region. —
N.** REGION, sphere, ground, soil, area,
realm, hemisphere, quarter, orb, circuit,
circle; pale &c. (limit) 233; compartment, department; clearing; domain,
tract, terrain, dominion, colony, commonwealth, territory, country, fatherland, motherland.

canton, county, shire, province, arrondissement [F.], mofussil [India], parish,
diocese, township, commune, ward,
wapentake [hist.], hundred, riding, lathe
[Kent, Eng.], soke [hist.], tithing,
bailiwick; principality, duchy, palatinate, archduchy, dukedom, kingdom,
empire.

precinct, arena, enceinte [F.], walk,
march, district, beat; patch, plot, inclosure, close, enclave, field, garth, court;
street &c. (abode) 189; paddock &c.
(inclosure) 232.

CLIME, climate, zone, meridian, latitude.

Adj. TERRITORIAL, local, parochial,
provincial, regional, insular.

182. [Limited space.] **Place. — N.**
PLACE, lieu, spot, whereabouts, point,
dot; niche, nook &c. (corner) 244; hole;
pigeonhole &c. (receptacle) 191; compartment; confine, premises, precinct,
station; area, courtyard, square, place
[F.], piazza [It.], plaza [Sp.], forum [L.],
agora [Gr.], hamlet, village &c. (abode)
189; pen &c. (inclosure) 232; countryside, location, site, locality &c. (situation) 183.

corners of the earth" [*Merchant of Venice*], from all points of the compass; to the four winds, to the uttermost parts of the earth.

ins and outs; every hole and corner.

Adv. SOMEWHERE, in some place, wherever it may be, here and there, in various places, *passim* [*L.*].

2. RELATIVE SPACE

183. Situation. — N. SITUATION, position, locality, locale (*properly*, local), status, latitude and longitude; footing, standing, standpoint, post; stage; aspect, attitude, posture, set [*colloq.*], pose.

PLACE, site, situs, station, seat, venue, whereabouts, environment, ground; bearings &c. (*direction*) 278; spot &c. (*limited space*) 182.

topography, geography, chorography; map &c. 554.

V. BE SITUATED, be situate, be located; lie; have its seat in.

Adj. SITUATE, situated; local, topical, topographical &c. *n.*

Adv. *in situ* [*L.*], *in loco* [*L.*]; here and there, *passim* [*L.*]; hereabouts, thereabouts, whereabouts; in place, here, there.

in –, amidst– such and such- -surroundings, – environs, – *entourage* [*F.*].

184. Location. — N. LOCATION, localization; lodgment; deposition, reposition; stowage; collocation; packing, lading; establishment, settlement, installation; fixation; insertion &c. 300.

anchorage, roadstead, mooring, encampment.

SETTLEMENT, plantation, colony, cantonment; situation; quarters, barracks; habitation &c. (*abode*) 189; "a local habitation and a name" [*M. N. D.*].

DOMESTICATION, cohabitation, colonization; endenization [*obs.*], naturalization.

V. PLACE, situate, locate, localize, make a place for, put, lay, set, seat, station, lodge, quarter, post, install; house, stow; establish, fix, pin, root; graft; plant &c. (*insert*) 300; shelve, pitch, camp, lay down, deposit, reposit, store, store away, cradle; moor, tether, picket; pack, tuck in; embed, imbed; vest, invest in.

BILLET ON, quarter upon, saddle with.

LOAD, lade, stevedore, freight; pocket, put up, bag.

185. Displacement. — N. DISPLACEMENT, elocation [*obs.*], heterotopy, transposition.

EJECTMENT &c. 297; exile &c. (*banishment*) 893.

REMOVAL &c. (*transference*) 270; unshipment, transshipment *or* transhipment, unplacement [*rare*], moving, shift.

MISPLACEMENT, dislocation &c. 61; fish out of water.

V. DISPLACE, displant, dislodge, disestablish; misplace, unplace [*rare*], translocate [*rare*], unseat, disturb, disniche; exile &c. (*seclude*) 893; ablegate [*obs.*], set aside, remove; take away, cart away; take off, draft off; lade &c. 184.

UNLOAD, empty &c. (*eject*) 297; transfer &c. 270; dispel.

VACATE; depart &c. 293.

Adj. DISPLACED &c. *v.;* unplaced, unhoused, unharbored, unestablished, unsettled; houseless, homeless, harborless [*archaic*]; out of place, out of a situation.

MISPLACED, out of its element.

INHABIT &c. (*be present*) 186; domesticate, colonize, found, people; take root, strike root; anchor; cast –, come to an- anchor; sit down, settle down; settle; take up one's -abode, – quarters; plant –, establish –, locate- oneself; have one's legal residence at; hang out one's shingle [*colloq.*]; squat, perch, hive, *se nicher* [*F.*], bivouac, burrow, get a footing; encamp, pitch one's tent; put up -at, – one's horses at; keep house.

NATURALIZE, endenizen [*rare*], adopt.

PUT BACK, replace &c. (*restore*) 660.

Adj. PLACED &c. *v.;* situate, posited, ensconced, imbedded, embosomed, rooted; domesticated; vested in, unremoved.

MOORED &c. *v.;* at anchor.

3. Existence in Space

186. Presence. — N. presence, presentness, occupancy, occupation; attendance.

permeation, pervasion; diffusion &c. (*dispersion*) 73.

whereness, ubiety, ubiquity, ubiquitariness; omnipresence.

bystander &c. (*spectator*) 444.

V. be present &c. *adj.; assister* [*F.*]; make one -of, - at; look on, attend, remain; find -, present- oneself; show one's face; fall in the way of, occur in a place; exist in space, lie, stand; occupy.

inhabit, dwell, reside, stay, sojourn, live, abide, lodge, bunk, room [*U. S.*], nestle, roost [*colloq.*], perch; take up one's abode &c. (*be located*) 184; tenant; people.

frequent, resort to, haunt; revisit.

pervade, permeate; be diffused through, be disseminated through; overspread, overrun; fill, run through; meet one at every turn.

Adj. present; occupying, inhabiting &c. *v.;* moored &c. 184; resiant [*obs.*], resident, residential, residentiary; domiciled.

ubiquitous, ubiquitary; omnipresent; universally present.

peopled, populous, full of people, inhabited.

Adv. here, there, where, everywhere, aboard, on board, at home, afield; on the spot; here there and everywhere &c. (*space*) 180; in presence of, before; under the eyes of, under the nose of; in the face of; *in propriâ personâ* [*L.*].

.•. *nusquam est qui ubique est* [Seneca].

187. [Nullibicity.] Absence. — N. nullibicity, nullibiety [*rare*], absence; awayness [*rare*], cut [*colloq.*]; inexistence &c. 2; nonresidence, absenteeism; nonattendance, alibi.

emptiness &c. *adj.;* void, vacuum; vacuity [*rare*], vacancy, voidness [*rare*], *tabula rasa* [*L.*]; exemption; hiatus &c. (*interval*) 198; lipotype.

truant, absentee.

nobody; nobody -present, - on earth; not a soul; no man, nix [*slang*].

V. be absent &c. *adj.;* keep away, keep out of the way; play truant, absent oneself, stay away; slip off, slip out, slip away; keep -, hold- aloof.

withdraw, make oneself scarce [*colloq.*], retreat, retire, vacate; go away &c. 293.

Adj. absent, not present, away, nonresident, gone, from home; missing; lost; wanting; omitted; nowhere to be found; inexistent &c. 2.

empty, void; vacant, vacuous; blank, null; untenanted, unoccupied, uninhabited; tenantless; desert, deserted; devoid; unhabitable, uninhabitable.

exempt from, not having.

Adv. without, minus, nowhere; elsewhere; neither here nor there; in default of; sans; behind one's back.

.•. the bird has flown; *non est inventus.*

"absence makes the heart grow fonder" [Bayley]; "absent in body but present in spirit" [*1 Corinthians v, 3*]; *absenti nemo ne nocuisse velit* [Propertius]; "Achilles absent was Achilles still" [Homer]; *aux absents les os; briller par son absence;* "conspicuous by his absence" [Russell]; "in the hope to meet shortly again and make our absence sweet" [B. Jonson].

188. Inhabitant. — N. inhabitant; resident, residentiary; dweller, indweller, habitant [*rare*]; addressee; occupier, occupant; householder, lodger, roomer [*U. S.*], inmate, tenant, incumbent, sojourner, *locum tenens* [*L.*], commorant; settler, squatter, backwoodsman, colonist; islander; denizen, citizen; burgher, oppidan, cockney, cit [*colloq.*], townsman, burgess; villager; cottager, cottier, cotter; compatriot; backsettler, boarder; hotel keeper, innkeeper; habitant; paying guest; planter.

native, indigene [*rare*], aborigines, autochthon (*pl.* autochthones), abo-

189. [Place of habitation, or resort.] Abode. — N. abode, dwelling, lodging, domicile, residence, address, habitation, where one's lot is cast, local habitation, berth, diggings [*colloq.*], seat, lap, sojourn, housing, quarters, headquarters, resiance [*obs.*], tabernacle, throne, ark.

home, fatherland, motherland, country; homestead, home stall [*Eng.*], fireside; hearth, hearthstone; chimney corner, ingleside; harem, seraglio, zenana; household gods, *lares et penates* [*L.*], roof, household, housing, *dulce domum* [*L.*], paternal domicile; native

riginal; newcomer &c. (*stranger*) 57.

American; Briton, Englishman, Britisher, John Bull; Canadian, Canuck [*slang*]; downeaster [*U. S.*]; Scot, Scotchman, Scotsman, Caledonian; Hibernian, Irishman, Paddywhack, Paddy, Mick, Teague, Greek *or* Grecian [*slang*]; Welshman, Cambrian, Taffy; Frenchman, Parleyvoo, Froggy [*slang*]; Chinaman, Celestial; Uncle Sam, Yankee, Brother Jonathan.

PEOPLE &c. (*mankind*) 372; colony, settlement; household; mir [*Russia*]; garrison, crew; population.

V. INHABIT &c. (*be present*) 186; endenizen [*rare*] &c. (*locate oneself*) 184.

Adj. INDIGENOUS: native, natal; autochthonal, autochthonous; British, English; American; Canadian; Irish, Hibernian; Scotch, Scottish; Welsh, Cambrian; French, Gallic; Chinese, Celestial, Sinæan, Sinaic *or* Sinic [*rare*], Chink [*slang*], Chinee [*slang*]; domestic; domiciliated, domiciled; naturalized, vernacular, domesticated; domiciliary; colonial.

OCCUPIED BY, in the occupation of; garrisoned by.

*** "For he might have been a Roosian, A Frenchman, Turk or Proosian, Or perhaps Italian! But in spite of all temptations To belong to other nations, He remains an Englishman" [Gilbert].

soil, native land, "God's own country," down home [*colloq.*]

quarter, parish &c. (*region*) 181.

RETREAT, haunt, resort; nest, nidus, snuggery [*colloq.*], arbor, bower &c. 191; lair, den, cave, hole, hiding place, cell, sanctum sanctorum, aerie, eyrie *or* eyry, rookery, hive; habitat, covert, perch, roost; nidification; *kala jagah* [*Hind.*].

CAMP, bivouac, encampment, cantonment; castrametation; barrack, casemate, casern *or* caserne; tent &c. 223.

TENEMENT, messuage, farm, farmhouse, grange, hacienda [*Sp. Amer.*], toft [*Scot., and dial. Eng.*].

COT, cabin, hut, chalet *or* châlet [*F.*], croft, shed, booth, stall, hovel, bothy *or* boothy, shanty, dugout [*U. S.*], wigwam; pen &c. (*inclosure*) 232; barn, bawn [*obs.*], kennel, sty, doghole, cote, coop, hutch; byre, cowhouse, cowshed, cowbyre; stable, dovecote, columbary, columbarium; shippen [*dial.*]; igloo *or* iglu [*Eskimo*], jacal; lacustrine –, lake –, pile- dwelling; log cabin, log house; shack [*colloq.*], shebang [*slang*], tepee, topek.

HOUSE, mansion, place, villa, cottage, box, lodge, hermitage, *rus in urbe* [*L.*], folly, rotunda, tower, château [*F.*], castle, pavilion, hotel, court, manor-house, messuage, hall, palace; kiosk, bungalow, chummery [*esp. Anglo-Indian*], casa

[*Sp., Pg. and It.*], country seat; apartment-, brownstone-, duplex-, frame-, shingle-, flat-, tenement- house; three-decker, monitor building [*U. S.*]; building &c. (*construction*) 161; room, chamber &c. (*receptacle*) 191; rents [*colloq. or cant, U. S.*], buildings, mews.

HAMLET, village, bustee *or* basti [*Hind.*], thorp *or* thorpe, dorp, kraal [*S. Africa*], rancho [*Sp. Amer.*].

TOWN, borough, burgh, ham [*now used only in compounds*], city, capital, metropolis; suburb; provincial town, county town, county seat; courthouse [*U. S.*]; ghetto.

STREET, place, terrace, parade, esplanade, alameda [*Sp.*], board walk, embankment, road, row, lane, alley, court, quadrangle, quad [*colloq.*], wynd [*dial.*], close, yard, passage.

square, polygon, circus, crescent, mall, piazza, arcade, colonnade, peristyle, cloister; gardens, grove, residences; block of buildings, market place, *place* [*F.*], plaza.

ANCHORAGE, roadstead, roads; dock, basin, wharf, quay, port, harbor.

ASSEMBLY ROOM, auditorium, concert hall, armory, gymnasium; cathedral, church, chapel, meetinghouse &c. (*temple*) 1000; parliament &c. (*council*) 696.

INN, hostel [*archaic*], hostelry [*archaic*], hotel, tavern, caravansary *or* caravanserai, xenodochium, dak bungalow [*India*], khan, hospice; public house, alehouse, pothouse, mughouse; gin palace; bar, barroom; barrel house [*slang, U. S.*], cabaret [*U. S.*], chophouse; club, clubhouse; cookshop, dive [*U. S.*], exchange [*euphemism, U. S.*]; grill room, saloon [*U. S.*], shebeen [*Irish and Scot.*]; coffeehouse, eating-house; canteen, restaurant, buffet, café, estaminet [*F.*], posada [*Sp.*]

ALMSHOUSE, poorhouse, townhouse [*U. S.*].

GARDEN, park, pleasure ground, pleasance *or* plaisance [*archaic*], demesne.

SANATORIUM. health resort, Hill station *or* the Hills [*India*], health retreat, sanitarium, spa, watering-place, pump room.

V. INHABIT &c. (*be present*) 186; take up one's abode &c. (*locate oneself*) 184.

Adj. URBAN, oppidan [*rare*], metropolitan; suburban; provincial, rural, rustic, agrestic, country, countrified, regional; domestic; cosmopolitan; palatial.

    *** *eigner Herd ist goldes Werth;* "even cities have their graves" [Longfellow]; *ubi libertas ibi patria;* "the herds are shut in byre and hut" [Kipling]; "My wants are few, I only wish a hut of stone (A *very plain* brown stone will do) That I may call my own" [Holmes].

190. [THINGS CONTAINED.] **Contents. — N.** CONTENTS; cargo, lading, freight, shipment, load, bale, burden, jag [*colloq.*]; cartload, shipload; cup of, basket of &c. (*receptacle*) 191; inside &c. 221; stuffing.

    V. LOAD, lade, ship, charge, weight, pile, fill, stuff.

191. Receptacle. — N. RECEPTACLE, container; inclosure &c. 232; recipient, receiver, reservatory [*obs.*].

COMPARTMENT; cell, cellule; follicle; hole, corner, niche, recess, nook; crypt, stall, pigeonhole, cove, oriel; cave &c. (*concavity*) 252; mouth.

CAPSULE, vesicle, cyst, pod, calyx, cancelli, utricle, bladder; pericarp, udder.

STOMACH, paunch, belly, venter, ventricle, ingluvies, crop, craw, maw, gizzard, breadbasket [*slang*], Little Mary [*slang*]; omasum, manyplies, abomasum, rumen, reticulum.

BAG, sac, sack, saccule, wallet, pocket, pouch, fob, sheath, scabbard, socket, cardcase, scrip [*archaic*], poke [*chiefly dial.*], knapsack, haversack, satchel, reticule, budget [*dial.*], net; ditty-bag, -box; housewife *or* hussif; saddlebags; portfolio; quiver &c. (*magazine*) 636.

CASE, chest, box, coffer, caddy, casket; pyx *or* pix, monstrance [*R. C. Ch.*]; caisson; desk, bureau, reliquary, shrine; trunk, portmanteau, bandbox, valise, grip *or* grip-sack [*colloq.*, *U. S.*], suitcase, handbag, Boston bag, school bag, brief case, traveling-bag, Gladstone *or* Gladstone bag; skippet, vasculum; boot, imperial [*now rare*]; *vache* [*F.*]; cage, manger, rack.

VESSEL, vase, bushel, barrel; canister, jar; pottle, basket, pannier; buck basket, clothes basket, hopper, maund [*obs.*], creel, cran *or* crane [*Scot.*], crate, cradle, bassinet, whisket *or* wisket [*dial. Eng.*]; *jardinière* [*F.*], *corbeille* [*F.*], hamper, dosser *or* dorser, tray, hod, scuttle, utensil; brazier; cuspidor, spittoon.

[FOR LIQUIDS] cistern &c. (*store*) 636; vat, caldron *or* cauldron, barrel, cask, puncheon, keg, rundlet, tun, butt, firkin, kilderkin, carboy, amphora, bottle, jar, decanter, ewer, cruse, carafe, crock, kit [*dial. Eng.*], canteen, flagon; demijohn; flask, flasket; stoup *or* stoop, noggin, vial, phial, cruet, caster; urn, epergne, salver, patella, *tazza* [*It.*], patera; piggin; biggin, percolator, coffeepot, coffee urn, teapot, tea urn, samovar; tig *or* tyg [*dial. Eng.*], nipperkin [*now rare*], pocket pistol [*slang*], tub, bucket, pail, skeel [*dial.*], pot, tankard, jug, pitcher, mug, pipkin; gallipot; matrass *or* mattrass, receiver, retort, alembic, bolthead, capsule, can, kettle; bowl, basin, jorum [*colloq.*], punch bowl, cup, goblet, chalice, tumbler, glass, rummer, horn, saucepan, skillet, posnet [*obs.*], tureen, stein.

bail, beaker, billy [*Australia*], cannikin *or* canakin; catch basin, catch drain; chatti *or* chatty [*India*], lota *or* lotah [*India*], mussuk *or* mussuck [*India*]; schooner [*U. S.*], spider, terrine, toby, *urceus* [*L.*].

PLATE, platter, dish, trencher, calabash, porringer, potager [*obs.*], saucer, pan, crucible; glassware, tableware; vitrics.

LADLE, dipper, tablespoon, spoon; shovel, trowel, spatula.

CUPBOARD, closet, commode, cellaret, chiffonier *or* chiffonnier, *chiffonnière* [*F.*], locker, bin, bunker, buffet, press, clothespress, safe, sideboard, drawer, chest of drawers, till, escritoire, scrutoire [*obs.*], secretary, *secrétaire* [*F.*], davenport, book-case, cabinet, canterbury; *étagère* [*F.*], vargueno, vitrine.

CHAMBER, apartment, room, cabin; office, court, hall, atrium; suite of rooms, apartment [U. S.], flat, story; saloon, *salon* [F.], parlor; by-room, cubicle; presence chamber; living-, sitting-, drawing-, reception-, state-room; best room [colloq.], keeping room [dial. Eng.]; gallery, cabinet, closet; pew, box; boudoir; adytum, sanctum; bedroom, dormitory; refectory, dining room, *salle-à-manger* [F.]; nursery, schoolroom; library, study; studio; billiard room, bathroom, smoking room; den; state room, tablinum, tenement.

attic, loft, garret, cockloft, clerestory; cellar, vault, hold, cockpit; cubbyhole; cook house; *entre-sol* [F.]; mezzanine *or* mezzanine floor; ground floor, *rez-de-chaussée* [F.], basement, kitchen, pantry, *bawarchi-khana* [Hind.], scullery, offices; storeroom &c. (*depository*) 636; lumber room; dairy, laundry, coach house; garage; hangar; outhouse, penthouse; lean-to.

PORTICO, porch, stoop [U. S.], veranda, lobby, court, hall, vestibule, corridor, passage; anteroom, antechamber; lounge; piazza [=veranda, U. S.].

BOWER, arbor, summerhouse, alcove, grotto, hermitage; conservatory, greenhouse.

LODGING &c. (*abode*) 189; bed &c. (*support*) 215.

CARRIAGE &c. (*vehicle*) 272.

Adj. capsular; saccular, sacculated; recipient; ventricular, cystic, vascular, vesicular, cellular, camerated, locular, multilocular, polygastric; gastric, stomachic, gasteral [*rare*]; marsupial; siliquose, siliquous.

SECTION II. DIMENSIONS

1. GENERAL DIMENSIONS

192. Size. — **N.** SIZE, magnitude, dimension, bulk, volume; largeness &c. adj.; greatness &c. (*of quantity*) 31; expanse &c. (*space*) 180; amplitude, mass; proportions.

CAPACITY; tonnage *or* tunnage; cordage; caliber *or* calibre; scantling [obs.].

CORPULENCE, obesity; plumpness &c. adj.; *embonpoint* [F.], corporation [colloq.], flesh and blood, lustihood; turgidity &c. (*expansion*) 194.

HUGENESS &c. adj.; enormity, immensity; monstrosity.

GIANT, Brobdingnagian, Antæus, Goliath, Polyphemus, Colossus, Titan, Titaness, Briareus, Norn, Hercules, Cyclops, Gog and Magog, Gargantua; monster, mammoth, cachalot, whale, porpoise, behemoth, leviathan, elephant, jumbo [colloq.], hippopotamus; colossus.

LUMP, bulk, block, loaf, mass, swad [slang, U. S.], clod, nugget, tun, cord, bushel; thumper [slang], whopper *or* whapper [colloq.], spanker [slang], strapper [slang]; "Triton among the minnows" [Coriolanus].

mountain, mound; heap &c. (*assemblage*) 72.

FULL-SIZE, life-size; largest portion &c. 50.

V. BE LARGE &c. adj.; become large &c. (*expand*) 194.

Adj. LARGE, big; great &c. (*in quan-*

193. Littleness. — **N.** LITTLENESS &c. adj.; smallness &c. (*of quantity*) 32; exiguity, inextension; parvitude [rare], parvity [obs.]; duodecimo; Elzevir edition, epitome; microcosm; rudiment; vanishing point; thinness &c. 203.

DWARF, pygmy *or* pigmy, Liliputian, Negrito, Negrillo; chit, fingerling [rare], Pigwiggen, pigwidgeon [now rare], urchin, elf; atomy, dandiprat [archaic], doll, puppet; Tom Thumb, hop-o'-my-thumb; manikin *or* mannikin; micromorph [rare], homunculus, dapperling.

MITE, insect, arthropod, ephemerid, ephemera, bug [pop., U. S.], larva, emmet, fly, midge, gnat, shrimp, minnow, worm, maggot, grub; tit, tomtit, runt, mouse, small fry; millet seed, mustard seed; barleycorn; pebble, grain of sand; molehill, button, bubble.

ATOM, monad, animalcule, animalculum (pl. animalcula), diatom, dyad, triad, tetrad, pentad, hexad, heptad, octad, molecule, microbe, germ, microörganism, bacterium (pl. bacteria), microphyte, microzyme, amœba, microzoa, entozoön (pl. entozoa), phytozoaria, infusoria.

PARTICLE &c. (*small quantity*) 32; point, micron; scintilla; fragment &c. (*small part*) 51; powder &c. 330; point of a pin, mathematical point; minutiæ &c. (*unimportance*) 643.

tity) 31; considerable, bulky, voluminous, ample, massive, massy; capacious, comprehensive, spacious &c. 180; mighty, towering, fine, magnificent.

STOUT, corpulent, fat, plump, squab, full, lusty, strapping [*colloq.*], bouncing; portly, burly, well-fed, full-grown; corn-fed, gram-fed [*Anglo-Ind.*]; stalwart, brawny, fleshy; goodly; in good -case, – condition; in condition; chopping, jolly; club-faced [*obs.*], chubby-faced.

large as life; plump as a -dumpling, – partridge; fat as -a pig, – a quail, – butter, – brawn, – bacon [*all colloq.*].

HULKY, hulking, unwieldy, lumpish, lubberly, gaunt, spanking [*slang.*], whacking [*colloq.*], whopping [*colloq.*], thumping [*colloq.*], thundering [*colloq.*], overgrown; puffy &c. (*swollen*) 194.

HUGE, immense, enormous, titanic, mighty; vast, vasty [*archaic*]; stupendous; monster, monstrous; gigantic; elephantine; giant, giantlike; colossal, Cyclopean, Brobdingnagian, Gargantuan; infinite &c. 105.

** "obesity is the mother of abstinence" [*Cynic's Calendar*]; "he was plump and he was chubby" [Gilbert].

194. Expansion. — N. EXPANSION,
dilation, expansibleness; increase &c. 35 -of size; enlargement, extension, augmentation; amplification, ampliation; aggrandizement, spread, increment, growth, development, pullulation [*rare*], swell, dilatation, rarefaction; turgescence *or* turgescency, turgidness, turgidity; dispansion [*obs.*]; obesity &c. (*size*) 192; hydrocephalus, hydrophthalmus; dropsy, tumefaction, intumescence, swelling, tumor, diastole, distension; puffing, puffiness; inflation; pandiculation.

dilatability, expansibility.

GROWTH, upgrowth; accretion &c. 35; germination, budding, gemmation.

bulb &c. (*convexity*) 250; plumper; superiority of size.

OVERGROWTH, overdistension; hypertrophy, tympany.

V. BECOME LARGER &c. (large &c. 192); expand, widen, enlarge, extend, grow, increase, incrassate, swell, gather; fill out; deploy, take open order, dilate, stretch, spread; mantle, wax; grow up,

MICROGRAPHY; micrometer, microscope, interferometer, vernier; scale.

V. BE LITTLE &c. *adj.;* lie in a nutshell; become small &c. (*decrease*) 36, (*contract*) 195.

Adj. LITTLE; small &c. (*in quantity*) 32; minute, diminutive, microscopic; inconsiderable &c. (*unimportant*) 643; exiguous, puny, runty [*U. S.*], tiny, wee [*colloq.*], petty, minikin [*obs.*], miniature, pygmy *or* pigmy, elfin; undersized; dwarf, dwarfed, dwarfish; spare, stunted, limited; cramp, cramped; pollard, Liliputian, Negritic, dapper, pocket; portative, portable; duodecimo; dumpy, squat; short &c. 201.

IMPALPABLE, intangible, evanescent, imperceptible, invisible, inappreciable, infinitesimal, homeopathic; rudimentary, rudimental; embryonic, vestigial.

ANIMALCULAR, amœbic, amœboid, diatomaceous, diatomic, microzoal, microbial, microbic, molecular, atomic, corpuscular.

SCANT, weazen [*obs.*], scraggy, scrubby; thin &c. (*narrow*) 203; granular &c. (*powdery*) 330; shrunk &c. 195; brevipennate.

Adv. in a small compass, in a nutshell; on a small scale.

195. Contraction. — N. CONTRACTION,
reduction, diminution; decrease &c. 36 -of size; defalcation, decrement; lessening, shrinking &c. *v.;* compaction [*rare*], tabes, collapse, emaciation, attenuation, tabefaction [*rare*], consumption, marasmus, atrophy; systole, syncopation, syncope; neck, hourglass.

COMPRESSION, condensation, constraint, astriction [*rare*], compactness; compendium &c. 596; squeezing &c. *v.;* strangulation; corrugation; constringency, astringency; astringents, sclerotics; contractibility, contractibleness, contractility, compressibility, compressibleness, coarctation.

inferiority in size.

V. BECOME SMALL, become smaller; lessen, decrease &c. 36; grow less, dwindle, shrink, contract, narrow, shrivel, syncopate, collapse, wither, lose flesh, wizen [*dial.*], fall away, waste, wane, ebb; decay &c. (*deteriorate*) 659.

BE SMALLER THAN, fall short of; not come up to &c. (*be inferior*) 34.

RENDER SMALLER, lessen, diminish,

spring up; bud, burgeon *or* bourgeon, shoot, sprout, germinate, put forth, vegetate, pullulate, open, burst forth; gain flesh, gather flesh; outgrow; spread like wildfire, overrun.

BE LARGER THAN; surpass &c. (*be superior*) 33.

RENDER LARGER &c. (large &c. 192); expand, spread, extend, aggrandize, distend, develop, amplify, spread out, widen, magnify, rarefy, inflate, puff, blow up, stuff, pad, cram, bloat; exaggerate; fatten.

Adj. EXPANDED &c. *v.;* larger &c. (large &c. 192); swollen; expansive; wide open, widespread; fan-shaped, flabelliform; overgrown, exaggerated, bloated, fat, turgid, tumid, hypertrophied, dropsical; pot-bellied, swag-bellied [*obs.*]; œdematous *or* edematous, corpulent, obese, puffy, pursy, blowzy, distended; patulous; bulbous &c. (*convex*) 250; full-blown, full-grown, full-formed;

contract, draw in, narrow, pucker, cockle, coarct *or* coarctate [*rare*]; boil down; deflate, exhaust, empty; constrict, constringe; condense, compress, squeeze, corrugate, crush, crumple up, warp, purse, purse up, pack, stow; pinch, tighten, strangle; cramp; dwarf, bedwarf; shorten &c. 201; circumscribe &c. 229; restrain &c. 751.

PARE, reduce, attenuate, rub down, scrape, file, grind, chip, shave, shear.

Adj. CONTRACTING &c. *v.;* astringent, constringent, shrunk, shrunken, tabescent, tabetic, contractible, contracted &c. *v.;* strangulated, tabid, wizened, weazen, weazeny [*colloq.*], corky, stunted; waning &c. *v.;* neap, compact, compacted.

UNEXPANDED &c. (expand &c. 194); contractile; compressible; smaller &c. (small &c. 193).

big &c. 192; abdominous, enchymatous, rhipidate; tumefacient, tumefying.

*** "Her waist is ampler than her life, For life is but a span" [Holmes]; "the more waist the less speed" [*Cynic's Calendar*].

---

196. Distance. — N. DISTANCE; space &c. 180; remoteness, farness; far cry to; longinquity [*rare*], elongation; easting, westing, drift, offing, background; remote region; removedness; parallax; reach, span, stride.

outpost, outskirt; horizon, sky line; aphelion; foreign parts, *ultima Thule* [*L.*], *ne plus ultra* [*L.*], antipodes; jumping-off place [*colloq.*], long range, giant's stride.

DISPERSION &c. 73.

V. BE DISTANT &c. *adj.;* extend to, stretch to, reach to, spread to, go to, get to, stretch away to; range, outreach, outlie [*rare*].

remain at a distance; keep –, stand- -away, – off, – aloof, – clear of.

Adj. DISTANT; far off, far away; remote, telescopic, distal, wide of; stretching to &c. *v.;* yon, yonder; ulterior; transmarine, transpontine, transatlantic, transalpine; tramontane; ultramontane, ultramundane; hyperborean, antipodean; inaccessible, out-of-the-way, God-forsaken [*colloq.*]; unapproached, unapproachable; incontiguous [*obs.*].

Adv. FAR OFF, far away; afar, -off; off; away; a -long, – great, – good- way off; **wide away**, beyond range, aloof; wide

197. Nearness. — N. NEARNESS &c. *adj.;* proximity, propinquity; vicinity, vicinage; neighborhood, adjacency, nighness [*archaic*], appropinquity [*rare*]; contiguity &c. 199.

short -distance, – step, – cut; earshot, close quarters, range, stone's throw; bowshot, gunshot, pistol shot; hair's breadth, span.

PURLIEUS, neighborhood, vicinage, environs, *alentours* [*F.*], suburbs, *faubourg* [*F.*], confines, *banlieue* [*F.*], borderland; whereabouts.

BYSTANDER, spectator; neighbor *or* neighbour, borderer.

APPROACH &c. 286; convergence &c. 290; perihelion.

V. BE NEAR &c. *adj.;* adjoin, abut, neighbor, hang about, trench on; border upon, verge upon; stand by, approximate, tread on the heels of, cling to, clasp, hug; huddle; hang upon the skirts of, hover over; burn [*colloq.*].

bring *or* draw near &c. 286; converge &c. 290; crowd &c. 72; place side by side &c. *adv.*

Adj. NEAR, nigh; close –, near- at hand; close, neighboring, vicinal, propinquent [*rare*]; bordering upon, contiguous, adjacent, adjoining; proximate,

of, clear of; out of -the way, – reach; abroad, yonder, farther, further, beyond; *outre mer* [*F.*], over the border, far and wide, "over the hills and far away" [Gay]; from pole to pole &c. (*over great space*) 180; to the -uttermost parts, – ends- of the earth; out of range, out of hearing, nobody knows where, *à perte de vue* [*F.*], out of the sphere of, wide of the mark; a far cry to.

APART, asunder; wide apart, wide asunder; *longo intervallo* [*L.*]; at arm's length.

, "distance lends enchantment" [Campbell]; "Across the hills and far away Beyond their utmost purple rim" [Tennyson].

proximal; at hand, warm [*colloq.*], handy; near the mark, near run; home, intimate.

Adv. NEAR, nigh; hard by, fast by; close to, close upon; hard upon; at the point of; next door to; within -reach – call, – hearing, – earshot, – range; within an ace of; but a step, not far from, at no great distance; on the -verge, – brink, – skirts- of; in the environs &c. *n.;* at one's -door, – feet, – elbow, – finger's end, – side; on the tip of one's tongue; under one's nose; within a stone's throw &c. *n.;* in sight of, in presence of; at close quarters; cheek by jowl, cheek to cheek, shoulder to shoulder; beside, alongside, side by side, *tête-à-tête* [*F.*]; in juxtaposition &c.

(*touching*) 199; yardarm to yardarm; at the heels of; on the confines of, at the threshold, bordering upon, verging to; in the way.

ABOUT; hereabout *or* hereabouts, thereabout *or* thereabouts; roughly, in round numbers; approximately, approximatively; as good as, well-nigh.

---

198. Interval. — N. INTERVAL, interspace; separation &c. 44; hiatus, cæsura; interruption, interregnum; interstice, intersection, lacuna.

parenthesis &c. (*interjacence*) 228; void &c. (*absence*) 187; incompleteness &c. 53.

CLEFT, break, gap, opening; hole &c. 260; chasm, mesh, crevice, chink, rime [*now rare*], creek, cranny, crack, chap, slit, fissure, scissure, rift, fault, flaw, breach, fracture, rent, gash, cut, leak, dike, ha-ha.

GORGE, defile, ravine, cañon, crevasse, abyss, abysm; gulf; inlet, frith, strait, gully, nullah [*India*]; pass; furrow &c. 259; *abra* [*Sp. Amer.*], *barranco* [*Sp.*]; clove [*U. S.*], gulch [*U. S.*], notch [*U. S.*], yawning gulf; *hiatus maxime deflendus* [*L.*], *hiatus valde deflendus* [*L.*].

V. GAPE &c. (*open*) 260; separate &c. 44.

199. Contiguity. — N. CONTIGUITY, contiguousness, contact, proximity, apposition, abuttal, juxtaposition, touching &c *v.;* abutment, osculation; meeting, appulse, appulsion, *rencontre* [*F.*], rencounter, syzygy, conjunction, conjugation, coincidence, coexistence; adhesion &c. 46.

BORDERLAND; frontier &c. (*limit*) 233; tangent; abutter.

V. BE CONTIGUOUS &c. *adj.;* join, adjoin, abut on, neighbor, border, march with; graze, touch, meet, osculate, come in contact, coincide; coexist; adhere &c. 46.

Adj. CONTIGUOUS; touching &c. *v.;* in contact &c. *n.;* conterminous, end to end, osculatory; pertingent [*obs.*]; tangential.

hand to hand; close to &c. (*near*) 197; with no interval &c. 198.

Adj. with an interval, far between; breachy, rimose, rimous, rimulose.
Adv. AT INTERVALS &c. (*discontinuously*) 70; *longo intervallo* [*L.*].

---

2. LINEAR DIMENSIONS

200. Length.— N. LENGTH, longitude, longness [*rare*], extent, span; mileage.

LINE, bar, rule, stripe, streak, spoke, radius.

LENGTHENING &c. *v.;* prolongation, production, protraction; tension, tensure [*obs.*]; extension.

201. Shortness. — N. SHORTNESS &c. *adj.;* brevity littleness &c. 193; a span.

SHORTENING &c. *v.;* abbreviation, abbreviature [*obs.*], abridgment, concision, retrenchment, curtailment, decurtation [*obs.*], epitomization, obtruncation [*rare*], condensation; reduction &c. (*con-*

[MEASURES OF LENGTH] line, nail, inch, hand, palm, foot, cubit, yard, ell, fathom, rood, pole, furlong, mile, knot, league; chain; arpent, handbreadth, *jornada* [*U. S.*], kos [*Hind.*], vara [*Sp. & Pg.*]; meter, kilometer, centimeter &c.

pedometer, odometer, odograph, viameter, viatometer, log [*naut.*], speedometer, telemeter, perambulator; scale &c. (*measurement*) 466.

V. BE LONG &c. *adj.;* stretch out, sprawl; extend to, reach to, stretch to; make a long arm, "drag its slow length along" [Pope].

RENDER LONG &c. *adj.;* lengthen, extend, elongate; stretch; prolong, produce [*now rare*], protract; let out, draw out, spin out; drawl.

ENFILADE, look along, view in perspective.

Adj. LONG, longsome [*archaic*]; elongate *or* elongated, longish, lengthy, wiredrawn, outstretched, extended; lengthened &c. *v.;* sesquipedalian &c. (*words*) 577; interminable, no end of [*colloq.*].

LINEAR, lineal; longitudinal, oblong.

LANKY, lank, slabsided [*slang, U. S.*], rangy; tall &c. 206; macrocolous, longlimbed.

as long as -my arm, - to-day and tomorrow; unshortened &c. (shorten &c. 201).

Adv. LENGTHWISE, at length, longitudinally, endlong [*archaic*], endways, endwise, along; tandem; in a line &c. (*continuously*) 69; in perspective.

from end to end, from stem to stern, from head to foot, from the crown of the head to the sole of the foot, from top to toe; fore and aft; over all.

*** "And he is lean and lank and brown as is the ribbed sea-sand" [Wordsworth].

traction) 195; epitome &c. (*compendium*) 596.

elision, ellipsis; conciseness &c. (*in style*) 572.

ABRIDGER, epitomist, epitomizer, obtruncator [*rare*].

V. BE SHORT &c. *adj.;* RENDER SHORT &c. *adj.;* shorten, curtail, abridge, abbreviate, take in, reduce; compress &c. (*contract*) 195; epitomize &c. 596.

CUT SHORT, retrench, obtruncate [*rare*], scrimp, cut, chop up, hack, hew; cut down, pare down; clip, dock, lop, prune, shear, shave, mow, reap, crop; snub; truncate, pollard, stunt, nip, check the growth of; foreshorten [*drawing*].

Adj. SHORT, brief, curt; compendious, compact; stubby, pudgy, tubby [*colloq.*], squatty, squidgy [*rare*], scrimp; shorn, stubbed; stumpy [*colloq.*], thickset, pug; chunky [*U. S.*], curtate, curtal [*archaic*], decurtate; *retroussé* [*F.*], turned up; scrub, stocky; squab, squabby; squat, squattish, dumpy; little &c. 193; curtailed of its fair proportions; short by; oblate; abbreviatory; concise &c. 572; summary.

Adv. SHORTLY &c. *adj.;* in short &c. (*concisely*) 572.

---

202. Breadth, Thickness. — N. BREADTH, width, latitude, amplitude; diameter, bore, caliber, radius; superficial extent &c. (*space*) 180.

THICKNESS, crassitude [*obs.*]; corpulence &c. (*size*) 192; dilatation &c. (*expansion*) 194.

V. BE BROAD &c. *adj.;* become *or* render broad &c. *adj.;* expand &c. 194; thicken, widen, calibrate.

Adj. BROAD, wide, ample, extended; discous, discoid; fanlike; outspread, outstretched; "wide as a church-door" [*Romeo and Juliet*]; latifoliate [*rare*], latifolious [*rare*].

THICK, dumpy, squab, squat, thickset, stubby &c. 201; thick as a rope.

203. Narrowness, Thinness. — N. NARROWNESS &c. *adj.;* closeness, exility [*rare*]; exiguity &c. (*little*) 193.

line; hair's -, finger's- breadth; strip, streak, vein.

THINNESS &c. *adj.;* tenuity; emaciation, marcor [*obs.*], macilence *or* macilency [*rare*].

shaving, slip &c. (*filament*) 205; thread paper, skeleton, shadow, scrag, atomy [*obs. or joc.*], anatomy [*archaic*], study in anatomy [*humorous*], spindleshanks [*humorous or contemptuous*], barebone, lantern jaws, mere skin and bone.

MIDDLE CONSTRICTION, stricture, coarctation [*med.*]; neck, waist, isthmus, wasp, hourglass; ridge, ghât *or* ghaut [*India*], pass; ravine &c. 198.

NARROWING, angustation, tapering; contraction &c. 195.

V. be narrow &c. *adj.;* narrow, taper, contract, &c. 195; render narrow &c. *adj.*

Adj. NARROW, close; slender, gracile, thin, fine; thread-like &c. (*filament*) 205; finespun, taper, slim, slight-made; scant, scanty; spare, delicate, incapacious; contracted &c. 195; unexpanded &c. (*expand* &c. 194); slender as a thread.

LEAN, emaciated, meager *or* meagre, gaunt, macilent; lank, lanky; weedy [*colloq.*], skinny; scrawny [*U. S.*], slinky [*dial.*]; starved, starveling; attenuated, shriveled, pinched, poor, peaked [*colloq.*], lathy [*colloq.*], skeletal, flatsided [*colloq.*], slabsided [*slang*, *U. S.*]; spindle-legged, spindle-shanked, spindling; coarctate, angustate, tabic, tabelic, tabid, extenuated, marcid [*obs.*], rawboned; herring-gutted [*colloq.*]; worn to a shadow, "lean as a rake" [Chaucer]; thin as a -lath, – whipping post, – wafer; hatchet-faced; lantern-jawed.

∗ "Pinch, a hungry, lean-faced villain, a mere anatomy" [*Comedy of Errors*].

204. Layer. — N. LAYER, stratum, course, bed, couch, coping, zone, substratum, floor, flag, stage, story, tier, slab, escarpment; table, tablet; dess [*Scot. & dial. Eng.*]; flagstone; board, plank; trencher, platter.

LEAF, lamina, lamella, sheet, flake, foil, wafer, scale, coat, peel, pellicle, membrane, film, lap, ply, slice, shive, cut, rasher, shaving, plate; overlay, integument &c. (*covering*) 223; eschar.

STRATIFICATION, lamination, delamination, foliation; scaliness, nest of boxes, coats of an onion.

V. SLICE, shave, pare, peel, skive; delaminate; plate, coat, veneer; cover &c. 223.

Adj. LAMELLAR, lamelliferous, lamellate *or* lamellated, lamelliform; laminate *or* laminated, laminiferous; micaceous; schistose, schistous; scaly, filmy, membranous, membranaceous, flaky, squamous; foliated, foliaceous; stratified, stratiform; tabular, discoid; spathic, spathose.

206. Height. — N. HEIGHT, altitude, elevation; eminence, pitch; loftiness &c. *adj.*; sublimity, celsitude [*rare*].

TALLNESS &c. *adj.*; stature, procerity [*rare*]; prominence &c. 250; apex, zenith, culmination.

COLOSSUS &c. (*size*) 192; giant, grenadier; giraffe, camelopard.

HEIGHT, mount, mountain; hill, *alto* [*Sp.*], butte [*U. S.*], monticule, monticle [*obs.*], fell [*obs. exc. in proper names*], knap; cape; headland, foreland; promontory; ridge, hogback *or* hog's-back, dune, rising -, vantage- ground; down; moor, moorland; Alp; uplands, highlands; heights &c. (*summit*), 210; knob, *loma* [*U. S.*], *pena* [*U. S.*], *picacho* [*Sp.*], tump

205. Filament. — N. FILAMENT, line; fiber, fibril; funicle, vein, hair, cobweb, capillary, ciliolum, capillament [*rare*], cilium, cirrus, barbel, strand, tendril, gossamer; hair stroke; veinlet, venula, venule.

beard &c. (*roughness*) 256; ramification.

THREAD, threadlet, harl, yarn, packthread, cotton, sewing silk.

STRING, twine, twist, whipcord, cord, rope, hemp, oakum, jute; tape, ribbon, wire.

STRIP, shred, slip, spill, list, tænia *or* tenia, band, fillet, fascia; ribbon, riband *or* riband [*archaic*], roll, lath, splinter, shiver, shaving; ligule *or* ligula.

Adj. FILAMENTOUS, filamentiferous, filaceous [*rare*], filiform; fibrous, fibrillous, fibrilliform, fibrilliferous; threadlike, wiry, stringy, ropy; capillary, capilliform; funicular, wire-drawn; anguilliform; flagelliform; barbate, hairy &c. (*rough*) 256; tæniate, tæniform, tænioid; venose, venous; ligulate *or* ligulated.

207. Lowness. — N. LOWNESS &c. *adj.*; debasement; prostration &c. (*horizontal*) 213; depression &c. (*concave*) 252; subjacency; lowlands.

GROUND FLOOR; *rez de chaussée* [*F.*]; street floor.

BASEMENT, basement floor, cellar; hold; base &c. 211.

[COMPARISONS] feet, heels; molehill.

LOW WATER; low -, ebb -, neap- tide.

V. BE LOW &c. *adj.*; lie low, lie flat; underlie; crouch, slouch, wallow, grovel; lower &c. (*depress*) 308.

Adj. LOW, neap, debased; lower, inferior, under, nether; lowest, nethermost, lowermost; flat, level with the ground; lying low &c. *v.*; crouched, sub-

[*dial.*]; knoll, hummock, hillock, barrow, mound; steeps, bluff, cliff, craig [*Scot.*], tor, peak, pike [*dial.*], clough [*obs.*]; escarpment, edge, ledge, brae [*Scot. & dial. Eng.*]; dizzy height.

TOWER, pillar, column, obelisk, monument, belfry, steeple, spire, minaret, campanile, turret, dome, cupola; pylon, *tourelle* [*F.*], barbican, martello tower; pyramid, pagoda, mole [*Rom. antiq.*].

ceiling &c. (*covering*) 223; upstairs.

POLE, pikestaff, maypole, flagstaff; mast, mainmast, topmast, topgallant mast.

HIGH WATER; high –, flood –, spring-tide.

HYPSOGRAPHY, hypsometry, hypsometer, altimeter, altimetry &c. (*angle*) 244; hypsophobia.

jacent, squat, prostrate &c. (*horizontal*) 213; depressed.

Adv. UNDER; beneath, underneath; below; down, downwards; adown, at the foot of; underfoot, underground; downstairs, belowstairs; at a low ebb; below par.

V. BE HIGH &c. *adj.*; tower, soar, command; hover; cap, culminate; overhang, hang over, impend, beetle; bestride, ride, mount; perch, surmount; cover &c. 223; rise above, overtop &c. (*be superior*) 33; stand on tiptoe.

BECOME HIGH &c. *adj.*; grow, grow higher, grow taller; upgrow; rise &c. (*ascend*) 305.

RENDER HIGH &c. *adj.*; heighten &c. (*elevate*) 307.

Adj. HIGH, elevated, eminent, exalted, lofty; tall; gigantic &c. (*big*) 192; Patagonian; towering, beetling, soaring, mountained, hanging [gardens]; elevated &c. 307; higher, superior, upper, supernal; highest &c. (*topmost*) 210; high-reaching, insessorial, perching; hill-dwelling, monticoline, monticolous.

tall as a –maypole, – poplar, – steeple; lanky &c. (*thin*) 203.

UPLAND, moorland; hilly, knobby [*U. S.*]; mountainous, alpine, subalpine, heaven-kissing; cloud-topt, cloud-capt, cloud-touching; aërial.

OVERHANGING &c. *v.*; incumbent, overlying; superincumbent, supernatant, superimposed; prominent &c. 250.

HYPSOGRAPHIC, hypsographical, hypsometric, hypsometrical.

Adv. ON HIGH, high up, aloft, up, above, aloof, overhead; airward; upstairs, above stairs; in the clouds; on tiptoe, on stilts, on the shoulders of; over head and ears; breast high.

over, upwards; from top to bottom &c. (*completely*) 52.

⁎ *è meglio cader dalle finistre che dal tetto.*

208. Depth. — N. DEPTH; deepness &c. *adj.*; profundity, depression &c. (*concavity*) 252.

PIT, shaft, hollow, well, crater; gulf &c. 198; deep, abyss, bowels of the earth, bottomless pit, hell.

SOUNDINGS, depth of water, water, draft *or* draught, submersion; plummet, sound, probe; sounding-rod, –line; lead; bathometer, bathymeter, bathymetry; benthos; submarine, U-boat; depth bomb.

V. BE DEEP &c. *adj.*; render deep &c. *adj.*; deepen.

SOUND, heave the lead, take soundings; dig &c. (*excavate*) 252; plunge &c. 310.

Adj. DEEP, deep-seated, deep-bosomed; profound, sunk, buried; submerged &c. 310; subaqueous, submarine, subterranean, subterrene [*obs.*], subterraneous; underground.

knee-deep, ankle-deep.

BOTTOMLESS, soundless, fathomless; unfathomed, unfathomable; abysmal; deep as a well; bathycolpian *or* bathukolpic *or* bathukolpian; deep-sea, benthal, benthopelagic; bathymetric, bathymetrical; bathypelagic, bathysmal; downreaching, yawning.

Adv. OUT OF ONE'S DEPTH; beyond one's depth; over head and ears.

⁎ "under the whelming tide Visit'st the bottom of the monstrous world" [Milton].

209. Shallowness. — N. SHALLOWNESS &c. *adj.*; shoals; mere scratch.

Adj. SHALLOW, slight, superficial; skin –, ankle –, knee- deep; depthless, just enough to wet one's feet; shoal, shoaly.

210. Summit. — N.

SUMMIT, top, vertex, apex, summity [obs.], zenith, pinnacle, acme, culmination, meridian, utmost height, ne plus ultra [L.], height, pitch, maximum, climax; culminating –, crowning –, turning- point; turn of the tide, fountainhead; watershed, water parting; sky, pole.

TIP, tiptop; crest, crow's nest, cap, truck, peak, nib; end &c. 67; crown, brow; head, nob [slang], noddle [colloq.], pate [now humorous or derog.]; capsheaf.

HIGH PLACES, heights.

topgallant mast, skyscraper; quarter deck, hurricane deck.

architrave, frieze, cornice, corona, coping, coping stone, zoöphorus, capital, epistyle, sconce, pediment, entablature; attic, loft, garret, housetop, upper story, roof.

V. CROWN, top, cap, crest, surmount; overtop &c. (be superior to) 33; culminate.

Adj. HIGHEST &c. (high &c. 206); top; topmost, overmost, uppermost; tiptop; culminating &c. v.; meridian, meridional; capital, head, polar, supreme, supernal, apical, culminant [rare], culminal [rare], topgallant, skyward.

Adv. ATOP, at the top of the tree; en flûte [F.]; à fleur d'eau [F.].

211. Base. — N.

BASE, basement; plinth, dado, wainscot; baseboard, mopboard [U. S.]; bedrock, hardpan [U. S.]; foundation &c. (support) 215; substructure, substratum, ground, earth, pavement, floor, paving, flag, carpet, ground floor, deck; footing, ground work, basis; hold, bilge, sump; culet.

BED, basin, channel, coulee [Western N. Amer.], cañon &c. (interval) 198.

BOTTOM, nadir, foot, sole, toe, hoof, keel, root; centerboard.

Adj. BOTTOM, undermost, nethermost; fundamental; founded on, based on, grounded on, built on.

headpiece, capstone, fastigium, larmier, tympanum; ceiling &c. (covering) 223.

212. Verticality. — N.

VERTICALITY; erectness &c. adj.; perpendicularity, aplomb; right angle, normal; azimuth circle.

CLIFF, steep, crag, bluff, palisades; wall, precipice.

ELEVATION, erection; square, plumb line, plummet.

V. BE VERTICAL &c. adj.; stand -up, – on end, – erect, – upright; stick up, cock up.

RENDER VERTICAL &c. adj.; set up, stick up, raise up, cock up; erect, rear, raise, pitch, raise on its legs.

Adj. VERTICAL, upright, erect, perpendicular, unrecumbent [rare], plumb, normal, straight, bolt upright; rampant; straight up; standing up &c. v.; rectangular orthogonal.

Adv. VERTICALLY &c. adj.; up, on end; up –, right- on end; à plomb [F.], endwise; on one's legs; at right angles.

213. Horizontality. — N.

HORIZONTALITY; flatness; level, plane; stratum &c. 204; dead level, dead flat; level plane.

RECUMBENCY; lying down &c. v.; reclination, decumbence or decumbency, discumbency [obs.]; proneness &c. adj.; accubation, supination, resupination, prostration; azimuth.

[LEVEL SURFACES] plain, floor, platform, bowling green; cricket ground; croquet -ground, – lawn; billiard table; terrace, estrade [rare], esplanade, parterre, table-land, plateau, ledge.

V. BE HORIZONTAL &c. adj.; lie, recline, couch; lie -down, – flat, – prostrate; sprawl, loll; sit down.

RENDER HORIZONTAL &c. adj.; lay, lay down, lay out; level, flatten, even, raze, equalize, smooth, align or aline.

prostrate, knock down, floor, fell, ground, drop, grass [slang]; cut –, hew –, mow- down.

Adj. HORIZONTAL, level, even, plane, flush; flat &c. 251; flat as a -billiard table, – bowling green; alluvial; calm, – as a mill pond; smooth, – as glass.

RECUMBENT, procumbent, accumbent, decumbent [bot.]; lying &c. v.; prone, supine, couchant, jacent [rare], prostrate, recubant [rare], resupinate.

Adv. HORIZONTALLY &c. adj.; on one's back, on all fours, on its beam ends.

214. Pendency. — N.

PENDENCY, dependency; suspension, hanging &c. v.

PENDANT, drop, eardrop, tassel, tippet,

215. Support. — N.

SUPPORT, ground, foundation, base, basis; terra firma [L.], bearing, fulcrum, bait [U. S.], caudex,

lobe, tail, train, flap, skirt, queue, pigtail, pendulum; hangnail.

peg, knob, button, hook, nail, stud, ring, staple, tenterhook; fastening &c. 45; spar, horse.

CHANDELIER, gaselier, electrolier.

V. BE PENDENT &c. *adj.*; hang, depend, swing, dangle, lower, droop: swag [*dial.*]; daggle, flap, trail, flow; beetle, jut, overhang.

SUSPEND. hang, sling, hook up, hitch, fasten to, append.

Adj. PENDENT, pendulous, pendulant [*rare*], decumbent, penduline [*rare*], pensile; hanging &c. *v.*; beetle; beetling, jutting over, overhanging, projecting; dependent; lowering; suspended &c. *v.*; loose, flowing.

HAVING A PENDANT &c. *n.*; tailed, caudate.

crib; *point d'appui* [*F.*], *pou sto* [*Gr.* πού στῶ], purchase, footing, hold, *locus-standi* [*L.*]; landing, – stage, – place; stage, platform; block; rest, resting place; groundwork, substratum, riprap, sustentation [*now rare*], sustention [*rare*], subvention; floor &c. (*basement*) 211.

SUPPORTER; aid &c. 707; prop, stand, anvil, fulciment [*obs.*]; cue rest, jigger [*slang*], monkey [*builders' slang*], hod; stay, shore, skid, rib, truss, bandage; sleeper; stirrup, stilts, shoe, sole, heel, splint, lap; bar, rod, boom, sprit, outrigger; ratline *or* ratlin *or* ratling.

PEDICLE, pedicel *or* pedicellus *or* pediculus, peduncle [*all bot.*], stalk.

board, ledge, shelf, hob, bracket, trivet, arbor, rack; mantel, mantelpiece, mantelshelf; slab, console; counter, dresser; flange, corbel; table, trestle; shoulder; perch; horse; easel, desk; clotheshorse, hatrack; retable, predella, teapoy.

STAFF, stick, crutch, alpenstock, baton, crosier, cross, crook, lituus [*Rom. antiq.*], caduceus, thyrsus, staddle; bourdon, cowlstaff [*archaic*], lathi [*Hind.*], maulstick *or* mahlstick.

POST, pillar, shaft, thill, column, pilaster; pediment, pedestal; plinth, shank, leg, socle *or* zocle; buttress, jamb, mullion, stile, abutment; baluster, banister, stanchion; balustrade; headstone.

FRAME, framework; scaffold, skeleton, beam, rafter, girder, lintel, joist, travis *or* traviss [*dial. Eng.*], trave, corner stone, summer, breastsummer *or* bressomer, summertree, transom; rung, round, step, sill; angle-rafter, hip-rafter; cantilever, modillion; crown-post, king-post; vertebra, modiolus.

columella, backbone; keystone; axle, axletree; axis; arch, mainstay.

trunnion, pivot, rowlock; peg &c. (*pendency*) 214; tiebeam &c. (*fastening*) 45; thole pin.

SEAT, throne, dais; divan, musnud *or* masnad [*Ar.*], guddee *or* gaddi [*Hind.*]; chair, bench, form, sofa, davenport, couch, day-bed, settee, stall; wingchair, armchair, easychair, elbow-chair, rocking-chair; *fauteuil* [*F.*], woolsack, ottoman, settle, squab, bench; long chair, long-sleeve chair [*Anglo-Ind.*], *chaise longue* [*F.*], morris chair; *lamba chauki* or *lamba kursi* [*Hind.*]; saddle, aparejo, panel *or* pannel, pillion; sidesaddle, packsaddle; pommel, horn.

STOOL, foldstool, *prie-dieu* [*F.*], hassock, footstool; tabouret; tripod.

BED, berth, pallet, tester-bed, crib, cot, hammock, shakedown, truckle-bed, trundle-bed, cradle, litter, stretcher, bedstead; four-poster, French bed; bunk, kip [*dial.*], palang [*Hind.*]; roost [*slang*]; bedding, bichhana [*Hind.*], mattress, paillasse; pillow, bolster; mat, rug, cushion.

Atlas, Herakles *or* Hercules; tortoise that supports the earth.

[IN ARCHITECTURE] atlas (*pl.* atlantes), telamon (*pl.* telamones), caryatid (*pl.* caryatids *or* caryatides).

V. BE SUPPORTED &c.; lie –, sit –, recline –, lean –, loll –, rest –, stand –, step –, repose –, abut –, bear –, be based &c. – on; have at one's back: bestride, bestraddle.

SUPPORT, bear, carry, hold, sustain, shoulder; hold up, back up, bolster up, shore up; uphold, upbear; brace, truss, cradle, pillow, prop; underprop, underpin, underset; riprap; bandage &c. 43.

give –, furnish –, afford –, supply –, lend- -support, – foundations; bottom, found, base, ground, embed, imbed.

MAINTAIN, keep on foot; aid &c. 707.

Adj. SUPPORTING, supported, &c. *v.*; Atlantean, columellar, columelliform; sustentative, sustentational; fundamental; dorsigerous.

HAVING A PEDICLE &c. *n.*; pedunculate, pedicellate.

Adv. STRADDLE, astride on.

*** "With Atlantean shoulders, fit to bear The weight of mightiest monarchies" [Milton].

---

216. Parallelism. — N. PARALLELISM, coextension, equidistance, concentricity; collimation.

V. BE PARALLEL &c. *adj.*; parallel, equal; collimate.

Adj. PARALLEL, coextensive, equidistant, collateral, concentric, concurrent; abreast, aligned, equal, even, alongside.

Adv. alongside &c. (*laterally*) 236.

217. Obliquity. — N. OBLIQUITY, inclination, incline, slope, slant, skew, thrawnness [*Scot. & dial. Eng.*]; crookedness &c. *adj.*; slopeness; leaning &c. *v.*; bevel, ramp, pitch, bezel, tilt; bias, list, twist, swag [*prov. Eng.*], sag, cant, lurch; distortion &c. 243; bend &c. (*curve*) 245; tower of Pisa.

ACCLIVITY, rise, ascent, gradient [*chiefly Brit.*], grade [*U. S.*], *khudd* [*Hind.*], glacis, rising ground, hill, bank, declivity, downhill, dip, fall, devexity [*obs.*]; gentle –, rapid- slope; easy -ascent, – descent; shelving beach; talus; *montagne Russe* [*F.*]; *facilis descensus Averni* [*L.*].

steepness &c. *adj.*; cliff, precipice &c. (*vertical*) 212; escarpment, scarp; chevron.

[MEASURE OF INCLINATION] clinometer; sine, cosine, cotangent, angle, hypothenuse.

diagonal; zigzag.

V. BE OBLIQUE &c. *adj.*; slope, slant, skew, lean, incline, shelve, stoop, decline, descend, bend, keel, careen, sag, swag [*dial.*], seel [*obs.*], slouch, cant, sidle.

RENDER OBLIQUE &c. *adj.*; sway, bias; slope, slant; incline, bend, crook; cant, tilt; distort &c. 243.

Adj. OBLIQUE, inclined; sloping &c. *v.*; tilted &c. *v.*; recubant [*rare*], recumbent, clinal, skew, askew, slant, bias, aslant, plagihedral, indirect, wry, awry; agee *or* ajee, thrawn [*both Scot. & dial. Eng.*], crooked; sinuous, zigzag, zigzaggy, chevrony; knock-kneed &c. (*distorted*) 243; bevel, out of the perpendicular; aslope; asquint, backhand *or* backhanded.

UPHILL, rising, ascending, acclivous.

DOWNHILL, falling, descending: hanging (as, *hanging* gardens), declining, declivitous, proclivous [*rare*], declivous, devex [*obs.*], synclinal, anticlinal.

STEEP, abrupt, precipitous, breakneck.

DIAGONAL; transverse, transversal; athwart, antiparallel; curved &c. 245; loxic, loxotic, loxodromic.

Adv. OBLIQUELY &c. *adj.*; on one side, all on one side; askew, askance *or* askant, awry, skew, skewed, edgewise, at an angle; sidelong, sideways; slopewise, slantwise; by a side wind.

---

218. Inversion. — N. INVERSION, eversion, subversion, reversion, retroversion, introversion; retroflexion; contraposition &c. 237; contrariety &c. 14; reversal; turn of the tide &c. (*reversion*) 145.

OVERTURN; somersault *or* summersault, somerset *or* summerset; *culbute* [*F.*] eversion [*archaic*]; revulsion; pirouette.

TRANSPOSITION, transposal, anastrophy, metastasis, hyperbaton, anastrophe; hysterology, hysteron proteron; hypallage, synchysis, tmesis, parenthesis; metathesis; palindrome; ectropion [*path.*]; invagination, intussusception.

pronation and supination.

V. BE INVERTED &c.; turn –, go –, wheel- -round, – about, – to the right-about [*colloq.*]; turn –, go –, tilt –, topple- over; capsize, turn turtle.

INVERT, subvert, retrovert, introvert; reverse; turn the cat in the pan [*obs*]; upturn, overturn, upset, overset, *bouleverser* [*F.*], evert [*archaic*]; turn topsy-turvy

&c. *adj.; culbuter* [*F.*]; transpose, put the cart before the horse, turn the tables; invaginate, intussuscept.

Adj. INVERTED &c. *v.;* wrong side -out, – up; inside out, upside down; bottom –, keel- upwards; supine, on one's head, topsy-turvy, *sens dessus dessous* [*F.*]; ectropic.

INVERSE; reverse &c. (*contrary*) 14; opposite &c. 237; palindromic *or* palindromical.

TOPHEAVY, unstable.

Adv. INVERSELY &c. *adj.;* hirdy-girdy; heels over head, head over heels.

219. Crossing. — N. CROSSING &c. *v.;* intersection, interdigitation; decussation, transversion; chiasm *or* chiasma; convolution &c. 248; level crossing [*Eng.*], grade crossing [*U. S.*].

NETWORK, reticulation, cancellation; inosculation, anastomosis, intertexture, mortise.

NET, plexus, plexure, web, mesh, twill, skein, Hippocrates's sleeve, sleave [*archaic*]; sieve, sifter, riddle rocker, screen, cradle; felt, lace; wicker; mat, matting; plait, trellis, wattle, lattice, grating, grille, gridiron, tracery, fretwork, filigree, reticle [*obs.*]; tissue, netting, moke [*dial. Eng.*]; rivulation.

cross, chain, wreath, braid, cat's cradle, knot; entanglement &c. (*disorder*) 59.

CRUCIFIX, cross, rood, crisscross, christcross, tau; crux.

[WOVEN FABRICS] cloth, linen, muslin, cambric, *toile* [*F.*], drill, homespun, silk, satin, broadcloth, tweed &c.

V CROSS, decussate; intersect, interlace, intertwine, intertwist, interweave, interdigitate, interlink, intercross [*rare*], crisscross, crossbar.

twine, entwine, weave, inweave, twist, wreathe; anastomose, inosculate, dovetail, splice, link.

MAT, plait, pleat, plat, braid, felt, twill; tangle, entangle, ravel; net, knot; dishevel, raddle.

Adj. CROSSING &c. *v.;* crossed, matted &c. *v.;* transverse; intersected, decussate *or* decussated; chiasmal.

CROSS, cross-shaped cruciform, crucial; netlike, retiform, reticular, reticulate; areolar, cancellate *or* cancellated, cancellous, latticed, grated, barred, streaked; textile; crossbarred, cruciate, secant; cruciferous; plexal, plexiform; anastomotic; web-footed, palmiped.

Adv. CROSS, thwart, athwart, transversely; at grade [*U. S.*]; crosswise, thwartwise [*rare*].

3. CENTRICAL DIMENSIONS[1]

1. General

220. Exteriority. — N. EXTERIORITY; outside, exterior; surface, superficies; skin &c. (*covering*) 223; superstratum; disk *or* disc; face, facet; extrados.

eccentricity; circumjacence &c. 227.

V. BE EXTERIOR &c. *adj.;* lie around &c. 227.

PLACE EXTERIORLY, place outwardly, place outside; put out, turn out.

EXTERNALIZE, objectize [*rare*], objectify, visualize, envisage, actualize.

Adj. EXTERIOR, external, extraneous; outer, outermost; outward, outlying, outside, outdoor, *alfresco* [*It.*]; round about &c. 227; extramural; extralimi-

221. Interiority. — N. INTERIORITY; inside, interior; interspace, subsoil, substratum; intrados.

contents &c. 190; substance, pith, marrow; backbone &c. (*center*) 222; heart, bosom, breast; abdomen.

vitals, viscera, entrails, bowels, belly, intestines, guts [*vulgar or tech.*], chitterlings, womb, lap [*obs.*], rectum, cæcum, ileum, duodenum, jejunum.

GLAND, glandule [*rare*], gland cell; thyroid, parotid, prostate; liver, kidney.

PENETRALIA, recesses, innermost recesses; cave &c. (*concavity*) 252.

ENTEROLOGY, enterotomy, enterop-

---

[1] That is, Dimensions having reference to a center.

tary, extramundane, extraterrene, extra-terrestrial, extraterritorial, exterritorial; extern [*rare*].

extraregarding; eccentric *or* eccentrical; outstanding; extrinsic &c. 6; ecdemic, exomorphic.

SUPERFICIAL, skin-deep; frontal, discoid.

Adv. EXTERNALLY &c. *adj.;* out, without, over, outwards, *ab extra* [*L.*], out of doors; *extra muros* [*L.*].

IN THE OPEN AIR; *sub Jove* [*L.*], *sub dio* [*L.*]; *à la belle étoile* [*F.*], *alfresco* [*It.*].

athy, enteritis, splanchnology; peristalsis, vermiculation.

INMATE, intern, inhabitant &c. 188.

V. BE INSIDE &c. *adj.;* be within &c. *adv.*

INCLOSE &c. (*circumscribe*) 229; intern embed *or* imbed &c. (*insert*) 300; place within, keep within.

Adj. INTERIOR, internal; inner, intern [*archaic*], intraneous [*rare*], intimate. inside, inward, intraregarding; inmost. innermost; deep-seated; intestine, intestinal, visceral, rectal, duodenal, splanchnic; subcutaneous; abdominal,

cœliac *or* celiac, endomorphic.

intracanal, intracellular, intralobular, intramarginal, intramolecular, intramundane, intraocular, intraseptal, intratelluric, intrauterine, intravascular, intravenous, intraventricular.

interstitial &c. (*interjacent*) 228; inwrought &c. (*intrinsic*) 5; inclosed &c. *v* HOME, inland, domestic, family, indoor, intramural, vernacular; endemic.

Adv. INTERNALLY &c. *adj.;* inwards, within, in, inly; herein, therein, wherein; *ab intra* [*L.*], withinside [*obs. or Scot.*]; indoors, within doors; at home, in the bosom of one's family.

222. Centrality. — **N.** CENTRALITY, centricalness, centricality, center *or* centre; middle &c. 68; focus &c. 74.

center of -gravity, – pressure, – percussion, – oscillation, – buoyancy &c.; metacenter.

CORE, kernel; nucleus, nucleolus; heart, pole, axis, bull's-eye, nave, hub, navel, umbilicus; marrow, pith; backbone; vertebra, vertebral column; hotbed.

CONCENTRATION &c. (*convergence*) 290; centralization; symmetry; metropolis.

V. BE CENTRAL &c. *adj.;* converge &c. 290.

RENDER CENTRAL, centralize, concentrate; bring to a focus.

Adj. CENTRAL, centrical; middle &c. 68; axial, pivotal, nuclear, nucleate, centric, focal, umbilical, concentric; middlemost; rachial, rachidial *or* rachidian; spinal, vertebral; metropolitan.

Adv. MIDDLE; midst; centrally &c. *adj.*

. "Boston State-house is the hub of the solar system" [Holmes].

223. Covering. — **N.** COVERING, cover, baldachin *or* baldaquin; canopy, *shamianah* [*Hind.*], tilt, awning, tent, marquee, marquise, wigwam, tepee, *tente d'abri* [*F.*], umbrella, parasol, sunshade; veil (*shade*) 424; shield &c. (*defense*) 717.

ROOF, ceiling, thatch, tile, pantile, tiling, slates, slating, leads, shingles; dome, cupola, mansard, hip roof; barrack [*U. S.*], plafond [*F.*], planchment [*U. S.*], tiling, shed &c. (*abode*) 189.

TOP, lid, covercle [*obs.*], door, operculum; bulkhead [*U. S.*].

224. Lining. — **N.** LINING, inner coating; coating &c. (*covering*) 223; stalactite, stalagmite.

FILLING, stuffing, wadding, padding, facing; bushing.

WAINSCOT, parietes, wall, brattice, sheathing.

V. LINE, stuff, incrust, wad, pad, fill, face, ceil, bush, wainscot, sheathe.

Adj. LINED &c. *v.*

WRAPPING, bandage, plaster, lint, dossil, pledget, finger stall.

COVERLET, counterpane, sheet, quilt, blanket, rug, drugget; housing; tidy, antimacassar, eiderdown quilt *or* eiderdown; comforter *or* comfortable *or* comfort [*all U. S.*] numdah [*Hind.*], pillowcase, pillowslip; linoleum, oilcloth; tarpaulin; saddle blanket, saddlecloth; tilpah [*U. S.*], apishamore [*U. S.*], poncho.

TEGMEN (*pl.* tegmina), integument, tegument; skin, pellicle, fleece, fell, fur, leather, lambskin, sable, miniver, beaver, ermine, shagreen, hide, coat, buff, pelt, peltry [*collective noun*]; cordwain [*archaic*]; robe, buffalo robe [*U. S.*].

CUTICLE, cutis, dermis, corium, scarfskin, epidermis, derm [*rare*], derma; ectoderm, epithelium, ecderon, ecteron, enderon.

EXUVIÆ, desquamation, slough, cast, cast-off skin.

CLOTHING &c. 225; mask &c. (*concealment*) 530.

PEEL, crust, bark, rind. cortex, husk, shell, epicarp, testa; eggshell, glume.

CAPSULE; sheath, sheathing; pod, cod [*dial.*], casing, case, theca; elytron; elytrum; involucrum; wrapping, wrapper; envelope, vesicle; cornhusk, cornshuck [*U. S.*].

DERMATOGRAPHY, dermatology, dermatogen, dermoplasty, dermatopathy, dermatophyte; conchology; testaceology.

VENEER, facing; pavement; imbrication, scale &c. (*layer*) 204; anointing &c. *v.*; ointment &c. (*grease*) 356; inunction; incrustation, superposition, obduction [*obs.*]; coating, paint, stain, engobe; varnish &c. (*resin*) 356a; ground, enamel, whitewash, plaster, stucco, roughcast, plasterwork, scagliola, compo; cerement; cerecloth, shroud.

V. COVER; superpose, superimpose; overlay, overspread; wrap &c. 225; incase, encase, enchase, face, case, veneer, pave, paper; tip, cap, bind; bulkhead, bulkhead in; clapboard [*U. S.*], shingle; imbricate.

overlie, overarch; endome [*rare*]; conceal &c. 528.

COAT, paint, stain, varnish, flat, incrust, encrust, crust, cement, roughcast, stucco, dab, plaster, tar; wash; besmear; bedaub; anoint, do over; gild, plate, japan, lacquer, lacker, enamel, whitewash; parget; lay it on thick.

Adj. COVERING &c. *v.*; cutaneous, dermal, cortical, cuticular, tegumentary, tegumental, tegmental, integumentary, integumental, epidermal *or* epidermic, endermic, epicarpal, testaceous, dermatopathic, dermatological, dermoplastic, dermatophytic, subcutaneous, hypodermic.

SCALY, squamate, squamiferous, squamous; covered &c. *v.*; imbricate, imbricated, loricate, loricated, armored, encuirassed, armor-plated, ironclad, under cover.

HOODED, cowled, cucullate *or* cucullated, tectiform, rooflike; vaginate.

SKINLIKE, dermic, dermoid, dermatoid, epidermoid, skinny.

---

225. Investment. — N. INVESTMENT; covering &c. 223; dress, clothing, raiment, drapery, costume, attire, guise, toilet, toilette, trim; habiliment; vesture, vestment; garment, garb, palliament [*obs.*], apparel, wardrobe, wearing apparel, clothes, things.

ARRAY; tailoring, millinery; best bib and tucker [*colloq.*]; finery &c. (*ornament*) 847; full dress &c. (*show*) 882; garniture; theatrical properties.

OUTFIT, equipment, trousseau; uniform, khaki, olive-drab, regimentals; continentals [*Am. hist.*]; canonicals &c. 999; livery, gear, harness, turn-out, accouterment, caparison, suit, rigging, trappings, traps [*colloq.*], slops, togs [*colloq. or slang*], toggery [*colloq.*]; masquerade.

DISHABILLE *or* deshabille, morning dress, tea gown, wrapper, negligee *or* négligé [*F.*], dressing gown, undress; kimono; shooting coat; smoking jacket;

226. Divestment. — N. DIVESTMENT; taking off &c. *v.*

NUDITY; bareness &c. *adj.*; undress; dishabille &c. 225; altogether; *tout ensemble* [*F.*]; nudation [*rare*], denudation; decortication, depilation, excoriation, desquamation, slough &c. 223; molting *or* moulting, exuviation; exfoliation; trichosis.

BALDNESS, hairlessness, alopecia.

V. DIVEST; uncover &c. (cover &c. 223); denude, bare, strip; disfurnish; undress, disrobe &c. (dress, enrobe &c. 225); uncoif; dismantle; put off, take off, cast off; doff.

PEEL, pare, decorticate, desquamate, slough, excoriate, skin, scalp, flay, bark, husk, rind; expose, lay open; exfoliate, molt *or* moult, exuviate, mew [*archaic*]; cast the skin.

Adj. DIVESTED &c. *v.*; bare, naked, nude; undressed, undraped, unclad, ungarmented, unclothed, unappareled,

mufti [*chiefly Eng.*]; rags, tatters, old
clothes; mourning, weeds; duds [*colloq.
or slang*]; slippers.

ROBE, tunic, paletot, habit, gown,
coat, frock, blouse, middy blouse *or*
middy, jumper, shirt waist, suit; one-
piece –, two-piece- suit; toga, smock,
frock; Prince Albert coat [*colloq.*]; frock–,
sack–, tail- coat.

DRESS SUIT, dress clothes, evening
dress, swallow-tailed coat [*colloq.*], clawhammer coat [*colloq.*]; dinner -coat, –
jacket; Tuxedo coat *or* Tuxedo [*colloq.*,
U. S.*]; glad rags [*slang, U. S.*].

CLOAK, pall [*archaic*], mantle, mantua,
mantelet *or* mantlet, sagum, shawl,
pelisse, wrapper; veil; cape, kirtle [*archaic*], plaid [*Scot.*], tippet, muffler,
comforter, balaklava helmet, haik, huke

unarrayed; exposed; in dishabille.

IN A STATE OF NATURE, in nature's
garb, in buff, in native buff, in birthday
suit; *in puris naturalibus* [*L.*]; with
nothing on, stark-naked; bare as the
back of one's hand.

out at elbows; threadbare, ragged,
callow, roofless; barefoot; bareback,
barebacked; leafless, napless, hairless.

BALD, hairless, depilous [*rare*], glabrous, glabrate, tonsured, beardless, bald
as a coot.

EXUVIAL, sloughy, desquamative, des-
quamatory.

*** "unaccommodated man is no more
but such a poor, bare, forked animal as thou
art" [*King Lear*].

[*obs.*], chlamys, mantilla, tabard, hous-
ing, horse cloth, burnoose *or* burnous, roquelaure; houpland [*hist.*]; surcoat,
overcoat, greatcoat; surtout, spencer; oilskins, slicker [*U. S.*], mackintosh,
waterproof, ulster, dreadnaught *or* dreadnought, wraprascal, poncho; pea-coat,
pea-jacket; cardinal, pelerine; chuddar *or* chadar [*Hind.*], jubbah [*Hind.*], py-
jamas *or* pajamas, pilot jacket, sweater, blazer, coatee, cardigan *or* cardigan
jacket; Mackinaw coat *or* Mackinaw; talma.

JACKET, vest, jerkin [*hist. or dial.*], chaqueta [*Sp.*], sontag, waistcoat, doublet,
gaberdine; stays, corsage, corset, *brassière* [*F.*], camisole, corselet, bodice; stomacher.

SKIRT, petticoat, farthingale, kilt, filibeg *or* philibeg, jupe, crinoline, bustle,
panier, apron, pinafore; bloomer, bloomers; *tablier* [*F.*].

LOIN CLOTH, dhoti [*Hindu*], lungi [*Burmese*]; G string.

TROUSERS, breeches, pantaloons, inexpressibles [*humorous*], trews [*Scot.*],
innominables [*humorous*], unmentionables [*humorous*], continuations [*slang*],
kicks [*slang*]; overalls, smalls [*colloq. or archaic*], smallclothes [*archaic*]; pants
[*colloq.*]; shintiyan; shorts; tights, drawers; knickerbockers, knickers [*colloq.*].

HEADDRESS, headgear, coiffure [*F.*], head, headcloths, chignon [*F.*]; chapeau
[*F.*], crush hat, opera hat; kaffiyeh [*Ar.*]; taj, tam-o'-shanter, topee *or* topi
[*India*], sola topi [*India*], puggree *or* pagri [*Hind.*]; sombrero, sundown [*U.
S.*], cap, hat, beaver, castor, bonnet, tile [*slang*], wide-awake, panama, leghorn; derby [*U. S.*], bowler [*Eng.*], billycock [*Eng.*]; wimple; nightcap, skullcap; mobcap, boudoir cap, Dutch cap; Salvation-Army bonnet; hood, coif,
capote, calash, kerchief, snood; crown &c. (*circle*) 247; pelt, wig, front, peruke,
periwig; caftan, turban, fez, tarboosh, shako, busby; kepi, forage cap, campaign hat, overseas cap, bearskin; helmet &c. 717; mask, domino.

BODY CLOTHES; linen; hickory shirt [*U. S.*]; shirt, O.-D. (olive-drab) shirt;
sark [*archaic or dial.*], smock, shift, chemise; nightgown, nightshirt; bed-gown,
sac de nuit [*F.*]; jersey; underclothing, underwaistcoat, undershirt, undervest,
chemisette, guimpe.

TIE, neckerchief, neckcloth; ruff, collar, cravat, stock, handkerchief, scarf;
bib, tucker; boa; girdle &c. (*circle*) 247; cummerbund [*India*], rumal [*Hind.*],
rabat [*F.*], rabato.

SHOE, pump, sneakers [*U. S.*], boot, slipper, sandal, galosh *or* galoshe, patten,
clog; high-low; Blucher –, Wellington –, Hessian –, jack –, top- boot; Oxford
-shoe, – tie; Balmoral; arctics, bootee, bootikin, brogan, brogue, chaparajos
[*Mex. Sp.*], chaps [*colloq.*], chivarras or chivarros [*Sp. Amer.*]; gums [*U. S.*],
larrigan [*N. Amer.*], rubbers; snowshoe, ski; stogy, veldtschoen [*Dutch*], legging,
puttee *or* putty, buskin, greave, galligaskin [*dial.*], moccasin, gambado, gaiter,
spatterdashes, spats, gamashes [*archaic or dial. Eng.*], gamache [*F.*]; antigropelos.

STOCKING, hose, gaskins [*obs. or dial.*], trunk hose, sock; hosiery.

GLOVE, gauntlet, mitten, mitt.

CUFF, wristband; sleeve.

BABY LINEN, swaddling clothes, layette.

[SUPPLIERS] clothier, tailor, snip [*slang*], tailoress, milliner, costumer, costumier, seamstress *or* sempstress, dressmaker, *modiste* [*F.*], habit-maker; breeches-maker; shoemaker, Crispin cordwainer, cobbler; hosier, hatter, glover, draper, linen draper, haberdasher, mercer; hairdresser, *friseur* [*F.*].

V. INVEST; cover &c. 223; envelop, lap, involve; inwrap *or* enwrap; wrap; fold up, wrap up, lap up, muffle up; overlap; sheathe, swathe, swaddle, roll up in, shroud, circumvest [*obs.*].

CLOTHE, vest [*rare*], array, dress, dight [*archaic*], bedight [*archaic*], drape, robe, enrobe, attire, apparel, tire [*archaic*], habilitate [*rare*], garb, enclothe, breech, coat, jacket, gown, accouter, rig, fit out; dizen, bedizen, deck &c. (*ornament*) 847; perk, equip, harness, caparison.

WEAR; don; put on, huddle on, slip on; mantle.

Adj. INVESTED &c. *v.*; habited; dight, dighted; barbed, barded; clad, *costumé* [*F.*], shod, *chaussé* [*F.*]; *en grande tenue* [*F.*] &c. (*show*) 882; *décolletée* [*F.*].

SARTORIAL, sartorian [*rare*].

. "the soul of this man is his clothes" [*All's Well*]; "a bird on a bonnet is worth ten on a plate" [*Cynic's Calendar*]; "clothes have made men of us; they are threatening to make clothes-screens of us" [Carlyle].

---

227. Circumjacence. — N. CIRCUM-JACENCE *or* circumjacency, circumfluence [*rare*], circumambience environment, encompassment; atmosphere, medium; surroundings, *entourage* [*F.*].

OUTPOST; border &c. (*edge*) 231; girdle &c. (*circumference*) 230; outskirts, boulevards, suburbs, purlieus, precincts, *faubourgs* [*F.*], environs, environment, entourage, *banlieue* [*F.*], neighborhood, vicinage, vicinity.

V. LIE AROUND &c. *adv.*; surround, beset, compass, encompass, environ, inclose *or* enclose, encircle, encincture [*rare*], circle, girdle, ensphere, hedge, embrace, circumvent, lap, gird; belt; begird, engird; skirt; twine round; hem in &c. (*circumscribe*) 229; beleaguer, invest, besiege, beset, blockade.

Adj. CIRCUMJACENT, circumambient, circumfluent; ambient; surrounding &c. *v.*; circumferential, suburban.

Adv. AROUND, about; without; on every side, on all sides; right and left, all round, roundabout.

228. Interjacence. — N. INTERJA-CENCE *or* interjacency, intercurrence, intervenience *or* interveniency [*rare*], interlocation, interdigitation, interpenetration; permeation.

INTERJECTION, interpolation, interlineation, interspersion, intercalation; embolism.

INTERVENTION, interference, interposition, intromission, intrusion, obtrusion; insinuation; insertion &c. 300; dovetailing; infiltration.

INTERMEDIUM, intermediary; go-between, interagent, middleman, intervener, mean, medium, bodkin [*colloq.*], intruder, interloper; parenthesis, episode, flyleaf.

PARTITION, septum, interseptum, phragma, septulum, mediastinum, diaphragm, midriff; dissepiment; party wall, panel, bulkhead, brattice, *cloison* [*F.*], perpend, halfway house.

V. LIE BETWEEN, come between, get between; intervene, slide in, interpenetrate, permeate.

PUT BETWEEN, introduce, import; throw in, wedge in, edge in, jam in, worm in, foist in, run in, plow in, work in; interpose, interject, intercalate, interpolate, interline, interleave, intersperse, interweave, interlard, interdigitate; let in, dovetail, splice, mortise; insinuate, smuggle; infiltrate, ingrain.

INTERFERE, put in an oar, thrust one's nose in; intrude, obtrude; have a finger in the pie; introduce the thin end of the wedge; thrust in &c. (*insert*) 300.

Adj. INTERJACENT, intervenient [*rare*], intervening &c. *v.*; intercalary, intercolumnar, intercostal, intercurrent, interfacial, intergrowth, interlineal, interlobular, interlocular, intermedial, intermediary, intermediate, intermaxillary, intermolecular, intermur dane, internasal, interneural, internodal, interoceanic, interosseal, interosseous, interplanetary, interpolar, interradial, interrenal, interscapular, interseptal, interstellar, interstitial, intervalvular, intervascular, interventricular, intervertebral; septal, embolismal.

parenthetical, episodic; mediterranean; intrusive; embosomed; merged.

MEAN, medium, mesne, middle, median.

Adv. BETWEEN, betwixt; 'twixt; among *or* amongst; amid, amidst; 'mid, 'midst; in the thick of; betwixt and between [*colloq.*]; sandwich-wise; parenthically, *obiter dictum* [*L.*].

229. Circumscription. — N. CIRCUMSCRIPTION, limitation, inclosure; confinement &c. (*restraint*) 751; circumvallation; encincture; envelope &c. 232.

V. CIRCUMSCRIBE, limit, bound, confine, inclose *or* enclose; surround &c. 227; compass about; imprison &c. (*restrain*) 751; hedge in, wall in, rail in; fence round, hedge round; picket; corral.

ENFOLD, bury, incase, pack up, enshrine, inclasp *or* enclasp; wrap up &c. (*invest*) 225; embay, embosom.

Adj. CIRCUMSCRIBED &c. *v.;* begirt, circumambient, girt, cinct [*rare*], circumcinct [*rare*], lapt; buried in, immersed in; embosomed, in the bosom of, imbedded, encysted, mewed up; imprisoned &c. 751; landlocked, in a ring fence.

230. Outline. — N. OUTLINE, circumference; perimeter, periphery; ambit, circuit, lines, *tournure* [*F.*], contour, profile, silhouette, relief, lineaments; bounds; coast line.

ZONE, belt, girth, band, baldric, zodiac, girdle, tire *or* tyre, cingle [*rare*], clasp, girt, girth; cordon &c. (*inclosure*) 232; circlet &c. 247.

V. OUTLINE, contour, delineate, silhouette, block, sketch, profile; circumscribe &c. 229.

Adj. OUTLINED &c. *v.;* circumferential, perimetric, perimetrical, peripheral.

231. Edge. — N. EDGE, verge, brink, brow, brim, margin, border, confine, skirt, rim, flange, side, mouth; jaws, chops, chaps, fauces; lip, muzzle.

SHORE, coast, strand, bank; bunder, bund [*both Oriental*], quay, wharf, dock, mole, landing.

FRINGE, flounce, frill, list, trimming, edging, skirting, hem, selvage *or* selvedge, welt; furbelow, valance; frame; exergue.

THRESHOLD, door, porch; portal &c. (*opening*) 260.

V. EDGE, border, skirt, fringe, marginate.

Adj. BORDER, marginal, skirting; labial, labiated, marginated.

232. Inclosure. — N. INCLOSURE *or* enclosure, envelope; case &c. (*receptacle*) 191; wrapper; girdle &c. 230.

pen, fold; sty, penfold, sheepfold; paddock, croft, pasture, wood lot; pound; corral; yard, compound; net, seine net.

FENCE &c. (*defense*) 717; pale, paling, balustrade, rail, railing, quickset hedge, park paling, circumvallation, *enceinte* [*F.*]; ring fence; wall; hedge, hedgerow; espalier.

BARRIER, barricade; gate, gateway; weir; bent, dingle [*U. S.*]; door, hatch, cordon; prison &c. 752.

DIKE *or* dyke, ditch, fosse, trench, drain, dugout, *tranchée* [*F.*], *coupure* [*F.*], moat.

V. INCLOSE *or* enclose; circumscribe &c. 229.

233. Limit. — N. LIMIT, boundary, bounds, confine, enclave, term, bourn *or* bourne, verge, curbstone, but [*Scot.*], pale; termination, terminus, terminal; stint, stent; frontier, precinct, marches; backwoods.

BOUNDARY LINE, landmark; line of -demarcation, - circumvallation; pillars of Hercules; Rubicon, turning point; *ne plus ultra* [*L.*]; sluice, floodgate.

V. LIMIT, bound, compass, confine, define, circumscribe, demarcate, delimit.

Adj. DEFINITE; conterminate [obs.], conterminable; terminable, limitable; terminal, frontier; bordering, border, limitary, boundary, limital [rare].

Adv. THUS FAR, – and no further.

₊ "The undiscover'd country from whose bourn No traveller returns" [Hamlet].

2. Special

234. Front — N FRONT; fore, fore part or forepart; foreground, forefront; face, disk or disc, frontage, façade, proscenium, facia, frontispiece; priority, anteriority; obverse (of a medal).

VAN, vanguard; advanced guard; fore-rank, front rank; outpost; first line; scout.

BROW, forehead, visage, physiognomy, phiz [colloq.], features, countenance, mug [slang]; metoposcopy; chin, mentum; rostrum, beak, bow, stem, prow, prore, jib, bowsprit.

pioneer &c. (precursor) 64; metoposcopist, physiognomist

V. FRONT, face, confront, breast, buck [slang, U. S.], brave, dare, defy oppose, outbrazen; bend forwards; come to the front, come to the fore; be or stand in front &c. adj.

Adj. FORE, forward, anterior, front, frontal; metopic

Adv. BEFORE in front, in the van, in advance; ahead right ahead· foremost, headmost in the foreground, in the lee of; before one's -face, – eyes: face to face, vis-à-vis [F.]; front à front [F.].

₊ formosa facies muta commendatio est [Syrus]; frons est animi janua [Cicero]; "human face divine" [Milton]; imago animi vultus est indices oculi [Cicero]; "sea of upturned faces" [Scott].

235. Rear. — N. REAR, back, posteriority; rear rank, rear guard, rearward [archaic]; background, hinterland.

occiput, nape; heels.

SPINE, backbone, rachis, spinal column, chine.

TAIL, scut, brush, appendage [humorous].

RUMP, croup, buttock, posteriors, fundament, bottom [colloq.], stern [colloq.], seat, backside [vulgar], breech, dorsum, tergum, loin; dorsal –, lumbar-region; hind quarters; aitchbone.

STERN, poop, counter, mizzenmast, postern door, tailpiece, after-part, heel-piece, crupper.

WAKE; train &c. (sequence) 281.

REVERSE; other side of the shield.

V. BE BEHIND &c. adv.; fall astern; bend backwards; bring up the rear; heel, tag, shadow, follow &c. (pursue) 622.

Adj. BACK, rear; hind, hinder, hind-most, hindermost; sternmost; postern, posterior; dorsal, after; caudal, tergal, neural, spinal, vertebral, lumbar; mizzen.

Adv. BEHIND; in the -rear, – background; behind one's back; at the -heels, – tail, – back- of; back to back.

after, aft, abaft, baft, astern, aback, rearward, hindward, backward.

₊ ogni medaglia ha il suo rovescio.

236. Laterality. — N. LATERALITY [rare]; side, flank, quarter, lee; hand; cheek, jowl or jole, wing; profile; temple, paries (pl. parietes), loin, haunch, hip; beam.

gable, gable-end; broadside; lee side.

points of the compass; East, sunrise, Orient, Levant; West, Occident, sunset; orientation.

V. FLANK, outflank; sidle; skirt, border, wing; orientate; be on one side &c. adv.

Adj. LATERAL, sidelong; collateral; parietal, flanking, skirting; flanked; sideling.

237. Contraposition. — N. CONTRAPOSITION, opposition; polarity; inversion &c. 218; opposite side; reverse, inverse; counterpart; antithesis.

ANTIPODES, opposite poles, North and South.

V. BE OPPOSITE &c. adj.; subtend.

Adj. OPPOSITE; reverse, inverse; converse; antipodal, diametrical, antithetic, counter, subcontrary; fronting, facing, diametrically opposite.

NORTHERN, north, northerly, north-ward, hyperborean, septentrional, boreal, polar, arctic.

SOUTHERN, south, southerly, meridi-

many-sided; multilateral, bilateral, trilateral, quadrilateral.

EASTERN, eastward, east, orient, oriental, auroral *or* aurorean; Levantine.

WESTERN, west, westerly, westward, occidental, Hesperian.

onal, southward, Austral, antarctic.

Adv. OVER, over the way, over against; against; face to face, *vis-à-vis* [*F.*]; as poles asunder.

Adv. SIDEWAYS *or* sideway, sidewise, sideling, sidelong; broadside on; on one side, abreast, alongside, beside, aside; by, by the side of; side by side; cheek by jowl &c. (*near*) 197; to windward, to leeward; laterally &c. *adj.*; right and left; on her beam ends.

*** "his cheek the map of days outworn" [Shakespeare].

---

238. Dextrality. — N. DEXTRALITY; right, right hand; dexter, offside, starboard.

Adj. DEXTRAL, dexterous *or* dextrous, right-handed; dexter, dextrorsal, dextrorse.

AMBIDEXTER, ambidextrous, ambidextral.

Adv. DEXTRAD, dextrally; ambidextrously.

239. Sinistrality. — N. SINISTRALITY, sinistration; left, left hand, south paw [*slang, U. S.*]; *sinistra* or *sinistra mano* [*music, It.*]; nearside, larboard, port.

Adj. LEFT-HANDED, sinister-handed [*obs.*], sinister, sinistral, sinistrorsal, sinistrorse, sinistrous, ambilevous [*rare*]; sinistrogyrate, sinistrogyric.

Adv. SINISTRAD, sinistrally, sinistrously.

SECTION III. FORM

1. GENERAL FORM

240. Form. — N. FORM, figure, shape; conformation, configuration; make, formation, frame, construction, cut, set, build, *tournure* [*F.*], outline, get-up [*colloq.*], trim, cut of one's jib [*colloq.*]; stamp, type, cast, mold *or* mould; fashion; contour &c. (*outline*) 230; structure &c. 329; plasmature [*obs.*].

FEATURE, lineament, turn; phase &c. (*aspect*) 448; posture, attitude, pose.

[SCIENCE OF FORM] morphology.

[SIMILARITY OF FORM] isomorphism; isomorph.

FORMATION, figuration, efformation [*rare*]; forming &c. *v.*; sculpture; plasmation [*rare*].

V. FORM, shape, figure, fashion, efform [*rare*], carve, cut, chisel, hew, cast; roughhew, roughcast; sketch; block out, hammer out; trim; lick -, put- into shape; model, knead, work up into, set, mold, sculpture; cast, stamp; build &c. (*construct*) 161.

Adj. FORMED &c. *v.*; structural, morphologic *or* morphological.

SHAPELY, well-proportioned, symmetrical, well-made, well-formed, comely, trim, neat.

[RECEIVING FORM] plastic, fictile; formative, impressible, creative.

[GIVING FORM] plasmatic, plasmic; protoplasmic.

[SIMILAR IN FORM] isomorphic, isomorphous.

241. [ABSENCE OF FORM.] **Amorphism. — N.** AMORPHISM, misproportion, informity [*rare*]; uncouthness; rough diamond; unlicked cub; *rudis indigestaque moles* [*L.*]; disorder &c. 59; deformity &c. 243.

DISFIGUREMENT, defacement; mutilation; deforming.

V. [DESTROY FORM] deface, disfigure, deform, mutilate, truncate; derange &c. 61; blemish, mar.

Adj. SHAPELESS, amorphous, formless; unshapely, misshapen, unsymmetrical, malformed, unformed, unhewn, unfashioned, unshapen; anomalous.

ROUGH, rude, Gothic, barbarous, rugged, scraggy, vandalic; in the rough.

*** "If shape it might be call'd that shape had none Distinguishable in member, joint, or limb" [*P. L.*].

242. [REGULARITY OF FORM.] **Symmetry.** — N. SYMMETRY, shapeliness, finish; beauty &c. 845; proportion, eurythmy or eurhythmy, eurythmics or eurhythmics, uniformity, parallelism; bilateral –, trilateral –, multilateral-symmetry; centrality &c. 222; radiation, regularity, evenness.

ARBORESCENCE, branching, ramification; arbor vitæ; peloria.

Adj. SYMMETRICAL, shapely, well set, finished; beautiful &c. 845; classic, chaste, severe.

REGULAR, uniform, radiate, radiated. balanced; equal &c. 27; parallel, coextensive.

ARBORESCENT, arboriform; dendriform, dendroid or dendroidal; branching; ramous, ramose; fern-shaped, filiciform, filicoid; subarborescent; papilionaceous.

243. [IRREGULARITY OF FORM.] **Distortion** — N. DISTORTION, detortion [rare], contortion, contortuosity, knot, warp, buckle, screw, twist; crookedness &c. (obliquity) 217; grimace; deformity: malformation, malconformation; harelip; monstrosity, misproportion, want of symmetry, anamorphosy, anamorphosis; ugliness &c. 846; talipes, clubfoot; teratology.

V. DISTORT, contort, twist, warp, buckle, screw, wrench, writhe, gnarl, wrest, writhe, make faces, deform, misshape.

Adj. DISTORTED &c. v.; out of shape, irregular, unsymmetric, anamorphous, awry, wry, askew, crooked; not true, not straight; on one side, crump [obs.], deformed; harelipped; misshapen, misbegotten; misproportioned, ill-proportioned; ill-made; grotesque, crooked as a ram's horn; camelbacked, humpbacked, hunchbacked, bunchbacked, crookbacked; bandy; bandylegged, bowlegged; bowkneed, knockkneed; splayfooted, taliped or talipedic, clubfooted; round-shouldered; snub-nosed; curtailed of one's fair proportions; stumpy &c. (short) 201; gaunt (thin) &c. 203; bloated &c. 194; scalene; simous.

Adv. all manner of ways.

*** crooked as a Virginia fence [U. S.]; "Then, since the heav'ns have shap'd my body so, Let hell make crook'd my mind to answer it" [Henry VI].

2. SPECIAL FORM

244. Angularity. — N. ANGULARITY, angularness; aduncity; angle, cusp, bend; fold &c. 258; notch &c. 257; fork, furculum, bifurcation.

elbow, knee, knuckle, ankle, groin, crotch, crutch; crane, fluke, scythe, sickle; zigzag.

CORNER, nook, recess, niche, oriel, coign (as in "coign of vantage").

RIGHT ANGLE &c. (perpendicular) 212; obliquity &c. 217; angle of 45 degrees, miter; acute –, obtuse –, salient –, reëntering –, spherical- angle.

ANGULAR -MEASUREMENT, – elevation, – distance, – velocity; trigonometry, goniometry; altimeter, pantometer, altimetry; clinometer, graphometer, goniometer; theodolite; transit or transit theodolite, sextant, quadrant; dichotomy.

triangle, trigon, wedge; rectangle, square, lozenge, diamond; rhomb, rhombus, rhomboid, rhombohedron, quadrangle, quadrilateral; parallelogram; quadrature; polygon, pentagon, hexagon, heptagon, octagon, oxygon, decagon.

Platonic bodies; cube, rhomboid; tetrahedron, pentahedron, hexahedron, octahedron, dodecahedron, icosahedron; prism, pyramid; parallelepiped or parallelepipedon; curb –, gambrel –, French –, mansard- roof.

V. FORK, furcate, divaricate, branch, ramify, bifurcate, bend, crinkle.

Adj. ANGULAR, bent, crooked, aduncous, adunc or aduncal, aduncate or aduncated, uncinated, aquiline, jagged, serrated; falciform, falcated; furcal, furcate, furcated, forked, bifurcate, crotched, zigzag, furcular, hooked; dove-tailed; knockkneed, crinkled, akimbo, kimbo [obs.], geniculated; oblique &c. 217.

' wedge-shaped, cuneiform; cuneate, multangular, oxygonal; triangular, trigonal, trilateral; quadrangular, quadrilateral, foursquare, rectangular, square; multilateral; polygonal &c. n.; cubical, rhombic or rhombical, rhomboidal, pyramidal.

245. Curvature. — N. CURVATURE, curvity [*rare*], curvation; incurvature, incurvity [*obs.*], incurvation; bend; flexure, flexion; conflexure [*obs.*]; crook, hook, bought [*obs.*], bending; deflexion, inflexion; concameration; arcuation, devexity [*obs.*], turn; deviation, detour *or détour* [*F.*], sweep; curl, curling; bough; recurvity [*rare*], recurvation [*rare*]; sinuosity &c. 248; aduncity.

CURVE, arc, arch, arcade, vault, bow, crescent, meniscus, half-moon, lunule, horseshoe, loop, crane neck; parabola, hyperbola; catacaustic, diacaustic; geanticline, geosyncline; catenarian, catenary, festoon; conchoid, cardioid; caustic; tracery; arched- ceiling, – roof; bay window, bow window.

V. BE CURVED &c. *adj.;* sweep, swag [*obs. or dial.*], sag; deviate &c. 279; turn; reënter.

RENDER CURVED &c. *adj.;* bend, curve, incurvate; deflect, inflect; crook; turn; round, arch, arcuate, arch over, embow, recurvate [*rare*], concamerate [*rare*]; bow, coil, curl, recurve, frizzle, friz *or* frizz.

Adj. CURVED &c. *v.;* curvate *or* curvated, lobiform; curviform, curvilineal *or* curvilinear; devex [*obs.*], devious; recurved, recurvous; crump [*obs.*]; bowed &c. *v.;* vaulted; geanticlinal, geosynclinal; bow-legged &c. (*distorted*) 243; oblique &c. 217; circular &c. 247.

BEAK-SHAPED, beaked, rostrate, rostriform, rostroid, rhamphoid.

BELL-SHAPED, campaniform, campanular, campanulous, campanulate.

BOAT-SHAPED, navicular, cymbiform, naviform, scaphoid.

BOW-SHAPED, arcuate *or* arcuated, arcual; arciform, arclike, embowed.

CRESCENT-SHAPED, crescent, crescentiform, crescentic, convexo-concave, sigmoid, semilunar, horned, meniscal, bicorn, bicornute *or* bicornuate, bicornuous [*rare*], bicorned *or* bicornous, semicircular.

HEART-SHAPED, cordiform, cardioid, cordate.

HELMET-SHAPED, galeiform, galeate, galeated, cassidiform.

HOOK-SHAPED, hooked, hooklike, unciform, uncate, uncinal, uncinate, hamulate, hamate, hamiform, hamose *or* .hamous [*both rare*]; unguiform, unguiculate *or* unguiculated; curvated, aduncate, aduncous, adunc.

KIDNEY-SHAPED, reniform.

LENS-SHAPED, lenticular, lentoid, lentiform, meniscal, meniscoid.

MOON-SHAPED, lunar, lunate *or* lunated, luniform, lunular, lunulate *or* lunulated, crescent-shaped (*q. v.*); Cynthian.

OAR-SHAPED, remiform [*rare*].

PEAR-SHAPED, pyriform; obconic.

SHELL-SHAPED, conchate, conchiform, conchylaceous [*rare*], conchoidal [*min.*].

SHIELD-SHAPED, scutate, scutiform, peltate, clypeate *or* clypeated, clypeiform.

SICKLE-SHAPED, falcate, falciform, falculate [*rare*].

TONGUE-SHAPED, linguiform, lingulate, ligulate.

TURNIP-SHAPED, napiform.

246. Straightness. — N. STRAIGHTNESS, rectilinearity, rectilinearness; directness; inflexibility &c. (*stiffness*) 323; straight –, bee –, right –, direct- line; short cut.

V. BE STRAIGHT &c. *adj.;* have no turning; not -incline, – bend, – turn, -- deviate- to either side; go straight; steer for &c. (*direction*) 278.

RENDER STRAIGHT, straighten, rectify; set –, put- straight; unbend, unfold, uncurl &c. 248; unravel &c. 219, unwrap.

Adj. STRAIGHT; rectilinear, rectilineal; direct, even, right, true, in a line; virgate, unbent &c. *v.;* undeviating, unturned, undistorted, unswerving; straight-lined, straight as an arrow &c. (*direct*) 278; inflexible &c. 323.

PERPENDICULAR, plumb, vertical, upright, erect.

247. [SIMPLE CIRCULARITY.] **Circularity. — N.** CIRCULARITY, roundness; rotundity &c. 249.

CIRCLE, circlet, ring, areola, hoop, roundlet, annulus, annulet, bracelet,

248. [COMPLEX CIRCULARITY.] **Convolution. — N.** CONVOLUTION, involution, circumvolution; winding &c. *v.;* wave, undulation, tortuosity, anfractuosity; sinuosity, sinuation, sinuousness,

armlet; ringlet; eye, loop, wheel; cycle, orb, orbit, rundle, zone, belt, cordon, band; contrate -, crown- wheel; hub, nave; sash, girdle, cestus, cest *or* ceste, cincture, baldric, fillet, fascia, wreath, garland; crown, corona, coronet, chaplet, snood, necklace, collar; noose, lasso.

ELLIPSE, oval, ovule; ellipsoid, cycloid, epicycloid, epicycle.

semicircle; quadrant, sextant, sector.

V. MAKE ROUND &c. *adj.;* round.

GO ROUND; encircle &c. 227; describe a circle &c. 311.

Adj. ROUND, rounded, circular, annular, orbicular, orbiculate *or* orbiculated; oval, ovate, obovate, ovoid, ovoidal [*rare*], elliptic, elliptical, egg-shaped; pear-shaped &c. 245; cycloidal &c. *n.;* spherical &c. 249; fasciate *or* fasciated.

** "I watched the little circles die" [Tennyson].

flexuosity, tortility; meandering, circuit, circumbendibus [*humorous*], twist, twirl, windings and turnings, ambagiousness, ambages; torsion; inosculation; reticulation &c. (*crossing*) 219; rivulation.

COIL, roll, curl, buckle, spiral, helix, corkscrew, worm, volute, whorl, rundle; tendril; scollop, scallop, escalop *or* escallop; kink; ammonite, snakestone.

serpent, snake, eel; maze, labyrinth.

V. BE CONVOLUTED &c. *adj.;* wind, twine, turn and twist, twirl; wave, undulate, meander; inosculate; entwine *or* intwine; twist, coil, roll; wrinkle, curl, crisp, twill; frizz, frizzle; crimp, crape, indent, scollop, scallop; wring, intort; contort; wreathe &c. (*cross*) 219.

Adj. CONVOLUTED; winding, twisted &c. *v.;* tortile, tortive [*obs.*]; wavy; undate *or* undated [*rare*], undulatory; circling, snaky, snakelike, serpentine, serpentiform, anguilliform, anguiform, anguilloid, anguillous, vermiform, vermicular; mazy, tortuous, sinuose, sinuous, sinuate, flexuous; undulating, undulated, wavy; anfractuous, reclivate [*rare*], rivulose, scolecoid; sigmoid, sigmoidal; spiriferous, spiroid.

wreathy, frizzly, *crêpé* [*F.*], buckled; raveled &c. (*in disorder*) 59.

INVOLVED, intricate, complicated, perplexed; labyrinthic, labyrinthian, labyrinthine; circuitous, ambagious; peristaltic; Dædalian; kinky, curly.

SPIRAL, coiled, helical; cochlear, cochleate, cochleous [*rare*]; screw-shaped; turbinated, turbiniform, turbinoid, turbinal.

Adv. in and out, round and round.

249. Rotundity. — N. ROTUNDITY; roundness &c. *adj.;* cylindricity; sphericality, sphericity, spheroidicity *or* spheroidity, globoseness, globosity, globularity, annularity, orotundity, orbiculation.

CYLINDER, cylindroid; barrel, drum; roll, roller; rouleau, column, rolling-pin, rundle.

CONE, conoid; pear-shape, egg-shape, bell-shape.

SPHERE, globe, ball, bowlder *or* boulder; spheroid, geoid, globoid, ellipsoid; oblong -, oblate- spheroid; drop, spherule, globule, vesicle, bulb, bullet, pellet, clew, pill, marble, pea, knob, pommel, horn, knot; oval &c. 247.

V. RENDER SPHERICAL &c. *adj.;* form into a sphere, sphere, roll into a ball; give rotundity &c. *n.;* round.

Adj. ROTUND; round &c. (*circular*) 247; cylindric *or* cylindrical, cylindroid *or* cylindroidal, columnar, vermiform, lumbriciform; conic, conical; spherical, spheroidal; globular, globous, globose; gibbous; fungiform, bulbous; *teres atque rotundus* [*L.*]; round as -an orange, - an apple, - a ball, - a billiard ball, - a cannon ball.

BEAD-SHAPED, beadlike, moniliform, monilated.

BELL-SHAPED, campaniform, campanulate, campanulous, campanular.

EGG-SHAPED, ovoid, oviform, ovoidal, ovate, globoid, globate *or* globated; obovate, obovoid [*both bot.*].

PEAR-SHAPED, pyriform.

RICE-SHAPED, riziform.

** "she is spherical, like a globe." [*Comedy of Errors.*]

3. Superficial Form

250. Convexity. — N. convexity, prominence, projection, swelling, gibbosity, bilge, bulge, protuberance, protrusion, excrescency; camber, cahot [*N. Amer.*], thank-ye-ma'am [*U. S.*], swell.

intumescence, tumidity; tumor *or* tumour; tubercle, tuberousness, tuberosity, carunculation, bubo.

excrescence, hump, hunch, bunch; knob, knur, knurl, gnarl, knot; bow, boss, embossment, bump, mamelon, clump; bulb, node, nodule, nodosity.

tooth, molar; lip, flange; tongue; withers, shoulder, back, dorsum; elbow.

process, apophysis, condyle.

wheel, hub, hubble [*U. S.*].

peg; button, stud; ridge, rib, trunnion, snag; sugar loaf &c. (*sharpness*) 253.

pimple, wen, whelk, papula, papule, pustule, pock, proud flesh, growth, sarcoma, caruncle, corn, wart, verruca, furuncle, polypus, fungus, fungosity, exostosis, bleb, blister, bulla, blain; boil &c. (*disease*) 655; air bubble, blob.

papilla, nipple, teat, pap, breast, dug, mammilla.

proboscis, nose, olfactory organ, neb, beak, snout, nozzle.

belly, corporation [*colloq.*], paunch, epigastrium, abdomen.

arch, cupola, dome, vault, beehive; balcony; eaves.

relief, relievo, cameo; low relief, bas-relief, basso-relievo *or* basso-rilievo [*It.*]; half relief, mezzo-relievo *or* mezzo-rilievo [*It.*]; high relief, alto-relievo *or* alto-rilievo [*It.*]; pilaster.

point of land, hill &c. (*height*) 206; cape, promontory, mull; foreland, headland; hummock, ledge, spur; naze, ness; mole, jetty, jutty.

V. be prominent &c. *adj.;* project, bulge, protrude, bag, belly, carunculate, pout, bouge [*obs.*], bunch; jut out, stand out, stick out, poke out; stick up, bristle up, start up, cock up, shoot up; swell over, hang over, bend over; beetle.

render prominent &c. *adj.;* raise 307; emboss, chase.

Adj. prominent, protuberant, protrusile, protrusive; undershot, underhung; projecting &c. *v.;* bossed, bossy, nodular, convex, bunchy; clavate, clavated, claviform; hummocky, *moutonné*

251. Flatness. — N. flatness &c *adj.;* smoothness &c. 255.

plane; level &c. 213; plate, platter, table, tablet, slab.

V. flatten; render flat; squelch [*colloq.*], squash [*colloq.*], fell; level &c 213.

Adj. flat, plane, even, flush, scutiform, discoid; complanate, flattish, homaloid; level &c. (*horizontal*) 213; flat as - a pancake, - a fluke, - a flounder, - a board, - my hand; smooth.

Adv. flat, flatly [*rare*], flatways, flatwise, lengthwise, horizontally.

252. Concavity. — N. concavity, depression, dip; hollow, hollowness; indentation, intaglio, cavity, vug *or* vugg *or* vugh, dent, dint, dimple, follicle, pit, sinus, antrum, alveolus, lacuna; honeycomb.

excavation, pit, sap, mine, shaft, colliery; caisson, *fougasse* [*F.*], countermine; trough &c. (*furrow*) 259; bay &c. (*of the sea*) 343.

cup, basin, crater, punch bowl; cell &c. (*receptacle*) 191; socket.

valley, vale, dale, dell, dingle, coomb *or* combe, bottom, slade [*obs.*], strath [*Scot.*], gill *or* ghyll [*Scot. & dial. Eng.*], glade, grove, glen, donga [*S. Africa*], nullah [*India*], park [*U. S.*].

cave, subterrane, cavern, cove; grot, grotto; alcove, blind alley, *cul-de-sac* [*F.*], hole, burrow, kennel, tunnel; gully &c. 198; arch &c. (*curve*) 245.

excavator, sapper, miner.

V. be concave &c. *adj.;* retire, cave in.

render concave &c. *adj.;* depress, dish, hollow; scoop, scoop out; gouge, dig, delve, excavate, dent, dint, mine, sap, undermine, burrow, tunnel, stave in.

Adj. depressed &c. *v.;* alveolate, alveolar, calathiform, cup-shaped, dishing; favaginous, faveolate, favose; scyphiform, scyphose; concave, hollow, vuggy, stove in; retiring; retreating; cavernous; porous &c. (*with holes*) 260; cellular, spongy, spongious; honeycombed; infundibular, infundibuliform, funnel-shaped, bell-shaped, campaniform, capsular; vaulted, arched.

[*F.*]; caruncular *or* carunculous, carunculate *or* carunculated; furuncular, fu-|

runculous, furunculoid; mammiform; papulous, papulose; hemispheric, bulbous; bowed, arched; bold; bellied; tuberous, tuberculous; tumorous; cornute, odontoid; lentiform, lenticular; gibbous; club-shaped, hubby [*U. S.*], hubbly [*U. S.*], knobby, papillose; saddle-shaped, selliform; subclavate, torose, ventricose, verrucose; excrescential.

SALIENT, in relief, raised, *repoussé* [*F.*]; bloated &c. (*expanded*) 194.

. "the knobbes sittynge on his chekes". [Chaucer].

---

253. Sharpness. — N. SHARPNESS &c *adj.*; acuity, acumination, mucronation; spinosity.

POINT, spike, spine, spiculum; needle, pin; prick, prickle; spur, rowel, barb; spit, cusp; horn, antler; snag; tag; thorn, bristle; Adam's needle, bear grass [*U. S.*], tine, yucca.

nib, tooth, tusk; spoke, cog, ratchet.

254. Bluntness. — N. BLUNTNESS &c *adj.*

V. BE *or* RENDER BLUNT &c. *adj.*; obtund, dull; take off the -point, – edge; unedge [*rare*], turn.

Adj. BLUNT, obtuse, dull, dullish, pointless, unpointed; unsharpened, bluff; edentate, toothless.

---

beard, cheval-de-frise (*pl.* chevaux-de-frise), porcupine, hedgehog, brier, bramble, thistle; comb; awn, beggar's lice, bur *or* burr, catchweed, cleavers *or* clivers, goose grass, hairif *or* hariff [*dial. Eng.*], flax comb, hatchel *or* hackle *or* heckle.

PEAK, crag, crest, *arête* [*F.*], cone, sugar loaf, pike, aiguille; spire, pyramid, steeple.

CUTTING-EDGE, knife-edge, blade, edge tool, cutlery, knife, penknife, whittle, razor; scalpel, bistoury, lancet; plowshare, colter; hatchet, ax *or* axe, pickax, mattock, pick, adz *or* adze, bill; billhook, cleaver, cutter; scythe, sickle, scissors, shears; sword &c. (*arms*) 727; wedge; bodkin &c. (*perforator*) 262; *belduque* [*F.*], bowie knife, paring knife; bushwhacker [*U. S.*]; drawing knife *or* drawknife, drawshave.

SHARPENER, hone, strop; grindstone, whetstone; novaculite; steel, emery.

V. BE SHARP &c. *adj.*; taper to a point; bristle with, acuminate.

RENDER SHARP &c. *adj.*; sharpen, point, aculeate, acuminate, whet, barb, spiculate, set, strop, grind.

CUT &c. (*sunder*) 44.

Adj. SHARP, keen; acute; acicular, aciform; aculeate *or* aculeated, acuminate *or* acuminated, pointed; tapering; mucronate *or* mucronated, mucronulate; spiked, spiky, peaked, salient; cusped, cuspidate *or* cuspidated; prickly, echinate *or* echinated, acanaceous, acanthophorous, spiny, spinous, spinulose, spinulescent, spinuliferous; apiculate *or* apiculated; thorny, bristling, muricate *or* muricated, corniculate, pectinate *or* pectinated, studded, thistly, briery; craggy &c. (*rough*) 256; snaggy, digitate *or* digitated, two-edged.

ARROW-SHAPED, arrowheaded, arrowy, sagittal, sagittate, sagittated, sagittiform.

BARBED, glochidiate, spurred, aristate, awned, awny, bearded, barbate, crestate, setarious, subulate, tetrahedral.

CONE-SHAPED, conic, conical, coniform [*rare*], pyramidal.

HORN-SHAPED, corniform, cornute *or* cornuted; crescent-shaped; horned, corniculate.

LANCE-SHAPED, lanceolate, lanciform.

REED-SHAPED, calamiform [*rare*], arundinaceous, reedy.

SCIMITAR-SHAPED, acinaciform.

SPEAR-SHAPED, hastate, hastiform [*rare*], lance-shaped (*q. v.*).

SPINDLE-SHAPED, fusiform.

STAR-SHAPED, stellate *or* stellated, stelliform, stellular, starlike, starry.

SWORD-SHAPED, gladiate, ensate, ensiform, xiphoid.

TOOTH-SHAPED, dentiform, toothlike, odontoid, dentoid.

KEEN-EDGED, cutting; sharp-edged, knife-edged; sharp –, keen- as a razor; sharp as a needle; sharpened &c. *v.*; set.

255. Smoothness. — N. SMOOTH-NESS &c. *adj.;* polish, gloss; lubricity, lubrication.

[SMOOTH SURFACES] bowling green &c. (*level*) 213; glass, ice, slide; asphalt, granolithic pavement, wood pavement, flags; down, velvet, silk, taffeta, satin, velveteen, velumen.

SMOOTHER; roller, steam roller; sand-paper, emery paper; flatiron, sadiron; burnisher, chamois *or* shammy, turpentine and beeswax.

V. SMOOTH, smoothen [*rare*]; plane; file; mow, shave; level, roll; macadamize; polish, burnish, sleek, planish, levigate, calender, glaze; iron, hot-press, mangle; lubricate &c. (*oil*) 332.

Adj. SMOOTH; polished &c. *v.;* leiodermatous, slick [*colloq.*], velutinous; even; level &c. 213; plane &c. (*flat*) 251; sleek, glossy; silken, silky; lanate, downy, velvety; glabrous, slippery, glassy, lubricous, oily, soft; unwrinkled; smooth as -glass, – ice, – monumental alabaster; – ivory, – satin, – velvet, – oil; slippery as an eel; woolly &c. (*feathery*) 256.

256. Roughness. — N. ROUGHNESS &c. *adj.;* tooth, grain, texture, ripple; asperity, rugosity, salebrosity [*obs.*], corrugation, nodosity, nodulation; arborescence &c. 242; pilosity.

HAIR, brush, beard, shag, mane, whiskers, moustache, imperial, tress, lock, curl, ringlet, fimbria, eyelashes, lashes, cilia, villi; lovelock; beaucatcher; curl paper; goatee; pɛpillote, scalp lock, scolding locks [*colloq.*], elf locks, mop, mat, thatch; fringe, toupee; hair shirt.

PLUMAGE, plumosity; plume, panache, crest; feather, tuft.

NAP, pile, floss, velvet, plush, fur, down, wool, fluff; byssus, moss, bur *or* burr.

V. BE ROUGH &c. *adj.;* go against the grain.

RENDER ROUGH &c. *adj.;* roughen, knurl, crinkle, ruffle, crisp, crumple, corrugate, engrail; roughcast; set on edge, stroke the wrong way, rub the fur the wrong way, rumple.

Adj. ROUGH, uneven; scabrous, knotted; rugged, rugose, rugous, rugulose; nodose, nodular, nodulated; knurled, cross-grained, knurly; asperous [*obs.*], crisp, salebrous [*obs.*], gnarled, gnarly, scraggly, scragged, scraggy; jagged; unkempt, unpolished, unsmooth, rough-hewn; craggy, cragged; crankling [*obs.*]; prickly &c. (*sharp*) 253; arborescent &c. 242; leafy, well-wooded.

FEATHERY, plumose, plumigerous.

HAIRY, bristly, hirsute, hispid, pappous *or* pappose, pileous, pilose, pilous; trichogenous, trichoid; tufted, ciliated, filamentous; crinose, crinite; bushy; villous, nappy; bearded, shaggy, shagged; setous [*obs.*], setose, setaceous, setiferous, setigerous, setiform; "like quills upon the fretful porcupine" [*Hamlet*]; rough as a -nutmeg grater, – bear.

DOWNY, velvety, flocculent, woolly, lanate, lanated, lanuginous, lanuginose; tomentose; fluffy.

FRINGED, befringed, fimbriate, fimbriated, fimbricate, laciniate *or* laciniated, laciniform, laciniose.

Adv. AGAINST THE GRAIN; the wrong way of the goods; in the rough; on edge.

** *cabello luengo y corto el seso;* "flesh like slag in a furnace, knobbed and withered and grey" [Kipling].

257. Notch. — N. NOTCH, dent, nick, cut; dimple; scotch, indent, indentation, denticulation, serration, serrature.

saw, tooth, crenel *or* crenelle, scallop *or* scollop; rickrack, picot edge, vandyke; depression; jag.

EMBRASURE, battlement, machicolation.

V. NOTCH, nick, pink, mill, score, cut, dent, indent, jag, scarify, scotch, crimp, scallop *or* scollop, crenulate, crenelate *or* crenellate, vandyke.

Adj. NOTCHED &c. *v.;* crenate *or* crenated; dentate *or* dentated, denticulate *or* denticulated, crenelated *or* crenellated, toothed, palmate *or* palmated, serriform, serrate *or* serrated, serrulate·

258. Fold. — N. FOLD, plicature, plication, pleat, plait, ply, crease; knife-pleat, knife-plait, box-pleat, box-plait; accordion pleat, accordion plait; tuck, gather; flexion, flexure, joint, elbow, double, doubling, duplicature, gather, wrinkle, rimple, crinkle, crankle, crumple, rumple, rivel [*archaic*], ruck, ruffle, dog's-ear, corrugation, frounce [*obs.*], flounce, lapel; pucker, crow's-feet.

V. FOLD, double, plicate, pleat, plait, crease, wrinkle, crinkle, crankle, curl, smock, shrivel, cockle up, cocker [*dial.*], rimple, rumple, frizzle, frounce [*archaic*], rivel [*archaic*], twill, corrugate, ruffle, crimple [*obs.*], crumple, pucker; turn -, double- -down, -under; dog's-ear, tuck, ruck, hem, gather.

Adj. FOLDED &c. *v.*

⁎ "not tricked and frounced as she was wont" [Milton].

---

259. Furrow. — N. FURROW, groove, rut, sulcus, scratch, streak, striæ, crack, score, incision, slit; chamfer, fluting; corduroy road, cradle hole [*sleighing*].

TRENCH, ditch, dike *or* dyke, moat, fosse, trough, channel, gutter, ravine &c. (*interval*) 198; depression, tajo [*U. S.*], thank-ye-ma'am [*U. S.*].

V. FURROW &c. *n.;* flute, groove, chamfer, carve, corrugate, cut, chisel, plow; incise, engrave, etch, enchase, mezzotint, crosshatch, hatch, grave, bite in.

Adj. FURROWED &c. *v.;* ribbed, striated, sulcated, fluted, canaliculate *or* canaliculated; bisulcous *or* bisulcate *or* bisulcated; canaliferous; unisulcate; trisulcate; corduroy; costate, rimiform [*rare*].

---

260. Opening. — N. OPENING, aperture, apertness [*archaic*]; hiation [*rare*], yawning, oscitance *or* oscitancy, dehiscence, patefaction [*obs.*], pandiculation; chasm &c. (*interval*) 198.

outlet, inlet; vent, venthole, blow-hole, airhole, spiracle; vomitory [*Rom. arch.*]; embouchure; orifice, mouth, sucker, muzzle, throat, gullet, weasand, wizen [*dial.*], nozzle; placket.

WINDOW, casement; embrasure, *abat-jour* [*F.*]; light; skylight, fanlight; lattice; bay window, bow window, oriel, dormer; lantern.

PORTAL, porch, gate, ostiary [*obs.*], postern, wicket, trapdoor, hatch, door; arcade; cellarway, driveway, gateway, doorway, hatchway, gangway; lich gate *or* lych gate [*archaic*].

WAY, path &c. 627; thoroughfare; channel, gully; passage, passageway.

TUBE, pipe, main; water pipe &c. 350; air pipe &c. 351; vessel, tubule, canal, gut, fistula; ajutage *or* adjutage; ostium; smokestack; chimney, flue, tap, funnel.

TUNNEL, mine, pit, adit, drift, shaft; gallery.

261. Closure. — N. CLOSURE, occlusion, blockade; shutting up &c. *v.;* obstruction &c. (*hindrance*) 706; embolism, embolus; contraction &c. 195; infarct, infarction; constipation, obstipation; blind -alley, - corner; keddah [*India*], *cul-de-sac* [*F.*]; cæcum; imperforation, imperviousness &c. *adj.;* impermeability; stopper &c. 263; operculum.

V. CLOSE, occlude, plug; block up, stop up, fill up, bung up, cork up, button up, stuff up, shut up, dam up; blockade; obstruct &c. (*hinder*) 706; bar, bolt, stop, seal, plumb; choke, throttle; ram down, dam, cram; trap, clinch; put to -, shut- the door; slam, clap, snap.

Adj. CLOSED &c. *v.;* shut, operculated; unopened, blank.

UNPIERCED, imporous, cæcal; embolic; infarcted, imperforate, impervious, impermeable; impenetrable; impassable, unpassable, invious [*obs.*]; pathless, wayless; untrodden.

TIGHT, unventilated, air-tight, water-tight, hermetically sealed; snug.

ALLEY, lane, mall, aisle, glade, vista.

BORE, caliber *or* calibre; pore; blind orifice; fulgurite, thunder tube.

HOLE, foramen; puncture, perforation; fontane *or* fontanelle; transforation; pinhole, keyhole, loophole, porthole, peephole, mousehole, pigeonhole; eye, eye of a needle; eyelet; slot.

POROUSNESS, porosity; sieve, strainer, colander *or* cullender; cribble, riddle, screen; honeycomb.

PERFORATION, apertion [*archaic*]; piercing &c. *v.;* terebration, empalement, pertusion [*obs.*], puncture, acupuncture, penetration.

OPENER, key, master key, *passepartout* [*F.*], clavis, open-sesame.

V. OPEN, ope [*poetic*], gape, yawn, hiate [*rare*], dehisce, bilge; fly open.

PERFORATE, pierce, empierce [*obs.*], tap, bore, drill; mine &c. (*scoop out*) 252; tunnel; transpierce, transfix; enfilade, impale, spike, spear, gore, spit, stab, pink, puncture, lance; trepan, trephine; stick, prick, riddle, punch; stave in.

cut a passage through; make way for, make room for.

UNCOVER, unclose, unrip, rip; lay –, cut –, rip –, throw- open.

Adj. OPEN; perforated &c. *v.;* perforate; wide open, patulous, agape, dehiscent, ringent; ajar, unclosed, unstopped; oscitant, gaping, yawning; patent.

TUBULAR, cannular, fistulous; pervious, permeable; foraminous; vesicular, vascular; porous, follicular, cribriform, honeycombed, infundibular *or* infundibulate, riddled; tubulose *or* tubulous, tubulate *or* tubulated; piped, tubate, tubiform.

OPENING &c. *v.;* aperient.

Int. open sesame! gangway! passageway!

*** "she open'd, but to shut Excell'd her power; the gates wide open stood" [*P. L.*].

262. Perforator. — **N.** PERFORATOR, piercer, borer, auger, chisel, gimlet, drill, wimble, awl, bradawl, scoop, terrier [*obs.*], corkscrew, dibble, trocar, trepan, trephine, probe, bodkin, needle, stylet, stiletto, broach, reamer, rimer, lancet; punch, puncheon; spikebit, gouge; spear &c. (*weapon*) 727; puncher; punching machine, punching press; punch pliers.

263. Stopper. — **N.** STOPPER, stopple; plug, cork, bung, spike, spill, spile, stopcock, tap, faucet; rammer; ram, ramrod; piston; stop-gap; wadding, stuffing, padding, stopping, dossil, pledget, sponge [*surg.*], tampion *or* tompion, tourniquet.

VALVE, vent peg, spigot, slide valve; cover &c. 223.

DOORKEEPER, gatekeeper, janitor, janitress [*fem.*], janitrix [*fem.*], *concierge* [*F.*], porter, portress [*fem.*], warder, beadle, tiler *or* tyler [*Freemasonry*], durwaun [*Hind.*], usher, guard, sentinel; beefeater, yeoman of the guard [*Eng.*]; Cerberus, watch dog, ostiary.

SECTION IV. MOTION

1. MOTION IN GENERAL

264. [SUCCESSIVE CHANGE OF PLACE.[1]] **Motion.** — **N.** MOTION, movement, motility, motivity; move; going &c. *v.;* mobility; movableness, motive power, motorium; laws of motion; mobilization.

stream, flow, flux, run, course, stir; conduction; evolution; kinematics; telekinesis.

RATE, pace, tread, step, stride, gait, port, footfall, cadence, carriage, velocity, angular velocity; clip [*colloq.*], progress, locomotion; journey &c. 266; voyage &c. 267; transit &c. 270.

RESTLESSNESS &c. (*changeableness*) 149; unrest.

V. BE IN MOTION &c. *adj.;* move, go,

265. Quiescence. — **N.** REST; stillness &c. *adj.;* quiescence; stagnation, stagnancy; fixity, immobility, catalepsy; indisturbance [*rare*]; quietism.

QUIET, tranquillity, calm; repose &c. 687; peace; dead calm, anticyclone; statue-like repose; silence &c. 403; not a breath of air, not a mouse stirring; not a leaf stirring; sleep &c. (*inactivity*) 683.

PAUSE, lull &c. (*cessation*) 142; stand, standstill; standing still &c. *v.;* lock; deadlock, dead stop, dead stand; full stop; fix; embargo.

RESTING PLACE; *gîte* [*F.*]; bivouac; home &c. (*abode*) 189; pillow &c. (*sup-*

[1] A thing cannot be said to *move* from one place to another, unless it passes in succession through every intermediate place; hence motion is only such a change of place as is *successive.* "Rapid, swift, &c., as thought" are therefore incorrect expressions.

hie, gang [*Scot. & dial. Eng.*], budge, stir, pass, flit; hover -round, – about; shift, slide, glide; roll, roll on; flow, stream, run, drift, sweep along; wander &c. (*deviate*) 279; walk &c. 266; change –, shift- one's -place, – quarters; dodge; keep going, keep moving.

PUT IN MOTION, set in motion; move; impel &c. 276; propel &c. 284; render movable, mobilize.

Adj. MOVING &c. *v.;* in motion; traveling, transitional, metabatic; motory [*rare*], motive; shifting, movable, mobile, motiferous, motile, motific [*rare*], motor, motorial, quicksilver, mercurial, unquiet; restless &c. (*changeable*) 149; nomadic &c. 266; erratic &c. 279.

telekinetic, kinematic *or* kinematical, evolutionary.

Adv. UNDER WAY; on the -move, – wing, – fly, – tramp, – march.

** eppur si muove [Galileo]; *es bildet ein Talent sich in der Stille, sich ein Charakter in dem Strom der Welt;* "she 'gan stir With a short uneasy motion" [Coleridge]; "pace came to him like a maiden with a lamp, a new and beautiful wonder" [Dunsany]; "those proud ones swaying home with mainyards backed and bows a cream of foam" [Masefield].

port) 215; haven &c. (*refuge*) 666; goal &c. (*arrival*) 292.

V. BE QUIESCENT &c. *adj.;* stand still, stand fast, stand firm, lie still; keep quiet, repose, rest one's bonnet on a chair [*dial., U. S.*], rest one's face and hands [*dial., U. S.*], hold the breath.

REMAIN, stay; stand, lie to, ride at anchor, remain *in situ*, tarry, mark time; bring to, heave to, lay to; pull up, draw up; hold, halt; stop, stop short; rest, pause, anchor; cast anchor, come to anchor; rest on one's oars; repose –, rest- on one's laurels; lie back on one's record; take breath; stop &c. (*discontinue*) 142.

VEGETATE, stagnate; *quieta non movere* [*L.*]; let alone, let well enough alone; abide, rest and be thankful; keep within doors, stay at home, go to bed, live the life of a clam.

dwell &c. (*be present*) 186; settle &c. (*be located*) 184; alight &c. (*arrive*) 292; stick, stick fast; stand, stand like a post; not stir a -peg, – step; stand like a stuck pig [*colloq.*]; be at a stand &c. *n.*

QUELL, becalm, hush, calm, still, stay, lull to sleep, lay an embargo on, put the brakes on.

Adj. QUIESCENT, still; motionless, moveless; fixed; stationary; immotile; at rest, at a stand, at a standstill, at anchor; stock-still; standing still &c. *v.;* sedentary, untraveled, stay-at-home; becalmed, stagnant, quiet; unmoved, undisturbed, unruffled; calm, restful; cataleptic; immovable &c. (*stable*) 150; sleeping &c. (*inactive*) 683; silent &c. 403; still as - a statue, – a post, – a stone, – a mouse, – death.

Adv. AT A STAND &c. *adj.; tout court* [*F.*]; at the halt.

Int. STOP! stay! avast! [*naut.*], halt! hold hard! whoa! hold! *sabr karo!* [*Hind.*], *arrêtez!* [*F.*], *halte!* [*F.*].

** requiescat in pace; Deus nobis hæc otia fecit [Vergil]; "the noonday quiet holds the hill" [Tennyson]; "the silence surged softly backward When the plunging hoofs were gone" [De La Mare]; "There is not wind enough to twirl The one red leaf" [Coleridge].

---

266. [LOCOMOTION BY LAND.] **Journey.** — **N.** TRAVEL; traveling &c. *v.;* wayfaring, campaigning, nomadization.

EXCURSION, journey, expedition, tour, trip, grand tour, *Wanderjahr* [*Ger.*], circuit, peregrination, discursion [*obs.*], ramble, pilgrimage, hadj *or* hajj [*Ar.*], trek [*S. Africa*], course, ambulation, march, walk, promenade, constitutional [*colloq.*], stroll, saunter, hike [*colloq.*], tramp, jog trot, turn, stalk, perambulation; outing, ride, drive, airing, jaunt.

nightwalking, noctambulation, noctambulism; somnambulism, sleep walking, somnambulation.

267. [LOCOMOTION BY WATER OR AIR.] **Navigation.** — **N.** NAVIGATION; volatility; aquatics; boating, yachting, cruising; ship &c. 273.

oar, scull, sweep, pole; paddle, screw, turbine; sail, canvas.

natation, swimming; fin, flipper, fish's tail.

AËRONAUTICS, aërostatics, aërostation, aërodonetics, aërial navigation, aëronautism; aëromechanics, aërodynamics, balloonery; balloon &c. 273; ballooning; aviation, airmanship; flying, flight, volitation; volplaning, planing [*colloq.*], hydroplaning, volplane, glide, dive,

RIDING, equitation, horsemanship; manège *or* manege, manage [*archaic*], ride and tie.

ROVING, vagrancy, pererration [*obs.*]; marching and countermarching; nomadism; vagabondism, vagabondage; hoboism [*U. S.*]; gadding; flit, flitting; migration; emigration, immigration, demigration [*obs.*], intermigration; *Wanderlust* [*Ger.*].

ITINERARY, plan, guide; handbook, roadbook; Baedeker, Bradshaw, Murray.

PROCESSION, parade, cavalcade, caravan, file, *cortège* [*F.*], column.

[ORGANS AND INSTRUMENTS OF LOCOMOTION] cycle, automobile, motor car &c. (*vehicle*) 272; trolley, locomotive; palanquin *or* palankeen, litter, dandy *or* dandi [*India*], jinrikisha *or* jinricksha; roller skates, skates, skis, snowshoes; legs, shanks, feet; pegs, pins, trotters [*colloq.*].

TRAVELER &c. 268.

STATION, stop, stopping place, terminal [*U. S.*], terminus, depot [*U. S.*], railway station, *gare* [*F.*].

V. TRAVEL, journey, course; take –, go- a journey; railroad [*U. S.*]; flit, take wing; migrate, emigrate, immigrate; trek [*S. Africa*]; scour –, traverse- the country; peragrate [*obs.*]; perambulate, circumambulate; tour, peregrinate, itinerate [*rare*], nomadize.

motor, motorcycle, bicycle, cycle [*colloq.*], spin, speed, burn up the road; trolley [*colloq.*]; go by -car, – trolley, – automobile, – rail, – train &c.

MOTORIZE, electrify.

WANDER, roam, range, prowl, rove, jaunt, ramble, stroll, saunter, hover, go one's rounds, straggle; gad, gad about; expatiate [*rare*]; patrol, pace up and down, traverse; take a walk &c. *n.;* go out for a walk &c. *n.;* have a run, take the air; noctambulate; somnambulate.

nose-dive, spin, looping the loop; wing' pinion, aileron.

VOYAGE, sail, cruise, passage, circumnavigation, periplus; headway, sternway, leeway; fairway.

MARINER &c. 269; AËRONAUT &c. 269a.

V. SAIL; put to sea &c. (*depart*) 293; take ship, weigh anchor, get under way; spread -sail, – canvas; gather way, have way on; make –, carry- sail; plow the -waves, – deep, – main, – ocean; ride the waves, ride the storm, buffet the waves, walk the waters.

NAVIGATE, warp, luff, scud, boom, kedge; drift, course, cruise, steam, coast; hug the -shore, – land; circumnavigate.

ROW, paddle, ply the oar, pull, scull, punt.

FLOAT, swim, skim, *effleurer* [*F.*], dive, wade.

[IN AËRONAUTICS] fly, soar, drift, hover, be wafted, aviate, volplane, plane [*colloq.*], glide, dive, fly over, nose-dive, spin, loop the loop, land; take wing, take a flight; wing one's flight, wing one's way.

Adj. SAILING &c. *v.;* seafaring, nautical, maritime, naval; seagoing, coasting; afloat; navigable; grallatorial *or* grallatory.

AËRONAUTIC, aëronautical, aërostatic *or* aërostatical, aëromechanic *or* aëromechanical, aërodynamic, aërial, volant, volitant, volatile, volitational.

AQUATIC, natatory, natatorial, natational.

Adv. UNDER -WAY, – sail, – canvas, – steam; on the wing.

⁎⁎ bon voyage; "spread the thin oar and catch the driving gale" [Pope]; "the waves bowed down before her like blown grain" [Masefield]; "like the eagle free Away the good ship flies" [Cunningham]; "As if it dodged a water-sprite, It plunged and tacked and reared" [Coleridge].

TAKE HORSE, ride, drive, trot, amble, canter, prance, fisk [*obs.*], frisk, *caracoler* [*F.*], caracole; gallop &c. (*move quickly*) 274.

WALK, march, step, tread, pace, plod, wend [*archaic*]; promenade; trudge, track, hoof it [*slang*], hike [*colloq.*], tramp; stalk, stride, straddle, strut, foot it, stump, bundle, bowl along, toddle; paddle; tread –, follow –, pursue- a path.

peg on, jog on, wag on, shuffle on; stir one's stumps [*colloq.*]; bend one's -steps, – course; make –, find –, wend –, pick –, thread –, plow- one's way.

GLIDE, slide, coast, skim, skate.

FILE OFF, march in procession, defile.

GO TO, repair to, resort to, hie to, betake oneself to.

Adj. TRAVELING &c. *v.;* ambulatory, itinerant, peripatetic, perambulatory, mundivagant [*rare*], roving, rambling, gadding, discursive, vagrant, migratory, nomadic; circumforanean [*obs.*], circumforaneous.

NIGHT-WANDERING, noctivagant [*rare*], noctambulistic, noctivagous, somnambulistic *or* somnambular, somnambulant.

SELF-MOVING, automobile, automotive, locomotive, locomobile, automatic.

WAYFARING, wayworn; travel-stained.

Adv. on foot, on horseback, on Shanks's mare; by the Marrowbone stage; *in transitu* &c. 270; *en route* &c. 282.

Int. come along! step on it! [*automobile cant*].

. "I will paddle it stoutly at your side With the tandem that nature gave me" [Holmes]; "I dislike feeling at home when I am abroad" [Shaw].

268. Traveler. — N.

TRAVELER, wayfarer, voyager, itinerant, passenger, transient, commuter, straphanger [*colloq.*].

tourist, excursionist, explorer, adventurer, mountaineer, Alpine Club; peregrinator, wanderer, rover, straggler, rambler; landsman, landlubber, horse marine; bird of passage; gadabout [*colloq.*], gadling [*obs.*]; vagrant, scatterling [*obs.*], landlouper *or* landloper, waifs and estrays, wastrel, stray; loafer, swagman *or* swagsman [*Australia*], tramp, vagabond, nomad, Bohemian, gypsy, Arab, Wandering Jew, hadji *or* hajji [*Ar.*], pilgrim, palmer; peripatetic; comers and goers, immigrant; *émigré* [*F.*], emigrant; runagate, runaway, renegade, fugitive, refugee; beachcomber; booly [*Irish hist.*]; globe-girdler, globetrotter [*colloq.*]; hobo [*U. S.*], runabout, trekker [*S. Africa*], camper, *zingaro* (*pl. zingari*) [*It.*].

SLEEPWALKER, somnambulist, somnambulator [*rare*], nightwalker, noctambulist.

COURIER, messenger, express, *estafette* [*F.*], runner; Mercury, Iris, Ariel; comet.

PEDESTRIAN, walker, foot passenger, hiker [*colloq.*], perigrinator [*rare*], tramper.

RIDER, horseman, horsewoman [*fem.*], equestrian, equestrienne [*fem.*], cavalier,

269. Mariner. — N.

MARINER, sailor, navigator; seaman, seafarer, seafaring man, sea dog [*colloq.*], hand, water dog [*colloq.*], shellback [*slang*]; Ancient Mariner, Flying Dutchman; dock walloper [*slang*]; Jack, Jack Tar *or* jack-tar, tar, jacky (*pl.* jackies) [*landsman's term*], shipman [*obs. or poet.*], gob [*slang*, *U. S.*]; salt, able seaman, A. B.; man-of-war's man, bluejacket, galiongee *or* galionji, marine, devil-dog [*slang*, *U. S.*], jolly [*slang*]; midshipman, middy [*colloq.*]; lascar, *mangee* or *manjhi* [*Hind.*], matelot [*F.*], captain, commander, master mariner, skipper; mate; boatman, ferryman, waterman, lighterman, bargeman, longshoreman; bargee, gondolier; oar, oarsman; rower; boatswain.

STEERSMAN, coxswain *or* cockswain, cox [*colloq.*], helmsman, wheelman, pilot, *patron* [*F.*]; crew.

. "the keen Eye-puckered, hard-case seamen, silent, lean" [Masefield].

269a. Aëronaut. — N.

AËRONAUT, aviator, aëroplanist, airman, airwoman, flyer, birdman [*colloq.*], birdwoman [*colloq.*], aviatress *or* aviatrix, aërial navigator, man-bird [*colloq.*], wizard of the air, monoplanist; pilot, observer, spotter [*mil. cant*], scout, bomber, ace; balloonist, Icarus.

jockey, roughrider, trainer, breaker, huntsman, whip, postilion *or* postillion, postboy.

DRIVER, coachman, Jehu [*humorous*], charioteer, carter, wagoner, drayman; cabman, cabdriver; *voiturier* [*F.*], *vetturino* [*It.*], *condottiere* [*It.*], gharry-wallah *or* gari-wala [*Hind.*], hackman, syce [*India*], truckman.

[RAILROAD] engine driver [*Brit.*], engineer [*U. S.*], fireman, stoker, conductor, guard [*Brit.*], motorman.

[AUTOMOBILE] driver, chauffeur, chauffeuse [*fem.*], automobilist, motorist, truck driver, mechanician; scorcher [*slang*], speed maniac, road hog [*slang*].

. "of the cannibals that each other eat, And anthropophagi, and men whose heads Do grow beneath their shoulders" [*Othello*].

270. Transference. — N. TRANSFER, transference; translocation, elocation [obs.]; displacement; metastasis, metathesis; removal; remotion; amotion; relegation; deportation, asportation, extradition, conveyance, draft; carrying, carriage; convection, conduction, contagion, infection; transfusion; transfer &c. (of property) 783.

TRANSIT, transition; passage, ferry, gestation; portage, porterage, freightage, carting, cartage; shoveling &c. v.; vection [obs.], vecture [obs.], vectitation [obs.]; shipment, freight, waftage; transmission, transport, transportation, transumption [rare], transplantation, translation; shifting, dodging; dispersion &c. 73; transposition &c. (interchange) 148; traction &c. 285; portamento [music, It.].

[THING TRANSFERRED] drift, alluvion, alluvium, detritus, deposit, moraine; deed, gift, bequest, legacy, lease; quitclaim; freight, cargo, mail, baggage, luggage [Brit.], goods [Brit.].

TRANSFEREE, grantee, assignee; donee, legatee, consignee, indorsee, devisee.

V. TRANSFER, transmit, transport, transplace, transplant, transfuse; convey, carry, bear, fetch and carry; carry over, ferry over; hand, pass, forward; shift; conduct, convoy, bring, fetch, reach; tote [U. S.].

SEND, delegate, consign, relegate, turn over to, deliver; ship, freight, embark; waft; shunt; transpose &c. (interchange) 148; displace &c. 185; throw &c. 284; drag &c. 285; mail, post.

LADLE, bail or bale, bucket, lade, dip, drip; shovel, decant, draft off.

Adj. TRANSFERRED &c. v.; drifted, movable; portable, portative; conductive, contagious, infectious; metastatic, metathetic or metathetical; transumptive [rare].

TRANSFERABLE, assignable, conveyable, devisable, bequeathable, negotiable, transmittible, transmissible; mailable [U. S.].

Adv. from hand to hand, from pillar to post; by freight, by rail, by steamer, by aëroplane, by trolley, by motor truck, by express, by mail, by special delivery.

on the way, by the way; on the road, on the wing; as one goes; in transitu [L.], en route [F.], chemin faisant [F.], en passant [F.], in mid-progress.

271. Carrier. — N. CARRIER, porter, red cap [U. S.], bearer, tranter [obs.], conveyer; cargador [P.I.], freighter, express, expressman; stevedore; coolie; conductor, chauffeur, truck driver; letter carrier, postman, man of letters [humorous], aërial mail-carrier.

BEAST OF BURDEN, beast, cattle, horse, steed, nag, palfrey, Arab, blood horse, thoroughbred, galloway, charger, courser, racer, hunter, jument [obs.], pony; Shetland, – pony; filly, colt, foal, barb, roan, jade, hack, bidet, pad, cob, tit [dial.], punch [dial.], roadster, goer; race –, pack –, draft –, cart –, dray –, post- horse; shelty or sheltie; garran or garron [Brit.], jennet or genet, bayard, mare, stallion, gelding; broncho or bronco, cayuse [U. S.]; creature, critter [rural U. S.]; cow pony, mustang, Narragansett, waler; stud.

ASS, donkey, jackass, burro [S. W. U. S.], cuddy [Scot. & dial. Eng.], moke [slang]; wild ass, onager.

mule, hinny; sumpter -horse, – mule; ladino [U. S.].

reindeer; camel, dromedary, llama, elephant; carrier pigeon.

Pegasus, Bucephalus, Rosinante or Rocinante, Alborak, Bayard, Incitatus, Kantaha, Veillantif, Vindictive, Black Bess, Kelpie or Kelpy.

[MEANS OF TRANSPORT] locomotive, motor, trolley, carriage &c. (vehicle) 272; ship &c. 273.

Adj. equine, asinine; electric, motor, express.

** "I was not made a horse; And yet I bear a burthen like an ass" [Richard II].

272. Vehicle. — N. VEHICLE, conveyance, carriage, caravan, car, van; wagon or waggon, wain [archaic], dray, cart, lorry.

cariole or carriole; truck, tram; limber, tumbrel or tumbril, pontoon; barrow;

273. Ship. — N. SHIP, vessel, sail; craft, bottom.

NAVY, marine, fleet, flotilla.

SHIPPING, man-of-war &c. (combatant) 726; transport, tender, storeship; merchant ship, merchantman; packet, liner;

wheelbarrow, handbarrow; perambulator; Bath –, wheel- chair; chaise; police van, patrol wagon, black Maria [*colloq.*, *U. S.*]; conestoga wagon *or* wain; jinrikisha *or* jinricksha, ricksha [*colloq.*], dearborn [*U. S.*], dump cart, hack, jigger [*U. S.*, horse car; *New Eng.*, heavy cart; *Eng.*, light cart]; kittereen, mail stage, manumotor, rig, rockaway, prairie schooner [*U. S.*], shay [*colloq.*], sloven [*Can.*], team, tonga [*India*], Cape cart [*S. Africa*], hackery [*India*], ekka [*India*]; gharri *or* gharry *or* gari [*India*]; gocart.

EQUIPAGE, turnout [*colloq.*]; coach, chariot, phaëton, mail phaëton, wagonette, break *or* brake, drag, curricle, tilbury, whisky [*obs.*], landau, barouche, victoria, brougham, clarence, calash, calèche [*F.*], britzka, araba [*Oriental*], kibitka; berlin; sulky, désobligeant [*F.*], sociable, vis-à-vis [*F.*], dormeuse [*F.*], jaunting –, outside- car; runabout; vettura [*It.*].

post chaise; diligence [*F.*], stage, stagecoach; mail –, hackney –, glasscoach; stage wagon; car, omnibus, bus [*colloq.*]; fly [*Eng.*], cabriolet, cab, hansom, four-wheeler, growler [*slang, Eng.*], droshki *or* drosky.

dogcart, trap [*colloq.*], whitechapel, buggy, char-à-bancs (*pl. chars-à-bancs*) [*F.*], shandrydan *or* shandradan [*Scot., Ir., & dial. Eng.*].

TEAM, pair, span, tandem, randem; spike team *or* spike [*U. S.*], unicorn; four-in-hand.

LITTER, palanquin *or* palankeen, sedan *or* sedan chair; palki, jampan, dandy *or* dandi, dooly *or* doolie, munchil [*all India*]; cacolet [*F.*]; tonjon [*Ceylon*], brancard, horse litter; stretcher, hurdle; ambulance.

SLED, bob, bobsled *or* bobsleigh [*U. S.*]; cutter [*U. S.*]; doubleripper, doublerunner [*U. S.*]; jumper [*U. S. & Can.*], sledge, sleigh, toboggan, cariole *or* carriole [*Can.*], pung [*U. S.*]; ski (*pl.* ski *or* skis), snowshoes, skates, roller skates.

CYCLE, monocycle, bicycle, tricycle, quadricycle, hydrocycle, tandem; machine [*colloq.*], wheel [*colloq.*], bike [*slang*]; safety bicycle *or* safety [*colloq.*], motor cycle *or* motorcycle; velocipede, hobbyhorse, draisine *or* draisene.

AUTOMOBILE, motor car *or* motorcar, limousine, sedan, touring car, roadster,

whaler, slaver, collier, coaster, freight-steamer, freighter, lighter; fishing –, pilot- boat; trawler, hulk; yacht; baggala; floating -hotel, – palace; ocean greyhound [*colloq.*].

ship, bark *or* barque; shipentine, four-masted bark *or* barque; brig, snow, hermaphrodite brig; brigantine, barkentine *or* barquentine, schooner; topsail –, fore-and-aft- schooner; fore-and-after [*colloq.*]; three-, four-, five-, six- masted schooner; chusse-marée [*F.*], sloop, cutter, revenue cutter [*U. S.*], corvet *or* corvette, clipper, foist [*obs.*], yawl, dandy, ketch, smack, lugger, barge, hoy, cat, catboat, buss; sailer, sailing vessel; windjammer [*colloq.*]; steamer, steamboat, steamship; mail –, paddle –, turbine –, screw- steamer; tug; line of steamers &c.

BOAT, pinnace, launch; lifeboat, longboat, jolly-boat, bumboat, flyboat, cockboat, ferry-boat, canal boat; ark, bully [*Nfld.*], bateau [*Can.*], broadhorn [*W. U. S.*], dory, drogher, dugout, Durham boat [*U. S.*], galiot *or* galliot, flatboat, shallop, gig, funny [*Eng.*], skiff, dinghy *or* dingey *or* dingy, scow, cockleshell, wherry, coble, punt, cog, lerret [*dial. Eng.*]; eight-, four-, pair- oar; randan; outrigger; float, raft, pontoon; ice-boat, ice-canoe, ice-yacht.

catamaran, coracle, gondola, caravel *or* carvel, felucca, caïque, canoe; galley, galley foist [*hist.*], bilander, dogger, hooker *or* howker [*obs.*]; argosy, carack *or* carrack [*hist.*], galleass *or* galliass, galleon; polacre *or* polacca, corsair, piragua, bunderboat [*India*], tartane, junk, lorcha, praam, proa *or* prahu, saic, sampan, xebec, dhow; dahabeah; nuggar; kayak, keel boat [*U. S.*], log canoe, pirogue; quadrireme, trireme; stern-wheeler [*U. S.*]; wanigan *or* wangan [*U. S.*], wharf boat; derelict.

[AËRONAUTICS] balloon; airship, aëroplane, airplane, aëro [*colloq.*], monoplane, biplane, triplane; avion [*F.*], aëronat, dirigible, zeppelin, zepp [*colloq.*]; air cruiser, battle –, bombing –, combatplane; two-seater, biplace [*F.*]; singleseater, monoplace [*F.*], aëroboat, aërobus, aëro-hydroplane, aëroyacht, flying boat; aircraft; hydroplane, aërodrome [*obsoles.*], air –, pilot –, captive –, fire-balloon; aërostat, Montgolfier; kite, parachute.

coupé, motor [colloq.], machine [colloq.], car [colloq.], auto [colloq.], locomobile, autocar, steamer, electric, runabout, coupelet, racer, torpedo; truck, tractor; taxicab, taxi [colloq.], taxicoach, motor bus or motorbus; flivver [slang], jitney [colloq.], tacot [F. mil. slang].

[ALLIED AUTOMOBILE TERMS] tonneau, chassis, hood, top, ignition, spark plug, sparking plug [Eng.], generator, distributor, magneto, self-starter, gear, gear box, differential, cylinder, manifold, intake, exhaust, carburetor or carburettor; four –, six –, eight –, twelve- cylinder; twin six, ammeter, speedometer, oil gauge, primer, clutch, universal joint, crank shaft, transmission, tire or tyre [Brit.], rim; gasoline or gasolene, petrol [Brit.]; trailer; garage; chauffeur &c. 268.

TRAIN; express, mail; accommodation –, passenger –, express –, special –, limited –, mail –, corridor –, parliamentary –, luggage [Brit.] –, freight –, goods [Brit.]- train; 1st-, 2d-, 3d-class- -train, – carriage, – compartment; rolling stock; cattle truck; car, coach, carriage [Brit.]; baggage –, freight –, chair –, drawing-room –, palace –, parlor –, Pullman –, sleeping- car; surface –, tram- car; trolley or trolley car [U. S. & Can.], electric car, electric [colloq.]; trollibus, trackless trolley; box car, box wagon; horse box [Brit.], horse car [U. S.]; lightning express; mail car, mail van [Brit.]; baggage car, luggage van [Brit.].

HAND CAR, trolley or trolly.

[UTENSILS & IMPLEMENTS] spoon, spatula, ladle, hod, hoe; spade, shovel, spaddle [obs.], loy [Ir. & U. S.]; spud; pitchfork.

Adj. VEHICULAR, curricular [rare], vehiculatory [rare]; ambulatory &c. (traveling) 266.

⁎ "Now in building of chaises, I tell you what, There is always somewhere a weakest spot" [Holmes].

[ALLIED AÉRONAUTICAL TERMS] fuselage, gondola, wings, ailes [F.], controls, aileron, lifting power, camouflage, rudder; tail, empennage [F.]; cabane, hangar; aëronaut &c. 269a.

Adj. MARINE, maritime, naval, nautical, seafaring, ocean-going; A1, A1 at Lloyd's; seaworthy.

AËRONAUTIC or aëronautical, aërial; airworthy; volant &c. 267.

Adv. AFLOAT, aboard; on board, on ship board; hard-a -lee, – port, – starboard, – weather.

⁎ "The hollow oak our palace is, Our heritage the sea" [Cunningham]; "all the marvelous beauty of their bows" [Masefield].

2. DEGREES OF MOTION

274. Velocity. — N. VELOCITY, speed, celerity; swiftness &c. adj.; rapidity, eagle speed, lightning speed; expedition &c. (activity) 682; pernicity [obs.]; acceleration; haste &c. 684.

SPURT, sprint, rush, dash, race, steeple chase; automobile race; Marathon race or Marathon; smart –, lively –, swift &c. adj. –, rattling [colloq.] –, spanking [slang] –, strapping [colloq.]- -rate, – pace; round pace; flying, flight.

PACE, gallop, canter, trot, round trot, run, scamper; hand –, full- gallop; swoop.

[COMPARISONS] lightning, light, electricity, wind; cannon ball, rocket, arrow, dart, hydrargyrum, quicksilver, Mercury; wireless, telegraph, express train; swallow flight; torrent.

eagle, antelope, courser, race horse, barb, gazelle, greyhound, hare, doe, squirrel, camel bird, swallow, chickaree, chipmunk, hackee [U. S.], ostrich.

275. Slowness. — N. SLOWNESS &c. adj.; languor &c. (inactivity) 683; drawl; creeping &c. v., lentor [rare].

jog-trot, dog-trot; amble, rack, pace, single-foot, walk; mincing steps; dead march, slow march, slow time.

RETARDATION; slackening &c. v.; delay &c. (lateness) 133; claudication [obs.].

SLOW GOER, slow coach [colloq.]; lingerer, loiterer, sluggard, tortoise, snail; poke [slang, U. S.]; dawdle &c. (inactive) 683.

V. MOVE SLOWLY &c. adv.; creep, crawl, lag, slug [dial.], walk, drawl, linger, loiter, saunter; plod, trudge, stump along, lumber; trail, drag; dawdle &c. (be inactive) 683; grovel, worm one's way, inch, inch along, steal along; jog on, rub on, toddle, waddle, wabble or wobble, wamble, traipse or trapes [dial. or colloq.], slouch, shuffle, halt, hobble, limp, claudicate [obs.], shamble: flag, falter, totter, stagger;

scorcher [*slang*], joy rider [*colloq.*], speed maniac.

Mercury, Ariel, Puck, Camilla, Harlequin.

[MEASUREMENT OF VELOCITY] velocimeter, speedometer, patent log, log, log line.

V. MOVE QUICKLY, trip, fisk [*obs.*]; speed, hie, hasten, spurt, sprint, post, spank, scuttle; scud, scuddle [*obs. or Scot.*], scurry, whiz; thunder -by, – on; scour, scour the plain; scamper; run, run like mad [*colloq.*], fly, race, run a race, cut away, shoot, tear, whisk, sweep, skim, brush; skedaddle [*colloq.*], cut and run [*colloq.*], cut along [*colloq.*], bowl along; scorch [*colloq.*]; rush &c. (*be violent*) 173; dash on, dash off, dash forward; bolt; trot, gallop, bound, flit, spring, dart, boom; march in -quick, – double- time; ride hard, get over the ground; give her the gas, step on her tail, run wide open [*all automobile cant*].

HURRY &c. (*hasten*) 684; bundle, bundle along; bundle on; accelerate, put on; quicken; quicken –, mend -one's pace; clap spurs to one's horse; make haste, make rapid strides, make forced marches, make the best of one's way; put one's best leg foremost, stir one's stumps [*slang*], wing one's way, set off at a score; carry sail, crowd sail; go off like a shot, go ahead, gain ground; outstrip the wind, fly on the wings of the wind.

KEEP UP WITH, keep pace with.

OUTSTRIP &c. 303; outmarch.

Adj. FAST, speedy, swift, rapid, quick,

mince, step short; march in slow time, march in funeral procession; take one's time; hang fire &c. (*be late*) 133.

RETARD, relax, slacken, check, moderate, rein in, curb; reef; strike –, shorten –, take in- sail; put on the drag, brake, apply the brake; clip the wings; reduce the speed; slacken speed, slacken one's pace, backwater, back pedal, throttle down, lose ground.

Adj. SLOW, slack; tardy; dilatory &c. (*inactive*) 683; gentle, easy; leisurely; deliberate, gradual; insensible, imperceptible; languid, sluggish, apathetic, phlegmatic, lymphatic; moderate, slow-paced, tardigrade [*rare*], snail-like; creeping &c. *v.*; reptatorial *or* reptatory.

DULL, slow [*colloq.*], prosaic, unentertaining, boresome, wearisome, uninteresting &c. (*dull*) 843.

Adv. SLOWLY &c. *adj.*; leisurely; *piano* [*It.*], *adagio* [*It.*], *largo* [*It.*], *larghetto* [*It.*], at half speed, under easy sail; at a -foot's, – snail's, – funeral- pace; dead slow [*colloq.*]; slower than- death, – cold molasses [*colloq.*], – a funeral; in slow time; with mincing steps, with clipped wings; *haud passibus æquis* [Vergil]; in low (gear *or* speed) [*automobiling*].

GRADUALLY &c. *adj.*; gradatim; by degrees, by slow degrees, by inches, by little and little; step by step; inch by inch, bit by bit, little by little, *seriatim* [*L.*], consecutively.

. *dum Roma deliberat Saguntum perit;* "that, like a wounded snake, drags its slow length along" [Pope].

Adj. FAST, speedy, swift, rapid, quick, fleet; nimble, agile, expeditious; express; active &c. 682; flying, galloping &c. *v.*; light-footed, nimble-footed; winged, eagle-winged, mercurial, electric, telegraphic; light-legged, light of heel; swift as an arrow &c. *n.*; quick as lightning &c. *n.*; quick as thought.[1]

Adv. SWIFTLY &c. *adj.*; with speed &c.*n.*; apace; at a great rate, at full speed, at railway speed; full drive, full gallop; posthaste, in full sail, tantivy; like a shot [*colloq.*], like greased lightning [*colloq.*]; trippingly; instantaneously &c. 113.

under press of -sail, – canvas, – sail and steam; *velis et remis* [*L.*], on eagle's wing, in double-quick time; with rapid strides, with giant strides, *à pas de géant* [*F.*], in seven-league boots; whip and spur; *ventre à terre* [*F.*]; as fast as one's -legs, – heels- will carry one; as fast as one can lay feet to the ground, at the top of one's speed; by leaps and bounds; with haste &c. 684; in high (gear *or* speed) [*automobiling*].

. *tempus fugit; vires acquirit eundo;* "I'll put a girdle round about the earth In forty minutes" [*M. N. D.*]; "swifter than arrow from the Tartar's bow" [*M. N. D.*]; "he was the sworn companion of the wind" [Dunsany].

[1]See note on 264.

3. Motion conjoined with Force

276. Impulse. — N. impulse, impulsion, impetus; momentum; push, pulsion, thrust, shove, jog, jolt, brunt, boom, booming, boost [*U. S.*], throw; explosion &c. (*violence*) 173; propulsion &c. 284.

clash, collision, occursion [*obs.*], encounter, appulsion, appulse, shock, crash, bump; impact; *élan* [*F.*]; charge &c. (*attack*) 716; percussion, concussion; beating &c. (*punishment*) 972.

blow, dint, stroke, knock, tap, rap, slap, smack, pat, dab; fillip; slam, bang; hit, whack, thwack; cuff &c. 972; squash, douse *or* dowse, whap [*dial.*], swap [*obs.*], punch, thump, pelt, kick, punce [*obs.*], calcitration; *ruade* [*F.*]; arietation [*obs.*]; cut, thrust, lunge, yerk [*obs.*]; cannon [*billiards, Brit.*], carom *or* carrom, clip [*slang*], jab, plug [*slang*], sidewinder [*slang, U.S.*], sidewipe [*slang, U.S.*].

hammer, sledge hammer, mall, maul [*archaic*], mallet, flail; ram, rammer; ramrod; battering-ram, monkey, tamper, tamping iron, pile driver, pile-driving engine, punch, bat; cant hook [*U. S. or dial. Eng.*]; cudgel &c. (*weapon*) 727; ax &c. (*sharp*) 253.

[Science of mechanical forces] mechanics, dynamics; kinematics, kinetics; dynamograph, dynamometer; seismometer.

V. impel, give an impetus &c. *n.*; push; start, give a start to, set going; drive, urge, boom; thrust, prod, foin [*archaic*]; cant; elbow, shoulder, jostle *or* justle, hustle, hurtle, shove, jog, jolt, encounter; run –, bump –, butt- against; knock –, run- one's head against; impinge; boost [*U. S.*]; bunt, carom *or* carrom, cannon [*billiards, Brit.*], clip [*slang*]; fan, -out; jab, plug [*slang*].

strike, knock, hit, tap, rap, slap, flap, dab, pat, thump, beat, bang, slam, dash; punch, thwack, whack; hit –, strike- hard; swap [*obs.*], batter, douse *or* dowse [*obs.*], tamp, baste, paste [*slang*], pelt, patter, buffet, belabor; fetch one a blow; poke at, pink, lunge, yerk [*obs.*]; kick, calcitrate; butt, strike at &c. (*attack*) 716; whip &c. (*punish*) 972.

collide; come –, enter- into collision; foul; fall –, run- foul of; telescope. throw &c. (*propel*) 284.

Adj. impulsive, impellent, propulsive, pulsive [*rare*], booming; dynamic, dynamical; kinetic, kinematic *or* kinematical; impelled &c. *v.*; impelling &c. *v.*

*** "a hit, a very palpable hit" [*Hamlet*].

277. Recoil. — N. recoil; reaction, retroaction; revulsion; rebound, ricochet, backlash, repercussion, recalcitration: kick, *contrecoup* [*F.*]; springing back &c. *v.*; elasticity &c. 325; reflexion, reflex, reflux; reverberation &c. (*resonance*) 408; rebuff, repulse; return.

ducks and drakes; boomerang; spring.

reactionary, reactionist, recalcitrant.

V. recoil, react; balk, jib; spring –, fly –, bound- back; rebound, reverberate, repercuss, recalcitrate; echo, ricochet.

Adj. recoiling &c. *v.*; refluent, repercussive, recalcitrant, reactionary, revulsive, retroactive.

Adv. on the recoil &c. *n.*

4. Motion with reference to Direction

278. Direction. — N. direction, bearing, course, set, trend, run, drift, tenor; tendency &c. 176; incidence; bending, trending &c. *v.*; dip, tack, aim, collimation; steering, steerage.

points of the compass, cardinal points; north, east, south, west; N by E, NNE, NE by N, NE, &c.

rhumb, azimuth, line of collimation.

line, path, road, range, quarter, line of march; alignment *or* alinement; air line, bee line; straight shot.

279. Deviation. — N. deviation; swerving &c. *v.*; obliquation [*obs.*], warp, refraction; flection *or* flexion; sweep; deflection, deflexure; declination.

diversion, digression, departure from, aberration, drift, sheer, divergence &c. 291; zigzag; detour &c. (*circuit*) 629; divagation, disorientation, exorbitation [*rare*].

[Desultory motion] wandering &c. *v.*; vagrancy, evagation [*obs.*]; bypaths and crooked ways; byroad.

V. TEND TOWARDS, bend towards, point towards; conduct to, go to; point -to, – at; bend, trend, verge, incline, dip, determine.

STEER FOR, steer towards, make for, make towards; aim at, level at; take aim; keep –, hold- a course; be bound for; bend one's steps towards; direct ··, steer –, bend –, shape- one's course; align one's march; go straight, – to the point; make a bee line; march -on, – on a point.

ascertain one's direction &c. *n.*; *s'orienter* [*F.*], see which way the wind blows; box the compass; take the air line.

Adj. DIRECTED &c. *v.*, – towards; pointing towards &c. *v.*; bound for; aligned with; direct, straight; undeviating, unswerving; straightforward; north, northern, northerly, &c. *n.*

DIRECTABLE, steerable, leadable, dirigible, guidable, aimable, determinable.

Adv. TOWARDS; on the -road, – high road- to; *en avant* [*F.*]; *versus* [*L.*], to; hither, thither, whither; directly; straight, – forwards, – as an arrow; point-blank; in a -bee, – direct, – straight- line -to, – for, – with; in a line with; full tilt at, as the crow flies.

before –, near –, close to –, against- the wind; windward, in the wind's eye.

THROUGH, *viâ* [*L.*], by way of; in all -directions, – manner of ways; *quaquaversum* [*L.*], from the four winds.

[MOTION SIDEWAYS, OBLIQUE MOTION] sidling &c. *v.*; gybe *or* jibe, tack, yaw [*all naut.*]; passage, right passage, left passage [*manège*]; echelon [*mil.*]; knight's move at chess.

V. DEVIATE, alter one's course, depart from, turn, trend; bend, curve &c. 245; swerve, heel, bear off; gybe *or* jibe, break, yaw, wear, sheer, tack [*all naut.*].

DEFLECT; intervert [*obs.*]; divert, divert from its course; put on a new scent; shift, shunt [*Brit.*], switch [*U. S.*], draw aside, crook, warp.

STRAY, straggle; sidle, edge; diverge &c. 291; tralineate [*obs.*], digress, wander; wind, twist, meander; veer, divagate; go astray, go adrift; lose one's way; ramble, rove, drift.

SIDETRACK; turn aside, turn a corner, turn away from; wheel, steer clear of; dodge; step aside, ease off, make way for, shy, jib.

GLANCE OFF, fly off at a tangent; wheel about, face about; turn –, face-to the right-about; echelon [*mil.*]; waddle &c. (*oscillate*) 314; go out of one's way &c. (*perform a circuit*) 629.

Adj. DEVIATING &c. *v.*; aberrant, errant; excursive, discursive; devious, desultory, loose; rambling; stray, erratic, vagrant, undirected; circuitous, roundabout, crooked, sidelong, indirect, zigzag; crab-like.

Adv. ASTRAY FROM, round about, all manner of ways; circuitously &c. 629.

wide of the mark; to the right about; OBLIQUELY, sideling, sidelong, like the knight's move [*chess*].
. "with Whom is no variableness, neither shadow of turning" [*Bible*].

280. [GOING BEFORE.] **Precession.** — **N.** PRECESSION, leading, heading; precedence &c. 62; priority &c. 116; the lead, *le pas* [*F.*]; van &c. (*front*) 234; precursor &c. 64.

V. PRECEDE, go before, go ahead, go in the van, go in advance; forerun, forego [*archaic*]; usher in, introduce, herald, head, take the lead; lead, lead the way, lead the dance; get –, have- the start; steal a march; get before, get ahead, get in front of; outstrip &c. 303; take precedence &c. (*first in order*) 62.

Adj. LEADING, precedent &c. *v.*; first, foremost.

Adv. IN ADVANCE, before, ahead, in the van; foremost, headmost; in front.

. *seniores priores.*

281. [GOING AFTER.] **Sequence.** — **N.** SEQUENCE; sequel; coming after &c. (*order*) 63, (*time*) 117; following; pursuit &c. 622; run [*cards*].

FOLLOWER, attendant, satellite, pursuer, shadow, dangler, train.

V. FOLLOW; pursue &c. 622; go after, fly after.

ATTEND, beset, dance attendance on, dog; tread in the steps of, tread close upon; be –, go –, follow- in the -wake, – trail, – rear- of; follow as a shadow; hang on the skirts of; tread –, follow- on the heels of; camp on the trail.

LAG, loiter, linger, get behind.

Adj. following &c. *v.*

Adv. BEHIND; in the rear &c. 235, in the train of, in the wake of; after &c. (*order*) 63, (*time*) 117.

282. [MOTION FORWARDS; PROGRESSIVE MOTION.] **Progression.** — N. PROGRESSION, progress, progressiveness; advancing &c. *v.*; advance, advancement; ongoing; flood tide, headway; march &c. 266; rise; improvement &c. 658.

V. ADVANCE; proceed, progress; get on, get along, get over the ground; gain ground; forge ahead; jog on, rub on, wag on [*obs.*], go with the stream; keep –, hold on– one's course; go –, move –, come –, get –, pass –, push –, press– -on, – forward, – forwards, – ahead; press onward *or* onwards, step forward; make –, work –, carve –, push –, force –, edge –, elbow– one's way; make -progress, – head, – way, – headway, – advances, – strides, – rapid strides &c. (*velocity*) 274; go ahead, shoot ahead; drive -on, – ahead; go full steam ahead; distance; make up leeway.

Adj. ADVANCING &c. *v.*; ongoing; progressive, profluent; advanced.

Adv. FORWARD, onward; forth, on, ahead, under way, *en route* for, on -one's way, – the way, – the road, – the high road- to; in progress, in mid-progress; *in transitu* [*L.*] &c. 270.

₊ *vestigia nulla retrorsum;* "westward the course of empire takes its way" [Berkeley].

283. [MOTION BACKWARDS.] **Regression.** — N. REGRESSION, regress, retrocession, retrogression, retrogradation, retroaction; *reculade* [*F.*], retreat, withdrawal, retirement, remigration; recession &c. (*motion from*) 287; recess [*obs.*]; crab-like motion.

REFLUX, refluence, backwater, regurgitation, ebb, return; resilience, resiliency; reflexion (*recoil*) 277; *volte-face* [*F.*].

COUNTERMOTION, countermovement, countermarch; veering, tergiversation, recidivation [*obs. exc. in criminology*], backsliding, fall; deterioration &c. 659; recidivism *or* recidivity, relapse.

turning point &c. (*reversion*) 145; climax.

V. RECEDE, regrade, return, revert, retreat, remigrate, retire; retrograde, retrocede; back, back out [*colloq.*], back down [*colloq.*], balk; crawfish [*slang, U. S.*], crawl [*slang*]; withdraw; rebound &c. 277; go –, come –, turn –, hark –, draw –, fall –, break –, get –, put –, run- back; lose ground; fall astern, drop astern; backwater, put about [*naut.*], take the back track; veer, veer round; double, wheel, countermarch; ebb, regurgitate; jib, shrink, shy.

turn tail, turn round, turn upon one's heel, turn one's back upon; retrace one's steps, dance the back step; sound –, beat- a retreat; go home.

Adj. RECEDING &c. *v.*; retrograde, retrogressive; regressive, refluent, reflex, recidivous, resilient; crab-like; contraclockwise, counterclockwise; balky; reactionary &c. 277.

Adv. BACK, backwards; reflexively, to the right-about; *à reculons* [*F.*], *à rebours* [*F.*].

₊ *revenons à nos moutons,* as you were.

284. [MOTION GIVEN TO AN OBJECT SITUATED IN FRONT.] **Propulsion.** — N. PROPULSION, projection; propelment; *vis a tergo* [*L.*], push &c. (*impulse*) 276; jaculation, ejaculation; ejection &c. 297; throw, fling, toss, shot, discharge, shy.

[SCIENCE OF PROPULSION] gunnery, ballistics, archery.

PROPELLER, screw, twin-screws, turbine.

MISSILE, projectile, ball, shot; spear, arrow; gun &c. (*arms*) 727; discus, quoit; brickbat.

285. [MOTION GIVEN TO AN OBJECT SITUATED BEHIND.] **Traction.** — N. TRACTION; drawing &c. *v.*; draft *or* draught, pull, haul; rake; "a long pull, a strong pull, and a pull all together"; towage, haulage.

V. DRAW, pull, haul, lug, rake, snake [*slang, U. S.*], trawl, draggle, drag, tug, tow, trail, train; take in tow.

WRENCH, jerk, twitch; yank [*U. S.*].

Adj. DRAWING &c. *v.*; tractile, tractive, tractional, ductile.

SHOOTER, shot; archer, toxophilite; bowman, rifleman, marksman, gun [*cant*], gunner, good shot, dead shot, crack shot; sharpshooter &c. (*combatant*) 726.

V. PROPEL, project, throw, fling, cast, pitch, chuck, toss, jerk, heave, shy, hurl; flirt, fillip.

dart, lance, tilt; ejaculate, jaculate [*rare*], fulminate, bolt, drive, sling, pitchfork.

send; send off, let off, fire off; discharge, shoot; launch, send forth, let fly; dash.

start; put -, set- in motion; set agoing, give a start to, give an impulse to; bundle, bundle off; impel &c. 276; trundle &c. (*set in rotation*) 312; expel &c. 297.

carry one off one's legs; put to flight.

Adj. propelled &c. *v.*; propelling &c. *v.*; propulsive, projectile, ballistic.

*** "When Ajax strives some rock's vast weight to throw" [Pope].

286. [Motion towards.] **Approach.** — **N.** approach, approximation, approximateness, appropinquation; access; appulse, appulsion; afflux, affluxion; advent &c. (*approach of time*) 121; pursuit &c. 622.

V. approach, approximate [*archaic*], appropinquate [*rare*]; near; get -, go -, draw- near; come, - near, - to close quarters; move towards, set in towards; drift; make up to [*dial. or slang*]; gain upon; pursue &c. 622; tread on the heels of; bear up; make land; hug the shore, hug the land.

Adj. approaching &c. *v.*; approximate, approximative; affluent; converging, connivent, convergent; impending, imminent &c. (*destined*) 152.

Adv. on the road.

Int. approach! come hither! here! come! come near! forward!

287. [Motion from.] **Recession.** — **N.** recession, retirement, withdrawal; retreat; regression, regress, retrogradation, retrocession &c. 283; departure, &c. 293; recoil &c. 277; flight &c. (*avoidance*) 623.

switch, by-pass, shunt [*Brit.*].

V. recede, go, move back, move from, retire, withdraw, retrograde, retrogress, regress, ebb; shrink; come -, move -, go -, get -, drift- away; depart &c. 293; retreat &c. 283; move off, stand off, sheer off, swerve from; fall back, stand aside; run away &c. (*avoid*) 623.

switch, shunt [*Brit.*], sidetrack, turn, remove.

Adj. receding &c. *v.*; recessive, retrogressive, regressive.

*** "remember Lot's wife" [*Bible*].

288. [Motion towards, actively.] **Attraction.** — **N.** attraction, attractiveness; attractivity; pull, drawing to, pulling towards, attrahent, adduction, magnetism, gravity, attraction of gravitation.

loadstone *or* lodestone, lodestar *or* loadstar, polestar, lode [*archaic*]; magnet, magnetite, siderite.

lure, bait, charm, decoy.

V. attract; adduct; draw -, pull -, drag- towards; pull, draw, magnetize, bait, trap, decoy, charm; adduce.

Adj. attracting &c. *v.*; attrahent, attractive, adducent, adductive.

*** *ubi mel ibi apes* [Plautus]; "the cynosure of neighboring eyes" [Milton]; "and Beauty draws us by a single hair" [Pope].

289. [Motion from, actively.] **Repulsion.** — **N.** repulsion; driving from &c. *v.*; repulse, abduction, retrusion [*rare*].

V. repel; push from, drive from &c. 276; chase, dispel; retrude [*rare*]; abduce [*obs.*], abduct; send away; repulse; repercuss.

keep at arm's length, turn one's back upon, give the cold shoulder; send -off, - away- with a flea in one's ear [*colloq.*]; send about one's business; send packing.

Adj. repellent, repulsive; repelling &c. *v.*; abducent, abductive, repercussive.

290. [Motion nearer to.] **Convergence.** — **N.** convergence *or* convergency, confluence, concourse, conflux, congress, concurrence, concentration; appulse, meeting; corradiation [*rare*].

assemblage &c. 72; resort &c. (*focus*) 74; asymptote.

291. [Motion further off.] **Divergence.** — **N.** divergence *or* divergency, divarication, ramification, forking; radiation; separation &c. (*disjunction*) 44; dispersion &c. 73; deviation &c. 279; aberration, declination.

V. diverge, divaricate, radiate; ram-

V. CONVERGE, concur; come together, unite, meet, fall in with; close with, close in upon; center *or* centre, center round, center in; enter in; pour in.

CONCENTRATE, bring into a focus; gather together, unite.

Adj. CONVERGING &c. *v.*; convergent, confluent, concurrent; centripetal; asymptotic *or* asymptotical; confluxible [*rare*].

ify; branch off, glance off, file off; fly off, fly off at a tangent; spread. scatter, disperse &c. 73; deviate &c. 279; part &c. (*separate*) 44.

Adj. DIVERGING &c. *v.*; divergent, divaricate, radiant, radial, centrifugal; aberrant; broadcast.

Adv. broadcast; *passim* [*L.*].

---

292. [TERMINAL MOTION AT.] **Arrival.** — **N.** ARRIVAL, advent; landing; debarkation, disembarkation.

RECEPTION, welcome; *vin d'honneur* [*F.*].

DESTINATION, bourn *or* bourne, goal; landing -place,- stage; bunder *or* bandar [*Pers. & India*]; resting place; harbor, haven, port; terminus, terminal; halting -place, - ground; home, journey's end; anchorage &c. (*refuge*) 666; completion &c. 729.

RETURN, recursion [*obs.*], remigration, reëntry.

MEETING, joining, rencounter, encounter, rejoining.

V. ARRIVE; get to, come to; come; reach, attain; come up, - with, - to; overtake; make, fetch; come from, hail from; complete &c. 729; join, rejoin.

visit, pitch one's tent; sit down &c. (*be located*) 184; get to one's journey's end; be in at the death; come -, get- -back, - home; return; come in &c. (*ingress*) 294; make one's appearance &c. (*appear*) 446; drop in; detrain; outspan, offsaddle [*both S. Africa*].

LIGHT, alight, dismount.

LAND, make land, cast anchor, put in, put into; go ashore, debark, disbark [*rare*], disembark

MEET; encounter, rencounter [*rare*], come in contact; come to hand; come at, come across; hit; come -, light -, pop [*colloq.*] -, bounce [*colloq.*] -, plump [*colloq.*] -, burst -, pitch- upon.

Adj. ARRIVING &c. *v.*; homeward bound, terminal.

Adv. HERE, hither.

Int. WELCOME! hail! all hail! good-day! good-morrow! come in and rest your bonnet on a chair! [*Southern U. S.*], *bienvenu!* [*F.*].

⁎⁎⁎ "Journeys end in lovers meeting, Every wise man's son doth know" [*Twelfth Night*].

293. [INITIAL MOTION FROM.] **Departure.** — **N.** DEPARTURE, decession [*rare*], decampment; embarkation; outset, start, headway, inspan [*S. Africa*], debouchment, debouch *or débouché* [*F.*]; removal; exit &c. (*egress*) 295; *congé* [*F.*], exodus, hegira, flight.

LEAVE-TAKING, valediction, adieu, farewell, good-by *or* good-bye, Godspeed, stirrup cup; valedictorian.

STARTING POINT, starting post; point -, place- of -departure, - embarkation; port of embarkation.

V. DEPART; go, go away, part [*archaic*], take one's departure, set out; set -, march -, put -, start -, be -, move -, get -, whip -, pack -, go -, take oneself-off; start, boun [*archaic*], issue, march out, debouch; go forth, sally forth; sally, set forward; be gone.

leave a place, quit, vacate, evacuate, abandon; go off the stage, make one's exit; retire, withdraw, remove; "use your legs" [*Merchant of Venice*]; vamose *or* vamoose [*slang, U. S.*], mizzle [*slang*], skip [*slang*], cut [*colloq. or slang*], go one's way, go along, go from home; take flight, take wing; spring, fly, flit, wing one's flight; fly away, whip away; strike tents, decamp; break camp, break away, break ground [*naut.*] walk one's chalks [*slang*], cut one's stick *or* cut stick [*slang*], cut and run [*colloq.*]; take leave; say -, bid- good-by &c. *n.*; disappear &c. 449; abscond &c. (*avoid*) 623; entrain; saddle, bridle, harness up, hitch up [*colloq.*], inspan [*S. Africa*]; "speed the parting guest" [*Pope*].

EMBARK; go on board, go aboard; set sail; put to sea, go to sea; sail, take ship; hoist the blue Peter; get under way, weigh anchor.

Adj. DEPARTING &c. *v.*; valedictory; outward bound.

Adv. HENCE, whence, thence; with a foot in the stirrup; on the wing, on the move.

Int. BEGONE! &c. (*ejection*) 297; cut! cut away! cut off! [*all colloq.*], away! to horse! boot! saddle! all aboard! busk and boun ye! [*archaic*].

FAREWELL! adieu! good-by *or* goodbye! good-day! *au revoir!* [*F.*], *vale!* [*L.*], fare you well! God bless you! Godspeed! *auf Wiedersehen!* [*G.*], *au plaisir de vous revoir!* [*F.*], *bon voyage!* [*F.*], *glückliche Reise!* [*G.*], *vive valeque!* [*L.*], bye-bye! [*colloq.*], be good! [*slang*], so long! [*slang*], come again!

₊ "See the shaking funnels roar, With the Peter at the fore" [Kipling]; "Boot! saddle! to horse and away!" [Browning].

294. [MOTION INTO.] **Ingress. — N.** INGRESS; entrance, entry; introgression, ingressiveness, influx, intrusion, inroad, incursion, invasion, irruption; ingression; penetration, interpenetration; illapse [*rare*], infiltration; insinuation &c. (*interjacence*) 228; insertion &c. 300.

IMMIGRATION, incoming, foreign influx; admission &c. (*reception*) 296.

IMPORT, importation; imports.

IMMIGRANT, visitor, incomer, newcomer, comeling [*archaic*], colonist, Buttinsky [*humorous*].

INLET; way in; mouth, door, &c. (*opening*) 260; barway; path &c. (*way*) 627; conduit &c. 350.

V. ENTER; go –, come –, pour –, flow –, creep –, slip –, pop –, break –, burst- -into, – in; have the entrée; set foot on; ingress [*obs.*]; burst –, break- in upon; invade, insinuate itself; interpenetrate, penetrate; infiltrate; find one's way –, wriggle –, worm oneself- into; intrude, butt in [*slang*] horn in [*slang, U. S.*].

give entrance to &c. (*receive*) 296, insert &c. 300.

Adj. INCOMING, inbound, ingressive, inward, entrant [*rare*]; entering &c. *v.*

295. [MOTION OUT OF.] **Egress. — N.** EGRESS, exit, issue; emersion, emergence; outbreak, outburst, proruption [*rare*], eruption; emanation; egression; evacuation, disemboguement, exudation, transudation; extravasation, perspiration, sweating, leakage, percolation, lixiviation, leaching, distillation, seep, oozing; gush &c. (*water in motion*) 348; outpour, outpouring; effluence, effusion; efflux, effluxion; drain; dribbling &c. *v.*; defluxion; drainage; outcome, output; outflow, discharge &c. (*excretion*) 299.

EXPORT, exportation; exports, shipments.

EMIGRATION, exodus &c. (*departure*) 293; expatriation, remigration.

EMIGRANT, migrant, redemptioner [*U. S.*], colonist, *émigré* [*F.*].

OUTLET, vent, spout, tap, sluice, floodgate; vomitory, outgate, sallyport; debouch [*mil.*], *débouché* [*F.*]; way out; mouth, door &c. (*opening*) 260; path &c. (*way*) 627; conduit &c. 350; airpipe &c. 351; pore, emunctory.

V. EMERGE, emanate, issue; egress; go –, come –, move –, pass –, pour –, flowout of; pass off, evacuate.

EXUDE, transude; leak; run, – out, – through; lixiviate, leach, percolate, transcolate [*obs.*]; egurgitate [*rare*]; strain, distill; perspire, sweat, drain, seep, ooze; filter, infiltrate, filtrate; dribble, gush, spout, flow out; well, – out; pour, trickle, &c. (*water in motion*) 348; effuse, extravasate, disembogue, discharge itself, debouch; come –, break forth; burst -out, – through; find vent; escape &c. 671.

Adj. EMERGENT, emerging, erumpent, eruptive, emanant, emanational, emanative, exudative, porous, pervious, leaky, sweaty, transudatory; effused &c. *v.*; outgoing, outbound, outward-bound.

PERCOLATIVE, oozing, gushing, transuding &c. *v.*; effluent, emunctory, effusive, excretory.

₊ "Like a child from the womb, like a ghost from the tomb, I arise" [Shelley].

296. [MOTION INTO, ACTIVELY.] **Reception. — N.** RECEPTION; admission, admittance, entrée, importation; initiation, introduction, intromission; immission, ingestion, imbibition, introception,

297. [MOTION OUT OF, ACTIVELY.] **Ejection. — N.** EJECTION, emission, effusion, rejection, expulsion, eviction, extrusion, detrusion, trajection; discharge.

EGESTION, evacuation, vomition;

absorption, resorbence, engorgement, ingurgitation, inhalation; suction, sucking; eating, drinking &c. (*food*) 298; insertion &c. 300; interjection &c. 228; introit.

V. GIVE ENTRANCE TO, give admittance to, give the entrée; introduce, usher, admit, initiate, intromit [*rare*], receive, import, bring in, immit [*rare*], open the door to, throw open, ingest, absorb, imbibe, instill, implant, infiltrate, induct, inhale; let in, take in, suck in; readmit, resorb, reabsorb; snuff up.

SWALLOW, ingurgitate; engulf, engorge; gulp; eat, drink &c. (*food*) 298.

Adj. INTRODUCTORY, introductive, initiatory, initiary [*rare*], preliminary, ingestive; imbibitory, introceptive, intromittent, intromissive; admissible; absorbent, resorbent; admitting &c. *v.*, admitted &c. *v.*

emesis, eruption, eruptiveness, eruptivity, voidance, disgorgement; ructation, eructation; bloodletting, venesection, phlebotomy, extravasation, paracentesis; expuition [*rare*], exspuition [*rare*]; tapping, drainage; emetic; vomiting; excretion &c. 299; clearance, clearage.

DISLODGMENT; deportation; banishment &c. (*punishment*) 972; rogue's march; relegation; extradition.

EJECTOR, bouncer [*slang, U. S.*], chucker-out [*slang*].

V. EJECT, reject; expel, discard; cut [*colloq.*], ostracize, send to Coventry, boycott; *chasser* [*F.*], banish &c. (*punish*) 972; bounce [*slang, U. S.*]; fire [*slang*], – out [*slang*]; throw &c. (284) -out, – up, – off, – away, – aside; push &c. (276) -out, – off, – away, – aside; shovel –, sweep- -out, – away; brush –, whisk –, turn –, send- -off, – away; discharge;

send –, turn –, cast- adrift; turn out, sack to [*slang*]; send packing, send about one's business, send to the right-about; strike off the roll &c. (*abrogate*) 756; turn out -neck and heels [*colloq.*], – head and shoulders, – neck and crop [*colloq.*]; pack off; send away with a flea in the ear [*colloq.*]; send to Jericho [*colloq.*]; bow out, show the door to. bundle out; throw overboard; give the

EVICT, oust, dislodge; turn out of -doors, – house and home; unhouse, unkennel; unpeople, dispeople; depopulate; relegate, deport.

LET OUT, give out, pour out, send out; dispatch *or* despatch, exhale, excern [*obs.*], excrete; embogue [*obs.*], disembogue; extravasate, shed, void, egest, evacuate; emit; open the -sluices, – floodgates; turn on the tap; give exit to, give vent to; extrude, detrude; effuse, spend, expend; pour forth; squirt, spurt *or* spirt, spill, slop; perspire &c. (*exude*) 295; breathe, blow &c. (*wind*) 349.

TAP, draw off; bale out, lade out; let blood, broach.

EMPTY; drain, - to the dregs; sweep off; clear, – off, – out, – away; suck, draw off; clean out, make a clean sweep of, clear decks, purge.

DISEMBOWEL, embowel [*rare*], disbowel [*rare*], eviscerate, gut.

ROOT OUT, root up, unearth; eradicate, averruncate [*obs.*]; weed out, get out; eliminate, get rid of, do away with, shake off; exenterate [*rare*].

VOMIT, spew, puke [*obs. or vulgar*], keck, retch; cast up, bring up; disgorge.

SALIVATE, ptyalize, expectorate, clear the throat, hawk, spit, sputter, splutter, slobber, drivel, slaver, slabber, drool.

BELCH, eruct, eructate.

UNPACK, unlade, unload, unship; break bulk; dump [*chiefly U. S.*].

EMERGE, ooze &c. 295; be let out.

Adj. EJECTIVE, emissive, extrusive; egestive; salivant; vomitive, vomitory; emitting, emitted &c. *v.*

Int. BEGONE! get you gone! get –, go- -away, – along, – along with you! go your way! away, – with! off with you! go! go about your business! be off! avaunt! aroint *or* aroynt! [*archaic*], allez-vous-en! [*F.*], jao! [*Hind.*], va-t'en! [*F.*], scoot! [*colloq.*], shoo! "get thee behind me, Satan!" [*Bible*].

112

298. [EATING.] **Food. — N.** EATING &c. *v.*; deglutition, gulp, epulation [*rare*], mastication, manducation [*rare*], rumination; gastronomy, gastrology, pantophagy, hippophagy, carnivorism, carnivorousness, herbivority [*rare*], vegetarianism, ichthyophagy; gluttony &c. 957.

carnivore; herbivore, vegetarian.

MOUTH, jaws, gob [*slang*], mandible, mazard, chaps, chops.

DRINKING &c. *v.*; potation, draft *or* draught, libation; compotation, symposium; carousal &c. (*amusement*) 840; drunkenness &c. 959.

FOOD, pabulum; aliment, nourishment, nutriment; sustenance, sustentation; nurture, subsistence, provender, corn, feed, fodder, provision, ration, keep, commons, board; commissariat &c. (*provisions*) 637; prey, forage, pasture, pasturage; fare, cheer; diet, dietary; regimen; belly timber [*facetious, dial.*], staff of life; bread, – and cheese; liquid diet, spoon victuals.

EATABLES, comestibles, victuals, edibles, ingesta; grub [*slang*], prog, [*slang*], meat; bread, breadstuffs; cereals, viands, cates [*obs.*], delicacy, dainty, creature comforts, creature, contents of the larder, fleshpots; festal board; ambrosia; good cheer, good living.

[BREADSTUFFS AND DESSERTS] biscuit, cracker [*chiefly U. S.*], bun, cooky *or* cookie [*U. S.*], doughnut, cruller, hard-tack, pilot bread, sea biscuit, pilot biscuit, ship biscuit, hoecake [*U. S.*], ashcake, corncake, corndodgers [*U. S.*], corndabs [*U. S.*], shortbread, scone, rusk, matzo [*Jewish*], chupatty [*India*], damper [*Australia*], flapjack [*U. S. or dial.*], waffle, pancake, griddlecake, pastry, *pâtisserie* [F.], pie, *pâté* [F.], pasty, patty, turnover, *vol-au-vent* [F.], apple dumpling, apple slump, apple dowdy [*U. S.*], pandowdy [*U. S.*], mince pie, pudding, supawn [*U. S.*], apple pie, blueberry pie, custard pie, lemon pie, pumpkin pie, squash pie, charlotte russe, plum pudding, tart, compote, apple fritters, *beignets de pommes* [F.], banana fritters, macaroon, meringue, marchpane *or* marzipan, *massepain* [F.], whipped cream, *crème fouettée* [F.], cake, *gâteau* [F.], stewed prunes, *pruneaux* [F.], stewed apples, *compote de pommes* [F.], blancmange, cornstarch [*U. S.*], jam, *confiture* [F.], Bar-le-Duc, red currant jelly, *gelée de groseilles* [F.], ice cream, *crème glacée* [F.], college ice, sundae [*U. S.*]; vanilla –, strawberry –, chocolate –, coffee –, Neapolitan –, country club-ice cream; banana royal, water ice, sherbet [*U. S.*]; sweets &c. 396; see FRUIT.

[CEREALS] hominy [*U. S.*], oatmeal, mush, hasty pudding, porridge, gruel, crowdie *or* crowdy [*Scot. & dial. Eng.*], atole [*Mex. Sp.*], samp [*U. S.*], hulled corn, frumenty.

[SOUPS] *potage* [F.], pottage, broth, *bouillon* [F.], gravy soup, *consommé* [F.], thick soup, *purée* [F.], bisque, mulligatawny, turtle soup, mock-turtle soup, oyster stew, oyster chowder, clam chowder, fish chowder, *julienne* [F.], *potage à la julienne* [F.], vermicelli soup, *potage au vermicelle* [F.], chowder, spoon-meat, trepang, ox-tail soup, gumbo, okra soup, stock, *bouillabaisse* [F.].

[FISH] *poisson* [F.], salmon, *saumon* [F.], sole, fried sole, *sole frite* [F.], shad, plaice, bluefish, whiting, *merlan* [F.], trout, *truite* [F.], mackerel, *maquereau* [F.], herring, *hareng* [F.], bloater, kipper, kippered herring, cod, *morue* [F.], sturgeon ("Albany beef"), sardines, haddock, *aiglefin* [F.], finnan haddie *or* haddock, scrod [*U. S.*], sturgeon roe, caviar *or* caviare, shad roe, tarpon, tuna, lobster, *homard* [F.], lobster à la King, lobster Newburg, periwinkles, prawns, shrimps, *crevettes* [F.], oysters, *huitres* [F.], oyster stew, blue points, sea slug, *bêche de mer* [F.], clams, eel, *anguille* [F.], crab, crab meat, soft-shell crab, crawfish *or* crayfish, *écrevisse* [F.].

[MEATS] *rôti* [F.], joint, *pièce de résistance* [F.], *relevé* [F.], hash, *réchauffé* [F.], stew, ragout, fricassee, mince, chow mein, chop suey [*U. S.*], salmis, fatling, barbecue, kickshaws, mincemeat, forcemeat, meat balls, croquettes, goulash *or* Hungarian goulash; condiment &c. 393; haggis [*Scot.*], bubble and squeak, pilau *or* pilaw [*India*], curry, aspic jelly; turtle, terrapin, diamond-back terrapin.

BEEF, *bœuf* [F.], porterhouse steak, boiled beef, bouilli, beef à la mode, beefsteak, roast beef, *rosbif* [F.], *bifteck* [F.], sirloin, rump, chuck.

VEAL, *veau* [F.], fricandeau, calf's head, *tête de veau* [F.], tongue, *langue* [F.], fried brains, *cervelle frite* [F.], sweetbread, *ris de veau* [F.], calf's liver, *foie de veau* [F.].

MUTTON, *mouton* [F.], mutton chop, *côtelette de mouton* [F.], plain chop, *côtelette au naturel* [F.], *côtelette à la maître d'hôtel* [F.], *côtelette à la jardinière* [F.]; broiled kidneys, *rognons à la brochette* [F.], lamb, *agneau* [F.], saddle, *selle* [F.].

PORK, *porc* [F.], pork chop, *côtelette de porc frais* [F.], sausage, *saucisson* [F.], Frankforter, hot dog [*slang, U. S.*], bacon, ham, *jambon* [F.], sucking pig, *cochon de lait* [F.], pig's knuckles, pig's feet, trotters, *pieds de cochon* [F.], crackling.

POULTRY, *volaille* [F.], capon, *chapon* [F.], poularde [F.], pigeon, fowl, broiler, chicken, *poulet* [F.], duck, *canard* [F.], muscovy duck, roast duck, *canard rôti* [F.], goose, *oie* [F.], turkey, *dinde* (*masc.* dindon) [F.], wing, *aile* [F.], leg, *cuisse* [F.], breast, *filet (of a goose)* [F.], *blanc (of a fowl)* [F.], drumstick.

GAME, venison, *chevreuil* [F.], hare, *lièvre* [F.], jugged hare, civet [F.], rabbit, *lapin* [F.], pheasant, *faisan* [F.], partridge, *perdrix* [F.], snipe, *bécasse* [F.], quail, *caille* [F.[, wild duck, *canard sauvage* [F.], canvasback, teal, *sarcelle* [F.], grouse, ricebird [*Southern U. S.*], pigeon, squab.

[EGGS] *œufs* [F.], boiled eggs, *œufs à la coque* [F.], fried eggs, *œufs sur le plat* [F.], poached eggs, *œufs pochés* [F.], scrambled eggs, *œufs brouillés* [F.], new-laid eggs, *œufs frais* [F.], buttered eggs, dropped eggs, shirred eggs, stuffed eggs, omelet, *omelette* [F.], soufflé or *soufflée* [F.].

[CHEESE DISHES] cheese, *fromage* [F.], cheesecake, *talmouse* [F.], cheese-mold, *moule à fromage* [F.], Welsh rabbit *or* Welsh rarebit [*an erroneous form*], *rôtie au fromage* [F.], golden buck, cheese straws, cheese fondue; cream –, cottage –, Neuchatel –, Swiss (*Schweizerkäse or Schweitzerkäse or Schweitzer*) –, Gruyère –, Emmenthaler –, Dutch –, Edam –, Roquefort –, Brie –, Limburg *or* Limburger –, Wensleydale- cheese.

[VEGETABLES] *légumes* [F.], greens, asparagus, *asperge* [F.], green peas, *petits pois* [F.], artichoke, *artichaut* [F.], cabbage, *chou* [F.], coleslaw, Brussels sprouts, *choux de Bruxelles* [F.], cauliflower, *chou-fleur* (*pl. choux-fleurs*) [F.], lettuce, *laitue* [F.], romaine, cos lettuce, *laitue romaine* [F.], lima beans, string beans, French beans, *haricots verts* [F.], kidney beans, *haricots blancs* [F.], baked beans, potatoes, *pommes de terre* [F.], yams, sweet potatoes, *patates* [F.], spinach, *épinards* [F.], endive, *chicorée* [F.], pumpkin, squash, sauerkraut, *choucroute* [F.], eggplant, oyster plant, salsify, *salsifis* [F.], tomato, *tomate* [F.], celery, *céleri* [F.], cress, *cresson* [F.], water cress, *cresson de fontaine* [F.], beets, beetroot [*Brit.*], *betterave* [F.], parsnips, *panais* [F.], turnip, *navet* [F.], radish, *radis or rave* [F.], horse radish, *raifort* [F.], onion, *oignon* [F.], scallion, shalot, *échalote* [F.], cucumber, *concombre* [F.], mushrooms, *champignons* [F.], rhubarb, truffles, succotash [*U. S.*].

[FRUIT] figs, *figues* [F.], raisins, nuts, *noisettes* [F.], almonds: *les quatres mendiants* [F.]; apple, *pomme* [F.], pear, *poire* [F.], alligator pear, avocado, apricot, *abricot* [F.], peach, *pêche* [F.], plantain, banana, breadfruit, grapefruit, mango, mangosteen, grapes, pineapple, *ananas* [F.], walnuts, *noix* [F.], orange, lemon, lime, cherries, *cerises* [F.], watermelon, currants, cranberry, loganberry, blueberry, blackberry, gooseberry, whortleberry, huckleberry, raspberry, strawberry.

TABLE, *cuisine*, bill of fare, menu, *table d'hôte* [F.], ordinary, *à la carte* [F.], cover, *couvert* [F.]; American plan, European plan.

MEAL, repast, feed [*archaic or colloq.*], spread [*colloq.*]; mess; dish, plate, course; side dish, *hors-d'œuvre* [F.], entrée, *entremets* [F.], remove, dessert [*in U. S., often includes pastry or pudding*]; regale; regalement, refreshment, entertainment; refection, collation, picnic, feast, banquet, junket; breakfast; lunch, luncheon; *déjeuner* [F.], *déjeuner à la fourchette* [F.]; bever [*dial.*], tiffin, dinner, supper, snack [*colloq.*], whet, bait [*dial.*]; potluck; hearty –, square –, substantial –, full- meal; blowout [*slang*]; light refreshment; *chota hazri, bara hazri, bara khana* [*all Hind.*].

MOUTHFUL, bolus, gobbet [*archaic*], tidbit, kickshaw, morsel, sop, sippet.

DRINK, beverage, liquor, broth, soup; potion, dram, draft *or* draught, drench, swill [*slang*]; nip, sip, sup, gulp.

[BEVERAGES] wine, spirits, liqueur, beer, ale, malt liquor, (Sir) John Barleycorn, stingo [*old slang*], heavy wet [*slang, Eng.*]; grog, toddy, flip, purl, punch, negus, cup, bishop, wassail; hooch [*slang, U. S.*], whisky *or* whiskey, the creature [*humorous*]; gin &c. (*intoxicating liquor*) 959; coffee, chocolate, cocoa, tea, "the cup that cheers but not inebriates"; bock –, lager –, Pilsener –, schenk –, near- beer; Brazil tea, cider, claret, ice water, maté, mint julep [*U. S.*].

RESTAURANT, eating house &c. 189.

V. EAT, feed, fare, devour, swallow, take; gulp, bolt, snap; fall to; dispatch *or* despatch, discuss [*colloq.*]; take –, get –, gulp- down; lay in, lick, pick, peck; tuck in [*slang*], gormandize &c. 957; bite, champ, munch, craunch *or* cranch, crunch, chew, masticate, nibble, gnaw, mumble.

live on; feed –, batten –, fatten –, feast- upon; browse, graze, crop, regale; carouse &c. (*make merry*) 840; lick one's chops [*colloq.*], make one's mouth water; eat heartily, do justice to, play a good knife and fork [*dial. Eng.*], banquet.

break bread, break one's fast; breakfast, lunch, dine, take tea, sup.

DRINK, – in, – up, – one's fill; quaff, sip, sup; suck, – up; lap; swig [*dial. or colloq.*], swill [*slang*], tipple &c. (*be drunken*) 959; empty one's glass, drain the cup; toss off, toss one's glass; wash down, crack a bottle [*colloq.*], wet one's whistle [*colloq.*].

CATER, purvey &c. 637.

Adj. EATABLE, edible, esculent, comestible, gustable, alimentary; cereal, cibarious [*rare*]; dietetic; culinary; nutritive, nutritious; gastric; succulent.

underdone, rare, *saignant* [F.]; well-done, *bien cuit* [F.]; overdone; with gravy, *au jus* [F.]; high [*of game*]; ripe [*of cheese*].

DRINKABLE, potable, potulent [obs.]; bibulous.

omnivorous, carnivorous, herbivorous, granivorous, graminivorous, phytivorous, phytophagous, ichthyophagous; omophagic, omophagous; pantophagous, xylophagous.

. "But hark! the chiming clocks to dinner call" [Pope]; "across the walnuts and the wine" [Tennyson]; "blesséd hour of our dinner!" [O. Meredith]; "now good digestion wait on appetite, and health on both!" [Macbeth]; "who can cloy the hungry edge of appetite?" [Richard II]; "sit down and feed and welcome to our table" [As You Like It]; "bachelor's fare: bread and cheese and kisses" [Swift]; "my dinner was noble and enough" [Pepys]; "we have met the enemy and they are ours" [Perry]; "the cry is still 'They come!'" [Macbeth]; "the stag at eve had drunk his fill" [Scott]; "my grief lies onward and my joy behind" [Shakespeare, Sonnets].

299. Excretion. — N. EXCRETION, discharge, emanation, ejection; exhalation, exudation, extrusion, secretion, effusion, extravasation, ecchymosis, evacuation, dejection, feces or fæces, defecation, cacation, excrement; bloody flux; cœliac (or celiac) flux; dysentery; perspiration, sweat; subation [obs.], exudation; diaphoresis; sewage; eccrinology.

hemorrhage, bleeding; outpouring &c. (egress) 295; menses, menstrual discharge, menstrual flow, catamenial discharge; leucorrhea or leucorrhœa, the whites.

EJECTA (pl.), saliva, spittle, sputum (pl. sputa); spit, rheum; ptyalism, salivation, catarrh; diarrhea or diarrhœa; egesta (pl.), excreta; lava; exuviæ &c. (uncleanness) 653

V. EXCRETE &c. (eject) 297; secrete, secern; emanate &c. (come out) 295.

Adj. EXCRETORY, fecal or fæcal, feculent, secretory.

EJECTIVE, eliminative, eliminant.

300. [FORCIBLE INGRESS.] Insertion. — N. INSERTION, infixion, implantation, introduction; embolism, interpolation, intercalation, interlineation, insinuation &c. (intervention) 228; planting &c. v.; injection, inoculation, importation, infusion; forcible ingress &c. 294; immersion; submersion, submergence, dip, plunge; bath &c. (water) 337; interment &c. 363.

ENEMA, clyster, glyster, lavage, lavement.

V. INSERT, introduce, intromit, put into, run into; import; inject; imbed, inlay, inweave; interject &c. 228; infuse, instill or instil, inoculate, impregnate, imbue, imbrue.

insert &c. itself; plunge in medias res [L.].

GRAFT, ingraft, engraft, bud, plant, implant; dovetail.

OBTRUDE; thrust in, stick in, ram in, stuff in, tuck in, press in, drive in, pop in, whip in, drop in, put in: impact; pierce &c. (make a hole) 260.

IMMERSE, immerge, merge; bathe, soak &c. (water) 337; dip, plunge &c. 310.
BURY &c. (inter) 363.
Adj. INSERTED &c. v.

301. [FORCIBLE EGRESS.] Extraction. — N. EXTRACTION; extracting &c. v.; removal, elimination, extrication, eradication, evulsion, extirpation, extermination; ejection &c. 297; export &c. (egress) 295; avulsion, wrench, forcible separation.

EXPRESSION, squeezing; distillation.

EXTRACTOR, corkscrew, forceps, pliers.

V. EXTRACT, draw; take out, draw out, pull out, tear out, pluck out, pick out, get out; wring from, wrench; extort; root –, weed –, grub –, rake- -up, – out; eradicate; pull –, pluck- up by the roots; averruncate [obs.]; unroot; uproot, pull up, extirpate, dredge.

EDUCE, elicit, evolve, bring forth, draw forth; extricate.

ELIMINATE &c. (eject) 297; eviscerate &c. 297; remove.

EXPRESS, squeeze out, press out, distill or distil.

Adj. EXTRACTED &c. v.

302. [Motion through.] **Passage. — N.** passage, transmission; permeation; penetration, interpenetration; transudation, infiltration; exosmosis *or* exosmose; osmosis *or* osmose, endosmosis, endosmose; intercurrence; ingress &c. 294; egress &c. 295; path &c. 627; conduit &c. 350; opening &c. 260; journey &c. 266; voyage &c. 267.

V. pass, pass through; perforate &c. (*hole*) 260; penetrate, permeate, thread, thrid [*archaic or dial.*], enfilade; go through, go across; go over, pass over; cut across; ford, cross; pass and repass, work; make –, thread –, worm –, force- one's way; make –, force- a passage; cut one's way through; find its -way, – vent; transmit, make way, clear the course; traverse, go over the ground.

Adj. passing &c. *v.;* intercurrent; endosmosmic, endosmotic, exosmotic *or* exosmic, osmotic.

Adv. en passant [*F.*] &c. (*transit*) 270.

---

303. [Motion beyond.] **Overrun. — N.** overrun, transcursion [*obs.*], transilience *or* transiliency [*rare*], transgression; trespass; inroad, advancement, intrusion, infraction, encroachment, infringement; extravagation [*obs.*], transcendence; redundance &c. 641.

V. surpass, transgress, pass; go beyond, go by; show in front, come to the front; shoot ahead of; steal a march upon, gain upon.

overstep, overpass, overreach, overgo, override, overleap, overjump, overskip, overlap, overshoot the mark; outstrip, outleap, outjump, outgo, outstep, outrun, outride, outrival, outdo; beat, beat hollow [*colloq.*]; distance; leave in the -lurch, – rear; throw into the shade; exceed, transcend, surmount; soar &c. (*rise*) 305.

encroach, trespass, infringe, intrude, invade, accroach [*rare*], advance upon, trench upon, intrench on; strain; stretch –, strain- a point; pass the Rubicon.

Adj. surpassing &c. *v.*

Adv. ahead, beyond the mark.

---

304. [Motion short of.] **Shortcoming. — N.** shortcoming, failure; falling short &c. *v.;* default, defalcation, delinquency; leeway; labor in vain, no go [*colloq.*]; fizzle [*colloq.*], dud [*slang*], slump [*colloq.*]; flash in the pan.

incompleteness &c. 53; imperfection &c. 651; insufficiency &c. 640; noncompletion &c. 730; failure &c. 732.

V. fall short, – of; come short. – of; stop short, – of; not reach; want; keep within -bounds, –the mark, – compass.

collapse, fail, break down, stick in the mud, flat out [*U. S.*], come to nothing; fall down, slump, fizzle out [*all colloq.*]; fall through, fall to the ground; cave in [*colloq.*], end in smoke, miss the mark; lose ground; miss stays [*naut.*]; miss one's moorings.

Adj. unreached; deficient; short, short of; minus; out of depth; perfunctory &c. (*neglect*) 460.

Adv. within the mark, within compass, within bounds; behindhand; *re infectâ* [*L.*]; to no purpose; far from it.

*** the bubble burst; "Oh, the little more, and how much it is! And the little less, and what worlds away!" [Browning].

---

305. [Motion upwards.] **Ascent. — N.** ascent, ascension; rising &c. *v.;* rise, upgrowth, upward flight, upgrade; leap &c. 309; grade [*U. S.*], gradient [*Eng.*], ramp, acclivity, hill &c. 217.

stairway, staircase, stair [*esp. in Scot.*], stairs; flight of -steps, – stairs; ladder, scaling ladder; Jacob's ladder, companionway, companion, companion ladder [*all naut.*]; escalator, elevator &c. 307.

[Comparisons] rocket, skyrocket, lark, skylark; Alpine Club.

V. ascend, rise, mount, arise, uprise; go up, get up, work one's way up, start

---

306. [Motion downwards.] **Descent. — N.** descent, descension [*rare*], inclination, declension, declination; decurrence [*rare*], downcome, comedown, downcast, setback, fall; falling &c. *v.;* slump [*colloq.*], drop, cadence; subsidence, lapse; downfall, tumble, slip, tilt, trip, lurch; *culbute* [*F.*], titubation, stumble; fate of -Icarus, – Phaëthon, – Lucifer.

avalanche, debacle, *débâcle* [*F.*], landslip [*Eng.*], landslide [*U. S.*], slide, snowslip, snowslide, glissade.

declivity, dip, decline, pitch, drop, down-grade.

up, spring up, shoot up; aspire, aim high.
plane, swim, float.

CLIMB, shin [colloq.], swarm [colloq.],
clamber, ramp [rare], scramble, escalade,
surmount; wind upward; scale, – the
heights.

TOWER, soar, hover, spire, go–, fly-
aloft; surge; leap &c. 309.

Adj. RISING &c. v.; upcast; scandent,
buoyant; supernatant, superfluitant·
excelsior.

Adv. UP, upward or upwards, skyward. heavenward, toward the empyrean; upturned; uphill.

₊ "Hark! hark! the lark at heaven's gate
sings" [Shakespeare]; "they climbed the steep
ascent of heaven" [Heber]; "Higher still and
higher, From the earth thou springest"
[Shelley].

ELEVATOR &c. 307.
STAIRWAY &c. 305.

V. DESCEND; go –, drop –, comedown; fall, gravitate. drop, slip, slide,
settle; decline, set, sink, droop, come
down a peg [colloq.], slump [colloq.].

GET DOWN, dismount, alight, light;
swoop, souse; stoop &c. 308; fall prostrate, precipitate oneself; let fall &c.
308.

TUMBLE, trip, stumble, titubate [rare],
lurch, pitch, swag, topple; topple –,
tumble- -down, – over; tilt, sprawl,
plump, plump down; come –, fall –,
get- a cropper [colloq. or slang].

Adj. STEEP, sloping, declivitous, declivous; beetling &c. (high) 206; bottomless &c. (deep) 208.

DESCENDING &c. v.; down, downcast;
descendent; decurrent, decursive; labent [rare], deciduous; nodding to its
fall.

    Adv. DOWNWARD or downwards, downhill.

₊ "from morn To noon he fell, from noon to dewy eve" [Milton].

---

307. Elevation. — N. ELEVATION;
raising &c. v.; erection, lift; sublevation,
upheaval; sublimation, exaltation;
prominence &c. (convexity) 250.

LEVER &c. 633; crane, derrick, wind-
lass, capstan, winch; dredge, dredger,
dredging machine.

ELEVATOR, ascenseur [F.], lift [chiefly
Eng.], dumb-waiter, escalator.

V. ELEVATE, raise, heighten, lift,
erect; set up, stick up, perch up, perk
up, tilt up; rear, hoist, heave; uplift,
upraise, uprear, upbear, upcast, uphoist, upheave; buoy, weigh, mount,
give a lift; exalt; sublimate; place –,
set- on a pedestal.

take up, drag up, fish up; dredge.

STAND UP, rise up, get up, jump up;
spring to one's feet; hold oneself up,
hold one's head up; draw oneself up to
his full height.

Adj. ELEVATED &c. v.; upturned,
retroussé [F.]; stilted, attollent, rampant.

Adv. on stilts, on the shoulders of, on
one's legs, on one's hind legs [colloq.].

₊ "He raised a mortal to the skies, She
drew an angel down" [Dryden].

308. Depression. — N. DEPRESSION;
lowering &c. v.; dip &c. (concavity) 252;
abasement; detrusion; reduction.

OVERTHROW, overset, overturn; upset; prostration, subversion, precipitation.

BOW; curtsy or curtsey, dip [colloq.],
bob, obedience [archaic], duck, genuflexion, kotow or kowtow [Chinese].
obeisance, salaam or salam.

V. DEPRESS, lower; let –, take- -down,
– down a peg [colloq.]; cast; let drop, let
fall; sink, debase, bring low, abase,
reduce, detrude, pitch, precipitate.

OVERTHROW, overturn, overset; upset,
subvert, prostrate, level, fell; down
[archaic or colloq.], cast down, take
down, throw down, fling down, dash
down, pull down, cut down, knock down,
hew down; raze, raze to the ground;
trample in the dust, pull about one's
ears; come off –, pull off- one's high
horse [slang]; come off –, get off- one's
perch [slang].

SIT, sit down, couch, squat; recline
&c. 213.

CROUCH, stoop, bend, cower.

BOW; curtsy or curtsey, genuflect,
bend –, bow- the -head, – knee; incline,
make obeisance, salaam or salam, prostrate oneself; bow down.

    Adj. DEPRESSED &c. v.; at a low ebb; prostrate &c. (horizontal) 213; detrusive.

₊ facinus quos inquinat æquat [Lucan]; "with looks Downcast and damp" [Milton].

309. Leap. — N. LEAP, jump, hop, spring, bound, vault, pole vault, leaping, saltation [rare].

CAPER; dance, curvet, caracole or caracol; gambade, gambado, gambol, frisk, prance, dido [colloq., U. S.], capriole, demivolt; buck, – jump; hop skip and jump; falcade.

[COMPARISONS] kangaroo, jerboa, chamois, goat, frog, grasshopper, flea; buckjumper; wallaby.

V. LEAP; jump -up, – over the moon; hop, spring, bound, vault, negotiate [cant], clear, ramp, trip, skip.

prance, dance, caper; buck, buckjump; curvet, caracole or caracol; foot it, bob, bounce, flounce, start; frisk &c. (amusement) 840; jump about &c. (agitation) 315; cut capers [colloq.], cut a dido [colloq., U. S.]; trip it on the light fantastic toe, dance oneself off one's legs, dance the soles off one's feet.

310. Plunge. — N. PLUNGE, dip, dive, nose dive [aviation], header [colloq.]; ducking &c. v.

SUBMERGENCE, submersion, immersion, engulfment [rare].

DIVER; diving bird, loon, auk, penguin, grebe, sea duck &c.

V. PLUNGE, dip, souse, duck; dive, plump; take a -plunge, – header [colloq.]; make a plunge, bathe &c. (water) 337; pitch.

SUBMERGE, submerse; immerse; douse or dowse, sink, engulf, send to the bottom; send to -Davy Jones's locker, – feed the fishes.

FOUNDER, welter, wallow; get out of one's depth; go to the bottom, go down like a stone.

Adj. PLUNGING &c. v.; submergible, submersible; soundable.

Adj. LEAPING &c. v.; saltatorial, saltatoric or saltatory; frisky, lively.

Adv. on the light fantastic toe.

⁎ di salto in salto; "From peak to peak, the rattling crags among, Leaps the live thunder" [Byron].

---

311. [CURVILINEAR MOTION.] Circuition. — N. CIRCUITION [archaic], circulation, volutation; turn, curvet; excursion; circumvention, circumnavigation, circumambulation, circumambience or circumambiency, circumflexion, circumfluence [rare], circummigration, circumvolation [rare]; Northwest Passage; wheel, gyre, ambit, compass, lap, circuit &c. 629.

turning &c. v.; wrench; evolution; coil, spiral, corkscrew.

V. TURN, bend, wheel; go about, put about [both naut.]; heel; go –, turn--round, – to the right-about; turn on one's heel.

CIRCLE, encircle, circumscribe; circuit; make –, describe- a -circle, – complete circle; go –, pass- through -180°, – 360°; circumnavigate, circumambulate, circumvent; "put a girdle round about the earth" [M. N. D.]; go the round, make the round of, circumvolate [rare], circumflex.

ROUND; turn –, round- a corner; double a point [naut.]; make a detour &c. (circuit) 629.

WIND, circulate, meander; whisk, twirl; twist &c. (convolution) 248.

WALLOW, welter, roll, volutate.

Adj. CIRCUITOUS; turning &c. v.; circumforaneous, circumfluent, roundabout; devious, deviatory; circumambient, circumflex, circumfluent, circumfluous, circumvolant, circumnavigable.

Adv. round about.

⁎ "throws his steep flight in many an aery wheel" [Milton].

---

312. [MOTION IN A CONTINUED CIRCLE.] Rotation. — N. ROTATION, revolution, gyration, circulation, roll; circumrotation, circumvolution [rare], circumgyration; circumfusion, circina-

313. [MOTION IN A REVERSE CIRCLE.] Evolution. — N. EVOLUTION, unfolding, development; evolvement; unfoldment; eversion &c. (inversion) 218.

V. EVOLVE; unfold, unroll, unwind,

tion [obs.], turbination, pirouette, convolution.

EDDY, vortex, whirlpool, swirl, gurge [rare]; verticity [obs.]; vertiginousness; whir, whirl; countercurrent; cyclone, tornado; surge; vertigo, dizzy round; maelstrom, Charybdis.

Ixion; Wheel of Fortune.

[COMPARISONS] wheel, screw, propeller, turbine, whirligig, rolling stone, windmill; treadmill, top, teetotum; roller; cogwheel, gear, gearwheel, flywheel; jack, smokejack, turnspit; gyroplane, gyroscope, gyrostat, gyrocar; caster.

axis, axle, spindle, pivot, pin, hinge, pole, swivel, gimbals, arbor, bobbin. spool, reel, mandrel.

[SCIENCE OF ROTATORY MOTION] trochilics, gyrostatics.

V. ROTATE; roll, roll along; revolve, spin; turn, turn round; circumvolve [rare], circumgyrate [rare], circumvolute, circumfuse, turbinate [rare], encircle; circulate, gurge [rare], swirl, gyre, gyrate, wheel, whirl, twirl, trundle, troll, bowl, roll up, furl.

box the compass; spin like a -top, – teetotum.

Adj. ROTATING &c. v.; rotatory, rotary; circumrotatory, trochilic, vertiginous, gyral, circumgyratory, circumvolutory, gyratory, gulfy; vorticular, vortical, vorticose; gyrostatic, gyroscopic.

Adv. ROUND AND ROUND, head over heels, like a horse in a mill, in circles, clockwise.

uncoil, untwist, unfurl, untwine, unravel; disentangle· develop.

Adj. EVOLUTIONAL, evolutionary; evolving &c. v.; evolved &c. v.

---

314. [RECIPROCATING MOTION, MOTION TO AND FRO.] **Oscillation. — N.** OSCILLATION; vibration, vibratility, libration; motion of a pendulum; nutation, circumnutation; undulation; pulsation; pulse, beat, throb; seismicity, seismism, seismology.

ALTERNATION; coming and going &c. v.; ebb and flow, flux and reflux, systole and diastole; libration -of the moon, – in latitude; ups and downs; crossruff [in cards].

FLUCTUATION; vacillation &c. (irresolution) 605.

SWING, wave, vibratiuncle [rare], beat, shake, wag, seesaw, teeter [U. S.]; dance, lurch, dodge.

ROCKING STONE, logan (or loggan) stone.

[INSTRUMENTS] vibroscope, vibrograph; seismograph, seismoscope.

V. OSCILLATE; nutate, vibrate, librate; undulate, wave; rock, sway, swing; pulsate, beat; wag, waggle; nod, bob, curtsy or curtsey, tick; play; wamble, wabble; dangle, swag [obs. or dial.].

fluctuate, dance, curvet, reel, quake; quiver, quaver; shake, flicker; wriggle; roll, toss, pitch; flounder, stagger, totter; move -, bob- up and down &c. adv.

ALTERNATE, pass and repass, shuttle, ebb and flow, come and go; vacillate &c. 605.

BRANDISH, shake, flourish; agitate &c. 315.

Adj. OSCILLATING &c. v.; oscillatory, undulatory, pulsatory, libratory; vibratory, vibrative, vibratile; seismic or seismical, seismal, seismographic, seismological; pendulous; shuttlewise.

Adv. TO AND FRO, up and down, backwards and forwards, back and forth, in and out, seesaw, zigzag, wibble-wabble [colloq.], in and out, from side to side, like buckets in a well.

---

315. [IRREGULAR MOTION.] **Agitation. — N.** AGITATION, stir, tremor, shake, ripple, jog, jolt, jar, jerk, shock, succussion, trepidation, quiver, quaver, dance, tarantella, tarantism; vellication, jactation, jactitation, quassation [rare]; shuffling &c. v.; twitter, flicker, flutter.

DISQUIET, perturbation, commotion, turmoil, turbulence; tumult, tumultuation [obs.]; hubbub, rout, bustle, fuss, racket.

TWITCHING, subsultus, floccillation, carphology *or* carphologia; staggers, megrims, epilepsy, fits; chorea, the jerks [*colloq.*], St. Vitus's dance, tilmus.

SPASM, throe, throb, palpitation, pitapatation [*humorous*], convulsion, paroxysm, seizure, grip, cramp.

DISTURBANCE &c. (*disorder*) 59; restlessness &c. (*changeableness*) 149.

FERMENT, fermentation; ebullition, effervescence, hurly-burly, *cahotage* or *cahotement* [*F.*], cahot [*Can.*]; tempest, storm, ground swell, heavy sea, whirlpool, vortex &c. 312; whirlwind &c. (*wind*) 349.

V. BE AGITATED &c.; shake; tremble, – like an aspen leaf; shake like a jelly, quiver, quaver, quake, shiver, twitter, twire [*obs.*], writhe, toss, jactitate [*rare*], shuffle, tumble, stagger, bob, reel, sway; wag, waggle; wriggle, – like an eel; dance, stumble, shamble, flounder, totter, flounce, flop, curvet, prance, cavort [*U. S.*]; squirm; bustle.

toss about, jump about; jump like a parched pea; shake like an aspen leaf; shake to its -center, – foundations; be the sport of the winds and waves; reel to and fro like a drunken man; move –, drive- from post to pillar and from pillar to post; keep between hawk and buzzard.

THROB, pulsate, beat, palpitate, go pitapat.

FLUTTER, flitter [*archaic*], flicker, bicker; twitch, vellicate.

FERMENT, effervesce, foam; boil, boil over; bubble, bubble up; simmer.

AGITATE, shake, convulse, toss, tumble, bandy, wield, brandish, flap, flourish, whisk, jerk, hitch, jolt; jog, joggle; jostle, buffet, hustle, disturb, stir, shake up, churn, jounce, wallop [*dial.*], whip.

Adj. AGITATED, tremulous; subsultory [*obs.*], desultory, successive, saltatorial, saltant, saltatoric *or* saltatory· quassative [*rare*]; shambling; giddy-paced, convulsive, jerky; effervescent, effervescive, vellicative, unquiet, restless, all of a twitter [*colloq.*], all of a flutter; shaking &c. *v.*

Adv. by fits and starts; subsultorily [*obs.*] &c. *adj.; per saltum* [*L.*]; hop, skip, and jump; in convulsions, in fits, in a flutter.

*** *tempête dans un verre d'eau;* "the tempestuous petticoat" [Herrick]; "with many a flirt and flutter" [Poe]; "the waves were not like water: they were like falling city walls" [Chesterton]; "Let the ether go surging 'Neath thunder and scourging Of wild winds unbound" [E. B. Browning].

CLASS III

Words relating to MATTER

Section I. MATTER IN GENERAL

316. Materiality. — N. materiality, materialness; corporeity, corporality; substantiality, substantialness, materialization, material existence, incarnation, flesh and blood, plenum; physical condition.

matter, body, substance, brute matter, protoplasm, plasma, stuff. element, principle, parenchyma, material, substratum, hyle, *corpus* [*L.*], pabulum; frame.

object, article, thing, something; still life; stocks and stones; *matériel* [*F.*]; materials &c. 635.

[Science of matter] physics; somatology, somatics; natural –, experimental- philosophy; physicism; physical science, *philosophie positive* [*F.*], materialism, hylism, hylicism, hylotheism, somatism, substantialism.

materialist; physicist; somatologist, somatist, corporealist [*rare*], hylicist, hylotheist, substantialist.

V. materialize, incorporate, substantiate, substantialize, insubstantiate [*rare*], incorporate, embody, incarnate, corporify [*obs.*].

Adj. material, bodily; corporeal, corporal; physical; somatic, somatoscopic; mundane &c. (*terrestrial*) 318; sensible, tangible, ponderable, palpable, substantial, somatologic *or* somatological; embodied, fleshly.

317. Immateriality. — N. immateriality, immaterialness; incorporeity, dematerialization, insubstantiality, incorporality, decarnation [*obs.*], unsubstantiation, unsubstantiality, spirituality; inextension; astral plane.

personality; I, myself, me.

ego, spirit &c. (*soul*) 450; astral body, etheric double, subliminal self, subconscious self, higher self.

immaterialism; spiritualism, spiritism, animism, Platonism; Platonic -Idea, – Ideal.

immaterialist, spiritualist, spiritist, animist, Platonist.

V. immaterialize, dematerialize, unsubstantialize [*rare*]; disembody, spiritualize.

Adj. immaterial, immateriate, incorporeal, incorporal, incorporate, unsubstantial, insubstantial, immateriate [*obs.*], spiritistic, animistic; unfleshly; supersensible; asomatous, unextended; unembodied, discarnate, bodiless, decarnate *or* decarnated, disembodied; extramundane, unearthly; pneumatoscopic; spiritual &c. (*psychical*) 450; Platonistic.

subjective, personal, nonobjective.

⁂ "there is a natural body, and there is a spiritual body" [*Bib.*]; "the Thee in Me who works behind The Veil" [Omar Khayyám — Fitzgerald].

neuter, unspiritual, materialistic *or* materialistical, hylic, hylotheistic *or* hylotheistical, parenchymatous.

objective, impersonal, nonsubjective.

⁂ "and the Word was made flesh and dwelt among us" [*Bible*]; "this muddy vesture of decay" [*M. of Venice*].

318. World. — N. world, creation, nature, universe; earth, globe, wide world; cosmos *or* kosmos; Midgard; terraqueous globe, sphere; macrocosm, megacosm; music of the spheres.

heavens, sky, welkin [*archaic*], empyrean; starry -cope, – heaven, – host; firmament, caelum [*L.*], hyaline, supersensible regions; *varuna* [*Skr.*]; vault –, canopy- of heaven; celestial spaces.

heavenly bodies, luminaries, stars, asteroids; nebulæ; galaxy, Milky Way, galactic circle, *via lactea* [*L.*].

sun, orb of day, day-star [*poetic*], Helios, Apollo, Phœbus &c. (*sun god*) 423;

photosphere, chromosphere; solar system; planet, planetoid; Venus, Aphrodite Urania, Hyades; comet; satellite; moon, orb of night, Diana, Luna, Phœbe, Cynthia, Selene, "glimpses of the moon" [*Hamlet*], silver-footed queen; aërolite, meteor; falling –, shooting- star; meteorite, uranolite.

constellation, zodiac, signs of the zodiac; Charles's Wain, The Dipper; Great Bear, Ursa Major; Little Bear, Ursa Minor; Southern Cross, Orion's Belt, Cassiopeia's Chair, Pleiades.

colures, equator, ecliptic, orbit.

[Science of heavenly bodies] astronomy; uranography, uranology; uranometry, cosmology, cosmography, cosmogony; eidouranion, orrery; geodesy &c. (*measurement*) 466; star-gazing; observatory; planetarium.

cosmologist, cosmographer, cosmogonist, geodesist, geographer; astronomer. star-gazer.

Adj. cosmic *or* cosmical, mundane; terrestrial, terrestrious [*obs.*], terraqueous, terrene, terreous, [*obs.*]; fluvioterrestrial, geodesic *or* geodesical, geodetic *or* geodetical, cosmogonal, cosmogonic, cosmographic *or* cosmographical; telluric, earthly, under the sun; sublunary, subastral.

solar, heliacal; lunar; empyreal, celestial, heavenly, sphery; starry, stellar, stellary, bespangled, sidereal; sideral, astral; nebular; uranic.

Adv. in all creation, on the face of the globe, here below, under the sun.

** *die Weltgeschichte ist das Weltgericht;* "earth is but the frozen echo of the silent voice of God" [Hageman]; "green calm below, blue quietness above" [Whittier]; "hanging in a golden chain this pendent World" [*Paradise Lost*]; "nothing in nature is unbeautiful" [Tennyson]; "silently as a dream the fabric rose" [Cowper]; "some touch of nature's genial glow" [Scott]; "this majestical roof fretted with golden fire" [*Hamlet*]; "through knowledge we behold the World's creation" [*Spenser*].

---

319. Gravity. — **N.** gravity, gravitation; weight; heft [*U. S. & dial. Eng.*], heaviness &c. *adj.;* specific gravity; ponderation [*rare*], ponderousness, ponderance [*rare*], ponderosity, pressure, load; burden *or* burthen; ballast, counterpoise; mass; lump –, mass –, weight-of.

[Comparisons] lead, millstone, mountain; Ossa on Pelion.

weighing, ponderation, trutination [*obs.*]; weights; avoirdupois –, troy –, apothecaries'- weight; grain, scruple, drachma, dram *or* drachm, ounce, pound, lb., arroba, load, stone, hundred-weight, cwt., ton, quintal, carat, penny-weight, tod; gram *or* gramme, decagram, hectogram, kilogram *or* kilo, myriagram, decigram, centigram, milligram.

[Weighing instrument] balance, scales steelyard, beam, weighbridge, spring balance.

[Science of gravity] statics.

V. be heavy &c. *adj.;* gravitate, weigh, press, cumber, load.

[Measure the weight of] weigh, counterweigh, scale [*rare*], poise.

Adj. weighty; weighing &c. *v.;* heavy, – as lead; ponderous, ponderable; lumpish, lumpy, cumbersome, burdensome; cumbrous, unwieldy, massive; static *or* statical.

incumbent, superincumbent.

320. Levity. — **N.** levity; lightness &c. *adj.;* imponderability, buoyancy, volatility; imponderables [*tech.*].

[Comparisons] feather, dust, mote, down, thistledown, flue, fluff, cobweb, gossamer, straw, cork, bubble; float, buoy; ether, air.

ferment, leaven, barm, yeast, zyme, enzyme, pepsin, diastase.

V. be light &c. *adj.;* float, swim, be buoyed up.

render light &c. *adj.;* lighten.

ferment, work, raise, leaven.

Adj. light, subtile, subtle, airy; imponderous, imponderable; astatic, weightless, ethereal, sublimated; gossamery; suberose *or* suberous, subereous; uncompressed, volatile; buoyant, floating &c. *v.;* foamy, frothy; portable.

light as -a feather, – thistledown, – air.

fermenting, fermentative, zymogenic, zymologic *or* zymological, diastatic, yeasty.

** "Trifles light as air" [*Othello*].

Section II. INORGANIC MATTER

1. Solid Matter

321. Density. — N. DENSITY, solidity; solidness &c. *adj.;* impenetrability, impermeability; incompressibility; imporosity; cohesion &c. 46; costiveness, constipation, consistence, spissitude.

specific gravity; hydrometer, areometer.

CONDENSATION; caseation; solidation [*obs.*], solidification, consolidation, concretion, coagulation; petrifaction &c. (*hardening*) 323; crystallinity, crystallizability, crystallization, precipitation; deposit, precipitate; inspissation; incrassation, crassitude; thickening &c. *v.*

INDIVISIBILITY, indiscerptibility, indissolvableness [*rare*], infrangibility, infrangibleness, indissolubility, indissolubleness.

SOLID BODY, mass, block, knot, lump; concretion, concrete, conglomerate; cake, stone, bone, gristle, cartilage.

CLOT, coagulum, casein, crassament [*obs.*], crassamentum, legumin, curd; clabber, bonnyclabber, clotted cream, Devonshire cream, grume.

SEDIMENT, lees, dregs, settlings.

V. BE DENSE &c. *adj.;* become *or* render solid &c. *adj.;* solidify, solidate; concrete, set, take a set, consolidate, congeal, coagulate; curd, curdle, cruddle [*dial.*], lopper; fix, clot, cake, candy, precipitate, deposit, cohere, crystallize; petrify &c. (*harden*) 323.

CONDENSE, thicken, inspissate, incrassate.

COMPRESS, squeeze, ram down, constipate [*rare*].

Adj. DENSE, solid; solidified &c. *v.;* caseate, caseous; pucka *or* pakka [*Hind.*], coherent, cohesive &c. 46; compact, close, serried, thickset; substantial, massive, lumpish; impenetrable, impermeable, imporous; incompressible; constipated, costive; crass, spiss [*obs.*], clabber, kern [*chiefly dial.*]; concrete &c. (*hard*) 323; knotted, knotty; gnarled; crystallitic, crystalline, crystallizable; thick, grumose, grumous, stuffy.

UNDISSOLVED, unmelted, unliquefied, unthawed.

INDIVISIBLE, indiscerptible, infrangible, indissolvable [*rare*], indissoluble, insoluble, infusible.

. "O, that this too too solid flesh would melt" [*Hamlet*].

322. Rarity. — N. RARITY; tenuity; absence of solidity &c. 321; subtility; subtilty; sponginess, compressibility.

rarefaction, rarefication [*rare*], expansion, dilatation, inflation, subtilization.

ether &c. (*gas*) 334.

V. RAREFY, expand, dilate, subtilize [*rare*], attenuate, thin.

Adj. RARE, subtile [*now rare*], subtle, thin, fine, tenuous, compressible, flimsy, slight; light &c. 320; cavernous, porous, spongy &c. (*hollow*) 252.

rarefied &c. *v.;* unsubstantial; uncompact, uncompressed; rarefiable, rarefactive, rarefactional.

. "melted into air, thin air" [*Tempest*]; "I pass through the pores of the ocean and shores" [Shelley, *Cloud*].

323. Hardness. — N. HARDNESS &c. *adj.;* rigidity; renitency *or* renitence; inflexibility, temper, callosity, durity [*obs.*].

INDURATION, petrifaction; lapidification, lapidescence [*rare*]; cornification, chondrification, vitrification, vitrescence, ossification; crystallization.

[COMPARISONS] stone, pebble, flint, marble, rock, fossil, crag, crystal, quartz, granite, adamant; bone, cartilage; calculus; hardware; heart of oak, block, board, deal board; iron, steel; cast –,

324. Softness. — N. SOFTNESS, pliableness &c. *adj.;* flexibility; pliancy, pliability; sequacity [*obs. in this sense*], malleability, ductility, ductibility, tractability, tractility, extensibility, extendibility; plasticity; inelasticity, flaccidity, laxity, flabbiness, flocculence; mollescence, mollification; softening &c. *v.*

[COMPARISONS] clay, alumina, argil; wax, putty, butter, dough, pudding; cushion, pillow, feather bed, down, eider down, padding, wadding.

decarbonized –, wrought- iron; nail; brick, concrete; cement; osmiridium, iridosmine or iridosmium.

V. HARDEN; render hard &c. *adj.;* stiffen, indurate, petrify, temper, ossify, vitrify, lithify, lapidify, cement.

Adj. HARD, rigid, stubborn, stiff, firm; starch, starched; stark, unbending, unlimber, renitent, unyielding; inflexible, tense; indurate, indurated; gritty, proof.

adamantine, adamantean; concrete, stony, rocky, granitic, calculous, lithic, vitrescent, vitrifiable, vitrescible, vitreous; horny, cornified, callous, corneous; bony, ossipid, osseous, ossific; cartilaginous; lapideous, lapidific or lapidifical [*rare*]; crystallized, crystalloid; hard as a -stone &c. *n.;* stiff as -buckram, – a poker.

V. SOFTEN; render soft &c. *adj.;* mollify, mellow, milden, tender [*rare*], gentle [*rare*], dulcify; relax, temper; mash, knead, massage, squash [*colloq.*].

BEND, yield, relent, relax, give.

Adj. SOFT, tender, supple; pliant, pliable; flexible, flexile; lithe, lithesome; lissom, limber, plastic; ductile, ductible [*rare*], tractile, tractable; malleable, extensile, extensible, lax, sequacious [*obs. in this sense*], inelastic; aluminous; remollient [*obs.*], mollient, mollescent, mollitious, mollified.

yielding &c. v.; flabby,| limp, flimsy.

flaccid, flocculent, downy; spongy, œdematous or edematous, medullary, doughy, clayey, argillaceous, mellow.

soft as -butter, – down, – silk, – putty, – a feather bed; yielding as wax; tender as a chicken.

** "smoothing the raven down Of darkness till it smil'd" [Milton].

---

325. Elasticity. — N. ELASTICITY, springiness, spring, resilience or resiliency, renitency, buoyancy, tensibility, tensibleness, tensility, extensibility; recoil, rebound, reflex.

[COMPARISONS] India rubber or india-rubber, caoutchouc, gum elastic, whalebone, baleen; turf, moss; balloon, battledore.

V. BE ELASTIC &c. *adj.;* spring back &c. (*recoil*) 277.

Adj. ELASTIC, tensile, tensible, springy, resilient, renitent, ductile, extensible, buoyant.

326. Inelasticity. — N. INELASTICITY &c. (*softness*) 324; want of –, absence of- elasticity &c. 325; irresilience.

Adj. INELASTIC &c. (*soft*) 324; irresilient.

---

327. Tenacity. — N. TENACITY, toughness, strength; cohesiveness, cohesion &c. 46; sequacity, sequaciousness [*both obs. in this sense*]; stubbornness &c. (*obstinacy*) 606; gumminess, glutinousness, viscidity &c. 352.

[COMPARISONS] leather; white leather or whiteleather, tawed leather; gristle, cartilage.

CLAW, talon, pincers, nippers, vise; bulldog.

V. BE TENACIOUS &c. *adj.;* resist fracture.

Adj. TENACIOUS, cohesive, tough, strong, resisting, adhesive, stringy, viscid, gummy, glutinous, gristly, cartilaginous, leathery, coriaceous, tough as whiteleather; stubborn &c. (*obstinate*) 606.

328. Brittleness. — N. BRITTLENESS &c. *adj.;* fragility, friability, frangibility, fissility [*rare*], frailty, cold-shortness; house of -cards, – glass.

V. BE BRITTLE &c. *adj.;* live in a glass house.

BREAK, crack, snap, split, shiver, splinter, crumble, crash, crush, break short, burst, fly, give way; fall to pieces; fall to dust; crumble -to, – into- dust.

Adj. BRITTLE, brash [*U. S.*], frangible, breakable, friable, delicate, shattery [*rare*], fragile, frail, gimcrack, shivery, fissile; splitting &c. *v.;* lacerable, splintery, crisp, crimp, short, brittle as glass, cold-short; crisp as celery.

** "mistress of herself though china fall" [Pope].

---

329. [STRUCTURE.] Texture. — N. STRUCTURE, organization, anatomy, frame, mold or mould, fabric, construction; framework, carcass, architecture; stratification, cleavage.

substance, stuff, compages, parenchyma; constitution, staple, organism.

[SCIENCE OF STRUCTURES] organology, osteology, myology, splanchnology neurology, angiology, adenology ; angiography, adenography, organography.

TEXTURE, intertexture, contexture; tissue, grain, web, surface; warp and -woof, – weft; gossamer, homespun, linsey-woolsey, frieze, fustian; satin, velvet; tooth, nap &c. (*roughness*) 256; fineness –, coarseness- of grain; dry goods.

[SCIENCE OF TEXTURES] histology.

Adj. STRUCTURAL, organic; anatomic *or* anatomical; splanchnic, splanchnological, visceral, adenological.

TEXTURAL, textile; fine-grained, coarse-grained, ingrained, ingrain; fine, delicate, subtile, subtle, gossamer, gossamery, filmy; coarse; homespun, linsey-woolsey.

330. Pulverulence. — N. [STATE OF POWDER.] PULVERULENCE; sandiness &c. *adj.;* efflorescence; friability, friableness, arenosity, sabulosity.

PARTICLE &c. (*smallness*) 32; powder, dust, sand, shingle; sawdust; grit; meal, bran, flour, farina, rice, paddy, spore, sporule; crumb, seed, grain; limature [*obs.*], filings, *débris* [*F.*], detritus, scobs, magistery, fine powder; flocculi.

smoke; cloud of -dust, – sand, – smoke; puff –, volume- of smoke; sand storm, dust storm.

[REDUCTION TO POWDER] pulverization, comminution, attenuation, granulation, disintegration, subaction, contusion, trituration, levigation, abrasion, detrition, multure limation; tripsis; filing &c. *v.*

[INSTRUMENTS FOR PULVERIZATION] mill, arrastra, gristmill, grater, rasp, file, pestle and mortar, nutmeg grater, teeth, grinder, grindstone, kern [*dial.*], quern, quernstone, millstone.

[SCIENCE] koniology.

V. COME TO DUST; be disintegrated, be reduced to powder &c.

PULVERIZE, comminute, granulate, triturate, levigate; reduce *or* grind to powder; scrape, file, abrade, rub down, grind, grate, rasp, pound, bray, bruise, contuse, contund [*rare*]; beat, crush, craunch *or* cranch, crunch, scranch [*colloq.*], crumble, disintegrate; attenuate &c. 195.

Adj. POWDERY, pulverulent, granular, mealy, floury, farinaceous, branny, furfuraceous, flocculent, dusty, sandy, sabulous, psammous; detrital, arenaceous, arenose, arenarious, gritty; efflorescent, impalpable; lentiginous, lepidote, sabuline; sporaceous, sporous.

PULVERABLE *or* pulverizable; friable, crumbly, shivery; pulverized &c. *v.;* attrite; in pieces.

*** "Though the mills of God grind slowly, yet they grind exceeding small" [Longfellow — from von Logau].

331. Friction. — N. FRICTION, attrition; rubbing &c. *v.;* attriteness, attritus, erasure; confrication [*obs.*], contrition [*obs.*]; affriction [*obs.*], abrasion, arrosion [*obs.*], limature [*obs.*], anatripsis, anatripsology, frication, rub; elbow grease [*colloq.*]; rosin; massage.

MASSEUR (*fem. masseuse*) [*F.*], massagist, rubber.

V. RUB, abrade, scratch, scrape, scrub, fray, rasp, graze, curry, scour, polish, rub out, raze, erase, gnaw; file, grind &c. (*reduce to powder*) 330; rosin; massage.

set one's teeth on edge.

Adj. ABRASIVE, anatriptic; attrite [*rare*], attritive [*obs.*].

*** "let the galled jade wince" [*Hamlet*].

332. [ABSENCE OF FRICTION. PREVENTION OF FRICTION.] **Lubrication. — N.** LUBRICATION, lubrification [*rare*], lubricity; anointment; oiling &c. *v.*

smoothness &c. 255; unctuousness &c. 355.

LUBRICANT, lubricator, synovia; glycerin, oil &c. 356; saliva; lather; ointment, salve, balm, unguent, unguentum [*pharm.*], lenitive, unction.

V. LUBRICATE, lubricitate [*obs.*]; oil, grease, lather, soap; wax; anoint; salivate.

Adj. LUBRICATED &c. *v.;* lubricous, lubricant, lubric [*rare*]; lenitive, synovial.

*** "a dinner lubricates business" [**Lord** Stowell — quoted by Boswell].

2. Fluid Matter

1. Fluids in General

333. Fluidity. — N. FLUIDITY, liquidity, liquefaction; liquidness &c. *adj.;* gaseity &c. 334; solution, chylifaction, serosity.

fluid, inelastic fluid; liquid, liquor; lymph, humor, juice, sap, serum, blood, gravy, rheum, ichor, sanies; chyle.

solubility, solubleness.

[SCIENCE OF LIQUIDS AT REST] hydrology, hydrostatics, hydrodynamics, hydrometry, hydrokinetics.

hydrometer, hydrophone, hydrostat, meter.

V. BE FLUID &c. *adj.;* flow &c. (*water in motion*) 348; liquefy &c. 335.

Adj. LIQUID, fluid, serous, juicy, succulent, sappy; ichorous; rheumy, chylous, sanious, lymphatic; fluent &c. (*flowing*) 348.

LIQUEFIED &c. 335; uncongealed; soluble.

HYDROLOGICAL, hydrostatic *or* hydrostatical, hydrodynamic *or* hydrodynamical, hydrometric *or* hydrometrical.

..* "that liquefaction of her clothes" [Herrick].

335. Liquefaction. — N. LIQUEFACTION; liquescence, liquescency; deliquescence; melting &c. (*heat*) 384; colliquation [*obs.*], colliquefaction [*obs.*]; thaw; solubleness, deliquation [*obs.*], liquation; lixiviation, dissolution.

SOLUTION, decoction, apozem [*rare*], infusion, flux; alloy; lixivium.

SOLVENT, diluent, resolvent, dissolvent, menstruum, alkahest.

V. RENDER LIQUID &c. 333; liquefy, run; deliquesce; melt &c. (*heat*) 384; solve; dissolve, resolve; liquate; hold in solution.

LEACH, lixiviate, percolate.

Adj. LIQUEFIED &c. *v.*, liquescent, liquefiable; deliquescent, soluble, dissoluble, dissolvable, colliquative; leachy, porous.

SOLVENT, diluent, resolutive, resolvent, dissolvent.

334. Gaseity. — N. GASEITY, gaseousness, vaporousness &c. *adj.;* flatulence *or* flatulency; volatility; aëration, aërification; gasification.

ELASTIC FLUID, gas, air, vapor *or* vapour, ether, steam, fume, reek, effluvium, flatus; cloud &c. 353; ammonia, ammoniacal gas; volatile alkali.

[SCIENCE OF ELASTIC FLUIDS] pneumatics, pneumatology, pneumatonomy, pneumatostatics; aërostatics, aërodynamics, aëroscopy, aërography, aërology, aëromechanics.

pneumatoscope, pneumatometer, gasometer, gas meter; air −, swimming-bladder, sound (*of a fish*).

V. GASIFY, aërify, aërate; emit vapor &c. 336.

Adj. GASEOUS, gasiform, aëriferous, aëriform, ethereal, aëry, aërial, airy, vaporous, volatile, evaporable, flatulent.

pneumatolytic, aërostatic *or* aërostatical, aërodynamic, aëromechanic.

336. Vaporization. — N. VAPORIZATION, volatilization; gasification; evaporation, vaporation [*rare*], vaporishness, vaporosity, atomization, distillation, cupellation, cohobation, sublimation, exhalation; volatility.

fumigation, steaming.

VAPORIZER, atomizer, spray, evaporator, cohobator, finestill, still, retort.

bay salt, chloride of sodium.

V. RENDER GASEOUS &c. 334; vaporize, volatilize, atomize, spray; distill, sublime, sublimate, evaporate, exhale, smoke, transpire, emit vapor, fume, reek, steam, fumigate; cohobate; finestill.

Adj. VOLATILE, evaporable, vaporizable, vaporific, vapory, vaporous, gaseous; volatilized &c. *v.;* reeking &c. *v.*

..* "and those who came to cough remained to spray" [*Cynic's Calendar*].

2. Specific Fluids

337. Water. — N. water, lymph; *aqua* [*L.*], *eau* [*F.*], flood, crystal [*poetic*], Adam's ale [*humorous*], *agua* [*Sp.*], *pani* [*Hind.*]; diluent, serum &c. 333.

washing &c. *v.;* immersion, mersion [*obs.*]; dilution, maceration, lotion; humectation, infiltration, spargefaction [*obs.*], affusion, irrigation, seepage [*U. S., dial. Eng. & Scot.*], balneation, bath.

deluge &c. (*water in motion*) 348; high water, flood tide, springtide.

sprinkler, sparger, aspergillum *or* aspergill, shower *or* shower bath, douche, enema; nozzle; atomizer &c. 336.

V. be watery &c. *adj.;* reek.

water, wet; moisten &c. 339; dilute, add water, dip, immerse; merge; soak, drouk [*Scot.*]; affuse [*rare*], immerge, douse *or* dowse, submerge; plunge, souse, duck, drown; steep, macerate, wash, sprinkle, sparge, humect *or* humectate [*rare*], lave, bathe, splash, swash, drench; dabble, slop, slobber, irrigate, inundate, deluge; infiltrate, percolate, seep [*dial. & U. S.*]; slosh; marinate *or* marinade, pickle.

inject, gargle; syringe, douche.

Adj. watery, aqueous, aquatic, hydrous, lymphatic; balneal; diluent, solvent, hydrotic *or* hydrotical; infiltrative, seepy; drenching &c. *v.;* diluted &c. *v.;* weak; wet &c. (*moist*) 339.

⁎⁎ the waters are out; "men really know not what good water's worth" [Byron].

338. Air. — N. air &c. (*gas*) 334; common –, atmospheric- air; atmosphere; aërosphere [*rare*].

the open, – air; sky, lift [*archaic*], welkin [*archaic*], the blue, blue serene, blue sky; cloud &c. 353.

weather, climate; rise and fall of the -barometer, – mercury.

isopiestic line, isobar.

exposure to the -air, – weather; ventilation.

[Science of air] aërology, aërometry, aëroscopy, aërography; meteorology, climatology; pneumatics; aëronautics; eudiometry; eudiometer, barometer, vacuometer, climatometer, aërometer, aëroscope; aneroid, baroscope, weatherglass, weathergauge, barograph.

aërostation &c. (*aëronautics*) 267; aëronaut &c. 269*a.*

weathervane, weathercock, vane, cock.

V. air, ventilate, perflate [*rare*]; fan &c. (*wind*) 349.

fly, soar, drift, hover; aviate &c. (*aëronautics*) 267.

Adj. containing air, flatulent, effervescent; windy &c. 349.

atmospheric, airy; aërial, aëriform; aëry, pneumatic.

meteorologic *or* meteorological, aërological, aërometric, eudiometric *or* eudiometrical, barometric *or* barometrical, barographic, baroscopic *or* baroscopical; isobaric, isopiestic; aërographic *or* aërographical; weatherwise.

Adv. in the open air, *à la belle étoile* [*F.*], in the open, out of the blue, under the stars, out of doors, outdoors; *al fresco* [*It.*]; *sub Jove* [*L.*], *sub dio* [*L.*].

⁎⁎ "heaven's sweetest air" [Shakespeare].

339. Moisture. — N. moisture; moistness &c. *adj.;* humidity, humectation; madefaction [*obs.*], dew; *serein* [*F.*]; marsh &c. 345.

hygrometry, hygrometer.

V. moisten, wet; humect *or* humectate [*rare*]; sponge, damp, bedew; imbue, imbrue, infiltrate, saturate; soak, sodden, seethe, sop, dampen; drench &c. (*water*) 337.

be moist &c. *adj.;* not have a dry thread; perspire &c. (*exude*) 295.

Adj. moist, damp; watery &c. 337; madid [*now rare*], undried, humid, wet,

340. Dryness. — N. dryness &c. *adj.;* siccity [*rare*], siccation, aridness, aridity, drought *or* drouth.

ebb tide, low water.

desiccation, exsiccation [*rare*], dehydration, insolation, anhydration, anhydromyelia [*med.*], evaporation, arefaction [*rare*], dephlegmation, drainage.

drier, desiccative, desiccator.

V. be *or* render dry &c. *adj.;* dry; dry up, soak up; sponge, swab, wipe. drain, parch, sear.

be fine, hold up; be bright and fair.

desiccate, exsiccate, dehydrate, an-

dank, muggy, dewy; roric; roriferous, rorifluent [*both rare*], roral [*obs*], rorid [*obs*.]; roscid [*rare*]; juicy.

SATURATED &c. *v.;* wringing wet; wet through, wet to the skin.

SODDEN, swashy [*dial*.], soppy, soggy, dabbled; reeking, dripping, soaking, droukit [*Scot*.], soft, sloppy, muddy; swampy &c. (*marshy*) 345; irriguous.

** "honest water, which ne'er left man i' the mire" [*Timon of Athens*]; "My lips were wet, my throat was cold, My garments all were dank" [Coleridge].

hydrate, evaporate, insolate, infumate, torrefy, siccate [*rare*], arefy.

Adj. DRY, arid; droughty, waterless, siccaneous [*rare*], siccate [*obs*.], aneroid, sear *or* sere, siccant [*rare*], siccific, desiccatory; adust, arescent; dried &c. *v.;* undamped; dephlegmatory; juiceless, sapless; corky; husky; rainless, without rain, fine; dry as -a bone, – dust, – a stick, – a mummy, – a biscuit; waterproof, watertight.

ANHYDROUS, desiccated, desiccate, anhydric, dehydrated, insolated.

** "with throats unslaked, with black lips baked" [Coleridge].

---

341. Ocean. — N. OCEAN, sea, main, deep, blue, brine, salt water, waters, waves, billows, high seas, offing, great waters, watery waste, "vasty deep" "briny deep," "swan-bath" [*A.-S.*], "swan-road" [*A.-S.*], "whale-path" [*A.-S.*], mere [*archaic*], herring pond *or* pond [*humorous for Atlantic*], hyaline, the Seven Seas, *kala pani* [*Hind.*]; wave, tide &c. (*water in motion*) 348; ocean basin; ocean lane, steamer track.

Neptune, Poseidon, Oceanus, Thetis, Triton, Naiad, Nereid; sea nymph, Siren, mermaid, merman; trident, dolphin.

OCEANOGRAPHY, hydrography; oceanographer, hydrographer.

Adj. OCEANIC, marine, maritime; pelagic, pelagian [*rare*], pelagious [*obs*.]; seaworthy, seagoing; hydrographic *or* hydrographical, oceanographic *or* oceanographical; bathybic, cotidal.

Adv. at sea, on sea; afloat; over-sea *or* over-seas, oceanward *or* oceanwards.

** "great Neptune's ocean" [*Macbeth*]; 'Listen! the mighty Being is awake! And doth with his eternal motions make A sound like thunder — everlastingly" [Wordsworth].

342. Land. — N. LAND, earth, ground, soil, dry land, *terra firma* [*L.*].

continent, mainland, main, peninsula, chersonese, delta; tongue –, neck- of land; isthmus, oasis; promontory &c. (*projection*) 250; highland &c. (*height*) 206.

REALTY, real estate &c. (*property*) 780; acres.

COAST, shore, scar *or* scaur, strand, beach; *playa* [*Sp*.]; bank, lea; seaboard, seaside, sea bank, seacoast, seabeach; seashore, rock-bound coast, iron-bound coast; loom of the land; derelict; innings; reclamation, made land, alluvium, alluvion; *ancon* [*S. W. U. S.*].

REGION &c. 181; home, fatherland &c. (*abode*) 189.

SOIL, glebe, clay, loam, marl, cledge [*dial. Eng.*], chalk, gravel, mold *or* mould, subsoil, clod, clot [*dial.*].

ROCK, crag, cliff.

GEOGRAPHY, geodesy, geology, geognosy, geogony, agriculture, agronomics, agronomy, geoponics, georgics.

GEOGRAPHER, geodesist, geologist, geognost.

LANDSMAN, landlubber, tiller of the soil; agriculturist &c. 371.

V. LAND, disembark, debark, come to land; set foot on -the soil, – dry land; come –, go- ashore.

Adj. EARTHY; continental, midland; terrene &c. (*world*) 318.

LITTORAL, riparian, riparial, riparious, ripicolous, ripuarian; alluvial.

LANDED, prædial *or* predial, territorial; geophilous.

GEOGRAPHIC *or* geographical, geodesic *or* geodesical, geodetic *or* geodetical, geognostic *or* geognostical, geologic *or* geological, geoponic; agricultural &c. 371.

Adv. ASHORE; on shore, on land, on dry land, on *terra firma* [*L.*].

343. Gulf. Lake. — N. GULF, gulph, bay, inlet, bight, estuary, arm of the sea, bayou [*U. S.*], fiord, armlet; frith *or* firth, ostiary [*obs.*], mouth; lagoon *or* lagune; indraft *or* indraught [*obs.*], cove, creek; natural harbor; roads; strait; narrows; euripus; sound, belt, gut, kyle [*Scot.*].

LAKE, loch [*Scot.*], lough, [*Ir.*], mere, tarn, plash, broad [*Eng.*], pond, pool, sump [*Scot. or dial. Eng.*], slab [*dial.*], linn *or* lin [*Scot.*], tank, puddle, well, artesian well; standing –, dead –, sheet of- water; fish –, mill- pond; ditch, dike *or* dyke, dam, race, mill race; reservoir &c. (*store*) 636; *alberca* [*Sp. Amer.*], hog wallow, buffalo wallow.

Adj. LACUSTRINE, lacustral.

344. Plain. — N. PLAIN, table-land, face of the country; open –, champaign-country; basin, downs, waste, weary waste, desert, wild, steppe, tundra, peneplain, pampas, savanna, prairie &c. (*grassland*) 367; heath, common, wold, veldt *or* veld, moor, moorland; bush plateau &c. (*level*) 213; campagna [*obs. as Eng.*], champaign, uplands, fell [*Brit.*]; reach, stretch, expanse; alkali flat, llano; mesa, mesilla [*U. S.*], *playa* [*Sp.*]; shaking –, trembling- prairie; *vega* [*Sp. Amer.*].

MEADOW, mead, haugh [*Scot. & dial. Eng.*], pasture, lea, ley *or* lay [*dial.*], pasturage, field.

LAWN, green, plat, plot, grassplat.

GREENSWARD, sward, turf, sod, grass; heather.

GROUNDS; *maidan* [*India*], park, common, campus [*U. S.*], *agostadero* [*Sp.*].
Adj. CHAMPAIGN, campestral, campestrial [*obs.*], campestrian, campestrine.
ALLUVIAL, fluvio-marine.
Adv. in the bush.

345. Marsh. — N. MARSH, swamp, morass, marish [*archaic*], peat bog, moss, fen, bog, quagmire, slough, sump [*Scot. or dial. Eng.*], bottoms, holm [*Eng.*], wash; mud, squash, slush; baygall [*U. S.*], *ciénaga* [*Sp.*], *jhil* [*India*], *vlei* [*S. Africa*].

Adj. MARSH, marshy, swampy, boggy, plashy, poachy, quaggy, soft; muddy, sloppy, squashy, spongy; paludal; moorish, moory; fenny, marish [*archaic*].

346. Island. — N. ISLAND, isle, islet, ait *or* eyot, holm, reef, atoll; archipelago; islander.

V. INSULATE, island, enisle [*rare*], isle [*rare*].

Adj. INSULAR, insulary [*rare*], seagirt; archipelagic.

3. Fluids in Motion

347. [FLUID IN MOTION.] **Stream.** —**N.** STREAM &c. (*of water*) 348, (*of air*) 349.
V. FLOW &c. 348; BLOW &c. 349.

348. [WATER IN MOTION.] **River. — N.** running water.

jet, swash, spurt *or* spirt, squirt, spout, splash, rush, gush, *jet d'eau* [*F.*]; sluice.

waterspout, waterfall; fall, cascade, force *or* foss [*dial. Eng.*], linn *or* lin [*Scot.*], gill *or* ghyll; Niagara; cataract, catadupe [*obs.*], cataclysm; debacle, inundation, deluge; chute, washout.

RAIN, rainfall; *serein* [*F.*]; plash, shower, scud [*dial.*]; downpour; downflow, pour, cloudburst, drencher; driving –, drenching- rain; predominance of Aquarius, reign of St. Swithin; drisk [*U. S.*], brash [*dial.*], mizzle [*dial.*], drizzle, stillicidium, dropping &c. *v.*;

349. [AIR IN MOTION.] **Wind. — N.** WIND, draught, flatus, afflatus, sufflation [*rare*], insufflation, perflation, inflation, afflation, indraft *or* indraught, efflation; air; breath, – of air; puff, whiff, whiffet, zephyr, blow, drift; aura; stream, current; undercurrent.

Æolus or Eolus, Boreas, Euroclydon, Eurus, Notus [*rare*], Zephyr *or* Zephyrus, Favonius; cave of Æolus *or* Eolus; Wabun (east wind), Kabibonokka (north wind), Shawondasee (south wind), Mudjekeewis (west wind) [*all four from Hiawatha*].

GUST, blast, breeze, capful of wind, fresh breeze, stiff breeze, keen blast, squall, half a gale, gale.

TRADE WIND, trades, monsoon.

rains, rainy season, monsoon, *bursat* or *barsat* [*Hind.*]; falling weather [*colloq.*].

HYETOLOGY, hyetography; hyetograph, rain chart.

STREAM, course, flux, flow, profluence; effluence &c. (*egress*) 295; defluxion; flowing &c. *v.;* current, tide, race, mill race, tide race.

spring; fount, fountain; rill, rivulet, rillet; streamlet, brooklet; branch [*U. S.*]; runnel, runlet; sike, burn [*both dial. Eng. & Scot.*], beck [*Eng.*], brook, river; reach; tributary.

body of water, torrent, rapids, flush, flood, swash; spring –, high –, flood –, full- tide; bore, eagre *or* hygre; fresh, freshet; indraft *or* indraught; ebb, refluence, reflux, undercurrent, undertow, eddy, vortex, gurge [*rare*], whirlpool, Charybdis, Maelstrom (*also* maelstrom), regurgitation, overflow, alluvion; confluence, corrivation [*obs.*].

WAVE, billow, surge, swell, ripple, *anerithmon gelasma* [*Gr.* ἀνήριθμον γέλασμα]; beach comber, riffle [*U. S.*], tidal wave, comber, chop, choppiness, roll, rollers, ground swell, surf, breakers, white horses; rough –, heavy –, cross –, long –, short -, choppy –, chopping- sea.

[SCIENCE OF FLUIDS IN MOTION] hydrodynamics; hydraulics, hydrostatics, hydrokinetics, hydromechanics, pegology, pluviometry.

[MEASURES] hyetometer, hyetometrograph, hydrodynamometer, nilometer, fluviometer, fluviograph, marigraph, hydrometer, hydrometrograph, udometer, ombrometer, rain gauge *or* gage, pluviometer, pluviograph.

IRRIGATION &c. (*water*) 337; pump; watering- pot, – cart; hydrant, standpipe, syringe, siphon, *mussuk* [*Hind.*].

WATER CARRIER, bheesty *or* bheestie [*India*], Water Bearer, Aquarius.

V. FLOW, run; meander; gush, pour, spout, roll, jet, well, issue; drop, drip, dribble, plash, spirtle, trill, trickle, distill, percolate; stream, gurge [*rare*], surge, swirl, overflow, inundate, deluge, flow over, splash, swash; guggle, murmur, babble, bubble, purl, gurgle, sputter, spurt, regurgitate; ooze, flow out &c. (*egress*) 295.

FLOW INTO, fall into, open into, drain into; discharge itself, disembogue.

[CAUSE A FLOW] pour; pour out &c.

STORM, tempest, hurricane, whirlwind, tornado, samiel, cyclone, typhoon, simoom *or* simoon, harmattan, sirocco, mistral, *bise* [*F.*], *tramontana* [*It.*], tramontane, levant, levanter; blizzard, barber [*Can.*], *candelia* [*Sp. Am.*], chinook, foehn, khamsin, norther, northeaster, northeast gale, *vendaval* [*Sp.*], wuther [*dial.*], willy-willy [*Austral.*].

WINDINESS &c. *adj.;* ventosity [*obs.*]; rough –, dirty –, ugly –, wicked –, foul –, stress of- weather; dirty sky, mare's-tail, mackerel sky; cloud &c. 353; thick –, black –, white- squall.

ANEMOGRAPHY, anemology, anemometry, aërology, aërography, aërodynamics.

WIND-GAUGE, anemometer, anemoscope, anemograph, anemometrograph; weathercock, weathervane, vane.

BREATHING, respiration, inspiration, inhalation, expiration, exhalation; blowing, fanning, &c. *v.;* ventilation; sneezing &c. *v.;* errhine; sternutation; hiccup *or* hiccough, eructation, catching of the breath; inspirator, respirator, ejector.

air pump, lungs, bellows, pulmotor, blowpipe; branchiæ, gills.

FAN, punkah *or* punka [*India*], flabellum, thermantidote, electric fan; *ventilabrum* [*L.*].

VENTILATOR, louver, aërator [*rare*], transom; airpipe &c. 351; hygrometer, psychrometer.

V. BLOW, waft; blow -hard, – great guns, – a hurricane &c. *n.;* storm; wuther [*dial.*], stream, issue.

RESPIRE, breathe, inhale, exhale; inspire, expire; puff; whiff, whiffle; gasp, wheeze; snuff, snuffle; sniff, sniffle; sneeze, cough, hiccup *or* hiccough; belch, eruct [*rare*].

FAN, ventilate; inflate, pump, perflate [*obs.*]; blow up.

WHISTLE, scream, roar, howl, sing, sing in the shrouds, growl.

Adj. WINDY, airy, æolian *or* eolian, borean, favonian; ventilative; blowing &c. *v.;* breezy, gusty, squally.

STORMY, tempestuous, blustering, cyclonic, typhonic; boisterous &c. (*violent*) 173.

ANEMOGRAPHIC, anemological, anemometric *or* anemometrical, aërologic *or* aërological, aërographic *or* aërographical, aërodynamic.

PULMONIC, pulmonary, pulmonate.

(*discharge*) 297; shower down; irrigate, drench &c. (*wet*) 337; spill, splash.

[STOP A FLOW] stanch *or* staunch; dam, dam up &c. (*close*) 261; obstruct &c. 706.

RAIN, - hard, – in torrents, – cats and dogs, – pitchforks [*both colloq.*]; pour, shower, sprinkle, pour with rain, drizzle, spit [*colloq.*], set in; mizzle.

Adj. FLUENT, deliquescent, defluent, profluent [*rare*], diffluent, affluent; tidal; flowing &c. *v.*; meandering, meandrous, meandry [*obs.*], flexuous, fluvial, fluviatile; streamy, streamful; choppy, rolling; stillicidious [*obs.*], stillatitious [*rare*]; hydragogue [*med.*].

RAINY, showery, pluvial [*rare*], pluvious, pluviose [*rare*], drizzly, drizzling, mizzly, wet; pluviometric *or* pluviometrical.

NASAL, errhine; sternutative, sternutatory.

FLATULENT, gassy, windy, ventose.

** "lull'd by soft zephyrs" [Pope]; "the storm is up and all is on the hazard" [*Julius Cæsar*]; "the winds were wither'd in the stagnant air" [Byron]; "while mocking winds are piping loud" [Milton]; "winged with red lightning and tempestuous rage" [*Paradise Lost*]; "the headsail's low-volleying thunder" [Kipling]; "that gay companion, the loudly laughing wind" [Dunsany].

** "for men may come and men may go but I go on forever" [Tennyson]; "that mountain floods should thunder as before" [Wordsworth]; "the immense and contemptuous surges" [Kipling]; "the heave and the halt and the hurl and the crash of the comber wind-hounded" [*ibid.*]; "rivers are moving roads" [Pascal].

350. [CHANNEL FOR THE PASSAGE OF WATER.] **Conduit. — N.** CONDUIT, channel, duct, watercourse, cañon *or* canyon, coulee *or* coulée [*geol.*], water gap, gorge, ravine, chasm; race; head -, tail- race; abito [*F. Amer.*], aboideau *or* aboiteau [*local Can.*], bito [*dial., U. S.*]; acequia [*Sp. Amer.*], acequiador [*Sp. Amer.*], arroyo; adit, aqueduct, canal, trough, gutter, pantile; flume, dike, main; gully, gullet [*rare*], gulch [*U. S.*], moat, ditch, drain, sewer, culvert, cloaca, sough [*dial. Eng.*], kennel, siphon; piscine, piscina; pipe &c. (*tube*) 260; funnel; tunnel &c. (*passage*) 627; water -, waste- pipe; emunctory, gully hole, spout, scupper; penstock, pentrough, weir, lock weir, floodgate, water gate, sluice, lock, valve; rose, rosehead; waterworks.

[FOR METAL] ingate, runner, tedge.

[ANATOMY] artery, vein, vena [*L.*], blood vessel, lymphatic, pore; aorta; intestines, bowels; small intestine, duodenum, jejunum, ileum; large intestine, cæcum, colon, rectum; esophagus *or* œsophagus, gullet; throat.

Adj. VASCULAR &c. (*with holes*) 260.

EXCRETORY, eliminative.

351. [CHANNEL FOR THE PASSAGE OF AIR.] **Air Pipe. — N.** AIR PIPE, air tube, air hole, blowhole, breathing hole, spiracle, touchhole, vent hole, spile hole, bung, bunghole; shaft, airway, air shaft, smokeshaft, flue, chimney, funnel, vent, ventage; ventiduct, ventilator; pipe &c. (*tube*) 260; blowpipe &c. (*wind*) 349.

nostril, nozzle, throat, weasand, bronchus (*pl.* bronchi), larynx, tonsils, windpipe, trachea.

LOUVER, Venetian blind, Venetian shutter, jalousie [*F.*], jhilmil [*India*].

ajutage; hose; gargoyle *or* gurgoyle;

3. IMPERFECT FLUIDS

352. Semiliquidity. — N. SEMILIQUIDITY; stickiness &c. *adj.*; viscidity, viscosity, mucidness, gummosis, emulsification, jellification; gummosity [*rare*], glutinosity [*rare*], mucosity; crassitude, spissitude; lentor [*now rare*]; pastiness; adhesiveness &c. (*cohesion*) 46; succulence *or* succulency; lactescence.

INSPISSATION, incrassation, crassamentum, coagulum; thickening.

[COMPARISONS] jelly, gelatin, carlock, ichthyocol. ichthyocolla, isinglass; mu-

353. [MIXTURE OF AIR AND WATER.] **Bubble, Cloud. — N.** BUBBLE; foam, froth, head, spume, scum, fume, lather, suds, spray, surf, yeast, barm, spoondrift *or* spindrift.

EFFERVESCENCE, fermentation; bubbling &c. *v.*; evaporation, exhalation, emanation.

CLOUDINESS &c. (*opacity*) 426; nebulosity &c. (*dimness*) 422.

CLOUD, vapor, fog, mist, haze, steam; scud, rack, nimbus; cumulus, nebula,

cus, pus, phlegm, pituite; lava; paste; library –, flour- paste; glair, starch, gluten, albumen, milk, cream, protein; treacle, rob, sirup *or* syrup, molasses; gum, size, glue, varnish, mastic, mucilage, fish glue; wax, beeswax; emulsion; gruel, porridge; *purée* [*F.*], soup.

squash, mud, slush, slime, ooze; moisture &c. 339; marsh &c. 345.

V. inspissate, incrassate; coagulate, gelatinate, gelatinize; jellify, jelly, jell [*colloq., U. S.*]; emulsify, thicken; mash, squash, churn, beat up.

Adj. semifluid, semiliquid; half-melted, half-frozen; milky, muddy &c. *n.;* lacteal, lactean [*rare*], lacteous, lactescent, lactiferous; emulsive, curdled, thick, succulent, uliginose *or* uliginous.

gelatinous, albuminous, mucilaginous, glutinous; gummous, spissated [*rare*], crass, tremelloid, tremellose, amylaceous, ropy, clammy, clotted; viscid, viscous; sticky, tacky; slab [*dial.*], slabby; lentous [*obs.*], pituitous; mucid, muculent, mucous.

. "lucent syrops tinct with cinnamon" [Keats].

354. Pulpiness. — N. pulpiness &c. *adj.;* pulp, paste, dough, sponge, batter, clotted cream, curd, pap, jam, pudding, poultice, grume.

V. pulp, pulpify [*rare*], mash, squash [*colloq.*], masticate, macerate; coagulate &c. 352.

Adj. pulpy &c. *n.;* pultaceous, grumous; baccate; [*of fruit*] fleshy, succulent.

. "crisp and juicy stalks Culled from the ocean's meadows" [Bryant].

meteor, woolpack, cirrus, curl cloud, thunderhead, stratus; cirro-stratus, cumulo-stratus; cirro-cumulus; mackerel sky, mare's-tail, colt's-tail, cat's-tail, cocktail, dirty sky; frost smoke.

[Science of clouds] nephology, nephelognosy, meteorology; nephoscope, nephelometer, nephograph.

V. bubble, boil, foam, spume, froth, mantle, sparkle, guggle, gurgle; effervesce, pop, ferment, fizzle; aërate.

cloud, overcast, overcloud, befog, becloud, adumbrate [*rare*], mist, fog, overshadow, shadow.

Adj. bubbling &c. *v.;* frothy, nappy [*obs.*], effervescent, sparkling, *mousseux* [*F.*], fizzy, heady, with a head on, with a collar on [*slang*], up [*colloq.*].

cloudy &c. *n.;* cirrous, cirrose; nubiferous, cumulous, thunderheaded; vaporous, nebulous, overcast.

nephological, nepheloscopic, nephelometric, meteorologic *or* meteorological.

. "the lowring element scowls o'er the darkened landscip" [*Paradise Lost*]; "stinging, ringing spindrift" [Kipling].

355. Unctuousness. — N. unctuousness &c. *adj.;* unctiousness [*rare*], unguent, unctuosity, lubricity; salve, cerate; ointment &c. (*oil*) 356; anointment; lubrication &c. 332.

V. oil, anoint, lubricate &c. 332; smear, salve, grease, lard, pinguefy.

Adj. unctuous, unctious [*rare*], unguentary, unguentous, oily, oleaginous, adipose, sebaceous, unguinous, fat, fatty, greasy; waxy, butyraceous, soapy, saponaceous, pinguid, lardaceous; slippery.

356. Oil. — N. oil, fat, butter, cream, grease, tallow, suet, lard, dripping, exunge [*obs.*], blubber; glycerin *or* glycerine, stearin, elain *or* elaine, olein, oleagine; coconut butter; soap; soft soap, wax, cerement; paraffin *or* paraffine, benzine, gasoline *or* gasolene, petrol, spermaceti, adipocere; petroleum, mineral –, rock –, crystal- oil; vegetable –, colza –, olive –, salad –, linseed –, cottonseed –, coconut –, palm –, nut- oil; animal –, neat's-foot –, train- oil; ointment, pomade, pomatum, unguent, liniment; amole, Barbados tar; fusel –, grain –, rape –, seneca- oil; hydrate of amyl, ghee *or* ghi [*India*], kerosene, naphtha.

356a. Resin. — N. resin, rosin, colophony, gum; lac, shellac *or* shell-lac, sealing wax; amber, ambergris; bitumen, pitch, tar; asphalt *or* asphaltum; camphor; varnish, copal, mastic, megilp *or* magilp, lacquer, japan, Brunswick black.

V. varnish &c. (*overlay*) 223; rosin, resin.

Adj. resinous, resiny, rosinous [*rare*], lacquered, japanned, camphorated, tarred, tarry, pitched, pitchy, gummed, gummy, gummous, waxed; bituminous, asphaltic, asphaltite.

Section III. ORGANIC MATTER

1. Vitality

1. Vitality in general

357. Organization. — N. ORGANIZATION, organized world, organized nature, living nature, animated nature; living beings; organic remains; organism, bion [*physiological individual*]; morphon [*morphological individual*]; biota, animal and plant life, fauna and flora.

FOSSILS, fossilization, lapidification, petrification, petrifaction, paleontology *or* palæontology, paleozoölogy *or* palæozoölogy; paleontologist *or* palæontologist.

[SCIENCE OF LIVING BEINGS] biology, natural history; [1]zoölogy &c. 368; botany &c. 369; physiology, anatomy, cytology, embryology, organic chemistry, morphology; promorphology, tectology; cell theory *or* cellular theory, evolution, metabolism; abiogenesis, spontaneous generation; archigenesis &c. (*production*) 161; biotaxy, ecology *or* œcology, ontogeny, phylogeny, polymorphism, oxidation, invagination, vertebration.

Darwinism, Lamarckism, neo-Lamarckism, Weismannism.

NATURALIST, biologist, zoölogist, botanist, bacteriologist, embryologist, Darwinian.

PROTOPLASM, plasma *or* plasm, cytoplasm, metaplasm, karyoplasm, bioplasm, trophoplasm, idioplasm; cell, proteid, protein, albumen, albumin, albuminoid; structure &c. 329; chromatin; centrosome, nucleolus, karyosome, vacuole, chromosome; protoplast, protozoan, amœba; karyaster, erythroblast, dysmeromorph, antherozoid.

OVUM, oösperm, zygote, oösphere, oöcyte, oœcium, ovicell, oögonium; oöphyte, oöspore, oögamy, heterogamy, isogamy, oögenesis; gamete, gametophore, gametophyte, sporophyte, sporocyte, sporocyst, sporocarp, cystocarp, sporogonium, sporozoite, gametangium, antheridium *or* antherid; macrospore, megasporangium; microspore, microsporangium; biophore; spermatozoid, zoöspore, macrogamete, microgamete, spermatozoön, spermatium, spermatia, spermatocyte, spermatogenesis, spermatophore, spermatozoid, spermatozooid; spermogonium, spermary, sperm gland, testis, testicle, ovary; germ cell, blastoderm, mesoblast *or* mesoplast, meroblast (*opp. to* holoblast); germinal matter, biogenesis *or* biogeny, germ plasm *or* germ plasma, zoöglœa, zooid.

V. ORGANIZE, systematize, form, arrange, construct.

FOSSILIZE, petrify, lapidify, mummify.

Adj. ORGANIC, organized; biotic, zooid, zooidal.

FOSSILIZED, petrified, petrifactive, lapidified; paleontologic, paleontological *or* palæontological, paleozoölogical *or* palæozoölogical.

PROTOPLASMIC, plasmatic *or* plasmic, cytoplasmic, metaplasmic, karyoplasmic, bioplasmic, trophoplasmic, idioplasmic; cellular, cellulous; proteid, proteinaceous, albuminous *or* albuminose, albuminoidal, structural; nuclear, nucleate, nucleolar, nucleolate *or* nucleolated; vacuolar, protoplastic, protozoan, amœbic, amœboid.

OVARIAN, oviferous, oviparous (*opp. to* viviparous), ovicular; oöphytic, oösporic, oösporous, oögamous, heterogamous (*opp. to* autogamous *or* isogamous); gamic, sporogenous; spermatic, spermatogenetic, spermatoid, spermatophoral, spermatozoal; blastodermic, mesoblastic (*opp. to* holoblastic), biogenetic, germinal; zoöglœic, zoöglœoid; unsegmentic, diœcious *or* diecious (*opp. to* monœcious *or* monecious).

358. Inorganization. — N. MINERAL KINGDOM, mineral world; unorganized –, inorganic –, brute –, inanimate- matter.

[SCIENCE OF THE MINERAL KINGDOM] mineralogy, geology, geognosy, geoscopy, metallurgy, metallography, lithology, petrology, oryctology [*obs.*], oryctography [*obs.*].

V. MINERALIZE; pulverize, turn to dust.

Adj. INORGANIC, inanimate, unorganized *or* inorganized, lithoid *or* lithoidal; azoic; mineral.

---

[1] The term *natural history* is also used as relating to all the objects in Nature whether organic or inorganic, and including, therefore, *mineralogy, geology, meteorology,* &c.

359. Life. — N. LIFE; vitality, viableness, viability; animation.

VITAL SPARK, vital flame, Promethean spark, lifeblood; respiration, wind; breath of life, breath of one's nostrils; Archeus *or* Archæus; *anima* [*L.*], *anima bruta* [*L.*], *anima divina* [*L.*], *anima mundi* [*L.*]; world -soul, – spirit, – principle; existence &c. 1.

VIVIFICATION; oxygen; vital -air, – force; life force; vitalization; revival; revivification &c. 163; Prometheus; Deucalion and Pyrrha; life to come &c. (*destiny*) 152.

"a short summer" [Johnson]; "a bubble" [Browne]; "a battle" [Aurelius]; "one dem'd horrid grind" [Dickens].

[SCIENCE OF LIFE] physiology, biology, ætiology *or* etiology, embryology; animal economy.

NOURISHMENT, staff of life &c. (*food*) 298.

V. LIVE; be alive &c. *adj.*; breathe, respire, suspire; subsist &c. (*exist*) 1; walk the earth; (a poor player that) "struts and frets his hour upon the stage" [*Macbeth*]; be spared.

BE BORN, see the light, come into the world; fetch –, draw- -breath, – the breath of life; breathe the vital air; quicken; revive; come to, – life.

GIVE BIRTH TO &c. (*produce*) 161; bring to life, put into life, vitalize; vivify, vivificate [*rare*]; reanimate &c. (*restore*) 660.

KEEP ALIVE, keep body and soul together, keep the wolf from the door; support life.

have nine lives like a cat.

Adj. LIVING, alive; in life, in the flesh, in the land of the living; on this side of the grave, above ground, breathing, quick, animated; animative; lively &c. (*active*) 682; alive and kicking [*colloq.*]; tenacious of life.

VITAL, vitalic; vivifying, vivified &c. *v.*; viable, zoëtic; Promethean.

Adv. *vivendi causâ* [*L.*].

360. Death. — N. DEATH; decease, demise; mortality; dying; passing -away, – of the soul; dissolution, departure, obit, release, rest, eternal rest, quietus, fall; loss, bereavement.

end &c. 67 –, cessation &c. 142 –, loss –, extinction –, ebb- of life &c. 359.

DEATH-WARRANT, deathwatch, death rattle, deathbed; stroke –, agonies –; shades –, valley of the shadow –, summons –, jaws –, hand –, bridge –, river- of death; Jordan, Jordan's bank, "one more river to cross"; last -breath, -gasp, – agonies; dying -day, – breath. – agonies; swan song, *chant du cygne* [*F.*]; *rigor mortis* [*L.*]; Stygian shore; "crossing the bar" [Tennyson]; the great adventure.

euthanasia, euthanasy [*rare*]; happy release, *bona mors* [*L.*]; break-up of the system; natural -death, – decay; sudden – , violent- death; untimely end, taking off [*colloq.*], watery grave; debt of nature; mortification, heart failure, suffocation, asphyxia; fatal disease &c. (*disease*) 655; deathblow &c. (*killing*) 361.

ANGEL OF DEATH, death's bright angel, Azrael; King -of terrors, – Death; Death, doom &c. (*necessity*) 601; "Hell's grim Tyrant" [Pope].

NECROLOGY, bills of mortality, obituary.

DEATH SONG &c. (*lamentation*) 839.

V. DIE, expire, perish; meet one's -death, – end; pass away, pass over, be taken; yield –, resign- one's breath; resign one's -being, – life; end one's -days, – life, – earthly career; breathe one's last; cease to -live, – breathe; depart this life; be no more &c. *adj.*; go off [*colloq.*], drop off [*colloq.*], pop off [*slang*]; lose –, lay down –, relinquish –, surrender- one's life; drop –, sink- into the grave; close one's eyes; fall –, drop- -dead, – down dead; break one's neck; give –, yield- up the ghost; be all over with one.

pay the debt to nature, shuffle off this mortal coil, take one's last sleep; go the way of all flesh; hand –, pass- -in one's checks, – in one's chips [*all slang*]; go over to the –, join the- -greater number, – majority, – great majority; join the choir invisible; awake to life immortal; come –, turn- to dust; give an obolus to

[*Macbeth*]; "a little gleam of time between two eternities" [Carlyle]; "the vital warmth that feeds my life" [Otway]; "Life, like a dome of many-coloured glass, Stains the white radiance of eternity" [Shelley]; "Life, a beauty chased by tragic laughter" [Masefield].

Charon; cross the Stygian ferry; go to one's long account, go to one's last home, go to Davy Jones's locker, go to glory [*colloq. or slang*]; receive one's death warrant, make one's will, step out [*colloq.*], die a natural death, go out like the snuff of a candle; come to an untimely end; catch one's death; go off the hooks, kick the bucket, hop the twig, turn up one's toes [*all slang*]; die a violent death &c. (*be killed*) 361.

die for one's country, make the supreme sacrifice, go West [*World War euphemism*].

Adj. DEAD, lifeless; deceased, demised, departed, defunct; late, gone, no more; exanimate [*rare*], inanimate; out of the world, taken off, released; bereft of life; stone dead; departed this life &c. *v.;* dead and gone; dead as -a doornail, – a doorpost, – mutton, – a herring, – nits [*all slang or colloq.*]; launched into eternity, gathered to one's fathers, numbered with the dead; born into a better world, born into the next world; gone to a better land; dying –, dead- in the Lord; asleep in Jesus; with the saints.

stillborn; mortuary; deadly &c. (*killing*) 361.

DYING &c. *v.;* moribund, morient [*obs.*]; Hippocratic; *in articulo* [*L.*], *in extremis* [*L.*]; in the -jaws, – agony- of death; going, – off; *aux abois* [*F.*]; on one's -last legs [*colloq.*], – deathbed; at the point of death, at death's door, at the last gasp; near one's end, given up, given over, booked [*slang*]; with one foot in –, tottering on the brink of- the grave.

Adv. *post obit* [*L.*], *post mortem* [*L.*].

*** Life -ebbs, – fails, – hangs by a thread; one's days are numbered, one's hour is come, one's race is run, one's doom is sealed; Death knocks at the door, Death stares one in the face; the breath is out of the body; the grave closes over one; *sic itur ad astra* [Vergil]; *de mortuis nil nisi bonum; dulce et decorum est ⅌᧐ patria mori* [Horace]; *honesta mors turpi vitâ potior* [Tacitus]; "in adamantine chains shall death be bound" [Pope]; *mors ultima linea rerum est* [Horace]; *omnia mors œquat* [Claudianus]; "spake the grisly Terror" [*Paradise Lost*]; "the lone couch of his everlasting sleep" [Shelley]; "the push of death has swung her into life" [Tagore]; "And Death is beautiful as feet of friend Coming with welcome at our journey's end" [Lowell]; "Why do we then shun Death with anxious strife? If Light can thus deceive, wherefore not Life?" [J. Blanco White].

361. [DESTRUCTION OF LIFE; VIOLENT DEATH.] **Killing.** — **N.** KILLING &c. *v.;* homicide, manslaughter, murder, assassination, trucidation [*obs.*], occision [*obs.*]; effusion of blood; blood, bloodshed; gore, slaughter, carnage, butchery; *battue* [*F.*]; bomb explosion, electrocution, shipwreck; gladiatorial combat; lapidation.

MASSACRE; fusillade, *noyade* [*F.*]; thuggism, thuggee, thuggery; saturnalia of blood, sacrifice to Moloch; organized massacre, *pogrom* [*Russia*].

WAR, warfare, "organized murder," *horrida bella* [*L.*], crusade, jihad *or* jehad [*Moham.*]; battle; war to the death &c. (*warfare*) 722; Armageddon; gigantomachy; deadly weapon &c. (*arms*) 727.

DEATHBLOW, finishing stroke, *coup de grâce* [*F.*], quietus; execution &c. (*capital punishment*) 972; judicial murder; martyrdom.

SUFFOCATION, strangulation, garrote *or* garrotte; hanging &c. *v.*

SLAYER, butcher, murderer, Cain, assassin, cutthroat, garroter *or* garrotter, bravo, Thug *or* thug, Moloch, matador, *sabreur* [*F.*]; *guet-apens* [*F.*]; gallows, executioner &c. (*punishment*) 975; man-eater, Apache, hatchet man [*U. S.*], highbinder [*U. S.*], gunman [*colloq., U. S.*], bandit, lapidator [*rare*].

regicide, parricide, fratricide, infanticide; feticide *or* fœticide, aborticide; uxoricide, vaticide [*these words ending in* -cide *refer to both doer and deed*].

SUICIDE, self-murder, self-destruction, *felo-de-se* (*pl. felos-de-se*), seppuku [*Jap.*], hara-kiri [*Jap.*], suttee, sutteeism, car of Jagannath *or* Juggernaut [*an erroneous assumption*]; immolation, holocaust.

FATAL ACCIDENT, violent death, casualty, disaster, calamity.

ACELDAMA (*often l.c.*), potter's field, field of blood.

[DESTRUCTION OF ANIMALS] slaughtering; phthiozoics;[1] sport, sporting; the chase, venery; hunting, coursing, shooting, fishing; pig-sticking.

sportsman, huntsman, fisherman; hunter, Nimrod.

shambles, slaughterhouse, *abattoir* [*F.*].

V. KILL, put to death, slay, shed blood; murder, assassinate, butcher, slaughter, victimize, immolate; massacre; take away –, deprive of- life; make away with, put an end to; dispatch *or* despatch; burke, settle [*colloq.*], do to death, do for [*colloq.*]; hunt.

shoot, – dead; blow one's brains out; brain, knock on the head, blackjack; drop in one's tracks; stone, lapidate; give –, deal- a deathblow; give the -quietus, – *coup de grâce* [*F.*].

STRANGLE, garrote *or* garrotte, hang, throttle, choke, stifle, suffocate, stop the breath, smother, asphyxiate, drown.

SABER *or* sabre; cut -down, – to pieces, – the throat; jugulate; stab, run through the body, bayonet; put to the -sword, – edge of the sword.

EXECUTE, behead, guillotine, hang, electrocute; bowstring &c. (*execute*) 972.

CUT OFF, nip in the bud, launch into eternity, send to one's last account, sign one's death warrant, strike the death knell of.

GIVE NO QUARTER, pour out blood like water; decimate; run amuck; wade knee-deep in blood; dye –, imbrue- one's hands in blood.

DIE A VIOLENT DEATH, welter in one's blood; dash –, blow- out one's brains; commit suicide; kill –, make away with –, put an end to- oneself; suicide [*colloq.*]; disembowel, commit hara-kiri.

Adj. MURDEROUS, slaughterous, sanguinary, sanguinolent, blood-stained, blood-thirsty; killing &c. *v.;* homicidal, red-handed; bloody, bloody-minded; ensanguined, gory, sanguineous.

MORTAL, fatal, lethal; deadly, deathly; mortiferous [*obs.*], lethiferous; unhealthy &c. 657; mutually destructive, internecine; suicidal.

SPORTING; piscatorial, piscatory.

Int. thumbs down! *habet! hoc habet!* [*L.*], let him have it!

*** dead men tell no tales; "assassination has never changed the history of the world" [Disraeli].

362. Corpse. — N. CORPSE, corse [*archaic*], carcass *or* carcase, cadaver, bones, skeleton, dry bones; defunct, relics, reliquiæ, remains, mortal remains, dust, ashes, earth, clay; mummy; carrion; food for -worms, – fishes; tenement of clay, "this mortal coil" [*Hamlet*]; "this too, too solid flesh" [*Hamlet*].

GHOST, shade, manes, phantom, specter *or* spectre, apparition, spirit, revenant, sprite [*archaic*], spook [*colloq.*].

ORGANIC REMAINS, fossils.

Adj. CADAVEROUS, cadaveric, corpse-like; unburied &c. 363.

363. Interment. — N. INTERMENT, burial, sepulture, entombment *or* in-tombment, inhumation, humation [*obs.*]; obsequies, exequies; funeral, wake.

CREMATION, burning; pyre, funeral pile.

FUNERAL RITE, funeral solemnity; knell, passing bell, death bell, funeral ring, tolling; dirge &c. (*lamentation*) 839; cypress; obit, dead march, muffled drum; elegy; funeral -oration, – sermon.

UNDERTAKER, mortician [*cant, U. S.*], funeral director.

MOURNER, mute, keener [*Ireland*], lamenter; pallbearer, bearer.

GRAVECLOTHES, shroud, winding sheet, cerecloth; cerements.

COFFIN, casket, shell, sarcophagus.

urn, cinerary urn; pall, bier, litter, hearse, catafalque.

BURIAL PLACE, grave, pit, sepulcher *or* sepulchre, tomb, vault, crypt, cata-comb, mausoleum, cenotaph, golgotha, house of death, narrow house, low green tent, low house, long home, last home; cemetery, necropolis; burial ground;

[1] Bentham, *Chrestomathia.*

graveyard, churchyard; God's acre; potter's field; cromlech, barrow, tumulus, cairn; ossuary; bonehouse, charnel-house, deadhouse; morgue, mortuary; lich gate; burning ghât *or* ghaut [*India*]; crematorium, crematory; mastaba *or* mastabah [*Egypt*], tope *or* stupa [*Buddhist*]; dokhma, Tower of Silence [*Parsee*].

GRAVEDIGGER, sexton, *fossoyeur* [*F.*].

MONUMENT, cenotaph, shrine; gravestone, headstone, tombstone; *memento mori* [*L.*]; hatchment, stone, marker, cross; epitaph, inscription.

NECROPSY, necroscopy, autopsy, *post mortem* examination *or post mortem* [*L.*].

EXHUMATION, disinterment.

V. INTER, bury; lay in -, consign to- the -grave, - tomb; entomb *or* intomb; inhume; hold -, conduct- a funeral; put to bed with a shovel [*colloq.*]; inurn; cremate.

lay out; embalm, mummify; toll the knell.

EXHUME, disinter, unearth.

Adj. FUNEREAL, funebrial [*now rare*], funeral, funerary, mortuary, sepulchral, cinerary; buried &c. *v.*; burial; elegiac; necroscopic *or* necroscopical.

Adv. *hic jacet* [*L.*], *ci-gît* [*F.*], *R. I. P.*; *in memoriam* [*L.*]; *post obit* [*L.*], *post mortem* [*L.*]; beneath the sod, under the sod, underground; at rest.

⁎⁎ *requiescat in pace; resurgam;* "the lone couch of his everlasting sleep" [Shelley]; "without a grave — unknell'd, uncoffin'd, and unknown [Byron]; "in the dark union of insensate dust" [Byron]; "the deep cold shadow of the tomb" [Moore]; "like one that wraps the drapery of his couch about him, and lies down to pleasant dreams" [Bryant].

2. Special Vitality

364. Animality. — N. ANIMALITY, animalism, animal life; animation, animalization, animalness.

CORPOREAL NATURE, human system; breath; flesh, flesh and blood; physique; strength &c. 159.

V. ANIMALIZE; incarnate, incarn [*rare*], incorporate.

Adj. FLESHLY, carnal, human, corporeal.

366. Animal. — N. ANIMAL KINGDOM, fauna, brute creation.

ANIMAL, creature, created being; creeping thing, living thing; dumb animal, dumb friend, dumb creature; brute, beast.

mammal, quadruped, bird, reptile, fish, crustacean, shellfish, mollusk, worm, insect, zoöphyte; plankton, nekton, benthos; animalcule &c. 193.

beasts of the field, fowls of the air, denizens of the day; flocks and herds, live stock, domestic animals; wild animals, *feræ naturæ* [*L.*], game.

[DOMESTIC ANIMALS] horse &c. (*beast of burden*) 271; cattle, kine, ox; bull, bullock; cow, milch cow, Alderney, Jersey, calf, heifer, shorthorn, yearling, steer. stot [*prov. Eng.*]; sheep; lamb, lambkin, ewe lamb, pet lamb; ewe, ram, tup, wether, tag [*prov. Eng.*], teg [*prov.*

365. Vegetation. — N. VEGETATION, vegetable life, vegetability [*obs.*], vegetativeness, vegetism, vegetality [*rare*]; herbage, flowerage.

V. VEGETATE, germinate, sprout, grow, shoot up, luxuriate, fungate; grow -rank, - lush, - like a weed; flourish &c. 367; cultivate.

Adj. VEGETATIVE, vegetal, vegetable; leguminous &c. 367.

LUXURIANT, rank, dense, lush, wild, jungly.

367. Vegetable. — N. VEGETABLE, vegetable kingdom; flora.

organism, plant, tree, shrub, bush, creeper, vine; herb, seedling, plantlet, exotic, annual, perennial, biennial, triennial; legume, pulse, vetch, greens; asparagus &c. (*vegetables*) 298.

FOLIAGE, leafage, verdure, foliation, frondescence [*rare*]; prefoliation, vernation; branch, bough, ramage, stem, tigella *or* tigelle *or* tigellum *or* tigellus; leaf, spray, leaflet, frond, foliole, bract, bractlet, bracteole, cotyledon, pad [*U. S.*], flag, petal, needle, sepal; spray &c. 51; petiole, petiolule, bine; shoot, tendril.

FLOWER, blossom, bud, burgeon, blow, blowth [*rare*]; floweret, floret, floscule, flowering plant; inflorescence, flowerage.

TREE, sapling, seedling, stand, pollard, dryad [*fig.*]; oak, elm, beech, birch,

Eng.]; pig, swine, boar, hog, sow; yak, zebu, Indian buffalo.

DOG, hound, canine; pup, puppy; whelp, cur [*contemptuous*].

house –, watch –, sheep –, shepherd's –, sporting –, hunting –, fancy –, lap –, toy-dog; collie; mastiff; bulldog, English bulldog, Boston bull, bull terrier, French bull; police dog, bloodhound, greyhound, staghound, deerhound, foxhound, coach dog, bandog, lurcher, Russian *or* Siberian wolfhound, boarhound, St. Bernard, husky *or* Eskimo dog; otter-hound; harrier, beagle, spaniel, pointer, setter, retriever, Newfoundland; water -dog, – spaniel; pug, poodle; turnspit; terrier; fox –, Airedale –, Yorkshire –, Irish –, Skye –, toy- terrier; Dandie Dinmont; dachshund, badger dog; brindle; Pomeranian, cocker spaniel, King Charles spaniel, toy spaniel, spitz dog; chow *or* chow-dog, Japanese poodle.

pariah dog, pye-dog *or* pie-dog [*India*]; mongrel, mut *or* mutt [*slang*].

FEMALE, bitch, slut, brach, brachet, lady [*euphemistic*].

CAT, feline, puss, pussy, grimalkin, tomcat *or* tom, gib [*rare*], Angora, Persian, Maltese, tortoiseshell, mouser; tabby; kitten, kit, catling, kitling [*dial.*].

[WILD ANIMALS] DEER, buck, doe, fawn, stag, hart, hind, roe, roebuck, caribou, elk, moose, reindeer, sambar, wapiti *or* American elk, mule deer, black-tailed deer *or* Virginia deer, fallow deer, red deer.

ANTELOPE, gazelle, nilghau, eland, gnu, hartebeest, springbok *or* springbuck, oryx, steinbok, ibex; American antelope *or* pronghorn, chamois, koodoo *or* kudu.

armadillo, peba, poyou, tatouay; wild ass' kiang, dziggetai, onager; bear, polar bear' grizzly bear, brown bear; beaver; bison, buffalo; musk ox, giraffe, okapi, tapir; wild boar; babiroussa *or* babirussa; ape, monkey, gorilla, marmoset, chimpanzee, lemur, baboon, orang-utan *or* orang-outang; kangaroo, opossum; wild horse, zebra; elephant, *hathi* [*Hind.*]; fox, reynard, Reynard, vixen [*fem.*], varmin *or* varmint [*dial.*], prairie fox, gray fox, red fox, arctic fox; dingo, coyote; wildcat, lynx, bobcat; skunk; hippopotamus, rhinoceros, lion, tiger &c. (*wild beast*) 913; squirrel, chipmunk, gopher, prairie dog, ferret, stoat, weasel, mongoose, raccoon *or* coon, bandicoot, rat, mouse; bat, flying mouse, flying phalanger, flying squirrel; flying fox, flying lemur, colugo.

LIZARD, saurian, iguana, eft, newt, chameleon, gecko, Gila monster, dragon, horned toad, horned lizard.

CROCODILIAN, crocodile, mugger *or* magar [*India*], gavial [*India*], alligator, cayman, American crocodile.

whale, sperm whale, baleen whale; shark, porpoise, walrus, seal, octopus, devilfish; swordfish; pike; salmon &c. (*food*) 298.

138

timber tree, pine, palm, spruce, fir, hemlock, yew, larch, cedar, savin *or* savine, juniper, chestnut, maple, alder, ash, myrtle, magnolia, walnut, olive, poplar, willow, linden, lime; apple &c. (*fruit trees*) 298; arboretum &c. 371.

banyan, teak, acacia, deodar, pipal *or* pipal tree; fig tree, eucalyptus, gum tree.

WOODLANDS, virgin forest, forest primeval, forest, wood, timberland, timber, wood lot; hurst, frith, holt [*poetic or dial.*], weald, wold [*obs.*], park, chase [*Eng.*], greenwood, grove, copse, coppice, *bocage* [*F.*], tope [*India*], clump of trees, thicket, spinet [*obs.*], spinney [*Eng.*], bosk, chaparral, *ceja* [*Texas*], motte [*local, U. S.*]; jungle, bush.

UNDERGROWTH, underwood, brushwood, brake, "the mid-forest brake" [Keats], boscage, scrub, palmetto barrens, bosch [*Dutch*]; heath, heather, fern, bracken, furze, gorse, whin, broom, genista, sedge, rush, bulrush, bamboo; weed, moss, foggage [*Scot.*], lichen, Iceland moss, mushroom, toadstool, fungus; turf, turbary, mold *or* mould.

GRASS, fog, second growth, second crop; herbage.

alfalfa, lucern *or* lucerne, alfilaria, clover, bent *or* bent grass, timothy, redtop *or* English grass, switch grass *or* black bent, blue grass, Kentucky blue grass, ribbon grass, meadow grass, spear grass, wire grass, blue joint, crab grass, bunch grass, meadow fescue, meadow foxtail, grama *or* mesquite grass, gama *or* sesame grass, sheep's fescue; cereal, wheat, barley, buckwheat, maize *or* Indian corn, oats, rice, rye.

GRASSLAND, greensward, green, lawn, sward, common, maidan [*India*], mead, meadow, pasture, pasturage, prairie, pampas, steppe, llano, savanna, campo, plain, field, campus [*U. S.*].

SEAWEED, alga (*pl.* algæ), fucus, fucoid, conferva (*pl.* confervæ), confervoid, wrack, dulse, kelp, rockweed, sea lettuce, gulfweed, sargasso, sargassum; plankton, benthos; Sargasso Sea.

V. VEGETATE, grow, flourish, bloom, flower, blossom; bud &c. (*expand*) 194; timber, retimber, coppice, copse; bush, plant, trim, cut.

Adj. VEGETABLE, vegetal, vegetive [*obs.*], vegetative, vegetarian; leguminous, herbaceous, herbal, botanic *or* botanical; arbory, arboreous, arborescent, arborical [*obs.*], arboreal, arboral; silvan *or* sylvan; treelike, dendriform,

[BIRDS] feathered tribes, feathered songster, singing bird, warbler, dicky-bird [colloq.].

canary, vireo, linnet, finch, goldfinch, brown thrasher, siskin, crossbill, aberdevine, chewink, peewee, lapwing [Scot.], titmouse or chickadee, nightingale, lark; magpie, cuckoo, mocking bird, catbird, laughing jackass, starling, mina or mina; bobolink, redbird, ricebird, cardinal bird, cowbird, crow, rook, jackdaw, raven; pigeon, dove, cushat, ringdove, wood pigeon; swan, cygnet, goose, gander, duck, drake, wild duck, mallard; flamingo, heron, crane, stork, kingfisher, sandpiper, lyre bird, robin, thrush, hermit thrush, veery, mavis, missel thrush, ouzel or ousel, blackbird, red-winged blackbird; kingbird, fly-catcher; woodpecker, flicker; sparrow, song sparrow, chipping sparrow, vesper sparrow; swallow, swift, martin, sand martin, oriole, bluebird, meadow lark; bird of paradise, parrot, parrakeet or parakeet; penguin, pelican; gull, sea gull, albatross, petrel, stormy petrel or Mother Carey's chicken, fulmar or Mother Carey's goose; ostrich, emu; owl, bird of night; hawk, vulture, buzzard, turkey buzzard; eagle, bird of freedom, bird of Jove.

dendritic or dendritical, dendroid; grassy, verdant, verdurous; floral, floreal [rare], lignose or lignous [rare], ligneous, lignescent, wooden, woody; bosky, cespitose, copsy; mossy, turfy, turf-like; fungous, fungiform, fungoid; tigellate, radiculose, radicular, radiciform, radiciflorous, rhizanthous, radicated; endogenous, exogenous; deciduous, evergreen.

NATIVE, domestic, indigenous, native-grown, home-grown.

ALGAL, fucoid, confervoid; planktonic, benthonic.

₊ "green-robed senators of mighty woods" [Keats]; "this is the forest primeval" [Longfellow]; "Poems are made by fools like me, But only God can make a tree" [Joyce Kilmer].

GAME, black game, black grouse, ruffed grouse, grouse, blackcock, duck, plover, rail, snipe; pheasant &c. 298.

POULTRY, fowl, cock, rooster, chanticleer, dunghill fowl, barndoor fowl, barnyard fowl, hen, Partlet, chicken, chick, chickabiddy; guinea fowl, guinea hen; peafowl, peacock, bird of Minerva, peahen.

[INSECTS] bee, honeybee, queen bee, drone; ant, white ant, termite; wasp, sawfly, locust, grasshopper, cicada, cicala, cricket; dragon fly, June fly, caddis fly; beetle; butterfly, moth; fly, May fly, thrips, aphid, bug; ant lion, hellgramite or hellgamite, earwig; springtail, podura, lepisma; buffalo bug, buffalo carpet beetle &c. (injurious insects) 913.

VERMIN, lice, cooties [slang], flies, fleas, cockroaches or roaches, water bugs or Croton bugs, bugs, bedbugs, Norfolk Howards [slang], mosquitoes; rats, mice, weasels.

SNAKE, serpent, viper; asp, adder, coral snake or harlequin snake, krait [India], cobra, cobra de capello, king cobra, rattlesnake or rattler, copperhead, constrictor, boa constrictor, boa, python, Kaa [Kipling], ophidian.

[MYTHOLOGICAL] dipsas (pl. dipsades), basilisk, cockatrice, amphiobæna, Python, Hydra.

salamander; griffin or griffon or gryfon; chimæra; Cerberus.

Adj. ANIMAL, zoic, zooid or zooidal, zoölogical.

equine; bovine, vaccine; canine; feline; fishy, piscatory, piscatorial; molluscous, vermicular; gallinaceous, rasorial, solidungulate, soliped; planktonic, nekteric, benthonic.

OPHIDIAN, ophiologic, ophiomorphous, reptilian, anguine, ophic [rare], snake-like, serpentiform [rare], viperine, colubrine.

₊ "The whole creation groaneth and travaileth" [Bible]; "Hark! hark! the lark at heaven's gate sings" [Cymbeline]; "the mavis singing Its love song to the morn" [Jefferys]; "those feathery things, the hounds" [Masefield]; "some crush-nosed human-hearted dog" [Browning].

---

368. [SCIENCE OF ANIMALS.] Zoölogy — N. ZOÖLOGY, zoönomy, zoögraphy, zoötomy; morphology, anatomy, histology, embryology; comparative anatomy, animal physiology, comparative physiology; mammalogy.

anthropology, anthropotomy, ornithology, ornithotomy, ichthyology, ich-

369. [SCIENCE OF PLANTS.] Botany. — N. BOTANY; physiological -, structural -, systematic- botany; phytography, phytology, phytotomy, phytobiology, phytogenesis or phytogeny, phytonomy, phytopathology; phytochemistry, phytochimy [obsoles.], vegetable chemistry; pomology; vegetable

thyotomy, herpetology, herpetotomy, ophiology, malaeology, helminthology, entomology, entomotomy; oryctology [obs.], paleontology or palæontology; mastology, vermeology; taxidermy.

zoÖLOGIST, zoÖgrapher, zoÖgraphist, zoÖtomist, anatomist, anthropotomist, morphologist, promorphologist, anthropologist, ornithologist, ornithotomist, ichthyologist, ichthyotomist, herpetologist, herpetotomist, ophiliologist, malacologist, helminthologist, entomologist, entomotomist; oryctologist [obs.], paleontologist or palæontologist; vermeologist, taxidermist.

[PRINCIPAL GROUPS] PROTOZOA (the simplest animals): Rhizopoda, rhizopod; Foraminifera, foraminifer; Radiolaria, radiolarian; Flagellata; Infusoria, infusorian; Gregarinæ, gregarine.

CŒLENTERA or CŒLENTERATA (sponges, corals, jellyfishes): Porifera, poriferan; Cnidaria, cnida; Spongiæ or Spongiaria or Spongiozoa, sponge, calcareous sponges, siliceous sponges; Anthozoa, anthozoan, coral polyps; Hydrozoa, hydrozoÖn, hydroid, medusa.

ECHINODERMATA (crinoids, starfishes, and sea urchins): Pelmatozoa, Asterozoa, Echinozoa; Cystidea or Cystoidea, cystid, cystidean; Crinoidea, stone lilies, crinoidean; Blastoidea, blastoid; Ophiuroidea or Ophiurioidea, brittle stars, ophiuroid or ophiurid; Asterioidea or Asteridea, starfishes, asteridian; Echinoidea, sea urchins, echinoid; Holothurioidea, sea cucumbers, holothurian, holothure.

VERMES (worms): Platyhelminthes or Plathelminthes, flatworms, platyhelminth; Rotifera, rotifer; Nemathelminthes or Nematelminthes, roundworms; Gephyrea, marine annelids, gephyrean, gephyreoid; Annelida, annelid, annelidan, anneloid.

MOLLUSCOIDEA (mollusk-like animals): Bryozoa or Polyzoa, sea mosses, bryozoan; Brachiopoda, lamp shells, brachiopod.

MOLLUSCA (mollusks): Pelecypoda or Lamellibranchia, bivalves, lamellibranch; Scaphopoda, tooth-shells or tusk-shells, scaphopod; Amphineura, chitons; Gastropoda, univalves, snails, gastropod; Cephalopoda, nautilus, cuttlefish, squid, octopus, cephalopod or cephalopode.

ARTHROPODA (articulates): Branchiata, Tracheata; Crustacea, crustacean; Trilobita, trilobite; Limuloidea or Xiphosura, horseshoe crab, limulus; Entomostraca, ostracoids, barnacles, entomostracan; Malacostraca, lobsters, crabs, malacostracan; Myriapoda, centipeds or centipedes, galleyworms, millipeds, myriapod; Arachnida or Arachnoidea, spiders, scorpions, mites, ticks, arachnid, arachnidan; Insecta, insects.

VERTEBRATA (vertebrate animals): Cyclostomata or Cyclostoma, lampreys; Pisces, fishes; Selachii, sharks, rays, selachian; Holocephali or Holocephala, chimæras, spooks; Dipnoï, lung-fishes; Teleostomi, ordinary fishes, ganoids, teleost, teleostean; Amphibia, amphibians, batrachians; Reptilia, reptiles; Aves, birds; Mammalia, mammals; Monotremata or Prototheria, monotremes; Marsupialia, marsupials, marsupialian or marsupian; Placentalia, placentals.

physiology, herborization, dendrology, mycology, fungology, algology; flora, Flora, Pomona; botanic garden &c. (garden) 371; hortus siccus [L.]; herbarium, herbal [obs.].

PHYTON, phytomer or phytomeron.

[PRINCIPAL GROUPS] THALLOGENS or THALLOPHYTES (thallus plants): algæ and algoid forms: Cyanophyceæ, blue-green algæ; Chlorophyceæ, green algæ; Phæophyceæ, brown algæ; Rhodophyceæ, red algæ.

fungi and fungoid forms: Schizomycetes, fission fungi, bacteria; Myxomycetes, slime molds; Phycomycetes, algæ fungi, water molds; Ascomycetes, sac fungi, lichen fungi; Basidiomycetes, basidium fungi, rusts, mushrooms.

BRYOPHYTES (moss plants): Hepaticæ, liverworts; Musci, mosses.

PTERIDOPHYTES (fern plants): Lycopodiales: Sigillaria, Stigmaria, Lepidodendra, fossil trees, lepidodendrid, lepidodendroid; Lycopodiaceæ; club mosses: Equisetales, calamites, Equisetacæ, horsetails, equisetum; Filicales: Cycadofilices, cycad ferns; Filices, ferns, filicoid.

SPERMATOPHYTES (seed plants): Gymnospermæ (naked-seeded plants): gymnosperm. Cycadales, cycads; Gnetales, gnetums; Ginkgoales, ginkgo (pl. ginkgoes); Coniferæ, cone-bearing evergreens, conifer.

Angiospermæ (covered-seeded plants): angiosperm; Monocotyledones, monocotyledon, cereals, palms, lilies, orchids, banana, pineapple &c., endogens; Dicotyledones: oak, apple, sunflower, pea, dicotyledon.

BOTANIST, phytologist, phytotomist, phytobiologist, dendrologist; mycologist, fungologist; phytopathologist, horticulturist &c. 371; herbalist, herbist, herbarist [obs.], herborist, herbarian; pomologist.

V. BOTANIZE, herborize.

Adj. BOTANIC or botanical, phytoid, dendroid or dendroidal, herbose or herbous, dendriform, dendritic or dendritical, dendrologous, herby, herbal; fungoid, fungous, mycologic or mycological, mycetoid, phytobiological, phytochemical, phytogenetic or phytogenous, pomological, horticultural.

thalloid, thalline; hepatic, musciform, muscoid, lycopodiaceous, lepidodendroid, equisetaceous, equisetiform, filicoid, filiciform, gymnospermous, cycadaceous, coniferous, angiospermous, angiospermatous, monocotyledonous, endogenous, dicotyledonous.

Adj. zoölogical, zoölogic; zoönomic; zoögraphical &c. *n.*

protozoan, rhizopodous; foraminiferous, foraminous, foraminated; radiolarian; flagellate; infusorial, infusory; gregarine.

cœlenterate, poriferan, spongiose *or* spongious, spongoid, spongiform; anthozoan, anthozoic, corallaceous, coralliferous, coralliform, coralligenous, coralligerous, coralloid, coralloidal; polyparous, polypean; hydrozoal, hydroid; medusiform, medusoid.

echinodermatous, echinodermal; pelmatozoan; crinoidal, crinoid; ophiuran, ophiuroid; asteridian; echinoid, holothurian.

vermicious, vermicular, vermiculate, vermiculose *or* vermiculous, vermiform; gephyrean, gephyreoid; annelid *or* annelidan, annelidous.

molluscoid, molluscoidal; bryozoan; brachiopod.

molluscan, molluscoid, molluscous; lamellibranch, lamellibranchiate, bivalvular, bivalvous, bivalved; gastropodous, univalve *or* univalved, univalvular; cephalopodic, cephalopodous, nautiloid.

arthropodal, articulate; branchial, branchiate, branchiferous; tracheate; crustacean, crustaceous; arachnoid, arachnoidal, arachnidan, arachnidial; insectile, insected.

vertebrate, vertebrated, vertebral; cyclostome, cyclostomous; piscatorial *or* piscatory, pisciform, piscine; amphibian, amphibial [*rare*], amphibious; batrachian, batrachoid; reptilian; avicular; mammalian, mammiferous.

370. [Economy or management of animals.] **Cicuration.** — **N.** cicuration [*obs.*], taming &c. *v.;* zoöhygiantics;[1] domestication, domesticity; manège *or* manege, veterinary art; farriery; breeding; pisciculture; apiculture.

menagerie, vivarium, zoölogical garden, zoo [*colloq.*]; bear pit; aviary; apiary, alvearium, alveary, beehive, hive; aquarium, fishery, fish hatchery, fish pond; swan pond, duck pond; incubator.

[Destruction of animals] phthisozoics[2] &c. (*killing*) 361.

[Keeper] herder, oxherd, neatherd, cowherd, grazier, drover, cowkeeper; shepherd, shepherdess; keeper, gamekeeper; trainer, breeder; bull whacker [*U. S.*], cowboy, cow puncher [*U. S.*], *vaquero* [*Sp. Amer.*]; horse trainer, broncho-buster [*slang*]; apiarian [*rare*], apiarist, apiculturist.

veterinarian, veterinary surgeon, vet [*colloq.*], horse doctor, horse leech [*rare*]; farrier [*obsoles. as veterinarian*], horseshoer.

inclosure, stable, barn, byre; cage &c. (*prison*) 752; hencoop, bird cage, coif, cauf; sheepfold &c. 232.

V. tame, domesticate, domesticize, acclimatize, breed, tend, corral, round up, break in, gentle, cicurate [*obs.*], break, bust [*slang, U. S.*], break to harness, train; ride, drive &c. (*take horse*) 266; cage, bridle, &c. (*restrain*) 751; guide, spur, prick, lash, goad, whip; trot, gallop &c. (*move quickly*) 274; bolt; yoke, harness, harness up [*colloq.*], hitch, hitch up [*colloq.*], cinch [*U. S.*].

371. [Economy or management of plants.] **Agriculture.** — **N.** agriculture, cultivation, husbandry, farming; georgics, geoponics; agronomy, agronomics, tillage, tilth, gardening, spade husbandry, vintage; horticulture, arboriculture, silviculture, forestry; floriculture; landscape gardening; viticulture.

husbandman, horticulturist, gardener, florist; agricultor [*rare*], agriculturist, agronomist, yeoman, farmer, cultivator, tiller of the soil, plowman *or* ploughman, reaper, sower; logger, lumberman [*U. S. & Can.*], lumberjack [*N. W. U. S.*], forester, woodcutter, pioneer, backwoodsman; granger [*U. S.*], habitant, *vigneron* [*F.*], viniculturist, vine-grower, vintager, viticulturist; Triptolemus.

garden; botanic –, winter –, ornamental –, flower –, kitchen –, market –, truck –, hop- garden; nursery; greenhouse, hothouse; conservatory, forcing house, cold-frame; bed, border, seed plot; grassplot *or* grassplat, lawn; parterre; shrubbery, plantation, avenue, arboretum, pinery, pinetum, orchard; vineyard, vinery, orangery.

field, meadow, mead, green, common, maidan [*India*]; park &c. (*pleasure ground*) 840; farm &c. (*abode*) 189.

V. cultivate, till, till the soil, farm, garden, sow, plant; reap, mow, cut; manure, dress the ground, dig, spade, delve, dibble, hoe, plow *or* plough, harrow, rake, weed, lop and top; backset [*U. S.*]; force, seed, turf, transplant, thin out, bed, prune, graft.

Bentham.   [2] Bentham.

GROOM, rub down, brush, currycomb; water, feed, fodder; bed, bed down, litter; drench, embrocate.

TEND STOCK, milk, shear; water &c. (*groom*) *v.*; herd; raise, bring up, bring up by hand.

hatch, incubate, sit, brood, cover.

swarm, hive.

Adj. PASTORAL, bucolic, rural; agricultural &c. 371.

TAME, domestic, domesticated, broken, gentle, docile.

Adj. AGRICULTURAL, agronomic, geoponic, georgic, agrestical [*obs.*], agrestian, prædial *or* predial; horticultural, viticultural.

ARABLE, plowable *or* ploughable, tillable.

RURAL, rustic, country, agrarian, pastoral, bucolic, Arcadian.

*** "The first farmer was the first man, and all historic nobility rests on possession and use of land" [Emerson].

---

372. Mankind. — N. MANKIND, man; human -race, – species, – kind. – nature; humanity, mortality, flesh, generation.

[SCIENCE OF MAN] anthropology, anthropogeny, anthropography, anthroposophy; ethnology, ethnography; anthropotomy, androtomy; humanitarianism.

HUMAN BEING; person, personage; individual, creature, fellow creature, mortal, body, somebody, one; such a one, some one; soul, living soul; earthling; party [*slang or vulgar*], head, hand; member, members of the cast, *dramatis personæ* [*L.*]; *quidam* [*L.*].

PEOPLE, persons, folk, public, society, world; community, – at large; general public; nation, nationality; state, realm; commonweal, commonwealth; republic, body politic; million &c. (*commonalty*) 876; population &c. (*inhabitant*) 188.

cosmopolite; lords of creation; ourselves.

Adj. HUMAN, mortal, personal, individual, national, civic, public, social; cosmopolitan; anthropoid.

*** "am I not a man and a brother?" [Wedgwood].

---

373. Man. — N. MAN, male, he; manhood &c. (*adolescence*) 131; gentleman, sir, master, dan [*archaic*], don, huzur [*India*], sahib [*India*]; yeoman, chap [*colloq.*], wight [*now chiefly jocose*], swain, fellow, blade, beau, gaffer [*dial. Eng.*], goodman [*archaic*]; husband &c. (*married man*) 903; boy &c. (*youth*) 129.

MISTER, Mr., *monsieur* (abbr. M., pl. MM. *or* Messrs.) [*F.*], *Herr* [*Ger.*], *signor* [*It.*, *used before name*], *signore* [*It.*], *signorino* [*It.*, *dim. of signore*], signior [*Eng. form*], seignior, *señor* [*Sp.*], *senhor* [*Pg.*]

[MALE ANIMAL] cock, drake, gander, dog, boar, stag, hart, buck, horse, entire horse, stallion; gib [*rare*], tom, tomcat; he-goat, billy-goat [*colloq.*]; ram, tup; bull, bullock; capon; ox, gelding; steer, stot [*prov. Eng.*].

Adj. MALE, he, masculine; manly, virile; unwomanly, unfeminine.

*** *hominem pagina nostra sapit* [Mar.]; *homo homini aut deus aut lupus* [Erasmus]; *homo vitæ commodatus non donatus est* [Syrus]; "When Adam dolve, and Eve span, Who was then the gentleman?" [John Ball].

374. Woman. — N. WOMAN, she, female, petticoat; skirt, jane [*both slang*].

FEMINALITY, femininity, femineity, feminacy, feminity, muliebrity; gynics.

WOMANKIND; womanhood &c. (*adolescence*) 131; the sex, the fair; fair sex, softer sex; weaker vessel.

dame [*archaic except as an elderly woman*], madam, mastress [Chaucer, *obs.*], lady, Donna, belle, matron, dowager, goody, gammer [*dial. Eng.*], memsahib [*Anglo-Ind.*], sahiba [*Hind.*], *bibi* [*Hind.*], frow, *vrouw* [*Du.*], good woman, goodwife [*archaic*]; squaw; wife &c. (*marriage*) 903; matronage, matronhood.

bachelor girl, new woman, suffragist, suffragette; spinster, old maid.

nymph, houri, wench, grisette; girl &c. (*youth*) 129.

MISTRESS, Mrs., *madame* (*pl. mesdames*) [*F.*], *Frau* [*Ger.*], *signora* [*It.*], *señora* [*Sp.*], *senhora* [*Pg.*]; miss, *mademoiselle* (*pl. mesdemoiselles*) [*F.*], *Fräulein* [*Ger.*], *signorina* [*It.*], *señorita* [*Sp.*], *señhorita* [*Pg.*].

[EFFEMINACY] betty, cot betty [*U. S.*], cotquean, henhussy, molly, mollycoddle, muff, old woman, tame cat [*all contemptuous*].

[FEMALE ANIMAL] hen; bitch, slut, brach, brachet; sow, doe, roe, mare; she-goat, nanny-goat [*colloq.*], nanny [*colloq.*]; ewe, cow; lioness, tigress; vixen.

HAREM, gynæceum *or* gynæcium, seraglio, zenana [*India*], purdah [*India*].

Adj. FEMALE, she; feminine, womanly, ladylike, matronly, girlish, maidenly; womanish, effeminate, unmanly; gynecic *or* gynæcic.

** "a perfect woman nobly planned" [Wordsworth]; "a lovely lady garmented in white" [Shelley]; *das Ewig-Weibliche zieht uns hinan* [Goethe]; "earth's noblest thing, a woman perfected" [Lowell]; *es de vidrio la mujer;* "she moves a goddess and she looks a queen" [Pope]; "the beauty of a lovely woman is like music" [G. Eliot]; *varium et mutabile semper femina* [Vergil]; "woman is the lesser man" [Tennyson].

2. SENSATION

1. *Sensation in general*

375. Physical Sensibility. — N. SENSIBILITY; sensitiveness &c. *adj.;* physical sensibility, feeling, impressibility, perceptivity, susceptibility, æsthetics *or* esthetics; moral sensibility &c. 822.

SENSATION, impression; consciousness &c. (*knowledge*) 490.

external senses.

V. BE SENSIBLE OF &c. *adj.;* feel, perceive; feel -keenly, - exquisitely.

RENDER SENSIBLE &c. *adj.;* sharpen, refine, excite, stir, cultivate, tutor.

IMPRESS, cause sensation; excite -, produce- an impression.

Adj. SENSIBLE, sensitive, sensuous; æsthetic *or* esthetic, perceptive, sentient; conscious &c. (*aware*) 490; alive, alive to impressions, answering quickly to, impressionable, responsive, easily affected, quick in response.

ACUTE, sharp, keen, vivid, lively, impressive, thin-skinned.

Adv. TO THE QUICK; on the raw [*slang*].

** "the touch'd needle trembles to the pole" [Pope].

376. Physical Insensibility. — N. INSENSIBILITY, physical insensibility; obtuseness &c. *adj.;* palsy, paralysis, anæsthesia *or* anesthesia, narcosis, narcotization, hypnosis, stupor, coma; twilight sleep, *Dämmerschlaf* [*Ger.*]; sleep &c. (*inactivity*) 683; moral insensibility &c. 823; hemiplegia, motor paralysis.

ANÆSTHETIC *or* anesthetic, anæsthetic agent; local -, general- anæsthetic; opium, ether, chloroform, chloral; nitrous oxide, laughing gas; exhilarating gas, protoxide of nitrogen; cocaine, novocain; refrigeration.

V. BE INSENSIBLE &c. *adj.;* have a -thick skin, - rhinoceros hide.

RENDER INSENSIBLE &c. *adj.;* blunt, cloy, satiate, pall, obtund, benumb, numb, deaden, freeze, paralyze; anæsthetize *or* anesthetize, put under the influence of chloroform &c. *n.;* put to sleep, hypnotize, stupefy, stun.

Adj. INSENSIBLE, unfeeling, senseless, impercipient, callous, thick-skinned, pachydermatous; hard, hardened; case-hardened; proof; obtuse, dull; anæsthetic *or* anesthetic; paralytic, palsied, numb, dead.

** "a dreary numbness pains My sense, as though of hemlock I had drunk" [Keats].

377. Physical Pleasure. — N. PLEASURE; physical -, sensual -, sensuous - pleasure; bodily enjoyment, animal gratification, delight, sensual delight, hedonism, sensuality; luxuriousness &c. *adj.;* dissipation, round of pleasure; titillation, gusto, creature comforts, comfort, ease; pillow &c. (*support*) 215; luxury, lap of luxury; purple and fine linen; bed of -down. - roses; velvet.

378. Physical Pain. — N. PAIN; suffering, sufferance [*rare*]; bodily -, physical- -pain, - suffering; mental suffering &c. 828; dolor *or* dolour, ache; aching &c. *v.;* smart; shoot, shooting; twinge, twitch, gripe, hurt, cut; sore, soreness; discomfort; headache, *malaise* [*F.*], megrim, migraine, cephalalgy, cephalalgia; otalgia, earache; ischiagra, lumbago, arthritis, neuritis, gout, podagra, rheu-

clover; cup of Circe &c. (*intemperance*) 954.

TREAT; diversion, entertainment, banquet, regalement, refreshment, regale; feast; delice [*obs.*]; dainty &c. 394; *bonne bouche* [*F.*].

SOURCE OF PLEASURE &c. 829; happiness, felicity, bliss, beatitude &c. (*mental enjoyment*) 827.

V. ENJOY, pleasure [*rare*]; feel –, experience –, receive- pleasure; relish; luxuriate –, revel –, riot –, bask –, swim –, wallow- in; feast on; gloat -over, – on; smack the lips; roll under the tongue.

live on the fat of the land, live in comfort &c. *adv.;* bask in the sunshine, *faire ses choux gras* [*F.*].

GIVE PLEASURE &c. 829; charm, delight, enchant.

Adj. ENJOYING &c. *v.;* luxurious, voluptuous, sensual, comfortable, cosy, snug, in comfort, at ease, in clover [*colloq.*].

AGREEABLE &c. 829; grateful, refreshing, comforting, cordial, genial; gratifying, titillative, sensuous; apolaustic, hedonic, hedonistic, palatable &c. 394; sweet &c. (*sugar*) 396; fragrant &c. 400; melodious &c. 413; lovely &c. (*beautiful*) 845.

Adv. IN COMFORT &c. *n.;* on a bed of roses &c. *n.;* at one's ease; on flowery beds of ease.

*** *ride si sapis* [Martial]; *voluptates commendat rarior usus* [Juvenal]; "the man who finds most pleasure for himself is often the man who least hunts for it" [Chesterton].

matism, sciatica, ischialgia; neuralgia, tic douloureux, toothache, odontalgia; stiffneck, torticollis.

SPASM, cramp; nightmare, ephialtes; kink, crick, stitch; convulsion, throe; throb &c. (*agitation*) 315; pang; colic; tormina, gripes.

sharp –, piercing –, throbbing –, grinding –, stabbing –, shooting –, gnawing –, burning- pain.

TORMENT, torture, agony, anguish, lancination, rack, cruciation, crucifixion, martyrdom; vivisection.

martyr, sufferer; toad under a harrow.

V. SUFFER; feel –, experience –, suffer –, undergo- pain &c. *n.;* ache, smart, bleed; tingle, shoot; twinge, twitch, lancinate; writhe, wince, make a wry face; sit on -thorns, – pins and needles.

PAIN, give pain, inflict pain; lacerate; hurt, chafe, sting, bite, gnaw, stab, grind, gripe; pinch, tweak; grate, gall, fret, prick, pierce, wring, convulse; torment, torture; rack, agonize; crucify; cruciate [*obs.*], excruciate, break on the wheel, put to the rack; flog &c. (*punish*) 972; grate on the ear &c. (*harsh sound*) 410.

Adj. IN PAIN &c. *n.*, in a state of pain; under the harrow; pained &c. *v.;* gouty, podagric, torminous, torminal.

PAINFUL; aching &c. *v.;* poignant, pungent, torturous, baleful [*rare*], biting; with exposed nerves, sore, raw.

*** "the foundation of all our pain is unbelief" [Amiel]; "like dull narcotics numbing pain" [Tennyson]; "pain pays the income of each precious thing" [Shakespeare].

2. Special Sensation

(1) Touch

379. [SENSATION OF PRESSURE.] **Touch.** — **N.** TOUCH; tact, taction, tactility; contact, tangency, tangence [*rare*], impact, attaint [*archaic*]; feeling, kiss, osculation, graze, glance, brush; lick, licking, lambency, palpation, palpability; contrectation [*rare*]; manipulation, palmation [*obs.*], contaction [*obs.*]; stereognosis; rubbing, kneading, massage.

[ORGAN OF TOUCH] hand, palm, finger, forefinger, thumb, paw, feeler, antenna; tongue, palpus.

V. TOUCH, feel, handle, finger, thumb, paw, fumble, grope, grabble; twiddle, tweedle [*obs. or dial.*]; pass –, run- the fingers over; stroke, palpate, palm, massage, rub, knead, manipulate, wield; throw out a feeler.

Adj. TACTUAL, tactile; tangible, palpable, tangent, contactual [*rare*], lambent; touching &c. *v.;* stereognostic.

380. Sensations of Touch. — N.
ITCHING &c. *v.;* formication; aura [*med.*].
TICKLING, titillation.

ITCH, scabies, psora, pruritus, prurigo
[*all med.*]; mange.

V. ITCH, tingle, creep, thrill, sting;
prick, prickle.
TICKLE, titillate.

Adj. ITCHING, tingling &c. *v.*
TICKLISH, titillative.

ITCHY, psoric, scabious, mangy;
creepy, crawly; prurient.

381. [INSENSIBILITY TO TOUCH.]
Numbness. — N. NUMBNESS &c. (*physical insensibility*) 376; anæsthesia *or*
anesthesia, narcosis, narcotization; pins
and needles [*colloq.*].

V. BENUMB &c. 376; stupefy, narcotize,
drug, deaden, paralyze.

Adj. NUMB; benumbed &c. *v.;* insensible, unfeeling, anæsthetic *or* anesthetic, deadened; intangible, impalpable; dazed, dazy [*rare*], comatose, torporific, narcotic, carotic.

(2) Heat

382. Heat. — N. HEAT, caloric; temperature, warmth, fervor, calidity [*obs.*],
torridity; incalescence *or* incalescency
[*rare*], incandescence; recalescence, decalescence; adiathermancy, athermancy,
diathermacy, diathermance *or* diathermancy *or* diathermaneity; phlogiston
[*old chem.*], phlogisis; thermogenesis;
liquation.

summer, dog days, canicule, canicular
days; baking &c. 384 –, white –, tropical
–, Afric –, Indian –, Bengal –, summer
–, blood- heat; sirocco, simoom *or*
simoon, hot wave, sun at noon, "the
bloody Sun, at noon" [Coleridge], vertical rays, broiling sun; insolation; warming &c. 384.

FLUSH, glow, blush, bloom, redness;
rubicundity; fever, hectic; febricity,
pyrexia.

FIRE, spark, scintillation, flash, flame,
blaze; bonfire; firework, pyrotechny;
wildfire; sheet of fire, lambent flame;
devouring element; pyrotechnics.

sun &c. (*luminary*) 423.

HOT SPRINGS, geysers; thermæ, hot
baths; Turkish –, electric –, Russian-
bath; steam.

FIRE WORSHIP, pyrolatry, sun worship, heliolatry, Sabæanism *or* Sabeanism
or Sabeism, Parsiism *or* Parseeism,
Zoroastrianism; pyrolator, heliolator,
Sabæan *or* Sabean, Parsi *or* Parsee,
Zoroastrian.

[SCIENCE OF HEAT] pyrology; thermology, thermotics; thermometer &c.
389.

V. BE HOT &c. *adj.;* glow, flush,
sweat, swelter, bask, smoke, reek, stew,
simmer, seethe, boil, burn, singe, scorch,
scald, grill, broil, blaze, flame; smolder
or smoulder; parch, fume, pant.

383. Cold. — N. COLD, coldness &c.
adj.; frigidity, gelidity, algidity, glaciation, gelidness [*rare*], frore [*poetic*], inclemency, fresco [*obs.*]; "a hard, dull
bitterness of cold" [Whittier].

winter; depth of –, hard- winter;
Siberia, Nova Zembla; Arctic, North
Pole; Antarctic, South Pole.

ICE; sleet; hail, hailstone; frost, rime,
hoarfrost; rime –, white –, hard –, black
–, sharp- frost; barf [*Hind.*], glaze [*U. S.*],
lolly [*N. Amer.*]; icicle, thick-ribbed ice;
iceberg, floe, berg, ice field, ice float *or*
ice floe, ice pack, glacier; nevé [*F.*],
sérac [*F.*]; pruina [*L. & It.*]; icequake.

SNOW, snowflake, snowdrift, fall of
snow, snowstorm, heavy fall; snowball,
snowslide, snowslip, snow avalanche.

[SENSATION OF COLD] chilliness &c.
adj.; chill; shivering &c. *v.;* goose flesh,
goose skin, rigor, horripilation, aching,
ache, chilblains, frostbite, chattering of
teeth.

V. BE COLD &c. *adj.;* shiver, starve
[*rare in U. S.*], quake, shake, tremble,
shudder, didder, quiver; perish with
cold; chill &c. (*render cold*) 385; horripilate, glaciate [*obs.*].

Adj. COLD, cool; chill, chilly; gelid,
frigid, frore [*poet.*], algid; fresh, keen,
bleak, raw, inclement, bitter, biting,
cutting, nipping, piercing, pinching;
clay-cold; starved &c. (*made cold*) 385;
shivering &c. *v.;* aguish, transi de froid
[*F.*], frostbitten, frost-bound, frost-
nipped.

cold as – a stone, – marble, – lead, –
iron, – a frog, – charity, – Christmas;
cool as -a cucumber, – custard.

ICY, glacial, ice-built, frosty, freezing,
wintry, brumal, hibernal, boreal, arctic,
Siberian, hiemal *or* hyemal; hyper-

HEAT &c. (*make hot*) 384; insolate, incandesce, recalesce.

THAW, fuse, melt, liquate, liquefy; give.

Adj. WARM, mild, genial, tepid, lukewarm, unfrozen; calid; warm as -toast, -wool.

HOT, heated, fervid, fervent; roasting, sweltry; reeking &c. *v.;* ardent, aglow; baking &c. 384; sunny, sunshiny, æstival *or* estival, canicular, torrid, tropical; thermal, thermic; calorific.

red -, white -, smoking -, burning &c. *v.* -, piping- hot; like -a furnace, - an oven; hot as -fire, - pepper; hot enough to roast an ox.

CLOSE, sultry, stifling, stuffy, suffocating, oppressive.

FIERY; incandescent, incalescent [*rare*]; candent, ebullient, glowing, smoking; live; on fire; blazing &c. *v.;* in flames, in a blaze; alight, afire, ablaze; unquenched; unextinguished; smoldering *or* smouldering; in a -heat, - glow, - perspiration, -sweat; sudorific; sweltering, sweltered; blood-hot, blood-warm; recalescent, decalescent, thermogenic, thermogenous, thermogenetic, thermotic *or* thermotical; pyrotechnic *or* pyrotechnical; phlogotic *or* phlogistic; pyrological.

[TRANSMITTING RADIANT HEAT] diathermic, diathermal, diathermanous.

[NOT TRANSMITTING RADIANT HEAT] athermanous, adiathermal, adiathermanous, adiathermic.

VOLCANIC, plutonic, igneous.

ISOTHERMAL, isothermic, isothermical.

FEVERISH, febrile, febricose [*rare*], febrific, febrifacient, pyretic, pyrexic [*rare*], inflamed, burning; in a fever.

** not a breath of air; "whirlwinds of tempestuous fire" [*P. L.*]; "the land where every weed is flaming and only man is black" [Chesterton].

borean, hyperborean [*rare*]; snow-bound, ice-bound; frozen out.

UNWARMED, unheated; unthawed.

LUKEWARM, tepid; warm &c. *adj.* 382.

ISOCHEIMAL, isocheimenal, isocheimic.

Adv. COLDLY, bitterly &c. *adj.; à pierre fendre* [*F.*]; with chattering teeth.

** "Ho! why dost thou shiver and shake, Gaffer Guy?" [Holcroft]; "Marian's nose looks red and raw" [*L. L. L.*].

---

384. Calefaction. — N. CALEFACTION, tepefaction, torrefaction; increase of temperature; heating &c. *v.;* melting, fusion; liquefaction &c. 335; burning &c. *v.;* combustion; incension [*obs.*], accension [*archaic*]; concremation, cremation; scorification; cautery, cauterization; ustulation [*rare*], calcination; incineration; carbonization; cupellation.

IGNITION, kindling, inflammation, adustion [*rare*], flagration [*obs.*], deflagration, conflagration; empyrosis, incendiarism; arson; *auto-da-fé* [*Pg.*], *auto-de-fe* [*Sp.*], the stake, burning at the stake; suttee.

INCENDIARY, arsonist, arsonite, *pétroleur* (*fem. pétroleuse*) [*F.*], pyromaniac, fire bug [*U. S.*].

BOILING &c. *v.;* coction, ebullition, ebullience *or* ebulliency, æstuation *or* estuation, elixation [*obs.*], decoction; ebullioscope, ebulliometer; hot spring, geyser.

385. Refrigeration. — N. REFRIGERATION, infrigidation, reduction of temperature; cooling &c. *v.;* congelation, conglaciation [*obs.*], glaciation, regelation; ice &c. 383; solidification &c. (*density*),321; ice box, ice chest; refrigerator &c. 387.

FIRE-EXTINGUISHER, *extincteur* [*F.*]; fire annihilator; amianthus, amianth, earth flax, mountain flax; asbestos, flexible asbestos; fireman, fire brigade, fire department, fire engine.

incombustibility, incombustibleness &c. *adj.*

V. COOL, fan, refrigerate, infrigidate, refresh, ice; congeal, freeze, glaciate; benumb, starve [*rare in U. S.*], pinch, chill, petrify, chill to the marrow, regelate, nip, cut, pierce, bite, make one's teeth chatter.

DAMP, slack; quench; put out, stamp out; extinguish.

go out, burn out, die.

CREMATORY, crematorium, burning ghat [*India*], incinerator, calcinatory; cupel; furnace &c. 386.

WRAP, blanket, flannel, wool, fur; muff, mittens, wristers; muffler, fascinator, comforter [*U. S.*], comfortable; ear-muffs, ear-flaps; shawl; wadding &c. (*lining*) 224; clothing &c. 225.

CAUTERANT, scorifier; match &c. (*fuel*) 388; caustic, lunar caustic, apozem, moxa; aqua fortis, aqua regia; catheretic, nitric acid, nitrochlorohydric acid, nitromuriatic acid, radium.

SUNSTROKE, *coup de soleil* [*F.*]; insolation [*rare*], siriasis, [*med.*]; sunburn, burn, ambustion [*rare*].

POTTERY, ceramics, crockery, porcelain, china; earthenware, stoneware; pot, mug, terra cotta, brick.

[PRODUCTS OF COMBUSTION] cinder, ash, scoriæ; embers, slag, clinker, coke, carbon, charcoal.

INFLAMMABILITY, combustibility, accendibility.

[TRANSMISSION OF HEAT] diathermance *or* diathermancy &c. 382; transcalency.

V. HEAT, warm, chafe, foment; make hot &c. 382; sun oneself, bask in the sun.

FIRE, set fire to, set on fire; kindle, enkindle, light, ignite, strike a light; apply the -match, – torch- to; rekindle, relume; fan –, add fuel to- the flame; poke –, stir –, blow- the fire; make a bonfire of; build a campfire.

MELT, thaw, fuse; liquefy &c. 335.

BURN, inflame, roast, toast, fry, grill, singe, parch, bake, torrefy, scorch; brand, cauterize, sear, burn in; corrode, char, carbonize, calcine, incinerate, calefy, calcinate [*rare*], tepefy, cupel, cupellate [*rare*], deflagrate [*chem.*]; smelt, scorify; reduce to ashes; burn to a cinder; commit –, consign- to the flames.

take –, catch- fire; blaze &c. (*flame*) 382.

BOIL, digest, stew, cook, seethe, ebullate [*rare*], scald, parboil, simmer; do to rags [*colloq.*].

Adj. HEATED &c. v.; molten, sodden; *réchauffé* [*F.*]; heating &c. v.; adust; ambustial [*rare*], calefactive, deflagrable [*chem.*], ustulate; calcinatory, cauterant; æstuous [*rare*] apozemial, scoriaceous; transcalent; burnt &c. v.; volcanic.

INFLAMMABLE, burnable, inflammatory, accendible, combustible.

DIATHERMIC, diathermal, diathermanous.

radioactive; salamandrine.

Adj. COOLED &c. *v.;* frozen out; cooling &c. *v.;* frigorific, infrigidative [*rare*], refrigerative [*rare*].

INCOMBUSTIBLE, asbestic, unflammable, uninflammable; fireproof; amianthine, amianthoid *or* amianthoidal.

---

386. Furnace. — N. FURNACE, stove; air-tight –, Franklin –, Dutch –, gas –, oil –, electric- stove; cookstove, cooker, oven, brick oven, tin oven, Dutch oven, range, kitchener [*Eng.*]; fireless- heater, – cooker; forge, fiery furnace; kiln, brickkiln, limekiln; tuyère, brasier, salamander, heater, warming pan, foot-stove, foot-warmer; radiator, register,

387. Refrigeratory. — N. REFRIGERATORY, refrigerator; frigidarium; cold storage; ice –, freezing –, refrigerating-machine; refrigerating plant; icehouse, ice pail, ice bag, ice box, ice chest, ice pack, cold pack; cooler, wine cooler.

REFRIGERANT, freezing mixture, ice, ammonia.

---

coil; boiler, caldron, seething caldron, pot; urn, kettle, frying-pan, stew-pan, spider, broiler, skillet, tripod, chafing-dish; retort, crucible, alembic, still; waffle irons; flatiron, sadiron; curling tongs; toasting fork, toaster.

galley, caboose *or* camboose; hothouse, conservatory, bakehouse, washhouse, laundry; athanor, hypocaust, reverberatory; volcano.

FIREPLACE, hearth, grate, firebox, andiron, firedog, fire-irons; poker, tongs, shovel, hob, trivet; damper, crane, pothooks, chains, turnspit, spit, gridiron.

HOT BATH; thermæ, calidarium, tepidarium, vaporarium, sudatorium [*all L.*]; sudatory; Turkish –, Russian – vapor –, electric –, sitz –, hip –, shower –, warm - bath; tub, lavatory.

388. Fuel. — N. FUEL, firing, combustible, coal, wallsend [*Eng.*], anthracite, blind coal, glance coal; bituminous –, egg –, stove –, nut –, pea- coal; culm, coke, carbon, briquette, slack, cannel coal *or* cannel, lignite, charcoal; turf, peat; oil, gas, natural gas, electricity; ember, cinder &c. (*products of combustion*) 384; ingle; portfire; fire-barrel, fireball, firebrand.

LOG, backlog, yule log *or* yule clog, firewood, fagot *or* faggot, kindling wood, kindlings, brushwood, bavin [*dial. Eng.*].

TINDER, touchwood; punk, German tinder, amadou; smudge [*U. S. & Can.*], pyrotechnic sponge.

FUMIGATOR, incense, joss-stick; sulphur, brimstone, disinfectant.

[ILLUMINANTS] candle &c. (*luminary*) 423; oil &c. (*grease*) 356.

brand, torch, fuse *or* fuze, wick; spill, match, safety match, lights [*chiefly Eng.*], light, lucifer, congreve, vesuvian, vesta, fusee *or* fuzee, locofoco [*obs., U. S.*], linstock [*obs. or hist.*].

V. coal, stoke; feed, fire &c. 384.

Adj. carbonaceous; combustible, inflammable; slow-burning, free-burning.

389. Thermometer. — N. THERMOMETER, thermometrograph, thermopile, thermostat, thermoscope; differential thermometer, telethermometer, pyrometer, calorimeter, radiomicrometer.

(3) Taste

390. Taste. — N. TASTE, flavor, gust [*archaic*], gusto, savor; *goût* [*F.*], relish; sapor [*obs.*], sapidity; twang [*dial. Eng.*], smack, smatch [*dial. Eng.*]; aftertaste, tang.

TASTING; degustation, gustation.

palate; tongue; tooth; stomach.

V. TASTE, savor, smatch [*dial. Eng.*], smack, flavor; tickle the palate &c. (*savory*) 394; smack the lips.

391. Insipidity. — N. INSIPIDITY; tastelessness &c. *adj.;* jejuneness.

V. BE TASTELESS &c. *adj.*

Adj. INSIPID; void of taste &c. 390; tasteless, gustless [*obs.*], unsavory, unflavored, jejune, savorless; ingustible [*obs.*], mawkish, milk and water, weak, stale, flat, vapid, *fade* [*F.*], wishy-washy [*colloq.*], mild; untasted.

Adj. SAPID, saporific, gustable, gustatory, gustative, tastable, savory, gustful, tasty; strong; flavored, spiced, tanged [*obs.*]; palatable &c. 394.

** "behold this cordial julep here, That flames and dances in his crystal bounds, With spirits of balmy fragrant syrups_mixed" [Milton].

392. Pungency. — N. PUNGENCY, piquancy, poignancy, *haut-goût* [*F.*], acrity [*obs.*], strong taste, twang [*dial. Eng.*], race, tang, nip, kick [*slang*].

SHARPNESS &c. *adj.;* acrimony, acridity; roughness &c. (*sour*) 392; unsavoriness &c. 395.

[PUNGENT ARTICLES] niter, saltpeter; mustard, cayenne, caviare; seasoning &c. (*condiment*) 393; brine; carbonate of ammonia; sal-ammoniac, sal-volatile; smelling salts; hartshorn.

DRAM, cordial, nip, toothful [*colloq.*], tickler [*colloq.*], bracer [*colloq.*], pick-me-up [*colloq.*], potion, liqueur, *pousse-café* [*F.*].

TOBACCO, Lady Nicotine, Nicotiana, nicotian [*rare*], nicotine; snuff, quid; cigar *or* segar, cigarette, fag [*slang*], cheroot, Trichinopoli cheroot, Trichi [*colloq.*], Havana *or* Habana [*Sp.*], Cuban tobacco; weed [*colloq.*]; fragrant –, Indianweed; Cavendish, fid [*dial.*], niggerhead *or* negro head, rappee, stogy, old soldier [*slang*].

V. BE PUNGENT &c. *adj.;* bite the tongue.

RENDER PUNGENT &c. *adj.;* season, spice, bespice, salt, pepper, pickle, brine, devil, curry.

USE TOBACCO, smoke, chew, inhale, take snuff.

Adj. PUNGENT, strong; high-flavored, full-flavored; high-tasted, high-seasoned; gamy, high; sharp, stinging, rough, piquant, racy; biting, mordant; spicy;

seasoned &c. *v.;* hot, – as pepper; peppery vellicative, vellicating, escharotic, meracious [*obs.*]; acrid, acrimonious, bitter; rough &c. (*sour*) 397; unsavory &c. 395.

SALT, saline, brackish, briny; salt as -brine, – a herring, – Lot's wife.

. "For thy sake, tobacco, I Would do anything but die" [Lamb]; "the man who smokes thinks like a sage and acts like a Samaritan" [Lytton]; "to win the secret of a weed's plain heart" [Lowell]; "Heaven's last, best gift, my ever new delight" [*P. L.*]; "divine in hookas, glorious in a pipe" [Byron]; "come, look not pale! observe *me!*" [B. Jonson]; "O thou weed, Who art so lovely fair and smell'st so sweet" [*Othello*]; "sweet to the world and grateful to the skies" [Pope].

393. Condiment. — N. CONDIMENT, flavoring, salt, mustard, pepper, cayenne, cinnamon, nutmeg, curry, seasoning, sauce, spice, relish, *sauce piquante* [*F.*], *sauce tartare* [*F.*], caviare, pot herbs, onion, sauce-alone, hedge garlic, garlic, pickle; achar [*Hind.*], allspice, appetizer; bell –, Jamaica –, red- pepper; horse-radish, capsicum, chutney, tabasco sauce *or* tabasco; cubeb, pimento.

V. SEASON &c. (*render pungent*) 392.

. "Stewed in brine, smarting in lingering pickle" [*Antony and Cleopatra*]; "'tis the sour sauce to the sweet meat" [Dryden]; "spiced dainties, every one, From silken Samarcand to cedar'd Lebanon" [Keats].

394. Savoriness. — N. SAVORINESS &c. *adj.;* nectareousness; relish, zest.

APPETIZER, *apéritif* [*F.*], *hors d'œuvre* [*F.*]

DELICACY, titbit, dainty, ambrosia, nectar, delice [*obs.*], *bonne-bouche* [*F.*]; game, turtle, venison; delicatessen.

V. BE SAVORY &c. *adj.;* tickle the -palate, – appetite; tempt the appetite, taste good, taste of something; flatter the palate.

render palatable &c. *adj.*

relish, like, smack the lips.

Adj. SAVORY, to one's taste, tasty, good, palatable, good-tasting, pleasing, nice, dainty, delectable; toothful [*obs.*], toothsome; gustful, appetizing, lickerish *or* liquorish [*rare*], delicate, delicious, exquisite, rich, luscious, ambrosial, ambroisan, nectareous, distinctive.

Adv. *per amusare la bocca* [*It.*].

. *cela se laisse manger;* "lickerish baits, fit to ensnare a brute" [Milton].

395. Unsavoriness. — N. UNSAVORINESS &c. *adj.;* amaritude [*rare*], acrimony, acritude [*obs.*], acridity, acridness, roughness &c. (*sour*) 397; acerbity, austerity.

gall and wormwood, rue, quassia, aloes, asafetida *or* asafœtida; hemlock; sickener; Marah.

V. BE UNPALATABLE &c. *adj.;* sicken, disgust, nauseate, pall, turn the stomach.

Adj. UNSAVORY, unpalatable, unsweet; ill-flavored; bitter, bitter as gall; amarulent [*obs.*], acrid, acrimonious; rough.

OFFENSIVE, repulsive, nasty; sickening &c. *v.;* nauseous; loathsome, fulsome; unpleasant &c. 830.

. "it's a strong stomach that has no turning" [*Cynic's Calendar*].

396. Sweetness. — N. SWEETNESS, dulcitude, saccharinity.

SUGAR, saccharin *or* saccharine, saccharose, crystallose; cane –, beet –, loaf –, lump –, granulated- sugar.

preserve, conserve, confiture [*obs.*], jam, julep; sugar candy, sugarplum; marmalade.

SWEETS, confectionery, caramel, lolly [*colloq.*], lollipop, bonbon, licorice, jujube, comfit, sweetmeat, confection, confectionery; honey, manna; apple butter, glucose, sucrose, dulcin [*chem.*],

397. Sourness. — N. SOURNESS &c, *adj.;* acid, acetosity, acerbity, acidity. subacidity; acescence *or* acescency; acetous fermentation.

[SOUR ARTICLES] vinegar, acetum, tartar, verjuice, crab, alum; acetic acid; lime, lemon, crab apple, chokeberry, chokecherry; unripe –, green fruit.

V. BE SOUR, turn sour &c. *adj.;* set the teeth on edge.

RENDER SOUR &c. *adj.;* acidify, acidulate, acetify, acetize [*are*], tartarize. ferment.

149

dulcite [*chem.*]; sirup *or* syrup, treacle, molasses, maple sirup *or* syrup, maple sugar; *mithai* [*India*], sorghum, taffy, butterscotch.

[Sweet beverages] nectar; hydromel, mead, metheglin, liqueur, sweet wine, *eau sucrée* [*F.*].

PASTRY, cake, pie, tart, puff, pudding.

DULCIFICATION, dulcoration [*obs.*], saccharification, saccharization, edulcoration.

V. BE SWEET &c. *adj.*

RENDER SWEET &c. *adj.;* sweeten, sugar, saccharize, saccharify, sugar off [*local, U. S. & Can.*]; edulcorate; dulcorate [*obs.*], dulcify [*obs.*]; candy; mull.

Adj. SWEET, sugary, saccharine, sacchariferous, saccharoid *or* saccharoidal; dulcet, candied, honied, luscious, cloying, honey-sweet, nectarious [*rare*], nectareous, nectareal, nectarous, nectarean, nectarian; melliferous; sweetened &c. *v.* sweet as -sugar, – honey.

⁎ "sweets to the sweet" [*Hamlet*]; "the daintiest last to make the end most sweet" [*Richard II*]; "lucent syrops, tinct with cinnamon" [Keats]; "a wilderness of sweets" [*P. L.*].

Adj. SOUR; acid, acidulous, acidulated; tart, crab, crabbed; acetous, acetose, acerb, acetic; sour as vinegar, sourish; acescent, subacid; hard, rough, unripe, green; astringent, styptic.

⁎ "Every white will have its blacke, And every sweet its soure" [Percy].

---

(4) *Odor*

398. Odor. — N. ODOR *or* odour, smell, odorament [*obs.*], scent, effluvium; emanation, exhalation; fume, essence, trail, nidor [*obs.*], redolence.

SCENT; sense of smell; act of smelling &c. *v.;* olfaction, olfactories.

V. HAVE AN ODOR &c. *n.;* smell, – of, – strong of; exhale, effluviate [*rare*]; give out a smell &c. *n.;* scent.

SMELL, scent; snuff, – up; sniff, nose, inhale.

Adj. ODOROUS, odorant [*rare*], odoriferous; smelling, strong-scented, effluvious, redolent, nidorous, pungent.

[RELATING TO THE SENSE OF SMELL] olfactory, olfactive, olfactible *or* olfactable; quick-scented.

⁎ "Sabean odours from the spicy shore Of Araby the Blest" [Milton]; "Smells are surer than sounds or sights To make your heart-strings crack" [Kipling].

---

399. Inodorousness. — N. INODOROUSNESS; absence –, want- of smell.

deodorization; deodorizer, deodorant.

V. BE INODOROUS &c. *adj.;* not smell. deodorize.

Adj. INODOROUS, inodorate [*obs.*], scentless; without –, wanting- smell &c. 398. deodorized, deodorizing.

---

400. Fragrance. — N. FRAGRANCE, aroma, redolence, incensation, thurification [*rare*], perfume, bouquet; sweet smell, sweet odor *or* odour, aromatic perfume, scent.

[COMPARISONS] agalloch *or* agallochum, agal-wood, eaglewood, aloes wood, sandalwood, cedar, champak, calambac *or* calambour, lign-aloes, linaloa; bayberry, bay leaf, balsam, fir balsam; wild clove, wild cinnamon, Jamaica bayberry, oil of myrcia, bay rum; horehound, Marrubium, mint, musk root, muskrat, napha water, olibanum.

PERFUMERY; incense, frankincense; musk, pastil *or* pastille; myrrh, perfumes of Arabia; attar *or* ottar *or* otto; bergamot, balm, civet, potpourri, pulvil [*obs.*]; tuberose, hyacinth, heliotrope, rose, jasmine, lily, lily of the valley, violet,

150

---

401. Fetor. — N. FETOR *or* fœtor; bad &c. *adj.* -smell, – odor *or* odour; stench, stink; foul odor, malodor *or* malodour, fetidness, mephitis, empyreuma; fustiness, mustiness &c. *adj.;* rancidity, reastiness *or* reasiness [*dial. Eng.*]; foulness &c. (*uncleanness*) 653.

[COMPARISONS] stoat, polecat, skunk, zoril; foumart *or* foulmart, fitchew, fitchet, peccary; asafetida *or* assafœtida; fungus, garlic, onion, leek, skunk cabbage; stinkpot, stinkball, stinker, stinkhorn, stinkbush, stinkstone, stinkweed, stinkwood.

V. HAVE A BAD SMELL &c. *n.;* smell, empyreumatize; stink, – in the nostrils, – like a polecat; smell strong &c. *adj.*, smell to heaven, stench [*obs.*], smell offensively.

Adj. FETID; strong-smelling; high,

arbutus, carnation, sweet pea, sweet grass, new-mown hay, lilac; pomade, pomatum, pomander, toilet water; *eau de cologne* [*F.*], cologne, cologne water.

BOUQUET, nosegay, posy [*archaic or colloq.*], boughpot or bowpot; *boutonnière* [*F.*], buttonhole [*colloq.*].

spray; wreath, garland, chaplet.

[SCENT CONTAINERS] smelling bottle, scent bottle, vinaigrette; scent bag, sachet; thurible, censer, incense burner, incensorium, incensory; atomizer, spray.

PERFUMER, *parfumeur* [*F.*]; thurifer.

V. BE FRAGRANT &c. *adj.;* have a perfume &c. *n.;* smell sweet, scent, perfume; embalm.

INCENSE, cense, thurificate, thurify [*rare*]; aromatize.

Adj. FRAGRANT, aromatic, redolent, spicy, balmy, scented; sweet-smelling, sweet-scented; perfumed, perfumatory [*rare*], perfumy, incense-breathing, thuriferous; fragrant –, sweet- as a rose, muscadine, ambrosial.

.*.* "a steam of rich-distilled perfumes" [Milton]; "die of a rose in aromatic pain" [Pope].

bad, strong, fulsome, offensive, gravelolent, noisome, rank, rancid, reasty or reasy [*dial. Eng.*], moldy or mouldy, tainted, musty, frowsty [*dial. Eng.*], fusty, frowsy or frouzy; olid, olidous [*obs.*]; nidorous [*rare*], smelling, stinking; putrid &c. 653; suffocating, mephitic; empyreumatic or empyreumatical.

---

(5) Sound

(i) SOUND IN GENERAL

402. Sound. — N. SOUND, noise; sonority, sonorosity [*obs.*], sonification, strain; accent, twang, intonation, tune, cadence; sonorescence, sonorousness &c. *adj.;* audibility; resonance &c. 408; voice &c. 580; phonation; aspirate; phonogram, ideophone; rough breathing.

[SCIENCE OF SOUND] acoustics, acoumetry, diacoustics, catacoustics, diaphonics, cataphonics, polycoustics, phonics, phonetics, phonology, phonography; telephony, radiophony, photophony; polyphony, homophony; phonetism; acoustician.

V. PRODUCE SOUND; sound, make a noise; give out sound, emit sound; phonate, consonate [*rare*], resound &c. 408.

PHONETICIZE, phonetize [*rare*].

Adj. SOUNDING; soniferous; sonorous, sonorescent; sonorific [*rare*]; sonorant, sonoric; resonant, audible, distinct; auditory, acoustic, acoustical, diacoustic, polycoustic; stertorous, ear-splitting.

PHONIC, phonetic; homophonic or homophonous (*opp. to* polyphonic); monodic, monophonic; sonant; ideophonous; phonocamptic [*rare*].

.*.* "a thousand trills and quivering sounds" [Addison]; *forensis strepitus;* "sing With notes angelical, to many a harp" [Milton]; "with the sound Of dulcet symphonies and voices sweet" [Milton]; "the trembling notes ascend the sky" [Dryden]; "beauty born of murmuring sound" [Wordsworth].

403. Silence. — N. SILENCE; stillness &c. (*quiet*) 265; peace, hush, lull; rest [*music*]; muteness &c. 581; solemn –, awful –, dead –, deathlike- silence; silence of the -tomb, – grave.

V. BE SILENT &c. *adj.;* hold one's tongue &c. (*not speak*) 585; whist [*dial. Eng.*].

RENDER SILENT &c. *adj.;* silence, still, hush; stifle, muffle, gag, stop; muzzle, put to silence &c. (*render mute*) 581.

Adj. SILENT; still, stilly; noiseless, quiet, calm, hush [*archaic*], echoless, speechless, soundless; hushed &c. *v.;* aphonic, surd, mute &c. 581.

SOLEMN, soft, awful, deathlike; silent as the -tomb, – grave; inaudible &c. (*faint*) 405.

Adv. SILENTLY &c. *adj.; sub silentio* [*L.*]; in –, in dead –, in perfect- silence.

Int. HUSH! silence! soft! whist! mum! sh! chut! tut! *pax!* [*L.*], *tais-toi!* [*F.*], hold your tongue! shut up! [*colloq.*], be quiet! be silent! be still! *chup!* [*Hind.*], *chup rao!* [*Hind.*], *tace!* [*L.*].

.*.* one might hear a -feather, – pin- drop; *grosse Seelen dulden still; le silence est la vertu de ceux qui ne sont pas sages; le silence est le parti le plus sûr de celui qui se défie de soi-même;* "silence more musical than any song" [C. G. Rossetti]; *tacent satis laudant;* "Silence, like a poultice comes To heal the blows of sound" [Holmes]; "quiet as a nun Breathless with adoration [Wordsworth]; "its grand orchestral silences" [E. B. Browning]; "thunders of white silence" [*ibid.*].

404. Loudness. — N. LOUDNESS, power; vociferation, uproariousness.

DIN, loud noise, clang, clangor, clatter, noise, bombilation, roar, uproar, racket, clutter, hullabaloo, pandemonium, hell let loose; outcry &c. 411; hubbub; explosion, detonation; bobbery, fracas, charivari.

BLARE, trumpet blast, flourish of trumpets, fanfare, tintamarre [*archaic*]; blast; peal, swell, larum [*archaic*], alarum, boom; resonance &c. 408.

lungs; stentor; megaphone; calliope, steam siren, steam whistle; watchman's rattle.

[COMPARISONS] artillery, cannon, guns, bombs, shells, barrage; thunder.

V. BE LOUD &c. *adj.;* peal, swell, clang, boom, thunder, fulminate, bombilate [*rare*], roar; resound &c. 408; speak up, shout &c. (*vociferate*) 411; bellow &c. (*cry as an animal*) 412.

CLATTER, clutter, racket, uproar [*rare*].

REND THE AIR, rend the skies; fill the air; din –, ring –, thunder- in the ear; pierce –, split –, rend- the -ears, – head; deafen, stun; *faire le diable à quatre* [*F.*]; make one's windows shake; awake the echoes, startle the echoes; give tongue.

Adj. LOUD, sonorous; high-sounding, big-sounding; deep, full, powerful, noisy, blatant, clangorous, multisonous; thundering, deafening &c. *v.;* trumpet-tongued; ear-splitting, ear-rending, ear-deafening; piercing; shrill &c. 410; obstreperous, rackety, uproarious; enough to wake the -dead, – seven sleepers; clamorous &c. (*vociferous*) 411;

Adv. LOUDLY &c. *adj.;* aloud; with – voice; lustily, in full cry.

****** the air rings with; "the deep dread-bolted thunder" [*Lear*]; "on their hinges grate Harsh thunder" [Milton]; "The trumpet's loud clangor excites us to arms" [Dryden].

405. Faintness. — N. FAINTNESS &c. *adj.;* faint sound, whisper, breath; undertone, underbreath; murmur, hum, buzz, purr, lap [*of waves*], plash; sough, moan, rustle, susurration [*rare*], tinkle; "still small voice."

HOARSENESS &c. *adj.*

SILENCER, muffler; soft pedal, damper; mute, *sordino* [*It.*], sordine [*all music*].

V. WHISPER, breathe; mutter &c. (*speak imperfectly*) 583; susurrate [*rare*].

MURMUR, purl, hum, gurgle, ripple, babble, flow; rustle, tinkle.

steal on the ear, melt in the air, float on the air.

MUFFLE, deaden, mute, subdue.

Adj. FAINT, scarcely –, barely –, just-audible; low, dull; stifled, muffled; inaudible; hoarse, husky; gentle, soft; floating; purling, flowing &c. *v.;* muttered; whispered &c. *v.;* liquid; soothing; dulcet &c. (*melodious*) 413; susurrant [*rare*], susurrous [*rare*].

Adv. IN A WHISPER, with bated breath, *sotto voce* [*It.*], between the teeth, aside; piano, pianissimo [*both music*], sordamente [*It.*], sordo [*It.*], *à la sourdine* [*F.*]; out of earshot; inaudibly &c. *adj.*

****** "the mingled notes came softened from below" [Goldsmith]; "the beetle winds His small but sullen horn" [Collins]; "A little noiseless noise among the leaves, Born of the very sigh that silence heaves" [Keats]; "'Twas whispered in heaven, 'twas muttered in hell, And echo caught faintly the sound as it fell" [Fanshawe].

stentorian, stentorophonic [*obs.*]. with one wild yell; at the top of one's -lungs, – voice.

(ii) SPECIFIC SOUNDS

406. [SUDDEN AND VIOLENT SOUNDS.] **Snap. — N.** SNAP &c. *v.;* toot, shout, yell, yap [*dial.*], yelp, bark; rapping &c. *v.*

REPORT, decrepitation, crepitation; thump, knock, clap, thud; burst, thunderclap, thunderburst, eruption, blowout [*tire*], explosion, discharge, detonation, firing, salvo, volley.

DETONATOR, bomb, gun, rifle; torpedo, squib, cracker, firecracker, popgun, rattle.

407. [REPEATED AND PROTRACTED SOUNDS.] **Roll. — N.** ROLL &c. *v.;* drumming &c. *v.;* berloque [*F.*], ululation, howl, bombilation, bombination, rumbling; dingdong; tantara, rataplan, ratatat, rubadub, tattoo; pitapat; quaver, clutter, brustle [*dial.*], charivari, racket; cuckoo; repetition &c. 104; peal of bells, devil's tattoo; drum fire, barrage; whirr, rattle, drone; reverberation &c. 408.

V. ROLL, drum, rataplan, boom; whirr,

V. SNAP, rap, tap, knock; click; clash; crack, crackle; crash; pop; slam, bang, clap; thump, toot, yap [*dial.*], yelp, bark, fire, explode, rattle, burst on the ear; crepitate, flump.

Adj. rapping &c. *v.;* crepitant.

Adv. SLAP-BANG *or* slam-bang [*colloq.*], bang [*colloq.*].

Int. BANG! crash!

rustle, tootle, clutter, roar, drone, rumble, rattle, clatter, patter, clack; bombinate, bombilate [*rare*].

hum, trill, shake; chime, peal, toll; tick, beat.

DRUM IN THE EAR, din in the ear.

Adj. ROLLING, &c. *v.;* monotonous &c. (*repeated*) 104; like a bee in a bottle.

*** "The double double double beat Of the thundering drum" [Dryden].

408. Resonance. — N. RESONANCE; ring &c. *v.;* ringing &c. *v.;* reflection *or* reflexion; clangor, bell-note, tintinnabulation, vibration, reverberation.

low -, base -, bass -, flat -, grave -, deep- note; bass; *basso* [*It.*], *basso profondo* [*It.*]; barytone *or* baritone, contralto; pedal point, organ point.

V. RESOUND, reverberate, reëcho; ring, sound, jingle *or* gingle, chink, clink; tink, tinkle; chime; gurgle &c. 405; plash, guggle, echo, ring in the ear.

408a. Nonresonance. — N. NONRESONANCE; mutescence; thud, thump, dead sound; muffled drums, cracked bell; damper, *sordino* [*It.*], sordine, mute; muffler, silencer.

V. MUFFLE, deaden, mute; sound dead; stop -, damp -, deaden-, the -sound, - reverberations; use *or* employ the *sordino* [*It.*] &c. *n.*

Adj. NONRESONANT, dead, mute; muffled &c. *v.*

Adj. RESONANT, reverberant, resounding &c. *v.;* tinnient [*obs.*], tintinnabula *or* tintinnabulary; deep -toned, -sounding, -mouthed; hollow, sepulchral; gruff &c. (*harsh*) 410.

*** "as when hollow rocks retain The sound of blustering winds" [Milton]; "The tintinnabulation that so musically wells From the bells" [Poe].

409. [HISSING SOUNDS.**] Sibilation. — N.** SIBILATION; zip; hiss &c. *v.;* sternutation; high note &c. 410.

goose, serpent, snake.

V. HISS, buzz, whiz, rustle; fizz, fizzle; wheeze, whistle, snuffle; squash; sneeze; sizz [*colloq.*], sizzle, swish.

Adj. SIBILANT; hissing &c. *v.;* wheezy; sternutative.

410. [HARSH OR HIGH SOUNDS.**] Stridor. — N.** STRIDOR, harshness, roughness, sharpness &c. *adj.;* raucousness, raucity; creak &c. *v.;* creaking &c. *v.;* discord, &c. 414; cacophony; cacoëpy.

HIGH NOTE, acute note; soprano, treble, tenor, alto, falsetto; *voce di testa* [*It.*], head voice, head tone; shriek, yell; cry &c. 411.

penny trumpet, piccolo, fife, whistle; penny -, willow- whistle; Panpipes, syrinx; pipes, bagpipes, doodlesack [*Scot.*].

V. GRATE, creak, saw, snore, jar, burr, pipe, twang, jangle, clank, clink; scream &c. (*cry*) 411; yelp &c. (*animal sound*) 412; buzz &c. (*hiss*) 409.

set the teeth on edge, *écorcher les oreilles* [*F.*]; pierce -, split- the -ears, - head; offend -, grate upon -, jar upon- the ear.

Adj. GRATING, creaking &c. *v.;* stridulous, strident, harsh, coarse, hoarse, horrisonant [*obs.*], raucous, metallic, horrisonous [*obs.*], rough, rude, jangly [*rare*], gruff, grum, sepulchral, hollow.

HIGH, sharp, acute, shrill; trumpet-toned; piercing, ear-piercing, high-pitched, high-toned; cracked; discordant &c. 414; cacophonous.

*** "with impetuous recoil and jarring sound" [Milton]; "Like sweet bells jangled, out of tune and harsh" [*Hamlet*].

411. Cry. — N. CRY &c. *v.;* voice &c. (*human*) 580; view halloo, yoicks [*both hunting*]; hubbub; bark &c. (*animal*) 412.

OUTCRY, vociferation, hullabaloo, chorus, clamor *or* clamour, hue and cry, plaint; lungs; Stentor, stentor.

V. CRY, roar, shout, bawl, brawl, halloo, halloa, yo-ho, yoick, whoop *or* hoop [*rare*], yell, bellow, howl, scream, screech, screak, shriek, shrill, squeak, squeal, squall, whine, pule, pipe, yap, yaup *or* yawp.

CHEER, huzza, hurrah; hoot.

MOAN, grumble, groan.

SNORT, snore; grunt &c. (*animal sounds*) 412.

VOCIFERATE; raise –, lift up- the voice; yell out, call out, sing out, cry out; exclaim; rend the air; make the welkin ring; split the -throat, – lungs; thunder –, shout- at the -top of one's voice, – pitch of one's breath; *s'égosiller* [*F.*]; strain the -throat, – voice, – lungs; give cry; give a cry &c.; clamor *or* clamour.

Adj. CLAMANT, clamorous; crying &c. *v.;* vociferous; stentorian &c. (*loud*) 404; open-mouthed; full-mouthed.

₊ "And with no language but a cry" [Tennyson]; "A solitary shriek, the bubbling cry Of some strong swimmer in his agony" [Byron].

412. [ANIMAL SOUNDS.] **Ululation.** — N. ULULATION, howling, mugiency [*obs.*], reboation [*rare*]; cry &c. *v.;* crying &c. *v.;* call, note, howl, bark, yelp, bow-wow, latration, belling; woodnote; insect cry, twittering, fritiniancy [*obs.*], drone; cuckoo.

V. ULULATE, howl, cry, roar, bellow, blare, rebellow, latrate, bark, yelp; bay, bay the moon; yap, growl, yarr [*obs.*], yawl [*dial.*], yaup *or* yawp, snarl, howl; grunt, gruntle; snort, squeak; neigh, bray; mew, mewl, purr, caterwaul, miaow; bleat, low, moo; troat [*rare*], croak, crow, screech, caw, coo, gobble, quack, cackle, gaggle, guggle; chuck, chuckle; cluck, clack; chirp, cheep, chirrup, chirk [*obs.*], peep, sing, pule, twitter, chatter, hoot, wail, cuckoo; hum, buzz; hiss, blatter, blat [*colloq.*].

Adj. ULULANT, crying &c. *v.;* blatant, latrant, remugient [*obs.*], mugient; deep-mouthed, full-mouthed; rebellowing, reboant [*rare*].

Adv. in full cry.

₊ "I will roar you as gently as any sucking dove; I will roar you, an 'twere any nightingale" [*M. N. D.*]; "Whose household words are songs in many keys" [Longfellow]; "With bark and whoop and wild halloo" [Scott].

(iii) MUSICAL SOUNDS

413. Melody. Concord. — N. MELODY, rhythm, measure; rime *or* rhyme &c. (*poetry*) 597.

[MUSICAL TERMS] pitch, timbre, intonation, tone, overtone.

orchestration, harmonization, modulation, phrasing, temperament, syncope, syncopation, preparation, suspension, solution, resolution.

staff *or* stave, line, space, brace; bar, rest; *appoggiato* [*It.*], *appoggiatura* [*It.*]; *acciaccatura* [*It.*], trill *or* shake, turn, *arpeggio* [*It.*].

NOTE, musical note, notes of a scale; sharp, flat, natural; high note &c. (*shrillness*) 410; low note &c. 408; interval; semitone; second, third, fourth &c.; diatessaron [*ancient music*].

breve, semibreve *or* whole note, minim *or* half note, crotchet *or* quarter note, quaver *or* eighth note, semiquaver *or* sixteenth note, demisemiquaver *or* thirty-second note; sustained note, drone, bourdon, burden.

414. Discord. — N. DISCORD, discordance; dissonance, cacophony, want of harmony, caterwauling; harshness &c. 410; charivari, shivaree [*dial., U. S.*], racket; consecutive fifths.

[CONFUSED SOUNDS] Babel, pandemonium; Dutch concert, cat's concert, marrowbones and cleavers [*all colloq.*].

V. BE DISCORDANT &c. *adj.;* jar &c. (*sound harshly*) 410; shivaree [*dial., U. S.*].

Adj. DISCORDANT, dissonant, absonant; out of tune, tuneless; unmusical, untunable; immelodious, unmelodious, unharmonious, inharmonious, unsweet [*rare*], singsong; cacophonous; harsh &c. 410; jarring.

₊ "Like sweet bells jangled, out of tune and harsh" [*Hamlet*]; "chromatic tortures soon shall drive them hence" [Pope].

SCALE, gamut; diapason; diatonic –, chromatic –, enharmonic- scale; key, clef, chords.

tonic; key -, leading -, fundamental- note; supertonic, mediant, dominant; pedal point, organ point; submediant, subdominant; octave, tetrachord; Dorian *or* Doric - mode, - tetrachord; major -, minor- -mode, - scale, - key; passage, phrase.

HARMONY, concord, emmeleia; euphony, euphonism; tonality; consonance; concent [*archaic*], concentus; part.

unison, unisonance; chime, homophony.

[SCIENCE OF HARMONY] harmony, harmonics; thorough bass, fundamental bass; counterpoint; faburden [*medieval music*].

OPUS (*pl. opera*) [*L.*], piece of music &c. 415.

COMPOSER, harmonist, contrapuntist.

V. HARMONIZE, chime, symphonize, transpose, orchestrate; blend, put in tune, tune, accord, string; be harmonious &c. *adj.*

Adj. HARMONIOUS, harmonic, harmonical; in concord &c. *n.*, in tune, in concert, in unison; unisonant, concentual *or* concentuous [*rare*], symphonizing, isotonic, homophonous, assonant; ariose, consonant.

MEASURED, rhythmic *or* rhythmical, diatonic, chromatic, enharmonic.

MELODIOUS, musical; melic; tuneful, tunable; sweet, dulcet, canorous; mellow, mellifluous; soft; clear, - as a bell; silvery; euphonious, euphonic *or* euphonical, symphonious; enchanting &c. (*pleasure-giving*) 829; fine-toned, silver-toned, full-toned, deep-toned.

Adv. HARMONIOUSLY &c. *adj.*

*** "the hidden soul of harmony" [Milton]; "we did keep time, sir, in our catches" [*Twelfth Night*]; "What harmony is this? My good friends, hark!" [*Tempest*]; "music is harmony, harmony is perfection, perfection is our dream, and our dream is heaven" [Amiel]; "From Harmony, from heavenly Harmony, This universal frame began" [Dryden].

415. Music. — N. MUSIC; strain, tune, air; melody &c. 413; piece of music, *morceau* [*F.*], rondo, rondeau, *pastorale* [*It.*], pastoral, cavatina, fantasia, *toccata* [*It.*], *toccatella* [*It.*], *toccatina* [*It.*], *capriccio* [*It.*], fugue, canon; potpourri, medley, incidental music; variations, roulade, cadenza, cadence, trill; serenade, *notturno* [*It.*], nocturne; *passamezzo* [*It.*]; staff *or* stave &c. 413.

INSTRUMENTAL MUSIC; orchestral score, full score; minstrelsy, tweedledum and tweedledee [*applied by Byrom to the feuds between Handel and Bononcini*]; band, orchestra &c. 416; composition, *opus* (*pl. opera*) [*L.*], movement, concert piece, concerted piece, symphony, *concerto* [*It.*], sonata, symphonic poem, tone poem; chamber music; overture, prelude, voluntary, *Vorspiel* [*Ger.*]; string quartet *or* quartette.

LIVELY MUSIC, polka, reel &c. (*dance*) 848; ragtime, jazz; syncopation; *allegro* &c. *adv.*

SLOW MUSIC, slow movement, Lydian measures; *adagio* &c. *adv.*; minuet; siren strains, soft music; lullaby, cradle song, *berceuse* [*F.*]; dump [*obs.*]; dirge &c. (*lament*) 839; pibroch, coronach [*Scot. & Ir.*], dead march, martial music, march; waltz &c. (*dance*) 840.

VOCAL MUSIC, vocalism; chaunt [*archaic*], chant; psalm, psalmody, hymnology; hymn; song &c. (*poem*) 597; oratorio, opera, operetta; canticle, cantata, lay, ballad, ditty, carol, pastoral, recitative *or* recitativo, *aria parlante* [*It.*], aria, arietta *or* ariette, canzonet; bravura, *coloratura* [*It.*], coloratura; virtuoso music, cantabile.

solo, duet, *duo* [*It.*], trio, terzetto, quartet *or* quartette, quintet *or* quintette, sestet *or* sextet, septet, double quartet, chorus; part song, descant, glee, madrigal, catch, round, chorale; antiphon, antiphony; accompaniment; inside part, second, alto, tenor, bass; score, piano score, vocal score; burden, bourdon, drone.

CONCERT, musicale, musical [*colloq.*], recital, chamber concert, popular concert *or* pop [*colloq.*], open-air concert, serenade, *aubade* [*F.*]; community singing, singsong [*colloq.*].

METHOD, *solfeggio* [*It.*], tonic sol-fa, solmization; sight -singing, - reading; reading at sight.

COMPOSER &c. 413; MUSICIAN &c. 416.

V. COMPOSE, write, set to music, arrange &c. 416; attune.
PERFORM, execute, play &c. 416.

Adj. MUSICAL; instrumental, vocal, choral, lyric, melodic, pure, operatic; classic, modern, orchestral, symphonic, contrapuntal, program; imitative, falsetto; harmonious &c. 413; Wagnerian.

Adv. *adagio; largo, larghetto, andante, andantino; alla cappella; maestoso, moderato; allegro, allegretto; spiritoso, vivace, veloce; presto, prestissimo; con brio; capriccioso; scherzo, scherzando; legato, staccato, crescendo, diminuendo, rallentando, affettuoso; arioso, parlante, cantabile; obbligato; pizzicato; desto* [all *It.*].

∗∗ "a snapp of musique" [Pepys]; "in notes by distance made more sweet" [Collins]; "like the faint exquisite music of a dream" [Moore]; "the music arose with its voluptuous swell" [Byron]; "music is the universal language of mankind" [Longfellow]; "music's golden tongue" [Keats]; "the speech of angels" [Carlyle]; "will sing the savageness out of a bear" [*Othello*]; "music hath charms to soothe the savage breast" [Congreve]; "lap me in soft Lydian airs" [Milton]; "what a voice was here now!" [Beaumont and Fletcher]; "I am never merry when I hear sweet music" [*M. of V.*].

416. Musician. [PERFORMANCE OF MUSIC.] — **N.** MUSICIAN, *artiste* [*F.*], virtuoso, performer, player, minstrel; bard &c. (*poet*) 597; accompanist, instrumentalist, organist, pianist, violinist, tweedledee [*Scot.*], fiddler, catgut scraper [*slang*]; flutist or flautist; harpist or harper, fifer, trumpeter, cornetist, piper, drummer; accordionist.

ORCHESTRA; string -orchestra, – quartet; strings, woodwind, brass; band, brass band, military band, German band, jazz band; street musicians, waits.

VOCALIST, melodist, singer, warbler; songster, chanter or chaunter [*archaic*]; *cantatore* [*It.*], *cantatrice* [*F.*], improvisator, *improvvisatore* or *improvisatore* [*It.*]; *improvvisatrice* or *improvisatrice* [*It.*], songstress, chantress or chauntress [*archaic*]; chorister; chorus singer.

choir or quire [*archaic*]; chorus; *Liedertafel* [*Ger.*], *Liederkranz* [*Ger.*]; choral -club, – society; singing -club, – society; festival chorus, eisteddfod [*Welsh*].

SONG BIRD, nightingale, philomel, lark, ringdove, bulbul, cuckoo, thrush, mavis.

[PATRONS] Orpheus, Apollo, Apollo Musagetes, the Muses, Polyhymnia, Erato, Euterpe, Terpsichore; Pierides, sacred nine, tuneful nine, tuneful quire [*archaic*]; Siren.

COMPOSER &c. 413.

CONDUCTOR, choirmaster, bandmaster, concert master or *Konzertmeister* [*Ger.*], drum major, song leader, precentor.

PERFORMANCE, execution, touch, expression.

V. PLAY, tune, tune up, pipe, pipe up, strike up, sweep the chords, fiddle, scrape [*derog.*], strike the lyre, beat the drum; blow –, sound –, wind- the horn; doodle [*Scot. or colloq.*]; toot, tootle, grind the organ; touch the guitar &c. (*instruments*) 417; twang, pluck, pick, paw the ivories [*slang*]; pound, thump; drum, thrum, strum, beat time.

EXECUTE, perform; accompany; sing –, play- a second.

COMPOSE, set to music, arrange, harmonize, orchestrate.

SING, chant or chaunt [*archaic*], intone, hum, warble, carol, yodel, chirp, chirrup, lilt, purl, quaver, trill, shake, twitter, whistle; sol-fa; do-re-mi.

have an ear for music, have a musical ear, have a correct ear, have absolute pitch.

Adj. MUSICAL; lyric, dramatic; *coloratura* [*It.*], bravura, florid, brilliant; playing &c. *v.*

Adv. *adagio* [*It.*], *andante* [*It.*] &c. (*music*) 415.

∗∗ "At last divine Cecilia came, Inventress of the vocal frame" [Dryden]; "He raised a mortal to the skies, She drew an angel down" [*ibid.*]; "the little fellow stood keeping time" [Pepys]; "blows out his brains upon the flute" [Browning].

417. Musical Instruments. — N. MUSICAL INSTRUMENTS; orchestra, band; string band, military band, brass band; orchestrion, orchestrina.

[STRINGED INSTRUMENTS] polychord, harp, lyre, lute, archlute, theorbo, cithara, cither, cittern or cithern, gittern, zither, psaltery, guitar, banjo, banjo-zither; rebec or rebeck, mandola, mandolin or mandoline, ukulele [*Hawaii*]; bandurria [*It.*], samisen [*Jap.*]; bina, vina [*India*].

violin, Cremona, Stradivarius; fiddle, kit; viol, vielle; viola, - *d'amore*, - *di gamba*; tenor, violoncello, bass viol or base viol; double bass or double base, *contrabasso* [*It.*], *violone* [*It.*]; bow, fiddlestick, strings, catgut.

piano or pianoforte; grand -, concert-grand -, baby-grand -, square -, upright - piano; harpsichord, monochord [*hist.*], clavichord, clarichord, manichord or manichordon, clavier, spinet, virginals, dulcimer; hurdy-gurdy, street piano, piano organ; pianette, pianino, piano player, player piano, player; Æolian (or Eolian) harp.

[WIND INSTRUMENTS] organ; church -, pipe -, reed- organ; seraphine or seraphina, harmonium, cabinet organ, American organ; harmoniphon [*obs.*], barrel organ, hand organ, melodeon, accordion, concertina; humming top.

flute, fife, piccolo, flageolet, clarinet or clarionet, bass clarinet, basset horn, *corno di bassetto* [*It.*], musette, oboe or hautboy, *cor anglais* [*F.*], English horn, *corno inglese* [*It.*], bassoon, double bassoon, *contrafagotto* [*It.*], serpent, bag-pipes, union pipes, doodlesack [*Scot.*]; ocarina, Panpipes or Pandean pipes; reed instrument; pipe, pitch-pipe; whistle; willow -, penny- whistle; calliope, siren or sirene; catcall.

horn, bugle, cornet, cornet-à-pistons, cornopean [*obs.*], clarion [*now chiefly poetic*], trumpet, trombone, tuba, bombardon, bass tuba, ophicleide; French horn, bugle horn, post horn, saxhorn, *Flügelhorn* [*Ger.*], alt horn or althorn, tenor horn, sackbut [*archaic*], euphonium.

[VIBRATING SURFACES] cymbals, bell, gong; drum, tambour, snare drum, side drum, tabor or tabour, taboret or tabouret, kettle drum, timpano (*pl.* timpani), timbal or tymbal, tom-tom or tam-tam, timbrel, tambourine, castanet, bones; musical glasses, musical stones; mouth organ, harmonica; sounding-board, *abat-voix* [*F.*]; rattle, watchman's rattle; phonograph, graphophone, gramophone, victrola [*trade-mark name*]; zambomba [*Sp.*].

[VIBRATING BARS] reed, tuning fork, triangle, jew's-harp, music box or musical box, harmonicon, xylophone.

MUTE, sourdine, *sordino* [*It.*], sordine, sordet, sourdet.

.*. "But that which did please me beyond anything in the whole world was the wind-musick" [Pepys]; "the vile squeaking of the wry-necked fife" [*M. of V.*]; "Bugles that whinnied, flageolets that crooned, And strings that whined and grunted" [Masefield].

(iv.) PERCEPTION OF SOUND

418. [SENSE OF SOUND.] Hearing. — N. HEARING &c. *v.;* audition, auscultation; audibility; acoustics &c. 402; eavesdropping.

acute -, nice -, delicate -, quick -, sharp -, correct -, musical- ear; ear for music.

EAR, auricle, pinna, concha, labyrinth, lug [*Scot.*], lobule or lobe, acoustic organs, auditory apparatus, eardrum, tympanum; malleus, incus, stapes, vestibule, cochlea, auditory nerve, Eustachian tube.

EAR TRUMPET, speaking trumpet; telephone, phonograph, microphone;

419. Deafness. — N. DEAFNESS, hardness of hearing, surdity [*obs.*], deaf ears; inaudibility, inaudibleness.

adder, beetle, slowworm, blindworm; deaf-mute.

DACTYLOLOGY, deaf-and-dumb alphabet.

V. BE DEAF &c. *adj.;* have no ear; shut -, stop -, close- one's ears; turn a deaf ear to.

RENDER DEAF, stun, deafen; split the -ears, - eardrum.

Adj. DEAF, earless, surd; hard -, dull- of hearing; deaf-mute; stunned, deaf-

gramophone, phonograph, victrola [*trade-mark name*], megaphone, phonorganon; dictagraph *or* dictograph [*trade-mark name*], dictophone [*trade-mark name*], audiphone, dentiphone; stethoscope; telephone &c. 527.

ened; stone deaf; deaf as -a post, – an adder, – a beetle, – a trunkmaker; inattentive &c. 458.

INAUDIBLE, out of -earshot, – hearing.

⁎ none so deaf as those that will not hear.

HEARER, auditor, auditory, audience, listener, eavesdropper.

OTOLOGY, otoscopy, auriscopy; otoscope, auriscope; otopathy, otography, otoplasty; otorrhea, tympanitis; otologist, aurist.

V. HEAR, overhear; hark, harken; list, listen; give –, lend –, bend- an ear; strain one's ears, attend to, give attention, catch a sound, prick up one's ears; give ear, give a hearing to, give audience to.

hang upon the lips of, be all ear, listen with both ears.

BECOME AUDIBLE; meet –, fall upon –, catch –, reach- the ear; be heard; ring in the ear &c. (*resound*) 408.

Adj. HEARING &c. *v.*; auditory, otic, aural, acoustic, acoustical, phonic; auriculate, auricular; auricled, eared; auditive.

Adv. *arrectis auribus* [*L.*]; all ears.

Int. HARK! hark ye! hear! list! listen! oyez *or* oyes! attend! attention! lend me your ears!

⁎ "he that hath ears to hear, let him hear" [*Bible*]; little pitchers have big ears; "And hear, like ocean on a western beach, The surge and thunder of the Odyssey" [Andrew Lang].

---

(6) *Light*

(i) LIGHT IN GENERAL

420. Light. — N. LIGHT, ray, beam, stream, gleam, streak, pencil; sunbeam, moonbeam; aurora, dawn.

day; sunshine; light of -day, – heaven; sun &c. (*luminary*) 423, daylight, broad daylight, noontide light; noontide, noonday.

glow &c. *v.*; afterglow, sunset glow; glimmering &c. *v.*; glint; glare; play –, glare –, flood- of light; phosphorescence, lambent flame.

HALO, glory, nimbus, aureola, aureole, gloriole [*rare*], aura.

SPARK, scintilla; facula; sparkling &c. *v.*; emication [*obs.*], scintillation, flash, blaze, coruscation, fulguration [*now rare*]; flame &c. (*fire*) 382; lightning, levin; *ignis fatuus* [*L.*] &c. (*luminary*) 423.

LUSTER *or* lustre, sheen, shimmer, reflection *or* reflexion; gloss, tinsel, spangle, brightness, brilliancy, splendor *or* splendour, effulgence, refulgence; fulgor, fulgidity [*rare*]; dazzlement, resplendence *or* resplendency, transplendency [*rare*], luminousness &c. *adj.*; luminosity; lucidity; nitency [*rare*]; radiance, radiation; irradiation, illumination.

421. Darkness. — N. DARKNESS &c adj.; tenebrosity, umbrageousness, dunness [*rare*], caliginousness, lightlessness, sootiness; blackness &c. (*dark color*) 431; obscurity, gloom, murk *or* mirk, murkiness *or* mirkiness, darksomeness; dusk &c. (*dimness*) 422.

Cimmerian –, Stygian –, Egyptian-darkness; night; midnight; dead of –, witching hour of –, witching time of-night; darkness visible; "darkness which may be felt" [*Bible*]; "the palpable obscure" [Milton]; "embalméd darkness" [Keats]; Erebus; "the jaws of darkness" [*M. N. D.*]; "sable-vested Night" [Milton].

SHADOW, shade, umbra, penumbra; skiagraphy *or* sciagraphy; skiagram *or* sciagram, skiagraph *or* sciagraph; radiograph.

OBSCURATION; obumbration [*rare*]; obtenebration [*rare*], offuscation [*obs.*], caligation [*obs.*], adumbration; extinction; eclipse, total eclipse; gathering of the clouds.

SHADING; distribution of shade; *chiaroscuro* [*It.*] &c. (*light*) 420.

V. BE DARK &c. *adj.*; be in darkness &c. *n.*

[SCIENCE OF LIGHT] optics; photology, photics; actinology, actinometry, radiology, heliology, radiometry, radioscopy, photometry, dioptrics, catoptrics; photography, photolithography, photomicography, phototelegraphy, radiotelegraphy; phototherapy, heliotherapy, radiotherapy; heliometry, heliography.

actinic rays, actinism; radioactivity, radium emanation, exradio; Röntgen rays, X-rays, ultra-violet rays; photometer &c. 445; heliometer, refractometer.

[DISTRIBUTION OF LIGHT] *chiaroscuro* or *chiaro-oscuro* [*It.*], clair-obscure, *clair-obscur* [*F.*], mezzotint, mezzotinto, half tone *or* half-tone, demitint, half tint; breadth, light and shade, black and white, tonality.

reflection, refraction, dispersion; refractivity.

ILLUMINANT, artificial light; gas &c. 423.

V. SHINE, glow, beam, glitter; glister, glisten; twinkle, gleam; flare, flare up; glare, shimmer, glimmer, flicker, sparkle, scintillate, coruscate, flash, blaze; be bright &c. *adj.*; reflect light, daze, dazzle, bedazzle, radiate, shoot out beams; fulgurate, phosphoresce.

clear up, brighten.

LIGHTEN, enlighten; levin; light, light up; irradiate, shine upon; give -, hang out a - light; cast -, throw -, shed- -luster, - light- upon; illume, illumine, illuminate; relume, strike a light; kindle &c. (*set fire to*) 384.

Adj. LUMINOUS, luminiferous; shining &c. *v.*; lucid, lucent, luculent, luciferous [*rare*], lucific [*rare*]; illuminate [*archaic*], illuminant, light, lightsome; bright, vivid, splendent, nitid, lustrous, shiny, beamy, scintillant, fulgurant, radiant, lambent; sheen [*dial. or poetic*], sheeny; glossy, burnished, glassy, sunny, orient, meridian; noonday, noontide; cloudless, clear; unclouded, unobscured.

garish; resplendent, transplendent [*rare*]; refulgent, effulgent, fulgid, fulgent, relucent, splendorous *or* splendrous, splendid, blazing, in a blaze, ablaze, rutilant, meteoric, phosphorescent; aglow.

bright as silver; light -, bright- as -day, - noonday, - the sun at noonday.

[SCIENTIFIC] actinic, radioactive; optic, optical, photologic *or* photological. helio-

DARKEN, obscure, shade; dim; tone down, lower; overcast, overshadow; cloud, cloud over, darken over, murk *or* mirk; eclipse; offuscate [*obs.*], obumbrate, obtenebrate [*rare*], obfuscate; adumbrate; cast into the shade; becloud, bedim, bedarken; cast -, throw -, spread- a -shade, - shadow, - gloom; "walk in darkness and in the shadow of death" [*Book of Common Prayer*].

EXTINGUISH, put out, blow out, snuff out, dout [*obs. or dial. Eng.*]

Adj. DARK, darksome, darkling; obscure, tenebrious, tenebrous, sombrous; pitch dark, pitchy; caliginous [*archaic*]; black &c. (*in color*) 431.

dark as -pitch, - the pit, - Erebus.

SUNLESS, lightless &c. (*see* sun, light, &c. 423); somber, dusky; unilluminated &c. (*see* illuminate &c. 420); nocturnal; dingy, lurid, gloomy; murky *or* mirky, murksome *or* mirksome, sooty, shady, umbrageous; overcast &c. (*dim*) 422; cloudy &c. (*opaque*) 426; darkened &c. *v.*

BENIGHTED; noctivagant, noctivagous.

Adv. in the -dark, - shade; at night, by night, through the night; darkling, darklings [*rare*].

** "in the dead vast and middle of the night" [*Hamlet*]; "brief as the lightning in the collied night" [*M. N. D.*]; "eldest Night and Chaos, ancestors of Nature" [*P. L.*]; "Empress of silence, and the queen of sleep" [*Marlowe*]; "Who could have thought such darkness lay concealed Within thy beams, O Sun" [*J. Blanco White*]; "the blackness of the noonday night" [*Longfellow*]; "the prayer of Ajax was for light" [*ibid.*].

422. Dimness. — N. DIMNESS &c. *adj.*; darkness &c. 421; paleness &c. (*light color*) 429.

HALF LIGHT, *demi-jour* [*F.*]; partial shadow, partial eclipse; "shadow of a shade" [*Æschylus*]; "shadows numberless" [*Keats*]; glimmer, glimmering; nebulosity, nebulousness, obnubilation [*rare*]; cloud &c. 353; eclipse.

TWILIGHT, aurora, dusk, nightfall, gloaming, gloam [*rare*], blind man's holiday, *entre chien et loup* [*F.*], *inter canem et lupem* [*L.*], shades of evening, crepuscule, cockshut time [*obs.*]; break of day, daybreak, dawn.

moonlight, moonbeam, moonglade, moonshine; owl's-light, starlight, candle-light, rushlight, firelight; farthing candle.

V. BE *or* GROW DIM &c. *adj.*; gloom; cloud over; flicker, twinkle, glimmer,

logical; photogenic, photographic; helio-
graphic; heliophagous.

.*. "a day for gods to stoop and men to
soar" [Tennyson]; "dark with excessive bright"
[*P. L.*]; "Hail holy light! offspring of heav'n
first-born" [*P. L.*]; "And noon lay heavy on
flower and tree" [Shelley].

---

loom, lower; fade; pale, "pale his uneffectual fire" [*Hamlet*].

RENDER DIM &c. *adj.;* dim, bedim,
obscure, shade, shadow; encompass
with -gloom, – shadow; darken, dark
[*archaic*], cloud, becloud, darkle.

Adj. DIM, dull, lackluster, dingy,
darkish, dusky, shorn of its beams; dark &c. 421.

FAINT, shadowed forth; glassy; cloudy; misty &c. (*opaque*) 426; blear; fuliginous:
nebulous, nebular, obnubilated [*rare*], obnubilous [*obs.*].

LURID, leaden, dun, dirty; overcast, muddy; looming &c. *v.*

TWILIGHT, crepuscular, crepusculous [*rare*], crepusculine [*rare*].

pale &c. (*colorless*) 429; confused &c. (*invisible*) 447.

.*. "now fades the glimmering landscape on the sight" [Gray]; "draw the gradual dusky
veil" [Collins]; "the lengthening shadows wait The first pale stars of twilight" [Holmes]; "fade
away into the forest dim" [Keats].

---

423. [SOURCE OF LIGHT.] **Luminary.**
— **N.** LUMINARY; light &c. 420; flame
&c. (*fire*) 382.

spark, scintilla; phosphorescence.

[HEAVENLY BODIES] sun, orb of day,
day-star [*poetic*], Aurora; star, orb,
meteor; falling star, shooting star;
blazing star, dog star, canicula, Sirius,
Aldebaran; constellation, galaxy, Milky
Way; pole star, Polaris; Cynosure;
anthelion; morning star, Lucifer, Phos-
phor, Phosphorus; Venus, Hesperus,
evening star; mock sun, parhelion, sun
dog *or* sundog, moon &c. 318.

SUN GOD, Helios, Titan, Phaëthon,
Phœbus, Apollo, Hyperion, Ra *or* Re
[*Egypt*], Shamash [*Babylon & Assyria*].

LIGHTNING, levin; chain –, fork –,
sheet –, summer- lightning.

PHOSPHORUS; *ignis fatuus* [*L.*]; Jack
o' –, Friar's- lantern; will-o'-the-wisp,

424. Shade. — N. SHADE; awning &c.
(*cover*) 223; parasol, sunshade, umbrella.

SCREEN, curtain, chick [*India*], purdah
[*India*], *portière* [*F.*]; shutter, blind,
Venetian blind, *jalousie* [*F.*].

gauze, veil, mantle, mask, yashmak
[*Turk.*].

cloud, mist; gathering of clouds;
smoke screen [*mil.*].

umbrage [*archaic*], glade; shadow &c.
421; ambush, covert.

BLINKERS, blinders; smoked glasses,
colored spectacles.

V. VEIL, &c. *v.;* draw a curtain; put
up –, close- a shutter; cast a shadow &c.
(*darken*) 421.

Adj. SHADY, umbrageous, shadowy,
bowery.

.*. "welcome, ye shades! ye bowery
thickets, hail" [Thomson].

---

firedrake, Fata Morgana, St. Elmo's fire, Castor and Pollux [*naut.*], corposant.
glowworm, firefly.

POLAR LIGHTS, northern lights, *aurora borealis* [*L.*], *aurora australis* [*L.*]; aurora;
zodiacal light.

[ARTIFICIAL LIGHT] gas, gaslight, electric light; headlight, searchlight, spotlight,
flashlight, limelight, calcium light, lamplight, lamp; lantern, lanthorn [*archaic*];
electric torch, dark lantern, bull's-eye; candle; wax –, tallow –, bayberry- candle;
farthing dip, tallow dip [*colloq.*]; bougie, taper, rushlight; oil &c. (*grease*) 356;
wick, burner; Argand, moderator, duplex; torch, flambeau, link, brand; gaselier,
chandelier, electrolier; candelabrum, girandole, sconce, luster *or* lustre, candlestick.

FIREWORK, Catherine wheel, Roman candle, fizgig; pyrotechnics.

SIGNAL LIGHT, rocket, balefire, beacon fire; lighthouse &c. (*signal*) 550.

PYRE, funeral pyre; death fire; corpse candle.

V. ILLUMINATE &c. (*light*) 420.

Adj. SELF-LUMINOUS; phosphoric, phosphorescent; radiant &c. (*light*) 420.

.*. "blossomed the lovely stars, the forget-me-nots of the angels" [Longfellow]; "the sentinel stars set their watch in the sky" [Campbell]; "and with joy the stars perform their shining"
[Arnold]; "the planets in their station list'ning stood" [*P. L.*]; "the Scriptures of the skies"
[Bailey]; "that orbed continent, the fire that severs day from night" [*Twelfth Night*]; "that
orbed maiden with white fire laden, Whom mortals call the Moon" [Shelley].

425. Transparency. — N. TRANSPAR-ENCY, transparence, translucence, trans-lucency, diaphaneity, diaphanousness; lucidity, pellucidity, limpidity; fluorescence; transillumination, translumination.

TRANSPARENT MEDIUM, glass, crystal, lymph, water, hyalite, hyaline.

V. BE TRANSPARENT &c. *adj.;* transmit light.

Adj. TRANSPARENT, pellucid, lucid, diaphanous; translucent, tralucent [*obs.*], limpid, clear, serene, crystalline, clear as crystal, pervious [*rare*], vitreous, transpicuous [*rare*], glassy, hyaline, hyaloid [*rare*], vitreform.

** "translucent syrops tinct with cinnamon" [Keats].

or cyprus [*hist.*], bombyx, thin silk; film; opaline, frosted glass; mist &c. (*cloud*) 353.

Adj. SEMITRANSPARENT, semipellucid, semidiaphanous, semiopacous [*obs.*], semiopaque; opalescent, opaline; pearly, milky; frosted, nacreous; hazy, misty.

V. CLOUD, frost, cloud over, frost over; become -pearly, – milky, – misty.

be opalescent &c. *adj.;* opalesce.

426. Opacity. — N. OPACITY; opaqueness &c. *adj.;* obfuscation, fuliginosity, nubilation.

film; cloud &c. 353.

V. BE OPAQUE &c. *adj.;* obstruct the passage of light; obfuscate, offuscate [*obs.*].

Adj. OPAQUE, impervious to light; adiaphanous; dim &c. 422; turbid, thick, muddy, opacous [*obs.*], obfuscated, fuliginous, cloudy, nubilous, nubilose [*obs.*], foggy, vaporous, nubiferous.

SMOKY, fumid [*obs.*], murky or mirky, smeared, dirty.

427. Semitransparency. — N. SEMI-TRANSPARENCY, opalescence, milkiness, pearliness.

[COMPARISONS] gauze, muslin, cypress; mica, mother-of-pearl, nacre, opal glass, opaline, frosted glass; mist &c. (*cloud*) 353.

(ii) SPECIFIC LIGHT

428. Color. — N. COLOR or colour, hue, tint, tinct [*archaic*], tinction, tinge, dye, complexion, shade, tincture, cast, livery, coloration, chromatism or chromism, glow, flush; tone, key.

pure –, positive –, primary –, primitive –, complementary- color; three primaries; spectrum, chromatic dispersion; broken –, secondary –, tertiary- color.

local color, coloring, keeping, tone, value, aërial perspective.

[SCIENCE OF COLOR] chromatics, spectrum analysis; chromatography, chromatology, chromatoscopy; chromatograph, chromatometer, chromatoscope, chromoscope, chromatrope, chromometer, colorimeter; prism, spectroscope, kaleidoscope.

PIGMENT, coloring matter, paint, dye, wash, distemper, stain, chromogen; medium; mordant; oil paint &c. (*painting*) 556.

V. COLOR or colour, dye, tinge, stain, tint, tinct [*archaic*], hue, tone, complexion [*rare*]; paint, wash, distemper, ingrain, grain, illuminate, emblazon, imbue; paint &c. (*fine art*) 556.

Adj. COLORED &c. *v.;* colorific, tingent [*rare*], tinctorial; chromatic, prismatic;

429. [ABSENCE OF COLOR.**] Achromatism. — N.** ACHROMATISM, achromatization; decoloration, decolorization, discoloration; pallor, pallidity; paleness &c. *adj.;* etiolation.

neutral tint, monochrome, black and white.

V. LOSE COLOR &c. 428; fade, fly, go, become colorless &c. *adj.;* turn pale; pale, fade out, bleach out; wan; fly, go.

DEPRIVE OF COLOR, decolor or decolour, decolorize or decolourize, whiten, bleach, tarnish, achromatize, blanch, etiolate, wash out, tone down.

Adj. COLORLESS; achromatic; uncolored &c. (*see* color &c. 428); etiolated; hueless, pale, pallid; pale-faced, anæmic or anemic, tallow-faced; faint, dull, cold, muddy, leaden, dun, wan, sallow, dead, dingy, ashy, ashen, ghastly, cadaverous, glassy, lackluster; discolored &c. *v.*

pale as -death, – ashes, – a witch, – a ghost, – a corpse.

LIGHT-COLORED, fair, blond, ash-blond; white &c. 430; tow-headed, tow-haired.

** "O pale, pale now those rosy lips I oft hae kissed sae fondly" [Burns].

full –, high –, rich –, deep- colored; double-dyed; polychromatic; chroma-
togenous; chromatophoric, chromatophorous; tingible.

BRIGHT, vivid, intense, deep; fresh, unfaded; rich, gorgeous; bright-colored,
gay.

GAUDY, florid; garish; showy, flaunting; flashy; many-colored, party-colored *or*
parti-colored, variegated; raw, crude; glaring, flaring; discordant, inharmonious.

MELLOW, harmonious, pearly, sweet, delicate, subtle, tender.

DULL, sad, somber *or* sombre, sad-colored, grave, gray, dark.

430. Whiteness. — N. WHITENESS &c.
adj.; whitishness, canescence; argent,
argentine.

ALBIFICATION, albication, albinism,
albinoism; leucopathy, leucoderma *or*
leucodermia [*med.*], dealbation, albescence, etiolation; lactescence.

[COMPARISONS] snow, paper, chalk,
milk, lily, ivory, silver, alabaster;
albata, eburin *or* eburine *or* eburite,
German silver, white metal, barium
sulphate, *blanc fixe* [*F.*], pearl white;
white lead, ceruse, carbonate of lead,
Paris white, zinc white, flake white,
Chinese white.

WHITEWASH, whiting, whitening, calcimine.

V. BE WHITE &c. *adj.*

RENDER WHITE &c. *adj.;* whiten,
bleach, blanch, etiolate, silver, besnow,
dealbate [*obs.*], albify [*rare*], frost.

WHITEWASH, calcimine, white.

Adj. WHITE; snow-white; snowy, niveous; candent, candid [*archaic*], frosted,
hoar, hoary; silvery, silver, argent,
argentine; canescent, chalky, cretaceous;
lactescent, milk-white, milky, marmoreal
or marmorean; albificative, albicant,
albescent; albinistic.

white as –a sheet, – driven snow,
– a lily, – silver; like ivory &c. *n.*

WHITISH, creamy, pearly, ivory, fair,
blond, ash-blond; blanched &c. *v.;*
high in tone, light.

*** "lawn as white as driven snow"
[Shakespeare]; "the white radiance of eternity"
[Shelley]; "the chief assertion of religious
morality is that white is a colour" [Chesterton].

431. Blackness. — N. BLACKNESS &c.
adj.; darkness &c. (*want of light*) 421;
swarthiness, swartness; lividity; dark
-color, – tone; *chiaroscuro* [*It.*] &c. 420.

nigrification [*rare*], nigrefaction [*obs.*],
nigrescence, denigration, infuscation
[*rare*].

[COMPARISONS] jet, ink, ebony, ebon
[*now poetic*], coal, pitch, soot, charcoal,
sloe; smut, smutch, smudge, smirch;
raven, crow.

NEGRO, negress, blackamoor, man of
color, colored man, colored woman,
nigger [*colloq., usually contemptuous*],
darky *or* darkey [*colloq.*], black, blacky
[*colloq.*], Ethiop, Ethiopian, buck *or*
buck nigger [*colloq., U. S.*], coon [*slang,
U. S.*], sambo [*colloq. or humorous*],
kala admi [*Hind.*], Melanesian, Hottentot, Pygmy, Bushman, Negrillo [*African
Pygmy*], Negrito [*Asiatic Pygmy*],
African, Mandingo, Senegambian, Sudanese, Papuan, blackfellow, Australian
aborigine.

[PIGMENTS] lamp –, ivory –, blue-
black; writing –, printing –, printer's –,
Indian- ink.

V. BE BLACK &c. *adj.*

RENDER BLACK &c. *adj.;* black,
blacken, infuscate [*rare*], denigrate,
nigrify; blot, blotch, smut, smudge,
smutch, smirch; darken &c. 421.

Adj. BLACK, sable, somber *or* sombre,
livid, dark, inky, ebon, atramentous,
jetty; coal-black, jet-black; fuliginous,
pitchy, sooty; *dhu* [*Ir. & Gaelic*], swart,
swarthy, dusky, dingy, murky *or* mirky;
blotchy, smudgy, smutty; nigrine [*rare*],
nigricant, nigrescent, Ethiopian, Ethi-
opic; low-toned, low in tone; of the deepest dye.

black as –jet &c. *n.*, – my hat, – a shoe, – a tinker's pot, – November, – the ace
of spades, – thunder, – midnight; nocturnal &c. (*dark*) 421; gray &c. 432; obscure
&c. 421.

Adv. in mourning.

*** "more black than ash-buds in the front of March" [Tennyson]; "cyprus black as e'er
was crow" [Shakespeare].

432. Gray. — N. GRAY *or* grey &c. *adj.;* neutral tint, silver, dove-color, pepper and salt, *chiaroscuro* [*It.*], grisaille.

grayness *or* greyness &c. *adj.*

[PIGMENTS] Payne's gray; black &c. 431.

V. RENDER GRAY &c. *adj.;* gray or grey.

Adj. GRAY *or* grey; iron-gray, dun, drab, dingy, leaden, livid, somber, sad, pearly, calcareous, limy, silver, silvery, silvered; French –, steel –, Quaker –, dapple- gray; dappled; dove-colored, *gorge-de-pigeon* [*F.*]; ashen, ashy, favillous; cinereous, cineritious; grizzly, grizzled; slate-colored, stone-colored, mouse-colored, ash-colored; cool.

433. Brown. — N. BROWN &c. *adj.;* brownness.

[PIGMENTS] bister *or* bistre, brown ocher *or* ochre, mummy, sepia, Vandyke brown.

V. RENDER BROWN &c. *adj.;* brown, tan, embrown, imbrown, bronze.

Adj. BROWN, adust [*rare*], castaneous, toast-brown, nut-brown, seal-brown, cinnamon, hazel, fawn, puce, musteline, musteloid, écru, *feuille-morte* [*F.*], tawny, fuscous, chocolate, maroon, tan, brunette, whitey-brown; fawn-colored, snuff-colored, liver-colored; brown as -a berry, – mahogany, – oak leaves; khaki.

REDDISH-BROWN, terra cotta, rufous, russet, russety, russetish, ferruginous, rust, foxy, bronze, coppery, copperish, copper-colored; bay, bayard, roan, sorrel, henna, auburn, chestnut, mahogany; rubiginous, rubiginose, rust-colored; lurid.

sun-burnt; tanned &c. *v.*

Primitive Colors [1]

434. Redness. — N. RED, scarlet, cardinal, cardinal red, vermilion, carmine, crimson, pink, rose, cerise, cherry, rouge, coquelicot, salmon, lake, maroon, carnation, *couleur de rose* [*F.*], *rose du Barry* [*F.*]; magenta, solferino, damask, flesh -color, – tint; color; fresh –, high-color; warmth; gules [*her.*].

REDNESS &c. *adj.;* rubescence, rubicundity, ruddiness, rubefaction, rubrication, rubification; erubescence, blush.

[COMPARISONS] ruby, *grenat* [*F.*], garnet, carbuncle; rust, iron mold *or* mould; rose, cardinal flower, lobelia; cardinal-bird, – grosbeak; redstart.

[DYES AND PIGMENTS] cinnabar, cochineal, red ocher *or* ochre, stammel, fuchsine *or* fuchsin, vermilion; ruddle, madder; Indian red, palladium red, light red, Venetian red; red ink, annatto *or* annotto, realgar, minium, red lead.

V. BE *or* BECOME RED &c. *adj.;* blush, flush, color, color up, mantle, redden.

435. Greenness. — N. GREEN &c. *adj.;* blue and yellow; vert [*her.*].

GREENNESS, verdancy, verdure, viridescence, viridity.

[COMPARISONS] emerald, malachite, chrysoprase, jasper, chrysolite *or* olivine, beryl; verd antique, verdigris, aquamarine; reseda, mignonette, absinthe, *crème de menthe* [*F.*].

[PIGMENTS] *terre verte* [*F.*], viridian, bice, verditer, verdine, celadon.

V. RENDER GREEN &c. *adj.;* green.

Adj. GREEN, verdant; glaucous, olive; green as grass; verdurous, citrine *or* citrinous, porraceous, olivaceous, smaragdine [*rare*].

emerald –, pea –, grass –, apple –, sea –, olive –, cucumber –, leaf –, Irish –, Kelly –, bottle- green.

GREENISH, virent [*rare*], virescent, viridescent [*rare*], chlorine; aquamarine, blue-green.

RENDER RED &c. *adj.;* redden, rouge, crimson, encrimson [*rare*], empurple; rubify [*rare*], rubricate; incarnadine; ruddle, rust.

Adj. RED &c. *n.,* reddish; incarnadine, sanguine, sanguineous, bloody, gory; coral, coralline, rosy, roseate; stammel, blood-red, laky, wine-red, wine-colored, vinaceous; incarmined [*rare*], rubiform [*rare*], rufous, rufulous, murrey, bricky, lateritious [*rare*]; rubineous, rubious, rubricate, rubricose; Pompeiian red; reddish-brown &c. 433.

[1] Roget's classification of colors has been retained, though it does not entirely accord with the theories of modern science.

rose-, ruby-, cherry-, claret-, flame-, flesh-, peach-, salmon-, brick-, rust-colored.

red as -fire, – blood, – scarlet, – a turkey cock, – a lobster; warm, hot.

RED-COMPLEXIONED, red-faced, florid, burnt, rubicund, ruddy, red, blowzed, blowzy, glowing, sanguine, blooming, rosy, hectic, flushed, inflamed; blushing &c. *v.;* erubescent, rubescent; reddened &c. *v.*

[OF HAIR] sandy, carroty, brick-red, Titian red, auburn, chestnut.

*** "like a lobster boil'd, the morn From black to red began to turn" [Butler]; "red as a rose is she" [Coleridge]; "And Marian's nose looks red and raw" [Shakespeare].

436. Yellowness. — N. YELLOW &c. *adj.;* or [*her.*]; yellowness &c. *adj.;* xanthocyanopia *or* xanthocyanopsia, xanthochroia.

[COMPARISONS] crocus, jonquil, saffron, topaz; xanthite; gold, gilding, gilt; yolk; jaundice, icterus; London fog.

[PIGMENTS] gamboge, fustic, massicot; cadmium –, chrome –, Indian –, king's –, lemon- yellow; orpiment, yellow ocher, Claude tint, aureolin; xanthein, xanthin; xanthophyll.

V. RENDER YELLOW &c. *adj.;* yellow, gild; jaundice.

Adj. YELLOW, aureate, golden, gold, gilt, gilded, flavous [*obs.*], citrine, citreous, lemon, fallow; fulvous, fulvescent, fulvid [*rare*]; sallow, lutescent, luteolous, luteous, tawny, cream, creamy, sandy; xanthic, xanthous; jaundiced; auricomous, ocherous *or* ochreous, ochery *or* ochry, flaxen, yellowish, buff, écru; icterine, icteritious *or* icteritous, icteroid; xanthochroid, yellow complexioned.

gold-, saffron-, citron-, lemon-, sulphur-, amber-, straw-, primrose-, cream-colored; xanthocarpous, xanthopous [*bot., rare*].

yellow as a -quincy, – guinea, – crow's foot; yellow as saffron.

437. Purple. — N. PURPLE &c. *adj.;* blue and red, bishop's purple; gridelin, amethyst; damson, heliotrope; purpure [*her.*].

LIVIDNESS, lividity.

V. RENDER PURPLE &c. *adj.;* purple, empurple.

Adj. PURPLE, violet, plum-colored, lavender, lilac, puce, mauve, purplish, purpurate [*archaic*], violaceous, hyacinthine, amethystine, magenta, solferino, heliotrope; livid.

438. Blueness. — N. BLUE &c. *adj.;* garter-blue; watchet [*obs.*]; blueness, bluishness; bloom.

[COMPARISONS] *lapis lazuli* [*L.*], sapphire, turquoise; indicolite.

[PIGMENTS] ultramarine, smalt, cobalt, cyanogen; Prussian –, syenite- blue; bice, indigo; zaffer.

V. RENDER BLUE &c. *adj.;* blue.

Adj. BLUE, azure, cerulean, cyanic; sky-blue, sky-colored, sky-dyed; navy blue, midnight blue, cadet blue, robin's-egg blue, baby blue, ultramarine, aquamarine, electric blue *or* electric, steel blue *or* steel; cerulescent; bluish; atmospheric, retiring; cold.

*** "Oh, yellow's forsaken, and green is forsworn, But blue is the sweetest color that's worn"; "Blue, darkly, deeply, beautifully blue" [Southey]; "colour'd with the heaven's own blue" [Bryant].

439. Orange. — N. ORANGE, red and yellow; old gold; gold color &c. *adj.*

[PIGMENTS] ocher *or* ochre, Mars orange, cadmium.

V. GILD, engild, deaurate [*rare*], warm.

Adj. ORANGE; ocherous *or* ochreous, ochery *or* ochry; henna, burnt orange; orange-, gold-, brass-, apricot- colored; warm, hot, glowing, flame-colored.

440. Variegation. — N. VARIEGATION; dichroism, trichroism; iridescence, irisation, play of colors, polychrome, maculation, spottiness, striæ.

[COMPARISONS] spectrum, rainbow, iris, tulip, peacock, chameleon, butterfly, zebra, leopard, jaguar, panther, cheetah, ocelot, ophite, nacre, mother-of-pearl, tortoise shell; opal, cymophane, marble; mackerel, mackerel sky; harlequin; Joseph's coat; tricolor.

CHECK, plaid, tartan, patchwork; marquetry, parquet, parquetry, mosaic, tesseræ. tessellation, checkerwork; chessboard, checkers *or* chequers.

V. VARIEGATE, stripe, streak, checker *or* chequer, fleck, bespeckle, speckle, besprinkle, sprinkle; stipple, maculate, dot, bespot; tattoo, inlay, tessellate. damascene; embroider, braid, quilt.

be variegated &c. *adj.*

Adj. VARIEGATED &c. *v.;* many-colored, many-hued; divers-colored, party-colored *or* parti-colored, dichromatic, polychromatic; bicolor, tricolor, versi-color; of all the colors of the rainbow, of all manner of colors; kaleidoscopic, nævose *or* nevose, dædal.

IRIDESCENT, opaline, opalescent, prismatic, nacreous, pearly, shot, *gorge-de-pigeon* [*F.*], chatoyant; irised, irisated, pavonine; tortoise-shell.

MOTTLED, pied, piebald, skewbald; motley, marbled, pepper-and-salt, paned, dappled, clouded, cymophanous.

CHECKERED *or* chequered, mosaic, tessellated, plaid.

SPOTTED, spotty; punctate *or* punctated [*rare*], powdered; speckled &c. *v.;* freckled, flea-bitten, studded; flecked, fleckered.

STRIATED, barred, veined; brinded, brindled, tabby; watered; strigose, strigillose, strigate, striolate; listed; embroidered &c. *v.*

. "to paint the rainbow's varying hues" (Scott]; "iris all hues, roses and jessamin" [*P.L.*]; "'Fly pride,' says the peacock" [*Comedy of Errors*]; "That royal bird, whose tail's a diadem" [Byron].

(iii) PERCEPTIONS OF LIGHT

441. Vision. — N. VISION, sight, optics, eyesight.

VIEW, look, espial, glance, ken, *coup d'œil* [*F.*]; glimpse, glint, peep, peek; gaze, stare, leer; perlustration [*rare*], contemplation; conspection [*obs.*], conspectuity [*obs.*]; regard, survey; inspection, introspection; reconnoissance, reconnaissance, speculation, watch, espionage, *espionnage* [*F.*]; autopsy; ocular -inspection, – demonstration; sight-seeing, globe-trotting [*colloq.*].

VIEWPOINT, standpoint, point of view; gazebo, loophole, belvedere, watch-tower.

FIELD OF VIEW; theater *or* theatre, amphitheater *or* amphitheatre, arena, vista, horizon; commanding view, bird's-eye view, panoramic view.

VISUAL ORGAN, organ of vision; eye; naked eye, unassisted eye; retina, pupil, iris, cornea, white; optics, orbs; saucer -, goggle -, gooseberry- eyes.

short sight &c. 443; clear -, sharp -, quick -, eagle -, piercing -, penetrating- -sight, – glance, – eye; perspicacity, discernment; catopsis.

[COMPARISON] eagle, hawk; cat, lynx, weasel; Argus.

EVIL EYE, blighting glance; basilisk, cockatrice.

[OPTICAL DEVICES] spectacles, eye-glass, lorgnette, monocle, reading glass, field glass, opera glass; telescope &c. 445; microscope, periscope.

V. SEE, behold, discern, perceive, have

442. Blindness. — N. BLINDNESS, sightlessness, benightedness, anopsia *or* anopsy, cecity, excecation [*obs.*], cataract, ablepsia *or* ablepsy [*rare*], prestriction [*obs.*]; dim-sightedness &c. 443; amaurosis, *gutta serena* ["drop serene" *of Milton*], teichopsia.

[TYPE FOR THE BLIND] Braille *or* Braille type, New York point, Gall's serrated type, Howe's American type *or* Boston type, Moon's type; Alston's Glasgow type, Lucas's type, Frere's type; string alphabet, writing stamps, noctograph.

V. BE BLIND &c. *adj.;* not see; lose sight of; have the eyes bandaged; grope in the dark.

NOT LOOK; close -, shut -, turn away -, avert- the eyes; look another way; wink &c. (*limited vision*) 443; shut the eyes to, be blind to; wink at, blink at.

RENDER BLIND &c. *adj.;* excecate [*obs.*], blind, blindfold; hoodwink, dazzle; put one's eyes out; throw dust into one's eyes; *jeter de la poudre aux yeux* [*F.*]; screen from sight &c. (*hide*) 528.

Adj. BLIND; eyeless, sightless, visionless; dark; stone-blind, stark-blind, sand-blind [*archaic*]; undiscerning; dim-sighted &c. 443.

blind as -a bat, – a buzzard, – a beetle, – a mole, – an owl; wall-eyed.

BLINDED &c. *v.*

Adv. BLINDLY, blindfold; darkly.

. "O dark, dark, dark, amid the blaze of noon" [Milton].

in sight, descry, sight, make out, discover, distinguish, recognize, spy, espy, ken [*archaic*]; get -, have -, catch- a -sight, - glimpse -of; command a view of; witness, contemplate, speculate; cast -, set- the eyes on; be a spectator of &c. 444; look on &c. (*be present*) 186; see sights &c. 455; see at a glance &c. 498.

LOOK, view, eye; lift up the eyes, open one's eye; look -at, – on, – upon, – over, – about one, – round; survey, scan, inspect; run the eye -over, – through; reconnoiter *or* reconnoitre, glance- round, – on, – over; turn -, bend- one's looks upon; direct the eyes to, turn the eyes on, cast a glance.

observe &c. (*attend to*) 457; watch &c. (*care*) 459; see with one's own eyes; watch for &c. (*expect*) 507; peep, peek, peer, pry, take a peep; play at bopeep.

look full in the face, look hard at, look intently; strain one's eyes; fix -, rivet- the eyes upon; stare, gaze; pore over, gloat on, gloat over; leer, ogle, glare; goggle; cock the eye, squint, gloat, look askance *or* askant.

Adj. OCULAR; seeing &c. *v.;* visual, optic *or* optical; ophthalmic.

CLEAR-SIGHTED &c. *n.;* clear-eyed, far-sighted; eagle-, hawk-, lynx-, keen-, Argus- eyed.

VISIBLE &c. 446.

Adv. VISIBLY &c. 446; in sight of, with one's eyes open.

AT SIGHT, at first sight, at a glance, at the first blush; *primâ facie* [*L.*].

Int. LOOK! &c. (*attention*) 457.

*** the scales falling from one's eyes; "an eye like Mars to threaten or command" [*Hamlet*]; "her eyes are homes of silent prayer" [Tennyson]; "looking before and after" [*Hamlet*]; "thy rapt soul sitting in thine eyes" [*Milton*].

443. Dim-sightedness. — N. [IMPERFECT VISION] dim -, dull -, half -, short -, near -, long -, double -, astigmatic -, failing- sight; dim &c. -sightedness; purblindness, monocularity, blearedness, lippitude; myopia, presbyopia; confusion of vision; astigmatism; color blindness, chromato-pseudoblepsis, Daltonism; day blindness, hemeralopia; snow blindness; xanthocyanopia *or* xanthocyanopsia; ophthalmia; cataract; nyctalopia, moon blindness.

SQUINT, cross-eye, strabismus, strabism, nystagmus; cast in the eye, swivel eye, cockeye, goggle-eyes; obliquity of vision.

WINKING &c. *v.;* nictitation, nictation; blinkard, albino.

DIZZINESS, swimming, scotomy *or* scotoma [*med.*].

[LIMITATION OF VISION] blinker, blinder; screen &c. (*hider*) 530.

[FALLACIES OF VISION] *deceptio visûs* [*L.*]; refraction, distortion, illusion, false light, anamorphosis, virtual image, spectrum, mirage, looming, phasma [*obs.*]; phantasm, phantasma, phantom; vision; specter *or* spectre, apparition, ghost; *ignis fatuus* [*L.*] &c. (*luminary*) 423; specter of the Brocken; magic mirror; magic lantern &c. (*show*) 448; mirror, lens &c. (*instrument*) 445.

V. BE DIM-SIGHTED &c. *n.;* see double; "see men as trees walking" [*Bible*]; have a mote in the eye, have a mist before the eyes, have a film over the eyes; see through a -prism, - glass darkly; wink, blink, nictitate, nictate; squint; look askance *or* askant, screw up the eyes, glare, glower.

DAZZLE, glare, swim, blur, loom.

Adj. DIM-SIGHTED &c., myopic, nearsighted, shortsighted; presbyopic; astigmatic; moon-, blear-, goggle-, gooseberry-, one- eyed; blind of one eye, monoculous *or* monocular *or* monoculate; half-blind, purblind; cockeyed [*colloq.*], dim-eyed, mole-eyed, mope-eyed [*obs.*]; dichroic.

blind as a bat &c. (*blind*) 442; winking &c. *v.*

444. Spectator. — N. SPECTATOR, beholder, observer, looker-on, onlooker, *assistant* [*F.*], viewer, gazer, witness, eye-witness, bystander, passer-by; sightseer; rubberneck [*slang, U. S.*].

spy, scout; sentinel &c. (*warning*) 668.

GRANDSTAND [*fig.*], bleachers [*fig., U. S.*], gallery, the gods [*slang*].

V. WITNESS, behold &c. (*see*) 441; look on &c. (*be present*) 186; rubber *or* rubberneck [*slang, U. S.*].

445. Optical Instruments. — N. OPTICAL INSTRUMENTS; lens, meniscus, magnifier; microscope, simple microscope *or* single microscope, compound microscope, projecting microscope, ultramicroscope; spectacles, glasses, barnacles [*colloq., Eng.*], gig lamps [*slang*], goggles, eyeglass, *pince-nez* [*F.*]; periscopic lens; telescope, glass, teinoscope, prism telescope; lorgnette, binocular; spyglass, opera glass, field glass; burning glass, convex lens.

prism; camera, hand camera, kodak [*trade name*], moving-picture machine; camera-lucida, camera-obscura; magic lantern &c. (*show*) 448; megascope; stereopticon; chromatrope, thaumatrope; stereoscope, pseudoscope, polyscope, kaleidoscope, kaleidophon *or* kaleidophone.

photometer, optometer, eriometer, actinometer, lucimeter, radiometer; abdominoscope, gastroscope, helioscope, polariscope, polemoscope, spectroscope, spectrometer.

MIRROR, reflector, speculum; looking-glass, pier-glass, cheval-glass; hand mirror.

OPTICS, optician; photography, photographer; optometry, optometrist; abdominoscopy; gastroscopy; microscopy, microscopist.

446. Visibility. — N. VISIBILITY, perceptibility, perceivability; conspicuousness, distinctness &c. *adj.;* conspicuity [*rare*]; appearance &c. 448; basset [*geol.*]; exposure; manifestation &c. 525; ocular -proof, – evidence, – demonstration; field of view &c.(*vision*) 441; periscopism.

V. BE *or* BECOME VISIBLE &c. *adj.;* appear, open to the view; meet –, catch the eye; basset [*geol.*], crop out; present –, show –, manifest –, produce –, discover –, reveal –, expose –, betray– itself; stand forth, stand out; materialize; show; arise; peep out, peer out; start up, spring up, show up [*colloq.*], turn up, crop up; glimmer, gleam, glitter, glow, loom; glare; burst forth; burst upon the -view, – sight; heave in sight [*naut. or colloq.*]; come in sight, come into view, come out, come forth, come forward; see the light of day; break through the clouds; make its appearance, show its face, appear to one's eyes, upon the stage, float before the eyes, speak for itself &c. (*manifest*) 525; attract the attention &c. 457; reappear; live in a glass house.

expose to view &c. 525.

Adj. VISIBLE, perceptible, perceivable, discernible, apparent; in view, in full view, in sight; exposed to view, *en évidence* [*F.*]; unclouded.

447. Invisibility. — N. INVISIBILITY, invisibleness, nonappearance, imperceptibility; indistinctness &c. *adj.;* mystery, delitescence *or* delitescency.

CONCEALMENT &c. 528; latency &c. 526.

V. BE INVISIBLE &c. *adj.;* be hidden &c. (*hide*) 528; lurk &c. (*lie hidden*) 526; escape notice.

RENDER INVISIBLE &c. *adj.;* conceal &c. 528; put out of sight.

not see &c. (*be blind*) 442; lose sight of.

Adj. INVISIBLE, imperceptible; undiscernible, indiscernible; unapparent, nonapparent; out of sight, not in sight; *à perte de vue* [*F.*], behind the -scenes, – curtain; viewless, sightless; unconspicuous, inconspicuous; unseen &c. (*see* see &c. 441); covert &c. (*latent*) 526; eclipsed, under an eclipse.

INDISTINCT; dim &c. (*faint*) 422; mysterious, dark, obscure, confused; indistinguishable, undiscernible *or* undiscernable, shadowy, indefinite, undefined; ill-defined, ill-marked; blurred, blurry, fuzzy, out of focus; misty &c. (*opaque*) 426; veiled &c. (*concealed*) 528; delitescent.

*** "full many a flower is born to blush unseen" [Gray].

DISTINCT, plain, clear, definite; obvious &c. (*manifest*) 525; well-defined, well-marked; in focus; recognizable, palpable, autoptic *or* autoptical; glaring, staring, conspicuous; stereoscopic *or* stereoscopical; in bold relief, in strong relief, in high relief.

PERISCOPIC *or* periscopical, panoramic.

Adv. BEFORE ONE; under one's -nose, – very eyes; before –, under– one's eyes; *à vue d'œil* [*F.*], in one's eye, *oculis subjecta fidelibus* [*L.*]; visibly &c. *adj.;* in sight of; *veluti in speculum* [*L.*].

448. Appearance. — N. APPEARANCE, phenomenon, sight, spectacle, show, premonstration [obs.], scene, species, view, coup d'œil [F.]; lookout, outlook, prospect, vista, perspective, bird's-eye view, scenery, landscape, seascape, picture, tableau; display, exposure, mise en scène [F.], rising of the curtain.

PHANTASM, phantom &c. (fallacy of vision) 443.

SPECTACLE, pageant; peep show, rareeshow, galanty (or gallanty) show; ombres chinoises [F.]; magic lantern, phantasmagoria, dissolving views; biograph, cinematograph, cinema [colloq., Brit.], moving pictures, movies [colloq.], photoplay, photodrama; panorama, diorama, cosmorama, georama; coup de théâtre [F.], jeu de théâtre [F.]; pageantry &c. (ostentation) 882; insignia &c. (indication) 550.

449. Disappearance. — N. DISAPPEARANCE, evanescence, eclipse, occultation; insubstantiality.

departure &c. 293; exit; vanishing, vanishment, vanishing point; dissolving views.

V. DISAPPEAR, vanish, dissolve, fade, melt away, pass, go, avaunt [obs.]; be gone &c. adj.; leave no trace, "leave not a rack behind" [Tempest]; go off the stage &c. (depart) 293; suffer –, undergo– an eclipse; retire from sight; be lost to view, be lost to sight, see no longer, fade away [slang], pass out of sight.

lose sight of.

efface &c. 552.

Adj. DISAPPEARING &c. v.; evanescent; missing, lost; lost to sight, lost to view; gone.

Int. VANISH! disappear! fade! [slang], beat it! [slang], avaunt! &c. (ejection) 297.

ASPECT, angle, phase, phasis, seeming; shape &c. (form) 240; guise, look, complexion, color, image, mien, air, cast, carriage, port, demeanor; presence, expression, first blush, face of the thing; point of view, light.

LINEAMENT, feature, trait, lines; outline, outside; contour, silhouette, face, countenance, visage, phiz [colloq.], cast of countenance, profile, tournure [F.], cut of one's jib [colloq.], outside &c. 220.

PHYSIOGNOMY, metoposcopy, phrenology; physiognomist, metoposcopist, phrenologist.

V. APPEAR; be or become visible &c., 446; seem, look, show; present –, wear –, carry –, have –, bear –, exhibit –, take –, take on –, assume– the -appearance, – semblance- of; look like; cut a figure, figure; present to the view; show &c. (make manifest) 525.

Adj. APPARENT, seeming, ostensible; on view.

Adv. APPARENTLY; to all seeming, to all appearance; ostensibly, seemingly, as it seems, on the face of it, primâ facie [L.]; at the first blush, at first sight; in the eyes of; to the eye.

₊ editio princeps; "this insubstantial pageant" [Tempest]; "all the world's a stage, And all the men and women merely players" [As You Like It]; "Look here, upon this picture, and on this" [Hamlet].

CLASS IV

WORDS RELATING TO THE INTELLECTUAL FACULTIES

DIVISION (I) FORMATION OF IDEAS

Section I. OPERATIONS OF INTELLECT IN GENERAL

450. Intellect. — N. INTELLECT, mind, understanding, reason, thinking principle; rationality; cogitative –, cognitive –, discursive –, reasoning –, intellectual-faculties; faculties, senses, consciousness, observation, percipience *or* percipiency, apperception, mentality, intelligence, intellection [*obs.*], intuition, association of ideas, instinct, conception, judgment, wits, parts, capacity, intellectuality, genius; brains, cognitive –, intellectual-powers; wit &c. 498; ability &c. (*skill*) 698; wisdom &c. 498; *Vernunft* [*Ger.*], *Verstand* [*Ger.*].

450a. Absence or **want of Intellect. —N.** ABSENCE OF INTELLECT, want of intellect &c. 450; apartments to let [*slang*], nobody home [*slang*], unintellectuality; imbecility &c. 499; brutality, brute instinct, brute force.

Adj. unendowed with –, void of– reason; unintelligent &c. (*imbecile*) 499.

EGO, soul, spirit, ghost [*archaic*], inner man, heart, breast, bosom, *penetralia mentis* [*L.*], *divina particula auræ* [*L.*], *anima divina* [*L.*], heart's core; psyche, pneuma, subconscious self, subliminal consciousness, supreme principle, the Absolute.

SEAT OF THOUGHT, organ of thought, sensorium, sensory, brain; head, head-piece; pate [*colloq.*], noddle [*colloq.*], skull, pericranium, cerebrum, cranium, brain pan, brain box, brain case, sconce [*colloq.*], upper story [*colloq.*].

[SCIENCE OF MIND] metaphysics; philosophy &c. 451; psychics; pneumatology, psychology, psychogenesis; noölogy, noöscopics, ideology; mental –, moral-philosophy; philosophy of the mind.

phrenology; craniology, cranioscopy; psychometry, psychophysics, psychanalysis *or* psycho-analysis.

IDEALITY, idealism; transcendentalism, immateriality &c. 317; universal -concept, – conception; mahat [*theos.*].

PSYCHICAL RESEARCH; telepathy, thought transference, thought reading; clair-audience; clairvoyance, mediumship; spiritualism &c. 992*a*.

metaphysician, philosopher, psychologist, psychometer, psychopath, psycho-physicist; psychic, medium, spiritist; adept, mahatma, yogi [*Hinduism*].

V. REASON, understand, think, reflect, cogitate, excogitate, conceive. judge, contemplate, meditate; ruminate &c. (*think*) 451.

NOTE, notice, mark; take -notice, – cognizance- of; be aware of, be conscious of; realize; appreciate; fancy &c. (*imagine*) 515.

Adj. [RELATING TO INTELLECT] intellectual, mental, rational, endowed with reason; subjective, noöscopic, psychological; cerebral; percipient, appercipient, animastic; brainy [*colloq.*].

HYPERPHYSICAL, superphysical; subconscious, subliminal; telepathic, clair-audient, clairvoyant; psychic *or* psychical, spiritual, ghostly; metaphysical, transcendental.

IMMATERIAL &c. 317.

₊ *cogito ergo sum; ens rationis; frons est animi janua* [Cicero]; *locos y niños dicen la verdad; mens sola loco non exulat* [Ovid]; "my mind is my kingdom" [Campbell]; "stern men with empires in their brains" [Lowell]; "the mind, the music breathing from her face" [Byron]; "thou living ray of intellectual Fire" [Falconer]; "the mental condition of the modern world . . . the condition in which all natural explanations have broken down and no supernatural explanation has been established" [Chesterton]; "Friends, fellow mortals, bearers of the ghost That burns, and breaks its lamp, but is not lost" [Masefield].

451. Thought. — N. THOUGHT; exercitation –, exercise- of the intellect; intellection; reflection, cogitation, consideration, meditation, study, lucubration, speculation, deliberation, pondering; head work, brainwork; cerebration; mentation, deep reflection; close study, application &c. (*attention*) 457.

association –, succession –, flow –, train –, current- of -thought, – ideas.

MATURE THOUGHT; afterthought, reconsideration, second thoughts; retrospection &c. (*memory*) 505; excogitation; examination &c. (*inquiry*) 461; invention &c. (*imagination*) 515.

thoughtfulness &c. *adj.*

ABSTRACTION, abstract thought, contemplation, musing; brown study &c. (*inattention*) 458; reverie *or* revery, depth of thought, workings of the mind, thoughts, inmost thoughts; self-counsel, self-communing, self-consultation.

[PHILOSOPHY] philosophical -opinions, – systems, – schools; the handmaid of theology, *ancilla theologiæ* [L.].

452. [ABSENCE OR WANT OF THOUGHT]. **Incogitance. — N.** INCOGITANCE *or* incogitancy, vacancy, inunderstanding, vacancy of mind, poverty of intellect &c. 499; thoughtlessness &c. (*inattention*) 458; inanity, fatuity, vacuity.

V. NOT THINK &c. 451; not think of; dismiss from the -mind, – thoughts &c. 451.

indulge in reverie &c. (*be inattentive*) 458.

put away thought; unbend –, relax –, divert- the mind; make the mind a blank, let the mind lie fallow.

Adj. VACANT, inane, unintellectual, nonunderstanding, unideal, unoccupied, unthinking, incogitant, incogitative, unreasoning, inconsiderate, thoughtless; absent &c. (*inattentive*) 458; diverted; irrational &c. 499; narrow-minded &c. 481.

UNTHOUGHT OF, undreamt of, unconsidered; off one's mind; incogitable, inconceivable, not to be thought of.

₊ *absence d'esprit; pabulum pictura pascit inani.*

ORIENTAL PHILOSOPHY: Vedânta *or* Uttara-Mîmâmsâ ["later investigation"]; Pûrva-Mîmâmsâ ["prior investigation"]; Sâmkhya– , Yoga –, Nyâya –, Vaisheshika- philosophy.

GREEK AND GRECO-ROMAN PHILOSOPHY: Ionian –, Pythagorean –, Eleatic- school; Atomism; Sophism *or* Sophistic philosophy.

Socratic –, Megarian *or* Eristic –, Elean- school; Cynic philosophy; Cyrenaic *or* Hedonistic school, Hedonism; Platonism; philosophy of the -Absolute, – Academy; Aristotelianism, philosophy of the Lyceum; Peripatetic school [historical formula: *concept, Idea, essence*].

Stoic philosophy, Stoicism, philosophy of the Porch; Epicureanism, philosophy of the Garden; Scepticism; Eclecticism.

Neo-Pythagoreanism; Neo-Platonism.

PATRISTIC PHILOSOPHY: Gnosticism, Manicheism; Alexandrian school; philosophy of the Ante-Nicene Fathers, philosophy of the Post-Nicene Fathers.

SCHOLASTIC PHILOSOPHY: Scholasticism; Eclecticism; Mysticism, Mystic philosophy; Pantheistic school, pantheism; Thomism, Scotism, voluntarism; Averroism.

MODERN PHILOSOPHY: Post-Reformation philosophy; Humanism, rationalism, political philosophy; Cartesianism; Spinozism; empiricism, moralism; idealistic philosophy, idealism; Leibnitzianism *or* Leibnizianism, Berkeleian philosophy, Berkeleyism; pan-phenomenalism.

modern German philosophy: Kantianism, Fichteanism, Schelling's philosophy, Hegelianism, Herbartianism, Schopenhauer's philosophy; neocriticism; Freudianism, Freudian theory; Einstein theory, relativism.

modern French philosophy: traditionalism; psychologico-spiritualistic school; Positivism; sociological school; Bergsonism.

modern English philosophy: associational psychology, utilitarianism, Darwinism, evolutionistic ethics; Spencerian philosophy; agnosticism, idealism, Neo-Hegelianism.

modern Italian philosophy: Vicoism, sensism, empiricism, criticism, idealism, ontologism, Neo-Scholasticism.

American philosophy: Transcendentalism, pragmatism, neo-voluntarism, new ethical movement; Neo-Hegelianism, Neo-Hegelian movement.

V. THINK, reflect, cogitate, excogitate, consider, reason, deliberate; bestow -thought, – consideration -upon; speculate, contemplate, meditate, ponder, muse, dream, ruminate; brood over, con over, study; mouse over [*U. S.*], mull over [*colloq., U. S.*], sweat over [*colloq.*]; bend –, apply- the mind &c. (*attend*) 457; digest, discuss, hammer at, hammer out, weigh, perpend [*archaic*]; realize, appreciate; fancy &c. (*imagine*) 515; trow [*archaic*].

rack –, ransack –, crack –, beat –, cudgel- one's brains; set one's -brain, – wits- to work; cerebrate, mentalize [*rare*].

harbor –, entertain –, cherish –, nurture- an idea &c. 453, take into one's head; bear in mind; reconsider.

TAKE INTO CONSIDERATION; take counsel &c. (*be advised*) 695; commune with oneself, bethink oneself; collect one's thoughts; revolve –, turn over –, run over- in the mind; chew the cud upon [*colloq.*], sleep upon; take counsel of –, advise with- one's pillow.

SUGGEST itself, present itself, occur; come –, get- into one's head; strike one, flit across the view, come uppermost, run in one's head; enter –, pass in –, cross, –, flash on –, flash across –, float in –, fasten itself on –, be uppermost in –, occupy- the mind; have in one's mind.

MAKE AN IMPRESSION; sink –, penetrate- into the mind; engross the thoughts.

Adj. THOUGHTFUL, pensive, meditative, reflective, cogitative, excogitative, museful, wistful, contemplative, speculative, deliberative, studious, sedate, introspective, Platonic, philosophical; thinking &c. *v.*

UNDER CONSIDERATION, in contemplation, under advisement.

ABSORBED, rapt; lost in thought &c. (*inattentive*) 458; engrossed in &c. (*intent*) 457.

Adv. all things considered, taking everything into -account, – consideration.

*** the mind being on the stretch; the -mind, – head- -turning, – running- upon; "divinely bent to meditation" [*Richard III*]; *en toute chose il faut considérer la fin;* "freshpluckt from bowers of never-failing thought" [O. Meredith]; "go speed the stars of Thought" [Emerson]; "in maiden meditation fancy-free" [*M. N. D.*]; "so sweet is zealous contemplation" [*Richard III*]; "the power of Thought is the magic of the Mind" [Byron]; "those that think must govern those that toil" [Goldsmith]; "thought is parent of the deed" [Carlyle]; "thoughts in attitudes'imperious" [Longfellow]; "thoughts that breathe and words that burn" [Gray]; *vivere est cogitare* [Cicero]; *Volk der Dichter und Denker;* "thinking is the function; living is the functionary" [Emerson].

---

453. [OBJECT OF THOUGHT.] **Idea.** —
N. IDEA, notion, conception, thought, apprehension, impression, perception, image, eidolon [*Gr. εἴδωλον*], sentiment, reflection, observation, consideration; abstract idea; archetype, formative notion; guiding –, organizing- conception; image in the mind, regulative principle.

VIEW &c. (*opinion*) 484; theory &c. 514; conceit, fancy; phantasy &c. (*imagination*) 515.

VIEWPOINT, point of view; aspect &c. 448; field of view.

*** "Like a poet hidden In the light of thought" [Shelley].

454. [SUBJECT OF THOUGHT, *νοήματα*].
Topic. — **N.** SUBJECT OF THOUGHT, material for thought; food for the mind, mental pabulum.

SUBJECT, subject matter; matter, *motif* [*F.*], theme, noemata [*Gr. νοήματα*], topic, what it is about, thesis, text, business, affair, matter in hand, argument; motion, resolution; head, chapter; case, point; proposition, theorem; field of inquiry; moot point, debatable point, point at issue, point in question; problem &c. (*question*) 461.

V. float –, pass- in the mind &c. 451.

Adj. THOUGHT OF; uppermost in the mind; *in petto* [*It.*].

Adv. UNDER CONSIDERATION, under advisement; in question, in the mind; at issue, up for discussion, before the house, on foot, on the docket, on the carpet, on the tapis, *sur le tapis* [*F.*]; relative to &c. 9.

Section II. Precursory Conditions and Operations

455. [Desire of knowledge.] **Curiosity.** — **N.** curiosity, curiousness; interest, thirst for knowledge, mental acquisitiveness; newsmongery, inquiring mind; inquisitiveness.

questioner, *enfant terrible* [F.], walking interrogation point [*humorous*], quidnunc.

busybody, newsmonger; Peeping Tom, Paul Pry, eavesdropper; gossip &c. (*news*) 532.

sight-seer, rubberneck [*slang, U. S.*],
V. be curious &c. *adj.;* take an interest in, stare, gape; prick up the ears, see sights, lionize; rubber *or* rubberneck [*slang, U. S.*].

pry, nose, search, ferret out, poke one's nose into.

Adj. curious, inquisitive, burning with curiosity, overcurious, nosey [*colloq.*]; inquiring &c. 461; prying; inquisitorial; agape &c. (*expectant*) 507.

⁎⁎ what's the matter? what next? little pitchers have big ears; "Curiosity is mere vanity. Most people want to know only in order to talk" [Pascal].

456. [Absence of curiosity.] **Incuriosity.** — **N.** incuriosity; incuriousness &c. *adj.;* apathy, insouciance &c. 866; indifference.

V. be incurious &c. *adj.;* have no curiosity &c. 455; be bored by, take no interest in &c. 823; mind one's own business, pursue the even tenor of one's way, glance neither to the right hand nor to the left.

Adj. incurious, uninquisitive, indifferent; impassive &c. 823; uninterested, bored.

⁎⁎ "eyes and no-eyes."

457. Attention. — **N.** attention; mindfulness &c. *adj.;* intentness, intentiveness [*rare*]; alertness; thought &c. 451; advertence *or* advertency; observance, observation; consideration, reflection, perpension [*obs.*]; heed; heedfulness; particularity; notice, regard &c. *v.;* circumspection &c. (*care*) 459; study, scrutiny; inspection, introspection; revision, revisal.

active –, diligent –, exclusive –, minute –, close –, intense –, deep –, profound –, abstract –, labored –; deliberate- -thought, – attention, – application, – study.

absorption of mind &c. (*abstraction*) 458.

minuteness, meticulosity, meticulousness, finicality, finicalness; circumstantiality, attention to detail.

indication, calling attention to &c. *v.*
V. be attentive &c. *adj.;* attend, advert to, observe, look, see, view, remark, notice, regard, take notice, mark; give –, pay- -attention, – heed- to; know what o'clock it is [*colloq.*], know the time of day [*colloq.*]; incline –, lend- an ear to; trouble one's head about; give a thought to, animadvert; occupy oneself with; contemplate &c. (*think of*) 451; look -at, – to, – after, – into, – over; see to; turn –, bend –, apply –, direct –, give- the -mind, – eye, –attention -to;

458. Inattention. — **N.** inattention, inconsideration, want of consideration; inconsiderateness &c. *adj.;* oversight; inadvertence *or* inadvertency, nonobservance, disregard.

supineness &c. (*inactivity*) 683; *étourderie* [F.]; want of thought; heedlessness &c. (*neglect*) 460; insouciance &c. (*indifference*) 866.

abstraction; absence of mind, absorption of mind; preoccupation, distraction, reverie *or* revery, brown study [*colloq.*], woolgathering, moonraking [*dial. Eng.*], pipe dream [*colloq.*], castle in the air, *château en Espagne* [F.], fancy, deep musing, fit of abstraction.

V. be inattentive &c. *adj.;* overlook, disregard; pass by &c. (*neglect*) 460; not observe &c. 457; think little of.

close –, shut- one's eyes to; pay no attention to; dismiss –, discard –, discharge- from one's -thoughts, – mind; drop the subject, think no more of; set –, turn –, put- aside: turn away from, turn one's attention from, turn a deaf ear to, turn one's back upon.

abstract oneself, dream, be somewhere else, be absent, be woolgathering, indulge in reverie *or* revery.

escape notice, escape attention; come in at one ear and go out at the other; forget &c. (*have no remembrance*) 506.

have an eye to, have in one's eye; bear in mind; take into -account, – consideration; keep in -sight, – view; have regard to, heed, mind, take cognizance of, entertain, recognize; make –, take- note of; note.

EXAMINE, – closely, – intently; scan, scrutinize, consider; give –, bend- one's mind to; overhaul, revise, pore over; inspect, review, pass under review; take stock of; get the gist of; fix –, rivet –, devote- the -eye, – mind, – thoughts, – attention- on *or* to; hear out, think out; mind one's business, attend to one's business.

EXAMINE CURSORILY; glance -at, – upon, – over; cast –, pass- the eyes over; run over, turn over the leaves, dip into, perstringe [*obs.*]; skim &c. (*neglect*) 460; take a cursory view of.

REVERT TO, hark back to; watch &c. (*expect*) 507, (*take care of*) 459; hearken *or* harken to, listen to; prick up the ears; have –, keep- the eyes open; come to the point.

MEET WITH ATTENTION; fall under one's -notice, – observation; be under consideration &c. (*topic*) 454.

catch –, strike- the eye; attract notice; catch –, awaken –, wake –, invite –, solicit –, attract –, claim –, excite –, engage –, occupy –, strike –, arrest –, fix –, engross –, absorb –, rivet- the -attention, – mind, – thoughts; be present to the mind, be uppermost in the mind.

CALL ATTENTION TO, bring under one's notice; point -out, – to, – at, –the finger at; lay the finger on, indigitate [*obs.*], indicate; direct attention to; show; put a mark upon &c. (*sign*) 550; call soldiers to "attention"; bring forward &c. (*make manifest*) 525.

call off –, draw off –, call away –, divert –, distract- the -attention, – thoughts, – mind; put out of one's head.

CONFUSE, disconcert, discompose, put out, perplex, bewilder, moider [*dial. Eng.*], fluster, flurry, rattle [*colloq.*], muddle, dazzle.

Adj. INATTENTIVE; unobservant, unmindful, unheeding, undiscerning; inadvertent; mindless, regardless, respectless; listless &c. (*indifferent*) 866; blind, deaf; hen-headed [*colloq.*], flighty, giddypated, giddy-headed, bird-witted; hand over head [*rare*]; cursory, percursory [*rare*], volatile, scatter-brained, harebrained; unreflecting, *écervelé* [*F.*], inconsiderate, offhand, thoughtless, dizzy, muzzy [*colloq.*], brainsick; giddy, – as a goose; wild, harum-scarum [*colloq.*], rantipole, heedless, careless &c. (*neglectful*) 460.

ABSTRACTED, absent, *distrait* [*F.*], woolgathering, moonraking [*dial. Eng.*], dazed, absent-minded, lost; lost –, wrapped- in thought; rapt, in the clouds, bemused, day-dreaming; dreaming of–, musing on- other things; preoccupied, engrossed &c. (*attentive*) 457; in a reverie &c. *n.;* off one's guard &c. (*inexpectant*) 508; napping; dreamy; caught napping.

DISCONCERTED, put out &c. *v.;* rattled [*colloq.*].

Adv. INATTENTIVELY, inadvertently &c. *adj.; per incuriam* [*L.*], *sub silentio* [*L.*].

Int. stand at ease, stand easy!

*** the attention wanders; one's wits gone a -woolgathering, – bird's nesting; it never entered into one's head; the mind running on other things; one's thoughts being elsewhere; had it been a bear it would have bitten you; *aliquando bonus dormitat Homerus* [Hor.].

Adj. ATTENTIVE, mindful, heedful, intentive [*rare*], advertent, all eyes and ears, observant, regardful; alive to, awake to; on the job [*colloq.*]; there with the goods [*colloq.*]; observing &c. *v.;* alert; taken up with, occupied with; engaged in, engrossed in, wrapped in; absorbed, rapt; breathless; preoccupied &c. (*inattentive*) 458; watchful &c. (*careful*) 459; intent on, open-eyed; breathless, undistracted, upon the stretch; on the watch &c. (*expectant*) 507.

steadfast &c. (*persevering*) 604a.

Int. SEE! look! look you! look to it! mark! lo! behold! soho! hark! hark ye! mind! look out! look alive! [*colloq.*]; look here! [*colloq.*]; halloo! observe! lo and behold! attention! *nota bene* [*L.*]; N.B.; *, †; I'd have you know! notice! O yes! Oyez! *dekko!* [*Hind.*], *ecco!* [*It.*], yo-ho! ho!

*** this is –, these are- to give notice; *dictum sapienti sat est; finem respice;* "Give every man thy ear, but few thy voice" [*Hamlet*].

459. Care. — [VIGILANCE.] — N. CARE, solicitude, heed, concern, reck [*poetic*], heedfulness &c. *adj.;* scruple &c. (*conscientiousness*) 939.

VIGILANCE; watchfulness &c. *adj.;* surveillance, eyes of a lynx, eyes of Argus, watch, vigil, lookout, watch and ward, *l'œil du maître* [*F.*].

espionage &c. (*reconnoitering*) 461; invigilation, watching.

ALERTNESS &c. (*activity*) 682; attention &c. 457; prudence &c., circumspection &c. (*caution*) 864; anxiety; forethought &c. 510; precaution &c. (*preparation*) 673; tidiness &c. (*order*) 58, (*cleanliness*) 652; accuracy &c. (*exactness*) 494; minuteness, meticulousness, meticulosity, circumstantiality, attention to detail.

WATCHER, watchdog &c. 664.

V. BE CAREFUL &c. *adj.;* reck [*archaic*]; take care &c. (*be cautious*) 864; pay attention to &c. 457; take care of; look -, see- -to, –after; keep an eye upon, keep a sharp eye upon, chaperon, matronize, play gooseberry; keep watch, keep watch and ward; mount guard, set watch, watch; keep in -sight, – view; mind, mind one's business.

look sharp, look about one; look with one's own eyes; keep a -good, – sharp-lookout; have all one's -wits, – eyes-about one; watch for &c. (*expect*) 507; keep one's eyes open, have the eyes open, sleep with one eye open; catch a weasel asleep.

do one's best &c. 682; mind one's Ps and Qs [*colloq.*], speak by the card, pick one's steps.

TAKE PRECAUTIONS &c. 673; protect &c. (*render safe*) 664.

Adj. CAREFUL, regardful, heedful; taking care &c. *v.;* particular; prudent &c. (*cautious*) 864; considerate; thoughtful &c. (*deliberative*) 451; provident &c. (*prepared*) 673; alert &c. (*active*) 682; sure-footed.

GUARDED, on one's guard; on the -*qui vive* [*F.*], – alert, – watch, – lookout; awake, broad awake, vigilant; watchful, wakeful, Argus-eyed, lynx-eyed; wide awake &c. (*intelligent*) 498; on the watch for &c. (*expectant*) 507.

SCRUPULOUS &c. (*conscientious*) 939; tidy &c. (*orderly*) 58, (*clean*) 652; accurate &c. (*exact*) 494; *cavendo tutus* [*L.*] &c. (*safe*) 664.

174

460. Neglect. — N. NEGLECT; carelessness &c. *adj.;* trifling &c. *v.;* negligence; omission, laches [*obs.*], deferment, procrastination, default; supineness &c. (*inactivity*) 683; conspiracy of silence; inattention &c. 458; nonchalance &c. (*insensibility*) 823; imprudence, recklessness &c. 863; slovenliness &c. (*disorder*) 59, (*dirt*) 653; improvidence &c. 674; noncompletion &c. 730; inexactness &c. (*error*) 495.

PARALEIPSIS *or* paralipsis [*rhet.*].

TRIFLER, waiter on Providence; Micawber; waster [*colloq.*], wastrel [*dial. Eng.*], drifter [*colloq.*], bum [*slang*, *U. S.*], hobo [*U. S.*], tramp, Knight of the Road [*humorous*], down-and-outer [*colloq.*], dead one [*slang*], stiff [*slang*], roustabout [*U. S.*], sundowner [*Australia*]; slacker.

V. BE NEGLIGENT &c. *adj.;* take no care of &c. (take care of &c. 459); neglect; let slip, let go; lay -, set -, cast -, put- aside; keep -, leave- out of sight; lose sight of.

DELAY, defer, procrastinate, postpone, adjourn, pigeonhole, tie up with red tape, shelve, stay, suspend, table, lay on the table.

OVERLOOK, disregard; pass over, pass by; let pass; blink; wink at, connive at; gloss over; take no -note, – notice, – thought, – account- of; pay no regard to; *laisser aller* [*F.*].

SCAMP; trifle, fribble; do by halves; slight &c. (*despise*) 930; play with, trifle with; slur; skimp [*dial. & colloq.*]; skim, – the surface; *effleurer* [*F.*]; take a cursory view of &c. 457; slur -, slip -, skip -, jump- over; pretermit, miss, skip, jump, cut [*colloq.*], omit, give the go-by to [*slang*], push aside, throw into the background, sink.

IGNORE, refuse to notice, shut one's eyes to, refuse to hear, turn a deaf ear to, leave out of one's calculation; not attend to &c. 457, not mind; not trouble -oneself, – one's head- -with, – about; forget &c. 506.

BE CAUGHT NAPPING &c. (*not expect*) 508; leave a loose thread; let the grass grow under one's feet.

RENDER NEGLECTFUL &c. *adj.;* put *or* throw off one's guard.

Adj. NEGLECTING &c. *v.;* unmindful, negligent, neglectful; heedless, careless,

Adv. CAREFULLY &c. *adj.;* with care, gingerly.

⁎⁎ *quis custodiet istos custodes?* "care will kill a cat" [Wither]; *ni bebas agua que no veas;* "O polished perturbation! golden care!" [*Henry IV*]; "the incessant care and labor of his mind" [*Henry IV*]; Heaven helps those who help themselves.

thoughtless, inconsiderate; perfunctory, remiss.

UNWARY, unwatchful, unguarded, incircumspect [*rare*], uncircumspect, off one's guard, offhand.

SUPINE &c. (*inactive*) 683; inattentive &c. 458; insouciant &c. (*indifferent*) 823; imprudent, reckless &c. 863; slovenly &c. (*disorderly*) 59, (*dirty*) 653; inexact &c. (*erroneous*) 495; improvident &c. 674.

NEGLECTED &c. *v.;* unheeded, uncared for, unperceived, unseen, unobserved, unnoticed, unnoted, unmarked, unattended to, unthought of, unregarded, unremarked, unmissed; shunted, shelved.

UNEXAMINED, unstudied, unsearched, unscanned, unweighed, unsifted, unexplored.

ABANDONED; buried in a napkin; hid under a bushel.

Adv. NEGLIGENTLY &c. *adj.;* hand over head [*obs.*], in any old way [*colloq.*], anyhow; in an unguarded moment &c. (*unexpectedly*) 508; *per incuriam* [*L.*]; when the cat is away.

Int. NEVER MIND, no matter, let it pass; it will be all the same a hundred years hence; *mañana* [*Sp.*].

⁎⁎ "procrastination is the thief of time" [Young].

461. Inquiry. [SUBJECT OF INQUIRY. Question.] — **N.** INQUIRY; request &c. 765; search, research, quest; pursuit &c. 622.

EXAMINATION, review, scrutiny, investigation, indagation [*obs.*]; perquisition, perscrutation [*rare*], pervestigation [*obs.*]; inquest, inquisition; exploration; exploitation, ventilation.

sifting; calculation, analysis, dissection, resolution, induction; Baconian method.

strict –, close –, searching –, exhaustive- inquiry; narrow –, strict-search; study &c. (*consideration*) 451.

scire facias [*L.*], *ad referendum* [*L.*]; trial.

QUESTIONING &c. *v.;* interrogation, interrogatory; interpellation; challenge, examination, third degree [*colloq.*], cross-examination, catechism, catechesis; feeler, Socratic method, zetetic philosophy; leading question; discussion &c. (*reasoning*) 476.

RECONNOITERING, reconnaissance *or* reconnoissance, prying &c. *v.;* espionage, *espionnage* [*F.*]; domiciliary visit, peep behind the curtain; lantern of Diogenes.

QUESTION, query, problem, poser, desideratum, point to be solved, porism; subject –, field- of -inquiry, – controversy; point –, matter- in dispute;

462. Answer. — **N.** ANSWER, response, reply, replication, riposte *or* ripost, subjoinder, rejoinder, retort, repartee; rescript, rescription [*archaic*]; antiphon, antiphony; acknowledgment; password; echo; counterstatement, counterblast, countercharge, contradiction.

[LAW] defense, plea, surrebutter, surrejoinder, reply, rejoinder, rebutter.

SOLUTION &c. (*explanation*) 522; discovery &c. 480a; rationale &c. (*cause*) 153; clew *or* clue &c. (*indication*) 550.

Œdipus; oracle &c. 513; return &c. (*record*) 551.

V. ANSWER, respond, reply, rebut, riposte *or* ripost, retort, rejoin; give answer, return for answer; acknowledge, echo.

[LAW] defend, plead, surrebut, surrejoin, rebut, reply.

EXPLAIN &c. (*interpret*) 522; solve &c. (*unriddle*) 522; discover &c. 480a; fathom, hunt out &c. (*inquire*) 461; satisfy, set at rest, determine.

Adj. ANSWERING &c. *v.;* responsive, respondent; antiphonal; Œdipean, oracular; conclusive.

Adv. FOR THIS REASON; because &c. (*cause*) 153; on the scent, on the right scent.

Int. eureka.

moot point; issue, question at issue; bone of contention &c. (*discord*) 713; plain –, fair –, open- question; enigma &c. (*secret*) 533; knotty point &c. (*difficulty*) 704; *quodlibet* [*L.*]; threshold of an inquiry.

INQUIRER, investigator, inquisitor, inspector, querist, examiner, probator, catechist; scrutator, scrutineer, scrutinizer; analyst; quidnunc &c. (*curiosity*) 455.

V. INQUIRE, seek, search; make inquiry &c. *n.;* look -for, – about for, – out for; scan, reconnoiter *or* reconnoitre, explore, sound, rummage, ransack, pry, peer, look round; look –, go- -over, – through; give the once-over [*slang*]; spy, overhaul. scratch the head, slap the forehead.

look –, peer –, pry- into every hole and corner; visit –, look- behind the scenes; nose, nose out, trace up; hunt out, fish out, ferret out; unearth; leave no stone unturned.

TRACK, seek a clew. *or* clue; hunt, trail, shadow, mouse, dodge, trace; follow the -trail, – scent; pursue &c. 662; beat up one's quarters; fish for; feel for &c. (*experiment*) 463.

INVESTIGATE; take up –, institute –, pursue –, follow up –, conduct –, carry on –, prosecute- an inquiry &c. *n.;* look at, look into; preëxamine; discuss, canvass, agitate.

EXAMINE, mouse over [*U. S.*], study, consider, calculate; dip –, dive –, delve –, go deep- into; make sure of, probe, sound, fathom; probe to the -bottom, – quick; scrutinize, analyze, anatomize, dissect, parse, resolve, sift, winnow; view –, try- in all its phases; thresh out.

BRING IN QUESTION, subject to examination, pose; put to the proof &c. (*experiment*) 463; audit, tax, pass in review; take into consideration &c. (*think over*) 451; take counsel &c. 695.

QUESTION, ask, demand; put –, propose –, propound –, moot –, start –, raise –, stir –, suggest –, put forth –, ventilate –, grapple with –, go into- a question.

INTERROGATE, put to the question, catechize, pump; cross-question, cross-examine; roast [*colloq.*], grill [*colloq.*], put through the third degree [*colloq.*]; dodge; require an answer; pick –, suck- the brains of; feel the pulse.

BE IN QUESTION &c. *adj.;* undergo examination.

Adj. INQUIRING &c. *v.;* inquisitive &c. (*curious*) 455; requisitive [*obs.*], requisitory; catechetical, inquisitorial, analytic; in search of, in quest of; on the lookout for, interrogative, zetetic; all-searching.

UNDETERMINED, untried, undecided, tentative; in question, in dispute, in issue, in course of inquiry; under -discussion, – consideration, – investigation &c. *n.;* *sub judice* [*L.*], moot, proposed; doubtful &c. (*uncertain*) 475.

Adv. WHAT? why? wherefore? *pourquoi?* [*F.*], *warum?* [*Ger.*], whence? whither? where? *quære?* [*L.*]; how comes it? how does it happen? how is it? what is the reason? what's the matter? what's in the wind? what's afoot? what's up? what's in the air? what is it all about? what on earth? when? who? *nicht wahr?* [*Ger.*].

463. Experiment. — N. EXPERIMENT; essay &c. (*attempt*) 675; analysis &c. (*investigation*) 461; docimasy, trial, tentative method, *tâtonnement* [*F.*].

VERIFICATION, probation, *experimentum crucis* [*L.*], proof, criterion, diagnostic, test, crucial test; assay, ordeal.

REAGENT, crucible, check, touchstone, pyx *or* pix [*Brit. mint*], curcuma paper, turmeric paper.

EMPIRICISM, rule of thumb.

FEELER; pilot –, messenger- balloon; pilot engine; scout; straw to show the wind.

SPECULATION, random shot, leap in the dark.

EXPERIMENTER, experimentist, experimentalist, assayer, analyst, analyzer; prospecter *or* prospector, Forty-Niner [*U. S.*], adventurer; speculator, gambler, stock gambler, plunger [*slang*].

V. EXPERIMENT; essay &c. (*endeavor*) 675; try, assay; make an experiment, make trial of; give a trial to; put upon –, subject to- trial; experiment upon; rehearse;

put –, bring –, submit- to the -test, – proof; prove, verify, test, touch, practice upon, try one's strength.

GROPE; feel –, grope- -for, – one's way; fumble, *tâtonner* [*F*.], *aller à tâtons* [*F*.]; put –, throw- out a feeler; send up a pilot balloon; see how the -land lies, – wind blows; consult the barometer; feel the pulse; fish for, bob for; cast –, beat- about for; angle, trawl, cast one's net, beat the bushes.

VENTURE; try one's fortune &c. (*adventure*) 675; explore &c. (*inquire*) 461.

Adj. EXPERIMENTAL, probative, probatory, probationary; analytic, docimastic *or* docimastical, speculative, tentative; empirical.

TRIED, tested, proved.

ON TRIAL, on examination, on *or* under probation, "on suspicion" [Elbert Hubbard], under suspicion; on one's trial.

464. Comparison. — N. COMPARISON, collation, contrast, parallelism, balance; identification; comparative –, relative- estimate.

simile, similitude, parallelization [*rare*]; allegory &c. (*metaphor*) 521.

V. COMPARE, – to, – with; collate, confront; place side by side &c. (*near*) 197; set –, pit- against one another; contrast, balance.

compare notes; institute a comparison; *parva componere magnis* [*L*.].

PARALLEL, parallelize; draw a parallel.

Adj. COMPARATIVE, relative, contrastive; metaphorical &c. 521.

COMPARED WITH &c. *v.*; comparable; judged by comparison.

Adv. RELATIVELY &c. (*relation*) 9; as compared with &c. *v.*

*** comparisons are odious; "comparisons are odorous" [*Much Ado*].

465. Discrimination. — N. DISCRIMINATION, distinction, differentiation, diagnosis, diorism; nice perception; perception –, appreciation- of difference; estimation &c. 466; nicety, refinement; taste &c. 850; critique, judgment; tact; discernment &c. (*intelligence*) 498; acuteness, penetration; *nuances* [*F*.].

TIP, pointer, dope [*slang*]; past performances, record.

V. DISCRIMINATE, distinguish, severalize [*obs*.]; separate; draw the line, sift; separate –, winnow- the chaff from the wheat; separate the wheat from the tares; separate the sheep from the goats; split hairs.

465a. Indiscrimination. — N. INDISCRIMINATION; indistinctness, indistinction; want of distinction, want of discernment, inability to discriminate; uncertainty &c. (*doubt*) 475.

V. NOT DISCRIMINATE &c. 465; overlook &c. (*neglect*) 460- a distinction; confound, confuse, jumble, jumble together, heap indiscriminately; swallow whole, judge in a lump, use loosely.

Adj. INDISCRIMINATE, indistinguishable, lacking distinction, undistinguished, undistinguishable; unmeasured; promiscuous, undiscriminating.

*** *valeat quantum valere potest.*

estimate &c. (*measure*) 466; tip, tip off, sum up, criticize; know which is which, know what's what [*colloq*.], know one's way about, know a thing or two, know what o'clock it is, know the time of day, have cut one's eyeteeth, know the ways of the world [*all colloq*.]; "know a hawk from a handsaw" [*Hamlet*].

take into -account, – consideration; give –, allow- due weight to; weigh carefully.

Adj. DISCRIMINATING &c. *v.*; dioristic *or* dioristical [*obs*.], critical, diagnostic, perceptive, discriminative, distinctive; nice, acute.

*** *il y a fagots et fagots; rem acu tetigisti; la critique est aisée et l'art est difficile;* "He could distinguish, and divide A hair 'twixt south and south-west side" [Butler].

466. Measurement. — N. MEASUREMENT, admeasurement, mensuration, metage, mete [*rare*] survey, valuation, appraisement, assessment, assize; estimate, estimation; dead reckoning [*naut*.]; reckoning &c. (*numeration*) 85; gauging &c. *v.*; horse power, candle power, candle foot, foot candle, volt ampere, kilowatt; foot pound, foot poundal, foot ton; velo

METROLOGY, weights and measures, compound arithmetic.

MEASURE, yard measure, standard, rule, foot rule, spirit level, plumb line; square, T-square, steel square, compass, dividers, calipers; gauge *or* gage, standard gauge, broad *or* wide gauge, narrow gauge; log, log-line, patent log [*naut.*]; meter, line, rod, check.

flood mark, high-water mark, load-line mark, Plimsoll mark; index &c. 550.

SCALE; graduation, graduated scale; nonius; vernier &c. (*minuteness*) 193; quadrant, theodolite, transit *or* transit theodolite, viagraph; scale, beam, steelyard, weighing machine, balance &c. (*weight*) 319; anemometer &c. (*wind*) 349; barometer &c. (*air*) 338; bathometer &c. (*depth*) 208; dynamometer &c. (*force*) 276; galvanometer &c. (*power*) 157; goniometer &c. (*angle*) 244; hyetometer &c. (*fluids in motion*) 348; landmark &c. (*limit*) 233; pedometer &c. (*length*) 200; photometer &c. (*optical instruments*) 445; radiometer &c. (*light*) 420; stethoscope &c. (*medical*) 662; thermometer &c. 389.

coördinates, ordinate and abscissa, polar coördinates, latitude and longitude, declination and right ascension, altitude and azimuth.

GEOMETRY, stereometry, planimetry, hypsometry, altimetry, hypsography, chorometry, chorography, topography, cartography; surveying, land surveying, geodesy, geodetics, geodæsia *or* geodesia, orthometry; cadastre *or* cadaster; cadastral survey, cadastration.

astrolabe, armillary sphere.

SURVEYOR, land surveyor; geometer, chorographer, topographer, cartographer.

V. MEASURE, meter, mete; value, assess, rate, appraise, estimate, form an estimate, set a value on; appreciate; standardize.

span, pace, step, inch, dial; caliper, divide, apply the compass &c. *n.*; gauge *or* gage; balance, poise, hold the scales; place in the beam, kick the beam; plumb, probe, sound, fathom; heave the -log, - lead; survey, plot, block in, block out, rule, draw to scale.

take an average &c. 29; graduate, calibrate.

Adj. MEASURING &c. *v.;* metric, metrical; measurable; geodetical, cadastral, hypsographic *or* hypsographical, hypsometric *or* hypsometrical, chorographic *or* chorographical, topographic *or* topographical, cartographic *or* car ographical.

. "For 'Is' and 'Is-not' though with Rule and Line, And 'Up-and-Down' by Logic I define" [Omar Khayyám — Fitzgerald].

Section III. MATERIALS FOR REASONING

467. Evidence [ON ONE SIDE.] — **N.** EVIDENCE; facts, premises, data, præcognitum (*pl.* præcognita), grounds; indication &c. 550; criterion &c. (*test*) 463.

TESTIMONY, testification; attestation; affirmation, declaration; deposition &c. 535; examination.

AUTHORITY, warrant, credential, diploma, voucher, certificate, docket; *testamur* [*L.*]; record &c. 551; muniments; document; *pièce justificative* [*F.*]; deed, warranty &c. (*security*) 771; autograph, handwriting, signature, seal &c. (*identification*) 550; exhibit; citation, reference, quotation; admission &c. (*assent*) 488.

WITNESS, indicator, eyewitness, earwitness, deponent; sponsor; cojuror, oath-helper [*hist.*], compurgator [*hist.*].

EVIDENCE IN CHIEF; oral -, docu-

468. [EVIDENCE ON THE OTHER SIDE.] **Counterevidence.** — **N.** COUNTEREVIDENCE; evidence on the other -side, - hand; disproof; refutation &c. 479; negation &c. 536; conflicting evidence.

plea &c. 617; vindication &c. 937; counter-protest; *tu quoque* [*L.*] argument; other side -, reverse- of the shield; *reductio ad absurdum* [*L.*].

V. COUNTERVAIL, oppose; rebut &c. (*refute*) 479; subvert &c. (*destroy*) 162; check, weaken; contravene; run counter; contradict &c. (*deny*) 536; tell another story, turn the scale, alter the case; turn the tables; cut both ways; prove a negative.

audire alteram partem [*L.*].

Adj. COUNTERVAILING &c. *v.;* contradictory, in rebuttal.

UNATTESTED, unauthenticated, un-

mentary –, hearsay –, external –, extrinsic –, internal –, intrinsic –, circumstantial –, cumulative –, *ex parte* [*L.*] –, presumptive –, collateral –, constructive- evidence; proof &c. (*demonstration*) 478; finger print, thumb print.

SECONDARY EVIDENCE; confirmation, corroboration, support; ratification &c. (*assent*) 488; authentication; compurgation [*hist.*], wager of law [*hist.*], comprobation [*obs.*].

WRIT, summons &c. (*lawsuit*) 696.

V. BE EVIDENCE &c. *n.;* evince, show, betoken, tell of; indicate &c. (*denote*) 550; imply, involve, argue, bespeak, breathe.

HAVE WEIGHT, carry weight; tell, speak volumes; speak for itself &c. (*manifest*) 525.

REST UPON, depend upon; repose on.

BEAR WITNESS &c. *n.;* give evidence &c. *n.;* testify, depose, witness, vouch for; sign, seal, undersign, set one's hand and seal, sign and seal, deliver as one's act and deed, certify, attest; acknowledge &c. (*assent*) 488.

CONFIRM, make absolute, ratify, corroborate, indorse *or* endorse, countersign, support, bear out, vindicate, uphold, warrant.

ADDUCE, attest, evidence, cite, quote; refer to, appeal to; call, call to witness; bring forward, bring on, bring into court; allege, plead; produce –, confront- witnesses; collect –, bring together –, rake up- evidence.

ESTABLISH; have –, make out- a case; authenticate, circumstantiate, substantiate, verify, make good, quote chapter and verse; bring home to, bring to book, bring off.

supported by evidence; supposititious, trumped up.

Adv. CONVERSELY, on the other hand, on the other side, in opposition; *per contra* [*L.*].

469. Qualification. — N. QUALIFICATION, limitation modification, coloring.

ALLOWANCE, grains of allowance, consideration, extenuating circumstances; mitigation.

CONDITION, proviso, exception; exemption; salvo [*rare*], saving clause; discount &c. 813; restriction.

V. QUALIFY, limit, modify, affect, leaven, take color from, give a color to, introduce new conditions, narrow, temper.

ALLOW FOR, make allowance for; admit exceptions, take into account; modulate.

TAKE EXCEPTION, file exceptions, object, raise objections, rise to a point of order.

Adj. QUALIFYING &c. *v.;* modificatory, extenuatory, mitigatory, lenitive, palliative; conditional; exceptional &c. (*unconformable*) 83.

HYPOTHETICAL &c. (*supposed*) 514; contingent &c. (*uncertain*) 475.

Adv. PROVIDED, – always; if, unless, but, yet; according as; conditionally, admitting, supposing; on the supposition of &c. (*theoretically*) 514; with the understanding, even, although, though, for all that, after all, at all events.

IF POSSIBLE &c. 470; with grains of allowance, *cum grano salis* [*L.*]; *exceptis excipiendis* [*L.*], wind and weather permitting.

SUBJECT TO; with this proviso &c. *n.*

Adj. EVIDENTIAL; showing &c. *v.;* indicative, indicatory; deducible &c. 478; grounded on, founded on, based on; first-hand, authentic, verificative, verifiable, veridical, cumulative, corroborative, confirmatory; significant, weighty, overwhelming, damning, conclusive.

oral, documentary, hearsay &c. (*evidence in chief*) *n.*

Adv. BY INFERENCE; according to, witness, *a fortiori* [*L.*]; still more, still less; *raison de plus* [*F.*]; in corroboration of &c. *n.;* *valeat quantum* [*L.*]; under seal, under one's hand and seal; at first hand, at second hand.

⁎⁎ *dictum de dicto;* "where are the evidence that do accuse me?" [*Richard III*]; "we must never assume that which is incapable of proof" [George Henry Lewes]; "litigious terms, fat contentions, and flowing fees" [Milton]; "I do not know the method of drawing up an indictment against an whole people" [Burke]; "Still you keep o' the windy side of the law" [*Twelfth Night*]; "Oh Sammy, Sammy, vy worn't there a alleybi!" [Dickens]; "A dog's obeyed in office" [*King Lear*].

Degrees of Evidence

470. Possibility. — N. POSSIBILITY, potentiality, potency; what may be, what is possible &c. *adj.;* compatibility &c. (*agreement*) 23.

PRACTICABILITY, feasibility, workability, workableness; practicableness &c. *adj.*

CONTINGENCY, chance &c. 156.

V. BE POSSIBLE &c. *adj.;* stand a chance; have a leg to stand on; admit of, bear.

RENDER POSSIBLE &c. *adj.;* put in the way of, bring to bear, bring together.

Adj. POSSIBLE; on the -cards, -dice; *in posse* [*L.*], within the bounds of possibility, conceivable, imaginable, credible; compatible &c. 23; likely.

PRACTICABLE, feasible, workable, performable, achievable; within -reach, -measurable distance; accessible, superable, surmountable; attainable, obtainable; contingent &c. (*doubtful*) 475.

Adv. POSSIBLY, by any possibility; perhaps, perchance, peradventure; may be, it may be, haply, mayhap.

IF POSSIBLE, wind and weather permitting, God willing, *Deo volente* [*L.*], D. V.; as luck may have it.

₊ *misericordia Domini inter pontem et fontem;* "the glories of the Possible are ours" [B. Taylor].

471. Impossibility. — N. IMPOSSIBILITY &c. *adj.;* what cannot be, what can never be; sour grapes; hopelessness &c. 859; infeasibility, infeasibleness, impracticality; discrepancy &c. (*disagreement*) 241.

[COMPARISONS] Canute (commanding the tide), Mrs. Partington (and her mop).

V. BE IMPOSSIBLE &c. *adj.;* have no chance whatever.

ATTEMPT IMPOSSIBILITIES; square the circle, find the elixir of life, discover the philosopher's stone, discover the grand panacea, find the fountain of youth, discover the secret of perpetual motion; wash a blackamoor white; skin a flint; make a silk purse out of a sow's ear, make bricks without straw; have nothing to go upon; weave a rope of sand, build castles in the air, *prendre la lune avec les dents* [*F.*], extract sunbeams from cucumbers, milk a he-goat into a sieve, catch a weasel asleep, *rompre l'anguille au genou* [*F.*], be in two places at once; gather grapes from thorns, fetch water in a sieve, catch wind in cabbage nets, fling eels by the tail, make cheese of chalk.

Adj. IMPOSSIBLE; not possible &c. 470; absurd, contrary to reason; at variance with the facts; unlikely; unreasonable &c. 477; incredible &c. 485; beyond the bounds of -reason, - possibility; from which reason recoils; visionary; inconceivable &c. (*improbable*) 473; prodigious &c (*wonderful*) 870; unimaginable, inimaginable [*obs.*], not to be thought of, unthinkable.

IMPRACTICABLE, unachievable; unfeasible, infeasible; insuperable; insurmountable *or* unsurmountable, unattainable, unobtainable; out of reach, out of the question; not to be had; beyond control; desperate &c. (*hopeless*) 859; incompatible &c. 24; inaccessible, uncomeatable [*colloq.*], impassable, impervious, innavigable, inextricable; self-contradictory.

out of -, beyond- one's -power, - depth, - reach, - grasp; too much for; *ultra crepidam* [*L.*].

₊ the grapes are sour; *non possumus; non nostrum tantas componere lites* [Vergil]; *chercher une aiguille dans une botte de foin; il a la mer à boire;* "few things are impossible to diligence and skill" [Johnson]; "it is not a lucky word, this same *impossible*" [Carlyle].

472. Probability. — N. PROBABILITY, likelihood; credibleness; likeliness &c. *adj.; vraisemblance* [*F.*], verisimilitude, plausibility; color, semblance, show of; presumption; presumptive -, circumstantial- evidence; credibility.

reasonable -, fair -, good -, favorable- -chance, - prospect; prospect; well-grounded hope; chance &c. 156.

473. Improbability. — N. IMPROBABILITY, unlikelihood; unfavorable -, bad -, ghost of a -, little -, small -, poor -, scarcely any -, no- chance; bare possibility; long odds; incredibility &c. 485.

V. BE IMPROBABLE &c. *adj.;* violate -, stretch- the probabilities; go beyond reason, strain one's credulity; run

V. BE PROBABLE &c. *adj.;* give –, lend-color to; point to; imply &c. *(evidence)* 467; bid fair &c. *(promise)* 511; stand fair for; stand –, run- a good chance; stand–, run- an even chance.

PRESUME, infer, venture, suppose, take for granted, think likely, dare say, flatter oneself; expect &c. 507; count upon &c. *(believe)* 484.

Adj. PROBABLE, likely, hopeful, to be expected, in a fair way.

PLAUSIBLE, specious, ostensible, colorable, *ben trovato* [*It.*], well-founded, reasonable, credible, easy of belief, presumable, presumptive, apparent.

Adv. PROBABLY &c. *adj.;* belike [*archaic*]; in all probability, in all likelihood; very –, most- likely; like enough; very like; ten &c. to one; apparently, seemingly, to all seeming, as like as not [*colloq.*], according to every reasonable expectation; *primâ facie* [*L.*]; to all appearance &c. *(to the eye)* 448.

∗ the chances are, the odds are; appearances –, chances- are in favor of; there is reason to -believe, – think, – expect; I dare say; dollars to doughnuts [*U. S.*]; all Lombard Street to a China orange.

counter to the laws of nature; have a small chance &c. *n.;* stand a poor show [*colloq.*].

Adj. IMPROBABLE, unlikely, contrary to all reasonable expectation; contrary to -fact, – experience; implausible, rare &c. *(infrequent)* 137; unheard of, inconceivable; unimaginable, inimaginable [*obs.*]; incredible &c. 485; more than doubtful.

Int. NOT LIKELY! no fear! [*chiefly Eng.*]; I ask you! [*slang*]; catch me! [*slang*].

∗ the chances are against; *aquila non capit muscas; pedir peras al olmo;* "Lest men suspect your tale untrue, Keep probability in view" [Gay].

474. Certainty. — N. CERTAINTY; necessity &c. 601; certitude, sureness, surety, assurance; dead –, moral- certainty; infallibleness &c. *adj.;* infallibility, reliability, reliableness; indubitableness, inevitableness, unquestionableness.

gospel, scripture, church, pope, court of final appeal; *res adjudicata,* [*L.*], *res judicata* [*L.*]; ultimatum.

FACT; positive fact, matter of fact; *fait accompli* [*F.*].

BIGOTRY, positiveness, dogmatism, dogmatization; fanaticism.

DOGMATIST, dogmatizer, doctrinaire, bigot, opinionist, Sir Oracle; dogmatic theorist; zealot, fanatic; *ipse dixit* [*L.*].

V. BE CERTAIN &c. *adj.;* stand to reason.

RENDER CERTAIN &c. *adj.;* insure *or* ensure, assure; clinch, make sure; determine, find out once for all, decide, set at rest, "make assurance double sure" [*Macbeth*]; know &c. *(believe)* 484; dismiss all doubt, admit of no doubt.

DOGMATIZE, lay down the law.

Adj. CERTAIN, sure; assured &c. *v.;* solid, well-founded.

UNQUALIFIED, absolute, positive, determinate, definite, clear, unequivocal, categorical, unmistakable, decisive, decided, ascertained.

475. Uncertainty. — N. UNCERTAINTY, incertitude, doubt; doubtfulness &c. *adj.;* dubiety, dubitation, dubitancy [*obs.*], dubiosity, dubiousness.

HESITATION, suspense, state of suspense; perplexity, embarrassment, dilemma, Morton's fork [*hist.*], bewilderment; botheration [*colloq.*]; puzzle, quandary; timidity &c. *(fear)* 860; vacillation &c. 605; aporia, diaporesis, indetermination; sealed orders.

VAGUENESS &c. *adj.;* haze, fog; obscurity &c. *(darkness)* 421; ambiguity &c. *(double meaning)* 520; contingency, double contingency, possibility upon a possibility; open question &c. *(question)* 461; *onus probandi* [*L.*], blind bargain, pig in a poke, leap in the dark, something or other; needle in a bottle of hay; roving commission.

FALLIBILITY; unreliability, unreliableness, untrustworthiness; precariousness &c. *adj.*

V. BE UNCERTAIN &c. *adj.;* wonder whether.

lose the -clew *or* clue, – scent; miss one's way, wander aimlessly, beat about, hang around.

not know -what to make of &c. *(unintelligibility)* 519, – which way to turn, – whether one stands on one's head or one's heels; float in a sea of doubt,

INEVITABLE, unavoidable, avoidless; ineluctable.

CONCLUSIVE, unimpeachable, undeniable, unquestionable; indefeasible, indisputable, incontestable, incontrovertible indubitable; irrefutable &c. (*proven*) 478; without power of appeal, inappealable, final.

INDUBIOUS; without –, beyond a –, without a shade or shadow of- -doubt, – question; past dispute; clear as day; beyond all -question, – dispute; undoubted, uncontested, unquestioned, undisputed; questionless, doubtless.

AUTHORITATIVE, authentic, official, governmental, curule.

sure as -fate, – death and taxes, – a gun [*colloq.*].

EVIDENT, self-evident, axiomatic; clear, – as day, – as the sun at noonday; apparent &c. (*manifest*) 525.

INFALLIBLE, unerring; unchangeable &c. 150; to be depended on, trustworthy, reliable, bound.

DOGMATIC, opinionative, opinionated, dictatorial, doctrinaire; fanatical, bigoted.

Adv. CERTAINLY &c. *adj.;* for certain, certes [*archaic*], sure, no doubt, doubtless, and no mistake [*colloq.*], *flagrante delicto* [*L.*]; sure enough, to be sure, of course, as a matter of course, *a coup sûr* [*F.*], *sans doute* [*F.*], questionless [*rare*], for a certainty, of a certainty, to a certainty; in truth &c. (*truly*) 494; at any rate, at all events; without fail; *coûte que coûte* [*F.*], *coûte qu'il coûte* [*F.*]; whatever may happen, if the worse come to the worst; come what may, come what will, happen what may, happen what will; sink or swim; rain or shine, live or die.

⁎⁎ cela va sans dire; there is -no question, – not a shadow of doubt; the die is cast &c. (*necessity*) 601; "facts are stubborn things" [Smollett].

hesitate, flounder; lose oneself, lose one's head; muddle one's brains.

RENDER UNCERTAIN &c. *adj.;* put out, pose, puzzle, perplex, embarrass; muddle, confuse, confound; bewilder, bother, moider [*dial.*], rattle [*colloq.*], nonplus, addle the wits, throw off the scent, keep in suspense, keep one guessing.

DOUBT, &c. (*disbelieve*) 485; hang in the balance, tremble in the balance; depend.

Adj. UNCERTAIN, unsure; casual; random &c. (*aimless*) 621; changeable, changeful &c. 149.

DOUBTFUL, dubious; dazed; insecure, unstable, indecisive; unsettled, undecided, undetermined; in suspense, open to discussion; controvertible; in question &c. (*inquiry*) 461.

VAGUE; indeterminate, indefinite; ambiguous, equivocal; undefined, undefinable, confused &c. (*indistinct*) 447; mysterious, cryptic, veiled, obscure, oracular.

PERPLEXING &c. *v.;* enigmatic, paradoxical, apocryphal, problematical, hypothetical; experimental &c. 463.

FALLIBLE, questionable, precarious, slippery, ticklish, debatable, disputable; unreliable, untrustworthy.

UNAUTHENTIC, unauthenticated, unauthoritative; unascertained, unconfirmed; undemonstrated; untold, uncounted.

CONTINGENT, contingent on, dependent on; subject to; dependent on circumstances; occasional; provisional.

in a state of uncertainty, on the horns of a dilemma, in a cloud, in a maze; bushed, off the track; derailed; ignorant &c. 491; afraid to say; out of one's reckoning, out of one's bearings, astray, adrift; at sea, at fault, at a loss, at one's wit's end, at a non-plus; puzzled &c. *v.;* lost, abroad, *désorienté* [*F.*]; distracted, distraught.

Adv. UNCERTAINLY &c. *adj.;* at random, until things straighten out, while things are so uncertain, in this state of suspense; *pendente lite* [*L.*]; *sub spe rati* [*L.*].

⁎⁎ Heaven knows; who can tell? who shall decide when doctors disagree? spargere voces in vulgum ambiguas [Vergill]; "he is no wise man who will quit a certainty for an uncertainty" [Johnson]; "a little philosophy inclineth man's mind to atheism, but depth in philosophy bringeth men's minds about to religion" [Bacon]; dum in dubio est animus paulo momento huc illuc impellitur [Terence]; "To-morrow is, ah, whose?" [Mulock]; "Unborn To-morrow and dead Yesterday" [Omar Khayyám—Fitzgerald]; "Gather ye rose-buds while ye may" [Herrick]; "Uncertainty! Fell demon of our fears! The human soul, That can support despair, supports not thee" [Mallet]; "There is such a choice of difficulties, that I own myself at a loss how to determine" [General James Wolfe—Dispatch to Pitt].

Section IV. REASONING PROCESSES

476. Reasoning. — N. REASONING; ratiocination, rationalism; dialectics, dialecticism, induction, generalization.

DISCUSSION, comment; ventilation; inquiry &c. 461.

ARGUMENTATION, controversy, debate; polemics, wrangling; contention &c. 720; logomachy, disputation, disceptation [*archaic*]; paper war.

LOGIC, art of reasoning.

process –, train –, chain- of reasoning; deduction, induction; synthesis, analysis.

argument; case, plea, *plaidoyer* [*F.*], opening; premise *or* premiss; lemma, proposition, terms, premises; postulate, data, starting point, principle; inference &c. (*judgment*) 480.

prosyllogism, syllogism; enthymeme, sorites, dilemma, *a fortiori* reasoning, *a priori* reasoning, *reductio ad absurdum* [*L.*], horns of a dilemma, *argumentum ad hominem* [*L.*], comprehensive argument; empirema, epagoge.

LOGICAL SEQUENCE; good case; correct –, just –, sound –, valid –, cogent –, irrefutable –, logical –, forcible –, persuasive –, persuasory [*rare*] –, consectary [*obs.*] –, conclusive &c. 478 –, subtle-reasoning; force of argument; strong -point, – argument.

ARGUMENTS, reasons, pros and cons.

REASONER, logician, dialectician; disputant; controversialist, controvertist; wrangler, arguer, debater, polemic, casuist, rationalist; scientist; eristic.

V. REASON, argue, discuss, debate, dispute, wrangle; argufy *or* argify [*dial.*], bandy -words, – arguments; chop logic; hold –, carry on- an argument; controvert &c. (*deny*) 536; canvass; comment –, moralize- upon; consider &c. (*examine*) 461.

TRY CONCLUSIONS; open a -discussion, - case; join –, be at- issue; moot; come to the point; stir –, agitate –, ventilate –, torture- a question; take up a -side, - case.

CONTEND, take one's stand upon, insist, lay stress on; infer &c. 480.

FOLLOW FROM &c. (*demonstration*) 478.

Adj. REASONING &c. *v.;* rational, ratiocinative, rationalistic; argumentative, controversial, dialectic, polemical;

477. [ABSENCE OF REASONING.] Intuition. [SPECIOUS REASONING.] **Sophistry. — N.** INTUITION, instinct, association; presentiment; rule of thumb.

SOPHISTRY, paralogy, perversion, casuistry, jesuitry, equivocation, evasion, mental reservation; chicane, chicanery; quiddit [*obs.*], quiddity; mystification; special pleading; speciousness &c. *adj.;* nonsense &c. 497; word fence, tongue fence; overrefinement, hairsplitting, quibbling &c. *v.*

false –, fallacious –, specious –, vicious- reasoning; begging of the question, *petitio principii* [*L.*], *ignoratio elenchi* [*L.*]; *post hoc ergo propter hoc* [*L.*]; *non sequitur* [*L.*], *ignotum per ignotius* [*L.*].

misjudgment &c. 481; false teaching &c. 538.

SOPHISM, solecism, paralogism; quibble, quirk, elench, elenchus, fallacy, *quodlibet* [*L.*], subterfuge, shift, subtlety, quillet [*archaic*]; inconsistency, antilogy; "a delusion, a mockery, and a snare" [Denman]; claptrap, mere words; "lame and impotent conclusion" [*Othello*].

meshes –, cobwebs- of sophistry; flaw in an argument; weak point, bad case.

SOPHIST, casuist, paralogist.

V. JUDGE INTUITIVELY, judge by intuition; hazard a proposition, talk at random.

PERVERT, quibble; equivocate, mystify, evade, elude; gloss over, varnish; misteach &c. 538; mislead &c. (*error*) 495; cavil, refine, subtilize, split hairs; misrepresent &c. (*lie*) 544.

reason ill, reason falsely &c. *adj.;* misjudge &c. 481; paralogize.

BEG THE QUESTION, reason in a circle, cut blocks with a razor, beat about the bush, play fast and loose, blow hot and cold, prove that black is white and white black, travel out of the record, *parler à tort et à travers* [*F.*], put oneself out of court, not have a leg to stand on.

Adj. INTUITIVE, instinctive, impulsive; independent of –, anterior to- reason; gratuitous, hazarded; unconnected.

ILLOGICAL, unreasonable, false, unsound, invalid; unwarranted, not following, incongruous, inconsequent, inconsequential; inconsistent; absonous

discursory, discursive; disputatious; log-omachic *or* logomachical; Aristotelian, eristic *or* eristical.

DEBATABLE, controvertible.

LOGICAL; syllogistic, soritical, epagogic, inductive, deductive, synthetic *or* synthetical, analytic *or* analytical; relevant &c. 23.

Adv. FOR, because, hence, whence, seeing that, since, sith [*archaic*], then, thence, so; for -that, – this, – which-reason; for as much as *or* forasmuch as, in as much as *or* inasmuch as; whereas, *ex concesso* [*L.*], considering, in consideration of; therefore, argal [*archaic*], wherefore; consequently, *ergo* [*L.*], thus, accordingly; *a priori* [*L.*]; *a fortiori* [*L.*].

FINALLY, in conclusion, in fine; after all, *au bout du compte* [*F.*], on the whole, taking one thing with another; pro and con; rationally &c. *adj.*

[*obs.*], absonant, unscientific; untenable, inconclusive, incorrect; fallacious, fallible; groundless, unproved.

SPECIOUS, sophistic *or* sophistical, jesuitic *or* jesuitical, casuistic *or* casuistical, paralogistic, paralogical; deceptive, illusive, illusory; hollow, plausible, *ad captandum* [*L.*], evasive; irrelevant &c. 10.

WEAK, feeble, poor, flimsy, loose, vague, irrational; nonsensical &c. (*absurd*) 497; foolish &c. (*imbecile*) 499; frivolous, pettifogging, quibbling; fine-spun, overrefined.

at the end of one's tether, *au bout de son latin* [*F.*].

Adv. INTUITIVELY &c. *adj.;* by intuition.

ILLOGICALLY &c. *adj.*

*** *non constat;* that goes for nothing; "My dear madam, nonsense can only be defended by nonsense" [Johnson — *Boswell's Life.*]

*** *ab actu ad posse valet consecutio; per troppo dibatter la verità si perde; troppo disputare la verità fa errare;* "Remembrance and reflection, how allied; What thin partitions sense from thought divide" [Pope]; "And many a Knot unravelled by the Road, But not the Master-knot of Human Fate" [Omar Khayyám — Fitzgerald]; "logic is mainly valuable wherewith to exterminate logicians" [Chesterton].

478. Demonstration. — N. DEMONSTRATION, proof, irrefragability; conclusiveness &c. *adj.;* apodeixis *or* apodixis, probation, comprobation [*obs.*].

logic of facts &c. (*evidence*) 467; *experimentum crucis* [*L.*] &c. (*test*) 463; argument &c. 476; rigorous –, absolute-establishment.

V. DEMONSTRATE, prove, establish, make good; show, evince &c. (*be evidence of*) 467; verify &c. 467; settle the question, reduce to demonstration, set the question at rest.

make out, – a case; prove one's point, have the best of the argument; draw a conclusion &c. (*judge*) 480.

FOLLOW, – of course; stand to reason; hold good, hold water [*colloq.*].

Adj. DEMONSTRATING &c. *v.,* demonstrative, demonstrable; probative, unanswerable, conclusive, convincing; apodeictic *or* apodictic, apodeictical *or* apodictical; irresistible, irrefutable, irrefragable, undeniable.

CATEGORICAL, decisive, crucial.

DEMONSTRATED &c. *v.;* proven; unconfuted, unanswered, unrefuted; evident &c. 474.

479. Confutation. — N. CONFUTATION, refutation; answer, complete answer; disproof, conviction, redargution, invalidation; exposure, exposition, *exposé* [*F.*], clincher [*colloq.*], retort, *reductio ad absurdum* [*L.*]; knock-down –; *tu quoque*- argument; sockdolager [*slang*, *U. S.*].

V. CONFUTE, refute; parry, negative, disprove, redargue, expose, show up, show the fallacy of, rebut, defeat; demolish &c. (*destroy*) 162; overthrow, overturn; scatter to the winds, explode, invalidate; silence; put –, reduce- to silence; clinch -an argument, – a question; give one a setdown [*colloq.*], stop the mouth, shut up; have, have on the hip, have the better of; confound [*archaic*], convince.

not leave a leg to stand on, cut the ground from under one's feet; smash all opposition; knock the bottom out of an argument [*colloq.*].

BE CONFUTED &c.; fail; expose –, show- one's weak point.

Adj. CONFUTABLE, confutative, refutable; confuting, confuted, &c. *v.;* capable of refutation.

DEDUCIBLE, consequential, consectary [*obs.*], inferential, following.

Adv. OF COURSE, in consequence, consequently, as a matter of course.

*** *probatum est;* there is nothing more to be said, Q.E.D., it must follow; *exitus acta probat;* "For now the field is not far off Where we must give the world a proof Of deeds, not words" [Butler]; "a thing that nobody believes cannot be proved too often" [Shaw].

condemned -on one's own showing, - out of one's own mouth; "hoist with his own petar" [*Hamlet*].

*** the argument falls to the ground; *cadit quæstio;* it does not hold water; *suo sibi gladio hunc jugulo* [Terence]; "thy speech bewrayeth thee" [*Bible*]; "Now, infidel, I have you on the hip" [*M. of V.*]; "Let us have faith that Right makes Might" [Lincoln].

Section V. RESULTS OF REASONING

480. Judgment. [CONCLUSION.] — **N.** JUDGMENT, decision, determination, finding, verdict, sentence, decree; *res adjudicata* [*L.*], *res judicata* [*L.*]; opinion &c. (*belief*) 484; good judgment &c. (*wisdom*) 498.

RESULT, conclusion, upshot; deduction, inference, ergotism [*obs.*], illation; corollary, porism; moral.

ESTIMATION, valuation, appreciation, judication; dijudication, adjudication; arbitrament, arbitrement, arbitration; assessment, ponderation [*rare*]; valorization.

ESTIMATE, award; review, criticism, critique, notice, report.

PLEBISCITE, plebiscitum, voice, casting vote; vote &c. (*choice*) 609.

ARBITER, arbitrator; judge, umpire; assessor, referee; inspector, inspecting officer; censor.

REVIEWER, critic; connoisseur; commentator &c. 524.

V. JUDGE, conclude, opine; come to -, draw -, arrive at- a conclusion; ascertain, determine, make up one's mind.

DEDUCE, derive, gather, collect, infer, draw an inference, make a deduction, weet [*obs.*], ween [*archaic*].

ESTIMATE, form an estimate, appreciate, value, count, assess, rate, rank, account; regard, consider, think of; look upon &c. (*believe*) 484; review; size up [*colloq.*].

DECIDE, settle; pass -, give- an opinion; try, pronounce, rule; pass -judgment, - sentence; sentence, doom, decree; find; give -, deliver- judgment; adjudge, adjudicate, judicate [*rare*]; arbitrate, award, report; bring in a verdict; make absolute, set a question at rest; confirm &c. (*assent*) 488.

hold the scales, sit in judgment; try a cause, hear a cause.

REVIEW, comment, criticize; pass

481. Misjudgment. — **N.** MISJUDGMENT, obliquity of judgment, warped judgment; miscalculation, miscomputation, misconception &c. (*error*) 495, hasty conclusion.

PRECONCEPTION, prejudgment, prejudication [*rare*], prejudice; foregone conclusion; prenotion, prevention [*Gallicism*], predilection, prepossession, preapprehension, presumption, presentiment, foreboding; fixed idea; *idée fixe* [*F.*], obsession, preconceived idea, *mentis gratissimus error* [*L.*]; fool's paradise.

PARTISANSHIP, *esprit de corps* [*F.*], party spirit, mob spirit, class prejudice, class consciousness, race prejudice, provincialism, clannishness, prestige.

QUIRK, shift, quibble, equivocation, evasion, subterfuge.

BIAS, warp, twist; hobby, whim, craze, fad, crotchet, partiality, infatuation, blind side, blind spot, mote in the eye.

one-sided -, partial -, narrow -, confined -, superficial- -views, - ideas, - conceptions, - notions; purblindness, *entêtement* [*F.*]; narrow mind; bigotry &c. (*obstinacy*) 606; *odium theologicum* [*L.*]; pedantry; hypercriticism.

DOCTRINAIRE &c. (*positive*) 474.

V. MISJUDGE, misestimate, misesteem, misthink, misconjecture, misconceive &c. (*error*) 495; fly in the face of facts; miscalculate, misreckon, miscompute.

overestimate &c. 482; underestimate &c. 483.

PREJUDGE, forejudge; presuppose, presume, prejudicate [*rare*], dogmatize; have a bias &c. *n.;* have only one idea; *jurare in verba magistri* [*L.*], run away with the notion; jump -, rush- to a conclusion; go off half-cocked [*colloq.*]; look only at one side of the shield; view with jaundiced eye, view through distorting spectacles; not see beyond one's nose;

under review &c. (*examine*) 457; investigate &c. (*inquire*) 461.

Adj. JUDGING &c. *v.;* judicious &c.
(*wise*) 498; determinate, conclusive, confirmatory.

CRITICAL, hypercritical, hairsplitting,
censorious.

Adv. ON THE WHOLE, all things considered, taking all this into consideration,
this being so, *quæ cum ita sint* [*L.*],
therefore, wherefore.

₊ "a Daniel come to judgment" [*Merchant
of Venice*]; "and stand a critic, hated yet
caress'd " [Byron]; "it is much easier to be
critical than to be correct" [Disraeli]; *la
critique est aisée et l'art est difficile;* "nothing
if not critical" [*Othello*].

dare pondus fumo [*L.*]; get the wrong
sow by the ear &c. (*blunder*) 699.

BIAS, warp, twist; give a -bias, – twist;
prejudice, prepossess.

Adj. MISJUDGING &c. *v.;* ill-judging,
wrong-headed; prejudiced, prepossessed;
jaundiced; shortsighted, purblind; partial, one-sided, superficial.

NARROW, narrow-minded, narrow-
souled; provincial, parochial, insular;
mean-spirited; confined, illiberal, intolerant, besotted, infatuated, fanatical,
entêté [*F.*], positive, dogmatic, dictatorial; pragmatic *or* pragmatical, egotistical, conceited; opinioned, opinionated, opinionate [*rare*], opinionative
[*rare*], opinative [*obs.*], opiniative [*obs.*];
self-opinionated; self-opinioned, wedded to an opinion, *opiniâtre* [*F.*]; bigoted &c.
(*obstinate*) 606; crotchety, fussy, impracticable; unreasonable, stupid &c. 499;
credulous &c. 486; warped.

MISJUDGED &c. *v.*

Adv. *ex parte* [*L.*].

₊ nothing like leather; the wish is father to the thought; "O most lame and impotent
conclusion" [*Othello*]; *poudre aux yeux* [*F.*]; "Stiff in opinions, always in the wrong" [Dryden].

480a. [RESULT OF SEARCH OR INQUIRY.] **Discovery.** — **N.** DISCOVERY, detection,
disenchantment; ascertainment, disclosure, find, revelation.

TROVER &c. 775.

V. DISCOVER, find, determine, evolve; fix upon; find -, trace -, make -, hunt -,
fish -, worm -, ferret -, dig -, root- out; fathom; bring out, draw out; educe, elicit,
bring to light; dig up, grub up, fish up; unearth, disinter.

SOLVE, resolve; unriddle, unravel, ravel, ravel out, unlock; pick -, open- the
lock; find a clew *or* clue to; interpret &c. 522; disclose &c. 529.

TRACE, get at; hit it, have it; lay one's -finger, – hands- upon; spot [*colloq.*], see
through a millstone [*colloq.*]; get -, arrive- at the -truth &c. 494; put the saddle
on the right horse, hit the right nail on the head.

SCENT, be near the truth, be warm [*colloq.*], burn [*colloq.*]; smoke, sniff, smell out,
smell a rat [*colloq.*].

SEE THROUGH, see daylight, see in its true colors, see the cloven foot; open the
eyes to; detect; catch, catch tripping.

MEET WITH; pitch -, fall -, light -, hit -, stumble -, pop- upon; come across; fall
in with.

RECOGNIZE, realize, verify, make certain of, identify.

Int. eureka! I have it! at last!

482. Overestimation. — **N.** OVER-
ESTIMATION &c. *v.;* exaggeration &c.
549; vanity &c. 880; optimism, pessimism.

much cry and little wool, much ado
about nothing; storm in a teacup; fine
talking; fine writing, rodomontade, gush
[*colloq.*], hot air [*slang*].

EGOISM, egotism, bombast, conceit,
swelled head [*slang*], megalomania.

EGOIST, egotist, megalomaniac; optimist, booster [*U. S.*], pessimist; Rodo-

483. Underestimation. — **N.** UNDER-
ESTIMATION; depreciation &c. (*detraction*) 934; pessimism; self-detraction,
self-depreciation; undervaluation, miosis, litotes [*rhet.*]; undervaluing &c. *v.;*
modesty &c. 881.

PESSIMIST, depreciator, knocker
[*slang*], crape-hanger [*slang*].

V. UNDERRATE, underestimate, undervalue, underreckon; depreciate; disparage &c. (*detract*) 934; not do justice
to; misprize, disprize; ridicule &c 856:

mont, Braggadochio, braggart, boaster,
braggadocio, swaggerer; hot-air artist
[*slang*], gas-bag [*slang*], wind-bag [*slang*].

V. OVERESTIMATE, overrate, overvalue, overprize, overweigh, overreckon,
overstrain, overpraise; estimate too
highly, attach too much importance to,
make mountains of molehills, catch at
straws; strain, magnify; exaggerate &c.
549; set too high a value upon; think –,
make- -much, – too much- of; outreckon.

have too high an opinion of oneself
&c. (*vanity*) 880.

EULOGIZE, panegyrize, optimize, gush
[*colloq.*], gush over [*colloq.*], boost [*U. S.*];
puff *or* puff up [*colloq.*]; extol, – to the
skies; make the -most, – best, – worst- of; make two bites of a cherry.
Adj. overestimated &c. *v.;* oversensitive &c. (*sensibility*) 822.

INFLATED, puffed up; grandiose, stilted, pompous, pretentious, megalomaniacal,
braggart, bombastic.

. all his geese are swans; parturiunt montes nascetur ridiculus mus [Horace].

pessimize; slight &c. (*despise*) 930;
neglect &c. 460; slur over.

make -light, – little, – nothing, – no
account- of; belittle, knock [*slang*],
slam [*slang*], run down [*colloq.*], minimize, think nothing of; set no store by,
set at naught; shake off like water from
a duck's back, shake off as dewdrops
from the lion's mane.

Adj. DEPRECIATING &c. *v.;* depreciative, depreciatory.

DEPRECIATED &c. *v.;* unappreciated,
unvalued, unprized.

. "All pessimism has a secret optimism
for its object" [Chesterton]; "pessimist —
a man who thinks everybody as nasty as
himself and hates them for it" [Shaw].

484. Belief. — N. BELIEF; credence;
credit; assurance; faith, trust, troth,
confidence, presumption, sanguine expectation &c. (*hope*) 858; dependence
on, reliance on.

CONVICTION, persuasion, convince-
ment, plerophory [*rare*], self-conviction;
certainty &c. 474; opinion, mind, view;
conception, thinking; impression &c.
(*idea*) 453; surmise &c. 514; conclusion
&c. (*judgment*) 480.

TENET, dogma, principle, persuasion,
views, way of thinking; popular belief
&c. (*assent*) 488.

firm –, implicit –, settled –, fixed –,
rooted –, deep-rooted –, staunch –, unshaken –, steadfast –, inveterate –, calm
–, sober –, dispassionate –, impartial –,
well-founded- -belief, – opinion &c.;
uberrima fides [*L.*].

DOCTRINE, system of opinions, school,
articles, canons; article –, declaration
–, profession- of faith; tenets, credenda,
creed, credo, thirty-nine articles &c.
(*orthodoxy*) 983a; gospel, gospel truth;
catechism; assent &c. 488; propaganda
&c. (*teaching*) 537.

CREDIBILITY &c. (*probability*) 472.

V. BELIEVE, credit; give -faith, –
credit, – credence- to; see, realize;
assume, receive; set down for, take for;
have it, take it; consider, esteem, presume.

count –, depend –, calculate –, pin

485. Unbelief. Doubt. — N. UN-
BELIEF, disbelief, misbelief; discredit,
miscreance *or* miscreancy [*archaic*]; infidelity &c. (*irreligion*) 989; wrangling,
ergotism [*rare*]; dissent &c. 489; change
of opinion &c. 484; retractation &c. 607.

DOUBT &c. (*uncertainty*) 475; skepticism *or* scepticism, misgiving, demur;
distrust, mistrust; misdoubt, suspicion,
jealousy, scruple, qualm; *onus probandi*
[*L.*].

INCREDIBILITY, incredibleness, incredulity, unbelievability.

AGNOSTIC, skeptic *or* sceptic; unbeliever &c. 487.

V. DISBELIEVE, discredit; not believe
&c. 484; misbelieve; refuse to admit &c.
(*dissent*) 489; refuse to believe &c. (*incredulity*) 487.

DOUBT; be doubtful &c. (*uncertain*)
475; doubt the truth of; be skeptical as
to &c. *adj.;* diffide [*obs.*], distrust, mistrust; suspect, smoke, scent, smell, smell
a rat [*colloq.*], have –, harbor –, enter-
tain- -doubts, – suspicions; have one's
doubts.

throw doubt upon, raise a question;
bring –, call- in question; question,
challenge; dispute; deny &c. 536; cause
–, raise –, start –, suggest –, awake- a
-doubt, – suspicion; cavil, wrangle,
ergotize [*rare*].

DEMUR, stick at, pause, hesitate, shy
at, scruple; stop to consider, waver.

187

one's faith –, reckon –, lean –, build –, rely –, rest- upon; cast one's bread upon the waters; lay one's account for; make sure of.

make oneself easy -about, – on that score; take on -trust, – credit; take for -granted, – gospel; allow –, attach- some weight to.

KNOW, – for certain; be in the know [*slang*]; have –, make- no doubt; doubt not; be –, rest- -assured &c. *adj.*; per- suade –, assure –, satisfy- oneself; make up one's mind.

CONFIDE IN, believe in, put one's trust in; give one credit for; place –, repose- implicit confidence in; take one's word for, take at one's word; place reliance on, rely upon, swear by, regard to.

THINK, hold; take, take it; opine, be of opinion, conceive, trow [*archaic*], ween [*archaic*], fancy, apprehend; have –, hold –, possess –, entertain –, adopt –, imbibe –, embrace –, get hold of –, hazard –, foster –, nurture –, cherish- -a belief, – an opinion &c. *n.*

hang in suspense, hang in doubt.

STAGGER, startle; shake –, stagger- one's -faith, – belief.

Adj. UNBELIEVING; skeptical *or* scepti- cal, incredulous –, skeptical- as to; dis- trustful of, shy of, suspicious of; doubt- ing &c. *v.*

DOUBTFUL &c. (*uncertain*) 475; dispu- table; unworthy –, undeserving- of -belief &c. 484; questionable; suspect [*archaic*], suspicious; open to -suspicion – doubt; staggering, hard to believe, incredible, unbelievable, not to be be- lieved, inconceivable.

FALLIBLE &c. (*uncertain*) 475; unde- monstrable; controvertible &c. (*untrue*) 495.

Adv. WITH CAUTION, *cum grano salis* [*L.*]; with grains of allowance.

⁎⁎ *fronti nulla fides; nimium ne crede colori* [Vergil]; *timeo Danaos et dona ferentes* [Vergil]; *credat Judæus Apella* [Hor.]; let those believe who may; *ad tristem partem strenua est suspicio* [Syrus].

view as, consider as, take as, hold as, conceive as, regard as, esteem as, deem as, look upon as, account as, set down as; surmise &c. 514.

get –, take- it into one's head; come round to an opinion; swallow &c. (*cre- dulity*) 486.

PERSUADE; cause to be believed &c. *v.*; satisfy, bring to reason, have the ear of, gain the confidence of, assure; convince, convict, convert; wean, bring round; bring –, win- over; indoctrinate &c. (*teach*) 537; cram down the throat; produce –, carry- conviction; bring –, drive- home to.

FIND CREDENCE, go down, pass current; be received &c. *v.*, be current &c. *adj.*; possess –, take hold of –, take possession of- the mind.

Adj. BELIEVING &c. *v.*; certain, sure, assured, positive, cocksure [*colloq.*], satis- fied, confident, unhesitating, convinced, secure.

under the impression; impressed –, imbued –, penetrated- with.

CONFIDING, trustful, suspectless [*obs.*], unsuspecting, unsuspicious, void of sus- picion; credulous &c. 486; wedded to.

BELIEVED &c. *v.*; accredited, putative; unsuspected, trusted, undoubted.

worthy of –, deserving of –, commanding- -belief, – confidence; credible, reli- able, trustworthy, to be depended on; satisfactory; probable &c. 472; fiducial, fiduciary; persuasive, impressive.

DOCTRINAL, relating to belief.

Adv. IN THE OPINION OF, in the eyes of; *me judice* [*L.*]; meseems [*archaic*], methinks [*archaic*]; to the best of one's belief; in my opinion, in my judgment, according to my belief; I dare say, I doubt not, I have no doubt, I am sure; cocksure, sure enough &c. (*certainty*) 474; depend –, rely- upon it; be –, rest- assured; I'll warrant you &c. (*affirmation*) 535.

⁎⁎ *experto credite* [Vergil]; *Fata viam invenient; Justitiæ soror incorrupta Fides;* "live to explain thy doctrine by thy life" [Prior]; "stands not within the prospect of belief" [*Macbeth*]; *tarde quæ credita lædunt credimus* [Ovid]; *vide et crede;* "One in whom persuasion and belief Had ripened into faith, and faith become A passionate intuition" [Wordsworth]; "faith, that lodestar of the ghost" [Masefield]; "Nothing is so firmly believed as that we least know" [Montaigne]; "Belief consists in accepting the affirmations of the soul; unbelief, in denying them" [Emerson].

486. Credulity. — N. CREDULITY, credulousness &c. *adj.;* gullibility, cullibility [*obs.*]; gross credulity, infatuation; self-delusion, self-deception; superstition; one's blind side; bigotry &c. (*obstinacy*) 606; hyperorthodoxy &c. 984; misjudgment &c. 481.

CREDULOUS PERSON &c. (*dupe*) 547.

V. BE CREDULOUS &c. *adj.; jurare in verba magistri* [*L.*]; follow implicitly; swallow, swallow whole, gulp down; take on trust; take for -granted, – gospel; take on faith; run away with -a notion, – an idea; jump –, rush- to a conclusion; think the moon is made of green cheese; take –, grasp- the shadow for the substance; catch at straws.

IMPOSE UPON &c. (*deceive*) 545.

Adj. CREDULOUS, gullible; easily deceived &c. 545; simple, green, soft, childish, silly, stupid; easily convinced; overcredulous, overconfident, overtrustful; easy to stuff [*slang*]; infatuated, superstitious; confiding &c. (*believing*) 484.

*** the wish is father to the thought; *credo quia impossibile* [Tertullian]; all is not gold that glitters; *no es oro todo lo que reluce; omne ignotum pro magnifico;* "And still they gazed, and still the wonder grew That one small head could carry all he knew" [Goldsmith].

487. Incredulity. — N. INCREDULITY. incredulousness; skepticism, freethought, Pyrrhonism; want of faith &c. (*irreligion*) 989; minimifidianism; unbelief &c. 485.

SUSPICIOUSNESS &c. *adj.;* scrupulosity; suspicion &c. (*unbelief*) 485; inconvincibility.

UNBELIEVER, skeptic *or* sceptic, miscreant [*archaic*], doubting Thomas, disbeliever, agnostic, infidel, misbeliever, nullifidian, minimifidian, zendik [*Oriental*], freethinker, Pyrrhonist &c. (*irreligion*) 989; heretic &c. (*heterodox*) 984.

V. BE INCREDULOUS &c. *adj.;* distrust &c. (*disbelieve*) 485; refuse to believe; shut one's eyes to, shut one's ears to; turn a deaf ear to; hold aloof; ignore, *nullius jurare in verba magistri* [*L.*].

Adj. INCREDULOUS, skeptical *or* sceptical, dissenting, unbelieving, inconvincible; hard of belief, shy of belief; suspicious, scrupulous, distrustful, disposed to doubt, indisposed to believe; heterodox.

*** "I'm from Missouri and I want to be shown"; "You call me misbeliever, cutthroat dog" [*M. of V.*]; "knowledge of divine things, for the most part, as Heraclitus says, is lost to us by incredulity" [Plutarch].

488. Assent. — N. ASSENT, assentment [*archaic*]; acquiescence, admission; nod; accord, concord, concordance; agreement &c. 23; affirmance, affirmation; recognition, acknowledgment, avowal, recognizance [*rare*], confession, confession of faith.

UNANIMITY, common consent, consensus, acclamation, chorus, *vox populi* [*L.*]; popular –, current- -belief, – opinion; public opinion; concurrence &c. (*of causes*) 178; coöperation &c. (*voluntary*) 709.

RATIFICATION, confirmation, corroboration, approval, acceptance, visa, *visé* [*F.*]; indorsement &c. (*record*) 551.

consent &c. (*compliance*) 762.

AFFIRMANT, assentant [*obs.*], professor [*esp. in relig.*], confirmist, consenter, covenantor, subscriber, indorser *or* endorser; upholder &c. (*auxiliary*) 711.

V. ASSENT; give –, yield –, nod-assent; acquiesce; agree &c. 23; receive, accept, accede, accord, concur, lend oneself to, consent, coincide, reciprocate, go with; be at one with &c. *adj.;* go along

489. Dissent. — N. DISSENT, nonconsent, discordance &c. (*disagreement*) 24; difference –, diversity- of opinion.

NONCONFORMITY &c. (*heterodoxy*) 984; protestantism, recusancy, schism; disaffection; secession &c. 624; recantation &c. 607.

DISSENSION &c. (*discord*) 713; discontent &c. 832; caviling, wrangling, ergotism [*rare*].

PROTEST; contradiction &c. (*denial*) 536; noncompliance &c. (*rejection*) 764.

DISSENTIENT, dissenter, noncontent *or* noncon *or* non con [*House of Lords*], nonjuror, nonconformist; sectary, separatist, recusant, schismatic, protestant; heretic &c. (*heterodoxy*) 984.

V. DISSENT, nonconsent, demur; call in question &c. (*doubt*) 485; differ in opinion, disagree, agree to differ; say no &c. 536; refuse -assent, – to admit; cavil, wrangle, ergotize [*rare*], protest, raise one's voice against, repudiate; contradict &c. (*deny*) 536.

have no notion of, differ *toto cœlo* [*L.*], revolt at, revolt from the idea.

with, chime in with, strike in with, close with; echo, enter into one's views, agree in opinion; vote for, give one's voice for; recognize; subscribe –, conform –, defer to; say -yes, – ditto, – amen, – aye- to.

go –, float –, swim– with the stream; float with the current; get on the band wagon [slang]; be in the fashion, join in the chorus; be in every mouth.

arrive at –, come to- -an understanding, – terms, – an agreement.

ACKNOWLEDGE, own, admit, allow, avow, confess; concede &c. (yield) 762; come round to; abide by; permit &c. 760.

CONFIRM, affirm; ratify, approve, indorse, visa, visé [F.], countersign; corroborate &c. 467.

Adj. ASSENTING &c. v.; of one -accord, – mind; of the same mind, affirmant, assentaneous [rare], assentant [obs.], at one with, agreed, acquiescent, content; willing &c. 602.

UNCONTRADICTED, unchallenged, unquestioned, uncontroverted.

carried –, agreed– -nem. con. [L.] &c. adv.; unanimous; agreed on all hands, carried by acclamation.

affirmative &c. 535.

shake the head, shrug the shoulders; look askance or askant.

SECEDE; recant &c. 607.

Adj. DISSENTING &c. v.; negative &c. 536; dissident, dissentient; unconsenting &c. (refusing) 764; noncontent; nonjuring; protestant, recusant; unconvinced, unconverted.

UNAVOWED, unacknowledged; out of the question.

UNWILLING &c. 603; extorted; discontented &c. 832.

SECTARIAN, sectary [rare], denominational, schismatic; heterodox; intolerant.

Adv. NO &c. 536; at variance with, at issue with; under protest.

Int. GOD FORBID! not for the world! I'll be hanged if! [colloq.]; not another word! no, sirree! [U. S.]; not if I know it! I beg to differ; never tell me! your humble servant [archaic], pardon me.

⁎ many men, many minds; quot homines tot sententiæ [Terence]; tant s'en faut; il s'en faut bien; "the dissidence of dissent and the protestantism of the Protestant religion" [Burke]; "I had no taste for what is called popular art, no respect for popular morality, no belief in popular religion, no admiration for popular heroics" [Shaw].

Adv. YES, yea, aye or ay, true; good; well; how true, very -well, – true; well and good; granted; even so, just so; to be sure, as you say, sure, surely, assuredly, "thou hast said"; truly, exactly, precisely, that's just it, indeed, certainly, certes [archaic], ex concesso [L.], of course, unquestionably, no doubt, doubtless.

BE IT SO; so be it, so let it be; so mote it be, with all one's heart; amen; willingly &c. 602.

AFFIRMATIVELY, in the affirmative.

UNANIMOUSLY, unâ voce [L.], by common consent, in chorus, to a man; with one -consent, – voice, – accord; nem. con. [L.]; nemine contradicente [L.], nemine dissentiente [L.], without a dissentient voice; as one man, one and all, on all hands.

⁎ avec plaisir; chi tace acconsente; "the public mind is the creation of the Master-Writers" [Disraeli].

490. Knowledge. — **N.** KNOWLEDGE; cognizance, cognition, cognoscence [obs.]; acquaintance, experience, ken, privity, insight, familiarity; comprehension, apprehension; recognition; appreciation &c. (judgment) 480; intuition; conscience, consciousness; perception, apperception, precognition; acroamatics.

system –, body- of knowledge; science, philosophy, pansophism, pansophy; acroama; theory, ætiology or etiology; circle of the sciences; pandect, doctrine, body of doctrine; cyclopedia or cyclopædia, encyclopedia or encyclopædia,

491. Ignorance. — **N.** IGNORANCE, nescience, tabula rasa [L.], illiteracy, unlearnedness, crass ignorance, ignorance crasse [F.]; unacquaintance; unconsciousness &c. adj.; darkness, blindness; incomprehension, inexperience, simplicity.

sealed book, terra incognita [L.], virgin soil, unexplored ground; dark ages.

unknown quantities; x, y, z.

[IMPERFECT KNOWLEDGE] smattering, superficiality, half-learning, shallowness, sciolism, glimmering; bewilderment &c. (uncertainty) 475; incapacity.

circle of knowledge; school &c. (*system of opinions*) 484.

tree of knowledge; republic of letters &c. (*language*) 560.

ENLIGHTENMENT, light; glimpse, inkling, glimmer, glimmering, dawn; scent, suspicion; impression &c. (*idea*) 453; discovery &c. 480a.

LEARNING, erudition, lore, scholarship, reading, letters; literature; book madness; book learning, bookishness; bibliomania, bibliclatry; information, general information; store of knowledge &c.; education &c. (*teaching*) 537; culture, *Kultur* [Ger.], cultivation, menticulture, attainments; acquirements, mental acquisitions; accomplishments; proficiency; practical knowledge &c. (*skill*) 698; liberal education, higher education; dilettantism; rudiments &c. (*beginning*) 66.

deep –, profound –, solid –, accurate –, acroatic –, acroamatic –, vast –, extensive –, encyclopedical- -knowledge, -learning; omniscience, pantology.

march of intellect; progress –, advance- of -science, – learning; schoolmaster abroad.

V. KNOW, ken [*dial.*], scan, wot [*archaic*]; wot of [*archaic*], be aware of &c. *adj.*; ween [*archaic*], weet [*obs.*], trow [*archaic*]; have, possess.

conceive; apprehend, comprehend; take, realize, understand, savvy [*slang, U. S.*], be wise to [*slang*], appreciate; fathom, make out; recognize, discern, perceive, see, get a sight of, experience.

KNOW FULL WELL; have –, possess-some knowledge of; be *au courant* [F.] &c. *adj.*; have in one's head, have at one's fingers' ends; know by -heart, – rote; be master of; *connaître le dessous des cartes* [F.], know what's what [*colloq.*] &c. 698.

DISCOVER &c. 480a; see one's way.

LEARN, come to one's knowledge &c. (*information*) 527.

Adj. KNOWING &c. *v.*; cognitive; acroamatic *or* acroamatical, apperceptive, appercipient.

AWARE OF, cognizant of, conscious of; acquainted with, made acquainted with; privy to, no stranger to; *au fait* [F.], *au courant* [F.]; in the secret; up to [*colloq.*], alive to; behind the -scenes, – curtain; let into; apprized of, informed of; undeceived.

[AFFECTATION OF KNOWLEDGE] pedantry, charlatanry, charlatanism; Philistine, *Philister* [Ger.].

V. BE IGNORANT &c. *adj.*; not know &c. 490; know -not, – not what, – nothing of; have no -idea, – notion, – conception; not have the remotest idea; not know chalk from cheese; not know a B from a -bull's foot, – battledore, – broomstick.

ignore, be blind to; keep in ignorance &c. (*conceal*) 528.

see through a glass darkly; have a film over the eyes, have a glimmering &c. *n.*; wonder whether; not know what to make of &c. (*unintelligibility*) 519; not pretend to say, not take upon oneself to say.

Adj. IGNORANT; nescient; unknowing, unaware, unacquainted, unapprized, unwitting, unweeting [*obs.*], unconscious; witless, weetless [*obs.*]; a stranger to; unconversant.

UNINFORMED, uncultivated, unversed, uninstructed, untaught, uninitiated, untutored, unschooled, unscholarly, unguided, unenlightened; Philistine; behind the age.

SHALLOW, superficial, green, rude, empty, half-learned, half-baked [*colloq.*], low-brow [*slang*]; illiterate; unread, uninformed, uneducated, unlearned, unlettered, unbookish; empty-headed; pedantic.

IN THE DARK; benighted, belated; blinded, blindfold; hoodwinked; misinformed; *au bout de son latin* [F.], at the end of his tether, at fault; at sea &c. (*uncertain*) 475; caught tripping, caught napping.

UNKNOWN, unapprehended, unexplained, unascertained, uninvestigated, unexplored, unheard of, unperceived; concealed &c. 528; novel.

Adv. IGNORANTLY &c. *adj.*; unawares; for anything one knows, for aught one knows; not that one knows.

Int. God –, Heaven –, the Lord –, dear [*dial.*] –, nobody- knows!

✲✲✲ "ignorance never settles a question" [Disraeli]; *quantum animis erroris inest!* [Ovid]; "small Latin and less Greek" [B. Jonson]; "that unlettered, small-knowing soul" [*Love's Labor's Lost*]; "there is no darkness but ignorance" [*Twelfth Night*]; "a little learning is a dangerous thing" [Pope]; "only are reputed wise For saying nothing" [*M. of V.*].

PROFICIENT IN, versed in, read in, forward in, strong in, at home in; **oo**nversant with, familiar with.

EDUCATED, erudite, instructed, learned, lettered; well-conned, well-informed, well-versed, well-read, well-grounded, well-educated; enlightened, shrewd, *savant* [*F.*], blue [*colloq.*], bluestocking, high-brow [*slang*], bookish, scholastic, solid, profound, deep-read, book-learned, ætiological *or* etiological, pansophic *or* pansophical; accomplished &c. (*skillful*) 698; omniscient; self-taught, self-educated, auto-didactic; self-made.

KNOWN &c. *v.;* ascertained, well-known, recognized, received, notorious, noted; proverbial; familiar, – as household words, – to every schoolboy; hackneyed, trite, commonplace.

KNOWABLE, cognizable, cognoscible.

Adv. to –, to the best of– one's knowledge; as every schoolboy knows.

*** one's eyes being opened &c. (*disclosure*) 529; *comprendre tout c'est tout pardonner; empta dolore docet experientia;* γνῶθι σεαυτόν; "half our knowledge we must snatch not take" [Pope]; *Jahre lehren mehr als Bücher;* "knowledge comes but wisdom lingers" [Tennyson]; "knowledge is power" [Bacon]; *les affaires font les hommes; nec scire fas est omnia* [Horace]; "the amassed thought and experience of innumerable minds" [Emerson]; *was ich nicht weiss macht mich nicht heiss;* "knowledge and timber shouldn't be much used till they are seasoned" [Holmes]; "only so much do I know as I have lived" [Emerson]; "And I see all of it, Only, I'm dying!" [Browning]; "Beyond the bounds our staring rounds, Across the pressing dark" [Kipling].

---

492. Scholar. — N. SCHOLAR, *savant* [*F.*], pundit *or* pandit [*India*], schoolman, professor, graduate, wrangler [*Cambridge Univ., Eng.*], academician, academist [*obs.*], doctor, fellow, don [*Eng. Univ. cant*], graduate, postgraduate, clerk [*archaic*]; *Artium Magister* [*L.*], A.M. *or* M.A., master of arts; *Artium Baccalaureus,* A.B. *or* B.A., bachelor of arts; bookman [*rare*], classicist, licentiate, gownsman; philosopher, philomath; scientist, connoisseur, sophist, sophister; linguist; etymologist, philologist; philologer [*now rare*]; lexicographer, glossographer, glossologist, lexicologist, scholiast, commentator, annotator; grammarian; *littérateur* [*F.*], *literati* [*L.*], *dilettanti* [*It.*], illuminati; munshi *or* moonshee [*India*], mullah [*Moslem*], moolvi [*India*], guru [*India*]; Hebraist, Hellenist, Græcist, Sanskritist; sinologist, sinologue.

BOOKWORM, *helluo librorum* [*L.*], bibliophile, bibliophilist, bibliomaniac, bluestocking [*colloq.*], *bas-bleu* [*F.*], high-brow [*slang*].

Admirable Crichton, Mezzofanti, "learned Theban" [*King Lear*], Dominie Sampson [*Guy Mannering*], Socrates.

LEARNED MAN, literary man; *homo multarum literarum* [*L.*]; man of -learning, – letters, – education, – genius; giant of learning, colossus of knowledge, prodigy.

ANTIQUARIAN, antiquary, archæologist, Assyriologist, Egyptologist, sage &c. (*wise man*) 500.

PEDANT, doctrinaire; pedagogue, Dr. Pangloss; pantologist; instructor &c. (*teacher*) 540.

STUDENT, learner, classman, senior, junior, sophomore, freshman, pupil, schoolboy &c. (*learner*) 541.

Adj. LEARNED &c. 490; brought up at the feet of Gamaliel.

*** "he was a scholar, and a ripe and good one" [*Henry VIII*]; "the manifold linguist" [*All's Well That Ends Well*]; "the office of the scholar is to cheer, to raise, to guide men by showing them facts amidst appearances" [Emerson]; "if it were only for a vocabulary, the scholar would be covetous of action" [*ibid.*]; "the modern literary artist is compounded of almost every man except the orator" [Chesterton]; "This man decided not to Live but Know" [Browning].

---

493. Ignoramus. — N. IGNORAMUS, illiterate, dunce, duffer, woodenhead [*colloq.*], bonehead [*slang*], solid ivory [*slang*], numskull [*colloq.*], wooden spoon [*Cambridge Univ., Eng., cant*]; no scholar.

SCIOLIST, smatterer, dabbler, half scholar; charlatan; wiseacre.

NOVICE, tenderfoot; greenhorn &c. (*dupe*) 547; plebe *or* pleb [*cant, U. S.*]; tyro &c. (*learner*) 541; lubber &c. (*bungler*) 701; fool &c. 501.

Adj. BOOKLESS, shallow, simple, lumpish, dull, dumb [*colloq., U. S.*], dense, crass, imbecile; wise in his own conceit; ignorant &c. 491.

*** "a wit with dunces and a dunce with wits" [Pope]; "Oh! these deliberate fools!" [*M. of V.*].

494. [OBJECT OF KNOWLEDGE.] **Truth.** — **N.** TRUTH, verity; fact, reality &c. (*existence*) 1; plain matter of fact; nature &c. (*principle*) 5; gospel; orthodoxy &c. 983a; authenticity; veracity &c. 543.

plain –, honest –, sober –, naked –, unalloyed –, unvarnished –, unqualified –, stern –, exact –, intrinsic- truth; *nuda veritas* [*L.*]; the very thing; not an illusion &c. 495; real Simon Pure; unvarnished tale; the truth, the whole truth and nothing but the truth; just the thing.

ACCURACY, exactitude; exactness, preciseness &c. *adj.*; precision, delicacy; rigor, mathematical precision, fidelity; clockwork precision &c. (*regularity*) 80; conformity to rule; nicety.

orthology; *ipsissima verba* [*L.*], the very words; realism.

V. BE TRUE &c. *adj.*, be the case; stand the test; have the true ring; hold good, hold true, hold water.

RENDER TRUE, prove true &c. *adj.*; substantiate &c. (*evidence*) 467.

GET AT THE TRUTH &c. (*discover*) 480a.

Adj. TRUE, real, actual &c. (*existing*) 1; veritable; certain &c.; 474; substantially –, categorically- true &c.; true -to the letter, – as gospel, – as steel, – to life, – to the facts; unimpeachable; veracious &c. 543; unrefuted, unconfuted; unideal, unimagined; realistic.

EXACT, accurate, definite, precise, well-defined, just, right, correct, strict, severe; close &c. (*similar*) 17; orthological, literal; rigid, rigorous; scrupulous &c. (*conscientious*) 939; religiously exact, punctual, punctilious, mathematical, scientific; faithful, constant, unerring; curious, particular, nice, meticulous, delicate, fine; clean-cut, clear-cut.

AUTHENTIC, genuine, legitimate; orthodox &c. 983a; official, *ex officio* [*L.*].

PURE, natural, sound, sterling, true-blue; unsophisticated, unadulterated, Simon-Pure [*colloq.*], unvarnished, uncolored; in its true colors.

VALID, well-grounded, well-founded; solid, substantial, pucka *or* pakka [*Hind.*], tangible; undistorted, undisguised; unaffected, unexaggerated, unromantic, unflattering.

Adv. TRULY &c. *adj.*; verily, indeed, in reality; in very truth, in fact, as a matter of fact, to state the facts; beyond -doubt, - question; with truth &c.

495. Error. — **N.** ERROR, fallacy; misconception, misapprehension, misunderstanding; aberration, aberrance *or* aberrancy; inexactness &c. *adj.*; laxity; misconstruction &c. (*misinterpretation*) 523; anachronism; miscomputation &c. (*misjudgment*) 481; *non sequitur* [*L.*] &c. 477; misstatement, misreport; mumpsimus.

MISTAKE; miss, fault, blunder, cross-purposes, oversight, misprint, erratum, corrigendum, slip, blot, flaw, loose thread; trip, stumble &c. (*failure*) 732; botchery &c. (*want of skill*) 699; slip of the tongue, *lapsus linguæ* [*L.*]; slip of the pen, *lapsus calami* [*L.*], clerical error; bull &c. (*absurdity*) 497; Spoonerism, Malapropism, Leiterism [*U. S.*], Mrs. Partington; haplography.

DELUSION, illusion; false –, warped –, distorted- -impression, – idea; bubble; self-deceit, self-deception; mists of error; exploded -notion, – idea, – superstition.

heresy &c. (*heterodoxy*) 984; hallucination &c. (*insanity*) 503; false light &c. (*fallacy of vision*) 443; dream &c. (*fancy*) 515; fable &c. (*untruth*) 546; bias &c. (*misjudgment*) 481; misleading &c. *v.*

V. BE ERRONEOUS &c. *adj.*

MISLEAD, misguide; lead astray, lead into error; cause error; beguile, misinform &c. (*misteach*) 538; delude; give a false -impression, – idea; falsify, misstate; deceive &c. 545; lie &c. 544.

ERR; be in error &c. *adj.*, be mistaken &c. *v.*; be deceived &c. (*duped*) 547; mistake, receive a false impression, deceive oneself; fall into –, lie under –, labor under- an error &c. *n.*; be in the wrong, blunder; misapprehend, misconceive, misunderstand, misreckon, miscount, miscalculate &c. (*misjudge*) 481.

play –, be- at cross purposes &c. (*misinterpret*) 523.

TRIP, stumble; lose oneself &c. (*uncertainty*) 475; go astray; fail &c. 732; be in the wrong box; take the wrong sow by the ear &c. (*mismanage*) 699; put the saddle on the wrong horse; reckon without one's host; take the shadow for the substance &c. (*credulity*) 486; dream &c. (*imagine*) 515.

Adj. ERRONEOUS, untrue, false, devoid of truth, faulty, erring, fallacious, apocryphal, unreal, ungrounded, groundless; unsubstantial &c. 4; heretical &c. (*heterodox*) 984; unsound; illogical &c. 477.

193

(*veracity*) 543; certainly &c. (*certain*) 474; actually &c. (*existence*) 1; in effect &c. (*intrinsically*) 5.

exactly &c. *adj.; ad amussim* or *adamussim* [*L.*], verbatim, *verbatim et literatim* [*L.*]; word for word, literally, *literatim* [*L.*], *totidem verbis* [*L.*], *sic* [*L.*], to the letter, chapter and verse, *ipsissimis verbis* [*L.*]; *ad unguem* [*L.*]; to an inch; to a -nicety, – hair, – tittle, – turn, – T; *au pied de la lettre* [*F.*]; neither more nor less; in every respect, in all respects; *sous tous les rapports* [*F.*]; at any rate, at all events; strictly speaking.

. the truth is, the fact is; *rem acu tetigisti; en suivant la verité; ex facto jus oritur; la verità è figlia del tempo; locos y niños dicen la verdad; nihil est veritatis luce dulcius* [Cicero]; *veritas nunquam perit* [Seneca]; *veritatem dies aperit* [Seneca]; "Tell the truth and shame the devil"; "Truth crushed to earth shall rise again, The eternal years of God are hers" [Bryant].

divine" [Pope]; "you lie — under a mistake" with a little aversion" [Sheridan]; "the village all have a half-warmed fish in our bosoms" [Spoonerism].

INEXACT, unexact, inaccurate, incorrect; indefinite &c. (*uncertain*) 475.

ILLUSIVE, illusory, delusive; mock, ideal &c. (*imaginary*) 515; spurious &c. 545; deceitful &c. 544; perverted.

CONTROVERTIBLE, unsustainable, unsustained, unauthentic, unauthenticated, untrustworthy.

EXPLODED, refuted, discarded.

MISTAKEN &c. *v.;* in error, under an error &c. *n.;* tripping &c. *v.;* out, out in one's reckoning; aberrant; beside –, wide of- -the mark, – the truth; astray &c. (*at fault*) 475; on -a false, – the wrong- -scent, – trail; in the wrong box; at cross-purposes, all in the wrong; all out [*colloq.*]; all abroad [*colloq.*], at sea, bewildered.

Adv. more or less.

. *errare est humanum; mentis gratissimus error* [Horace]; "on the dubious waves of error tost" [Cowper]; "to err is human, to forgive" [Shelley]; "'tis safest in matrimony to begin that voted the earth was flat" [Kipling]; "we

496. Maxim. — N.
MAXIM, aphorism; apothegm *or* apophthegm; dictum, saying, adage, saw, proverb, epigram, gnomic saying, gnome, sentence, mot [*Gallicism*], motto, word, byword, bromidium [*slang*], commonplace, moral, phylactery, protasis [*rare*].

wise –, sage –, received –, admitted –, recognized- maxim &c.; true –, common –, hackneyed –, trite –, commonplace- saying &c.

AXIOM, theorem, scholium, truism, postulate.

PRINCIPLE, principia; profession of faith &c. (*belief*) 484; settled principle, formula; reflection &c. (*idea*) 453; conclusion &c. (*judgment*) 480; golden rule &c. (*precept*) 697.

Adj. APHORISTIC, aphorismic, aphorismatic, proverbial, phylacteric; axiomatic *or* axiomatical, gnomic *or* gnomical.

Adv. as the saying is, as they say, as it was said by them of old.

. "Full of wise laws and modern instances" [*As You Like It*].

497. Absurdity. — N.
ABSURDITY, absurdness &c. *adj.;* imbecility &c. 499; alogy [*obs.*], comicality, nonsense, paradox, inconsistency; stultiloquy [*rare*], stultiloquence [*rare*], stultification, futility, nugacity.

BLUNDER, muddle, bull; Irishism, Hibernicism; anticlimax, bathos; sophism &c. 477.

FARCE, galimatias, burlesque, parody, fiddle-faddle [*colloq.*], amphigory *or* amphigouri, rhapsody; farrago &c. (*disorder*) 59; *bêtise* [*F.*]; extravagance, romance; sciamachy.

PUN, sell [*colloq.*], catch [*colloq.*], verbal quibble, macaronic composition, limerick, joke.

JARGON, slipslop [*colloq.*], gibberish, balderdash, bombast, claptrap, fustian, twaddle &c. (*no meaning*) 517; exaggeration &c. 549; moonshine, stuff; mare's-nest, quibble, self-delusion.

TOMFOOLERY, vagary, mummery, monkeyshine [*slang, U. S.*], monkey trick, *boutade* [*F.*], frisk, practical joke, escapade.

V. PLAY THE FOOL &c. 499; stultify, blunder, muddle; employ absurdity &c. *n.;* rhapsodize; romance, sell [*slang*], fiddle-faddle [*colloq.*]; talk nonsense, *parler à tort et à travers* [*F.*]; *battre la campagne* [*F.*]; *anemolia bazein* [*Gr.* ἀνεμώλια βάζειν]; be absurd &c. *adj.;* frisk, caper, joke, play practical jokes.

BE THE FOOL, be the goat [*colloq.*], bite [*colloq.*].

Adj. ABSURD, nonsensical, farcical, preposterous, egregious, senseless, inconsistent, stultiloquent [*rare*], stulty [*obs.*], ridiculous, extravagant, quibbling; self-annulling, self-contradictory; paradoxical, macaronic *or* maccaronic, punning.

burlesque, foolish &c. 499; sophistical &c. 477; unmeaning &c. 517; amphigoric; without rime or reason; fantastic *or* fantastical, rhapsodic *or* rhapsodical, bombastic, high-flown.

Int. fiddledeedee! pish! pho *or* phoh! [*rare*], pooh! pooh-pooh! bah! stuff and nonsense! fiddle-faddle! bosh! rats! [*slang*], come off! [*slang*], "in the name of the Prophet — figs!" [Horace Smith].

. *credat Judæus Apella* [Horace]; tell it to the marines; "A little nonsense now and then Is relished by the wisest men" [*Anon.*]; "Say 'Boo!' to you — 'pooh-pooh!' to you" [Gilbert].

Faculties

498. Intelligence. Wisdom. — N.
INTELLIGENCE, capacity, comprehension, understanding; cuteness [*colloq.*], sabe [*slang, U. S.*], savvy [*slang, U. S.*]; intellect &c. 450; nous [*colloq.*], docity [*dial.*], parts, sagacity, mother wit, wit, *esprit* [*F.*], gumption [*colloq.*], quick parts, grasp of intellect; acuteness &c. *adj.;* acumen, longheadedness, arguteness, subtility, subtlety, penetration, perspicacy [*obs.*], perspicacity, discernment, due sense of, good judgment; discrimination &c. 465; cunning &c. 702; refinement &c. (*taste*) 850.

HEAD, brains, gray matter [*colloq.*], brain-stuff [*colloq.*], headpiece, upper story [*colloq.*], long head.

eagle -eye, – glance; eye of a lynx, eye of a hawk.

WISDOM, sapience, sense; good-, common -, horse – [*colloq., U. S.*], plain-sense; clear thinking, rationality, reason; reasonableness &c. *adj.;* judgment, solidity, depth, profundity, caliber *or* calibre; enlarged views; reach -, compass- of thought; enlargement of mind.

GENIUS, lambent flame of intellect, inspiration, *Geist* [*Ger.*], fire of genius, heaven-born genius, soul; talent &c. (*aptitude*) 698.

[WISDOM IN ACTION] prudence &c. 864; vigilance &c. 459; tact &c. 698; foresight &c. 510; sobriety, self-possession, *aplomb* [*F.*], ballast, mental poise, balance.

a bright thought, an inspiration, not a bad idea.

V. BE INTELLIGENT &c. *adj.;* have all one's wits about one; be brilliant, be witty, scintillate, coruscate; understand &c. (*intelligible*) 518; catch –, take in- an idea; take a -joke, – hint.

499. Imbecility. Folly. — N. IMBECILITY; want of intelligence &c. 498, want of intellect &c. 450; shallowness, unwisdom, silliness, foolishness &c. *adj.;* morosis, incapacity, vacancy of mind, poverty of intellect, clouded perception, poor head; apartments –, rooms –, space- to let [*all slang*]; nobody home [*slang*]; stupidity, insulsity [*rare*], stolidity; hebetude, dull understanding, meanest capacity, shortsightedness; incompetence &c. (*unskillfulness*) 699.

BIAS &c. 481; infatuation &c. (*insanity*) 503; one's weak side.

SIMPLICITY, puerility, babyhood; senility, dotage, anility, second childishness, fatuousness, fatuity; idiocy, idiotism, jobbernowlism [*colloq., Eng.*], driveling, driveling idiocy; senile dementia.

FOLLY, frivolity, irrationality, trifling, ineptitude, nugacity, futility, inconsistency, lip wisdom, conceit; sophistry &c. 477; giddiness &c. (*inattention*) 458; eccentricity &c. 503; extravagance &c. (*absurdity*) 497; rashness &c. 863.

act of folly &c. 699.

V. BE IMBECILE &c. *adj.;* have no -brains, – sense &c. 498; have a screw loose [*colloq.*].

TRIFLE, drivel, *radoter* [*F.*], dote, ramble &c. (*madness*) 503; play the -fool, – monkey; take leave of one's senses; not see an inch beyond one's nose; stultify oneself &c. 699; talk nonsense &c. 497.

Adj. [APPLIED TO PERSONS] UNINTELLIGENT, unintellectual, unreasoning; mindless, witless, reasonless, brainless; half-baked [*colloq.*], having no head &c. 498; not bright &c. 498; inapprehensive, thick [*colloq.*].

blockish, unteachable; Bœotian, Bœotic; bovine; ungifted, undiscerning, un-

PENETRATE; see through, see at a
glance, see with half an eye, see far
into, see through a millstone [colloq.];
discern &c. (descry) 441; foresee &c.
510.

DISCRIMINATE &c. 465; know what's
what [colloq.] &c. 698; listen to reason.

Adj. [APPLIED TO PERSONS] INTELLI-
GENT, quick of apprehension, keen,
acute, alive, brainy [colloq.], awake,
bright, quick, sharp; quick-, keen-,
clear-, sharp- -eyed, -sighted, -witted;
wide-awake; canny or cannie [archaic
or dial.], sly, pawky [dial.], shrewd,
astute; clear-headed; farsighted &c.
510; discerning, perspicacious, penetrating, piercing; argute; nimble-witted,
needle-witted; sharp as a needle; alive
to &c. (cognizant) 490; clever &c. (apt)
698; arch &c. (cunning) 702; pas si bête
[F.]; acute &c. 682.

WISE, sage, sapient [often in irony],
sagacious, reasonable, rational, sound,
in one's right mind, sensible, abnormis
sapiens [L.], judicious, strong-minded.

IMPARTIAL, unprejudiced, unbiased,
unbigoted, unprepossessed; undazzled,
unperplexed; of unwarped judgment,
equitable, fair.

COOL; cool-, long-, hard-, strong-
headed; long-sighted, calculating,
thoughtful, reflecting; solid, deep, profound.

PRUDENT &c. (cautious) 864; sober,
staid, solid; considerate, politic, wise
in one's generation; watchful &c. 459;
provident &c. (prepared) 673; in advance of one's age; wise as -a serpent,
– Solomon, – Solon, – Nestor, –Mentor.
oracular; heaven-directed, heaven-
born.

[APPLIED TO ACTIONS] WISE, sensible,
reasonable, judicious; well-judged, well-
advised; prudent, politic; expedient &c.
646.

⁎ aut regem aut fatuum nasci oportet;
"but with the morning cool reflection came"
[Scott]; flosculi sententiarum; les affaires font
les hommes; más vale saber que haber; más vale
ser necio que porfiado; nemo solus sapit [Plau-
tus); nosce te; γνῶθι σεαυτόν; nullum magnum
ingenium sine mixtura demertiæ fuit [Seneca,
from Aristotle]; sapere aude [Horace]; victrix
fortunæ sapientia [Juvenal]; "wisdom is the
principal thing; therefore, get wisdom; and
with all thy getting get understanding" [Bible];
"genius is always sufficiently the enemy of
genius by over-influence" [Emerson]; "I may
not deal with wisdom, being a king" [Masefield].

196

enlightened, unwise, unphilosophical:
apish, simious, simian.

weak-, addle-, puzzle-, blunder-,
muddle- [colloq.], jolter-, jolt-, chowder-,
pig-, beetle-, buffle- [obs.], chuckle-,
mutton-, gross- headed; maggot-pated
[obs.], beef-headed, beef-witted, fat-
headed, fat-witted.

WEAK-MINDED, feeble-minded; dull-,
shallow-, lack- brained; rattle- brained,
-headed; sap-head [colloq.], muddy-
brained, addle-brained; half-, lean-,
short-, shallow-, dull-, blunt- witted;
shallow-, clod-, addle- pated; dim-,
short- sighted; thick-skulled; thick-
headed; weak in the upper story
[colloq.], inapprehensible, nutty [slang],
batty [slang], balmy in the crumpet
[slang], loony or luny [slang].

SHALLOW, borné [F.], weak, wanting,
soft [colloq.], sappy, spoony or spooney
[slang]; dull, – as a beetle.

STUPID, heavy, insulse [rare], obtuse,
blunt, stolid, doltish; asinine; inapt &c.
699; prosaic &c. 843; hebetudinous,
hebetate, hebete [rare].

CHILDISH, childlike; infantine, infantile,
babyish, babish; puerile, senile, anile;
simple &c. (credulous) 486; old-womanish.

IMBECILE, fatuous, idiotic, driveling;
blatant, babbling; vacant; sottish; bewildered &c. 475.

FOOLISH, silly, senseless, irrational,
insensate, nonsensical, inept; maudlin.

NARROW-MINDED &c. 481; bigoted &c.
(obstinate) 606; giddy &c. (thoughtless)
458; rash &c. 863; eccentric &c. (crazed)
503.

[APPLIED TO ACTIONS] FOOLISH, unwise, injudicious, improper, unreasonable, without reason, ridiculous, silly,
stupid, asinine; ill-imagined, ill-advised,
ill-judged, ill-devised; mal entendu [F.];
inconsistent, irrational, unphilosophical;
extravagant &c. (nonsensical) 497;
sleeveless [obs.], idle; useless &c. 645;
inexpedient &c. 647; frivolous &c.
(trivial) 643.

⁎ Davus sum non Œdipus; "a fool's bolt
is soon shot" [Henry V]; clitellæ bovi sunt im-
positæ [Cicero]; "fools rush in where angels fear
to tread" [Pope]; il n'a ni bouche ni éperon;
"the bookful blockhead, ignorantly read"
[Pope]; "to varnish nonsense with the charms
of sound" [Churchill]; "And duller should'st
thou be than the fat weed That roots itself in
ease on Lethe wharf" [Hamlet]; "men are so
necessarily foolish that not to be a fool is
merely a varied freak of folly" [Pascal].

500. Sage. — **N.** SAGE, wise man; master mind, master spirit of the age; longhead, thinker, philosopher.

AUTHORITY, oracle, mentor, luminary, shining light, *esprit fort* [*F.*], *magnus Apollo* [*L.*], Solon, Solomon, Buddha, Confucius, Mentor, Nestor, the Magi; Seven Wise Men of Greece, Seven Sages, Philosophical Pleiad; "second Daniel."

savant [*F.*], pundit &c. (*scholar*) 492; wiseacre [*archaic or ironical*]; expert &c. 700; wizard &c. 994.

Adj. VENERABLE, venerated, reverenced, revered, honored, looked up to; authoritative, wise, oracular; erudite &c. (*knowledge*) 490; *emeritus* [*L.*].

⁎⁎ *barbâ tenus sapientes;* "O wise young judge, how I do honor thee" [*M. of V.*].

501. Fool. — **N.** FOOL, idiot, tomfool, wiseacre, simpleton, Simple Simon, moron, gaby [*colloq.*], witling, dizzard [*obs.*], donkey, ass; ninny, ninny hammer, chowderhead [*dial.*], jolterhead or jolthead, mutt [*slang*], chucklehead [*colloq.*], dolt, booby, tomnoddy, loony or luny [*slang*], looby, hoddy-doddy [*obs.*], noddy, nonny [*dial.*], noodle, nizy [*obs.*], owl, goose, imbecile; *radoteur* [*F.*], nincompoop [*colloq.*], *badaud* [*F.*], zany [*Eng.*]; trifler, babbler; pretty fellow; natural, *niais* [*F.*].

child, baby, infant, innocent, milksop, sop.

oaf, lout, loon or lown [*dial.*]; bullhead, blunderhead, addle-pate, addlebrain, addlehead [*all colloq.*]; blockhead, dullhead, bonehead [*slang*], rattlepate, dullard, doodle [*obs.*], calf [*colloq.*], colt, buzzard [*obs.*], block, put, stick [*colloq.*], stock, numps [*obs.*], tony [*obs.*]; loggerhead, beetlehead, grosshead [*obs.*], muttonhead [*colloq.*], noodlehead, giddyhead [*colloq.*], numskull [*colloq.*], thickhead [*colloq.*], thick skull; lackbrain, shallowbrain; halfwit, lackwit; dunderpate; lunkhead [*U. S.*].

sawney [*dial. Eng.*], clod, clodhopper; clodpoll, clodpate, clotpole or clotpoll [*obs.*], clotpate [*obs.*], soft or softy [*colloq. or slang*], saphead [*slang*], bull calf [*colloq.*], spoony or spooney [*slang*], gawk, gawky, gowk, Gothamite, lummox [*dial.*], rube [*U. S.*]; men of Bœotia, wise men of Gotham.

un sot à triple étage [*F.*], sot [*Scot.*], jobbernowl [*colloq., Eng.*], changeling [*archaic*], mooncalf, *gobe-mouches* [*F.*].

greenhorn &c. (*dupe*) 547; dunce &c. (*ignoramus*) 493; lubber &c. (*bungler*) 701; madman &c. 504; solid ivory.

one who -will not set the Thames on fire, – did not invent gunpowder, – does not exactly scintillate; *qui n'a pas inventé la poudre* [*F.*]; no conjuror; no Solomon.

DOTARD, driveler; old fogy or fogey [*colloq.*], old woman; crone, grandmother; cotquean [*archaic*], henhussy, betty [*contempt*].

⁎⁎ *fortuna favet fatuis; les fous font les festins et les sages les mangent; nomina stultorum parietibus hærent; stultorum plena sunt omnia* [Cicero]; "a fool and his money are soon parted"; "where ignorance is bliss, 'tis folly to be wise" [Gray]; "Cruel children, crying babies All grow up as geese and gabies, Hated, as their age increases, By their nephews and their nieces" [Stevenson]; "a rosebud need not have a mind" [Masefield]; "you may lead an ass to knowledge, but you cannot make him think" [*Cynic's Calendar*].

502. Sanity. — **N.** SANITY; soundness &c. *adj.;* rationality, normalcy, normality, sobriety, lucidity, lucid interval; senses, sober senses, common sense, horse sense [*colloq.*], sound mind, *mens sana* [*L.*].

V. BE SANE &c. *adj.;* retain one's senses, – reason.

BECOME SANE &c. *adj.;* come to one's senses, sober down, cool down, get things into proportion, see things in proper perspective.

RENDER SANE &c. *adj.;* bring to one's senses, sober; bring to reason.

Adj. SANE, rational, normal, whole-

503. Insanity. — **N.** INSANITY, lunacy; madness &c. *adj.*, mania, rabies, furor, mental alienation, aberration, amentia, paranoia; dementation, dementia, demency [*rare*], morosis, idiocy; *dementia a potu* [*L.*], delirium tremens, D. T.'s, the horrors [*colloq.*]; phrenitis, frenzy, raving, incoherence, wandering, delirium, calenture of the brain, delusion, hallucination; lycanthropy; brain storm.

DERANGEMENT; disordered -reason, – intellect; diseased –, unsound –, abnormal- mind; unsoundness.

VERTIGO, dizziness, swimming, sunstroke, *coup de soleil* [*F.*], siriasis.

some, right-minded, reasonable, *compos mentis* [*L.*], of sound mind; sound, sound-minded; lucid.

self-possessed; sober, sober-minded.

in one's -sober senses, – right mind; in possession of one's faculties.

Adv. SANELY &c. *adj.;* in reason, within reason, within bounds; according to the dictates of -reason, – common sense; in the name of common sense.

*** *Quisnam igitur sanus? Qui non stultus* [*Horace*].

ODDITY, eccentricity, twist, monomania; fanaticism, infatuation, craze; kleptomania, dipsomania; hypochondriasis &c. (*low spirits*) 837; melancholia, hysteria.

screw –, tile –, slate- loose; bee in one's bonnet, rats in the upper story, bats in the belfry, bee in the head [*all colloq.*].

dotage &c. (*imbecility*) 499.

V. BE *or* BECOME INSANE &c. *adj.;* lose one's senses, – reason, – faculties, – wits; go mad, run mad; rave, dote, ramble, wander; drivel &c. (*be imbecile*) 499; have a screw loose &c. *n.*, have a devil; *avoir le diable au corps* [*F.*]; lose one's head &c. (*be uncertain*) 475.

DERANGE; render *or* drive mad &c. *adj.;* madden, dementate [*rare*], addle the wits, derange the head, infatuate, befool; turn the brain, turn one's head.

Adj. INSANE, mad, lunatic; crazy, crazed, *aliéné* [*F.*], *non compos mentis* [*L.*], not right, dement [*rare*], dementate, cracked [*colloq.*], touched; bereft of reason; all-possessed, unhinged, unsettled in one's mind; insensate, reasonless, beside oneself, demented, maniacal, daft; frenzied, frenetic *or* frenetical; possessed, – with a devil; deranged, far gone, maddened, moonstruck; shatterpated, shatterbrained; madbrained, scatterbrained, crack-brained; off one's head.

Corybantic, dithyrambic; rabid, giddy, vertiginous, wild; haggard, mazed; flighty; distracted, distraught; bewildered &c. (*uncertain*) 475.

mad as a -March hare, – hatter; of unsound mind &c. *n.;* touched –, wrong –, not right- in one's -head, – mind, – wits, – upper story [*colloq.*]; out of one's -mind, – senses, – wits; not in one's right mind; nutty [*slang*].

ODD, fanatical, infatuated, eccentric; hypochondriac, hyppish [*rare*], hipped *or* hypped [*colloq.*], hippish [*colloq.*].

DELIRIOUS, light-headed, incoherent, rambling, doting, wandering; frantic, raving, stark mad, stark staring mad.

IMBECILE, silly, &c. 499.

Adv. like one possessed.

*** the mind having lost its balance; the reason under a cloud; *tête exaltée; tête montée; ira furor brevis est; omnes stultos insanire* [Horace]; "great wits are sure to madness near allied" [Dryden]; "moping melancholy and moon-struck madness" [Milton]; "And moody madness laughing wild Amid severest woe" [Gray]; "Though this be madness, yet there is method in't" [*Hamlet*]; "no excellent soul is exempt from a mixture of madness" [Aristotle]; "Fetter strong madness in a silken thread" [*Much Ado About Nothing*]; "That he is mad, 'tis true, 'tis true, 'tis pity; And pity 'tis 'tis true [*Hamlet*]; "we are not ourselves When nature, being oppress'd, commands the mind To suffer with the body" [*King Lear*].

504. Madman. — **N.** MADMAN, lunatic, maniac, bedlamite, candidate for Bedlam, raver, phrenetic, madcap; energumen [*eccl. antiq.*]; automaniac, monomaniac, dipsomaniac, kleptomaniac, paranoiac; hypochondriac &c. (*low spirits*) 837; crank [*colloq.*], Tom o' Bedlam; nut [*slang*].

DREAMER &c. 515; rhapsodist, seer, highflyer *or* highflier [*obs.*], enthusiast, fanatic, *fanatico* [*It.*], *exalté* [*F.*], Don Quixote, Ophelia, Madge Wildfire.

IDIOT &c. 501.

*** "The lunatic, the lover, and the poet Are of imagination all compact" [*M. N. D.*]; "There is a pleasure, sure, In being mad, which none but madmen know" [Dryden]; "O, what a noble mind is here o'erthrown!" [*Hamlet*]; "who knows of madness whether it is divine or whether it be of the pit" [Dunsany].

Section VI. EXTENSION OF THOUGHT

1. To the Past

505. Memory. — N. MEMORY, remembrance; retentivity, retention, retentiveness; tenacity; *veteris vestigia flammæ* [*L.*]; tablets of the memory; readiness.

retentive –, tenacious –, trustworthy –, capacious –, faithful –, correct –, exact –, ready –, prompt- memory; Memory's halls, Memory's pictures.

RECOLLECTION, reminiscence, recognition, recurrence, rememoration [*rare*], rememorance [*rare*]; retrospect, retrospection; "that inward eye" [Wordsworth]; afterthought.

REMINDER; suggestion &c. (*information*) 527; prompting &c. *v.;* hint, token of remembrance, memento, souvenir, keepsake, relic, memorandum (*pl.* memoranda); remembrancer, flapper; memorial &c. (*record*) 551; commemoration &c. (*celebration*) 883.

things to be remembered, memorabilia.

MNEMONICS; art of –, artificial- memory; *memoria technica* [*L.*]; mnemotechnics, mnemotechny; Mnemosyne.

AIDS TO MEMORY, jogger [*colloq.*], memorandum book, notebook, promptbook, engagement book.

FAME, celebrity, renown, reputation &c. (*repute*) 873.

V. REMEMBER, mind [*obsoles.*], rememorate [*rare*]; retain the -memory, - remembrance- of; keep in view.

have –, hold –, bear –, carry –, keep–, retain- in *or* in the -thoughts, – mind, – memory, – remembrance; be in –, live

506. Oblivion. — N. OBLIVION; forgetfulness &c. *adj.;* obliteration &c. (552) of –, insensibility &c. (823) to- the past.

short –, treacherous –, loose –, slippery –, failing- memory; decay –, failure –, lapse- of memory; mind –, memory- like a sieve; untrustworthy memory; waters of -Lethe, - oblivion; amnesia.

AMNESTY, general pardon.

V. FORGET; be forgetful &c. *adj.;* fall –, sink- into oblivion; have a short memory &c. *n.*, have no head.

forget one's own name, have on the tip of one's tongue, come in at one ear and go out at the other.

slip –, escape –, fade from –, die away from- the memory; lose, lose sight of.

EFFACE &c. (552) –, discharge- from the memory; unlearn; consign to -oblivion, - the tomb of the Capulets; think no more of &c. (*turn the attention from*) 458; cast behind one's back, wean one's thoughts from; let bygones be bygones &c. (*forgive*) 918.

Adj. FORGOTTEN &c. *v.;* unremembered, past recollection, bygone, out of mind; buried –, sunk- in oblivion; clean forgotten; gone out of one's -head, - recollection.

FORGETFUL, oblivious, mindless, Lethean; insensible &c. (823) to the past; heedless.

** non mi ricordo; the memory -failing, - deserting one, - being at (*or* in) fault.

in –, remain in –, dwell in –, haunt –, impress- one's -memory, – thoughts, – mind.

sink in the mind; run in the head; not be able to get it out of one's head; be deeply impressed with; rankle &c. (*revenge*) 919.

recognize, bethink oneself, recall, call up, conjure up, retrace; look –, trace-back, – backwards; think upon, look back upon; review; call –, recall –, bringto -mind, – remembrance; carry one's thoughts back; rake up the past.

redeem from oblivion; keep the -memory alive, – wound green; *tangere ulcus* [*L.*]; keep the memory green, keep up the memory of; commemorate &c. (*celebrate*) 883.

RECOLLECT, recur to the mind; flash on the mind, flash across the memory.

REMIND; suggest &c. (*inform*) 527; prompt; put –, keep- in mind; fan the embers; call up, summon up; renew; *infandum renovare dolorem* [*L.*]; task –, tax –, jog –, flap –, refresh –, rub up –, awaken- the memory; pull by the sleeve; bring back to the memory, put in remembrance, memorialize.

MEMORIZE, commit to memory; con, – over; fix –, rivet –, imprint –, impress –, stamp –, grave –, engrave –, store –, treasure up –, bottle up –, embalm –, bury –, enshrine- in the memory; load –, store –, stuff –, burden- the memory with; get –, have –, learn –, know –, say –, repeat- by -heart, – rote; get –, drive- into one's head; bury in the mind; say one's lesson; repeat, – like a parrot; have at one's fingers' ends.

make a note of &c. (*record*) 551.

Adj. REMEMBERING, remembered &c. *v.;* mindful, reminiscential; alive in memory; retained in the memory &c. *v.;* pent up in one's memory; fresh; green, – in remembrance; still vivid, rememorant [*rare*]; not –, never -to be erased, – to be forgotten; unforgettable *or* unforgetable; enduring, – in memory; unforgotten, present to the mind; within one's memory &c. *n.;* indelible; uppermost in one's thoughts; memorable &c. (*important*) 642; suggestive.

Adv. BY HEART, *par cœur* [F.], by rote; without book, *memoriter* [L.].

IN MEMORY OF; *in memoriam* [L.]; *memoriâ in æternâ* [L.].

*** *manet altâ mente repostum* [Vergil]; *forsan et hœc olim meminisse juvabit* [Vergil]; *absens hœres non erit; beatœ memoriœ:* "briefly thyself remember" [*Lear*]; *mendacem memorem esse oportet* [Quintilian]; "memory, the warder of the brain" [*Macbeth*]; *parsque est meminisse doloris* [Ovid]; "To live in hearts we leave behind, Is not to die" [Campbell]; *vox audita perit littera scripta manet; monumentum œre perennius* [Horace]; "Music, when soft voices die, Vibrates in the memory; Odours, when sweet violets sicken, Live within the sense they quicken" [Shelley]; "Lest we forget" [Kipling]; "They flash upon that inward eye Which is the bliss of solitude" [Wordsworth].

2. To the Future

507. Expectation. — N. EXPECTATION, expectance, expectancy; anticipation, contingency, contingent, reckoning, calculation; foresight &c. 510; contemplation, prospection.

PROSPECT, lookout [*chiefly Eng.*], perspective, horizon, vista; destiny &c. 152; futures [*stock exchange*].

SUSPENSE, waiting, abeyance; curiosity &c. 455; anxious –, ardent –, eager –, breathless –, sanguine- expectation; torment of Tantalus.

ASSURANCE, confidence, presumption, reliance; hope &c. 858; trust &c. (*belief*) 484; prognosis [*med.*], prognostic, prognostication; auspices &c. (*prediction*) 511.

V. EXPECT; look -for, – out for, – forward to; hope for, anticipate; have in -prospect, – contemplation; keep in view; contemplate, promise oneself; not wonder at *or* if &c. 870.

WAIT FOR, tarry for, lie in wait for, watch for, bargain for; keep a -good, – sharp -lookout for; await; stand at "attention," abide, mark time, bide one's time, watch.

prick up one's ears, hold one's breath.

FORESEE &c. 510; prepare for &c. 673; forestall &c. (*be early*) 132; count upon &c. (*believe in*) 484; think likely &c. (*probability*) 472; bargain for; make one's mouth water.

PREDICT, prognosticate, forecast; lead one to expect &c. (*predict*) 511; have in store for &c. (*destiny*) 152.

508. Inexpectation. — N. INEXPECTATION [*rare*], nonexpectation; unforeseen contingency, the unforeseen; false expectation &c. (*disappointment*) 509; miscalculation &c. 481.

SURPRISE, sudden burst, thunderclap, blow, shock; bolt out of the blue; surprisement [*rare*], astoundment [*rare*], astonishment, mazement [*rare*], amazement; wonder &c. 870; eye opener.

V. NOT EXPECT &c. 507; be taken by surprise; start; miscalculate &c. 481; not bargain for; come –, fall- upon.

BE UNEXPECTED &c. *adj.;* come unawares &c. *adv.;* turn up, pop [*colloq.*], drop from the clouds; come –, burst –, flash –, bounce –, steal –, creep- upon one; come –, burst- like a -thunderclap, -thunderbolt; take –, catch- -by surprise, – unawares; catch napping, catch off one's guard; yach [*S. Africa*].

SURPRISE, startle, take aback [*colloq.*], electrify, stun, stagger, take away one's breath, throw off one's guard; pounce upon, spring, spring upon, spring a mine upon; stound [*archaic*], astound; astonish &c. (*strike with wonder*) 870.

Adj. NONEXPECTANT, inexpectant; surprised &c. *v.;* unwarned, unaware; off one's guard; inattentive &c. 458.

UNEXPECTED, unanticipated, unlooked for, unforeseen, unhoped for; dropped from the clouds; beyond –, contrary to –, against- expectation; out of one's reckoning; unheard of &c. (*exceptional*)

Adj. EXPECTANT; expecting &c. *v.*; in expectation &c. *n.;* on the watch &c. (*vigilant*) 459; open-eyed, open-mouthed; agape, gaping, all agog; on tenterhooks, on tiptoe, on the tiptoe of expectation; *aux aguets* [*F.*]; ready, prepared, provided for, provisional, provident; curious &c. 455; looking forward to; on the rack.

EXPECTED &c. *v.*; long expected, foreseen; in prospect &c. *n.;* prospective, future, forward [*com.*], coming; in one's eye, in view, on the horizon; impending &c. (*destiny*) 152.

Adv. EXPECTANTLY; on the watch &c. *adj.*; in the event of; as a possible contingency; with muscles tense, on edge [*colloq.*]; with eyes –, with ears -strained; with ears pricked forward; *arrectis auribus* [*L.*]; with breathless expectation &c. *n.*, with bated breath.

SOON, shortly, forthwith, anon [*archaic*], presently; prospectively &c. 121.

** we shall see; *nous verrons;* "expectation whirls me round" [*Troilus and Cressida*].

83, startling; sudden &c. (*instantaneous*) 113.

Adv. UNEXPECTEDLY, abruptly, plump, pop, *à l'improviste* [*F.*], unawares; without -notice, – warning, – saying "by your leave"; like a thief in the night, like a thunderbolt; like a lightning flash; in an unguarded moment; suddenly &c. (*instantaneously*) 113.

Int. heydey! &c. (*wonder*) 870; do tell! [*colloq., U. S.*].

** little did one -think, – expect; nobody would ever -suppose, – think, – expect; who would have thought? it beats the Dutch; it is the unexpected that happens.

509. [FAILURE OF EXPECTATION.] **Disappointment. — N.** DISAPPOINTMENT; blighted hope, disillusion, balk; blow; slip 'twixt cup and lip; nonfulfillment of one's hopes; sad –, bitter- disappointment; trick of fortune; afterclap; false –, vain-expectation; miscalculation &c. 481; fool's paradise; much cry and little wool.

V. BE DISAPPOINTED; look blank, look blue [*colloq.*]; look *or* stand aghast &c. (*wonder*) 870; find to one's cost; laugh on the wrong side of one's mouth [*colloq.*], laugh out of the other corner of the mouth [*colloq.*]; find one a false prophet.

DISAPPOINT; crush –, dash –, balk –, disappoint –, blight –, falsify –, defeat –, not realize- one's -hope, – expectation; balk, jilt, bilk; play one -false, – a trick; dash the cup from the lips; tantalize; dumfounder *or* dumbfounder, dumfound *or* dumbfound, disillusion, disillusionize; come short of; dissatisfy, make dissatisfied, disgruntle.

Adj. DISAPPOINTED &c. *v.*; disconcerted, aghast; disgruntled; out of one's reckoning; short of expectations.

** the mountain brought forth a mouse; *parturiunt montes nascetur ridiculus mus* [Horace]; *dis aliter visum* [Vergil]; the bubble burst; one's countenance falling.

510. Foresight. — N. FORESIGHT, prospicience, prevision, long-sightedness, farsightedness; anticipation; providence &c. (*preparation*) 673.

FORETHOUGHT, forecast; predeliberation, presurmise; foregone conclusion &c. (*prejudgment*) 481; prudence &c. (*caution*) 864.

FOREKNOWLEDGE, precognition, prescience, prenotion, presentiment; second sight; sagacity &c. (*intelligence*) 498; antepast, prelibation; prophasis [*med.*], prognosis [*med.*].

PROSPECT &c. (*expectation*) 507; foretaste; prospectus &c. (*plan*) 626.

V. FORESEE; look -forwards to, – ahead, – beyond; scent from afar; feel it in one's bones [*colloq.*]; look –, pry –, peep- into the future.

see one's way; see how the -land lies, – wind blows, – cat jumps [*colloq.*].

ANTICIPATE; expect &c. 507; be beforehand &c. (*early*) 132; predict &c. 511; foreknow, forejudge, forecast; surmise; have an eye to the -future, – main chance; *respicere finem* [*L.*]; keep a sharp lookout &c. (*vigilance*) 459; forewarn &c. 668.

Adj. FORESEEING &c. *v.*; prescient, anticipatory; farseeing, farsighted, long-sighted; sagacious &c. (*intelligent*) 498; weatherwise; provident &c. (*prepared*) 673; on the lookout, – for; prospective &c. 507.

Adv. against the time when; for a rainy day.

** *cernit omnia Deus vindex; mihi cura futuri.*

511. Prediction. — N. PREDICTION, announcement; program *or* programme &c. (*plan*) 626; premonition &c. (*warning*) 668; prognosis, prognostic, presage, presagement, precurse [*obs.*], prophecy, vaticination, mantology [*rare*], prognostication, premonstration [*obs.*]; augury, auguration [*obs.*], ariolation [*obs.*], hariolation [*obs.*], foreboding, aboding [*obs.*], abode [*obs.*], bode [*obs.*], bodement, abodement; omniation [*obs.*], auspice (*pl.* auspices), forecast; omen &c. 512; horoscope, nativity; sooth [*obs.*], soothsaying, fortune-telling; divination.

adytum, oak of Dodona; cave of the Cumæan Sibyl, Sibylline leaves, Sibylline books; tripod of the Pythia.

prefiguration, prefigurement; prototype, type.

[DIVINATION BY THE STARS] astrology, astromancy, horoscopy, genethlialogy, judicial *or* mundane astrology.

ORACLE, prophet, seer &c. 513.

[MEANS OF DIVINATION] crystal, ink, tea leaves, cards; Hallowe'en -nuts, mirror; divining-rod, wych-hazel *or* witch-hazel; hand of glory; wax image; teraphim; shadows &c. [*see footnote*]; spell, charm &c. 993.

sorcery, magic, necromancy &c. 992; heteroscopic divination.[1]

V. PREDICT, prognosticate, prophesy, vaticinate, divine, foretell, soothsay, augurate, tell fortunes; cast a horoscope, cast a nativity; advise; forewarn, prewarn &c. 668.

presage, augur, bode, abode [*obs.*], forebode; foretoken, betoken; prefigure, prefigurate, augurate [*rare*], ariolate [*rare*], figure [*obs.*], forecast, precurse, portend; preshow, foreshow, foreshadow; shadow forth, typify, pretypify, ominate [*obs.*], signify, point to.

hold out –, raise –, excite- -expectation, – hope; bid fair, promise, lead one to expect; be the precursor &c. 64.

HERALD, usher in, premise, announce; lower.

Adj. PREDICTING &c. *v.;* predictive, prophetic, fatidic *or* fatidical, precursal, precurrent, presageful, vaticinal, oracular, fatiloquent [*rare*], haruspical; Sibylline; weatherwise.

OMINOUS, portentous; augurous, augurial, augural, precursive, precursory, auspicial, auspicious; prescious [*rare*], prescient, monitory, extispicious [*obs.*], premonitory, significant of, pregnant with, big with the fate of.

*** "If you can look into the seeds of time, And say which grain will grow and which will not" [Macbeth]; "coming events cast their shadows before" [Campbell]; *dicamus bona verba;* "there buds the promise of celestial worth" [Young].

---

[1] The following terms, expressive of different forms of divination, have been collected from various sources, and are here given as a curious illustration of bygone superstitions:
Divination *by oracles*, theomancy; *by the Bible*, Bibliomancy; *by ghosts*, psychomancy; *by crystal gazing*, crystallomancy; *by shadows or manes*, sciomancy; *by appearances in the air*, aëromancy, chaomancy; *by the stars at birth*, genethliacs; *by meteors*, meteoromancy; *by winds*, austromancy; *by sacrificial appearances*, aruspicy (*or* haruspicy), hieromancy, hieroscopy; *by the entrails of animals sacrificed*, extispicy, hieromancy; *by the entrails of a human sacrifice*, anthropomancy; *by the entrails of fishes*, ichthyomancy; *by sacrificial fire*, pyromancy; *by redhot iron*, sideromancy; *by the smoke from the altar*, capnomancy; *by mice*, myomancy; *by birds*, orniscopy, ornithomancy; *by a cock picking up grains*, alectryomancy (*or* alectoromancy); *by snakes*, ophiomancy; *by herbs*, botanomancy; *by water*, hydromancy; *by fountains*, pegomancy; *by a wand*, rhabdomancy; *by dough of cakes*, crithomancy; *by meal*, aleuromancy, alphitomancy; *by salt*, halomancy; *by lead*, molybdomancy; *by dice*, cleromancy; *by arrows*, belomancy; *by a balanced hatchet*, axinomancy; *by a balanced sieve*, coscinomancy; *by a suspended ring*, dactyliomancy; *by dots made at random on paper*, geomancy; *by precious stones*, lithomancy; *by pebbles*, pessomancy; *by pebbles drawn from a heap*, psephomancy; *by mirrors*, catoptromancy; *by writings in ashes*, tephramancy; *by dreams*, oneiromancy; *by the hand*, palmistry, chiromancy; *by nails reflecting the sun's rays*, onychomancy; *by finger rings*, dactylomancy; *by numbers*, arithmancy; *by drawing lots*, sortilege; *by passages in books*, stichomancy; *by the letters forming the name of the person*, onomancy, nomancy; *by the features*, anthroposcopy; *by the mode of laughing*, geloscopy; *by ventriloquism*, gastromancy; *by walking in a circle*, gyromancy; *by dropping melted wax into water*, ceromancy; *by currents*, bletonism; *by the color and peculiarities of wine*, œnomancy; *by the shoulder blade*, scapulimancy *or* scapulomancy, omoplatoscopy.

512. Omen. — N. OMEN, portent, presage, prognostic, augury, auspice; sign &c. (*indication*) 550; harbinger &c. (*precursor*) 64; yule candle, yule log *or* clog.

bird of ill omen; halcyon birds; signs of the times; gathering clouds, thunder, lightning, rainbow, comet, shooting star; rain of blood, warning &c. 668.

prefigurement &c. 511; adytum &c. 511.

Adj. ILL-BODING, ill-omened, inauspicious.

₊ *auspicium melioris œvi.*

513. Oracle. — N. ORACLE; prophet, seer, soothsayer, augur, medium, clairvoyant, palmist, fortune teller, prophetess, sibyl, witch, geomancer, haruspice *or* aruspice, haruspex *or* aruspex; Sibyl; python, pythoness, Pythia; Pythian oracle, Delphian (*or* Delphic) oracle; Monitor, Sphinx, Tiresias, Cassandra, Sibylline leaves; oak –, oracle- of Dodona; sorcerer &c. 994; interpreter &c. 524.

WEATHER PROPHET, weather sharp [*slang*], weather bureau, Old Probabilities *or* Old Prob. [*humorous nickname for U. S. weather bureau*]; Old Moore, Zadkiel.

₊ "it is not enough for a prophet to believe in his message; he must believe in its acceptability" [Chesterton].

Section VII. CREATIVE THOUGHT

514. Supposition. — N. SUPPOSITION, assumption, supposal, supposableness [*rare*], suppositality [*obs.*], postulation [*rare*], condition, presupposition, hypothesis, postulate, postulatum, theory, data; proposition, position; thesis, theorem; proposal &c. (*plan*) 626; assumed premise.

bare –, vague –, loose- -supposition, – suggestion; conceit; conjecture; guess, guesswork; rough guess, shot [*colloq.*]; conjecturality [*rare*], suggestiveness, presurmise, surmise, suspicion, inkling, suggestion, association of ideas, hint; presumption &c. (*belief*) 484; divination, speculation.

THEORIST, theorizer, speculatist [*rare*], speculator, notionalist, hypothesist, hypothetist [*rare*], doctrinaire, doctrinarian.

V. SUPPOSE, conjecture, surmise, suspect, guess, divine; theorize; presume, presuppose; assume, fancy, wis [*archaic*], take it; give a guess, speculate, believe, dare say, take it into one's head, take for granted.

PROPOUND, propose, put forth; start, put a case, submit, move, make a motion; hazard –, venture –, throw out –, put forward- a -suggestion, – conjecture, – supposition; hypothesize.

SUGGEST, allude to, hint, put it into one's head.

suggest itself &c. (*thought*) 451; run in the head &c. (*memory*) 505; marvel - wonder- -if, – whether.

Adj. SUPPOSING &c: *v.;* given, mooted, postulatory [*now rare*]; assumed &c. *v.;* suppositive, supposititious; gratuitous, speculative, conjectural, conjecturable, hypothetical, theoretical, academic, supposable, presumptive, putative; suppositional, suppositionary.

SUGGESTIVE, allusive, stimulating.

Adv. IF, if so be; an [*archaic*]; on the supposition &c. *n.; ex hypothesi* [*L.*], in case, in the event of; if that [*archaic*], so that, whether; quasi, as if, provided; perhaps &c. (*by possibility*) 470; for aught one knows.

515. Imagination. — N. IMAGINATION, originality, invention; fancy; inspiration; verve.

warm –, heated –, excited –, sanguine –, ardent –, fiery –, boiling –, wild –, bold –, daring –, playful –, lively –, fertile- -imagination, – fancy.

"mind's eye" [*Hamlet*]; "the mind's internal heaven" [Wordsworth]; "such stuff as dreams are made on " [*Tempest*].

IDEALITY, idealism; romanticism, utopianism, castle-building; dreaming; frenzy *or* phrensy, ecstasy; calenture &c. (*delirium*) 503; reverie *or* revery, brown study, pipe dream, daydream, trance; somnambulism.

conception, *Vorstellung* [*Ger.*], excogitation, "a fine frenzy" [*M. N. D.*]; cloudland, dreamland; flight −, fumes- of fancy; "thick-coming fancies" [*Macbeth*]; creation −, coinage- of the brain; imagery; word painting.

FANTASY, conceit, figment, myth, dream, vision, shadow, chimera; phantasm, phantasy, fancy; maggot, whim, whimwham, whimsey *or* whimsy, vagary, rhapsody, romance, gest *or* geste, extravaganza; "air-drawn dagger" [*Macbeth*], bugbear, nightmare; flying Dutchman, great sea serpent, man in the moon, castle in the air, castle in Spain, *château en Espagne* [*F.*], pleasure dome of Kubla Khan, Utopia; Heavenly City, New Jerusalem; Atlantis, Happy Valley [Johnson], millennium, fairyland; land of Prester John, kingdom of Micomicon; Estotiland *or* Estotilandia [Milton]; Laputa; Cockagne, Lubberland; Arabian nights; *le pot au lait* [*F.*]; pot of gold at the foot of the rainbow; dream of Alnaschar &c. (*hope*) 858; golden dream.

CREATIVE WORKS] work of fiction &c.(*novel*) 594; poetry &c. 597; play, tragedy, comedy &c. (*drama*) 599; sonata &c. (*music*) 415.

ILLUSION &c. (*error*) 495; phantom &c. (*fallacy of vision*) 443; *Fata Morgana* [*L.*] &c. (*ignis fatuus*) 423; vapor &c. (*cloud*) 353; stretch of the imagination &c. (*exaggeration*) 549; mythogenesis.

IDEALIST, romanticist, visionary; mopus [*slang*], romancer, daydreamer, dreamer; somnambulist; rhapsodist &c. (*fanatic*) 504; castle-builder, fanciful projector; "sweetest Shakespeare, Fancy's child" [Milton].

V. IMAGINE, fancy, conceive; idealize, realize; dream, − of; "gives to airy nothing a local habitation and a name" [*M. N. D.*].

set one's wits to work; strain −, crack- one's invention; rack −, ransack −, cudgel- one's brains; excogitate.

give -play, − the reins, − a loose [*obs.*]- to the- -imagination, − fancy; tilt at windmills; indulge in rêverie.

conjure up a vision; fancy −, represent −, picture −, figure- to oneself; *vorstellen* [*Ger.*]; "see visions and dream dreams" [*Bible*].

float in the mind; suggest itself &c. (*thought*) 451.

CREATE, originate, devise, invent, make up, coin, fabricate; improvise, strike out something new.

Adj. IMAGINED &c. *v.; ben trovato* [*It.*]; air-drawn, air-built.

IMAGINATIVE; imagining &c. *v.*; original, inventive, creative, fertile, productive, ingenious.

EXTRAVAGANT, romantic, high-flown, flighty, preposterous; rhapsodic *or* rhapsodical; fanatic, enthusiastic, Utopian, Quixotic.

IDEAL, unreal; in the clouds, *in nubibus* [*L.*]; unsubstantial &c. 4; illusory &c. (*fallacious*) 495; fictitious, theoretical, hypothetical.

fanciful; fabulous, legendary, mythic *or* mythical, mythological, chimerical; imaginary, visionary; dream-beset, dream-ridden, dreamy, entranced, notional, fancy, fantastical, high-fantastical, fantasied, maggoty, made of empty air, vaporous, whimsical; fairy, fairylike.

** "a change came o'er the spirit of my dream" [Byron]; *ægri somnia vana; delphinum appingit sylvis in fluctibus aprum* [Horace]; "your old men shall dream dreams; your young men shall see visions" [*Bible*]; "fancy light from fancy caught" [Tennyson]; "imagination rules the world" [Napoleon]; *l'imagination gallope, le jugement ne va que le pas; musæo contingens cuncta lepore* [Lucretius]; "He is a dreamer; let us leave him: pass" [*Julius Cæsar*]; "For he on honey-dew hath fed And drunk the milk of Paradise" [Coleridge]; "Forms more real than living man, Nurslings of immortality" [Shelley]; *tous songes sont mensonges; Wahrheit und Dichtung;* "magic casements, opening on the foam Of perilous seas, in faëry lands forlorn" [Keats]; "O sweet Fancy! let her loose" [*ibid.*]; "the centre of every man's existence is a dream" [Chesterton]; "this is visionary mania" [Galsworthy].

DIVISION (II) COMMUNICATION OF IDEAS

Section I. NATURE OF IDEAS COMMUNICATED

516. [IDEA TO BE CONVEYED.] **Meaning.** [THING SIGNIFIED.] — **N.** MEANING; signification, significance; sense, expression; import, purport; implication, connotation, essence, force; drift, tenor, spirit, bearing, coloring; scope.

allusion &c. (*latency*) 526; suggestion &c. (*information*) 527; interpretation, acceptation &c. 522; acceptance [*rare*].

general –, broad –, substantial –, colloquial –, literal –, primary –, accepted –, essential –, plain –, simple –, natural –, unstrained –, true &c. (*exact*) 494 –, honest &c. 543 –, *primâ facie* [*L.*] &c. (*manifest*) 525- meaning.

LITERALITY; literal –, obvious –, real- -meaning, – sense, – interpretation.

EQUIVALENT MEANING; interchangeable word, figure of speech &c. 521; equivalent, synonym &c. 522.

THING SIGNIFIED, matter, subject, subject matter, substance, sum and substance; gist &c. 5; argument, text.

V. MEAN, signify, connote, denote, express; import, purport; convey, imply, breathe, indicate, bespeak, bear a meaning, bear a sense; tell of, speak of; touch on; point to, allude to; drive at; involve &c. (*latency*) 526; declare &c. (*affirm*) 535.

understand by &c. (*interpret*) 522.

SYNONYMIZE, express by a synonym; paraphrase, state differently.

Adj. MEANING &c. *v.;* expressive, suggestive, allusive; significant, significative, significatory; pithy; meaningful; full of –, pregnant with- meaning; explicit &c. 525.

declaratory &c. 535; intelligible &c. 518.

LITERAL, metaphrastic *or* metaphrastical, word-for-word, verbatim; exact, real.

SYNONYMOUS; tantamount &c.(*equivalent*) 27.

IMPLIED &c. (*latent*) 526; understood, tacit.

Adv. TO THAT EFFECT; that is to say &c. (*being interpreted*) 522.

VERBATIM, literally; evidently, apparently, from the context.

517. [ABSENCE OF MEANING.] **Unmeaningness.** — **N.** UNMEANINGNESS &c. *adj.;* scrabble, scribble, scrawl, pothooks.

empty sound, dead letter, *vox et præterea nihil* [*L.*]; "a tale Told by an idiot, full of sound and fury, Signifying nothing" [*Macbeth*]; "weasel words" [Roosevelt]; "sounding brass or a tinkling cymbal" [*Bible*].

NONSENSE, jargon, gibberish, jabber, mere words, hocus-pocus, fustian, rant, bombast, balderdash, palaver, patter [*cant or colloq.*], flummery, verbiage, babble, *bavardage* [*F.*], *baragouin* [*F.*], platitude, *niaiserie* [*F.*]; inanity; flapdoodle [*colloq.*]; rigmarole, rodomontade; truism; *nugæ canoræ* [*L.*]; twaddle, twattle, fudge, trash; poppy-cock [*U. S.*]; stuff, – and nonsense; bosh [*colloq.*], rubbish, moonshine, wish-wash [*slang*], fiddle-faddle [*colloq.*]; absurdity &c. 497; imbecility, folly &c. 499; unintelligibleness, ambiguity, vagueness &c. (*unintelligibility*) 519.

V. MEAN NOTHING; be unmeaning &c. *adj.;* twaddle, quibble, jabber, rant, rodomontade, palaver, babble, fiddle-faddle [*colloq.*].

SCRIBBLE, scrawl, scrabble, scratch.

Adj. UNMEANING; meaningless, senseless; nonsensical &c. 497; void of sense &c. 516.

inexpressive, unexpressive; vacant; not significant &c. 516; insignificant.

TRASHY, washy, wishy-washy [*colloq.*], inane, wash [*obs.*], rubbishy, vague, trumpery, trivial, fiddle-faddle [*colloq.*], twaddling, quibbling.

UNMEANT, not expressed; tacit &c. (*latent*) 526.

INEXPRESSIBLE, undefinable, ineffable, unutterable, incommunicable.

Int. FUDGE! stuff! stuff and nonsense! bosh! fiddle-faddle! [*colloq.*]; poppy-cock! oh! la-la! [*F.*]; rubbish! fiddledeedee! &c. 497.

∗∗∗ "To varnish nonsense with the charms of sound" [Churchill]; "the spirits of the wise sit in the clouds and mock us" [*II Henry IV*].

518. Intelligibility. — N. INTELLIGI-
BILITY; clearness, clarity, explicitness
&c. *adj.;* lucidity, comprehensibility,
perspicuity; legibility, plain speaking
&c. *(manifestation)* 525; precision &c.
494; *phonanta sunetoisi* [*Gr.* φωνᾶντα
συνετοῖσι], a word to the wise.

V. BE INTELLIGIBLE &c. *adj.;* speak
for itself, speak volumes; tell its own
tale, lie on the surface.

RENDER INTELLIGIBLE &c. *adj.;* popularize, simplify, clear up; elucidate &c.
(explain) 522.

UNDERSTAND, comprehend; take, – in;
catch, grasp, follow, collect, master,
make out; see with half an eye, see
daylight, see one's way [*all colloq.*];
enter into the ideas of; come to an understanding.

Adj. INTELLIGIBLE; clear, clear as
-day, – noonday, – crystal; lucid; perspicuous, transpicuous; luminous, transparent.

easily understood, easy to understand, for the million, intelligible to the
meanest capacity, popularized.

PLAIN, distinct, clear-cut, hard-hitting, to the point, explicit; positive;
definite &c. *(precise)* 494.

unambiguous, unequivocal, unmistakable &c. *(manifest)* 525, unconfused;
legible, recognizable; obvious &c. 525.

GRAPHIC, telling, vivid; expressive &c.
(meaning) 516; illustrative &c. *(explanatory)* 522.

Adv. in plain -terms, – words, – English; hitting the nail on the head.

₊ he that runs may read &c. *(manifest)*
525; "that wayfaring men, though fools, should
not err therein" [*Bible*].

519. Unintelligibility. — N. UNIN-
TELLIGIBILITY, incomprehensibility, imperspicuity [*rare*]; inconceivableness,
unknowability, unknowableness, vagueness &c. *adj.;* obscurity; ambiguity &c.
520; doubtful meaning; uncertainty &c.
475; perplexity &c. *(confusion)* 59;
spinosity; *obscurum per obscurius* [*L.*];
mystification &c. *(concealment)* 528;
latency &c. 526; transcendentalism.

pons asinorum [*L.*], asses' bridge;
double Dutch, high Dutch [*slang*],
Greek, Hebrew, Choctaw; jargon &c.
(unmeaning) 517.

ENIGMA, riddle &c. *(secret)* 533; paradox; *dignus vindice nodus* [*L.*]; sealed
book; steganography, cryptography,
freemasonry.

V. BE UNINTELLIGIBLE &c. *adj.;* require explanation &c. 522; have a doubtful meaning, pass comprehension.

RENDER UNINTELLIGIBLE &c. *adj.;*
conceal &c. 528; darken &c. 421; confuse &c. *(derange)* 61; mystify, perplex
&c. *(bewilder)* 475.

NOT UNDERSTAND &c. 518; lose, – the
clew; miss; not know what to make of,
be able to make nothing of, give it up;
not be able to -account for, – make
head or tail of; be at sea &c. *(uncertain)*
475; wonder &c. 870; see through a
glass darkly &c. *(ignorance)* 491.

not understand one another; play at
cross-purposes &c. *(misinterpret)* 523.

Adj. UNINTELLIGIBLE, unaccountable,
undecipherable, undiscoverable, unknowable, unfathomable; incognizable,
inexplicable, inscrutable; inapprehensible, incomprehensible; insolvable, insoluble; impenetrable.

PUZZLING, as Greek to one, unex-
plained, paradoxical, enigmatic *or* enigmatical, indecipherable, illegible.

OBSCURE, crabbed, imperspicuous [*rare*], dark, muddy, clear as mud [*colloq.*],
seen through a mist, dim, nebulous, shrouded in mystery; undiscernible &c. *(invisible)* 447; misty &c. *(opaque)* 426; hidden &c. 528; latent &c. 526; mysterious;
mystic, mystical, acroamatic *or* acroamatical, metempiric *or* metempirical; transcendental; occult, esoteric, recondite, abstruse.

INDEFINITE &c. *(indistinct)* 447; perplexed &c. *(confused)* 59; undetermined,
vague, loose, ambiguous.

INCONCEIVABLE, inconceptible [*obs.*]; searchless; above –, beyond –, past-
comprehension; beyond one's depth; unconceived.

INEXPRESSIBLE, unutterable, ineffable, undefinable, incommunicable.

520. [HAVING A DOUBLE SENSE.] **Equivocalness. — N.** EQUIVOCALNESS &c. *adj.;*
equivocation; double meaning &c. 516; ambiguity, *double entente* [*F., often erron.*
double-entendre], pun, paragram [*rare*], *calembour* [*F.*], quibble, equivoque *or* equi-
voke, anagram; conundrum &c. *(riddle)* 533; word play &c. *(wit)* 842; homonym,

homonymy; amphiboly, amphibologism, amphilogism *or* amphilogy [*rare*], anagrammatism, ambilogy, ambiloquy [*obs.*].

Sphinx, Delphic oracle.

EQUIVOCATION &c. (*duplicity*) 544; white lie, mental reservation &c. (*concealment*) 528; paltering.

V. EQUIVOCATE &c. (*palter*) 544; anagrammatize; be equivocal &c. *adj.*; have two meanings &c. 516.

Adj. EQUIVOCAL, ambiguous, amphibolous [*obs.*], doubtful, amphibolic, ambiloquent [*obs.*], ambiloquous, homonymic, homonymous; double-tongued &c. (*lying*) 544; enigmatical, indeterminate.

---

521. Metaphor. — N. FIGURE OF SPEECH; *façon de parler* [*F.*], way of speaking, colloquialism.

phrase &c. 566; figure, trope, metaphor, tralatition, metonymy, enallage, catachresis, synecdoche, antonomasia; satire, irony, figurativeness &c. *adj.*; image, imagery, metathesis, metalepsis, type, anagoge, simile.

PERSONIFICATION, prosopopœia, allegory, allegorization, apologue, parable, fable.

INFERENCE, implication, deduction, allusion, adumbration; euphemism, euphuism, application.

V. EMPLOY METAPHOR &c. *n.*; personify, allegorize, fable, adumbrate, shadow forth, apply, allude to.

Adj. METAPHORICAL, tropical, tralatitious, figurative, catachrestic *or* catachrestical, antonomastic *or* antonomastical, typical, parabolic *or* parabolical, allegoric *or* allegorical, allusive, referential, anagogic *or* anagogical; euphuistic *or* euphuistical, euphemistic *or* euphemistical, ironic, ironical; colloquial.

Adv. AS IT WERE; so to -speak, – say, – express oneself; in a manner of speaking [*colloq.*].

⁎⁎ mutato nomine de te fabula narratur [Horace].

---

522. Interpretation. — N. INTERPRETATION, definition; explanation, explication; solution, answer; rationale; plain –, simple –, strict- interpretation; meaning &c. 516; *mot d'énigme* [*F.*]; clew &c. (*indication*) 550.

symptomatology, semeiology *or* semiology, diagnosis, prognosis; metoposcopy, physiognomy; paleography &c. (*philology*) 560; oneirology.

TRANSLATION; rendering, rendition; reddition; literal –, free- translation; key; secret; *clavis* [*L.*], crib, pony [*U. S.*].

COMMENT, commentary; exegesis; expounding, exposition; hermeneutics; inference &c. (*deduction*) 480; illustration, exemplification; gloss, annotation, scholium, note; enucleation, elucidation, dilucidation [*obs.*]; *éclaircissement* [*F.*].

acception [*obs.*], acceptation, acceptance; light, reading, lection, construction, version.

EQUIVALENT, – meaning &c. 516; synonym, pœcilonym, polyonym [*rare*]; paraphrase, metaphrase; convertible terms, apposition.

523. Misinterpretation. — N. MISINTERPRETATION, misapprehension, misdoubt, misconception, misunderstanding, misacception [*obs.*], misconstruction, misapplication; catachresis; eisegesis; cross-reading, cross-purposes; mistake &c. 495.

MISREPRESENTATION, perversion, misstatement, exaggeration &c. 549; false -coloring, – construction; abuse of terms; play upon words, *jeu de mots* [*F.*], pun, parody, travesty; falsification &c. (*lying*) 544.

V. MISINTERPRET, misapprehend, misunderstand, misconceive, misjudge, misdeem, misdoubt, misspell, mistranslate, misconstrue, misapply; mistake &c. 495.

MISREPRESENT, pervert; explain wrongly, misstate; garble &c. (*falsify*) 544; distort, detort [*obs.*]; travesty, play upon words; stretch –, strain –, twist –, wrench –, wring –, wrest- the -sense, – meaning; explain away; put a -bad, – wrong, – erroneous, – false- construction on; give a false coloring; look through dark –, rose-colored- spectacles.

dictionary &c. 562; polyglot.

PREDICTION &c. 511; chiromancy or cheiromancy, palmistry; astrology.

V. INTERPRET, explain, define, construe, translate, render; do into, turn into; transfuse the sense of.

find out &c. (480a)- -the meaning of &c. 516; read; spell out, make out; decipher, unravel, disentangle; find the key of, enucleate, resolve, solve; consignify [rare]; read between the lines.

ELUCIDATE, account for; find -, tell-the cause of &c. 153; throw -, shed--light, -new light, - fresh light- upon; clear up.

BE OUT; be -, play- at cross-purposes; be off [slang], be 'way off [slang].

Adj. MISINTERPRETED &c. v.; eisegetical, catachrestic or catachrestical; untranslated, untranslatable.

CONFUSED, tangled, snarled, mixed, dazed, perplexed, bewildered, rattled [slang], benighted.

Adv. AT CROSS-PURPOSES, at sixes and sevens [colloq.]; à tort et à travers [F.]; all balled up [colloq.], in a maze.

⁎ "there are no secrets better kept than the secrets that everybody guesses" [Shaw].

illustrate, exemplify; unfold, expound, comment upon, annotate; popularize &c. (render intelligible) 518.

UNDERSTAND BY; take -, understand -, receive -, accept- in a particular sense; put a construction on, be given to understand.

Adj. EXPLANATORY, expository; explicative, explicatory; exegetical; construable; hermeneutic or hermeneutical, interpretive, interpretative, commentarial, commentatorial, inferential, illustrative, exemplificative, exemplificational, annotative, scholiastic, elucidative; symptomatological; paleographic or paleographical.

EQUIVALENT &c. 27; paraphrastic, consignificative [rare], consignificant, synonymous, pœcilonymic, polyonymal [rare], polyonymic [rare].

metaphrastic, literal &c. 516; polyglot.

Adv. IN EXPLANATION &c. n.; that is to say, id est [L.], videlicet [L.], to wit, namely, in other words.

LITERALLY, strictly speaking: in -plain, - plainer- -terms, - words, - English; more simply.

⁎ "one must be an inventor to read well" [Emerson].

524. Interpreter. — N. INTERPRETER (fem. interpretress), translator, expositor, expounder, exponent, explainer; demonstrator.

COMMENTATOR, scholiast, annotator; metaphrast, paraphrast; glossarist, prolocutor.

SPOKESMAN, speaker, mouthpiece, foreman of the jury; mediator, delegate, exponent, representative, diplomatic agent, ambassador, plenipotentiary; advocate, judge, Supreme Court.

GUIDE, dragoman, courier, valet de place [F.], cicerone, showman, barker [colloq.], oneirocritic; Œdipus, Joseph; oracle &c. 513.

Section II. MODES OF COMMUNICATION

525. Manifestation. — N. MANIFESTATION, unfoldment, unfolding; plainness &c. adj.; plain speaking; expression; showing &c. v.; exposition, demonstration, séance, materialization; exhibition, production; display, show-down [slang], show, showing off [colloq.]; premonstration [obs.].

[THING SHOWN] exhibit, exhibition, exposition, show [colloq.], performance.

INDICATION &c. (calling attention to)

526. Latency. — N. LATENCY, inexpression; hidden -, occult- meaning; obscurity &c. (unintelligibility) 519; occultness, mystery, cabala or cabbala, cabalism, occultism, mysticism, symbolism, anagoge; silence &c. (taciturnity) 585; concealment &c. 528; more than meets the -eye, - ear; Delphic oracle; le dessous des cartes [F.], undercurrent; "something rotten in the state of Denmark" [Hamlet].

457; publicity &c. 531; disclosure &c. 529; openness &c. (*honesty*) 543, (*artlessness*) 703; *épanchement* [*F.*]; saliency, prominence.

V. MAKE *or* RENDER MANIFEST &c. *adj.;* materialize; bring -forth, – forward, – to the front, – into view; give notice; express; represent, set forth, evidence, exhibit; show, – up; expose; produce; hold up –, expose- to view; set –, place –, lay- before -one, – one's eyes; tell to one's face; trot out [*colloq.*], put through one's paces [*colloq.*], show one's paces, show off [*colloq.*]; show forth, unveil, bring to light, display, demonstrate, unroll; lay open; draw out, bring out; bring out in strong relief; call –, bring- into notice; hold up the mirror to; wear one's heart upon his sleeve; show one's -face, – colors; manifest oneself; speak out; make no -mystery, – secret- of; unfurl the flag; proclaim &c. (*publish*) 531.

indicate &c. (*direct attention to*) 457; disclose &c. 529; translate, transcribe, decipher, decode; elicit &c. 480*a*.

BE MANIFEST &c. *adj.;* appear &c. (*be visible*) 446; transpire &c. (*be disclosed*) 529; speak for itself, stand to reason; stare one in the face, loom large, appear on the horizon, rear its head; give -token, – sign, – indication of; tell its own tale &c. (*intelligible*) 518; go without saying, be self-evident.

Adj. MANIFEST, apparent; salient, striking, demonstrative, prominent, in the foreground, notable, pronounced.

FLAGRANT; notorious &c. (*public*) 531; arrant; stark-staring; unshaded, glaring.

PLAIN, clear, defined, definite, distinct, conspicuous &c. (*visible*) 446; obvious, evident, unmistakable, conclusive, indubitable, not to be mistaken, palpable, self-evident, autoptic *or* autoptical; intelligible &c. 518; clear as -day, – daylight, – noonday; plain as -a pikestaff [*colloq.*], – the sun at noonday, – the nose on one's face [*colloq.*], – way to parish church [*colloq.*].

ostensible; open, – as day; overt, patent, express, explicit; naked, bare, literal, downright, undisguised, exoteric.

UNRESERVED; frank, plain-spoken &c. (*artless*) 703.

BAREFACED, brazen, bold, shameless, daring, flaunting, *risqué* [*F.*], loud.

snake in the grass &c. (*pitfall*) 667; secret &c. 533.

darkness, invisibility, imperceptibility.

ALLUSION, insinuation, inference, implication; innuendo &c. 527; adumbration.

LATENT INFLUENCE, invisible government, power behind the throne, friend at court, wire-puller [*colloq.*], kingmaker; "a destiny that shapes our ends" [*Hamlet*].

V. BE LATENT &c. *adj.;* lurk, smolder *or* smoulder, underlie, make no sign; escape -observation, – detection, – recognition; lie hid &c. 528.

laugh in one's sleeve; keep back &c. (*conceal*) 528.

INVOLVE, imply, implicate, connote, import, understand, allude to, infer, leave an inference; mysticize [*rare*], symbolize; whisper &c. (*conceal*) 528.

Adj. LATENT; lurking &c. *v.;* secret, occult, anagogic *or* anagogical, cabalistic *or* cabalistical, symbolic, esoteric, recondite, veiled, symbolic, cryptic *or* cryptical; mystic, mystical; implied &c. *v.;* dormant; abeyant.

unapparent, unknown, unseen &c. 441; in the background; invisible &c. 447; indiscoverable, dark; impenetrable &c. (*unintelligible*) 519; unspied, unsuspected.

undeveloped, unsolved, unexplained, untraced, undiscovered &c. 480*a*, untracked, unexplored, uninvented.

UNEXPRESSED, unmentioned, unpronounced, unsaid, unwritten, unpublished, unbreathed, untalked of, untold &c. 527, unsung, unexposed, unproclaimed, undisclosed &c. 529, not expressed, tacit.

INDIRECT, crooked, inferential; by inference, by implication; implicit; constructive; allusive, covert, muffled; steganographic; understood, underhand, underground; concealed; under cover &c. 528; delitescent.

Adv. SECRETLY &c. 528; by a side wind; *sub silentio* [*L.*]; in the background; behind the scenes, behind one's back; on the tip of one's tongue; between the lines; by a mutual understanding; *sub rosa* [*L.*]; below the surface.

*** "thereby hangs a tale" [*As You Like It*]; *tacitum vivit sub pectore vulnus* [Vergil].

MANIFESTED &c. *v.;* disclosed &c. 529; capable of being shown, producible; unconcealable.

Adv. MANIFESTLY, openly &c. *adj.;* before one's eyes, under one's nose [*colloq.*], under one's very eyes, to one's face, face to face, above board, cards on the table, *cartes sur table* [*F.*], on the stage, in open court, in the open streets, in plain sight, in the open, at the cross-roads, in the market place, in market overt; in the face of -day, – heaven; in- broad –, open- daylight; without reserve; at first blush, *primâ facie* [*L.*], on the face of; in set terms.

*** *cela saute aux yeux;* he that runs may read; you can see it with half an eye; it needs no ghost to tell us; the meaning lies on the surface; *cela va sans dire; res ipsa loquitur;* "clothing the palpable and familiar" [Coleridge]; *fari quæ sentiat; volto sciolto i pensieri stretti.*

---

527. Information. — N. INFORMATION, advisement [*archaic*], enlightenment, acquaintance, knowledge &c. 490; publicity &c. 531.

mention; acquainting &c. *v.;* instruction &c. (*teaching*) 537; outpouring; intercommunication, communicativeness.

INTIMATION, communication, notice, notification, enunciation, annunciation, announcement, *communiqué* [*F.*]; representation, round robin, presentment.

REPORT, advice, monition; news &c. 532; return &c. (*record*) 551; account &c. (*description*) 594; statement &c. (*affirmation*) 535; case, estimate, specification.

DISPATCH *or* despatch, message, wire [*colloq.*], cable [*colloq.*], telegram &c. (*news*) 532; telephone, phone [*colloq.*], radiophone, wireless telephone, telegraphone.

INFORMANT, authority, teller, annunciator, harbinger, herald, intelligencer [*now rare*], reporter, exponent, mouthpiece; spokesman &c. (*interpreter*) 524; informer, eavesdropper, delator, detective, bull [*slang, U. S.*], sleuth [*colloq.*]; *mouchard* [*F.*], spy, newsmonger; messenger &c. 534; *amicus curiæ* [*L.*].

GUIDE, *valet de place* [*F.*], cicerone, pilot, guidebook, handbook; *vade mecum* [*L.*], manual; map, plan, chart, gazetteer; itinerary &c. (*journey*) 266.

HINT, suggestion, innuendo, inkling, whisper, passing word, word in the ear, subaudition, subauditur, cue, byplay; gesture &c. (*indication*) 550; gentle –, broad- hint; *verbum sapienti* [*L.*]; word to the wise; insinuation &c. (*latency*) 526.

V. TELL; inform, – of; acquaint, – with; impart, – to; make acquainted with, apprise, advise, enlighten, awaken.

let fall, mention, express, intimate, represent, communicate, make known; publish &c. 531; notify, signify, specify,

528. Concealment. — N. CONCEALMENT; hiding &c. *v.;* occultation, mystification.

reticence, reserve, reservation; mental reservation, aside; *arrière pensée* [*F.*], suppression, evasion, white lie, misprision; silence &c. (*taciturnity*) 585; suppression of truth &c. 544; underhand dealing; closeness, secret veness &c. *adj.;* mystery.

seal of secrecy; freemasonry; screen &c. 530; disguise &c. 530; masquerade; masked battery; hiding place &c. 530.

CRYPTOGRAPHY, steganography; cipher, code, cable code; sympathetic ink, palimpsest.

STALKING, still-hunt, hunt.

STEALTH, stealthiness; obreption [*obs.*]; slyness &c. (*cunning*) 702.

SECRECY, latitancy [*rare*], latitation [*obs.*]; seclusion &c. 893; privacy, secretness, hugger-mugger [*archaic*]; disguise, incognito (*fem.* incognita).

MYSTICISM, occultism, supernaturalism; esotericism, esoterics, esotery.

LATENCY &c. 526; snake in the grass; secret &c. 533; stowaway; blind baggage [*slang*].

MASQUERADER, masker, mask, domino.

V. CONCEAL, hide, secrete, put out of sight; lock up, seal up, bottle up.

cover, screen, cloak, veil, shroud; cover up one's tracks; screen from -sight, – observation; draw the veil; draw –, close- the curtain; curtain, shade, eclipse, throw a veil over; becloud, bemask; mask, camouflage, disguise; ensconce, muffle; befog; whisper.

keep- from, – back, – to oneself; keep -snug, – close, – secret, – dark; bury; sink, suppress; keep -from, – out of- -view, – sight; keep in –, throw into- the -shade, – background; stifle, hush up, smother, withhold, reserve; fence with a question; ignore &c. 460.

convey the knowledge of; retail, render an account; give an account &c. (*describe*) 594; state &c. (*affirm*) 535.

let one know, have one know; give one to understand; give notice; set -, lay -, put- before; point out, put into one's head; put one in possession of; instruct &c. (*teach*) 537; direct the attention to &c. 457.

ANNOUNCE, annunciate; report, – progress; bring –, send –, leave –, writeword; telegraph, wire [*colloq.*], telephone, phone [*colloq.*].

DISCLOSE &c. 529; show cause; explain &c. (*interpret*) 522.

HINT; give an inkling of; give –, drop –, throw out- a hint; insinuate; allude to, make allusion to; glance at; tip off [*slang*], give one a tip [*colloq.*]; tip the wink [*slang*] &c. (*indicate*) 550; suggest, prompt, give the cue, breathe; whisper, – in the ear.

BERATE, scold, chide, strafe [*colloq.*], score [*colloq., U. S.*], dress down [*colloq.*], reprove, trim [*slang*], rate; give one a -bit, –piece- of one's mind; tell one -plainly, – once for all; speak volumes.

UNDECEIVE, unbeguile; set right, correct, open the eyes of, disabuse.

BE INFORMED OF &c.; know &c. 490; learn &c. 539; get scent of, gather from; sleuth [*colloq.*]; awaken to, open one's eyes to; become -alive, – awake- to; hear, understand; come to one's -ears, – knowledge; reach one's ears; overhear &c. (*hear*) 418; get wise to [*slang*].

Adj. INFORMED &c. *v.; communiqué* [*F.*]; informational, advisory, intelligential; reported &c. *v.;* published &c. 531.

expressive &c. 516; explicit &c. (*open*) 525, (*clear*) 518; plain-spoken &c. (*artless*) 703.

DECLARATORY, declarative, enunciative, nunciative [*rare*], annunciative [*rare*], enunciatory, insinuant [*rare*]; oral, nuncupative [*said of oral wills*], nuncupatory [*obs.*]; expository; communicative, communicatory.

Adv. FROM INFORMATION RECEIVED; according to -reports, – suggestion, – rumor; from notice given; by the underground route; as a matter of -general information, – common report; in the air; according to –, from- what one can gather.

.˙. a little bird told me; "foul whisperings are abroad" [*Macbeth*].

CODE, codify; use a -code, – cipher.

KEEP A SECRET, keep one's own counsel; hold one's tongue &c. (*silence*) 585; make no sign, not let it go further; not breathe a -word, – syllable- about; not let the right hand know what the left is doing; hide one's light under a bushel, bury one's talent in a napkin.

HOODWINK; keep –, leave- in -the dark, – ignorance; blind, – the eyes; blindfold, mystify; puzzle &c. (*render uncertain*) 475; bamboozle &c. (*deceive*) 545.

BE CONCEALED &c. *v.;* suffer an eclipse; occult, retire from sight, couch; hide oneself; lie -hid, – in ambush, – perdu, – snug, – low [*colloq.*], – close; latitate [*obs.*]; seclude oneself &c. 893; lurk, sneak, skulk, slink, prowl, gumshoe [*slang, U. S.*]; steal -into, – out of, – by, – along; play at -bopeep, – hide and seek; hide in holes and corners; stillhunt.

Adj. CONCEALED &c. *v.;* hidden; secret, latitant [*rare*], recondite, mystic, mystical, cabalistic *or* cabalistical, occult, dark; cryptic *or* cyptical, private, privy, *in petto* [*It.*], auricular, clandestine, close, close-mouthed, inviolate; tortuous.

behind a screen &c. 530; under -cover, – an eclipse; in ambush, in hiding, in disguise; in a -cloud, – fog, – mist, – haze, – dark corner; in the -shade, – dark; clouded, wrapt in clouds; invisible &c. 447; buried, underground, perdu; secluded &c. 893.

UNDISCLOSED &c. 529, untold &c. 527; covert &c. (*latent*) 526; mysterious &c. (*unintelligible*) 519.

INVIOLABLE, irrevealable, confidential; esoteric; not to be spoken of.

FURTIVE, obreptitious, stealthy, feline; skulking &c. *v.;* surreptitious, underhand, hole and corner [*colloq.*]; sly &c. (*cunning*) 702; secretive, clandestine, evasive; reserved, reticent, uncommunicative, buttoned up; close, – as wax; taciturn &c. 585.

Adv. SECRETLY &c. *adj.;* in secret, in private, in one's sleeve, in holes and corners [*colloq.*]; in the dark &c. *adj.*

januis clausis [*L.*], with closed doors, *à huis clos* [*F.*]; hugger-mugger, in hugger-mugger [*archaic*], *à la dérobée* [*F.*], under the -cloak of, – rose, – table; *sub rosâ* [*L.*], *en tapinois* [*F.*], in the background, aside, on the sly [*colloq.*], with bated breath, sotto voce, in a whisper, without beat of drum, *à la sourdine* [*F.*].

BEHIND THE VEIL; beyond -mortal ken, – the grave, – the veil; hid from mortal vision; into the -eternal secret, – realms supersensible, – supreme mystery.

CONFIDENTIALLY &c. *adj.*; in –, in strict- confidence; between -ourselves, – you and me; *entre nous* [*F.*], *inter nos* [*L.*], under the seal of secrecy; *à couvert* [*F.*].

UNDERHAND, by stealth, like a thief in the night; stealthily &c. *adj.*; behind -the scenes, – the curtain, – one's back, – a screen &c. 530; incognito; *in camerâ* [*L.*].

⁎ it must go no further, it will go no further; "tell it not in Gath" [*Bible*]; nobody the wiser; *alitur vitium vivitque tegendo;* "let it be tenable in your silence still" [*Hamlet*]; "but let concealment, like a worm i' the bud, Feed on her damask cheek" [*Twelfth Night*]; "mysticism . . . a transcendent form of common sense" [Chesterton].

529. Disclosure. — N. DISCLOSURE;
retection [*obs.*]; unveiling &c. *v.*; deterration [*obs.*], revealment, revelation; divulgement, divulgation [*rare*], divulgence, exposition, exposure, publication, *exposé* [*F.*], whole truth; telltale &c. (*news*) 532.

bursting of a bubble; *dénouement* [*F.*].

ACKNOWLEDGMENT, avowance, avowal; confession, confessional; shrift.

NARRATOR &c. 594; talebearer &c. 532.

V. DISCLOSE, discover, dismask [*obs.*]; draw –, draw aside –, lift –, raise –, lift up –, remove –, tear- the -veil, – curtain; unmask, unveil, unfold, uncover, unseal, unkennel; take off –, break- the seal; lay open, lay bare; expose; open, – up; bare, bring to light; evidence; make -clear, – evident, – manifest; evince.

raise –, drop –, lift –, remove –, throw off- the mask; expose; lay open; undeceive, unbeguile; disabuse, set right, correct, open the eyes of; *désillusionner* [*F.*].

530. Ambush. [MEANS OF CONCEAL-MENT.] — N. AMBUSH, ambuscade; stalking-horse; lurking-hole, -place; secret path, back stairs; retreat &c. (*refuge*) 666.

HIDING PLACE, hidlings [*Scot. & dial. Eng.*]; secret -place, – drawer; recess, hole, cubbyhole, hidie-hole [*Scot.*], holes and corners; closet, crypt, adytum, abditory [*rare*], *oubliette* [*F.*]; safe, safedeposit box, safety-deposit box.

SCREEN, cover, shade, blinker; veil, curtain, blind, purdah [*India*], cloak, cloud.

MASK, visor *or* vizor, vizard [*archaic*], disguise, masquerade dress, domino.

PITFALL &c. (*source of danger*) 667; trap &c. (*snare*) 545.

V. AMBUSH, ambuscade; lie in ambush &c. (*hide oneself*) 528; lie in wait for; set a trap for &c. (*deceive*) 545.

Adv. *aux aguets* [*F.*]; *januis clausis* [*L.*] &c. 528.

DIVULGE, reveal, break [*obs.*]; let into the secret; reveal the secrets of the prison house; tell &c. (*inform*) 527; squeal [*slang*]; breathe, utter, blab, peach [*slang*]; let -out, – fall, – drop, – slip, – the cat out of the bag [*colloq.*], come out with it [*colloq.*], come it [*slang*], betray; tell tales, – out of school; come out with; give vent to, give utterance to; open the lips, blurt out, vent, whisper about; speak out &c. (*make manifest*) 525; break the news; make public &c. 531; unriddle &c. (*find out*) 480*a*; split.

ACKNOWLEDGE, allow, concede, grant, admit, own, confess, avow, throw off all disguise, turn inside out, make a clean breast; show one's -hand, – cards; unburden –, disburden- one's mind, – conscience, – heart; open –, lay bare –, give one a piece of [*colloq.*]- one's mind; unbosom oneself, "own the soft impeachment" [Sheridan]; say –, speak- the truth; turn informer; turn -King's, – Queen's, – State's- evidence; acknowledge the corn [*slang, U. S.*].

BE DISCLOSED &c.; transpire, come to light; come in sight &c. (*be visible*) 446; become known, escape the lips; come out, ooze out, creep out, leak out, peep out, crop out, crop forth, crop up; show its -face, – colors; discover &c. itself; break through the clouds, flash on the mind; come to one's ears &c. 527.

Adj. DISCLOSED &c. *v.*; revelative, revelatory, revelational, expository, confessional, confessionary, confessory.

Int. out with it! 'fess up! [*slang*]; open up! [*colloq*].

⁎ the murder is out; a light breaks in upon one; the scales fall from one's eyes; the eyes are opened; "do good by stealth, and blush to find it fame" [Pope].

531. Publication. — **N.** PUBLICATION; public announcement &c. 527; promulgation, propagation, proclamation, pronouncement, *pronunciamiento* [*Sp.*], pronunciamento, edict, encyclical; circulation, indiction [*rare*], edition, impression, imprint.

PUBLICITY, notoriety, currency, flagrancy, cry, hue and cry, *bruit* [*F.*]; bruit, oyez *or* oyes, *vox populi* [*L.*]; report &c. (*news*) 532; telegram, cable [*colloq.*] &c. 532; telegraphy; publisher &c. *v.*

THE PRESS, the Fourth Estate, public press, newspaper, journal, gazette, daily, weekly, monthly, quarterly, annual; magazine.

ADVERTISEMENT, ad., placard, bill, flyer [*cant*], leaflet, handbill, *affiche* [*F.*], broadside, broadsheet, poster; circular, - letter; manifesto; notice &c. 527; program *or* programme.

V. PUBLISH; make -public, - known &c. (*information*) 527; speak of, talk of; broach, utter; put forward; circulate, propagate, promulgate; spread, - abroad; rumor, diffuse, disseminate, evulgate [*obs.*]; put -, give -, send- forth; emit, edit, get out; issue; bring -, lay -, drag- before the public; give -out, - to the world; report, cover [*newspaper cant*]; put -, bandy -, hawk -, buzz -, whisper -, bruit -, blaze- about; drag into the -open day, - limelight [*colloq.*], throw the spotlight on [*colloq.*]; voice, bruit.

PROCLAIM, herald, blazon; blaze -, noise- abroad; sound a trumpet; trumpet -, thunder- forth; give tongue; announce with -beat of drum, - flourish of trumpets; proclaim -from the housetops, - at Charing Cross, - at the crossroads, - at the market cross.

raise a -cry, - hue and cry, - report; set news afloat.

telegraph, cable, wireless [*colloq.*], broadcast, wire [*colloq.*].

ADVERTISE, placard; post, - up; *afficher* [*F.*], publish in the Gazette, send round the crier, cry abroad.

BE PUBLISHED &c.; be *or* become public &c. *adj.*; come out; go -, fly -, buzz -, blow- about; get -about, - abroad, - afloat, - wind; find vent; see the light; go forth, take air, acquire currency, pass current; go the rounds, go the round of the newspapers, go through the length and breadth of the land; *virum volitare per ora* [*L.*]; pass from mouth to mouth; spread; run -, spread- like wildfire.

Adj. PUBLISHED &c. *v.*; current &c. (*news*) 532; in circulation, public; notorious; flagrant, arrant; open &c. 525; trumpet-tongued; encyclic *or* encyclical, proclamatory, annunciatory, promulgatory; exoteric.

TELEGRAPHIC, cabled, radiotelegraphic, telegraphed, wireless; radiophonic.

Adv. PUBLICLY &c. *adj.*; in public, in open court, with open doors; in the -limelight, - spotlight [*both colloq.*]; for publication.

Int. Oyez! Oyes! notice!

** notice is hereby given; this is -, these are- to give notice; *nomina stultorum parietibus hærent; semel emissum volat irrevocabile verbum;* "thou god of our Idolatry, the Press!" [Cowper]; "report me and my cause aright To the unsatisfied" [*Hamlet*]; "A chiel's amang ye takin' notes And, faith, he'll prent it!" [Burns].

532. News. — **N.** NEWS; information &c. 527; piece -, budget- of -news, - information; intelligence, tidings; beat *or* scoop [*newspaper cant*], story, copy [*cant*], print, letterpress.

fresh -, stirring -, old -, stale- news; glad tidings; old -, stale- story; chestnut [*slang*].

MESSAGE, word, advice, aviso, dispatch *or* despatch; telegram, cable [*colloq.*], wire [*colloq.*], radio [*colloq.*], radiogram, wireless telegram, wireless [*colloq.*], marconigram, pneumatogram, communication, errand, embassy; bulletin; broadcast.

533. Secret. — **N.** SECRET; dead -, profound- secret; arcanum, mystery; latency &c. 526; Asian mystery; sealed book, secrets of the prison house; *le dessous des cartes* [*F.*].

ENIGMA, riddle, puzzle, nut to crack, conundrum, charade, rebus, logogriph; monogram, anagram, anagrammatism; Sphinx; *crux criticorum* [*L.*].

MAZE, labyrinth. meander [*usually in pl.*], Hyrcynian wood; intricacy.

PROBLEM &c. (*question*) 461; paradox &c. (*difficulty*) 704; unintelligibility &c. 519; *terra incognita* [*L.*] &c. (*ignorance*) 491.

REPORT, rumor, hearsay, on-dit, flying rumor, news stirring, cry, buzz, bruit, fame; talk, *oui-dire* [*F*.], scandal, eavesdropping; town –, table- -talk, – gossip; tittle-tattle; canard, topic of the day, idea afloat.

NARRATOR &c. (*describe*) 594; newsmonger, scandalmonger; busybody, talebearer, telltale, gossip, tattler, blab, babbler, tattletale, chatterer; informer, squealer [*slang*].

Adj. SECRET &c. (*concealed*) 528; involved &c. 248; labyrinthian, labyrinthine, labyrinthic *or* labyrinthical, mazy, meandrous.

ENIGMATIC *or* enigmatical, anagrammatic *or* anagrammatical, monogrammatic, logographic, cryptic *or* cryptical.

. "she was more mystical than Woman" [Dunsany].

V. TRANSPIRE &c. (*be disclosed*) 529; rumor &c. (*publish*) 531.

Adj. RUMORED; publicly –, currently- -rumored, – reported; many-tongued; rife, current, floating, afloat, going about, in circulation, in every one's mouth, all over the town.

HAVING NEWS VALUE, newsy [*colloq*.], snappy [*slang*].

Adv. AS THEY SAY; as the story -goes, – runs; it is said.

BY TELEGRAPH, by cable, by radio [*colloq*.], by wireless [*colloq*.].

. "airy tongues that syllable men's names" [Milton]; "Master! master! news, old news, and such news as you never heard of" [*Taming of the Shrew*]; ' Some tell, some hear, some judge of news, some make it" [Dryden].

534. Messenger. — N. MESSENGER, angel, envoy, emissary, legate, delegate, nuncio, internuncio, intermediary, go-between; ambassador &c. (*diplomatist*) 758.
Gabriel, Hermes, Mercury, Iris, Ariel.
marshal, flag bearer, herald, crier, trumpeter, bellman, pursuivant, *parlementaire* [*F*.], apparitor.

COURIER, runner, dak *or* dawk [*India*], estafette *or* estafet, commissionaire; errand boy, chore boy, newsboy.

MAIL; post, post office; letter bag, mail bag; postman, mail-man, letter carrier; mail train, mail boat, mailer; aërial mail; carrier pigeon.

TELEGRAPH, cable [*colloq*.], wire [*colloq*.], radiotelegraph, wireless telegraph, wireless [*colloq*.], radio [*colloq*.].

TELEPHONE, phone [*colloq*.], radio-telephone, radiophone, wireless telephone.

REPORTER, newspaperman, journalist; gentleman –, representative- of the Press; penny-a-liner; hack writer, special –, war –, own- correspondent; spy, scout; informer &c. 527.

535. Affirmation. — N. AFFIRMATION, affirmance, statement, allegation, assertion, predication, predicate [*logic*], declaration, word, averment; confirmation.

ASSEVERATION, adjuration, swearing, oath, affidavit; deposition &c. (*record*) 551; avouchment, avouch [*rare*], assurance; protest, protestation; profession; acknowledgment &c. (*assent*) 488; legal pledge, pronouncement; solemn -averment, – avowal, – declaration.

VOTE, voice; ballot, suffrage; *vox populi* [*L*.].

REMARK, observation; position &c. (*proposition*) 514; saying, dictum, sentence, *ipse dixit* [*L*.].

POSITIVENESS, emphasis, peremptoriness; dogmatism &c. (*certainty*) 474; weight.

536. Negation. — N. NEGATION, abnegation; denial; disavowal, disclaimer; abjuration; contradiction, contravention; recusation, protest; recusancy &c. (*dissent*) 489; flat –, emphatic- -contradiction, – denial; *démenti* [*F*.].

QUALIFICATION &c. 469; repudiation &c. 610; recantation, revocation; retractation &c. 607; rebuttal; confutation &c. 479; refusal &c. 764; prohibition &c. 761.

V. DENY; contradict, contravene; controvert, give denial to, gainsay, negative, shake the head.

deny -flatly, – peremptorily, – emphatically, – absolutely, – wholly, – entirely; give the lie to, belie.

DISCLAIM, disown, disaffirm, disavow, abjure, forswear, abnegate, renounce;

DOGMATIST &c. 887.

V. ASSERT; make an assertion &c. *n.;* have one's say; say, affirm, predicate, declare, state; protest, profess; acknowledge &c. *(assent)* 488.

put forth, put forward; advance, allege, propose, propound; announce &c. 527; enunciate, broach, set forth, hold out, maintain, contend, pronounce, pretend.

DEPOSE, depone, aver, avow, avouch, asseverate, swear, rap [*archaic slang*], affirm; make –, take one's- oath; make –, swear –, put in- an affidavit; take one's Bible oath, kiss the book, vow, *vitam impendere vero* [*L.*]; swear till -one is black in the face, – all's blue [*both colloq.*]; be sworn, call Heaven to witness; vouch, warrant, certify, assure; swear by bell, book, and candle; attest &c. *(evidence)* 467; adjure &c. *(put to one's oath)* 768.

EMPHASIZE; swear by &c. *(believe)* 484; insist upon, take one's stand upon; lay stress on; assert -roundly, – positively; lay down, – the law; raise one's voice, dogmatize, have the last word; rap out; repeat; reassert, reaffirm.

recant &c. 607; revoke &c. *(abrogate)* 756.

DISPUTE, impugn, traverse, rebut, join issue upon; bring *or* call in question &c. *(doubt)* 485; give (one) the lie in his throat.

REPUDIATE &c. 610; set aside, ignore &c. 460; rebut &c. *(confute)* 479; qualify &c. 469; refuse &c. 764.

Adj. DENYING &c. *v.;* denied &c. *v.;* revocatory, abjuratory, abnegative [*rare*], contradictory; negative, negatory; recusant &c. *(dissenting)* 489; at issue upon.

Adv. NO, nay, not, nowise, noways; not a -bit, – whit, – jot; not at all, not in the least, not so; no such thing; nothing of the -kind, – sort; quite the contrary, *tout au contraire* [*F.*], far from it; *tant s'en faut* [*F.*]; on no account, in no respect; by no means, by no manner of means; negatively.

** there never was a greater mistake; I know better; *non hæc in fœdera.*

Adj. AFFIRMATIVE; asserting &c. *v.;* declaratory, predicatory, predicative, predicational, pronunciatory, pronunciative, *soi-disant* [*F.*]; positive; unmistakable, clear; certain &c. 474; express, explicit &c. *(patent)* 525; absolute, emphatic, flat, broad, round, pointed, marked, distinct, decided, assertive, insistent, confident, trenchant, dogmatic, definitive, formal, solemn, categorical, peremptory; unretracted.

PREDICABLE, affirmable, attributable.

Adv. AFFIRMATIVELY &c. *adj.;* in the affirmative.

with emphasis, ex-cathedra, without fear of contradiction.

I must say, indeed, i' faith, let me tell you, why, give me leave to say, marry [*archaic*], you may be sure, I'd have you know; upon my -word, – honor; by my troth, egad [*euphemism*], I assure you; by jingo, by Jove, by George &c. [*all colloq.*]; troth, seriously, sadly [*obs.*]; in –, in sober- -sadness, – truth, – earnest; of a truth, truly, pardie *or* perdy [*archaic*]; in all conscience, upon oath; be assured &c. *(belief)* 484; yes &c. *(assent)* 488; I'll -warrant, – warrant you, – engage, – answer for it, – be bound, – venture to say, – take my oath; in fact, forsooth, joking -aside, – apart; in all -soberness, – seriousness; so help me God; not to mince the matter.

** quoth he; *dixi.*

537. Teaching. — **N.** TEACHING &c. *v.;* pedagogics, pedagogy; instruction; edification; education; tuition; tutorship, tutorage, tutelage; direction, guidance; opsimathy [*rare*].

PREPARATION, qualification, training, schooling &c. *v.;* discipline; exercise, exercitation, drill, practice.

PERSUASION, proselytism, propagan-

538. Misteaching. — **N.** MISTEACHING, misinformation, misintelligence, misguidance, misdirection, mispersuasion [*archaic*], misinstruction, misleading &c. *v.;* perversion; false –, dangerousteaching; sophistry &c. 477; college of Laputa; the blind leading the blind.

V. MISINFORM, misteach, misdescribe, misdirect, misguide, misinstruct, mis-

dism, propaganda; indoctrination, inculcation, inoculation, initiation.

LESSON, lecture, sermon, homily, harangue, disquisition; apologue, parable; discourse, prelection or prælection, preachment; explanation &c. (interpretation) 522; chalk talk [colloq.].

Chautauqua -system, – course; lyceum [U. S.].

exercise, task; curriculum; course, – of study; grammar, three R's; A. B. C. &c. (beginning) 66.

[EDUCATION] elementary –, primary –, grammar school –, common school –, high school –, secondary –, technical –, college –, collegiate –, military –, university –, liberal –, classical –, academic –, religious –, denominational –, moral –, secular- education; propædeutics, moral tuition; the humanities, humanism, humane studies.

normal –, kindergarten- -course, – training; vocational -training, – therapeutics; Montessori system.

PHYSICAL EDUCATION, physical drill, gymnastics, calisthenics, eurythmics or eurhythmics; sloyd.

V. TEACH, instruct, edify, school, tutor; cram [colloq.], grind [colloq.], prime, coach; enlighten &c. (inform) 527.

inculcate, indoctrinate, inoculate, infuse, instill, infix, ingraft or engraft, infiltrate; imbue, impregnate, implant; graft, sow the seeds of, disseminate, propagate.

give an idea of; put up to [slang]; put in the way of; set right.

sharpen the wits, enlarge the mind; give new ideas, open the eyes, bring forward, "teach the young idea how to shoot" [Thomson]; improve &c. 658.

direct, guide; direct attention to &c. (attention) 457; impress upon the -mind, – memory; beat into, – the head; convince &c. (belief) 484.

EXPOUND &c. (interpret) 522; lecture; read –, give- a -lesson, – lecture, – sermon, – discourse; incept [Cambridge Univ., Eng.]; hold forth, preach; prelect or prælect, sermonize, moralize; point a moral.

TRAIN, discipline; bring up, – to; educate, form, ground, prepare, qualify, drill, exercise, practice, habituate, familiarize with, nurture, drynurse, breed, rear, take in hand; break, – in; tame;

correct; pervert; put on a false –, throw off the- scent; deceive &c. 545; mislead &c. (error) 495; misrepresent; lie &c. 544; spargere voces in vulgum ambiguas [Vergil], preach to the wise, teach one's grandmother to suck eggs [colloq.].

RENDER UNINTELLIGIBLE &c. 519; bewilder &c. (uncertainty) 475; mystify &c. (conceal) 528; unteach [archaic].

Adj. MISTEACHING &c. v.; unedifying.

‡ piscem natare doces.

539. Learning. — N. LEARNING; acquisition of -knowledge &c. 490, – skill &c. 698; acquirement, attainment; mental cultivation, edification, scholarship, erudition; acquired knowledge, lore; wide –, general- information; wide reading; self-instruction; study, grind [colloq.], reading, perusal; inquiry &c. 461.

docility &c. (willingness) 602; aptitude &c. 698.

APPRENTICESHIP, prenticeship [obs. or colloq.], pupilage, tutelage, novitiate.

EXAMINATION, matriculation; responsions or smalls [Oxford Univ.], previous examination or little go [Cambridge Univ., Eng.], moderations or mods. [Oxford Univ.], final examination, finals, greats [Oxford Univ.], great go, tripos [both Cambridge Univ., Eng.].

TRANSLATION, crib [student cant]; pony, trot, horse [all student slang, U. S.].

V. LEARN; acquire –, gain –, receive –, take in –, drink in –, imbibe –, pick up –, gather –, get –, obtain –, collect –, glean- -knowledge, – information, – learning.

acquaint oneself with, master; make oneself -master of, – acquainted with; grind [college slang], cram or cram up [colloq.], get up, coach up [colloq.]; learn by -heart, – rote.

read, spell, peruse; con; run –, pore –, thumb- over; wade through, run through, plunge into, dip into; glance –, run the eye- -over, – through; turn over the leaves.

STUDY; be studious &c. adj.; consume –, burn- -the midnight oil; mind one's book, bury oneself in.

go to -school, – college, – the university, – the 'varsity [colloq.]; serve an (or one's) apprenticeship, serve one's time; learn one's trade; be informed &c. 527; be taught &c. 537.

preinstruct; initiate, graduate; inure &c. (*habituate*) 613.

put to nurse, send to school.

Adj. EDUCATIONAL; scholastic, academic, doctrinal; disciplinal, disciplinary, instructive, instructional, hortatory, homiletic *or* homiletical, pedagogic *or* pedagogical, didactic; teaching &c. *v.*; taught &c. *v.*; propædeutic *or* propædeutical; propagative; cultural, humanistic, humane; pragmatic *or* pragmatical, practical, utilitarian; naturalistic, psychological, scientific, sociological, eclectic, coeducational.

. the schoolmaster abroad; *a bovi majori discit arare minor; adeo in teneris consuescere multum est* [Vergil]; *docendo discimus; quæ nocent docent; qui docet discit;* "sermons in stones and good in everything" [*As You Like It*]; "We will our youth lead on to higher fields" [*II Henry IV*].

Adj. STUDIOUS; industrious &c. 682; scholastic, scholarly, well read, widely read, well posted [*colloq.*], erudite, learned; full of -information, – learning, – lore.

TEACHABLE; docile &c. (*willing*) 602; apt &c. 698.

Adv. at one's books; *in statu pupillari* [L.] &c (*learner*) 541.

. "a lumber-house of books in every head" [Pope]; *ancora imparo!* "hold high converse with the mighty dead" [Thomson]; "lash'd into Latin by the tingling rod" [Gay]; "the more a man looks at a thing, the less he can see it, and the more a man learns a thing the less he knows it" [Chesterton]; "Macaulay is like a book in breeches" [Sydney Smith]; "learning without thought is labor lost; thought without learning is perilous" [Confucius]; "words of learned length and thundering sound" [Goldsmith].

---

540. Teacher. — N. TEACHER, trainer, preceptor, instructor, institutor [*obs.*], master, tutor, director, coryphæus [*Oxford Univ.*], dry nurse [*slang*], coach [*colloq.*], crammer [*colloq.*], grinder [*college slang, Eng.*], don [*Univ. cant*]; governor [*obs.*], bear leader [*humorous*]; governess, duenna; disciplinarian.

professor, lecturer, reader, prelector *or* prælector, prolocutor, preacher; chalk talker, *khoja* [*Turk.*], munshi *or* moonshee [*Moham.*]; pastor &c. (*clergy*) 996; schoolmaster, dominie, usher [*Brit.*], pedagogue, abecedarian; schoolmistress, dame [*rare*], kindergartner, monitor, pupil teacher.

GUIDE; expositor &c. 524; guru [*Hindu*]; mentor &c. (*adviser*) 695; pioneer, apostle, missionary, propagandist; example &c. 22.

PROFESSORSHIP &c. (*school*) 542.

TUTELAGE &c. (*teaching*) 537.

Adj. PEDAGOGIC *or* pedagogical, preceptorial, tutorial, professorial; scholastic &c. 537.

. *qui docet discit.*

541. Learner. — N. LEARNER, scholar, student, alumnus (*fem.* alumna, *pl.* alumni), *élève* [F.], pupil, schoolboy, schoolgirl; questionist, questioner, inquirer; monitor, prefect; beginner, tyro, abecedarian, alphabetarian.

UNDERGRADUATE, undergrad. [*colloq.*], freshman, fresh *or* freshie [*slang*], plebe [*West Point cant*], sophomore, soph [*colloq.*], junior, senior; commoner; pensioner, sizar [*both Cambridge Univ., Eng.*]; exhibitioner, scholar [*winner of a scholarship*], fellow commoner [*Eng. Univ.*], demy [*Magdalene Coll., Oxford*]; junior, sophister *or* soph, senior sophister *or* soph, sophister, questionist [*all Eng. Univ.*].

graduate student, post-graduate student.

CLASS, form, grade, room; promotion, graduation, remove; pupilage &c. (*learning*) 539.

DISCIPLE, chela [*India*], follower, apostle, proselyte.

fellow student, *condiscipulus* [L.], condisciple, classmate, schoolmate, schoolfellow, fellow pupil.

NOVICE, recruit, tenderfoot [*slang or colloq.*], neophyte, inceptor, *débutant* [F.], catechumen, probationer; apprentice, prentice [*obs. or colloq.*], articled clerk.

Adj. *in statu pupillari* [L.], in leading strings, pupillary, monitorial; abecedarian, rudimentary; probationary, probatory, probational; sophomoric *or* sophomoral [U. S.].

. "schoolboy, with his satchel And shining morning face, creeping like snail Unwillingly to school" [*As You Like It*].

542. School. — N. SCHOOL, academy, lyceum, *Gymnasium* [*Ger.*], *lycée* [*F.*], palæstra *or* palestra, seminary, college, educational institution, institute; university, 'varsity [*colloq.*], *Alma Mater* [*L.*].

[GENERAL] day –, boarding –, preparatory *or* prep [*colloq.*, *U. S.*] –, elementary –, common –, denominational –, secondary –, endowed –, free –, continuation –, convent –, art –, music –, military –, naval –, technical –, library –, secretarial –, business –, correspondence- school; kindergarten, nursery, day nursery, nursery school, *crèche* [*F.*]; Sunday –, Sabbath -, Bible- school; reform school, reformatory; teachers' training college; university extension -lectures, – course.

[BRITISH] primary –, infant –, dame [*hist.*] –, voluntary –, government –, Board –, higher grade –, National –, mission –, missionary –, British and Foreign –, state-aided –, grant-in-aid –, middle-class –, County Council –, training –, normal –, grammar –, collegiate –, high –, upper –, modern –, lower –, County –, County high –, Cathedral –, municipal secondary-, municipal technical –, Friends' –, coeducational *or* dual –, Polytechnic –, King Henry VIII's –, King Edward's –, Queen Elizabeth's –, Queen Mary's –, merchant guild –, Blue-Coat- school; Christ's Hospital; public school (*as* Eton, Harrow, Rugby &c.); school of art, school of arts and crafts, trade school; Royal Naval College, Royal Military Academy (Woolwich), Royal Military College (Sandhurst); training ship for -royal navy, – mercantile marine; College of Preceptors; Royal Academy –, London College –, Trinity College- of Music; Royal College of Organists.

[UNITED STATES] district –, grade –, parochial –, public –, primary –, grammar –, junior high –, high –, Latin- school; private –, technological –, normal –, kindergarten training- school; summer school; military academy (West Point); naval academy (Annapolis); college, fresh-water college [*colloq.* or *slang*, *U. S.*], State university; graduate school, post-graduate school.

CLASS, division, form &c. 541; seminar *or* seminary.

CLASS ROOM, room, school room, recitation room, lecture room, lecture hall, theater *or* theatre, amphitheater *or* amphitheatre.

DESK, reading desk, ambo, pulpit, forum, stage, rostrum, platform, hustings, tribune.

SCHOOLBOOK, textbook, hornbook; grammar, primer, abecedary [*rare*], abecedarium, New England Primer, rudiments, manual, *vade mecum* [*L.*]; encyclopedia *or* encyclopædia; cyclopedia *or* cyclopædia; Lindley Murray, Cocker; dictionary, lexicon, thesaurus.

PROFESSORSHIP, associate professorship, lectureship, readership, fellowship, tutorship, instructorship; chair.

DIRECTORATE, board, syndicate; College Board, Board of Regents (N. Y.), School Board, Council of Education; Board of Education; Board –, Prefect- of Studies; Textbook Committee; propaganda.

Adj. SCHOLASTIC, academic, collegiate; educational, palæstral *or* palestral, cultural; gymnastic, athletic, physical, eurythmic.

Adv. ex-cathedra.

543. Veracity. — N. VERACITY; truthfulness, frankness &c. *adj.*; truth, soothfastness [*archaic*], sooth [*archaic*], veridicality, sincerity, candor, honesty, fidelity; plain dealing, *bona fides* [*L.*]; love of truth; probity &c. 939; ingenuousness &c. (*artlessness*) 703.

the truth the whole truth and nothing but the truth; honest –, unvarnished –, sober- truth &c. (*fact*) 494; unvarnished tale; light of truth.

V. SPEAK THE TRUTH, tell the truth; speak on oath; speak without -equivocation, – mental reservation; speak by the card; paint in its –, show oneself in one's- true colors; make a clean breast

544. Falsehood. — N. FALSEHOOD, falseness; falsity, falsification; deception &c. 545; untruthfulness; untruth &c. 546; guile; lying &c. *v.*, misrepresentation; mendacity, perjury, false swearing; forgery, invention, fabrication; subreption; covin [*archaic*].

perversion –, suppression- of truth; *suppressio veri* [*L.*]; perversion, distortion, false coloring; exaggeration &c. 549; prevarication, equivocat on, shuffling, fencing, evasion, fraud; *suggestio falsi* [*L.*] &c. (*lie*) 546; mystification &c. (*concealment*) 528; simulation &c. (*imitation*) 19; dissimulation, dissembling; deceit; *blague* [*F.*].

&c. (*disclose*) 529; speak one's mind &c. (*be blunt*) 703; not lie &c. 544, not deceive &c. 545.

Adj. TRUTHFUL, true; veracious, veridical; scrupulous &c. (*honorable*) 939; sincere, candid, frank, open, straightforward, unreserved; open-, frank-, true-, simple- hearted; soothfast [*archaic*], truth-telling, honest, trustworthy; undissembling &c. (dissemble &c. 544); guileless, pure; truth-loving; unperjured; true-blue, as good as one's word; one's word one's bond; unaffected, unfeigned, *bonâ fide* [L.]; outspoken, ingenuous &c. (*artless*) 703; undisguised &c. (*real*) 494.

Adv. TRULY &c. (*really*) 494; in plain words &c. 703; in –, with –, of a –, in good- truth; as the dial to the sun, as the needle to the pole; honor bright [*colloq.*]; troth; in good -sooth, – earnest; soothfast [*archaic*], unfeignedly, with no nonsense, in sooth, sooth to say, *bonâ fide* [L.], *in foro conscientiæ* [L.]; without equivocation; *cartes sur table* [F.], from the bottom of one's heart; by my troth &c. (*affirmation*) 535.

*** *di il vero e affronterai il diavolo; Dichtung und Wahrheit; esto quod esse videris; magna est veritas et prævalet;* "*that golden key that opes the palace of eternity*" [Milton]; *veritas odium parit; veritatis simplex oratio est; verité sans peur.*

SHAM, pretense, pretending, malingering.

DUPLICITY, double dealing, insincerity, tartufism *or* tartuffism, hypocrisy, cant, humbug, fake [*colloq. or slang*]; casuistry, jesuitism, jesuitry; pharisaism; Machiavelism, "organized hypocrisy"; lip -homage, – service; mouth honor; hollowness; mere -show, – outside; crocodile tears, mealy-mouthedness, quackery; charlatanism, charlatanry; gammon [*colloq.*], buncombe *or* bunkum, flam: bam [*slang*], flimflam, cajolery, flattery; Judas kiss; perfidy &c. (*bad faith*) 940; *il volto sciolto i pensieri stretti* [It.].

UNFAIRNESS &c. (*dishonesty*) 940; artfulness &c. (*cunning*) 702; missatement &c. (*error*) 495.

V. BE FALSE &c. *adj.*, be a liar &c. 548; speak falsely &c. *adv.*; tell a lie &c. 546; lie, fib; lie like a trooper; swear falsely, forswear, perjure oneself, bear false witness.

FALSIFY, misstate, misquote, miscite, misreport, misrepresent; belie, pervert, distort; put a false construction upon &c. (*misinterpret*) 523.

PREVARICATE, equivocate, quibble; palter, – to the understanding; *répondre en Normand* [F.]; trim, shuffle, fence, mince the truth, beat about the bush, blow hot and cold [*colloq.*], play fast and loose.

GARBLE, gloss over, disguise, give a color to; give –, put- a -gloss, – false coloring- upon; color, varnish, cook [*colloq.*], doctor [*colloq.*], dress up, embroider; exaggerate &c. 549; *blague* [F.].

FABRICATE, invent, trump up, get up; forge, fake [*slang*], hatch, concoct; romance &c. (*imagine*) 515; cry "wolf!"

DISSEMBLE, dissimulate; feign, assume, put on, pretend, make believe; act the old soldier [*colloq.*], play possum; play -false, – a double game; coquet; act –, play- a part; affect &c. 855; simulate, pass off for; counterfeit, sham, make a show of; malinger; say the grapes are sour.

cant [*dial. Eng.*], play the hypocrite, sham Abram *or* Abraham, *faire pattes de velours* [F.], put on the mask, clean the outside of the platter, lie like a conjuror; hand out –, hold out –, sail under- false colors; "commend the poisoned chalice to the lips" [*Macbeth*]; *spargere voces in vulgum ambiguas* [Vergil]; deceive &c. 545.

Adj. FALSE, deceitful, mendacious, unveracious, fraudulent, dishonest; faithless, truthless, untruthful, trothless [*archaic*]; unfair, uncandid; hollow-hearted; evasive; uningenuous, disingenuous; hollow, insincere, *Parthis mendacior* [L.]; forsworn.

collusive, collusory [*obs.*]; artful &c. (*cunning*) 702; perfidious &c. 940; spurious &c. (*deceptive*) 545; untrue &c. 546; falsified &c. *v.;* covinous.

HYPOCRITICAL, canting, jesuitical, pharisaical; tartufish *or* tartuffish; Machiavellic, Machiavellian *or* Machiavelian; double, -tongued, -handed, -minded, -hearted, -dealing; two-faced, double-faced; Janus-faced; smooth -faced, -spoken, -tongued; plausible; mealy-mouthed; affected &c. 855.

Adv. FALSELY &c. *adj.; à la Tartufe* [*F.*]; with a double tongue; slily &c. (*cunning*) 702.

. *blandæ mendacia linguæ; falsus in uno falsus in omnibus;* "I give him joy that's awkward at a lie" [Young]; *la mentira tiene las piernas cortas* [*Sp.*]; "O what a goodly outside falsehood hath!" [*M. of V.*]; "look like the innocent flower, But be the serpent under 't" [*Macbeth*]; "a Hair perhaps divides the False and True" [Omar Khayyám – Fitzgerald]; "sin has many tools, but a lie is the handle which fits them all" [Holmes].

545. Deception. — N. DECEPTION; falseness &c. 544; untruth &c. 546; imposition, imposture; fraud, deceit, guile; fraudulence, fraudulency; covin [*archaic*]; knavery &c. (*cunning*) 702; misrepresentation &c. (*falsehood*) 544; bluff; straw-bail, straw-bid [*U. S.*]; spoof [*slang*]; hocus-pocus, *escamoterie* [*F.*], jockeyship; trickery, coggery [*obs.*], pettifoggery, sharp practice, chicanery; *supercherie* [*F.*], cozenage, circumvention, ingannation [*obs.*], collusiveness, collusion; treachery &c. 940; practical joke.

DELUSION, gullery [*archaic*]; juggling, jugglery; sleight of hand, legerdemain; prestigiation [*obs.*], prestidigitation; magic &c. 992; conjuring, conjuration.

TRICK, cheat, wile, blind, feint, plant [*slang*], bubble, fetch, catch [*dial.*], chicane, artifice, reach [*obs.*], bite [*obs., colloq.*], juggle, hocus [*archaic*]; thimble-rig, card sharping, artful dodge, swindle; tricks upon travelers; trapan *or* trepan [*archaic*]; stratagem &c. (*artifice*) 702; fake [*colloq. or slang*], hoax; theft &c. 791; ballot-box stuffing [*U. S.*], barney [*slang*], bunko *or* bunco, bunko game; confidence -trick, – game; brace -, drop -, gum -, panel -, shell -, skin- game [*all slang*]; gold brick [*colloq., U. S.*].

SNARE, trap, pitfall, Cornish hug, decoy, gin; springe, springle [*obs.*]; noose, hook; bait, decoy duck, stool pigeon, tub to the whale, baited trap, *guet-apens* [*F.*]; cobweb, net, meshes, toils, mouse trap, birdlime; Dionæa, Venus's flytrap; ambush &c. 530; trapdoor, sliding panel, false bottom; spring net, spring gun; mask, masked battery; mine; flytrap; green goods [*U. S.*]; panel house.

DISGUISE, disguisement; false colors, masquerade, mummery, borrowed plumes; wolf in sheep's clothing &c. (*deceiver*) 548; *pattes de velours* [*F.*].

SHAM; mockery &c. (*imitation*) 19; copy &c. 21; counterfeit, make-believe, forgery, fraud; lie &c. 546; "a delusion, a mockery, and a snare" [Denman], hollow mockery; whited -, painted- sepulcher; jerry-building, jerryism [*builders' cant*]; man of straw.

TINSEL, paste, false jewelry, scagliola, ormolu, mosaic gold, brummagem, German silver, albata, paktong, white metal, Britannia metal, paint.

ILLUSION &c. (*error*) 495; *ignis fatuus* [*L.*] &c. 423; mirage &c. 443.

V. DECEIVE, take in, Machiavellize; defraud, cheat, jockey, do [*slang, Eng.*], *escamoter* [*F.*], cozen, diddle [*dial.*], nab [*slang*], chouse [*colloq.*], bite [*colloq.*], play one false, bilk, cully, jilt [*obs.*], pluck [*rare*], swindle, victimize; abuse; mystify; blind, – one's eyes; blindfold, hoodwink; throw dust into the eyes, "keep the word of promise to the ear and break it to the hope" [*Macbeth*].

impose -, practice -, play -, put -, palm -, foist- upon; snatch a verdict; bluff, – off; bunko *or* bunco, four-flush [*slang*]; gum [*slang, U. S.*], spoof [*slang*], stuff (a ballot box) [*U. S.*].

CIRCUMVENT, overreach; outreach, outwit, outmaneuver *or* outmanœuvre, steal a march upon, give the go-by to [*slang*], leave in the lurch.

INSNARE, ensnare; set -, lay- a -trap, - snare- for; bait the hook, forelay [*obs.*], spread the toils, lime; decoy, waylay, lure, beguile, delude, inveigle; trapan *or* trepan [*archaic*]; kidnap; let in, hook in; trick; entrap *or* intrap, nick, springe [*rare*], nousel *or* nousle [*obs.*]; blind a trail, enmesh *or* immesh; shanghai, crimp; catch, - in a trap; sniggle, entangle, illaqueate [*rare*], balk, trip up; throw a tub to a whale, hocus.

FOOL, befool, practice on one's credulity, dupe, gull, hoax, bamboozle [*colloq.*]; hum [*slang or colloq.*], humbug, gammon [*colloq.*], stuff up [*slang*], stuff [*slang*], sell [*slang*]; play a -trick, - practical joke- upon one; fool to the top of one's bent, send on a fool's errand; make -game, - a fool, - an April fool, - an ass- of; trifle with, cajole, flatter; come over &c. (*influence*) 615; gild the pill, make things pleasant, divert, put a good face upon; dissemble &c. 544.

LIVE BY ONE'S WITS; cog [*rare*], cog the dice; play at hide and seek; obtain money under false pretenses &c. (*steal*) 791; conjure, juggle, practice chicanery; deacon [*U. S.*]; jerry-build; pass by trickery, play off, palm off, foist off, fob off [*archaic*].

MISLEAD &c. (*error*) 495; lie &c. 544; misinform &c. 538; betray &c. 940.

BE DECEIVED &c. 547.

Adj. DECEPTIVE, deceptious [*rare*], deceitful, covinous [*law*]; delusive, delusory; illusive, illusory; deceived &c. *v.*; deceiving &c. *v.*; cunning &c. 702; prestigious [*obs.*], prestigiatory [*obs.*]; elusive, insidious, *ad captandum vulgus* [*L.*].

MAKE-BELIEVE; untrue &c. 546; mock, sham, counterfeit, snide [*slang*], pseudo, spurious, so-called, pretended, feigned, trumped-up, bogus [*colloq.*], scamped, fraudulent, tricky, factitious, artificial, bastard; surreptitious, illegitimate, contraband, adulterated, sophisticated; unsound, rotten at the core; colorable; disguised; meretricious; jerry-built, jerry [*builders' cant*]; tinsel, pinchbeck, plated; catchpenny; brummagem; simulated &c. 544.

Adv. under -false colors, – the garb of, – cover of; over the left [*slang*].

⁎ *fronti nulla fides;* "ah that deceit should steal such gentle shapes" [*Rich. III*]; "a quicksand of deceit" [*Henry VI*]; *decipimur specie recti* [Hor.]; *falsi crimen; fraus est celare fraudem; lupus in fabula;* "so smooth, he daubed his vice with show of virtue" [*Rich. III*]; "there are but two classes of men, the righteous, who think themselves to be sinners, and the sinners, who think themselves righteous" [Pascal].

546. Untruth. — N. UNTRUTH, falsehood, lie, story, thing that is not, fib, bounce, crammer [*slang*], tarradiddle *or* taradiddle [*colloq. or dial. Eng.*], whopper *or* whapper [*colloq.*], jhuth [*Hind.*].

FABRICATION, forgery, invention; misstatement, misrepresentation, perversion, falsification, gloss, *suggestio falsi* [*L.*]; exaggeration &c. 549.

fiction; fable, nursery tale; romance &c. (*imagination*) 515; absurd –, untrue –, false –, trumped up- -story, – statement; thing devised by the enemy; canard; shave [*slang, Eng.*], sell [*colloq.*], hum, [*slang*], yarn [*colloq.*], fish story [*colloq.*], traveler's tale, Canterbury tale, cock-and-bull story, fairy tale, fake, press-agent's yarn [*colloq.*], hot air [*slang*], claptrap.

myth, moonshine, bosh [*colloq.*], all my eye and Betty Martin [*colloq.*], all my eye [*colloq.*], mare's-nest, farce.

HALF TRUTH, white lie, pious fraud; mental reservation &c. (*concealment*) 528; irony.

PRETENSE, pretext; false plea &c. 617; subterfuge, evasion, shift, shuffle, make-believe; sham &c. (*deception*) 545; profession, empty words; Judas kiss &c. (*hypocrisy*) 544; disguise &c. (*mask*) 530.

V. RING UNTRUE; have a -false meaning, – hidden meaning, – false appearance; be an untruth &c. *n.*; lie &c. 544.

FEIGN, pretend, sham, counterfeit, gammon [*colloq.*], make-believe.

Adj. UNTRUE, false, trumped up; void of –, without- foundation; fictive, far from the truth, false as dicer's oaths; unfounded, *ben trovato* [*It.*], invented, fabulous, fabricated, fraudulent, forged; fictitious, factitious, supposititious, surreptitious; illusory, elusory; evasive, satiric *or* satirical, ironical; *soi-disant* [*F.*] &c. (*misnamed*) 565.

⁎ *se non e vero e ben trovato;* "where more is meant than meets the ear" [Milton]; "a lie in time saves nine" [*Cynic's Calendar*].

547. Dupe. — N. DUPE, gull, gudgeon, *gobemouche* [*F.*], cully, victim, April fool; jay, sucker, pigeon, cull [*all slang*]; laughingstock &c. 857; simple Simon, flat [*colloq.*], greenhorn; fool &c. 501; puppet, cat's-paw.

V. BE DECEIVED &c. 545, be the dupe

548. Deceiver. — N. DECEIVER &c. (deceive &c. 545); dissembler, hypocrite; sophist, Pharisee, Jesuit, Mawworm, Pecksniff, Joseph Surface, Tartufe *or* Tartuffe, Janus; serpent, snake in the grass, cockatrice, Judas, wolf in sheep's clothing; jilt; shuffler.

of; fall into a trap; swallow –, nibble at- the bait; bite; catch a Tartar.

Adj. CREDULOUS &c. 486.

MISTAKEN &c. (*error*) 495.

liar &c. (*lie* &c. 544); Tom Pepper, Machiavel, Machiavelist; story-teller; perjurer, false witness, *menteur à triple étage* [*F*.], Scapin; bunko steerer, carpet-bagger, capper [*all slang, U. S.*], faker [*slang*], fraud, four-flusher [*slang*], confidence man, horse coper [*Eng*.], ringer [*slang*], spieler [*colloq., Australasia*]; straw bidder [*U. S.*]; crimp; decoy duck, stool pigeon; rogue, knave, cheat; swindler &c. (*thief*) 792; jobber, gypsy.

IMPOSTOR, pretender, malingerer, humbug; adventurer, adventuress; Cagliostro, Fernam Mendez Pinto; ass in lion's skin &c. (*bungler*) 701; actor &c. (*stage player*) 599.

QUACK, charlatan, mountebank, saltimbanco [*obs.*], *saltimbanque* [*F*.], *blagueur* [*F*.], empiric, quacksalver [*now rare*], medicaster.

CONJUROR, juggler, trickster, prestidigitator, necromancer, sorcerer, magician; wizard, mage [*archaic*], medicine man, shaman.

. "saint abroad and a devil at home" [Bunyan].

549. Exaggeration. — N. EXAGGERATION; expansion &c. 194; hyperbole, stretch, strain, coloring; high coloring, caricature, *caricatura* [*It*.]; extravagance &c. (*nonsense*) 497; Baron Munchausen; Munchausenism; men in buckram, yarn [*colloq.*], fringe, embroidery, traveler's tale; fish story [*colloq.*], gooseberry [*slang*].

storm –, tempest- in a teacup; much ado about nothing &c. (*overestimation*) 482; puffery &c. (*boasting*) 884; rant &c. (*turgescence*) 577.

false coloring &c. (*falsehood*) 544; aggravation &c. 835.

FIGURE OF SPEECH, *façon de parler* [*F*.]; stretch of -fancy, – the imagination; flight of fancy &c. (*imagination*) 515.

V. EXAGGERATE, magnify, pile up, aggravate; amplify &c. (*expand*) 194; optimize; overestimate &c. 482; hyperbolize; overcharge, overstate, overdraw, overlay, overshoot the mark, overpraise; make much of, make the most of; strain, – a point; stretch, – a point; go great lengths; spin a long yarn [*colloq.*]; draw –, pull –, use –, shoot with- a (*or* the) longbow [*colloq.*]; deal in the marvelous.

out-Herod Herod, run riot, talk at random.

OVERCOLOR, heighten; color -highly, – too highly; *broder* [*F*.], embroider, be flowery; flourish; color &c. (*misrepresent*) 544; puff &c. (*boast*) 884.

UNDERRATE, pessimize, underestimate &c. 483.

Adj. EXAGGERATED &c. *v.;* overwrought; bombastic &c. (*magniloquent*) 577; hyperbolical, on stilts; fabulous, extravagant, preposterous, egregious, *outré* [*F*.], highflying.

. *excitabat enim fluctus in simpulo* [Cicero]; "exaggeration is to paint a snake and add legs" [*Chinese proverb*]; "there is no one who does not exaggerate" [Emerson].

Section III. MEANS OF COMMUNICATING IDEAS

1. *Natural Means*

550. Indication. — N. INDICATION; symbolism, symbolization; symptomatology, semeiology *or* semiology, semeiotics *or* semiotics, pathognomy; *Zeitgeist* [*Ger*.], sign of the times.

MEANS OF RECOGNITION; lineament, feature, trait, trick, earmark, characteristic, diagnostic; divining rod; cloven hoof; footfall.

SIGN, symbol; index, indice [*obs.*], indicator, point, pointer; exponent, note, token, symptom; dollar mark; type, figure, emblem, cipher, device; representation &c. 554.

MOTTO, epigraph, epitaph, posy [*archaic*].

GESTURE, gesticulation; pantomime; wink, glance, leer; nod, shrug, beck; touch, nudge; grip, freemasonry; telegraphy, byplay, dumb show; cue; hint &c. 527.

TRACK, spoor, trail, footprint, scent; clew *or* clue, key.

DACTYLOLOGY, dactylography, dactylonomy, dactyliomancy, chirology [*rare*], chiromancy, palmistry; finger print, Bertillon system.

SIGNAL, signal post, rocket, blue light, red light; watch fire, watchtower; telegraph, semaphore, flagstaff; fiery cross; calumet, peace pipe; heliograph; guidon; headlight, searchlight, flashlight, spotlight.

MARK, line, stroke, score, stripe, streak, scratch, tick, dot, point, notch, nick, blaze; red letter, sublineation, underlining, jotting; print; imprint, impress, impression; note, annotation.

[MAP DRAWING] hachure, contour line; isobar, isopiestic line, isobaric line; isotherm, isothermal line; latitude, longitude, meridian, equator.

[TYPOGRAPHY] dash, hyphen, parentheses, brackets *or* crotchets, apostrophe, interrogation *or* interrogation point, exclamation *or* exclamation point; acute -, grave- accent; long *or* macron, short *or* breve, diæresis, caret, brace, ellipsis, leaders, asterisk, dagger *or* obelisk, double dagger, section, parallels, paragraph, index, asterism, cedilla, guillemets [*rare*], quotation marks *or* quotes [*colloq.*], tilde, circumflex.

[FOR IDENTIFICATION] badge, criterion; countercheck, countermark, countersign, counterfoil, stub, duplicate, tally; label, ticket, billet, letter, counter, check, chip, chop [*Oriental*], dib [*slang*]; broad arrow; government mark; totem; tessera, card, bill; witness, voucher; stamp; *cachet* [*F.*]; trade -, hall- mark; signature; address -, visiting- card; *carte de visite* [*F.*]; credentials &c. (*evidence*) 467; attestation; hand, handwriting, sign manual; cipher; monogram; seal, sigil, signet; autograph, autography; finger print; paraph, brand; superscription; indorsement *or* endorsement; title, heading, docket; tonsure, scalp lock; mortar board [*colloq.*], cap and gown, hood; caste mark; *mot de passe* [*F.*], *mot du guet* [*F.*]; passeparole *or* passparole [*obs.*], shibboleth; watchword, catchword, password; sign, countersign, pass, dueguard, grip; open-sesame; timbrology [*rare*].

INSIGNIA; banner, banneret; banderole, bandrol *or* bannerol; flag, colors, streamer, standard, eagle, vexillum, labarum, oriflamme *or* oriflamb; figurehead; ensign; pennant, whip *or* coach-whip, pennon, burgee, blue peter, jack, ancient [*rare*], gonfalon, union jack; "Old Glory" [*colloq., U. S.*], quarantine flag; yellow flag, yellow jack; tricolor, *drapeau tricolore* [*F.*], stars and stripes; half-masted flag, union down; red flag; bunting.

HERALDRY, crest; arms, coat of arms; armorial bearings, hatchment; escutcheon *or* scutcheon, achievement, shield, supporters; livery, uniform; cockade, brassard, epaulet, chevron; garland, chaplet, fillet [*antiq.*], love knot, favor.

[OF LOCALITY] beacon, beacon fire, cresset, cairn, post, staff, flagstaff, hand, pointer, vane, cock, weathercock, weathervane; guide-, hand-, finger-, directing-, sign- post; pillars of Hercules, pharos; balefire, signal fire; *l'Etoile du Nord* [*F.*], North Star, polestar, Polaris; landmark, seamark; lighthouse, balize [*rare*], lodestar *or* loadstar; cynosure, guide; address, direction, name; sign, signboard.

[OF THE FUTURE] warning &c. 668; omen &c. 512; prefigurement &c. 511.

[OF THE PAST] trace, record &c. 551.

[OF DANGER] warning &c. 668; fire alarm, burglar alarm; alarm &c. 669.

[OF AUTHORITY] scepter &c. 747.

[OF TRIUMPH] trophy &c. 733.

[OF QUANTITY] gauge &c. 466.

[OF DISTANCE] milestone, milepost; mileage ticket; milliary [*Rom. antiq.*].

[OF DISGRACE] brand, fool's cap, mark of Cain, stigma, stripes, broad arrow.

[FOR DETECTION] check, time clock, telltale; test &c. (*experiment*) 463.

NOTIFICATION &c. (*information*) 527; advertisement &c. (*publication*) 531.

CALL, word of command; bugle call, trumpet call; bell, alarum, cry; battle -, rallying- cry; reveille, taps [*Brit.*], last post [*U. S.*]; sacring bell, Sanctus bell, angelus; pibroch, keen [*Ir.*], coronach [*Scot. & Ir.*], dirge.

V. INDICATE; be the sign of &c. *n.*; denote, betoken; argue, testify &c. (*evidence*) 467; bear the impress of &c. *n.*; connote, connotate, signify.

represent, stand for; typify &c. (*prefigure*) 511; symbolize.

MARK; put an indication, put a mark &c. *n.;* note, tick,! stamp, nick, earmark; blaze; label, ticket, docket; dot, spot, score, dash, trace, chalk.

PRINT, imprint, impress; engrave, stereotype, electrotype, lithograph; prove, pull, reprint.

MAKE A SIGN &c. *n.;* signalize; give –, hang out- a signal; beck [*archaic*], beckon; nod; wink, glance, leer, nudge, shrug, tip the wink [*slang*]; gesture, gesticulate; raise –, hold up- the -finger, – hand; saw the air, "suit the action to the word" [*Hamlet*].

wave –, unfurl –, hoist –, hang out- a banner &c. *n.;* wave -the hand, – a kerchief; give the cue &c. (*inform*) 527; show one's colors; give –, sound- an alarm; beat the drum, sound the trumpets, raise a cry.

sign, seal, attest &c. (*evidence*) 467; underscore, underline &c. (*give importance to*) 642; call attention to &c. (*attention*) 457; give notice &c. (*inform*) 527.

Adj. INDICATIVE, indicatory; indicating &c. *v.* connotative, denotative; diacritical, representative, typical, symbolic *or* symbolical, pantomimic, pathognomonic *or* pathognomonical, symptomatic, semeiotic *or* semiotic, sematic, ominous, characteristic, significant, significative, demonstrative, diagnostic, exponential, emblematic, armorial; individual &c. (*special*) 79.

KNOWN BY, recognizable by; indicated &c. *v.;* pointed, marked.

[CAPABLE OF BEING DENOTED] denotable; indelible.

Adv. SYMBOLICALLY &c. *adj.;* in token of; in dumb show, in pantomime.

⁎⁎ *ecce signum; ex ungue leonem; ex pede Herculem; vide ut supra; vultus ariete fortior; vera incessu patuit dea* [Vergil].

551. Record. — N.

TRACE, vestige, relic, remains; scar, cicatrix; footstep, footmark, footprint; pug [*India*], track, mark, wake, trail, scent, *piste* [*F.*].

MONUMENT, hatchment, achievement; escutcheon *or* scutcheon; slab, tablet, trophy, obelisk, pillar, column, monolith; memorial; memento &c. (*memory*) 505; testimonial, medal, Congressional medal; cross, Victoria cross *or* V. C., iron cross [*Ger.*]; ribbon, garter; commemoration &c. (*celebration*) 883.

RECORD, note, minute; register, registry; roll &c. (*list*) 86; chartulary *or* cartulary, diptych, Domesday book; *catalogue raisonné* [*F.*]; entry, memorandum, indorsement *or* endorsement, inscription, copy, duplicate, docket; notch &c. (*mark*) 550; muniments; deed &c. (*security*) 771; document; deposition, *procés verbal* [*F.*]; affidavit; certificate &c. (*evidence*) 467.

notebook, memorandum book, pocketbook, commonplace book, portfolio; bulletin, bulletin board, score board, score sheet, totalizator [*racing*]; card index, file, letter file, pigeonholes; *excerpta* [*L.*], excerpt, extract, adversaria, jottings, dottings.

newspaper, daily, gazette &c. (*publication*) 531; magazine.

calendar, ephemeris, diary, log, log book *or* logbook, journal, daybook, ledger, cashbook, petty cashbook.

ARCHIVE, scroll, state paper, return, bluebook *or* blue book; almanac *or* almanack, gazetteer, Almanach de Gotha, Statesman's Year-book, Whitaker's Almanack; census report; statistics &c. 86; *compte rendu* [*F.*]; Acts –, Transactions –, Proceedings- of; Hansard's Debates; Congressional Records: minutes, chronicle, annals; legend; history, biography &c. 594.

552. [SUPPRESSION OF SIGN.] Obliteration. — N.

OBLITERATION, erasure, rasure [*rare*]; cancel, cancellation; circumduction [*rare*], deletion, blot; *tabula rasa* [*L.*]; effacement, extinction.

V. EFFACE, obliterate, erase, rase [*rare*], expunge, cancel, dele; blot –, take –, rub –, scratch –, strike –, wipe –, wash –, sponge- out; wipe off, rub off; wipe away; deface, render illegible; draw the pen through, rule out, apply the sponge.

BE EFFACED &c.; leave no trace &c. 550; "leave not a rack behind" [*Tempest*].

Adj. OBLITERATED &c. *v.;* leaving no trace; intestate; unrecorded, unregistered, unwritten; printless, out of print.

Int. dele; out with it!

⁎⁎ *delenda est Carthago* [Cato].

REGISTRATION; registry, enrollment *or* enrolment, tabulation; entry, booking; signature &c. (*identification*) 550; recorder &c. 553; journalism.

MECHANICAL RECORD, recording instrument; gramophone, phonograph &c. 418; seismograph, seismometer; speedometer, pedometer, patent log [*naut.*]; ticker, tape; time clock; anemometer &c. (*measurement*) 466; turnstile; cash register; votograph.

V. RECORD; put –, place– upon record; chronicle, calendar, excerpt, hand down to posterity; keep up the memory &c. (*remember*) 505; commemorate &c. (*celebrate*) 883; report &c. (*inform*) 527; commit to –, reduce to– writing; put –, set down– –in writing, – in black and white; put –, jot –, take–, write–, note –, set-down; note, minute, put on paper; take –, make– a –note, – minute, – memorandum; summarize, make a return; mark &c. (*indicate*) 550; sign &c. (*attest*) 467.

ENTER, book; post, post up; insert, make an entry of; mark off, tick off; register, list, docket, enroll, inscroll; file &c. (*store*) 636.

Adv. ON RECORD, on file; in one's -good books, – bad books.

** *exegi monumentum ære perennius* [Horace]; "read their history in a nation's eyes" [Gray]; "records that defy the tooth of time" [Young].

553. Recorder. — N. RECORDER, notary, clerk; registrar, registrary [*obs.*], register; prothonotary; amanuensis, secretary, recording secretary, stenographer, scribe, babu [*India*], remembrancer, bookkeeper, *custos rotulorum* [*L.*], Master of the Rolls.

ANNALIST, historian, historiographer, chronicler; biographer &c. (*narrator*) 594; antiquary &c. (*antiquity*) 122; memorialist.

JOURNALIST, newspaperman, reporter, interviewer, pressman [*cant*], publicist, author, editor.

** "the journalists are now the true kings and clergy" [Carlyle].

554. Representation. — N. REPRESENTATION, depiction, depicture; imitation &c. 19; illustration, delineation, depictment; imagery, portraiture, iconography; design, designing; art, fine arts; painting &c. 556; sculpture &c. 557; engraving &c. 558.

PHOTOGRAPHY; radiography, X-ray photography, skiagraphy; spectroheliography, photospectroheliography.

PERSONATION, personification; impersonation; drama &c. 599.

DRAWING, picture, sketch, draft *or* draught; tracing; copy &c. 21.

PHOTOGRAPH, photo [*colloq.*], daguerreotype, talbotype, calotype; heliotype, heliograph; print, cabinet, *carte de visite* (*pl. cartes de visite*) [*F.*], ping-pong [*cant*], snapshot.

555. Misrepresentation. — N. MISREPRESENTATION, misstatement, falsification, caricatura [*obs.*], exaggeration; daubing &c. *v.;* bad likeness, daub, scratch; imitation, effigy.

DISTORTION, anamorphosis, anamorphoscope; Claude Lorrain –, concave –, convex– mirror.

BURLESQUE, travesty, parody, take-off, caricature, extravaganza.

V. MISREPRESENT, distort, overdraw, exaggerate, daub; falsify, understate, overstate, stretch.

BURLESQUE, travesty, parody, caricature.

Adj. MISREPRESENTED &c. *v.;* bluesky [*U. S.*].

IMAGE, likeness, icon, portrait; striking likeness, speaking likeness; very image; effigy, facsimile.

FIGURE, figurehead; puppet, doll, figurine, aglet *or* aiglet, manikin, mannequin, lay figure, model, marionette, fantoccini, waxwork, bust; statue, statuette, hieroglyph.

hieroglyphic, anaglyph, diagram, monogram.

MAP, plan, chart; ground plan, projection, elevation; atlas; outline, scheme; view &c. (*painting*) 556; ichnography, cartography.

RADIOGRAM, radiogram, scotograph, skiagraph *or* sciagraph, skiagram *or* sciagram, X-ray photograph, X-ray [*colloq.*]; spectrogram, spectroheliogram, photospectroheliogram.

DELINEATOR, draftsman *or* draughtsman; artist &c. 559; photographer, radiographer, X-ray photographer, skiagrapher, daguerreotypist.

V. REPRESENT, delineate, depict, depicture, portray, picture, limn, take –, catch- a likeness &c. *n.;* hit off, photograph, daguerreotype; snapshot; figure; shadow -forth, – out; adumbrate; body forth; describe &c. 594; trace, copy; mold *or* mould.

illustrate, symbolize; paint &c. 556; carve &c. 557; engrave &c. 558.

PERSONATE, personify, impersonate, dress up [*colloq.*], assume a character, pose as, act; play &c. (*drama*) 599; mimic &c. (*imitate*) 19; hold the mirror up to nature.

Adj. REPRESENTING &c. *v.*, representative; illustrative; represented &c. *v.;* imitative, figurative; iconic, like &c. 17; graphic &c. (*descriptive*) 594.

Renaissance, trecento, quattrocento, cinquecento, Directoire, Moyen Age.

⁎ "Passionless eyes, long dead, that judged and glared" [Masefield].

556. Painting and Black and White. — N. PAINTING; depicting; drawing &c. *v.;* design; perspective; *chiaroscuro* &c. (*light*) 420; composition; treatment; arrangement, values, atmosphere, tone, technique.

historical –, portrait –, miniature –, landscape –, marine –, flower –, poster –, interior –, scene- painting; scenography.

pallet, palette; easel; brush, pencil, stump; black lead, charcoal, crayons, chalk, pastel; paint &c. (*coloring matter*) 428; water-, body-, oil- color; oils, oil paint; varnish &c. 356a; priming; *gouache* [*F.*], tempera, distemper, fresco, water glass; enamel; encaustic painting; mosaic; tapestry, batik; sun painting.

STYLE, school; the grand style, high art, *genre* [*F.*], portraiture; futurist, cubist, vorticist; ornamental art &c. 847; monochrome, polychrome; grisaille.

[SCHOOLS OF PAINTING] Italian –, Bolognese –, Florentine –, Milanese –, Modena –, Parma –, Neapolitan –, Paduan –, Roman –, Umbrian –, Venetian –, British –, Dutch –, Flemish –, French –, German –, Spanish- School; School of Raphael &c.

PICTURE, painting, piece, tableau, canvas; oil painting &c.; fresco, cartoon; easel –, cabinet- picture; drawing, draft *or* draught; pencil &c. drawing, water-color drawing; still life; sketch, outline, study.

PORTRAIT &c. (*representation*) 554; whole –, full –, half- length; three-quarters profile; head; miniature; shade, silhouette; profile.

VIEW, landscape, seascape, sea view, seapiece; scene, prospect; interior; panorama, bird's-eye view, diorama.

PICTURE GALLERY, art gallery, art museum, pinacotheca; studio, *atelier* [*F.*].

PHOTOGRAPHY, skiagraphy, radiography &c. 554; photograph, radiograph &c. 554; scenograph.

V. PAINT, design, limn, draw, sketch, pencil, scratch, shade, stipple, hatch, dash off, chalk out, square up; color, dead color, wash, varnish; draw in pencil &c. *n.;* paint in oils &c. *n.;* stencil; depict &c. (*represent*) 554.

Adj. PICTORIAL, graphic; painted &c. *v.;* picturesque, genre; historical &c. *n.;* monochrome, polychrome; scenographic; futurist, cubist, vorticist; in the grand style; painty, pastose.

pencil, oil &c. *n.*

Adv. in pencil &c. *n.*

⁎ *fecit, delineavit;* *mutum est pictura poema;* "art is the perfection of nature" [Sir Thomas Browne]; "the canvas glow'd beyond ev'n nature warm" [Goldsmith]; "greater completion marks the progress of art, absolute completion usually its decline" [Ruskin].

557. Sculpture. — N. SCULPTURE, insculpture [*obs.*]; carving &c. *v.;* statuary, anaglyptics, ceramics.

marble, bronze, terra cotta; ceramic ware, pottery, porcelain, china, earthenware; cloisonné, enamel, faïence, satsuma.

RELIEF, relievo; basso-relievo *or* bassorilievo [*It.*], low relief, bas-relief; alto-relievo *or* alto-rilievo [*It.*], high relief; mezzo-relievo *or* mezzo-rilievo [*It.*]; glyph, intaglio, anaglyph; medal, medallion; cameo.

[SCHOOLS OF SCULPTURE] Æginetan -, Attic -, Chian -, Pergamene -, Rhodian -, Samian -, Sicyonian- School.

STATUE &c. (*image*) 554; cast &c. (*copy*) 21; glyptotheca.

[STATUES] Apollo Belvedere, Venus of Melos *or* Milo, Cnidian Aphrodite, Venus de' Medici, Dying Gaul, Farnese Hercules, Laocoön, Niobe, Silenus and Infant Bacchus, Theseus, Centaur and Eros, Niké *or* Winged Victory of Samothrace, The Wrestlers, Michelangelo's David, Mercury taking Flight, Rodin's The Thinker.

V. SCULPTURE, carve, cut, chisel, model, mold; cast.

Adj. SCULPTURED &c. *v.;* in relief, glyptic, anaglyphic, anaglyptic, ceroplastic, ceramic; Parian; marble &c. *n.;* xanthian.

558. Engraving. — N. ENGRAVING, chalcography, glyptography; line -, mezzotint -, stipple -, chalk- engraving; dry point, bur; etching, aquatint *or* aquatinta; chiseling; plate -, copperplate -, steel -, half-tone -, process -, wood- engraving; xylography, lignography, glyptography, cerography, lithography, chromolithography, photolithography, zincography, glyphography.

graver, burin, etching point, style; plate, stone, wood block, negative; die, punch, stamp.

PRINTING; plate -, copperplate -, anastatic -, color -, lithographic- printing; type printing &c. 591; three-color process.

IMPRESSION, print, engraving, plate; steel-plate, copperplate; etching; aquatint, mezzotint, lithotint; cut, woodcut; stereotype, graphotype, autotype, heliotype; xylograph, lignograph, glyptograph, cerograph, lithograph, chromolithograph, photolithograph, zincograph, glyphograph; process.

illustration, illumination; half tone; photogravure; rotogravure [*trade name*]; vignette, initial letter, *cul de lampe* [*F.*], tailpiece.

V. ENGRAVE, grave, insculp [*rare*], stipple, scrape, etch; bite, bite in; lithograph &c. *n.;* print.

Adj. ENGRAVED &c. *v.;* insculptured, glyptographic; "insculp'd upon" [*Merchant of Venice*].

₊ *sculpsit; imprimit.*

559. Artist. — N. ARTIST; painter, limner, drawer, sketcher, designer, engrave chalcographer, glyptographer, graver, line engraver, draftsman *or* draughtsman copyist; enameler *or* enameller, enamelist *or* enamellist; cartoonist, caricaturist.

historical -, landscape -, marine -, flower -, portrait -, genre -, miniature -, scene- painter; carver, chaser, modeler, *figuriste* [*F.*], statuary, sculptor.

Phidias, Praxiteles, Apelles, Raphael, Michelangelo, Titian; Royal Academician.

₊ "Dead he is not, but departed, — for the artist never dies" [Longfellow]; "Around the mighty master come The marvels which his pencil wrought" [Whittier].

2. Conventional Means

1. Language generally

560. Language. — N. LANGUAGE; phraseology &c. 569; speech &c. 582; tongue, lingo [*chiefly humorous or contemptuous*], vernacular; mother -, vulgar -, native-tongue; household words; King's *or* Queen's English; dialect, brogue, patois &c. 563; idiom, idiotism.

confusion of tongues, Babel; *pasigraphie* [*F.*], pasigraphy; universal language, Volapük, Esperanto, Ido; pantomime &c. (*signs*) 550.

LINGUISTICS, lexicology, philology, glossology, glottology, comparative philology; Grimm's law, Verner's law; comparative grammar, phonetics; chrestomathy; paleology *or* palæology, paleography *or* palæography.

onomatopœia, betacism, mimmation, myatism, nunnation.

LITERATURE, letters, polite literature, *belles lettres* [*F.*], muses, humanities, *litteræ humaniores* [*L.*], republic of letters, dead languages, classics; genius -, spirit -, idiom- of a language; scholarship &c. (*knowledge*) 490.

LINGUIST &c. (*scholar*) 492.

V. EXPRESS, say, express by words &c. 566.

Adj. LINGUAL, linguistic; dialectic; vernacular, current; bilingual; diglot, hexaglot, polyglot; literary; colloquial, slangy.

₊ "syllables govern the world" [Selden]; "Literature is the Thought of thinking Souls" [Carlyle].

561. Letter. — N. LETTER; character; hieroglyphic &c. (*writing*) 590; type &c. (*printing*) 591; capitals; digraph, trigraph; ideogram, ideograph; majuscule, *majusculæ* [*L.*]; minuscule, *minusculæ* [*L.*]; alphabet, ABC, abecedary, christcross-row *or* crisscross-row [*obs. or dial. Eng.*].

consonant, vowel; diphthong, triphthong; mute, surd, sonant, liquid, labial, palatal, cerebral, dental, guttural; guna, vriddhi [*Skr. gram.*].

SYLLABLE; monosyllable, dissyllable, polysyllable; affix, prefix, suffix.

SPELLING, orthography; phonography, phonetic spelling, phonetics; anagrammatism, metagrammatism.

CIPHER, monogram, anagram; acrostic, double acrostic.

V. spell, orthographize [*rare*]; gunate; transliterate.

CIPHER, decipher; code, decode; make -, construct- acrostics; design monograms; play anagrams; use -, invent- ciphers.

Adj. LITERAL; alphabetical, abecedarian; syllabic; majuscular, minuscular; uncial &c. (*writing*) 590.

PHONETIC, voiced, tonic, sonant; voiceless, surd; mute, labial, palatal, cerebral, dental, guttural, liquid.

562. Word. — N. WORD, term, vocable; name &c. 564; phrase &c. 566; root, etymon; derivative; part of speech &c. (*grammar*) 567; ideophone.

DICTIONARY, lexicon, vocabulary, word book, index, glossary, thesaurus, gradus, delectus, concordance; Rosetta stone.

[SCIENCE OF LANGUAGE] etymology, derivation, glottology *or* glossology, terminology, orismology; translation; pronunciation, orthoëpy; paleology &c. (*philology*) 560; lexicography.

LEXICOGRAPHER, lexicologist, etymologist, orthoëpist, verbarian; glossographer &c. (*scholar*) 492.

VERBOSITY, verbiage, wordiness; loquacity &c. 584.

V. vocalize; etymologize, derive, philologize; index; translate.

Adj. VERBAL, literal; titular, nominal.

[SIMILARLY DERIVED] conjugate, paronymous; derivative.

VERBOSE, wordy &c. 573; loquacious &c. 584.

Adv. VERBALLY &c. *adj.*; *verbatim* [*L.*] &c. (*exactly*) 494.

₊ "in the beginning was the Word" [*Bible*]; "the artillery of words" [Swift].

563. Neology. — N. NEOLOGY, neologism; newfangled expression; caconym; barbarism; archaism, black letter, monkish Latin; corruption, missaying, antiphrasis; pseudology; idioticon.

PLAY UPON WORDS, paronomasia; word play &c. (*wit*) 842; *double-entente* [*F.*] &c. (*ambiguity*) 520; palindrome, paragram, clinch [*now rare*], pun; abuse of -language, – terms.

DIALECT, brogue, patois, provincialism, broken English, Anglicism, Briticism, Gallicism, Scotticism, Hibernicism, Americanism; Gypsy lingo, Romany.

LINGUA FRANCA, pidgin *or* pigeon English; Chinook, Hindustani, kitchen Kaffir, Swahili, Haussa, Volapük, Esperanto, Ido.

JARGON, dog Latin, gibberish; confusion of tongues, Babel; babu English, chi-chi [*Anglo-India*].

colloquialism &c. (*figure of speech*) 521; byword; technicality, lingo, slang, cant, argot, *bat* [*Hind.*], macaronics, St. Giles's Greek, thieves' Latin, peddler's French, flash tongue, Billingsgate, Wall Street slang.

PSEUDONYM &c. (*misnomer*) 565; Mr.

So-and-so; "Sergeant What-is-name" [Kipling]; what d'ye call 'em, what's his name, thingummy, thingamabob, thingummybob [*all colloq.*]; *je ne sais quoi* [*F.*]. NEOLOGIST, coiner of words.

V. coin words; Americanize, Anglicize, Gallicize; sling the bat [*slang, Anglo-Ind.*].

Adj. neologic, neological; archaic, rare, obsolescent; obsolete &c. (*old*) 124; colloquial, dialectal, dialectic *or* dialectical; slang, cant, flash, barbarous; *Anglice* [*NL.*].

564. Nomenclature. — N. NOMEN-
CLATURE; naming &c. *v.;* nuncupation
[*obs.*], nomination [*obs.*], baptism; orismology; onomatopœia; antonomasia.

NAME; appellation, appellative; designation; title; head, heading; caption;
denomination; by-name; nickname &c.
565; epithet; what one may -well, –
fairly, – properly, – fitly- call.

style, proper name; prænomen, agnomen, cognomen; patronymic, surname;
cognomination; eponym; compellation,
description, synonym, antonym; empty
-title, – name; title, handle to one's
name; namesake.

TERM, expression, noun; byword; convertible terms &c. 522; technical term;
cant &c. 563.

V. NAME, call, term, denominate,
designate, style, entitle, clepe [*archaic*],
dub [*colloq. or humorous*], christen, baptize, nickname, characterize, specify,
define, distinguish by the name of;
label &c. (*mark*) 550.

BE CALLED &c. *v.;* take –, bear –, go
(*or* be known) by –, go (*or* pass) under –, rejoice in- the name of; hight [*archaic*],
yclept *or* ycleped [*archaic or humorous*].

Adj. NAMED &c. *v.;* known as; nuncupatory [*obs.*], nuncupative [*obs.*]; cog-
nominal, titular, nominal, orismological.

⁎⁎ "beggar'd all description" [*Antony and Cleopatra*]; "what's in a name? That which
we call a rose By any other name would smell as sweet" [*Romeo and Juliet*].

565. Misnomer. — N. MISNOMER; *lucus a non lucendo* [*L.*]; Mrs. Malaprop;
what d'ye call 'em &c. (*neologism*) 563.

NICKNAME, *sobriquet* [*F.*] *or* soubri-
quet, pet name, little name, by-name;
assumed -name, – title; alias; *nom de
course* [*F.*], *nom de theâtre* [*F.*], stage
name; *nom de guerre* [*F.*], *nom de plume*
[*English formation*], pen name, pseudonym; pseudonymity, pseudonymous-
ness.

V. MISNAME, miscall, misterm; call
out of one's name [*colloq.*], nickname;
assume -a name, – an alias; take an
-alias, – assumed name.

Adj. MISNAMED &c. *v.;* pseudony-
mous; *soi-disant* [*F.*]; self-called, self-
styled, self-christened; so-called, quasi.

NAMELESS, anonymous; without a –,
having no- name; innominate, unnamed; unacknowledged; pseudo, bastard.

Adv. in no sense; by whatever name,
under any name.

---

566. Phrase. — N. PHRASE, expression, locution, set phrase; sentence, paragraph;
figure of speech &c. 521; idiom, idiotism; turn of expression; style.

paraphrase &c. (*synonym*) 522; euphemism; euphuism; periphrase &c. (*circumlocution*) 573; motto &c. (*proverb*) 496; phraseology &c. 569.

V. EXPRESS, phrase; word, word it; give -words, – expression -to; voice; arrange
in –, clothe in –, put into –, express by- words; couch in terms; find words to
express; speak by the card; call, denominate, designate, dub.

Adj. expressed &c. *v.;* idiomatic; stylistic.

Adv. in -round, – set, – good set- terms; in set phrases; by the card.

---

567. Grammar. — N. GRAMMAR, accidence, syntax, analysis, praxis, punctuation; parts of speech; jussive; syllabi-
cation *or* syllabification, paradigm,
syllepsis, synopsis; inflection, case, declension, conjugation; *jus et norma
loquendi* [*L.*]; Lindley Murray &c.
(*schoolbook*) 542; correct style, philology
&c. (*language*) 560.

V. parse, analyze *or* analyse, conjugate, decline; punctuate, syllabicate,
syllabize.

Adj. grammatical, syntactic *or* syn-
tactical, inflectional; synoptic.

568. Solecism. — N. SOLECISM; bad
–, false –, faulty- grammar; grammatical
blunder; *faux pas* [*F.*], error, slip; slip
of the pen, *lapsus calami* [*L.*]; slip of the
tongue, *lapsus linguæ* [*L.*]; slipslop; bull,
Hibernianism; barbarism, impropriety.

V. SOLECIZE *or* solecise, commit a
solecism; use -bad, – faulty- grammar;
murder the King's (*or* Queen's) English;
speak –, write- out of the idiom; break
Priscian's head.

Adj. UNGRAMMATICAL; incorrect, inaccurate, faulty; improper, incongruous;
solecistic *or* solecistical; slipslop.

569. Style. — **N.** STYLE, diction, phraseology, wording; manner, strain; composition; mode of expression, idiom, choice of words; mode of speech, literary power, ready pen, pen of a ready writer; grand style, grand manner; command of language &c. (*eloquence*) 582; authorship, artistry; *la morgue littéraire* [*F.*].

V. WORD; express by words &c. 566; write; apply –, employ- the file.

. *le style c'est de l'homme* [Buffon]; "style is the dress of thoughts" [Chesterfield].

Various Qualities of Style

570. Perspicuity. — **N.** PERSPICUITY &c. (*intelligibility*) 518; plain speaking &c. (*manifestation*) 525; definiteness, definition; exactness &c. 494; explicitness, lucidness, lucidity, limpidity, clearness.

Adj. LUCID &c. (*intelligible*) 518; limpid, pellucid, clear; explicit &c. (*manifest*) 525; exact &c. 494.

. "Clear conception leads naturally to clear and correct expression" [Boileau].

571. Obscurity.— **N.** OBSCURITY &c. (*unintelligibility*) 519; involution, crabbedness, confusion; hard words; ambiguity &c. 520; unintelligibility, unintelligibleness; vagueness &c. 475, inexactness &c. 495; what d'ye call 'em &c. (*neologism*) 563; darkness of meaning.

Adj. OBSCURE &c. *n.;* crabbed; involved, confused.

. "full of sound and fury, Signifying nothing" [*Macbeth*].

572. Conciseness. — **N.** CONCISENESS &c. *adj.;* brevity, "the soul of wit," laconicism *or* laconism; ellipsis; syncope; abridgment &c. (*shortening*) 201; compression &c. 195; epitome &c. 596; monostich; Spartans; Tacitus.

PORTMANTEAU-WORD [Lewis Carroll]; brunch [breakfast+lunch], squarson [squire+parson]; slithy, *adj.* [slimy+lithe], torrible, *adj.* [torrid+horrible], crowzy, *adj.* [crowded+cozy].

V. BE CONCISE &c. *adj.;* telescope, laconize; condense &c. 195; abridge &c. 201; abstract &c. 596; come to the point.

Adj. CONCISE, brief, short, terse, close; to the point, exact; neat, compact; compressed, condensed, pointed; laconic, curt, pithy, trenchant, summary; pregnant; compendious &c. (*compendium*) 596; succinct; elliptical, epigrammatic, crisp; sententious.

Adv. CONCISELY &c. *adj.;* briefly, summarily; in brief, in short, in a word, in few words; for the sake of brevity, for shortness' sake; to come to the point, to make a long story short, to cut the matter short, to be brief; it comes to this, the long and short of it is, the gist is.

. *brevis esse laboro obscurus fio* [Horace].

573. Diffuseness. — **N.** DIFFUSENESS &c. *adj.;* amplification &c. *v.;* dilating &c. *v.;* verbosity, wordiness; verbiage, cloud of words, *copia verborum* [*L.*]; flow of words &c. (*loquacity*) 584; looseness.

TAUTOLOGY, battology, polylogy [*obs.*], perissology [*obs.*]; pleonasm, exuberance, redundance; thrice-told tale; prolixity, longiloquence, longsomeness, circumlocution, ambages [*rare*], periphrase, periphrasis, roundabout phrases; episode; expletive; penny-a-lining; richness &c. 577; padding [*editor's cant*]; drivel, twaddle, drool.

V. BE DIFFUSE &c. *adj.;* run out on, descant, expatiate, enlarge, dilate, amplify, expand, inflate, pad [*editor's cant*]; launch out, branch out; rant.

MAUNDER, prose; harp upon &c. (*repeat*) 104; dwell on, insist upon.

DIGRESS, ramble, *battre la campagne* [*F.*], beat about the bush, perorate, spin a long yarn, protract; spin –, swell –, draw- out; battologize *or* battalogize; drivel, twaddle, drool.

Adj. DIFFUSE, profuse; wordy, verbose, largiloquent [*obs.*], copious, exuberant, pleonastic, lengthy; long, longsome, long-winded, longspun, long drawn out; spun out, protracted, prolix, diffusive, prosing, maundering; circumlocutory, periphrastic, ambagious *or* ambaguious, ambagitory, roundabout; digressive; discursive, excursive; loose; rambling, episodic; flatulent, frothy.

Adv. DIFFUSELY &c. *adj.;* at large, *in extenso* [*L.*]; about it and about.

. "Thou sayest an undisputed thing In such a solemn way" [Holmes].

574. Vigor. — N. VIGOR, power, force; boldness, raciness &c. *adj.;* intellectual force; spirit, punch [*slang*], point, piquancy; verve, ardor, enthusiasm, glow, fire, warmth; strong language; gravity, weight, sententiousness.

LOFTINESS, elevation, sublimity, grandeur.

ELOQUENCE; command of words, command of language.

Adj. VIGOROUS, nervous, powerful, forcible, forceful, mordant, biting, trenchant, incisive, graphic, impressive; sensational.

SPIRITED, lively, glowing, sparkling, racy, bold, slashing, crushing; pungent, piquant, full of pep [*slang*], having punch [*slang*], full of point, pointed, pithy; sententious.

LOFTY, elevated, sublime, poetic, grand, weighty, ponderous; eloquent.

VEHEMENT, petulant, passionate, burning, impassioned.

Adv. in -glowing, – good set, – no measured- terms; with his heart on fire; like a ton of bricks [*colloq.*].

*** "thoughts that breathe and words that burn" [Gray].

575. Feebleness. — N. FEEBLENESS &c. *adj.;* enervation, flaccidity, vapidity, poverty, frigidity.

Adj. FEEBLE, bald, tame, meager *or* meagre, insipid, watery, nerveless, jejune, vapid, trashy, cold, frigid, poor, dull, dry, languid; colorless, enervated; prosing, prosy, prosaic, unvaried, monotonous, weak, washy, wishy-washy [*colloq.*], sloppy, sketchy, slight; careless, slovenly, loose, disjointed, disconnected, lax; slipshod, slipslop; inexact; puerile, childish; flatulent; rambling &c. (*diffuse*) 573.

576. Plainness. — N. PLAINNESS &c. *adj.;* simplicity, *simplex munditiis* [Hor.], lack of ornamentation, severity; plain -terms, – English; Saxon English; household words.

V. SPEAK PLAINLY, waste no words, call a spade a spade; plunge *in medias res* [*L.*]; come to the point.

Adj. PLAIN, simple; unornamented, unadorned, unvarnished; homely, homespun; neat; severe, chaste, pure, Saxon; commonplace, matter-of-fact, natural, prosaic, sober, unimaginative.

DRY, unvaried, monotonous &c. 575.

Adv. POINT-BLANK; in plain -terms, words, – English; in common parlance.

577. Ornament. — N. ORNAMENT; floridness &c. *adj.;* turgidity, turgescence *or* turgescency; altiloquence [*obs.*], grandiloquence, magniloquence, declamation, teratology [*obs.*]; well-rounded periods; elegance &c. 578; orotundity.

inversion, antithesis, alliteration, paronomasia; trope; figurativeness &c. (*metaphor*) 521.

flourish; flowers of -speech, – rhetoric; frills, – of style; euphuism, euphemism.

BOMBAST, big-sounding words, high-sounding words; macrology, *sesquipedalia verba* [*L.*], sesquipedalian words, sesquipedality, sesquipedalianism, Alexandrine; inflation, pretension; rant, fustian, highfalutin' [*slang, U. S.*], buncombe *or* bunkum [*U. S.*], balderdash; prose run mad; fine writing; purple patches; Minerva press.

PHRASEMONGER, euphuist, euphemist; word coiner.

V. ORNAMENT, overlay with ornament, overcharge, overload; euphuize, euphemize; buncomize [*colloq.*]; smell of the lamp.

Adj. ORNATE; ornamented &c. *v.;* beautified &c. 847; florid, rich, flowery; euphuistic, euphemistic; sonorous; high- big- sounding; inflated, swelling, tumid; turgid, turgescent; pedantic, pompous, stilted; orotund; high-flown, high-flowing, highfalutin' [*slang, U. S.*]; sententious, rhetorical, declamatory; grandiose; grandiloquent; magniloquent; altiloquent [*obs.*]; sesquipedal, sesquipedalian; Johnsonian, mouthy; bombastic; fustian; frothy, flashy, flamboyant.

antithetical, alliterative; figurative &c. 521; artificial &c. (*inelegant*) 579.

Adv. *ore rotundo* [*L.*], with rounded phrase.

*** "to gild refinéd gold, to paint the lily, to throw a perfume on the violet" [*King John*]; "make all the little fishes talk like big whales" [Goldsmith, of Johnson — *Boswell's Life*]; "in the end never died, but passed away at her residence" [Dunsany].

578. Elegance. — N. ELEGANCE, distinction, clarity, purity, grace, felicity, ease; gracefulness, readiness &c. *adj.;* concinnity, concinnation [*rare*], euphony; balance, rhythm, symmetry, proportion, taste, good taste, restraint, nice discrimination, propriety, correctness; Attic salt, Atticism, classicalism, classicism.

well-rounded –, well-turned –, flowing- periods; the right word in the right place; antithesis &c. 577.

PURIST, classicist, stylist.

V. FLOW -SMOOTHLY, – with ease; discriminate nicely, display elegance &c. *n.;* point an antithesis, round a period.

Adj. ELEGANT, polished, classic *or* classical, classicistic, concinnous [*rare*], correct, Attic, Ciceronian, artistic; chaste, pure, Saxon, academic *or* academical.

graceful, easy, readable, fluent, flowing, tripping; unaffected, natural, unlabored; mellifluous, euphonious; euphemistic; symmetrical, balanced, restrained; rhythmic *or* rhythmical.

579. Inelegance. — N. INELEGANCE, impurity, vulgarity; want of –, poor –, bad- taste; stiffness &c. *adj.;* "unlettered Muse" [Gray]; cacology, cacography, poor diction, poor choice of words; loose –, slipshod- construction; want of balance, ill-balanced sentences; barbarism; slang &c. 563; solecism &c. 568; mannerism &c (*affectation*) 855; euphuism, Marinism, Gongorism; fustian &c. 577; cacophony; words that -break the teeth, – dislocate the jaw.

CACOGRAPHER, barbarian; euphuist, Marinist, Gongorist.

V. BE INELEGANT &c. *adj.;* employ inelegance &c. *n.*

Adj. INELEGANT, graceless, ungraceful; harsh, abrupt; dry, stiff, cramped, formal, *guindé* [*F.*]; forced, labored; artificial, mannered, ponderous; awkward, uncourtly, unpolished; turgid &c. 577; affected, euphuistic; barbarous, uncouth, grotesque, rude, crude, halting, cacographic *or* cacographical; offensive to ears polite; vulgar, tasteless.

FELICITOUS, happy, neat; well –, neatly- -put, – expressed.

*** "true ease in writing comes from art, not chance" [Pope]; "whoever wishes to obtain an English style . . . must give his days and nights to the volumes of Addison" [Johnson – *Boswell's Life*]; "elegant as simplicity" [Cowper].

2. Spoken Language

580. Voice. — N. VOICE; vocality; organ, lungs, bellows; good –, fine –, powerful &c. (*loud*) 404 –, musical &c. 413- voice; intonation; tone &c. (*sound*) 402- of voice.

UTTERANCE; vocalization; cry &c. 411; strain, prolation [*archaic*]; exclamation, ejaculation, vociferation, ecphonesis; enunciation, articulation; articulate sound, distinctness; clearness, – of articulation; stage whisper; delivery, attack.

ACCENT, accentuation; emphasis, stress; broad –, strong –, pure –, native –, foreign- accent; pronunciation; orthoëpy; euphony &c. (*melody*) 413; polyphonism, polyphony.

[WORDS SIMILARLY PRONOUNCED] homonyms.

VENTRILOQUISM *or* ventriloquy, ventrilocution, gastriloquism *or* gastriloquy [*rare*]; ventriloquist, gastriloquist [*rare*].

[SCIENCE OF VOICE], phonology; &c. (*sound*) 402.

581. Aphonia. — N. APHONIA *or* aphony; dumbness &c. *adj.;* obmutescence [*rare*]; absence –, want- of voice; dysphonia *or* dysphony; silence &c. (*taciturnity*) 585; raucity; harsh voice &c. 410, unmusical voice &c. 414; quaver, quavering; falsetto, "childish treble"; deaf-mutism, deaf-muteness, deaf-dumbness, mute, dummy, deaf-mute.

V. SPEAK LOW, speak softly; whisper &c. (*faintness*) 405; keep silence &c. 585.

SILENCE; render -mute, – silent; muzzle, muffle, suppress, smother, gag, strike dumb, dumfound *or* dumbfound dumfounder *or* dumbfounder, mum [*obs.*], drown the voice, put to silence, stop one's mouth, cut one short.

stick in the throat.

Adj. APHONOUS, nonvocal, aphonic, dumb, mute, deaf and dumb, deaf-dumb; mum; obmutescent [*rare*], tongue-tied; breathless, tongueless, voiceless, speechless, wordless; mute as a -fish,

V. SPEAK, utter, breathe; give utterance, give tongue; cry &c. (*shout*) 411; ejaculate, rap out; vocalize, prolate [*obs.*], articulate, enunciate, pronounce, accentuate, aspirate, deliver, emit; whisper, murmur, whisper in the ear; ventriloquize.

Adj. VOCAL, phonetic, oral; ejaculatory, articulate, articulated, distinct, enunciative, accentuated, aspirated; euphonious &c. (*melodious*) 413; whispered.

VENTRILOQUOUS, ventriloquistic, gastriloquial [*rare*], gastriloquous [*rare*].

*** "how sweetly sounds the voice of a good woman" [Massinger]; "the organ of the soul" [Longfellow]; "thy voice is a celestial melody" [Longfellow]; "speak in a monstrous little voice" [*M. N. D.*]; "I was never so bethump'd with words" [*King John*].

582. Speech. — N. SPEECH, faculty of speech; locution, talk, parlance, verbal intercourse, prolation [*archaic*], oral communication, word of mouth, parole, palaver, prattle.

ORATION, recitation, delivery, say [*colloq.*], speech, lecture, prelection *or* prælection, harangue, sermon, tirade, formal speech, peroration; speechifying; soliloquy &c. 589; allocution &c. 586; interlocution &c. 588; salutatory [*U. S.*]; screed; valedictory [*U. S.*].

ORATORY, elocution, eloquence, rhetoric, declamation; grandiloquence, multiloquence, talkativeness; burst of eloquence; facundity [*obs.*]; flow –, command– of -words, – language; *copia verborum* [*L.*]; power of speech, gift of the gab [*colloq.*]; *usus loquendi* [*L.*].

SPEAKER &c. v.; spokesman; prolocutor, interlocutor; mouthpiece, Hermes; orator, oratrix, oratress; Demosthenes, Cicero; rhetorician, lecturer, preacher, prelector *or* prælector; elocutionist, reciter, reader [*U. S.*]; spellbinder; stump –, platform– orator; speechmaker, patterer, monologist, monologuist, improvisator, *improvvisatore* or *improvisatore* [*It.*], *improvvisatrice* or *improvisatrice* [*It.*].

V. SPEAK, – of; say, utter, pronounce, deliver, give utterance to; utter –, pour-

– stockfish, – mackerel; silent &c. (*taciturn*) 585; muzzled; inarticulate, inaudible.

CROAKING, raucous, hoarse, husky, dry, hollow, sepulchral, hoarse as a raven; rough.

Adv. WITH BATED BREATH, with the finger on the lips; *sotto voce* [*It.*]; in a -low tone, – cracked voice, – broken voice; in broken tones, aside, in an aside.

Int. MUM! hush! sh! silence! whist! whisht! [*dial.*]; *chut*! &c. (*silence*) 403.

*** *vox faucibus hæsit* [Vergil]; "there is a homely old adage which runs: 'Speak softly and carry a big stick; you will go far'" [Roosevelt].

583. [IMPERFECT SPEECH.] Stammering. — N. INARTICULATENESS; stammering &c. *v.*; hesitation &c. *v.*; impediment in one's speech; titubancy [*obs.*], traulism [*obs.*]; whisper &c. (*faint sound*) 405; lisp, drawl, tardiloquence [*rare*]; nasal -tone, – accent; twang; falsetto &c. (*want of voice*) 581; cacology, cacoëpy; broken -voice, – accents, – sentences; brogue &c. 563.

SLIP OF THE TONGUE, *lapsus linguæ* [*L.*].

V. STAMMER, stutter, hesitate, falter, hammer [*obs. or dial. Eng.*], balbutiate [*obs.*], balbucinate [*obs.*], haw, hum and haw, be unable to put two words together.

MUMBLE, mutter, maund [*obs.*], maunder; whisper &c. 405; mince, lisp; jabber, gabble, gibber; splutter, sputter; muffle, mump; drawl, mouth; croak; speak thick, speak through the nose; talk incoherently, quaver, snuffle, clip one's words.

MURDER THE LANGUAGE, murder the King's (*or* Queen's) English; mispronounce, missay [*rare*].

Adj. INARTICULATE; stammering &c. *v.*; guttural, throaty, nasal; tremulous; affected; stertorous; cacoëpistic.

Adv. *sotto voce* &c. (*faintly*) 405.

forth; breathe, let fall, come out with; rap out, blurt out; have on one's lips; have at the -end, – tip- of one's tongue.

soliloquize &c. 589; tell &c. (*inform*) 527; speak to &c. 586; talk together &c. 588.

BREAK SILENCE; open one's - lips, –mouth; lift –, raise- one's voice; give tongue, wag the tongue [*colloq.*]; talk, outspeak; put in a word or two.

DECLAIM, hold forth; make –, deliver- a speech &c. *n.;* speechify [*derisive or humorous*], harangue, stump [*colloq., U. S.*], flourish, spout, rant, recite, lecture, prelect *or* prælect, sermonize, discourse, be on one's legs; have –, say- one's say; expatiate &c. (*speak at length*) 573; speak one's mind, go on the –, take the-stump [*U. S.*].

BE ELOQUENT &c. *adj.;* have a tongue in one's head, have the gift of the gab [*colloq.*] &c. *n.*

PASS ONE'S LIPS, escape one's lips; fall from the -lips, – mouth.

Adj. ORAL, lingual, phonetic, not written, nuncupative [*of wills*], unwritten; speaking &c., spoken &c. *v.;* outspoken, facund [*archaic*].

ELOQUENT, oratorical, rhetorical, elocutionary, declamatory; grandiloquent &c. 577; talkative &c. 584; Ciceronian, Tullian.

Adv. ORALLY &c. *adj.;* by word of mouth, *vivâ voce* [*L.*], from the lips of; from his own mouth.

*** quoth –, said- he &c.; "action is eloquence" [*Coriolanus*]; "pour the full tide of eloquence along" [Pope]; "she speaks poignards and every word stabs" [*Much Ado About Nothing*]; "speech is but broken light upon the depth of the unspoken" [G. Eliot]; "to try thy eloquence now 'tis time" [*Antony and Cleopatra*]; "Language most shows a man; speak that I may see thee" [B. Jonson].

---

584. Loquacity. — N. LOQUACITY, loquaciousness, effusion; talkativeness &c. *adj.;* garrulity; multiloquence, much speaking.

GABBLE, gab [*colloq.*], jaw [*low*], hot air [*slang*]; jabber, chatter; prate, prat-tle, cackle, clack; twaddle, twattle, rattle, *caquet* [*F.*], *caqueterie* [*F.*], blab-ber, *bavardage* [*F.*], bibble-babble, gibble-gabble; small talk &c. (*converse*) 588; Babel.

FLUENCY, flippancy, volubility, flow-ing tongue; flow, – of words; *flux de -bouche, – mots* [*F.*]; *copia verborum* [*L.*], *cacoëthes loquendi* [*L.*]; *furor loquendi* [*L.*]; verbosity &c. (*diffuseness*) 573; gift of the gab &c. (*eloquence*) 582.

TALKER; chatterer, chatterbox; bab-bler &c. *v.;* rattle; "agreeable rattle" [Goldsmith]; ranter; sermonizer, proser, driveler *or* driveller, blatherskite [*colloq., U. S.*], blab, jaw-box [*slang*], gas-bag [*slang*], wind-bag [*slang*], hot-air artist [*slang*]; gossip &c. (*converse*) 588; mag-pie, jay, parrot, poll *or* polly; *moulin à paroles* [*F.*].

V. BE LOQUACIOUS &c. *adj.;* talk glibly, pour forth, patter; prate, palaver, prose, maunder, chatter, blab, gush, prattle, clack, jabber, jaw [*low*], shoot one's mouth off [*slang*]; blather, blatter, blether; rattle, – on; twaddle, twattle; babble, gabble; outtalk; talk oneself -out of breath, – hoarse; talk –, run on- like a mill race; have one's tongue hanging in the middle and wagging at both ends; talk the hind legs off a mule, talk one deaf and dumb, clack like a hen, go on forever; expatiate &c. (*speak at length*) 573; gossip &c. (*converse*) 588; din in the ears &c. (*repeat*) 104; talk at random, talk nonsense &c. 497; be hoarse with talking.

585. Taciturnity. — N. SILENCE, muteness, obmutescence [*rare*], laconism, laconicism, taciturnity, pauciloquy, cos-tiveness [*obs.*], curtness; reserve, reti-cence &c. (*concealment*) 528.

MAN OF FEW WORDS; Spartan, Laco-nian.

V. BE SILENT &c. *adj.;* keep silence; hold one's -tongue, – peace; not speak &c. 582; say nothing; seal –, close –, put a padlock on- the -lips, – mouth; put a bridle on one's tongue; keep one's tongue between one's teeth; make no sign, not let a word escape one; keep a secret &c. 528; have not a word to throw at a dog, not have a word to say; lay –, place- the finger on the lips; render mute &c. 581.

stick in one's throat.

Adj. SILENT, mute, mum; silent as a -post, – stone, – the grave &c. (*still*) 403; dumb &c. 581; unconversable.

TACITURN, laconic, pauciloquent, con-cise, sententious, sparing of words; close, close-mouthed, close-tongued; costive [*obs.*], inconversable [*obs.*], curt; reserved; reticent &c. (*concealing*) 528.

Int. SILENCE! tush! mum! hush! *chut!* [*F.*], hist! tut! not another word! stop right there! be still! *chup!* [*Hind.*].

*** *cave quid dicis quando et cui; volto sciolto i pensieri stretti.*

Adj. LOQUACIOUS, talkative, garrulous, linguacious [obs.], multiloquent or multiloquous; chattering &c. v.; chatty &c. (sociable) 892; declamatory &c. 582; open-mouthed.

FLUENT, voluble, glib, flippant; long-tongued, long-winded &c. (diffuse) 573.

Adv. GLIBLY &c. adj.; trippingly on the tongue.

*** the tongue running -fast, – loose, – on wheels; all talk and no cider; "foul whisperings are abroad" [Macbeth]; "the parrot is forever polishing his beak, however clean it may be" [Pascal]; "what a spendthrift is he of his tongue!" [Tempest]; "a loose tongue is just as unfortunate an accompaniment for a nation as for an individual" [Roosevelt]; "His talk was like a charge of horse" [Masefield]; "Another flood of words! A very torrent" [B. Jonson]; "It would talk, — Lord! how it talked!" [Beaumont and Fletcher].

---

586. Allocution. — N. ALLOCUTION, alloquy [obs.], address; smoke talk, chalk talk [both colloq.]; speech &c. 582; vocation, salutation, salutatory [U. S.];

PLATFORM &c. 542; plank [politics].

AUDIENCE &c. (interview) 588.

[FEIGNED DIALOGUE] dialogism.

V. ADDRESS, speak to, accost, make up to [colloq.], apostrophize, appeal to, invoke; hail, salute; call to, halloo.

lecture &c. (make a speech) 582; preach, sermonize, harangue, spellbind.

TAKE ASIDE, take by the button; talk to in private.

Int. soho! halloo! hey! hist! hi!

---

587. Response &c. see ANSWER 462.

apostrophe, interpellation, appeal, invocation, salutation, salutatory [U. S.]; word in the ear.

---

588. Interlocution. — N. INTERLOCUTION; collocution, colloquy, converse, conversation, confabulation, confab [colloq.], chin-music [slang], talk, discourse, verbal intercourse; oral communication, commerce; dialogue, duologue, trialogue.

"the feast of reason and the flow of soul" [Pope]; mollia tempora fandi [L.].

CHAT, causerie [F.], chitchat; small –, table –, tea-table –, town –, village –, idle-talk; tattle, gossip, tittle-tattle; babble, babblement; tripotage [F.], cackle, prittle-prattle, on dit [F.]; talk of the -town, - village.

CONFERENCE, parley, interview, audience, pourparler [F.]; tête-à-tête [F.]; reception, conversazione [It.]; congress &c.

HALL OF AUDIENCE, durbar [India], auditorium, assembly room.

DEBATE, palaver, logomachy, war of words, controversy, newspaper war.

TALKER, gossip, tattler; Paul Pry; tabby [colloq.], chatterer &c. (loquacity) 584; interlocutor &c. (spokesman) 582; conversationist, conversationalist, dialogist.

V. CONVERSE, talk together, confabulate; dialogue, dialogize; hold -, carry on -, join in -, engage in- a conversation; put in a word; shine in conversation; bandy words; parley; palaver; chat, gossip, tattle; prate &c. (loquacity) 584; powwow [U. S.].

CONFER WITH, discourse with, commune with, commerce with; hold -converse, - conference, - intercourse; talk it over; be closeted with; talk with one in private, talk with one tête-à-tête [F.].

Adj. CONVERSING &c. v.; interlocutory; conversational, conversable; discursive or discoursive [obs.]; chatty &c. (sociable) 892; colloquial, confabulatory, tête-à-tête [F.].

*** "with thee conversing I forget all time" [Paradise Lost]; "Discourse, the sweeter banquet of the mind" [Pope].

---

589. Soliloquy. — N. SOLILOQUY, monology, monologue, apostrophe; monology.

SOLILOQUIST, monologist, monologuist, monologian, soliloquizer; speaker &c. 582; Dr. Johnson, Coleridge.

V. SOLILOQUIZE, monologize, monologuize, say -, talk- to oneself; rehearse a speech, address an imaginary audience; address the four walls; say aside, think aloud, apostrophize.

Adj. SOLILOQUIZING &c. v.; monologic or monological; apostrophic, apostrophal [rare].

Adv. ASIDE, apart.

(council) 696; powwow [U. S.].

3. Written Language

590. Writing. — **N.** WRITING &c. *v.;* chirography, stelography [*rare*], monography, stylography, cerography, graphology; pencraft, penmanship; quill driving [*humorous*]; typewriting.

stroke -, dash- of the pen; *coup de plume* [*F.*]; line; headline; pen and ink.

MANUSCRIPT, MS., writing, *litteræ scriptæ* [*L.*]; these presents [*law*].

CHARACTER, letter &c. 561; uncial writing, cuneiform character, arrowhead, contraction; Ogham, runes; hieroglyphic, hieratic, demotic, Hebrew, Greek, Cyrillic, Roman; Arabic, Persian, Naskhi *or* Neskhi, Shikasta, Nasta'lik *or* Ta'lik; Brahmi, Devanagari, Nagari; Chinese; script.

SHORTHAND; stenography, brachygraphy, tachygraphy; secret writing, writing in cipher; cryptography, steganography; phonography, pasigraphy, polygraphy [*rare*], logography.

COPY; transcript, rescript; rough -, fair- copy; rough draft.

HANDWRITING; signature, sign manual, mark, autograph, monograph, holograph; hand, fist [*colloq.*].

CALLIGRAPHY; good -, running -, flowing -, cursive -, Italian -, slanting -, perpendicular -, round -, copybook -, fine -, legible -, bold- hand.

CACOGRAPHY, *griffonage* [*F.*], *barbouillage* [*F.*]; bad -, cramped -, crabbed -, illegible- hand; scribble &c. *v.; pattes de mouche* [*F.*], fly tracks; ill-formed letters; pothooks and hangers.

STATIONERY; pen, reed, quill, goose quill; pencil, style, stylograph, stylographic pen, fountain pen; paper, foolscap, parchment, vellum, papyrus, tablet, block, pad, notebook, memorandum book, copybook, commonplace-book; slate, marble, pillar, table; blackboard; ink-bottle, inkhorn, inkpot, inkstand, inkwell; typewriter.

COMPOSITION, authorship; *cacoëthes scribendi* [*L.*]; graphomania; lucubration, production, work, preparation; screed, article, paper, pamphlet; book &c. 593; essay, theme, thesis; novel, textbook, poem, book of poems, book of verse; compilation, anthology; piece of music, *morceau* [*F.*] &c. (*musical composition*) 415.

591. Printing. — **N.** PRINTING; block -, type- printing; linotype, monotype; plate printing &c. (*engraving*) 558; the press &c. (*publication*) 531; composition.

PRINT, letterpress, text, matter; live -, standing -, dead- matter; copy; context, page, column, note, section; catchword; running head, running title; signature; justification; dummy.

folio &c (*book*) 593; copy, impression, pull, proof, revise, advance sheets; author's -, galley -, page -, plate -, press- proof; press revise.

TYPOGRAPHY; stereotype, electrotype; matrix; font *or* fount; pi *or* pie; roman, italics; capitals &c (*letters*) 561, caps., small caps., upper case, lower case; logotype; type-bar. type-slug; type-body; em, en; type measure. type scale; type casting, type metal, type mold, typograph; type foundry, letter foundry; composing stick, stick; composing -frame, - rule, - stand; foot stick; chase, form, galley, measure, scale, case, boxes; gauge, gauge pin, feed gauge, guide, dabber, gutter, gutter stick; brayer, boss, batter, bank; bearer, guard; bed, blanket, tympan, turtle, platen, bevel, burr, frame, frisket, gripper; quadrat, quad; quoin, slug, slur, ratchet, reglet; guillotine, rounce, cylinder; overlay, underlay, sinkage, macule; platen press, perfecting machine; printing-press, printing-machine; presswork; sheet work; off-cut, off-print; set-off; off-set, smut; turn, turned letter; bookplate, bookstamp, colophon; composing room, press room.

SPACE, 3-em, thick space; 4-em, 5-em, thin space; 6-em, hair space; patent space.

METAL TYPE, body, shank, face, shoulder, counter, serif *or* ceriph, stem, beard, groove, feet.

STYLES OF TYPE: Old English, Black Letter, German Text, Gothic, Antique, Clarendon, Boldface *or* Full-face, French Elzevir, Caslon Old Style, Ionic, Script, Typewriter.

POINT SYSTEM: 4½ point (diamond), 5 pt. (pearl), 5½ pt. (agate *or* ruby), 6 pt. (nonpareil), 7 pt. (minion), 8 pt. (brevier), 9 pt. (bourgeois), 10 pt. (long primer), 11 pt. (small pica), 12 pt. (pica), 14 pt. (English), 16 pt. (Columbian), 18 pt. (great primer).

PRINTER, compositor, reader, proof reader; printer's devil; copyholder.

V. PRINT; compose; put -, go- to press; pass -, see- through the press; publish &c. 531; bring out; appear in -, rush into- print; set up, stick [*cant*], make-up, impose, justify, macule *or* mackle, mortise, offset, overrun, rout.

DISTRIBUTE, pi *or* pie, pi a form.

Adj. TYPOGRAPHICAL &c. *n.;* printed &c. *v.;* in type; solid in galleys; kerned, deckle-edged; boldfaced *or* full-faced; pied.

transcription &c. (*copy*) 21; inscription &c. (*record*) 551; superscription &c. (*indication*) 550.

WRITER, scribe, amanuensis, scrivener, secretary, clerk, penman, copyist, transcriber, quill driver [*humorous*]; stenographer, brachygrapher, tachygrapher, phonographer, logographer, cipherer, cryptographer *or* cryptographist, steganographist; typewriter, typist; writer for the press &c. (*author*) 593; chirographer, cerographist; monographist, graphomaniac; calligraphist, calligrapher; cacographer; graphologist.

V. WRITE, pen, typewrite, type [*colloq.*]; copy, engross; write out, – fair; transcribe; scribble, scrawl, scrabble, scratch; interline; take down in -shorthand, – longhand; spoil –, stain- paper [*humorous*]; note down; write down &c. (*record*) 551; sign &c. (*attest*) 467; enface.

COMPOSE, indite, draw up, draft, formulate; dictate; inscribe, throw on paper, dash off; manifold.

take up the pen, take pen in hand; shed –, spill –, dip one's pen in- ink.

Adj. writing &c. *v.*; written &c. *v.*; in writing, in black and white; under one's hand.

uncial, runic, cuneiform, hieroglyphic *or* hieroglyphical, arrowhead &c. *n.*

STENOGRAPHIC, phonographic, brachygraphic, cryptographic, pasigraphic, logographic, tachygraphic; stenographical &c.

Adv. *currente calamo* [*L.*]; pen in hand; with the pen of a ready writer; that "the wayfaring men, though fools, shall not err therein" [*Bible*].

*** *audacter et sincere; le style est l'homme même;* "nature's noblest gift — my gray goose quill" [Byron]; *scribendi recte sapere et principium et fons* [Horace]; "that mighty instrument of little men" [Byron]; "the pen became a clarion" [Longfellow].

592. Correspondence. —N. CORRESPONDENCE, letter, epistle, note, billet, written communication, post card *or* postcard, postal [*U. S.*], postal card; missive, circular, favor, *billet-doux* [*F.*]; chit *or* chitty [*India*], letter card [*Brit.*], picture post card; dispatch *or* despatch; bulletin, these presents [*law*]; rescript, rescription [*archaic*]; post &c. (*messenger*) 534.

LETTER WRITER, epistolarian, correspondent, writer, communicator; author, contributor.

V. CORRESPOND, – with; write to, send a letter to; drop a line to [*colloq.*]; start –, begin –, keep up- a correspondence; deluge with -letters, – post cards; communicate by -writing, – letter; let one know by -post, – mail; dispatch *or* despatch, circularize, follow up, bombard; reply, reply by return mail, communicate.

Adj. EPISTOLARY, epistolarian.

*** *furor scribendi.*

593. Book.— N. BOOK, booklet; writing, work, volume, tome, opuscule *or* opuscle, opusculum; tract, tractate, treatise, *livret* [*F.*], brochure, monograph, pamphlet, codex, libretto; handbook, manual, enchiridion; novel &c. (*composition*) 590; circular, publication; the press &c. 531; chapbook.

part, issue, number, *livraison* [*F.*]; album, portfolio; periodical, serial, magazine, ephemeris, annual, journal.

PAPER, bill, sheet, broadsheet; leaf, leaflet; fly leaf, page; quire, ream.

PASTEBOARD, cardboard, strawboard, millboard, binder's board; carton.

MAKE-UP, bastard title, title, printer's imprint, subtitles, dedication, preface, contents, list of plates *or* illustrations, errata, introduction, text; chapter, section, head, article, paragraph, passage, clause; recto, verso *or* reverso; supplement, appendix, index.

[SIZES] folio, quarto (4to *or* 4°); octavo (8vo), cap 8vo, demy 8vo, imperial 8vo, medium 8vo, royal 8vo, post 8vo, pott 8vo, crown 8vo, foolscap 8vo; duodecimo, twelvemo *or* 12mo; sextodecimo, sixteenmo *or* 16mo; octodecimo, eighteenmo *or* 18mo.

BOOKBINDING, bibliopegy; folding, stitching, wire-stitching; tooling; blind –, gold- tooling; binder's title; case, cover; quarter –, half –, three-quarters- bound book; full leather.

[BINDING MATERIALS] paper, paper boards, buckram, cloth, skiver, roan, pigskin, Russia, Turkey morocco, levant morocco, seal, parchment, vellum.

WORK OF REFERENCE, encyclopedia *or* encyclopædia, cyclopedia *or* cyclopædia, dictionary, thesaurus, concordance, anthology; compilation.

WRITER, author, *littérateur* [*F.*], essayist; pen, scribbler, the scribbling race;

literary hack, Grub-street writer; adjective jerker [*slang*], hack writer, hack, ghost [*cant*], ink slinger [*slang*]; journalist, publicist, writer for –, gentleman of –, representative of- the press; reporter, correspondent; war –, special- correspondent; knight of the -plume, – pen, – quill [*all humorous*]; penny-a-liner; editor, subeditor, reviser, diaskeuast; scribe &c. 590; playwright &c. 599; poet &c. 597.

THE TRADE, publisher, bookseller; book -salesman, – agent, – canvasser, – solicitor.

bibliopole, bibliopolist, book collector; bookbinder, bibliopegist; bookworm &c. 492; bibliologist, bibliographer, bibliophile, bibliognost, librarian, bibliothec.

bookstore, bookshop, bookseller's shop, *librairie* [*F.*], publishing house.

LIBRARY, bibliotheca, public library, lending library.

KNOWLEDGE OF BOOKS, bibliography, bibliology; book learning &c. (*knowledge*) 490; bookselling, bibliopolism.

₊ "among the giant fossils of my past" [E. B. Browning]; *craignez tout d'un auteur en courroux;* "for authors nobler palms remain" [Pope]; "I lived to write and wrote to live" [Rogers]; "look in thy heart and write" [Sidney]; "there is no Past so long as Books shall live" [Bulwer-Lytton]; "the public mind is the creation of the Master-Writers" [Disraeli]; "volumes that I prize above my dukedom" [*Tempest*]; "the true University of these days is a Collection of Books" [Carlyle].

594. Description. — N. DESCRIPTION, account, statement, report; *exposé* [*F.*] &c. (*disclosure*) 529; specification, particulars; summary of facts; brief &c. (*abstract*) 596; return &c. (*record*) 551; *catalogue raisonné* [*F.*] &c. (*list*) 86; guidebook &c. (*information*) 527.

delineation &c. (*representation*) 554; sketch, pastel, vignette, monograph; minute –, detailed –, particular –, circumstantial –, graphic- account; narration, recital, rehearsal, relation.

NARRATIVE, history; memoir, memorials; annals &c. (*chronicle*) 551; saga; tradition, legend, story, tale, historiette; personal narrative, journal, letters, biography, autobiography, life; obituary, necrology; adventures, fortunes, experiences, confessions; anecdote, ana.

historiography, chronography; historic Muse, Clio.

WORK OF FICTION, novel, romance, short story; detective -story, – yarn; "grue" [Stevenson]; fairy –, nursery- tale; fable, parable, apologue, allegory; dime novel, penny dreadful, shilling shocker [*slang*].

RELATOR &c. *v.; raconteur* [*F.*]; historiographer, chronographer, historian &c. (*recorder*) 553; biographer, fabulist, novelist, story-teller, romancer, spinner of yarns, teller of tales, anecdotist, word-painter; writer &c. 593.

V. DESCRIBE; set forth &c. (*state*) 535; draw a picture, picture; portray &c. (*represent*) 554; characterize, analyze, give words to, narrate, relate, recite, recount, sum up, run over, recapitulate, rehearse, fight one's battles over again; harrow up the soul, hold one breathless, novelize, romance.

unfold &c. (*disclose*) 529- a tale; tell; give –, render- an account of; report, make a report, draw up a statement; throw into -essay form, – book form; stick to the facts, show life as it is; historicize.

DETAIL, particularize, itemize; enter into –, descend to- -particulars, – details.

Adj. DESCRIPTIVE, graphic, narrative, epic, suggestive, well-drawn; historic *or* historical, historiographical, chronographic *or* chronographical, biographic *or* biographical, autobiographical; traditive [*esp., from ancestors to descendants*], traditional, traditionary; legendary, mythical, fabulous; anecdotic, storied; described &c. *v.;* romantic, idealistic; realistic, true to life; expository.

₊ *furor scribendi;* "to hold, as 'twere, the mirror up to nature" [*Hamlet*].

595. Dissertation. — N. DISSERTATION, treatise, essay; thesis, theme; tract, tractate, tractation [*obs.*]; discourse, memoir, disquisition, lecture, sermon, homily, pandect, digest; excursus.

investigation &c. (*inquiry*) 461; study &c. (*consideration*) 451; discussion &c. (*reasoning*) 476; exposition &c. (*explanation*) 522.

COMMENTARY, commentation, review, critique, criticism, article; leader, leading article; editorial; running commentary.

COMMENTATOR, critic, essayist, pamphleteer, publicist, reviewer, leader writer, editor, annotator.

V. COMMENT, explain, interpret, criticize, illuminate; dissert [rare] –, descant –, write –, touch- upon a subject; treat of –, take up –, ventilate –, discuss –, deal with –, go into –, canvass –, handle –, do justice to- a subject; show the true inwardness of.

Adj. DISQUISITIONAL, disquisitive, disquisitionary [rare]; expository, commentarial, commentatorial, critical.

DISCURSIVE, discoursive, digressive, desultory.

596. Compendium. — N. COMPENDIUM, compend, abstract, *précis* [F.], epitome, *multum in parvo* [L.], analysis, pandect, digest, sum and substance, brief, abridgment, *abrégé* [F.], summary, *aperçu* [F.], draft, minute, note; excerpt, extract; synopsis, textbook, conspectus, outlines, syllabus, contents, heads, prospectus.

ALBUM; scrap –, note –, memorandum –, commonplace- book.

FRAGMENTS, ana, extracts, *excerpta* [L.], cuttings; fugitive -pieces, – writings; *spicilegium* [L.], flowers, anthology, miscellany, collectanea, analects *or* analecta; compilation.

RECAPITULATION, *résumé* [F.], review.

ABBREVIATION, abbreviature; contraction; shortening &c. 201; compression &c. 195.

V. ABRIDGE, abstract, epitomize, summarize; make –, prepare –, draw –, compile- an abstract &c. n.; abbreviate &c. (*shorten*) 201; condense &c. (*compress*) 195.

COMPILE &c. (*collect*) 72; note down, collect, edit.

RECAPITULATE, review, skim, run over, sum up.

Adj. COMPENDIOUS, synoptic, analectic; *abrégé* [F.], abridged &c. v.; abbreviatory; analytic *or* analytical; variorum.

Adv. IN SHORT, in epitome, in substance, in few words.

✶✶✶ it lies in a nutshell; "infinite riches in a little room" [Marlowe]; "in small proportions we just beauties see" [Jonson].

597. Poetry. — N. POETRY, poetics, poesy, Muse, tuneful Nine, Apollo, Apollo Musagetes, Calliope, Parnassus, Helicon, Pierides, Pierian spring; inspiration, fire of genius, coal from off the altar.

POEM; epic, epic poem; epopee *or* epopœia, epos, ode, epode, idyl *or* idyll, lyric, eclogue, pastoral, bucolic, georgic, dithyramb *or* dithyrambus, anacreontic, sonnet, roundelay, rondeau, rondel, roundel, rondelet; triolet, sestina, virelay, ballade, cento, ghazal *or* ghazel, madrigal, monody, elegy; amœbæum, palinode.

dramatic –, didactic –, narrative –, lyric –, satirical- poetry; satire, opera.

ANTHOLOGY, posy [archaic], garland, miscellany, *disjecta membra poetæ* [L.].

SONG, ballad, lay; love –, drinking –, war –, sea- song; lullaby, *aubade* [F.]; music &c. 415; nursery rhymes.

[BAD POETRY] doggerel, Hudibrastic verse; macaronics, macaronic verse; "not poetry, but prose run mad" [Pope].

VERSIFICATION, riming *or* rhyming, making verses; prosody; scansion, scanning, orthometry [rare].

598. Prose. — N. PROSE, prosaism, prosaicness, prosaicism [rare]; poetic prose; history &c. (*description*) 594.

PROSE WRITER, essayist, monographer, monographist, novelist; *raconteur* [F.] &c. 594.

V. PROSE; write -prose, – in prose.

Adj. PROSAIC, prosy, prosal [obs.]; unpoetical.

rimeless *or* rhymeless, unrimed *or* unrhymed, in prose, not in verse.

✶✶✶ "prose, — words in their best order" [Coleridge].

239

canto, stanza, distich, verse, line, couplet, triplet, quatrain; strophe, antistrophe; refrain, chorus, burden; octave, sextet.

VERSE, rime *or* rhyme, assonance, crambo [*contemptuous*], meter, measure, foot,
numbers, strain, rhythm; ictus, beat, accent; accentuation &c. (*voice*) 580;
iambus, iambic, iamb; dactyl, spondee, trochee, anapest &c.; hexameter, pentameter; Alexandrine; anacrusis, antispast, blank verse, Leonine verse, runes,
alliteration; *bout-rimé* [*F.*].

elegiacs &c. *adj.;* elegiac &c. *adj.* -verse, – meter *or* metre, – poetry.

POET, minor poet; genius, maker [*obs.*], creator; poet laureate; laureate; bard,
lyrist, scald *or* skald, scop [*hist.*], idylist *or* idyllist, sonneteer, rhapsodist, epic
[*obs.*], epic poet, dithyrambic, satirist, troubadour, trouvère; minstrel; minnesinger,
Meistersinger; jongleur, improvisator *or improvvisatore* [*It.*] *or improvisatore;*
versifier, rimer *or* rhymer, rimester *or* rhymester; ballad monger, runer; poetaster; *genus irritabile vatum* [*L.*].

V. POETIZE, sing, "lisp in numbers" [Pope], build the stately rime, sing deathless songs, make immortal by verse; satirize; compose epic &c. *adj.*- poetry;
string verses together, cap rimes, poeticize, versify, make verses, rime *or* rhyme,
scan.

produce -lame verses, – limping meters, – halting rime.

Adj. POETIC *or* poetical; lyric *or* lyrical; tuneful; epic; dithyrambic &c. *n.;*
metrical; acatalectic, catalectic; elegiac, iambic, dactylic, spondaic *or* spondaical,
trochaic, anapestic; amœbæic, Melibean, scaldic *or* skaldic; Ionic, Sapphic, Alcaic,
Pindaric, Pierian.

*** "a poem round and perfect as a star" [Alex. Smith]; *Dichtung und Wahrheit; furor
poeticus;* "his virtues formed the magic of his song" [Hayley]; "I do but sing because I
must" [Tennyson]; "I learnt life from the poets" [de Staël]; *licentia vatum; mutum est
pictura poema;* "O for a muse of fire!" [*Henry V*]; "sweet food of sweetly uttered knowledge"
[Sidney]; "the true poem is the poet's mind" [Emerson]; *Volk der Dichter und Denker;*
"wisdom married to immortal verse" [Wordsworth]; "Unlock my heart with a sonnet-key"
[Browning].

599. The Drama. — N. THE DRAMA, the stage, the theater *or* theatre, the play;
theatricals, dramaturgy, histrionic art, mimography, buskin, sock, cothurnus,
Melpomene and Thalia, Thespis.

PLAY, drama, stageplay, piece, five-act play, tragedy, comedy, opera, vaudeville,
comedietta, *lever de rideau* [*F.*], curtain raiser, interlude, afterpiece, exode [*Rom.
antiq.*], farce, *divertissement* [*F.*], extravaganza, burletta, harlequinade, pantomime,
burlesque, *opéra bouffe* [*F.*], ballet, spectacle, masque, *drame* [*F.*], *comédie drame*
[*F.*]; melodrama; *comédie larmoyante* [*F.*]; emotional -drama, – play; sensation
drama; tragi-comedy; light –, genteel –, low –, farce- comedy, comedy of manners,
farcical-comedy; monodrama, monodram *or* monodrame, monologue, duologue,
dialogue; trilogy; charade, *proverbe* [*F.*]; mystery, miracle play, morality play.

ACT, scene, tableau, curtain; introduction, induction [*archaic*], exposition, expository scenes; prologue, epilogue; libretto, book, text; prompter's copy.

PERFORMANCE, representation, show [*colloq.*], *mise en scène* [*F.*], stage setting,
stagery [*obs.*], stagecraft, *jeu de théâtre* [*F.*]; acting; gesture &c. 550; impersonation
&c. 554; stage business, gag, patter, slap-stick [*slang*], buffoonery.

THEATER *or* theatre, playhouse, opera house; music hall; amphitheater *or* amphi-
theatre, circus, hippodrome; moving-picture theater, moving pictures, movies [*colloq.*],
cinematograph *or* cinema [*colloq., Brit.*]; puppet show, fantoccini; marionettes.
Punch and Judy.

AUDITORY, auditorium, front of the house, front [*colloq. and professional*], stalls
[*chiefly Eng.*], orchestra seats *or* orchestra, pit [*chiefly Eng.*], parquet, orchestra
circle, boxes, balcony, gallery, peanut gallery [*slang*]; dressing rooms, greenroom.

SCENERY; back scene, flat; drop, drop scene; wing, screen, coulisse, side scene,
transformation scene, curtain, act drop; proscenium; fire curtain, asbestos curtain.

STAGE, movable stage, scene, the boards; trap, mezzanine floor; flies; floats, footlights; limelight, spotlight, colored light; orchestra.

theatrical costume, theatrical properties, props [*theat. cant*].

CAST, *dramatis personæ* [*L.*], persons in the play; rôle, part, character; repertoire, repertory, *répertoire* [*F.*].

ACTOR, player; stage –, strolling- player; barnstormer, stager [*rare*], old stager; masker, masquer [*rare*], mime, mimer, mimic, mimester [*rare*]; *artiste* [*F.*], performer, star, headliner; comedian, tragedian, *tragédienne* [*F.*], Thespian, Roscius, ham [*slang*], hamfatter [*slang*]; utility, general utility, utility man.

BUFFOON, pantomimist, clown, *farceur* [*F.*], *buffo (pl. buffi*) [*It.*], grimacer, pantaloon, harlequin, columbine; punch, punchinello, *pulcinella* [*It.*].

mummer, guiser [*Eng. & Scot.*], guisard [*Scot.*], gysart [*obs.*], masque [*obs.*], mask.

mountebank, Jack Pudding; tumbler, posture master, acrobat; contortionist; ballet dancer, ballet girl; *coryphée* [*F.*], *danseuse* [*F.*]; chorus girl, chorus singer.

COMPANY; first tragedian, prima donna, leading lady; lead; leading man, protagonist; *jeune premier* [*F.*], *débutant (fem. débutante*) [*F.*]; light –, genteel –, low- comedian; walking gentleman *or* lady [*obsoles.*], *amoroso* [*It.*], juvenile lead, juvenile; heavy lead, heavy; heavy father, *ingénue* [*F.*], *jeune veuve* [*F.*], soubrette, *farceur (fem. farceuse*) [*F.*].

MUTE, figurant, figurante, walking part, supernumerary, super [*theat. cant*], supe [*theat. cant*].

manager; stage –, actor –, acting- manager; *entrepreneur* [*F.*], impresario; angel [*slang*].

[THEATER STAFF] property man, prop [*theat. cant*]; costumer, costumier, wigmaker, make-up artist; sceneshifter, grip [*U. S.*], stage hand, stage carpenter, machinist, electrician, chief electrician; prompter, call boy; advance agent, publicity agent.

DRAMATIST, playwright, playwriter; dramatic -author, – writer; mimographer, mimist [*obs.*]; dramatic critic.

AUDIENCE, auditory, house; orchestra &c. *n.;* gallery, the gods [*colloq.*], gallery gods [*colloq.*].

V. ACT, play, perform; put on the stage, dramatize, stage, produce, set; personate &c. 554; mimic &c. (*imitate*) 19; enact; play –, act –, go through –, perform a part; rehearse, spout, gag [*slang*], patter [*slang*], rant; strut and fret one's hour upon the stage; tread the -stage, – boards; make one's début, take a part, come out; star; supe [*slang*].

Adj. DRAMATIC; theatric *or* theatrical; scenic, histrionic, comic, tragic, buskined, cothurned; farcical, tragi-comic, melodramatic, operatic; stagy *or* stagey; spectacular, stellar, all-star [*cant*]; stagestruck.

Adv. ON THE STAGE, on the boards; in the limelight, in the spotlight; before the floats, before the footlights, before the curtain, before an audience; behind the scenes.

** *fere totus mundus exercet histrionem* [Petronius Arbiter]; "suit the action to the word, the word to the action" [*Hamlet*]; "the play's the thing" [*Hamlet*]; "is there no play, To ease the anguish of a torturing hour?" [*M. N. D.*]; "If it be true that good wine needs no bush, 'tis true that a good play needs no epilogue" [*As You Like It*]; "Come, sit down, every mother's son, and rehearse your parts" [*M. N. D.*]; "let gorgeous Tragedy In sceptred pall come sweeping by" [Milton]; "There's a dearth of wit in this dull town, While silly plays so savourily go down" [Dryden]; "Thus they jog on, still tricking, never thriving, And murd'ring plays, which still they call reviving" [*ibid.*]; "the monuments of vanished minds" [*ibid.*]; "to wake the soul by tender strokes of art" [Pope]; "For we that live to please must please to live" [Johnson]; "the players are my pictures and their scenes my territories" [Steele]; " 'The world's a stage,' — as Shakespeare said one day; The stage a world — was what he meant to say" [Holmes].

CLASS V

WORDS RELATING TO THE VOLUNTARY POWERS[1]

DIVISION (I) INDIVIDUAL VOLITION

Section I. VOLITION IN GENERAL

1. *Acts of Volition*

600. Will. — N. WILL, volition, conation, volitiency, velleity; *liberum arbitrium* [*L.*]; will and pleasure, free will; freedom &c. 748; discretion; choice, inclination, intent, purpose, voluntarism; option &c. (*choice*) 609; voluntariness; spontaneity, spontaneousness; originality.

WISH, desire, pleasure, mind, frame of mind &c. (*inclination*) 602; intention &c. 620; predetermination &c. 611; self-control &c. determination &c. (*resolution*) 604; force of will, will power, autocracy, bossiness [*colloq.*, *U. S.*].

V. WILL, list [*archaic*]; see fit, think fit; determine &c. (*resolve*) 604; enjoin; settle &c. (*choose*) 609; volunteer.

HAVE A WILL OF ONE'S OWN; do what one chooses &c. (*freedom*) 748; have it all one's own way; have one's will, have one's own way; use –, exercise-one's discretion; take –upon oneself, – one's own course, – the law into one's own hands; do of one's own accord, do upon one's own authority, do upon one's own responsibility; take responsibility, boss [*colloq.*], take the bit between one's teeth; originate &c. (*cause*) 153.

Adj. VOLUNTARY, volitional, willful *or* wilful; free &c. 748; optional; discretional, discretionary; volitient, volitive; volunteer, voluntaristic; dictatorial, bossy [*colloq.*, *U. S.*].

minded &c. (*willing*) 602; prepense &c. (*predetermined*) 611; intended &c. 620; autocratic; unbidden &c. (bid &c. 741); spontaneous; original &c. (*causal*) 153; unconstrained.

Adv. VOLUNTARILY &c. *adj.*; at will, at pleasure; *à volonté* [*F.*], *à discrétion*

601. Necessity. — N. INVOLUNTARINESS; instinct, blind impulse; inborn –, innate- proclivity; native –, natural-tendency; natural impulse, predetermination.

NECESSITY, necessitation, necessitarianism, obligation; compulsion &c. 744; subjection &c. 749; stern –, hard –, dire –, imperious –, inexorable –, iron –, adverse- -necessity, – fate; *anagke* [*Gr.* ἀνάγκη], what must be.

DESTINY, destination; fatality, fate, kismet, doom, foredoom, election, predestination; preordination, foreordination; lot, fortune; fatalism; inevitableness &c. *adj.*; spell &c. 993.

FATES, Parcæ, Sisters three, book of fate; God's will, Heaven, will of Heaven; star, stars; planet, planets; astral influence; wheel of Fortune, Ides of March, Hobson's choice.

LAST SHIFT, last resort; *dernier ressort* [*F.*]; *pis aller* &c. (*substitute*) 147; necessaries &c. (*requirement*) 630.

NECESSARIAN, necessitarian; fatalist; automaton, pawn.

V. LIE UNDER A NECESSITY; be fated, be doomed, be destined &c., be in for, be under the necessity of; be obliged, be forced, be driven; have no -choice, – alternative; be one's fate to &c. *n.*; be pushed to the wall, be driven into a corner, be unable to help, be swept on, be drawn irresistibly.

DESTINE, doom, foredoom, devote; predestine, preordain; cast a spell &c. 992; necessitate; compel &c. 744.

BE DECREED, be determined, be destined &c., be written; be written in the -book of fate, – stars.

[1] Conative powers or faculties as distinguished from cognition and feeling [Hamilton].

[*F.*]; *al piacere* [*It.*]; *ad libitum* [*L.*], *ad arbitrium* [*L.*]; as one thinks proper, as it seems good to; *a beneplacito* [*It*].

of one's own -accord, – free will; on one's own responsibility; *proprio* –, *suo* –, *ex mero- motu* [*L.*]; out of one's own head; by choice &c. 609; purposely &c. (*intentionally*) 620; deliberately &c. 611.

> ** *stet pro ratione voluntas; sic volo sic jubeo; beneficium accipere libertatem est vendere; Deus vult; was man nicht kann meiden muss man willig leiden;* "Sir, we *know* the will is free, and there's an end on't" [Johnson].

Adj. NECESSARY, necessarian, neces sitarian; needful &c. (*requisite*) 630.

FATED; destined &c. *v.;* fateful, big with fate; set apart, devoted, elect.

COMPULSORY &c. (*compel*) 744; uncontrollable, inevitable, unavoidable, indefeasible, irresistible, irrevocable, inexorable, binding; avoidless, resistless.

INVOLUNTARY, instinctive, automatic, blind, mechanical; unconscious, unwitting, unthinking; unintentional &c. (*undesigned*) 621; spellbound; impulsive &c. 612.

Adv. NECESSARILY &c. *adj.;* of necessity, of course; *ex necessitate rei* [*L.*]; needs must; perforce &c. 744; *nolens volens* [*L.*]; will he nil he, will I nill I, willy-nilly, *bon gré mal gré* [*F.*]; willing or unwilling, *coûte que coûte* [*F.*]; compulsorily, by compulsion, by force.

faute de mieux [*F.*]; by stress of; if need be; *que faire?* [*F.*].

> ** it cannot be helped; there is no -help for, – helping- it; it -will, – must, – must needs- be, – be so, – have its way; the die is cast; *jacta est alea; che sarà sarà;* "it is written"; one's days are numbered, one's fate is sealed; *Fata obstant; dis aliter visum; actus me invito factus, non est meus actus; aujourd'hui roi demain rien; quisque suos patimur manes* [Vergil]; "but helpless pieces of the game He plays Upon this chequer-board of nights and days" [Omar Khayyám — Fitzgerald]; "the ball no question makes of ayes and noes" [*ibid.*]; *necessità il c'induce e non diletto* [Dante]; "There's a divinity that shapes our ends, Rough-hew them how we will" [*Hamlet*].

602. Willingness. — N.
WILLINGNESS, voluntariness &c. *adj.;* willing mind, heart.

DISPOSITION, inclination, liking, turn, propensity, propension, propenseness, leaning, animus; frame of mind, humor, mood, vein; bent &c. (*turn of mind*) 820; *penchant* [*F.*] &c. (*desire*) 865; aptitude &c. 698.

DOCILITY, docibleness [*rare*], docibility [*rare*], appetency, tractability, tractableness, persuadability, persuadableness, persuasibleness, persuasibility; pliability &c. (*softness*) 324.

GENIALITY, cordiality; goodwill; alacrity, readiness, zeal, enthusiasm, earnestness, forwardness; eagerness &c. (*desire*) 865.

ASSENT &c. 488; compliance &c. 762; pleasure &c. (*will*) 600.

LABOR OF LOVE, self-appointed task, volunteering; gratuitous service; social service, welfare work.

VOLUNTEER, unpaid worker, amateur, voluntary [*rare*]; social worker, welfare worker.

V. BE WILLING &c. *adj.;* incline, lean to, mind, propend [*rare*], had as lief, would as lief; lend –, give –, turn- a willing ear; have -a, – half a, – a great-mind to; hold to, cling to; desire &c. 865.

603. Unwillingness. — N.
UNWILLINGNESS &c. *adj.;* indisposition, indisposedness, disinclination, aversation [*rare*], aversion; averseness &c. (*dislike*) 867; nolleity [*rare*], nolition [*rare*]; renitence *or* renitency; reluctance; indifference &c. 866; backwardness &c. *adj.;* slowness &c. 275; want of -alacrity, – readiness; indocility &c. (*obstinacy*) 606.

SCRUPULOUSNESS, scrupulosity; qualms –, twinge- of conscience; delicacy, demur, scruple, qualm, shrinking, recoil; hesitation &c. (*irresolution*) 605; fastidiousness &c. 868.

DISSENT &c. 489; refusal &c. 764.

FORCED LABOR, unwilling service, peonage; compulsion &c. 744; slacker.

V. BE UNWILLING &c. *adj.;* nill [*archaic*]; dislike &c. 867; grudge, begrudge; not find it in one's heart to, not have the stomach to.

DEMUR, stick at, scruple, stickle; hang fire, run rusty [*colloq.*], go stale; give up, let down [*slang*]; pull back, be a dead weight, be a passenger in the boat, not pull fair, shirk, slack, shy [*dial. Eng.*], fight shy of, get by [*slang*], duck [*slang*]; recoil, shrink, swerve; hesitate &c. 605; avoid &c. 623.

OPPOSE &c. 708; dissent &c. 489; refuse &c. 764.

ACQUIESCE &c. (*assent*) 488; see think- -good, – fit, – proper; comply with &c. 762.

swallow –, nibble at- the bait; swallow bait, hook, and sinker; swallow bait and all; gorge the hook; have –, make- no scruple of; make no bones of [*colloq.*]; jump at, catch at; go in for, go in at [*both colloq.*]; take up, plunge into, have a go at [*colloq.*]; meet halfway.

VOLUNTEER, offer, proffer; offer oneself &c. 763.

Adj. WILLING, minded, fain, disposed, inclined, favorable; favorably -minded, -inclined, -disposed; well-disposed, lief [*archaic*], nothing loth; in the -vein, – mood, – humor, – mind.

READY, forward, earnest, eager, zealous, enthusiastic; bent upon &c. (*desirous*) 865; predisposed, desirous, propense.

DOCILE; persuadable, persuasible; suasible, amenable, easily persuaded, facile, easy-going; tractable &c. (*pliant*) 324; genial, gracious, cordial, cheering, hearty; content &c. (*assenting*) 488.

VOLUNTARY, gratuitous, spontaneous; unasked &c. (ask &c. 765); unforced &c. (*free*) 748.

Adv. WILLINGLY &c. *adj.;* fain, freely, as lief, heart and soul; with pleasure, with all one's heart, with open arms; with good will, with right good will; *de bonne volonté* [*F.*], *ex animo* [*L.*], *con amore* [*It.*], heart in hand, nothing loath, without reluctance, of one's own accord, graciously, with a good grace; without demur.

à la bonne heure [*F.*]; by all means, by all manner of means; to one's heart's content; yes &c. (*assent*) 488.

Int. SURELY! sure! with pleasure! of course! delighted!

Adj. UNWILLING; not in the vein, loath *or* loth, shy of, disinclined, indisposed, averse, reluctant, not content; renitent, opposed; adverse &c. (*opposed*) 708; laggard, backward, remiss, slack, slow to; indifferent &c. 866; scrupulous; squeamish &c. (*fastidious*) 868; repugnant &c. (*dislike*) 867; restiff [*obs.*], restive; demurring &c. *v.;* unconsenting &c. (*refusing*) 764; involuntary &c. 601; grudging, forced; irreconcilable.

Adv. UNWILLINGLY &c. *adj.;* grudgingly, with a heavy heart; with -a bad, – an ill- grace; against –, sore against- -one's wishes, – one's will, – the grain; *invita Minerva* [*L.*]; *à contre cœur* [*F.*]; *malgré soi* [*F.*]; in spite of -one's teeth, – oneself; *nolens volens* [*L.*] &c. (*necessity*) 601; perforce &c. 744; under protest; no &c. 536; if I must I must; not if one can help it; not for the world; far be it from me.

---

604. Resolution. — N. DETERMINATION, will; iron will, unconquerable will; will of one's own, decision, resolution; backbone; clear grit, grit [*U. S. & Can.*]; sand [*slang*]; strength of -mind, – will; resolve &c. (*intent*) 620; intransigence *or* intransigency, *intransigeance* [*F.*]; firmness &c. (*stability*) 150; energy, manliness, vigor; resoluteness &c. (*courage*) 861; zeal &c. 682; desperation; devotion, devotedness.

SELF-CONTROL, *aplomb* [*F.*], mastery over self, self-mastery, self-command, self-possession, self-reliance, self-government, self-restraint, self-conquest, self-denial; moral -courage, – fiber, – strength.

TENACITY, perseverance &c. 604a; obstinacy &c. 606; game, pluck; fighting cock, game cock; bulldog; British lion.

IRRECONCILABLE, intransigent, *in-*

605. Irresolution. — N. IRRESOLUTION, infirmity of purpose, indecision, indetermination, undetermination [*rare*], instability; loss of will power, abulia, abulomania; unsettlement; uncertainty &c. 475; demur, suspense; hesitating &c. *v.,* hesitation, hesitancy; wabble *or* wobble; revocability, vacillation; changeableness &c. 149; fluctuation; alternation &c. (*oscillation*) 314; caprice &c. 608; lukewarmness, Laodiceanism.

FICKLENESS, levity, *légèreté* [*F.*]; pliancy &c. (*softness*) 324; weakness; timidity &c. 860; cowardice &c. 862; half measures.

WAVERER, shilly-shally, ass between two bundles of hay; shuttlecock, butterfly, feather, piece of thistledown; house built on sand; doughface [*U. S.*]; turncoat, opportunist, Vicar of Bray, Dite Deuchars; Laodicean; timeserver &c. 607.

transigeant [*F*.], bitter-ender [*colloq*.]; fighting minority, militant remnant.

V. HAVE DETERMINATION &c. *n.;* know one's own mind; be resolved &c. *adj.;* make up one's mind; will, resolve, determine; decide &c. (*judgment*) 480; form –, come to- a -determination, – resolution, – resolve; conclude, fix, seal, determine once for all, bring to a crisis, drive matters to an extremity; take a decisive step &c. (*choice*) 609; take upon oneself &c. (*undertake*) 676.

STEEL ONESELF, devote oneself to, give oneself up to; throw away the scabbard, kick down the ladder, nail one's colors to the mast, set one's back against the wall, burn one's bridges, grit one's teeth, set one's teeth, set one's jaw, take the bit in one's mouth, put one's foot down, take one's stand, stand firm &c. (*stability*) 150; stand no nonsense, not listen to the voice of the charmer; insist upon, make a point of; set one's heart upon, set one's mind upon.

BUCKLE TO; buckle oneself; put –, lay –, set- one's shoulder to the wheel; put one's heart into; run the gauntlet, make a dash at, take the bull by the horns; rush –, plunge- *in medias res* [*L*.]; go in for [*colloq*.].

STICK AT NOTHING; make short work of &c. (*activity*) 682; not stick at trifles; go all lengths, go the limit [*slang*], go the whole hog [*slang*], go it blind [*slang*]; go down with one's colors flying; die game; persist &c. (*persevere*) 604a; go through fire and water, "ride in the whirlwind and direct the storm" [Addison].

Adj. RESOLVED &c. *v.;* determined; strong-willed, strong-minded; resolute &c. (*brave*) 861; self-possessed, earnest, serious; decided, definitive, peremptory, unhesitating, unflinching, unshrinking; firm, iron, game, plucky, tenacious, gritty [*U. S*.], indomitable, game to the backbone, game to the last; inexorable, relentless, not to be -shaken, – put down; *tenax propositi* [*L*.]; obstinate &c. 606; steady &c. (*persevering*) 604a.

UNBENDING, unyielding; set –, bent –, intent- upon; grim, stern; inflexible &c. (*hard*) 323; cast-iron, irrevocable, irreversible; not to be deflected; firm as Gibraltar.

steeled –, proof- against; *in utrumque paratus* [*L*.].

Adv. RESOLUTELY &c. *adj.;* in earnest, in good earnest; seriously, joking apart, earnestly, heart and soul; on one's mettle; manfully, like a man; with a high -heart, – courage, – hand; with a strong hand &c. (*exertion*) 686.

AT ALL RISKS, at all hazards, at all events; at any -rate, – risk, – hazard,

V. BE IRRESOLUTE &c.; *adj.;* hang –, keep- in suspense; leave *ad referendum;* think twice about, pause; dawdle &c. (*inactivity*) 683; remain neuter; dilly-dally, hesitate, boggle, hover, dacker *or* daiker [*dial. Eng. & Scot*.], wabble *or* wobble [*colloq*.], shilly-shally, hum and haw, demur, not know one's own mind; debate, balance; dally with, coquet with; will and will not, *chasser-balancer* [*F*.]; go halfway, compromise, make a compromise; be thrown off one's balance, stagger like a drunken man; be afraid &c. 860; let "I dare not" wait upon "I would" [*Macbeth*]; falter, waver.

VACILLATE &c. 149; change &c. 140; retract &c. 607; fluctuate; pendulate; alternate &c. (*oscillate*) 314; keep off and on, play fast and loose; blow hot and cold &c. (*caprice*) 608; turn one's coat.

SHUFFLE, palter, blink, shirk, trim.

Adj. IRRESOLUTE, infirm of purpose, palsied, drifting, double-minded, half-hearted; undecided, unresolved, undetermined; shilly-shally, wabbly *or* wobbly; fidgety, tremulous; hesitating &c. *v.;* off one's balance; abulic; at a loss &c. (*uncertain*) 475.

VACILLATING &c. *v.;* unsteady &c. (*changeable*) 149; unsteadfast, fickle, unreliable, irresponsible, unstable, unstable as water, without ballast; capricious &c. 608; volatile, frothy; light, lightsome, lightminded; giddy; fast and loose.

WEAK, feeble-minded, frail; timid &c. 860; cowardly &c. 862; dough-faced [*U. S*.]; facile; pliant &c. (*soft*) 324; unable to say "no," easy-going.

REVOCABLE, reversible.

Adv. IRRESOLUTELY &c. *adj.;* irresolvedly; in faltering accents; off and on; on the sands; from pillar to post; seesaw &c. 314.

** "the brave man chooses while the coward stands aside" [Lowell]; "to have twa minds is as confusing as twins" [Barrie]; "how happy could I be with either!" [Gay].

−price, − cost, − sacrifice; *à bis ou à blanc* [*F.*], cost what it may; *coûte que coûte* [*F.*]; *à tort et à travers* [*F.*]; once for all; neck or nothing; survive or perish, live or die; rain or shine.

∗ spes sibi quisque; celui qui veut celui-là peut; chi non s'arrischia non guadagna; frangas non flectes; manu forti; tentanda via est;* "that bent like perfect steel, to spring again and thrust" [Lowell — *of Lincoln*]; "free peoples can escape being mastered by others only by being able to master themselves" [Roosevelt]; "if the single man plant himself indomitably on his instincts and there abide, the huge world will come round to him" [Emerson]; "yours is a thoroughbred heart: you don't scream and cry every time it's pinched" [Shaw].

604a. Perseverance. — N. PERSEVERANCE; continuance &c. (*inaction*) 143; permanence &c. (*absence of change*) 141; firmness &c. (*stability*) 150.

constancy, steadiness; singleness −, tenacity- of purpose; persistence, plodding, patience; sedulity [*rare*] &c. (*industry*) 682; pertinacy [*obs.*], pertinacity, pertinaciousness; iteration &c. 104.

GRIT, bottom, game, pluck, stamina, backbone, sand [*slang*]; indefatigability, indefatigableness; tenacity, staying power, endurance; bulldog courage.

V. PERSEVERE, persist; hold -on, − out; die in the last ditch, be in at the death; stick to, cling to, adhere to; stick to one's text; keep on, carry on, hold on; keep to −, maintain- one's -course, − ground; go all lengths, go through fire and water; bear up, keep up, hold up; plod; stick to work &c. (*work*) 686; continue &c. 143; follow up; die in harness, die at one's post.

Adj. PERSEVERING, constant; steady, steadfast; undeviating, unwavering, unfaltering, unswerving, unflinching, unsleeping, unflagging, undrooping; steady as time; unintermitting, unremitting; plodding; industrious &c. 682; strenuous &c. 686; pertinacious; persisting, persistent.

solid, sturdy, stanch *or* staunch, true to oneself; unchangeable &c. 150; unconquerable &c. (*strong*) 159; indomitable, game to the last, indefatigable, untiring, unwearied, never tiring.

Adv. WITHOUT FAIL; through evil report and good report, through thick and thin, through fire and water; *per fas et nefas* [*L.*]; sink or swim, at any price, *vogue la galère* [*F.*]; rain or shine, fair or foul, in sickness and in health.

∗ never say die; vestigia nulla retrorsum; aut vincere aut mori; la garde meurt et ne se rend pas; tout vient à temps pour qui sait attendre;* "If you can force your heart and nerve and sinew To serve your turn long after they are gone, And so hold on when there is nothing in you Except the Will which says to them: 'Hold on!' . . . Yours is the Earth, and everything that's in it" [Kipling]; "Man, the marvellous thing, that in the dark Works with his little strength to make a light" [Masefield].

606. Obstinacy. — N. OBSTINATENESS &c. *adj.;* obstinacy, tenacity; cussedness [*U. S.*]; perseverance &c. 604a; immovability; old school; inflexibility &c. (*hardness*) 323; obduracy, obduration [*rare*], obdurateness, doggedness, dogged resolution; resolution &c. 604; ruling passion; blind side.

self-will, contumacy, perversity; pervicaciousness [*rare*], pervicacy [*obs.*], pervicacity [*obs.*]; indocility [*obs.*].

BIGOTRY, intolerance, dogmatism; opiniatry [*obs.*], opiniativeness [*rare*]; impersuasibility, impersuadableness; intractableness, incorrigibility; fixed idea &c. (*prejudgment*) 481; fanaticism, zealotry, infatuation, monomania; opinionatedness, opinionativeness.

BIGOT, opinionist [*obs.*], opinionatist [*obs.*], opiniator [*obs.*], opinator [*obs.*];

607. Tergiversation. — N. TERGIVERSATION, tergiversating, recantation; palinode, palinody [*rare*]; renunciation; abjuration, abjurement; defection &c. (*relinquishment*) 624; going over &c. *v.;* apostasy; retraction, retractation; withdrawal; disavowal &c. (*negation*) 536; revocation, revokement [*rare*], reversal; repentance &c. 950; *redintegratio amoris* [*L.*].

change of -mind, − intention, − purpose; afterthought.

coquetry, flirtation; vacillation &c. 605.

recidivism, recidivation, backsliding; *volte-face* [*F.*].

TURNCOAT, turn-tippet [*obs.*]; rat [*cant*], apostate, renegade, pervert, deserter, backslider; recidivist; crawfish [*slang, U. S.*], mugwump [*U. S.*]; black-

stickler, dogmatist, zealot, enthusiast, fanatic, bitter-ender [colloq.]; mule.

V. BE OBSTINATE &c. adj.; stickle, take no denial, fly in the face of facts; opinionate [rare], be wedded to an opinion, hug a belief; have one's own way &c. (will) 600; persist &c. (persevere) 604a; have –, insist on having– the last word.

DIE HARD, die fighting, fight to the last ditch, fight against destiny, not yield an inch, stand out.

Adj. obstinate, tenacious, stubborn, obdurate, casehardened; inflexible &c. (hard) 323; balky; immovable, not to be moved; inert &c. 172; unchangeable &c. 150; inexorable &c. (determined) 604; mulish, obstinate as a mule, pig-headed.

dogged; sullen, sulky; unmoved, uninfluenced, unaffected.

WILLFUL or wilful, self-willed, perverse; resty [dial. Eng.], restive, pervicacious [rare], ungovernable, wayward, refractory, unruly; heady, headstrong; entêté [F.]; contumacious; crossgrained.

arbitrary, dogmatic, positive, bigoted, opinionated, opinionative, opinionate [obs.], opinioned, opiniative [rare]; prejudiced &c. 481; creed-bound; prepossessed, infatuated; stiff-backed, stiffnecked, stiff-hearted; hard-mouthed, hidebound; unyielding; impervious, impracticable, impersuasible, impersuadable, unpersuadable; untractable, intractable; incorrigible, deaf to advice, impervious to reason; crotchety &c. 608.

Adv. obstinately &c. adj.; with set jaw, with sullen mouth; no surrender.

⁎ non possumus; no surrender; ils n'ont rien appris ni rien oublié; other people are obstinate, I am firm; "lest any foreigner should alter their laws, which are bad, but not to be altered by mere aliens" [Dunsany].

leg, scab [slang]; proselyte, convert.

TIMESERVER, time-pleaser; timist [obs.], Vicar of Bray, trimmer, ambidexter; double dealer; weathercock &c. (changeable) 149; Janus; coquet, flirt.

V. TERGIVERSATE, veer round, wheel round, turn round; change one's- mind, – intention, – purpose, – note; abjure, renounce; withdraw from &c.(relinquish) 624; turn a pirouette; go over –, pass –, change –, skip- from one side to another; go to the right-about; box the compass, shift one's ground, go upon another tack.

APOSTATIZE, change sides, go over, rat [cant], tourner casaque [F.], recant, retract; revoke; rescind &c. (abrogate) 756; recall; forswear, unsay; come -over, – round- to an opinion.

BACK DOWN, draw in one's horns, eat one's words; eat –, swallow- the leek; swerve, flinch, back out of, retrace one's steps, crawfish, crawl [both slang, U. S.]; think better of it; come back –, return- to one's first love; turn over a new leaf &c. (repent) 950.

TRIM, shuffle, play fast and loose, blow hot and cold, coquet, flirt, be on the fence, straddle, hold with the hare but run with the hounds; nager entre deux eaux [F.], wait to see how the -cat jumps, – wind blows.

Adj. CHANGEFUL &c. 149; irresolute &c. 605; ductile, slippery as an eel, trimming, ambidextrous, timeserving; coquetting &c. v.

revocatory, reactionary.

⁎ "a change came o'er the spirit of my dream" [Byron]; "They are not constant, but are changing still" [Cymbeline]; "Was ever feather so lightly blown to and fro as this multitude?" [II Henry VI].

---

608. Caprice. — N. CAPRICE, fancy, humor; whim, whimsey or whimsy, whimwham, crotchet, capriccio [It.], quirk, freak, maggot, fad, vagary, prank, fit, flimflam, escapade, boutade [obs.], wild-goose chase; capriciousness &c. adj.; kink.

V. BE CAPRICIOUS &c. adj.; have a maggot in the brain; take it into one's head, take the bit in one's teeth; strain at a gnat and swallow a camel; blow hot and cold; play fast and loose, play fantastic tricks; tourner casaque [F.].

Adj. CAPRICIOUS; erratic, eccentric, fitful, hysterical; full of whims &c. n.; maggoty; inconsistent, fanciful, fantastic, whimsical, crotchety, kinky [U. S.], particular, humorsome, freakish, skittish, wanton, wayward; contrary; captious; unreasonable, unrestrained, undisciplined, not amenable to reason, arbitrary; unconformable &c. 83; penny wise and pound foolish; fickle &c. (irresolute) 605; frivolous, sleeveless [obs.], giddy, volatile.

Adv. BY FITS, by fits and starts, without rime or reason, at one's own sweet will; without counting the cost.

⁎ nil fuit unquam sic impar sibi; the deuce is in him.

609. Choice. — N. CHOICE, option; discretion &c. (*volition*) 600; preoption; alternative; dilemma, *embarras de choix* [*F.*]; adoption, coöptation; novation [*law*]; decision &c. (*judgment*) 480.

ELECTION, poll, ballot, vote, division, voice, suffrage, cumulative vote; plebiscitum, plebiscite, *vox populi* [*L.*], popular decision, referendum; electioneering; voting &c. *v.;* elective franchise; straight ticket, ticket [*U. S.*]; ballot-box.

SELECTION, excerption, gleaning, eclecticism; *excerpta* [*L.*]; gleanings, cuttings, scissors and paste; pick &c. (*best*) 650.

PREFERENCE, prelation [*rare*]; predilection &c. (*desire*) 865; Apple of Discord; choice of Hercules; Scylla and Charybdis; good and evil.

V. OFFER FOR ONE'S CHOICE, set before; hold out –, present –, offer- the alternative; put to the vote.

CHOOSE, elect; coöpt, coöptate [*rare*]; take –, make- one's choice; make choice of, fix upon; use –, exercise –, one's- -discretion, – option; adopt, take up, embrace, espouse.

settle; decide &c. (*adjudge*) 480; list &c. (*will*) 600; make up one's mind &c. (*resolve*) 604.

VOTE, poll, hold up one's hand, give a (*or* the) voting sign; divide.

SELECT; pick, – and choose; pick –, single- out; excerpt, cull, glean, winnow; sift –, separate –, winnow- the chaff from the wheat; pick up, pitch upon; pick one's way; indulge one's fancy.

set apart, mark out for; mark &c. 550.

PREFER; have rather, had (*or* would) as lief; fancy &c. (*desire*) 865; reserve, set one's seal upon; be persuaded &c. 615.

TAKE A DECIDED STEP, take a decisive step; commit oneself to a course; pass –, cross- the Rubicon; cast in one's lot with; take for better or for worse.

Adj. OPTIONAL; coöptative; discretional &c. (*voluntary*) 600; at choice, on approval.

CHOOSING &c. *v.;* eclectic; preferential.

CHOSEN &c. *v.;* choice &c. (*good*) 648; elect, select, popular.

Adv. OPTIONALLY &c. *adj.;* at pleasure &c. (*will*) 600; either, – the one or the other; or; at the option of; whether or not; once for all; for one's money.

BY CHOICE, by preference; in preference; rather, before.

609a. Absence of Choice. — N. NO CHOICE, Hobson's choice; first come first served; necessity &c. 601; not a pin to choose &c. (*equality*) 27; any, the first that comes; that or nothing.

NEUTRALITY, indifference; indecision &c. (*irresolution*) 605.

V. BE NEUTRAL &c. *adj.;* have no -preference, – choice; waive, not vote; abstain –, refrain, -from voting; leave undecided; "make a virtue of necessity" [*Two Gentlemen*].

Adj. NEUTRAL, neuter; indifferent; undecided &c. (*irresolute*) 605.

Adv. EITHER &c. (*choice*) 609.

*** "The Ball no question makes of Ayes and Noes, But Right or Left, as strikes the Player, goes" [Omar Khayyám — Fitzgerald]; "hanging and wiving goes by destiny" [*Merchant of Venice*].

610. Rejection. — N. REJECTION, repudiation, exclusion; refusal &c. 764; declination, declinature, withdrawal; averseness.

V. REJECT; set –, lay- aside; give up; decline &c. (*refuse*) 764; exclude, except; pluck up, spurn, cast out.

REPUDIATE, scout, set at naught; fling –, cast –, throw –, toss- -to the winds, – to the dogs, – overboard, – away; send to the right-about; disclaim &c. (*deny*) 536; discard &c. (*eject*) 297, (*have done with*) 678.

Adj. REJECTED &c. *v.;* rejectaneous [*obs.*], rejectitious [*obs.*], declinatory; not chosen &c. 609, not to be thought of; out of the question; "declined with thanks."

Adv. NEITHER, neither the one nor the other; no &c. 536.

*** *non hæc in fœdera.*

611. Predetermination. — N. PREDETERMINATION, predestination, preordination, premeditation, predeliberation; foregone conclusion; *parti pris* [*F.*];

612. Impulse. — N. IMPULSE, sudden thought; impromptu, improvisation; inspiration, flash, spurt.

IMPROVISOR, extemporizer, *improvvisa-*

resolve, propendency [*obs.*]; intention &c. 620; project &c. 626; fate, foredoom, necessity.

SCHEDULE, list, calendar, docket [*U. S.*], slate [*pol. cant, U. S.*], register, roster, poll, muster, draft, *cadre* [*F.*], panel.

V. PREDETERMINE, predestine, preordain, premeditate, preresolve, preconcert; resolve beforehand.

LIST, schedule, docket [*U. S.*], slate [*U. S.*], register, poll, empanel, draft.

Adj. PREMEDITATED &c. *v.;* predesigned; prepense, advised, studied, designed, calculated; aforethought; intended &c. 620; foregone.

WELL-LAID, well-devised, well-weighed; maturely considered; cut-and-dried, slated [*pol. cant, U. S.*]; cunning.

Adv. ADVISEDLY &c. *adj.;* with premeditation, deliberately, all things considered, with eyes open, in cold blood; intentionally &c. 620.

.•. "With Earth's first Clay They did the Last Man knead [Omar Khayyám — Fitzgerald].

tore or *improvisatore* [*It.*]; creature of impulse.

V. flash on the mind.

IMPROVISE, extemporize; say what comes uppermost, say what comes first into one's head; act on the spur of the moment, rise to the occasion; spurt.

Adj. EXTEMPORANEOUS, impulsive, indeliberate [*rare*]; snap; improvised, improvisate, improviso, improvisatory; unpremeditated; unmeditated, improvisatorial, improvisatory, *improvisé* [*F.*]; unprompted, unguided; natural, unguarded; spontaneous &c. (*voluntary*) 600; instinctive &c. 601.

Adv. EXTEMPORE, extemporaneously; offhand, impromptu, *a l'improviste* [*F.*]; on the spur of the -moment, - occasion.

.•. "To its own impulse every creature stirs" [Arnold].

---

613. Habit. — N. HABIT, habitude, habituation, assuetude [*obs.*], assuefaction [*obs.*]; wont; run, way; habitual attitude, habitual state of mind, habitual course.

common -, general -, natural -, ordinary- -course, - run, - state- of things; matter of course; beaten -path, - track, - ground.

cacoëthes; bad -, confirmed -, inveterate -, intrinsic &c. (5)- habit; addictedness, addiction, trick.

CUSTOM, use, usage, prescription, immemorial usage, practice; prevalence, observance; conventionalism, conventionality; mode, fashion, vogue; etiquette &c. (*gentility*) 852; order of the day, cry; conformity &c. 82; consuetude, dastur *or* dustoor [*India*].

one's old way, old school, *veteris vestigia flammæ* [*L.*]; *laudator temporis acti* [*L.*].

RULE, standing order, precedent, routine; red tape, red-tapism; pipe clay; rut, groove.

ADDICT, habitué, habitual [*colloq.*], frequenter, case [*slang*], hard case [*slang*], the limit [*slang*].

INUREMENT; training &c. (*education*) 537; seasoning, hardening; radication; second nature, acclimatization; knack &c. (*skill*) 698.

614. Desuetude. — N. DESUETUDE, disusage; obsolescence, disuse &c. 678; want of -habit, - use, - practice; inusitation [*rare*]; newness to; new brooms.

NONPREVALENCE; infraction of usage &c. (*unconformity*) 83; "a custom more honored in the breach than the observance" [*Hamlet*].

V. BE UNACCUSTOMED &c . *adj.;* leave off -, cast off -, break off -, cure oneself of -, wean oneself from -, shake off -, violate -, break through -, infringe- -a habit, - a custom, - a usage; break one's -chains, - fetters; do old things in a new way, give an original touch, give a new dress to old ideas; disuse &c. 678; wear off.

Adj. UNACCUSTOMED, unused, unwonted, unseasoned, uninured, unhabituated, untrained; new, fresh, original; impulsive &c. *adj.* 612; green &c. (*unskilled*) 699; unhackneyed.

UNCONVENTIONAL, unfashionable; dissident, protestant; unusual &c. (*unconformable*) 83; nonobservant; disused &c. 678.

Adv. CONTRARY TO -CUSTOM, - usage, - convention; for once, just once; "this time doesn't count."

.•. exceptions prove the rule.

V. BE WONT &c. *adj.*

fall into a custom &c. (*conform to*) 82; tread -, follow- the beaten -track, - path; *stare super antiquas vias* [*L.*]; move in a rut, run on in a groove, go round like a horse in a mill, go on in the old jog-trot way; get wound up in red tape.

HABITUATE, inure, harden, season, caseharden; accustom, familiarize; naturalize, acclimatize; keep one's hand in; train &c. (*educate*) 537.

get into the -way, - knack- of; learn &c. 539; cling to, adhere to; repeat &c. 104; acquire -, contract -, fall into- a -habit, - trick; addict oneself to, take to, accustom oneself to.

BE HABITUAL &c. *adj.*; prevail; come into use, become a habit, take root; gain upon one, grow upon one.

Adj. HABITUAL; accustomary, customary; prescriptive; accustomed &c. *v.*; of -daily, - everyday- occurrence; consuetudinary; wonted, usual, general, ordinary, common, frequent, every day, household, jog-trot; well-trodden, well-known; familiar, vernacular, trite, commonplace, conventional, regular, set, stock, established, stereotyped; prevailing, prevalent; current, received, acknowledged, recognized, accredited; of course, admitted, understood.

CONFORMABLE &c. 82; according to -use, - custom, - routine; in vogue, in fashion; fashionable &c. (*genteel*) 852.

WONT; used to, given to, addicted to, attuned to, habituated to &c. *v.*; in the habit of; *habitué* [*F.*]; at home in &c. (*skillful*) 698; seasoned; imbued with, soaked in, permeated with, never free from; devoted to, wedded to.

HACKNEYED, fixed, rooted, deep-rooted, ingrafted *or* engrafted, permanent, inveterate, besetting, naturalized; ingrained &c. (*intrinsic*) 5.

Adv. HABITUALLY &c. *adj.*; always &c. (*uniformly*) 16.

AS USUAL, as is one's wont, as things go, as the world goes, as the sparks fly upwards; as you were [*mil.*]; *more suo* [*L.*], *more solito* [*L.*]; *ex more* [*L.*].

AS A RULE, for the most part; generally &c. *adj.*; most -often, - frequently.

. cela s'entend; abeunt studia in mores; adeo in teneris consuescere multum est; consuetudo quasi altera natura [Cicero]; hoc erat in more majorum; "how use doth breed a habit in a man!" [*Two Gentlemen*]; magna est vis consuetudinis; morem fecerat usus [Ovid]; "Custom, like Winter, is the king of all" [Masefield].

2. *Causes of Volition*

615. Motive. — N. MOTIVE, springs of action.

REASON, ground, call, principle; by-end, by-purpose; mainspring, *primum mobile* [*L.*], keystone; the why and the wherefore; *pro* and *con*, reason why; secret motive, ulterior motive; *arrière pensée* [*F.*]; intention &c. 620.

INDUCEMENT, consideration; attraction; loadstone; magnet, magnetism, magnetic force; allectation [*obs.*], allective [*obs.*], temptation, enticement, *agacerie* [*F.*], allurement, witchery; bewitchment, bewitchery; charm; spell &c. 993; fascination, blandishment, cajolery; seduction, seducement; honeyed words, voice of the tempter, song of the Sirens; forbidden fruit, golden apple.

PERSUASIBILITY, persuasibleness, persuadability, persuadableness; attract-

615a. Absence of Motive. — N. ABSENCE OF MOTIVE; caprice &c. 608; chance &c. (*absence of design*) 621.

V. SCRUPLE &c. (*be unwilling*) 603; have no motive.

Adj. AIMLESS &c. (*chance*) 621; without rime or reason.

Adv. CAPRICIOUSLY, out of mere caprice.

616. Dissuasion. — N. DISSUASION, dehortation [*rare*], expostulation, remonstrance; deprecation &c. 766.

DISCOURAGEMENT, dehortative [*rare*], monitory, damper, wet blanket; contra-indicant.

CURB &c. (*means of restraint*) 752; constraint &c. (*restraint*) 751; check &c. (*hindrance*) 706.

RELUCTANCE &c. (*unwillingness*) 603; contraindication.

ability; impressibility, susceptibility; softness; persuasiveness, attractiveness; tantalization.

INFLUENCE, prompting, dictate, instance; impulse, impulsion; incitement, incitation; press, insistence, urge [*rare*], instigation; provocation &c. (*excitation of feeling*) 824; inspiration; persuasion, suasion; encouragement, advocacy; exhortation, hortation; advice &c. 695; solicitation &c. (*request*) 765; lobbyism; pull [*slang*].

INCENTIVE, stimulus, spur, fillip, whip, goad, ankus [*India*], rowel, provocative, whet, dram.

BRIBE, lure; decoy, decoy duck; bait, trail of a red herring; bribery and corruption; sop, sop to Cerberus.

TEMPTER, seducer, seductor, seductress; prompter, suggester, coaxer, wheedler, Siren, Circe, vampire [*colloq.*], vamp [*slang*]; instigator, *agent provocateur* [*F.*]; lobbyist; firebrand, incendiary.

V. DISSUADE, dehort [*rare*], cry out against, remonstrate, expostulate, warn, contraindicate.

DISINCLINE, indispose, shake, stagger; dispirit; discourage, dishearten, disenchant; deter; hold back, keep back &c. (*restrain*) 751; render averse &c. 603; repel; turn aside &c. (*deviation*) 279; wean from; act as a drag &c. (*hinder*) 706; throw cold water on, damp, cool, chill, blunt, calm, quiet, quench; deprecate &c. 766.

Adj. DISSUADING &c. *v.*; dissuasive; dehortatory [*rare*], dehortative [*rare*], expostulatory; monitive [*obs.*], monitory, monitorial.

DISSUADED &c. *v.*; admonitory; uninduced &c. (induce &c. 615); unpersuadable &c. (*obstinate*) 606; averse &c. (*unwilling*) 603; repugnant &c. (*dislike*) 867.

V. INDUCE, move; draw, draw on; bring in its train, give an impulse to &c. *n.*; inspire; put up to [*slang*], prompt, call up; attract, beckon.

STIMULATE &c. (*excite*) 824; spirit, spirit up, inspirit; rouse, arouse, animate, incite, provoke, instigate, set on, actuate; act upon, work upon, operate upon; encourage; pat –, clap- on the -back, – shoulder.

set an example, set the fashion; keep in countenance, back up.

INFLUENCE, weigh with, bias, sway, incline, dispose, predispose, turn the scale, inoculate; lead, – by the nose; have –, exercise –, influence- -with, – over, – upon; go –, come- round one [*colloq.*]; turn the head, magnetize; lobby [*chiefly U. S.*].

PERSUADE; prevail -with, – upon; overcome, carry; bring round, bring to one's senses; draw –, win – , gain –, talk- over; come over [*colloq.*]; procure, enlist, engage; invite, court.

TEMPT, seduce, overpersuade, entice, allure, captivate, fascinate, bewitch, carry away, charm, conciliate, wheedle, coax, lure, vamp [*slang*]; inveigle; tantalize; cajole &c. (*deceive*) 545.

BRIBE, tamper with, suborn, grease the palm, bait with a silver hook, gild the pill, make things pleasant, put a sop into the pan, throw a sop to, bait the hook.

ENFORCE, force; impel &c. (*push*) 276; propel &c. 284; whip, lash, goad, spur, prick, urge; egg on, hound on, hurry on; drag &c. 285; exhort; advise &c. 695; call upon &c., press &c. (*request*) 765; advocate.

BE PERSUADED &c.; yield to temptation, come round [*colloq.*]; concede &c. (*consent*) 762; obey a call; follow -advice, – the bent, – the dictates of; act on principle.

Adj. IMPULSIVE, motive; persuasive, persuasory [*rare*], hortative, hortatory; protreptical [*obs.*]; inviting, tempting, &c. *v.*; suasive, suasory [*obs.*], irresistible, seductive, attractive; fascinating &c. (*pleasing*) 829; provocative &c. (*exciting*) 824.

INDUCED &c. *v.*; disposed; persuadable &c. (*docile*) 602; spellbound; instinct –, taken –, smitten- with; inspired by &c. *v.*

Adv. BECAUSE, therefore &c. (*cause*) 155; from this motive, from that motive; for this reason, for that reason; for; by reason of, for the sake of, on the score of, on account of; out of, from, as, forasmuch as.

for all the world; on principle.

⁎⁎⁎ fax mentis incendium gloriæ; "temptation hath a music for all ears" [Willis]; "to beguile many and be beguiled by one" [*Othello*].

617. [Ostensible motive, ground, or reason.] **Plea.** — **N.** plea, pretext; allegation, advocation [*archaic*]; ostensible -motive, – ground, – reason; excuse &c. (*vindication*) 937; color; gloss, guise.

handle, peg to hang on; room, *locus standi* [*L.*]; stalking-horse, *cheval de bataille* [*F.*], cue.

loophole, starting-hole [*obs.*]; hole to creep out of, come-off [*colloq.*], way of escape.

pretense &c. (*untruth*) 546; put-off, subterfuge, dust thrown in the eye; blind; moonshine; mere –, shallow- pretext; lame -excuse, – apology; tub to a whale; false plea, sour grapes; makeshift, shift, white lie; special pleading &c. (*sophistry*) 477; soft sawder [*slang*] &c. (*flattery*) 933.

V. plead, allege; shelter oneself under the plea of; creep out of; tell a white lie; excuse &c. (*vindicate*) 937; color, gloss over, lend a color to; furnish a handle &c. *n.;* make a pretext of, make a handle of; use as a plea &c. *n.;* take one's stand upon, make capital out of; pretend &c. (*lie*) 544.

Adj. advocatory [*rare*], excusing; ostensible &c. (*manifest*) 525; alleged, apologetic; pretended &c. 545.

Adv. ostensibly; under the plea of, under the pretense of.

3. *Objects of Volition*

618. Good. — **N.** good, benefit, advantage; improvement &c. 658; greatest –, supreme- good; interest, service, behoof, behalf; weal [*archaic*]; main chance, *summum bonum* [*L.*]; commonwealth [*now rare*], commonweal *or* common weal; "consummation devoutly to be wished" [*Hamlet*]; gain, boot [*archaic*]; profit, harvest.

boon &c. (*gift*) 784; good turn; blessing, benison; world of good; piece of good -luck, – fortune; nuts [*now slang*], prize, windfall, godsend, waif, treasure-trove.

good fortune &c. (*prosperity*) 734; happiness &c. 827.

[Source of good] goodness &c. 648; utility &c. 644; remedy &c. 662; pleasure giving &c. 829.

V. benefit, profit, advantage, serve, help, avail, boot [*archaic*], good [*obs.*], do good to.

gain, prosper, flourish, thrive &c. 734.

Adj. commendable &c. 931; useful &c. 644; good &c., beneficial &c. 648.

Adv. well, aright, satisfactorily, favorably, not amiss; all for the best; to one's advantage &c. *n.;* in one's favor, in one's interest &c. *n.*

** so far so good; *magnum bonum;* "so shines a good deed in a naughty world" [*M. of V.*]; "from seeming evil still educing good" [Thomson]; "And learn the luxury of doing good" [Goldsmith]; "worthiest by being good, Far more than great or high" [Milton].

619. Evil. — **N.** evil, ill, harm, hurt, mischief, nuisance; machinations of the devil, Pandora's box, ills that flesh is heir to; mental suffering &c. (*pain*) 828.

[Evil spirit] demon &c. 980.

[Cause of evil] bane &c. 663.

[Production of evil] badness &c. 649; painfulness &c. 830; evildoer &c. 913.

blow, buffet, stroke, scratch, bruise, wound, gash, mutilation; mortal -blow, – wound; *immedicabile vulnus* [*L.*]; damage, loss &c. (*deterioration*) 659.

disadvantage, prejudice, drawback.

disaster, accident, casualty; mishap &c. (*misfortune*) 735; bad job [*colloq.*], devil to pay [*colloq.*]; calamity, bale [*chiefly poetic*], woe, fatal mischief, catastrophe, tragedy; ruin &c. (*destruction*) 162; adversity &c. 735.

outrage, wrong, injury, foul play; bad turn, ill turn; disservice; spoliation &c. 791; grievance, crying evil.

V. disserve, do disservice to, harm, injure, hurt.

be in trouble &c. (*adversity*) 735.

Adj. disastrous, bad &c. 649; awry, out of joint; disadvantageous; disserviceable, injurious, harmful.

Adv. amiss, wrong, ill, to one's cost.

** "man is born unto trouble as the sparks fly upward" [*Bible*]; "the evil that men do lives after them" [*Julius Cæsar*]; "broken with the storms of state" [*Henry VIII*]; "one only good, namely, knowledge; and one only evil, namely, ignorance" [Diogenes Laertius].

Section II. Prospective Volition[1]

1. *Conceptional Volition*

620. Intention. — N. intention, intent, intentionality; purpose; *quo animo* [*L.*]; project &c. 626; undertaking &c. 676; predetermination &c. 611; design, ambition.

contemplation, mind, animus, view, purview [*law*], proposal; study; look-out.

object, aim, end; final cause; *raison d'être* [*F.*]; *cui bono* [*L.*]; "the be-all and the end-all" [*Macbeth*]; drift &c. (*meaning*) 516; tendency &c. 176; destination, mark, point, butt, goal, target, bull's-eye, quintain; prey, quarry, game.

decision, determination, resolve; fixed –, set –, settled- purpose; ultimatum; resolution &c. 604; wish &c. 865; *arrière pensée* [*F.*]; motive &c. 615.

[study of final causes] teleology.

V. intend, purpose, design, mean; have to; propose to oneself; harbor a design; have in -view, – contemplation, – one's eye; have *in petto* [*It.*]; have an eye to.

bid for, labor for; be after, aspire to *or* after, endeavor after; be at, aim at, drive at, point at, level at; take aim; set before oneself; study to.

contemplate, meditate; take upon oneself &c. (*undertake*) 676; take into one's head; think of, dream of, talk of; premeditate &c. 611; compass [*legal*], calculate; destine, destinate; propose.

project &c. (*plan*) 626; have a mind to &c. (*be willing*) 602; desire &c. 865; pursue &c. 622.

Adj. intended &c. *v.*; intentional, advised, express, determinate; prepense &c. 611; bound for; intending &c. *v.*; disposed, inclined, minded; bent upon &c. (*earnest*) 604; at stake; on the -anvil, – tapis; in view, in prospect, in the breast of; *in petto* [*It.*]; teleological.

Adv. intentionally &c. *adj.*; advisedly, wittingly, knowingly, designedly, purposely, on purpose, by design, studiously, pointedly; with intent &c. *n.*; deliberately &c. (*with premeditation*) 611; with one's eyes open, in cold blood.

for; with a view to, with an eye to; in order -to, – that; to the end that,

621. [Absence of purpose.] Chance.[2] — N. chance &c. 156; lot, fate &c. (*necessity*) 601; luck; good luck &c. (*good*) 618; hoodoo, jinx [*slang*], jadoo *or* jadu [*Hind.*]; voodoo, voodooism; swastika *or* swastica, fylfot, gammadion; wheel of chance, Fortune's wheel; mascot.

speculation, venture, mere –, random- shot; blind bargain, leap in the dark; pig in a poke &c. (*uncertainty*) 475; fluke [*sporting cant*], potluck, flyer [*slang*], flutter [*slang*]; futures.

gambling, game of chance; drawing lots; sortilege, sortition [*obs.*]; *sortes, – Vergilianæ* [*L.*]; *rouge et noir* [*F.*], hazard, ante, chuck-a-luck *or* chuck-luck, crack-loo [*U. S.*]; craps; faro, faro bank; roulette, pitch and toss, chuck-farthing, cup tossing, heads or tails, cross and pile [*archaic*], dice, dice box, poker-dice; fan-tan [*Chinese*].

wager; gamble, risk, stake, pyramid, plunge; bet, betting; gambling; the turf.

gambling house, gaming house, gambling den, pool room, betting-house; bucket shop; joint [*slang*]; totalizator, totalizer [*slang*]; hell; betting ring; Wall Street, Stock Exchange, curb, curb market.

gambler, gamester, dicer, sport [*cant*], punter, plunger, speculator, hazarder, bookmaker, bookie [*colloq.*], man of the turf; pool shark [*colloq.*], adventurer.

V. chance &c. (*hap*) 156; stand a chance &c. (*be possible*) 470.

toss up; cast –, draw- lots; leave –, trust- -to chance, – to the chapter of accidents; tempt fortune; chance it, take one's chance; run –, incur –, encounter- the -risk, – chance; stand the hazard of the die.

speculate, try one's luck, set on a cast, raffle, put into a lottery, buy a pig in a poke, shuffle the cards.

risk, venture, hazard, stake; ante; lay, – a wager; make a bet, wager, bet, gamble, game, play for; play at chuck-farthing; play the ponies [*slang*]; play craps &c.

Adj. fortuitous &c. 156; uninten-

---

[1] That is, volition having reference to a future object.   [2] See note on 156.

with the intent that; for the purpose of, with the view of, in contemplation of, on account of.

in pursuance of, pursuant to; *quo animo* [*L.*]; to all intents and purposes.

** "hell is paved with good intentions" [Johnson]; *sublimi feriam sidera vertice* [Horace].

tional, unintended; accidental; not meant; undesigned, unpurposed; unpremeditated &c. 612; never thought of.

INDISCRIMINATE, promiscuous; undirected, random; aimless, driftless, designless, purposeless, causeless; without purpose.

POSSIBLE &c. 470.

Adv. CASUALLY &c. 156; unintentionally &c. *adj.*; unwittingly.

INCIDENTALLY, *en passant* [*F.*], by the way.

at random, at a venture, at haphazard; as luck would have it; in luck; out of luck; by chance, by good fortune; as it may happen.

Int. what luck! better luck next time!

** *acierta errando; dextro tempore;* "fearful concatenation of circumstances" [D. Webster]; "fortuitous combination of circumstances" [Dickens]; *le jeu est le fils d'avarice et le père du désespoir;* "the happy combination of fortuitous circumstances" [Scott]; "the fortuitous or casual concourse of atoms" [Bentley]; "a fool must now and then be right by chance" [Cowper]; "fortune is unstable, while our will is free" [Laertius].

622. [PURPOSE IN ACTION.] **Pursuit.**
— **N.** PURSUIT; pursuing &c. *v.*; prosecution; pursuance; enterprise &c. (*undertaking*) 676; business &c. 625; adventure &c. (*essay*) 675; quest &c. (*search*) 461; scramble, hue and cry, game; hobby; still-hunt.

CHASE, hunt, *battue* [*F.*], race, steeplechase, hunting, coursing; venation [*obs.*], venery; fox chase, fox hunting; sport, sporting; shooting, angling, fishing, hawking; shikar [*India*].

PURSUER; hunter, huntsman, the field; shikari [*India*], sportman, Nimrod; hound &c. 366.

V. PURSUE, prosecute, follow; run –, make –, be –, hunt –, prowl- after; shadow; carry on &c. (*do*) 680; be absorbed in; engage in &c. (*undertake*) 676; set about &c. (*begin*) 66; endeavor &c. 675; court &c. (*request*) 765; seek &c. (*search*) 461; aim at &c. (*intention*) 620; follow the trail &c. (*trace*) 461; fish for &c. (*experiment*) 463; press on &c. (*haste*) 684; run a race &c. (*velocity*) 274.

tread a path; take –, hold- a course; shape –, direct –, bend- one's -steps, – course; play a game; fight –, elbow- one's way; follow up; take to, take up; go in for; ride one's hobby.

CHASE, give chase, still-hunt, stalk, shikar [*India*], course, dog, hunt, hound; tread –, follow- on the heels of, &c. (*sequence*) 281; start game.

RUSH UPON; rush headlong &c. (*violence*) 173; ride at, run full tilt at; make a leap at, jump at, snatch at; run down.

623. [ABSENCE OF PURSUIT.] **Avoidance.** — **N.** AVOIDANCE, evasion, elusion; seclusion &c. 893.

avolation [*obs.*], flight; escape &c. 671; retreat &c. 287; recoil &c. 277; departure &c. 293; rejection &c. 610.

ABSTENTION, abstinence; forbearance; refraining &c. *v.*; inaction &c. 681; neutrality.

SHIRKER &c. *v.*; slacker [*colloq.*], shirk, quitter [*U. S.*], eye servant, truant; fugitive, refugee, runaway, runagate, deserter, renegade, backslider; maroon.

V. ABSTAIN, refrain, spare, not attempt; not do &c. 681; maintain the even tenor of one's way.

ESCHEW, keep from, let alone, have nothing to do with; keep –, stand –, hold- -aloof, – off; take no part in, have no hand in.

AVOID, shun; steer –, keep- clear of; fight shy of; keep one's distance, keep at a respectful distance; keep –, get- out of the way; evade, elude, turn away from; set one's face against &c. (*oppose*) 708; deny oneself.

SHRINK; hang –, hold –, draw- back; recoil &c. 277; retire &c. (*recede*) 287; flinch, blink, blench, shy, shirk, dodge, parry, make way for, give place to.

BEAT A RETREAT; turn tail, turn one's back; take to one's heels; run, run away, run for one's life; maroon; cut and run [*colloq.*]; be off, – like a shot; fly, flee, fly –, flee –, run away- from; take flight, take to flight; desert, elope; make off, scamper off, sneak off, shuffle off, sheer

Adj. PURSUING &c. *v.;* in quest of &c. (*inquiry*) 461; in pursuit, in full cry, in hot pursuit; on the scent.

Adv. AFTER; in pursuance of &c. (*intention*) 620.

Int. tallyho! yoicks! soho!

off; break –, burst –, tear oneself –, slip –, slink –, steal- -away, – away from; slip cable, part company, turn on one's heel; sneak out of, play truant, give one the go-by [*slang*], give leg bail [*slang*], take French leave, slope [*slang*], decamp, flit, bolt, abscond, levant [*slang, Eng.*], skedaddle [*dial. or slang, U. S.*], absquatulate [*U. S.*], cut one's stick [*slang*], walk one's chalks [*slang*], show the heels, show a clean (*or* light) pair of heels, make oneself scarce [*slang*]; escape &c. 671; go away &c. (*depart*) 293; abandon &c. 624; reject &c. 610.

lead one a dance, lead one a pretty dance; throw off the scent, play at hide and seek.

Adj. AVOIDING &c. *v.;* neutral; unsought, unattempted; shy of &c. (*unwilling*) 603; elusive, evasive; fugitive, runaway; shy, wild.

Adv. LEST, in order to avoid.

Int. forbear! keep off! hands off! *sauve qui peut!* [*F.*], devil take the hindmost!

⁎ "things unattempted yet in prose or rhyme" [*Paradise Lost*].

624. Relinquishment. — N. RELINQUISHMENT, abandonment: desertion, defection, secession, withdrawal; cave of Adullam; *nolle prosequi* [*L.*].

discontinuance &c. (*cessation*) 142; renunciation &c. (*recantation*) 607; abrogation &c. 756; resignation &c. (*retirement*) 757; desuetude &c. 614; cession &c. (*of property*) 782.

V. RELINQUISH, give up, abandon, desert, forsake, leave in the lurch; go back on [*colloq.*]; depart –, secede – withdraw- from; back out of [*colloq.*], back down from [*colloq.*]; leave, quit, take leave of, bid a long farewell; vacate &c. (*resign*) 757.

RENOUNCE &c. (*abjure*) 607; forego, have done with, drop; nol-pros [*law*]; disuse &c. 678; discard &c. 782; wash one's hands of; drop all idea of.

BREAK OFF, leave off; desist; stop &c. (*cease*) 142; hold one's hand, stay one's hand; quit one's hold; give over, shut up shop; throw up the -game, – cards.

give up the -point, – argument; pass to the order of the day, move the previous question, table, table the motion.

Adj. UNPURSUED; relinquished &c. *v.;* relinquishing &c. *v.*

Int. avast! &c. (*stop*) 142.

⁎ *aufgeschoben ist nicht aufgehoben; entbehre gern was du nicht hast.*

625. Business. — N. BUSINESS, occupation, employment, undertaking; pursuit &c. 622; what one is doing, what one is about; affair, concern, matter, case.

TASK, matter in hand, irons in the fire; thing to do, agendum (*pl.* agenda), work, job, chore [*U. S.*], errand, commission, mission, charge, care; duty &c. 926.

exercise; work &c. (*action*) 680; avocation, hobby; press of business &c. (*activity*) 682.

FUNCTION, part, rôle, cue; province, lookout [*colloq.*], department, capacity, sphere, orb [*now rare*], field, line; walk, – of life; beat, round, routine; race, career.

OFFICE, place, post, chargeship, incumbency, living; situation, berth, billet, appointment, employ [*rare*], service &c. (*servitude*) 749; engagement; undertaking &c. 676.

VOCATION, calling, profession, cloth, faculty; industry, art; industrial arts; craft, mystery [*obs.*], handicraft; trade &c. (*commerce*) 794.

V. OCCUPY ONESELF WITH; pass –, employ –, spend- one's time in; employ oneself -in, – upon; concern oneself with; make it one's business &c. *n.;* undertake &c. 676; enter a profession; betake oneself to, turn one's hand to; have to do with &c. (*do*) 680.

be about, be doing, be engaged in, be employed in, be occupied with, be at work on; have one's hands in, have in hand; have on one's -hands, – shoulders; bear the burden; have one's hands full &c. (*activity*) 682.

PLY ONE'S TASK, ply one's trade; drive a trade; carry on –, do –, transact-
-business, – a trade &c. *n.;* keep a shop; labor in one's vocation; pursue the even
tenor of one's way; attend to business, attend to one's work.

OFFICIATE, serve, act; act one's part, play one's part; do duty; serve –, discharge –, perform- the -office, – duties, – functions- of; hold –, fill- -an office,
– a place, – a situation; hold a portfolio.

BE IN THE HANDS OF, be on the stocks, be on the anvil; pass through one's hands.

Adj. BUSINESSLIKE; workaday; professional, vocational; official, functional; humming, busy &c. (*actively employed*) 682.

IN HAND, on hand; on *or* in one's hands; afoot; on foot, on the anvil; going on;
acting.

Adv. IN THE COURSE OF BUSINESS, all in the day's work; professionally &c. *adj.*

*** "a business with an income at its heels" [Cowper]; *amoto quæramus seria ludo* [Horace];
par negotiis neque supra [Tacitus]; "why not have a bit of romance in business when it costs
nothing?" [Shaw].

626. Plan. — **N.** PLAN, scheme, design, project, proposal, proposition, suggestion;
resolution, motion; precaution &c. (*provision*) 673; deep-laid &c. (*premeditated*) 611-
plan &c.; germ &c. (*cause*) 153.

SYSTEM &c. (*order*) 58; organization &c. (*arrangement*) 60.

OUTLINE, sketch, skeleton, draft *or* draught, *ébauche* [F.], *brouillon* [F.]; rough
-cast, – draft *or* draught, – copy; copy; proof, revise.

forecast, program *or* programme, prospectus; *carte du pays* [F.]; card; bill, protocol; order of the day, memoranda, list of agenda; bill of fare &c. (*food*) 298; base
of operations; platform, plank, slate [*U. S.*], ticket [*U. S.*].

rôle; policy &c. (*line of conduct*) 692.

CONTRIVANCE, invention, expedient, receipt, nostrum, artifice, device; pipelaying
[*U. S.*]; stratagem &c. (*cunning*) 702; trick &c. (*deception*) 545; alternative, loophole; shift &c. (*substitute*) 147; last shift &c. (*necessity*) 601, gadget.

MEASURE, step; stroke, – of policy; masterstroke; trump, trump card, courtcard;
cheval de bataille [F.], great gun; *coup, – d'état* [F.]; clever –, bold –, good- -move,
– hit, – stroke; bright -thought, – idea; great idea.

INTRIGUE, cabal, plot, conspiracy, complot, machination; underplot, counterplot;
mine, countermine.

SCHEMER, schemist [*rare*], schematist [*obs.*]; strategist, machinator; Machiavellian,
Machiavellist, conspirator; intrigant &c. (*cunning*) 702.

PROJECTOR, promoter, designer &c. *v.;* organizer, founder (*fem.* foundress), author,
artist, builder.

V. PLAN, scheme, design, frame, contrive, project, forecast, sketch; devise, invent
&c. (*imagine*) 515; set one's wits to work &c. 515; spring a project; fall upon, hit
upon; strike –, chalk –, cut –, lay –, map- out; lay down a plan; shape –, mark-
out a course; predetermine &c. 611; concert, preconcert, preëstablish; prepare &c.
673; hatch, – a plot; concoct; take -steps, – measures.

SYSTEMATIZE, organize; cast, recast, arrange &c. 60; digest, mature.

PLOT; counterplot, mine, countermine, dig a mine; lay a train; intrigue &c.
(*cunning*) 702.

Adj. PLANNED &c. *v.;* strategic *or* strategical.

PLANNING &c. *v.;* in course of preparation &c. 673; under consideration, on the
tapis, on the carpet, on the table.

*** "a mighty maze! but not without a plan" [Pope]; "lofty designs must close in like effects"
[Browning].

627. Method. [PATH.] — **N.** METHOD, way, manner, wise [*rare, exc. in phrases*],
gait, form, mode, fashion, tone, guise; *modus operandi* [L.]; procedure &c. (*line of
conduct*) 692.

PATH, road, route, course; line of way, line of road; trajectory, orbit, track, beat,
tack.

STEPS; stair, staircase; flight of -steps, - stairs; ladder, stile; perron.

BRIDGE, footbridge, viaduct, pontoon, stepping-stone, plank, gangway; drawbridge.

pass, ford, ferry, tunnel; pipe &c. 260.

MEANS OF ACCESS, adit, entrance, approach, passage, cloister, covered way, lobby, corridor, aisle; alley, lane, vennel [*Scot. & dial. Eng.*], avenue, artery, channel; gateway &c. (*opening*) 260; door, backdoor, backstairs; secret passage; covert way.

ROADWAY, express; thoroughfare; highway, macadam, parkway, boulevard; turnpike -, royal -, state -, coach- road; broad -, King's -, Queen's- highway; beaten -track, - path; horse -, bridle- -road, - track, - path; walk, *trottoir* [*F.*], footpath, pathway, pavement, flags, sidewalk, by-road, crossroad; by -, cross- -path, - way; cut; short cut & (*mid-course*) 628; *carrefour* [*F.*]; private -, occupation- road; highways and byways; railroad, railway, trolley track, tramroad, tramway; towpath; causeway; street &c. (*abode*) 189; stairway, gangway; speedway; canal &c. (*conduit*) 350.

Adv. HOW; in what way, in what manner; by what mode; so, thus, in this way, after this fashion.

ONE WAY OR ANOTHER, anyhow; somehow or other &c. (*instrumentality*) 631; by way of; *viâ* [*L.*]; *in transitu* [*L.*] &c. 270; on the high road to, on the way to.

° *hæ tibi erunt artes;* "the noblest prospect which a Scotchman ever sees is the high-road that leads him to England" [Johnson].

---

628. Mid-course. — N. MID-COURSE, midway [*rare*], middle way, middle course; moderation; mean &c. 29; middle &c. 68; *juste milieu* [*F.*], *mezzo termine* [*L.*], golden mean, *ariston metron* [*Gr.* ἄριστον μέτρον], *aurea mediocritas* [*L.*]; fifty-fifty [*colloq.*].

SHORTCUT, crosscut; straight &c. (*direct*) 278 -course, - path; great-circle sailing.

COMPROMISE, half measures, half-and-half measures; neutrality.

*°***V.** KEEP THE GOLDEN MEAN; keep in -, steer -, preserve- -a middle, - an even- course; avoid both Scylla and Charybdis; go straight &c. (*direct*) 278.

COMPROMISE, make a compromise, go fifty-fifty [*colloq.*], concede half, go halfway.

Adj. NEUTRAL, average, even, evenly balanced; impartial, moderate; straight &c. (*direct*) 278.

Adv. MIDWAY, in the mean; in moderation.

° *medium tenuere beati; est modus in rebus* [Horace]; "moderation is the virtue best adapted to the dawn of prosperity" [Pitt].

629. Circuit. — N. CIRCUIT, roundabout way, digression, detour, circumbendibus [*humorous*], circumambience, circumambiency, circumambulation, ambages, loop; winding &c. (*circuition*) 311; zigzag &c. (*deviation*) 279.

V. GO ROUND ABOUT, circumambulate, perform a circuit, make a circuit, go out of one's way; make a detour; meander &c. (*deviate*) 279.

lead a pretty dance; beat about, - the bush; make two bites of a cherry.

Adj. CIRCUITOUS, circumambient, circumambulatory, indirect, roundabout; zigzag &c. (*deviating*) 279; backhanded.

Adv. IN A ROUNDABOUT WAY; by a side wind, by an indirect course; from pillar to post.

° the longest way round is the shortest way home.

---

630. Requirement. — N. REQUIREMENT, need, wants, necessities; necessaries, - of life; stress, exigency, pinch, *sine quâ non* [*L.*], matter of necessity; case of need, case of life or death.

desideratum &c. (*desire*) 865; want &c. (*deficiency*) 640.

NEEDFULNESS, essentiality, necessity, indispensability, urgency, prerequisite; the least one can -do, - require.

REQUISITION &c. (*request*) 765 (*exaction*) 741; run; demand for, call for.

CHARGE, claim, command, injunction, mandate, order, precept, ultimatum.

V. REQUIRE, need, want, have occasion for; not be able to do without, not able to dispense with; prerequire.

BE NECESSARY &c. *adj.*; stand in need of; lack &c. 640; desiderate; desire &c. 865.

RENDER NECESSARY, necessitate, create a necessity for, call for, put in requisition; make a requisition &c. (*ask for*) 765, (*demand*) 741.

Adj. NECESSARY; required &c. *v.*; requisite, needful, imperative, essential, indispensable, prerequisite; called for; in demand, in request.

in want of; destitute of &c. 640.

URGENT, exigent, pressing, instant, crying, absorbing.

Adv. OF NECESSITY; *ex necessitate rei* [*L.*] &c. (*necessarily*) 601; out of -stern necessity, - bitter need; at a pinch.

⁎⁎ there is no time to lose; it cannot be -spared, - dispensed with; *mendacem memorem esse oportet* [Quintilian]; *necessitas non habet legem; nec tecum possum vivere nec sine te* [Martial]; needs must when the devil drives; "necessity has no law" [Rabelais]; "necessity's sharp pinch" [*Lear*]; "Socrates said, 'those who want fewest things are nearer to the gods'" [Diogenes Laertius].

2. *Subservience to Ends*

1. *Actual Subservience*

631. Instrumentality.— N. INSTRUMENTALITY; aid &c. 707; subservience *or* subserviency, intermediacy, intermediation, mediation, intervention, medium, intermedium, intermediary, interagent, intermediate, mediating agency, vehicle, hand; agency &c. 170.

minister, handmaid; midwife, *accoucheur* [*F.*], *accoucheuse* [*fem., F.*], obstetrician; servant, slave, maid, valet; friend at court; go-between; cat's-paw; stepping-stone.

KEY, master -, pass -, latch- key; "open sesame"; passport, *passe-partout* [*F.*], safe-conduct; pull [*slang*], influence.

INSTRUMENT &c. 633; expedient &c. (*plan*) 626; means &c. 632.

V. SUBSERVE, minister, mediate, intervene, intermediate, come -, go- between; interpose; pull the -strings, - wires; use one's influence; be instrumental &c. *adj.*; pander to; officiate; tend.

Adj. INSTRUMENTAL; useful &c. 644; ministerial, subservient, serviceable; mediatorial, intermedial, intermediary, intermediate, intervening; conducive.

Adv. THROUGH, by, *per* [*L.*]; whereby, thereby, hereby; by the agency of &c. 170; by dint of; by *or* in virtue of; through the medium of &c. *n.*; along with; on the shoulders of; by means of &c. 632; by *or* with the aid of &c. (*assistance*) 707.

SOMEHOW; *per fas et nefas* [*L.*]; by fair means or foul; somehow or other; by hook or by crook.

⁎⁎ "man is thy most awful instrument In working out a pure intent" [Wordsworth].

632. Means. — N. MEANS, resources, wherewithal, ways and means; capital &c. (*money*) 800; revenue, income; stock in trade &c. 636; provision &c. 637; reserve, remnant, last resource, a shot in the locker [*colloq.*]; appliances &c. (*machinery*) 633; means and appliances; conveniences; cards to play; expedients &c. (*measures*) 626; two strings to one's bow; wheels within wheels; sheet anchor &c. (*safety*) 666; aid &c. 707; medium &c. 631.

V. PROVIDE THE WHEREWITHAL; find -, have -, possess- means &c. *n.*; have something laid by, - for a rainy day; have powerful friends, have friends at court; have something to draw on; beg, borrow, or steal.

Adj. INSTRUMENTAL &c. 631; MECHANICAL &c. 633.

RELIABLE, trustworthy, efficient; honorable &c. (*upright*) 939.

Adv. BY MEANS OF, with; by -what, - all, - any, - some- means; wherewith, herewith, therewith; wherewithal.

how &c. (*in what manner*) 627; through &c. (*by the instrumentality of*) 631; with *or* by the aid of &c. (*assistance*) 707; by the agency of &c. 170.

⁎⁎ "my extremest means Lie all unlock'd to your occasions" [*M. of V.*].

633. Instrument. — N. MACHINERY, mechanism, engineering.

INSTRUMENT, organ, tool, implement, utensil, machine, engine, lathe, gin, mill; air –, caloric –, heat –, steam –, internal-combustion- engine; motor.

EQUIPMENT, gear, tackle, tackling; rigging, apparatus, appliances; plant, *matériel* [*F.*]; harness, trappings, fittings, accouterments *or* accoutrements, impedimenta; equipment, equipage; appointments, furniture, upholstery; chattels; paraphernalia &c. (*belongings*) 780.

MECHANICAL POWERS; mechanical -advantage, – movements, – contrivances; leverage; fulcrum lever, crow, crowbar, gavelock [*Scot. & dial. Eng.*], jemmy, jimmy, marline spike *or* marlinspike, handspike, arm, limb, wing; oar, paddle &c. (*navigation*) 267.

wheel and axle; wheelwork, clockwork; rolling contact; epicyclic train; revolving lever; wheels within wheels; pinion, crank, winch; cam; capstan &c. (*lift*) 307; wheel &c. (*rotation*) 312; bevel gearing, spur gearing, universal joint; fly wheel, governor, turbine, water wheel; pump, lift-pump, force-pump, hydraulic ram.

pulley, crane, derrick; belt, open belt, crossed belt; cone pulley, stepped speed pulley.

inclined plane; wedge; screw; jack; spring, mainspring; can hook, glut, heald, heddle, loom, shuttle, jenny, parbuckle, sprag.

[TOOLS &c.] hammer &c. (*impulse*) 276; edge tool &c. (*cut*) 253; turnscrew, screw driver *or* screwdriver; borer &c. 262; vise, teeth, &c. (*hold*) 781; nail, rope &c. (*join*) 45; peg &c. (*hang*) 214; support &c. 215; spoon &c. (*vehicle*) 272; arms &c. 727.

handle, hilt, haft *or* heft, shaft, shank, blade, trigger, tiller, rudder, helm, treadle, pedal, key; knocker.

Adj. INSTRUMENTAL &c. 631.

MECHANICAL, machinal [*rare*]; brachial; propulsive, driving, hoisting, elevating, lifting.

useful, labor-saving, ingenious; simple; complicated; well made, well fitted, sharp, in good order, well equipped.

⁎⁎⁎ "the tools to him that can handle them" [Carlyle]; "there is no jesting with edge tools" [Beaumont and Fletcher]; a good workman is known by his tools.

634. Substitute. — N. SUBSTITUTE &c. 147; proxy, alternate, understudy; deputy &c. 759; *badli* [*Hind.*].

⁎⁎⁎ "man, proud man, Drest in a little brief authority" [*M. for M.*]; "a substitute shines brightly as a king, until a king be by" [*M. of V.*].

635. Materials. — N. MATERIAL, raw material, stuff, stock, staple; ore.

[BUILDING MATERIAL] marble, granite, limestone, freestone, sandstone, brown stone; stone, metal, brick, bricks and mortar; chinking, mortar, lime, chunam [*India*], clay, plaster, daubing, concrete, cement, reënforced concrete; unburnt brick, adobe; composition, compo; slates, tiles; whitewash &c. 223.

wood, timber, clapboard, shingle, shake, puncheon, log, rafter, beam, joist; two-by-four, three-by-four; post, upright, stud, lath; wall board.

MATERIALS; supplies, munition, fuel, grist, household stuff; crockery &c. 384; pabulum &c. (*food*) 298; oilcloth, linoleum; ammunition &c. (*arms*) 727; contingents; relay, reënforcement; baggage &c. (*personal property*) 780; means &c. 632.

FABRICS, calico, cambric, cashmere, linen, cotton, wool, silk; muslin, lawn, voile, gingham, dimity, broadcloth, homespun, serge, tweed, crêpe de chine, chiffon, satin, velvet.

Adj. raw &c. (*unprepared*) 674; finished; wooden &c. *n.;* adobe.

⁎⁎⁎ "all the means of action — The shapeless masses, the materials — Lie everywhere about us" [Longfellow]; "The carpenter dresses his plank — the tongue of his fore-plane whistles its wild ascending lisp" [Whitman].

636. Store. — **N.** STOCK, fund, mine, vein, lode, quarry; spring; fount, fountain; well, wellspring [*obs. exc. fig.*]; orchard, garden, farm; milch cow; hen.

STOCK IN TRADE, supply; heap &c. (*collection*) 72; treasure; reserve, *corps de réserve* [*F.*], reserve fund, nest egg, savings, *bonne bouche* [*F.*].

CROP, harvest, vintage, yield, product, gleaning.

STORE, accumulation, hoard; mow, rick, stack; lumber; relay &c. (*provision*) 637.

STOREHOUSE, storeroom, store closet; depository, depot, cache, repository, reservatory [*obs.*], repertory; repertorium [*rare*]; promptuary, warehouse, godown [*Oriental*], entrepôt [*F.*], magazine; buttery, larder, spence [*dial. Eng.*]; garner, granary, grain elevator, silo; cannery, safe-deposit vault, stillroom, bank &c. (*treasury*) 802; armory; arsenal; dock; freight yard, train shed, car-barn, power station; stable, barn, byre, cowhouse; piggery; hen house; fish hatchery; hothouse, conservatory.

quiver, bandoleer; coffer &c. (*receptacle*) 191.

RESERVOIR, cistern, *aljibar* [*Sp. Am.*], tank, pond, mill pond; gasometer.

[COLLECTIONS] library, public library, library of Congress, British Museum, Bodleian, Bibliothek; gallery, art gallery, picture gallery, Louvre, museum, Madame Tussaud's, zoölogical garden, zoo [*colloq.*], aquarium, menagerie.

WORK OF REFERENCE, dictionary, lexicon, encyclopedia *or* encyclopædia, cyclopedia *or* cyclopædia, thesaurus, atlas, concordance, anthology.

CONSERVATION; storing &c. *v.;* storage.

file, letter file, card index, portfolio, budget; photographic -plate, – film; memory.

V. STORE; put by, lay by, set by; stow away; set apart, lay apart; store up, hoard up, treasure up, lay up, heap up, put up, garner up, save up; bank; cache; accumulate, amass, hoard, fund, garner, save.

RESERVE; keep back, hold back; husband, – one's resources.

DEPOSIT; stow, stack, load; harvest; heap, collect &c. 72; lay in store &c. *adj.;* keep, file [papers]; lay in &c. (*provide*) 637; preserve &c. 670.

Adj. STORED &c. *v.;* in store, in reserve, in ordinary; spare, supernumerary.

Adv. for a rainy day, for a nest egg, to fall back upon; on deposit.

⁎ *adde parvum parvo magnus acervus erit;* "cast thy bread upon the waters" [*Bible*].

---

637. Provision. — **N.** PROVISION, supply; grist, – to the mill; subvention &c. (*aid*) 707; resources &c. (*means*) 632; groceries, grocery.

providing &c. *v.;* purveyance; reénforcement; commissariat.

PROVENDER &c. (*food*) 298; ensilage; viaticum; ration; emergency –, ironration.

CATERER, purveyor, provider, commissary, quartermaster, steward; purser, housekeeper, manciple, feeder, batman, victualer *or* victualler, comprador *or* compradore [*China*]; innkeeper, landlord, innholder, mine host, khansamah [*India*], *restaurateur* [*F.*]; grocer, green grocer, huckster, fishmonger, provision merchant; sutler &c. (*merchant*) 797.

PROVISION SHOP, provision store, meat shop, fish store; market, public market; grocery [*U. S.*], – shop, – store.

V. PROVIDE; make -provision, – due provision for; lay in, – a stock, – a store.

---

638. Waste. — **N.** CONSUMPTION, expenditure, exhaustion; dispersion &c. 73; ebb; leakage &c. (*exudation*) 295; loss &c. 776; wear and tear; waste; prodigality &c. 818; misuse &c. 679; wasting &c. *v.;* rubbish &c. (*useless*) 645.

V. CONSUME, spend, expend, use, swallow up; exhaust; impoverish; spill, drain, empty, deplete; disperse &c. 73.

cast –, fool –, muddle –, throw –, fling –, fritter- away; burn the candle at both ends, waste; squander &c. 818.

LABOR IN VAIN &c. (*useless*) 645; "waste its sweetness on the desert air" [Gray]; cast pearls before swine; employ a steam engine to crack a nut, waste powder and shot, break a butterfly on a wheel; cut blocks with a razor, pour water into a sieve, tilt at windmills.

RUN TO WASTE; ebb; leak &c. (*run out*) 295; melt away, run dry, dry up; spoil.

SUPPLY, suppeditate [*obs.*]; furnish; find, find one in; arm.

cater, victual, provision, purvey, forage; beat up for; stock, – with; make good, replenish; fill, – up; recruit, feed.

STORE, have in –store, – reserve; keep, keep by one; have to fall back upon; store &c. 636; provide against a rainy day &c. (*economy*) 817; conserve, keep, preserve, lay by, gather into barns.

⁎ "soul, thou hast much goods laid up for many years" [*Bible*].

639. Sufficiency. — N.

SUFFICIENCY, adequacy, enough, wherewithal, *quantum sufficit* [*L.*], satisfaction, competence; no less.

MEDIOCRITY &c. (*average*) 29.

FILL; fullness &c. (*completeness*) 52; plenitude, plenty; abundance; copiousness &c. *adj.*; amplitude, galore [*rare*], lots [*colloq.*], profusion; full measure; "good measure, pressed down, and shaken together, and running over" [*Bible*].

LUXURIANCE &c. (*fertility*) 168; affluence &c. (*wealth*) 803; fat of the land; "a land flowing with milk and honey" [*Bible*]; cornucopia; horn of -plenty, – Amalthæa; mine &c. (*stock*) 636.

OUTPOURING; flood &c. (*great quantity*) 31; tide &c. (*river*) 348; repletion &c. (*redundance*) 641; satiety &c. 869.

RICH MAN &c. (*wealth*) 803; financier, banker, creditor &c. 805; plutocrat.

V. BE SUFFICIENT &c. *adj.*; suffice; do, just do [*both colloq.*], satisfy, pass muster; have enough &c. *n.*; eat –, drink –, have- one's fill; roll in, swim in; wallow in &c. (*superabundance*) 641; wanton.

ABOUND, exuberate, teem, flow, stream, rain, shower down; pour, pour in; swarm; bristle with; superabound.

RENDER SUFFICIENT &c. *adj.*; replenish &c. (*fill*) 52.

Adj. SUFFICIENT, enough, adequate, up to the mark, commensurate, competent, satisfactory, valid, tangible.

MODERATE &c. (*temperate*) 953; measured.

AMPLE; full &c. (*complete*) 52; plenty, plentiful, plenteous; plenty as blackberries; copious, abundant; abounding &c. *v.*; replete, enough and to spare, flush; chock-full or choke-full; well-stocked, well-provided; liberal; unstinted, unstinting; stintless; without

Adj. WASTED &c. *v.*; gone to waste, useless, rendered useless, made unavailable; run to seed; dried up; at a low ebb.

WASTEFUL &c. (*prodigal*) 818; penny wise and pound foolish.

⁎ *magno conatu magnas nugas; le jeu ne vaut pas la chandelle;* "idly busy rolls their world away" [Goldsmith]; "Time wasted is existence, used is life" [Young]; "O, call back yesterday, bid time return" [*Richard II*].

640. Insufficiency. — N.

INSUFFICIENCY, inadequacy, inadequateness; incompetence &c. (*impotence*) 158; deficiency &c. (*incompleteness*) 53; imperfection &c. 651; shortcoming &c. 304; paucity; stint; scantiness &c. (*smallness*) 32; none to spare; bare subsistence.

SCARCITY, dearth; want, need, lack, poverty, exigency; inanition, starvation, famine, drought or drouth.

DOLE, mite, pittance; short -allowance, – commons; half rations; banyan day; fast day, Lent.

DEPLETION, emptiness, poorness &c. *adj.*; vacancy, flaccidity; ebb tide; low water; "a beggarly account of empty boxes" [*Rom. and Jul.*]; indigence &c. 804; insolvency &c. (*nonpayment*) 808.

POOR MAN, pauper &c. 804; bankrupt &c. (*nonpayment*) 808.

MISER, niggard &c. (*parsimony*) 819.

V. BE INSUFFICIENT &c. *adj.*; not suffice &c. 639; kick the beam; come short of &c. 304; run dry.

WANT, lack, need, require; caret [*L.*]; be in want &c. (*poor*) 804; live from hand to mouth.

RENDER INSUFFICIENT &c. *adj.*; drain of resources; impoverish &c. (*waste*) 638; stint &c. (*begrudge*) 819; put on short -allowance, – commons.

do insufficiently &c. *adv.*; scotch the snake.

Adj. INSUFFICIENT, inadequate; too little &c. 32; not enough &c. 639; unequal to; incompetent &c. (*impotent*) 158; perfunctory &c. (*neglect*) 460; deficient &c. (*incomplete*) 53; wanting &c. *v.*; imperfect &c. 651; ill-furnished, ill-provided, ill-stored, ill-off.

SHORT OF, out of, destitute of, devoid of, bereft of &c. 789, denuded of; slack, at a low ebb; empty, vacant, bare; dry, drained.

stint; unsparing, unmeasured; lavish &c. 641; wholesale.

unexhausted; unwasted; exhaustless, inexhaustible.

RICH; luxuriant &c. (*fertile*) 168; affluent &c. (*wealthy*) 803; wantless; big with &c. (*pregnant*) 161.

Adv. SUFFICIENTLY, amply &c. *adj.*; full; in abundance &c. *n.*; with no sparing hand; to one's heart's content, *ad libitum* [L.], without stint; to the good.

** "cut and come again" [Crabbe]; das Beste ist gut genug; "scatter plenty o'er a smiling land" [Gray].

UNPROVIDED, unsupplied, unfurnished; unreplenished, unfed; unstored, untreasured; empty-handed.

MEAGER *or* meagre, poor, thin, scrimp, sparing, stunted, spare, stinted; starved, starveling, emaciated, undernourished, underfed, half-starved, famine-stricken, famished; jejune.

SCARCE; not to be had, – for love or money, – at any price; scurvy; stingy &c. 819; at the end of one's tether; without resources &c. 632; in want &c. (*poor*) 804; in debt &c. 806; scant &c. (*small*) 32.

Adv. insufficiently &c. *adj.*; in default of, for want of; failing.

** semper avarus eget [Horace]; "a needy, hollow-eyed, sharp-looking wretch" [M. for M.]; "thou art weighed in the balances, and art found wanting" [Bible].

641. Redundance. — N. REDUNDANCE; too much, too many; superabundance, superfluity, superfluence [*obs.*], supersaturation; nimiety [*rare*], transcendency, exuberance, profuseness; profusion &c. (*plenty*) 639; repletion, enough in all conscience, *satis superque* [L.], lion's share; more than enough &c. 639; plethora, engorgement, congestion, load, surfeit, sickener; turgescence &c. (*expansion*) 194; overdose, overmeasure, oversupply, overflow; inundation &c. (*water*) 348; avalanche, deluge.

pleonasm &c. (*diffuseness*) 573; too many irons in the fire; *embarras de richesses* [F.]; embarrassment of riches; money to burn [*colloq.*].

ACCUMULATION &c. (*store*) 636; heap &c. 72; drug, – in the market; glut; crowd; burden.

EXCESS, surplus, overplus; epact; margin; remainder &c. 40; duplicate; surplusage, expletive; work of supererogation; bonus, bonanza [U. S.].

LUXURY; extravagance &c. (*prodigality*) 818; exorbitance, lavishment; intemperance &c. 954.

V. SUPERABOUND, overabound; know no bounds, swarm; meet one at every turn; creep with, bristle with; overflow; run –, flow –, well –, brim- over; run riot; overrun, overstock, overlay, overcharge, overdose, overfeed, overburden , overload, overdo, overwhelm, overshoot the mark &c. (*go beyond*) 303; surcharge, supersaturate, gorge, glut, load, drench, whelm, inundate, deluge, flood; drug, – the market; hepatize.

send –, carry– -coals to Newcastle, – owls to Athens; teach one's grandmother to suck eggs [*colloq.*]; *pisces natare docere* [L.]; kill the slain, butter one's bread on both sides, put butter upon bacon; employ a steam engine to crack a nut &c. (*waste*) 638.

wallow in; roll in &c. (*plenty*) 639; remain on one's hands, hang heavy on hand, go a-begging *or* go begging; exaggerate &c. 549.

CLOY, choke, accloy [*archaic*], suffocate; pile up, lay on thick; lay it on, – with a trowel; impregnate with; lavish &c. (*squander*) 818.

Adj. REDUNDANT; too much, too many; exuberant, inordinate, superabundant, excess, overmuch, replete, profuse, lavish; prodigal &c. 818; exorbitant; overweening; extravagant; overcharged &c. *v.*; supersaturated, drenched, overflowing; running -over, – to waste, – down.

CRAMMED –, filled- to overflowing; gorged, stuffed, smothered, ready to burst; dropsical, turgid, plethoric; full-blooded, hæmatose *or* hematose; obese &c. 194.

SUPERFLUOUS, unnecessary, needless, supervacaneous [*obs.*], uncalled for, to spare, in excess; over and above &c. (*remainder*) 40; *de trop* [F.]; adscititious &c. (*additional*) 37; supernumerary &c. (*reserve*) 636; on one's hands, spare, duplicate, supererogatory, expletory, expletive; *un peu fort* [F.].

Adv. OVER AND ABOVE; over much, too much; too far; over, too; without –, beyond –, out of- measure; with . . . to spare; over head and ears; over one's head; up to one's -eyes, - ears; extra; beyond the mark &c. (*overrun*) 303; *acervatim* [*L.*].

. it never rains but it pours; *fortuna multis dat nimium nulli satis;* "to gild refined gold, to paint the lily, to throw a perfume on the violet" [Shakespeare].

2. Degree of Subservience

642. Importance. — **N.** IMPORTANCE, consequence, moment, prominence, consideration, mark, materialness, materiality.

greatness &c. 31; superiority &c. 33; notability &c. (*repute*) 873; weight &c. (*influence*) 175; value &c. (*goodness*) 648; usefulness &c. 644.

IMPORT, significance, concern; emphasis, interest.

GRAVITY, seriousness, solemnity; no joke, no laughing matter; pressure, urgency, stress; matter of life and death.

MEMORABILIA, notabilia, great doings; red-letter day.

SALIENT POINT, outstanding feature; great -thing, - point; main chance, "the be-all and the end-all" [*Macbeth*]; cardinal point; substance, gist &c. (*essence*) 5; sum and substance, gravamen, head and front; important –, principal –, prominent –, essential- part; half the battle; *sine quâ non* [*L.*]; breath of one's nostrils &c. (*life*) 359; cream, salt, core, kernel, heart, nucleus; key, keynote; keystone; corner stone; trump card &c. (*device*) 626.

CHIEF, top sawyer, first fiddle, prima donna, triton among the minnows; "it" [*U. S.*]; the only pebble on the beach [*U. S.*]; burra (*or* bara) sahib [*India*]; bigwig &c. 875.

V. BE IMPORTANT &c. *adj.;* be somebody, be something; import, signify, matter, be an object; carry weight &c. (*influence*) 175; make a figure &c. (*repute*) 873; be in the ascendant, come to the front, lead the way, take the lead, play first fiddle, throw all else into the shade; lie at the root of; deserve –, merit –, be worthy of- -notice, – regard, – consideration.

VALUE; attach –, ascribe –, give- importance &c. *n.*- to; care for; set store -upon, – by; mark &c. 550; mark with a white stone, underline; write –, put –, print- in -italics, – capitals, – large letters, – large type, – bold-faced type,

643. Unimportance. — **N.** UNIMPORTANCE, insignificance, nothingness, immateriality.

TRIVIALITY, levity, frivolity, fribble; paltriness &c. *adj.;* poverty; smallness &c. 32; vanity &c. (*uselessness*) 645; matter of indifference &c. 866; no object.

NOTHING, – to signify, – worth speaking of, – particular, – to boast of, – to speak of; small –, no great –, trifling &c. *adj.*- matter; mere joke, mere nothing; hardly –, scarcely- anything; nonentity, small beer, cipher; no great shakes [*colloq.*], *peu de chose* [*F.*]; child's play.

TOY, plaything, popgun, paper pellet, gimcrack, gewgaw, bauble, trinket, bagatelle, kickshaw, knickknack, whimwham, trifle, "trifles light as air" [*Othello*].

TRUMPERY, trash, rubbish, stuff, *fatras* [*F.*], frippery; "leather or prunello" [Pope]; fiddle-faddle [*colloq.*], finglefangle; chaff, drug, froth, bubble, smoke, cobweb; weed; refuse &c. (*inutility*) 645; scum &c. (*dirt*) 653.

JOKE, jest, snap of the fingers, snap of one's thumb; fudge &c. (*unmeaning*) 517; fiddlestick, pack of nonsense, mere farce.

TRIFLE, straw, pin, fig, fico [*archaic*], button, rush; bulrush, feather, half-penny, farthing, brass farthing, doit, peppercorn, iota, tinker's dam (*or* damn), continental [*U. S.*], jot, mote, rap, pinch of snuff, old song; cent, mill, picayune [*colloq.*]; pai, pice [*both India*]; pistareen, red cent [*U. S.*].

nine days' wonder, *ridiculus mus* [*L.*]; flash in the pan &c. (*impotence*) 158; much ado about nothing &c. (*overestimation*) 482; tempest –, storm- in a teapot.

MINUTIÆ, details, minor details, small fry; dust in the balance, feather in the scale, drop in the ocean, fleabite, pin prick, molehill.

V. BE UNIMPORTANT &c. *adj.;* not matter &c. 642; go for –, matter –,

– letters of gold; accentuate, emphasize, lay stress on.

MAKE MUCH OF; make -a fuss, – a stir, – a piece of work, – much ado- about.

Adj. IMPORTANT; of importance &c. *n.;* momentous, material; to the point; not to be -overlooked, – despised, – sneezed at [*colloq.*]; egregious; weighty &c. (*influential*) 175; of note &c. (*repute*) 873; notable, prominent, salient, signal; memorable, remarkable; worthy of -remark, – notice; never to be forgotten; stirring, eventful.

in the front rank, first-rate, A1 *or* A number 1 [*colloq.*], first chop [*Anglo-Ind. & colloq.*]; superior &c. 33; considerable &c. (*great*) 31; marked &c. *v.;* rare &c. 137.

GRAVE, serious, earnest, noble, grand, solemn, impressive, commanding, imposing.

URGENT, pressing, critical, instant.

PARAMOUNT, essential, vital, all-absorbing, radical, cardinal, chief, main, prime, primary, principal, leading, capital, foremost, overruling; of vital &c. importance.

SIGNIFICANT, telling, trenchant, emphatic, pregnant; *tanti* [*L.*].

Adv. IN THE MAIN; materially &c. *adj.;* above all, in the first place, before everything else; *kat' exochen* [*Gr.* κατ' ἐξοχήν], *par excellence* [*F.*], to crown all.

** expende Hannibalem! [Juvenal]; *delenda est Carthago!* [Cato]; "first cast out the beam out of thine own eye" [*Bible*]; "we talked about all those great things for which literature is too small and only life large enough" [Chesterton].

signify- -little, – nothing, – little or nothing; not matter a straw &c. *n.*

make light of &c. (*underestimate*) 483; catch at straws &c. (*overestimate*) 482; tumble –, stumble- over one's shadow; make mountains out of molehills, make much ado about nothing.

Adj. UNIMPORTANT; of -little, – small, – no- -account, – importance &c. 642; immaterial; nonessential, unessential, irrelevant, not vital, uninteresting; indifferent, amateurish.

SUBORDINATE &c. (*inferior*) 34; mediocre &c. (*average*) 29; passable, fair, respectable, tolerable, commonplace; uneventful, mere, common; ordinary &c. (*habitual*) 613; inconsiderable, soso *or* so-so, insignificant, nugatory, inappreciable.

TRIFLING, trivial; slight, slender, light, flimsy, frothy, idle; puerile &c. (*foolish*) 499; airy, shallow; weak &c. 160; powerless &c. 158; frivolous, petty, niggling; peddling, piddling, fribbling, fribble, inane, ridiculous, farcical; finical, finicking *or* finicky *or* finikin, mincing, fiddle-faddle [*colloq.*], namby-pamby, wishy-washy [*colloq.*], milk and water, insipid.

PALTRY, poor, pitiful; contemptible &c. (*contempt*) 930; sorry, mean, meager *or* meagre, shabby, miserable, wretched, vile, scrubby, scrannel [*archaic*], weedy, niggardly, scurvy, beggarly, worthless, twopenny-halfpenny, two-for-a-cent, two-by-four [*colloq., U. S.*], cheap, trashy, catchpenny, gimcrack, trumpery; one-horse [*U. S.*].

not worth -the pains, – while, – mentioning, – speaking of, – a thought, – a curse, – a cent, – a rap, – a hair, – a straw &c. *n.;* beneath contempt, below par; not up to -sample, – specification; beneath-, unworthy of- -notice, – regard – consideration; *de lanâ caprinâ* [*L.*]; vain &c. (*useless*) 645.

Adv. SLIGHTLY &c. *adj.;* rather, somewhat, pretty well, fairly, fairly well, tolerably.

FOR AUGHT ONE CARES; it matters not, it does not signify; it is of no -consequence, – importance.

Int. NO MATTER! pish! tush! tut! pshaw! pugh! pooh, -pooh! fudge! bosh! humbug! fiddlestick, – end! fiddledeedee! never mind! *n'importe!* [*F.*]; what signifies! what matter! what boots it! what of that! what's the odds! a fig for! stuff! nonsense! stuff and nonsense!

** magno conatu magnas nugas; le jeu ne vaut pas la chandelle; elephantus non capit murem; tempête dans un verre d'eau; "why beholdest thou the mote that is in thy brother's eye?" [*Bible*]; "very trifles comfort, because very trifles grieve us" [Pascal]; "Come, gentlemen, we sit too long on trifles" [*Pericles*]; "These little things are great to little men" [Goldsmith]; "Seeks painted trifles and fantastic toys, And eagerly pursues imaginary joys" [Akenside]; "Trifles unconsciously bias us for or against a person from the very beginning" [Schopenhauer].

644. Utility. — N. UTILITY; usefulness &c. *adj.;* efficacy, efficiency, adequacy; service, use, stead, avail, boot [*archaic*]; help &c. (*aid*) 707; applicability &c. *adj.;* subservience &c. (*instrumentality*) 631; function &c. (*business*) 625; value; worth &c. (*goodness*) 648; money's worth; productiveness &c. 168; *cui bono* &c. (*intention*) 620; utilization &c. (*use*) 677; step in the right direction.

COMMONWEAL *or* common weal; commonwealth [*now rare*]; public -good, - service, - interest; utilitarianism &c. (*philanthropy*) 910; public servant.

V. BE USEFUL &c. *adj.;* avail, serve; subserve [*rare*] &c. (*be instrumental to*) 631; conduce &c. (*tend*) 176; answer -, serve- -one's turn, - a purpose.

ACT A PART &c. (*action*) 680; perform -, discharge -a function &c. 625; do -, render- -a service, - good service, - yeoman's service; bestead, stand one in good stead; be the making of; help &c. 707.

BENEFIT &c. (*do good*) 648; bear fruit &c. (*produce*) 161; bring grist to the mill; profit, remunerate.

find one's -account, - advantage- in; reap the benefit of &c. (*be better for*) 658.

RENDER USEFUL &c. (*use*) 677.

Adj. USEFUL; of use &c. *n.;* serviceable, proficuous [*obs.*], good for; subservient &c. (*instrumental*) 631; conducive &c. (*tending*) 176; subsidiary &c. (*helping*) 707.

ADVANTAGEOUS &c. (*beneficial*) 648; profitable, gainful, remunerative, worth one's salt; valuable; invaluable, beyond price, of general utility; prolific &c. (*productive*) 168.

ADEQUATE; efficient, efficacious; effective, effectual; expedient &c. 646.

APPLICABLE, usable, available, ready, handy, at hand, tangible; commodious, adaptable; of all work.

Adv. USEFULLY &c. *adj.*

FOR USE, for service; in the public service; for the good of the -people, - public, - service; *pro bono publico* [*L.*].

⁂ "life, like every other blessing, derives its value from its use alone" [Johnson].

645. Inutility. — N. INUTILITY; uselessness &c. *adj.;* inefficacy, futility; ineptitude, inaptitude; inadequacy &c. (*insufficiency*) 640; unfitness; inefficiency &c. (*incompetence*) 158; unskillfulness &c. 699; disservice; unfruitfulness &c. (*unproductiveness*) 169; labor -in vain, - lost, - of Sisyphus; lost -trouble, - labor; work of Penelope; Penelope's web; sleeveless [*obs.*] -, bootless- errand; wild-goose chase, mere farce.

REDUNDANCE, supererogation &c. 641; tautology &c. (*repetition*) 104.

WORTHLESSNESS; vanity, *vanitas vanitatum* [*L.*], inanity, nugacity; triviality &c. (*unimportance*) 643.

worthless residue, *caput mortuum* [*L.*, *old chem.*]; waste paper, dead letter; blunt tool.

RUBBISH, junk, lumber, litter, odds and ends, cast-off clothes; button top; shoddy; rags, orts [*archaic*], leavings, dross, trash, refuse, sweepings, scourings, offscourings, waste, rubble, *débris* [*F.*]; chaff, stubble, broken meat; dregs &c. (*dirt*) 653; weeds, tares; rubbish heap, dust hole; *rudera* [*L.*], deads, slag.

IDLER; *fruges consumere natus* [Horace] &c. (*drone*) 683.

V. BE USELESS &c. *adj.;* go a-begging &c. (*redundant*) 641; fail &c. 732.

LABOR IN VAIN; seek -, strive- after impossibilities; use vain efforts, roll the stone of Sisyphus, beat the air, lash the waves, *battre l'eau avec un bâton* [*F.*], *donner un coup d'épée dans l'eau* [*F.*], fish in the air, milk the ram, drop a bucket into an empty well, pour water into a sieve, sow the sand; bay the moon; preach -, speak- to the winds; whistle jigs to a milestone; kick against the pricks, *se battre contre des moulins* [*F.*]; lock the stable door when the steed is stolen &c. (*too late*) 135; hold a farthing candle to the sun; cast pearls before swine &c. (*waste*) 638; carry coals to Newcastle &c. (*redundance*) 641; wash a blackamoor white &c. (*impossible*) 471.

RENDER USELESS &c. *adj.;* dismantle, dismast, dismount, disqualify, disable; unrig [*chiefly naut.*]; hamstring, hock *or* spike guns, clip the wings; put out of gear; throw a wrench in the machinery, throw a monkey-wrench into the works.

hough, cripple, lame &c. (*injure*) 659;

Adj. USELESS, inutile, nugatory, inefficacious, futile, unavailing, bootless; inoperative &c. 158; inadequate &c. (*insufficient*) 640; inservient [*obs.*], inept, inefficient &c. (*impotent*) 158; of no avail &c. (*use*) 644; ineffectual &c. (*failure*)

732; incompetent &c. (*unskillful*) 699; "weary, stale, flat, and unprofitable" [*Hamlet*]; superfluous &c. (*redundant*) 641; dispensable; thrown away &c. (*wasted*) 638; abortive &c. (*immature*) 674.

WORTHLESS, valueless, unsalable; not worth a straw &c. (*trifling*) 643; dear at any price.

VAIN, empty, inane; gainless, profitless, fruitless; unserviceable, unprofitable; ill-spent; effete, barren, sterile, impotent, worn out; unproductive &c. 169; *hors de combat* [*F.*], past work &c. (*impaired*) 659; obsolete &c. (*old*) 124; fit for the dust hole; good for nothing; of no earthly use; not worth -having, – powder and shot; leading to no end, uncalled for; unnecessary, unneeded, superfluous.

Adv. USELESSLY &c. *adj.*; to -little, – no, – little or no- purpose.

Int. *cui bono?* [*L.*]; what's the good! what's the use!

. *actum ne agas; chercher une aiguille dans une botte de foin; tanto buon che val niente;* "like sending them ruffles, when wanting a shirt" [Sorbienne]; "one might as well expect the Astronomer Royal to tell the time in a catacomb" [Shaw].

---

646. [SPECIFIC SUBSERVIENCE.] **Expedience. — N.** EXPEDIENCE *or* expediency, desirability, desirableness &c. *adj.*; fitness &c. (*agreement*) 23; utility &c. 644; propriety; opportunism; advantage, opportunity; pragmatism, pragmaticism; a working proposition.

high time &c. (*occasion*) 134; suitable time *or* season, tempestivity [*obs.*].

V. BE EXPEDIENT &c. *adj.*; suit &c. (*agree*) 23; befit; suit –, befit- the -time, – season, – occasion; produce the goods [*colloq.*].

CONFORM &c. 82.

Adj. EXPEDIENT; desirable, advisable, acceptable; convenient; worth while, meet; fit, fitting; due, proper, eligible, seemly, becoming; befitting &c. *v.*; opportune &c. (*in season*) 134; *in loco* [*L.*]; suitable &c. (*accordant*) 23; applicable &c. (*useful*) 644.

PRACTICAL, practicable, effective, pragmatic, pragmatical.

Adv. CONVENIENTLY &c. *adj.*; in the nick of time; in the right place.

. *operæ pretium est;* "the end must justify the means" [Prior]; "too fond of the Right to pursue the Expedient" [Goldsmith — *of Burke*]; "Principle is ever my motto, not expediency" [Disraeli]; "expediency is the science of exigencies" [Kossuth].

647. Inexpedience. — N. INEXPEDIENCE *or* inexpediency, undesirability, undesirableness &c. *adj.*; discommodity, impropriety; unfitness &c. (*disagreement*) 24; inutility &c. 645; disadvantage, disadvantageousness, inconvenience, inadvisability.

V. BE INEXPEDIENT &c. *adj.*; come amiss &c. (*disagree*) 24; embarrass &c. (*hinder*) 706; put to inconvenience.

Adj. INEXPEDIENT, undesirable; unadvisable [*rare*], inadvisable, unsuitable, troublesome, objectionable; inapt, ineligible, inadmissible, inconvenient; incommodious, discommodious; disadvantageous; inappropriate, unfit &c. (*inconsonant*) 24.

ILL-CONTRIVED, ill-advised; unsatisfactory; unprofitable &c., inept &c. (*useless*) 645; inopportune &c. (*unseasonable*) 135; out of –, in the wrong-place; improper, unseemly.

CLUMSY, awkward; cumbrous, cumbersome; lumbering, unwieldy, hulky; unmanageable &c. (*impracticable*) 704; impedient &c. (*in the way*) 706.

UNNECESSARY &c. (*redundant*) 641.

. it will never do; it doesn't pay; the game is not worth the candle; "he has paid dear, very dear, for his whistle" [Franklin].

---

648. [CAPABILITY OF PRODUCING GOOD. GOOD QUALITIES.] **Goodness. — N.** GOODNESS &c. *adj.*; excellence, merit; virtue &c. 944; value, worth, price.

SUPEREXCELLENCE, supereminence, quintessence; superiority &c. 33; perfection &c. 650; *coup de maître* [*F.*]; masterpiece, *chef d'œuvre* [*F.*], prime, flower, cream, *élite* [*F.*], pick, nonesuch [*now rare*], A1 *or* A number 1 [*colloq.*], *nonpareil*

649. [CAPABILITY OF PRODUCING EVIL. BAD QUALITIES.] **Badness. — N.** HURTFULNESS &c. *adj.*; virulence.

BANE &c. 663; plague spot &c. (*insalubrity*) 657; evil star, ill wind; hoodoo [*colloq.*], jinx [*slang*], *jadu* [*Hind.*], Jonah; snake in the grass, skeleton in the closet; *amari aliquid* [*L.*]; thorn in the -side, – flesh.

MALIGNITY, damnability, damnifica-

[*F*], *crême de la crême* [*F.*], flower of the flock, cock of the roost, salt of the earth; champion; prodigy, wonder, best ever [*colloq.*].

GEM, – of the first water; *bijou* [*F.*], precious stone, jewel, pearl, diamond, ruby, brilliant, treasure; tidbit, good thing; *rara avis* [*L.*], one in a thousand.

BENEFICENCE &c. 906.

GOOD MAN &c. 948.

V. BE BENEFICIAL &c. *adj.;* produce *or* do good &c. 618; profit &c. (*be of use*) 644; benefit; confer a benefit &c. 618.

produce a good effect; be the making of, do a world of good, make a man of; do a good turn, confer an obligation; improve &c. 658.

do no harm, break no bones.

BE GOOD &c. *adj.;* be pure gold, be all wool; be the real -thing, – article; look good to [*colloq.*]; excel, transcend &c. (*be superior*) 33; bear away the bell.

stand the -proof, – test; pass muster, pass an examination.

VIE, challenge comparison, emulate, rival.

Adj. BENEFICIAL, valuable, of value; serviceable &c. (*useful*) 644; advantageous, profitable, edifying; salutary &c. (*healthful*) 656.

HARMLESS, hurtless; unobnoxious; innocuous, innocent, inoffensive.

FAVORABLE; propitious &c. (*hope-giving*) 858; fair.

GOOD, good as gold; excellent; better; superior &c. 33; above par; nice, fine; genuine &c. (*true*) 494.

CHOICE, best, select, picked, elect, *recherché* [*F.*], rare, priceless; unparagoned [*rare*], matchless, peerless, unequaled *or* unequalled, unparalleled &c. (*supreme*) 33; superlatively &c. (33)-good; bully [*slang*], crackajack [*slang*], gilt-edge *or* gilt-edged [*colloq.*]; superfine, superexcellent; of the first water; first-rate, first-class; high-wrought, exquisite, very best, crack [*colloq.*], prime, tip-top [*colloq.*], capital, cardinal; standard &c. (*perfect*) 650; inimitable.

ADMIRABLE, estimable; praiseworthy &c. (*approve*) 931; pleasing &c. 829; *couleur de rose* [*F.*], precious, of great price; costly &c. (*dear*) 814; worth -its weight in gold, – a king's ransom; priceless, invaluable, inestimable, precious as the apple of the eye.

SATISFACTORY, up to the mark,

tion, damnifying; malevolence &c. 907; tender mercies [*irony*].

ILL-TREATMENT, annoyance, molestation, abuse, oppression, persecution, outrage; misusage &c. 679; *damnum* [*L.*], scathe; injury &c. (*damage*) 659; knockout drops [*U. S.*].

BADNESS &c. *adj.;* peccancy, abomination; painfulness &c. 830; pestilence &c. (*disease*) 655; guilt &c. 947; depravity &c. 945.

BAD MAN &c. 949; evildoer &c. 913.

V. BE HURTFUL &c. *adj.;* cause –, produce –, inflict –, work –, do- evil &c. 619; damnify, endamage, hurt, harm, scathe; injure &c. (*damage*) 659; pain &c. 830.

WRONG, aggrieve, oppress, persecute; trample –, tread –, bear hard –, put-upon; overburden; weigh -down, – heavy on; victimize; run down, run hard; thwart; molest &c. 830.

MALTREAT, abuse; ill-use, illtreat; buffet, bruise, scratch, maul; smite &c. (*scourge*) 972; do violence, do a mischief; stab, pierce, outrage.

DO MISCHIEF, do harm, make mischief; bring –, lead –, get- into trouble; hoodoo [*colloq., U. S.*].

DESTROY &c. 162.

Adj. HURTFUL, harmful, scathful [*obs. or dial.*], scatheful, baneful, baleful, injurious, deleterious, detrimental, noxious, pernicious, mischievous, full of mischief, mischief-making, malefic, malignant, nocuous, noisome; prejudicial; disserviceable, disadvantageous; wide-wasting.

UNLUCKY, sinister; obnoxious; untoward, disastrous.

OPPRESSIVE, burdensome, onerous; malign &c. (*malevolent*) 907.

CORRUPTING &c. (*corrupt* &c. 659); virulent, venomous, envenomed, corrosive; poisonous &c. (*morbific*) 657; deadly &c. (*killing*) 361; destructive &c. (*destroying*) 162; inauspicious &c. 859.

BAD, ill, arrant, as bad as bad can be, dreadful; horrid, horrible; dire; rank, peccant, foul, fulsome; rotten, rotten at the core.

UNSATISFACTORY, indifferent; injured &c. deteriorated &c. 659; exceptionable, below par &c. (*imperfect*) 651; ill-contrived, ill-disposed, ill-conditioned.

DEPLORABLE, wretched, sad, grievous, lamentable, pitiful, pitiable, woeful &c.

unexceptionable, unobjectionable; tidy [*colloq.*].

in -good, – fair- condition; unspoiled, fresh; sound &c. (*perfect*) 650.

Adv. BENEFICIALLY &c. *adj.;* well &c. 618; for one's benefit.

*** "jewels five words long" [Tennyson]; "long may such goodness live!" [Rogers]; "the luxury of doing good" [Goldsmith]; "seek Virtue: she alone is free" [Milton]; "before virtue the immortal gods have put the sweat of man's brow" [Hesiod].

---

650. Perfection. — N.

PERFECTION; perfectness &c. *adj.;* indefectibility; impeccancy, impeccability.

PARAGON, pink, *beau ideal* [F.]; pink –, acme- of perfection; *ne plus ultra* [L.]; summit &c. 210.

[COMPARISONS] *cygne noir* [F.]; Phœnix *or* Phenix; black tulip, *tulipe noir* [F.]; philosopher's stone; Koh-i-noor.

MODEL, standard, pattern, mirror, Admirable Crichton; trump, brick, corker, caution, humdinger [*all slang*]; "the observed of all observers" [*Hamlet*], very prince of.

Bayard, *chevalier sans peur et sans reproche* [F.]; Roland, Sidney.

MASTERPIECE, masterstroke, prize-winner, prize; superexcellence &c. (*goodness*) 648; transcendence &c. (*superiority*) 33.

V. BE PERFECT &c. *adj.;* transcend &c. (*be supreme*) 33.

PERFECT, bring to perfection, ripen, mature; consummate, crown, put the finishing touch to (*or* upon); complete &c. 729; put in trim &c. (*prepare*) 673; maturate [*rare*].

Adj. PERFECT, faultless; indefective [*rare*], indeficient [*rare*], indefectible; immaculate, spotless, impeccable; free from imperfection &c. 651; unblemished, uninjured &c. 659; sound, – as a roach; in perfect condition; scathless [*obs. or dial.*], scatheless, intact, harmless; seaworthy &c. (*safe*) 644; right as a trivet; *in se ipso totus teres atque rotundus* [Hor.]; consummate &c. (*complete*) 52; finished &c. 729; complete in itself; well-rounded.

(*painful*) 830; mean &c. (*paltry*) 643.

EVIL, wrong; depraved &c. 945; shocking; reprehensible &c. (*disapproved*) 932.

HATEFUL, – as a toad; abominable, vile, base, villainous, detestable, execrable, cursed, accursed, confounded; damned, damnable, damnatory, damnific [*rare*]; infernal; diabolic &c. (*malevolent*) 907.

INADVISABLE, unadvisable [*rare*] &c. (*inexpedient*) 647; unprofitable &c. (*useless*) 645; incompetent &c. (*unskillful*) 699; irremediable &c. (*hopeless*) 859.

Adv. BADLY &c. *adj.;* wrong, ill; to one's cost; where the shoe pinches; with malignity &c. *n.*

*** bad is the best; if the worst come to the worst; *herba mala presto cresco;* "wrongs unredressed or insults unavenged" [Wordsworth]; "one only evil, namely, ignorance" [Socrates]; "the love of money is the root of all evil" [*Bible*].

---

651. Imperfection. — N.

IMPERFECTION; imperfectness &c. *adj.;* deficiency; inadequacy &c. (*insufficiency*) 640; peccability, defection, peccancy &c. (*badness*) 649; immaturity &c. 674.

FAULT, defect, "little rift within the lute" [Tennyson], weak point; screw loose; flaw &c. (*break*) 70; gap &c. 198; twist &c. 243; taint, attainder; *mésalliance* [F.], bar sinister; hole in one's coat; blemish &c. 848; weakness &c. 160; shortcoming &c. 304; drawback; seamy side.

HALF BLOOD, drop of black blood, touch of the tar-brush [*colloq.*].

MEDIOCRITY; no great -shakes, – catch [*both colloq.*]; not much to boast of; one-horse shay; one-horse town; peanut -politics, – policy.

V. BE IMPERFECT &c. *adj.;* rot before it ripens, bear within it the seeds of decay; have a defect &c. *n.;* lie under a disadvantage; spring a leak.

not pass muster, barely pass muster; fall short &c. 304.

Adj. IMPERFECT; not perfect &c. 650; deficient, defective; faulty, unsound, tainted, specked; mutilated; out of order; out of tune, cracked; leaky; sprung; warped &c. (*distort*) 243; lame; injured &c. (*deteriorated*) 659; peccant &c. (*bad*) 649; frail &c. (*weak*) 160; inadequate &c. (*insufficient*) 640; crude &c. (*unprepared*) 674; incomplete &c. 53; found wanting; below par; short-handed; below –, under- its full -strength, – complement.

BEST &c. (*good*) 648; model, standard; inimitable, unparagoned [*rare*], unparalleled &c. (*supreme*) 33; superhuman, divine; beyond all praise &c. (*approbation*) 931; *sans peur et sans reproche* [*F.*].

Adv. TO PERFECTION; perfectly &c. *adj.*; *ad unguem* [*L.*]; clean, – as a whistle; with a finish; to the limit.

*** "let us go on unto perfection" [*Hebrews vi, 1*]; "the perfection of art is to conceal art" [Quintilian]; "the glass of fashion and the mould of form" [*Hamlet*].

INDIFFERENT, middling, ordinary, mediocre; average &c. 29; soso *or* so-so; *couci-couci* [*F.*], milk-and-water; tolerable, fair, passable; pretty -well, – good; rather –, moderately- good; good –, well- enough; decent; not bad, not amiss; unobjectionable, admissible, bearable, better than nothing.

SECONDARY, inferior; second-rate, second best; one-horse [*U. S.*]; two-by-four [*U. S.*].

Adv. ALMOST &c.; to a limited extent, rather &c. 32; pretty, moderately; only, might be worse.

considering, all things considered, enough;

*** *surgit amari aliquid;* "with all my imperfections on my head" [*Hamlet*]; "Frailty, thy name is woman" [*ibid.*].

---

652. Cleanness. — N. CLEANNESS &c. *adj.*; purity; cleaning &c. *v.*; purification, defecation &c. *v.*; purgation, lustration; abstersion [*rare*], detersion; aspersion, asperges [*R. C. Ch.*]; epuration [*rare*], mundation [*obs.*], ablution, lavation, colature [*obs.*]; disinfection &c. *v.*; drainage, sewerage.

BATH, bathroom, swimming pool, natatorium, swimming bath, public bath, baths, bathhouse, hot bath &c. 386; lavatory; laundry, washhouse.

CLEANER, washerwoman, laundress, dhobi [*India*], laundryman, washerman; scavenger, sweeper; mehtar (*fem.* mehtrani), bhangi [*all India*]; mud lark [*slang*]; crossing –, street- sweeper, white wings [*local, U. S.*]; dustman; sweep.

brush; broom, besom, vacuum cleaner, carpet sweeper; mop, swab, – hose; scraper; rake, shovel; sieve, riddle, screen, filter; blotter.

napkin, serviette, cloth, maukin [*obs.*], malkin [*obs.*], handkerchief, towel, sudary, sudarium, face cloth, wash cloth; doily *or* doyley, bib; carving cloth, tablecloth; duster, sponge.

MAT, doormat, rug, drugget, cover.

[CLEANSING AGENTS] wash, lotion, detergent, soap, purifier &c. *v.*; disinfectant; benzene, benzine, benzol, benzolin; bleaching powder, chloride of lime; lye, buck.

DENTIFRICE, tooth paste, tooth powder; mouth wash.

CATHARTIC, purgative, aperient, deobstruent, laxative.

V. BE *or* RENDER CLEAN &c. *adj.*

CLEAN, cleanse; mundify [*obs.*], rinse,

653. Uncleanness.— N. UNCLEANNESS &c. *adj.*; impurity; immundity [*rare*], immundicity [*rare*], mucidness, impurity &c. (of mind) 961.

DEFILEMENT, contamination &c. *v.*; defœdation [*obs.*]; soilure, soiliness [*obs.*]; abomination; taint, tainture [*obs.*]; fetor &c. 401.

LOUSINESS, pediculosis, pediculation, phthiriasis [*med.*].

DECAY; putrescence, putrefaction; corruption; mold *or* mould, must, mildew, dry rot, mucor [*rare*], caries [*med.*], rubigo [*obs.*].

SLOVENRY; slovenliness &c. *adj.*; squalor.

DOWDY, drab, slut, malkin *or* mawkin [*obs. or dial. Eng.*], slattern, sloven, slammerkin [*obs.*], slammock *or* slummock [*dial.*], drabble-tail, draggle-tail, mud lark [*slang*], dustman, sweep; beast, pig.

DIRT, filth, soil, slop; dust, cobweb, flue; smoke, soot, smudge, smut, grime, raff [*dial.*], riffraff; sossle *or* sozzle [*dial.*].

DREGS, sordes, grounds, lees; argol; sediment, settlement; heeltap; dross, drossiness; mother [*obs.*], precipitate, *scoriæ* [*L.*], ashes, cinders, recrement, slag; scum, froth.

USELESS REFUSE, hogwash [*colloq.*], swill, garbage, ditch water, dishwater, bilge-water; rinsings, cheeseparings; sweepings &c. 645; outscourings, offscourings, offscum; *caput mortuum* [*L.*], residuum, sprue, dross, clinker, draff; scurf, scurfiness; exuviæ; furfur, dandruff; tartar, fur.

spawn, offal, gurry [*U. S.*]; carrion;

wring, flush, full, wipe, mop, sponge, scour, swab, scrub.

wash, lave &c. (*water*) 337; launder, buck; absterge [*rare*], deterge; decrassify; clear, purify; depurate, spurate [*rare*], despumate, defecate; purge, expurgate, elutriate, lixiviate, edulcorate, clarify, refine, rack; percolate, separate, strain, filter, filtrate, drain.

SIFT, winnow, sieve, bolt, screen, riddle; pick, weed.

COMB, rake, scrape, rasp; hackle, heckle, card.

SWEEP, brush, brush up, whisk, broom, vacuum [*colloq*.].

rout –, clear –, sweep &c.- out; make a clean sweep of, clean house, spruce up [*colloq*.].

DISINFECT, fumigate, ventilate, deodorize; whitewash.

Adj. CLEAN, cleanly; pure; immaculate; spotless, stainless, taintless, trig [*dial*.], without a stain, unstained, unspotted, unsoiled, unsullied, untainted, uninfected; sweet, – as a nut.

NEAT, spruce, tidy, trim, jimp *or* gimp [*Scot. & dial. Eng*.], clean as a new penny, like a cat in pattens; cleaned &c. *v*.; kempt [*archaic*].

ABSTERGENT, detergent, depurative, abstersive [*rare*], cathartic, cleansing, purifying.

Adv. NEATLY &c. *adj*.; clean as a whistle.

⁎ cleanliness is next to godliness; "I'll purge and leave sack and live cleanly" [Shakespeare]; "wash me and I shall be whiter than snow" [*Bible*]; "cleanliness is not next to godliness nowadays, for cleanliness is made an essential and godliness is regarded as an offence" [Chesterton].

slough, peccant humor, pus, matter, suppuration.

DUNG, ordure, lienteria; feces *or* fæces, excrement, feculence; excreta &c. 299; sewage, sewerage [*rare in this sense*]; fertilizer, muck; coprolite; guano, manure, compost.

[RECEPTACLES] dunghill, colluvies [*med*.]; mixen, midden [*both archaic or dial. Eng*.], bog, laystall [*obs*.]; cesspool; sump [*Scot. & dial. Eng*.], sough [*dial. Eng*.], cloaca, Cloaca Maxima; sink, drain, sewer, common sewer; Cloacina; dust hole; glory hole [*colloq*.].

WATER-CLOSET, w. c., toilet [*colloq*.], *cabinet d'aisance* [*F*.], latrine, backhouse, necessary, privy, jakes [*rare*], Mrs. Jones; head [*naval slang*].

STY, pigsty, lair, den, Augean stable, sink of corruption; slum, rookery.

MUD, mire, quagmire, alluvium, silt, sludge, slime, slush, slosh [*dial*.], sposh [*U. S*.].

VERMIN, louse, flea, nit, bug, chinch; lice &c. 366.

V. BE *or* BECOME UNCLEAN &c. *adj*.; rot, putrefy, fester, rankle, reek; stink &c. 401; mold *or* mould, molder *or* moulder; go bad &c. *adj*.

wallow in the mire; slobber, slabber.

RENDER UNCLEAN &c. *adj*.; dirt, dirty; soil, smoke, tarnish, slaver, spot, smear; daub, blot, blur, smudge, smutch, smirch; begrease; drabble, dabble, daggle, spatter, slubber [*dial*.]; besmear &c., bemire, beslime, begrime, befoul; splash, stain, distain [*archaic*], maculate, sully, pollute, defile, debase, contaminate, taint, leaven; corrupt &c. (*injure*) 659; cover with dust &c. *n*.; drabble in the mud; roil.

Adj. UNCLEAN, dirty, filthy, grimy; soiled &c. *v*.; not to be handled -without gloves, – with kid gloves; dusty, snuffy, smutty, sooty, smoky; thick, turbid, dreggy; slimy; mussy [*U. S*.].

LOUSY, pedicular, pediculous.

UNCLEANLY, slovenly, slatternly, untidy, sluttish, dowdy, draggle-tailed, drabble-tailed; uncombed, unkempt, unscoured, unswept, unwiped, unwashed, unstrained, unpurified; squalid; lutose, slammocky *or* slummocky [*dial*.], sossly *or* sozzly [*dial*.], sloppy [*colloq*.].

OFFENSIVE, nasty, coarse, foul, impure, abominable, beastly, reeky, reechy [*dial. Eng*.]; fetid &c. 401.

moldy *or* mouldy, musty, fusty, mildewed, rusty, moth-eaten, mucid, rancid, bad, gone bad, lentiginous *or* lentiginose, touched, reasty [*dial. Eng*.], rotten, corrupt, tainted, high, flyblown, maggoty; putrid, putrefactive, putrescent, putrefied; saprogenic *or* saprogenous; purulent, carious, peccant; fecal, feculent; stercoraceous, excrementitious; scurfy, impetiginous; gory, bloody; rotting &c. *v*.; rotten as -a pear, – cheese.

crapulous &c. (*intemperate*) 954; beastlike; gross &c. (*impure in mind*) 961; fimetarious, fimicolous.

Int. pah! faugh! ugh!

*** "they that touch pitch will be defiled" [*Much Ado About Nothing*]; "if dirt was trumps, what hands you would hold!" [Lamb]; "sluts are good enough to make a sloven's porridge" [*old proverb*].

654. Health. — N. HEALTH, sanity; soundness &c. *adj.*; vigor; good –, perfect –, excellent –, rude –, robust- health; bloom, *mens sana in corpore sano* [*L.*]; Hygeia; incorruption, incorruptibility; valetude [*obs.*]; good state –, clean bill- of health; eupepsia *or* eupepsy, euphoria *or* euphory; convalescence, upgrade; strength, poise.

V. BE IN HEALTH &c. *adj.*; be bursting with -vigor, – pep [*slang*]; never feel better; bloom, flourish.

keep body and soul together, keep on one's legs; enjoy -good, – a good state of- health; have a clean bill of health.

RETURN TO HEALTH; recover &c. 660; get better &c. (*improve*) 658; take a -new, – fresh- lease of life; convalesce, be convalescent; add years to one's life; recruit; restore to health; cure &c. (*restore*) 660.

Adj. HEALTHY, healthful; in health &c. *n.*; well, sound, whole, strong, blooming, hearty, hale, fresh, green, florid, flush, hardy, stanch *or* staunch, brave, robust, vigorous, weatherproof.

on one's legs; sound as a -roach, – bell; fresh as -a daisy, – a rose, – April; walking on air; hearty as a buck; in -fine, – high- feather; in good case, in full bloom; pretty bobbish [*dial. or slang*]; bursting with -health, – vigor; in fine fettle; chipper [*colloq.*, *U. S.*]; tolerably well, as well as can be expected.

UNSCATHED, uninjured, unmaimed, unmarred, untainted; sound of wind and limb, without a scratch, safe and sound.

SANITARY &c. (*health-giving*) 656; sanatory &c. (*remedial*) 662.

*** "health that snuffs the morning air" [Grainger]; *non est vivere sed valere vita* [Martial].

655. Disease. — N. DISEASE; illness, sickness &c. *adj.*; ailing &c. *v.*; "the thousand natural shocks That flesh is heir to" [*Hamlet*]; "all ills that men endure" [Cowley]; morbidity, morbosity [*obs.*]; infirmity, ailment, indisposition; complaint, disorder, malady, distemperature [*archaic*]; valetudinarianism; loss of health, delicacy, delicate health, invalidity, invalidism, invalescence [*rare*]; malnutrition, want of nourishment, cachexia *or* cachexy; prostration, decline, collapse; decay &c. 659.

VISITATION, attack, seizure, stroke, fit, epilepsy, apoplexy, bloodstroke; palsy, paralysis, motor paralysis, sensory paralysis, hemiplegia, paraplegia *or* paraplegy; *paralysis agitans* [*L.*], shaking palsy, Parkinson's disease; shock; shell-shock [*common during World War*].

TAINT, virus, pollution, infection, contagion; septicæmia *or* septicemia, blood poisoning, pyæmia *or* pyemia, septicity; epidemic; sporadic, endemic; plague, pestilence.

FEVER, calenture; inflammation; ague; intermittent –, remittent –, congestive –, pernicious- fever; malaria, malarial fever; dengue *or* dandy fever, breakbone fever; yellow fever, yellow jack; typhoid *or* typhoid fever, enteric fever; typhus; eruptive fever; scarlet fever, scarlatina; smallpox, variola; varioloid; vaccinia, cow pox; varicella, chicken pox; rubeola, measles.

ERUPTION, rash, brash, breaking out; canker rash; dartre, exanthema *or* exanthem; scabies, itch, psora; pox; eczema, tetter, psoriasis; lichen, papular rash; lichen tropicus, prickly heat; impetigo; erythema; erysipelas, St. Anthony's fire; urticaria, hives, nettlerash; herpes; herpes zoster, shingles; herpes circinatus, ringworm; miliaria, pemphigus, rupia.

SORE, canker, ulcer, fester, boil, gumboil; pimple &c. (*swelling*) 250; carbuncle; gathering; abscess, imposture *or* imposthume [*obsoles.*], aposteme; Rigg's disease, pyorrhea *or* pyorrhœa; chancre; peccant humor; proud flesh;

corruption; enanthem *or* enanthema, gangrene; mortification, sphacelus, sphacelation; slough, caries, necrosis; cancer, carcinoma; tumor, leprosy.

HEART DISEASE, carditis, peric‥ditis, endocarditis, valvular lesion; hypertrophy –, dilatation –, atrophy –, fatty degeneration- of the heart; angina pectoris.

WASTING DISEASE, marasmus, emaciation, atrophy; consumption, white plague, tuberculosis, T.B. [*med. cant*], phthisis; pulmonary –, galloping- consumption; pulmonary phthisis, phthisipneumonia, pneumonia; chlorosis, green sickness; anæmia *or* anemia; leucocythænia *or* leucocythenia.

THROAT DISEASE, laryngitis, tonsillitis, quinsy, cynanche; bronchitis, diphtheria, whooping cough, pertussis; thrush, canker.

OOLD, cough; rheum; catarrh, hay fever; influenza, grippe or grip; rose cold.

INDIGESTION, dyspepsia, poor digestion, pyrosis, water qualm; cardialgia, heartburn; seasickness, *mal de mer* [*F.*]; nausea; giddiness, vertigo; constipation, autointoxication.

EYE DISEASE, trachoma, conjunctivitis, pink eye; cataract, caligo, pin-and-web, *gutta serena* [*L.*].

VENEREAL DISEASE, pox, syphilis; gonorrhea or gonorrhœa, blennorrhea or blennorrhœa, blennorrhagia.

[VARIOUS DISEASES] headache &c. (*physical pain*) 378; goiter or goitre, bronchocele, struma, tracheocele; lockjaw, tetanus, trismus; diarrhea or diarrhœa, dysentery, bloody flux, flux, issue. hemorrhage; hemorrhoids, piles; cholera, cholera morbus, Asiatic cholera [*colloq., Eng.*] cholera infantum, summer complaint; colic; jaundice, icterus; apnœa; asthma; king's evil, scrofula; rickets, rachitis; appendicitis; gall-stones, biliary calculus, stone; hernia, rupture; varicosis, varicose veins; arteriosclerosis, hardening of the arteries; neuritis; nervous prostration; St. Vitus's dance, chorea; neurasthenia; sciatica; rheumatism, arthritis, lumbago; dropsy, œdema or edema; elephantiasis; beriberi [*bo h tropical*]; locomotor ataxia; paresis, softening of the brain; bubonic plague; black death; leprosy, elephantiasis Græcorum; sleeping sickness.

fatal &c. (*hopeless*) 859 –disease &c.; dangerous illness, churchyard cough; general breaking up, break-up of the system.

[DISEASE OF MIND] idiocy &c. 499; insanity &c. 503.

MARTYR TO DISEASE; cripple; "the halt, the lame, and the blind"; valetudinary, valetudinarian; invalid, patient, case.

sick-room, sick-chamber; hospital &c. 662.

[SCIENCE OF DISEASE] pathology, pathogeny, etiology, nosology, nosography, nosogeny, therapeutics; diagnostics, symptomatology, semeiology, semeiography, prognosis, diagnosis; clinic, polyclinic.

[VETERINARY] anthrax, splenic fever, woolsorter's disease, charbon, milzbrand, malignant pustule, quarter evil, quarter ill, Texas fever, blackwater, murrain. bighead; blackleg, black quarter; cattle plague, glanders, milk sickness; rinderpest, foot-and-mouth disease, hog cholera; epizoötic; heaves, rot, sheep rot; scabies, mange, distemper.

V. BE or FEEL ILL &c. *adj.;* ail, suffer, labor under, be affected with, complain of; droop, flag, languish, halt; sicken, peak, pine, dwindle; gasp; drop down in one's tracks; waste away, fail, lose strength, lose one's grip.

keep one's bed; lay by, lay up; be laid by the heels; lie helpless, – on one's back.

fall a victim to –, be stricken by –, take –, catch- -a disease &c. *n.*, – an infection; break out.

MALINGER, feign sickness &c. (*falsehood*) 544.

Adj. AILING &c. *v.;* ill, ill of; taken ill, seized with; indisposed, unwell, sick, squeamish, poorly, seedy [*colloq.*]; affected –, afflicted- with illness; laid up, confined, bedridden, invalided, in hospital, on the sick list; out of health, out of sorts [*colloq.*], under the weather [*U. S.*]; valetudinary.

UNSOUND, unhealthy; morbose [*obs.*], healthless, infirm, chlorotic, unbraced, cranky [*dial. Eng.*], sickly, weakly, weakened &c. (*weak*) 160; drooping, flagging; lame, halt, crippled, halting; *hors de combat* [*F.*] &c. (*useless*) 645.

touched in the wind, broken-winded, spavined, gasping.

DISEASED, morbid, tainted, vitiated, peccant, contaminated, poisoned, septic, septical, tabetic, tabid, mangy, leprous, cankered; rotten, – to, – at- the core; withered; palsied, paralytic; dyspeptic; luetic, pneumonic, pulmonic, phthisic or phthisical, consumptive, tubercular, tuberculous, rachitic; syntectic or syntectical, varicose.

DECREPIT; decayed &c. (*deteriorated*) 659; incurable &c. (*hopeless*) 859; in declining health; in a bad way, in danger, prostrate; moribund &c. (*death*) 360.

EPIDEMIC, epizoötic [*of animals*]; zymotic, contagious; morbific &c. 657.

* "in sickness and in health" [*marriage service*]; "tie up the knocker; say I'm sick, I'm dead" [Pope]; "the whole head is sick, and the whole heart faint" [*Bible*]; "diseases desperate grown By desperate appliance are reliev'd, Or not at all" [*Hamlet*]; "this sickness doth infect The very life-blood of our enterprise" [*I Henry IV*]; "That dire disease, whose ruthless power Withers the beauty's transient flower" [Goldsmith]; "a malady Preys on my heart that med'cine cannot reach" [Maturin]; "The best of remedies is a beefsteak Against sea-sickness; try it, sir, before You sneer" [Byron].

656. Salubrity. — N. SALUBRITY, salubriousness, wholesomeness, healthfulness; healthiness &c. *adj.;* Hygeia, Æsculapius.

fine -air, – climate; eudiometer.

[PRESERVATION OF HEALTH] hygiene; valetudinarianism; pure air, exercise, nourishment, tonic; immunity; sanitarium, sanatorium; valetudinarian, sanitarian.

V. BE SALUBRIOUS &c. *adj.;* make for health, conduce to health; be good for, agree with; assimilate &c. 23.

Adj. SALUBRIOUS, salutary, salutiferous [*rare*]; wholesome; healthy, healthful; sanitary, prophylactic; benign, bracing, tonic, invigorating, good for, nutritious; hygeian, hygienic; Hygeian.

sanative &c. (*remedial*) 662; restorative &c. (*reinstate*) 660; useful &c. 644.

INNOXIOUS, innocuous, innocent; harmless, uninjurious, uninfectious; immune.

658. Improvement. — N. IMPROVEMENT, amelioration, melioration, betterment; mend, amendment, emendation; mending &c. *v.;* advancement; advance &c. (*progress*) 282; ascent &c. 305; promotion, preferment; elevation &c. 307; increase &c. 35.

CULTIVATION, culture, march of intellect, menticulture; race-culture, acculturation, civilization; culture zone; eugenics.

REFORM, reformation; revision, radical reform; second thoughts, correction, *limæ labor* [*L.*], refinement, elaboration; purification &c. 652; repair &c. (*restoration*) 660; recovery &c. 660.

REVISE, revised edition, new edition, new issue.

REFORMER, reformist, progressive, radical.

V. IMPROVE; be –, become –, getbetter; mend, amend.

advance &c. (*progress*) 282; ascend &c. 305; increase &c. 35; fructify, ripen, mature; pick up, come about, rally, take a favorable turn; turn over a new leaf, turn the corner; raise one's head, have sown one's wild oats; recover &c. 660.

PROFIT BY; be better &c. *adj.*, be improved by; turn to -right, – good, – best- account; reap the benefit of; make good use of, make capital out of; place to good account.

657. Insalubrity. — N. INSALUBRITY, insalubriousness; unhealthiness &c. *adj.;* plague spot; malaria &c. (*poison*) 663; death in the pot, contagion; poisonousness, toxicity.

V. BE INSALUBRIOUS &c. *adj.;* disagree with; shorten one's days.

Adj. INSALUBRIOUS; unhealthy, unwholesome; noxious, noisome; morbific *or* morbifical, morbiferous; mephitic, septic, azotic, deleterious; pestilent, pestiferous, pestilential; virulent, venomous; envenomed, poisonous, toxic, toxiferous, narcotic; deadly &c. (*killing*) 361.

INNUTRITIOUS, unnutritious [*rare*], undigestible [*rare*], indigestible, ungenial; uncongenial &c. (*disagreeing*) 24.

CONTAGIOUS, infectious, catching, taking, communicable, inoculable, epidemic, zymotic, sporadic, endemic, pandemic; epizoötic [*of animals*].

659. Deterioration. — N. DETERIORATION, debasement; wane, ebb; recession &c. 287; retrogradation &c. 283; decrease &c. 36.

DEGENERACY, degeneration, degenerateness; degradation; depravation, depravement [*rare*], depravedness; devolution; depravity &c. 945; demoralization, retrogression; masochism.

IMPAIRMENT, inquination [*obs.*], injury, damage, loss, detriment, delaceration [*obs.*], outrage, havoc, inroad, ravage, scathe, scath [*dial.*], perversion, prostitution, vitiation, discoloration, pollution, defœdation, poisoning, venenation [*rare*], leaven, contamination, canker, corruption, adulteration, alloy.

DECLINE, declension, declination; decadence *or* decadency; falling off &c. *v.;* caducity [*rare*], senility, decrepitude.

DECAY, dilapidation, ravages of time, wear and tear; erosion, corrosion, moldiness *or* mouldiness; rottenness; moth and rust, dry rot, blight, marcescence, marasmus, atrophy, collapse; disorganization; *délabrement* [*F.*] &c. (*destruction*) 162; aphid, aphis (*pl.* aphides), plant louse; vine fretter, vine grub; gypsy (*or* gipsy) moth; buffalo carpet beetle &c. (*injurious insects*) 913.

WRECK, mere wreck, honeycomb, *magni nominis umbra* [*L.*], jade, rackabones [*U. S.*], skate [*U. S.*]; **tacky** *or*

RENDER BETTER, improve, mend, amend, better; ameliorate, meliorate, relieve; correct; repair &c. (*restore*) 660; doctor &c. (*remedy*) 662; purify &c. 652; decrassify.

improve –, refine- upon; rectify; enrich, mellow, elaborate, fatten.

REFRESH, revive; put –, infuse- new blood into; invigorate &c. (*strengthen*) 159; reinvigorate, recruit, renew, make over, revivify, freshen.

PROMOTE, cultivate, advance, forward, enhance; bring forward, bring on; foster &c. 707.

TOUCH UP, rub up, brush up, furbish up, bolster up, vamp up, brighten up, warm up; polish, cook, make the most of, set off to advantage; prune; put in order &c. (*arrange*) 60.

REVISE, edit, redact, digest, review, make corrections, make improvements &c. *n.*

REFORM, remodel, reorganize; build -afresh, – anew; reclaim, civilize; lift, uplift, inspire; new-model.

view in a new light, think better of, appeal from Philip drunk to Philip sober.

PALLIATE, mitigate; lessen &c. (36) an evil.

Adj. BETTER, – off, – for; all the better for; better advised; improving &c. *v.;* progressive, improved &c. *v.*

REFORMATORY, emendatory; reparatory &c. (*restorative*) 660; remedial &c. 662.

CORRIGIBLE, improvable, curable; accultural.

Adv. ON CONSIDERATION, on reconsideration, on second thoughts, on better advice; on the mend, on the upgrade; *ad melius inquirendum* [L.].

⁎ *urbem latericiam invenit marmoream reliquit;* "to look up and not down, to look forward and not back, to look out and not in, and to lend a hand " [Hale].

tackey [*Southern U. S.*], plug [*slang or colloq., U. S.*].

V. DETERIORATE; be –, become- -worse, – deteriorated &c. *adj.;* have seen better days, degenerate, fall off; wane &c. (*decrease*) 36; ebb; retrograde &c. 283; decline, droop; go down &c. (*sink*) 306; go downhill, go on from bad to worse, go farther and fare worse; jump out of the frying pan into the fire; avoid Scylla and fall into Charybdis.

run to -seed, – waste; swale [*obs.*], sweal [*obs.*]; lapse, be the worse for; sphacelate; break, break down; spring a leak, crack, start; shrivel &c. (*contract*) 195; fade, go off, wither, molder *or* moulder, rot, rankle, decay, go bad; go to –, fall into- decay; fall "into the sere, the yellow leaf" [*Macbeth*]; rust, crumble, shake; totter, – to its fall; perish &c. 162; die &c. 360.

[RENDER LESS GOOD] deteriorate; weaken &c. 160; put back; taint, infect, contaminate, poison, empoison, envenom, canker, corrupt, exulcerate [*obs.*], pollute, vitiate, inquinate [*obs.*], debase, embase [*obs.*]; denaturalize, leaven; deflower, debauch, defile, deprave, degrade; ulcerate; stain &c. (*dirt*) 653; discolor; alloy, adulterate, sophisticate, tamper with, prejudice.

PERVERT, prostitute, demoralize, brutalize; render vicious &c. 945.

EMBITTER, acerbate, exacerbate, aggravate.

INJURE, impair, labefy [*rare*], damage, harm, hurt, shend, scath [*dial.*], scathe, spoil, mar, despoil, dilapidate, waste; overrun; ravage; pillage &c. 791.

wound, stab, pierce, maim, lame, surbate [*obs.*], cripple, hock *or* hough, hamstring, hit between wind and water, scotch, mangle, mutilate, disfigure, blemish, deface, warp.

BLIGHT, rot; corrode, erode; wear away, wear out; gnaw, – at the root of; sap, mine, undermine, shake, sap the foundations of, break up; disorganize, dismantle, dismast; destroy &c. 162.

DAMNIFY &c. (*aggrieve*) 649; do one's worst; knock down; deal a blow to; play -havoc, – sad havoc, – the mischief [*colloq.*], – the deuce [*colloq.*], – the very devil [*colloq.*]- -with, – among; decimate.

Adj. DETERIORATED &c. *v.;* altered, – for the worse; unimproved &c. (improve &c. 658); injured &c. *v.;* sprung; withering, spoiling &c. *v.;* on the -wane, – decline; tabid; degenerate; worse; the –, all the- worse for; out of -repair, – tune; imperfect &c. 651; the worse for wear; battered; weathered, weather-beaten; stale, *passé* [F.], shaken, dilapidated, frayed, faded, wilted, shabby, secondhand, threadbare; worn, – to- -a thread, – a shadow, – the stump, – rags; reduced, – to a skeleton; far-gone; tacky [*colloq. or slang*].

DECAYED &c. *v.;* moth-eaten, worm-eaten; mildewed, rusty, moldy *or* mouldy, spotted, seedy [*colloq.*], time-worn, moss-grown; discolored; effete, wasted, crumbling, moldering *or* mouldering, rotten, cankered, blighted, marcescent, tainted; depraved &c. (*vicious*) 945; decrepit; broken-down; done, – for, – up [*all colloq.*]; worn-out, used up [*colloq.*]; fit for the -dust hole, – waste-paper basket; past work &c. (*useless*) 645.

AT A LOW EBB, in a bad way, on one's last legs; undermined, deciduous; nodding to its fall &c. (*destruction*) 162; tottering &c. (*dangerous*) 665; past cure &c. (*hopeless*) 859; washed out, run down; fatigued &c. 688; unprogressive, improgressive [*rare*], backward, stagnant, behind the times; retrograde &c. (*retrogressive*) 283; deleterious &c. 649.

Adv. ON THE DOWN GRADE, on the downward track; beyond hope.

⁂ *ægrescit medendo;* "what a falling off was there!" [*Hamlet*]; "oh, what a fall was there, my countrymen!" *Julius Cæsar*]; *fuimus Troës, fuit Ilium* [Vergil].

---

660. Restoration. — N. RESTORATION, restoral [*rare*], restorance [*obs.*]; reinstatement, replacement, rehabilitation, reëstablishment, reconstitution, reconstruction; reproduction &c. 163; renovation, renewal; revival, revivement [*rare*], reviviscence *or* revivescence; refreshment &c. 689; resuscitation, reanimation, revivification, reviction [*obs.*]; reorganization.

reaction; redemption &c. (*deliverance*) 672; restitution &c. 790; relief &c. 834.

recurrence &c. (*repetition*) 104; *réchauffé* [*F.*], *rifacimento* [*It.*].

RENAISSANCE, renascence, rebirth, second youth, rejuvenescence, rejuvenation, new birth; regeneration, regeneracy, regenerateness, regenesis, palingenesis, reconversion; resurgence, resurrection.

REDRESS, retrieval, reclamation, recovery; convalescence; resumption, *résumption* [*F.*]; sanativeness.

CURE, recure [*obs.*], sanation [*obs.*]; healing &c. *v.;* redintegration; rectification; instauration; cicatrization; disinfection; delousing, delousement.

REPAIR, repairing, reparation, mending; recruiting &c. *v.;* tinkering.

MENDER, doctor, physician, surgeon; priest, clergyman, pastor; carpenter, joiner, plumber, tinker, cobbler; reviver, revivor [*rare*], renewer, *vis medicatrix* [*L.*] &c. (*remedy*) 662.

CURABLENESS, curability, reparability, restorableness, retrievability, recoverability, recoverableness.

V. RETURN TO THE ORIGINAL STATE; recover, rally, revive; come to, come round, come to oneself; pull through, weather the storm, be oneself again; get -well, – round, – the better of, – over – up, – about; rise from -one's ashes, – the grave; resurge, resurrect; survive &c. (*outlive*) 110; resume, reappear; come to, – life again; live again, rise again.

HEAL, heal over, skin over, cicatrize; right itself, heal itself.

RESTORE, put back, place *in statu quo* [*L.*]; reinstate, replace, reseat, rehabilitate, reëstablish, reëstate, reinstall.

RECONSTRUCT, rebuild, reorganize, reconstitute; convert, reconvert; recondition, renew, renovate; regenerate; rejuvenate.

---

661. Relapse. — N. RELAPSE, lapse; falling back &c. *v.;* retrogradation &c. (*retrogression*) 283; deterioration &c. 659.

[RETURN TO, OR RECURRENCE OF, A BAD STATE] backsliding, recidivation [*obs.*]; recidivism, recidivity; recrudescence.

V. RELAPSE, lapse; fall –, slide –, slip –, sink- back; have a relapse, be overcome, be overtaken, yield again to, fall again into; return; retrograde &c. 283; recidivate [*rare*]; fall off &c. 659- again.

Adj. BACKSLIDING, relapsing &c. *v.;* recidivous, recidivistic, recrudescent, retrograde.

REDEEM, reclaim, recover, retrieve; rescue &c. (*deliver*) 672.

CURE, heal, remedy, doctor, physic, medicate; redress, recure; break of; bring round, set on one's legs.

RESUSCITATE, revive, reanimate, revivify, recall to life; reproduce &c. 163; warm up; reinvigorate, refresh &c. 689.

REDINTEGRATE, make whole; recoup &c. 790; make good, make all square; rectify; put -, set- -right, - to rights, - straight; set up, correct; put in order &c. (*arrange*) 60; refit, recruit; fill up, - the ranks; reinforce.

REPAIR, mend; put in repair, put in thorough repair; retouch, botch, vamp, tinker, cobble; do up, patch up, plaster up, vamp up; darn, finedraw, heelpiece; stop a gap, stanch *or* staunch, calk *or* caulk, careen, splice, bind up wounds.

Adj. RESTORED &c. *v.;* redivivus, redivivous [*rare*], reviviscible, convalescent; in a fair way; none the worse; rejuvenated; renascent.

RESTORING &c. *v.;* restorative, recuperative; sanative, sanatory; reparative, reparatory; curative, remedial.

RESTORABLE, recoverable, remediable, retrievable, curable, sanable [*rare*].

Adv. *in statu quo* [*L.*[; as you were.

⁎ *revenons à nos moutons; vestigia nulla retrorsum* [Horace]; "physician, heal thyself" [*Bible*]; 'with healing in his wings" [*Bible*]; "Richard's himself again!" [Cibber].

---

662. Remedy. — N. REMEDY, help, redress; anthelmintic, vermifuge, helminthagogue; antifebrile, febrifuge; antipoison, antidote, mithridate [*old pharm.*], theriaca *or* theriac, counterpoison; antispasmodic; lithagogue; bracer, pick-me-up [*colloq.*], stimulant, tonic; abirritant, prophylactic, antiseptic, germicide, bactericide, corrective, restorative; alterant, alterative; cathartic &c. 652; specific; emetic, carminative.

MATERIA MEDICA, pharmacy, pharmacology, pharmaceutics, acology, posology, dosology [*rare*]; pathology &c. 655; pharmacopœia.

NARCOTIC, nepenthe *or* nepenthes, opium, morphine, cocaine, hashish, bhang, ganja, dope [*slang*]; sedative &c. 174.

CURE; partial -, attempted -, radical -, perfect -, certain- cure; sovereign remedy, panacea, cure-all, catholicon.

PHYSIC, medicine, simples, drug, potion, draft *or* draught, dose, pill, bolus, electuary; lincture *or* linctus; medicament; pharmacon.

NOSTRUM, recipe, receipt, prescription; elixir, *elixir vitæ* [*L.*], balm, balsam, cordial, tisane, ptisan.

agueweed, boneset; arnica, benzoin, cream of tartar, bitartrate of potash, calomel, mercurous chloride; catnip, catmint; Epsom salts; feverroot *or* feverwort, feverweed, friar's balsam; Indian sage; ipecac *or* ipecacuanha; Peruvian

663. Bane. —N. BANE, curse, hereditary evil, thorn in the flesh; *bête noir* [*F.*], bugbear; evil &c. 619; hurtfulness &c. (*badness*) 649; painfulness &c. (*cause of pain*) 830; scourge &c. (*punishment*) 975; *damnosa hereditas* [*L.*]; white elephant.

rust, worm, helminth, moth, "moth and rust " [*Bible*], fungus, mildew; dry rot; canker, cankerworm; cancer; viper &c. (*evildoer*) 913; demon &c. 980.

STING, fang, thorn, tang [*dial. Eng.*], bramble, brier *or* br ar, nettle.

POISON, leaven, virus, venom; arsenic, Prussic acid, antimony, tartar emetic, strychnine, tannin *or* tannic acid, nicotine; miasma *or* miasm, effluvium, mephitis, stench; fetor &c. 401; malaria, azote [*rare*], nitrogen, coal gas, illuminating gas, natural gas, gas, poison gas, mustard gas, chlorine, tear gas, lachrymose gas; sewer gas; pest.

Albany hemp, arsenious -oxide, - acid; bichloride of mercury; carbonic acid, - gas; choke damp, black damp, fire damp, afterdamp, marsh gas, methane; cyanide of potassium, carbolic acid, corrosive sublimate; hydrocyanic acid, hydrocyanide; nux vomica, ratsbane.

toxicant, intoxicant, deliriant, delirifacient, hemlock, hellebore, nightshade, deadly nightshade, belladonna, henbane, aconite; banewort, opium, bhang [*India*], ganja [*India*], hemp, cannabin, hashish; Upas tree.

bark, Jesuits' bark, cinchona, quinine *or* quinin, sassafras, yarrow.

SALVE, ointment, cerate, oil, lenitive, palliative, lotion, embrocation, liniment.

harquebusade *or* arquebusade, traumatic, vulnerary, pepastic, maturative, maturant, suppurative; eyewater, collyrium; cosmetic; depilatory.

POULTICE, cataplasm, vesicatory, plaster, *emplastrum* [*L.*], epithem, sinapism.

compress, pledget; bandage &c. (*support*) 215.

[SCIENCE OF POISONS] toxicology.

Adj. BANEFUL &c. (*bad*) 649; poisonous &c. (*unwholesome*) 657.

⁎ *bibere venenum in auro;* "my bane and antidote are both before me" [Addison]; "this even-handed justice Commends the ingredients of our poisoned chalice To our own lips" [*Macbeth*]; die "like a poisoned rat in a hole" [Swift].

TREATMENT, medical treatment, regimen, diet; dietary, dietetics; *vis medicatrix* [*L.*]; *vis naturæ* [*L.*]; *médecine expectante* [*F.*]; bloodletting, bleeding, venesection, phlebotomy, cupping, sanguisuge, leeches; operation, the knife [*colloq.*], surgical operation; major operation; electrolysis, electrolyzation.

HEALING ART, leechcraft [*archaic*], practice of medicine, therapeutics; allopathy, homeopathy *or* homœopathy, osteopathy, eclecticism, heteropathy; gynecology, gyniatrics, gynecological therapeutics; pediatrics *or* pædiatrics; surgery, chirurgery [*archaic*]; orthopedics *or* orthopædics, orthopedia *or* orthopædia, orthopraxy, orthopraxis, orthopedic surgery; sarcology, organotherapy; hydrotherapy, hydropathy, cold-water cure; faith cure, faith healing, mind cure, psychotherapy, psychotherapeutics; Christian Science, Eddyism; radiotherapy, heliotherapy, serotherapy, serum therapy; aërotherapy, pneumatotherapy; vocational therapy; dentistry, surgical dentistry; midwifery, obstetrics, tocology.

HOSPITAL, infirmary, clinic, *hôpital* [*F.*], general hospital, *hotel-Dieu* [*F.*]; special hospital (cancer, children's, dental, fever, maternity *or* lying-in, ophthalmic &c); pesthouse, lazarhouse, lazaretto, lazaret; lock hospital [*Eng.*]; *maison de santé* [*F.*]; *Hôtel des Invalides* [*F.*]; sanatarium, sanitarium, sanatorium, springs, baths, spa, pump room, well; hospice; asylum, home; Red Cross; ambulance.

dispensary, dispensatory, drug store, chemist's shop [*Brit.*].

DOCTOR, physician, leech [*archaic*], medical man, disciple of Æsculapius; medical –, general– practitioner; medical attendant, specialist; surgeon, chirurgeon [*archaic*].

consultant, operator; interne, anæsthetist *or* anesthetist; aurist, oculist, dentist, dental surgeon; osteopath, osteopathist; orthopedist *or* orthopædist; gynecologist, obstetrician; Christian Science practitioner, faith healer; medical student, medic [*colloq. or slang, U. S.*]; *accoucheur* (*fem. accoucheuse*) [*F.*], midwife; nurse; graduate –, trained –, district –, practical –, monthly-nurse; sister, nursing sister; dresser, bonesetter, apothecary, druggist, chemist [*Brit.*], pharmacopolist, pharmaceutist, pharmacist, pharmaceutical chemist, pharmacologist; Æsculapius, Hippocrates, Galen; *masseur* (*fem. masseuse*) [*F.*], massagist, rubber.

[INSTRUMENTS] stethoscope, stethometer, stethograph, respirometer, spirometer, pneumometer, spirograph, pneumatograph, pneumatometer, pulmotor.

V. APPLY A REMEDY &c. *n.;* doctor [*colloq.*], dose, physic, nurse, minister to, attend, dress the wounds, plaster, poultice; strap, splint, bandage; prevent &c. 706; relieve &c. 834; palliate &c. 658; heal, cure, "kill or cure," work a cure, remedy, stay (disease), snatch from the jaws of death; restore &c. 660; drench with physic; consult, specialize, operate, anæsthetize *or* anesthetize; straighten, mold *or* mould; deliver; extract, fill, stop; transfuse, bleed, cup, let blood; electrolyze.

manicure; pedicure; shampoo; massage, rub.

Adj. REMEDIAL; restorative &c. 660; corrective, palliative, healing; sanatory, sanative; prophylactic; salutiferous &c. (*salutary*) 656; medical, medicinal; therapeutic, hypnotic, neurotic, chirurgical [*archaic*], surgical, epulotic [*obs.*], paregoric, tonic, corroborant, roborant; analeptic, balsamic, anodyne, narcotic, sedative, lenitive, demulcent, emollient; detersive, detergent; abstersive, disinfectant; febrifugal, antifebrile; alterative; traumatic, vulnerary.

allopathic, homeopathic *or* homœopathic, eclectic, hydropathic, heteropathic; aperient, laxative, cathartic, purgative; septic; aseptic, antiseptic, antiluetic, antisyphilitic; anthelmintic, vermifugal; chalybeate, deobstruent; purifying, cleansing, depurative, depuratory; electrolytic *or* electrolytical.

DIETETIC, dietary, alimentary; nutritious, nutritive; digestive, digestible, peptic.

REMEDIABLE, curable; antidotal, alexipharmic, alexiteric.

*** *aux grands maux les grands remèdes; temporis ars medicina fere est* [Ovid]; "physicians mend or end us, *Secundum artem*" [Byron]; "troubled with thick-coming fancies" [*Macbeth*]; "the remedy is worse than the disease" [Dryden]; "throw physic to the dogs, I'll none of it" [*Macbeth*]; "the best doctors in the world are Doctor Diet, Doctor Quiet, and Doctor Merryman" [Swift]; "Divine presenter of the healing rod" [Browning].

3. Contingent Subservience

664. Safety. — N. SAFETY, security, surety, impregnability; invulnerability, invulnerableness &c. *adj.;* danger -past, – over; storm blown over; coast clear; escape &c. 671; means of escape; blow-, safety-, snifting- valve; safeguard, palladium; sheet anchor; rock, tower.

GUARDIANSHIP, wardship, wardenship; tutelage, custody, safe-keeping; preservation &c. 670; guardship [*obs.*], protection, auspices.

PROTECTOR, guardian; warden, warder; preserver, life saver, custodian, duenna, chaperon, third person.

safe-conduct, escort, convoy; guard, shield &c. (*defense*) 717; guardian angel; tutelary -god, – deity, – saint; *genius loci* [L.].

WATCHDOG, bandog; Cerberus.

WATCHMAN, patrolman, policeman, police officer, officer [*colloq.*], "the finest" [*local, U. S.*]; cop, copper, peeler, bobby [*all slang*], blue coat [*colloq.*], constable, roundsman [*U. S.*], *gendarme* [*F.*], military police; detective,· tec [*slang*], bull [*slang, U. S.*], spotter [*slang*]; sheriff, deputy; sentinel, sentry, scout &c. (*warning*) 668.

ARMED FORCE, garrison, life guard, State guard, militia, regular army, navy; volunteer; marine &c. 726; battleship, man-of-war &c. 726.

[MEANS OF SAFETY] refuge &c., anchor &c. 666; precaution &c. (*preparation*) 673; guard, guard rail, hand rail; bulkhead, watertight compartment, safety appliance; bolt, hasp &c. (*pin*) 45; cyclone cellar, dugout, bombproof dug-out; quarantine, *cordon sanitaire* [*F.*].

[SENSE OF SECURITY] confidence &c. 858.

JUDGE, justice, judiciary, magistrate, beak [*slang, Eng.*], justice of the peace, J. P.; deemster [*Isle of Man*], hakim [*Oriental*]; chancellor &c. 967.

V. BE SAFE &c. *adj.;* keep one's head above water, tide over, save one's bacon [*colloq.*]; ride out –, weather- the storm; light upon one's feet; bear a

665. Danger. — N. DANGER, peril, insecurity, jeopardy, risk, hazard, venture, precariousness, slipperiness; instability &c. 149; defenselessness &c. *adj.*

exposure &c. (*liability*) 177; vulnerability; vulnerable point, heel of Achilles; forlorn hope &c. (*hopelessness*) 859.

[DANGEROUS COURSE] leap in the dark &c. (*rashness*) 863; road to ruin, *facilis descensus Averni* [Vergil], hairbreadth escape.

[APPROACH OF DANGER] cause for alarm; source of danger &c. 667; rock -, breakers- ahead; storm brewing; clouds -in the horizon, – gathering; warning &c. 668; alarm &c. 669.

[SENSE OF DANGER] apprehension &c. 860.

V. BE IN DANGER &c. *adj.;* be exposed to –, run into –, incur –, encounter-danger &c. *n.;* run a risk; lay oneself open to &c. (*liability*) 177; lean on –, trust to- a broken reed; feel the ground sliding from under one, have to run for it; have the -chances, – odds- against one.

hang by a thread, totter; tremble on the verge; totter on the brink; sleep -, stand- on a volcano; sit on a barrel of gunpowder, live in a glass house.

ENDANGER; bring -, place -, put- in -danger &c. *n.;* expose to danger, imperil; be proscribed; have one's name on the danger list; be overdue [*naut.*], be despaired of; be under sentence of death; jeopard, jeopardize; put one's head in the lion's mouth; beard the lion in his den; compromise; sail too near the wind &c. (*rash*) 863.

threaten &c. (909) danger; run one hard; lay a trap for &c. (*deceive*) 545.

ADVENTURE, risk, hazard, venture, stake, set at hazard; run the gauntlet &c. (*dare*) 861; engage in a forlorn hope.

Adj. IN DANGER &c. *n.;* endangered

278

charmed life; escape &c. 671; possess nine lives.

PROTECT, watch over; make *or* render safe &c. *adj.*; take care of &c. (*care*) 459; preserve &c. 670; cover, screen, shelter, shroud, flank, ward; take charge of; guard &c. (*defend*) 717; garrison; man the -garrison, – lifeboat; secure &c. (*restrain*) 751; intrench *or* entrench, mine, countermine; dig in; fence round &c. (*circumscribe*) 229; house, nestle, ensconce.

ESCORT, support, accompany, convoy.

WATCH, mount guard, patrol, go on one's beat; do –, perform- sentry go; scout, spy.

TAKE PRECAUTIONS &c. (*prepare for*) 673; "make assurance double sure" [*Macbeth*] &c. (*caution*) 864; take up a loose thread; reef, take in a reef, make all snug, have an anchor to windward, double reef topsails.

seek safety; take –, find- shelter &c. 666; run into port.

Adj. SAFE, secure, sure; in safety, in security; in shelter, in harbor, in port; in the shadow of a rock; on *terra firma* [L.]; on the safe side; under the -shield of, – shade of, – wing of, – shadow of one's wing; under cover, under lock and key; out of -danger, – the meshes, – harm's way; on sure ground, at anchor, high and dry, above water; unthreatened, unmolested; protected &c. *v.*; *cavendo tutus* [L.]; panoplied &c. (*defended*) 717.

safe and sound &c. (*preserved*) 670; harmless; scatheless &c. (*perfect*) 650; unhazarded; not dangerous &c. 665.

snug, seaworthy, airworthy; watertight, weathertight, weatherproof, waterproof, fireproof; bombproof, shellproof.

DEFENSIBLE, tenable, proof against, invulnerable; unassailable, unattackable; "founded upon a rock" [*Bible*], impregnable, imperdible [*obs.*]; inexpugnable.

PROTECTING &c. *v.*; guardian, tutelary; preservative &c. 670; trustworthy &c. 939.

&c. *v.*; fraught with danger; dangerous, hazardous, perilous, periculous [*obs.*], parlous [*archaic*], unsafe, unprotected &c. (safe, protect &c. 664); insecure, untrustworthy, unreliable; built upon sand, on a sandy basis; unsound, speculative, wild-cat.

DEFENSELESS, guardless, fenceless [*archaic*], harborless, unsheltered, unshielded; vulnerable, expugnable, exposed; open to &c. (*liable*) 177.

aux abois [F.], at bay, with one's back to the wall; on the wrong side of the wall, on a lee shore, on the rocks.

PRECARIOUS, critical, ticklish; slippery, slippy; hanging by a thread &c. *v.*; with a halter round one's neck; between -the hammer and the anvil, – Scylla and Charybdis, – two fires; on the edge, brink, *or* verge of -a precipice, – a volcano, – an abyss, -a pit; in the lion's den, on slippery ground, under fire; not out of the wood; in the condemned cell, under sentence of death; at stake, in question.

UNWARNED, unadmonished, unadvised; unprepared &c. 674; off one's guard &c. (*inexpectant*) 508.

TOTTERING, unstable, unsteady; shaky, top-heavy, tumble-down, ramshackle, crumbling, water-logged; helpless, guideless; in a bad way; reduced to –, at- the last extremity; trembling in the balance; nodding to its fall &c. (*destruction*) 162.

THREATENING &c. 909; ominous, illomened; alarming &c. (*fear*) 860; explosive; poisonous; venomous &c. (*insalubrious*) 657; rotten at the core.

ADVENTUROUS &c. (*rash*) 863, (*bold*) 861.

Int. STOP! look! listen! look out! look alive! look slippy! [*colloq.*]; below there! 'ware heads! beware! take care! *prenez garde!* [F.].

※ *incidit in Scyllam qui vult vitare Charybdim; nam tua res agitur paries dum proximus ardet;* "out of this nettle, danger, we pluck this flower, safety" [*King Henry IV*]; "pleased with the danger, when the waves went high He sought the storms" [Dryden].

Adv. *ex abundante cautelâ* [L.]; with impunity.

Int. ALL'S WELL! all clear! all serene! [*slang*]; safety first! at rest! at ease!

※ *salva res est; suave mari magno; à cowert; e terra alterius spectare laborem* [Lucretius]; *Dieu vous garde;* "safe through a thousand perils brought" [Montgomery]; "early and provident fear is the mother of safety" [Burke]; "be of good cheer: it is I; be not afraid" [*Bible*]; "he who fights and runs away May live to fight another day" [Goldsmith]; "Astoundingly tricephalate, Waits Cerberus, the mutt of Hades" [Don Marquis].

666. [MEANS OF SAFETY.] Refuge. —
N. REFUGE, sanctuary, retreat, fastness, stronghold, fortress, castle, acropolis; keep, last resort; ward; prison &c. 752; asylum, ark, home, refuge for the destitute; almshouse; hiding place &. (*ambush*) 530; *sanctum sanctorum* [*L.*] &c. (*privacy*) 893.

ANCHORAGE, roadstead; breakwater, mole, port, haven; harbor, – of refuge; seaport; pier, jetty, embankment, quay, wharf, landing place; bund, bunder [*both Oriental*]; water wing [*arch.*].

COVERT,, shelter, screen, lee wall, wing, shield, umbrella; dashboard, dasher [*U. S.*], splashboard, mud guard *or* mudguard, wheel guard.

wall &c. (*inclosure*) 232; fort &c. (*defense*) 717.

ANCHOR, sheet anchor, sacred anchor [*Gr. & Rom. antiq.*], kedge *or* kedge anchor; Trotman's –, Martin's –, mushroom- anchor; killick; grapnel, grappling iron; mainstay; support &c. 215; check &c. 706; ballast.

MEANS OF ESCAPE &c. (*escape*) 671; lifeboat, swimming belt, cork jacket, life preserver, buoy, breeches buoy; parachute, plank, stepping-stone.

SAFEGUARD &c. (*protection*) 664.

jury mast; vent-peg; safety -valve, – lamp; lightning -rod, – conductor.

V. SEEK *or* FIND SAFETY &c. 664; seek –, take –, find- refuge &c. *n.*; claim sanctuary; throw oneself into the arms of; break for the tall timber [*U. S.*], break for the woods; fly to, reach in time; make port, make the harbor; anchor in the roadstead; crouch in the lee of; reach -shelter, – home, – running water.

BAR THE GATE, let the portcullis down; lock –, bolt –, make fast- the door; raise the drawbridge.

** bibere venenum in auro; valet anchora virtus; "ein feste Burg ist unser Gott" — a mighty fortress is our God [Luther].

---

667. [SOURCE OF DANGER.] Pitfall. —
N. rocks, reefs, coral reef, sunken rocks, snags; sands, quicksands; syrt [*rare*], syrtis [*rare*]; Goodwin sands, sandy foundation; slippery ground; breakers, shoals, shallows, bank, shelf, flat, lee shore, ironbound coast, rockbound coast; rock –, breakers- ahead; derelict.

ABYSS, abysm, pit, void, chasm, crevasse.

WHIRLPOOL, eddy, vortex, gurge [*rare*], rapids, undertow; current, tide gate, tide race, maelstrom; eagre, bore, tidal wave.

PITFALL; ambush &c. 530; trapdoor; trap &c. (*snare*) 545; mine, masked battery, spring-gun.

PEST, ugly customer, dangerous person, *le chat qui dort* [*F.*]; crouching tiger; incendiary, firebug [*slang*]; firebrand; hornet's nest.

sword of Damocles; wolf at the door, snake in the grass, snake in one's bosom, death in the -cup, – pot; latency &c. 526.

** latet anguis in herbâ [Vergil]; *proximus ardet Ucalegon* [Vergil]; "O Thou, who didst with pitfall and with sin Beset the Road I was to wander in" [Omar Khayyám — Fitzgerald].

---

668. Warning. — N. WARNING, caution, caveat; notice &c. (*information*) 257; premonition, premonishment [*rare*]; prediction &c. 511; symptom, contraindication, lesson, dehortation; admonition, monition; alarm &c. 669.

handwriting on the wall, *tekel upharsin* [*Heb.*], yellow flag; red flag, red light, fog-signal, fog-horn; siren; monitor, warning voice, Cassandra, signs of the times, Mother Cary's chickens, stormy petrel, bird of ill omen, gathering clouds, cloud no bigger than a man's hand, clouds in the horizon, death watch, death lights &c. (*premonitions*) 992a.

WATCHTOWER, beacon, signal post; lighthouse &c. (*indication of locality*) 550.

SENTINEL, sentry; watch, watchman; watch and ward; watchdog, bandog, house dog; patrol, vedette, picket, bivouac, scout, spy, spial [*obs.*]; advanced –, rear-guard; lookout, flagman.

CAUTIOUSNESS &c. 864.

V. WARN, caution; forewarn, prewarn; admonish, forebode, premonish [*rare*]; give -notice, – warning; menace &c. (*threaten*) 909; put on one's guard; sound the alarm &c. 669; croak.

BEWARE, ware [*dial.*]; take -warning, – heed at one's peril; look out, keep one's wits about one; keep watch and ward &c. (*care*) 459.

Adj. WARNING &c. *v.;* premonitory, monitory, cautionary, admonitory, admonitive [*rare*]; ominous, threatening, lowering, minatory &c. (*threat*) 909; symptomatic, sematic [*biol.*].

WARNED &c. *v.;* on one's guard &c. (*careful*) 459, (*cautious*) 864.

Adv. with alarm, on guard, after due warning, with one's eyes open; *in terrorem* [*L.*].

Int. BEWARE! ware! take care! mind –, take care- what you are about! mind! look out! watch your step!

*** *ne reveillez pas le chat qui dort; fanum habet in cornu; caveat actor; le silence du peuple est la leçon des rois; verbum sat sapienti; un averti en vaut deux;* "by the pricking of my thumbs, Something wicked this way comes" [*Macbeth*]; "cold-pausing Caution's lesson scorning" [Burns].

669. [INDICATION OF DANGER.] **Alarm. — N.** ALARM; alarum, larum [*archaic*], alarm bell, tocsin, *alerte* [*F.*], beat of drum, sound of trumpet, note of alarm, hue and cry, fiery cross; signal of distress; flag at -half-mast, – half-staff; blue lights; war cry, war whoop; warning &c. 668; fog signal, fog bell, fog horn, siren; yellow flag; danger signal; red light, red flag; fire bell, fire alarm, still alarm; burglar alarm; watchman's rattle, police whistle.

FALSE ALARM, cry of wolf; bugbear, bugaboo.

V. ALARM; give –, raise –, sound –, turn in –, beat- the *or* an -alarm &c. *n.;* warn &c. 668; ring the tocsin; *battre la générale* [*F.*]; cry wolf; half-mast.

Adj. ALARMED; warned; alarming &c. *v.*

Int. *sauve qui peut!* [*F.*]; *qui vive?* [*F.*]; who goes there?

*** "the trumpet's loud clangor Excites us to arms" [Dryden].

670. Preservation. — N. PRESERVATION; safe-keeping; conservation &c. (*storage*) 636; maintenance, support, sustentation [*rare*], conservatism; economy; *vis conervatrix* [*L.*]; salvation &c. (*deliverance*) 672.

[MEANS OF PRESERVATION] prophylaxis; preserver, preservative; hygiastics, hygiantics [*both rare*]; hygiene, hygienics; cover, drugget; *cordon sanitaire* [*F.*]; ensilage; dehydration, anhydration, evaporation; drying, putting up, canning, pickling; tinned goods [*chiefly Brit.*], canned goods; kyanization.

[SUPERSTITIOUS REMEDIES] charm &c. 993.

V. PRESERVE, maintain, keep, sustain, support; keep -up, – alive; not willingly let die; nurse; cure &c. (*restore*) 660; save, rescue; be –, make- safe &c. 664; take care of &c. (*care*) 459; guard &c. (*defend*) 717; bank, bank up, shore up.

embalm, dry, cure, salt, pickle, season, kyanize, bottle, pot, tin [*chiefly Brit.*], can; dehydrate, anhydrate, evaporate; husband &c. (*store*) 636.

HOLD ONE'S OWN; *stare super antiquas vias* [Bacon]; hold –, stand- one's ground &c. (*resist*) 719.

Adj. PRESERVING &c. *v.;* conservative; prophylactic; preservatory, preservative; hygienic.

PRESERVED &c. *v.;* unimpaired, unbroken, uninjured, unhurt, unsinged, unmarred; safe, – and sound; intact, with a whole skin, without a scratch.

*** *nolumus leges Angliæ mutari;* "thrift, thrift, Horatio" [*Hamlet*]; "the back door robs the house" [Herbert]; "a man he seems of cheerful yesterdays And confident tomorrows" [Wordsworth].

671. Escape. — N. ESCAPE, scape [*obs.*]; avolation [*obs.*], elopement, flight; evasion &c. (*avoidance*) 623; retreat; narrow –, hairbreadth- escape; close call [*colloq.*], close shave, near shave [*colloq.*]; come off, impunity.

[MEANS OF ESCAPE] loophole &c. (*opening*) 260; path &c. 627; secret -chamber, passage; refuge &c. 666; vent, – peg; safety valve; drawbridge, fire escape.

reprieve &c. (*deliverance*) 672; liberation &c. 750.

REFUGEE &c. (*fugitive*) 623.

V. ESCAPE, scape [*archaic*]; make –, effect –, make good- one's escape; break jail; get off, get clear off, get well out of; *échapper belle* [*F.*], save one's bacon [*colloq.*], make a get-away [*slang*]; weather the storm &c. (*safe*) 664; escape scot-free.

ELUDE &c., make off &c. (*avoid*) 623; march off &c. (*go away*) 293; give one the slip; slip through the -hands, – fingers; slip the collar, wriggle out of; break loose, break from prison; break – slip –, get- away; find vent, find a hole to creep out of.

Adj. escaping, escaped &c. *v.;* stolen away, fled; scot-free.

. the bird has flown; "I am escaped with the skin of my teeth" [*Bible*].

672. Deliverance. — N. DELIVERANCE, extrication, rescue, ransom; reprieve, reprieval [*rare*], respite; armistice, truce; liberation &c. 750; emancipation; redemption, redeemableness, salvation; exemption; day of grace; riddance; jail (*or* gaol) delivery.

V. DELIVER, extricate, rescue, save, free, liberate, set free, release, emancipate, redeem, ransom; bring -off, – through; *tirer d'affaire* [*F.*], get the wheel out of the rut, snatch from the jaws of death, come to the rescue; rid; retrieve &c. (*restore*) 660; be –, get- rid of.

Adj. saved &c. *v.;* extricable, redeemable, rescuable.

Int. to the rescue! a rescue! saved!

. "in the course of justice, none of us Should see salvation: we do pray for mercy" [*Merchant of Venice*].

3. *Precursory Measures*

673. Preparation. — N. PREPARATION; providing &c. *v.;* provision, providence; anticipation &c. (*foresight*) 510; precaution, preconcertedness, preconcertion, predisposition; forecast &c. (*plan*) 626; rehearsal, note of preparation; dissemination, propaganda.

groundwork, first stone, cradle, stepping-stone; foundation, first rung, scaffold &c. (*support*) 215; scaffolding, *échafaudage* [*F.*].

ELABORATION; ripening &c. *v.;* maturation, evolution; perfection; concoction, digestion; gestation, hatching, incubation, sitting.

[PUTTING IN ORDER] arrangement &c. 60; clearance; adjustment &c. 23; tuning; equipment, outfit, accouterment *or* accoutrement, armament, array.

[PREPARATION OF MEN] training &c. (*education*) 537; inurement &c. (*habit*) 613; novitiate.

[PREPARATION OF FOOD] cooking, cookery, culinary art; brewing.

[PREPARATION OF THE SOIL] tilling, plowing *or* ploughing, sowing, semination, cultivation.

[STATE OF BEING PREPARED] preparedness, readiness, ripeness, mellowness; maturity; *un impromptu fait à loisir* [*F.*].

[PREPARER] preparer, trainer, coach; teacher &c. 540; pioneer; *avant-courrier* [*F.*], *avant-coureur* [*F.*]; *voortrekker*

674. Nonpreparation. — N. NONPREPARATION, unpreparedness; absence of –, want of- preparation; inculture [*obs.*], inconcoction [*obs.*], improvidence.

IMMATURITY, crudity; rawness &c. *adj.;* abortion; disqualification.

[ABSENCE OF ART] nature, state of nature; virgin soil, unweeded garden; rough diamond; neglect &c. 460.

rough copy &c. (*plan*) 626; germ &c. 153; raw material &c. 635.

improvisation &c. (*impulse*) 612.

V. BE UNPREPARED &c. *adj.;* want –, lack- preparation; lie fallow; *s'embarquer sans biscuits* [*F.*]; live from hand to mouth.

[RENDER UNPREPARED] dismantle &c. (*render useless*) 645; undress &c. 226.

EXTEMPORIZE, improvise; cook up, fix up, vamp.

SURPRISE, drop in upon [*colloq.*], pay a surprise visit, drop in [*colloq.*], give a surprise party, take potluck with; take –, catch- unawares; take by surprise, call informally.

Adj. UNPREPARED &c. (prepare &c. 673); without preparation &c. 673; incomplete &c. 53; rudimental, embryonic, abortive; immature, unripe, *kutcha* or *kachcha* [*Hind.*]; callow, unfledged, unhatched, unnurtured, raw, green, crude; coarse; rough, rough́cast, roughhewn; in the rough; rough-edged, unhewn, un-

[*Dutch*]; prophet; forerunner &c. (*precursor*) 64; sappers and miners, pavior, navvy; packer, stevedore, longshoreman; warming pan.

V. PREPARE; get –, make– ready; predispose, address oneself to, get under weigh; make preparations, settle preliminaries, get up, sound the note of preparation.

set *or* put in order &c. (*arrange*) 60; forecast &c. (*plan*) 626; prepare –, plow –, dress- the ground; till –, cultivate- the soil; sow the seed, lay a train, dig a mine; lay –, fix- the -foundations, – basis, – groundwork; dig the foundations, erect the scaffolding; lay the first stone &c. (*begin*) 66.

ROUGHHEW; cut out work; block out, hammer out; lick into shape &c. (*form*) 240.

ELABORATE, mature, ripen, mellow, season, bring to maturity; nurture &c. (*aid*) 707; hatch, cook, brew; temper, anneal, smelt; barbecue; dry, cure, salt, smoke, infumate [*rare*]; maturate.

EQUIP, arm, man; fit out, fit up; furnish, rig, dress, garnish, betrim, accouter *or* accoutre, array, fettle [*dial. Eng.*], fledge; dress up, furbish up, brush up, vamp up; refurbish; sharpen one's tools, trim one's -tackle, - foils; set, prime, attune; whet the -knife, - sword; wind up, screw up; adjust &c. (*fit*) 27; put in -trim, - train, - gear, - working order, - tune, - a groove for, - harness; pack, stow away, stow down, stow, load, store.

formed, unfashioned, unwrought, unlabored, unblown; indigested, undigested; unmellowed, unseasoned, unleavened; uncooked, unboiled, unconcocted; unpolished, uncut, deckle-edged.

UNTAUGHT, uneducated, untrained, untutored, undrilled, unexercised; unlicked; precocious, premature.

FALLOW, unsown, untilled, uncultivated.

NATURAL, *in puris naturalibus* [*L.*], in a state of nature; undressed; in dishabille, *en déshabillé* [*F.*], in negligee.

UNFITTED, disqualified, unqualified, ill-digested; unbegun, unready, unarranged, unorganized, unfurnished, unprovided, unequipped, untrimmed; out of -gear. – kilter *or* kelter [*colloq.*], – order; dismantled &c. *v.*

SHIFTLESS, improvident, unthrifty, thriftless, thoughtless, unguarded; happy-go-lucky; slack, remiss; caught napping &c. (*inexpectant*) 508; unpremeditated &c. 612.

Adv. INADVERTENTLY, by surprise, without premeditation; extempore &c. 612.

PREPARE FOR &c.; train &c. (*teach*) 537; inure &c. (*habituate*) 613; breed; rehearse; make provision for; take -steps, – measures, – precautions; provide, provide against; beat up for recruits; open the door to &c. (*facilitate*) 705.

set one's house in order, make all snug; clear decks, clear for action; close one's ranks; shuffle the cards.

PREPARE ONESELF; serve an apprenticeship &c. (*learn*) 539; lay oneself out for, get into harness, gird up one's loins, buckle on one's armor, *reculer pour mieux sauter* [*F.*], prime and load, shoulder arms, get up steam; put the horses to, harness, harness up [*colloq.*], hitch up [*colloq.*].

guard against, make sure against; forearm, make sure, prepare for the evil day, have a rod in pickle, have a bone to pick, provide against a rainy day, feather one's nest; lay in provisions &c. 637; make investments; keep on foot, keep going.

BE PREPARED, be ready &c. *adj.*; hold oneself in readiness, watch and pray, keep one's powder dry, lie in wait for &c. (*expect*) 507; anticipate &c. (*foresee*) 510; *principiis obstare* [*L.*]; *venienti occurrere morbo* [*L.*].

Adj. PREPARING &c. *v.*; in preparation, in course of preparation, in agitation, in embryo, in hand, in train; afoot, afloat; on foot, on the stocks, on the anvil; under consideration &c. (*plan*) 626; in consultation; brewing, hatching, forthcoming, brooding; in store for, in reserve.

precautionary, provident; preparative, preparatory; provisional, inchoate, under revision; under advisement; preliminary &c. (*precedent*) 62.

PREPARED &c. *v.*; in readiness; ready, – to one's hand, ready made; cut and dried; made to one's hand, ready cut, made to order, at one's elbow, ready for use, all ready; handy, on the table; in gear; running -smoothly, – sweetly; in working -order, – gear; snug; in practice.

in full feather, in best bib and tucker [*colloq.*]; in –, at- harness; in the saddle, in arms, in battle array, in war paint; up in arms; armed -at all points, – to the teeth, – *cap à pie* [*F.*]; sword in hand; booted and spurred.

in utrumque paratus [Vergil], *semper paratus* [*L.*]; on the alert &c. (*vigilant*) 459; at one's post.

RIPE, mature, mellow; pucka *or* pakka [*Hind.*]; practiced &c. (*skilled*) 698; labored, elaborate, high-wrought, smelling of the lamp, worked up.

Adv. IN PREPARATION, in anticipation of; afoot, astir, abroad; abroach.

*** *a bove majori discit arare minor;* "looking before and after"[*Hamlet*], *si vis pacem para bellum;* "there is a divinity that shapes our ends, Roughhew them how we will" [*Hamlet*].

675. Essay. — N. ESSAY, trial, endeavor, attempt; aim, struggle, venture, adventure, speculation, *coup d'essai* [*F.*], *début* [*F.*]; probation &c. (*experiment*) 463.

V. TRY, essay; experiment &c. 463; endeavor, strive; tempt, attempt, make an attempt; venture, adventure, speculate, take one's chance, tempt fortune; try one's -fortune, – luck, – hand; use one's endeavor; feel –, grope –, pick- one's way.

try hard, push, make a bold push, use one's best endeavor; do one's best &c. (*exertion*) 686.

Adj. ESSAYING &c. *v.;* experimental &c. 463; tentative, empirical, problematic *or* problematical, probationary.

Adv. EXPERIMENTALLY &c. *adj.;* on trial, at a venture; by rule of thumb.

if one may be so bold.

*** *aut non tentaris aut perfice* [Ovid]; *chi non s'arrischia non guadagna;* I'll try anything once.

676. Undertaking. — N. UNDERTAKING; compact &c. 769; adventure, venture, engagement &c. (*promise*) 768; enterprise, emprise *or* emprize [*archaic*]; pilgrimage; matter in hand &c. (*business*) 625; move; first move &c. (*beginning*) 66.

V. UNDERTAKE; engage –, embark- in; launch –, plunge- into; volunteer; apprentice oneself to; engage &c. (*promise*) 768; contract &c. 769; take upon -oneself, – one's shoulders; devote oneself to &c. (*determination*) 604.

TAKE UP, take on, take in hand; tackle [*colloq.*]; set –, go- about; set –, fall- -to, – to work; launch forth; break the ice; set up shop; put in -hand, – execution; set forward; break the neck of a -day's work, – business; be in for [*colloq.*]; put one's hand to; betake oneself to, turn one's hand to, go to do; be in the midst of; begin &c. 66; broach, institute &c. (*originate*) 153; put –, lay- one's -hand to the plow, – shoulder to the wheel.

have in hand &c. (*business*) 625; have many irons in the fire &c. (*activity*) 682.

Adj. UNDERTAKING &c. *v.;* on the anvil &c. 625; available, receptive; full of pep [*slang*], energetic; adventurous, venturesome.

Int. here goes! shoot! [*colloq.*].

*** "Nowher so besy a man as he ther n'as, And yet he semed besier than he was" [Chaucer]; "So many worlds, so much to do!" [Tennyson].

677. Use. — N. USE, employ; exercise, exercitation; application, appliance; adhibition, disposal; consumption; agency &c. (*physical*) 170; usufruct; usefulness &c. 644; benefit; recourse, resort, avail; pragmatism, pragmaticism.

[CONVERSION TO USE] utilization, utility, service, wear.

[WAY OF USING] usage, employment, *modus operandi* [*L.*].

678. Disuse. — N. DISUSE; forbearance, abstinence; relinquishment &c. 782; desuetude &c. (*want of habit*) 614; disusage.

V. NOT USE; do without, dispense with, let alone, not touch, forbear, abstain, spare, waive, neglect; keep back, reserve.

DISUSE; lay up, lay by, lay on the shelf, lay up in a napkin; shelve; set –,

USER, consumer, purchasing public, buying public; market, public demand, popular demand, demand.

V. USE, make use of, employ, put to use; apply; put in -action, – operation, – practice; set in motion, set to work.

PLY, work, wield, handle, manipulate; play, play off; exert, exercise, practice, avail oneself of, profit by; resort to, lay one's hand to, fall back upon, have recourse to, recur to, take to [colloq.], take up, betake oneself to; take up with, take advantage of; lay one's hands on, try.

RENDER USEFUL &c. 644; mold or mould; turn to -account, – use; convert to use, utilize; administer; work up; call –, bring- into play; put into requisition; call –, draw- forth; press –, enlist- into the service; task, tax, put to task; bring to bear upon, devote, dedicate, consecrate, apply, adhibit, dispose of; make a handle of, make a cat's-paw of.

FALL BACK UPON, make a shift with; make the most of, make the best of.

CONSUME, use up, devour, swallow up; absorb, expend; wear, outwear.

Adj. IN USE; used &c. v.; well-worn, well-trodden.

USEFUL &c. 644; subservient &c. (instrumental) 631; utilitarian, pragmatic or pragmatical.

*** "busy people are never busybodies" Cynic's Calendar].

put –, lay- aside; leave off, have done with; supersede; discard &c. (eject) 297; dismiss, give warning.

THROW ASIDE &c. (relinquish) 782; make away with &c. (destroy) 162; cast –, heave –, throw- overboard; cast to the -dogs, – winds; dismantle &c. (render usless) 645.

lie –, remain- unemployed &c. adj.

Adj. NOT USED &c. v.; unemployed, unapplied, undisposed of, unspent, unexercised, untouched, untrodden, unessayed, ungathered, unculled; uncalled for, not required.

DISUSED &c. v.; done with, run down, worn out, not worth saving.

Int. no use!

679. Misuse. — N. MISUSE, misusage, misemployment, misapplication, misappropriation.

ABUSE, profanation, prostitution, desecration; waste &c. 638.

V. MISUSE, misemploy, misapply, misappropriate.

DESECRATE, abuse, profane, prostitute.

OVERTASK, overtax, overwork, overdrive; squander &c. 818; waste &c. 638.

cut blocks with a razor, employ a steam engine to crack a nut; catch at a straw.

Adj. MISUSED &c. v.

*** ludere cum sacris; "who first misuse, then cast their toys away" [Cowper].

Section III. VOLUNTARY ACTION

1. Simple Voluntary Action

680. Action. — N. ACTION, performance; doing &c. v.; perpetration; exercise, exercitation; movement, operation, evolution, work, employment; labor &c. (exertion) 686; praxis [L.], execution; procedure &c. (conduct) 692; handicraft; business &c. 625; agency &c. (power at work) 170.

DEED, act, overt act, stitch, touch, gest or geste; transaction, job, doings, dealings, proceeding, measure, step, maneuver or maneuvre, manœuver or manœuvre, bout, passage, move, stroke, blow; coup, – de main, – d'état [F.]; tour de force [F.] &c. (display) 882; feat, exploit; achievement &c. (completion) 729; handiwork, craftsmanship, work-

681. Inaction. — N. INACTION, passiveness, abstinence from action; watchful waiting; noninterference; Fabian –, laisser-aller [F.] –, laisser-faire [F.] –, conservative- policy; neglect &c. 460.

INACTIVITY &c. 683; stagnation, vegetation, loafing, loaf; rest &c. (repose) 687; quiescence &c. 265; want of occupation, unemployment, inoccupation; idle hours, idle hands, time hanging on one's hands, dolce far niente [It.]; shore duty; interregnum; sinecure; soft snap, soft thing, cinch [all three slang].

V. NOT DO, not act, not attempt; be inactive &c. 683; abstain from doing, do nothing, hold, spare; not stir –, not move –, not lift- a -finger, – hand,

manship; manufacture; stroke of policy &c. (*plan*) 626.

ACTOR &c. (*doer*) 690.

V. DO, perform, execute; achieve &c. (*complete*) 729; transact, enact; commit, perpetrate, inflict; exercise, prosecute, carry on, work, practice, play.

EMPLOY ONESELF, ply one's task; officiate, have in hand &c. (*business*) 625; labor &c. 686; be at work; pursue a course; shape one's course &c. (*conduct*) 692.

ACT, operate; take action, take steps; strike a blow, lift a finger, stretch forth one's hand; take in hand &c. (*undertake*) 676; put oneself in motion; put in practice; carry into execution &c. (*complete*) 729; act upon.

BE AN ACTOR &c. 690; take -, act -, play -, perform- a part in; participate in; have a -hand in, - finger in the pie; have to do with; be a party to, be a participator in; bear -, lend- a hand; pull an oar, run in a race; mix oneself up with &c. (*meddle*) 682.

BE IN ACTION; come into operation &c. (*power at work*) 170.

Adj. IN ACTION; doing &c. *v.;* acting; in harness; up to one's ears in work; in the midst of things; on duty; at work; operative; in operation &c. 170.

Adv. in the -act, - midst of, - thick of; red-handed, *in flagrante delicto* [*L.*]; while one's hand is in; while one is at it.

** "action is eloquence" [*Coriolanus*]; actions speak louder than words; *actum ne agas* [Terence]; "awake, arise, or be forever fall'n" [*Paradise Lost*]; *dii pia facta vident* [Ovid]; *faire sans dire; fare fac; fronte capillata post est occasio calva;* "our deeds are sometimes better than our thoughts" [Bailey]; "we live in deeds not years" [*ibid.*]; "the great end of life is not knowledge but action" [Huxley]; "thought is the soul of act" [R. Browning]; *vivre ce n'est pas respirer c'est agir;* "our nature is movement; absolute stillness is death" [Pascal].

- foot, - peg; fold one's -arms, - hands; leave -, let- alone; let be, let pass, let things take their course, let it have its way, let well alone, let well enough alone; *quieta non movere* [*L.*]; *stare super antiquas vias* [*L.*]; rest and be thankful, live and let live; lie -, rest- upon one's oars; *laisser aller* [*F.*], *laisser faire* [*F.*]; stand aloof; refrain &c. (*avoid*) 623; keep oneself from doing; remit -, relax- one's efforts; desist &c. (*relinquish*) 624; stop &c. (*cease*) 142; pause &c. (*be quiet*) 265.

WAIT, lie in wait, bide one's time, take time, tide it over.

cool -, kick- one's heels; while away the -time, - tedious hours; pass -, fill up -, beguile- the time; talk against time; waste time &c. (*inactive*) 683.

lie by, lie on the shelf, lie idle, lie to, lie fallow; keep quiet, slug [*obs.*]; have nothing to do, whistle for want of thought; twiddle one's thumbs.

UNDO, do away with; take down, take to pieces; destroy &c. 162.

Adj. NOT DOING &c. *v.;* not done &c. *v.;* undone; passive; unoccupied, unemployed; out of -employ, - work, - a job; uncultivated, fallow; *désœuvré* [*F.*].

Adv. AT A STAND, *re infectâ* [*L.*], *les bras croisés* [*F.*], with folded arms; with the hands -in the pockets, - behind one's back; *pour passer le temps* [*F.*].

Int. STOP! &c. 142; hands off! so let it be! enough! no more! bas! [*Hind.*].

** *cunctando restituit rem;* "inaction is cowardice" [Emerson].

---

682. Activity. — **N.** ACTIVITY; briskness, liveliness &c. *adj.;* animation, life, vivacity, spirit, verve, pep [*slang*], dash, go [*colloq.*], energy; snap, vim.

SMARTNESS, nimbleness, agility; quickness &c. *adj.;* velocity &c. 274; alacrity, promptitude; dispatch *or* despatch, expedition; haste &c. 684; punctuality &c. (*early*) 132.

EAGERNESS, zeal, ardor, enthusiasm, *perfervidum ingenium* [*L.*], *empressement* [*F.*], earnestness, intentness; *abandon* [*F.*]; vigor &c. (*physical energy*) 171;

683. Inactivity. — **N.** INACTIVITY; inaction &c. 681; inertness &c. 172; obstinacy &c. 606.

lull &c. (*cessation*) 142; quiescence &c. 265; rust, rustiness.

IDLENESS, remissness &c. *adj.;* sloth, indolence, indiligence [*rare*]; dawdling &c. *v.;* ergophobia, otiosity, hoboism [*U. S.*].

dull work; pottering; relaxation &c. (*loosening*) 47; Castle of Indolence.

LANGUOR; dullness &c. *adj.;* segnity [*obs.*], segnitude [*obs.*], lentor; sluggish-

devotion &c. (*resolution*) 604; exertion &c. 686.

INDUSTRY, assiduity; assiduousness &c. *adj.;* sedulity [*rare*], sedulousness; laboriousness; drudgery &c. (*labor*) 686; painstaking, diligence; perseverance &c. 604*a*; indefatigation [*obs.*]; businesslike habits, habits of business.

VIGILANCE &c. 459; wakefulness; sleeplessness, restlessness; insomnia; pervigilium, *insomnium* [L.]; racketing.

BUSTLE, hustle [*colloq.*], movement, stir, fuss, ado, bother, fidget, fidgetiness; flurry &c. (*haste*) 684.

OFFICIOUSNESS; dabbling, meddling; interference, interposition, intermeddling; butting in [*slang*], horning in [*slang*], intrusiveness, minding others' business, not minding one's own business; tampering with, intrigue.

PRESS OF BUSINESS, no sinecure, plenty to do, a great deal doing [*colloq.*], a lot going on [*colloq.*], many irons in the fire, great doings, busy hum of men, the madding crowd, the thick of things, battle of life, thick of the action.

MAN OF ACTION, busy bee; new broom; sharp fellow, blade; devotee, enthusiast, fanatic, zealot, hummer [*slang*], hustler [*colloq.*], humdinger [*slang*, U. S.], rustler [*slang*, U. S.]; live wire, human dynamo [*both colloq.*], live man [U. S.].

MEDDLER, intermeddler, intriguer, intrigant *or* intriguant, telltale, busybody, pickthank [*archaic*].

V. BE ACTIVE &c. *adj.;* busy oneself in; stir, stir about, stir one's stumps [*colloq.*]; bestir –, rouse- oneself; speed, hasten, peg away, lay about one, bustle, fuss; raise –, kick up- a dust; push; make a -fuss, – stir; go ahead, push forward; fight –, elbow- one's way; make progress &c. 282; toil &c. (*labor*) 686; moil, drudge, plod, persist &c. (*persevere*) 604*a*; keep up the ball; keep the pot boiling.

look sharp; have all one's eyes about one &c. (*vigilance*) 459; rise, arouse oneself, hustle [*colloq.*], push [*colloq.*], get up early, be about, keep moving, steal a march, catch a weasel asleep, kill two birds with one stone; seize the opportunity &c. 134; lose no time, not lose a moment, make the most of one's time, not suffer the grass to grow under one's feet, improve the shining hour, make short work of; dash off; make haste &c.

ness &c. (*slowness*) 275; procrastination &c. (*delay*) 133; torpor, torpidity, torpescence; stupor &c. (*insensibility*) 823; somnolence; drowsiness &c. *adj.;* nodding &c. *v.;* oscitation, oscitancy; pandiculation, hypnotism, lethargy; statuvolence *or* statuvolism; sand in the eyes, heaviness, heavy eyelids.

SLEEP, slumber; sound –, heavy –, balmy- sleep; Morpheus; Somnus; coma, trance, catalepsy, hypnosis, ecstasis, dream; hibernation; nap, doze, snooze [*colloq. or dial.*], siesta, wink of sleep, forty winks [*colloq.*]; snore; hypnology.

[CAUSE OF INACTIVITY] lullaby, *berceuse* [F.], *Schlummerlied* [Ger.]; anæsthesia *or* anesthesia, anæsthetic *or* anesthetic, opiate, sedative &c. 174.

IDLER, drone, dawdle [*rare*], dawdler; stiff, dead one [*both slang*], mopus [*obs.*], do-little, *fainéant* [F.], dummy, sleeping partner; afternoon farmer; truant &c. (*runaway*) 623; bummer [U. S.], bum [*slang*, U. S.], Weary Willie [*colloq.*], tramp, sundowner [*slang*, *Austral.*], hobo [U. S.], fakir *or* fakeer [*Moham.*], sunyasi [*Hind.*]; beggar, cadger [*slang*], lounge lizard [*slang*, U. S.], lounger, lazzarone, loafer; lubber, lubbard [*rare*]; slow coach &c. (*slow*) 275; opium –, lotus- eater; slug; laggard, sluggard; slumberer, the Dustman, the Sandman; the Fat Boy in Pickwick; dormouse, marmot; waiter on Providence, *fruges consumere natus* [L.]; Mr. Micawber.

V. BE INACTIVE &c. *adj.;* do nothing &c. 681; move slowly &c. 275; let the grass grow under one's feet; take one's time, dawdle, drawl, lag, hang back, slouch; loll, lollop [*colloq.*, *Brit.*], lounge, poke, loaf, loiter; go to sleep over; sleep at one's post, *ne battre que d'une aile* [F.].

take it easy, take things as they come; lead an easy life, vegetate, swim with the stream, eat the bread of idleness; loll in the lap of -luxury, – indolence; waste –, consume –, kill –, lose-time; burn daylight, waste the precious hours.

DALLY, dilly-dally; idle –, trifle –, fritter –, fool- away time; spend –, take-time in; peddle, piddle; potter, putter [U. S.], dabble, faddle [*dial. Eng.*], fribble, fiddle-faddle.

SLEEP, slumber, be asleep; hibernate; oversleep; sleep like a -top, – log, – dormouse; sleep -soundly, – heavily;

684; do one's best, take pains &c. (*exert oneself*) 686; do –, work- wonders; have a lot of -kick [*colloq.*], – pep [*slang*].

have many irons in the fire, have one's hands full, have much on one's hands; have other -things to do, – fish to fry; be busy; not have a moment -to spare, – that one can call one's own.

HAVE ONE'S FLING, run the round of; go all lengths, stick at nothing, run riot.

OUTDO; overdo, overact, overlay, weigh down, overshoot the mark; make a toil of a pleasure.

HAVE A HAND IN &c. (*act in*) 680; take an active part, put in one's oar, have a finger in the pie, mix oneself up with, trouble one's head about, intrigue; agitate.

MEDDLE, tamper with, intermeddle, interfere, interpose; obtrude; poke –, thrust- one's nose in; butt in, horn in [*both slang*].

Adj. ACTIVE, brisk, – as a lark, – as a bee; lively, animated, vivacious; alive, – and kicking [*colloq.*]; frisky, spirited, stirring.

nimble, – as a squirrel; agile; light-footed, nimble-footed; featly tripping.

QUICK, prompt, yare [*archaic*], instant, ready, alert, spry [*colloq. & dial.*], sharp, smart; fast &c. (*swift*) 274; capable, smart as a steel trap, no sooner said than done &c. (*early*) 132; quick as a lamplighter, expeditious; awake, broad awake; go-ahead, live [*U. S.*], hustling [*colloq.*]; wide-awake &c. (*intelligent*) 498.

FORWARD, eager, ardent, strenuous, zealous, enterprising, in earnest; resolute &c. 604.

INDUSTRIOUS, assiduous, diligent, sedulous, notable [*obsoles. in this sense*], painstaking; intent &c. (*attention*) 457; indefatigable &c. (*persevering*) 604*a*; unwearied, never weary, sleepless, unsleeping, never tired; plodding, hard-working &c. 686; businesslike.

BUSTLING; restless, – as a hyena; fussy, fidgety, pottering; busy as a hen with one chicken.

WORKING, at work, on duty, in harness; up in arms; on one's legs, at call; up and -doing, – stirring; laboring, workday, workaday.

BUSY, occupied; hard at work, hard at it; up to one's ears in, full of business; busy as a -bee, – housewife.

MEDDLING &c. *v.*; meddlesome, pushing, officious, overofficious, *intrigant* [*F.*].

doze, drowse, snooze [*colloq. or dial.*], nap; take a nap &c. *n.*; dream; snore; settle –, go –, go off- to sleep; drop off [*colloq.*]; fall asleep, drop asleep; close –, seal up- -the -eyes, – eyelids; weigh down the eyelids; get sleepy, nod, yawn; go to bed, turn in, hit the hay [*slang*], rest in the arms of Morpheus.

LANGUISH, expend itself, flag, hang fire; relax.

RENDER IDLE &c. *adj.*; sluggardize; mitigate &c. 174.

Adj. INACTIVE; motionless &c. 265; unoccupied &c. (*doing nothing*) 681.

INDOLENT, lazy, slothful, idle, lusk [*obs.*], remiss, slack, inert, torpid, torpescent, sluggish, otiose, languid, supine, heavy, dull, leaden, lumpish; drony, dronish; lazy as Ludlam's dog.

dilatory, laggard; lagging &c. *v.*; slow &c. 275; rusty, flagging; fiddle-faddle; pottering &c. *v.*; shilly-shally &c. (*irresolute*) 605.

exanimate [*now rare*], soulless; listless; lackadaisical, maudlin.

SLEEPING &c. *v.*; asleep; fast –, dead –, sound- asleep; in a sound sleep; sound as a top, dormant, comatose; in the -arms, – lap- of Morpheus.

SLEEPY, sleepful [*rare*], full of sleep, oscitant, dozy, drowsy, somnolent, torpescent; lethargic *or* lethargical, somnifacient; statuvolent, statuvolic; heavy, heavy with sleep; nappy, somnific, somniferous; soporose *or* soporous, soporific, soporiferous; hypnotic; balmy, dreamy; unawakened, unwakened.

sedative &c. 174.

Adv. INACTIVELY &c. *adj.*; at leisure &c. 685; with half-shut eyes, half asleep; in dreams, in dreamland.

*** the eyes begin to draw straws; "bankrupt of life yet prodigal of ease" [Dryden]; "better fifty years of Europe than a cycle of Cathay" [Tennyson]; "idly busy rolls their world away" [Goldsmith]; "the mystery of folded sleep" [Tennyson]; "the timely dew of sleep" [Milton]; "thou driftest gently down the tides of sleep" [Longfellow]; "tired Nature's sweet restorer, balmy sleep" [Young]; "slumber lay so deep Even her hands upon her lap Seemed saturate with sleep" [De La Mare].

ASTIR, stirring; agoing, afoot; on foot; in full swing; eventful; on the alert &c. (*vigilant*) 459.

Adv. ACTIVELY &c. *adj.;* featly [*archaic*]; with life and spirit, with might and main &c. 686, with haste &c. 684, with wings; full tilt, *in mediis rebus* [*L.*].

Int. be –, look- -alive, – sharp! move on! push on! keep moving! go ahead! stir your stumps! [*colloq.*]; *age quod agis!* [*L.*], *jaldi!* [*Hind.*], *jaldi karo!* [*Hind.*], step lively!

*** *carpe diem* &c. (*opportunity*) 134; *nulla dies sine lineâ* [Pliny]; *nec mora nec requies* [Vergil]; the plot thickens; *veni vidi vici* [Suetonius]; *abends wird der Faule fleissig; dictum ac factum* [Terence]; *schwere Arbeit in der Jugend ist sanfte Ruhe im Alter;* "the busy hum of men" [Milton]; "they shall run and not be weary; they shall walk and not faint [*Bible*]; "Life, not the daily coil, but as it is Lived in its beauty in eternity" [Masefield].

684. Haste. — N.

HASTE, urgency, dispatch *or* despatch, acceleration, spurt *or* spirt, forced march, rush, scurry *or* skurry, scuttle, dash; velocity &c. 274; precipitancy, precipitation, precipitousness &c. *adj.;* impetuosity; *brusquerie* [*F.*]; hurry, drive, scramble, bustle, fuss, fidget, flurry, flutter, splutter.

V. HASTE, hasten; make haste, make a dash &c. *n.;* hurry –, dash –, whip –, push –, press- -on, – forward; hurry, scurry *or* skurry, scuttle along, bundle on, dart to and fro, bustle, flutter, scramble; plunge, – headlong; dash off; rush &c. (*violence*) 173; express, railroad [*colloq., U. S.*].

BESTIR ONESELF &c. (*be active*) 682; lose -no time, – not a moment, – not an instant; make short work of; make the best of one's -time, – way.

be precipitate &c. *adj.;* jump at, be in haste, be in a hurry &c. *n.;* have -no time –, have not a moment- -to lose, – to spare; work against time, work under pressure.

QUICKEN &c. 274; accelerate, expedite, put on, precipitate, urge, whip, spur, flog, goad.

Adj. HASTY, hurried, brusque; scrambling, cursory, precipitate, headlong, furious, boisterous, impetuous, hot-headed; feverish, fussy; pushing.

IN HASTE, in a hurry &c. *n.;* in hot haste, in all haste; breathless, pressed for time, hard pressed, urgent.

Adv. WITH HASTE, with all haste, with breathless speed; in haste &c. *adj.;* apace &c. (*swiftly*) 274; amain; all at once &c. (*instantaneously*) 113; at short notice &c., immediately &c. (*early*) 132; posthaste; by cable, by telegraph, by wireless [*colloq.*], by aëroplane, by return mail, by steam [*colloq.*], by forced marches.

HASTILY, precipitately &c. *adj.;* helter-skelter, hurry-skurry, holus-bolus; slap-dash, slap-bang; full-tilt, full-drive; heels over head, head and shoulders, headlong, *à corps perdu* [*F.*].

BY FITS AND STARTS, by spurts; hop skip and jump.

Int. RUSH! immediate! urgent! look alive! *jaldi karo!* [*Hind.*]; get a move on! [*colloq.*], get a wiggle on! [*colloq.*]; quickmarch! [*mil.*], double! [*mil.*]; gallop! charge! [*mil.*].

*** *sauve qui peut,* devil take the hindmost, no time to be lost; sharp is the word; no sooner said than done &c. (*early*) 132; a word and a blow; *maggiore frétta minore átto; ohne Hast aber ohne Rast* [Goethe's motto]; "stand not upon the order of your going" [*Macbeth*]; "swift, swift, you dragons of the night" [*Cymbeline*].

685. Leisure. — N.

LEISURE; convenience; spare -time, – hours, - moments; vacant hour; time, – to spare, – to burn [*slang, U. S.*], – on one's hands; holiday &c. (*rest*) 687; *otium cum dignitate* [*Cic.*]; ease.

V. HAVE LEISURE &c. *n.;* take one's -time, – leisure, – ease; repose &c. 687; move slowly &c. 275; while away the time &c. (*inaction*) 681; be master of one's time, be an idle man; *desipere in loco* [*L.*].

*** time hanging heavy on one's hands; *eile mit Weile;* my time is at your disposal; "retiréd Leisure That in trim gardens takes his pleasure" [Milton]; "Shall I not take mine ease in mine inn?" [Shakespeare].

686. Exertion. — N. EXERTION, effort, strain, tug, pull, stress, throw, stretch, struggle, spell, spurt or spirt; stroke -, stitch- of work.

"a long pull, a strong pull, and a pull all together"; dead lift; heft [dial.]; wear and tear; ado; toil and trouble; uphill -, hard -, warm- work; harvest time.

EXERCISE, exercitation, practice, play, gymnastics, field sports; breather [colloq.], racing, running, jumping, riding &c.

LABOR, work, toil, travail [rare], manual labor, sweat of one's brow, swink [obs.], operoseness, drudgery, slavery, fag [colloq., Eng.], faggery, fagging, hammering; limæ labor [L.]; operosity [obs.], operoseness.

trouble, pains, duty; resolution &c. 604; energy &c. (physical) 171.

WORKER, plodder, laborer, drudge, fagger, fag [Eng. schools], slave; man of action &c. 682; agent &c. 690; Samson, Hercules.

V. EXERT ONESELF; exert -, tax- one's energies; use exertion.

LABOR, work, toil, moil, sweat, fag, swink [archaic], toil and moil, drudge, slave, drag a lengthened chain, wade through, strive, strain; make -, stretch- a long arm; pull, tug, ply; ply -, tug at- the oar; do the work; take the laboring oar.

bestir oneself (be active) 682; take trouble, trouble oneself.

WORK HARD; rough it; put forth -one's strength, - a strong arm; fall to work, bend the bow; buckle to, set one's shoulder to the wheel &c. (resolution) 604; work like a -horse, - cart horse, - dog, - galley slave, - coal heaver, - Briton; labor -, work- day and night; redouble one's efforts; do double duty; work double -hours, - tides; sit up, burn the candle at both ends, burn the midnight oil; stick to &c. (persevere) 604a; work -, fight- one's way; lay about one, hammer at.

DO ONE'S BEST, do one's level best, do one's utmost; take pains; do the best one can, do all one can, do all in one's power, do as much as in one lies, do what lies in one's power; use one's -best, - utmost- endeavor; try one's- -best, - utmost; play one's best card; put one's -best, - right- leg foremost; put one's best foot foremost; have one's whole soul in his work, put all one's strength into, strain every nerve; spare no -efforts, -pains; go all lengths; go through fire and water &c. (resolution) 604; move heaven and earth, leave no stone unturned.

Adj. laboring &c. v.

LABORIOUS, hefty [colloq., U. S.], operose, elaborate; strained; toilsome, troublesome, wearisome, burdensome; uphill; herculean, gymnastic, palæstric or palestric, athletic.

HARDWORKING, painstaking, strenuous, energetic, never idle.

hard at work, on the stretch, on the move, on the jump, on the dead jump, on the run.

Adv. LABORIOUSLY &c. adj.; lustily; pugnis et calcibus [L.]; with might and main, with all one's might, with a strong hand, with sledge hammer, with much ado; to the best of one's abilities, totis viribus [L.], vi et armis [L.], manibus

687. Repose. — N. REPOSE, rest, silken repose; sleep &c. 683.

relaxation, breathing time; halt, stay, pause &c. (cessation) 142; respite.

DAY OF REST, dies non [L.], Sabbath, Lord's day, Sunday, First Day, holiday, red-letter day; gala day &c. (amusement) 840; vacation, recess.

V. REPOSE; rest, rest and be thankful; take rest, take one's ease.

lie down; recline, recline on a bed of down, recline on an easychair; go to -rest, - bed, - sleep &c. 683.

RELAX, unbend, slacken; take breath &c. (refresh) 689; rest upon one's oars; pause &c. (cease) 142; stay one's hand.

take a holiday, shut up shop; lie fallow &c. (inaction) 681.

Adj. REPOSING &c. v.; unstrained.

HOLIDAY, festal, ferial [rare]; sabbatic or sabbatical.

Adv. at rest.

⁎ "the best of men have ever loved repose" [Thomson]; "to repair our nature with comforting repose" [Henry VIII]; "The nightly mercy of the eventide" [Masefield].

pedibusque [*L.*], tooth and nail, *unguibus et rostro* [*L.*], hammer and tongs, heart and soul; through thick and thin &c. (*perseverance*) 604a.

by the sweat of one's brow, *suo Marte* [*L.*].

*** *aide-toi, le ciel t'aidera;* "and still be doing, never done" [Butler]; *buen principio la mitad es hecha; cosa ben fatta è fatta due volte;* "it is better to wear out than to rust out" [Bp. Horne]; *labor omnia vincit* [Vergil]; "labor, wide as the earth, has its summit in Heaven" [Carlyle]; *le travail du corps délivre des peines de l'esprit; manu forti; ora et labora;* "I wish to preach . . . the doctrine of the strenuous life" [Roosevelt]; "Sorrow of soul in toil, that brings delight" [Masefield].

688. Fatigue. — N. FATIGUE; weariness &c. 841; yawning, drowsiness &c. 683; lassitude, tiredness, fatigation [*obs.*], sweat.

SHORTNESS OF BREATH; anhelation [*rare*], dyspnœa *or* dyspnea, panting, labored breathing.

FAINTNESS, fainting, swoon, goneness, exhaustion, collapse, prostration, deliquium, syncope, lipothymy.

V. BE FATIGUED &c. *adj.;* yawn &c. (*get sleepy*) 683; droop, sink, flag; lose breath, lose wind; gasp, pant, puff, blow, drop, swoon, faint, succumb.

FATIGUE, tire, bore, weary, irk [*chiefly impersonal, as,* it irks me], flag, jade, harass, exhaust, knock up, wear out, bleed white, prostrate.

TAX, task, strain; overtask, overwork, overburden, overtax, overstrain, fag, fag out.

Adj. FATIGUED &c. *v.;* weary &c. 841; drowsy &c. 683; drooping &c. *v.;* haggard; toilworn, wayworn; footsore, surbated [*obs.*], weather-beaten; faint; done, done up, used up, knocked up [*all colloq.*]; bushed [*slang or dial., Amer.*]; exhausted, prostrate, spent; overtired, overspent, overfatigued; unrefreshed, unrestored.

ready to drop, all in [*slang*], more dead than alive, dog-weary, dog-tired, walked off one's legs, tired to death, on one's last legs, played out, *hors de combat* [*F.*].

WORN, worn out; battered, shattered, pulled down, seedy [*colloq.*], enfeebled, altered.

BREATHLESS, windless; short of –, out of -breath, – wind; blown, puffing and blowing; short-breathed; anhelose; broken-winded, short-winded; dyspnœal *or* dyspneal, dyspnœic *or* dyspneic.

*** "weary and old with service" [*Henry VIII*]; "the weariness, the fever, and the fret" [Keats]; "When Ajax strives some rock's vast weight to throw, The line too labours and the words move slow" [Pope].

689. Refreshment. — N. RECUPERATION; recovery of strength &c. 159; refreshing, bracing &c. *v.;* restoration, revival &c. 660; repair, refection, refocillation [*obs.*], refreshment, regale, regalement, bait; relief &c. 834.

V. REFRESH; brace &c. (*strengthen*) 159; reinvigorate; air, freshen up, recruit; repair &c. (*restore*) 660; fan, refocillate [*obs.*]; refresh the inner man; get better, raise one's head; recover –, regain –, renew- one's strength &c. 159; perk up.

BREATHE, respire; drink in the ozone; draw –, take –, gather –, take a long –, regain –, recover- breath.

RECUPERATE; come to oneself &c. (*revive*) 660; feel like a giant refreshed.

Adj. REFRESHING &c. *v.;* recuperative &c. 660.

REFRESHED &c. *v.;* untired, unwearied.

*** "they that wait upon the Lord shall renew their strength; they shall mount up with wings as eagles" [*Bible*].

690. Agent. — N. AGENT, doer, actor, performer, perpetrator, operator; executor, executrix; practitioner, worker, old stager; mediary, medium, reagent.

minister &c. (*instrument*) 631; representative &c. (*commissioner*) 758, (*deputy*) 759; factor, steward.

SERVANT &c. 746; factotum, general, maid-of-all-work, servant-of-all-work, do-all [*colloq.*].

[COMPARISONS] bee, ant, working bee, termite, white ant; laboring oar; shaft horse.

WORKMAN, artisan; craftsman, handicraftsman; mechanic, operative; workingman, laboring man; hewers of wood and drawers of water, laborer, navvy [*Eng.*];

hand, man, day laborer, journeyman, hack; mere tool &c. 633; beast of burden, drudge, fag; lumper, stevedore, roustabout [U. S.].

maker, artificer, *artifex* [L.], artist, wright, manufacturer, architect, contractor, builder, mason, bricklayer, smith, forger, Vulcan; carpenter; platelayer; blacksmith, locksmith, sailmaker, tailor, cordwainer, wheelwright.

machinist, mechanician, engineer, electrician, plumber, gasfitter.

WORKWOMAN, charwoman, seamstress *or* sempstress, needlewoman, laundress, washerwoman, "Madonna of the tubs" [Phelps].

COWORKER, associate, fellow worker, coöperator, colleague, *confrère* [F.]; party to, participator in, *particeps criminis* [L.], *dramatis personæ* [L.]; *personnel* [F.].

. *quorum pars magna fui* [Vergil]; *faber est quisque fortunæ suæ.*

691. Workshop. — N. WORKSHOP, workhouse; laboratory, manufactory, armory, arsenal, mill, factory, *usine* [F.], mint, loom; cabinet, bureau, studio, *atelier* [F.]; hive, hive of industry; plant; hothouse, hotbed; kitchen; alveary, beehive; bindery, forcing pit, nailery, dock, dockyard, slip, yard, wharf; foundry *or* foundery, forge, furnace; vineyard, orchard, nursery, truck garden, truck farm, farm.

melting pot, crucible, caldron *or* cauldron, mortar, alembic; matrix.

2. Complex Voluntary Action

692. Conduct. — N. CONDUCT, behavior; deportment, comportment; carriage, *maintien* [F.], demeanor, guise, bearing, manner, observance.

course -, line- of -conduct, - action, – proceeding; rôle; process, ways, practice, procedure, *modus operandi* [L.]; method &c., path &c. 627.

DEALING, transaction &c. (*action*) 680; business &c. 625.

POLICY, polity; tactics, game, generalship, statesmanship, seamanship; strategy, strategics; plan &c. 626.

MANAGEMENT, government &c. (*direction*) 693; stewardship, husbandry; housekeeping, housewifery; *ménage or* menage; *régime or* regime, regimen, economy, economics; political economy.

CAREER, life, course, walk, province, race, record; execution, manipulation, treatment; campaign.

V. TRANSACT, execute; dispatch *or* despatch, proceed with, discharge; carry -on, – through, – out, – into effect; work out; go through, get through; enact; put into practice; officiate &c. 625.

bear -, behave -, comport -, demean -, carry -, conduct -, acquit- oneself.

run a race, lead a life, play a game; take -, adopt- a course; steer -, shape- one's course; play one's part, play one's cards; shift for oneself; paddle one's own canoe; bail one's own boat.

conduct; manage &c. (*direct*) 693.

DEAL WITH, have to do with; treat, handle a case; take -steps, - measures.

Adj. CONDUCTING &c. *v.;* directive, strategic *or* strategical, methodical, businesslike, practical, executive; economic.

. "it is their care that the wheels run truly" [Kipling].

693. Direction. — N. DIRECTION; management, managery [obs.]; government, gubernation [obs.], conduct, legislation, regulation, guidance; bossism [slang, U. S.]; legislature; steerage, pilotage; reins, - of government; helm, rudder, needle, compass; guiding star, lodestar *or* loadstar, polestar; cynosure.

ministry, ministration; administration; stewardship, proctorship; chair; agency.

SUPERVISION, superintendence; surveillance, oversight; eye of the master; control, charge; auspices; board of control &c. (*council*) 696; command &c. (*authority*) 737.

STATESMANSHIP; statecraft, kingcraft, queencraft; premiership, senatorship; director &c. 694; seat, portfolio.

V. DIRECT, manage, govern, conduct; order, prescribe, cut out work for; head, lead; lead the way, show the way; take the lead, lead on; regulate, guide, steer, pilot; take the helm, be at the helm; have –, handle –, hold –, take- the reins; drive, tool [*cant*], tackle.

SUPERINTEND, supervise; overlook, oversee, control, keep in order, look after, see to, legislate for; administer, ministrate [*obs.*]; matronize; patronize; have the -care, – charge- of; have –, take- the direction; pull the -strings, – wires; rule &c. (*command*) 737; be the guiding force; have –, hold- -office, – the portfolio; preside, – at the board; take –, occupy –, be in- the chair; pull the stroke oar.

Adj. DIRECTING &c. *v.*; executive, gubernatorial, supervisory; hegemonic *or* hegemonical; predominant; statesmanlike.

Adv. IN CHARGE OF, under the guidance of, under the auspices of; in control of, at the helm, at the head of.

694. Director. — N. DIRECTOR, manager, governor, rector [*rare*], controller, comptroller; superintendent, supervisor; intendant; overseer, overlooker; supercargo, husband [*archaic*], inspector, foreman, ganger [*Eng.*], visitor, ranger, surveyor, ædile *or* edile [*Rom. hist.*], moderator, monitor, taskmaster; master &c. 745; leader, ringleader, agitator, demagogue, corypheus, conductor, fugleman, precentor, bellwether; *caporal* [*F.*], choregus, collector, file leader, flugelman, linkboy.

GUIDING STAR &c. (*guidance*) 693; adviser &c. 695; guide &c. (*information*) 527; pilot; helmsman; steersman, steersmate [*obs.*]; wire-puller.

DRIVER, whip, jehu [*humorous*], charioteer; coachman, carman, cabman; postilion, *vetturino* [*It.*], muleteer, *arriero* [*Sp.*], teamster; whipper-in; chauffeur, motorman, engine-driver.

HEAD, headman, chief, principal, president, speaker; chair, chairman; captain &c. (*master*) 745; superior; mayor &c. (*civil authority*) 745; vice-president, prime minister, premier, vizier *or* vizir, grand vizier, eparch.

OFFICER, functionary, minister, official, red-tape, red-tapist, bureaucrat; Jack in office; office bearer, office holder; person in authority &c. 745.

STATESMAN, strategist, legislator, lawgiver, politician, statist [*rare*], statemonger; Minos, Draco; arbiter &c. (*judge*) 967; boss [*slang, U. S.*], political dictator, power behind the throne, kingmaker; secretary, – of state; Reis Effendi; vicar &c. (*deputy*) 759; board &c. (*council*) 696.

STEWARD, factor; agent &c. 758; bailiff, middleman; clerk of works; landreeve; factotum, major-domo, seneschal, housekeeper, shepherd; croupier; proctor, procurator, curator, librarian.

Adv. *ex officio.*

⁎⁎ "drest in a little brief authority" [Shakespeare]; "it is excellent To have a giant's strength; but it is tyrannous To use it as a giant" [*ibid.*].

695. Advice. — N. ADVICE, counsel, adhortation [*obs.*]; word to the wise; suggestion, submonition [*obs.*], recommendation, advocacy; advisement [*archaic*]; consultation.

EXHORTATION &c. (*persuasion*) 615; expostulation &c. (*dissuasion*) 616; admonition &c. (*warning*) 668; guidance &c. (*direction*) 693.

INSTRUCTION, charge, injunction; Governor's –, President's- message; King's –, Queen's- speech; message, speech from the throne.

ADVISER, prompter; counsel, counselor; monitor, mentor, Nestor, sage, wise man, wise woman; *magnus Apollo* [*L.*], senator; teacher &c. 540; yogi *or* yogin; physician, leech [*archaic*]; archiater; arbiter &c. (*judge*) 967.

GUIDE, manual, chart &c. (*information*) 527.

CONSULTATION, conference, *pourparler* [*F.*], parley, powwow [*U. S.*]; reference, referment.

V. ADVISE, counsel; give -advice, – counsel, – a piece of advice; suggest, prompt, submonish [*obs.*], recommend, prescribe, advocate; exhort &c. (*persuade*) 615.

ENJOIN, enforce, charge, instruct, call; call upon &c. (*request*) 765; dictate.

EXPOSTULATE &c. (*dissuade*) 616; admonish &c. (*warn*) 668.

ADVISE WITH; lay heads –,consult- together; compare notes; hold a council, deliberate, be closeted with.

CONFER, consult, refer to, call in; follow, follow implicitly; take –, follow- advice; be advised by, have at one's elbow, take one's cue from.

Adj. RECOMMENDATORY; hortative &c. (*persuasive*) 615; dehortatory &c. (*dissuasive*) 616; admonitory &c. (*warning*) 668; consultative; dictatory, dictatorial; didactic.

Int. go to!

* * "give every man thine ear but few thy voice" [*Hamlet*]; "I am Sir Oracle, And when I ope my lips, let no dog bark!" [*M. of V.*]; "I pray thee cease thy counsel" [*Much Ado About Nothing*]; "my guide, philosopher and friend" [Pope]; "'twas good advice and meant, my son be good" [Crabbe]; *verbum sat sapienti; vive memor lethi* (or *leti*); "we ask advice but we mean approbation" [Colton].

696. Council.— **N.** COUNCIL, committee, subcommittee, comitia [*Rom. hist.*], privy council, court, chamber, cabinet, board, bench, staff.

junta, divan, musnud, sanhedrin *or* sanhedrim [*Jewish antiq.*], amphictyonic council [*Gr. hist.*]; syndicate; court of appeal &c. (*tribunal*) 966; board of -control, – works; county council, local board, parish council, common council, town meeting; board of overseers; zemstvo [*Russ.*].

[ECCLESIASTICAL] convocation, synod, congregation, church, chapter, directory, vestry, consistory, conventicle, conclave, convention, classis.

LEGISLATURE, parliament, congress, national council, states-general, diet.

Duma [*Russia*], Storthing *or* Storting [*Norway*], Rigsdag [*Denmark*], Riksdag [*Sweden*], Cortes [*Spain*], Reichsrath *or* Reichsrat [*Austria*], Volksraad [*Dutch*]; Dail Eireann [*Sinn Fein*]; witan, witenagemot *or* witenagemote [*Anglo-Saxon hist.*].

UPPER HOUSE, upper chamber, first chamber, senate, *senatus* [*Rom. hist.*], legislative council, House of Lords, House of Peers; Bundesrath *or* Bundesrat [*Ger.*], federal council, Lagting [*Nor.*], Landsthing [*Den.*].

LOWER HOUSE, lower chamber, second chamber, house of representatives, House of Commons, the house, legislative assembly, chamber of deputies; Odelsting [*Nor.*], Folkething [*Den.*], Reichstag [*Ger.*].

ASSEMBLY, plenum, caucus, clique; meeting, sitting, séance, *camarilla* [*Sp.*], conference, hearing, session, palaver, *pourparler* [*F.*], durbar [*India*]; quorum; council fire [*N. Am.*], powwow [*U. S.*].

[REPRESENTATIVES] congressman, M. C., senator, representative; member, – of parliament, M. P.; representative of the people; assemblyman, councilor.

Adj. curule, congressional, senatorial, parliamentary; synodic *or* synodical.

697. Precept. — N. PRECEPT, direction, instruction, charge; prescript, prescription; recipe, receipt; golden rule; maxim &c. 496.

rule, canon, law, code, *corpus juris* [*L.*], *lex scripta* [*L.*], convention; unwritten law; canon law; act, statute, rubric, stage direction, regulation; model, form, formula, formulary; technicality; nice point, fine point, norm.

order &c. (*command*) 741.

698. Skill. — N. SKILL, skillfulness *or* skilfulness, address; dexterity, dexterousness *or* dextrousness, adroitness, expertness &c. *adj.*; proficiency, competence, craft; callidity [*rare*], callidness, facility, knack, trick, sleight; mastery, mastership; excellence, panurgy [*rare*]; ambidexterity, ambidextrousness; sleight of hand &c. (*deception*) 545.

seamanship, airmanship, marksmanship, horsemanship; rope-dancing; tightrope –, slack-rope- walking.

699. Unskillfulness. — N. UNSKILLFULNESS *or* unskilfulness &c. *adj.*; want of skill &c. 698; incompetence *or* incompetency; inability, infelicity, indexterity [*rare*], clumsiness, inaptitude &c. *adj.*; inexperience; disqualification, unproficiency; quackery.

FOLLY, stupidity &c. 499; indiscretion &c. (*rashness*) 863; thoughtlessness &c. (*inattention*) 458, (*neglect*) 460; sabotage [*F.*].

MISMANAGEMENT, misconduct, mis-

ACCOMPLISHMENT, acquirement, attainment; art, science; finish, finished execution, technique, technic, practical -, technical- knowledge; technology.

WORLD WISDOM, knowledge of the world, *savoir faire* [*F.*]; tact; mother wit &c. (*sagacity*) 498; discretion &c. (*caution*) 864; finesse; craftiness &c. (*cunning*) 702; management &c. (*conduct*) 692; self-help.

CLEVERNESS, talent, ability, ingenuity, capacity, parts, talents, faculty, endowment, forte, turn, gift, genius; intelligence &c. 498; sharpness, readiness &c. (*activity*) 682; invention &c. 515; aptness, aptitude; turn for, capacity for, genius for; felicity, capability, *curiosa felicitas* [*L.*], qualification, habilitation.

PROFICIENT, expert, adept &c. 700.

MASTERPIECE, masterwork, *coup de maître* [*F.*,] *chef d'œuvre* [*F.*], *tour de force* [*F.*]; good stroke &c. (*plan*) 626.

V. BE SKILLFUL &c. *adj.*; excel in, be master of; have a turn for &c. *n.*

KNOW WHAT'S WHAT, know- a hawk from a handsaw, – what one is about, – on which side one's bread is buttered, – what's o'clock, – what o'clock it is, – the time of day, – a thing or two, – the ropes; have cut one's -eyeteeth, – wisdom teeth; see through a millstone; be up to [*all colloq.*].

see one's way, see where the wind lies, see which way the wind blows; have all one's wits about one, have one's hand in; *savoir vivre* [*F.*]; *scire quid valeant humeri quid ferre recusent* [*L.*].

look after the main chance; cut one's coat according to one's cloth; live by one's wits; exercise one's discretion, feather the oar, sail near the wind; stoop to conquer &c. (*cunning*) 702; play one's cards well, play one's best card; hit the right nail on the head, put the saddle on the right horse.

TAKE ADVANTAGE OF, make the most of; profit by &c. (*use*) 677; make a hit &c. (*succeed*) 731; make a virtue of necessity; make hay while the sun shines &c. (*occasion*) 134.

Adj. SKILLFUL *or* skilful, dexterous *or* dextrous, adroit, expert, apt, handy, quick, deft, ready, slick [*slang*], smart &c. (*active*) 682; proficient, good at, up to, at home in, master of, a good hand at, *au fait* [*F.*[, thoroughbred, masterly,

feasance; inexpedience, bad policy, impolicy; maladministration; misrule, misgovernment, misapplication, misdirection.

ABSENCE OF RULE, rule of thumb; bungling &c. *v.;* failure &c. 732; screw loose; too many cooks.

BLUNDER &c. (*mistake*) 495; *étourderie* [*F.*], *gaucherie* [*F.*], act of folly, *balourdise* [*F.*], bungle, botch, botchery; bad job, sad work.

sprat sent out to catch a whale, butterfly broken on a wheel, tempest in a teacup, storm in a teacup, much ado about nothing, wild-goose chase.

BUNGLER &c. 701; fool &c. 501; hen with its head cut off [*colloq.*].

V. BE UNSKILLFUL *or* unskilful, &c. *adj.;* not see an inch beyond one's nose; blunder, bungle, muff [*esp., baseball*], boggle, fumble, botch, mar, spoil, bitch [*obs.*], flounder, stumble, trip; hobble &c. 275; put one's foot in it [*colloq.*]; make a -mess, – hash, – sad work- of [*all colloq.*]; overshoot the mark.

play tricks with, play Puck; mismanage, misconduct, misdirect, misapply, missend.

ACT FOOLISHLY; stultify -, make a fool of -, commit- oneself; play the fool; put oneself out of court; lose one's -head, – senses, – cunning; begin at the wrong end; do things by halves &c. (*not complete*) 730; make two bites of a cherry; play at cross-purposes; strain at a gnat and swallow a camel &c. (*caprice*) 608; put the cart before the horse; lock the stable door when the horse is stolen &c. (*too late*) 135.

not know what one is about, not know one's own interest, not know on which side one's bread is buttered; stand in one's own light, quarrel with one's bread and butter, throw a stone in one's own garden, kill the goose which lays the golden eggs, pay dear for one's whistle, cut one's own throat, burn one's fingers; knock -, run- one's head against a stone wall; bring the house about one's ears; have too many -eggs in one basket (*imprudent*) 863, – irons in the fire.

cut blocks with a razor; hold a farthing candle to the sun &c. (*useless*) 645; fight with -, grasp at- a shadow; catch at straws, lean on a broken reed, reckon without one's host, pursue a wild-goose chase; go on a fool's errand,

crack [*colloq.*], crackajack [*slang*], accomplished; conversant &c. (*knowing*) 490.

EXPERIENCED, practiced, skilled; up in, well up in; in practice; competent, efficient, qualified, capable, fitted, fit for, up to the mark, up and coming [*dial., U.S.*], trained, initiated, prepared, primed, finished.

CLEVER, cute [*colloq.*], able, ingenious, felicitous, gifted, talented, endowed; inventive &c. 515; shrewd, sharp &c. (*intelligent*) 498; cunning &c. 702; alive to, up to snuff [*slang*], not to be caught with chaff; discreet.

neat-handed, fine-fingered, nimble-fingered, ambidextrous, sure-footed; cut out for [*colloq.*], fitted for.

technical, artistic, scientific, dædalian, shipshapelike, workmanlike, businesslike, statesmanlike.

Adv. SKILLFULLY *or* skilfully &c. *adj.*; well &c. 618; artistically; with skill, with fine techique, with consummate skill; *secundum artem* [*L.*], *suo Marte* [*L.*]; to the best of one's abilities &c. (*exertion*) 686; like a machine.

٭٭ *ars celare artem; artes honorabit; celui qui veut celui-là peut; c'est une grande habileté que de savoir cacher son habileté; expertus metuit* [Horace]; *es bildet ein Talent sich in der Stille sich ein Charakter in dem Strom der Welt;* "heart to conceive, the understanding to direct, or the hand to execute" [Junius].

go on a sleeveless errand [*obs.*]; go further and fare worse; fail &c. 732.

MISTAKE &c. 495; take the shadow for the substance &c. (*credulity*) 486; bark up the wrong tree; be in the wrong box, aim at a pigeon and kill a crow; take -, get- -the wrong pig by the tail, – the wrong sow by the ear, – the dirty end of the stick [*all colloq.*]; put the saddle on the wrong horse, put a square thing into a round hole, put new wine into old bottles; lose one's way, miss one's way; fall into a trap, catch a Tartar.

Adj. UNSKILLFUL *or* unskilful &c. 698; unskilled, inexpert; bungling &c. *v.;* awkward, clumsy, unhandy, lubberly, *gauche* [*F.*], maladroit; left-handed, heavy-handed; slovenly, slatternly; gawky.

adrift, at fault.

INAPT, unapt; inhabile [*obs.*]; untractable, unteachable; giddy &c. (*inattentive*) 458; inconsiderate &c. (*neglectful*) 460; stupid &c. 499; inactive &c. 683; incompetent; unqualified, disqualified, ill-qualified; unfit; quackish; raw, green, inexperienced, rusty, out of practice.

UNACCUSTOMED, unused, untrained &c. 537, uninitiated, unconversant &c. (*ignorant*) 491; unbusinesslike, unpractical, shiftless; unstatesmanlike.

ILL-ADVISED, unadvised, misadvised; ill-devised, ill-imagined, ill-judged, ill-contrived, ill-conducted; unguided, mis-

guided; misconducted, foolish, wild; infelicitous; penny wise and pound foolish &c. (*inconsistent*) 608.

٭٭ one's fingers being all thumbs; the right hand forgets its cunning; *il se noyerait dans une goutte d'eau; incidit in Scyllam qui vult vitare Charybdim;* out of the frying pan into the fire; *non omnia possumus omnes* [Vergil].

---

700. Proficient. — **N.** PROFICIENT, expert, adept; dab, dabster [*both colloq. or dial.*], connoisseur &c. (*scholar*) 492; master, – hand; top sawyer, prima donna, *première danseuse* [*F.*], first fiddle, *chef de cuisine* [*F.*]; protagonist; past master; mahatma.

nice -, good -, clean- hand; practiced -, experienced- -eye, – hand; marksman; good -, dead -, crack- shot [*colloq.*]; ropedancer, ropewalker, funambulist; contortionist, acrobat; conjuror &c. (*deceiver*) 548; wizard &c. 994.

PICKED MAN; medallist, prizeman, honorsman.

701. Bungler. — **N.** BUNGLER; blunderer, blunderhead; marplot, fumbler, lubber, clown, lout, duffer [*colloq.*]; stick, poor stick, odd stick [*all colloq.*]; bad -, poor- -hand, – shot; butter-fingers [*colloq.*], fumble-fist [*colloq.*].

no conjuror; flat, muff, muffer, slow coach [*all colloq.*]; looby, swab [*slang & dial.*], doit, yokel [*Eng.*], clod; awkward squad, novice, greenhorn, *blanc-bec* [*F.*], galoot [*slang*].

fish out of water, ass in lion's skin, jackdaw in peacock's feathers; quack &c. (*deceiver*) 548; Lord of Misrule, Abbot of Unreason [*both obs. or hist.*].

VETERAN; old -stager, – campaigner, – soldier, – file, – hand; man of business, man of the world.

GENIUS; master -mind, – head, – spirit.

PANTOLOGIST, Admirable Crichton, Jack of all trades; prodigy of learning, walking encyclopedia, mine of information.

MAN OF CUNNING; cunning –, sharp- -blade, – fellow; diplomatist, diplomat, Machiavellian; politician, jobber; tactician, strategist.

PECULATOR, forger, coiner; cracksman &c. 792.

LANDLUBBER, fresh-water sailor, fair-weather sailor, horse marine.

SLOVEN, slattern, traipse *or* trapes [*obs. or dial. Eng.*], slut.

*** *il n'a pas invent∂ la poudre;* he will never set the Thames on fire; *acierta errando; aliquis in omnibus nullus in singulis;* "They called us the seasick scull'ry maids, An' we called 'em the Ass-Marines" [Kipling].

702. Cunning. — N. CUNNING, craft;
cunningness, craftiness &c. *adj.;* subtlety, subtilty, subtility [*rare*]; the cunning of the -serpent, – Old Boy [*slang*]; artificiality; maneuvering *or* manœuvring &c. *v.;* temporization; circumvention.

CHICANE, chicanery; sharp practice, knavery, jugglery; concealment &c. 528; guile, a nigger in the woodpile [*colloq.*], doubling, duplicity &c. (*falsehood*) 544; foul play.

DIPLOMACY, politics; Machiavellianism *or* Machiavellism; gerrymander, jobbery, back-stairs influence.

ARTIFICE, art, device, machination; plot &c. (*plan*) 626; maneuver, stratagem, dodge, artful dodge, wile; trick, trickery &c. (*deception*) 545; ruse, *ruse de guerre* [*F.*]; finesse, side blow, thin end of the wedge, shift, go-by [*colloq.*], subterfuge, evasion; white lie &c. (*untruth*) 546; juggle, *tour de force* [*F.*]; tricks -of the trade, – upon travelers; gold brick [*colloq., U. S.*], imposture, deception; *espièglerie* [*F.*]; net, trap &c. 545.

SCHEMER, trickster, keener [*Western U. S.*], Philadelphia lawyer [*colloq., U. S.*]; sly boots [*humorous*], fox, reynard; intriguer, intrigant; repeater [*U. S. politics*], floater [*U. S.*]; man of cunning &c. 700; horse trader; Indian giver [*colloq., U. S.*].

Ulysses, Machiavelli *or* Machiavel.

703. Artlessness. — N. ARTLESSNESS
&c. *adj.;* inartificiality, unsophistication; nature, simplicity; innocence &c. 946; *bonhomie* [*F.*], *naiveté* [*F.*], *abandon* [*F.*], candor, sincerity; singleness of -purpose, – heart; honesty &c. 939; plain speaking; *épanchement* [*F.*].

rough diamond, matter-of-fact man; *le palais de vérité* [*F.*]; *enfant terrible* [*F.*].

V. BE ARTLESS &c. *adj.;* be round with one [Shakespeare]; look one in the face; wear one's heart upon one's sleeve for daws to peck at; think aloud; speak -out, – one's mind; be free with one, call a spade a spade; tell the truth, the whole truth, and nothing but the truth.

Adj. ARTLESS, natural, pure, native, confiding, simple, plain, inartificial, untutored, unsophisticated, *ingénu* [*F.*], unaffected, naïve; sincere, frank; open, – as day; candid, ingenuous, guileless; unsuspicious, honest &c. 939; childlike; innocent &c. 946; Arcadian; undesigning, straightforward, unreserved, aboveboard; simple-minded, single-minded; frank-, open-, single-, simple- hearted.

MATTER-OF-FACT, free-spoken, plain-spoken, outspoken, blunt, downright, direct, unpoetical; unflattering, untrimmed, unvarnished.

Adv. IN PLAIN -WORDS, – English; without mincing the matter; not to mince the matter &c. (*affirmation*) 535.

*** *Davus sum non Œdipus* [Terence]; *libe-ravi animam meam;* "as frank as rain on cherry-blossoms" [E. B. Browning].

V. BE CUNNING &c. *adj.;* have cut one's eyeteeth; contrive &c. (*plan*) 626; live by one's wits; maneuver *or* manœuvre; intrigue, gerrymander, finesse, double, temporize, stoop to conquer, *reculer pour mieux sauter* [*F.*], circumvent, steal a march upon; outdo, get the better of, snatch a thing from under one's nose, have a nigger in the wood-pile [*colloq.*]; overreach &c. 545; throw off one's guard; surprise &c. 508; snatch a verdict; waylay, undermine, introduce the thin end of the wedge; be too much for, be too deep for, sell a gold brick to [*colloq., U. S.*], give the go-by to [*slang*];

play a deep game, play tricks with; flatter, make things pleasant; have an ax to grind.

Adj. CUNNING, crafty, artful; skillful *or* skilful &c. 698; subtle, subtile, feline, vulpine; cunning as a -fox, – serpent; deep, – laid; profound; designing, contriving; intriguing &c. *v.;* strategic, diplomatic, politic, Machiavellian *or* Machiavelian, timeserving; artificial; tricky, tricksy [*rare*], wily, sly, slim [*S. Africa*], insidious, stealthy; underhand &c. *(hidden)* 528; subdolous [*obs.*], double-faced, double-tongued, shifty, deceptive; deceitful &c. 545; crooked; arch, pawky [*Scot. & dial. Eng.*], shrewd, acute; sharp, – as a needle; canny *or* cannie, astute, leery [*slang*], knowing, up to snuff, [*slang*] too clever by half, not to be caught with chaff.

Adv. CUNNINGLY &c. *adj.;* slily, on the sly [*colloq.*], by a side wind.

. diamond cut diamond; *à bis ou à blanc; fin contre fin;* "something is rotten in the state of Denmark" [*Hamlet*].

Section IV. ANTAGONISM

1. *Conditional Antagonism*

704. Difficulty. — N. DIFFICULTY; hardness &c. *adj.;* impracticability &c. *(impossibility)* 471; tough –, hard –, uphill- work; hard –, Herculean –, Augean- task; task of Sisyphus, Sisyphean labor, tough job [*colloq.*], tough proposition [*colloq.*], teaser [*colloq.*], rasper [*slang*], dead weight, dead lift.

DILEMMA, embarrassment; deadlock; perplexity &c. *(uncertainty)* 475; intricacy; entanglement &c. 59; cross fire; awkwardness, delicacy; delicate ground, thin ice, ticklish card to play, knot, Gordian knot, *dignus vindice nodus* [*L.*], net, meshes, maze; coil &c. *(convolution)* 248; crooked path; involvement; hard road to travel.

VEXED QUESTION, *vexata quæstio* [*L.*], poser; puzzle &c. *(riddle)* 533; nice –, delicate –, subtle –. knotty- point; paradox; hard –, nut to crack; bone to pick, crux, *pons asinorum* [*L.*], where the shoe pinches.

QUANDARY, nonplus, strait, pass, pinch, rub, pretty pass, stress, brunt; critical situation, crisis; trial, emergency, exigency, scramble.

scrape, hobble, slough, quagmire, hot water [*colloq.*], hornet's nest; sea –, peck- of troubles; pretty kettle of fish [*colloq.*]; pickle, stew, imbroglio, mess, muddle, botch, fuss, bustle, ado; false position; stand; deadlock, dead set; fix, horns of a dilemma, *cul de sac* [*F.*], blind alley; hitch; stumblingblock &c. *(hindrance)* 706.

V. BE DIFFICULT &c. *adj.;* run one hard, go against the grain, try one's patience, put one out; put to one's

705. Facility. — N. FACILITY, ease; easiness &c. *adj.;* capability; feasibility &c. *(practicability)* 470; flexibility, pliancy &c. 324; smoothness &c. 255; disencumbrance, disentanglement; deoppilation [*obs.*]; permission &c. 760.

plain –, smooth –, straight- sailing; mere child's play, holiday task; cinch, snap [*both slang, U. S.*].

ALL CLEAR, smooth water, fair wind; smooth –, royal- road; clear -coast, – stage, – course; straight course; *tabula rasa* [*L.*]; full play &c. *(freedom)* 748.

V. BE EASY &c. *adj.;* go on –, run-smoothly; have full play &c. *n.;* go –, run- on all fours [*colloq.*]; hit on all -four, – six, – eight, – twelve (cylinders) [*automobile cant*]; obey the helm, work well, work smoothly, work like a machine.

flow –, swim –, drift –, go- with the--stream, – tide; see one's way; have it all one's own way, have the game in one's own hands; walk over the course, win at a canter, win at a walk, win hands down [*colloq.*]; make little of, make light of, make nothing of; be at home in &c. *(skillful)* 698.

RENDER EASY &c. *adj.;* facilitate, smooth, ease, popularize; lighten, – the labor; free, clear; disencumber, disembarrass, disentangle, disengage; deobstruct, unclog, extricate, unravel, unknot; get the links out of; untie –, cut- the knot; disburden, unload, exonerate, emancipate, free from, deoppilate [*obs.*]; humor &c. *(aid)* 707; lubricate &c. 332; relieve &c. 834.

-shifts, – wit's end; go hard with one, try one; pose, perplex &c. (*uncertain*) 475; pother, bother, nonplus, gravel [*colloq.*], bring to a deadlock; be impossible &c. 471; be in the way of &c. (*hinder*) 706.

BE IN DIFFICULTY &c. *n.;* meet with –, labor under –, get into –, plunge into –, struggle with –, contend with –, grapple with- difficulties; labor under a disadvantage; fish in troubled waters, buffet the waves; swim against the -current, – stream; scud under bare poles; have much ado with, have a hard time of it; come to the -push, – pinch; bear the brunt; grope in the dark, lose one's way, weave a tangled web, walk on eggshells, walk among eggs.

get into a scrape &c. *n.;* bring a hornet's nest about one's ears; be put to one's shifts; flounder, boggle [*local, U. S.*], struggle; not know which way to turn &c. (*uncertain*) 475; *perdre son latin* [*F.*]; stick -at, – in the mud, – fast; come to a -stand, – deadlock; get all -balled up [*slang*], – snarled up, – tangled up, – wound up; hold the wolf by the ears.

RENDER DIFFICULT &c. *adj.;* enmesh, encumber, embarrass, ravel, entangle; put a spoke in the wheel &c. (*hinder*) 706; spike one's guns; lead a wild-goose chase, lead a pretty dance.

leave a hole to creep out of, leave a loophole, leave the matter open; give the reins to, give full play, give full swing; make way for; open the -door to, – way; prepare –, smooth –, clear- the -ground, – way, – path, – road; make all clear for, pave the way, bridge over; permit &c. 760.

Adj. EASY, facile; feasible &c. (*practicable*) 470; easily -managed, – accomplished; within reach, accessible, easy of access, for the million, open to.

MANAGEABLE, wieldy [*rare*], toward, towardly, tractable; submissive; yielding, ductile; suant *or* suent [*local U. S. & prov. Eng.*]; tractable &c. (*docile*) 602, pliant &c. (*soft*) 324; glib [*obs.*], slippery; smooth &c. 255; on friction wheels, on velvet.

UNBURDENED, disburdened, disencumbered, disembarrassed; exonerated; unloaded, unobstructed, untrammeled; unrestrained &c. (*free*) 748; at ease, light.

at home, quite at home; in one's element, in smooth water.

Adv. EASILY &c. *adj.;* readily, smoothly, swimmingly, with no effort, on easy terms, single-handed, with one hand tied behind one's back.

⁎⁎⁎ touch and go; "Custom hath made it in him a property of easiness" [*Hamlet*].

Adj. DIFFICULT, not easy, hard, tough [*colloq.*]; troublesome, toilsome, irksome; operose, laborious, onerous, arduous, Herculean, formidable; sooner –, more easily-said than done; difficult –, hard- to deal with; ill-conditioned, crabbed; not to be handled with kid gloves, not made with rose water.

AWKWARD, unwieldy, unmanageable; intractable, stubborn &c. (*obstinate*) 606; perverse, refractory, plaguy [*colloq.*], trying, thorny, rugged; knotted, knotty; invious [*obs.*]; pathless, trackless; labyrinthine &c. (*convoluted*) 248; intricate, complicated &c. (*tangled*) 59; impracticable &c. (*impossible*) 471; not feasible &c. 470; desperate &c. (*hopeless*) 859.

EMBARRASSING, perplexing &c. (*uncertain*) 475; delicate, ticklish, critical, uncertain, thorny, set with thorns; beset with –, full of –, surrounded by –, entangled by –, encompassed with- difficulties.

UNDER A DIFFICULTY; in a box; in difficulty, in hot water [*colloq.*], in the suds [*colloq.*], in the soup [*slang*], in a cleft stick, in a fix [*colloq.*], in the wrong box, in a scrape &c. *n.*, in deep water, in a fine pickle [*colloq.*], *in extremis* [*L.*]; between -two stools, – Scylla and Charybdis; on the horns of a dilemma; on the rocks; surrounded by -shoals, – breakers, – quicksands; at cross-purposes; not out of the wood.

reduced to straits; hard –, sorely- pressed; run hard; pinched, put to it, straitened; hard up [*slang*]; hard put to it, hard set [*both colloq.*]; put to one's shifts; puzzled, at a loss, &c. (*uncertain*) 475; at the end of one's tether, at one's wits' end, at a nonplus, at a standstill; graveled, nonplused *or* nonplussed, stranded, aground; stuck -, set- fast; out, put out, out in one's reckoning; up a tree, at bay, *aux abois* [*F.*], driven -into a corner, – from post to pillar, – to extremity, –

to one's wit's end, – to the wall; *au bout de son Latin* [*F.*]; out of one's depth; thrown out.

ACCOMPLISHED WITH DIFFICULTY; hard-fought, hard-earned.

Adv. WITH DIFFICULTY, with much ado; hardly &c. *adj.;* uphill; upstream; against the -stream, – grain; *à rebours* [*F.*]; *invitâ Minervâ* [*L.*]; in the teeth of; at a pinch, upon a pinch; at long odds.

*** "ay, there's the rub" [*Hamlet*]; *hic labor hoc opus* [Vergil]; things are come to a pretty pass; *ab inconvenienti; ad astra per aspera; aucun chemin de fleurs ne conduit à la gloire.*

2. *Active Antagonism*

706. Hindrance. — N. PREVENTION, preclusion, obstruction, stoppage; embolus, clot, embolism; interruption, interception, interclusion [*obs.*], hindrance, impedition [*obs.*]; retardment, retardation; embarrassment, oppilation [*obs.*], striction, constriction, coarctation, stricture, restriction; infarct, infarction; restraint &c. 751; inhibition &c. 761; blockade &c. (*closure*) 261.

INTERFERENCE, interposition; obtrusion; discouragement, discountenance; disapproval, disapprobation, opposition.

IMPEDIMENT, let [*archaic*], obstacle, obstruction, knot, knag; check, hitch, *contretemps* [*F.*], screw loose, grit in the oil; stumbling-block, stumbling-stone; lion in the path; snag; snags and sawyers [*U. S.*], sawyer [*U. S.*], planter [*local, U. S.*]

BAR, stile, barrier; turnstile, turnpike; gate, portcullis; beaver dam; barricade &c. (*defense*) 717; wall, dead wall, breakwater, groin *or* groyne; bulkhead, block, buffer; stopper &c. 263; boom, dam, weir.

CHECK; encumbrance *or* incumbrance; clog, skid, shoe, spoke, brake; drag anchor, drag sail, drag sheet, drift sail, sea anchor, floating anchor; anchor; mushroom –, sheet –, kedge- anchor; kedge, bower; checkrein, bearing rein; bit, snaffle, curb, curb bit; drag, – chain, – weight; load, burden, fardel [*obs.*], onus, millstone round one's neck, impedimenta; dead weight; lumber, pack; nightmare, ephialtes, incubus, old man of the sea; remora [*surg.*]; stay, stop; preventive, prophylactic.

DRAWBACK, objection; difficulty &c. 704; insuperable &c. (471) obstacle; trail of a red herring; estoppel [*law*]; ill wind; head wind &c. (*opposition*) 708; trammel, tether &c. (*means of restraint*) 752; holdback, counterpoise.

DAMPER, wet blanket, hinderer, marplot, kill-joy, crape-hanger [*slang*], dog

707. Aid. — N. AID, aidance, assistance, help, opitulation [*obs.*], succor; support, lift, advance, furtherance, promotion; coadjuvancy &c. (*coöperation*) 709.

PATRONAGE, auspices, championship, countenance, favor, interest, advocacy.

SUSTENANCE, sustentation [*rare*], maintenance, alimentation, nutrition, nourishment; eutrophy; manna in the wilderness; food &c. 298; means &c. 632; subsidy, bounty, subvention.

MINISTRY, ministration; subministration [*obs.*], accommodation.

RELIEF, rescue; help at a dead lift; supernatural aid; *deus ex machinâ* [*L.*].

SUPPLIES, reënforcements, succors, contingents, recruits; support &c. (*physical*) 215; adjunct, ally &c. (*helper*) 711.

V. AID, assist, help, succor, lend one's aid; come to the aid of &c. *n.;* contribute, subscribe to; bring –, give –, furnish –, afford –, supply aid &c. *n.;* give –, stretch –, lend –, bear –, hold out- a -hand, – helping hand; give one a -lift, – cast, – turn; take by the hand, take in tow; help a lame dog over a stile, lend wings to.

relieve, rescue; set up, set agoing, set on one's legs; bear –, pull- through; give new life to, be the making of; reënforce, recruit; set –, put –, push- forward; give -a lift, – a shove, – an impulse- to; promote, further, forward, advance; speed, expedite, quicken, hasten.

SUPPORT, sustain, uphold, prop, hold up, bolster.

NOURISH, nurture, nurse, cradle, dry nurse, suckle, foster, cherish, put out to nurse; manure, cultivate, force; foment; feed –, fan- the flame.

SERVE; do service to, tender to, pander to; administer to, subminister to [*obs.*], minister to; tend, attend, wait on; take care of &c. 459; entertain; smooth the bed of sickness.

in the manger, Buttinsky [*humorous*, *U. S.*]; usurper, interloper; opponent &c. 710; filibusterer [*U. S.*].

V. HINDER, impede, filibuster [*U. S.*], impedite [*obs.*], embarrass.

AVERT, keep off, stave off, ward off; obviate; antevert [*obs.*]; turn aside, draw off, prevent, forfend *or* forefend [*archaic*], nip in the bud; retard, slacken, check, let [*archaic*]; counteract, counter-check; preclude, debar, foreclose, estop [*law*]; inhibit &c. 761; shackle &c. (*restrain*) 751; restrict.

OBSTRUCT, stop, stay, bar, bolt, lock; block, – up; choke off; belay, barricade; block –, stop- the way; forlay *or* forelay [*obs.*], dam up &c. (*close*) 261; put on the brake &c. *n.;* scotch –, lock –, put a spoke in- the wheel; put a stop to &c. 142; traverse, contravene; interrupt, intercept; oppose &c. 708; hedge -in, – round; cut off; interclude [*obs.*].

INTERFERE, interpose, intermeddle &c. 682.

ENCUMBER *or* incumber; cramp, hamper; clog, – the wheels; cumber; handicap; choke; saddle with, load with; overload, overlay, overwhelm; lumber, trammel, tie one's hands, put to inconvenience; incommode, discommode; discompose; hustle [*colloq.*], corner, drive into a corner.

RUN FOUL OF, fall foul of; cross the path of, break in upon.

THWART, frustrate, disconcert, balk, foil; faze, feeze *or* feaze [*U. S.*]; baffle, snub, override, circumvent; defeat &c. 731; spike guns &c. (*render useless*) 645; spoil, mar, clip the wings of; cripple &c. (*injure*) 659; put an extinguisher on; damp; dishearten &c. (*dissuade*) 616;

OBLIGE, accommodate, consult the wishes of; humor, cheer, encourage.

SECOND, stand by; back, – up; pay the piper, abet; work for, make interest for, stick up for [*colloq.*], stick by, take up the cudgels for; take up –, espouse –, adopt- the cause of; advocate, beat up for recruits, press into the service; squire [*colloq.*], give moral support to, keep in countenance, countenance, patronize, take up; lend one's name to; lend oneself to, lend one's countenance to; smile upon, shine upon; favor, befriend, take in hand, enlist under the banners of; side with &c. (*coöperate*) 709.

be of use to; subserve &c. (*instrument*) 631; benefit &c. 648; render a service &c. (*utility*) 644; conduce &c. (*tend*) 176.

Adj. AIDING &c. *v.;* auxiliary, adjuvant, helpful; coadjuvant &c. 709; subservient, ministrant, ancillary, accessary, accessory, subsidiary.

FRIENDLY, amicable, favorable, propitious, well-disposed; neighborly; obliging &c. (*benevolent*) 906; at one's beck.

Adv. WITH *or* BY THE AID OF &c. *n.;* on –, in- behalf of; in aid of, in the service of, in favor of, in the name of, in furtherance of; on account of; for the sake of, on the part of; *non obstante* [*L.*].

Int. HELP! save us! to the rescue! this way! *à moi!* [*F.*].

⁎⁎ *alterum alterius auxilio eget* [Sallust]; "God befriend us as our cause is just" [*Henry IV*]; "God helps those who help themselves" [Sidney]; "put your trust in God; but mind to keep your powder dry" [*ascribed to* Cromwell].

discountenance, throw cold water on; steal one's thunder; cut the ground from under one, take the wind out of one's sails, undermine; be –, stand- in the way of; act as a drag; hang like a millstone round one's neck.

Adj. HINDERING &c. *v.;* obstructive, obstruent; intrusive, meddlesome; impeditive, impedient; intercipient [*obs.*]; prophylactic &c. (*remedial*) 662; impedimentary, impedimental.

in the way of, unfavorable; onerous, burdensome; cumbrous, cumbersome; obtrusive.

HINDERED &c. *v.;* windbound, water-logged, heavy laden; hard pressed.

UNASSISTED &c. (*see* assist &c. 707); single-handed, alone; deserted &c. 624; unseconded.

Adv. IN THE WAY, with everything against one, with one's wheels clogged, through all obstacles; with many difficulties, under many difficulties.

⁎⁎ *occurrent nubes;* "he that wrestles with us strengthens our nerves and sharpens our skill. Our antagonist is our helper" [Burke.]

708. Opposition. — N. OPPOSITION, antagonism; oppugnancy, oppugnation [*rare*]; impugnation, impugnment, contrariousness [*rare*], contrariness, contrariety; contravention; counteraction &c. 179; counterplot.

resistance &c. 719; restraint &c. 751; hindrance &c. 706; absence of aid &c. 707.

cross fire, cross current, undercurrent, head wind.

CLASHING, collision, conflict, discord, want of harmony; filibuster [*U. S.*], filibusterism.

COMPETITION, two of a trade, rivalry, emulation, race, contest; tug of war.

V. OPPOSE, counteract, run counter to; withstand &c. (*resist*) 719; control &c. (*restrain*) 751; hinder &c. 706; antagonize, oppugn, fly in the face of, go dead against, kick against, cross, kick at, fall out with, fall foul of; set -, pit- against; face, confront, cope with; make a -stand, - dead set- against; set -oneself, - one's face- against; protest -, vote -, raise one's voice- against; disfavor, turn one's back upon; set at naught, slap in the face, slam the door in one's face.

THWART, be -, play- at cross-purposes; counterwork, countermine; over-thwart.

ENCOUNTER, stem, breast; stem -, breast- the -tide, - current, - flood; buffet the waves; beat up against, make head against; grapple with; kick against the pricks &c. (*resist*) 719; contend with *or* against &c. 720; do battle with *or* against &c. (*warfare*) 722.

CONTRADICT, contravene; belie; go -, run -, beat -, militate- against; come in conflict with.

COMPETE, emulate &c., 720; rival, spoil one's trade, force out, drive one out of business.

Adj. OPPOSING, opposed &c. *v.*; adverse, antagonistic, oppugnant, over-thwart; contrary &c. 14; at variance &c. 24; at issue, at war with, in controversy with, in opposition; " agin' the government."

in hostile array, front to front, with crossed bayonets, at daggers drawn; up in arms; resistant &c. 719.

UNFAVORABLE, unpropitious, unfriendly, hostile, inimical, cross; filibusterous.

302

709. Coöperation. — N. COÖPERATION; coadjuvancy, coadjutorship, coadjument [*rare*], coagency, coefficiency; concert, concurrence, complicity, coadministration, coaction; participation · union &c. 43; coefficacy; combination &c. 48; collusion, collusiveness.

ASSOCIATION, alliance, colleagueship, joint stock, copartnership, pool, gentleman's agreement; cartel; confederation &c. (*party*) 712; coalition, federation, fusion; a long pull a strong pull and a pull all together; logrolling [*chiefly U. S.*], quid pro quo [*L.*], freemasonry.

UNANIMITY &c. (*assent*) 488; *esprit de corps* [*F.*], party spirit; clanship, partisanship; concord &c. 714; synergy, synergism.

V. COÖPERATE, concur; conduce &c· 178; combine, coadjute, coadjuvate, coact [*rare*], unite one's efforts; keep -, draw -, pull -, club -, hand -, hold -, league -, band -, be banded- together; pool; stand -, put- shoulder to shoulder; act in concert, join forces, fraternize, cling to one another; vote solidly, vote in blocks; conspire, concert, lay one's heads together; confederate, make an agreement with, be in league with; collude, understand one another, play into the hands of, hunt in couples.

SIDE WITH, take sides with, go along with, go hand in hand with, join hands with, make common cause with, strike in with, unite with, join with, mix oneself up with, take part with, cast in one's lot with; join -, enter into-partnership with; rally round, flock to, follow the lead of; come to, pass over to, come into the views of; be -, row -, sail- in the same boat; sail on the same tack.

PARTICIPATE, be a party to, lend oneself to; chip in [*colloq.*], have a -hand in, - finger in the pie; take -, bear- part in; second &c. (*aid*) 707; take the part of, play the game of; espouse a -cause, - quarrel.

Adj. COÖPERATING &c. *v.*; in coöperation &c. *n.*, in league &c. (*party*) 712; coadjuvant, coadjutant, coadjutive, coactive, coalitional, hand in glove with; dyed in the wool; synergetic, synergistic.

FAVORABLE TO &c. 707; unopposed &c. 708.

COMPETITIVE, emulous, cut-throat; in rivalry with, in friendly rivalry.

Adv. AGAINST, *versus* [*L.*], counter to, in conflict with, at cross-purposes, cross, contrariwise, unfavorably.

against the -grain, – current, – stream, – wind, – tide; with a head-wind; with the wind -ahead, – in one's teeth.

IN SPITE, in despite, in defiance; in the -way, – teeth, – face- of; across; athwart, overthwart; where the shoe pinches; in one's teeth.

THOUGH &c. 30; even; *quand même* [*F.*]; *per contra* [*L.*].

⁎ *nitor in adversum;* "take arms against a sea of troubles, And by opposing end them" [*Hamlet*]; "I have no words, My voice is in my sword" [*Macbeth*].

Adv. UNANIMOUSLY, as one man &c. 488; shoulder to shoulder, in coöperation with.

⁎ *due teste valgono più che una sola;* "we must all hang together, or assuredly we shall all hang separately" [Franklin, July 4, 1776]; "I shall know that your good is mine; ye shall know that my strength is yours" [Kipling].

---

710. Opponent. — N. OPPONENT, antagonist, adversary, oppugnant [*rare*]; adverse party, opposition; enemy &c. 891; assailant.

OPPOSITIONIST, obstructive; brawler; wrangler, brangler [*rare*], disputant; filibuster [*U. S.*], filibusterer [*U. S.*], extremist, bitter-ender [*U. S.*], irreconcilable, obstructionist, "willful men."

MALCONTENT; demagogue, reactionist; anarchist, anarch; Jacobin, Fenian, Sinn Feiner, Red; Industrial Workers of the World, I. W. W.

RIVAL, competitor, contestant, entrant; the field.

⁎ "each brave foe was in his heart a friend" [Homer]; "He that wrestles with us strengthens our nerves and sharpens our skill. Our antagonist is our helper" [Burke].

711. Auxiliary. — N. AUXILIARY; recruit; assistant; adjuvant, adjutant; *ayudante* [*Sp. Amer.*], co-aid; adjunct; help, helper, helpmate, helping hand; colleague, partner, mate, confrère, coöperator; coadjuvant, coadjutant, coadjutator [*rare*], coadjutor, coadjutrix, collaborator.

ALLY; friend &c. 890; confidant (*fem.* confidante), *fidus Achates* [*L.*], *alter ego* [*L.*], pal [*slang*], chum [*colloq.*], mate, comate.

aide-de-camp [*F.*], secretary, clerk, associate, marshal; right-hand, right-hand man; candleholder, bottle-holder [*colloq.*]; handmaid; servant &c. 746.

PUPPET, cat's-paw, creature, jackstraw, tool; jackal; *âme damnée* [*F.*]; satellite, adherent; parasite, dependent, client [*Rom. hist.*].

CONFEDERATE; complice [*archaic*], accomplice; accessory, – after the fact; *particeps criminis* [*L.*]; *socius criminis* [*L.*].

UPHOLDER; votary; sectarian, sectary; seconder, backer, supporter, abettor, advocate, partisan, champion, patron, friend at court, mediator; angel [*slang*].

FRIEND IN NEED, jack at a pinch, special providence, *deus ex machinâ* [*L.*], guardian angel, fairy godmother, tutelary genius.

⁎ a friend in need is a friend indeed; "of every friendless name the friend" [Johnson]; "the best-condition'd and unwearied spirit In doing courtesies" [*Merchant of Venice*].

---

712. Party. — N. PARTY, faction, denomination, class, communion, side, crew, team; band, horde, posse, phalanx; caste, family, gens [*Rom. hist.*], clan &c. 166.

Confederates, Conservatives, Democrats, Federalists, Federals, Liberals, Radicals, Republicans, Socialists, Tories, Whigs &c.

COMMUNITY, body, fellowship, solidarity; freemasonry; party spirit &c. (*coöperation*) 709; fraternity, sodality, confraternity, sorority; *familistère* [*F.*], familistery; brotherhood, sisterhood.

FRATERNAL ORDER, Freemasons, Knights Templars, Odd Fellows, Knights of Pythias; Royal Arcanum &c.

GANG, tong [*Chin.*]; Camorra, Kuklux, Kuklux Klan, Molly Maguires, Fenians, Sinn Feiners, Bolsheviki, Bolshevists, Industrial Workers of the World, I. W. W., Luddites; ring, machine; Tammany, – Hall [*U. S.*]; junto, cabal, camarilla, brigue [*obs.*].

CLIQUE, knot, circle, set, coterie; club, casino.

CORPORATION, corporate body, guild; establishment, company, copartnership, partnership, cahoot [*slang*]; firm, house; joint concern, joint-stock company; combine [*colloq., U. S.*], trust; holding company, merger.

SOCIETY, association; institute, institution; union; trades union; league, syndicate, alliance; *Verein, Bund, Zollverein* [*all Ger.*]; combination; *Turnverein* [*Ger.*]; *Liedertafel* &c. (*singing societies*) 416; league –, alliance- offensive and defensive; coalition; federation; confederation, confederacy.

STAFF; cast, *dramatis personæ* [*L.*].

V. UNITE, join; band together; club together &c. (*coöperate*) 709; found a -firm, – house; cement –, form- a party &c. *n.;* associate &c. (*assemble*) 72; federate, federalize, go cahoots [*slang*], go fifty-fifty [*slang*].

Adj. IN LEAGUE, in partnership, in alliance &c. *n.*

bonded –, banded –, linked &c. (*joined*) 43- together; embattled; confederated, federative, joint, corporate, organized, enleagued, leagued, syndicated; clubbable *or* clubable, fraternal, Masonic, institutional, denominational; cliquish, cliquy *or* cliquey; union-made.

Adv. SIDE BY SIDE, hand in hand, shoulder to shoulder, *en masse* [*F.*], in the same boat.

⁎⁎ "to party gave up what was meant for mankind" [Goldsmith — *of Burke*]; "he left not faction, but of it was left" [Dryden — *of Buckingham*].

---

713. Discord. — N. DISCORD, disaccord, dissidence, dissonance; disagreement &c. 24; jar, clash, break, shock; jarring, jostling &c. *v.;* screw loose.

VARIANCE, difference, dissension, misunderstanding, cross-purposes, odds, *brouillerie* [*F.*]; division, split, rupture, disruption, division in the camp, house divided against itself, "rift within the lute" [*Tennyson*], disunion, breach; schism &c. (*dissent*) 489; feud, faction.

POLEMICS; litigation; strife &c. (*contention*) 720; warfare &c. 722; outbreak, open rupture, breaking off of negotiations, recall of ambassadors, declaration of war.

QUARREL, dispute, tiff, bicker, *tracasserie* [*F.*], squabble, altercation, barney [*slang*], *démêlé* [*F.*], snarl, spat [*colloq. or dial.*], towrow [*Scot. & dial Eng.*], words, high words; wrangling &c. *v.;* jangle, brabble [*archaic*], brabblement [*archaic*], cross questions and crooked answers, snip-snap [*rare*]; family jars.

BROIL, brawl, row [*colloq.*], racket, hubbub, rixation [*obs.*]; embroilment, embranglement, imbroglio, ꞏfracas, breach of the peace, piece of work, scrimmage, rumpus [*colloq.*]; breeze [*colloq.*], squall; riot, disturbance &c. (*disorder*) 59; commotion &c. (*agitation*) 315; bear garden, Donnybrook Fair.

SUBJECT OF DISPUTE, ground of quarrel, battle ground, disputed point; bone -of contention, – to pick; apple

714. Concord. — N. CONCORD, accord, harmony, symphony; homologue, homology, correspondence; agreement &c. 23; sympathy &c. (*love*) 897; response; union, unison, unity; bonds of harmony; peace &c. 721; unanimity &c. (*assent*) 488; league &c. 712; happy family.

rapprochement [*F.*], reunion; amity &c. (*friendship*) 888; alliance, *entente cordiale* [*F.*], good understanding, conciliation, arbitration.

PEACEMAKER, intercessor, interceder, propitiator, mediator.

V. AGREE &c. 23; accord, harmonize with, blend in with; fraternize; be concordant &c. *adj.;* go hand in hand; run parallel &c. (*concur*) 178; understand one another; pull together &c. (*coöperate*) 709; put up one's horses together, sing in chorus.

SIDE WITH, sympathize with, go with, chime in with, fall in with; come round [*colloq.*]; be pacified &c. 723; assent &c. 488; enter into the -ideas, – feelings- of; reciprocate.

hurler avec les loups [*F.*]; go –, swim- with the stream; get on the band wagon [*slang*].

SMOOTH, pour oil on the troubled waters; keep in good humor, render accordant, put in tune; come to an understanding, meet halfway; keep the peace, remain at peace; mediate, intercede.

of discord, *casus belli* [*L.*]; question at issue &c. (*subject of inquiry*) 461; vexed question, *vexata quæstio* [*L*], brand of discord.

CONTENTIOUSNESS &c. *adj.;* enmity &c. 889; hate &c. 898; troublous times; cat-and-dog life; Kilkenny cats; disputant &c. 710; strange bedfellows.

V. DISAGREE; be discordant &c. *adj.;* disaccord, come amiss &c. 24; clash, jar, jostle, pull different ways, conflict, have no measures with, misunderstand one another; live like cat and dog; differ; dissent &c. 489; have a bone to pick with, have a crow to pluck with.

QUARREL, fall out, dispute; litigate; controvert &c. (*deny*) 536; squabble, tiff, spat [*colloq. or dial.*], altercate, row [*colloq.*], brabble, wrangle, jangle, brangle, bicker, nag; spar &c. (*contend*) 720; have words with &c. *n.;* fall foul of.

split; break –, break squares –, part company– with; declare war, try conclusions; join –, put in– issue; pick a quarrel, fasten a quarrel on; sow –, stir up– dissension &c. *n.;* embroil, entangle, disunite, widen the breach; rub one's fur the wrong way; get one all het up [*dial.*]; get one hot under the collar [*colloq.*]; set at odds, set together by the ears; set –, pit– against.

get into hot water, fish in troubled waters, brawl; kick up a –row, – dust [*colloq.*]; turn the house out of window.

Adj. DISCORDANT, dissident; disagreeing &c. *v.;* out of tune, dissonant, harsh, grating, jangling, unmelodious, inharmonious, ajar; on bad terms, dissentient &c. 489; unreconciled, unpacified; inconsistent, contradictory, incongruous, discrepant.

QUARRELSOME, unpacific; gladiatorial, controversial, polemic, disputatious; factious; litigious, litigant.

AT STRIFE, at odds, at loggerheads, at daggers drawn, at variance, at issue, at cross-purposes, at sixes and sevens, at feud, at high words; up in arms, heated, het up [*dial.*], hot under the collar [*colloq.*], together by the ears, in hot water, embroiled; torn, disunited.

** quot homines tot sententiæ [Terence]; no love lost between them, *non nostrum tantas componere lites* [Vergil]; *Mars gravior sub pace latet* [Claudius]; "She was no sister to the hen, But fierce and minded to be queen" [Masefield]; "above the pitch, out of tune, and off the hinges" [Rabelais].

Adj. CONCORDANT, congenial; agreeing &c. *v.;* in accord &c. *n.;* harmonious, united, cemented; banded together &c. 712; allied; friendly &c. 888; fraternal; conciliatory; at one with; of one mind &c. (*assent*) 488.

at peace, in still water; tranquil &c. (*pacific*) 721.

Adv. UNANIMOUSLY, without a dissentient voice; with one voice &c. (*assent*) 488; in concert with, hand in hand; on one's side.

Int. make it unanimous! are you with us?

** commune periculum concordiam parit; "every expansion of civilization makes for peace" [Roosevelt].

715. Defiance. — N. DEFIANCE; daring &c. *v.;* dare, defial, defi [*slang*]; "dare, dare, and double-dare" [*child's challenge*]; challenge, cartel; threat &c. 909; war cry, war whoop.

V. DEFY, dare, beard; brave &c. (*courage*) 861; bid defiance to; bite the thumb at; set at defiance, set at naught; hurl defiance at; dance the war dance; snap the fingers at, laugh to scorn; disobey &c. 742.

show –fight, – one's teeth, – a bold front; bluster, look big, stand with arms akimbo; double –, shake– the fist; threaten &c. 909.

CHALLENGE, call out; throw –, fling– down the –gauntlet, – gage, – glove.

Adj. DEFIANT; defying &c. *v.;* with arms akimbo; rebellious, bold, insolent, reckless, contemptuous, greatly daring, regardless of consequences.

Adv. IN DEFIANCE OF, in the teeth of; under one's very nose; in open rebellion.

Int. do your worst! come if you dare! come on! marry come up! [*archaic or dial.*], hoity toity!

** noli me tangere; nemo me impune lacessit; "And dar'st thou then To beard the lion in his den, The Douglas in his hall?" [Scott].

716. Attack. — **N.** ATTACK; assault,
- and battery; onset, onslaught, charge.

base of operations, point of attack;
echelon; open order; close formation.

AGGRESSION, offense; incursion, inroad, invasion; irruption; outbreak;
bucking, estapade [*manège*], *ruade* [*F.*],
kicking, kick; punch &c. (*impulse*)
276; *coup de main* [*F.*]; sally, sortie,
camisade *or* camisado [*archaic*], raid,
foray; run at, run against; dead set at.

STORM, storming; boarding, escalade;
siege, investment, obsession [*obs.*], bom-
bardment, cannonade, barrage; zero
hour.

battue [*F.*], razzia, dragonnade *or*
dragoonade; devastation &c. 162; *éboulement* [*F.*].

FIRE, volley; direct –, ricochet –,
plunging –, rolling –, horizontal –,
vertical –, platoon –, file- fire; fusilade;
fire of demolition, percussion fire; sharpshooting, broadside; raking ·–, cross-
fire; volley of grapeshot, *feu d'enfer*
[*F.*].

CUT, THRUST, lunge, pass, passado
[*obs.*], stoccado *or* stoccata [*archaic*],
carte (*or* quarte) and tierce, home
thrust; *coup de bec* [*F.*].

ASSAILANT, aggressor, invader; sharpshooter, dead shot, fusilier, dragoon,
Uhlan.

V. ATTACK, assault, assail; set upon,
fall upon; charge, impugn, break a lance
with, enter the lists.

SHOW FIGHT, come on; assume –, take-
the offensive; be –, become- the aggressor; strike the first blow, throw the
first stone at, fire the first shot; lift a
hand –, draw the sword- against; take
up the cudgels; advance –, march-
against; march upon, invade, harry.

strike at, poke at, thrust at; aim –,
deal- a blow at; give –, fetch- one a
-blow, – kick; have a -cut, – shot, –
fling, – shy- at; be down upon, pounce
upon; fall foul of, pitch into [*colloq.*],
launch out against; bait, slap on the
face; make a -thrust, – pass, – set, –
dead set- at; bear down upon.

close with, come to close quarters,
bring to bay, come to blows.

ride full tilt against; let fly at, dash
at, run a tilt at, rush at, tilt at, run at,
fly at, hawk at, have at, let out at;
make a -dash, – rush at; attack tooth
and nail; strike home; drive –, press-

717. Defense. — **N.** DEFENSE *or*
defence, protection, guard, ward; shield-
ing &c. *v.;* propugnation [*obs.*]; preservation &c. 670; guardianship.

SELF-DEFENSE, self-preservation; resistance &c. 719.

SAFEGUARD &c. (*safety*) 664; screen
&c. (*shelter*) 666, (*concealment*) 350;
fortification; munition, muniment; bulwark, fosse, trench, mine, countermine,
dugout; moat, ditch, intrenchment *or*
entrenchment, vallation, rampart, scarp,
escarp, counterscarp, vanfoss; dike *or*
dyke; parapet, sunk fence, haha, embankment, mound, mole, bank; earthwork, fieldwork; fence, wall, dead wall,
contravallation *or* countervallation; paling &c. (*inclosure*) 232; palisade, stock-
ade, stoccado [*obs.*], laager [*S. Africa*],
sangar [*India*]; barrier, barricade; boom;
portcullis, *chevaux de frise* [*F.*]; abatis *or*
abattis, barbed wire entanglements,
vallum [*Rom. antiq.*], circumvallation,
merlon, battlement, glacis; casemate;
buttress, abutment; shore &c. (*support*)
215.

breastwork, banquette, mantelet *or*
mantlet, tenaille *or* tenail, ravelin,
curtain, demilune, half-moon; bastion,
demibastion, redan; vauntmure [*rare*];
faussebraie *or* . faussebraye, advanced
work, hornwork, lunette, outwork; barbican, redoubt, sconce, fortalice; lines.

machicolation, bartizan, loophole,
balistraria [*ancient fortification*]; postern
gate, sally port.

STRONGHOLD, hold, fastness; asylum
&c. (*refuge*) 666; keep, donjon, citadel,
capitol, castle; tower, – of strength;
fortress, propugnaculum, fort, kila
[*India*]; barracoon, barrack; pah *or*
pa [*N. Z.*]; peel, peel tower, peelhouse;
rath [*Ir. antiq.*]; martello tower, block-
house, wooden walls.

[PROTECTIVE DEVICES] buffer, fender,
cowcatcher [*U. S.*]; apron, mask, gauntlet, thimble; armor *or* armour, shield,
buckler, scutum [*Rom. antiq.*], target,
targe [*archaic*], ægis, breastplate, cuirass,
backplate, habergeon, mail, coat of
mail, brigandine, hauberk, lorica, helm
[*archaic*], armet, basinet *or* bassinet,
sallet *or* salade, greave, jambe, heaume,
morion, cabasset, beaver, visor *or* vizor;
face guard, helmet, casque, casquetel,
siege cap, headpiece; steel helmet,
tin -helmet, – hat [*soldiers' cant*];

one hard; be hard upon, run down, strike at the root of.

lay about one, run amuck.

FIRE UPON, fire at, fire a shot at; draw a bead on [*U. S.*]; shoot at, pop at, level at, let off a gun at; open fire, pepper, bombard, shell, pour a broadside into; fire a volley, fire red-hot shot; spring a mine.

STONE, lapidate, pelt; throw - a stone, – stones - at; hurl -at, – against, – at the head of; rock [*U. S.*].

BESET, besiege, beleaguer; lay siege to, invest, open the trenches, plant a battery, sap, mine; storm, board, scale the walls, go over the top.

cut and thrust, bayonet, give one the bayonet; butt; kick, strike &c. (*impulse*) 276; horsewhip, whip &c. (*punish*) 972.

Adj. ATTACKING &c. *v.*; aggressive, offensive, incursive, invasive, irruptive, obsidional.

up in arms; amuck.

Adv. ON THE OFFENSIVE, on the war-path, amuck, over the top; at bay.

Int. "up and at them!"

∗∗∗ "the din of arms, the yell of savage rage, the shriek of agony, the groan of death" [Southey]; "their fatal hands no second stroke intend" [*Paradise Lost*]; "thirst for glory quells the love of life" [Addison].

camail, neckguard; *Pickelhaube* [*Ger.*]; spiked helmet; shako &c. (*dress*) 225; bearskin; vambrace, rerebrace, cubitière; sollerets, pédieux; panoply, caparison, housings; chamfron *or* chamfrain; truncheon &c. (*weapon*) 727; carapace, shell; spines, needles.

DEFENDER, protector; Defender of the Faith, *fidei defensor* [*L.*], guardian &c. (*safety*) 664; bodyguard, champion; knight-errant, Paladin; propugnator *or* propugner *or* propugnor [*obs.*]; picket; garrison.

V. DEFEND, forfend *or* forefend [*archaic*], fend [*archaic*]; shield, screen, shroud; engarrison, garrison, man; fence round &c. (*circumscribe*) 229; fence, intrench *or* entrench; arm, harness [*archaic*], accouter *or* accoutre; guard &c. (*keep safe*) 664; guard against; take care of &c. (*vigilance*) 459; bear harmless; fend –, keep –, ward –, beat- off; hinder &c. 706.

REPEL, parry, propugn [*obs.*], put to flight; give a warm reception to [*ironical*]; hold – keep- at -bay, – arm's length.

RESIST INVASION, stand siege; be –, stand –, act- on the defensive; show fight; maintain –, stand- one's ground; stand by; hold one's own; bear –, stand-the brunt; fall back upon, hold, stand in the gap.

Adj. DEFENDING &c. *v.*; defensive; mural; armed, – at all points, – cap-a-pie, – to the teeth; panoplied; accoutered *or* accoutred, harnessed [*archaic*], "in complete steel" [*Hamlet*]; iron-plated, ironclad; loopholed, castellated, machicolated, casemated; defended &c. *v.*; proof against, ball-proof, bullet-proof; protective.

Adv. DEFENSIVELY; on the defensive; in defense; in self-defense; at bay, *pro aris et focis* [*L.*].

Int. NO SURRENDER! "*ils ne passeront pas!*" "they shall not pass!" [*the French at Verdun*].

∗∗∗ defense not defiance; *Dieu défend le droit;* "Millions for defence, but not a cent for tribute" [Pinkney].

---

718. Retaliation. — N. RETALIATION, reprisal, talion [*rare*], retort; counterstroke, counterblast, counterplot, counterproject; retribution, *lex talionis* [*L.*]; reciprocation &c. (*reciprocity*) 12.

REQUITAL, desert; tit for tat, give and take, blow for blow, *quid pro quo* [*L.*], a Roland for an Oliver, measure for measure, diamond cut diamond, an eye for an eye, boomerang, the biter bit, a game at which two can play; reproof valiant, retort courteous.

recrimination &c. (*accusation*) 938;

719. Resistance. — N. RESISTANCE, stand, front, oppugnation [*rare*], oppugnance, oppugnancy; opposition &c. 708; renitency, renitence, reluctance [*archaic*], reluctation [*rare*], recalcitrance *or* recalcitrancy, recalcitration; repugnance, repulsion; kicking &c. *v.*

REPULSE, rebuff, snub.

INSURRECTION &c. (*disobedience*) 742; strike; turnout [*colloq.*], lockout; barringout; *levée en masse* [*F.*], Jacquerie [*F. hist.*]; rebellion; boycott; riot &c. (*disorder*) 59.

revenge &c. 919; compensation &c. 30; reaction &c. (recoil) 277.

V. RETALIATE, retort, turn upon; pay, pay off, pay back; pay in -one's own, – the same- coin; cap, match; reciprocate &c. 148; turn the tables upon, return the compliment; give a *quid pro quo* &c. n., give as much as one takes; give as good as was sent; exchange blows; give and take, exchange fisticuffs; be quits, be even with; pay off old scores.

serve one right, be hoist on one's own petard, throw a stone in one's own garden, catch a Tartar.

Adj. RETALIATING &c. *v.;* retaliatory, retaliative, retributive, recriminatory, reciprocal; talionic [*rare*].

Adv. IN RETALIATION; *en revanche* [*F.*].

⁎⁎ *mutato nomine de te fabula narratur* [Horace]; *par pari refero* [Terence]; *tu quoque;* you're another; *suo sibi gladio hunc jugulo; à beau jeu beau retour; litem lite resolvere* [adap'ed from Horace]; "curses, like chickens, come home to roost."

V. RESIST; not submit &c. 725; repugn [*obs.*], reluctate [*rare*], oppugn, withstand; stand up -, strive -, bear up -, be proof -, make head- against; stand, – firm, – fast, – one's ground, – the brunt of, – out; hold -one's ground, – one's own, – out; stick it out [*colloq.*].

FACE, confront, breast the -wave, – current; stem the -tide, – torrent; grapple with; show a bold front &c. (*courage*) 861; present a front, make a stand, take one's stand.

OPPOSE &c. 708; kick, – against; recalcitrate, kick against the pricks; fly in the face of; lift the hand against &c. (*attack*) 716; withstand -an attack, – a siege, – the onset; rise up in arms &c. (*war*) 722; strike, turn out; draw up a round robin &c. (*remonstrate*) 932; put one's foot down; boycott; revolt &c. (*disobey*) 742; make a riot.

prendre le mors aux dents [*F.*], take the bit between the teeth; sell one's life dearly, die hard, keep at bay; repel, repulse.

Adj. RESISTING &c. *v.;* oppugnant, resistive, resistant; refractory &c. (*disobedient*) 742; repugnant; recalcitrant, renitent, repulsive, repellent; up in arms.

PROOF AGAINST; unconquerable &c. (*strong*) 159; stubborn, unconquered; indomitable &c. (*persevering*) 604a; unyielding &c. (*obstinate*) 606.

Int. HANDS OFF! keep off!

NEVER SAY DIE! stick it! [*colloq.*]; show what you're made of! give 'em hell! [*colloq.*]; "up, Guards, and at them!" [Wellington — *at Waterloo, as alleged*].

---

720. Contention. —**N.** CONTENTION, strife; contest, contestation; struggle; belligerency; opposition &c. 708.

CONTROVERSY, polemics; debate &c. (*discussion*) 476; war of words, logomachy, litigation; paper war; high words &c. (*quarrel*) 713; sparring &c. *v.*

COMPETITION, rivalry; corrivalry, corrivalship; agonism [*obs.*], *concours* [*F.*], match, race, tug of war, horse racing, heat, dash, steeple chase, point-to-point race, handicap; regatta; field day; sham fight, Derby day; turf, sporting, bullfight, tauromachy [*rare*], gymkhana [*orig. Anglo-Indian*]; boat race, torpids [*Oxford Univ.*].

pugilism, boxing, fisticuffs, spar, mill [*cant*], set-to [*colloq.*], round, bout, event; prize fighting; quarterstaff, single stick; gladiatorship, gymnastics; wrestling; catch-as-catch-can -, Greco-Roman (*or* Græco-Roman) -, Cornish -, Westmorland and Cumberland- style [of wrestling]; jujutsu (*also* jujitsu, jiujutsu, jiujitsu), *samo* [*Jap.*], *kooshti* [*Hind.*]; athletics, athletic sports; games of skill &c. 840.

721. Peace. — **N.** PEACE; amity &c. (*friendship*) 888; pacifism; harmony &c. (*concord*) 714; tranquillity &c. (*quiescence*) 265; truce &c. (*pacification*) 723; pipe of peace, calumet.

piping time of peace, quiet life; neutrality.

V. BE AT PEACE; keep the peace &c. (*concord*) 714; make peace &c. 723; pacify; be a pacifist.

Adj. PACIFIC; peaceable, peaceful; calm, tranquil, untroubled, halcyon; bloodless; neutral, pacifistic, "too proud to fight" [Woodrow Wilson].

⁎⁎ the storm blown over; the lion lies down with the lamb; "all quiet on the Potomac"; *paritur pax bello* [Nepos]; "peace hath her victories no less renowned than war" [Milton]; "the peace of fact is not the peace of principle" [Amiel]; "peace is a goddess only when she comes with sword girt on thigh" [Roosevelt].

FRACAS &c. (*discord*) 713; clash of arms; tussle, scuffle, broil, fray; affray, affrayment [*obs.*]; velitation [*obs.*]; luctation [*rare*], colluctation [*obs.*], shindy [*colloq.*], brigue [*obs.*], brabble, scramble, *mêlée* [*F.*], scrimmage, stramash [*dial. or slang*], free-for-all [*cant*]; free –, stand up –, hand to hand –, running- fight.

CONFLICT, skirmish; encounter, rencounter, rencontre, collision, affair, brush, fight; sharp contest, hard knocks; battle, – royal; combat, action, engagement, just *or* joust, tournament; tilt, tilting; tourney, lists; pitched battle; guerrilla (*or* guerilla) –, irregular- warfare; bush-fighting.

deeds –, feats- of arms; pugnacity; combativeness &c. *adj.*; bone of contention &c. 713.

death struggle, struggle for life or death, Armageddon.

NAVAL ENGAGEMENT, naumachia *or* naumachy, sea fight.

DUEL, duello [*rare*], single combat, *monomachia* [*L.*] *or* monomachy, satisfaction, *passage d'armes* [*F.*], passage of arms, affair of honor; triangular duel; hostile meeting, digladiation [*archaic*]; appeal to arms &c. (*warfare*) 722.

V. CONTEND; contest, strive, struggle, scramble, wrestle; spar, square [*colloq.*]; exchange -blows, – fisticuffs; fib [*slang, Eng.*], jostle *or* justle, tussle, tilt, box, stave [*obs. or dial.*], fence; skirmish; pickeer [*obs.*]; fight &c. (*war*) 722; wrangle &c. (*quarrel*) 713.

contend &c. with; grapple –, engage –, close –, buckle [*obs.*] –, bandy –, try conclusions –, have a brush &c. *n.* –, tilt- with; encounter, fall foul of, pitch into [*colloq.*], clapperclaw [*archaic or dial.*], run a tilt at; oppose &c. 708; reluct.

compete –, cope –, vie –, race- with; outvie, emulate, rival; run a race.

contend &c. for, stipulate for, stickle for; insist upon, make a point of.

JOIN ISSUE, come to blows; be at –, fall to –, go to- loggerheads; set to, come to the scratch, pull a gun [*slang*], exchange shots, measure swords, meet hand to hand; take up the -cudgels, – glove, – gauntlet; tourney, just *or* joust, enter the lists; couch one's lance; give satisfaction; appeal to arms &c. (*warfare*) 722.

lay about one; break the peace.

Adj. CONTENDING &c. *v.*; at loggerheads, at war, at issue.

CONTENTIOUS, combative, bellicose, belligerent, unpeaceful; warlike &c. 722; quarrelsome &c. 901; pugnacious, pugilistic; tauromachian *or* tauromachic [*rare*]; gladiatorial.

ATHLETIC, gymnastic, palæstral *or* palestral, palæstric *or* palestric; competitive, rival.

*** *a verbis ad verbera;* a word and a blow; "a very pretty quarrel as it stands" [Sheridan]; *commune periculum concordiam parit; lis litem generat;* "litigious terms, fat contentions, and flowing fees" [Milton].

---

722. Warfare. — N. WARFARE; fighting &c. *v.*; hostilities; war, arms, the sword; Mars, Bellona, grim-visaged war, *horrida bella* [*L.*]; bloodshed.

appeal to -arms, – the sword; ordeal –, wager- of battle; *ultima ratio regum* [*L.*], arbitrament of the sword, declaration of war.

battle array, campaign, crusade, expedition; mobilization; state of siege; battlefield &c. (*arena*) 728; warpath.

ART OF WAR, rules of war, the war game, tactics, strategy, castrametation; generalship, soldiership; military evolutions, ballistics, gunnery; aviation; chivalry; gunpowder, shot, shell, poison gas.

723. Pacification. — N. PACIFICATION, conciliation; reconciliation, reconcilement, shaking of hands, calumet, peace pipe; accommodation, arrangement, adjustment; terms, compromise; amnesty, deed of release.

PEACE OFFERING; olive branch; calumet, – of peace; overture, preliminaries of peace.

TRUCE, armistice; suspension of -arms, – hostilities; truce of God; breathing time; convention; *modus vivendi* [*L.*]; flag of truce, white flag, *parlementaire* [*F.*], cartel.

hollow truce, *pax in bello* [*L.*]; drawn battle.

V. PACIFY, tranquillize, compose;

battle, conflict &c. (*contention*) 720; service, campaigning, active service, tented field; kriegspiel *or Kriegsspiel* [*Ger.*], fiery cross, trumpet, clarion, bugle, pibroch, slogan; war cry, war whoop; battle cry, beat of drum, *rappel* [*F.*], tom-tom; word of command; password, watchword; *passage d'armes* [*F.*].

war to the -death, – knife; *guerre à -mort, – outrance* [*F.*]; open –, trench –, guerrilla (*or* guerilla) –, internecine –, civil- war (*or* warfare).

WAR MEDAL, military medal, Victoria Cross, V. C., *croix de guerre* [*F.*], *médaille militaire* [*F.*], iron cross [*Ger.*].

WAR NEWS, war bulletin, war extra; war correspondent.

V. ARM; prepare for war; raise –, mobilize- troops; raise up in arms; take up the cudgels &c. 720; take up –, fly to –, appeal to- -arms, – the sword; draw –, unsheathe- the sword; dig up the -hatchet, – tomahawk.

WAR, make war, go to war, declare war, wage war, "let slip the dogs of war" [*Julius Cæsar*]; cry havoc; kindle –, light- the torch of war; raise one's banner, send round the fiery cross, hoist the black flag; throw –, fling- away the scabbard; take the field; take the law into one's own hands; do –, give –, join –, engage in –, go to- battle; flesh one's sword; set to, fall to, engage, measure swords with, draw the trigger, cross swords; come to -blows, – close quarters; fight; combat; contend &c. 720; battle with, break a lance with.

SERVE; enroll, enlist; see –, be on- -service, – active service; campaign; wield the sword, shoulder a musket, smell powder, be under fire; spill blood, imbrue the hands in blood; be on the warpath.

carry on -war, – hostilities; keep the field; fight the good fight; take by storm; go over the top [*colloq.*]; fight -it out, – like devils, – one's way, – hand to hand; cut one's way -out, – through; sell one's life dearly.

Adj. ARMED, – to the teeth, – cap-a-pie; sword in hand; contending, contentious &c. 720; in –, under –, up in- arms; at war with; bristling with arms; in battle array, in open arms, in the field; embattled; battled.

WARLIKE, belligerent, combative, armigerous, bellicose, martial, unpacific, unpeaceful; military, militant; soldier like, soldierly, chivalrous; strategical, civil, internecine; irregular, guerrilla *or* guerilla.

Adv. *flagrante bello* [*L.*], in the thick of the fray, in the cannon's mouth; at the sword's point, at the point of the bayonet.

Int. TO ARMS! *væ victis!* [*L.*]· to your tents O Israel! *c'est la guerre!* [*F.*].

.*. the battle rages; *à la guerre comme à la guerre; bis peccare in bello non licet; jus gladii;* "my voice is still for war" [Addison]; "my sentence is for open war" [Milton]; "pride, pomp, and circumstance of glorious war" [*Othello*]; "the cannons have their bowels full of wrath" [*King John*]; "the cannons . . . spit forth their iron indignation" [*ibid.*]; "the fire-eyed maid of smoky war" [*I Henry IV*]; *silent leges inter arma* [Cicero]; "O war! thou son of hell Whom angry heavens do make their minister" [*II Henry VI*]; "So frowned the mighty combatants that hell Grew darker at their frown" [*P. L.*]; "Nothing except a battle lost can be half so melancholy as a battle won" [Wellington]; "Charge, Chester, charge! On, Stanley, on!" [Scott]; "There never was a good war or a bad peace" [Franklin]; "Battle's magnificently stern array!" [Byron]; "But stay, I do not like Undue assassination" [Gilbert]; *si vis pacem para bellum;* "hard hitting is the best parry" [Roosevelt]; "If I should die, think only this of me: That there's some corner of a foreign field That is for ever England" [Rupert Brooke].

allay &c. (*moderate*) 174; reconcile, propitiate, placate, conciliate, meet halfway, hold out the olive branch, heal the breach, make peace, restore harmony, bring to terms.

MAKE UP A QUARREL; settle –, arrange –, accommodate- -matters, – differences; set straight; *tantas componere lites* [*L.*]; come to -an understanding, – terms; bridge over, hush up; make it up, make matters up; shake hands; mend one's fences [*U. S.*].

raise a siege; put up –, sheathe- the sword; bury the hatchet, lay down one's arms, turn swords into plowshares; smoke the calumet, close the temple of Janus; keep the peace &c. (*concord*) 714; be pacified &c.; come round.

Adj. CONCILIATORY, pacificatory; composing &c. *v.;* pacified &c. *v.;* accommodative.

.*. *requiescat in pace;* "to see great Hector in his weeds of peace" [*Troilus and Cressida*]; "Health, peace, and many a bloodless year To fight his battles o'er" [Holmes].

724. Mediation. — N. MEDIATION, mediatorship, mediatization, mediatorialism; intervention, interposition, interference, intermeddling, intercession; parley, negotiation, arbitration; flag of truce &c. 723; good offices, peace offering; diplomatics [*rare*], diplomacy; compromise &c. 774.

MEDIATOR, intercessor, peacemaker, make-peace, negotiator, go-between; diplomatist &c. (*consignee*) 758; moderator; propitiator; umpire, arbitrator.

V. MEDIATE, mediatize; intercede, interpose, interfere, intervene; step in, negotiate; meet halfway; arbitrate, propitiate; agree to arbitration; submit; *componere lites* [*L.*].

Adj. MEDIATORY, mediatorial, negotiable; mediating &c. *v.;* propitiatory, diplomatic.

725. Submission. — N. SUBMISSION, yielding, acquiescence, compliance, submittal, submissiveness, deference, nonresistance; obedience &c. 743.

SURRENDER, cession, capitulation, resignation, backdown [*colloq.*]; passing under the yoke, laying down one's arms, delivering up the keys (of the city &c.), handing over one's sword.

OBEISANCE, homage, kneeling, genuflexion, curtsy *or* curtsey, kotow [*Chinese*], salaam *or* salam [*Oriental*], prostration.

V. SUBMIT, succumb, yield, bend, stoop, accede, relent, resign, defer to.

SURRENDER, – at discretion; cede, capitulate, come to terms, retreat, beat a retreat; lay down –, deliver up- one's arms; lower –, haul down –, strike- one's -flag, – colors; draw in one's horns &c. (*humility*) 879; give -way, – ground, – in, – up; cave in [*colloq.*]; suffer judgment by default; bend, – to one's yoke, – before the storm; reel back; bend –, knuckle- -down, – to, – under; knock under.

HUMBLE ONESELF; eat -dirt, – crow, – the leek, – humble pie; bite –, lick- the dust; be –, fall- at one's feet; crouch before, throw oneself at the feet of; swallow the -leek, – pill; kiss the rod; turn the other cheek; *avaler les couleuvres* [*F.*], gulp down.

pocket the affront; make the best of, make a virtue of necessity; grin and abide, grin and bear it, shrug the shoulders, resign oneself; submit with a good grace &c. (*bear with*) 826.

YIELD OBEISANCE; obey &c. 743; kneel to, bow to, pay homage to, cringe to, truckle to; bend the -neck, – knee; kneel, fall on one's knees, bow submission, curtsy *or* curtsey, kotow [*Chinese*].

Adj. SUBMISSIVE, resigned, crouching, prostrate; downtrodden; surrendering &c. *v.;* down on one's marrowbones [*slang*]; on one's bended knee; nonresisting, unresisting; pliant &c. (*soft*) 324; humble &c. 879; undefended.

UNTENABLE, indefensible, insupportable, unsupportable.

*** have it your own way; it can't be helped; amen &c. (*assent*) 488; *da locum melioribus; tempori parendum.*

726. Combatant. — N. COMBATANT; disputant, controversialist, polemic, litigant, belligerent; competitor, rival, corrival; fighter, assailant; champion, Paladin; mosstrooper, swashbuckler, fire eater, duelist, swordsman, *sabreur* [*F.*], *beau sabreur* [*F.*]; athlete, wrestler, boxer.

bully, bludgeon man, rough, rowdy, ruffian, tough [*colloq., U. S.*], gunman [*colloq., U. S.*], Thug *or* thug; terrorist &c. 887; fighting man, prize fighter, pugilist, bruiser, the fancy [*now rare*], gladiator, fighting-cock, gamecock.

SOLDIER, warrior, brave, man at arms, guardsman, *gendarme* [*F.*]; campaigner, veteran; redcoat, military man, Rajput; armiger, esquire, knight; Amazon.

Janizary *or* Janissary; myrmidon; Mameluke *or* Mamaluke, spahi *or* spahee, bashi-bazouk [*Turk.*], Cossack, Croat, Pandor; irregular, free lance, franc-tireur, tirailleur, guerrilla *or* guerilla, *condottiere* [*It.*], mercenary; bushwhacker, companion; Hessian.

private, – soldier; Tommy Atkins [*Brit.*], doughboy [*slang, U. S.*], rank and file, peon, sepoy [*India*], *légionnaire* |*F*.], legionary, food for powder, fodder for cannon, *Kannonenfutter* [*Ger*.]; spearman, pikeman; archer, bowman; halberdier; musketeer, carabineer, rifleman, sharpshooter, jäger *or* yager, skirmisher; grenadier, fusileer, infantryman, foot soldier, footman [*rare*], light infantryman, chasseur, zouave; artilleryman, gunner, cannoneer, bombardier [*hist*.], matross [*obs*.]; engineer; sapper, – and miner; cavalryman, trooper, sowar [*India*], dragoon; light –, heavydragoon; heavy, cuirassier, hussar, lancer; recruit, rookie [*slang*, *U. S*.], conscript, drafted man, enlisted man.

officer &c. (*commander*) 745; subaltern, ensign, standard bearer.

HORSE AND FOOT; cavalry, horse, light horse, mounted rifles; infantry, foot, light infantry, rifles; artillery, horse artillery, field artillery, gunners; military train.

ARMED FORCE, troops, soldiery, military, forces, Sabaoth, host, the army, standing army, regulars, the line, troops of the line, militia, national guard, state guard [*U. S*.], bodyguard, yeomanry, volunteers, trainband, fencibles [*hist*.]; auxiliary, *bersagliere* [*It*.]; *garde -nationale*, – *royale* [*F*.]; minuteman [*Am. hist*.]; auxiliary - reserve- forces; reserves, *posse comitatus* [*L*.], posse; guards, yeomen of the guard, beefeaters [*Eng*.], life guards, household troops, Horse Guards, Foot Guards; Swiss guards.

LEVY, draft *or* draught; raw levies, awkward squad; Landwehr, Landsturm.

ARMY, *corps d'armée* [*F*.], army corps; host, division, battalia [*rare*], sotnia [*Russ*.], column, wing, detachment, garrison, flying column, brigade, regiment, corps, battalion, squadron, company, battery, subdivision, section, platoon, squad; picket, guard, rank, file; legion, phalanx, cohort, maniple, manipulus [*Rom. hist*.]; cloud of skirmishers.

WAR HORSE, charger, destrer *or* destrier [*archaic*].

NAVY, first line of defense, wooden walls, naval forces, fleet, flotilla, armada, squadron; man-of-war's man &c. (*sailor*) 269; marines.

MAN-OF-WAR, line-of-battle ship, ship of the line, battleship, warship, ironclad, war vessel, war castle, H.M.S., U.S.S.; superdreadnought, dreadnought, cruiser; armored –, protected- cruiser; torpedo-boat, – destroyer; destroyer, torpedocatcher, gunboat; submarine, submersible, U-boat; submarine chaser; mine layer, sweeper; turret ship, ram, monitor, floating battery; first-rate, frigate, sloop of war, corvet *or* corvette; bomb vessel; flagship, guard ship, privateer; troopship, transport, tender, store-ship, catamaran [*obs*.], fire boat.

AËROPLANE, airplane, aëro [*colloq*.], *avion* [*F*.], Fokker, dirigible, blimp [*cant*]; zeppelin &c. (*aëronautics*) 273.

*** "They left the peaceful river. The cricket field, the quad, The shaven lawns of Oxford, To seek a bloody sod" [W. M. Letts]; "They who to Glory's fanning This streamer have unfurled, The men whose joy is manning, The men who man the world!" [William Watson].

727. Arms. — N. ARMS, arm, weapon, deadly weapon; armament, armature; panoply, stand of arms; armor &c. (*defense*) 717; armory &c. (*store*) 636; *apparatus belli* [*L*.]; gunnery; ballistics &c. (*propulsion*) 284.

SIDE ARMS, *armes blanches* [*F*.], sword; good –, trusty –, naked- sword; cold steel, naked steel, steel, blade, brand [*archaic*]; broadsword, Toledo, Ferrara, claymore, glaive [*archaic*] *or* glave [*obs*.]; saber *or* sabre, cutlass, hanger, bilbo, falchion, scimitar *or* cimeter [*obs*.], whinyard [*obs*.], rapier, tuck [*hist*.], foil, yataghan (*also* ataghan, attaghan); dagger, poniard, baselard, dirk, stiletto, katar *or* kuttar [*India*], stylet; skean, skean dhu [*Scot*.]; creese *or* kris; dudgeon [*archaic*], bowie knife; bayonet, sword bayonet, sword stick.

AX *or* AXE, battle ax, Lochaber ax, adaga, poleax *or* poleaxe, halberd *or* halbert, gisarme, tomahawk, bill, black bill, brown bill, partisan.

SPEAR, lance, pike, spontoon, assagai *or* assegai, javelin, jereed *or* jerid, dart, shaft, bolt, reed, arrow; harpoon, gaff, eelspear; weet-weet, womerah, throwing stick, throw stick, boomerang; oxgoad, ankus.

CLUB, war club, waddy [*Austral*.], mace, truncheon, staff, bludgeon, cudgel, shillalah *or* shillelagh, handstaff, quarterstaff; bat, cane, stick, walking-stick, knuckle duster; billy, life-preserver, blackjack, sandbag.

BOW, crossbow, arbalest, ballista *or* balista *or* balister [*obs*.], trebuchet *or* trebucket, catapult, sling; battering-ram &c. (*impulse*) 276.

FIREARMS; gun, piece; artillery, ordnance; siege –, battering- train; park, battery;

cannon, gun of position, heavy gun, fieldpiece, field gun, mountain gun, siege gun, seacoast gun; mortar, howitzer, carronade, culverin, basilisk [obs.]; falconet, jingal, swivel, swivel gun, pedrero or pederero, *bouche à feu* [F.], smooth bore, rifled cannon; Armstrong –, Lancaster –, Paixhans –, Whitworth –, Parrott –, Krupp –, Vickers –, Benet-Mercié –, Gatling –, Maxim –, machine- gun; pompom, *mitrailleuse* [F.]; "seventy-five" [*French rapid-fire* 75 mm. *field gun*]; Lewis gun; auto-rifle, ten-pounder; flame-thrower, *Flammenwerfer* [Ger.], *lance-flamme* [F.].

SMALL ARMS; musketry; musket, firelock, fowling piece, rifle, fusil [obs. or hist.], escopette or escopet, carbine, blunderbuss, musketoon, Brown Bess, matchlock, harquebus or arquebus, caliver, hackbut or hagbut, shotgun, petronel [hist.]; small bore; breechloader, muzzle-loader; gunflint, gunlock; Minié –, Enfield –, Flobert –, Westley Richards –, Snider –, Martini-Henry –, Lee-Metford –, Lee-Enfield –, Mauser –, Mannlicher –, Springfield –, magazine- rifle; needle gun, *chassepot* [F.]; wind gun, air gun; automatic -gun, – pistol; automatic; revolver, repeater; shooting iron [slang, U. S.], shooter [colloq., U. S.], six-shooter [U. S.], gun [U. S. and colloq. for revolver or pistol], pistol, pistolet [obs.].

MISSILE, bolt, projectile, shot, ball; grape; grape –, canister –, bar –, cannon –, langrage or langrel –, round –, chain- shot; slung shot; shrapnel, *mitraille* [F.], grenade, hand grenade, rifle grenade; shell, high-explosive shell, *obus explosif* [F.], bomb, depth bomb, smoke bomb, gas bomb; bullet; dumdum –, man-stopping –, explosive –, expanding- bullet; petard; infernal machine, torpedo; carcass, rocket; congreve, – rocket; slug, stone, rock, brickbat.

thunderbolt, levin- -bolt, – brand; stroke, stroke of lightning, thunderstone [obs. or dial. Eng.].

AMMUNITION; powder, – and shot; explosive; gunpowder, "villanous saltpetre" [Hen. IV.]; guncotton, pyroxylin or pyroxyline, dynamite, melinite, cordite, gelignite, lyddite, nitroglycerin or nitroglycerine, trinitrotoluol, trinitrotoluine, T.N.T.; cartridge; ball cartridge, cartouche, fireball; poison gas, mustard gas, chlorine gas, tear gas &c.

⁎ *en flûte; nervos belli pecuniam infinitam;* "his sword which he called Mouse because it was swift and nimble" [Dunsany].

728. Arena. — N. ARENA, field, platform; scene of action, theater or theatre, walk, course; hustings; stage, boards &c. (*playhouse*) 599; amphitheater or amphi-theatre, Coliseum, Colosseum; Flavian amphitheater, hippodrome, circus, race course, *corso* [It.], turf, cockpit, bear garden, gymnasium, palæstra or palestra, ring, lists; tilt-yard, tilting ground; *Campus Martius* [L.], *Champ de Mars* [F.]; campus [U. S.], playing field, playground.

BATTLE FIELD, battle ground; field of -battle, – slaughter; No Man's Land [World War]; "over there" [used in America, esp. of the Western Front], "out there" [corresponding term in Eng.]; theater –, seat- of war; Aceldama, camp; the enemy's camp.

TRYSTING PLACE &c. (*place of meeting*) 74.

⁎ "My race being run, I love to watch the race" [Masefield].

Section V.   RESULTS OF VOLUNTARY ACTION

729. Completion. — N. COMPLETION; accomplishment, achievement, fulfill-ment or fulfilment; performance, exe-cution; dispatch or despatch, consum-mation, culmination; finish, conclusion; limit, effectuation; close &c. (*end*) 67; terminus &c. (*arrival*) 292; winding up; *finale* [It.], *dénouement* [F.], catastrophe, issue, upshot, result; final –, last –, crowning –, finishing- -touch, – stroke;

730. Noncompletion. — N. NON-COMPLETION, nonfulfillment or nonful-filment, shortcoming &c. 304; incom-pleteness &c. 53; drawn -battle, – game: work of Penelope; Sisyphean -labor, – toil, – task.

NONPERFORMANCE, inexecution; neg-lect of execution; neglect &c. 460.

V. NOT COMPLETE &c. 729; leave un-finished &c. adj., leave undone; neglect

last finish, *coup de grâce* [F.]; crowning of the edifice; coping stone, copestone, keystone; missing link &c. 53; super-structure, *ne plus ultra* [L.], work done, *fait accompli* [F.].

elaboration; finality; completeness &c. 52.

V. COMPLETE, perfect; effect, effectu-ate; accomplish, achieve, compass, con-summate, hammer out; bring to -ma-turity, - perfection; elaborate.

DO, execute, make; go -, get- through; work out, enact; bring -about, - to bear, - to pass, - through, - to a head.

dispatch *or* despatch, knock off [*col-loq.*], finish off, polish off; make short work of; dispose of, set at rest; per-form, discharge fulfill *or* fulfil, realize; - into effect, - into execution; make good; be as good as one's word.

&c. 460; let alone, let slip; lose sight of.

FALL SHORT OF &c. 304; do things by halves, scotch the snake not kill it; hang fire; be slow to; collapse &c. 304.

Adj. INCOMPLETE &c. 53; not com-pleted &c. *v.;* uncompleted, unfinished, unaccomplished, unperformed, unexe-cuted; sketchy; addle, muddled, sterile.

in progress, in hand, on the stocks, in preparation, moving, getting along, going on, proceeding; on one's hands; on the anvil.

Adv. *re infectâ* [L.]; without -, lacking- -the final touches, - the finishing stroke.

put in -practice, - force; carry -out, - into effect, - into execution; make good; be as good as one's word.

DO THOROUGHLY, not do by halves, go the whole hog [*colloq.*]; drive home, be in at the death &c. (*persevere*) 604*a;* carry through, deliver the goods [*colloq.*, *U. S.*], play out, exhaust; fill the bill [*colloq.*, *U. S.*].

FINISH, bring to a close &c. (*end*) 67; wind up, stamp, clinch, seal, set the seal on, put the seal to; give the final touch &c. *n.* to; put the -last, - finishing-touch to; crown, crown all; cap.

ripen, culminate; come to a -head, - crisis; come to its end; die a natural death, die of old age; run its course, run one's race; touch -, reach -, attain-the goal; reach &c. (*arrive*) 292; get in the harvest.

Adj. COMPLETING, final; concluding, conclusive; crowning &c. *v.;* exhaustive, elaborate, complete, mature, perfect, consummate, thorough.

DONE, completed &c. *v.;* done for [*colloq.*], sped, wrought out; highly wrought &c. (*preparation*) 673; thorough &c. 52; ripe &c. (*ready*) 673.

Adv. COMPLETELY &c. (*thoroughly*) 52; to crown all, out of hand; with absolute -perfection, - finish; as a last stroke; as a fitting climax.

*** the race is run; *actum est; finis coronat opus; consummatum est; c'en est fait;* it is all over; the game is played out, the bubble has burst; *aussitôt dit aussitôt fait; aut non tentaris aut perfice* [Ovid]; "Life is as just as Death; Life pays its debt" [Masefield].

---

731. Success. — N. SUCCESS, success-fulness; speed; advance &c. (*progress*) 282.

trump card; hit, stroke; lucky -, for-tunate -, good- -hit, - stroke; bold stroke, masterstroke; ten-strike [*colloq.*, *U. S.*]; *coup de maître* [F.], checkmate; half the battle, prize; profit &c. (*acquisi-tion*) 775.

continued success; good fortune &c. (*prosperity*) 734; time well spent.

MASTERY, advantage over; upper hand, whip hand; ascendancy, expunga-tion [*obs.*], conquest, victory, walkover [*colloq.*], subdual; subjugation &c. (*sub-jection*) 749; triumph &c. (*exultation*) 884; proficiency &c. (*skill*) 698; a feather in one's cap [*colloq.*].

VICTOR, victress [*rare*], victrix [*rare*],

732. Failure. — N. FAILURE, unsuc-cess, nonsuccess, nonfulfillment *or* non-fulfilment; dead failure, successlessness; abortion, miscarriage; *brutum fulmen* [L.] &c. 158; labor in vain &c. (*inutility*) 645; no go [*colloq.*]; inefficacy; ineffica-ciousness &c. *adj.;* vain -, ineffectual -, abortive- -attempt, - efforts; flash in the pan, "lame and impotent conclu-sion" [*Othello*]; frustration; slip 'twixt cup and lip &c. (*disappointment*) 509.

BLUNDER &c. (*mistake*) 495; fault, omission, miss, oversight, slip, trip, stumble, claudication [*obs.*]; footfall; false -, wrong- step; *faux pas* [F.], titubation, *bévue* [F.], *faute* [F.], lurch; botchery &c. (*want of skill*) 699; scrape, mess, muddle, botch, fiasco, breakdown; flunk [*colloq.*, *U. S.*].

conqueror, master, champion, winner; master of the -situation, - position.

V. SUCCEED; be successful &c. *adj.;* gain one's -end, - ends; crown with success.

gain -, attain -, carry -, secure -, win- -a point, - an object; get there [*slang, U. S.*]; manage to, contrive to; accomplish &c. (*effect, complete*) 729; do -, work- wonders; make a go of it [*colloq.*].

come off -well, - successfully, - with flying colors; make short work of; take -, carry- by storm; bear away the bell; win one's spurs, win the battle; win -, carry -, gain- the -day, - prize, - palm; have the best of it, have it all one's own way, have the game in one's own hands, have the ball at one's feet, have one on the hip; walk over the course; carry all before one, remain in possession of the field; score a success.

make progress &c. (*advance*) 282; win -, make -, work -, find- one's way; speed; strive to some purpose; prosper &c. 734; drive a roaring trade; make profit &c. (*acquire*) 775; reap -, gather- the -fruits, - benefit of, - harvest; strike oil [*slang, U. S.*], make one's fortune, get in the harvest, turn to good account; turn to account &c. (*use*) 677.

TRIUMPH, be triumphant; gain -, obtain- -a victory, - an advantage; chain victory to one's car.

surmount -, overcome -, get over- -a difficulty, - an obstacle &c. 706; *se tirer d'affaire* [*F.*]; make head against; stem the -torrent, - tide, - current; weather -the storm, - a point; turn a corner, keep one's head above water, tide over; master; get -, have -, gain- the -better of, - best of, - upper hand, - ascendancy, - whip hand, - start of; distance; surpass &c. (*superiority*) 33.

DEFEAT, conquer, vanquish, discomfit; euchre [*slang*]; overcome, overthrow, overpower, overmaster, overmatch, overset, override, overreach; outwit, outdo, outflank, outmaneuver *or* outmanœuvre, outgeneral, outvote; take the wind out of one's adversary's sails; beat, beat hollow [*colloq.*], lick [*colloq.*], rout, drub, floor, worst, lick to a frazzle [*colloq.*]; put -down, - to flight, - to the rout, - *hors de combat* [*F.*], - out of court.

settle [*colloq.*], do for [*colloq.*], break the -neck of, - back of; capsize, sink,

MISHAP &c. (*misfortune*) 735; split, collapse, smash, blow, explosion.

REPULSE, rebuff, defeat, rout, overthrow, discomfiture; beating, drubbing; quietus, nonsuit, subjugation; checkmate, stalemate, fool's mate.

losing game, *affaire flambée* [*F.*]

FALL, downfall, ruin, perdition; wreck &c. (*destruction*) 162; deathblow; bankruptcy &c. (*nonpayment*) 808.

VICTIM, prey; bankrupt; flunker [*colloq., U. S.*], flunky *or* flunkey [*cant, U. S.*].

V. FAIL; be unsuccessful &c. *adj.;* not succeed &c. 731; make vain efforts &c. *n.;* do -, labor -, toil- in vain; flunk [*colloq., U. S.*]; lose one's labor, take nothing by one's motion; bring to naught, make nothing of; wash a blackamoor white &c. (*impossible*) 471; roll the stone of Sisyphus &c. (*useless*) 645; do by halves &c. (*not complete*) 730; lose ground &c. (*recede*) 283; fall short of &c. 304; go to -the wall, - the dogs, - pot [*colloq.*], lick -, bite- the dust; be defeated &c. 731; have the worst of it, lose the day, come off second best, lose; not have a leg to stand on; fall a prey to; succumb &c. (*submit*) 725.

MISS, - one's aim, - the mark, - one's footing, - stays [*naut.*]; slip, trip, stumble; make a slip &c., *n.;* make a blunder &c. 495, make a mess of, make a botch of; bitch it [*obs.*], miscarry, abort, go up like a rocket and come down like the stick, reckon without one's host; get the wrong -pig by the tail, - sow by the ear [*colloq.*] &c. (*blunder, mismanage*) 699.

FLOUNDER, falter; limp, halt, hobble, titubate; fall, tumble; lose one's balance; fall to the ground, fall between two stools; stick in the mud, run aground, split upon a rock; run -, knock -, dash- one's head against a stone wall; break one's back; break down, sink, drown, founder, have the ground cut from under one; get into -trouble, - a mess, - a scrape; come to grief &c. (*adversity*) 735.

COME TO NOTHING, end in smoke; flat out [*colloq., U. S.*]; fall -to the ground, - through, - dead, - stillborn, - flat; slip through one's fingers; hang fire, misfire, flash in the pan, collapse; topple down &c. (*descent*) 305; go to wrack and ruin &c. (*destruction*) 162.

shipwreck, drown, swamp; subdue; subjugate &c. (*subject*) 749; reduce; make
the enemy bite the dust; victimize, roll'
in the dust, trample under foot, put an
extinguisher upon.

CHECKMATE, silence, quell, nonsuit,
upset, confound, nonplus, stalemate,
trump; baffle &c. (*hinder*) 706; circumvent, elude; trip up, – the heels of; drive
-into a corner, – to the wall; run hard,
put one's nose out of joint [*colloq.*].

AVAIL; answer, – the purpose; prevail,
take effect, do, turn out well, work well,
take [*colloq.*], tell, bear fruit; hit it, hit
the mark, hit the right nail on the head;
nick it; turn up trumps, make a hit;
find one's account in.

Adj. SUCCESSFUL; prosperous &c. 734;
succeeding &c. *v.;* triumphant; flushed
-, crowned- with success; victorious;
set up [*colloq.*]; in the ascendant; unbeaten &c. (*see* beat &c. *v.*); well-spent;
felicitous, effective, in full swing.

Adv. SUCCESSFULLY &c. *adj.;* with flying colors, in triumph, swimmingly; *à
merveille* [*F.*], beyond all hope; to some
-, to good- purpose; to one's heart's
content.

. *veni vidi vici;* the day being one's own;
one's star in the ascendant; *omne tulit punctum;
bis vincit qui se vincit in victoria; cede repug-
nanti cedendo victor abibis* [Ovid]; *chacun est
l'artisan de sa fortune; dies faustus; l'art de
vaincre est celui de mépriser la mort; omnia
vincit amor;* "peace hath her victories no less
renowned than war" [Milton]; "the race by
vigor not by vaunts is won" [Pope]; *vincit qui
patitur; vincit qui se vincit;* "Is there anything
in life so disenchanting as attainment?"
[Stevenson].

GO AMISS, go wrong, go cross, go hard
with, go on a wrong tack; go on -, come
off -, turn out -, work- ill; take a wrong
turn, take an ugly turn, be all over with,
be all up with; explode; dash one's
hopes &c. (*disappoint*) 509; defeat the
purpose; sow the wind and reap the
whirlwind, jump out of the frying pan
into the fire.

Adj. UNSUCCESSFUL, successless, stick-
it [*Scot.*]; failing, tripping &c. *v.;* at
fault; unfortunate &c. 735.

ABORTIVE, sterile, impotent, addle,
stillborn; fruitless, bootless; ineffectual,
ineffective; inefficient &c. (*impotent*)
158; inefficacious; lame, hobbling, *décousu* [*F.*]; insufficient &c. 640; unavailing &c. (*useless*) 645; of no effect.

STRANDED, aground, grounded,
swamped, cast away, wrecked, foun-
dered, capsized, shipwrecked, nonsuited;
foiled; defeated &c. 731; struck -,
borne -, broken- down; downtrodden;
overborne, overwhelmed; all up with
[[*colloq.*]; plowed *or* ploughed [*Eng.
Univ. cant*], plucked [*college cant*].

UNDONE, lost, ruined, broken; bankrupt &c. (*not paying*) 808; played out;
done up, done for [*both colloq.*]; dead-
beat [*colloq.*], ruined root and branch,
flambé [*F.*], knocked on the head; destroyed &c. 162.

FRUSTRATED, thwarted, crossed, unhinged, disconcerted, dashed; thrown
-off one's balance, – on one's back, –
on one's beam ends; unhorsed, in a
sorry plight; hard hit; stultified, befooled, dished [*colloq.*], hoist on one's
own petard; victimized, sacrificed.

wide of the mark &c. (*error*) 495; out of one's reckoning &c. (*inexpectation*)
508; left in the lurch; thrown away &c. (*wasted*) 638; unattained; uncompleted
&c. 730.

Adv. UNSUCCESSFULLY &c. *adj.;* to little or no purpose, in vain, *re infectâ* [*L.*].

. the bubble has burst, "the game is up" [*Cymbeline*]; all is lost; the devil to pay; *parturiunt montes* &c. (*disappointment*) 509; *dies infaustus; tout est perdu hors l'honneur;* "Trust
still to Life, the day is not yet old" [Masefield].

---

733. Trophy. — **N.** TROPHY; medal, prize, palm, laurel, laurels, bays, crown,
chaplet, wreath, civic crown; insignia &c. 550; eulogy, citation; scholarship;
feather in one's cap &c. (*honor*) 873; garland; triumphal arch; Victoria Cross,
Congressional medal, *croix de guerre* [*F.*], *médaille militaire* [*F.*], Iron Cross; Car-
negie medal, Nobel prize; blue ribbon; red ribbon of the Legion of Honor; decoration &c. 877.

TRIUMPH &c. (*celebration*) 883; flying colors &c. (*show*) 882.

. *monumentum ære perennius* [Hor.]; "for valor"; "Now are our brows bound with victorious
wreaths" [*Richard III*]; "'Tis deeds must win the prize" [*Taming of the Shrew*]; "It is a conquest
for a prince to boast of" [*I Henry IV*].

734. Prosperity. — **N.** PROSPERITY, welfare, well-being; affluence &c. (*wealth*) 803; success &c. 731; thrift, roaring trade; good –, smiles of - fortune; blessings, godsend; bed of roses; fat of the land, milk and honey, loaves and fishes, fleshpots of Egypt.

LUCK; good –, run of- luck; sunshine; fair -weather, – wind; fair wind and no favor; palmy –, bright –, halcyon-days; piping times, tide, flood, high tide.

GOLDEN AGE, golden time, *Saturnia regna* [*L.*], Saturnian age.

MAN OF SUBSTANCE, made man, lucky dog, *enfant gâté* [*F.*], spoiled child of fortune.

UPSTART, parvenu, *nouveau riche* [*F.*], *narikin* [*Jap.*], skipjack [*dial. Eng.*], mushroom.

V. PROSPER, thrive, flourish; be prosperous &c. *adj.;* drive a roaring trade; go on -well, – smoothly, – swimmingly; sail before the wind, swim with the tide; run -smooth, – smoothly, – on all fours [*colloq.*].

rise –, get on- in the world; work –, make- one's way; look up; lift –, raise-one's head, make one's fortune, feather one's nest, make one's pile [*slang*].

flower, blow, blossom, bloom, fructify, bear fruit, fatten, batten.

keep oneself afloat; keep –, hold-one's head above water; light –, fall-on one's -legs, – feet; drop into a good thing; bear a charmed life; bask in the sunshine; have a good (*or* fine) time of it; have a run, – of luck; have the good fortune &c. *n.* to; take a favorable turn; live -on the fat of the land, – in clover, – on velvet.

Adj. PROSPEROUS; thriving &c. *v.;* in a fair way, buoyant; well off, well to do, well to live [*archaic*], set up [*colloq.*], well to do in the world; at one's ease; rich &c. 803; in good case; in full feather, in high feather; fortunate, lucky, in luck; born with a silver spoon in one's mouth, born under a lucky star; on the sunny side of the hedge.

palmy, halcyon; agreeable &c. 829; *couleur de rose* [*F.*].

AUSPICIOUS, propitious, providential.

Adv. PROSPEROUSLY &c. *adj.;* swimmingly; as good luck would have it; beyond all -expectation, – hope; be-

735. Adversity. — **N.** ADVERSITY, evil &c. 619; failure &c. 732; bad – ill –, evil –, adverse –, hard- -fortune, – hap, – luck, – lot; frowns of fortune; evil -dispensation, – star, – genius; ups and downs of life; the sport of fortune; broken fortunes; hard -case, – lines, – life; sea –, peck- of troubles; hell upon earth; slough of despond.

pressure of the times, iron age, evil day, time out of joint; hard –, bad –, sad- times; rainy day, cloud, dark cloud, gathering clouds, ill wind; affliction &c. (*painfulness*) 830; bitter -pill, – draft (*or* draught), – cup; care.

TROUBLE, hardship, curse, blight, blast, load, pressure, humiliation.

MISFORTUNE, misventure [*archaic*], mishap, mischance, misadventure, disaster, calamity, catastrophe; accident, casualty, cross, blow, trial, sorrow, visitation, infliction, reverse, check, *contretemps* [*F.*], pinch, rub; backset, comedown, setback.

DOWNFALL, fall; losing game; falling &c. *v.;* ruination, ruinousness, undoing; extremity; ruin &c. (*destruction*) 162.

V. BE ILL OFF &c. *adj.;* go hard with; fall on evil, – days; go on ill; not prosper &c. 734.

COME TO GRIEF, go downhill, go to rack and ruin &c. (*destruction*) 162, go to the dogs [*colloq.*]; fall, – from one's high estate; decay, sink, decline, go down in the world; have seen better days; bring down one's gray hairs with sorrow to the grave; be all over with, be all up with [*colloq.*]; bring a wasp's (*or* hornet's) nest about one's ears.

Adj. UNFORTUNATE, unblest, unhappy, unlucky, unprosperous, improsperous [*obs.*]; hoodooed [*colloq., U. S.*], Jonahed [*slang*], jinxed [*slang*], luckless, hapless; out of luck; in trouble, in a bad way, in an evil plight; under a cloud; clouded; ill off, badly off; in adverse circumstances; poor &c. 804; behindhand, down in the world, decayed, undone; on the road to ruin, on its last legs, on the wane; in one's utmost need.

ILL-FATED, ill-starred, ill-omened; planet-struck, devoted, doomed; inauspicious, unauspicious [*rare*], ominous, sinister, unpropitious; unfavorable; born -under an evil star, – with a wooden ladle in one's mouth.

yond one's deserts; beyond the dreams of avarice.

. one's star in the ascendant; all for the best; one's course runs smooth.

chacun est l'artisan de sa fortune; donec eris felix multos numerabis amicos [Ovid]; *felicitas multos habet amicos; felix se nescit amari* [Lucan]; "good luck go with thee" [*Henry V*]; *nulli est homini perpetuum bonum* [Plautus]; "the lines are fallen unto me in pleasant places; yea, I have a goodly heritage" [*Bible*].

ADVERSE, untoward; disastrous, calamitous, ruinous, dire, deplorable.

Adv. if the worst come to the worst, as ill luck would have it, from bad to worse, out of the frying pan into the fire.

. one's star is on the wane; one's luck turns, one's luck fails; the game is up, one's doom is sealed, the ground crumbles under one's feet, *sic transit gloria mundi, tant va la cruche à l'eau qu' à la fin elle se casse.*

"adversity's sweet milk, philosophy" [*Romeo and Juliet*]; *amici probantur rebus adversis; bien vengas mal si vienes solo;* εὐτυχῶν μὲν μέτριος ἴσθι ἀτυχῶν δὲ φρόνιμος [Periander]; *gaudet tentamine virtus; curæ leves loquuntur ingentes stupent; res est sacra miser* [Ovid]; *sempre il mal non vien per nuocere; væ victis* [Livy]; "sweet are the uses of adversity" [*As You Like It*]; "the man who complains of the crumpled rose leaf very often has his flesh full of thorns" [Chesterton]; "in the shadow of a great affliction" [Whittier].

736. Mediocrity. — N. MEDIOCRITY; golden mean &c. (*mid-course*) 628, (*moderation*) 174; moderate -, average- circumstances; respectability.

middle classes, *bourgeoisie* [*F.*].

V. strike the golden mean; preserve a middle course &c. 628.

jog on, get along [*colloq.*], get by [*slang*]; go -, get on- -fairly, - quietly,- peaceably, - tolerably, - respectably.

Adj. MIDDLING, *comme ci comme ça* [*F.*], soso *or* so-so, fair, fair to middling [*colloq.*], medium, moderate, mediocre, ordinary; second -, third -, fourth- rate.

Adv. with nothing to brag about.

. "High hopes die on a warm hearthstone" [Kipling]; "No characteristic trait had he Of any distinctive kind" [Gilbert]; "contentment is the smother of invention" [*Cynic's Calendar*].

Division (II) INTERSOCIAL VOLITION[1]

Section I. GENERAL INTERSOCIAL VOLITION

737. Authority. — N. AUTHORITY; influence, patronage, power, preponderance, credit, prestige, prerogative, jurisdiction; right &c. (*title*) 924.

divine right, dynastic rights, authoritativeness; royalty, regality, imperiality [*rare*]; absoluteness, absolutism, despotism, tyranny; *jus nocendi* [*L.*]; *jus divinum* [*L.*].

COMMAND, empire, sway, rule; dominion, domination; sovereignty, supremacy, suzerainty; kinghood, kingship; lordship, headship; chiefdom; patriarchy, patriarchate; leadership, hegemony; seigniory; mastery, mastership, masterdom; government &c. (*direction*) 693; dictation, control.

hold, grasp; grip, gripe; reach; iron sway &c. (*severity*) 739; fangs, clutches, talons; rod of empire &c. (*scepter*) 747.

REIGN, *régime* [*F.*], dynasty; directorship, dictatorship; protectorate, protec-

738. [ABSENCE OF AUTHORITY] Laxity. — N. LAXITY; laxness, looseness, slackness; toleration &c. (*lenity*) 740; freedom &c. 748.

ANARCHY, interregnum; relaxation; loosening &c. *v.;* remission; dead letter, *brutum fulmen* [*L.*], misrule; license, licentiousness; insubordination &c. (*disobedience*) 742; mob rule, mob law, mobocracy, ochlocracy; lynch law &c. (*illegality*) 964, nihilism, reign of violence.

[DEPRIVATION OF POWER] dethronement, impeachment, deposition, abdication; usurpation.

V. BE LAX &c. *adj.; laisser faire* [*F.*], *laisser aller* [*F.*]; hold a loose rein; give the reins to, give rope enough, give a loose to [*obs.*], give a free course to, give free rein to; tolerate; relax; misrule.

go beyond the length of one's tether; have one's -swing, - fling; act without -instructions, - authority; act on one's

---

[1] Implying the action of the will of one mind over the will of another.

torship; caliphate, pashalic, electorate; presidency, presidentship; administration; consulship, proconsulship; prefecture; seneschalship; magistrature, magistracy.

[GOVERNMENTS] empire; monarchy; limited -, constitutional- monarchy; aristarchy, aristocracy; oligarchy, democracy, demagogy; heteronomy; republic; thearchy; diarchy, duarchy, duumvirate; triarchy, triumvirate; heterarchy [obs.]; autocracy, monocracy.

representative government, constitutional government, vox populi [L.], home rule, dominion rule [Brit.], colonial government; self-government, autonomy, self-determination; republicanism, federalism; socialism; collectivism; pantisocracy; imperium in imperio [L.]; bureaucracy; beadledom, Bumbledom; stratocracy [rare], martial law; military -power, - government; feodality, feodatory, feudal system, feudalism.

GYNOCRACY, gynarchy, gynecocracy or gynæcocracy, matriarchy, matriarchate, metrocracy; petticoat government.

[VICARIOUS AUTHORITY] commission &c. 755; deputy &c. 759; permission &c. 760.

STATE, realm, commonwealth, country, power, polity, body politic, posse comitatus [L.]; toparchy.

RULER; person in authority &c. (master) 745; judicature &c. 965; cabinet &c. (council) 696; seat of -government, - authority; headquarters.

usurper, tyrant, jack-in-office.

[ACQUISITION OF AUTHORITY] accession; installation &c. 755; usurpation.

V. AUTHORIZE &c. (permit) 760; warrant &c. (right) 924; dictate &c. (order) 741; have -, hold -, possess -, exercise -, exert -, grasp -, seize -, wrest -, wield- -authority &c. n.

RULE, sway, command, control, administer; govern &c. (direct) 693; lead, preside over, reign; possess -, be seated on -, occupy -, seize- the throne; sway -, wield- the scepter or sceptre; wear the crown.

be at the head of &c. adj.; hold -, be in -, fill an- office; hold- , occupy- a post; be master &c. 745.

DOMINATE; have -, get- the -upper, - whip- hand; gain a hold upon, preponderate, dominate, rule the roast; boss [colloq., chiefly U. S.]; override, overrule, overawe; lord it over, hold in hand, keep under, make a puppet of, lead by the nose, turn round one's little finger, bend to one's will, hold one's own, wear the breeches [colloq.]; have the ball at one's feet, have it all one's own way, have the game in one's own hand, have on the hip, have under one's thumb; be master of the situation; take the lead, play first fiddle, set the fashion; give the law to; carry with a high hand; lay down the law; "ride in the whirlwind and direct the storm" [adapted from Addison]; rule with a rod of iron &c. (severity) 739.

ASSUME AUTHORITY &c. n.; ascend -, mount- the throne; take the reins, - into one's hand; assume the reins of government; take -, assume the- command.

BE GOVERNED BY, be in the power of; be under the -rule of, - dominion of.

Adj. RULING &c. v.; regnant, at the head, dominant, paramount, supreme, predominant, preponderant, in the ascendant, influential; gubernatorial; imperious; authoritative, executive, administrative, clothed with authority, official, bureaucratic, departmental, ex officio [L.], imperative, peremptory, overruling, absolute; hegemonic or hegemonical; arbitrary; compulsory &c. 744; stringent.

at one's command; in one's power, in one's grasp; under control; authorized &c. (due) 924.

SOVEREIGN; regal, royal, royalist, monarchical, kingly; dynastic, imperial,

own responsibility, usurp authority, undermine the authority of.

DETHRONE, depose; abdicate.

Adj. LAX, loose; slack; remiss &c. (careless) 460; weak.

RELAXED; licensed; reinless, unbridled; anarchic or anarchical, nihilistic; "agin the government"; unauthorized &c. (unwarranted) 925; adespotic, undespotic; not imperious &c. (ruling) 737.

. "when the cat's away the mice will play" [prov.]; "Pleasant it is for the little tin gods When great Jove nods" [Kipling].

imperialistic; princely; feudal; aristocratic, autocratic; oligarchic &c. *n.;* democratic, republican.

Adv. in the name of, by the authority of, at one's command, *de par le Roi* [*F.*], in virtue of; under the auspices of, in the hands of.

at one's pleasure; by a dash (*or* stroke) of the pen; at one's nod; by lifting one's finger; *ex mero motu* [*L.*]; *ex cathedrâ* [*L.*].

. the gray mare the better horse; "every inch a king" [*Lear*]; "a dog's obeyed in office" [*ibid.*]; *cada uno tiene su alguazil; le Roi le veut; regibus esse manus an nescis longas; regnant populi;* "the demigod Authority" [*Measure for Measure*]; "off with his head! so much for Buckingham" [Cibber]; "the right divine of kings to govern wrong" [Pope]; "uneasy lies the head that wears a crown" [*Henry IV*]; "government of the people, by the people, for the people" [Lincoln]; "quack remedies . . . are generally as noxious to the body politic as to the body corporal" [Roosevelt].

---

739. Severity. — N. SEVERITY; strictness, harshness &c. *adj.;* rigor, stringency, austerity; inclemency &c. (*pitilessness*) 914*a;* arrogance &c. 885; precisianism, formalism.

ARBITRARY POWER; absolutism, despotism; dictatorship, autocracy, tyranny, domineering, domination, oppression; assumption, usurpation; inquisition, reign of terror, martial law; iron -heel, – rule, – hand, – sway; tight grasp; brute -force, – strength; coercion &c. 744; strong –, tight- hand.

BUREAUCRACY, red-tapism, pipe-clay, officialism; hard -lines, – measure; tender mercies [*ironical*]; sharp practice.

TYRANT, disciplinarian, precisian, martinet, stickler, bashaw, despot, the Grand Panjandrum himself, hard master, Draco, oppressor, inquisitor, extortioner, harpy, vulture; Accipitres, Raptores, raptors [*obs.*], birds of prey.

V. BE SEVERE &c. *adj.*

740. Lenity. — N. LENITY, lenitence, lenitency; moderation &c. 174; tolerance, toleration; mildness, gentleness; favor; indulgence, indulgency [*rare*], clemence [*obs.*], clemency, mercy, forbearance, quarter; compassion &c. 914.

V. BE LENIENT &c. *adj.;* tolerate, bear with; *parcere subjectis* [*L.*], spare the vanquished, give quarter.

INDULGE; allow one to -go his own gait, – have his own way, spoil.

Adj. LENIENT; mild, – as milk; gentle, soft; tolerant, indulgent, easy, moderate, complaisant, unconcerned, easy-going; clement &c. (*compassionate*) 914; forbearing; long-suffering.

. "lenity has almost always wisdom and justice on its side" [Ballou]; "He was the mildest manner'd man That ever scuttled ship or cut a throat" [Byron]; "Sweet mercy is nobility's true badge" [*Coriolanus*]; "Nothing emboldens sin so much as mercy" [*Timon of Athens*].

ARROGATE, assume, usurp, take liberties; domineer, bully &c. 885; tyrannize; wrest the law to one's advantage; inflict, wreak, stretch a point, put on the screw; be hard upon; bear –, lay- a heavy hand on; be down upon [*slang*], come down upon [*colloq.*]; illtreat; deal hardly with, deal hard measure to; rule with a rod of iron, chastise with scorpions; dye with blood; oppress, override; trample –, tread- -down, – upon, – under foot; crush under an iron heel, ride roughshod over; rivet the yoke; hold –, keep- a tight hand; force down the throat; coerce &c. 744; give no quarter &c. (*pitiless*) 914*a.*

Adj. SEVERE; strict, hard, harsh, dour [*Scot.*], rigid, stiff, stern, rigorous, uncompromising, exacting, exigent, *exigeant* [*F.*], inexorable, inflexible, obdurate, austere, hard-headed, hard-shell [*colloq.*, *U. S.*], relentless, Spartan, Draconian, stringent, strict, prudish, precise, puritanical, strait-laced, searching, unsparing, ironhanded, peremptory, absolute, positive, arbitrary, imperative; coercive &c. 744; tyrannical, extortionate, grinding, withering, oppressive, inquisitorial; inclement &c. (*ruthless*) 914*a;* cruel &c. (*malevolent*) 907; haughty, arrogant &c. 885; precisian, formal, punctilious.

Adv. SEVERELY &c. *adj.;* with a -high, – strong, – tight, – heavy- hand.

at the point of the -sword, – bayonet.

. *quidquid delirant reges plectuntur Achivi* [Horace]; *manu forti; ogni debole ha sempre il suo tiranno;* "the King's argument was that anything that had a head could be beheaded" [Carroll].

741. Command. — **N.** COMMAND, order, ordinance, act, fiat, *hukm* [*Hind.*], bidding, dictum, hest, behest, call, beck, nod.

DISPATCH *or* despatch, message, direction, injunction, charge, instructions; appointment, fixture.

DEMAND, exaction, imposition, requisition, claim, reclamation, revendication [*rare*]; ultimatum &c. (*terms*) 770; request &c. 765; requirement.

DECREE, dictate, dictation, mandate, caveat, *senatus consultum* [*L.*]; precept; prescript, rescript, writ, ordination, bull, edict, decretal, dispensation, prescription, brevet, placet, *placitum* [*L.*], ukase, firman, hatti-sherif, hatti-humayoun (*or* humayun), warrant, passport, mittimus, mandamus, summons, subpœna, *nisi prius* [*L.*], interpellation, citation; word, – of command; *mot d'ordre* [*F.*]; bugle –, trumpet- call; beat of drum, tattoo; order of the day; enactment &c. (*law*) 963; plebiscite &c. (*choice*) 609.

V. COMMAND, order, decree, enact, ordain, dictate, direct, give orders.

issue a command; make –, issue –, promulgate- -a requisition, – a decree, – an order &c. *n.;* give the -word of command, – word, – signal; call to order; give –, lay down- the law; assume the command &c. (*authority*) 737; remand.

PRESCRIBE, set, appoint, mark out; set –, prescribe –, impose- a task; set to work, put in requisition.

BID, enjoin, charge, call upon, instruct; require, – at the hands of; exact, impose, tax, task; demand; insist on &c. (*compel*) 744.

CLAIM, lay claim to, revendicate [*rare*], reclaim.

CITE, summon, avoke; call for, send for; subpœna; beckon.

BE ORDERED &c.; receive an order &c. *n.*

Adj. COMMANDING &c. *v.;* authoritative &c. 737; decretory, decretive, decretal; callable; imperative, jussive; decisive, final, without appeal; interpellative, demanded, commanded &c. *v.*

Adv. in a commanding tone; by a -stroke, – dash- of the pen; by order, at beat of drum, on the first summons, to order, at the word of command; by -command, – order, – decree- of; as required, as requested, as ordered, as commanded.

⁎⁎ the decree is gone forth; *sic volo sic jubeo; le roi le veut; boutez en avant.*

742. Disobedience. — **N.** DISOBEDIENCE, insubordination, contumacy; infraction, infringement; violation, noncompliance; nonobservance &c. 773.

REVOLT, rebellion, mutiny, outbreak, rising, uprising, insurrection, *émeute* [*F.*], riot, tumult &c. (*disorder*) 59; strike &c. (*resistance*) 719; barring out; defiance &c. 715.

mutinousness &c. *adj.;* mutineering; sedition, treason; high –, petty –, misprision of- treason; præmunire *or* premunire; *lèse-majesté* [*F.*]; violation of law &c. 964; defection, secession, Sinn Fein; revolution; overthrow –, overturn- of -government, – authority; *sabotage* [*F.*], sans-culottism, bolshevism.

INSURGENT, mutineer, rebel, revolter, rioter, traitor, *Carbonaro* [*It.*], sansculotte, red republican, *bonnet rouge* [*F.*], communist, Fenian, Sinn Feiner, Red, Bolshevist, *frondeur* [*F.*], seceder, Secessionist [*esp.*, *U.S. hist.*] *or* Secesh [*colloq. or slang*, *U.S.*]; apostate, renegade, runaway, runagate; brawler, an-

743. Obedience. — **N.** OBEDIENCE; observance &c. 772; compliance; submission &c. 725; subjection &c. 749; nonresistance; passiveness, passivity, resignation.

ALLEGIANCE, loyalty, fealty, homage, deference, devotion; constancy, fidelity.

SUBMISSIVENESS, submissness [*obs.*]; ductility &c. (*softness*) 324; obsequiousness &c. (*servility*) 886.

V. BE OBEDIENT &c. *adj.;* obey, bear obedience to; submit &c. 725; comply, answer the helm, come at one's call; do one's bidding, do what one is told, do suit and service; attend to orders; serve -faithfully, – loyally, – devotedly, – without question; give -loyal, – devoted-service; be resigned to, be submissive to.

follow, – the lead of, – to the world's end; serve &c. 746; play second fiddle.

Adj. OBEDIENT, law-abiding, complying, compliant; loyal, faithful, devoted; at one's -call, – command, – orders, – beck and call; under beck and call, under control.

archist, demagogue; Spartacus, Masaniello, Wat Tyler, Jack Cade; ringleader.

V. DISOBEY, violate, infringe; shirk, slide out of, slack; set at defiance &c. (*defy*) 715; set authority at naught, run riot, fly in the face of; take the law into one's own hands; kick over the traces; refuse to support, bolt [*U. S. politics*].

turn -, run- restive; champ the bit; strike &c. (*resist*) 719; rise, - in arms; secede; mutiny, rebel.

Adj. DISOBEDIENT; uncomplying, uncompliant; unsubmissive, unruly, ungovernable; breachy, insubordinate, impatient of control; restive, restiff [*obs.*], refractory, contumacious; recusant &c. (*refuse*) 764; recalcitrant; resisting &c. 719; lawless, riotous, mutinous, seditious, insurgent, revolutionary, sansculottic, secessionist.

unobeyed, disobeyed; unbidden.

. *seditiosissimus quisque ignavus* [Tacitus]; "unthread the rude eye of rebellion" [*King John*]; "revolution is the larva of civilization" [Hugo]; "there is little hope of equity where rebellion reigns" [Sidney]; "rebellion to tyrants is obedience to God" [*epitaph to John Bradshaw*].

restrainable; resigned, passive; submissive &c. 725; henpecked; pliant &c. (*soft*) 324.

unresisted, unresisting.

Adv. OBEDIENTLY &c. *adj.;* as you please, if you please; in compliance with, in obedience to; at your -command, - orders, - service.

. to hear is to obey; "theirs not to make reply, theirs not to reason why" [Tennyson]; "Obedience, bane of all genius, virtue, freedom, truth" [Shelley]; "obedience is the mother of success" [Æschylus]; "And art made tongue-tied by authority" [Shakespeare].

744. Compulsion. — **N.** COMPULSION, coercion, coaction, constraint; restraint &c. 751; duress, enforcement, press, conscription; eminent domain.

force; brute -, main -, physical- force; the sword, *ultima ratio* [*L.*]; club -, lynch -, mob- law, *argumentum baculinum* [*L.*], le droit du plus fort [*F.*]; the force of -might, - right; martial law.

necessity &c. 601; *force majeure* [*F.*], spur of necessity, Hobson's choice.

V. COMPEL, force, make, drive, coerce, constrain, enforce, necessitate, oblige.

force upon, press; cram -, thrust -, force- down the throat; say it must be done, make a point of, insist upon, take no denial; put down, dragoon.

extort, wring from; put -, turn- on the screw; drag into; bind, - over; pin-, tie- down; require, tax, put in force; commandeer; restrain &c. 751.

Adj. COMPELLING &c. *v.;* coercive, coactive; inexorable &c. 739; compulsory, compulsatory; obligatory, stringent, peremptory, binding.

forcible, not to be trifled with; irresistible &c. 601; compelled &c. *v.;* fain to.

Adv. FORCIBLY; by force &c. *n.,* by force of arms; on compulsion, perforce; *vi et armis* [*L.*], under the lash; at the point of the -sword, - bayonet; by a strong arm.

under protest, in spite of, in one's teeth; against one's will &c. 603; *nolens volens* [*L.*] &c. (*of necessity*) 601; by stress of -circumstances, - weather; under press of; *de rigueur* [*F.*].

745. Master. — **N.** MASTER, *padrone* [*It.*], lord, - paramount; commander, commandant, captain, chief, chieftain; paterfamilias [*Rom. law*], patriarch; sahib [*India*], bara (*or* burra) sahib [*India*], sirdar, sheik; head, senior, governor, ruler, dictator; leader &c. (*director*) 694; boss, baas [*Dutch*]; cockarouse [*obs.*], sachem, sagamore, werowance.

lord of the ascendant; cock of the -walk, - loft, - midden [*archaic*], - roost; gray mare; mistress.

POTENTATE; liege, - lord; suzerain,

746. Servant. — **N.** SERVANT, retainer, follower, henchman, servitor, domestic, menial, help [*local, U. S.*], lady help [*Brit.*], employee *or* employé; *attaché* [*F.*], official.

SUBJECT, liege, liegeman; people, "my people."

RETINUE, suite, *cortège* [*F.*], staff, court; office force, clerical staff, clerical force, workers, associate workers, employees, the help [*esp., U. S.*].

ATTENDANT, squire, usher, donzel [*obs.*], apprentice, prentice [*colloq. or dial.*]; page, buttons [*colloq.*], footboy;

overlord, overking, sovereign, monarch, autocrat, despot, tyrant, oligarch.

crowned head, emperor, king, anointed king, majesty, imperator, protector, president, stadholder *or* stadtholder, judge.

cæsar, kaiser, czar *or* tsar, sultan, soldan [*obs.*], grand Turk, caliph, imam *or* imaum, shah, padishah, sophi, mogul, great mogul, khan, lama, pendragon, tycoon, mikado, inca, cazique; voivode *or* waywode, hospodar, landamman; sayid *or* sayyid, cacique, czarevitch, grand seignior.

prince, duke &c. (*nobility*) 875; archduke, doge, elector; seignior; landgrave, margrave; maharajah, rajah, emir, nizam, nawab &c. (*Indian ruling chiefs*) 875.

empress, queen, sultana, czarina *or* tsarina, princess, infanta, duchess, margravine; czarevna *or* tsarevna, czarina; maharani, rani [*both Hindu*], begum [*Moham.*]; rectoress *or* rectress, rectrix.

REGENT, viceroy, exarch, palatine, khedive, beglerbeg *or* beylerbey, three-tailed bashaw, pasha *or* bashaw, bey *or* beg, dey, shereef *or* sherif, tetrarch, satrap, mandarin, nabob, burgrave; laird &c. (*proprietor*) 779; commissioner, deputy commissioner, collector, woon *or* wun [*Burmese*].

THE AUTHORITIES, the powers that be, the government, "them above" [Eliot]; staff, *état major* [*F.*], aga, official, man in office, person in authority; sirkar *or* sircar; Sublime Porte.

[MILITARY AUTHORITIES] marshal, field marshal, *maréchal* [*F.*], generalissimo; commander-in-chief, seraskier [*Turk.*], hetman [*Cossack*]; general, brigadier general, brigadier, lieutenant general, major general, colonel, lieutenant colonel, major, captain, ressaldar *or* risaldar [*India*], subahdar *or* subadar [*India*]; centurion, lieutenant, jemadar [*India*], sublieutenant, officer, staff officer, aide-de-camp, brigade major, adjutant, ensign, cornet, cadet, subaltern; non-commissioned officer; sergeant, -major; color sergeant; top-sergeant [*U. S.*], havildar [*India*]; corporal, -major; lance corporal, acting corporal; naik [*India*]; drum major; captain general, knight marshal.

[CIVIL AUTHORITIES] mayor, mayoralty; *maire* [*F.*], prefect, chancellor,

trainbearer, cupbearer; waiter, tapster, butler, livery servant, lackey, footman, flunky *or* flunkey [*colloq.*]; bearer [*Anglo-Ind.*], boy [*any colored male servant, as in the Orient, South Africa, &c.*]; hamal [*India*], scout [*Oxford Univ.*], gyp [*Camb. Univ.*], valet, *valet de chambre* [*F.*]; equerry, groom; jockey, hostler *or* ostler, orderly, messenger, gillie *or* gilly, caddie *or* caddy, herdsman, swineherd; barkeeper, bartender, barkeep [*U. S.*]; boots [*Brit.*]; cad [*Eng. Univ. cant*], bell boy, bell-hop [*slang*], tiger, chokra [*India*], boy; counterjumper [*colloq.*]; khansamah *or* khansaman [*India*], khitmutgar [*India*]; yardman, journeyman.

bailiff, castellan *or* castellain, seneschal, chamberlain, major-domo, groom of the chambers.

secretary; under –, assistant- secretary; stenographer, clerk; subsidiary; agent &c. 758; subaltern; underling, understrapper; man.

MAID, maidservant; girl, help [*local, U. S.*], handmaid; confidant (*fem.* confidante), *confident* (*fem. confidente*) [*F.*]; lady's maid, abigail, soubrette, amah [*Oriental*], biddy [*colloq.*], *bonne* [*F.*], ayah [*India*]; nurse-, nursery-, house-, parlor-, waiting-, chamber-, kitchen-, scullery- maid; *femme* –, *fille- de chambre* [*F.*]; *chef de cuisine* [*F.*], *cordon bleu* [*F.*], cook, scullion, Cinderella; pot-walloper; maid-, servant- of all work; slavey [*slang, Eng.*], general servant [*Brit.*], general housework maid [*U. S.*], general [*colloq.*]; washerwoman, laundress, bedmaker; charwoman &c. (*worker*) 690.

DEPENDENT *or* dependant, hanger-on, led friend [*obs.*], satellite; parasite &c. (*servility*) 886; led captain; *protégé* [*F.*], ward, hireling, mercenary, puppet, man of straw, creature; serf, vassal, slave, negro, helot; bondsman, bondswoman; bondslave; *âme damnée* [*F.*], odalisque *or* odalisk, ryot, *adscriptus glebæ* [*L.*], villein *or* villain [*hist.*], churl *or* ceorl [*hist.*]; beadsman *or* bedesman; sizar *or* sizer [*Camb. & Dublin Univs.*], pensioner, pensionary; client.

badge of slavery; bonds &c. 752.

V. SERVE, minister to, help, coöperate; wait –, attend –, dance attendance –, fasten oneself –, pin oneself- upon; squire, valet, tend, hang on the sleeve of; chore [*dial., U. S.*], do the chores

archon [*Gr.*], provost, magistrate, syndic; alcalde [*Sp.*], alcaide *or* alcaid; burgomaster, *corregidor* [*Sp.*], seneschal, alderman, warden, constable, portreeve; lord mayor; officer &c. (*executive*) 965; diwan *or* dewan [*India*]; hakim; *fonctionnaire* [*F.*].

[NAVAL AUTHORITIES] admiral, admiralty; rear-, vice-, port- admiral; commodore, captain, commander, lieutenant; skipper, master, mate, navarch [*Gr. antiq.*].

** *da locum melioribus; der Fürst ist der erste Diener seines Staats;* "lord of thy presence and no land beside" [*King John*]; "Duty, not joy, is all a prince's share" [Masefield].

[*colloq.*], char [*dial. Eng.*], do for [*colloq.*], fag.

Adj. SERVICEABLE, useful, helpful; coöperative.

SERVING &c. *v.;* in the train of; in one's -pay, – employ; at one's call &c. (*obedient*) 743; in bonds.

SERVILE, slavish, vernile [*rare*]; subject, thrall, bond; subservient, obsequious, base, fawning, truckling, sycophantic *or* sycophantical, sycophantish [*rare*], parasitic, cringing.

** "art thou less a slave because thy master lo es and caresses thee?" [Pascal]; "How happy is he born and taught That serveth not another's will" [Wotton].

747. [INSIGNIA OF AUTHORITY.] **Scepter.** — **N.** [REGAL] scepter *or* sceptre, rod of empire; orb; pall; robes of -state, – royalty; ermine, purple; crown, coronet, diadem, cap of maintenance; triple plume, Prince of Wales's feathers; uræus, flail [*both Egyptian*]; signet, seal.

[ECCLESIASTICAL] tiara, triple crown; ring, keys; miter *or* mitre, crozier, crook, staff; cardinal's hat; bishop's -apron, – sleeves, – lawn, – gaiters, – shovel hat; fillet.

[MILITARY] epaulet *or* epaulette, star, bar, eagle, crown [*Brit.*], oak leaf, Sam Browne belt; chevron, stripe.

caduceus; Mercury's -staff, – rod, – wand; mace, fasces, ax *or* axe, truncheon, staff, baton, wand, rod; staff –, rod- -of office, – of authority; insignia –, ensign –, emblem –, badge- of authority; flag &c. (*insignia*) 550; regalia; toga, mantle, decoration; title &c. 877; portfolio.

THRONE, Peacock throne [*Chinese*], musnud *or* masnad [*Ar.*]; raj-gaddi, gaddi *or* guddee [*India*], divan; wool-sack, chair; dais &c. (*seat*) 215.

TALISMAN, amulet, charm, sign.

HELM; reins &c. (*means of restraint*) 752.

748. Freedom. — **N.** FREEDOM, liberty, independence; license &c. (*permission*) 760; eleutherism [*rare*]; facility &c. 705.

SCOPE, range, latitude, play; free –, full- -play, – scope; free field and no favor; swing, full swing, elbowroom, margin, rope, wide berth; Liberty Hall.

FRANCHISE, denization; prerogative &c. (*dueness*) 924.

freeman, freedman, liveryman [*London guilds*], citizen, denizen.

IMMUNITY, exemption; emancipation &c. (*liberation*) 750; affranchisement, enfranchisement; right, privilege.

AUTONOMY, self-government, liberalism, free trade; self-determination; noninterference &c. 706; Monroe Doctrine [*U. S.*].

FREE LAND, freehold; alod *or* allod, alodium *or* allodium; frankalmoign *or*

749. Subjection. — **N.** SUBJECTION; dependence, dependency; subordination; thrall, thralldom *or* thraldom, enthrallment *or* enthralment, subjugation, bondage, serfdom; feudalism, feudality; vassalage, villenage *or* villeinage, slavery, enslavement, involuntary servitude; conquest.

SERVICE; servitude, servitorship; tendence, employ, tutelage, clientship; liability &c. 177; constraint &c. 751; oppression &c. (*severity*) 739; yoke &c. (*means of restraint*) 752; submission &c. 725; obedience &c. 743.

V. BE SUBJECT &c. *adj.;* be *or* lie at the mercy of; depend –, lean –, hang-upon; fall a prey to, fall under; play second fiddle.

be a -mere machine, – puppet, – doormat, – football; not dare to say one's soul is his own; drag a chain.

frankalmoigne [*Eng. law*], tenure in (*or* by) free alms [*Eng. law*]; dead hand, mortmain [*law*].

INDEPENDENT, free lance, freethinker, free trader *or* freetrader; bushwhacker [*U. S.*].

V. BE FREE &c. *adj.;* have -scope &c. *n.,* – the run of, – one's own way, – a will of one's own, – one's fling; do what one -likes, – wishes, – pleases, – chooses; go at large, feel at home, paddle one's own canoe; stand on one's rights; stand on one's own legs; shift for oneself.

TAKE A LIBERTY; make free with, make oneself quite at home; use a freedom; take leave, take French leave.

FREE, liberate, set free &c. 750; give the reins to &c. (*permit*) 760; allow –, give -scope &c. *n.* to; give a horse his head.

make free of; give the -freedom of, – franchise; enfranchise, affranchise.

laisser faire [F.], *laisser aller* [F.]; live and let live; leave to oneself; leave *or* let alone, mind one's own business.

Adj. FREE, – as air; out of harness, independent, at large, loose, scot-free; left -alone, – to oneself.

UNCONSTRAINED, unbuttoned, unconfined, unrestrained, unchecked, unprevented, unhindered, unobstructed, unbound, uncontrolled, untrammeled, uncaught; in full swing.

UNSUBJECT, ungoverned, unenslaved, unenthralled, unchained, unshackled, unfettered, unreined, unbridled, uncurbed, unmuzzled, unvanquished.

UNRESTRICTED, unlimited, unconditional; absolute; with unlimited -power, – opportunity; discretionary &c. (*optional*) 600.

unassailed, unforced, uncompelled.

serve &c. 746; obey &c. 743; submit &c. 725.

SUBJUGATE, subject, tame, break in; master &c. 731; tread -down, – under foot; weigh down; drag at one's chariot wheel; reduce to -subjection, – slavery; enthrall *or* enthral, inthrall *or* inthral, bethrall, enslave, lead captive; take into custody &c. (*restrain*) 751; rule &c. 737; drive into a corner, hold at the sword's point; keep under; hold in -bondage, – leading strings, – swaddling clothes; have at one's -apron strings, – beck and call; have in one's pocket.

Adj. SUBJECT, dependent, subordinate; feudal, feudatory; in subjection to, servitorial [*rare*], under control; in leading strings, in harness; subjected, thrall [*archaic*]; servile, slavish &c. 746; enslaved &c. *v.;* constrained &c. 751; downtrodden; overborne, overwhelmed; under the lash, on the hip, led by the nose, henpecked; the -puppet, – sport, – plaything- of; under one's -orders, – command, – thumb; used as a doormat, treated like dirt under one's feet; a slave to; at the mercy of; in the -power, – hands, – clutches- of; at the feet of; in one's pocket; tied to one's apron strings; at one's beck and call &c. (*obedient*) 743; liable &c. 177; parasitical; stipendiary.

Adv. UNDER; under -orders, – the heel, – command; at one's orders; with no -mind, – will, – soul- of one's own.

*** "slaves — in a land of light and law" [Whittier]; "base in kind, and born to be a slave" [Cowper]; "Subjection, but requir'd with gentle sway" [Milton]; "the parrot of other men's thinking" [Emerson]; "La Belle Dame sans Mercy Hath thee in thrall" [Keats].

UNBIASED, unprejudiced, uninfluenced; spontaneous.

FREE AND EASY; at –, at one's- ease; *dégagé* [F.], quite at home; beyond all bounds; wanton, rampant, irrepressible.

EXEMPT; freed &c. 750; freeborn; autonomous, freehold, alodial *or* allodial; eleutherian [*rare*].

GRATUITOUS, gratis &c. 815; for nothing, for love.

UNCLAIMED, going a-begging.

Adv. freely &c. *adj.; ad libitum* [L.] &c. (*at will*) 600; with no restraint &c. 751.

*** *ubi libertas ibi patria;* "For what avail the plough or sail, Or land or life, if freedom fail?" [Emerson]; "We must be free or die who speak the tongue That Shakespeare spake" [Wordsworth]; "Oh! let me live my own, and die so too!" [Pope]; "He is the freeman whom the truth makes free, And all are slaves besides" [Cowper]; "Where liberty dwells, there is my country" [Franklin]; "liberty exists in proportion to wholesome restraint" [Daniel Webster]; "The God who gave us life gave us liberty at the same time" [Thomas Jefferson].

750. Liberation. — N. LIBERATION, disengagement, release, enlargement, emancipation, disenthrallment *or* disenthralment, Emancipation Proclamation; affranchisement, enfranchisement; manumission; discharge, dismissal.

DELIVERANCE &c. 672; redemption, extrication, acquittance, absolution; acquittal &c. 970; escape &c. 671.

V. LIBERATE, free; set free, set at liberty; render free, emancipate, release; enfranchise, affranchise; manumit; enlarge; demobilize, disband, discharge, disenthrall *or* disenthral, disinthrall *or* disinthral, dismiss; let go, let loose, let out, let slip; cast -, turn- adrift; deliver &c. 672; absolve &c. (*acquit*) 970.

UNFETTER &c. 751, untie &c. 43; loose &c. (*disjoin*) 44; loosen, relax; unbolt, unbar, unclose, uncork, unclog, unhand, unbind, unchain, unharness; disengage, disentangle; clear, extricate, unloose; reprieve.

BECOME FREE; gain -, obtain -, acquire- one's -liberty &c. 748; get rid of, get clear of; deliver oneself from; shake off the yoke, slip the collar; break loose, break prison; tear asunder one's bonds, cast off trammels; escape &c. 671.

Adj. LIBERATED &c. *v.;* out of harness &c. (*free*) 748; foot-loose; breathing free air again; one's own master again.

Adv. AT LARGE, at liberty; adrift.

Int. unhand me! let me go! reprieve! go in peace! free!

*** "In giving freedom to the slave we assume freedom to the free" [Lincoln]; "Over my head his arm he flung Against the world" [Browning].

751. Restraint. — N. RESTRAINT; hindrance &c. 706; coercion &c. (*compulsion*) 744; cohibition [*rare*], constraint, repression; discipline, control.

limitation, restriction, protection, monopoly; prohibition &c. 761; economic pressure.

CONFINEMENT, restringency [*obs.*], durance, duress; imprisonment; incarceration, coarctation [*obs.*], entombment, mancipation [*obs.*], thrall; thralldom &c. (*subjection*) 749; durance vile, limbo, captivity; blockade; detention camp; quarantine station.

ARREST, arrestation [*rare*], arrestment, custody.

KEEP, care, charge, ward.

curb &c. (*means of restraint*) 752; *lettres de cachet* [*F.*].   .

REPRESSIONIST, monopolist, protectionist.

PRISONER &c. 754.

V. RESTRAIN, check; put -, lay- under restraint, put under arrest; enthrall *or* enthral, inthrall *or* inthral, bethrall *or* bethral; restrict; debar &c. (*hinder*) 706; constrain; coerce &c. (*compel*) 744: curb, control; hold -, keep- -back, - from, - in, - in check, - within bounds; hold in -leash, - leading strings; withhold.

repress, suppress ; keep under ; smother; pull in, rein in; hold, - fast; keep a tight hand on; prohibit &c. 761; inhibit, cohibit.

FASTEN &c. (*join*) 43; enchain, fetter, shackle; entrammel, trammel; bridle, muzzle, hopple, gag, pinion, manacle, handcuff, tie one's hands, hobble, bind, bind hand and foot; swathe, swaddle;

pin down, tether; picket; tie, - up, - down; peg -out, - down; keep [*archaic*], secure; forge fetters.

CONFINE; shut -up, - in; clap up, lock up, box up, mew up, bottle up, cork up, seal up, button up; hem in, bolt in, wall in, rail in; impound, pen, coop; inclose &c. (*circumscribe*) 229; cage; incage *or* encage; close the door upon, cloister; imprison, jug [*slang*], immure; incarcerate, entomb; clap -, lay- under hatches; put in -irons, - a strait-waistcoat; throw -, cast- into prison; put into bilboes.

ARREST; take -up, - charge of, - into custody; restringe [*rare*], cohibit [*rare*]; take -, make- -prisoner, - captive; captivate [*rare*]; lead -captive, - into captivity; send -, commit- to prison; commit; give in -charge, - custody; subjugate &c. 749.

Adj. RESTRAINED, constrained; imprisoned &c. *v.;* pent up; jammed in, packed in, wedged in; under -restraint, - lock and key, - hatches; in swaddling clothes; on parole; serving -, doing- time [*colloq. or slang*]; in irons, in the guardhouse; in custody &c. (*prisoner*) 754; cohibitive [*rare*]; mancipatory [*Rom. law*]; coactive &c. (*compulsory*) 744.

icebound, windbound, weatherbound; "cabined, cribbed, confined" [*Macbeth*]; in lob's pound, laid by the heels.

STIFF, restringent [obs.], narrow, prudish, strait-laced, hidebound, barkbound.

Adv. UNDER RESTRAINT, under discipline; in prison, in jail, in durance vile, in confinement; behind bars; in captivity, during captivity; under arrest; under prohibition; within limits, within bounds.

*** "Checked like a bondman" [*Julius Cæsar*]; "you forget yourself To hem me in" [*ibid.*]; "her cabin'd ample spirit" [Arnold].

752. [MEANS OF RESTRAINT.] **Prison.** — **N.** PRISON, prisonhouse; jail *or* gaol, cage, coop, den, cell; stronghold, fortress, keep, donjon, dungeon, Bastille, *oubliette* [*F.*], bridewell [*Eng.*], jug [*slang*], house of correction, hulks, tollbooth, panopticon, penitentiary, state prison, guardroom, lockup, roundhouse [*archaic*], watch-house [*obs. or Scot.*], station house, station [*colloq.*], sponging house; house of detention, black hole, pen [*also slang for penitentiary*], fold, pinfold *or* penfold, pound; inclosure &c. 232; penal settlement; bilboes, stocks, limbo *or* limbus, quod [*slang*]; calaboose [*local, U. S.*], choky *or* chokey [*Anglo-Ind. or slang, Eng.*]; *chauki, thana* [*both India*]; workhouse [*U. S.*; *in England, a workhouse is a poorhouse*], reformatory, reform school; debtor's prison, college [*slang, Eng.*].

Tower, Newgate, Fleet, Marshalsea; King's (*or* Queen's) Bench; Sing Sing, the Tombs.

[RESTRAINING DEVICES] shackle, bond, gyve, fetter, trammel, irons, pinion, manacle, handcuff, strait-waistcoat, hopples; vise *or* vice; bandage, splint, strap.

yoke, collar, halter, harness; muzzle, gag, bit, curb, snaffle, bridle; rein, reins; bearing rein; martingale; leading string; tether, picket, band, guy, chain; cord &c. (*fastening*) 45; cavesson, hackamore [*Western U. S.*], jaquima [*S. W. U. S.*], headstall, lines [*U. S. & dial. Eng.*], ribbons [*colloq.*]; brake.

BAR, bolt, lock, padlock; rail, paling, palisade; wall, fence, barrier, barricade. drag &c. (*hindrance*) 706.

Adj. imprisoned &c. (*restrained*) 751.

*** "I am forbid To tell the secrets of my prison house" [*Hamlet*]; "Brightest in dungeons, Liberty! thou art" [Byron]; "Stone walls do not a prison make Nor iron bars a cage" [Lovelace].

753. Keeper. — **N.** KEEPER, custodian, *custos* [*L.*], ranger, gamekeeper, warder, jailer *or* gaoler, turnkey, castellan, guard; watch, watchdog, watchman, night watchman, Charley *or* Charlie [*Brit.*]; chokidar [*Anglo-Ind.*], durwan [*Anglo-Ind.*], hayward; sentry, sentinel, watch and ward; *concierge* [*F.*], coastguard.

ESCORT, bodyguard; convoy.

GUARDIAN, protector, governor, duenna; governess &c. (*teacher*) 540; nurse, *bonne* [*F.*], amah [*Oriental*], ayah [*India*].

*** "Am I my brother's keeper?" [*Bible*].

754. Prisoner. — **N.** PRISONER, convict, captive, *détenu* [*F.*], collegian [*slang, Eng.*], close prisoner.

JAILBIRD *or* gaolbird, ticket-of-leave man [*Brit.*], *chevronné* [*F.*].

V. stand committed; be imprisoned &c. 751.

Adj. IMPRISONED &c. 751; in prison, in quod [*slang*], in durance vile, in limbo, in custody, in charge, in chains; behind bars; under lock and key, under hatches. on parole.

*** "Dweller in yon dungeon dark" [Burns].

755. [VICARIOUS AUTHORITY.] **Commission.** — **N.** COMMISSION, delegation; consignment, assignment; proxy, power of attorney, procuration; deputation, legation, mission, embassy; agency, agentship; clerkship.

errand, charge, brevet, diploma, exequatur, permit &c. (*permission*) 760.

APPOINTMENT, nomination, return; charter; ordination; installation, inauguration, investiture; accession, coronation, enthronement.

756. Abrogation. — **N.** ABROGATION, annulment, nullification; *vacatur* [*L.*]; *nolle prosequi* [*L., law*]; canceling &c. *v.*; cancel; revocation, revokement; repeal, rescission, defeasance.

DISMISSAL, *congé* [*F.*], demission [*obs.*]; bounce [*slang, U. S.*]; deposal, deposition; dethronement; disestablishment; disendowment; secularization, deconsecration; sack [*slang*], walking-papers, walking-ticket [*both colloq.*], yellow cover [*slang*].

REGENCY, regentship; vicegerency.

viceroy &c. 745; consignee &c. 758; deputy &c. 759.

V. COMMISSION, delegate, depute; consign, assign; charge; intrust *or* entrust; commit, – to the hands of; authorize &c. (*permit*) 760.

put in commission, accredit, engage, hire, bespeak, appoint, name, nominate, return, ordain; install, induct, inaugurate, invest, crown; enroll, enlist; give power of attorney to; employ, empower; set –, place- over; send out.

BE COMMISSIONED, be accredited; represent, stand for; stand in the -stead, – place, – shoes- of.

Adj. commissioned &c. *v.*

Adv. INSTEAD OF; in one's -stead, – place; as proxy for; *per procurationem* [*L.*], *in loco parentis* [*L.*].

abolition, abolishment; dissolution.

COUNTERORDER, countermand; repudiation, retractation; recantation &c. (*tergiversation*) 607.

abolitionist, prohibitionist.

V. ABROGATE, annul, cancel; destroy &c. 162; abolish; revoke, repeal, rescind, reverse, retract, recall; overrule, override; set aside; disannul, dissolve, quash, nullify, make void, nol-pros [*law*], declare null and void; disestablish, disendow; deconsecrate.

countermand, counterorder; do away with; sweep –, brush- away; throw overboard, throw to the dogs; scatter to the winds, cast behind.

DISCLAIM &c. (*deny*) 536; ignore, repudiate; recant &c. 607; divest oneself, break off.

DISMISS, discard; cast –, turn- -off, – out, – adrift, – out of doors, – aside, – away; send off, send away, send about one's business; discharge, get rid of &c. (*eject*) 297; bounce [*slang, U. S.*]; fire, fire out, sack [*all slang*].

cashier; break; oust; unseat, unsaddle; unthrone, dethrone, disenthrone, depose, uncrown; unfrock, strike off the roll; disbar, disbench.

BE ABROGATED &c.; receive its quietus.

Adj. ABROGATED &c. *v.; functus officio* [*L.*].

Int. get along with you! begone! go about your business! away with!

757. Resignation. — **N.** RESIGNATION, retirement, abdication; renunciation, retractation, retraction, renunciance [*rare*], disclamation, disclaimer, abjuration; abandonment, relinquishment.

V. RESIGN; give up, throw up; lay down, throw up the cards, wash one's hands of, abjure, renounce, forego, disclaim, retract; deny &c. 536.

ABROGATE &c. 756; desert &c. (*relinquish*) 624; get rid of &c. 782.

VACATE, – one's seat; abdicate; accept the stewardship of the Chiltern Hundreds [*Eng.*]; retire; tender –, pass in –, hand in- one's resignation.

Adj. ABDICANT; resigning &c *v.; renunciatory, renunciant [*rare*], abjuratory, disclamatory [*rare*], retractive.

** "Othello's occupation's gone" [*Othello*]; "few die and none resign" [Jefferson].

758. Consignee. — **N.** CONSIGNEE, trustee, nominee; committee.

functionary, placeman, curator; treasurer &c. 801; agent, factor, reeve [*Eng. hist.*], steward, gomashta [*India*], bailiff, clerk, secretary, attorney, solicitor, proctor, broker, dalal [*India*], dubash [*India*]; insurer, underwriter, commission agent, auctioneer, one's man of business; factotum &c. (*director*) 694; caretaker; garnishee; under agent, employé; servant &c. 746.

negotiator, go-between; middleman; walking delegate [*trade-unions*].

DELEGATE; commissary, commissioner; emissary, envoy, commissionaire; messenger &c. 534.

DIPLOMATIST, diplomat *or* diplomate, *corps diplomatique* [*F.*], embassy; ambassador *or* embassador, diplomatic agent, representative, resident, consul, legate, nuncio, internuncio, *chargé d'affaires* [*F.*], *attaché* [*F.*]; vicegerent &c. (*deputy*) 759; plenipotentiary.

SALESMAN, traveler, bagman, *commis voyageur* [*F.*], traveling salesman, commercial traveler, drummer [*U. S.*], traveling man; agent for (firm *or* commodity); touter [*colloq.*], barker [*colloq*].

REPORTER; newspaper –, own –, war –, special- correspondent.

** "Diplomacy: lying in state" [*Cynic's Calendar*].

759. Deputy. — N. DEPUTY, substitute, proxy, *locum tenens* [*L.*], *badli* [*Hind.*], delegate, representative, next friend [*law*], *prochein ami* [*F. law*], surrogate, secondary; vice-president, vice-chairman, vice [*colloq.*].

regent, vicegerent, vizier, minister, vicar; premier &c. (*director*) 694; chancellor, prefect, provost, warden, lieutenant, archon [*antiq.*], consul, proconsul [*Rom. antiq.*]; viceroy &c. (*governor*) 745; ambassador; commissioner &c. 758; plenipotentiary, plenipotent; *alter ego* [*L.*].

TEAM, eight, nine, eleven; captain, champion.

V. BE DEPUTY &c. *n.;* stand –, appear –, hold a brief –, answer- for; represent; stand –, walk- in the shoes of; stand in the stead of.

DELEGATE, depute, empower, commission, substitute, ablegate [*R. C. Ch.*], accredit.

Adj. ACTING; vice, viceregal; accredited to; delegated &c. *v.;* representative, plenipotent [*rare*], consular, proconsular.

Adv. IN BEHALF OF, in the place of, as representing, by proxy.

Section II. SPECIAL INTERSOCIAL VOLITION

760. Permission. — N. PERMISSION, leave; allowance, sufferance; tolerance, toleration; liberty, law, license, concession, grace; indulgence &c. (*lenity*) 740; favor, dispensation, exemption, release; connivance; vouchsafement.

authorization, warranty [*law*], accordance, admission.

PERMIT, warrant, brevet, precept, sanction, authority, firman; *hukm* [*Hind.*]; pass, passport; furlough, license, *carte blanche* [*F.*], ticket of leave; grant, charter, patent.

V. PERMIT; give permission &c. *n.,* give power; let, allow, admit; suffer, bear with, tolerate, recognize; concede &c. 762; accord, vouchsafe, favor, humor, gratify, indulge, stretch a point; wink at, connive at; shut one's eyes to.

grant, empower, charter, enfranchise, privilege, confer a privilege, license, authorize, warrant; sanction; intrust &c. (*commission*) 755.

give *carte blanche* [*F.*], give the reins to, give scope to &c. (*freedom*) 748; leave -alone, – it to one, – the door open; open the -door to, – floodgates; give a loose to [*obs.*].

ask –, beg –, crave –, request- -leave, – permission.

LET OFF; absolve &c. (*acquit*) 970; release, exonerate, dispense with.

Adj. PERMITTING &c. *v.;* permissive, indulgent.

PERMITTED &c. *v.;* patent, chartered, permissible, allowable, lawful, legitimate, legal; legalized &c. (*law*) 963; licit; unforbid [*archaic*], unforbidden; unconditional.

Adv. PERMISSIBLY, licitly; by –, with –, on- leave &c. *n.;* *speciali gratiâ* [*L.*]; under favor of; *pace* [*L.*]; *ad libitum* [*L.*] &c. (*freely*) 748, (*at will*) 600; by all means &c. (*willingly*) 602; yes &c. (*assent*) 488.

avec permission; brevet d'invention; "Who has no will but by her high permission" [Burns].

761. Prohibition. — N. PROHIBITION, inhibition; veto, disallowance; interdict, interdiction; injunction; embargo, ban, taboo *or* tabu, proscription; *index expurgatorius* [*L.*], restriction &c. (*restraint*) 751; hindrance &c. 706; forbidden fruit; Maine law, Volstead Act, 18th amendment [*all U. S.*].

V. prohibit, inhibit; forbid, put one's veto upon, disallow; bar; debar &c. (*hinder*) 706, forfend *or* forefend [*archaic*].

RESTRAIN &c. 751; keep -in, – within bounds; cohibit [*rare*], withhold, limit, circumscribe, clip the wings of, restrict; interdict, taboo *or* tabu; put –, place- under -an interdiction, – the ban; proscribe; exclude, shut out; shut –, bolt –, show- the door; warn off; dash the cup from one's lips; forbid the banns.

Adj. PROHIBITIVE, prohibitory; proscriptive; restrictive, exclusive; forbidding &c. *v.*

PROHIBITED &c. *v.;* not permitted &c. 760; unlicensed, contraband, under the ban of, taboo *or* tabu; illegal &c. 964; unauthorized, not to be thought of.

Adv. on no account &c. (*no*) 536.

Int. forbid it heaven! &c. (*deprecation*) 766.

HANDS OFF! keep off! hold! stop! avast!

*that will never do; "I would fain die a dry death" [Tempest].

762. Consent. — N. CONSENT; assent &c. 488; acquiescence; approval &c. 931; compliance, agreement, concession; yieldance [*obs.*], yieldingness; accession, acknowledgment, acceptance, agnition [*obs.*].

settlement, adjustment, ratification, confirmation.

permit &c. (*permission*) 760; promise &c. 768.

V. CONSENT; assent &c. 488; yield assent, admit, allow, concede, grant, yield; come over, come round; give into, acknowledge, agnize [*archaic*], give consent, comply with, acquiesce, agree to, fall in with, accede, accept, embrace an offer, close with, take at one's word, have no objection.

satisfy, meet one's wishes, settle, come to terms &c. 488; not refuse &c. 764; turn a willing ear &c. (*willingness*) 602; jump at; deign, vouchsafe; promise &c. 768.

Adj. CONSENTING &c. *v.*; compliant, agreeable [*colloq.*], willing, eager; agreed &c. (*assent*) 488; unconditional.

Adv. YES &c. (*assent*) 488; by all means &c. (*willingly*) 602; if you please, as you please; be it so, so be it, well and good, of course.

⁂ *chi tace acconsente;* "Barkis is willin" [Dickens]; "silence gives consent" [Goldsmith]; "And whispering, 'I will ne'er consent.' — consented" [Byron].

---

763. Offer. — N. OFFER, proffer, presentation, tender, bid, overture; proposal, proposition; motion, invitation; candidature, candidacy; offering &c. (*gift*) 784.

V. OFFER, proffer, present, tender; bid; propose, move; make a motion, make advances; start; invite, hold out, place in one's way; put -, place- at one's disposal; put in one's power, make possible, put forward.

hawk about; offer for sale &c. 796; press &c. (*request*) 765; go a-begging; lay at one's feet.

VOLUNTEER, come forward, be a candidate; offer -, present- oneself; stand for, bid for; seek; be at one's service.

BRIBE &c. (*give*) 784; grease the palm [*slang*].

Adj. OFFERING, offered &c. *v.*; in the market, for sale, to let, disengaged, on hire; at one's disposal.

⁂ "Take the goods the gods provide thee" [Dryden]; "The gods to-day stand friendly" [*Julius Cæsar*].

764. Refusal. — N. REFUSAL, rejection; noncompliance, incompliance; denial; declining &c. *v.*; declension; declinature; peremptory -, flat -, point blank- refusal; repulse, rebuff; discountenance, disapprobation.

NEGATION, recusancy, abnegation, protest, disclamation, renunciation, disclaimer; dissent &c. 489; revocation &c. 756.

V. REFUSE, reject, deny, decline; nill [*archaic*], turn down [*slang*], abnegate, negate, negative; refuse -, withhold- one's assent; shake the head; close the -hand, - purse; grudge, begrudge, be slow to, hang fire; pass [*at cards*].

STAND ALOOF, be deaf to; turn a deaf ear to, turn one's back upon; set one's face against, discountenance, not hear of, have nothing to do with, wash one's hands of, forswear, set aside, cast behind one; not yield an inch &c. (*obstinacy*) 606.

RESIST, cross; not grant &c. 762; repel, repulse; shut -, slam- the door in one's face; rebuff; send -back, - to the right about, - away with a flea in the ear [*colloq.*]; deny oneself, not be at home to; discard &c. (*repudiate*) 610; rescind &c. (*revoke*) 756; disclaim, protest; dissent &c. 489.

Adj. REFUSING &c. *v.*; restive, restiff [*obs.*]; recusant; uncomplying, noncompliant, incompliant, unconsenting; declinatory, uncomplaisant, disclamatory [*rare*], negatory, protestant; not willing to hear of, deaf to.

REFUSED &c. *v.*; ungranted, out of the question, not to be thought of, impossible.

Adv. NO &c. 536; on no account, not for the world; no thank you; your humble servant [*ironically*], bien obligé [*F.*], not on your life! [*U. S.*].

⁂ "one refusal no rebuff" [Byron]; "'Tis fine to see them scattering refusals And wild dismay" [*ibid.*]; "he who begs timidly courts a refusal" [Seneca].

765. Request. — N. REQUEST, requisition; claim &c. (*demand*) 741; petition, suit, prayer; begging letter, round robin.

motion, overture, application, canvass, address, appeal, apostrophe; imprecation; rogation [*eccl.*]; proposal, proposition.

orison &c. (*worship*) 990; incantation &c. (*spell*) 993.

mendicancy, mendicat on [*rare*]; asking, begging &c. *v.*; postulation, solicitation, invitation, entreaty, importunity, supplication, instance, impetration, imploration, obsecration, obtestation, invocation, interpellation.

V. REQUEST, ask, beg, crave, sue, pray, petition, solicit, invite, pop the question [*colloq.*], make bold to ask; beg leave, beg a boon; apply to, call to,

766. [NEGATIVE REQUEST.**] Deprecation. — N.** DEPRECATION, expostulation; intercession, mediation, protest, remonstrance.

V. DEPRECATE, protest, expostulate, enter a protest, intercede for; remonstrate.

Adj. DEPRECATORY, expostulatory, intercessory, mediatorial.

deprecated, protested.

UNSOUGHT, unbesought; unasked &c. (*see* ask &c. 765).

Int. GOD FORBID! cry you mercy! forbid it Hea ven! Heaven forfend (*or* forefend)! Hea ven forbid! far be it from! hands off! &c. (*prohibition*) 761.

. "Woodman, spare that tree! Touch not a single bough!" [Morris]; "Be to her virtues very kind; Be to her faults a little blind" [Prior].

put to; call upon, call for; make –, address –, p refer –, put up- a -request, – prayer, – petition; make -application, – a requisition; ask –, trouble- one for; claim &c. (*demand*) 741; offer up prayers &c. (*worship*) 990; whistle for [*colloq.*].

bespeak, canvass, tout [*cant, Eng.*], make interest, court; seek, bid for &c. (*offer*) 763; publish the banns.

ENTREAT, beseech, plead, supplicate, beg hard, implore; conjure, adjure; obsecrate [*rare*], apostı́ ophize, obtest [*rare*]; cry to, kneel to, appeal to; invoke, evoke; impetrate, imprecate, ply, press, urge, beset, importune, dun, tax, clamor for; cry aloud, cry for help; fall on one's knees; throw oneself at the feet of; come down on one's marrowbones [*slang or humorous*].

beg from door to door, send the hat round, go a-begging; mendicate [*rare*], mump, cadge [*dial. or slang, Eng.*], beg one's bread.

dance attendance on, besiege, knock at the door.

Adj. REQUESTING &c. *v.*; precatory, suppliant, supplicant, supplicatory, invocative, invocatory, invitatory, imprecatory, rogatory; postulatory [*rare*], postulant; obsecratory [*rare*], obsecrationary [*rare*]; imploratory [*rare*], mendicant, mendicatory [*obs.*].

IMPORTUNATE, clamorous, urgent, solicitous; cap in hand; on one's -knees, – bended knees, – marrowbones [*slang or humorous*].

Adv. PLEASE, prithee, do, pray; be so good as, be good enough; have the goodness, vouchsafe, will you, I pray thee, if you please.

Int. for- God's, – heaven's – goodness', – mercy's- sake! we beseech thee to hear us! help! save me!

. *Dieu vous garde; dirige nos Domine;* "urge them while their souls Are capable of this ambition" [*King John*].

767. Petitioner. — N. PETITIONER, solicitor, applicant, suppliant, supplicant, suitor, candidate, claimant, postulant, aspirant, competitor, bidder; place hunter, pothunter, prizer [*archaic*].

SALESMAN, drummer [*U. S.*]; bagman &c. 758; canvasser.

BEGGAR, mendicant, mumper, sturdy beggar, panhandler [*slang*], cadger.

HOTEL RUNNER [*cant, U. S.*], touter [*colloq.*], runner [*cant, U. S.*], steerer [*U. S.*], tout [*cant, Eng.*]; barker [*colloq.*].

SYCOPHANT, parasite &c. (*servility*) 886.

. "Homer himself must beg if he wants means" [Burton]; "A beggar through the world am I" [Lowell]; "His house was known to all the vagrant train" [Goldsmith]; "Beggars must be no choosers" [Beaumont and Fletcher]; "Of others take a sheaf, of me a grain! Of me a grain!" [*Anon.*].

Section III. Conditional Intersocial Volition

768. Promise. — N. PROMISE, undertaking, word, troth, plight, pledge, parole, word of honor, vow; oath &c. (*affirmation*) 535; profession, assurance, warranty, guarantee, insurance, obligation; contract &c. 769; stipulation.

ENGAGEMENT, preëngagement; affiance; betrothal, betrothment; marriage -contract, - vow; plighted faith, troth-plight [*Scot. or dial.*], gage d'amour [*F.*].

V. PROMISE; give a promise &c. *n.;* undertake, engage; make -, form- an engagement; enter into *or* on an engagement; bind -, tie -, pledge -, commit -, take upon- oneself; vow; swear &c. (*affirm*) 535, give -, pass -, pledge -, plight- one's -word, - honor, - credit, - troth; betroth, plight faith, take the vows, trothplight [*Scot. or dial.*].

ASSURE, warrant, guarantee; covenant &c. 769; avouch, vouch for; attest &c. (*bear witness*) 467.

hold out an expectation; contract an obligation; become bound to, become sponsor for; answer for, be answerable for; secure; give security &c. 771; underwrite.

ADJURE, administer an oath, put to one's oath, swear a witness.

Adj. PROMISING &c. *v.;* promissory; votive; under hand and seal, upon oath, upon the Book; upon -, on- affirmation.

PROMISED &c. *v.;* affianced, pledged, bound; committed, compromised; in for it [*colloq.*].

Adv. as true as I live; in all soberness; upon my honor; my word for it; my head upon it; I call God to witness; as one's head shall answer for; *ex voto* [*L.*].

** his word is his bond; in for a penny in for a pound; "Indeed, indeed, Repentance oft before I swore — but, was I sober when I swore?" [Omar Khayyám — Fitzgerald]; "Thy promises are like Adonis' gardens, That one day bloom'd, and fruitful were the next" [*I Henry VI*].

768a. Release from engagement.— N. RELEASE &c. (*liberation*) 750.

Adj. ABSOLUTE; unconditional &c. (*free*) 748.

---

769. Compact. — N. COMPACT, contract, specialty, bundobast [*India*], deal [*colloq.*], agreement, bargain; affidation [*rare*], pact, paction [*chiefly Scot.*], bond, covenant, indenture [*law*].

stipulation, settlement, convention; compromise, cartel.

negotiation &c. (*bargaining*) 794; diplomacy &c. (*mediation*) 724; negotiator &c. (*agent*) 758.

TREATY, protocol, concordat, *Zollverein* [*Ger.*], *Sonderbund* [*Ger.*], charter, Magna Charta *or* Magna Carta, pragmatic sanction.

RATIFICATION, completion, signature, seal, sigil, signet, bond.

V. CONTRACT, covenant, agree for; engage &c. (*promise*) 768; indent.

NEGOTIATE, treat, stipulate, make terms; bargain &c. (*barter*) 794.

CONCLUDE, close, close with, complete; make -, strike- a bargain; come to -terms, - an understanding; compromise &c. 774; set at rest; settle; confirm, ratify, clinch *or* clench, subscribe, underwrite; indorse, endorse, put the seal to; sign, seal &c. (*attest*) 467; take one at one's word, bargain by inch of candle.

Adj. CONTRACTUAL, complete; agreed &c. *v.;* conventional; under hand and seal; signed, sealed, and delivered.

Adv. AS AGREED UPON, as promised, as contracted for; according to the -contract, - bargain, - agreement.

** *caveat emptor;* "'Tis not in the bond" [*M. of V.*]; "an honest man's word is as good as his bond" [Cervantes].

---

770. Conditions. — N. CONDITIONS, terms; articles, - of agreement; memorandum; clauses, provisions; proviso &c. (*qualification*) 469; covenant, stipulation, obligation, ultimatum, *sine quâ non* [*L.*]; *casus fœderis* [*L.*].

V. CONDITION, make it a condition, stipulate, insist upon, make a point of; bind, tie up; fence in, hedge in, have a string to it [*colloq.*]; make –, come to- -terms &c. (*contract*) 769.

Adj. CONDITIONAL, provisional, guarded, fenced, hedged in.

Adv. CONDITIONALLY &c. (*with qualification*) 469; provisionally, *pro re natâ* [*L.*], on condition; with a string to it [*colloq.*], with a reservation.

771. Security. — N. SECURITY; guaranty, guarantee; gage, warranty, bond, tie, pledge, *vadium vivum* [*L.*], plight [*rare*], mortgage, *vadium mortuum* [*L.*], debenture, hypothec [*Rom. & civil law*], hypothecation, bill of sale, lien, pawn, pignoration; real security; vadium, collateral, bail; parole &c. (*promise*) 768.

stake, deposit, earnest, handsel *or* hansel, handsale, caution [*Scot. law*].

PROMISSORY NOTE; bill, – of exchange; I.O.U.; personal security, covenant.

ACCEPTANCE, indorsement *or* endorsement, signature, execution, stamp, seal.

SPONSOR, surety, bail, replevin; mainpernor, mainprise *or* mainprize [*hist. law*]; hostage; godchild, godfather, godmother; sponsion, sponsorship.

RECOGNIZANCE; deed –, covenant- of indemnity.

AUTHENTICATION, verification, warrant, certificate, voucher, docket *or* doquet [*obs.*]; record &c. 551; probate, attested copy.

acquittance, quittance; discharge, release; receipt.

MUNIMENTS, title deed, instrument; deed, deed poll, indenture; specialty; insurance; charter &c. (*compact*) 769; charter poll; paper, parchment, settlement, will, testament, last will and testament, codicil.

V. GIVE SECURITY, give bail, give substantial bail; go bail; handsel *or* hansel, pawn, put in pawn, pledge, put up the spout [*slang*], impawn *or* empawn [*obs.*], spout [*slang*], impignorate, mortgage, hypothecate.

GUARANTEE, warrant, assure; accept, indorse *or* endorse, underwrite, insure.

EXECUTE, stamp; sign, seal &c. (*evidence*) 467.

LET, set *or* sett [*Scot. law*]; grant –, take –, hold- a lease; hold in pledge; lend on security &c. 787.

Adj. PLEDGED, pawned &c. *v.;* secure; impignorate, pignorative [*rare*], in pawn, up the spout [*slang*]; at stake, on deposit, as earnest.

SPONSORIAL, sponsional [*rare*]; as sponsor &c. *n.*

LET, leased; held in pledge.

*** *bonis avibus;* "gone where the woodbine twineth"; "where there's a will there's a lawsuit" *Cynic's Calendar*].

772. Observance. — N. OBSERVANCE, performance, compliance, acquiescence, concurrence; obedience &c. 743; fulfillment *or* fulfilment, satisfaction, discharge; acquittance, acquittal.

ADHESION, acknowledgment; fidelity &c. (*probity*) 939; exact &c. 494- observance; unswerving fidelity to.

V. OBSERVE, comply with, respect, acknowledge, abide by; cling to, adhere to, be faithful to, act up to; meet, fulfill *or* fulfil; carry out, carry into execution; execute, perform, keep, satisfy, discharge; do one's office.

KEEP FAITH WITH; perform –, fulfill –, discharge –, acquit oneself of- an obligation; make good; make good –, keep- one's -word, – promise; redeem one's pledge; stand to one's engagement.

Adj. OBSERVANT, faithful, true, loyal;

773. Nonobservance. — N. NONOBSERVANCE &c. 772; evasion, inobservance, failure, omission, neglect, laches [*law*], casualness, slackness, laxness, laxity, informality.

lawlessness; disobedience &c. 742; bad faith &c. 940.

INFRINGEMENT, infraction; violation, transgression; piracy.

RETRACTATION, repudiation, nullification; protest; forfeiture.

V. EVADE, fail, neglect, omit, elude, give the go-by to [*slang*], cut [*colloq.*], set aside, ignore; shut –, close- one's eyes to.

INFRINGE, transgress, violate, pirate, break, trample under foot, do violence to, drive a coach and four (*or* six) through.

DISCARD, protest, repudiate, fling to

honorable &c. 939; true as the dial to the sun, true as the needle to the pole; punctual, punctilious, scrupulous, meticulous; literal &c. (*exact*) 494; as good as one's word.

Adv. FAITHFULLY &c. *adj.;* to the letter.

*_*_* *ignoscito sæpe alteri nunquam tibi; tempori parendum;* "to God, thy country, and thy friend be true" [Vaughan]; "he that sweareth to his own hurt, and changeth not" [*Bible*].

the winds, set at naught, nullify, declare null and void; cancel &c. (*wipe off*) 552.

RETRACT, go back from, be off, forfeit, go from one's word, palter; stretch a point, strain a point.

Adj. VIOLATING &c. *v.;* lawless, transgressive; elusive, evasive, slack, lax, casual, slippery; nonobservant.

unfilfilled &c. (*see* fulfill &c. 772).

774. Compromise. — **N.** COMPROMISE, commutation, composition; middle term, *mezzo termine* [*It.*]; compensation &c. 30; abatement of differences, adjustment, mutual concession.

V. COMPROMISE, commute, compound; take the mean; split the difference, meet one halfway, give and take; come to terms &c. (*contact*) 769; submit to arbitration, abide by arbitration; patch up, bridge over, arrange; straighten out, adjust, adjust differences; agree; make the best of, make a virtue of necessity; take the will for the deed.

*_*_* "all government, — indeed every human benefit and enjoyment, every virtue and every prudent act, — is founded on compromise and barter" [Burke].

Section IV. Possessive Relations[1]

1. *Property in general*

775. Acquisition. — **N.** ACQUISITION; gaining &c. *v.;* obtainment, procuration, procurement; purchase, descent, inheritance; gift &c. 784.

RECOVERY, retrieval, revendication [*rare*], replevin; redemption, salvage, trover; find, *trouvaille* [*F.*], foundling.

GAIN, thrift; money-making, money-grubbing; lucre, filthy lucre, loaves and fishes, fleshpots of Egypt, the main chance, pelf; emolument &c. (*remuneration*) 973.

PROFIT, earnings, winnings, innings, pickings, perquisite, accruement [*obs.*], net profit; avails; income &c. (*receipt*) 810; proceeds, produce, product; outcome, output; return, fruit, crop, harvest; second crop, aftermath; benefit &c. (*good*) 618.

PRIZE, sweepstakes, trick, pool; kitty, jack pot, pot; wealth &c. 803.

[FRAUDULENT ACQUISITION] subreption; obreption; stealing &c. 791.

V. ACQUIRE, get, gain, win, earn, obtain, procure, gather; collect &c. (*assemble*) 72; pick, pick up; glean.

find; come –, pitch –, light- upon; come across, come at; scrape -up, – together; get in, reap and carry, net,

776. Loss. — **N.** LOSS, perdition, deperdition [*archaic*]; forfeiture, lapse.

privation, bereavement; deprivation &c. (*dispossession*) 789; riddance; damage, squandering, waste.

V. LOSE; incur –, experience –, meet with- a loss; miss; mislay, let slip, allow to slip through the fingers; be deprived of; be without &c. (*exempt*) 777a; forfeit, pay with.

SQUANDER; get rid of &c. 782; waste &c. 638.

BE LOST, lapse.

Adj. LOSING &c. *v.;* not having &c. 777a.

DEPRIVED OF; shorn of, deperdite [*rare*], denuded, bereaved, bereft, minus [*colloq., exc. in math.*], cut off; dispossessed &c. 789; rid of, quit of; out of pocket.

LOST &c. *v.;* long lost; irretrievable &c. (*hopeless*) 859; off one's hands.

Int. FAREWELL TO! adieu to! good riddance.

*_*_* "Farewell! a long farewell, to all my greatness!" [*Henry VIII*]; "by losing rendered sager" [Byron]; "all is lost save honor" [*misquoted remark of Francis I*].

bag, sack, bring home, secure; derive, draw, get in the harvest.

get hold of, get between one's finger and thumb, get into one's hand, get at; take –, come into –, enter into- possession.

---

[1] That is, relations which concern property.

PROFIT; make –, draw– profit; turn to -profit, – account; make capital out of, make money by; obtain a return, reap the fruits of; reap –, gain- an advantage; turn -a penny, – an honest penny; make the pot boil, bring grist to the mill; make –, coin –, raise- money; raise funds, raise the wind [*slang*]; fill one's pocket &c. (*wealth*) 803.

realize, clear; treasure up &c. (*store*) 636; produce &c. 161; take &c. 789.

receive &c. 785; come by, come in for; inherit; step into, – a fortune, – the shoes of; succeed to.

RECOVER, get back, regain, retrieve, revendicate [*rare*], replevin, replevy, redeem, come by one's own.

BE PROFITABLE &c. *adj.*; pay, answer.

accrue &c. (*be received*) 785.

Adj. ACQUISITIVE, productive, profitable, advantageous, gainful, remunerative, paying, lucrative, acquiring, acquired &c. *v.*

Adv. in the way of gain; for money; at interest.

*** *lucri causa;* "Getting and spending we lay waste our powers" [Wordsworth]; "the greatest possession is self-possession" [*Cynic's Calendar*].

777. Possession. — N. POSSESSION, seizin *or* seisin; ownership &c. 780; occupancy; hold, holding; tenure, tenancy, feodality, feodatory, feud *or* feod, fief, fee, fee tail, fee simple; dependency; villenage *or* villeinage; socage, chivalry, knight service.

bird in hand, *uti possidetis* [L.], chose in possession [*rare*].

EXCLUSIVE POSSESSION, impropriation, monopoly, retention &c. 781; prepossession, preoccupancy; nine points of the law; corner, usucapion *or* usucaption [*Rom. law*], prescription.

FUTURE POSSESSION, heritage, inheritance, heirship, reversion, fee; primogeniture, ultimogeniture.

V. POSSESS, have, hold, occupy, enjoy; be possessed of &c. *adj.*; have in hand &c. *adj.*; own &c. 780; command.

INHERIT; come to, come in for.

MONOPOLIZE, engross, forestall, regrate, impropriate, appropriate, usucapt [*Rom. law*], have all to oneself; corner; have a firm hold of &c. (*retain*) 781; get into one's hand &c. (*acquire*) 775.

BELONG TO, appertain to, pertain to; be in one's possession &c. *adj.*; vest in.

Adj. POSSESSING &c. *v.*; worth; possessed of, seized of, master of, usucapient [*Rom. law*]; in possession of; endowed –, blest –, instinct –, fraught –, laden –, charged- with.

POSSESSED &c. *v.*; on hand, by one; in hand, in store, in stock; unsold, unshared; in one's -hands, – grasp, – possession; at one's command, at one's disposal; one's own &c. (*property*) 780.

*** *entbehre gern was du nicht hast; meum et tuum; tuum est;* "possession is eleven points in the law" [Cibber].

777a. Exemption. — N. EXEMPTION; absence &c. 187; exception, immunity, privilege, release.

V. NOT HAVE &c. 777; be without &c. *adj.*; excuse.

Adj. DEVOID OF, exempt from, without, unpossessed of, unblest with; immune from.

NOT HAVING &c. 777; unpossessed; untenanted &c. (*vacant*) 187; without an owner. UNOBTAINED, unacquired.

778. [JOINT POSSESSION.] Participation. — N. PARTICIPATION; cotenancy, joint tenancy; occupancy –, possession –, tenancy- in common; joint –, common- stock; copartnership, partnership; communion; community of -possessions, – goods; communization, communalization; communism, communalism, collectivism, socialism; coöperation &c. 709.

snacks [*obs.*], coportion [*obs.*], picnic, hotchpot *or* hotchpotch, hodgepodge; coheirship, coparcenary *or* coparceny; gavelkind.

PARTICIPATOR, sharer, copartner, partner; shareholder; cotenant, joint tenant; tenants in common; coheir, coparcener.

COMMUNIST, communitarian, communalist, collectivist, socialist.

V. PARTICIPATE, partake; share, share in; come in for a share; go shares, go snacks [*obs.*], go cahoots [*slang*], halve; share and share alike.

join in; have a hand in &c. (*coöperate*) 709.

COMMUNIZE, communalize; have –, possess –, be seized- -in common, – as joint tenants &c. *n.*

Adj. PARTAKING &c. *v.*

COMMUNISTIC, communalistic, socialistic; coöperative, profit-sharing.

Adv. IN COMMON, share and share alike; on shares.

779. Possessor. — N. POSSESSOR, holder; occupant, occupier; tenant; person *or* man in possession &c. 777; renter, lodger, lessee, underlessee; zamindar *or* zemindar [*India*]; ryot [*India*]; tenant -on sufferance, – at will, – from year to year, – for years, – for life.

OWNER; proprietor, proprietress, proprietary; impropriator, master, mistress, lord.

LANDHOLDER, landowner, landlord, landlady; lord -of the manor, – paramount; heritor [*Scots law*], laird [*Scot.*], vavasor *or* vavasour [*feud. law*]; landed gentry, mesne lord; planter.

BENEFICIARY, *cestui que* (or *qui*) *trust* [*law*], mortgagor.

GRANTEE, feoffee, feoffee in trust, releasee, devisee; legatee, legatary [*rare*].

TRUSTEE; holder &c. of the legal estate; mortgagee.

right owner, rightful owner.

[FUTURE POSSESSOR] heir, – apparent, – presumptive; inheritor, reversioner; remainder-man; heiress, inheritress, inheritrix.

. " 'Twas mine, 'tis his, and has been slave to thousands" [*Othello*].

780. Property. — N. PROPERTY, possession, seizin *or* seisin; tenure &c. (*possession*) 777; *suum cuique* [*L.*], *meum et tuum* [*L.*].

OWNERSHIP, proprietorship, lordship; seigniory *or* seignory *or* seigneury, seignoralty; empire &c. (*dominion*) 737.

ESTATE, interest, stake, right, title, claim, demand, holding; vested –, contingent –, beneficial –, equitable- interest; use, trust, benefit; legal –, equitable- estate.

absolute interest, paramount estate, freehold; fee, – simple, – tail; estate -in fee, – in tail, – tail; estate in tail -male, – female, – general.

term, limitation, lease, settlement, strict settlement, particular estate; estate -for life, – for years, – *pur autre vie* [*F.*]; remainder, reversion, expectancy, possibility.

DOWER, dowry, jointure, appanage *or* apanage, inheritance, heritage, patrimony, alimony; legacy &c. (*gift*) 784; Falcidian law, paternal estate, thirds.

ASSETS, belongings, means, resources, circumstances; wealth &c. 803; money &c. 800; what one -is worth, – will cut up for [*colloq.*]; estate and effects.

REALTY, land, lands, *prædium* [*L.*]; landed –, real- -estate, – property; tenements; hereditaments; corporeal –, incorporeal- hereditaments; acres; ground &c. (*earth*) 342; acquest, mesestead [*archaic*], messuage, toft [*Scot. & dial. Eng.*].

manor, honor [*Eng. feudal law*], domain, demesne; farm, plantation, hacienda [*Sp. Am.*]; alodium *or* allodium &c. (*free*) 748; feoff, fief, feud *or* feod, zamindari *or* zemindari [*India*], arado [*S. W. U. S.*], rancho [*S. W. U. S.*], ranch.

freeholds, copyholds, leaseholds; folkland [*O. Eng. law*].

chattels real; fixtures, plant, heirloom; easement; right of -common, – user.

TERRITORY, state, kingdom, principality, realm, empire, protectorate, dependency, sphere of influence, mandate.

PERSONALTY; personal -property, – estate, – effects; chattels, goods, effects, movables; stock, – in trade; things, traps [*colloq.*], chattels personal, rattletraps, paraphernalia; equipage &c. 633; parcels [*Eng.*], appurtenances.

IMPEDIMENTA; luggage, baggage; bag and baggage; pelf; cargo, lading.

INCOME &c. (*receipts*) 810; rent roll; maul and wedges [*U. S.*].

patent, copyright; chose in action; credit &c. 805; debt &c. 806.

V. POSSESS &c. 777; be the possessor of &c. 779; own; have for one's -own, - very own; come in for, inherit; enfeoff.

savor of the realty.

BELONG TO; be one's property &c. *n.*; pertain to, appertain to.

Adj. ONE'S OWN; landed, prædial *or* predial, manorial, alodial *or* allodial; seigniorial *or* seigneurial; freehold, copyhold, leasehold; feudal *or* feodal; hereditary, entailed, real, personal.

Adv. TO ONE'S CREDIT, to one's account; to the good.

to one and -his heirs for ever, – the heirs of his body, – his heirs and assigns, – his executors, administrators and assigns.

*** "Is it not lawful for me to do what I will with mine own?" [*Bible*].

---

781. Retention. — N. RETENTION; retaining &c. *v.*; keep [*archaic*], detention, custody; tenacity, firm hold, grasp, gripe, grip, iron grip; bond &c. (*vinculum*) 45.

CLUTCHES, tongs, forceps, tenaculum, pincers, nippers, pliers, vise, hook.

fangs, teeth, claws, talons, nail, unguis, tentacle.

paw, hand, finger, wrist, fist, nieve *or* nief [*archaic or dial.*].

CAPTIVE &c. 754; bird in hand.

V. RETAIN, keep; hold, – fast, – tight, – one's own, – one's ground; clinch, clench, clutch, grasp, gripe, hug, have a firm hold of.

SECURE, withhold, detain; hold –, keep- back; keep close; husband &c. (*store*) 636; reserve; have –, keep- in stock &c. (*possess*) 777; entail, tie up, settle.

Adj. RETENTIVE, tenacious; retaining &c. *v.*

UNFORFEITED, undeprived, undisposed, uncommunicated.

INCOMMUNICABLE, inalienable; in mortmain; in strict settlement.

*** *uti possidetis.*

782. Relinquishment. — N. RELINQUISHMENT, abandonment &c. (*of a course*) 624; renunciation, expropriation, dereliction; cession, surrender, dispensation; resignation &c. 757; riddance.

DERELICT &c. *adj.*; jetsam *or* jettison; abandoned farm [*U. S.*]; waif, foundling.

V. RELINQUISH, give up, surrender, yield, cede; let go, let slip; spare, drop, resign, forego, renounce, abandon, expropriate, give away, dispose of, part with; lay -aside, – apart, – down, – on the shelf *&* (*disuse*) 678; set aside, put aside; make away with, cast behind; discard, cast off, dismiss; maroon.

cast –, throw –, pitch –, fling- -away, – aside, – overboard, – to the dogs; cast –, throw –, sweep- to the winds; put –, turn –, sweep- away; jettison.

quit one's hold.

SUPERSEDE, give notice to quit, give warning; be *or* get rid of; be *or* get quit of; eject &c. 297.

rid –, disburden –, divest –, dispossess- oneself of; wash one's hands of.

DIVORCE, unmarry [*rare*]; cut off, desert, disinherit; separate.

Adj. RELINQUISHED &c. *v.*; cast off, derelict; unowned, disowned, disinherited, divorced; unappropriated, unculled; left &c. (*residuary*) 40.

Int. away with!

*** "dismiss'd without a parting pang" [Cibber]; "He cast off his friends as a huntsman, his pack" [Goldsmith].

2. *Transfer of Property*

783. Transfer. — N. TRANSFER, conveyance, assignment, alienation, abalienation; demise, limitation; conveyancing; transmission &c. (*transference*) 270; enfeoffment, bargain and sale, lease and release; exchange &c. (*interchange*) 148; barter &c. 794; substitution &c. 147.

SUCCESSION, reversion; shifting use, shifting trust; devolution.

V. TRANSFER, convey; alien, alienate; assign; enfeoff; grant &c. (*confer*) 784; consign; make over, hand over; pass, hand, transmit, negotiate; hand down; exchange &c. (*interchange*) 148.

CHANGE HANDS, change from one to another; devolve, succeed; come into possession &c. (*acquire*) 775.

DISINHERIT; abalienate [*rare*]; dispossess &c. 789; substitute &c. 147.

Adj. ALIENABLE, negotiable, transferable, reversional, transmissive; inherited.

Adv. BY TRANSFER &c. *n.*; on lease.

---

784. Giving. — N. GIVING &c. *v.*; bestowal, bestowment, donation; presentation, presentment; accordance; concession, cession; delivery, consignment, dispensation, communication, endowment; investment, investiture; award.

CHARITY, almsgiving, liberality, generosity.

[THING GIVEN] gift, donation, present, *cadeau* [*F.*]; fairing; free gift, boon, favor, benefaction, grant, offering, oblation, sacrifice, immolation.

GRACE, act of grace, bonus.

ALLOWANCE, contribution, subscription, subsidy, tribute, subvention.

BEQUEST, legacy, devise, will, dotation, dot, appanage *or* apanage, dowry, dower; voluntary -settlement, - conveyance &c. 783; amortization.

GRATUITY, lagniappe *or* lagnappe [*Louisiana*], pilon [*S. W. U. S.*]; alms, largess, bounty, dole, sportule [*obs.*], donative, help, oblation, offertory, honorarium, Peter pence, sportula, Christmas box, Easter offering, vails [*rare*], *douceur* [*F.*], drink money, tip, hand out [*slang*], *pourboire* [*F.*], *Trinkgeld* [*G*], baksheesh *or* bakshish, cumshaw [China], dash *or* dashee [Africa]; fee &c. (*recompense*) 973; consideration.

BRIBE, bait, ground bait; peace offering; handsel *or* hansel; boodle [*slang*], graft [*colloq.*], grease [*slang*].

785. Receiving. — N. RECEIVING &c. *v.*; acquisition &c. 775; reception &c. (*introduction*) 296; suscipiency [*rare*], acceptance, admission.

RECIPIENT, receiver, suscipient [*rare*], accipient; assignee, devisee; legatee, legatary; grantee, feoffee, donee, relessee, lessee.

BENEFICIARY, sportulary [*obs.*], stipendiary; pensioner, pensionary; almsman.

INCOME &c. (*receipt*) 810.

V. RECEIVE; take &c. 789; acquire &c. 775; admit.

POCKET; take in, catch, touch; put into one's -pocket, - purse; accept; take off one's hands.

BE RECEIVED; come in, come to hand; pass -, fall- into one's hand; go into one's pocket; fall to one's -lot, - share; come -, fall- to one; accrue; have given &c. (784) to one.

Adj. RECEIVING &c. *v.*; recipient, suscipient [*rare*]; stipendiary, stipendarian, pensionary.

RECEIVED &c. *v.*; given &c. 784; secondhand.

NOT GIVEN, unbestowed &c. (*see* give, bestow &c. 784).

*** "it is more blessed to give than to receive" [*Bible*]; "presents, I often say, endear absents" [Lamb].

GIVER, grantor &c. *v.*; donor, almoner, testator, feoffer, settlor [*law*]; investor, subscriber, contributor; Fairy Godmother [*or l. c.*].

V. DELIVER, hand, pass, put into the hands of; hand -, make -, deliver -, pass -, turn- over; assign dower.

PRESENT, give away, dispense, dispose of; give -, deal -, dole -, mete -, squeeze-out; fork out, shell out [*both slang*].

make a present; allow, contribute, subscribe, furnish its quota.

PAY &c. 807; render, impart, communicate.

CONCEDE, cede, yield, part with, shed, cast; spend &c. 809; sacrifice, immolate.

GIVE, bestow, donate [*chiefly U. S.*], confer, grant, accord, award, assign; offer &c. 763.

INTRUST, consign, vest in.

INVEST, endow, settle upon; bequeath, leave, devise.

FURNISH, supply, help; administer to, minister to; afford, spare; accommodate with, indulge with, favor with; shower down upon; lavish, pour on, thrust upon.

BRIBE, tip; tickle -, grease- the palm [slang].

Adj. GIVING &c. v.; given &c. v.; allowed, allowable; concessional; communicable.

CHARITABLE, eleemosynary, sportulary [obs.], tributary; gratis &c. 815; donative.

Adv. AS A FREE GIFT &c. n.; in charity; toward the endowment fund.

Int. don't mention it! not another word! glad to do it!

⁎ *auctor pretiosa facit; ex dono; res est ingeniosa dare* [Ovid]; freely ye have received; freely give" [Bible]; "the gift without the giver is bare" [Lowell]; "rich gifts wax poor when givers prove unkind" [Hamlet]; "To him who gives is given Corn, water, wine, the world, the starry heaven" [Masefield]; "Money makes the mayor go" [Cynic's Calendar]; "But the jingling of the guinea helps the hurt that Honor feels" [Tennyson].

786. Apportionment. — N. APPORTIONMENT, allotment, consignment, assignment, allocation, appointment; appropriation; dispensation, distribution; division, deal; partition, repartition, administration.

PORTION, dividend, contingent, share, allotment, lot, measure, dose; dole, meed, pittance; *quantum* [L.], ration; ratio, proportion, quota, modicum, mess, allowance.

V. APPORTION, divide; distribute, administer, dispense; billet, allot, allocate, detail, cast, share, mete; portion -, parcel -, dole- out; deal, carve.

partition, assign, appropriate, appoint.

PARTICIPATE, come in for one's share &c. 778.

Adj. apportioning &c. v.; apportioned &c. v.; respective.

Adv. respectively, each to each; by lot; in equal shares.

787. Lending. — N. LENDING &c. v.; loan, advance, accommodation, feneration [obs.]; mortgage &c. (security) 771; investment.

PAWNSHOP, spout [slang], *mont de piété* [F.], my uncle's [slang].

LENDER, pawnbroker, money lender, usurer, Shylock.

V. LEND, advance, accommodate with; lend on security; loan; pawn &c. (security) 771.

INVEST; intrust; place -, put- out to interest; place, put; embark, risk, venture, sink, fund.

LET, lease, set *or* sett [Scot. law], sublet, sublease, underlet; demise.

Adj. LENDING &c. v.; lent &c. v.; come across (or down) with the needful [slang].

Adv. in advance; on loan, on security.

⁎ "It is a very good world to live in, To lend, or to spend, or to give in" [attributed to Earl of Rochester]; "the ruthless usurer's gold" [Bulwer-Lytton].

789. Taking. — N. TAKING &c. v.; reception &c. (taking in) 296; deglutition &c. (taking food) 298; appropriation, prehension [chiefly zoöl.], prensation [obs.]; capture, caption; apprehension, deprehension [obs.]; abreption [obs.], seizure; abduction, ablation; subtraction &c. (subduction) 38; abstraction, ademption; androlepsia or androlepsy.

788. Borrowing. — N. BORROWING, pledging, pawning, putting up the spout [slang].

borrowed plumes; plagiarism &c. (thieving) 791.

V. BORROW, desume [obs.]; pawn, put up the spout [slang], patronize my uncle [slang].

raise -, take up- money; raise the wind [slang]; get the -dough, - needful [both slang]; fly a kite, borrow of Peter to pay Paul; run into debt &c. (debt) 806.

HIRE, rent, farm; take a -lease, - demise; take -, hire- by the -hour, - mile, - year &c.

APPROPRIATE, adopt, apply, imitate, make use of, take; plagiarize, pirate.

replevy.

Adj. borrowed &c. v.

⁎ "Neither a borrower nor a lender be" [Hamlet]; "borrowing dulls the edge of husbandry" [ibid.]; "Who goes a borrowing Goes a sorrowing" [Tusser].

790. Restitution. — N. RESTITUTION, return; rendition, reddition; restoration, reinstatement, reinvestment, recuperation; rehabilitation &c. (reconstruction) 660; reparation, atonement; compensation, indemnification.

RECOVERY &c. (getting back) 775; release, replevin, replevy, redemption; reversion; remitter.

DISPOSSESSION; deprivation, deprivement; bereavement; divestment; disinheritance, disherison; distraint, distress, attachment, execution; sequestration, confiscation; eviction &c. 297.

RAPACITY, rapaciousness, extortion, predacity; bloodsucking, vampirism; theft &c. 791.

RESUMPTION; reprises [law], reprisal; recovery &c. 775.

CLUTCH, swoop, wrench; grip &c. (retention) 781; haul, take, catch; scramble.

TAKER, captor, capturer; extortioner or extortionist; vampire.

V. TAKE, catch, hook, nab [obs. or slang], bag, sack, pocket, put into one's pocket; receive; accept.

REAP, crop, cull, pluck; gather &c. (get) 775; draw.

V. RESTORE, return; give –, carry –, bring- back; render, – up; give up; let go, unclutch; disgorge, regorge; regurgitate; recoup, reimburse, compensate, indemnify, reinvest, reinstate, remit, rehabilitate; repair &c. (make good) 660.

RECOVER &c. (get back) 775; redeem; take back again; revest, revert.

Adj. RESTORING &c. v.; recuperative &c. 660; compensatory, indemnificatory; reversionary, redemptive, revertible.

Adv. in full restitution; as partial compensation; to atone for.

⁎⁎⁎ suum cuique; "He was ever precise in promise-keeping" [M. for M.]; "words pay no debts" [Troilus and Cressida]; "Who never promiseth but he means to pay" [I Henry IV].

APPROPRIATE, impropriate [Eng. eccl. law]; assume, possess oneself of; take possession of; commandeer [colloq.]; lay –, clap- one's hands on [colloq.]; help oneself to; make free with, dip one's hands into, lay under contribution; intercept; scramble for; deprive of.

SEIZE, abstract; take –, carry –, bear- -away, – off; adeem [law]; hurry off –, run away- with; abduct; steal &c. 791; ravish; pounce –, spring- upon; swoop to, swoop down upon; take by -storm, – assault; snatch, reave [archaic].

snap up, nip up, whip up, catch up; kidnap, crimp, capture, lay violent hands on.

get –, lay –, take –, catch –, lay fast –, take firm- hold of; lay by the heels, take prisoner; fasten upon, grapple, embrace, grip, gripe, clasp, grab [colloq.], make away with, clutch, collar, throttle, take by the throat, claw, clinch, clench, make sure of.

CATCH AT, jump at, make a grab at, snap at, snatch at; reach, make a long arm [colloq.], stretch forth one's hand.

DISSEIZE or disseise; take from, take away from; deduct &c. 38; retrench &c. (curtail) 201; dispossess, ease one of, away –, wrench –, wrest –, wring- inherit, cut off with a shilling; oust &c. fiscate; sequester, sequestrate; accroach; plume. snatch from one's grasp; tear –, tear from; extort; deprive of, bereave; dis- (eject) 297; divest; levy, distrain, confiscate; usurp; despoil, strip, fleece, shear, displume.

ABSORB &c. (suck in) 296; draw off; suck, – like a leach, – the blood of; impoverish, eat out of house and home; drain, – to the dregs; gut, dry, exhaust, swallow up.

RETAKE, resume; recover &c. 775.

Adj. TAKING &c. v.; privative, prehensile; predacious or predaceous, predal [obs.], predatory, wolfish, lupine, rapacious, raptorial; ravening, ravenous; parasitic; all-devouring, all-engulfing.

bereft &c. 776.

Adv. at one fell swoop.

⁎⁎⁎ give an inch and take an ell.

791. Stealing. — **N.** STEALING &c. v.; theft, thievery, robbery, direption [rare]; abstraction, appropriation; plagiary [rare], plagiarism, autoplagiarism; rape, depredation; kidnaping or kidnapping.

PILLAGE, spoliation, plunder, sack, sackage [rare], rapine, brigandage, latrociny [obs.], latrocinium [Rom. law], highway robbery, holdup [slang, U. S.]; raid, foray, razzia; piracy, privateering, buccaneering; filibustering, filibusterism; burglary, housebreaking; abaction, cattle stealing, cattle lifting [*colloq.*], horse stealing; automobile –, car- stealing.

BLACKMAIL, badger game [*cant*], Black Hand [*U. S.*].

PECULATION, embezzlement; fraud &c. 545; larceny, petty larceny, pilfering, shoplifting.

THIEVISHNESS, rapacity, predacity, predaciousness; kleptomania.

Alsatia; Whitefriars; den of Cacus, den of thieves.

LICENSE TO PLUNDER, letters of marque.

V. STEAL, thieve, rob, purloin, pilfer, filch, prig [*cant*], bag, nim [*obs.*], crib [*colloq.*], cabbage, palm; abstract; appropriate, plagiarize.

disregard the distinction between *meum* and *tuum*.

ABDUCT, convey away, carry off, kidnap, crimp, impress, press [*rare*]; make –, walk –, run- off with; run away with; spirit away, seize &c. (*lay violent hands on*) 789.

PLUNDER, pillage, rifle, sack, loot, ransack, spoil, spoliate, despoil, strip, sweep, gut, forage, levy blackmail, pirate, pickeer [*obs.*], maraud, lift cattle [*colloq.*], poach, smuggle, run; badger [*cant*], bunko *or* bunco; hold up; bail up, stick up [*both colloq. or slang, Austral.*], filibuster.

SWINDLE, peculate, embezzle; sponge, mulct, rook, bilk, pluck, pigeon [*slang*], thimblerig; diddle [*colloq. or dial.*], fleece; defraud &c. 545; obtain under false pretenses; live by one's wits.

rob –, borrow of- Peter to pay Paul; set a thief to catch a thief.

Adj. THIEVING &c. *v.*; thievish, light-fingered, furacious [*rare*]; furtive; piratical; predacious *or* predaceous, predal [*obs.*], predatory; raptorial &c. (*rapacious*) 789.

STOLEN &c. *v.*

*** *sic vos non vobis.*

792. Thief. — N. THIEF, robber, *homo trium literarum* [*L.*], spoiler, depredator, pillager, marauder; pilferer, rifler, filcher, plagiarist; harpy, shark [*slang*], land rat [*cant*], land pirate, land shark, falcon; smuggler, poacher; abductor, badger [*cant*], kidnaper *or* kidnapper; *chor* [*Hind.*], crook [*slang*], lifter, skin [*slang*], contrabandist, hawk; hold-up, jackleg, rustler [*all three slang, U. S.*]; spieler [*colloq., Austral.*], sandbagger, sneak thief, strong-arm man [*U. S.*].

PIRATE, corsair, viking, sea king, buccaneer, privateer; Paul Jones.

BRIGAND, bandit, freebooter, thug, dacoit [*India*]; rover, ranger, pickeerer [*obs.*], picaroon, filibuster, rapparee [*Ir.*]; cattle thief, abactor; bushranger, mosstrooper [*hist.*], Bedouin; wrecker; highwayman, footpad, sturdy beggar, knight of the road.

Dick Turpin, Claude Duval, Jonathan Wild, Macheath, Nevison.

PICKPOCKET, dip [*slang*], cutpurse, pickpurse [*rare*], light-fingered gentry; sharper; card sharper, card cheat, Greek; thimblerigger; bunkoman *or* buncoman, rook [*slang*], welsher [*slang*], blackleg [*colloq.*], leg [*slang, Eng.*], diddler [*colloq. or slang*], defaulter; Autolycus, Jeremy Diddler, Robert Macaire, Artful Dodger, trickster; swell mob [*slang*], *chevalier d'industrie* [*F.*]; shoplifter.

SWINDLER, duffer [*Eng.*], peculator; forger, coiner, smasher [*cant, Eng.*], counterfeiter; fence, receiver of stolen goods.

BURGLAR, housebreaker, yeggman *or* yegg [*slang*], cracksman [*slang*], magsman [*slang*]; sneak thief; second-story -thief, – man; Bill Sikes, Jack Sheppard.

*** "he stole nothing smaller than the moomoo's egg" [Dunsany]; "a promising young robber, the lieutenant of his band" [Gilbert].

793. Booty. — N. BOOTY, spoil, plunder, prize, loot, swag [*cant*]; perquisite, boodle [*polit. cant*], graft [*colloq.*], pork barrel [*polit. cant, U. S.*], pickings; *spolia opima* [*L.*], prey; blackmail; stolen goods.

Adj. LOOTING, plundering, spoliative, manubial [*obs.*].

3. *Interchange of Property*

794. Barter. — N. BARTER, exchange, scorse [*obs.*], truck system; interchange &c. 148.

a Roland for an Oliver, *quid pro quo* [*L.*], commutation, composition; Indian gift [*colloq., U. S.*].

TRADE, commerce, mercature [*obs.*], buying and selling, bargain and sale; traffic, business, nundination [*obs.*], custom, shopping; commercial enterprise, speculation, jobbing, stockjobbing, agiotage, brokery.

dealing, transaction, negotiation, bargain.

free trade [*opp. to* protection].

V. BARTER, exchange, truck, scorse [*obs.*], swap *or* swop [*colloq. & dial.*]; interchange &c. 148; commutate &c. (*sub titute*) 147; compound for.

TRADE, traffic, buy and sell, give and take, nundinate [*obs.*]; carry on –, ply –, drive- a trade; be in -business, – the city; keep a shop, deal in, employ one's capital in.

trade –, deal –, have dealings- with; put through a deal with; have truck with; transact –, do- business with; open –, have –, keep- an account with.

BARGAIN; drive –, make- a bargain; negotiate, bid for; haggle, stickle, – for; higgle, dicker [*U. S.*], chaffer, huckster, cheapen, beat down; underbid; outbid; ask, charge; strike a bargain &c. (*contract*) 769.

SPECULATE; give –, bait with- a sprat to catch a -herring, – mackerel; buy low and sell high, buy in the cheapest and sell in the dearest market; stag the market [*London Stock Exchange*], rig the market [*Exchange cant*].

Adj. COMMERCIAL, mercantile, trading; interchangeable, marketable, staple, in the market, for sale; at a bargain, marked down.

wholesale, retail.

Adv. across the counter; in the marts of trade; on the Rialto, on 'change.

⁎ *cambio non è furto;* "a business with an income at its heels" [Cowper]; "bad is the trade that must play fool to sorrow" [*King Lear*]; "Traffic's thy god; and thy god confound thee!" [*Timon of Athens*]; "What news on the Rialto?" [*Merchant of Venice*].

795. Purchase. — N. PURCHASE, emption [*rare*]; buying, purchasing, shopping; preëmption, refusal.

coemption [*Rom. law*]; bribery; slave trade.

BUYER, purchaser, emptor [*law*], co-emptor, vendee; client, customer, clientele, clientage; patron, employer.

V. BUY, purchase, invest in, regrate, procure; rent &c. (*hire*) 788; repurchase, buy in.

make –, complete- a purchase; buy over the counter; pay cash for; charge, – to one's account.

shop, market, go a-shopping.

keep in one's pay, bribe, suborn; pay &c. 807; spend &c. 809.

Adj. purchased &c. *v.;* emptorial, coemptional, coemptive; cliental.

⁎ *caveat emptor.*

796. Sale. — N. SALE, vent [*rare*], vend [*Eng.*], disposal; auction, roup [*Scot.*], outcry, vendue, Dutch auction; custom &c. (*traffic*) 794.

SALA BLENESS, salability, marketability, vendibility, vendibleness.

SELLER, vender, vendor; consigner; *institor* [*L.*]; rouping wife [*Scot.*]; merchant &c. 797; auctioneer.

SALESMA NSHIP, selling ability.

V. SELL, vend, dispose of, make a sale, effect a sale; sell over the counter, sell at [*esp. U. S.*] auction, sell by [*esp. Brit.*] auction, vendue, roup [*Scot.*], outcry; put up to (*or* at) auction; bring to (*or* under) the hammer; offer –, put up- for sale; hawk, bring to market; wholesale [*colloq.*]; dump, unload, place; offer &c. 763; undersell; dispense, retail; deal in &c. 794; sell -off, – out; turn into money, realize.

let; mortgage &c. (*security*) 771.

Adj. FOR SALE, under the hammer, in the market.

SALABLE, marketable, vendible, staple, merchantable; in demand, popular.

UNSALABLE &c., unpurchased, unbought; on the shelves, shelved, on one's hands.

⁎ *chose qui plaît est à demi vendue.*

797. Merchant. — N. MERCHANT, trader, dealer, monger, chandler, salesman; money changer, changer [*archaic*]; regrater; shopkeeper, shopman; tradesman, tradespeople, tradesfolk.

RETAILER; chapman, hawker, huckster, higgler; peddler *or* pedlar, colporteur, cadger, Autolycus; sutler, vivandière; costerman, costermonger; tallyman [*rare*], canvasser, solicitor [*U. S.*]; cheap Jack, *camelot* [*F.*]; faker [*slang*]; vintner; greengrocer, groceryman, haberdasher.

MONEY-LENDER, cambist, usurer, moneyer [*obs.*], banker; money-changer, money-broker.

JOBBER; broker &c. (*agent*) 758; buyer &c. 795; seller &c. 796; bear, bull [*Stock Exchange*].

CONCERN, house, corporation; firm &c. (*partnership*) 712.

*** "a merchant of great traffic through this world" [*Taming of the Shrew*].

798. Merchandise. — N. MERCHANDISE, ware, commodity, effects, goods, article, stock, produce, staple commodity; stock in trade &c. (*store*) 636; cargo &c. (*contents*) 190.

*** "I sometimes wonder what the vintners buy One half so precious as the stuff they sell" [Omar Khayyám — Fitzgerald].

799. Mart. — N. MART, market, marketplace; fair, bazaar, staple, exchange, stock exchange, Wheat Pit [*Chicago*]; 'change, bourse, curb, hall, guildhall; tollbooth [*Scot. & dial. Eng.*], customhouse; Tattersall's.

SHOP, stall, booth; wharf; office, chambers, countinghouse, bureau; counter *or* compter [*obs.*].

STORE &c. 636; department store, finding store [*U. S.*], grindery warehouse, warehouse, wareroom; depot, interposit [*rare*], entrepôt [*F.*], emporium, establishment.

market overt, open market.

*** "To business that we love we rise betime, And go to't with delight." [*Antony and Cleopatra*].

4. *Monetary Relations*

800. Money. — N. MONEY, finance; money -matters, – market; accounts &c. 811; funds, treasure; capital, stock; assets &c. (*property*) 780; wealth &c. 803; supplies, ways and means, wherewithal *or* wherewith, sinews of war, almighty dollar, cash.

SOLVENCY, responsibility, reliability, solidity, soundness.

SUM, amount; balance, balance sheet; sum total; proceeds &c. (*receipts*) 810.

CURRENCY, circulating medium, specie, coin, piece, hard cash; dollar, sterling; pounds, shillings, and pence, £ s. d.; guinea; gold mohur [*India*]; eagle, double eagle; pocket, breeches pocket [*colloq.*], wallet, roll, purse; money in hand; *argent comptant* [*F.*], ready [*colloq.*], ready money; Federal –, fractional –, postal- currency; bottom dollar [*colloq.*]; checks, chips.

[SLANG TERMS] the needful, rhino, brass, blunt, dust, mopus, tin, salt, chink, dough, jack, moss, rock, dibs, slug [*Calif.* 1849]; buzzard dollar, spondulics, long green; barrel, pile, wad.

PRECIOUS METALS, gold, silver, copper, bullion, ingot, bar, nugget.

PETTY CASH, pocket money, pin money, spending money, change, small coin; long bit, short bit, two bits, quarter [*all U. S.*]; dime, nickel, cent, red cent [*colloq., U. S.*]; doit, stiver, rap, mite, farthing, sou, penny, shilling, tester, groat, rouleau.

WAMPUM, wampumpeag, seawan *or* seawant, roanoke, cowrie.

GREAT WEALTH, money to burn [*colloq.*]; power –, mint –, barrel –, raft- of money [*all colloq.*]; good –, round –, lump- sum; plum (=£100,000) [*rare slang*]; million, millions, thousands; crore (=ten million rupees, written *Rs.* 1,00,00,000) [*India*]; lac *or* lakh, lac of rupees (=100,000 rupees, written *Rs.* 1,00,000) [*India*].

[SCIENCE OF COINS] numismatics, numismatology, chrysology.

PAPER MONEY; money –, postal –, post office- order; note, – of hand; bank –, promissory- note; I O U, bond; bill, – of exchange; draft, check [*esp. U. S.*] *or* cheque [*esp. Brit.*], hundi [*India*], order, warrant, coupon, debenture, exchequer bill, assignat, greenback [*U. S.*]; blueback [*U. S.*], shinplaster [*slang, U. S.*].

remittance &c. (*payment*) 807; credit &c. 805; liability &c. 806.

drawer, drawee; obligor, obligee.

COUNTERFEIT –, false –, bad- money; queer [*slang*], base coin, flash note, slip [*obs.*], kite [*slang*]; fancy stocks; Bank of Elegance.

COUNTERFEITER, coiner, moneyer, forger.

V. TOTAL, amount to, come to, mount up to.

TOUCH THE POCKET; draw, draw upon; back; indorse &c. (*security*) 771; discount &c. 813.

ISSUE, utter, circulate; fiscalize, monetize, remonetize.

DEMONETIZE, deprive of standard value; cease to issue.

COIN, counterfeit, forge; circulate bad money, shove the queer [*slang*].

Adj. MONETARY, pecuniary, crumenal [*obs.*], fiscal, financial, sumptuary, numismatical; sterling; nummary.

SOLVENT, sound, substantial, good, reliable, responsible, solid, having a good rating; able to pay -20 shillings to the pound, – 100 cents to the dollar.

٭ *barbarus ipse placet dummodo sit dives* [Ovid]; *argumentum ad crumenam; nervos belli pecuniam infinitam* [Cicero]; *redet Geld so schweigt die Welt; Geld regiert die Welt;* "this bank-note world" [Halleck]; "get to live; Then live and use it" [Herbert]; "Get money; still get money, boy; No matter by what means" [B. Jonson]; "Money brings honor, friends, conquest, and realms" [Milton]; "the image of it gives me content already" [*Measure for Measure*].

801. Treasurer. — N. TREASURER; bursar, purser, purse bearer; cash keeper, banker; depositary; questor *or* quæstor [*Rom.*], receiver, liquidator, steward, trustee, accountant, expert accountant, Accountant General, almoner *or* almner, paymaster, cashier, teller; cambist; money changer &c. (*merchant*) 797.

financier, Chancellor of the Exchequer, Secretary of the Treasury, minister of finance.

802. Treasury. — N. TREASURY, bank, exchequer, almonry, fisc *or* fiscus, hanaper; kutcherry *or* cutcherry *or* kachahri [*India*], bursary; strong box, stronghold, strong room; coffer; chest &c. (*receptacle*) 191; safe; depository &c. 636; cash register, cash box, money-box, till, tiller.

PURSE, money-bag, portemonnaie, pocketbook, wallet; purse strings; pocket, breeches pocket.

sinking fund; stocks; public –, parliamentary- -stocks, – funds, – securities; Consols, *crédit mobilier* [*F.*]; bonds, government bonds, Liberty bonds [*U. S.*], three per cents; gilt-edged securities.

803. Wealth. — N. WEALTH, riches, fortune, handsome fortune, opulence, affluence; good –, easy- circumstances; independence; competence &c. (*sufficiency*) 639; solvency &c. 800.

capital, money; round sum; great wealth &c. (*treasure*) 800; mint of money, mine of wealth, bonanza, El Dorado, Pactolus, Golconda, Potosi, Philosopher's Stone; the Golden Touch.

long –, full –, well lined –, heavy-purse; purse of Fortunatus; *embarras de richesses* [*F.*].

pelf, Mammon, lucre, filthy lucre; loaves and fishes, fleshpots of Egypt.

MEANS, resources, substance, command of money; property &c. 780; income &c. 810.

804. Poverty. — N. POVERTY, indigence, penury, pauperism, destitution, want; need, neediness; lack, necessity, privation, distress, difficulties, wolf at the door.

STRAITS; bad –, poor –, needy –, embarrassed –, reduced –, straightened- circumstances; slender –, narrow- means; hand-to-mouth existence, *res angusta domi* [*L.*], low water [*slang, U. S.*], impecuniosity.

MENDICITY, beggary, mendicancy; broken –, loss of- fortune; insolvency &c. (*nonpayment*) 808.

empty -purse, – pocket; light purse; "a beggarly account of empty boxes" [*Romeo and Juliet*].

POOR MAN, pauper, mumper, mendi-

PROVISION, maintenance, livelihood; dowry, alimony.

RICH MAN, moneyed man, warm man [old slang], man of substance; capitalist, millionaire, tippybob [slang], Nabob, Crœsus, Midas, Plutus, Dives, Timon of Athens; Danaë.

timocracy, plutocracy.

V. BE RICH &c. adj.; roll -, wallow-in -wealth, - riches; have money to burn [colloq.].

AFFORD, well afford; command -money, - a sum; make both ends meet, hold one's head above water.

BECOME RICH &c. adj.; fill one's pocket &c. (treasury) 802; feather one's nest, make a fortune; make money &c. (acquire) 775.

enrich, imburse [rare].

worship Mammon, worship the golden calf.

Adj. WEALTHY, rich, affluent, opulent, moneyed, worth a great deal; well-to-do, well off; warm [old slang]; well -, provided for.

made of money; rich as - Crœsus; rolling in -riches, - wealth; having a power of money &c. (great wealth) 800.

flush, - of -cash, - money, - tin [slang]; in funds, in cash, in full feather.

SOLVENT &c., 800; pecunious [rare], out of debt, all straight.

⁎ one's ship coming in.

amour fait beaucoup mais argent fait tout; aurea rumpunt tecta quietem [Seneca]; *magna servitus ist magna fortuna;* "mammon, the least erected spirit that fell from Heaven" [*Paradise Lost*]; *opum furiata cupido* [Ovid]; *vera prosperità è non aver necessità; wie gewonnen so zerronnen; O senza brama sicura ricchezza!* [Dante]; "whose plenty made him pore" [Spenser]; "base wealth preferring to eternal praise" [Homer]; "an incarnation of fat dividends" [Sprague].

cant, beggar, starveling; *pauvre diable* [F.], fakir *or* fakeer [*India*], sunyasi [*India*], schnorrer [*Yiddish*].

V. BE POOR &c. adj.; want, lack, starve, live from hand to mouth, have seen better days, go down in the world, come upon the parish; go to -the dogs, - the almshouse, - the poorhouse, - rack and ruin; not have a -penny &c. (money) 800, - shot in one's locker; beg one's bread, - from door to door; *tirer le diable par la queue* [F.]; run into debt &c. (debt) 806.

RENDER POOR &c. adj.; impoverish; reduce, - to poverty; pauperize, fleece, ruin, bring on the parish.

Adj. POOR, indigent; poverty-stricken; badly -, poorly -, ill- off; poor as -a rat, - a church mouse, - Job, - Job's turkey [colloq.]; fortuneless, dowerless, moneyless, penniless; unportioned, unmoneyed; impecunious; out -, short-of -money, - cash; without -, not-worth- a rap &c. (money) 800; *qui n'a pas le sou* [F.], out of pocket, hard up; out at -elbows, - heels; seedy [colloq.], in rags, barefooted; beggarly, beggared, destitute ∴ fleeced, stripped; bereft, bereaved; reduced.

IN WANT &c. n.; needy, necessitous, distressed, pinched, straitened; put to one's -shifts, - last shifts; unable to -keep the wolf from the door, - make both ends meet; embarrassed, under hatches; involved &c. (in debt) 806; insolvent &c. (not paying) 808.

Adv. *in formâ pauperis* [L.].

⁎ *zonam perdidit;* "a penniless lass wi' a lang pedigree" [Lady Nairne]; *á pobreza no hay vergüenza;* "he that is down can fall no lower" [Butler]; *poca roba poco pensiero;* "steep'd . . . in poverty to the very lips" [*Othello*]; "the short and simple annals of the poor" [Gray]; "the beggarly last doit" [Cowper]; "I am as poor as Job, my lord, but

not so patient" [*II Henry IV*]; "I only ask that Fortune send A *little* more than I can spend" [Holmes]; "I enjoyed the immunities of impecuniosity with the opportunities of a millionaire" [Shaw].

---

805. Credit. — N. CREDIT, trust, tick [colloq.], strap [slang], score, tally, account.

PAPER CREDIT, letter of credit, circular note; duplicate; mortgage, lien, debenture, floating capital; draft, *lettre de créance* [F.], securities.

CREDITOR, lender, lessor, mortgagee; dun, dunner; usurer.

806. Debt. — N. DEBT, obligation, liability, indebtness, debit, score.

ARREARS, deferred payment, deficit, default; insolvency &c. (nonpayment) 808; bad debt.

INTEREST; premium; usance [obs.], usury; floating -debt, - capital.

DEBTOR, debitor [obs.], mortgagor; defaulter &c. 808; borrower.

V. CREDIT, accredit, intrust *or* entrust; keep –, run up– an account with.

place to one's –credit, – account; give –, take– credit; fly a kite [*com. slang*]; have one's credit good for.

Adj. ACCREDITED; of good credit, of unlimited credit; well rated; credited, crediting.

Adv. on credit &c. *n;* to the account of, to the credit of; *à compte* [*F*].

*** "we think ourselves unsatisfied Till he hath found a time to pay us" [*I Henry IV*]; "doubt not of the day" [*III Henry VI*].

V. BE IN DEBT &c. *adj.;* owe; incur –, contract– a debt &c. *n.;* run up –a bill, – a score, – an account; go on tick [*colloq.*]; borrow &c. 788; run –, get-into debt; be over head and ears in debt; be in difficulties; outrun the constable.

ANSWER FOR, go bail for; back one's note.

Adj. LIABLE, chargeable, answerable for.

INDEBTED, in debt, in embarrassed circumstances, in difficulties; encumbered *or* incumbered, involved; in-volved –, plunged –, deep –, over head and ears- in debt; deeply involved; fast tied up; insolvent &c. (*not paying*) 808; minus [*colloq.*], out of pocket.

UNPAID; unrequited, unrewarded; owing, due, in arrear, outstanding.

*** *æs alienum debitorem leve gravius inimicum facit;* "neither a borrower nor a lender be" [*Hamlet*]; "he that has no credit owes no debts!" [Middleton]; "Knowing how the debt grows, I will pay it" [*Comedy of Errors*]; "My lord, vouchsafe me a word with you" [*Hamlet*].

---

807. Payment. — N. PAYMENT, defrayment; discharge; acquittance, quit-tance; settlement, clearance, liquidation, satisfaction, reckoning, arrangement.

ACKNOWLEDGMENT, release; receipt, – in full, – in full of all demands; voucher.

REPAYMENT, reimbursement, retribution; pay &c. (*reward*) 973; money paid &c. (*expenditure*) 809.

READY MONEY &c. (*cash*) 800; stake, remittance, installment *or* instalment.

PAYER, liquidator &c. 801.

V. PAY, defray, make payment; pay -down, – on the nail [*slang*], – ready money, – at sight, – in advance; cash, honor a bill, acknowledge; redeem; pay in kind.

pay one's -way, – shot, – footing; pay -the piper, – sauce for all [*both colloq.*], – costs; come down with the needful [*slang*]; shell –, fork- out [*both slang*]; come down with, – the dust [*both slang*]; tickle –, grease- the palm [*both colloq.*]; expend &c. 809; put down, lay down.

DISCHARGE, settle, quit [*archaic*], ac-quit oneself of; foot the bill [*colloq.*, *U. S.*]; account with, reckon with, settle with, be even with, be quits with; strike a balance; settle –, balance –, square- accounts with; quit scores [*archaic*]; wipe –, clear- off old scores; satisfy; pay in full; satisfy –, pay in full- all demands; clear, liquidate; pay -up, – old debts.

REPAY, refund, reimburse, retribute [*obs.*]; make compensation &c. 30; disgorge, make repayment.

Adj. PAYING &c. paid &c. *v.;* owing nothing, out of debt, all straight, all

808. Nonpayment. — N. NONPAY-MENT; default, defalcation; protest, re-pudiation; application of the sponge; whitewashing.

INSOLVENCY, bankruptcy, failure; in-sufficiency &c. 640; run upon a bank; overdrawn account.

waste paper bonds; dishonored –, protested- bills; bogus check *or* cheque.

DEFAULTER, bankrupt, insolvent debtor, lame duck [*slang*], man of straw; welsher *or* welcher, stag [*obs.*], levanter, ab-sconder.

V. NOT PAY &c. 807; fail, break, stop payment; become -insolvent, – bank-rupt; be gazetted; have one's check -dishonored, – protested.

pay under protest; button up one's pockets, draw the purse strings; apply the sponge; pay over the left shoulder [*colloq.*], get whitewashed; swindle &c. 791; run up bills, fly kites [*com. slang*].

PROTEST, dishonor, repudiate, nullify.

Adj. NOT PAYING; in debt &c. 806; behindhand, in arrear; beggared &c., (*poor*) 804; unable to make both ends meet, minus [*colloq.*], worse than nothing.

INSOLVENT, bankrupt, in the gazette, gazetted, ruined.

UNPAID &c. (*outstanding*) 806; gratis &c. 815; unremunerated.

346

clear, clear of encumbrance, clear of debt, above water; unowed, never indebted; solvent &c. 800.

Adv. to the tune of [*colloq.*]; on the nail [*slang*], money down, cash down, cash on delivery, C.O.D.

****** "You'll pay me altogether? Will I live?" [*II Henry IV*]; "Defer no time, delays have dangerous ends" [*I Henry VI*]; "he . . . prays your speedy payment" [*Timon of Athens*].

---

809. Expenditure. — N. EXPENDITURE, money going out; outgoings, outlay; expenses, disbursement; prime cost &c. (*price*) 812; circulation; run upon a bank.

[MONEY PAID] payment &c. 807; pay &c. (*remuneration*) 973; bribe &c. 973; fee, footing, garnish [*obs.*]; subsidy; tribute; contingent, quota; donation, gift &c. 784.

investment; purchase &c. 795.

DEPOSIT, pay in advance, earnest, handsel *or* hansel, installment *or* instalment.

V. EXPEND, spend; run –, get-through; pay, disburse; ante, ante up [*both poker*]; pony up [*slang, U. S.*]; open –, loose –, untie- the purse strings, lay out, shell out [*slang*], fork out [*slang*]; bleed; make up a sum, invest, sink money.

fee &c. (*reward*) 973; pay one's way &c. (*pay*) 807; subscribe &c. (*give*) 784; subsidize; bribe.

Adj. EXPENDING, expended &c. *v.*; sumptuary, lavish, free, free with one's money, liberal; beyond one's income.

EXPENSIVE, costly, dear, high-priced, precious, high.

****** *vectigalia nervos esse reipublicæ* [Cicero].

810. Receipt. — N. RECEIPT, value received, money coming in; income, incomings [*rare*], revenue, return, proceeds; gross receipts, net profit; earnings &c. (*gain*) 775; *accepta* [*L.*], avails.

RENT, rent roll; rental, rentage [*obs.*], rack-rent.

PREMIUM, bonus; sweepstakes, tontine, prize, drawings, hand-out [*slang*].

PENSION, annuity; jointure &c. (*property*) 780; alimony, pittance; emolument &c. (*remuneration*) 973.

V. RECEIVE &c. 785; get, have an income of, be in receipt of, have coming in; take money; draw from, derive from; acquire &c. 775; take &c. 789; have in prospect.

YIELD, bring in, afford, pay, return; accrue &c. (*be received from*) 785.

Adj. RECEIVING, received &c. *v.*; well-paying, remunerative, interest-bearing; well –, profitably- invested; profitable &c. (*gainful*) 775.

Adv. at interest; within one's income.

---

811. Accounts. — N. ACCOUNTS, accompts [*archaic*]; business –, commercial –, monetary- arithmetic; statistics &c. (*numeration*) 85; money matters, finance, budget, bill, score, reckoning, account.

BOOKKEEPING, audit, single entry, double entry; computation, calculation, casting up.

ACCOUNT BOOK, books, ledger; day –, cash –, petty-cash –, pass- book; journal; debtor and creditor –, cash –, running- account; account current; balance, – sheet; *compte rendu* [*F.*], account settled; *acquit* [*F.*], assets, expenditure, liabilities, outstanding accounts; profit and loss -account, – statement; receipts; receipt -in full, – in part, – on account.

ACCOUNTANT, auditor, actuary, bookkeeper; financier &c. 801; accounting party; chartered accountant [*Eng.*], expert accountant [*U. S.*], certified accountant [*U. S.*], bank examiner.

V. KEEP ACCOUNTS, enter, post, post up, book, credit, debit, carry over; take stock; tot up [*colloq.*], add, add up; balance –, make up –, square –, settle –, wind up –, cast up- accounts; make accounts square.

bring to book, audit, examine the books, tax.

FALSIFY, surcharge; falsify –, garble- an account; cook –, doctor- an account [*both colloq.*].

Adj. monetary &c. 800; accountable, accounting; statistical; entered &c. *v.*

812. Price. — N. PRICE, amount, cost, expense, prime cost, charge, figure, demand, damage [*colloq.*], fare, hire; wages &c. (*remuneration*) 973.

DUES, duty, toll, tax, impost, tariff, cess, sess [*obs.*], tallage *or* tailage [*Old Eng. law*], levy; *abkari* [*India*], capitation, capitation tax, poll tax; doomage [*U. S.*], *likin* [*Chinese*], gabel *or* gabelle, salt tax; gavel [*Old Eng. law*], octroi [*F.*], custom, excise, assessment, taxation, benevolence [*hist.*], forced loan; tenths [*hist.*], tithe, exactment, ransom, salvage, towage; brokerage, wharfage, freightage.

WORTH, rate, value, par value, valuation, appraisement, money's worth; penny &c. -worth; price current, market price, quotation, current quotation; what it will fetch &c. *v.*

bill &c. (*account*) 811; shot, scot, scot and lot.

V. PRICE; bear -, set -, fix- a price; appraise, assess, doom [*U. S.*], charge, demand, ask, require, exact, run up; distrain; run up a bill &c. (*debt*) 806; have one's price; liquidate.

AMOUNT TO, come to, mount up to; stand one in [*colloq.*], put one back [*slang*].

FETCH, sell for, cost, bring in, yield, afford.

Adj. PRICED &c. *v.*; to the tune of, *ad valorem* [*L.*]; dutiable, taxable, assessable; mercenary, venal.

₊ no penny no paternoster; *point d'argent point de Suisse;* no longer pipe no longer dance; no song no supper.

813. Discount. — N. DISCOUNT, abatement, concession, reduction, depreciation, allowance, qualification, set-off, drawback, poundage, agio, percentage; rebate, rebatement, backwardization [*Eng.*], backwardation [*Eng.*], contango [*Eng. Stock Exchange*]; salvage; tare [*com.*], tare and tret.

V. DISCOUNT, bate, rebate, abate, deduct, strike off, mark down, reduce, take off, allow, give, make allowance; depreciate.

Adj. DISCOUNTING &c. *v.*; concessional; marked down; depreciative.

Adv. AT A DISCOUNT, at a bargain, below par.

---

814. Dearness. — N. DEARNESS &c. *adj.*; high -, famine -, fancy- price; overcharge; extravagance; exorbitance, extortion; heavy pull upon the purse.

V. BE DEAR &c. *adj.*; cost much, cost a pretty penny [*colloq.*]; rise in price, look up.

OVERCHARGE, bleed [*colloq.*], skin [*slang*], fleece, extort.

pay too much, pay through the nose [*colloq.*], pay too dear for one's whistle [*colloq.*].

Adj. DEAR; high, - priced; of great price, expensive, costly, precious, dear bought; unreasonable, extravagant, exorbitant, extortionate.

at a premium; not to be had, - for love or money; beyond price, above price; priceless, of priceless value.

Adv. DEAR, dearly; at great cost, at heavy cost, at a high price, *à grands frais* [*F.*].

₊ prices looking up; *le jeu ne vaut pas la chandelle; le coût en ôte le goût; vel prece vel pretio;* "Since you are dear-bought, I will love you dear" [*Merchant of Venice*]; "But bless you, it's dear — it's dear!" [Browning].

815. Cheapness. — N. CHEAPNESS, low price; depreciation; bargain, *bon marché* [*F.*]; good penny &c. -worth; drug in the market.

[ABSENCE OF CHARGE] gratuity; free -quarters, - seats, -admission; free lunch; run of one's teeth [*slang*]; nominal price, peppercorn rent; labor of love.

DEADHEAD [*colloq.*], dead beat [*slang*], beat [*slang*], sponger.

V. BE CHEAP &c. *adj.*; cost little; come down -, fall- in price; be marked down.

buy for a mere nothing, buy at a bargain, buy dirt-cheap, buy for an old song; have one's money's worth; beat down, cheapen.

Adj. CHEAP; low, - priced; moderate, reasonable; inexpensive *or* unexpensive; well -, worth the money; *magnifique et pas cher* [*F.*]; good -, cheap- at the price; dirt-cheap, dog-cheap; cheap as dirt, cheap and nasty [*colloq.*]; peppercorn; catchpenny.

REDUCED, half-price, depreciated, shopworn, marked down, unsalable.

GRATUITOUS, gratis, free, for nothing;

costless, expenseless; without charge, not charged, untaxed; scot-free, shot-free, rent-free; free of -cost, - expense; complimentary, honorary, unbought, unpaid for.

Adv. AT A BARGAIN, for a mere song; at cost price, at prime cost, at a reduction; on the cheap [*colloq., Eng.*]; *bon marché* or *à bon marché* [*F.*].

*** "ill ware is never cheap" [Herbert]; "cheapest is the dearest" [*proverb*].

816. Liberality. — N. LIBERALITY, generosity, munificence; bounty, bounteousness, bountifulness; hospitableness, hospitality; charity &c. (*beneficence*) 906; open -, free- hand; open -, large-, free- heart; enough and to spare.

CHEERFUL GIVER, free giver, patron; benefactor &c. 912.

V. BE LIBERAL &c. *adj.*; spend -, bleed- freely; shower down upon; open one's purse strings &c. (*disburse*) 809; spare no expense, give *carte blanche* [*F.*]; give with both hands; give the coat off one's back; keep open house, fill one's house with guests.

Adj. LIBERAL, free, generous; charitable &c. (*beneficent*) 906; hospitable; bountiful, bounteous, ample, handsome; unsparing, ungrudging; unselfish; open-, free-; full- handed; open-, large-, free-hearted; munificent, princely.

Adv. LIBERALLY &c. *adj.*; ungrudgingly; with open hands, with both hands.

*** "handsome is that handsome does" [Goldsmith]; "good measure, pressed down, and shaken together, and running over" [*Bible*]; "it snewed in his hous of mete and drynke" [Chaucer]; " 'Tis Heaven alone that is given away, 'Tis only God may be had for the asking" [Lowell].

818. Prodigality. — N. PRODIGALITY, prodigence [*obs.*], wastefulness, wastry or wastrie [*Scot.*], unthriftiness, waste; profusion, profuseness; extravagance; squandering &c. *v.*; lavishness.

pound-foolishness, pound-folly, penny wisdom.

PRODIGAL, spendthrift, wastethrift, wastrel [*dial. Eng.*], waster, high roller [*slang, U. S.*], squanderer, spender, spendall, scattergood [*archaic*]; locust; Prodigal Son; Timon of Athens.

V. BE PRODIGAL &c. *adj.*; squander, lavish, sow broadcast; blow in [*slang*]; pay through the nose &c. (*dear*) 814; spill, waste, dissipate, exhaust, drain, eat out of house and home, overdraw, outrun the constable; run out, run through; misspend; throw good money after bad, throw the helve after the

817. Economy. — N. ECONOMY, frugality; thrift, thriftiness; care, husbandry, good housewifery, savingness, retrenchment.

SAVINGS; prevention of waste, save-all; parsimony &c. 819.

V. BE ECONOMICAL &c. *adj.*; practice economy, economize, save; retrench, cut down expenses; cut one's coat according to one's cloth, make both ends meet, keep within compass, meet one's expenses, keep one's head above water, pay one's way; husband &c. (*lay by*) 636; save -, invest- money; put out to interest; provide -, save- -for, - against- a rainy day; feather one's nest; look after the main chance [*colloq.*].

Adj. ECONOMICAL, frugal, careful, thrifty, saving, chary, spare, sparing; parsimonious &c. 819; sufficient; plain.

Adv. SPARINGLY &c. *adj.*; *ne quid nimis* [*L.*].

*** *adde parvum parvo magnus acervus erit; magnum est vectigal parsimonia* [Cicero]; "though on pleasure she was bent, She had a frugal mind" [Cowper]; "Gars auld claes look amaist as weel's the new" [Burns].

819. Parsimony. — N. PARSIMONY, parcity [*obs.*]; parsimoniousness, stinginess &c. *adj.*; stint; illiberality, avarice, tenacity, avidity, rapacity, extortion, malversation, venality, cupidity; lack of prodigality &c. 818; selfishness &c. 943; *auri sacra fames* [*L.*]; cheeseparings and candle ends.

MISER, niggard, churl, screw, skinflint, skin [*slang*], codger [*dial. Eng.*], money-grub [*slang*], muckworm, scrimp [*colloq.*], pinchgut [*obs. or vulgar*], lickpenny, hunks [*colloq.*], curmudgeon, harpy, extortioner, usurer, Hessian[*U.S.*]; pinchfist, pinchpenny [*obs*].

Harpagon, Euclio, Silas Marner, Daniel Dancer.

V. BE PARSIMONIOUS &c. *adj.*; grudge, begrudge, stint, pinch, gripe, screw, dole out, hold back, withhold, starve, fam-

hatchet; burn the candle at both ends; make ducks and drakes of one's money; fool –, potter –, muddle –, fritter –, throw- away one's money; squander one's substance in riotous living; spend money like water; pour water into a sieve, kill the goose that lays the golden eggs; *manger son blé en herbe* [*F.*].

Adj. PRODIGAL, profuse, thriftless, unthrifty, improvident, wasteful, losel, extravagant, lavish, dissipated, over-liberal; full-handed &c. (*liberal*) 816; overpaid.

penny-wise and pound-foolish.

Adv. with an unsparing hand; money burning one's pocket.

Int. keep the change! hang expense!

⁂ amor nummi; facile largiri de alieno; wie gewonnen so zerronnen; les fous font les festins et les sages les mangent; "spendthrift alike of money and of wit" [Cowper]; "squandering wealth was his peculiar art" [Dryden]; "How pleasant it is to have money!" [Clough].

ish, live upon nothing, skin a flint [*colloq.*], pinch a sixpence till it squeaks.

drive a bargain, cheapen, beat down; stop one hole in a sieve; have an itching palm, grasp, grab.

Adj. PARSIMONIOUS, penurious, stingy, miserly, mean, shabby, peddling, penny wise, near, near as the bark on a tree, niggardly, close; close-handed, close-fisted, fast-handed [*obs.*], hard-fisted, straithanded [*obs.*], tight-fisted; tight [*colloq.*], sparing; chary; grudging, griping &c. *v.*; illiberal, ungenerous, churlish, hidebound, sordid, mercenary, venal, covetous, usurious, avaricious; greedy, extortionate, rapacious; underpaid.

Adv. with a sparing hand.

⁂ desunt inopiæ multa avaritiæ omnia [Syrus]; "hoards after hoards his rising raptures fill" [Goldsmith]; "the unsunn'd heaps of miser's treasures" [Milton]; "a crusty old fellow, as close as a vise" [Hawthorne]; "all these men have their price" [Walpole].

CLASS VI

WORDS RELATING TO THE SENTIENT AND MORAL POWERS

SECTION I. AFFECTIONS IN GENERAL

820. Affections. — N. CHARACTER, qualities, disposition, affections, nature, spirit, tone; temper, temperament; diathesis, idiosyncrasy; cast –, habit –, frame- of -mind, – soul; predilection, turn; natural –, turn of mind; bent, bias, predisposition, proneness, proclivity, propensity, propenseness, propension, propendency [*obs.*]; vein, humor, mood, grain, mettle, backbone; sympathy &c. (*love*) 897.

SOUL, heart, breast, bosom, inner man; heart's -core, – strings, – blood; heart of hearts, *penetralia mentis* [*L.*]; secret and inmost recesses of the heart, cockles of one's heart; inmost- heart, – soul.

PASSION, pervading spirit; ruling –, master- passion; *furore* [*It.*], furor; fullness of the heart, heyday of the blood, flesh and blood, flow of soul.

ENERGY, fervor, fire, verve, force.

V. have *or* possess character &c. *n.;* be of a character &c. *n.;* be affected &c. *adj.;* breathe energy &c. *n.*

Adj. CHARACTERIZED, affected, formed, molded *or* moulded, cast; attemperate, attempered, tempered; framed.

PRONE, predisposed, disposed, inclined; having a bias &c. *n.;* tinctured –, imbued –, penetrated –, eaten up- with.

INBORN, inbred, ingrained; deep-rooted, ineffaceable, inveterate; congenital, dyed in the wool, implanted by nature, inherent, in the grain.

Adv. in one's heart &c. *n.;* at heart; heart and soul &c. 821; in the vein, in the mood.

*** the ruling passion strong in death; "the Divinity that stirs within us" [Addison]; "that dread apocalypse of soul" [E. B. Browning]; "how paint to the sensual eye what passes in the holy-of-holies of man's soul?" [Carlyle]; "build thee more stately mansions, O my soul" [Holmes]; "character is an historical fruit, and the result of a man's biography" [Amiel]; "One master-passion in the breast. Like Aaron's serpent, swallows all the rest" [Pope].

821. Feeling. — N. FEELING; suffering &c. *v.;* endurance, tolerance, sufferance, experience, response; sympathy &c. (*love*) 897; impression, inspiration, affection, sensation, emotion, pathos, deep sense.

WARMTH, glow, unction, gusto, vehemence, fervor, fervency; heartiness, cordiality; earnestness, eagerness; *empressement* [*F.*], gush [*colloq.*], ardor, zeal, passion, enthusiasm, verve, *furore* [*It.*], furor, fanaticism; excitation of feeling &c. 824; fullness of the heart &c. (*disposition*) 820; passion &c. (*state of excitability*) 825; ecstasy &c. (*pleasure*) 827.

STATE OF EXCITEMENT; blush, suffusion, flush; hectic, hectic fever, hectic flush; tingling, thrill, turn, shock; agitation &c. (*irregular motion*) 315; quiver, heaving, flutter, flurry, fluster, twitter, tremor; throb, throbbing; pulsation, palpitation, panting; trepidation, perturbation, ruffle, hurry of spirits, pother, stew [*colloq.*], ferment.

V. FEEL; receive an impression &c. *n.;* be impressed with &c. *adj.;* entertain –, harbor –, cherish- -feeling &c. *n.*

RESPOND; catch the -flame, – infection; enter into the spirit of.

BEAR, suffer, support, sustain, endure, thole [*obs. or dial.*], aby *or* abye; brook;

351

abide &c. (*be composed*) 826; experience &c. (*meet with*) 151; taste, prove; labor –, smart- under; bear the brunt of, brave, stand.

BE AGITATED, be excited &c. 824; swell, glow, warm, flush, blush, crimson, change color, mantle; darken, whiten, pale; turn -color, – pale, – red, – black in the face; tingle, thrill, heave, pant, throb, palpitate, go pitapat, tremble, quiver, flutter, twitter; shake &c. 315; blench, stagger, reel; look -blue, – black; wince, draw a deep breath.

impress &c. (*excite the feelings*) 824.

Adj. FEELING &c. *v.*; sentient; sensuous, sensorial, sensory; emotive, emotional; of *or* with feeling &c. *n.*

LIVELY, quick, smart, strong, sharp, acute, cutting, piercing, incisive; keen, – as a razor; trenchant, pungent, racy, piquant, poignant, caustic.

IMPRESSIVE, deep, profound, indelible; deep-felt, homefelt, heart-felt; swelling, soul-stirring, heart-expanding, electric, thrilling, rapturous, ecstatic; pervading, penetrating, absorbing.

EARNEST, wistful, eager, breathless; fervent, fervid, gushing [*colloq.*], warm, passionate, warm-hearted, hearty, cordial, sincere, zealous, enthusiastic, glowing, ardent, burning, red-hot, fiery, flaming; boiling, – over.

RABID, raving, feverish, fanatical, hysterical; impetuous &c. (*excitable*) 825; overmastering.

IMPRESSED –, moved –, touched –, affected –, penetrated –, seized –, imbued &c. 820- with; devoured by; wrought up &c. (*excited*) 824; struck all of a heap [*colloq.*]; rapt; in a quiver &c. *n.*; enraptured &c. 829.

the heart -big, – full, – swelling, – beating, – pulsating, – throbbing, – thumping, – beating high, – melting, – overflowing, -bursting, – breaking.

Adv. HEARTILY, heart and soul, from the bottom of cne's heart, *ab imo pectore* L.]; *de profundis* [*L.*]; at heart, *con amore* [*It.*], devoutly, over head and ears.

⁂ "We should count time by heart-throbs" [Bailey]; "give me that man That is not passion's slave, and I will wear him In my heart's core" [*Hamlet*].

822. Sensibility. — N. SENSIBILITY, sensibleness, sensitiveness; moral sensibility; impressibility, affectibility; susceptibleness, susceptibility, susceptivity; mobility; vivacity, vivaciousness; tenderness, softness; sentimentality, sentimentalisn.

excitability &c. 825; fastidiousness &c. 868; physical sensibility &c. 375; sensitive plant.

SORE POINT, sore place; quick, raw; where the shoe pinches.

V. BE SENSIBLE &c. *adj.*; have a tender, – warm, – sensitive- heart; be all heart.

take to heart, treasure up in the heart; shrink, wince, blench, quiver.

"die of a rose in aromatic pain" [Pope]; touch to the quick; touch –, flick one- on the raw.

Adj. SENSIBLE, sensitive; impressible, impressionable; susceptive, susceptible; alive to, impassionable, gushing [*colloq.*]; warm-hearted, tender-hearted, softhearted; tender, soft, maudlin, sentimental, romantic; enthusiastic, impassioned, highflying, spirited, mettle-

823. Insensibility. — N. INSENSIBILITY, insensibleness; want of sensibility &c. 823; moral insensibility; inertness, inertia, *vis inertiæ* [*L.*]; impassibility, impassibleness; inappetency, apathy, phlegm, dullness, hebetude, supineness, insusceptibility, unimpressibility, lukewarmness.

COLDNESS; cold -fit, – blood, – heart; coolness; frigidity, *sang-froid* [*F.*], stoicism, imperturbation &c. (*inexcitability*) 826; nonchalance, unconcern, dry eyes; insouciance &c. (*indifference*) 866; recklessness &c. 863; callousness, callosity, obtundity, brutification; heart of stone, blood and iron, stock and stone, marble, deadness.

neutrality; quietism, vegetation.

TORPOR, torpidity; obstupefaction [*obs.*], lethargy, coma, trance; sleep &c. 683; inanimation [*rare*], suspended animation; stupor, stupefaction; paralysis, palsy; numbness &c. (*physical insensibility*) 376; analgesia.

stoic, Indian, man of iron, pococurante, pococurantist; the Fat Boy in Pickwick.

some, vivacious, lively, expressive, mobile, tremblingly alive; excitable &c. 825; oversensitive, without skin, thin-skinned; fastidious &c. 868.

Adv. SENSIBLY &c. *adj.;* to the quick, on the raw, to the inmost core.

⁎⁎ mens æqua in arduis; "let the galled jade wince" [*Hamlet*]; "the bravest are the tenderest" [Taylor]; "If she could weep, they said, She could love, they said" [Dunsany].

TRIFLER, dabbler, dilettante, sciolist &c. 493.

V. BE INSENSIBLE &c. *adj.;* have a rhinoceros hide; show insensibility &c. *n.;* not mind, not care, not be affected by; have no desire for &c. 866; have –, feel –, take– no interest in; *nil admirari* [*L.*]; not care a straw &c. (*unimportance*) 643 for; disregard &c. (*neglect*) 460; set at naught &c. (*make light of*) 483; turn a deaf ear to &c. (*inattention*) 458; vegetate.

RENDER INSENSIBLE, render callous; blunt, obtund, numb, benumb, paralyze, chloroform, deaden, hebetate, stun, stupefy; brutify, brutalize.

INURE; harden, harden the heart; steel, caseharden, sear.

Adj. INSENSIBLE, unconscious; impassive, impassible; blind to, deaf to, dead to; obtundent, insusceptible *or* unsusceptible, unimpressionable, unimpressible; passionless, spiritless, heartless, soulless, unfeeling; unmoral.

APATHETIC, unemotional, leucophlegmatic [*obs.*], phlegmatic; dull, frigid; cold cold-blooded, cold-hearted; cold as charity; flat, obtuse, inert, supine, sluggish, torpid, torpedinous [*rare*], torporific; sleepy &c. (*inactive*) 683; languid, half-hearted, tame; numb, numbed; comatose; anæsthetic &c. 376; stupefied, chloroformed, palsy-stricken.

INDIFFERENT, lukewarm, Laodicean, careless, mindless, regardless; inattentive &c. 458; neglectful &c. 460; disregarding.

UNCONCERNED, nonchalant, pococurante, insouciant, *sans souci* [*F.*]; unambitious &c. 866.

UNAFFECTED, unruffled, unimpressed, uninspired, unexcited, unmoved, unstirred, untouched, unshocked, unstruck; unblushing &c. (*shameless*) 885; unanimated; vegetative.

CALLOUS, thick-skinned, pachydermatous, impervious; hard, hardened; inured, casehardened; steeled –, proof- against; imperturbable &c. (*inexcitable*) 826; unfelt.

Adv. INSENSIBLY &c. *adj.;* *æquo animo* [*L.*], without being -moved, – touched, – impressed; in cold blood; with dry eyes, with withers unwrung.

Int. never mind! it is of no consequence &c (*unimportant*) 642; it cannot be helped! it is all the same!

⁎⁎ "But och! it hardens a' within, And petrifies the feelin'" [Burns]; "that repose Which stamps the caste of Vere de Vere" [Tennyson]; "if he is content with a vegetable love" [Gilbert].

824. Excitation. — N. EXCITATION OF FEELING; mental –, excitement; suscitation [*obs.*], suscitability [*obs.*], galvanism, high pressure, stimulation, piquancy, provocation, inspiration, calling forth, infection; animation, agitation, perturbation; subjugation, fascination, intoxication, enravishment, ravishment, entrancement; unction, impressiveness &c. *adj.*

trial of temper, *casus belli* [*L.*], irritation &c. (*anger*) 900; passion &c. (*state of excitability*) 825; thrill &c. (*feeling*) 821; repression of feeling &c. 826.

emotional appeal, melodrama; great moment, crisis; sensationalism, yellow journalism.

V. EXCITE, affect, touch, move, impress, strike, interest, animate, inspire, impassion, smite, infect; stir –, fire –, warm- the blood; set astir; awake, wake; awaken, waken; call forth; evoke, provoke; raise up, summon up, call up, wake up, blow up, get up, light up; raise; get up the steam, rouse, arouse, stir, fire, kindle, enkindle, illumine, illuminate, apply the torch, set on fire, inflame.

STIMULATE; exuscitate *or* exsuscitate [*both obs.*], suscitate [*obs.*]; inspirit; spirit up, stir up, work up; infuse life into, give new life to; bring –, introduce- new blood; quicken; sharpen, whet; work upon &c. (*incite*) 615; hurry on, give a fillip, fillip, put on one's mettle.

fan the -fire, – flame; blow the coals, stir the embers; fan, fan into a flame; foster, heat, warm, foment, raise to a fever heat; keep up, keep the pot boiling; revive, rekindle; rake up, rip up.

intoxicate, overwhelm, overpower, *bouleverser* [*F.*], upset, turn one's head; fascinate; enrapture &c. (*give pleasure*) 829.

PENETRATE, pierce; stir –, play on –, come home to- the feelings; touch -a string, – a chord, – the soul, – the heart; go to one's heart, go through one, open the wound, turn the knife in the wound; touch to the quick; possess –, pervade –, imbue –, penetrate –, imbrue [*obs.*] –, absorb –, affect –, disturb- the soul; rivet the attention; sink into the -mind, – heart; absorb; prey on the mind.

AGITATE, perturb, ruffle, fluster, flutter, flurry, shake, disturb, startle, shock, stagger; give one a -shock, – turn; strike all of a heap [*colloq.*], strike dumb, stun, astound, electrify, galvanize, petrify.

IRRITATE, sting; cut; cut to the -heart, – quick; try one's temper; fool to the top of one's bent, pique; infuriate, madden, make one's blood boil; lash into fury &c. (*wrath*) 900.

BE EXCITED &c. *adj.*; flash up, flare up; catch the infection; thrill &c. (*feel*) 821; mantle; work oneself up; seethe, boil, simmer, foam, fume, flame, rage, rave; run mad &c. (*passion*) 825; run amuck.

Adj. EXCITED &c. *v.*; wrought up, on the *qui vive*, astir, sparkling; in a -quiver &c. 821, – fever, – ferment, – blaze, – state of excitement; in hysterics; black in the face, overwrought; hot, red-hot, flushed, feverish; all of a -flutter, – twitter; all in a pucker [*colloq.*]; with quivering lips, with trembling lips, with twitching lips, with tears in one's eyes.

RAGING, flaming; boiling, – over; ebullient, seething; foaming, – at the mouth; fuming; stung to the quick; on one's high ropes; on one's high horse; carried away by passion, wild, raving, frantic, mad, amuck, distracted, beside oneself, out of one's wits, ready to burst, *bouleversé* [*F.*], demoniacal.

LOST, *éperdu* [*F.*], tempest-tossed; haggard; ready to sink.

EXCITING &c. *v.*; impressive, warm, glowing, fervid, swelling, imposing, spirit-stirring, thrilling; high-wrought; soul-stirring, soul-subduing; heart-stirring, heart-swelling, heart-thrilling; agonizing &c. (*painful*) 830; telling, sensational, melodramatic, hysterical; overpowering, overwhelming; more than flesh and blood can bear; yellow.

piquant &c. (*pungent*) 392; spicy, appetizing, stinging, provocative, *provoquant* [*F.*], tantalizing.

Adv. at a critical -moment, – period, – point; under a sudden strain; with heart-interest [*cant*]; with plenty of pep [*slang*], with a punch [*slang*]; till one is black in the face.

** the heart -beating high, – going pitapat, – leaping into one's mouth; the blood -being up, – boiling in one's veins; the eye -glistening, – "in a fine frenzy rolling" [*M. N. D.*].

"the Powers That stir men's spirits, waking or asleep, To thoughts like planets and to acts like flowers" [Masefield]; "I ha' harpit ye up to the throne o' God" [Kipling]; "I tried to force a note that was beyond its power, that is why the harp-string is broken" [Tagore]; "my senses swooned in ecstasy" [*ibid.*].

---

825. [EXCESS OF SENSITIVENESS.] **Excitability.** — N. EXCITABILITY, impetuosity, vehemence; boisterousness &c. *adj.*; turbulence; impatience, intolerance, non-endurance; irritability &c. (*irascibility*) 901; itching &c. (*desire*) 865; wincing; disquiet, disquietude; restlessness; fidgets, fidgetiness; agitation &c. (*irregular motion*) 315.

TREPIDATION, perturbation, ruffle, hurry, fuss, flurry, fluster, flutter; pother, stew [*colloq.*], ferment; whirl;

826. Inexcitability. — N. INEXCITABILITY, imperturbability, inirritability; even temper, tranquil mind, dispassion; toleration, tolerance, patience.

PASSIVENESS &c. (*physical inertness*) 172; hebetude, hebetation; impassibility &c. (*insensibility*) 823; stupefaction.

CALMNESS &c. *adj.*; composure, placidity, indisturbance, imperturbation, *sang-froid* [*F.*], coolness, tranquillity, serenity; quiet, quietude; peace of mind, mental calmness.

buck fever [*colloq.*]; **stage fright**; hurry-scurry *or* hurry-skurry; thrill &c. (*feeling*) 821; state –, fever- of excitement; transport.

PASSION, excitement, flush, heat; fever, fever-heat; fire, flame, fume, blood boiling; tumult; effervescence, ebullition; boiling, – over; whiff, gust, storm, tempest; scene, breaking out, burst, fit, paroxysm, explosion, outbreak, outburst; agony.

FURY; violence &c. 173; fierceness &c. *adj.*; rage, furor, *furore* [*It.*], desperation, madness, distraction, raving, delirium; frenzy *or* phrensy, hysterics; intoxication; tearing –, raging- passion; towering rage; anger &c. 900.

FIXED IDEA, *l'idée fixe* [*F.*], monomania; fascination, infatuation, fanaticism; Quixotism, Quixotry; *tête montée* [*F.*].

V. BE IMPATIENT &c. *adj.*; not be able to bear &c. 826; bear ill, wince, chafe, champ the bit; be in a stew [*colloq.*] &c. *n.*; be out of all patience, fidget, fuss, not have a wink of sleep; toss, – on one's pillow.

FUME, rage, foam; lose one's temper &c. 900; break out, burst out, fly out; go –, fly- -off, – off at a tangent; explode; flare up, flame up, fire up, burst into a flame, take fire, fire, burn; stew [*colloq.*]; boil, – over; rave, rant, tear; go –, run- -wild, – mad; go into hysterics; run riot, run amuck; *battre la campagne* [*F.*], *faire le diable à quatre* [*F.*]; play the deuce [*slang*]; raise -Cain, – the mischief, – the devil [*all slang*].

Adj. EXCITABLE, easily excited, in an excitable state; startlish, mettlesome, high-mettled, skittish; high-strung; irritable &c. (*irascible*) 901; impatient, intolerant; moody, maggoty-headed.

FEVERISH, febrile, hysterical; delirious, mad.

UNQUIET, mercurial, electric, galvanic, hasty, hurried, restless, fidgety, fussy; chafing &c. *v.*

VEHEMENT, demonstrative, violent, wild, furious, fierce, fiery, hot-headed, madcap.

OVERZEALOUS, enthusiastic, impassioned, fanatical; rabid &c. (*eager*) 865.

RAMPANT, clamorous, uproarious, turbulent, tempestuous, tumultuary, boisterous.

IMPULSIVE, impetuous, passionate,

EQUANIMITY, poise, staidness &c. *adj.*; gravity, sobriety, quietism, Quakerism; philosophy, stoicism, command of temper; self-possession, self-control, self-command, self-restraint; presence of mind.

RESIGNATION, submission &c. 725; sufferance, supportance, endurance, longsufferance, forbearance, longanimity, fortitude; patience of Job, "patience on a monument" [*Twelfth Night*], "patience sovereign o'er transmuted ill" [Johnson]; moderation; repression –, subjugation- of feeling; restraint &c. 751; tranquillization &c.(*moderation*)174.

V. BE COMPOSED &c. *adj.*

laisser faire [*F.*], *laisser aller* [*F.*]; take things -easily, – as they come; take it easy, rub on [*colloq.*], live and let live; take -easily, – coolly, – in good part; *æquam servare mentem* [*L.*].

ENDURE; bear, – well, – the brunt; go through, support, brave, disregard; tolerate, suffer, stand, bide; abide, aby *or* abye; bear with, put up with, take up with, abide with; acquiesce; submit &c. (*yield*) 725; submit with a good grace; resign –, reconcile- oneself to; brook, digest, eat, swallow, pocket, stomach; carry on, carry through; make light of, make the best of, make "a virtue of necessity" [Chaucer]; put a good face on, keep one's countenance; check &c. 751- oneself.

COMPOSE, appease &c. (*moderate*) 174; propitiate; repress &c. (*restrain*) 751; render insensible &c. 823; overcome –, allay –, repress- one's excitability &c. 825; master one's feelings; make -oneself, – one's mind- easy; set one's mind at -ease, – rest; calm –, cool- down; gentle, tame, thaw, grow cool.

BE BORNE, be endured, be swallowed; go down.

Adj. INEXCITABLE, imperturbable; unsusceptible &c. (*insensible*) 823; dispassionate, unpassionate, cold-blooded, unirritable, inirritable; enduring &c. *v.*; stoical, Platonic, philosophic, staid, stayed [*obs.*], sober, – minded; grave; sober –, grave- as a judge; sedate, demure, cool-headed, level-headed.

EASY-GOING, peaceful, placid, calm; quiet, – as a mouse; tranquil, serene; cool, – as -a cucumber, – custard [*both colloq.*]; undemonstrative.

COMPOSED, collected; temperate &c.

uncontrolled, uncontrollable, ungovernable, irrepressible, stanchless *or* staunchless, inextinguishable, burning, simmering, volcanic, ready to burst forth.

excited, exciting &c. 824.

Adv. in confusion, pell-mell; in trepidation &c. *n.*

Int. pish! pshaw! horrors!

⁎⁎ *noli me tangere;* "filled with fury, rapt, inspir'd" [Collins]; *maggiore frètta minore átto;* "For joy he was as a song" [Dunsany]; "on with the dance! let joy be unconfined" [Byron]; "whispering with white lips, 'The foe! They come! They come!' " [*ibid.*]; "quiet to quick bosoms is a hell" [*ibid.*]; "all is not bold that titters" [*Cynic's Calendar*].

(*moderate*) 174; unexcited, unstirred, unruffled, undisturbed, unperturbed, unimpassioned.

MEEK, tolerant; patient, – as Job; unoffended; unresisting; submissive &c. 725; tame; content, resigned, chastened, subdued, lamblike; gentle, – as a lamb; *suaviter in modo* [*L.*]; mild, – as mother's milk; soft as peppermint; armed with patience, bearing with, clement, longsuffering, forbearant, longanimous.

Adv. "like patience on a monument smiling at grief" [*Twelfth Night*]; *æquo animo* [*L.*], in cold blood &c. 823; more in sorrow than in anger.

Int. patience! and shuffle the cards.

⁎⁎ it will all be the same one hundred years hence; this too will pass; "adversity's sweet milk, philosophy" [*Romeo and Juliet*]; *mens æqua in arduis; philosophia stemma non inspicit* [Seneca];¹ *quo me cumque rapit tempestas deferor hospes* [Horace]; "they also serve who only stand and wait" [Milton]; "Patience, thou young and rose-lipp'd cherubin" [*Othello*]; "the mildest curate going" [Gilbert].

Section II. PERSONAL AFFECTIONS¹

1. Passive Affections

827. Pleasure. — N. PLEASURE, gratification, enjoyment, fruition, delectation, oblectation [*rare*]; relish, zest; gusto &c. (*physical pleasure*) 377; satisfaction &c. (*content*) 831; complacency.

WELL-BEING; good &c. 618; snugness, comfort, ease; cushion &c. 215; *sans souci* [*F.*], mind at ease.

JOY, gladness, delight, glee, cheer, sunshine; cheerfulness &c. 836.

TREAT, refreshment; amusement &c. 840; luxury &c. 377.

HAPPINESS, felicity, bliss; beatitude, beatification; enchantment, transport, rapture, ravishment, ecstasy; *summum bonum* [*L.*]; paradise, elysium &c. (*heaven*) 981; third –, seventh- heaven; unalloyed happiness &c.; hedonics, hedonism.

mens sana in corpore sano [Juvenal]. honeymoon; palmy –, halcyon- days; golden -age, – time; Eden, Paradise; Dixie, Dixie land *or* Dixie's land; *Saturnia regna* [*L.*], Arcadia, Cockaigne, happy valley, Agapemone.

V. BE PLEASED &c. 829; oblectate [*rare*]; feel –, experience- pleasure &c. *n.;* joy; enjoy –, hug- oneself; be in clover [*colloq.*] &c. 377, be in elysium &c. 981; tread on enchanted ground; fall –, go- into raptures.

828. Pain. — N. PAIN, mental suffering, dolor, suffering, sufferance [*rare*], ache; smart &c. (*physical pain*) 378; passion.

DISPLEASURE, dissatisfaction, discomfort, discomposure, disquiet; *malaise* [*F.*], inquietude, uneasiness, vexation of spirit; taking [*colloq.*]; discontent &c. 832.

DEJECTION &c. 837; weariness &c. 841; anhedonia.

ANNOYANCE, irritation, worry, infliction, visitation; plague, bore; bother, botheration [*colloq.*], stew [*colloq.*], vexation, mortification, chagrin, *esclandre* [*F.*]; *mauvais quart d'heure* [*F.*].

CARE, anxiety, solicitude, trouble, trial, ordeal, fiery ordeal, shock, blow, cark [*archaic*], dole [*archaic*], fret, burden, load.

GRIEF, sorrow, distress, affliction, woe, bitterness, heartache; carking cares [*archaic*]; concern; heavy –, aching –, bleeding –, broken- heart; heavy affliction, gnawing grief.

MISERY, unhappiness, infelicity, tribulation, wretchedness, desolation; despair &c. 859; extremity, prostration, depth of misery; slough of despond &c. (*adversity*) 735; peck –, sea- of troubles; "the thousand natural shocks that

---

¹ Or those which concern one's own state of feeling.

feel at home, breathe freely, bask in the sunshine.

ENJOY, like, relish; be pleased with &c. 829; receive –, derive- pleasure &c. *n.*- from; take pleasure &c. *n.*- in; delight in, rejoice in, indulge in, luxuriate in; gloat over &c. (*physical pleasure*) 377; love &c. 897; take to, take a fancy to [*both colloq.*]; have a liking for; enter into the spirit of; take in good part; treat oneself to, solace oneself with.

Adj. PLEASED &c. 829; not sorry; glad, gladsome; pleased as Punch; pleased as a child with a new toy.

HAPPY, blest, blessed, blissful, beatified; happy as -a clam at high water [*U. S.*], – a king, – the day is long; thrice happy, *ter quaterque beatus* [*L.*]; enjoying &c. *v.*; joyful &c. (*in spirits*) 836; hedonic.

in a blissful state, in paradise &c. 981, in raptures, in ecstasies, in a transport of delight.

COMFORTABLE &c. (*physical pleasure*) 377; at ease; in clover [*colloq.*]; content &c. 831; *sans souci* [*F.*].

OVERJOYED, entranced, enchanted; raptured, enraptured, enravished, ravished, transported; fascinated, captivated.

with a joyful face, with sparkling eyes.

PLEASING &c. 829; ecstatic, beatific *or* beatifical; painless, unalloyed, without alloy, cloudless.

Adv. HAPPILY &c. *adj.*; with pleasure &c. (*willingly*) 602; with glee &c. *n.*

⁎⁎* one's heart leaping with joy.

"a wilderness of sweets" [*P. L.*]; "I wish you all the joy that you can wish" [*M. of V.*]; *jour de ma vie;* "joy ruled the day and love the night" [Dryden]; "joys season'd high and tasting strong of guilt" [Young]; "oh happiness, our being's end and aim!" [Pope]; "there is a pleasure that is born of pain" [O. Meredith]; "throned on highest bliss" [*P. L.*]; *vedi Napoli e poi muori; zwischen Freud und Leid ist die Brücke nicht weit.*

flesh is heir to" [*Hamlet*] &c. (*evil*) 616; miseries of human life; the iron entering the soul; "unkindest cut of all" [*Julius Cæsar*].

NIGHTMARE, ephialtes, incubus.

ANGUISH, pang, agony, torture, torment; crucifixion, martyrdom, rack; purgatory &c. (*hell*) 982; hell upon earth; iron age, reign of terror.

SUFFERER, victim, prey, martyr, object of compassion, wretch, shorn lamb.

V. SUFFER, ail; feel –, suffer –, experience –, undergo –, bear –, endure- pain &c. *n.*, smart, ache &c. (*physical pain*) 378; bleed; be the victim of.

labor under afflictions; bear –, stagger under –, take up- the cross; quaff the bitter cup, have a bad time of it; fall on evil days &c. (*adversity*) 735; go hard with, come to grief, fall a sacrifice to, drain the cup of misery to the dregs, "sup full of horrors" [*Macbeth*].

FRET, chafe, sit on thorns, be on pins and needles, wince, worry oneself, be in a taking [*colloq.*], fret and fume; take on [*colloq.*], take to heart; cark [*archaic*].

GRIEVE; mourn &c. (*lament*) 839; yearn, repine, pine, droop, languish, sink; give way; despair &c. 859; heartscald [*dial. Eng.*]; break one's heart; weigh upon the heart &c. (*inflict pain*) 830.

Adj. PAINED, afflicted; in –, in a state of –, full of- pain &c. *n.*; suffering &c. *v.*; worried, displeased &c. 830; aching, griped, sore &c. (*physical pain*) 378; on the rack, in limbo; between hawk and buzzard.

UNEASY, uncomfortable, ill at ease; in a taking, in a way [*both colloq.*]; disturbed; discontented &c. 832; out of humor &c. 901*a*; weary &c. 841.

UNFORTUNATE &c. (*hapless*) 735; to be pitied, doomed, devoted, accursed, undone, lost, stranded; fey [*obs.*]; victimized, a prey to, ill-used.

UNHAPPY, infelicitous, poor, wretched, miserable, woe-begone; cheerless &c. (*dejected*) 837; careworn; heavy laden, stricken, crushed.

concerned, sorry; sorrowing, sorrowful; cut up [*colloq.*], chagrined, horrified, horror-stricken; in –, plunged in –, a prey to- grief &c. *n.*; in tears &c. (*lamenting*) 839; steeped to the lips in misery; heartstricken, heartbroken, heart-scalded [*dial. Eng.*]; broken-hearted; in despair &c. 859.

⁎⁎* *hæret lateri lethalis arundo* [Vergil]; one's heart bleeding; "the iron entered into his soul" [*Book of Common Prayer*]; "down, thou climbing sorrow" [*Lear*]; "mirth cannot move a soul in agony" [*Love's Labor's Lost*]; *nessun maggior dolore che ricordarsi del tempo felice nella miseria;* "sorrow's crown of sorrow is remembering happier things" [Tennyson]; "the Niobe of Nations" [Byron].

829. [CAPABILITY OF GIVING PLEAS-
URE.] **Pleasurableness. — N.** PLEAS-
URABLENESS, pleasantness, agreeable-
ness &c. *adj.;* pleasure giving, jucundity
[*rare*], jocundity, delectability; amusement &c. 840; goodness &c. 648; manna
in the wilderness, land flowing with
milk and honey, "the shadow of a great
rock in a weary land" [*Bible*]; flowery
beds of ease; fair weather.

treat; regale &c. (*physical pleasure*)
377; sweets &c. (*sugar*) 396; dainty,
bonne bouche [*F.*], titbit *or* tidbit; sweets,
sweetmeats, nuts, *sauce piquante* [*F.*],
salt, savor; a sight for sore eyes
[*colloq.*].

ATTRACTION &c. (*motive*) 615; attractiveness, attractability [*rare*], attract-
ableness; invitingness &c. *adj.;* charm,
fascination, captivation, enchantment,
witchery, seduction, winning ways,
amenity, amiability; winsomeness; loveliness &c. (*beauty*) 845; sunny side,
bright side.

V. DELIGHT, charm, becharm, imparadise; gladden &c. (*make cheerful*) 836;
win –, gladden –, rejoice –, warm the
cockles of- the heart; do one's heart
good; bless, beatify; take, captivate,
fascinate; enchant, entrance, enrapture,
transport, bewitch, ravish, enravish.

cause –, produce –, create –, give –,
afford –, procure –, offer –, present –,
yield- pleasure &c. 827.

PLEASE, satisfy, gratify, – desire &c.
865; slake, satiate, quench; indulge,
humor, flatter, tickle; tickle the palate
&c. (*savory*) 394; regale, refresh; enliven; treat; amuse &c. 840; take –,
tickle –, hit- one's fancy; meet one's
wishes.

ATTRACT, allure &c. (*move*) 615; stimulate &c. (*excite*) 824; interest.

MAKE THINGS PLEASANT, make everyone feel happy, popularize, gild the pill,
sweeten; smooth –, pour oil upon- the
troubled waters.

Adj. PLEASURABLE, causing pleasure
&c. *v.;* lætificant; pleasure-giving; pleasing, pleasant, amiable, agreeable, grateful, gratifying; lief *or* leef [*obs.*], acceptable; dear, beloved; welcome, – as the
roses in May; welcomed; favorite; to
one's taste, – mind, – liking; satisfactory &c. (*good*) 648.

REFRESHING; comfortable; cordial; genial; glad, gladsome; sweet, delectable,

830. [CAPABILITY OF GIVING PAIN.]
Painfulness. — N. PAINFULNESS &c.
adj.; trouble, care &c. (*pain*) 828; trial,
affliction, infliction; cross, blow, stroke,
burden, load, curse; bitter -pill, –
draft *or* draught, – cup; cup –, waters-
of bitterness.

ANNOYANCE, grievance, nuisance, vexation, mortification, sickener [*rare*],
worry, bore, bother, pother, hot water,
"sea of troubles" [*Hamlet*], hornet's
nest, plague, pest.

source of -irritation, – annoyance;
wound, sore subject, skeleton in the
closet; thorn in -the flesh, – one's side;
where the shoe pinches, gall and wormwood; fly in the ointment; worm at the
heart of the rose; crumpled rose-leaf;
pea in the shoe.

cancer, ulcer, sting, thorn; canker &c.
(*bane*) 663; scorpion &c. (*evildoer*) 913;
dagger &c. (*arms*) 727; scourge &c.
(*instrument of punishment*) 975; carking
care [*archaic*], canker worm of care.

mishap, misfortune &c. (*adversity*)
735; *désagrément* [*F.*], *esclandre* [*F.*], rub.

sorry sight, heavy news, provocation;
affront &c. 929; "head and front of
one's offending" [*Othello*].

INFESTATION, molestation; malignity
&c. (*malevolence*) 907.

V. PAIN, hurt, wound; cause –, occasion –, give –, bring –, induce –, produce
–, create –, inflict- pain &c. 828.

pinch, prick, gripe &c. (*physical
pain*) 378; pierce, lancinate, cut.

hurt –, wound –, grate upon –, jar
upon- the feelings; wring –, pierce –,
lacerate –, break –, rend- the heart;
make the heart bleed; tear –, rend- the
heartstrings; draw tears from the eyes;
add a nail to one's coffin.

SADDEN; make unhappy &c. 828;
plunge into sorrow, grieve, fash [*Scot.*],
afflict, distress; cut up [*colloq.*], cut to
the heart.

ANNOY, incommode, displease, discompose, trouble, disquiet; faze [*U. S.*],
feeze *or* feaze [*colloq., U. S. & dial. Eng.*],
disturb, cross, thwart, perplex, molest;
tease, tire, irk, vex, mortify, wherret
[*obs.*], worry, plague, bother, pester,
bore, pother, harass, harry, badger,
heckle [*Brit.*], bait, beset, infest, persecute, importune.

TORMENT, wring, harrow, torture;
bullyrag; put to the -rack, – question;

nice, dainty; delicate, delicious; dulcet; luscious &c. 396; palatable &c. 394.

LUXURIOUS, voluptuous; sensual &c. 377.

ATTRACTIVE &c. 615; inviting, prepossessing, engaging; winning, winsome; taking, fascinating, captivating, killing [colloq.]; seducing, seductive; heart-robbing; alluring, enticing; appetizing &c. (exciting) 824; cheering &c. 836; bewitching; enchanting, entrancing, enravishing.

DELIGHTFUL, charming, felicitous, exquisite; lovely &c. (beautiful) 845; ravishing, rapturous; heartfelt, thrilling, ecstatic, beatific or beatifical, seraphic; empyrean; paradisaic or paradisaical; elysian &c. (heavenly) 981.

PALMY, halcyon, Saturnian.

Adv. TO ONE'S DELIGHT, to one's heart's content, in utter satisfaction; at one's ease; in clover; in heaven, in paradise, in elysium; from a full heart.

*** *decies repetita placebit;* "charms strike the sight but merit wins the soul" [Pope]; "sweetness and light" [Swift]; "when you speak, sweet, I'd have you do it ever" [*Winter's Tale*].

break on the wheel, rack, scarify; cruciate [obs.], crucify; convulse, agonize; barb the dart; plant a - dagger in the breast, - thorn in one's side.

IRRITATE, provoke, sting, nettle, try the patience, pique, fret, roil, rile [colloq. & dial.], tweak the nose, chafe, gall; sting -, wound -, cut- to the quick; aggrieve, affront, enchafe [obs.], enrage, ruffle, sour the temper; give offense &c. (resentment) 900.

MALTREAT, bite, snap at, assail; smite &c. (punish) 972; bite the hand that feeds one.

REPEL, revolt; sicken, disgust, nauseate; disenchant, offend, shock, stink in the nostrils; go against -, turn- the stomach; make one sick, set the teeth on edge, go against the grain, grate on the ear; stick in one's -throat, - gizzard [colloq.]; rankle, gnaw, corrode, horrify, appal, freeze the blood; make the flesh creep, make the hair stand on end; make the blood -curdle, - run cold; make one shudder.

HAUNT, haunt the memory; weigh -, prey- on the -heart, - mind, - spirits; bring one's gray hairs with sorrow to the grave.

Adj. PAINFUL, causing pain, hurting &c. v.; hurtful &c. (bad) 649; dolorific or dolorifical, dolorous.

UNPLEASANT, unpleasing, displeasing, disagreeable, unpalatable, bitter, distasteful, unpleasing, uninviting, unwelcome, undesirable, undesired; obnoxious; unacceptable, unpopular, thankless.

UNTOWARD, unsatisfactory, unlucky, inauspicious, ill-starred, uncomfortable.

DISTRESSING; afflicting, afflictive; joyless, cheerless, comfortless, dismal, disheartening; depressing, depressive; dreary, melancholy, grievous, piteous, woeful, rueful, mournful; deplorable, pitiable, lamentable, sad, affecting, touching, pathetic.

IRRITATING, provoking, stinging, annoying, aggravating [colloq.], exasperating, mortifying, galling; unaccommodating, invidious, vexatious; troublesome, tiresome, irksome, wearisome; plaguing, plaguesome, plaguy [colloq.]; awkward.

IMPORTUNATE; teasing, pestering, bothering, harassing, worrying, tormenting, carking [archaic].

INSUFFERABLE, intolerable, insupportable, unbearable, unendurable; past bearing; not to be -borne, - endured; more than flesh and blood can bear; enough to -drive one mad, - provoke a saint, - make a parson swear [colloq.], - try the patience of Job.

SHOCKING, terrific, grim, appalling, crushing; dreadful, fearful, frightful; thrilling, tremendous, dire; heartbreaking, heart-rending, heart-wounding, heart-corroding, heart-sickening; harrowing, rending.

ODIOUS, hateful, execrable, repulsive, repellent, abhorrent; horrid, horrible, horrific, horrifying; offensive; nauseous, nauseating; disgusting, sickening, revolting; nasty; loathsome, loathful; fulsome; vile &c. (bad) 649; hideous &c. 846.

ACUTE, sharp, sore, severe, grave, hard, harsh, cruel, biting, caustic; cutting, corroding, consuming, racking, excruciating, searching, searing, grinding, grating, agonizing; envenomed; catheretic, pyrotic.

CUMBROUS, cumbersome, burdensome, onerous, oppressive.

DESOLATING, withering, tragical, disastrous, calamitous, ruinous.

Adv. PAINFULLY &c. *adj.;* with pain &c. 828; deuced *or* deucedly [*slang*]; under torture, in agony, out of the depths.

Int. woe's me! alas! that I had ever been born! *hinc illæ lacrimæ!* [Terence].

* *surgit amari aliquid;* the place being too hot to hold one; the iron entering into the soul; "he jests at scars that never felt a wound" [*Romeo and Juliet*]; "I must be cruel only to be kind" [*Hamlet*]; "what deep wounds ever closed without a scar?" [Byron]; "every despot must have one disloyal subject to keep him sane" [Shaw]; "Upon the bitter iron there is peace" [Masefield].

831. Content. — N. CONTENT, contentment, contentedness; complacency, satisfaction, entire satisfaction, ease, heart's ease, peace of mind; serenity &c. 826; cheerfulness &c. 836; ray of comfort; comfort &c. (*well-being*) 827.

PATIENCE, moderation, endurance; conciliation, reconciliation; resignation &c. (*patience*) 826; quietism.

waiter on Providence; quietist.

V. BE CONTENT &c. *adj.;* rest satisfied, rest and be thankful; take the good the gods provide, let well enough alone, feel oneself at home, hug oneself, lay the flattering unction to one's soul.

take up with, take in good part; assent &c. 488; be reconciled to, make one's peace with; get over it; take heart, take comfort; put up with &c. (*bear*) 826.

RENDER CONTENT &c. *adj.;* set at ease, comfort; set one's -heart, – mind- at -ease, – rest; speak peace; conciliate, reconcile, win over, propitiate, disarm, beguile; content, satisfy; gratify &c. 829.

BE TOLERATED &c. 826; go down, go down with [*colloq.*], do.

Adj. CONTENT, contented; satisfied &c. *v.;* at ease, at one's ease, at home; with the mind at ease, *sans souci* [*F.*], *sine curâ* [*L.*], easy-going, not particular; conciliatory; unrepining, of good comfort; resigned &c. (*patient*) 826; cheerful &c. 836.

SERENE &c. 826; unafflicted, unvexed, unmolested, unplagued; at rest; snug, comfortable; in one's element; not easily perturbed; imperturbable.

SATISFACTORY, adequate, commensurate, sufficient, ample, equal to; satisfying.

Adv. to one's heart's content; *à la bonne heure* [*F.*]; all for the best.

Int. amen &c. (*assent*) 488; very well!

360

832. Discontent. — N. DISCONTENT, discontentment; dissatisfaction; "the winter of our discontent" [*Henry VI*]; dissent &c. 489; querulousness &c. (*lamentation*) 839; hypercriticism.

DISAPPOINTMENT, mortification; cold comfort; regret &c. 833; repining, taking on [*colloq.*] &c. *v.;* inquietude, vexation of spirit, soreness; heartburning, heart-grief.

MALCONTENT, grumbler, growler, grouch [*slang*], croaker, *laudator temporis acti* [*L.*]; censurer, complainer, faultfinder, murmurer.

The Opposition; Bitter-Enders [*U. S. politics*], Die-Hards; cave of Adullam; indignation meeting.

V. BE DISCONTENTED &c. *adj.;* quarrel with one's bread and butter; repine; regret &c. 833; wish one to Jericho, wish one at the bottom of the Red Sea; take on [*colloq.*], take to heart; shrug the shoulders; make a wry face, pull a long face; knit one's brows; look blue, look black, look black as thunder, look blank, look glum.

GRUMBLE, take ill, take in bad part; fret, chafe, make a piece of work [*colloq.*], croak; lament &c. 839.

CAUSE DISCONTENT &c. *n.;* dissatisfy, disappoint, mortify, put out [*colloq.*], disconcert; cut up; dishearten.

Adj. DISCONTENTED; dissatisfied &c. *v.;* unsatisfied, ungratified; dissident; dissentient &c. 489; malcontent, exigent, exacting, hypercritical.

REPINING &c. *v.;* regretful &c. 833; down in the mouth &c. (*dejected*) 837.

GLUM, sulky; in high dudgeon, in a fume, in the sulks, in the dumps, in bad humor; sour, sour as a crab; sore as a crab [*colloq.*]; soured, sore; out of humor, out of temper.

DISAPPOINTING &c. *v.;* unsatisfactory.

Adv. FROM BAD TO WORSE, out of the

all the better! so much the better! well and good! it will do! that will do! it cannot be helped! done! content! i' faith! [*archaic*]; better and better! good! good for you! put it thar, pard! [*colloq.*].

*** nothing comes amiss.

"a heart with room for every joy" [Bailey]; *ich habe genossen das irdische Glück ich habe gelebt und geliebet* [Schiller]; "nor cast one longing, ling'ring look behind' [Gray]; "shut up in measureless content" [*Macbeth*]; "swee are the thoughts that savor of content" [R. Greene]; "their wants but few, their wishes all confined" [Goldsmith]; "man wants but little here below" [*Bible*]; "Little I ask; my wants are few; I only wish a house of stone, (A *very plain* brown stone will do,) That I may call my own [*Holmes*]; "Too grateful for the blessing lent Of simple tastes and mind content!" [*ibid.*].

frying pan into the fire, in the depths of despair.

Int. so much the worse! that's bad! couldn't be worse! worse and worse!

*** that –, it– will never do; *curtæ nescio quid semper abest rei* [Horace]; *ne Jupiter quidem omnibus placet;* "poor in abundance, famished at a feast" [*Young*]; "no tears but o' my shedding" [*Merchant of Venice*].

833. Regret. — **N.** REGRET, repining; homesickness, nostalgia; *mal du pays* [F.], *maladie du pays* [F.]; lamentation &c. 839; penitence &c. 950.

BITTERNESS, heartburning.

laudator temporis acti [L.] &c. (*discontent*) 832.

V. REGRET, deplore; bewail &c. (*lament*) 839; repine, cast a longing lingering look behind; rue, rue the day; repent &c. 950; *infandum renovare dolorem* [L.]. prey –, weigh –, have a weight– on the mind; leave an aching void.

Adj. REGRETTING &c. *v.;* regretful; homesick.

REGRETTED &c. *v.;* much to be regretted, regrettable; lamentable &c. (*bad*) 649.

Int. what a pity! hang it *or* hang it all! [*colloq.*].

*** "'tis true 'tis pity; And pity 'tis 'tis true" [*Hamlet*]; 'sigh'd and look'd and sigh'd again" [Dryden]; "bombazine would have shown a deeper sense of her loss" [Gaskell]; "I am a lone, lorn creetur' and every think goes contrairy with me" [*Mrs. Gummidge, in David Copperfield*].

834. Relief. — **N.** RELIEF; deliverance; refreshment &c. 689; easement, softening, alleviation, mitigation, palliation, soothing; lullaby, cradle-song, *berceuse* [F.].

SOLACE, consolation, comfort, encouragement; crumb of comfort, balm in Gilead.

LENITIVE, palliative, restorative &c. (*remedy*) 662; stupe, poultice, fomentation, assuasive; cushion &c. 215.

V. RELIEVE, ease, alleviate, mitigate, palliate, soothe; salve; soften, – down; foment, stupe, poultice; assuage, allay, abirritate.

remedy; cure &c. (*restore*) 660; refresh; pour balm into, pour oil on.

smooth the ruffled brow of care, temper the wind to the shorn lamb, lay the flattering unction to one's soul.

CHEER, comfort, console; enliven; encourage, bear up, pat on the back, give comfort, set at ease; gladden –, cheer– the heart; inspirit, invigorate.

DISBURDEN &c. (*free*) 705; take off a load of care.

BE RELIEVED; breathe more freely, draw a long breath; take comfort; dry the eyes, dry the tears, wipe the eyes, wipe away the tears; pull oneself together.

Adj. RELIEVING &c. *v.;* consolatory, soothing; assuaging, assuasive; balmy, balsamic; lenitive, palliative; anodyne &c. (*remedial*) 662; curative &c. 660.

*** "here comes a man of comfort" [*Measure for Measure*].

835. Aggravation. — **N.** AGGRAVATION, heightening; exacerbation; exasperation; overestimation &c. 482; exaggeration &c. 549.

V. AGGRAVATE, render worse, heighten, embitter, sour; exacerbate, acerbate, exasperate, envenom; enrage, provoke, tease.

add fuel to the –fire, – flame; fan the flame &c. (*excite*) 824; go from bad to worse &c. (*deteriorate*) 659.

Adj. AGGRAVATED &c. *v.;* worse, unrelieved; aggravable [*obs.*], aggravative, aggravating &c. *v.*

Adv. out of the frying pan into the fire, from bad to worse, worse and worse.

Int. so much the worse! *tant pis!* [F.].

*** "When sorrows come, they come not single spies, But in battalions" [*Hamlet*]; "One woe doth tread upon another's heel, So fast they follow" [*ibid.*].

836. Cheerfulness. — N. CHEERFUL-
NESS &c. *adj.;* geniality, gayety, *L'Allegro* [*It.*], cheer, good humor, spirits;
high spirits, animal spirits, flow of
spirits; glee, high glee, light heart; sunshine of the -mind, – breast; *gaieté de
cœur* [*F.*], *bon naturel* [*F.*].

LIVELINESS &c. *adj.;* life, alacrity,
vivacity, animation, *allégresse* [*F.*]; jocundity, joviality, jollity; levity; jocularity &c. (*wit*) 842.

MIRTH, merriment, hilarity, exhilara-
tion; laughter &c. 838; merrymaking
&c. (*amusement*) 840; heyday, rejoicing
&c. 838; marriage bell.

nepenthe *or* nepenthes, lotus; Euphrosyne.

OPTIMISM &c. (*hopefulness*) 858; self-
complacency; hedonics, hedonism.

V. BE CHEERFUL &c. *adj.;* have the
mind at ease, smile, put a good face
upon, keep up one's spirits; view the
bright side of the picture, view things
en couleur de rose [*F.*]; look through rose-
colored spectacles; *ridentem dicere verum*
[*L.*], cheer up, brighten up, light up,
bear up; take heart, cast away care,
drive dull care away, perk up; keep a
stiff upper lip [*slang*].

REJOICE &c.; 838; carol, chirp, chirrup,
lilt; frisk, rollic, give a loose to mirth
[*obs.*].

CHEER, enliven, elate, exhilarate, gladden, inspirit, animate, raise the spirits,
inspire; put in good humor; cheer –,
rejoice- the heart; delight &c. (*give
pleasure*) 829.

Adj. CHEERFUL; happy &c. 827;
cheery, of good cheer, smiling; blithe;
in spirits, in good spirits; breezy, bully
[*slang*], chipper [*colloq., U. S.*]; in high
-spirits, – feather; happy as -the day is
long, – a king; gay, gay as a lark;
allegro [*It.*]; debonair *or* debonaire, light,
lightsome, lighthearted; buoyant, bright,
free and easy, airy; jaunty *or* janty,
rollicky [*colloq.*], canty [*Scot. & dial.
Eng.*], "crouse an' canty" [Burns];
hedonic; riant; sprightly, sprightful;
spry; spirited, spiritful [*rare*], lively,
animated, vivacious; brisk, – as a bee;
sparkling; sportive; full of -play, –
spirit; all alive.

sunny, palmy; hopeful &c. 858.

MERRY, – as a -cricket, – grig, – marriage bell; joyful, joyous, jocund, jovial;
jolly, – as a thrush, – as a sand-boy;

837. Dejection. — N. DEJECTION; de-
jectedness &c. *adj.;* depression, prosternation [*obs.*], mopishness, damp; lowness –, depression- of spirits; weight –,
oppression –, damp- on the spirits; low
–, bad –, drooping –, depressed- spirits;
heart sinking; heaviness –, failure- of
heart.

heaviness &c. *adj.;* infestivity, gloom;
weariness &c. 841; *tœdium vitœ* [*L.*], disgust of life; *mal du pays* [*F.*] &c. (*regret*)
833; anhedonia.

MELANCHOLY; sadness &c. *adj.; Il
Penseroso* [*Old It.*], melancholia, dismals,
blue devils [*colloq.*], blues [*colloq.*], mopes,
lachrymals *or* lacrimals, mumps, dumps
[*chiefly humorous*] doldrums, vapors
[*archaic*], megrims, spleen [*obsoles.*],
horrors, hypochondriasis, hypochondria,
hyps [*colloq.*], jawfall [*rare*], pessimism;
la maladie sans maladie [*F.*], despondency, slough of Despond; disconsolate-
ness &c. *adj.;* hope deferred, blank
despondency; voiceless woe.

PROSTRATION, prostration of soul;
broken heart; despair &c. 859; cave of
despair, cave of Trophonius.

GRAVITY; demureness &c. *adj.;* solemnity; long face, grave face.

HYPOCHONDRIAC, seek-sorrow, self-
tormentor, *heautontimorumenos* [*Gr.*],
malade imaginaire [*F.*], *médecin tant pis*
[*F.*]; croaker, pessimist; mope, mopus
[*dial. Eng. & slang*], damper, wet blanket
crape-hanger [*slang*], Job's comforter.

[CAUSE OF DEJECTION] affliction &c.
830; sorry sight; *memento mori* [*L.*];
deathwatch, death's-head, skeleton at
the feast.

V. BE DEJECTED &c. *adj.;* grieve;
mourn &c. (*lament*) 839; take on [*colloq.*],
give way, lose heart, despond, droop,
sink.

LOWER, look downcast, frown, pout;
hang down the head; pull –, make- a
long face; laugh on the wrong side of
the mouth; grin a ghastly smile; look
blue, look like a drowned man; lay to
heart, take to heart.

MOPE, brood over; fret; sulk; pine,
pine away; yearn; repine &c. (*regret*)
833; despair &c. 859.

refrain from laughter, keep one's
countenance; be *or* look grave &c. *adj.;*
repress a smile, keep a straight face.

DEPRESS, discourage, dishearten, dispirit; damp, hyp [*colloq.*], dull, deject,

blithesome; gleeful, gleesome; hilarious, rattling [*colloq.*].

WINSOME, bonny, hearty, buxom.

PLAYFUL, playsome; *folâtre* [F.], playful as a kitten, tricksy, frisky, frolicsome; gamesome; jocose, jocular, waggish; mirth-loving, laughter-loving, abderian; mirthful, rollicking.

ELATE, elated; exulting, jubilant, flushed; rejoicing &c. 838; cock-a-hoop.

CHEERING, inspiriting, exhilarating; cardiac *or* cardiacal; pleasing &c. 829; palmy, flourishing, halcyon.

Adv. CHEERFULLY &c. *adj.*; cheerily, with good cheer; with a cheerful &c. heart; with relish, with zest; on the crest of the wave.

Int. NEVER SAY DIE! come! cheer up! hurrah! &c. 838; "hence loathed melancholy!" begone dull care! away with melancholy!

✱ "a merry heart goes all the day" [*A Winter's Tale*]; "as merry as the day is long" [*Much Ado*]; *ride si sapis* [Martial]; "as merry as cards, suppers, wine, and old women can make us" [Goldsmith].

lower, sink, dash, knock down, unman, prostrate, break one's heart; frown upon; cast a gloom on, cast a shade on; sadden; damp -, dash -, wither- one's hopes; weigh -, lie heavy -, prey- on the -mind, - spirits; damp -, dampen -, depress- the spirits.

Adj. CHEERLESS, joyless, spiritless, uncheerful, uncheery, unlively; unhappy &c. 828; melancholy, dismal, somber, dark, gloomy, *triste* [F.], clouded, murky, lowering, frowning, lugubrious, funereal, mournful, lamentable, dreadful.

DREARY, flat; dull, - as -a beetle, - ditchwater; depressing &c. *v.*; damp [*archaic*].

DOWNCAST, downhearted, mopy [*colloq.*], "melancholy as a gib cat" [*I Henry IV*]; a prey to melancholy; "besieged with sable-coloured melancholy" [*L. L. L.*]; down in the mouth [*colloq.*], down on one's luck [*colloq.*]; heavy-hearted; in the -dumps, - suds [*colloq.*], - sulks, - doldrums; in doleful dumps, in bad humor; sullen; mumpish, dumpish, mopish, moping; moody, glum; sulky

&c. (*discontented*) 832; out of -sorts, - humor, - heart, - spirits; ill at ease, low-spirited, in low spirits, a cup too low; weary &c. 841; discouraged, disheartened, desponding, chapfallen *or* chopfallen, jawfallen [*rare*], hypped [*colloq.*], hyppish [*rare*]; crestfallen.

SAD, pensive, *pensieroso* [It.], tristful; dolesome, doleful; woe-begone, lachrymose, in tears, melancholic, hypochondriacal, bilious, jaundiced, atrabilious, saturnine, splenetic; lackadaisical.

SERIOUS, sedate, staid, earnest; grave, - as -a judge, - an undertaker, - a mustard pot [*colloq.*]; sober, solemn, demure; grim, grim-faced, grim-visaged; rueful, wan, long-faced.

DISCONSOLATE, inconsolable, forlorn, comfortless, desolate, *désolé* [F.], sick at heart; soul-sick, heartsick; *au désespoir* [F.]; in despair &c. 859; lost.

OVERCOME; broken-down, borne-down, bowed-down; heartstricken &c. (*mental suffering*) 828; cut up [*colloq.*], dashed, sunk; unnerved, unmanned; downfallen, downtrodden; broken-hearted; careworn.

Adv. SADLY &c. *adj.*; with a long face, with tears in one's eyes.

✱ the countenance falling; the heart failing one, the heart sinking within one; "a plague of sighing and grief" [*Henry IV*]; "thick-ey'd musing and curs'd melancholy" [*Henry IV*]; "melancholy is the pleasure of being sad" [Victor Hugo]; "the sickening pang of hope deferred" [Scott]; "Our sincerest laughter With some pain is fraught" [Shelley].

838. [EXPRESSION OF PLEASURE.] **Rejoicing.** — **N.** REJOICING, exultation, triumph, jubilation, heyday, flush, reveling *or* revelling; merrymaking &c. (*amusement*) 840; jubilee &c. (*celebration*) 883; pæan, *Te Deum* [L.] &c. (*thanksgiving*) 990; congratulation &c. 896.

SMILE, simper, smirk, grin; broad grin, sardonic grin.

LAUGHTER, giggle, titter, snicker,

839. [EXPRESSION OF PAIN.] **Lamentation.** — **N.** LAMENTATION, lament, wail, complaint, plaint, murmur, mutter, grumble, groan, moan, whine, whimper, sob, sigh, suspiration, deep sigh; frown, scowl.

CRY &c. (*vociferation*) 411; scream, howl; outcry, wail, wail of woe.

WEEPING &c. *v.*; tear; flood of tears, fit of crying, lachrymation [*rare*], crying;

snigger, crow, cheer, chuckle, shout; Homeric laughter; horse -, hearty-laugh; guffaw; burst -, fit -, shout -, roar -, peal- of laughter; cachinnation; Kentish fire.

risibility; derision &c. 856; "sport that wrinkled Care derides" [Milton].

Momus; Democritus the Abderite; rollicker.

CHEER, huzza, hurrah or hurra, cheering; shout, yell [U. S. & Can.], college yell; tiger [colloq.].

V. REJOICE; thank -, bless- one's stars; congratulate oneself, hug oneself; rub -, clap- one's hands; smack the lips, fling up one's cap; dance, skip; sing, carol, chirrup, chirp; hurrah or hurra; cry for joy, leap with joy, skip for joy; exult &c. (boast) 884; triumph; hold jubilee &c. (celebrate) 883; sing a Te Deum, sing a pæan of triumph; make merry &c. (sport) 840.

SMILE, simper, smirk; grin, - like a Cheshire cat [colloq.]; mock, laugh in one's sleeve.

LAUGH, - outright; giggle, titter, snigger, snicker, crow, smicker [obs.], chuckle, cackle; burst out; burst into a roar of laughter, burst into a fit of laughter; shout, split [colloq.], roar.

shake -, split -, hold both- cne's sides; roar -, shake -, nearly die -, die-with laughter.

raise laughter &c. (amuse) 840.

Adj. REJOICING &c. v.; jubilant, exultant, triumphant; flushed, elated; laughing &c. v.; risible; ready to -burst, - split, - die with laughte [all colloq.]; convulsed with laughter; shaking like a jelly with -laughter, - suppressed merriment [both colloq.].

laughable &c. (ludicrous) 853.

Adv. LAUGHINGLY; on a broad grin, in fits of laughter, amid peals of laughter; in triumph; in mockery; with a -roar, - peal, - outburst- of laughter.

Int. HURRAH! huzza! three cheers! hip, hip, hurrah! aha! hail! tolderolloll! Heaven be praised! tant mieux! [F.], so much the better! good enough! tra-la-la!

. the heart leaping with joy; "laugh? I thought I should a' died!" [Chevalier]; ce n'est pas être bien aisé que de rire; "Laughter holding both his sides" [Milton]; θάλαττα! θάλαττα! le roi est mort, vive le roi; "with his eyes in flood with laughter" [Cymbeline].

melting mood; "weeping and gnashing of teeth" [Bible].

plaintiveness &c. adj.; languishment; condolence &c. 915.

MOURNING, weeds [colloq.], widow's weeds, willow, cypress, crape, deep mourning; sackcloth and ashes; lachrymatory, tear bottle, lachrymals or lacrimals; knell &c. 363; dump [obs.], death song, dirge, coronach [Scot. & Ir.], nenia, requiem, elegy, epicedium; threne [rare], menody, threnody; jeremiad or jeremiade, ululation, keen [Ir.], ullalulla [Ir.].

MOURNER, keener [Ir.]; grumbler &c. (discontent) 832; Niobe; Heraclitus, Jeremiah, Mrs. Gummidge.

V. LAMENT, mourn, deplore, grieve, keen [Ir.], weep over; bewail, bemoan; condole with &c. 915; fret &c. (suffer) 828; wear -, go into -, put on- mourning; wear -the willow, - sackcloth and ashes; infandum renovare dolorem [Vergil] &c. (regret) 833; give sorrow words.

SIGH; give -, heave -, fetch- a sigh; "waft a sigh from Indus to the pole" [Pope]; sigh "like furnace" [As You Like It]; wail.

CRY, weep, sob, greet [archaic or Scot.], blubber, snivel, bibber, whimper, pule; pipe, pipe one's eye [both slang, orig. naut.]; drop -, shed- -tears, - a tear; melt -, burst- into tears; fondre en larmes [F.], cry oneself blind, cry one's eyes out; yammer [dial.].

scream &c. (cry out) 411; mew &c. (animal sounds) 412; groan, moan, whine, yelp, howl, yell, ululate; roar; roar -, bellow- like a bull; cry out lustily, rend the air.

SHOW SIGNS OF GRIEF; frown, scowl, make a wry face, gnash one's teeth, wring one's hands, tear one's hair, beat one's breast, roll on the ground, burst with grief.

COMPLAIN, murmur, mutter, grumble, growl, clamor, make a fuss about, croak, grunt, maunder [obs.]; deprecate &c. (disapprove) 932.

cry out before one is hurt, complain without cause.

Adj. LAMENTING &c. v.; in mourning, in sackcloth and ashes; ululant, ululative [obs.], clamorous; crying -, lamenting- to high heaven, sorrowing, sorrowful &c. (unhappy) 828; mournful, tearful; lachrymose, lachrymal or lacrimal, lachrymatory, plaintive, plaintful; querulous, querimonious; in the melting mood.

IN TEARS, with tears in one's eyes; with moistened eyes, with watery eyes; bathed –, dissolved- in tears; "like Niobe, all tears" [*Hamlet*].

elegiac, epicedial, threnetic *or* threnetical.

Adv. *de profundis* [*L.*], *les larmes aux yeux* [*F.*].

Int. ALAS! alack! heigh-ho! O dear! ah me! woe is me! lackadaisy! well a day! lack a day! alack a day! wellaway! alas the day! *O tempora, O mores!* [*L.*]; what a pity! *miserabile dictu!* [*L.*]; too true!

** tears standing in the eyes, tears starting from the eyes; eyes -suffused, – swimming, – brimming, – overflowing- with tears; "if you have tears prepare to shed them now" [*Julius Cæsar*]; *interdum lacrymæ pondera vocis habent* [Ovid]; "strangled his language in his tears" [*Henry VIII*]; "tears such as angels weep" [*Paradise Lost*]; "she wept, she blubbered, and she tore her hair" [Swift]; "laughter is at all ages the natural recognition of destruction, confusion, and ruin" [Shaw].

---

840. Amusement. — N. AMUSEMENT, entertainment, diversion, divertisement, *divertissement* [*F.*]; reaction, relaxation, solace; pastime, *passe-temps* [*F.*], sport; labor of love; pleasure &c. 827.

FUN, frolic, merriment, jollity, joviality, jovialness; heyday; laughter &c. 838; jocosity, jocoseness; drollery, buffoonery, tomfoolery; mummery, mumming, masquing, pageant; pleasantry; wit &c. 842; quip, quirk.

PLAY; game, game of romps; gambol, romp, prank, antic, frisk, rig [*obs. or dial.*], lark [*colloq.*], spree, skylarking, vagary, monkey trick, *fredaine* [*F.*], escapade, *échappée* [*F.*], bout, *espièglerie* [*F.*]; practical joke &c. (*ridicule*) 856.

[DANCE STEPS] *gambade* [*F.*], gambado, *pas* [*F.*]; pigeonwing, heel-and-toe, buck-and-wing, shuffle, double shuffle; *chassé* [*F.*], *coupé* [*F.*], grapevine, &c.

[DANCES] dance, hop [*colloq.*], stag dance, shindig [*slang, U. S.*]; ball; *bal, bal masqué, bal costumé* [all *F.*], masquerade, masquerade ball, cornwallis [*U. S.*]; mistletoe-bough dance; Dance of Death, *danse macabre* [*F.*]; interpretative dance, step dance, sand dance, *pas seul* [*F.*], skirt dance, folk dance; Morisco *or* morice [*obs.*], morris dance, saraband, fandango, bolero, tarantella, boutade, gavot *or* gavotte, minuet, *allemande* [*F.*], rigadoon, fling, Highland fling, Highland schottische, strathspey, reel, jig, hornpipe, sword dance, breakdown, cakewalk; kantikoy, snake dance; country dance, Scotch reel, Virginia reel, Sir Roger de Coverley, Portland ˡancy; ballet &c. (*drama*) 599; ragtime [*colloq.*] &c. (*music*) 415; jazz [*slang*]; nautch [*India*].

SQUARE DANCE, quadrille, Lancers, cotillion *or* cotillon [*F.*], German.

ROUND DANCE, waltz, *valse* [*F.*], polka, mazurka, galop, gallopade *or* galopade, schottische, one-step, two-step, fox-trot, turkey-trot; shimmy.

danse du ventre [*F.*], *chonchina* [*Jap.*], cancan.

841. Weariness. — N. WEARINESS, defatigation [*obs.*], ennui, boredom; lassitude &c. (*fatigue*) 688; drowsiness &c. 683.

DISGUST, nausea, loathing, sickness; satiety &c. 869; *tædium vitæ* [*L.*] &c. (*dejection*) 837.

TEDIUM, wearisomeness, tediousness &c. *adj.*; heavy hours, dull work, monotony, twice-told tale; "the enemy" [*time*].

BORE, buttonholer, proser, dry-asdust, fossil [*colloq.*], wet blanket; pill, stiff [*both slang*].

V. WEARY; tire &c. (*fatigue*) 688; bore; bore –, weary –, tire- -to death, – out of one's life, – out of all patience; set –, send- to sleep; buttonhole.

PALL, sicken, nauseate, disgust; harp on the same string; drag its -slow, – weary- length along.

never hear the last of; be tired &c. *adj.* of *or* with; yawn; die with *ennui*.

Adj. WEARYING &c. *v.*; wearing; wearisome, tiresome, irksome; uninteresting, stupid, bald, devoid of interest, jejune, dry, monotonous, dull, arid, tedious, humdrum, mortal [*colloq.*], flat; prosy, prosing; slow; soporific, somniferous, dormitive, opiate.

DISGUSTING &c. *v.*; unenjoyed.

WEARY; tired &c. *v.*; drowsy &c. (*sleepy*) 683; uninterested, flagging, used up, worn out, *blasé* [*F.*], life-weary, weary of life; sick of.

Adv. WEARILY &c. *adj.*; *usque ad nauseam* [*L.*].

** time hanging heavily on one's hands; *toujours perdrix; crambe repetita;* "Weary of myself and sick of asking What I am and what I ought to be" [Arnold].

DANCER, *danseur* (*fem. danseuse*) [*F.*], *première danseuse* [*F.*], ballet dancer; geisha [*Jap.*]; nautch girl, bayadere [*both India*]; clog -, step -, skirt -, figure-dancer; figurant (*fem.* figurante), Morisco [*obs.*], morris dancer; terpsichorean [*colloq.*]; Terpsichore.

FESTIVITY, merrymaking; party &c. (*social gathering*) 892; revels, revelry, reveling *or* revelling, carnival, Saturnalia, jollification [*colloq.*], junket, picnic.

fête champêtre [*F.*], lawn party, garden party, regatta, field day, *fête* [*F.*], festival, gala, gala day; feast, banquet &c. (*food*) 298; regale, symposium, high jinks [*colloq.*], carouse, carousal, brawl; wassail; wake; bust [*slang*], tear [*slang*]; *Turnerfest* [*Ger.*]; gymkhana [*orig. Anglo-Ind.*]; treat; *ridotto* [*It.*], drum [*obs. or hist.*], kettledrum [*colloq.*], rout [*archaic*]; tea party, tea, tea fight [*slang*]; *Kaffee-Klatsch* [*Ger.*]; concert &c. (*music*) 415; show [*colloq.*]; play &c. (*drama*) 599; randy [*dial.*]; clambake, fish fry, beefsteak fry, squantum, donation party [*all U. S.*]; bat, bum [*both slang, U. S.*], jamboree [*slang*].

ROUND OF PLEASURE, dissipation, a short life and a merry one, racketing, holiday making.

rejoicing &c. 838; jubilee &c. (*celebration*) 883.

FIREWORKS, *feu-de-joie* [*F.*], firecrackers, bonfire.

HOLIDAY, red-letter day, play day; high days and holidays; high holiday, Bank holiday [*Eng.*]; May day, Derby day [*Eng.*]; Easter Monday, Whitmonday, Twelfth Night, Halloween; Christmas &c. 138; Dewali [*Hindu*], Holi *or* Hoolee [*Hindu*]; Bairam, Muharram [*both Moham.*]; wayzgoose [*Printers*], beanfeast [*Eng.*]; Arbor -, Declaration -, Independence -, Labor -, Memorial *or* Decoration -, Thanksgiving- Day; Washington's -, Lincoln's -, King's- birthday; Empire Day [*Brit.*]; Mardi gras, *mi-carême* [*F.*], feria [*S. W. U. S.*], fiesta [*Sp.*].

PLACE OF AMUSEMENT, theater *or* theatre; concert -hall, - room; ballroom, dance hall, assembly room; moving-picture -, cinema- theater; movies [*colloq.*]; music hall; vaudeville -theater, - show; circus, hippodrome.

park, pleasance *or* plaisance [*archaic*]; arbor; garden &c. (*horticulture*) 371; pleasure-, play-, cricket-, croquet- archery-, polo-, hunting- ground; tennis-, racket-, squash-, badminton- court; bowling- green, -alley; croquet lawn, rink, glaciarium, ice rink, skating rink; golf links, race course, athletic field, stadium; gymnasium, swimming -pool, - bath; billiard room, pool room, casino, shooting gallery; flying horses, roundabout, merry-go-round; swing; *montagne Russe* [*F.*]; aërial railway, scenic railway, roller coaster, chutes, flying boats, etc.

Vauxhall, Ranelagh, Hurlingham; Lord's, Epsom, Newmarket, Doncaster, Sandown Park, Henley, Cowes, Mortlake [*all in Eng.*]; Coney Island; Brooklands, Sheepshead Bay, Belmont Park, Saratoga; New London, Forest Hills, Longwood [*all in U. S.*]; Monte Carlo; Longchamps [*France*]; Flemington [*Melbourne, Australia*].

[SPORTS AND GAMES] athletic sports, track events, gymnastics; archery, rifle shooting; tournament, pugilism &c. (*contention*) 720; sporting &c. 622; horse racing, the turf; water polo; aquatics &c. 267.

skating, ice skating, roller skating, sliding; cricket, tennis, lawn tennis, pallone, rackets, squash, fives, trap bat and ball, badminton, battledore and shuttlecock, pall-mall, croquet, golf, curling, hockey, shinny *or* shinney; polo, football, Rugby, rugger [*colloq.*]; association, soccer [*colloq.*]; tent pegging, tilting at the ring, quintain, greasy pole; knur (*or* knurr) and spell [*Eng.*]; quoits, discus; hammer -, horseshoe- throwing; putting the -weight, - shot; hurdling; leapfrog; sack -, potato -, obstacle -, three-legged- race; hop skip and jump; French and English, tug of war; rounders, baseball, basket ball, pushball, captain ball; lacrosse; tobogganing.

blind-man's buff, hunt the slipper, hide and seek, kiss in the ring; snapdragon; cross questions and crooked answers, twenty questions, what's my thought? charades, crambo, dumb crambo, crisscross, proverbs, *bouts rimés* [*F.*]; hopscotch, jackstones, mumble-the-peg *or* mumblety-peg; ping-pong, tiddledywinks, tipcat.

billiards, pool, pyramids, bagatelle; bowls, skittles, ninepins, American bowls; tenpins [*U. S.*], tivoli.

chess, draughts, checkers *or* chequers, backgammon, dominoes, halma, dice, craps, crap shooting, crap game, "negro golf," "indoor golf" [*both humorous*]; merelles, nine men's morris, gobang, "the royal game of goose" [Goldsmith]; fox and geese; lotto *or* loto &c.[1]

CARDS; whist, rubber; round game; loo, cribbage, *bésique* [*F.*], euchre, cutthroat euchre, railroad euchre; drole, écarté, picquet, all fours, quadrille, omber *or* ombre, reverse, Pope Joan, commit; boston, *vingt et un* [*F.*], quinze, thirty-one, put, speculation, connections, brag, cassino, lottery, commerce, snip-snap-snorem, lift smoke, blind hookey, Polish bank, Earl of Coventry, napoleon *or* nap [*colloq.*]; banker, penny-ante, poker, jack pot; blind -, draw -, straight -, stud-

---

[1] A curious list of games is given in Sir Thomas Urquhart's translation of Rabelais. — *Life of Gargantua*, book i, chapter 22.

poker; bluff; bridge, – whist; auction; monte, reversis, squeezers, old maid, fright, beggar-my-neighbor, goat, hearts, patience, solitaire, pairs.

court cards; ace, king, queen, knave, jack, joker; bower; right –, left- bower; dummy; hand; trump; face cards, diamonds, hearts, clubs, spades; pack, deck; flush, full-house, straight, three of a kind, pair, *misère* [F.] &c.

TOY, plaything, bauble; doll &c. (*puppet*) 554; teetotum; knickknack &c. (*trifle*) 643; magic lantern &c. (*show*) 448; peep-, puppet-, raree-, galanty *or* gallanty-, Punch-and-Judy- show; marionettes; toy-shop; "quips and cranks and wanton wiles, nods and becks and wreathed smiles" [Milton].

SPORTSMAN (*fem.* sportswoman), hunter, Nimrod.

archer, toxophilite; cricketer, footballer, ball-players &c.

GAMESTER (*fem.* gamestress), sport, gambler; dicer, punter, plunger.

REVELER *or* reveller, carouser; master of the -ceremonies, – revels; *arbiter elegantiarum* [L.]; *arbiter bibendi* [L.].

DEVOTEE, enthusiast, follower, fan [*slang, U. S.*], rooter [*slang or cant, U. S.*]; turfman.

V. AMUSE, entertain, divert, enliven; tickle, – the fancy; titillate, raise a smile, put in good humor; cause –, create –, occasion –, raise –, excite –, produce –, convulse with- laughter; set the table in a roar, be the death of one.

CHEER, rejoice; recreate, solace; please &c. 829; interest; treat, regale.

AMUSE ONESELF; game; play, – a game, – pranks, – tricks; sport, disport, toy, wanton, revel, junket, feast, carouse, banquet, make merry, drown care; drive dull care away; frolic, gambol, frisk, romp; caper; dance &c. (*leap*) 309; keep up the ball; run a rig, sow one's wild oats, have one's fling, take one's pleasure; paint the town red [*slang*]; see life; *desipere in loco* [Horace], play the fool.

make –, keep- holiday; go a-Maying.

while away –, beguile- the time; kill time, dally.

Adj. AMUSING, entertaining, diverting &c. *v.*; recreative, lusory; pleasant &c. (*pleasing*) 829; laughable &c. (*ludicrous*) 853; witty &c. 842; festive, festal; jovial, jolly, jocund, roguish, rompish; playful, – as a kitten; sportive, ludibrious [*obs.*].

AMUSED &c. *v.*; "pleased with a rattle, tickled with a straw" [Pope].

Adv. "on the light fantastic toe" [Milton], at play, in sport.

Int. *vive la bagatelle!* [F.], *vogue la galère!* [F.], come on fellows! "hail, hail, the gang's all here!" some party! [*slang*].

*** *Deus nobis hæc otia fecit; dum vivimus vivamus; dulce est desipere in loco* [Horace]; "(every room) hath blazed with lights and brayed with minstrelsy" [*Timon of Athens*]; *misce stultitiam consiliis brevem* [Horace]; "Foot it featly here and there" [*Tempest*]; "The grass stoops not, she treads on it so light" [*Venus and Adonis*]; "He capers, he dances, he has eyes of youth" [*Merry Wives*]; "Fleet the time carelessly as they did in the golden world" [*As You Like It*]; "therefore put you in your best array!" [*ibid.*]; "A very merry, dancing, drinking, Laughing, quaffing and unthinking time" [Dryden]; "a clear fire, a clean hearth, and the rigour of the game" [Lamb]; "Patience, and shuffle the cards" [Cervantes]; "Lady, wherefore talk you so?" [*I Henry VI*]; "they laugh that win" [*Othello*].

---

842. Wit. — N. WIT, wittiness; Attic -wit, – salt; Atticism; salt, *esprit* [F.], point, fancy, whim, humor *or* humour, drollery, pleasantry.

BUFFOONERY, fooling, farce, tomfoolery; shenanigan [*slang, U. S.*], harlequinade &c. 599; broad -farce, – humor; fun, *espiéglerie* [F.]; *vis comica* [L.].

JOCULARITY; jocosity, jocoseness; facetiousness; waggery, waggishness; whimsicality; comicality &c. 853.

SMARTNESS, ready wit, banter, persiflage, *badinage* [F.], retort, repartee, *quid pro quo* [L.]; ridicule &c. 856.

FACETIÆ, quips and cranks; jest,

843. Dullness. — N. DULLNESS *or* dulness, heaviness, flatness; infestivity &c. 837, stupidity &c. 499; want of originality; dearth of ideas.

prose, matter of fact; heavy book, *conte à dormir debout* [F.]; commonplace, platitude.

V. BE DULL &c. *adj.*; hang fire, fall flat; platitudinize, prose, take *au sérieux* [F.], be caught napping.

RENDER DULL &c. *adj.*; damp, depress, throw cold water on, lay a wet blanket on; fall flat upon the ear.

Adj. DULL, – as ditch water; jejune, dry, unentertaining, uninteresting, un-

joke, capital joke; *canoræ nugæ* [L.]; standing -jest, – joke; conceit, quip, quirk, crank, quiddity [*rare*], *concetto* [*It.*], *plaisanterie* [*F.*], brilliant idea; merry –, bright –, happy- thought; sally; flash, – of wit, – of merriment; scintillation; *mot*, – *pour rire* [*F.*]; witticism, smart saying, *bon mot* [*F.*], *jeu d'esprit* [*F.*], epigram; jest book; dry joke, *quodlibet* [*L.*], cream of the jest.

WORD-PLAY, *jeu de mots* [*F.*], play upon words; pun, punning; *double entente* [*F.*] &c. (*ambiguity*) 520; quibble, verbal quibble; conundrum &c. (*riddle*)

lively, heavy-footed, elephantine; slow' of comprehension; insipid, tasteless, slow as cold molasses [*colloq.*], logy [*U. S.*]; unimaginative; insulse; dry as dust; prosy, prosing, prosaic; matter-of-fact, commonplace, platitudinous, pointless; "weary, stale, flat, and unprofitable" [*Hamlet*].

STUPID, slow, flat, humdrum, monotonous; melancholic &c. 837; stolid &c. 499; plodding.

*** *Davus sum non Œdipus;* "fain would I write but that I fear to pall" [*Cynic's Calendar*].

533; anagram, acrostic, double acrostic, trifling, idle conceit, turlupinade [*obs.*].

OLD JOKE, Joe Miller, chestnut [*slang*]; hoary-headed -joke, – jest; joke –, jest-with whiskers [*humorous*].

V. JOKE, jest, cut jokes; crack a joke, get off a joke; pun; perpetrate a -joke, – pun; make fun of, make merry with; set the table in a roar &c. (*amuse*) 840; tell a good -story, – yarn.

RETORT, flash back, flash, scintillate; banter &c. (*ridicule*) 856; *ridentem dicere verum* [*L.*]; joke at one's expense.

Adj. WITTY, Attic; clever, keen, keen-witted, brilliant, pungent; quick-witted, nimble-witted; smart, jocular, jocose, funny, waggish, facetious, whimsical, humorous; playful &c. 840; merry and wise; pleasant, sprightly, cute [*colloq.*], *spirituel* [*F.*], sparkling, epigrammatic, full of point, *ben trovato* [*It.*]; comic &c. 853.

Adv. in joke, in jest, for the jest's sake, in sport, in play.

*** *adhibenda est in jocando moderatio;* "gentle dullness ever loves a joke" [Pope]; "leave this keen encounter of our wits" [*Richard III*].

844. Humorist. — N. HUMORIST, wag, wit, reparteeist, epigrammatist, punster; *bel esprit* [*F.*], life of the party; joker, jester, Joe Miller, *drôle de corps* [*F.*], galliard *or* gaillard [*archaic*], spark; *bon diable* [*F.*]; *persifleur* [*F.*], banterer, "Agreeable Rattle" [Goldsmith].

buffoon, *farceur* [*F.*], merry-andrew, mime, tumbler, acrobat, mountebank, charlatan, posture master, harlequin, punch, punchinello, *pulcinella* [*It.*], Scaramouch, clown; wearer of the -cap and bells, – motley; motley fool; pantaloon, gypsy; jack-pudding [*archaic*], Jack-in-the-green; jack-a-dandy [*unconscious humorist*]; zany; madcap, pickle-herring, witling, caricaturist, grimacer, grimacier.

*** "I never dare to write As funny as I can" [Holmes].

2. DISCRIMINATIVE AFFECTIONS

845. Beauty. — N. BEAUTY, beautifulness, pulchritude; the beautiful, *to kalon* [*Gr.* τὸ καλόν].

beauty unadorned; form, elegance, grace, *belle tournure* [*F.*]; symmetry &c. 242; concinnity, delicacy, refinement, charm, *je ne sais quoi* [*F.*], *nescio quid* [*L.*], style.

comeliness, fairness &c. *adj.;* polish, gloss; good effect, good looks; trigness.

BLOOM, brilliancy, radiance, splendor *or* splendour, gorgeousness, magnificence; sublimity, sublimification [*obs.*].

846. Ugliness. — N. UGLINESS &c. *adj.;* deformity, inelegance; acomia, baldness, alopecia; disfigurement &c. (*blemish*) 848; want of symmetry, inconcinnity [*rare*], "uglification" [Carroll]; distortion &c. 243; squalor &c. (*uncleanness*) 653.

FORBIDDING COUNTENANCE, vinegar aspect, hanging look, wry face, face that would stop a clock [*colloq.*]; *spretæ injuria formæ* [Vergil].

EYESORE, object, figure, sight [*colloq.*], fright, octopus. specter *or* spectre.

BEAU IDEAL, *le beau idéal* [*F.*]; Venus, Aphrodite, Hebe, the Graces, Peri, Houri, Cupid, Apollo, Hyperion, Adonis, Antinous, Narcissus, Astarte; Helen of Troy, Cleopatra; Venus of Milo, Apollo Belvedere.

[COMPARISONS] butterfly; flower, flow'ret gay; garden, anemone, asphodel, buttercup, crane's-bill, daffodil, lily, lily of the valley, ranunculus, rose, rhododendron, windflower.

the flower of, the pink of; *bijou* [*F.*]; jewel &c. (*ornament*) 847; work of art.

LOVELINESS, pleasurableness &c. 829.

BEAUTIFYING, beautification [*rare*]; landscape gardening; decoration &c. &c. 847; calisthenics, physical culture.

[SCIENCE OF THE PERCEPTION OF BEAUTY] callæsthetics.[1]

V. BE BEAUTIFUL &c. *adj.;* shine, beam, bloom; become one &c. (*accord*) 23; set off, become, grace.

RENDER BEAUTIFUL &c. *adj.;* beautify; polish, burnish; gild &c. (*decorate*) 847; set out.

"snatch a grace beyond the reach of art" [Pope].

Adj. BEAUTIFUL, beauteous, handsome; pretty; lovely, graceful, elegant, exquisite, flowerlike, delicate, dainty, refined.

COMELY, fair, personable, seemly [*obs.*], decent [*archaic*], proper [*archaic or dial.*], bonny, good-looking; well-favored, well-made, well-formed, well-proportioned, shapely; symmetrical &c. (*regular*) 242; harmonious &c. (*color*) 428; sightly, fit to be seen.

bright, bright-eyed; rosy-cheeked, cherry-cheeked; rosy, ruddy; blooming, in full bloom.

goodly, dapper, tight, jimp *or* gimp [*Scot. & dial. Eng.*], jaunty *or* janty, trig, natty [*orig. slang*], quaint [*archaic*], trim, tidy, neat, spruce, smart, tricksy [*rare*].

BRILLIANT, shining; beamy, beaming; sparkling, radiant, splendid, resplendent, dazzling, glowing; glossy, sleek; rich, gorgeous, superb, magnificent, grand, fine, sublime.

ARTISTIC *or* artistical, æsthetic; picturesque, pictorial; *fait à peindre* [*F.*], well-varied; curious.

enchanting &c. (*pleasure-giving*) 829; attractive &c. (*inviting*) 615; becoming &c. (*accordant*) 23; ornamental &c. 847; of consummate art.

scarecrow, hag, harridan, satyr, witch, toad, baboon, monster, Caliban, Æsop; *monstrum horrendum informe ingens cui lumen ademptum* [Vergil].

V. BE UGLY &c. *adj.;* look ill, grin horribly a ghastly smile, grin through a horse collar [*colloq.*], make faces.

RENDER UGLY &c. *adj.;* deface; disfigure, defigure [*obs.*], deform, uglify [*rare*], spoil; distort &c. 243; blemish &c. (*injure*) 659; soil &c. (*render unclean*) 653.

Adj. UGLY, — as -sin, — a toad, — a scarecrow, — a dead monkey; plain, coarse; homely &c. (*unadorned*) 849; ordinary, unornamental, inartistic; unsightly, unseemly, uncomely, unshapely, unlovely; sightless [*obs.*], seemless [*obs.*], not fit to be seen; unbeauteous, unbeautiful, beautiless.

BALD, bald-headed, acomous, hairless, *chauve* [*F.*], depilous [*rare*], glabrous [*bot.*]; smooth-faced, beardless, whiskerless, clean-shaven.

MISSHAPEN, misproportioned; shapeless &c. (*amorphous*) 241; monstrous; gaunt &c. (*thin*) 203; dumpy &c. (*short*) 201; curtailed of its fair proportions; ill-made, ill-shaped, ill-proportioned; crooked &c. (*distorted*) 243.

UNPREPOSSESSING, hard-featured, hard-visaged; ill-favored, hard-favored, evil-favored; ill-looking; squalid, haggard; grim, grim-faced, grim-visaged; grisly, ghastly; ghostlike, deathlike; cadaverous, gruesome *or* grewsome.

uncouth, ungainly, graceless, inelegant; ungraceful, stiff; rugged, rough, gross, rude, awkward, clumsy, slouching, rickety, gawky, lumping, lumpish, lumbering, hulking *or* hulky, unwieldy.

REPELLENT, forbidding, frightful, hideous, odious, uncanny, repulsive; horrid, horrible; shocking &c. (*painful*) 830.

foul &c. (*dirty*) 653; dingy &c. (*colorless*) 429; gaudy &c. (*color*) 428; tarnished, smeared, besmeared, bedaubed, disfigured &c. *v.;* discolored, spotted, spotty.

SHOWY, specious, pretentious, garish &c. (*ostentatious*) 882.

paintable, well-composed, well-grouped,

[1] Whewell, *Philosophy of the Inductive Sciences.*

PERFECT, unspotted, spotless &c. 650; immaculate; undeformed, undefaced.
PASSABLE, presentable, tolerable, not amiss.

*** *auxilium non leve vultus habet* [Ovid]; "beauty born of murmuring sound" [Wordsworth]; "flowers preach to us if we will hear" [C. G. Rossetti]; "Winter makes water solid, yet the spring, That is but flowers, is a stronger thing" [Masefield]; "butterflies, the souls of summer hours" [*ibid.*]; *gratior ac pulchro veniens in corpore virtus* [Vergil]; "none but the brave deserve the fair" [Dryden]; "thou who hast the fatal gift of beauty" [Byron]; "Was this the face that launch'd a thousand ships?" [Marlowe].

847. Ornament. — N.

ORNAMENT, ornamentation, ornamental art; ornature [*rare*], ornateness, ornation [*rare*], adornment, decoration, embellishment; architecture.

GARNISH, polish, varnish, French polish, gilding, japanning, lacquer, ormolu, enamel; *champlevé* ware, *cloisonné* ware; cosmetics.

[ORNAMENTATION] pattern, diaper, powdering, paneling, graining, inlaid work, pargeting; detail; texture &c. 329; richness; tracery, molding *or* moulding, fillet, listel, strapwork, *coquillage* [F.], flourish, *fleur-de-lis* [F.], arabesque, fret, anthemion; egg and -tongue, – dart; astragal, zigzag, acanthus, cartouche; pilaster &c. (*projection*) 250; bead, beading; frostwork, tooling; Moresque, Morisco.

embroidery, broidery [*archaic*], needlework, brocade, brocatel *or* brocatelle, bugles, beads, galloon, lace, fringe, border, insertion, *motif* [F.], edging, trimming; trappings; drapery, overdrapery, hanging, tapestry, arras; millinery, ermine; *drap d'or* [F.].

wreath, festoon, garland, chaplet, flower, nosegay, bouquet, posy [*archaic or colloq.*]; "daisies pied and violets blue" [L. L. L.].

tassel, knot; shoulder knot, epaulet *or* epaulette, aglet *or* aiglet, aigulet [*rare*], frog; star, rosette, bow; feather, plume, panache, aigret *or* aigrette; fillet, snood.

JEWELRY *or* jewellery, *bijouterie* [F.] *or* bijoutry; tiara, crown, coronet, diadem; jewel, *bijou* [F.], trinket, locket, necklace, bracelet, bangle; armlet, anklet, earring, nose-ring, carcanet [*archaic*], chain, chatelaine, brooch, torque.

GEM, precious stone; diamond, brilliant; pearl; sapphire, Oriental topaz, lapis lazuli; ruby, balas *or* balais *or* balas ruby; emerald, beryl, aquamarine, alexandrite; opal, fire opal, girasol *or* girasole; garnet, carbuncle; amethyst, plasma; turquoise *or* turquois; topaz; coral; chalcedony, agate, onyx, sard, sardonyx, chrysoprase, carnelian, cat's-eye, jasper; heliotrope, bloodstone; hyacinth, jacinth, zircon, jargon *or* jargoon; chrysolite, peridot; spinel *or* spinelle, spinel ruby; moonstone, sunstone.

848. Blemish. — N.

BLEMISH, disfigurement, deformity; adactylism; defect &c. (*imperfection*) 651; flaw, maculation; injury &c. (*deterioration*) 659; spots on the sun; eyesore.

stain, blot, spot, spottiness; speck, speckle, blur, freckle, mole, macula, macule, patch, blotch, birthmark; blobber lip, blubber lip, harelip; blain, tarnish, smudge; dirt &c. 653; scar, wem [*obs.*], wen; pustule; whelk; excrescence, pimple &c. (*protuberance*) 250; burn, blister, roughness.

V. DISFIGURE &c. (*injure*) 659; uglify [*rare*]; render ugly &c. 846.

Adj. DISFIGURED; discolored; imperfect &c. 651; blobber-lipped *or* blubber-lipped, harelipped; chapped, specked, speckled, freckled, pitted, bloodshot, bruised; injured &c. (*deteriorated*) 659.

849. Simplicity. — N.

SIMPLICITY, plainness, homeliness; undress, nudity, beauty unadorned; chasteness, chastity, restraint, severity, naturalness, unaffectedness.

V. BE SIMPLE &c. *adj.*

RENDER SIMPLE &c. *adj.;* simplify, reduce to simplicity, strip of ornament, chasten, restrain.

Adj. SIMPLE, plain, homelike, homish, homely, homespun [*fig.*], ordinary, household.

unaffected, natural, native; inartificial &c. (*artless*) 703; free from -affectation, – ornament; *simplex munditiis* [Horace]; *sans façon* [F.], *en déshabillé* [F.].

chaste, inornate, severe.

UNADORNED, unornamented, undecked, ungarnished, unarranged, untrimmed, unvarnished.

bald, flat, blank, dull.

SIMPLE-MINDED, childish, credulous &c. 486.

*** *veritatis simplex oratio est;* "Nothing is more simple than greatness; indeed, to be simple is to be great" [Emerson].

FRIPPERY, finery, gewgaw, knickknack, gimcrack, tinsel, spangle, clinquant, pinchbeck, paste; excess of ornament &c. (*vulgarity*) 851; gaud, pride, show, ostentation.

illustration, illumination, vignette; *fleuron* [*F.*]; headpiece, tailpiece, *cul-de-lampe* [*F.*]; purple patches, flowers of rhetoric &c. 577.

VIRTU, article of virtu, piece of virtu, work of art, bric-a-brac, curio; rarity, a find.

V. ORNAMENT, embellish, enrich, decorate, adorn, beautify; adonize [*rare*], dandify.

garnish, furbish, polish, gild, varnish, whitewash, enamel, japan, lacquer, paint, grain.

spangle, bespangle, bead, embroider, work; chase, tool, emboss, fret; emblazon, blazon, illuminate; illustrate.

SMARTEN, trim, dizen, bedizen, prink, prank; trick up, trick out, fig out; deck, bedeck, dight [*archaic*], bedight [*archaic*], array; titivate *or* tittivate [*colloq.*], spruce up [*colloq.*]; smarten up, dress, dress up; powder.

become &c. (*accord with*) 23.

Adj. ORNAMENTED, beautified &c. *v.*; ornate, rich, gilt, begilt, tessellated, inlaid, festooned; *champlevé* [*F.*], *cloisonné* [*F.*], topiary [*rare*].

SMART, gay, tricksy [*rare*], flowery, glittering; new-gilt, new-spangled; fine; fine as -a Mayday queen, – fivepence, – a carrot fresh scraped, – a fiddle [*all colloq.*]; pranked out, bedight [*archaic*], well-groomed.

in full dress &c. (*fashion*) 852; *en grande -tenue*, – *toilette* [*F.*]; in one's best bib and tucker, in Sunday best, *endimanché* [*F.*]; dressed to advantage.

SHOWY, flashy; gaudy &c. (*vulgar*) 851; garish *or* gairish, splendiferous [*obs. or humorous*], gorgeous.

ORNAMENTAL, decorative; becoming &c. (*accordant*) 23.

** "The first spiritual want of a barbarous man is Decoration" [Carlyle].

850. [GOOD TASTE.] **Taste. — N.**
TASTE; good –, refined –, cultivated-taste; delicacy, refinement, fine feeling, gust, gusto, tact, finesse; nicety &c. (*discrimination*) 465; *to prepon* [*Gr.* τὸ πρέπον], polish, elegance, grace.

ARTISTIC QUALITY, virtu; dilettante-ism, virtuosity, connoisseurship, fine art of living; fine art; culture, cultivation.

"caviare to the general" [*Hamlet*].

[SCIENCE OF TASTE] æsthetics.

MAN OF TASTE &c.; connoisseur, judge, critic, conoscente, virtuoso, amateur, dilettante; Aristarchus, Corinthian; Aristotle, Stagirite; Petronius, *arbiter elegantiæ* [*L.*], *arbiter elegantiarum* [*L.*].

euphemist, purist, precisian.

V. DISPLAY TASTE &c. *n.*; appreciate, judge, criticize, discriminate &c. 465.

Adj. IN GOOD TASTE, tasteful, unaffected, pure, chaste, classical, Attic, cultivated; attractive, charming, dainty; æsthetic, artistic.

refined, tasty [*colloq.*]; prim, precise, formal, prudish; elegant &c. 578; euphemistic.

TO ONE'S TASTE, to one's mind; after

851. [BAD TASTE.] **Vulgarity. — N.**
VULGARITY, vulgarism; barbarism, Vandalism, Gothicism; *mauvais goût* [*F.*], bad taste; want of tact; ungentleman-liness, ungentlemanlikeness; ill-breeding &c. (*discourtesy*) 895.

coarseness &c. *adj.*; indecorum, loud behavior [*colloq.*], misbehavior; *gaucherie* [*F.*], awkwardness; boorishness &c. *adj.*; homeliness, rusticity.

LOWNESS, low life, *mauvais ton* [*F.*]; brutality; blackguardism, rowdyism, ruffianism; ribaldry; slang &c. (*neology*) 563.

BAD JOKE, *mauvaise plaisanterie* [*F.*], poor joke, joke in bad taste; practical joke.

[EXCESS OF ORNAMENT] gaudiness, tawdriness, gingerbread, false ornament, cheap jewelry; flashy -clothes, – dress; finery, frippery, trickery, tinsel, gewgaw, clinquant.

VULGARIAN, rough diamond; clown &c. (*commonalty*) 876; Goth, Vandal, Bœotian; snob, cad [*colloq.*], gent [*humorous or vulgar*]; parvenu &c. 876; frump [*colloq.*], dowdy; slut, slattern &c. 653; tomboy, hoyden, cub, unlicked cub

one's fancy; *comme il faut* [F.]; *tiré à quatre épingles* [F.].

Adv. ELEGANTLY &c. *adj.;* with quiet elegance; with elegant simplicity; without ostentation.

** nihil tetigit quod non ornavit [from Johnson's epitaph on Goldsmith]; *chacun à son goût; oculi picturâ tenentur aures cantibus* [Cicero]; "Be not the first by whom the new are tried, Nor get the last to lay the old aside" [Pope]; "The life of man is stronger than good taste" [Masefield].

852. Fashion. — N. FASHION, style, *ton* [F.], *bon ton* [F.], society; good -, polite- society; *monde* [F.]; drawing-room, civilized life, civilization, town, *beau monde* [F.], high life, court; world; fashionable -, gay- world; height -, pink -, star -, glass- of fashion; "the glass of fashion and the mould of form" [*Hamlet*]; Vanity Fair; Mayfair; show &c. (*ostentation*) 822.

MANNERS, breeding &c. (*politeness*) 894; air, demeanor &c. (*appearance*) 448; *savoir faire* [F.]; gentlemanliness, gentility, decorum, propriety, *bienséance* [F.]; conventions of society; Mrs. Grundy; dictates of -Society, - Mrs. Grundy; convention, conventionality, the proprieties; punctiliousness, punctilio, form, formality; etiquette, point of etiquette.

MODE, vogue, style, the latest thing, *dernier cri* [F.], the go [*colloq.*], the rage &c. (*desire*) 865; prevailing taste; dress &c. 225; custom &c. 613.

LEADER OF FASHION; *arbiter elegantiarum* [L.] &c. (*taste*) 850; man -, woman- of -fashion, - the world; clubman, clubwoman; upper ten thousand &c. (*nobility*) 875; upper ten [*colloq.*]; *élite* [F.] &c. (*distinction*) 873; smart set [*colloq.*]; the four hundred [*U. S.*].

V. BE FASHIONABLE &c. *adj.*, be the rage &c. *n.;* have a run, pass current.

V. be vulgar &c. *adj.;* misbehave; talk -, smell of the- shop; show a want of -tact, - consideration; be a vulgarian &c. *n.*

Adj. IN BAD TASTE, vulgar, unrefined, coarse, indecorous, ribald, gross; unseemly, unbeseeming, unpresentable; *contra bonos mores* [L.]; ungraceful &c. (*ugly*) 846; dowdy; slovenly &c. (*dirty*) 653; ungenteel, shabby genteel; low &c. (*plebeian*) 876.

extravagant, monstrous, horrid; shocking &c. (*painful*) 830.

ILL-MANNERED, ill-bred, underbred, snobbish, uncourtly; uncivil &c. (*discourteous*) 895; ungentlemanly, ungentlemanlike; unladylike, unfeminine; wild, wild as a hawk, wild as an unbacked colt.

UNCOUTH, unkempt, uncombed, untamed, unlicked, unpolished, plebeian; incondite [*rare*]; heavy, rude, awkward; homely, homespun, homebred; provincial, countrified, rustic; boorish, clownish; savage, brutish, blackguard, blackguardly, rowdyish, rowdy.

barbarous, barbaric, Gothic, heathenish, tramontane, outlandish; uncultivated; Bohemian; unclassical, doggerel *or* doggrel.

OBSOLETE &c. (*antiquated*) 124; out of fashion, old-fashioned, out of date, unfashionable.

NEWFANGLED &c. (*unfamiliar*) 83; fantastic, fantastical, odd &c. (*ridiculous*) 853; particular; affected &c. 855.

TAWDRY, gaudy, meretricious, brummagem [*slang*], bedizened, tricked out; obtrusive, flaunting, loud, crass, showy, flashy, garish.

** "it is considered more withering to accuse a man of bad taste than of bad ethics" [Chesterton]; "On with the dance! Let joy be unrefined!" [*Cynic's Calendar*].

follow -, keep up with -, conform to -, fall in with- the fashion &c. *n.;* go with the stream &c. (*conform*) 82; be on (*or* get on) the band wagon [*slang*], be in the swim [*colloq.*]; *savior -vivre, - faire* [F.]; keep up appearances, behave oneself.

set the fashion, bring into fashion; give a tone to society, cut a figure in society [*colloq.*]; brush shoulders with -the nobility, - royalty; appear -, be presented- at court.

keep one's -automobile, - car, - carriage, - yacht, - house in town [*Eng.*], - cottage at Newport [*U. S.*]; be a member of the best clubs.

Adj. FASHIONABLE; in fashion &c. *n.; à la mode* [F.], *comme il faut* [F.]; admitted -, admissible- in society &c. *n.;* presentable; punctilious, decorous, conventional &c. (*customary*) 613; genteel; well-bred, well-mannered, well-behaved, well-spoken; gentlemanlike, gentlemanly; ladylike; civil, polite &c. (*courteous*) 894.

dashing, jaunty *or* janty, showy, spirited, fast.

POLISHED, refined, thoroughbred, gently bred, courtly; *distingué* [F.], distinguished, aristocratic *or* aristocratical; unselfconscious, self-possessed, poised, easy, frank, unconstrained, unembarrassed, *dégagé* [F.].

MODISH, stylish, swell [*slang*], *récherché* [F.]; newfangled &c. (*unfamiliar*) 83; all the rage, all the go [*colloq.*].

in -court, – full, – evening- dress; *en grande tenue* [F.] &c. (*ornament*) 847.

Adv. FASHIONABLY &c. *adj.;* for fashion's sake; in fear of Mrs. Grundy; in the latest -style, – mode.

Int. it isn't done!

*** à la française, à la parisienne; à l'anglaise, à l'américaine; autre temps autre mœurs; chaque pays a sa guise; il faut souffrir pour être belle; "*the fashion Doth wear out more apparel than the man" [*Much Ado*]; "Custom, the ass man rides, will plod for years, But laughter kills him and he dies at tears" [Masefield].*

853. Ridiculousness. — N. RIDICULOUSNESS &c. *adj.;* comicality, oddity &c. *adj.;* drollery; farce, comedy; burlesque &c. (*ridicule*) 856; buffoonery &c. (*fun*) 840; frippery; amphigory *or* amphigouri, doggerel (*or* doggrel) verses; bull, Irish bull, Hibernicism, Hibernianism, Spoonerism; absurdity &c. 497.

fustian, extravagance, bombast &c. (*unmeaning*) 517; anticlimax, bathos; monstrosity &c. (*unconformity*) 83; laughingstock &c. 857; screamer *or* scream [*slang*].

V. BE RIDICULOUS &c. *adj.;* pass from the sublime to the ridiculous; make one laugh; play the fool, make a fool of oneself, commit an absurdity; ride –, play- the goat [*colloq.*].

MAKE RIDICULOUS, make a goat of [*colloq.*], make a fool of, play a joke on.

Adj. RIDICULOUS, ludicrous, comic *or* comical, drollish, waggish, quizzical, droll, funny, laughable, risible, farcical, screaming; serio-comic, serio-comical; tragi-comic, tragi-comical; *pour rire* [F.].

ODD, grotesque; whimsical, – as a dancing bear; fanciful, fantastic, queer, rum [*slang*], quaint, bizarre; eccentric &c. (*unconformable*) 83; strange, outlandish, out-of-the-way, baroque, rococo; awkward &c. (*ugly*) 846.

EXTRAVAGANT, *outré* [F.], monstrous, preposterous, absurd, bombastic, inflated, stilted, burlesque, mock heroic.

TRIVIAL, doggerel *or* doggrel, gimcrack, contemptible &c. (*unimportant*) 643.

DERISIVE, ironical &c. 856.

*** risum teneatis amici? [*Horace*]; rideret Heraclitus; du sublime au ridicule il n'y a qu'un pas [*Napoleon*]; "*Oh, let's be kings in a humble way" [Gilbert]; "I know it is a sin For me to sit and grin At him here" [Holmes].*

854. Fop. — N. FINE GENTLEMAN, fop, swell [*colloq.*], dandy, exquisite, coxcomb, beau, macaroni [*hist.*]; blade, blood, buck [*archaic*], man about town, fast man, *roué* [F.]; fribble, jemmy [*obs.*], spark, popinjay, puppy [*contemptuous*], prig, *petit maître* [F.]; jackanapes, jack-a-dandy, jessamy [*obs.*], man milliner; carpet knight; masher [*vulgar or slang*], dude [*colloq.*].

FINE LADY, belle, flirt, coquette, toast.

855. Affectation. — N. AFFECTATION; affectedness &c. *adj.;* acting a part &c. *v.;* pretense &c. (*falsehood*) 544, (*ostentation*) 882; boasting &c. 884; charlatanism, quackery, shallow profundity.

pretension, airs, pedantry, pedantism, purism, precisianism, stiffness, formality, buckram; prunes and prisms; euphuism; teratology &c. (*altiloquence*) 577.

prudery, demureness, mock modesty, *minauderie* [F.], sentimentalism; *mauvaise honte* [F.], false shame.

mannerism, *simagrée* [F.], grimace.

FOPPERY, dandyism, man millinery, coxcombry, coquetry, puppyism, conceit.

AFFECTER *or* affector, performer, actor; pedant, pedagogue, doctrinaire, purist, euphuist, mannerist; grimacier [*rare*]; lump of affectation, *précieuse ridicule* [F.], *bas bleu* [*F.*], blue stocking, poetaster; prig; charlatan &c. (*deceiver*) 548; *petit maître* [*F.*] &c. (*fop*) 854; flatterer &c. 935; coquette, prude, puritan, precisian, formalist.

V. AFFECT, act a part, put on; give oneself airs &c. (*arrogance*) 885; boast &c. 884; coquet; simper, mince, attitudinize, pose; flirt a fan; languish; euphuize; overact, overdo.

Adj. AFFECTED, full of affectation, pretentious, pedantic, stilted, stagy, theatrical, big-sounding, *ad captandum* [*L.*]; canting, insincere; not natural, unnatural; self-conscious; mannered, *maniéré* [*F.*]; artificial; overwrought, overdone, overacted; euphuistic &c. 577.

STIFF, starch, formal, prim, smug, demure, *tiré à quatre épingles* [*F.*], quakerish, puritanical, prudish, pragmatical.

PRIGGISH, conceited, coxcomical, foppish, dandified, finical, finicking *or* finicky *or* finikin; mincing, simpering, namby-pamby, sentimental, languishing.

*** "conceit in weakest bodies strongest works" [*Hamlet*].

856. Ridicule. — N. RIDICULE, derision; sardonic -smile, – grin; irrision [*obs.*], snicker *or* snigger, grin, twit [*rare*]; scoffing &c. (*disrespect*) 929; mockery, quiz, banter, irony, persiflage, raillery, chaff, *badinage* [*F.*]; quizzing &c. *v.;* asteism.

SQUIB, satire, skit, quip, quib [*obs.*].

BURLESQUE, parody, travesty, *travestie* [*F.*]; farce &c. (*drama*) 599; caricature.

BUFFOONERY &c. (*fun*) 840; practical joke, horseplay, roughhouse [*slang*].

V. RIDICULE, deride; laugh at, grin at, smile at; snicker *or* snigger; laugh in one's sleeve; banter, rally, chaff, joke, twit, quiz, poke fun at, roast [*slang*], guy [*colloq.*, *U. S.*], jolly [*colloq.*], rag [*slang*, *Eng.*]; haze [*U. S.*]; tehee *or* teehee; fleer; play upon, play tricks upon; get the laugh on [*slang*]; fool, – to the top of one's bent; show up.

turn into ridicule; make merry with; make -fun, – game, – a fool, – an April fool- of; rally; scoff &c. (*disrespect*) 929.

BURLESQUE, satirize, parody, caricature, travesty.

BE RIDICULOUS &c. 853; raise a laugh &c. (*amuse*) 840; play the fool, make a fool of oneself.

Adj. DERISIVE, derisory, mock; sarcastic, ironical, quizzical, burlesque, Hudibrastic, Rabelaisian; scurrilous &c. (*disrespectful*) 929.

Adv. IN RIDICULE &c. *n.;* as a joke, to raise a laugh.

Int. "What fools these mortals be!" [*M. N. D.*].

857. [OBJECT AND CAUSE OF RIDICULE.] **Laughingstock. — N.** LAUGHINGSTOCK, jesting-stock, gazing-stock; butt, game, fair game; April fool &c. (*dupe*) 547; original, oddity; queer –, odd- fish [*colloq.*], figure of fun [*colloq.*]; quiz, square toes; old fogy *or* fogey [*colloq.*].

monkey; buffoon &c. (*jester*) 844; pantomimist &c. (*actor*) 599.

JEST &c. (*wit*) 842.

*** *dum vitant stulti vitia in contraria currunt* [Horace].

3. PROSPECTIVE AFFECTIONS

858. Hope. — N. HOPE, hopes; desire &c. 865; fervent hope, sanguine expectation, trust, confidence, reliance; faith &c. (*belief*) 484; affiance, assurance; secureness, security; reassurance.

good -omen, – auspices; promise, well-grounded hopes; good –, bright- prospect; clear sky.

HOPEFULNESS, buoyancy, optimism, enthusiasm, heart of grace, aspiration; assumption, presumption; anticipation &c. (*expectation*) 507.

859. [ABSENCE, WANT, OR LOSS OF HOPE.] **Hopelessness. — N.** HOPELESSNESS &c. *adj.;* despair, desperation; despondency &c. (*dejection*) 837; pessimism.

hope deferred, dashed hopes; vain expectation &c. (*disappointment*) 509.

airy hopes &c. 858; bad -job, – business; gloomy –, clouds on the –, black spots in the- horizon; dark future; slough of Despond, cave of Despair; *immedicabile vulnus* [*L.*].

OPTIMIST, utopist [*rare*], utopian.

DAYDREAM, castles in the air, *châteaux en Espagne* [*F.*], *le pot au lait* [*F.*], Utopia, millennium; golden dream; dream of Alnaschar; airy hopes, fool's paradise; mirage &c. (*fallacies of vision*) 443; fond hope.

RAY OF HOPE; beam –, gleam –, glimmer –, dawn –, flash –, star- of hope; cheer; bit of blue sky, silver lining of the cloud, bottom of Pandora's box, balm in Gilead.

MAINSTAY, anchor, sheet anchor; staff &c. (*support*) 215; heaven &c. 981.

V. HOPE, trust, confide, rely on, put one's trust in, lean upon; pin one's hope upon, pin one's faith upon &c. (*believe*) 484.

feel –, entertain –, harbor –, indulge –, cherish –, feed –, foster –, nourish –, encourage –, cling to –, live in- hope &c. *n.;* see land; feel –, rest- -assured, – confident &c. *adj.*

hope for &c. (*desire*) 865; anticipate; presume; promise oneself; expect &c. (*look forward to*) 507.

BE HOPEFUL &c. *adj.;* look on the bright side of, view on the sunny side, *voir en couleur de rose* [*F.*], make the best of it, hope for the best; hope against hope; put -a good, – a bold, – the best-face upon; keep one's spirits up; take heart, – of grace; be of good -heart, – cheer; flatter oneself, "lay the flattering unction to one's soul" [*Hamlet*].

catch at a straw, hope against hope, count one's chickens before they are hatched.

ENCOURAGE, hearten, inspirit; give –, inspire –, raise –, hold out- hope &c. *n.;* raise expectations; encourage, cheer, assure, reassure, buoy up, embolden; promise, bid fair, augur well, be in a fair way, look up, flatter, tell a flattering tale.

Adj. HOPEFUL, confident; hoping &c. *v.;* in hopes &c. *n.;* secure &c. (*certain*) 484; sanguine, in good heart, buoyed up, buoyant, elated, flushed, exultant, enthusiastic; heartsome [*chiefly Scot.*]; utopian.

FEARLESS; free from –, exempt from- -fear, – suspicion, – distrust, – despair; unsuspecting, unsuspicious, undespairing, self-reliant; dauntless &c. (*courageous*) 861.

PROPITIOUS, promising; probable, on

FORLORN HOPE, *enfant perdu* (*pl. enfants perdus*) [*F.*]; goner [*slang*]; gone -case, – coon [*slang*, *U. S.*].

PESSIMIST, Job's comforter; hypochondriac &c. 837; bird of bad omen, bird of ill omen.

V. DESPAIR; lose –, give up –, abandon –, relinquish- -all hope, – the hope of; give up, give over; yield to despair; falter; despond &c. (*be dejected*) 837; *jeter le manche après la cognée* [*F.*].

shatter one's hopes; inspire –, drive to- despair &c. *n.;* disconcert; dash –, crush –, destroy- one's hopes; dash the cup from one's lips; undermine one's foundation; take away one's last hope.

Adj. HOPELESS, desperate, despairing, gone, in despair, *au désespoir* [*F.*], forlorn; inconsolable &c. (*dejected*) 837; broken-hearted.

out of the question, not to be thought of; impracticable &c. 471; past -hope, – cure, – mending, – recall; at one's last gasp &c. (*death*) 360; given up, given over.

UNDONE, ruined; incurable, cureless, immedicable, remediless, beyond remedy; incorrigible; irreparable, irremediable, irrecoverable, irreversible, irretrievable, irreclaimable, irredeemable, irrevocable, immitigable.

UNPROPITIOUS, unpromising, inauspicious, ill-omened, threatening, clouded over, lowering, ominous.

*** "*lasciate ogni speranza voi ch' entrate*" [Dante]; its days are numbered; the worst come to the worst; "no change, no pause, no hope, yet I endure" [Shelley]; "O dark, dark, dark. amid the blaze of noon" [Milton].

860. Fear. — N. FEAR, timidity, diffidence, want of confidence; apprehensiveness, fearfulness &c. *adj.;* solicitude, anxiety, care, apprehension, misgiving; feeze [*colloq.*, *U. S.*]; mistrust &c. (*doubt*) 485; suspicion, qualm; hesitation &c. (*irresolution*) 605.

TREPIDATION, flutter, fear and trembling, perturbation, tremor, quivering, shaking, trembling, throbbing heart, palpitation, ague fit, cold sweat; nervousness, restlessness &c. *adj.;* inquietude, disquietude, heartquake; abject fear &c. (*cowardice*) 862; mortal funk [*colloq.*], heartsinking, despondency; despair &c. 859.

batophobia, hypsophobia; claustrophobia; agoraphobia.

the high road to; within sight of -shore, – land; of –, full of- promise; of good omen; auspicious, *de bon augure* [*F.*]; reassuring; encouraging, cheering, inspiriting, looking up, bright, roseate, *couleur de rose* [*F.*], rose-colored.

Adv. hopefully &c. *adj.*

Int. God speed! good luck!

*** *nil desperandum* [Horace]; never say die, *dum spiro spero, latet scintillula forsan,* all is for the best, *spero meliora;* "the wish being father to the thought" [*Henry IV*]; "hope told a flattering tale"; *rusticus expectat dum defluat amnis; at spes non fracta; ego spem pretio non emo* [Terence].

en Dieu est ma fiance; "hope! thou nurse of young desire" [Bickerstaff]; *in hoc signo spes mea; in hoc signo vinces; la speranza è il pan de' miseri; l'espérance est le songe d'un homme éveillé;* "the mighty hopes that make us men" [Tennyson]; "the sickening pang of hope deferred" [Scott].

FRIGHT, affright [*archaic*], affrightment [*archaic*], boof [*slang, U. S.*], alarm, dread, awe, terror, horror, dismay, consternation, panic, scare, panic fear, panic terror; "terror by night" [*Bible*]; chute [*N. U. S.*], stampede [*of horses*].

INTIMIDATION, terrorism, reign of terror; terrorist.

[OBJECT OF FEAR] bugbear, bugaboo, scarecrow; hobgoblin &c. (*demon*) 980; nightmare, Gorgon, mormo [*obs.*], ogre, Hurlothrumbo, raw head and bloody bones, fee-faw-fum, *bête noire* [*F.*], *enfant terrible* [*F.*].

ALARMIST &c. (*coward*) 862.

V. FEAR, stand in awe of; be afraid &c. *adj.;* have qualms &c. *n.;* apprehend, sit upon thorns, eye askance; distrust &c. (*disbelieve*) 485.

hesitate &c. (*be irresolute*) 605; falter, funk [*colloq.*], cower, crouch; skulk &c. (*cowardice*) 862; take fright, take alarm; start, wince, flinch, shy, shrink, blench; fly &c. (*avoid*) 623.

grow pale, turn pale, stand aghast; be in a daze; not dare to say one's soul is one's own.

TREMBLE, shake; shiver, – in one's shoes; shudder, flutter; shake –, tremble- -like an aspen leaf, – all over; quake, quaver, quiver, quail.

FRIGHTEN, fright, affright, terrify; inspire –, excite- -fear, – awe; raise apprehensions; bulldoze [*colloq., U. S.*], faze [*colloq. or dial.*], feeze or feaze [*dial. Eng. & colloq. U. S.*]; give –, raise –, sound- an alarm; alarm, startle, scare, cry "wolf," disquiet, dismay, astound; frighten from one's propriety; frighten out of one's -wits, – senses, – seven senses; awe; strike all of a heap [*colloq.*], strike an awe into, strike terror; harrow up the soul, appall *or* appal, unman, petrify, horrify; pile on the agony.

make one's -flesh creep, – hair stand on end, – blood run cold, – teeth chatter; take away –, stop- one's breath; make one tremble &c.

DAUNT, put in fear, intimidate, cow, daunt, overawe, abash, deter, discourage; browbeat, bully; threaten &c. 909; terrorize, put in bodily fear.

HAUNT, obsess, beset, besiege; prey –, weigh- on the mind.

Adj. AFRAID, fearful, timid, timorous, nervous, diffident, coy, faint-hearted, tremulous, shaky, afraid of one's shadow, apprehensive, restless, fidgety; more frightened than hurt.

fearing &c. *v.;* frightened &c. *v.;* in fear, in a fright &c. *n.;* haunted with the fear of &c. *n.;* afeard [*obs. or dial.*].

aghast; awe-struck, awe-stricken; horror-struck, horror-stricken; terror-struck, terror-stricken; panic-struck, panic-stricken; frightened to death, white as a sheet; pale, – as -death, – ashes, – a ghost; breathless, in hysterics.

INSPIRING FEAR &c. *v.;* alarming; formidable, redoubtable; perilous &c. (*danger*) 665; portentous; fearful, dread, dreadful, fell, dire, direful, shocking, frightful, terrible, terrific, tremendous; horrid, horrible, horrific, ghastly, awful, awe-inspiring; revolting &c. (*painful*) 830; Gorgonian, Gorgon-like.

Adv. *in terrorem* [*L.*].

Int. "angels and ministers of grace defend us!" [*Hamlet*].

*** *ante tubam trepidat; horresco referens,* one's heart failing one, *obstupui steteruntque comœ et vox faucibus hœsit* [Vergil].

"a dagger of the mind" [*Macbeth*]; *expertus metuit* [Horace]; "letting 'I dare not' wait upon 'I would'" [*Macbeth*]; "fain would I climb but that I fear to fall" [Raleigh]; "fear is the parent of cruelty" [Froude]; "Gorgons and hydras and chimeras dire" [*Paradise Lost*], *omnia tuta timens* [Vergil]; "our fears do make us traitors" [*Macbeth*].

861. [ABSENCE OF FEAR.] **Courage.** —
N. COURAGE, bravery, valor *or* valour;
resoluteness, boldness &c. *adj.;* spirit,
daring, gallantry, intrepidity, prowess,
heroism, chivalry; contempt –, defiance-
of danger; derring-do [*pseudo-archaic*];
audacity; rashness &c. 863; dash; defiance &c. 715; confidence, self-reliance.

manhood, manliness, nerve, pluck,
mettle, game; heart, – of grace; spunk
[*colloq.*], grit, virtue, hardihood, fortitude; firmness &c. (*stability*) 150; heart
of oak; bottom, backbone &c. (*preseverance*) 604a; resolution &c. (*determination*) 604; tenacity, bulldog courage.

EXPLOIT, feat, deed, act, achievement;
heroic, –deed, – act; bold stroke.

BRAVE MAN, man of courage, man of
mettle; a man; hero, demigod, paladin;
Hercules, Theseus, Perseus, Achilles,
Hector; Bayard, *chevalier sans peur et
sans reproche;* Lancelot, Sir Galahad.

BRAVE WOMAN, heroine, Amazon,
Joan of Arc.

[COMPARISONS] lion, tiger, panther,
bulldog; gamecock, fighting-cock.

DARE-DEVIL, fire eater &c. 863.

V. BE COURAGEOUS &c. *adj.;* dare,
venture, make bold; face –, front –,
affront –, confront –, brave –, defy –,
despise –, mock- danger; look in the
face; look -full, – boldly, – danger-
in the face; face; meet, meet in front;
brave, beard; defy &c. 715.

bell the cat, take the bull by the
horns, beard the lion in his den, march
up to the cannon's mouth, go through
fire and water, run the gantlet *or*
gauntlet.

NERVE oneself; take –, muster –,
summon up –, pluck up- courage; take
heart; take –, pluck up- heart of grace;
hold up one's head, screw one's courage
to the sticking place; come -to, – up to-
the scratch; stand, – to one's guns, –
fire, – against; bear up, – against; hold
out &c. (*persevere*) 604a.

put a bold face upon; show –, present-
a bold front; show fight; face the
music.

HEARTEN; give –, infuse –, inspire- courage; reassure, encourage, embolden,
inspirit, cheer, nerve, put upon one's mettle, rally, raise a rallying cry; pat on the
back, make a man of, keep in countenance.

Adj. COURAGEOUS, brave, valiant, valorous, gallant, intrepid, spirited, spiritful;
high-spirited, high-mettled, mettlesome, plucky; manly, manful, resolute, stout,
stout-hearted; iron-hearted, lion-hearted; heart of oak; Penthesilean.

bold, bold-spirited; daring, audacious; fearless, dauntless, aweless, dreadless

862. [EXCESS OF FEAR.] **Cowardice.** —
N. COWARDICE, pusillanimity; cowardli-
ness &c. *adj.;* timidity, effeminacy.

poltroonery, baseness, dastardness,
dastardy, abject fear, funk [*colloq.*];
Dutch courage [*colloq.*]; fear &c. 860;
white feather, faint heart; cold feet
[*slang, U. S.*], yellow streak [*slang*].

COWARD, poltroon, dastard, sneak,
recreant; shy –, dunghill- cock; coistril
or coistril [*archaic*], milksop, white-liver
[*colloq.*], nidget [*obs.*], one that cannot
say "Bo" to a goose; slink [*Scot. & dial.
Eng.*], cur [*contemptuous*], craven, caitiff;
Bob Acres, Jerry Sneak.

ALARMIST, terrorist, pessimist; sheep
in wolf's clothing.

SHIRKER, slacker; runagate &c. (*fugitive*) 623.

V. QUAIL &c. (*fear*) 860; be cowardly
&c. *adj.*, be a coward &c. *n.;* funk
[*colloq.*], cower, skulk, sneak; flinch,
shy, fight shy, slink, turn tail; run away
&c. (*avoid*) 623; show the white feather.

Adj. COWARDLY, coward, fearful, shy,
timid, timorous, skittish; poor-spirited,
spiritless, soft, effeminate; weak-minded;
infirm of purpose &c. 605; weak-, faint-,
chicken-, hen-, pigeon- hearted; white-,
lily-, milk- livered; smock-faced; unable to say "Bo" to a goose.

DASTARD, dastardly, base, craven,
sneaking, dunghill, recreant; unwarlike,
unsoldierlike; "in face a lion but in
heart a deer"; "more like a rabbit than
a robber."

UNMANNED; frightened &c. 860.

Adv. with fear and trembling, in fear
of one's life, in a blue funk [*colloq.*];
"with groanings that cannot be uttered"
[*Bible*].

Int. *sauve qui peut!* [*F.*], devil take
the hindmost!

₊ *ante tubam trepidat,* one's courage oozing
out; *degeneres animos timor arguit* [Vergil];
"Thou wear a lion's hide! doff it for shame,
And hang a calf's skin on those recreant limbs"
[*King John*]; "the coward stands aside, Doubt-
ing in his abject spirit, till his Lord is crucified"
[Lowell].

[obs.]; undaunted, unappalled, undismayed, unawed, unblenched, unabashed, unalarmed, unflinching, unshrinking, unblenching, unapprehensive; confident, self-reliant; bold as -a lion, - brass [colloq.].

ENTERPRISING, adventurous, venturous, venturesome, dashing, chivalrous; soldierly &c. (warlike) 722; heroic.

FIERCE, savage; pugnacious &c. (bellicose) 720.

STRONG-MINDED, strong-willed, hardy, doughty [archaic or humorous]; firm &c. (stable) 150; determined &c. (resolved) 604; dogged, indomitable &c. (persevering) 604a.

upon one's mettle; up to the scratch; reassured &c. v.; unfeared, undreaded.

*** one's blood being up; courage sans peur; fortes fortuna adjuvat [Terence]; "have I not in my time heard lions roar" [Taming of the Shrew]; "I dare do all 'that may become a man" [Macbeth]; male vincetis sed vincite [Ovid]; omne solum forti patria; "self-trust is the essence of heroism" [Emerson]; stimulos dedit æmula virtus [Lucan]; "strong and great, a hero" [Longfellow]; teloque animus præstantior omni [Ovid]; "there is always safety in valor" [Emerson]; virtus ariete fortior; "the way to avoid death is not to have too much aversion to it" [Chesterton].

863. Rashness. — N. RASHNESS &c. adj.; temerity, want of caution, imprudence, indiscretion; overconfidence, presumption, audacity; precipitancy, precipitation, impetuosity; levity; foolhardihood, foolhardiness; heedlessness, thoughtlessness &c. (inattention) 458; carelessness &c. (neglect) 460; desperation; Quixotism, knight-errantry; fire eating.

gaming, gambling; blind bargain, leap in the dark, fool's paradise; too many eggs in one basket.

DESPERADO, rashling [obs.], madcap, daredevil, Hotspur, Hector; scapegrace, enfant perdu [F.]; Don Quixote, knight-errant, Icarus; adventurer; dynamiter or dynamitard; fire eater, bully, bravo.

GAMBLER, gamester &c. (chance) 621.

V. BE RASH &c. adj.; stick at nothing, play a desperate game; run into danger &c. 665; play with -fire, - edge tools; donner tête baissée [F.]; knock one's head against a wall &c. (be unskillful) 699; kick against the pricks; rush on destruction; tempt Providence, go on a forlorn hope.

carry too much sail, sail too near the wind, ride at single anchor, go out of one's depth; go to sea in a sieve.

take a leap in the dark; buy a pig in a poke; bet against a dead certainty.

count one's chickens before they are hatched; reckon without one's host; catch at straws; trust to -, lean on- a broken reed.

Adj. RASH, incautious, indiscreet, injudicious, imprudent, improvident, temerarious; uncalculating, impulsive; heedless; careless &c. (neglectful) 460;

864. Caution. — N. CAUTION; cautiousness &c. ad;.; discretion, prudence, cautel [obs.], heed, circumspection, calculation, deliberation.

foresight &c. 510; vigilance &c. 459; warning &c. 668.

worldly wisdom; "safety first," Fabian policy, "watchful waiting."

COOLNESS &c. adj.; self-possession, self-command; presence of mind, sang-froid [F.], well-regulated mind.

V. BE CAUTIOUS &c. adj.; take -care, - heed, - good care; have a care; mind, mind what one is about; be on one's guard &c. (keep watch) 459; "make assurance double sure" [Macbeth].

think twice, look before one leaps, keep one's eye peeled [slang], keep one's weather eye open [colloq.]; count the cost, look to the main chance; cut one's coat according to one's cloth; feel one's -ground, - way; see how the land lies &c. (foresight) 510; pussy-foot [Roosevelt]; wait to see how the cat jumps; bridle one's tongue; reculer pour mieux sauter [F.] &c. (prepare) 673; let well enough alone, ne pas reveiller le chat qui dort [F.]; let sleeping dogs lie.

keep out of -harm's way, - troubled waters; keep at a respectful distance, stand aloof; keep -, be- on the safe side.

ANTICIPATE; bespeak &c. (be early) 132.

LAY BY; husband one's resources &c. 636.

WARN, caution &c. 668.

Adj. CAUTIOUS, wary, guarded, guardful [rare]; on one's guard &c. (watchful) 459; gingerly, precautious [rare], sus-

without ballast, head over heels, heels over head; giddy &c. (*inattentive*) 458.

RECKLESS, wanton, wild, madcap, desperate, devil-may-care, death-defying; hot-blooded, hot-headed, hot-brained; headlong, headstrong; break-neck, foolhardy, harebrained, precipitate.

overconfident, overweening; venturesome, venturous, adventurous, Quixotic; fire-eating.

UNEXPECTED; off one's guard &c. (*inexpectant*) 508.

Adv. posthaste, *à corps perdu* [*F.*], hand over head [*rare*], *tête baissée* [*F.*], headforemost; happen what may.

₊ neck or nothing, the devil being in one; *non semper temeritas est felix* [Livy]; *paucis temeritas est bono multis malo* [Phædrus]; "I am reckless what I do to spite the world" [*Macbeth*]; "I tell thee, be not rash; a golden bridge Is for a flying enemy" [Byron].

picious, leery [*slang*]; *cavendo tutus* [*L.*]; *in medio tutissimus* [*L.*]; vigilant; careful, heedful, cautelous [*obs.*], stealthy, chary, shy of; circumspect, prudent, canny [*Scot.*], safe, noncommittal, discreet, politic; sure-footed &c. (*skillful*) 698.

UNENTERPRISING, unadventurous, cool, steady, self-possessed; overcautious.

Adv. cautiously &c. *adj.*

Int. have a care! look out! danger! mind your eye! [*colloq.*]; stop! look! listen! *cave canem!* [*L.*].

₊ *timeo Danaos et dona ferentes* [Vergil]; *festina lente.*

ante victoriam ne canas triumphum; "give every man thine ear but few thy voice" [Hamlet]; *il rit bien qui rit le dernier; ni firmes carta que no leas ni bebas agua que no veas; nescit vox missa reverti* [Horace]; "love all, trust a few" [*All's Well*]; *noli irritare leones;* safe bind safe find; "the cautious seldom err" [Confucius].

865. Desire. — N. DESIRE, wish, fancy, fantasy; inclination, leaning, bent, mind, animus, partiality, *penchant* [*F.*], predilection; propensity &c. 820; willingness &c. 602; liking, love, fondness, relish.

longing, hankering, yearning, coveting; aspiration, ambition, vaulting ambition; eagerness, zeal, ardor, *empressement* [*F.*], breathless impatience, solicitude, anxiety, overanxiety; impetuosity &c. 825.

NEED, want, exigency, urgency, necessity.

APPETITE, appetition, appetence, appetency; sharp appetite, keenness, hunger, stomach, twist; thirst, thirstiness; drought *or* drouth, mouth-watering.

edge of -appetite, – hunger; torment of Tantalus; sweet tooth [*colloq.*], lickerish (*or* liquorish) tooth; longing –, wistful –, sheep's- eyes.

AVIDITY, greed, greediness, covetousness, ravenousness &c. *adj.;* grasping, craving, canine appetite, rapacity; voracity &c. (*gluttony*) 957.

PASSION, rage, furor, frenzy, mania, manie [*obs.*]; itching palm; inextinguishable desire; itch, itching, prurience, cacoëthes, cupidity, lust, concupiscence; kleptomania, dipsomania; monomania, *idée fixe* [*F.*].

[OF ANIMALS] heat, rut, œstrus.

[PERSON DESIRING] lover, amateur,

866. Indifference. — N. INDIFFERENCE, neutrality; unconcern, insouciance, nonchalance; want of -interest, – earnestness; anorexia *or* anorexy, inappetence *or* inappetency; apathy &c. (*insensibility*) 823; supineness &c. (*inactivity*) 683; disdain &c. 930; recklessness &c. 863; inattention &c. 458; coldness &c. *adj.;* anaphrodisia.

ANAPHRODISIAC *or* antaphrodisiac; lust-quencher, passion-queller.

V. BE INDIFFERENT &c. *adj.;* stand neuter; take no interest in &c. (*insensibility*) 823; have no desire for &c. 865, have no taste for, have no relish for; not care for; care nothing -for, – about; not care a -straw &c. (*unimportance*) 643 -about, – for; not mind.

set at naught &c. (*make light of*) 483; spurn &c. (*disdain*) 930.

Adj. INDIFFERENT, cold, frigid, lukewarm; cool, – as a cucumber; neutral, unconcerned, insouciant, phlegmatic, pococurantish, pococurante, easy-going, devil-may-care, careless, listless, lackadaisical; half-hearted, unambitious, unaspiring, undesirous, unsolicitous, unattracted, inappetent, all one to.

UNATTRACTIVE, unalluring, undesired, undesirable, uncared for, unwished, unvalued.

insipid &c. 391.

Adv. for aught one cares; with utter indifference.

votary, devotee, aspirant, solicitant, candidate; cormorant &c. 957; parasite, sycophant.

[OBJECT OF DESIRE] desideratum, desideration; want &c. (*requirement*) 630; "a consummation devoutly to be wish'd" [*Hamlet*]; attraction, magnet, loadstone, lure, allurement, fancy, temptation, seduction, fascination, prestige, height of one's ambition, idol; whim, whimsey *or* whimsy, whimwham; maggot; hobby, hobbyhorse [*rare*].

Fortunatus's cap; wishing -cap, - stone, - well; love potion; aphrodisiac.

V. DESIRE; wish, wish for; be desirous &c. *adj.;* have a longing &c. *n.;* hope &c. 858.

care for, affect, like, list [*archaic*]; take to, cling to, take a fancy to; fancy; prefer &c. (*choose*) 609; have an eye to, have a mind to; find it in one's heart &c. (*be willing*) 602; have a fancy for, set one's eyes upon; cast sheep's eyes upon, look sweet upon [*colloq.*]; take into one's head, have at heart, be bent upon; set one's cap at [*colloq.*], set one's heart upon, set one's mind upon; covet.

hunger -, thirst -, crave -, lust -, itch -, hanker -, run mad- after; raven for, die for; burn to; sigh -, cry -, gape -, gasp -, pine -, pant -, languish -, yearn -, long -, be on thorns -, hopefor; aspire after; catch at, grasp at, jump at.

woo, court, ogle, solicit; fish for, whistle for, put up for [*slang*].

WANT, miss, need, lack, desiderate, feel the want of; would fain -have, - do; would be glad of.

HUNGER; be hungry &c. *adj.;* have a good appetite, play a good knife and fork [*colloq.*].

ATTRACT, allure; cause -, create -, raise -, excite -, provoke- desire; whet the appetite; appetize, titillate, take one's fancy, tempt; hold out -temptation, - allurement; tantalize, make one's mouth water, *faire venir l'eau à la bouche* [*F.*].

GRATIFY DESIRE &c. (*give pleasure*) 829.

Adj. DESIROUS; desiring &c. *v.;* orectic, appetitive; inclined &c. (*willing*) 602; partial to [*colloq.*]; fain, wishful, longing, wistful; optative; anxious, curious; at a loss for, sedulous, solicitous.

Int. NEVER MIND! who cares! it's all one to me!

⁎⁎ "Let the world slide, let the world go; A fig for care, and a fig for woe!" [Heywood]; "I care for nobody, no, not I, If no one cares for me" [Bickerstaff].

867. Dislike. — N. DISLIKE, distaste, disrelish, disinclination, displacency [*rare*].

reluctance; backwardness &c. (*unwillingness*) 603.

REPUGNANCE, disgust, queasiness, nausea, loathing, loathfulness [*rare*], aversion, averseness, aversation [*obs.*], abomination, antipathy, abhorrence, horror; mortal -, rooted- -antipathy, - horror; hatred, detestation; hate &c. 898; animosity &c. 900.

hydrophobia, canine madness; xenophobia, batophobia &c. (*nervousness*) 860; Anglophobia, Germanophobia, Slavophobia &c.

sickener; gall and wormwood &c. (*unsavory*) 395; shuddering, cold sweat.

V. DISLIKE, mislike, disrelish; mind, object to; would rather not, not care for; have -, conceive -, entertain -, take- -a dislike, - an aversion- to; have no -taste, - stomach- for; shrug the shoulders at, shudder at, turn up the nose at, look askance at; make a -mouth, - wry face, - grimace; make faces.

shun, avoid &c. 623; eschew; withdraw -, shrink -, recoil - from; not be able to -bear, - abide, - endure.

LOATHE, nauseate, wamble [*obs. or dial. Eng.*], abominate, detest, abhor; hate &c. 898; take amiss &c. 900; have enough of &c. (*be satiated*) 869.

CAUSE DISLIKE, excite dislike; disincline, repel, sicken; make sick, render sick; turn one's stomach, nauseate, disgust, shock, stink in the nostrils; go against the -grain, - stomach; stick in the throat; make one's blood run cold &c. (*give pain*) 830; pall.

Adj. DISLIKING &c. *v.;* averse to, loath *or* loth, adverse; shy of, sick of, out of conceit with; disinclined; heartsick, dogsick; queasy.

DISLIKED &c. *v.;* uncared for, unpopular, out of favor; repulsive, repugnant, repellent; abhorrent, insufferable, fulsome, nauseous, loathsome, loathful [*rare*], offensive; disgusting &c. *v.;* disagreeable &c. (*painful*) 830.

eager, avid, keen; burning, fervent, ardent; agog; all agog; breathless; impatient &c. (*impetuous*) 825; bent –, intent –, set- -on, – upon; mad after, *enragé* [*F.*], rabid, dying for, devoured by desire.

aspiring, ambitious, vaulting, sky-aspiring, high-reaching.

CRAVING, hungry, sharp-set, peckish [*colloq.*], ravening, with an empty stomach, esurient, lickerish, thirsty, athirst, parched with thirst, pinched with hunger, famished, dry, droughty *or* drouthy; hungry as a -hunter, – hawk, – horse, – church mouse.

GREEDY, – as a hog; overeager, voracious; ravenous, – as a wolf; open-mouthed, covetous, rapacious, grasping, extortionate, exacting, sordid, *alieni appetens* [*L.*]; insatiable, insatiate, unquenchable, quenchless; omnivorous.

unsatisfied, unsated, unslaked.

DESIRABLE; desired &c. *v.;* in demand, popular; pleasing &c. (*giving pleasure*) 829; appetizing, appetible; tantalizing.

Adv. FAIN; with eager appetite; wistfully &c. *adj.*

Int. would that! would it were! O for! if only! *esto perpetua!* [*L.*].

⁎ the wish being father to the thought; *sua cuique voluptas; hoc erat in votis,* the mouth watering, the fingers itching; *aut Cæsar aut nullus.*

"Cassius has a lean and hungry look" [*Julius Cæsar*]; "hungry as the grave" [Thomson]; "I was born to other things" [Tennyson]; "not what we wish but what we want" [Merrick]; "such joy ambition finds" [*P. L.*]; "the sea hath bounds but deep desire hath none" [*Venus and Adonis*]; *ubi mel ibi apes;* "let us pay with our bodies for our souls' desire" [Roosevelt].

UNEATABLE, inedible, inesculent [*rare*], unappetizing, unsavory.

Adv. TO SATIETY, to one's disgust; *usque ad nauseam* [*L.*].

Int. faugh! foh! ugh!

⁎ *non libet;* "more abhorr'd Than spotted livers in the sacrifice" [*Troilus and Cressida*]; "I find no abhorring in my appetite" [Donne].

868. Fastidiousness. — N. FASTIDIOUSNESS &c. *adj.;* nicety, meticulosity, hypercriticism, difficulty in being pleased; *friandise* [*F.*], epicurism, *omnia suspendens naso* [*L.*].

DISCRIMINATION, discernment, perspicacity, perspicaciousness [*rare*], keenness, sharpness, insight.

EPICURE, gourmet.

[EXCESS OF DELICACY] prudery, prudishness, primness.

V. BE FASTIDIOUS &c. *adj.;* split hairs; hunt for the crumpled rose-leaf.

mince the matter; turn up one's nose at &c. (*disdain*) 930; look a gift horse in the mouth, see spots on the sun; see the mote in one's brother's eye.

DISCRIMINATE, have nice discrimination; have exquisite taste; be discriminative &c. *adj.*

Adj. FASTIDIOUS, nice, delicate, *délicat* [*F.*]; meticulous, finicking *or* finicky *or* finikin, exacting, finical; difficult, dainty, lickerish, squeamish, thin-skinned; queasy; hard –, difficult- to please; querulous; particular, scrupulous; censorious &c. 932; hypercritical; overcritical.

PRUDISH, strait-laced, prim.

DISCRIMINATIVE, discriminating, discerning, discriminant [*rare*], judicious,

keen, sharp, perspicacious.

⁎ *noli me tangere;* "you are idle, shallow things: I am not of your element" [*Twelfth Night*].

869. Satiety. — N. SATIETY, satisfaction, saturation, repletion, glut, surfeit; cloyment [*obs.*], satiation; weariness &c. 841.

spoiled child; *enfant gâté* [*F.*]; too much of a good thing, *toujours perdrix* [*F.*]; a diet of cake; *crambe repetita* [Juvenal].

V. SATE, satiate, satisfy, saturate; cloy, quench, slake, pall, glut, gorge, surfeit; bore &c. (*weary*) 841; tire &c. (*fatigue*) 688; spoil.

have enough of, have quite enough of, have one's fill, have too much of; be satiated &c. *adj.*

Adj. SATIATED &c. *v.;* overgorged; gorged with plenty, overfed; *blasé* [*F.*], used up [*colloq.*], sick of, heartsick.

Int. ENOUGH! hold! *eheu jam satis!* [*L.*].

⁎ "mitigate the ennui of a crushing satiety" [Shaw]; "I feel the old convivial glow (unaided) o'er me stealing" [Holmes].

4. CONTEMPLATIVE AFFECTIONS

870. Wonder. — N. WONDER, marvel; astonishment, amazement, wonderment, bewilderment; amazedness &c. *adj.*; admiration, awe; stupor, stupefaction, stound [*obs.*], fascination; sensation; surprise &c. (*inexpectation*) 508.

note of admiration; thaumaturgy &c. (*sorcery*) 992.

V. WONDER, marvel, admire; be surprised &c. *adj.*; start; stare; open –, rub –, turn up- one's eyes; gloar [*obs.*]; gape, open one's mouth, hold one's breath; look –, stand- -aghast, – agog; look blank &c. (*disappointment*) 509; *tomber des nues* [*F.*]; not believe one's -eyes, – ears, – senses; not be able to account for &c. (*unintelligible*) 519; not know whether one stands on one's head or one's heels.

ASTONISH, surprise, amaze, astound; dumfound *or* dumbfound, dumfounder *or* dumbfounder, startle, dazzle; daze; strike, – with -wonder, – awe; electrify; stun, stupefy, petrify, confound, bewilder, flabbergast [*colloq.*]; stagger, throw on one's beam ends, fascinate, turn the head, take away one's breath, strike dumb; make one's -hair stand on end, – tongue cleave to the roof of one's mouth; make one stare.

TAKE BY SURPRISE, take unawares &c. (*be unexpected*) 508.

BE WONDERFUL &c. *adj.*; beggar –, baffle- description; stagger belief.

Adj. ASTONISHED, surprised &c. *v.*; aghast, all agog, breathless, agape; openmouthed; awe-, thunder-, moon-, planet- struck; spellbound; lost in -amazement, – wonder, – astonishment; struck all of a heap [*colloq.*], unable to believe one's senses; like a duck in -a fit, – thunder [*both colloq.*].

WONDERFUL, wondrous; surprising &c. *v.*; unexpected &c. 508; unheard of; mysterious &c. (*inexplicable*) 519; miraculous.

monstrous, prodigious, stupendous, marvelous; inconceivable, incredible, inimaginable [*obs.*], unimaginable; strange &c. (*uncommon*) 83; passing strange.

striking &c. *v.*; overwhelming; wonder-working.

INDESCRIBABLE, inexpressible, ineffable; unutterable, unspeakable.

Adv. WONDERFULLY &c. *adj.*; fearfully; for a wonder, in the name of wonder; strange to say; *mirabile dictu* [*L.*], *mirabile visu* [*L.*]; to one's great surprise.

WITH WONDER &c. *n.*, with gaping mouth, with open eyes, with upturned eyes; with the eyes starting out of one's head.

Int. LO! lo and behold! O! heyday! halloo! what! indeed! really! surely! humph! hem! good -lack, – heavens, – gracious! gad so! welladay! dear me! only think! lackadaisy! my stars! my goodness! gracious goodness! goodness gracious! mercy on us! heavens and earth! God bless me! bless us! bless my heart! odzookens! *O gemini!* adzooks! hoity-toity! strong! Heaven save –, bless- the mark! can such things be! zounds! 'sdeath! what on earth! what in the world! who would have thought it! &c. (*inexpectation*) 508; you don't say so! what do you say to that! *nous verrons!* [*F.*], how now! where am I? fancy! do tell! [*U. S.*], *Ciel!* [*F.*]; what do you know? [*slang, U. S.*]; what do you know about that! [*slang, U. S.*]; well, I'll be jiggered! [*colloq.*].

*** *vox faucibus hæsit;* one's hair standing on end; "oppress'd with awe And stupid at the wondrous things he saw" [Dryden]; "this is wondrous strange" [*Hamlet*]; "all wonder is the effect of novelty upon ignorance" [Johnson]; "wonder is involuntary praise" [Young]; "That is ever the difference between the wise and the unwise: the latter wonders at what is unusual; the wise man wonders at the usual" [Emerson]; "the world will never starve for want of wonders, but only for want of wonder" [Chesterton].

871. [ABSENCE OF WONDER.] Expectance. — N. EXPECTANCE, expectancy &c. (*expectation*) 507.

IMPERTURBABILITY. imperturbableness, imperturbation, *sang-froid* [*F.*], calmness, unruffled calm, coolness, coldbloodedness, hardheadedness, steadiness, lack of nerves, want of imagination, practicality.

nothing out of the ordinary.

V. EXPECT &c. 507; not be surprised, not wonder &c. 870; *nil admirari* [*L.*], make nothing of; take it coolly; be unamazed &c. *adj.*; display imperturbability &c. *n.*

Adj. EXPECTING &c. *v.*; unamazed, astonished at nothing; *blasé* [*F.*] &c. (*weary*) 841; expected &c. *v.*; foreseen.

IMPERTURBABLE, nerveless, cool, coolheaded, unruffled, calm, steady, hardheaded, practical, unimaginative.

common, ordinary &c. (*habitual*) 613.

Int. no wonder! of course! why not?

872. Prodigy. — N. PRODIGY, phenomenon, wonder, wonderment, marvel, miracle; freak, freak of nature, *lusus naturæ* [*L.*], monstrosity; monster &c. (*unconformity*) 83; curiosity, infant prodigy, lion, sight, spectacle; *jeu –, coup- de théâtre* [*F.*]; gazingstock; sign; St. Elmo's -fire, – light; portent &c. 512.

what no words can paint; wonders of the world; *annus mirabilis* [*L.*]; *dignus vindice nodus* [*L.*].

DETONATION; bursting of a -shell, – bomb, – mine; volcanic eruption, peal of thunder; thunderclap, thunderbolt, thunderstone [*obs. or dial. Eng.*].

'' *⁎⁎⁎ natura il fece e poi roppe la stampa;* "A schoolboy's tale, the wonder of an hour!" [Byron]; "Stones have been known to move and trees to speak" [*Macbeth*]; "'Twas strange, 'twas passing strange; 'Twas pitiful, 'twas wondrous pitiful" [*Othello*].

5. EXTRINSIC AFFECTIONS[1]

873. Repute. — N. REPUTE, reputation; distinction, mark, name, figure; good –, high- repute; note, notability, notoriety, *éclat*, "the bubble reputation" [*As You Like It*], vogue, celebrity; fame, famousness; renown; popularity, *aura popularis* [*L.*]; approbation &c. 931; credit, *succès d'estime* [*F.*], prestige, talk of the town; name to conjure with.

account, regard, respect; reputability [*rare*], reputableness &c. *adj.;* respectability &c. (*probity*) 939; good -name, – report; fair name.

DIGNITY; stateliness &c. *adj.;* solemnity, grandeur, splendor, nobility, majesty, sublimity; glory, honor; luster &c. (*light*) 420; illustriousness &c. *adj.*

RANK, standing, brevet rank, precedence, *pas* [*F.*], station, place, status; position, – in society; order, degree, *locus standi* [*L.*], caste, condition.

graduation, university degree, baccalaureate, doctorate, doctorship; scholarship, fellowship.

EMINENCE; greatness &c. *adj.;* height &c. 206; importance &c. 642; preëminence, supereminence; high mightiness, primacy; top of the -ladder, – tree; elevation; ascent &c. 305; superexaltation, exaltation, dignification [*rare*], aggrandizement; dedication, consecration, enthronement.

CELEBRITY, worthy, hero, man of mark, great card, lion, *rara avis* [*L.*], notability, somebody; "the observed of all observers" [*Hamlet*]; classman; man of rank &c. (*nobleman*) 875; pillar of the -state, – church; "a mother in Israel" [*Bible*].

chief &c. (*master*) 745; first fiddle &c. (*proficient*) 700; scholar, *savant* [*F.*] &c. 492; cynosure, mirror; flower, pink,

874. Disrepute. — N. DISREPUTE, discredit; ill-, bad- -repute, -name, -odor, -favor; disapprobation &c. 932; ingloriousness, derogation, abasement, debasement; abjectness &c. *adj.;* degradation, dedecoration [*rare*]; "a long farewell to all my greatness" [*Henry VIII*]; odium, obloquy, opprobrium, ignominy.

dishonor, disgrace, shame, crying –, burning- shame; humiliation; scandal, baseness, vileness; turpitude &c. (*improbity*) 940; infamy.

STIGMA, brand, reproach, imputation, slur, stain, blot, spot, blur; *scandalum magnatum* [*L.*], badge of infamy, blot in one's escutcheon; bend sinister, bar sinister, champain, point champain [*her.*]; byword of reproach; object of scorn, hissing [*archaic*]; Ichabod.

tarnish, taint, defilement, pollution. *argumentum ad verecundiam* [*L.*]; sense of shame &c. 879.

V. BE INGLORIOUS &c. *adj.;* incur disgrace &c. *n.;* have –, earn- a bad name; put –, wear- a halter round one's neck; disgrace –, expose- oneself.

play second fiddle; lose caste; "pale his uneffectual fire" [*Hamlet*]; recede into the shade; fall from one's high estate; keep in the background &c. (*modesty*) 881; be conscious of disgrace &c. (*humility*) 879; look -blue, – foolish, – like a fool; cut a -poor, – sorry- figure; laugh on the wrong side of the mouth [*colloq.*]; make a sorry face, go away with a flea in one's ear [*colloq.*], slink away.

CAUSE SHAME &c. *n.;* shame, disgrace, put to shame, dishonor; throw –, cast –, fling –, reflect- dishonor &c. *n.* upon; be a reproach to &c. *n.;* derogate from.

tarnish, stain, blot, sully, taint; dis-

[1] Or personal affections derived from the opinions or feelings of others.

383

pearl; paragon &c. (*perfection*) 650; "the choice and master spirits of this age" [*Julius Cæsar*]; *élite* [*F*.]; star, sun, constellation, galaxy.

ORNAMENT, honor, feather in one's cap, halo, aureole, nimbus; halo –, blaze-of glory; "blushing honors" [*Henry VIII*]; laurels &c. (*trophy*) 733.

POSTHUMOUS FAME, memory, niche in the temple of fame; celebration, canonization, enshrinement, glorification; immortality, immortal name; *magni nominis umbra* [Lucan].

V. GLORY IN; be conscious of glory; be proud of &c. (*pride*) 878; exult &c. (*boast*) 884; be vain of &c. (*vanity*) 880.

BE DISTINGUISHED &c. *adj.*; shine &c. (*light*) 420; shine forth, figure; cut a figure, cut a dash [*colloq*.], make a splash [*colloq*.].

SURPASS, outshine, outrival, outvie, outjump, eclipse; throw –, cast- into the shade; overshadow.

RIVAL, emulate, vie with.

GAIN *or* ACQUIRE HONOR &c. *n.*; live, flourish, glitter; flaunt; play first fiddle &c. (*be of importance*) 642; bear the -palm, – bell; lead the way, take precedence, take the wall of [*obs*.]; gain –, win- -laurels, – spurs, – golden opinions &c. (*approbation*) 931; graduate, take one's degree, pass one's examination; win a -scholarship, – fellowship.

make -a, – some- -noise, – noise in the world; leave one's mark, exalt one's horn, star, have a run, be run after; be lionized, come into vogue, come to the front; raise one's head.

HONOR; give –, do –, pay –, render- honor to; accredit, pay regard to, dignify, glorify; sing praises to &c. (*approve*) 931; look up to; exalt, aggrandize, elevate, nobilitate [*archaic*]; enthrone, signalize, immortalize, deify, exalt to the skies; hand one's name down to posterity.

consecrate; dedicate to, devote to; enshrine, inscribe, blazon, lionize, blow the trumpet, crown with laurel.

confer *or* reflect honor on &c. *n.*; shed a luster on; redound to one's honor, ennoble.

Adj. DISTINGUISHED, *distingué* [*F*.], noted; of note &c. *n.*; honored &c. *v.*; popular; fashionable &c. 852; remarkable &c. (*important*) 642; notable, notorious; celebrated, renowned, in every one's mouth, talked of, famous, famed, far-famed; conspicuous, to the front; foremost; in the -front rank, – ascendant.

credit; degrade, debase, defile; beggar; expel &c. (*punish*) 972.

STIGMATIZE, vilify, defame, slur, cast a slur upon, impute shame to, brand, post, hold up to shame, send to Coventry; tread –, trample- under foot; show up [*colloq*.], drag through the mire, heap dirt upon; reprehend &c. 932.

bring low, put down, snub; take down; take down a peg, – lower, – or two [*colloq*.].

OBSCURE, eclipse, outshine, take the shine out of [*colloq*.]; throw –, cast- into the shade; overshadow; leave –, put- in the background; push into a corner, put one's nose out of joint [*colloq*.]; put out, put out of countenance.

DISCONCERT, upset, throw off one's center, discompose; put to the blush &c. (*humble*) 879.

Adj. DISGRACED &c. *v.*; blown upon; "shorn of its beams" [Milton], shorn of one's glory; overcome, downtrodden; loaded with shame &c. *n.*; in bad repute &c. *n.*; out of -repute, – favor, – fashion, – countenance; at a discount; under -a cloud, – an eclipse; unable to show one's face; in the -shade, – background; out at elbows, down in the world, down on one's uppers [*colloq*.], down and out.

inglorious, nameless, renownless, obscure, unknown to fame, unnoticed, unnoted, unhonored, unglorified.

DISCREDITABLE, shameful, disgraceful, disreputable, despicable; questionable; unbecoming, unworthy, derogatory; degrading, humiliating, *infra dignitatem* [*L*.], dedecorous [*rare*]; scandalous, infamous, too bad, unmentionable, ribald, opprobrious; arrant, shocking, outrageous, notorious.

ignominious, scrubby, dirty, abject, vile, beggarly, pitiful, low, mean, petty, shabby; base &c. (*dishonorable*) 940.

Adv. to one's shame be it spoken.

Int. SHAME! fie! for shame! *proh pudor!* [*L*.]; *O tempora! O mores!* [*L*.]; ough! *sic transit gloria mundi!* [*L*.].

*** *fama malum quo non velocius ullum* [Vergil].

in good odor; in favor, in high favor; reputable, respectable, creditable.

IMPERISHABLE, deathless, immortal, never fading, fadeless, *ære perennius* [*L.*], time-honored.

ILLUSTRIOUS, glorious, splendid, brilliant, radiant; bright &c. 420; full-blown; honorific.

EMINENT, prominent; high &c. 206; in the zenith; at the -head of, – top of the tree; peerless, of the first water; superior &c. 33; supereminent, preëminent.

great, dignified, proud, noble, honorable, worshipful, lordly, grand, stately, august, princely, imposing, solemn, transcendent, majestic, sacred, sublime, heaven-born, heroic, *sans peur et sans reproche* [*F.*]; sacrosanct.

Int. HAIL! all hail! *ave!* [*L.*], *viva!* [*It.*], *vive!* [*F.*], long life to! glory –, honor be to!

⁎ one's name being in every mouth; one's name living for ever; *sic itur ad astra, fama volat, aut Cæsar aut nullus;* none but himself could be his parallel; *palmam qui meruit ferat* [Nelson's motto]; "above all Greek above all Roman fame" [Pope]; *cineri gloria sera est* [Martial]; "great is the glory for the strife is hard" [Wordsworth]; *honor virtutis præmium* [Cicero]; *immensum gloria calcar habet* [Ovid]; "the glory dies not and the grief is past" [Brydges]; *vivit post funera virtus;* "not to know me argues yourselves unknown" [Milton].

---

875. Nobility. — N. NOBILITY, rank, condition, distinction, optimacy [*rare*], blood, *pur sang* [*F.*], birth, high descent, order; quality, gentility; blue blood of Castile; "all the blood of all the Howards" [Pope]; caste of "Vere de Vere" [Tennyson]; *ancien régime* [*F.*].

high life, *haut monde* [*F.*]; upper classes, upper ten [*colloq.*], upper ten thousand; the four hundred [*U. S.*]; *élite* [*F.*], aristocracy, great folks; fashionable world &c. (*fashion*) 852.

personage –, man- of -distinction, – mark, – rank; notables, notabilities; celebrity, bigwig [*humorous*], magnate, great man, star; big bug, big gun, great gun [*colloq.*]; gilded rooster [*slang*, *U. S.*]; *magni nominis umbra* [Lucan]; "every inch a king" [*Lear*].

[THE NOBILITY] peerage, baronage; house of -lords, – peers; lords, – temporal and spiritual; noblesse; knightage.

peer, noble, nobleman; lord, lording [*archaic*], lordling; grandee, magnifico, hidalgo; daimio, samurai, *shizoku* [*Jap.*]; don; aristocrat, swell [*colloq.*], three-tailed bashaw; gentleman, squire, squireen [*humorous,Eng.*], patrician; laureate.

gentry, gentlefolk; squirarchy *or* squirearchy, better sort, magnates, primates, optimates; pantisocracy.

king &c. (*master*) 745; atheling [*hist.*]; prince, duke, marquis, earl, viscount, baron, thane [*hist.*], banneret, baronet, knight, chevalier, count, armiger, esquire, laird [*Scot.*]; signior, seignior; *signor* [*It.*], *señor* [*Sp.*], *senhor* [*Pg.*]; boyar *or* boyard [*Russ.*]; effendi, sheik

876. Commonalty. — N. COMMONALTY, democracy; obscurity; low -condition, – life, – society, – company; *bourgeoisie* [*F.*]; mass of -the people, – society; Brown, Jones, and Robinson; Tom, Dick, and Harry; "the four million" [O. Henry]; the peepul [*humorous*]; lower –, humbler- -classes, – orders; vulgar –, common- herd; rank and file, *hoc genus omne* [*L.*]; the -many, – general, – crowd, – people, – populace, – multitude, – million, – masses, – mobility [*humorous*], – other half, - peasantry; king Mob; proletariat; *fruges consumere nati* [*L.*], demos [*Gr.* δῆμος], *hoi polloi* [*Gr.* οἱ πολλοί], great unwashed; man in the street.

RABBLE, – rout; chaff, rout, horde, canaille; scum –, residuum –, dregs- of -the people, – society; mob, swinish multitude, *fæx populi* [*L.*]; trash; *profanum* –, *ignobile- vulgus* [*L.*]; vermin, raff, riffraff, rag-tag and bobtail; small fry.

COMMONER, one of the people, democrat, plebeian, republican, proletary, proletarian, *proletaire, roturier* [*F.*], John Smith, Mr. Snooks, *bourgeois* [*F.*], *épicier* [*F.*], Philistine, cockney; grisette, demimonde, demimondaine.

PEASANT, countryman, boor, carl *or* carle [*Scot. or archaic*], churl; villain *or* villein [*obs. or rare*], serf; *terræ filius* [*L.*], kern *or* kerne [*Ir.*], gossoon [*Anglo-Ir.*]; tike *or* tyke [*archaic or dial.*], ryot [*India*], fellah [*Ar. pl.* fellahin *or* fellaheen]; docker, stevedore, longshoreman; swain, clown, hind [*Eng.*], clod, clodhopper,

or sheikh, emir, shereef *or* sherif, pasha, sahib; palsgrave [*Ger. hist.*], waldgrave, margrave; vavasor [*feudal law*].

empress, queen, princess, duchess, marchioness, viscountess, countess; lady, doña [*Sp.*], dona [*Pg.*[; *signora* [*It.*], señora [*Sp.*], senhora [*Pg.*]; dame; memsahib.

[INDIAN RULING CHIEFS] raja, rana, rao, rawal, rawat, rai, raikwar, raikbar, raikat; maharaja, maharana, maharao &c.; Gaekwar [*lit.* cowherd; *Baroda*]; maharaja bahadur, raja bahadur, rai (*or* rao) bahadur; rai (*or* rao) sahib; jám, thakur [*all Hindu titles*].

nawab, wali, sultan, ameer *or* amir, mir, mirza, mian, khan; Nizam, nawab bahadur, khan bahadur, khan sahib [*all Moham. titles*].

sirdar *or* sardar, diwan *or* dewan [*both Hindu and Moham. titles*].

[HONORIFICS] shahzada ["King's son"], kumar *or* kunwar ["prince"]; mirza [*when appended it signifies* "prince"; *when prefixed*, "Mr."]; arbab ["lord"]; malik ["master"]; khanzada ["son of a khan"]; huzur *or* huzoor ["the presence"].

[FEMALE TITLES] rani, maharani [*Hindu*]; sultana, malikah, begum *or* begam [*Moham.*].

shahzadi, kumari *or* kunwari, raj-kumari, malikzadi, khanam [*all equivalent to* "princess"].

[RANK OR OFFICE] kingship, dukedom, marquisate, earldom; viscountship, viscounty, viscountcy; lordship, baronetcy, knighthood, donship.

V. be noble &c. *adj.*

Adj. NOBLE, exalted; of rank &c. *n.*; princely, titled, patrician, aristocratic; highborn, well-born; of gentle blood; genteel, *comme il faut* [*F.*], gentleman-like, courtly &c. (*fashionable*) 852; highly respectable.

Adv. in high quarters.

** *Adel sitzt im Gemüthe nicht im Geblüte; adelig und edel sind zweierlei; noblesse oblige.*

877. Title. — N. TITLE, honor; knighthood &c. (*nobility*) 875.

highness, excellency, grace, lordship, worship; reverence; reverend; esquire, sir, master, Mr., *signor* [*It.*], señor [*Sp.*], &c. 373; *Mein Herr* [*Ger.*], mynheer; your –, his- honor; serene highness.

madam, *madame* [*F.*] &c. (*mistress*) 374; empress, queen &c. 875.

DECORATION, laurel, palm, wreath, garland, bays, medal, ribbon, riband, blue ribbon, red ribbon, cordon, cross, crown, coronet, star, garter, fleece; feather, – in one's cap; epaulet *or* epaulette, chevron, *fourragère* [*F.*], colors, cockade; livery; order, arms, coat of arms, shield, escutcheon *or* scutcheon, crest; reward &c. 973; handle to one's name.

hobnail, yokel [*Eng.*], bogtrotter, bumpkin; plowman *or* ploughman, plowboy *or* ploughboy; chuff, hayseed [*slang*], rustic, lunkhead [*colloq., U. S.*], loon [*archaic*], rube [*slang, U. S.*], chawbacon [*slang*], tiller of the soil; hewers of wood and drawers of water; sons of Martha; groundling [*obs.*], gaffer, put, cub, Tony Lumpkin [Goldsmith], looby, lout, underling; gamin, street Arab, mudlark.

ROUGH, rowdy, roughneck [*slang*], ruffian, tough [*colloq., U. S.*], potwallopper [*slang*], scullion, slubberde-gullion [*obs.*], vulgar –, low- fellow; cad.

UPSTART, parvenu, skipjack [*dial. Eng.*]; nobody, – one knows; *hesterni quirites* [*L.*], *pessoribus orti* [*L.*]; *bourgeois gentilhomme* [*F.*]; *novus homo* [*L.*], snob, gent [*vulgar or humorous*], mushroom, no one knows who, adventurer; *nouveau riche* (*pl. nouveaux riches; fem. nouvelles riches*) [*F.*].

VAGABOND, beggar, gaberlunzie [*Scot.*], beadsman *or* bedesman [*Scot.*], muckworm, *sans-culotte* [*F.*], tatterdemalion, caitiff, ragamuffin, pariah, outcast of society, tramp, bezonian [Shakespeare], panhandler [*slang*], sundowner [*Austral.*], bum [*slang, U. S.*], hobo [*U. S.*]; chiffonier *or* chiffonnier [*rare*], ragman, ragpicker, sweeper, sweep, scrub.

wench, slut, quean, Cinderella.

BARBARIAN, Goth, Vandal, Hottentot, Zulu, savage, Yahoo; unlicked cub, rough diamond.

barbarousness, barbarism, savagery; Bœotia; Philistinism; parvenuism, parvenudom.

V. BE IGNOBLE &c. *adj.*, be nobody &c. *n.*; be of (*or* belong to) the common herd &c. *n.*

Adj. IGNOBLE, common, mean, low, base, vile, sorry, scrubby, beggarly; below par; no great shakes &c. (*unimportant*) 643; homely, homespun, vulgar, low-minded; snobbish, parvenu, low bred; menial, underling, servile.

PLEBEIAN, proletarian; of -low, – mean- -parentage, – origin, – extraction; lowborn, baseborn, earthborn; mushroom, dunghill, risen from the ranks; unknown to fame, obscure, untitled.

RUSTIC, country, uncivilized; loutish, boorish, clownish, churlish, brutish, raffish; rude, unpolished, unlicked.

BARBAROUS, barbarian, barbaric, barbaresque [De Quincey].
COCKNEY, born within sound of Bow bells.
Adv. below the salt.

* *dummodo sit dives Barbarus ipse placet* [Ovid]; "The play, I remember, pleased not the million; 'twas caviare to the general" [*Hamlet*]; "he who meanly admires mean things is a snob" [Thackeray].

878. Pride. — N. PRIDE; haughtiness &c. *adj.;* high notions, hauteur; vainglory, crest; arrogance &c. (*assumption*) 885; self-importance, pomposity, pompousness; side [*slang*], swank [*dial. Eng.*], swagger, toploftiness [*colloq.*].

proud man, highflyer *or* highflier; fine gentleman; fine lady, *grande dame* [*F.*].

DIGNITY, self-respect, *mens sibi conscia recti* [Vergil].

V. BE PROUD &c. *adj.;* put a good face on; look one in the face; stalk abroad, perk, perk up, perk oneself up; think no small beer of oneself [*colloq.*]; think no small potatoes of oneself [*colloq.*]; presume, swagger, strut; rear –, lift up –, hold up- one's head; hold one's head high, look big, take the wall; "bear like the Turk no rival near the throne" [Pope]; carry with a high hand; ride the –, mount on one's- high horse; set one's back up, bridle, toss the head; give oneself airs &c. (*assume*) 885; boast &c. 884.

pride oneself on; glory in, take a pride in; pique –, plume –, hug- oneself; stand upon, be proud of; not hide one's light under a bushel, not put one's talent in a napkin; not think small beer of oneself [*colloq.*] &c. (*vanity*) 880.

Adj. DIGNIFIED; stately, proud-crested, lordly, baronial; lofty-minded, high-souled, high-minded, high-mettled, high-plumed, high-flown, high-toned.

PROUD, haughty, lofty, high, mighty, swollen, puffed up, flushed, blown; vainglorious; purse-proud, fine; proud as -a peacock, – Lucifer; bloated with pride.

SUPERCILIOUS, disdainful, bumptious, magisterial, imperious, high-handed, high and mighty, overweening, consequential; pompous, toplofty [*colloq.*]; arrogant &c. 885; unblushing &c. 880.

STIFF, stiff-necked; starched, perked up, stuck up [*colloq.*]; in buckram, strait-laced; prim &c. (*affected*) 855.

ON ONE'S DIGNITY; on one's -high horse, – tight ropes, – high ropes; on stilts; *en grand seigneur* [*F.*].

879. Humility. — N. HUMILITY, humbleness, meekness, lowness, lowliness, lowlihood; abasement, self-abasement; submission &c. 725; resignation.

modesty, timidity &c. 881; verecundity [*obs.*], blush, suffusion, confusion; sense of -shame, – disgrace; humiliation, mortification; letdown, setdown.

CONDESCENSION; affability &c. (*courtesy*) 894.

V. BE HUMBLE &c. *adj.;* deign, vouchsafe, condescend; humble oneself, demean oneself [*colloq.*]; stoop, – to conquer; carry coals; submit &c. 725; submit with a good grace &c. (*brook*) 826; yield the palm.

lower one's -tone, – note; sing small [*colloq.*], draw in one's horns [*colloq.*], sober down; hide one's -face, – diminished head; not dare to show one's face, take shame to oneself, not have a word to say for oneself; feel –, be conscious of- -shame, – disgrace; be humiliated, be put out of countenance, be shamed, be put to the blush &c. *v.;* receive a snub; eat humble pie, eat crow, eat dirt; drink the cup of humiliation to the dregs.

blush for, blush up to the eyes; redden, change color; color up; hang one's head, look foolish, feel small.

RENDER HUMBLE; humble, humiliate; let –, set –, take –, tread –, frown-down; snub, abash, abase, make one sing small [*colloq.*], strike dumb; teach one his distance; take down a peg, – lower; throw –, cast- into the shade &c. 874; stare –, put- out of countenance; put to the blush; confuse, ashame [*rare*], shame, mortify, disgrace, crush; send away with a flea in one's ear [*colloq.*].

get a setdown.

Adj. HUMBLE ,lowly, meek; modest &c. 881; humble-minded, sober-minded; unoffended; submissive &c. 725; servile &c. 886.

CONDESCENDING; affable &c. (*courteous*) 894.

HUMBLED &c. *v.;* bowed down, resigned; abashed, ashamed, dashed; out

Adv. with head erect; *de haut en bas* [*F.*]; with nose in air, with nose turned up; with a sneer, with curling lip.

. *odi profanum vulgus et arceo* [Horace].
"a duke's revenues on her back" [*Henry VI*]; "disdains the shadow which he treads on at noon" [*Coriolanus*]; "pride in their port, defiance in their eye" [Goldsmith].

Adv. HUMBLY; with downcast eyes, with bated breath, on bended knee; on all fours; with one's tail between one's legs.

UNDER CORRECTION, with due deference.

⁻*.* I am your -obedient, – very humble- servant; my service to you; *da locum melioribus* [Terence]; *parvum parva decent* [Horace]; "humility is a virtue all preach, none practice" [Selden].

880. Vanity. — N. VANITY; conceit, conceitedness; self-conceit, self-complacency, self-confidence, self-sufficiency, self-esteem, self-love, self-approbation, self-praise, self-glorification, self-laudation, self-gratulation, self-applause, self-admiration; *amour propre* [*F.*]; selfishness &c. 943.

PRETENSIONS, airs, affected manner, mannerism; egoism, egotism, priggism, priggishness; coxcombery, gaudery, vainglory, elation; pride &c. 878; ostentation &c. 882; assurance &c. 885.

vox et præterea nihil [*L*].

EGOIST, egotist; peacock; coxcomb &c. 854; Sir Oracle &c. 887.

V. BE VAIN &c. *adj.*; be vain of; pique oneself &c. (*pride*) 878; lay the flattering unction to one's soul.

have -too high, – an overweening-opinion of -oneself, – one's talents; blind oneself as to one's own merit; not think small beer of oneself [*colloq.*]; strut; put oneself forward; fish for compliments; give oneself airs &c. (*assume*) 885; boast &c. 884.

RENDER VAIN &c. *adj.*; inspire with vanity &c. *n.*; inflate, puff up, turn one's head.

Adj. VAIN, – as a peacock; conceited, overweening, pert, forward; vainglorious, high-flown; ostentatious &c. 882; puffed up, inflated, flushed.

self-satisfied, self-confident, self-sufficient, self-flattering, self-admiring, self-applauding, self-glorious, self-opinionated; *entêté* [*F.*] &c. (*wrong-headed*)

of countenance; down in the mouth; down on one's -knees, – marrowbones [*colloq.*], – uppers [*colloq.*]; humbled in the dust, brow-beaten; chapfallen, crestfallen; dumfoundered *or* dumbfoundered, flabbergasted [*colloq.*], struck all of a heap [*colloq.*]; shorn of one's glory &c. (*disrepute*) 874.

881. Modesty. — N. MODESTY; humility &c. 879; diffidence, timidity; retiring disposition; unobtrusiveness; bashfulness &c. *adj.*; *mauvaise honte* [*F.*]; blush, blushing; verecundity [*obs.*]; self-knowledge.

reserve, constraint; demureness &c. *adj.*; "blushing honors" [*Henry VIII*]. [COMPARISON] violet.

V. BE MODEST &c. *adj.*; retire, reserve oneself; give way to; draw in one's horns &c. 879; hide one's face.

keep private, keep in the background, keep one's distance; pursue the noiseless tenor of one's way, "do good by stealth and blush to find it fame" [Pope], hide one's light under a bushel; cast sheep's eyes.

Adj. MODEST, diffident; humble &c. 879; timid, timorous, bashful; shy, nervous, skittish, coy, sheepish, shamefaced, blushing, overmodest.

unpretending, unpretentious; unobtrusive, unassuming, unostentatious, unboastful, unaspiring; poor in spirit; deprecative, deprecatory.

reserved, constrained, demure.

ABASHED, ashamed; out of countenance &c. (*humbled*) 879.

Adv. MODESTLY &c. *adj.*; quietly, privately; without -ceremony, – beat of drum; *sans façon* [*F.*].

. "not stepping o'er the bounds of modesty" [*Romeo and Juliet*]; "thy modesty's a candle to thy merit" [Fielding].

481; wise in one's own conceit, pragmatical [*rare*], overwise, pretentious, priggish; egotistic *or* egotistical; *soidisant* [*F.*] &c. (*boastful*) 884; arrogant &c. 885; assured.

UNABASHED, unblushing, unconstrained, unceremonious; free and easy.

Adv. VAINLY &c. *adj.*

. "how we apples swim!" [Swift]; "prouder than rustling in unpaid-for silk" [*Cymbeline*]; "the fuming vanities of earth" [Wordsworth]; "How many saucy airs we meet, From Temple Bar to Aldgate Street!" [Gay]; "Vain? Let it be so! Nature was her teacher" [Holmes].

882. Ostentation. — N. OSTENTATION, display, show, *coup d' œil* [*F.*], flourish, parade, *étalage* [*F.*], pomp, magnificence, splendor, pageantry, array, state, solemnity; dash [*colloq.*], splash [*colloq.*], splurge [*colloq.*], glitter, strut, pomposity, pompousness; pretense, pretensions, showing off; fuss; grand doings.

DEMONSTRATION, flying colors; flourish of trumpets &c. (*celebration*) 883; pageant, spectacle, exhibition, exposition, procession, turnout [*colloq.*], set out; grand function; fête, gala, field day, review, march past, promenade, "insubstantial pageant" [*Tempest*].

coup de théâtre [*F.*], stage effect, stage trick; claptrap; *mise en scène* [*F.*], *tour de force* [*F.*], *chic* [*colloq.*, *F.*].

DRESS; court –, full –, evening –, ball –, fancy- dress; tailoring, millinery, man millinery, frippery; foppery, equipage.

CEREMONY, ceremonial, ritual, form, formality, etiquette, puncto [*obs.*], punctilio, punctiliousness, starchedness, stateliness.

mummery, solemn mockery, mouth honor; tomfoolery; attitudinarianism.

ATTITUDINARIAN; fop &c. 854; no modest violet.

V. BE OSTENTATIOUS &c. *adj.*; come forward, put oneself forward, attract attention, star; make –, cut- a -figure, – dash, – splash, – splurge [*all colloq.*]; strut; blow one's own trumpet; have no false modesty; figure; make a show, – display; glitter.

SHOW OFF, show one's paces; parade, march past; display, exhibit, put forward, hold up; trot out [*slang*], hand out; sport [*colloq.*], brandish, blazon forth; dangle, – before the eyes; cry up &c. (*praise*) 931; *prôner* [*F.*], flaunt, emblazon, prink, set off, mount, have framed and glazed.

put on the mask; put a -good, – smiling- face upon; clean the outside of the platter &c. (*disguise*) 544.

Adj. OSTENTATIOUS, showy, dashing, pretentious, jaunty *or* janty, grand, pompous, high-sounding; turgid &c. (*big-sounding*) 577; garish *or* gairish; gaudy, – as a -peacock, – butterfly, – tulip; flaunting, flashing, flaming, glittering; gay &c. (*ornate*) 847.

splendid, magnificent, sumptuous, palatial.

THEATRICAL, theatric, dramatic, spectacular, scenic, scenical; dramaturgic *or* dramaturgical.

CEREMONIAL, ritual, ritualistic; solemn, stately, majestic, formal, stiff, ceremonious, punctilious, starched, starchy.

en grande tenue [*F.*], in one's best bib and tucker [*colloq.*], in one's Sunday best, *endimanché* [*F.*], *chic* [*colloq.*, *F.*].

Adv. with flourish of trumpet, with beat of drum, with flying colors, with a brass band; at the head of the procession; with no false modesty.

ad captandum vulgus [*L.*].

. *honores mutant mores;* "Hell is paved with big pretensions" [*Cynic's Calendar*].

883. Celebration. — N. CELEBRATION, solemnization, commemoration, ovation, triumph; lionization.

inauguration, installation, presentation; coronation; *début* [*F.*], coming out [*colloq.*]; Lord Mayor's show [*London, Eng.*]; harvest-home, husking bee, quilting bee; birthday, anniversary, biennial, triennial &c.; centenary, centennial; bicentenary, bicentennial; tercentenary, tercentennial &c.; "the day we celebrate"; red-letter day; trophy &c. 733; jubilation, laudation, pæan *or* pean; *Te Deum* &c. (*thanksgiving*) 990; festivity, festival; fête &c. 882; Forefathers' Day [*U. S.*], Independence Day, "the Glorious Fourth" [*U. S.*]; holiday &c. 840.

triumphal arch, bonfire; salute, salvo, salvo of artillery; *feu de joie* [*F.*], flourish of trumpets, fanfare, colors flying, illuminations.

[WEDDING ANNIVERSARIES] *wooden* wedding [5th], *tin* wedding [10th], *crystal* wedding [15th], *china* wedding [20th], *silver* wedding [25th], *golden* wedding [50th], *diamond* wedding [60th].

JUBILEE, 50th anniversary; diamond jubilee, 60th anniversary.

V. CELEBRATE, keep, signalize, do honor to, commemorate, solemnize, hallow; keep high festival, keep holiday; mark with a red letter.

PLEDGE, drink to, toast; hob and nob, hobnob with; present.

INAUGURATE, install, instate, induct, chair.

rejoice &c. 838; kill the fatted calf, hold jubilee; roast an ox, serve up the Thanksgiving turkey, serve up the Christmas goose; fire a salute, dip the colors, present arms; paint the town red [*colloq.*]; maffick [*colloq., Eng.*].

Adj. CELEBRATING &c. *v.;* commemorative, celebrated, immortal; solemn, jubilant; kept, kept in remembrance.

Adv. IN HONOR OF, in commemoration of, in celebration of, in memory of; as a toast.

Int. HAIL! all hail! "see the conquering hero comes!" "Hail! hail! the gang's all here!"

₊ "I drink to the general joy of the whole table" [*Macbeth*]; "God bless thy lungs, good Knight" [*II Henry IV.*]; "One flag, one land, one heart, one hand, One nation evermore!" [Holmes]; "A broadside for our Admiral, Load every crystal gun" [*ibid.*]; "ere we depart we'll share a bounteous time" [*Timon of Athens*]; "they are ever forward In celebration of this day" [*Henry VIII*]; "less noise, less noise!" [*II Henry IV*]; "The yearly course that brings this day about Shall never see it but a holiday" [*King John*]; "Lest we forget" [Kipling].

---

884. Boasting. — N. BOASTING &c. *v.;* boast, vaunt, crake [*obs.*], pretense, pretensions, cock-a-hoopness, braggadocio, braggadocianism, puff [*colloq.*], puffery; flourish, fanfaronade; gasconade, bluff, highfaluting *or* highfalutin, *blague* [*F.*]; side [*slang, Eng.*], swagger, jingoism, spread-eagleism [*U. S.*]; brag, braggartism *or* braggardism, braggartry, bounce, rant, bluster, bravado, buncombe *or* bunkum [*cant or slang, U. S.*]; jactation, jactitation, jactancy; venditation [*obs.*], vaporing, rodomontade, bombast, gas [*slang*], hot air [*slang*], fine talking, tall talk, tall story [*both colloq.*], fish story [*humorous*]; magniloquence, teratology [*obs.*], heroics; chauvinism; exaggeration &c. 549; vanity &c. 880; *vox et præterea nihil* [*L.*]; much cry and little wool, *brutum fulmen* [*L.*].

exultation, gloriation [*obs.*], glorification; flourish of trumpets; triumph &c. 883.

BOASTER, braggart, braggadocio, fanfaron, pretender, bluffer, blower [*slang, U. S.*], blower of his own trumpet, windbag [*slang*], hot-air artist [*slang*], Fourth of July orator; Thraso, Gascon; chauvinist, jingo, jingoist; blusterer, swaggerer &c. 887; charlatan, trumpeter; puppy &c. (*fop*) 854.

V. BOAST, make a boast of, brag, vaunt, puff, show off, flourish, crake [*obs.*], crack, trumpet, strut, swagger, *blague* [*F.*], gasconade, vapor; blow [*slang*], fourflush [*slang*], bluff; talk big, draw the long bow, speak for Buncombe; *faire claquer son fouet* [*F.*], blow one's own trumpet; put on side [*slang, Eng.*], swank [*dial. Eng.*]; let the American eagle scream, sing "Rule, Britannia," indulge in jingoism; *se faire valoir* [*F.*], take merit to oneself, make a merit of; holloa before one is out of the wood.

EXULT; crow, crow over [*both colloq.*], triumph, glory, jubilate, rejoice, maffick [*colloq., Eng.*], throw up one's cap, yell oneself hoarse, cheer.

gloat, gloat over; chuckle; neigh.

Adj. BOASTING &c. *v.;* magniloquent, flaming, thrasonic [*rare*], thrasonical, stilted, gasconading, braggart, boastful, pretentious; vainglorious &c. (*conceited*) 880; highfaluting *or* highfalutin; spread-eagle [*colloq. & humorous, U. S.*].

ELATE, elated, jubilant, triumphant, exultant; in high feather; flushed, – with victory; cock-a-hoop, cock-a-hoopish; on stilts [*colloq.*].

vaunted &c. *v.*

Adv. VAUNTINGLY &c. *adj.;* in triumph; with a blare of trumpets.

₊ "God, I thank thee that I am not as other men are" [*Bible*]; *facta non verba;* "The empty vessel makes the greatest sound" [*Henry V*]; "What cracker is this same, that deafs our ears With this abundance of superfluous breath?" [*King John*]; "every braggart shall be found an ass" [*All's Well*]; "Cæsar's thrasonical brag of 'I came, saw, and overcame' " [*As You Like It*]; "Where boasting ends, there dignity begins" [Young].

885. [Undue assumption of superiority.] Insolence. — **N.** insolence,
brashness, brazenness, malapertness;
haughtiness &c. *adj.;* arrogance, airs;
bumptiousness, toploftiness [*colloq.*], assumption, presumption; assumption of
infallibility; contumely, disdain, insult; overbearance, domineering &c. *v.;*
bluster, swagger, swaggering &c. *v.;*
bounce; terrorism; tyranny &c. 739;
beggar on horseback; usurpation.

impertinence, cheek [*colloq. or slang*],
nerve [*slang*], nerviness [*slang*], sauce
[*colloq.*], abuse; sauciness &c. *adj.;* flippancy, dicacity [*obs.*], petulance [*rare
in this sense*], procacity [*rare*].

impudence, self-assertion, assurance,
audacity, hardihood; front, face, brass,
gall [*slang*]; shamelessness &c. *adj.;*
effrontery, hardened front, face of
brass.

jingoism, chauvinism; *Kultur* [*Ger.*],
"might is right," *Macht ist Recht* [*Ger.*].

malapert, saucebox &c. (*blusterer*)
887.

jingo, jingoist, chauvinist; fire eater
[*colloq.*]; boaster &c. 884.

V. be insolent &c. *adj.;* bluster, vapor, swagger, swell, give oneself airs,
snap one's fingers, kick up a dust
[*colloq.*]; swear &c. (*affirm*) 535; rap out
oaths; roister.

arrogate, assume, presume; make
bold, make free; take a liberty, give an
inch and take an ell.

outface, outlook, outstare, outbrazen,
outbrave; stare out of countenance;
brazen out; lay down the law; teach
one's grandmother to suck eggs [*colloq.*];
assume a lofty bearing; talk big, look big,
put on big looks, act the *grand seigneur;*
mount –, ride- the high horse; toss the
head, carry with a high hand; tempt
Providence; want snuffing [*colloq.*].

domineer, bully, dictate, hector;
lord it over; *traiter –, regarder- de haut
en bas* [*F.*]; exact; snub, huff, beard,
fly in the face of; put to the blush; bear
–, beat- down; browbeat, intimidate;
trample –, tread- -down, – under foot;
dragoon, ride roughshod over; bulldoze
[*colloq., U. S.*], terrorize.

Adj. insolent, haughty, arrogant,
imperious, magisterial, dictatorial, arbitrary; high-handed, high and mighty;
contumelious, supercilious, overbearing,
toplofty [*colloq.*], toploftical [*rare*], in-

886. Servility. — N. servility; slavery &c. (*subjection*) 749; obsequiousness
&c. *adj.;* subserviency; abasement, prostration, prosternation [*obs.*]; genuflection
&c. (*worship*) 990; toadeating; fawning
&c. *v.;* tufthunting, timeserving, flunky-
ism *or* flunkeyism; sycophancy &c.
(*flattery*) 933; humility &c. 879.

sycophant, parasite; toad, toady,
toadeater, tufthunter; snob, flunky *or*
flunkey, lapdog, spaniel, lick-spit, lick-
spittle, smell-feast, *Græculus esuriens*
[*L.*], hanger on, *cavalier* (or *cavaliere*)
servente [*It.*], led captain, carpet knight;
timeserver, fortune hunter, Vicar
of Bray, Sir Pertinax MacSycophant,
pickthank; flatterer &c. 935; doer of
dirty work; *âme damnée* [*F.*], tool;
reptile; slave &c. (*servant*) 746; *homme
de cour* [*F.*], courtier; beat [*slang*], dead
beat [*slang*], doughface [*slang, U. S.*];
heeler, ward heeler [*both polit. cant,
U. S.*]; jackal, sponge, sponger, sucker
[*slang*], tagtail, truckler.

V. cringe, bow, stoop, kneel, bend
the knee; fall on one's knees, prostrate
oneself; worship &c. 990.

fawn, crouch, cower, sneak, crawl,
sponge, truckle, toady, truckle to,
grovel, lick the feet of, lick one's shoes,
make a doormat of oneself, kiss the hem
of one's garment; be servile &c. *adj.*

pay court to; feed on, fatten on,
batten on, dance attendance on, follow
at heel, pin oneself upon, hang on the
sleeve of, *avaler les couleuvres* [*F.*], keep
time to, fetch and carry, do the dirty
work of.

go with the stream, follow the crowd,
worship the rising sun, hold with the
hare and run with the hounds; get on
the band wagon; be a timeserver &c. *n.*

Adj. servile, obsequious; supple, –
as a glove; soapy [*slang*], oily, pliant,
cringing, abased, dough-faced [*colloq.*],
fawning, slavish, groveling, reptilian,
sniveling, mealy-mouthed; beggarly,
sycophantic, parasitical; abject, prostrate, down on one's marrowbones
[*jocular or slang*]; base, mean, sneaking;
crouching &c. *v.;* timeserving.

Adv. with servility &c. *n.;* hat –,
cap- in hand; "in a bondman's key"
[*M. of V.*]; "with bated breath and
whispering humbleness" [*ibid*].

Int. so please you! as my lord wills!
don't mind me!

tolerant, domineering, overweening, high-flown; precocious, assuming, would-be, bumptious.

pert, flippant, fresh [slang, U. S.], brash, cavalier, saucy, forward, impertinent, malapert; impudent, audacious, presumptuous.

BRAZEN, bluff, shameless, aweless, unblushing, unabashed; bold-faced, bare-faced, brazen-faced; dead –, lost- to shame.

BLUSTERING, swaggering, hectoring, rollicking, roistering, vaporing, free and easy, devil-may-care, jaunty or janty; thrasonic [rare], thrasonical, fire-eating [colloq.]; "full of sound and fury" [Macbeth].

JINGO, jingoistic, chauvinistic.

Adv. INSOLENTLY &c. adj.; with nose in air; with arms akimbo; de haut en bas [F.]; with a high hand; ex cathedra [L.].

. one's bark being worse than his bite; "beggars mounted run their horse to death" [III Henry VI]; quid times? Cæsarem vehis [Plutarch].

887. Blusterer. — N. BLUSTERER, swaggerer, vaporer, roisterer, brawler; fanfaron; braggart &c. (boaster) 884; bully, terrorist, rough, ruffian, rough-neck [slang], tough [colloq., U. S.], rowdy, bulldozer [colloq., U. S.], roarer [slang, obs.], slang-whanger [slang], larrikin [Austral. & Eng.]; hoodlum [colloq.], hooligan [slang], Mohock, Mohawk [rare], Drawcansir, swashbuckler, Captain Bobadil, Sir Lucius O'Trigger, Thraso, Pistol, Parolles, Bombastes Furioso, Hector, Chrononhotonthologos; jingo; desperado, dare-devil, fire eater [colloq.]; fury &c. (violent person) 173.

puppy &c. (fop) 854, jackanapes, bantam-cock; malapert, saucebox [colloq.]; minx, hussy.

DOGMATIST, doctrinaire, Sir Oracle, stump orator &c. 582; prig, Jack-in-office.

SECTION III. SYMPATHETIC AFFECTIONS

1. SOCIAL AFFECTIONS

888. Friendship. — N. FRIENDSHIP, amity; friendliness &c. adj.; brotherhood, fraternity, sodality, confraternity; sorority, sorosis, sisterhood; harmony &c. (concord) 714; peace &c. 721.

firm –, staunch –, intimate –, familiar –, bosom –, cordial –, tried –, devoted –, lasting –, fast –, sincere –, warm –, ardent- friendship.

cordiality, fraternization, association, entente cordiale [F.], good understanding, rapprochement [F.], sympathy, fellow-feeling, response, welcomeness; affection &c. (love) 897; partiality, favoritism; good will &c. (benevolence) 906.

acquaintance, introduction, familiarity, intimacy, intercourse, fellowship, knowledge of.

V. BE FRIENDLY &c. adj., be friends &c. 890, be acquainted with &c. adj.; know; have the ear of; keep company with &c. (sociality) 892; hold communication with, have dealings with, sympathize with; have a leaning to; bear good will &c. (benevolent) 906; love &c. 897; make much of; befriend &c. (aid) 707; introduce to.

set one's horses together; have the latchstring out [U. S.]; hold out –, extend-

889. Enmity. — N. ENMITY, hostility, antagonism; unfriendliness &c. adj.; discord &c. 713; bitterness, rancor; heartburning; animosity &c. 900; malevolence &c. 907.

alienation, estrangement; dislike &c. 867; aversion, hate &c. 898.

V. BE UNFRIENDLY &c. adj.; keep –, hold- at arm's length; be at loggerheads; bear malice &c. 907; fall out; take umbrage &c. 900; harden the heart, alienate, estrange.

Adj. UNFRIENDLY, inimical, hostile; at enmity, at variance, at daggers drawn, at open war with; up in arms against; in bad odor with.

on bad terms, not on speaking terms; cool, cold, cold-hearted; estranged, alienated, disaffected, irreconcilable.

. "To be wroth with one we love Doth work like madness in the brain" [Coleridge].

the right hand of -friendship, – fellowship; become friendly &c. *adj.;* make friends &c. (890) with; break the ice, be introduced to; pick up acquaintance; make –, scrape- acquaintance with; get into favor, gain the friendship of.

shake hands with, strike hands with, fraternize, sororize [*rare*], embrace; receive with open arms, throw oneself into the arms of; meet halfway, take in good part.

Adj. FRIENDLY, amicable, amical; well-affected, unhostile, neighborly; brotherly, fraternal, sisterly, sororal [*rare*]; ardent, devoted, sympathetic, harmonious, hearty, cordial, warm-hearted.

friends with, at home with, hand in hand with; on -good, – friendly, – amicable, – cordial, – familiar, – intimate- -terms, – footing; on speaking terms, on visiting terms, on one's visiting list; in one's good -graces, – books.

acquainted, familiar, intimate, thick, hand and glove, hail fellow well met, free and easy; welcome.

Adv. AMICABLY &c. *adj.;* with open arms, *à bras ouverts* [*F.*]; *sans cérémonie* [*F.*]; arm in arm.

*** *amicitia semper prodest* [Seneca]; "a mystic bond of brotherhood makes all men one" [Carlyle]; "friendship is love without either flowers or veil" [Hare]; *vulgus amicitias utilitate probat* [Ovid].

---

890. Friend. — **N.** FRIEND, – of one's bosom; *alter ego* [*L.*], other self; intimate, confidant (*masc.*), confidante (*fem.*), confident; best –, bosom –, fastfriend; *amicus usque ad aras* [*L.*], *fidus Achates* [*L.*]; *persona grata* [*L.*]; wellwisher; neighbor *or* neighbour, acquaintance.

favorer, fautor [*rare*], patron, backer, Mæcenas; tutelary saint, good genius, advocate, partisan, sympathizer; ally; friend in need &c. (*auxiliary*) 711.

ASSOCIATE, consociate, compeer, comrade, mate, companion, *camarade* [*F.*], confrère [*F.*], colleague, comate, copemate *or* copesmate [*obs.*]; partner; side-partner, copartner, consort; old –, crony; chum [*colloq.*], pal [*slang*], buddy [*slang*, *World War*]; playfellow, playmate, schoolfellow; bedfellow, bunkie [*colloq.*, *U. S.*], bedmate, chamberfellow; classfellow, classman, classmate; roommate, shopmate, shipmate, messmate; fellow –, boon –, pot- companion; fellow-man, stable companion; best man, bridesmaid, maid of honor.

[FAMOUS FRIENDSHIPS] Pylades and Orestes, Castor and Pollux, Achilles and Patroclus, Diomedes and Sthenalus, Hercules and Iolaus, Theseus and Pirithoüs, Epaminondas and Pelopidas, Nisus and Euryalus, Damon and Pythias, David and Jonathan, Christ and the beloved disciple; Soldiers Three, the Three Musketeers.

par nobile fratrum [*L.*, *often ironical*]; *Arcades ambo* [*L.*].

HOST, hostess (*fem.*), Amphitryon, Boniface.

GUEST, visitor, frequenter, habitué, *protégé* [*F.*].

COMPATRIOT; fellow –, countryman; fellow townsman, townie [*slang*].

Int. "Thank God for a trusty chum!" [Kipling].

*** *amici probantur rebus adversis; ohne Bruder kann man leben nicht ohne Freund;* "best friend, my well-spring in the wilderness" [G. Eliot]; *conocidos muchos amigos pocos;* "friend more divine than all divinities" [G. Eliot]; *vida sin amigo muerte sin testigo;* "to each a man that knows his naked soul" [Kipling]; "friends who make salt sweet and blackness bright" [Masefield].

891. Enemy. — **N.** ENEMY; antagonist; foe, foeman; open –, bitterenemy; opponent &c. 710; backfriend [*obs.*], copemate *or* copesmate [*obs.*], "dearest foe"; mortal -aversion, – antipathy; snake in the grass.

PUBLIC ENEMY, enemy to society; anarchist, seditionist, traitor, traitress (*fem.*).

*** every hand being against one; "he makes no friend who never made a foe" [Tennyson].

---

892. Sociality. — **N.** SOCIALITY, sociability, sociableness &c. *adj.;* social intercourse, consociation, intercourse, intercommunion; consortship, companionship, comradeship, fellowship; urban-

893. Seclusion. Exclusion. — **N.** SECLUSION, privacy, retirement, eremitism, anchoretism, anchoritism, reclusion, recess: suspension; snugness &c. *adj.;* concealment, delitescence; rustication,

ity &c. (*courtesy*) 894; intimacy, familiarity; clubbability *or* clubability `[colloq.]`, clubbism; *esprit de corps* [F.]; *morale* [F.].

CONVIVIALITY; good- fellowship, – company; joviality, jollity, *savoir vivre* [F.], *joie de vivre* [F.], festivity, festive board, walnuts and wine, merrymaking; loving cup; hospitality, heartiness; cheer; "the feast of reason and the flow of soul" [Pope].

WELCOME, welcomeness, greeting; hearty –, warm –, welcome- reception; hearty welcome; hearty –, warm-greeting; the glad hand [*slang*].

BOON COMPANION; good –, jolly-fellow; *bon enfant* [F.], bawcock [*archaic*], crony, *bon vivant* [F.]; a good mixer [*colloq., U. S.*]; a j'iner [*colloq., U. S.*].

social –, family- circle; family hearth; circle of acquaintance, coterie, society, company; club &c. (*association*) 712.

SOCIAL GATHERING, social reunion; assembly &c. (*assemblage*) 72; barbecue [*U. S.*]; bee; corn-husking [*U. S.*], corn-shucking [*U. S.*]; husking, husking-bee [*U. S.*]; hen party [*colloq.*]; house raising, house-warming, hanging of the crane; infare *or* infair [*Scot & dial., U. S.*]; smoker, – party [*both colloq.*]; Dutch treat [*colloq., U. S.*]; stag, – party [*both colloq.*]; sociable [*U. S.*], tamasha [*Hind.*], party, entertainment, reception, levee, at home, *conversazione* [*It.*], *soirée* [F.], matinée; evening –, morning –, afternoon –, garden –, coming-out [*colloq.*] –, surprise- party; *partie carrée* [F.]; kettledrum, drum, drum major, rout [*archaic*], tempest, hurricane; *ridotto* [*It.*]; ball, hunt ball, dance, dinner dance, festival &c. (*amusement*) 840.

[SOCIAL MEALS] breakfast, wedding breakfast, hunt breakfast; luncheon, lunch; picnic lunch, basket lunch, picnic; tea, afternoon tea, five o'clock tea, cup of tea, dish of tea [*esp. Brit.*], *thé dansant* [F.], coming-out tea [*colloq.*]; tea party, tea fight [*slang*]; dinner, potluck, bachelor dinner, stag dinner [*colloq.*], hunt dinner; church supper, high tea; banquet &c. 298.

VISIT, visiting; round of visits; call, morning call; interview &c. (*interlocution*) 588; assignation; tryst, trysting place; appointment.

V. be sociable &c. *adj.*; know; be acquainted &c. *adj.*; associate with, sort with, consort with, keep company with, walk hand in hand with; eat off the same trencher, club together, consort, bear one company, join; consociate [*rare*], intercommunicate, intercommune [*rare*], make acquaintance with &c. (*friendship*) 888; make advances, fraternize, embrace.

rus in urbe [L.], ruralism, rurality [*rare*], solitude; solitariness &c. (*singleness*) 87; isolation; "splendid isolation"; loneliness &c. *adj.*; estrangement from the world, voluntary exile; aloofness.

depopulation, desertion, desolation; wilderness &c. (*unproductive*) 169; howling wilderness; rotten borough, Old Sarum [*Eng.*].

RETREAT, cell, hermitage, cloister; convent &c. 1000; *sanctum sanctorum* [L.], study, library, den [*colloq.*].

EXCLUSION, excommunication, banishment, exile, ostracism, proscription; economic pressure; cut, cut direct; dead cut.

UNSOCIABILITY, unsociableness, dissociability, dissociality; inhospitality, inhospitableness &c. *adj.*; domesticity, self-sufficiency, Darby and Joan.

RECLUSE, hermit, eremite, anchoret *or* anchorite, anchorist [*obs.*]; santon; stylite, pillarist, pillar-saint [*all Ch. hist.*]; St. Simeon Stylites; caveman, cave-dweller, troglodyte, Timon of Athens, solitarian [*obs.*], solitaire, ruralist [*obs.*], disciple of Zimmermann, closet cynic, cynic, Diogenes.

OUTCAST, pariah, leper; outsider, rank outsider; castaway, pilgarlic [*low*], wastrel [*dial. Eng.*], losel, foundling; wilding.

V. BE *or* LIVE SECLUDED &c. *adj.*; keep –, stand –, hold oneself- -aloof, – in the background; keep snug; shut oneself up; deny oneself, seclude oneself; creep into a corner, rusticate, dissocialize; retire, – from the world; hermitize; take the veil; abandon &c. 624; sport one's oak [*Univ. slang, Eng.*].

EXCLUDE, repel; cut, – dead; refuse to -associate with, – acknowledge; send to Coventry, look cool –, turn one's back –, shut the door- upon; blackball, excommunicate, exile, expatriate; banish, outlaw, maroon, ostracize, proscribe, cut off from, keep at arm's length, draw a cordon round, boycott, embargo, blockade, isolate.

DEPOPULATE, dispeople, unpeople; desolate, devastate.

Adj. SECLUDED, sequestered, retired, delitescent, private, by; in a backwater; out of the world, out of the way; "the world forgetting by the world forgot" [Pope].

UNSOCIABLE, unsocial, dissocial, inhospitable, cynical, inconversable [*obs.*],

VISIT, pay a visit; interchange -visits, – cards; call at, call upon; leave a card; drop in, look in, look one up, beat up one's quarters [colloq.].

RECEIVE HOSPITALITY; be –, feel –, make oneself- at home with; make free with; crack a bottle with; take potluck with; live at free quarters; find the latchstring out [U. S.].

ENTERTAIN; give a party &c. n.; be at home, see one's friends, keep open house, do the honors; receive, – with open arms; welcome; give a warm reception &c. n. to; kill the fatted calf.

Adj. SOCIABLE, companionable, clubbable or clubable [colloq.], clubbish; conversable, cozy or cosy or cosey, chatty, conversational; convivial, festive, festal, jovial, jolly, hospitable.

welcome, – as roses in May; fêted, entertained.

free and easy, hail fellow well met, familiar, intimate, consociate, consociated; associated with &c. v.; on visiting terms, acquainted; social, neighborly.

international, cosmopolitan; gregarious.

Adv. SOCIABLY &c. adj.; en famille [F.], in the family circle; on terms of intimacy; in the social whirl; sans -façon, – cérémonie [F.], arm in arm.

⁎ "a crowd is not company" [Bacon]; "be bright and jovial among your guests to-night" [Macbeth]; "his worth is warrant for his welcome" [Two Gentlemen]; "let's be red with mirth" [Winter's Tale]; "welcome the coming speed the parting guest" [Pope]; "we have heard the chimes at midnight" [II Henry IV]; "'tis grievous parting with good company" [George Eliot]; "O go not yet!" [II Henry VI]; "and now subscribe your names" [L. L. L.]; "drink a health to me for I must hence" [Taming of the Shrew]; "Stand not upon the order of your going, But go at once" [Macbeth].

unclubbable or unclubable [colloq.], sauvage [F.]; hermitical, eremitic or eremitical, anchoretic or anchoretical, anchoritic or anchoritical, anchoretish, anchoritish, troglodytic.

snug, domestic, stay-at-home.

EXCLUDED &c. v.; unfrequented, unvisited, unintroduced, uninvited, unwelcome; on the fringe of society; under a cloud, left to shift for oneself; deserted, – in one's utmost need; unfriended, friendless, kithless, homeless, desolate, lorn, forlorn; solitary, lonely, lonesome, isolated, single, estranged; derelict, outcast, outside the gates, "yammering at the bars"; banished &c. v.; under an embargo.

UNINHABITED, unoccupied, untenanted, tenantless, abandoned; uninhabitable.

⁎ noli me tangere.

"among them but not of them" [Byron]; "and homeless near a thousand homes I stood" [Wordsworth]; "far from the madding crowd's ignoble strife" [Gray]; "makes a solitude and calls it peace" [Byron]; magna civitas magna solitudo; "never less alone than when alone" [Rogers]; "O sacred solitude! divine retreat!" [Young]; "Alone as the last man on earth" [Galsworthy].

---

894. Courtesy. — N. COURTESY; respect &c. 928; good- manners, – behavior, – breeding; manners; politeness &c. adj.; bienséance [F.], urbanity, comity, gentility, breeding, gentle breeding, cultivation, culture, polish, presence; civility, civilization; amenity, suavity; good temper, good humor, amiability, easy temper, complacency, soft tongue, mansuetude [archaic]; condescension &c. (humility) 879; affability, complaisance; compliance, prévenance [F.], amiability, gallantry, chivalry; fine flower of -courtesy, – chivalry.

pink of courtesy, pink of politeness; flower of knighthood, chevalier sans peur et sans reproche, Bayard, Sidney, "a verray parfit gentil knight" [Chaucer], Chesterfield; Launcelot, Gawaine,

895. Discourtesy. — N. DISCOURTESY; ill-breeding; ill –, bad –, ungainly- manners; tactlessness; uncourteousness &c. adj.; rusticity, inurbanity; illiberality, incivility, displacency [obs.]; lack or want of courtesy &c. 894; disrespect &c. 929; procacity [obs.], impudence, misbehavior, barbarism, barbarity; brutality, brutishness, brutification, blackguardism, conduct unbecoming a gentleman, grossièreté [F.], brusquerie [F.], vulgarity &c. 851.

BAD TEMPER, ill temper; peevishness, surliness; churlishness &c. adj.; spinosity, perversity; moroseness &c. (sullenness) 901a.

sternness &c. adj.; austerity; moodishness, captiousness &c. 901; cynicism; tartness &c. adj.; acrimony, acerbity, virulence, asperity.

Colonel Newcome; "gentle Shakespeare" [Ben Jonson].

compliment; fair -, soft -, sweet- words; honeyed phrases, ceremonial; salutation, reception, presentation, introduction, *accueil* [*F.*], greeting, recognition; welcome, abord [*obs.*], respects, *devoir* [*F.*], duty [*archaic*], regards, remembrances; kind -regards, - remembrances; deference, love, best love, empty encomium, flattering remark, hollow commendation; salaams.

[FORMS OF GREETING] obeisance &c. (*reverence*) 928; bow, curtsy *or* curtsey, scrape, salaam, kotow *or* kowtow [*China*], bowing and scraping; kneeling; genuflection &c. (*worship*) 990; obsequiousness &c. 886; capping, pulling the forelock, making a leg [*colloq.*], shaking hands, &c. *v.;* grip of the hand; embrace, hug, squeeze, kiss, buss, smack; salute, accolade; loving cup, *vin d'honneur* [*F.*], pledge; love token &c. (*endearment*) 902.

mark of recognition, nod; "nods and becks and wreathed smiles" [Milton]; valediction &c. 293; condolence &c. 915.

V. BE COURTEOUS &c. *adj.;* show courtesy &c. *n.*

mind one's P's and Q's [*colloq.*], behave oneself, be all things to all men, conciliate, speak one fair, take in good part; do the amiable [*colloq.*]; look as if butter would not melt in one's mouth; mend -, mind- one's manners.

DO THE HONORS, usher, usher in, receive, greet, hail, bid welcome; welcome, - with open arms; shake hands; hold out -, press -, squeeze- the hand; bid Godspeed; speed the parting guest; cheer, serenade.

visit, wait upon, present oneself, pay one's respects, pay a visit &c. (*sociability*) 892; dance attendance on &c. (*servility*) 886; pay attentions to; do homage to &c. (*respect*) 928; give *or* send one's regards to &c. *n.*

SALUTE; embrace &c. (*endearment*) 902; kiss, - hands; drink to, pledge, hob and nob; move to [*colloq.*], nod to; smile upon.

uncover, cap; touch -, raise -, lift -, take off- the hat; doff the cap; tip the hat to [*slang*]; pull the forelock; present arms; make way for; bow, make one's bow, make a leg scrape, curtsy *or* curtsey,

scowl, black looks, frown; sulks, short answer, rebuff; hard words, contumely; unparliamentary language, personality.

bear, bruin, grizzly, grizzly bear; brute, blackguard, beast; unlicked cub; frump [*colloq.*], crosspatch [*colloq.*]; grouch, old grouch [*both slang*]; saucebox &c. 887; crooked stick.

V. BE RUDE &c. *adj.;* insult &c. 929; treat with discourtesy; take a name in vain; make bold with, make free with; take a liberty; stare out of countenance, ogle, point at, put to the blush.

CUT; turn one's back upon, turn on one's heel; give the cold shoulder; keep at -a distance, - arm's length; look -cool, - coldly, - black- upon; show the door to, send away with a flea in the ear [*colloq.*].

LOSE ONE'S TEMPER &c. (*resentment*) 900; mump [*dial.*], sulk &c. 901*a;* frown, scowl, glower, pout; snap, snarl, growl.

RENDER RUDE &c. *adj.;* brutalize, brutify.

Adj. DISCOURTEOUS, uncourteous, uncourtly; ill-bred, ill-mannered, ill-behaved, ill-conditioned, unbred; unmannerly, unmannered, impolite, unpolite; uncivil, ungracious, unceremonious, cool; unpolished, uncivilized, ungenteel; ungentlemanlike, ungentlemanly; unladylike; blackguard; vulgar &c. 851; dedecorous [*obs.*]; foul-mouthed, foul-spoken; abusive.

pert, forward, obtrusive, impudent, rude, saucy, procacious [*archaic*], brash; flippant &c. (*insolent*) 885.

repulsive; uncomplaisant, unaccommodating, unneighborly, ungallant; inaffable; ungentle, ungainly, rough, rugged, bluff, blunt, gruff; churlish, boorish, bearish; brutal, brusque, stern, harsh, austere; cavalier.

BAD-TEMPERED, ill-tempered, ill-humored; out of -temper, - humor; crusty, tart, sour, crabbed, sharp, short, trenchant, sarcastic, biting, doggish, currish, caustic, virulent, bitter, acrimonious, venomous, contumelious; snarling &c. *v.;* surly, - as a bear; perverse; grim, sullen &c. 901*a;* peevish &c. (*irascible*) 901; bristling, thorny, spinose, spinous.

Adv. DISCOURTEOUSLY &c. *adj.;* with discourtesy &c. *n.,* with a bad grace.

..* "You are rude; I pretend not to perceive it" [Martial].

bow and scrape, bob a curtsy, kneel; bow –, bend- the knee; salaam, kotow or kowtow [China]; prostrate oneself &c. (worship) 990.

RENDER POLITE &c. adj.; polish, rub off the -corners, – rough edges; cultivate, civilize, humanize.

Adj. COURTEOUS, polite, civil, mannerly, urbane; well-behaved, well-mannered, well-bred, well-brought up; gently bred; of gentle -manners, – breeding; good-mannered, polished, civilized, cultivated; refined &c. (taste) 850; gentlemanlike &c. (fashion)852; gallant, chivalrous, chivalric; on one's good (or best) behavior.

ingratiating, winning; gentle, mild; good-humored, cordial, gracious, amiable, tactful, affable, familiar; neighborly; obliging, complaisant, complacent, conciliatory.

BLAND, suave; fine –, fair –, soft- spoken; honey-mouthed, honey-tongued; oily, oily-tongued, unctuous; obsequious &c. 886.

Adv. COURTEOUSLY &c. adj.; with a good grace; with open arms, with outstretched arms, à bras ouverts [F.]; suaviter in modo [L.], with perfect courtesy, in good humor.

Int. HAIL! welcome! well met! ave! [L.]; all hail! good -day, – morrow, – morning, – evening, – afternoon, – night! sweet dreams! Godspeed! pax vobiscum! [L.]; all good go with you! may your shadow never be less!

₊ rien de plus estimable que la cerémonie; "the very pink of courtesy" [Romeo and Juliet].

896. Congratulation. — **N.** CONGRATULATION, gratulation, felicitation; salute &c. 894; condolence &c. 915; compliments of the season; good wishes, best wishes.

V. CONGRATULATE, gratulate, felicitate; give joy, wish one joy; compliment; tender –, offer- one's congratulations; wish many happy returns of the day, wish a merry Christmas and a happy new year.

congratulate oneself &c. (rejoice) 838.

Adj. CONGRATULATORY, gratulatory.

₊ "I wish you all the joy that you can wish" [Merchant of Venice].

897. Love. — **N.** LOVE, affection, sympathy, fellow-feeling; tenderness &c. adj.; heart, brotherly love; charity, good will; benevolence &c. 906; attachment; fondness &c. adj.; liking; inclination &c. (desire) 865; regard, dilection [obs.], admiration, fancy.

yearning, eros [Gr. ἔρως], tender passion, amour; gyneolatry; gallantry, passion, flame, devotion, fervor, enthusiasm, transport of love, rapture, enchantment, infatuation, adoration, idolatry.

mother love, maternal love, natural affection, storge [Gr. στοργή].

attractiveness, charm; popularity; idol, favorite &c. 899.

god of love, Cupid, Venus, Eros, Kama [Hindu]; myrtle; turtle dove, sparrow; cupid amoretto; true lover's knot; love -token, – suit, – affair, – tale, – story; the old story, plighted love; courtship &c. 902; amourette; free-love.

LOVER, suitor, fiancé [F.], follower [colloq.], admirer, adorer, wooer, amoret [obs.], amorist, beau, sweetheart, inamorato, swain, young man [colloq.], flame [colloq.], love, truelove: leman [archaic],

898. Hate. — **N.** HATE, hatred, vials of hate; "Hymn of Hate."

disaffection, disfavor; alienation, estrangement, coolness; enmity &c. 889; animosity &c. 900; malice &c. 907; implacability &c. (revenge) 919.

umbrage, pique, grudge, dudgeon, spleen, bitterness, bitterness of feeling; ill blood, bad blood; acrimony.

repugnance &c. (dislike) 867; odium, unpopularity; detestation, abhorrence, loathing, execration, abomination, aversion, antipathy; demonophobia, gynephobia, negrophobia; Anglophobia &c. 867.

OBJECT OF HATRED, an abomination, an aversion, bête noire [F.]; enemy &c. 891; bitter pill; source of annoyance &c. 830.

V. HATE, detest, abominate, abhor, loathe; recoil at, shudder at; shrink from, view with horror, hold in abomination, revolt against, execrate; scowl &c. 895; disrelish &c. (dislike) 867.

owe a grudge; bear spleen, bear a grudge, bear malice &c. (malevolence) 907; conceive an aversion to.

Lothario, gallant, paramour, captive; *amoroso, cavaliere servente, cicisbeo, caro sposo* [*all It.*].

LADYLOVE, sweetheart, mistress, inamorata, idol, darling, duck, Dulcinea, angel, goddess, *cara sposa* [*It.*]; betrothed, affianced, *fiancée* [*F.*].

flirt, coquette, amorette.

pair of turtledoves; abode of love; Agapemone [*Ch. hist.*].

V. LOVE, like, affect, fancy, care for, take an interest in, be partial to, sympathize with; affection; be in love with &c. *adj.*; have –, entertain –, harbor –, cherish- a love for &c. *n.*; regard, revere; take to, bear love to, be wedded to; set one's affections on; burn; adore, idolize, love to distraction, *aimer éperdument* [*F.*]; dote- on, – upon.

make much of, feast one's eyes on; hold dear, prize; hug, cling to, cherish, caress, fondle, pet.

take a fancy to, look sweet upon [*colloq.*]; become enamored &c. *adj.*; fall in love with, lose one's heart; desire &c. 865.

EXCITE LOVE; win –, gain –, secure –, engage- the -love, – affections, – heart; take the fancy of; have a place in –, wind round- the heart; attract, attach, endear, charm, fascinate, captivate, bewitch, seduce, enamor, enrapture, turn the head.

EXCITE HATRED, provoke hatred &c. *n.*; be hateful &c. *adj.*; stink in the nostrils; estrange, alienate, repel, set against, sow dissension, set by the ears, envenom, incense, irritate, rile [*dial.* or *colloq.*], ruffle, vex, roil; horrify &c. 830.

Adj. HATING &c. *v.*; abhorrent; averse from &c. (*disliking*) 867; set against; bitter &c. (*acrimonious*) 895; implacable &c. (*revengeful*) 919.

UNLOVED, unbeloved, unlamented, undeplored, unmourned, uncared for, unendeared, unvalued; disliked &c. 867.

crossed in love, forsaken, rejected, lovelorn, jilted.

HATEFUL, obnoxious, odious, abominable, repulsive, offensive, shocking; disgusting &c. (*disagreeable*) 830; reprehensible.

invidious, spiteful; malicious &c. 907.

insulting, irritating, provoking.

[MUTUAL HATE] at daggers drawn; not on speaking terms &c. (*enmity*) 889; at loggerheads.

** no love lost between; "In time we hate that which we often fear" [*Antony and Cleopatra*]; "I like a good hater" [Johnson]; "Heaven has no rage like love to hatred turned" [Congreve]; "There are glances of hatred that stab and raise no cry of murder" [G. Eliot].

get into favor; ingratiate –, insinuate –, worm- oneself; propitiate, curry favor with, pay one's court to, *faire l'aimable* [*F.*], set one's cap at [*colloq.*], coquet, flirt.

Adj. LOVING &c. *v.*; fond of; taken with [*colloq.*], struck with [*colloq.*], smitten, bitten [*colloq.*]; attached to, wedded to; enamored; charmed &c. *v.*; in love; lovesick; over head and ears in love.

affectionate, tender, sweet upon [*colloq.*], sympathetic, amorous, amatory; fond, erotic, uxorious, ardent, passionate, rapturous, devoted, motherly.

LOVED &c. *v.*; beloved, well beloved, dearly beloved; dear as the apple of one's eye, nearest to one's heart; dear, precious, darling, pet, little; favorite, popular.

congenial; to –, after- one's -mind, – taste, – fancy, – own heart; in one's good graces &c. (*friendly*) 888.

LOVABLE, adorable, lovely, sweet, attractive, seductive, winning, winsome, charming, engaging, interesting, enchanting, captivating, fascinating, bewitching, amiable; seraphic *or* seraphical, angelic, like an angel.

** *amantes amentes* [Terence]; *credula res amor est* [Ovid]; *militat omnis amasius* [Ovid]; *omnia vincit amor* [Vergil]; *si vis amari ama* [Seneca]; "the sweetest joy, the wildest woe" [Bailey]; "Affection is a coal that must be cool'd; Else, suffer'd, it will set the heart on fire" [*Venus and Adonis*]; "Affection lights a brighter flame Than ever blazed by art" [Cowper].

899. Favorite. — N. FAVORITE, pet, fondling, cosset, minion [*rare*], idol, jewel, spoiled child, *enfant gâté* [*F.*]; led captain; crony; apple of one's eye, man after one's own heart; *persona grata* [*L.*].

love, dear, darling, duck, honey, jewel; mopsy *or* mopsey, moppet; sweetheart &c. (*love*) 897.

general –, universal- favorite; idol of the people; matinée idol.

900. Resentment. — **N.** RESENTMENT, displeasure, animosity, anger, wrath, ire, indignation; exasperation, vexation, bitter resentment, wrathful indignation.

pique, umbrage, huff, miff [*colloq.*], soreness, dudgeon, acerbity, virulence, bitterness, acrimony, asperity, spleen, gall; heartburning, heart-swelling; rankling.

ill -, bad- -humor, – temper; irascibility &c. 901; scowl &c. 895; sulks &c. 901*a*; ill blood &c. (*hate*) 898; revenge &c. 919.

IRRITATION; warmth, bile, choler, fume, pucker [*colloq.*], dander [*colloq.*], ferment, excitement, ebullition; angry mood, taking [*colloq.*], pet, tiff, passion, fit, tantrum [*colloq.*].

RAGE, fury; towering -rage, – passion; *acharnement* [*F.*], desperation, burst, explosion, paroxysm, storm; violence &c. 173; fire and fury; vials of wrath; gnashing of teeth, hot blood, high words.

FURIES, Erinyes (*sing.* Erinys), Eumenides; Alecto, Megæra, Tisiphone.

[CAUSE OF UMBRAGE] affront, provocation, offense; indignity &c. (*insult*) 929; grudge; crow to -pluck, – pick, – pull; red rag, last straw, sore subject, *casus belli* [*L.*]; ill turn, outrage.

buffet, blow, slap in the face, box on the ear, rap on the knuckles.

V. RESENT; take -amiss, – ill, – to heart, – offense, – umbrage, – huff, – exception; not take it as a joke; *ne pas entendre raillerie* [*F.*]; take in bad part, take in ill part.

pout, knit the brow, frown, scowl, lower, snarl, growl, gnarl, gnash, snap; redden, color; look black, look black as thunder, look daggers; bite one's thumb; show -, grind- one's teeth; champ the bit.

BE ANGRY; fly -, fall -, get- into a -rage, – passion; fly off the handle [*slang*], fly off at a tangent; let one's angry passions rise; bridle up, bristle up, froth up, fire up, flare up; foam at the mouth; open -, pour out- the vials of one's wrath.

chafe, mantle, fume, kindle, fly out, take fire; boil, – over; boil with- indignation, – rage; rage, storm, foam; hector, bully, bluster; vent one's -rage, spleen; lose one's temper; have a fling at; kick up a -row, – dust, – shindy [*all slang*]; cut up rough [*slang*], stand on one's hind legs, stamp the foot; stamp -, quiver -, swell -, foam- with rage; burst with anger; raise -Cain, – the devil, – Ned, – the mischief, – the roof [*all slang*]; breathe fire and fury; breathe revenge.

bear malice &c. (*revenge*) 919.

CAUSE ANGER, raise anger; affront, offend; give -offense, – umbrage; anger; hurt the feelings; insult, discompose, fret, ruffle, roil, heckle [*Brit.*], nettle, huff, pique; excite &c. 824; irritate, stir the blood, stir up bile; sting, – to the quick; rile [*dial. or colloq.*], provoke, chafe, wound, incense, inflame, wrath [*obs.*], make one hot under the collar [*slang*], enrage, aggravate, add fuel to the flame, fan into a flame, widen the breach, envenom, embitter, exasperate, infuriate, kindle wrath; stick in one's crop *or* gizzard [*colloq.*]; rankle &c. 919; hit -, rub -, sting -, strike- on the raw.

put out of -countenance, – humor; put (*or* get) one's monkey up [*slang or colloq., Eng.*], put (*or* get) one's back up; raise one's -gorge, – dander [*colloq.*], – choler; work up into a passion, make one's blood boil, make the ears tingle, throw into a ferment, madden, drive one mad; lash into -fury, – madness; fool to the top of one's bent; set by the ears; bring a hornet's nest about one's ears.

Adj. ANGRY, wroth, irate, ireful, wrathful; cross &c. (*irascible*) 901; Achillean; sulky &c. 901*a*; bitter, virulent; acrimonious &c. (*discourteous*) &c. 895; offended &c. *v.*; waxy [*slang, Eng.*], wrought, worked up; indignant, hurt, sore; set against.

warm, burning; boiling, – over; fuming, raging, hot under the collar [*slang*]; *acharné* [*F.*]; foaming, – at the mouth; convulsed with rage; fierce, wild, rageful, furious, mad with rage, fiery, infuriate, rabid, savage; relentless &c. 919; violent &c. 173.

flushed with -anger, – rage; in a- huff, – stew [*colloq.*], – fume, – pucker [*dial. or colloq.*], – wax [*slang*], – passion, – rage, – fury, – taking [*colloq.*]; on one's high ropes [*colloq.*], up in arms; in high dudgeon.

Adv. ANGRILY &c. *adj.;* in the height of passion; in the heat of -passion, – the moment; in an ecstasy of rage.

Int. *tantæne animis cælestibus iræ!* [Vergil]; marry come up! zounds! 'sdeath!

** one's blood being up, one's back being up, one's monkey being up [*slang or colloq., Eng.*]; *fervens difficili bile jecur;* the gorge rising, eyes flashing fire; the blood -rising, – boiling; *hæret lateri lethalis arundo* [Vergil]; "beware the fury of a patient man" [Dryden]; *furor arma ministrat* [Vergil]; *ira furor brevis est* [Horace]; *quem Jupiter vult perdere dementat prius;* "What, drunk with choler? stay and pause awhile" [*I Henry IV*].

901. Irascibility. — N. IRASCIBILITY, irascibleness, temper; crossness &c. *adj.;* susceptibility, procacity [*rare*], petulance, irritability, tartness, acerbity, acrimony, asperity, protervity [*rare*]; huff &c. (*resentment*) 900; a word and a blow; pugnacity &c. (*contentiousness*) 720; excitability &c. 825; bad –, fiery –, crooked –, irritable &c. *adj.*- temper; *genus irritabile* [L.], hot blood.

ill humor &c. (*sullenness*) 901a; churlishness &c. (*discourtesy*) 895.

Sir Fretful Plagiary; brabbler, Tartar; shrew, vixen, virago, termagant, dragon, scold, Xanthippe *or* Xantippe, Kate the Shrew; porcupine; spitfire; fire eater &c. (*blusterer*) 887; fury &c. (*violent person*) 173.

V. BE IRASCIBLE &c. *adj.;* have a temper &c. *n.,* have a devil in one, be possessed of the devil, have the temper of a fiend; brabble [*archaic or dial.*]; fire up &c. (*be angry*) 900.

Adj. IRASCIBLE, bad-tempered, ill-tempered, irritable, susceptible; excitable &c. 825; thin-skinned &c. (*sensitive*) 822; fretful, fidgety; on the fret.

hasty, overhasty, quick, warm, hot, testy, touchy, techy *or* tetchy; like -touchwood, – tinder, – a barrel of gunpowder; huffy, pettish, petulant, querulous, captious, moody, moodish; fractious, peevish, *acariâtre* [F.].

QUARRELSOME, contentious, disputatious; pugnacious &c. (*bellicose*) 720; cantankerous [*colloq.*], exceptious [*rare*], cross-grained; waspish, snappish, peppery, fiery, passionate, choleric, shrewish; "sudden and quick in quarrel" [*As You Like It*]; restive &c. (*perverse*) 901a; churlish &c. (*discourteous*) 895; cross, – as -crabs, – a bear with a sore head, – a cat, – a dog, – two sticks, – the tongs [*all colloq.*]; sore, sore as a crab [*colloq.*].

in a bad temper; sulky &c. 901a; angry &c. 900; resentful, resentive; vindictive &c. 919.

Int. pish!

** *à vieux comptes nouvelles disputes; quamvis tegatur proditur vultu furor* [Seneca]; *vino tortus et irâ* [Horace]; "What sudden anger's this?" [Henry VIII].

901a. Sullenness. — N. SULLENNESS &c. *adj.;* morosity, spleen; churlishness &c. (*discourtesy*) 895; irascibility &c. 901; moodiness &c. *adj.;* perversity; obstinacy &c. 606; torvity [*obs.*], thorniness, spinosity; crabbedness &c. *adj.*

ill –, bad- -temper, – humor; sulks, dudgeon, mumps, dumps [*humorous*], doleful dumps [*colloq. or humorous*], vapors [*archaic*], glooming, doldrums, fit of the sulks, bouderie, black looks, scowl; grouch [*slang*]; huff &c. (*resentment*) 900.

V. BE SULLEN &c. *adj.;* sulk; frown, scowl, lower, glower, pout, have a hangdog look, glout [*rare or dial.*], grouch [*slang*], grout [*U. S.*].

Adj. SULLEN, sulky; ill-tempered; ill-humored, ill-affected, ill-disposed; grouty [*colloq., U. S.*]; in -an ill, – a bad, – a shocking- -temper, – humor; out of -temper, – humor; naggy [*colloq.*], torvous [*obs.*], crusty, crabbed, sour, sore, sore as a crab; surly &c. (*discourteous*) 895.

moody, moodish, spleenish, spleeny, spleenful, splenetic, cankered; cross, crossgrained; perverse, wayward, humorsome; restive, restiff [*rare*], malignant, refractory, ungovernable, cantankerous, intractable, exceptious [*rare*], sinistrous [*obs.*], deaf to reason, unaccommodating, rusty [*dial. Eng.*], froward, cussed [*vulgar or euphemistic, U. S.*], curst [*archaic or dial.*].

grumpy, glum, grim, grum, morose, frumpish [*obs.*]; in the sulks &c. *n.;* out of sorts; scowling, glowering, growling, grouchy [*slang*]; peevish &c. (*irascible*) 901; dogged &c. (*stubborn*) 606.

** "Gathering her brows like gathering storm, Nursing her wrath to keep it warm" [Burns].

902. [Expression of affection.] **Endearment. — N.** endearment, caress, blandishment, blandiment [obs.]; épanchement [F.], fondling, billing and cooing, dalliance, caressing, embrace, salute, kiss, buss, smack, osculation, deosculation [obs.].

courtship, wooing, suit, addresses, the soft impeachment; love-making; calf love [colloq.]; amorous glances, ogle, side-glance, sheep's eyes, goo-goo eyes [slang, U. S.]; serenading, caterwauling.

flirting &c. v.; flirtation, gallantry; coquetry, spooning [slang].

true lover's knot, plighted love, engagement, betrothal; marriage &c. 903; honeymoon; love tale, love token; love letter, billet-doux [F.]; posy [archaic]; valentine. Strephon and Chloe, 'Arry and 'Arriet.

flirt, coquette; male flirt, philanderer; spoon [slang].

V. caress, fondle, pet, dandle; pat, – on the -head, – cheek; chuck under the chin, smile upon, coax, wheedle, cosset, coddle, cocker, make much of, cherish, foster, kill with kindness.

clasp, hug, cuddle; fold to the heart, press to the bosom; fold –, strain- in one's arms; take to one's arms; snuggle, nestle, nuzzle; embrace, kiss, buss, smack, blow a kiss; salute &c. (courtesy) 894.

make love, bill and coo, spoon [slang], toy, dally, flirt, coquet, gallivant or galavant; philander; pay one's -court, – addresses, – attentions- to; serenade; court, sweetheart [colloq. or dial.], woo; set one's cap at or for [colloq.]; be or look sweet upon [colloq.]; ogle, cast sheep's eyes upon, make goo-goo eyes at [slang, U. S.], faire les yeux doux [F.].

fall in love with, fall over head and ears in love with; win the affections &c. (love) 897; die for.

propose; make –, have- an offer; pop the question [colloq.]; become engaged, become betrothed; plight one's -troth, – faith.

Adj. caressing &c. v.; "sighing like furnace" [As You Like It]; love-sick, spoony or spooney [slang].

caressed &c. v.

⁎ "faint heart ne'er won fair lady"; "kisses honeyed by oblivion" [G. Eliot].

903. Marriage. — N. marriage, matrimony, wedlock, union, intermarriage, miscegenation, marriageability; vinculum matrimonii [L.], nuptial tie, nuptial knot; match; betrothment &c. (promise) 768

married state, coverture, bed, cohabitation.

wedding, nuptials, Hymen, bridal, espousals, spousals; leading to the altar &c. v.; nuptial benediction, epithalamium; sealing.

torch –, temple- of Hymen; saffron -veil, – robe; hymeneal altar; honeymoon.

bridesmaid, maid of honor, matron of honor; usher, best man, bridesman, groomsman; bride, bridegroom.

married man, neogamist [obs.], Benedict, partner, spouse, mate, yokemate, husband, man, consort, baron [old law & her.], goodman [archaic or dial.], old man.

married woman, wife, wife of one's bosom, wedded wife, rib [dial. & sportive], helpmeet, helpmate, better half,

904. Celibacy. — N. celibacy, singleness, single blessedness; bachelorhood, bachelorship; misogamy, misogyny.

virginity, pucelage [rare], maidhood [rare], maidenhood, maidenhead.

unmarried man, bachelor, Cœlebs, agamist, old bachelor; misogamist, misogynist; monk, priest, celibate, religious.

unmarried woman, spinster, maid, maiden; virgin, feme sole [law], old maid; bachelor-girl, girl-bachelor; nun, sister, vestal, vestal virgin; Diana, St. Agnes.

V. live single, enjoy single blessedness, keep bachelor hall.

Adj. unmarried, unwedded; wifeless, spouseless; single, celibate, virgin.

⁎ "Is the single man therefore blessed? No!" [As You Like It]; "a man is all in the way in the house" [Gaskell].

905. Divorce. Widowhood. — N. divorce, divorcement; separation, judicial separation, separate maintenance;

gray mare, goodwife [*archaic or dial.*], old woman [*vulgar*].

feme, – covert [*law*]; lady [*obs. or uncultivated*]; squaw; matron, matronship, matronage, matronhood.

MARRIED COUPLE, man and wife, wedded pair, wedded couple, Darby and Joan, Philemon and Baucis.

AFFINITY, soul-mate; spiritual wife, spiritual husband.

[KINDS OF MARRIAGE] monogamy, monogyny; bigamy, digamy, deuterogamy; trigamy; polygamy, polygyny, polyandry, polyandrism; Mormonism, spiritual wifery (*or* wifeism); levirate.

harem, seraglio; Mormon.

monogamist, monogynist, bigamist &c.; Turk, Bluebeard.

unlawful –, left-handed –, morganatic –, ill-assorted- marriage; *mésalliance* [*F.*], *mariage de convenance* [*F.*].

MARRIAGE BROKER, matchmaker, professional matchmaker, schatchen [*Yiddish*]; matrimonial -agency, – agent, – bureau.

V. MARRY, wive, take to oneself a wife; be married, be spliced [*colloq.*]; go off, go to the world [*obs.*], pair off; wed, espouse, lead to the hymeneal altar, take "for better for worse," give one's hand to, bestow one's hand upon.

marry, join, handfast [*archaic*]; couple &c. (*unite*) 43; be made one; tie the nuptial knot; give away, give in marriage; seal; affy, affiance; betroth &c. (*promise*) 768; publish –, call –, proclaim –, bid- the banns, be asked in church.

remarry, rewed; intermarry, interwed.

Adj. MARRIED &c. *v.;* one, one bone and one flesh.

MARRIAGEABLE, nubile.

ENGAGED, betrothed, affianced.

MATRIMONIAL, marital, conjugal, connubial, wedded; nuptial, hymeneal, spousal, bridal; monogamous &c.

separatio a -mensâ et thoro, – vinculo matrimonii [*L.*].

WIDOWHOOD, viduity [*rare*], viduage, viduation, weeds; viduate [*eccl.*].

widow, relict, dowager; divorcée; grass widow.

widower; grass widower; cuckold.

V. live separate; separate, divorce, disespouse [*obs.*], put away; wear the horns.

⁎⁎⁎ the gray mare the better horse; "a world-without-end bargain" [*L. L. L.*]; "marriages are made in Heaven" [Tennyson]; "render me worthy of this noble wife" [*Julius Cæsar*]; *si qua voles apte nubere nube pari* [Ovid]; "He for God only, she for God in him" [Milton]; "Look down, you gods, And on this couple drop a blessed crown!" [*Tempest*]; "procure the vicar To stay for me at church twixt twelve and one" *Merry Wives*]; "good luck Shall fling her old shoe after" [Tennyson]; "Now sighs steal out and tears begin to flow!" [Pope].

2. DIFFUSIVE SYMPATHETIC AFFECTIONS

906. Benevolence. — N. BENEVOLENCE, Christian charity; God's love, God's grace; good will; philanthropy &c. 910; unselfishness &c. 942.

good -nature, – feeling, – wishes; kindness, kindliness &c. *adj.;* lovingkindness, benignity, brotherly love, charity, humanity, kindly feelings, fellow-feeling, sympathy; goodness –, warmth- of heart; warm-heartedness, bonhomie *or* bonhommie, kind-heartedness; amiability, milk of human kindness, tenderness; love &c. 897; friendship &c. 888; toleration, consideration; mercy &c. (*pity*) 914.

CHARITABLENESS &c. *adj.;* bounty, almsgiving; good works, beneficence, generosity; "the luxury of doing good" [Goldsmith].

907. Malevolence. — N. MALEVOLENCE, bad intent, bad intention, unkindness, diskindness [*obs.*]; ill-nature, ill-will, ill-blood, bad blood; enmity &c. 889; hate &c. 898; malice, – prepense, – aforethought; malignance, malignancy, malignity; maliciousness &c. *adj.;* spite, despite; resentment &c. 900.

uncharitableness &c. *adj.;* incompassion [*rare*], incompassionateness [*rare*] &c. 914*a;* gall, venom, rancor, rankling, virulence, mordacity, acerbity; churlishness &c. (*discourtesy*) 895; hardness of heart, heart of stone, obduracy; evil eye, cloven -foot, – hoof.

ill turn, bad turn; affront &c. (*disrespect*) 929; bigotry, intolerance, tender mercies [*ironical*]; "unkindest cut of all" [*Julius Cæsar*].

acts of kindness, a good turn; good
-, kind- -offices, - treatment.

PHILANTHROPIST, "one who loves his
fellow-men" [Hunt], salt of the earth;
good Samaritan, sympathizer, wellwisher, *bon enfant* [F.]; altruist.

V. BE BENEVOLENT &c. *adj.;* have
one's heart in the right place, bear good
will; wish well, wish Godspeed; view -,
regard- with an eye of favor; take in
good part; take -, feel- an interest in;
be -, feel- interested- in; have a fellow-
feeling for, sympathize with, feel for;
fraternize &c. (*be friendly*) 888.

enter into the feelings of others,
practice the Golden Rule, do as you
would be done by, meet halfway.

treat well; give comfort, smooth the
bed of death; do good, do a good turn;
benefit &c. (*goodness*) 648; render a
service, render assistance, give one a
hand, be of use; aid &c. 707.

Adj. BENEVOLENT, kind, kindly, well-
meaning, amiable, cordial; obliging, accommodating, indulgent, gracious, complacent, good-humored; tender, considerate; warm-hearted, kind-hearted,
tender-hearted, large-hearted, broadhearted, soft-hearted; merciful &c. 914.

good-natured, well-natured, spleenless
[*rare*]; sympathizing, sympathetic; complaisant &c. (*courteous*) 894; well-meant,
well-intentioned, kindly meant.

full of natural affection, fatherly,
motherly, brotherly, sisterly; paternal, maternal, fraternal; sororal [*rare*];
friendly &c. 888.

CHARITABLE, beneficent, philanthropi-
cal, generous, humane, benignant, bounteous, bountiful.

Adv. WITH GOOD WILL, with a good
intention [*rare*], with the best intentions; out of deepest sympathy; in a
burst of generosity.

Int. GODSPEED! good luck! all good
luck go with you! count on me!

⁎ "act a charity sometimes" [Lamb];
"a tender heart, a will inflexible" [Long-
fellow]; *de mortuis nil nisi bonum;* "kind hearts
are more than coronets" [Tennyson]; *quando
amigo pide no hay mañana;* 'the social smile,
the sympathetic tear" [Gray]; "in kindness
preferring one another" [*Bible*]; "Who gives
himself with his alms feeds three — Himself,
his hungering neighbor, and Me" [Lowell].

CRUELTY, cruelness &c. *adj.;* brutality,
savagery, ferity, ferocity; outrage, atrocity, ill-usage, persecution; barbarity,
inhumanity, immanity [*obs.*], trucu-
lence, ruffianism; Inquisition, torture,
vivisection.

V. BE MALEVOLENT &c. *adj.;* bear -,
harbor- -spleen, - a grudge, - malice;
betray -, show- the cloven foot; hurt
&c. (*physical pain*) 378; annoy &c. 830;
injure, harm, wrong; do harm to, do
an ill office to; outrage; disoblige,
malign, plant a thorn in the breast;
turn and rend one.

molest, worry, harass, haunt, harry,
bait, tease; throw stones at; play the
devil with; hunt down, dragoon, hound;
persecute, oppress, grind, maltreat, illtreat, ill-use, misuse.

wreak one's malice on, do one's worst,
break a butterfly on the wheel; dip -,
imbrue- one's hands in blood; show no
quarter, have no mercy &c. 914a.

Adj. MALEVOLENT, unbenevolent, unbenign; ill-disposed, ill-intentioned, ill-
natured, ill-conditioned, ill-contrived;
evil-minded, evil-disposed, black-browed;
malicious, malign, malignant; rancorous,
spiteful, despiteful, treacherous, morda-
cious, caustic, bitter, envenomed, acrimonious, virulent; unamiable, uncharitable;
maleficent, venomous, grinding, galling.

harsh, disobliging, unkind, unfriendly,
ungracious, inofficious [*obs.*], invidious;
churlish &c. (*uncourteous*) 895; surly,
sullen &c. 901a.

COLD-BLOODED, cold-hearted; black-
hearted, hard-hearted, flint-hearted,
marble-hearted, stony-hearted, hard of
heart, cold, unnatural; ruthless &c.
(*unmerciful*) 914a; relentless &c. (*revengeful*) 919.

CRUEL, brutal, brutish, savage; savage
as a -bear, - tiger; ferine, ferocious,
feral, inhuman; barbarous, fell, untamed,
tameless, truculent, incendiary; blood-
thirsty &c. (*murderous*) 361; atrocious;
bloody-minded; fiendish, fiendlike; demoniac *or* demoniacal; diabolic *or* diabolical, devilish, infernal, hellish, Tartarean *or* Tartareous, Satanic.

Adv. MALEVOLENTLY &c. *adj.;* with
bad intent &c. *n.;* with the ferocity of
a tiger.

⁎ cruel as death; "hard unkindness' alter'd eye" [Gray]; *homo homini lupus* [Plautus];
mala mens malus animus [Terence]; "rich gifts wax poor when givers prove unkind" [*Hamlet*];
"sharp-tooth'd unkindness" [*Lear*].

908. Malediction. — **N.** MALEDICTION, malison, curse, imprecation, denunciation, execration; anathema, – maranatha; maranatha [a *misinterpretation*]; ban, proscription, excommunication, commination, thunders of the Vatican, fulmination; aspersion, disparagement, vilification, vituperation.

ABUSE; foul –, bad –, strong –, unparliamentary- language; billingsgate, sauce [*colloq.*]; blackguardism &c. (*discourtesy*) 895; evil speaking; cursing &c. *v.;* profane swearing, oath; foul invective, ribaldry, rude reproach, scurrility, threat &c. 909; more bark than bite; invective &c. (*disapprobation*) 932.

V. CURSE, accurse, imprecate, damn; curse with bell, book, and candle; invoke –, call down- curses on the head of; call down curses upon one's devoted head; devote to destruction.

execrate, beshrew [*archaic*], scold; anathematize &c. (*censure*) 932; hold up to execration, denounce, proscribe, excommunicate, fulminate, thunder against; curse up hill and down dale; threaten &c. 909.

SWEAR, curse and swear; swear like a trooper; fall a-cursing, rap out an oath, swear at, damn.

Adj. MALEDICTORY, imprecatory; cursing, cursed &c. *v.*

Int. woe to! beshrew! [*archaic*], *ruat cœlum!* [L.], woe betide! ill betide! confusion seize! damn! confound! blast! curse! devil take! hang! out with! a plague upon! out upon! aroynt! *honi soit!* [F.], *parbleu!* [F.].

*** *delenda est Carthago;* "Ruin seize thee, ruthless king" [Gray].

909. Threat. — **N.** THREAT, menace; defiance &c. 715; abuse, minacity *rare*], minaciousness, intimidation; denunciation; fulmination; commination &c. (*curse*) 908; gathering clouds &c. (*warning*) 668.

V. THREATEN, threat, menace; snarl, growl, gnarl, mutter, bark, bully.

defy &c. 715; intimidate &c. 860; keep –, hold up –, hold out- *in terrorem* [L.]; shake –, double –, clinch- the fist at; thunder, talk big, fulminate, use big words, bluster, look daggers.

Adj. THREATENING, menacing, minatory, minacious, comminatory, abusive; *in terrorem* [L.]; ominous &c. (*predicting*) 511; defiant &c. 715; under the ban.

Int. *vœ victis!* at your peril! do your worst! look out!

*** *nemo me impune lacessit;* "an eye like Mars, to threaten and command" [*Hamlet*].

910. Philanthropy. — **N.** PHILANTHROPY, altruism, humanity, humanitarianism, universal benevolence, eudæmonism *or* eudemonism, *deliciæ humani generis* [L.].

PUBLIC WELFARE, commonwealth [*now rare*], commonweal *or* common weal [*now rare*]; socialism, communism; Fourierism, phalansterism *or* phalansterianism, Saint Simonianism; cosmopolitanism, utilitarianism, the greatest happiness of the greatest number, social science, sociology.

PUBLIC SPIRIT, patriotism, civism, nationality, love of country, *amor patriæ* [L.].

CHIVALRY, knight errantry; generosity &c. 942.

PHILANTHROPIST, eudæmonist *or* eudemonist, utilitarian, Benthamite, socialist, communist, cosmopolite, citizen of the world, *amicus humani generis* [L.]; altruist &c. 906; "little friend of all the world" [Kipling]; knight errant; patriot.

Adj. PHILANTHROPIC, altruistic, humanitarian, utilitarian, cosmopolitan; public-

911. Misanthropy. — **N.** MISANTHROPY, incivism; egotism &c. (*selfishness*) 943; moroseness &c. 901*a;* cynicism; want of patriotism &c. 910.

MISANTHROPE, misanthropist, egotist, cynic, man hater, Timon, Diogenes.

woman hater, misogynist.

Adj. MISANTHROPIC, antisocial, unpatriotic; egotistical &c. (*selfish*) 943; morose &c. 901*a.*

*** "no man is a true American who hates another country more than he loves his own" [Roosevelt]; "the worst thing about cynicism is its truth" [*Cynic's Calendar*].

spirited, patriotic; humane, large-hearted &c. (*benevolent*) 906; chivalric, chivalrous; generous &c. 942.

Adv. *pro bono publico* [*L.*]; *pro aris et focis* [Cicero].

** *humani nihil a me alienum puto* [Terence]; *omne solum forti patria* [Ovid]; *un bienfait n'est jamais perdu;* "mine is that great country which shall never take toll from the weakness of others" [Galsworthy].

912. Benefactor. — N. BENEFACTOR, savior, protector, good genius, tutelary saint, guardian angel, good Samaritan; friend in need, "a very present help in time of trouble" [*Bible*]; fairy godmother; *pater patriæ* [*L.*]; salt of the earth &c. (*good man*) 948; auxiliary &c. 711.

913. [MALEFICENT BEING.] Evildoer — N. EVILDOER, evil worker, malfeasor; wrongdoer &c. 949; mischiefmaker, marplot; oppressor, tyrant; firebrand, incendiary, fire bug [*U. S.*], pyromaniac, arsonist &c. 384; anarchist, nihilist, destroyer, Vandal, iconoclast, terrorist; Attila, scourge of the human race.

bane &c. 963; torpedo, bomb, U-boat.

SAVAGE, brute, ruffian, barbarian, semibarbarian, caitiff, desperado; Apache, gunman, hoodlum [*colloq.*], plug-ugly [*slang, U. S.*], Redskin, tough [*colloq., U. S.*], Mohock, Mohawk [*rare*], bludgeon man, bully, rough, hooligan [*slang*], larrikin [*Austral. & Eng.*], ugly customer, dangerous classes; thief &c. 792; butcher, hangman; cutthroat &c. (*killer*) 361.

WILD BEAST, tiger, leopard, panther, hyena, catamount [*U. S.*], catamountain, lynx, cougar, jaguar, puma; bloodhound, hellhound, sleuth-hound; gorilla; vulture.

cockatrice, adder; snake, – in the grass; serpent, cobra, asp, rattlesnake, anaconda; boa; viper &c. (*snake*) 366; *alacrán* [*Sp. Amer.*], alligator, cayman, crocodile, mugger *or* magar [*Hind.*]; Gila monster; octopus.

[INJURIOUS INSECTS] buffalo carpet beetle, cucumber flea beetle, elm-tree beetle, striped cucumber beetle, gypsy (*or* gipsy) moth, brown-tail moth, flat-headed apple-tree borer, peach-tree borer, round-headed apple-tree borer, squash vine borer, bedbug, harlequin cabbage bug, potato bug, buffalo bug, rose bug, squash bug, tent caterpillar; curculio, weevil, snout beetle, billbeetle, billbug, plum curculio; horn fly, white grub, San José scale, onion maggot, clover-seed midge, grain weevil, bollworm, cankerworm, cutworm, fall webworm, tobacco worm, tomato worm, wireworm; white ant, scorpion, hornet, mosquito, locust, Colorado beetle.

HAG, hellhag, beldam, Jezebel.

MONSTER; fiend &c. (*demon*) 980; devil incarnate, demon in human shape; Frankenstein's monster; cannibal, anthropophagus, anthropophagist; bloodsucker, vampire, ogre, ghoul.

harpy, siren, vampire [*colloq.*], vamp [*slang*]; Furies, Eumenides.

** *fœnum habet in cornu;* "Tremble thou wretch, That hast within thee undivulged crimes, Unwhipp'd of justice" [*King Lear*]; "From the fury of the Northmen, Good Lord, deliver us."

3. SPECIAL SYMPATHETIC AFFECTIONS

914. Pity. — N. PITY, compassion, commiseration; bowels, – of compassion; sympathy, fellow-feeling, tenderness, soft-heartedness, yearning, forbearance, humanity, mercy, clemency; leniency &c. (*lenity*) 740; exorability, exorableness; charity, ruth, long-suffering.

melting mood; *argumentum ad misericordiam* [*L.*]; quarter, grace, *locus pœnitentiæ* [*L.*].

SYMPATHIZER; advocate, friend, par-

914a. Pitilessness. — N. PITILESSNESS &c. *adj.;* inclemency, inexorability, inflexibility, incompassion [*rare*], hardness of heart; want of pity &c. 914; severity &c. 739; malevolence &c. 907.

V. BE PITILESS &c. *adj.;* turn a deaf ear to; claim one's "pound of flesh" [*M. of V.*]; have no –, shut the gates of-mercy &c. 914; give no quarter.

Adj. PITILESS, merciless, ruthless, bowelless; unpitying, unmerciful, inclement; grim-faced, grim-visaged; un-

tisan, patron, wellwisher, defender, champion.

V. PITY; have -, show -, take- pity &c. *n.;* commiserate, compassionate; condole &c. 915; sympathize; feel for, | compassionate, incompassionate [*rare*], uncompassioned; inflexible, relentless, inexorable; unrelenting &c. 919; harsh &c. 739; cruel &c. 907.

be sorry for, yearn over; weep, melt, thaw, enter into the feelings of.

forbear, relent, relax, give quarter, wipe the tears, *parcere subjectis* [*L.*]; give a *coup de grâce* [*F.*], put out of one's misery; be cruel to be kind.

RAISE *or* EXCITE PITY &c. *n.;* touch, soften, melt, melt the heart; appeal, - to one's better feelings; propitiate, disarm.

SUPPLICATE &c. (*request*) 765; ask for mercy &c. *n.;* cry for quarter, beg one's life, kneel; deprecate.

Adj. PITYING &c. *v.;* pitiful, compassionate, sympathetic, touched.

merciful, clement, ruthful; humane; humanitarian &c. (*philanthropic*) 910; tender, tender-hearted; soft, soft-hearted; unhardened; lenient &c. 740; exorable, forbearing; melting &c. *v.;* weak.

Int. for pity's sake! mercy! have -, cry you- mercy! God help you! poor -thing, - dear, - fellow! woe betide! *quis talia fando temperet a lachrymis!* [Vergil].

.*.* one's heart bleeding for; *haud ignara mali miseris succurrere disco* [Vergil]; "a fellow feeling makes one wondrous kind" [Garrick]; *onor di bocca assai giova e poco costa*; "Taught by that Power that pities me, I learn to pity them" [Goldsmith].

915. Condolence. — N. CONDOLENCE; lamentation &c. 839; sympathy, conso lation.

V. CONDOLE WITH, console, sympathize; express -, testify- pity; afford-, supply-consolation; lament with &c. 839; express sympathy for, feel for, send one's condolences; feel -grief, - sorrow- in common with; share one's sorrow.

.*.* "the human heart Finds nowhere shelter but in human kind" [G. Eliot], "pity and need Make all flesh kin. There is no caste in blood" [Edwin Arnold].

4. RETROSPECTIVE SYMPATHETIC AFFECTIONS

916. Gratitude. — N. GRATITUDE, gratefulness, thankfulness; feeling of -, sense of- obligation.

acknowledgment, recognition, thanksgiving, giving thanks; thankful good will.

THANKS, praise, benediction; pæan; *Te Deum* &c. (*worship*) 990; grace, - before meat, - after meat; thank offering; requital.

V. BE GRATEFUL &c. *adj.;* thank; give -, render -, return -, offer -, tender-thanks &c. *n.;* acknowledge, requite.

feel -, be -, lie- under an obligation; *savoir gré* [*F.*]; not look a gift horse in the mouth; never forget, overflow with gratitude; thank -, bless- one's stars; fall on one's knees.

Adj. GRATEFUL, thankful, obliged, beholden, indebted to, under obligation·

Int. THANKS! many thanks! gramercy! much obliged! thank you! thank Heaven! Heaven be praised!

917. Ingratitude. — N. INGRATITUDE, thanklessness, oblivion of benefits, unthankfulness.

"benefits forgot" [*As You Like It*]; thankless task, thankless office.

V. BE UNGRATEFUL &c. *adj.;* feel no obligation, owe one no thanks, forget benefits; look a gift horse in the mouth.

Adj. UNGRATEFUL, unmindful, unthankful; thankless, ingrate, wanting in gratitude, insensible of benefits.

forgotten; unacknowledged, unthanked, unrequited, unrewarded; ill-requited; ill-rewarded.

Int. thank you for nothing! "*et tu Brute!*" [*Julius Cæsar*].

.*.* "ingratitude! thou marble-hearted fiend" [*Lear*]; "this was the most unkindest cut of all" [*Julius Cæsar*]; "hearts unkind, kind deeds With coldness still returning" [Wordsworth].

.*.* "Now, God be praised, the day is ours" [Macaulay]; "the still small voice of gratitude" [Gray]; "Alas! the gratitude of men Hath often left me mourning" [Wordsworth]; "a lively sense of favors to come."

918. Forgiveness. — N. FORGIVE-NESS, pardon, condonation, grace, remission, absolution, amnesty, oblivion; indulgence; reprieve.

conciliation; reconcilement; reconciliation &c. (*pacification*) 723; propitiation.

longanimity, placability; *amantium iræ* [*L.*]; *locus pœnitentiæ* [*L.*]; forbearance.

EXONERATION, excuse, quittance, release, indemnity; bill -, act-, covenant -, deed- of indemnity; exculpation &c. (*acquittal*) 970.

V. FORGIVE, - and forget; pardon, condone, think no more of, let bygones be bygones, shake hands; forget an injury; bury the hatchet; drown all unkindness; start afresh, make a new start.

let off [*colloq.*], remit, absolve, give absolution; blot out one's -sins, - offenses, - transgressions, - debts; wipe the slate clean; reprieve; acquit &c. 970.

EXCUSE, pass over, overlook; wink at &c. (*neglect*) 460; bear with; allow for, make allowances for; let one down easily, not be too hard upon, pocket the affront.

CONCILIATE, propitiate, placate; beg -, ask -, implore- pardon &c. *n.;* make up a quarrel &c. (*pacify*) 723; let the wound heal.

Adj. FORGIVING, placable, conciliatory. forgiven &c. *v.;* unresented, unavenged, unrevenged.

Int. have mercy! cry you mercy! forgive and forget!

** veniam petimusque damusque vicissim [Horace]; more in sorrow than in anger; *tout comprendre c'est tout pardonner;* "the offender never pardons" [Herbert]; "Good to forgive, Best to forget" [Browning]; "to err is human, to forgive, divine" [Pope]; "the sin That neither God nor man can well forgive" [Tennyson].

919. Revenge. — N. REVENGE, revengement [*rare*], vengeance; avengement, avengeance [*obs.*], sweet revenge, vendetta, death feud, blood for blood; eye for an eye, tooth for a tooth, retaliation &c. 718; day of reckoning.

rancor, vindictiveness, immitigability; implacability; malevolence &c. 907; ruthlessness &c. 914a.

AVENGER, vindicator [*obs.*], Nemesis, Eumenides.

V. REVENGE, avenge, vindicate [*obs.*]; take revenge, have one's revenge; breathe -revenge, - vengeance; wreak one's -vengeance, - anger; cry quittance; give no quarter, take no prisoners.

have accounts to settle, have a crow to pluck, have a rod in pickle.

keep the wound green; nurse one's revenge, harbor -revenge, - vindictive feeling; bear malice; rankle, rankle in the breast.

HAVE AT A DISADVANTAGE, have on the hip, have the upper hand, have at one's mercy.

Adj. REVENGEFUL, vengeful, vindictive, rancorous; pitiless &c. 914a; ruthless, rigorous, avenging, retaliative, grudgeful [*rare*].

unforgiving, unrelenting; inexorable, stony-hearted, implacable, relentless, remorseless.

RANKLING, immitigable; *æternum servans sub pectore vulnus* [*L.*].

** manet cicatrix; manet altâ mente repostum; dies iræ dies illa; "in high vengeance there is noble scorn" [G. Eliot ; *inhumanum verbum est ultio* [Seneca]; *malevolus animus abditos dentes habet* [Syrus]; "revenge is sweet — especially to women" [Byron]; "Revenge, at first though sweet, Bitter ere long back on itself recoils" [Milton]; 'Vengeance is in my heart, death in my hand" [*Titus Andronicus*]; "I will feed fat the ancient grudge I bear him" [*M. of V.*]; "vengeance is mine; I will repay, saith the Lord" [*Bible*].

920. Jealousy. — N. JEALOUSY, jealousness; jaundiced eye; distrust, mistrust, misdoubt, heartburn; envy &c. 921; doubt, envious suspicion, suspicion; "green-eyed monster" [*Othello*]; yellows; Juno.

V. BE JEALOUS &c. *adj.;* view with jealousy, view with a jealous eye, view with a jaundiced eye; grudge, begrudge.

doubt, distrust, mistrust, suspect, misdoubt, heartburn [*obs.*]; jealouse [*obs. or Scot. & dial. Eng.*].

Adj. JEALOUS, jealous as a Barbary pigeon; jaundiced, yellow-eyed, envious; beside oneself with -jealousy, - envy.

** "Jealousy is cruel as the grave" [*Bible*]; "in jealousy there is more self-love than love" [La Rochefoucauld]; "For jealousy dislikes the world to know it" [Byron]; "the injur'd lover's hell" [*Paradise Lost*].

921. Envy. — **N.** ENVY; enviousness &c. *adj.;* rivalry; *jalousie de métier* [*F.*]; ill-will, spite; jealousy &c. 920.

V. ENVY, covet, grudge, begrudge, burst with envy, break the tenth commandment.

Adj. ENVIOUS, invidious, covetous, grudging, begrudged; belittling; *alieni appetens* [*L.*].

*** "base envy withers at another's joy" [Thomson]; *cæca invidia est* [Livy]; *multa petentibus desunt multa* [Horace]; *summa petit livor* [Ovid]; "for envy is a kind of praise" [Gay]; "Envy, to which th' ignoble mind's a slave, Is emulation in the learn'd or brave" [Pope].

SECTION IV. MORAL AFFECTIONS

1. MORAL OBLIGATIONS

922. Right. — **N.** RIGHT; what ought to be, what should be; what is fit &c. *adj.;* fitness &c. *adj.; summum jus* [*L.*].

JUSTICE, equity; equitableness &c. *adj.;* propriety; fair play, square deal [*colloq.*], impartiality, measure for measure, give and take, *lex talionis* [*L.*].

scales of justice, evenhanded justice, karma; *suum cuique* [*L.*]; clear stage –, fair field- and no favor; retributive justice, nemesis.

Astræa, Nemesis, Themis, Rhadamanthus.

morals &c. (*duty*) 926; law &c. 963; honor &c. (*probity*) 939; virtue &c. 944.

V. BE RIGHT &c. *adj.;* stand to reason.

see justice done, see one righted, see fair play; do justice to; recompense &c. (*reward*) 973; hold the scales even, give and take; serve one right, put the saddle on the right horse; give every one his due, give the devil his due; *audire alteram partem* [*L.*].

DESERVE &c. (*be entitled to*) 924.

Adj. RIGHT, good; just, reasonable; fit &c. 924; equal, equable, equitable; evenhanded, fair, square, fair and square.

LEGITIMATE, justifiable, rightful; as it should be, as it ought to be; lawful &c. (*permitted*) 760, (*legal*) 963.

DESERVED &c. 924.

Adv. RIGHTLY &c. *adj.; à –, au- bon droit* [*F.*], in justice, in equity, in reason.

without -distinction of, – regard to, – respect to- persons; upon even terms.

Int. all right!

923. Wrong. — **N.** WRONG; what ought not to be, what should not be *malum in se* [*L.*]; unreasonableness grievance; shame.

INJUSTICE; unfairness &c. *adj.;* iniquity, foul play, partiality, leaning, favor, favoritism, nepotism; partisanship, party spirit; undueness &c. 925; unlawfulness &c. 964.

robbing Peter to pay Paul &c. *v.;* the wolf and the lamb; vice &c. 945.

V. BE WRONG &c. *adj.;* cry to heaven for vengeance.

DO WRONG &c. *n.;* be inequitable &c. *adj.;* favor, lean towards; encroach; impose upon; reap where one has not sown; give an inch and take an ell; rob Peter to pay Paul.

Adj. WRONG, wrongful; bad, too bad; unjust, unfair, inequitable, unequitable, unequal, partial, one-sided; injurious.

UNJUSTIFIABLE, unreasonable, unallowable, unwarrantable, objectionable, improper, unfit; unjustified &c. 925; illegal &c. 964; iniquitous; immoral &c. 945.

in the wrong, – box; in bad [*slang*], in wrong [*slang*].

Adv. WRONGLY &c. *adj.*

Int. this is too bad! it will not do!

*** "a custom more honored in the breach than the observance" [*Hamlet*]; "Truth forever on the scaffold, Wrong forever on the throne" [Lowell]; "stiff in opinions, always in the wrong" [Dryden]; "To do a great right, do a little wrong" [*Merchant of Venice*].

*** *Dieu et mon droit;* "in equal scale weighing delight and dole" [*Hamlet*]; *justitia suum cuique distribuit* [Cicero]; *justitiæ soror incorrupta fides; justitia virtutum regina;* "thrice is he armed that hath his quarrel just" [*II Henry VI*]; "Sir, I would rather be right than be president" [Henry Clay]; "Heaven itself has ordained the right" [Washington]; "righteousness is at the bottom of all things" [Phillips Brooks].

924. Dueness. — **N.** dueness, right, droit [law], due, privilege, prerogative, prescription, title, claim, pretension, demand, birthright.

immunity, license, liberty, franchise; vested -interest, – right.

sanction, authority, warranty [law], charter, licitness, warrant &c. (permission) 760; constitution &c. (law) 963; tenure; bond &c. (security) 771.

deserts, merits, dues; all that is coming to one [colloq.].

claimant, appellant; plaintiff &c. 938.

V. be due to &c. adj.; be the due of &c. n.; have -right, – title, – claim- to; be entitled to; have a claim upon; belong to &c. (property) 780.

deserve, merit, be worthy of, richly deserve.

demand, claim; call upon one for, come upon one for, appeal to for; revendicate [rare], revindicate, reclaim; exact; insist -on, – upon; challenge; take one's stand, make a point of, require, lay claim to; assert, assume, arrogate.

make good; substantiate; vindicate a -claim, – right; fit –, qualify- for; make out a case.

use a right, assert, enforce, put in force, lay under contribution.

entitle; give or confer a right; authorize &c. 760; sanction, sanctify, legalize, ordain, prescribe, allot.

give every one his due &c. 922; pay one's dues; have one's -due, – rights; stand upon one's rights.

Adj. having a right to &c. v.; entitled to; claiming; deserving, meriting, worthy of.

privileged, allowed, sanctioned, warranted, authorized; ordained, prescribed, constitutional, chartered, enfranchised.

prescriptive, presumptive, absolute, indefeasible, unalienable, inalienable,

925. [Absence of right.] Undueness. — **N.** undueness &c. adj.; malum prohibitum [L.]; impropriety; illegality &c. 964.

falseness &c. adj.; emptiness –, invalidity- of title; illegitimacy.

loss of right, disfranchisement, forfeiture.

assumption, usurpation, tort [law], violation, breach, encroachment, presumption, seizure; stretch, exaction, imposition, lion's share.

usurper, pretender, impostor.

V. be undue &c. adj.; not be due &c. 924.

infringe, encroach, trench on, exact; arrogate, – to oneself; give an inch and take an ell; stretch –, strain- a point; usurp, violate, do violence to; get under false pretenses, sail under false colors.

disentitle, disfranchise, disqualify; invalidate.

relax &c. (be lax) 738; misbehave &c. (vice) 945; misbecome.

Adj. undue; unlawful &c. (illegal) 964; unconstitutional, illicit, unauthorized, unwarranted, unallowed, unsanctioned, unjustified; disentitled, unentitled; disqualified, unqualified; unprivileged, unchartered.

undeserved, unmerited, unearned; unfulfilled.

forfeited, disfranchised.

illegitimate, bastard, spurious, false; usurped, tortious [law].

improper; unmeet, unfit, unbefitting, unseemly, unbecoming, misbecoming, seemless [obs.]; contra bonos mores [L.]; not the thing, out of the question, not to be thought of; preposterous, pretentious, would-be.

⁎ filius nullius; "an honour snatch'd with boisterous hands" [II Henry VI].

imprescriptible, inviolable, unimpeachable, unchallenged; sacrosanct.

due to, merited, deserved, condign [archaic, except of punishment], richly deserved.

right, fit, fitting, correct, proper, meet, befitting, becoming, seemly; decorous; creditable, up to the mark, right as a trivet; just –, quite- the thing; selon les règles [F.]; square, unexceptionable, equitable &c. 922; due, en règle [F.].

lawful, licit, legitimate, legal; legalized &c. (law) 963; allowable &c. (permitted) 760.

Adv. duly; as is -right, – fitting, – just; unexceptionably; ex officio [L.], de jure [L.]; by right, by divine right; jure divino [L.], Dei gratiâ [L.], in the name of.

⁎ civis Romanus sum [Cicero]; à chaque saint sa chandelle; "render to Cæsar the things that are Cæsar's" [Bible].

926. Duty. — N. DUTY, what ought to be done, moral obligation, accountableness, liability, onus, responsibility; bounden –, imperative- duty; call, -- of duty; accountability.

allegiance, fealty, tie; engagement &c. (*promise*) 768; part; function, calling &c. (*business*) 625.

OBSERVANCE, fulfillment, discharge, performance, acquittal, satisfaction, redemption; good behavior.

MORALITY, morals, decalogue; case of conscience; conscientiousness &c. (*probity*) 939; conscience, inward monitor, still small voice within, sense of duty, tender conscience; the hell within [*P. L.*].

PROPRIETY, fitness; dueness &c. 924; seemliness, amenableness, amenability, decorum, *to prepon* [*Gr.* τὸ πρέπον]; the thing, the proper thing; the -right, - proper- thing to do.

[SCIENCE OF MORALS] ethics, ethology [*obs. in this sense*]; deontology, aretology [*obs.*]; moral –, ethical- philosophy; casuistry, polity.

V. BE THE DUTY OF, be incumbent on &c. *adj.;* be responsible &c. *adj.;* behoove, become, befit, beseem; belong to, pertain to; fall to one's lot; devolve on; lie upon, lie on one's head, lie at one's door; rest with, rest on the shoulders of.

take upon oneself &c. (*promise*) 768; be –, become- -bound to, – sponsor for; incur a responsibility &c. *n.;* be –, stand –, lie- under an obligation; stand responsible for; have to answer for; owe it to oneself.

enter upon –, perform –, observe –, fulfill –, discharge –, adhere to –, acquit oneself of –, satisfy- -a duty, – an obligation; act one's part, redeem one's pledge, do justice to, be at one's post; do duty; do one's duty &c. (*be virtuous*) 944.

927. Dereliction of Duty. — N. DERELICTION OF DUTY; fault &c. (*guilt*) 947; sin &c. (*vice*) 945; nonobservance, nonperformance, noncoöperation; indolence, neglect, relaxation, infraction, violation, transgression, failure, evasion; eyeservice; dead letter.

SLACKER, loafer, time-killer; eyeserver, eyeservant; striker; noncoöperator.

V. VIOLATE; break, break through; infringe; set aside, set at naught; encroach upon, trench upon; trample -on, – under foot; slight, get by [*slang*], neglect, evade, renounce, forswear, repudiate; wash one's hands of; escape. transgress, fail.

call to account &c. (*disapprobation*) 932.

. "There never was a bad man that had ability for good service" [Burke].

927a. Exemption. — N. EXEMPTION, freedom, irresponsibility, immunity, liberty, license, release, quitclaim [*law*]; exoneration, excuse, dispensation, absolution, franchise [*obs.*], renunciation, discharge; exculpation &c. 970.

V. EXEMPT, release, acquit, discharge, quitclaim [*law*], remise, remit; free, set at liberty, let off [*colloq.*], pass over, spare, excuse, dispense with, give dispensation, license; stretch a point; absolve &c. (*forgive*) 918; exonerate &c. (*exculpate*) 970; save the necessity.

be exempt &c. *adj.*

Adj. EXEMPT, free, immune, at liberty, scot-free; released &c. *v.;* unbound, unencumbered; irresponsible, not responsible, unaccountable, not answerable; excusable.

. *bonis nocet quisquis pepercerit malis* [Syrus]; "The charter of thy worth gives thee releasing" [Shakespeare].

be on one's good behavior, mind one's P's and Q's; walk the straight path.

IMPOSE A DUTY &c. *n.;* enjoin, require, exact; bind, – over; saddle with, prescribe, assign, call upon, look to, oblige.

Adj. OBLIGATORY, binding; imperative, peremptory; stringent &c. (*severe*) 739; behooving &c. *v.;* incumbent on, chargeable on; under obligation; obliged by, bound by, tied by; saddled with.

due to, beholden to, bound to, indebted to; tied down; compromised &c. (*promised*) 768; in duty bound.

AMENABLE, liable, accountable, responsible, answerable.

RIGHT, meet &c. (*due*) 924; moral, ethical, casuistical, conscientious, ethological.

Adv. with a safe conscience, as in duty bound, on good behavior, on one's own responsibility, at one's own risk, *suo periculo* [*L.*]; *in foro conscientiæ* [*L.*]; *quamdiu se bene gesserit* [*L.*]; at one's post.

. *dura lex sed lex; dulce et decorum est pro patria mori; honos habet onus; leve fit quod bene fertur onus* [Ovid]; *loyauté m'oblige;* "simple duty hath no place for fear" [Whittier]; "stern daughter of the voice of God" [Wordsworth]; "there is a higher law than the Constitution" [Wm. Seward]; "So nigh is grandeur to our dust, So near is God to man, When Duty whispers low, *Thou must*, The youth replies, *I can!*" [Emerson]; "labor to keep alive in your breast that little spark of celestial fire — conscience" [George Washington]; "Thus conscience does make cowards of us all" [*Hamlet*]; "And voices that we thought were fled Arise and call us, and we come" [Noyes].

2. MORAL SENTIMENTS

928. Respect. — **N.** RESPECT, regard, consideration; courtesy &c. 894; attention, deference, reverence, honor, esteem, estimation, veneration, admiration; approbation &c. 931.

HOMAGE, fealty, obeisance, genuflection, kneeling, prostration; obsequiousness &c. 886; salaam, kotow *or* kowtow [*Chinese*], bow, presenting arms, salute.

RESPECTS, regards, duty, *devoirs* [*F.*], *égards* [*F.*].

devotion &c. (*piety*) 987.

V. RESPECT, regard; revere, reverence; hold in reverence, honor, venerate, hallow; esteem &c. (*approve of*) 931; think much of; entertain –, bear-respect for; look up to, defer to; have –, hold- a high opinion of; pay attention to, pay respect to &c. *n.;* do *or* render honor to; do the honors, hail; show courtesy &c. 894; salute, present arms.

do *or* pay homage to; pay tribute to, kneel to, bow to, bend the knee to; fall down before, prostrate oneself, kiss the hem of one's garment; worship &c. 990.

keep one's distance, make room, observe due decorum, stand upon ceremony.

COMMAND RESPECT, inspire respect; awe, impose, overawe, dazzle.

Adj. RESPECTING &c. *v.;* respectful, deferential, decorous, reverential, obsequious, ceremonious, bareheaded, cap in hand, on one's knees; prostrate &c. (*servile*) 886.

RESPECTED &c. *v.;* in high –esteem, – estimation; time-honored, venerable, *emeritus* [*L.*].

Adv. IN DEFERENCE TO; with all respect, with due respect, with the highest respect; with submission.

excusing the liberty; saving your -grace, – presence; *salva sit reverentia* [*L.*]; *pace tanti nominis* [*L.*].

929. Disrespect. — **N.** DISRESPECT, disesteem, disestimation; disfavor, disrepute, want of esteem, low estimation, disparagement &c. (*dispraise*) 932, (*detraction*) 934; irreverence; slight, neglect; *spretæ injuria formæ* [Vergil], superciliousness &c. (*contempt*) 930.

indignity, vilipendency [*obs.*], contumely, affront, dishonor, insult, outrage, discourtesy &c. 895; practical joking; scurrility, scoffing; sibilation, hiss, hissing, hoot, irrision [*rare*], derision; mockery; irony &c. (*ridicule*) 856; sarcasm.

GIBE *or* jibe, flout, jeer, scoff, gleek [*obs.*], fleer, taunt, sneer, quip, fling, twit, wipe [*dial. or slang*], slap in the face.

V. TREAT WITH DISRESPECT &c. *n.;* hold in disrespect &c. (*despise*) 930; misprize, disregard, slight, undervalue, humiliate, depreciate, trifle with, set at naught, pass by, push aside, overlook, turn one's back upon, laugh in one's sleeve; be disrespectful &c. *adj.;* be discourteous &c. 895; set down, browbeat.

dishonor, desecrate; insult, affront, outrage.

speak slightingly of; disparage &c. (*dispraise*) 932; vilipend, call names; throw –, fling- dirt; throw mud at; make ride the rail, drag through the mud, point at, indulge in personalities; make mouths [*archaic*], make faces; bite the thumb; take –, pluck- by the beard; toss in a blanket, tar and feather.

DERIDE, have *or* hold in derision; scoff, barrack [*dial. Eng. & Austral.*], sneer, laugh at, snigger, ridicule, gibe *or* jibe, mock, jeer, taunt, twit, niggle, gleek [*obs.*], gird, flout, fleer; roast [*colloq.*], guy [*colloq.*], rag [*dial. Eng. & college slang*], smoke [*old slang*]; turn into ridicule; burlesque &c. 856; laugh to scorn &c.

Int. hail! all hail! *hoch!* [*Ger.*]; *esto perpetua!* [*L.*], may your shadow never be less!

. "and pluck up drowned honor by the locks" [*I Henry IV*]; "honor pricks me on" [*ibid.*]; "his honor rooted in dishonor stood" [Tennyson].

(*contempt*) 930; lead one a dance, have a fling at, scout, hiss, hoot, mob.

fool; make game of, make a fool of, make an April fool of; play a practical joke.

Adj. DISRESPECTFUL; aweless, irreverent; disparaging &c. 934; insulting &c. *v.*; supercilious &c. (*scornful*) 930; rude, derisive, sarcastic; scurrile, scurrilous, contumelious, contemptuous, insolent, disdainful.

UNRESPECTED, unworshiped, unenvied, unsaluted; unregarded, disregarded.

Adv. DISRESPECTFULLY &c. *adj.*

. "old friends pass me as if I were a wall" [Galsworthy].

930. Contempt. — N. CONTEMPT, disdain, scorn, sovereign contempt; despisal [*rare*], despiciency [*obs.*], despisement [*rare*]; vilipendency [*obs.*], contumely; slight, sneer, spurn, byword; despect [*rare*].

contemptuousness &c. *adj.*; scornful eye; smile of contempt; derision &c. (*disrespect*) 929.

[STATE OF BEING DESPISED] despisedness.

V. DESPISE, contemn, scorn, disdain, feel contempt for, view with a scornful eye; disregard, slight, not mind; pass by &c. (*neglect*) 460; look down upon; hold -cheap, – in contempt, – in disrespect; think nothing of, think small beer of [*colloq.*]; make light of; underestimate &c. 483; esteem slightly, esteem of small or no account; take no account of, care nothing for; set no store by; not care a straw &c. (*unimportance*) 643; set at naught, laugh in one's sleeve, snap one's fingers at, shrug one's shoulders, turn up one's nose at, pooh-pooh, "damn with faint praise" [Pope].

sneeze at, whistle at, sneer at; curl up one's lip, toss the head, *traiter de haut en bas* [*F.*]; laugh at &c. (*be disrespectful*) 929; point the finger of –, hold up to –, laugh to- scorn; scout, hoot, flout, hiss, scoff at.

SPURN, turn one's back upon, turn a cold shoulder upon; tread –, trample- -upon, – under foot; kick; fling to the winds &c. (*repudiate*) 610; send away with a flea in the ear [*colloq.*].

Adj. CONTEMPTUOUS, disdainful, scornful, withering, contumelious, supercilious, cynical, haughty, cavalier; derisive; with the nose in air, *de haut en bas* [*F.*].

CONTEMPTIBLE, despicable; pitiable; pitiful &c. (*unimportant*) 643; despised &c. *v.*; downtrodden; unenvied.

Adv. CONTEMPTUOUSLY &c. *adj.*

Int. a fig for &c. (*unimportant*) 643; bah! pooh! pshaw! never mind! away with! hang it! fiddledeedee!

. "a dismal universal hiss, the sound of public scorn" [*Paradise Lost*]; "I had rather be a dog and bay the moon than such a Roman" [*Julius Cæsar*]; "as if I was next door's dog" [Shaw]; "This is my private hell" [Galsworthy]; "there are many men who feel a kind of twisted pride in cynicism" [Roosevelt].

931. Approbation. — N. APPROBATION, approval, approvement [*obs.*], bepraisement, sanction, advocacy; nod of approbation; esteem, estimation, good opinion, golden opinions, admiration; love &c. 897; appreciation, regard, account, popularity, *kudos* [*Gr.* κῦδος], credit; repute &c. 873.

commendation, praise, laud, laudation; good word; meed -, tribute- of praise; encomium, eulogy, eulogium, *éloge* [*F.*], panegyric, blurb [*slang*];

932. Disapprobation. — N. DISAPPROBATION, disapproval, improbation [*obs.*], disesteem, displacency [*rare*]; odium; dislike &c. 867; black list, blackball, ostracism, boycott; index expurgatorius.

DISPARAGEMENT, depreciation, disvaluation, dispraise, discommendation; detraction &c. 934; denunciation; condemnation &c. 971; animadversion, reflection, stricture, objection, exception, criticism; blame, censure, obloquy; sar-

homage, hero worship; benediction, blessing, benison.

APPLAUSE, plaudit, clap; clapping, – of hands; acclaim, acclamation; cheer; pæan, hosanna; shout –, peal –, chorus –, thunders- of -applause &c.; prytaneum.

WINNER, prize winner, best seller, corker [slang], peach [slang], oner [slang], the real thing [colloq.], the goods [slang].

V. APPROVE, approbate,[1] think good of, think much of, think well of, think highly of; esteem, value, prize; set great store by.

honor, hold in esteem, look up to, admire; like &c. 897; be in favor of, wish Godspeed; hail, hail with satisfaction, do justice to, appreciate.

stand up for, stick up for [colloq.], uphold, hold up, countenance, sanction; clap –, pat- on the back; keep in countenance, indorse or endorse; give credit, recommend; mark with a white -mark, – stone.

COMMEND, belaud, praise, laud, compliment, pay a tribute, bepraise; clap, – the hands; applaud, cheer, acclaim, acclamate [rare], encore; panegyrize, eulogize, boost [colloq., U. S.], root for [slang, U. S.], cry up, prôner [F.], puff; extol, – to the skies; magnify, glorify, exalt, swell, make much of; flatter &c. 933; bless, give a blessing to; have –, say- a good word for; speak -well, –highly, – in high terms- of; sing –, sound –, chant –, resound- the praises of; sing praises to; cheer –, applaud- to the -echo, – very echo.

redound to the -honor, – praise, – credit- of; do credit to; deserve -praise &c. n.; recommend itself; pass muster.

BE PRAISED &c.; receive honorable mention; be in favor with, be in high favor with; ring with the praises of, win golden opinions, gain credit, find favor with, stand well in the opinion of; laudari a laudato viro [L.].

Adj. APPROVING &c. v.; in favor of; lost in admiration; commendatory, complimentary, benedictory, laudatory, panegyrical, eulogistic, encomiastic, acclamatory, lavish of praise, uncritical.

APPROVED, praised &c. v.; uncensured, unimpeached; popular, in good odor; in high esteem &c. (respected) 928; in favor, in high favor.

donic -grin, – laugh; sarcasm, satire, insinuation, innuendo; bad –, poor –, left-handed- compliment.

sneer &c. (contempt) 930; taunt &c. (disrespect) 929; cavil, carping, censoriousness; hypercriticism &c. (fastidiousness) 868.

REPREHENSION, remonstrance, expostulation, reproof, reprobation, admonition, increpation [archaic], reproach; rebuke, reprimand, castigation, jobation [colloq.], lecture, curtain lecture, blowup [colloq.]; blowing up, trimming, wigging, dressing, dressing down [all colloq.]; rating, scolding, correction, set down, rap on the knuckles, coup de bec [F.], rebuff; slap, slap on the face; home thrust, hit; frown, scowl, black look.

diatribe, jeremiad or jeremiade, tirade, philippic.

chiding, upbraiding &c. v.; exprobration [rare], personal remarks, abuse, vituperation, invective, objurgation, contumely; hard –, cutting –, bitter-words; evil-speaking; bad language &c. 908; personality.

CLAMOR, outcry, hue and cry; hiss, hissing, sibilation, catcall; execration &c. 908.

V. DISAPPROVE; dislike &c. 867; lament &c. 839; object to, take exception to; be scandalized at, think ill of; view with -disfavor, – dark eyes, – jaundiced eyes; nil admirari [L.], disvalue, improbate [obs.].

frown upon, look grave; bend –, knit-the brows; shake the head at, shrug the shoulders; turn up the nose &c. (contempt) 930; look askance, look black upon; look with an evil eye; make a wry face at, make a mouth at [archaic], set one's face against.

BLAME; lay –, cast- blame upon; censure, fronder [F.], reproach, pass censure on, reprobate, impugn, impeach; disbar, unfrock.

accuse &c. 938; impeach, denounce; hold up to -reprobation, – execration; expose, brand, gibbet, stigmatize; show up, pull up [both colloq.]; take up; cry "shame" upon; be outspoken; raise a hue and cry against.

REPREHEND, chide, admonish; berate, betongue; bring –, call- -to account, – over the coals [colloq.], – to order; take

---

[1] Obsolete in England except in legal writings, but surviving in the United States chiefly in a technical sense for license. C. O. S. M.

PRAISEWORTHY, commendable, of estimation; deserving –, worthy of-praise &c. *n.;* good &c. 648; meritorious, estimable, creditable, unimpeachable; beyond all praise.

Adv. COMMENDABLY, with credit, to admiration; well &c. 618; with three times three.

Int. hear hear! good for you! do it again! bully for you! [*slang*], well done! fine! bravo! *bravissimo!* [*It.*], *euge!* [*Gr. & L.*], *macte virtute!* [*L.*], so far so good! that's right! quite right! one cheer more! may your shadow never be less! *esto perpetua!* [*L.*], long life to! *viva!* [*It.*], *evviva!* [*It.*], Godspeed! *valete et plaudite!* [*L.*], *encore!* [*F.*], *bis!* [*L. & F.*].

₊ *probatum est; tacent satis laudant;* "servant of God, well done!" [*Paradise Lost*]; "I have bought Golden opinions from all sorts of people" [*Macbeth*]; "How his silence drinks up this applause!" [*Troilus and Cressida*]; "we are the Jasons, we have won the fleece" [*M. of V.*]; "O well done! I commend your pains" [*Macbeth*]; "right noble is thy merit" [*Richard II*].

to task, haul over the coals [*colloq.*], reprove, lecture, bring to book; read a -lesson, – lecture- to; rebuke, correct; reprimand, chastise, castigate, lash, trounce; trim, blow up, give it to, give one fits, give it to one, lay out [*all si colloq.*]; *laver la tête* [*F.*], overhaul.

remonstrate, expostulate, recriminate.

execrate &c. 908; exprobate [*rare*], speak daggers, vituperate; abuse, – like a pickpocket; tongue-lash [*colloq.*], scold, rate, objurgate, upbraid, fall foul of; jaw [*low*]; rail, – at, – in good set terms; bark at, yelp at, anathematize, call names; call by -hard, – ugly- names; avile [*obs.*], revile, vilify, vilipend, bespatter; clapperclaw [*archaic*]; rave –, thunder –, fulminate- against; load with reproaches.

DECRY, cry down, run down, frown down; exclaim –, protest –, inveigh –, declaim –, cry out –, raise one's voice-against; clamor, hiss, hoot, catcall, mob; backbite; ostracize, blacklist, boycott, blackball; draw up –, sign- a round robin.

take down, set down; snub, snap one up, give a rap on the knuckles; throw a stone -at, – in one's garden; have a fling at, have a snap at; have words with, pluck a crow with; give one a wipe [*dial. or slang*]; give one a lick with the rough side of the tongue [*colloq.*].

animadvert upon, reflect upon; glance at; cast -reflection, – reproach – a slur-upon; insinuate, "damn with faint praise" [Pope]; "hint a fault and hesitate dislike" [Pope]; not to be able to say much for.

DISPARAGE, depreciate, knock [*colloq., U. S.*], dispraise, discommend [*rare*], deprecate, speak ill of, not speak well of; condemn &c. (*find guilty*) 971; scoff at, point at; twit, taunt &c. (*disrespect*) 929; sneer at &c. (*despise*) 230; satirize. lampoon; defame &c. (*detract*) 934; depreciate, find fault with, criticize, cut up; pull –, pick- to pieces; take exception; cavil; peck at, nibble at, carp at; be censorious &c. *adj.;* pick -holes, – a hole, – a hole in one's coat; make a fuss about.

INCUR BLAME, excite disapprobation, scandalize, shock, revolt; get a bad name, forfeit one's good opinion, be under a cloud, come under the ferule, bring a hornet's nest about one's ears.

take blame, stand corrected; have to answer for.

Adj. DISAPPROVING &c. *v.;* disparaging, condemnatory, damnatory, denunciatory, reproachful, abusive, objurgatory, clamorous, vituperative; defamatory &c. 934.

satirical, sarcastic, sardonic, cynical, dry, sharp, cutting, biting, severe, withering, trenchant, hard upon; censorious, critical, captious, carping, hypercritical·scandalized; fastidious &c. 868; sparing of –, grudging -praise.

DISAPPROVED, chid &c. *v.;* in bad odor, blown upon, unapproved; unblest; at a discount, exploded; weighed in the balance and found wanting.

unlamented, unbewailed, unpitied.

BLAMEWORTHY, reprehensible &c. (*guilt*) 947; to –, worthy of- blame; answerable, uncommendable, exceptionable, not to be thought of; bad &c. 649; vicious &c. 945.

Adv. REPROACHFULLY &c. *adj.;* with a wry face.

Int. it is too bad! it won't do! it will never do! it isn't done! marry come up! [*archaic or dial.*], Oh! come! 'sdeath! [*archaic*].

forbid it Heaven! God forbid! Heaven forbid! out upon it! fie upon it! away with! tut! *O tempora! O mores!* [*L.*]; shame! fie, – for shame! out on you!

tell it not in Gath!

∗∗∗ "The poorest way to face life is to face it with a sneer" [Roosevelt]; "defamed by every charlatan" [Tennyson]; "willing to wound, and yet afraid to strike" [Pope]; "Compound for sins they are inclined to By damning those they have no mind to" [Butler]; "Of whom to be disprais'd were no small praise" [Milton]; "Censure is the tax a man pays to the public for being eminent" [Swift]; "There is no defense against reproach except obscurity" [Addison].

---

933. Flattery. — N. FLATTERY, adulation, gloze [*rare*]; blandishment [*rare*], blandiloquence; cajolery; fawning, wheedling &c. |*v.;* captation, coquetry, obsequiousness, sycophancy, flunkeyism, toadyism, toadeating, tufthunting; snobbishness.

incense, honeyed words, flummery, buncombe *or* bunkum [*cant or slang*]; blarney, butter, soft soap, soft sawder [*all colloq.*]; rose water.

voice of the charmer, mouth honor; lip homage; euphemism; unctuousness &c. *adj.*

V. FLATTER, praise to the skies, puff; wheedle, cajole, glaver [*obs. or dial.*], coax; fawn, – upon; humor, gloze [*now rare*], soothe, pet, coquet, slaver, butter [*colloq.*], jolly [*slang or colloq.*]; bespatter, beslubber, beplaster, beslaver; lay it on thick, overpraise; cog [*obs.*], collogue [*obs. in this sense*]; truckle to, pander *or* pandar to, pay court to; court; creep into the good graces of, curry favor with, hang on the sleeve of; fool to the top of one's bent; lick the dust.

lay the flattering unction to one's soul, gild the pill, make things pleasant.

overestimate &c. 482; exaggerate &c. 549.

Adj. FLATTERING &c. *v.;* adulatory; mealy-mouthed, honey-mouthed, honeyed, smooth, smooth-tongued; soapy [*slang*], oily, unctuous, blandiloquous, specious; fine-, fair- spoken; plausible, servile, sycophantic, fulsome; courtierly, courtierlike.

Adv. ad captandum.

∗∗∗ "for ne'er Was flattery lost on Poet's ear" [Scott]; "Lay not that flattering unction to your soul" [*Hamlet*]; "Flatter and praise, commend, extol their graces" [*Two Gentlemen*]; "Our praises are our wages" [*Winter's Tale*]; "The sweeter sound of woman's praise" [Macaulay]; "And wrinkles, the d——d democrats, won't flatter" [Byron].

934. Detraction. — N. DETRACTION, disparagement, depreciation, vilification, obloquy, scurrility, scandal, defamation, aspersion, traducement [*rare*], slander, calumny, obtrectation [*obs.*], evil-speaking, backbiting, *scandalum magnatum* [*L.*].

sarcasm, cynicism; criticism (*disapprobation*) 932; invective &c. 932; envenomed tongue; *spretæ injuria formæ* [*L.*].

PERSONALITY, libel, lampoon, skit [*Scot. & dial.*], squib, pasquil, pasquinade; *chronique scandaleuse* [*F.*], roorback [*U. S.*].

DETRACTOR &c. 936.

V. DETRACT, derogate, decry, depreciate, disparage; run down, cry down; back-cap [*U. S.*]; belittle; pessimize; sneer at &c. (*contemn*) 930; criticize, pull to pieces, pick a hole in one's coat, asperse, cast aspersions, blow upon, bespatter, blacken, vilify, vilipend, avile [*obs.*]; give a dog a bad name, brand, malign; backbite, libel, lampoon, traduce, slander, defame, calumniate, bear false witness against; speak ill of behind one's back.

muckrake; fling dirt &c. (*disrespect*) 929; anathematize &c. 932; dip the pen in gall, view in a bad light.

Adj. DETRACTING &c. *v.;* defamatory, traducent [*rare*], detractory, derogatory, disparaging, libelous; scurrile, scurrilous, abusive; foul-spoken, foul-tongued, foul-mouthed; slanderous, calumnious, calumniatory; sarcastic, sardonic, satirical, cynical.

∗∗∗ "Damn with faint praise, assent with civil leer; And without sneering, teach the rest to sneer" [Pope]; another lie nailed to the counter; "cut men's throats with whisperings" [B. Jonson]; "foul whisperings are abroad" [*Macbeth*]; "soft-buzzing slander" [Thomson]; "virtue itself 'scapes not calumnious strokes" [*Hamlet*]; "ill-will never said well" [*Henry V*].

935. Flatterer. — N. FLATTERER, adulator, eulogist, euphemist; optimist, encomiast, laudator, booster [*colloq., U. S.*], whitewasher.

toady, toadeater, sycophant, courtier, flattercap [*obs. or dial. Eng.*], pickthank [*archaic or dial.*], Damocles, Sir Pertinax MacSycophant; **flatteur** [*F.*], *prôneur* [*F.*]; puffer, *claqueur* [*F.*], claquer; tout, touter [*both colloq.*], claw-back [*obs. or dial. Eng.*], slaverer; doer of dirty work; parasite, hanger-on &c. (*servility*) 886.

Adj. flattering &c. 933.

*** *pessimum genus inimicorum laudantes* [Tacitus]; "But when I tell him he hates flatterers, He says he does, being then most flattered" [*Julius Cæsar*].

936. Detractor. — N. DETRACTOR, reprover; censor, censurer; cynic, critic, caviler, carper, word-catcher, *frondeur* [*F.*], barracker [*dial. Eng. & Austral.*].

defamer, knocker [*colloq., U. S.*], backbiter, slanderer, Sir Benjamin Backbite, lampooner, satirist, traducer, libeler, calumniator, dearest foe, Thersites; Zoilus; good-natured friend [*satirical*]; reviler, vituperator, castigator; shrew &c. 901; muckraker.

DISAPPROVER, *laudator temporis acti* [Horace].

Adj. black-mouthed, abusive &c. 934.

*** "You know who the critics are? — the men who have failed in literature and art" [Disraeli]; "Oh, you chorus of indolent reviewers!" [Tennyson].

937. Vindication. — N. VINDICATION, justification, warrant; exoneration, exculpation, disculpation; acquittal &c. 970; whitewashing.

EXTENUATION, palliation, palliative, softening, mitigation.

PLEA &c. 617; apology, gloss, varnish; salvo [*rare*], excuse, extenuating circumstances; allowance, - to be made; *locus pœnitentiæ* [*L.*]; reply, defense *or* defence; recrimination &c. 938.

APOLOGIST, vindicator, justifier; defendant &c. 938.

TRUE BILL, justifiable charge.

V. JUSTIFY, warrant; be an excuse for &c. *n.*; lend a color, furnish a handle; vindicate, exculpate, disculpate [*rare*]; acquit &c. 970; clear, set right, exonerate, whitewash; clear the skirts of.

EXTENUATE, palliate, excuse, soften, apologize, varnish, slur, gloze; put a -gloss, - good face- upon; mince; gloss over, bolster up, help a lame dog over a stile.

ADVOCATE, defend, plead one's cause; stand up for, stick up for [*colloq.*], speak up for; contend for, speak for; bear out, keep in countenance, support; plead &c. 617; say in defense; plead ignorance; confess and avoid, propugn [*obs.*], put in a good word for.

take the will for the deed, make allowance for, do justice to; give one his due, give the Devil his due.

make good; prove the truth of, prove one's case; be justified by the event.

Adj. VINDICATIVE, vindicatory, vindicated, vindicating &c. *v.;* palliative;

938. Accusation. — N. ACCUSATION, charge, imputation, slur, inculpation, exprobration [*rare*], delation; crimination, incrimination, accrimination [*obs.*], recrimination; *tu quoque* argument; invective &c. 932.

denunciation, denouncement [*archaic*]; libel, challenge, citation, arraignment, impeachment, appeachment [*obs.*], indictment, bill of indictment, true bill; lawsuit &c. 969; condemnation &c. 971.

gravamen of a charge, head and front of one's offending, *argumentum ad hominem* [*L.*]; scandal &c. (*detraction*) 934; *scandalum magnatum* [*L.*].

ACCUSER, prosecutor, plaintiff, complainant, libelant, delator, informant, informer.

ACCUSED, defendant, prisoner, respondent, corespondent; litigant; panel.

V. ACCUSE, charge, tax, impute, twit, taunt with, reproach; brand with reproach; stigmatize, slur; cast a stone at, cast a slur on; criminate, incriminate, inculpate, implicate; call to account &c. (*censure*) 932; take to -blame, - task; put in the black book.

inform against, indict, denounce, arraign; impeach, appeach [*obs.*]; have up, show up [*colloq.*], pull up [*colloq.*]; challenge, cite, lodge a complaint; prosecute, bring an action against &c. 969; blow upon [*colloq.*], squeal [*slang*].

charge with, saddle with; lay to one's -door, - charge; lay the blame on, bring home to; cast -, throw- in one's teeth; cast the first stone at.

exculpatory, disculpatory, apologetic.

EXCUSABLE, defensible, pardonable; venial, veniable [obs.]; specious, plausible, justifiable.

. "honi soit qui mal y pense"; "good wine needs no bush" [As You Like It]; "The lady doth protest too much, methinks" [Hamlet]; "apologies only account for that which they do not alter" [Disraeli].

[slang], in stir [slang], in the house of detention.

ACCUSABLE, imputable, indefensible, inexcusable, unpardonable, unjustifiable; vicious &c. 845.

Int. look at home! tu quoque [L.] &c. (retaliation) 718.

. qui s'excuse s'accuse; "the breath of accusation kills an innocent name" [Shelley]; "thou canst not say I did it" [Macbeth].

have –, keep- a rod in pickle for; have a crow to pluck with.

trump up a charge.

Adj. ACCUSING &c. v.; accusatory, accusative, imputative, denunciatory, recriminatory, criminatory.

ACCUSED &c. v.; suspected; under -suspicion, – a cloud, – surveillance.

IN CUSTODY, in detention, in the lock-up, in the watch-house, in the jug

3. MORAL CONDITIONS

939. Probity. — N. PROBITY, integrity, rectitude; uprightness &c. adj.; honesty, faith; honor; bonne foi [F.], good faith, bona fides [L.]; purity, grace; clean hands.

constancy; faithfulness &c. adj.; fidelity, loyalty, incorruption [archaic], incorruptibility; trustworthiness &c. adj.; truth, candor, singleness of heart; veracity &c. 543; tender conscience &c. (sense of duty) 926.

fairness &c. adj.; fair play, justice, equity, impartiality, principle.

court of honor, a fair field and no favor; argumentum ad verecundiam [L.].

PUNCTILIOUSNESS, punctilio, delicacy, nicety, scrupulosity, scrupulousness &c. adj.; scruple; point, – of honor; punctuality [rare in this sense].

dignity &c. (repute) 873; respectability, respectableness &c. adj.

MAN OF HONOR, man of his word, gentleman, gentilhomme [F.], fidus Achates [L.], preux chevalier [F.], galantuomo [It.]; true-penny, trump [slang], brick [slang or colloq.], true Briton; white man [slang, U. S.].

V. BE HONORABLE &c. adj.; deal -honorably, – squarely, – impartially, – fairly; speak the truth &c. (veracity) 543; draw a straight furrow; tell the truth and shame the Devil, vitam impendere vero [L.]; show a proper spirit, make a point of; do one's duty &c. (virtue) 944; play the game [colloq.].

redeem one's pledge &c. 926; keep –, be as good as- one's -promise, – word; keep faith with, not fail.

940. Improbity. — N. IMPROBITY, dishonesty, dishonor; deviation from rectitude; disgrace &c. (disrepute) 874; fraud &c. (deception) 545; lying &c. 544; mouth honor &c. (flattery) 933; bad faith, mala fides [L.], Punic faith, Punica fides [L.]; infidelity; faithlessness &c. adj.; Judas kiss, betrayal; perfidy; perfidiousness &c. adj.; treachery, double dealing; unfairness &c. adj.

breach of -promise, – trust, – faith; prodition [obs.], disloyalty, divided allegiance, hyphenated allegiance [cant], treason, high treason; apostacy &c. (tergiversation) 607; nonobservance &c. 773.

shabbiness &c. adj.; villainy; baseness &c. adj.; abjection, debasement, degradation, turpitude, moral turpitude, laxity, trimming, shuffling.

KNAVERY, roguery, rascality, foulplay; jobbing, jobbery, graft [colloq.], venality, nepotism; corruption, job, shuffle, fishy transaction; barratry [law], sharp practice, heads I win tails you lose.

V. BE DISHONEST &c. adj.; play false; break one's -word, – faith, – promise; jilt, betray, forswear; shuffle &c. (lie) 544; play with marked cards, cheat at cards, live by one's wits, sail near the wind.

disgrace –, dishonor –, lower –, demean [colloq.] –, degrade- oneself; derogate, stoop, grovel, sneak, lose caste; sell oneself, squeal [slang], go back on [colloq.], go over to the enemy; seal one's infamy.

give and take, *audire alteram partem*
[L.], give the Devil his due, put the
saddle on the right horse.

redound to one's honor.

Adj. UPRIGHT; honest, – as daylight;
veracious &c. 543; virtuous &c. 944;
noble, honorable, reputable, respectable; fair, right, just, equitable, impartial, evenhanded, square; fair –, open-
and aboveboard; white [*slang*, *U. S.*].

inviolable, inviolate, unviolated, unbroken, unbetrayed; unbought, unbribed.

constant, – as the northern star; faithful, loyal, staunch; true, – blue, – to
one's colors, – to the core, – as the
needle to the pole; "marble-constant"
[*Antony and Cleopatra*]; true-hearted,
trusty, trustworthy; as good as one's
word, to be depended on, incorruptible,
honest as the day.

manly, straightforward &c. (*ingenuous*) 703; frank, candid, open-hearted.

CONSCIENTIOUS, tender-conscienced,
right-minded, high-principled, high-
minded, scrupulous, religious, strict;
nice, punctilious, overscrupulous, correct, punctual.

STAINLESS, unstained, untarnished,
unsullied, untainted, unperjured, uncor-
rupt, uncorrupted; innocent &c. 946;
pure, undefiled, undepraved, undebauched; *integer vitœ scelerisque purus*
[Horace]; *justus et tenax propositi*
[Horace]; supramundane, unworldly.

chivalrous, jealous of honor, *sans peur
et sans reproche* [F.]; high-spirited.

Adv. HONORABLY &c. *adj.; bonâ fide*
[L.]; on the square [*colloq.*], in good
faith, in all honor, by fair means, *foro
conscientiœ* [L.], with clean hands.

Adj. DISHONEST, dishonorable; unconscientious, unscrupulous; fraudulent &c.
545; knavish; disgraceful &c. (*disreputable*) 974; wicked &c. 945.

false-hearted, disingenuous; unfair,
one-sided; double, double-hearted,
double-tongued, double-faced; timeserving, crooked, tortuous, insidious,
Machiavellian, dark, slippery; fishy
[*colloq.*], questionable.

INFAMOUS, arrant, foul, base, vile,
low, ignominious, blackguard, perfidious,
treacherous, perjured; hyphenated
[*cant*].

contemptible, abject, mean, shabby,
little, paltry, dirty, scurvy, scabby,
sneaking, groveling, scrubby, rascally,
barratrous [*law*], pettifogging; corrupt,
venal; debased, mongrel; beneath one.

low-minded, low-thoughted, base-
minded.

DEROGATORY, degrading, undignified,
indign [*obs.*], unbecoming, unbeseeming, unbefitting, *infra dignitatem* [L.],
ungentlemanly, ungentlemanlike; unknightly, unchivalric, unmanly, unhandsome; recreant, inglorious.

FAITHLESS, of bad faith, false, unfaithful, disloyal; untrustworthy; trustless,
trothless [*archaic*], lost to shame, dead
to honor.

Adv. DISHONESTLY &c. *adj.; malâ fide*
[L.]; like a thief in the night, by crooked
paths, by foul means.

Int. *O tempora! O mores!* [Cicero].

⁎⁎ *corruptissimâ republicâ plurimæ leges*
[Tacitus], "And seem a saint, when most I
play the devil" [*Richard III*]; "Crooked
counsels and dark politics" [Pope]; "Honor is
without profit — in most countries" [*Cynic's
Calendar*].

Int. on my honor! honor bright! [*colloq.*]; by my faith!

⁎⁎ "a face untaught to feign" [Pope]; *bene qui latuit bene vixit* [Ovid]; *mens sibi conscia
recti; probitas laudatur et alget* [Juvenal]; *fidelis ad urnam;* "his heart as far from fraud as heaven
from earth" [*Two Gentlemen*]; *loyauté m'oblige; loyauté n'a honte;* "what stronger breastplate than
a heart untainted?" [*Henry VI*]; "among the faithless, faithful only he" [Milton].

941. Knave. — **N.** KNAVE, rogue, villain; Scapin, rascal; Lazarillo de Tormes;
bad man &c. 949; blackguard &c. 949; barrator *or* barrater [*law*], shyster [*U. S.*].

TRAITOR, betrayer, archtraitor, conspirator, Judas, Catiline; reptile, serpent, snake
in the grass, wolf in sheep's clothing, sneak, Jerry Sneak, squealer [*slang*], telltale,
mischief-maker; trimmer, renegade &c. (*tergiversation*) 607; truant, recreant,
slacker; sycophant &. (*servility*) 886.

⁎⁎ "O villain, villain, smiling, damned villain" [*Hamlet*]; "Thou little valiant, great in villainy!" [*King John*]; "he's been true to *one* party, and that is himself" [Lowell]; "Just for a
handful of silver he left us, Just for a riband to stick in his coat" [Browning]; "His honor rooted
in dishonor stood, And faith unfaithful left him falsely true" [Tennyson].

942. Disinterestedness. — N. DIS-
INTERESTEDNESS &c. *adj.;* generosity;
liberality, liberalism; altruism; benevolence &c. 906; elevation, loftiness of purpose, exaltation, magnanimity; chivalry,
chivalrous spirit, heroism, sublimity.

SELF-DENIAL, self-abnegation, self-
sacrifice, self-devotion, self-immolation,
self-control &c. (*resolution*) 604; stoicism,
devotion; martyrdom, suttee.

labor of love.

[COMPARISONS] Good Shepherd, Good
Samaritan, Bishop Bienvenu [Victor
Hugo], Great Heart.

V. BE DISINTERESTED &c. *adj.;* make
a sacrifice, lay one's head on the block;
put oneself in the place of others, do as
one would be done by, do unto others
as we would men should do unto us.

Adj. DISINTERESTED, unselfish, self-
denying, self-sacrificing, self-devotional.

MAGNANIMOUS, noble-minded, high-
minded; princely, handsome, great,
high, elevated, lofty, exalted, spirited,
stoical, great-hearted, large-hearted;
generous, liberal; chivalrous, heroic, sublime.

unbought, unbribed; uncorrupted &c.
(*upright*) 939.

⁎⁎ non vobis solum; "Earth changes, but
thy soul and God stand sure" [Browning];
"A courage terrible to see, And mercy for his
enemy" [Masefield]; "Love took up the harp
of Life, and smote on all the chords with
might; Smote the chord of Self, that, trembling,
pass'd in music out of sight" [Tennyson].

943. Selfishness. — N. SELFISHNESS
&c. *adj.;* self-love, self-indulgence, self-
worship, self-seeking, self-interest; egotism, egoism; *amour propre* [*F.*] &c.
(*vanity*) 880; nepotism; charity that
begins at home.

worldliness &c. *adj.;* world wisdom.
illiberality; meanness &c. *adj.*

SELF-SEEKER, timeserver, time-
pleaser, tuft-hunter, fortune hunter;
jobber, worldling; egotist, egoist, monopolist, nepotist; dog in the manger,
canis in praesepi [*L.*], "foes to nobleness,"
temporizer, hyphenate [*cant*], trimmer;
hog, road-hog, end-seat hog [*colloq.*].

V. BE SELFISH &c. *adj.;* please -, indulge -, pamper -, coddle- oneself; consult one's own -wishes, - pleasure; look
after one's own interest; feather one's
nest; take care of number one, have an
eye to the main chance, know on which
side one's bread is buttered; give an
inch and take an ell.

Adj. SELFISH, self-seeking, self-indulgent, self-interested; wrapt up in self,
centered in self; egotistic *or* egotistical,
egoistic *or* egoistical.

ILLIBERAL, mean, ungenerous, narrow-
minded; mercenary, venal; covetous &c.
819.

WORLDLY, unspiritual, earthly, earthly
-minded, mundane, worldly-minded;
worldly-wise; timeserving.

interested; *alieni appetens sui profusus*
[Sallust].

Adv. UNGENEROUSLY &c. *adj.;* to
gain some private ends, from selfish motives, from interested motives.

⁎⁎ après nous le déluge; "the fine Felicity and flower of wickedness" [Browning]; "I to
myself am dearer than a friend" [*Two Gentlemen*]; "The wretch, concentred all in self" [Scott].

---

944. Virtue. — N. VIRTUE; virtuous-
ness &c. *adj.;* morality; moral rectitude;
integrity &c. (*probity*) 939; nobleness
&c. 873.

merit, worth, desert, excellence, credit;
self-control &c. (*resolution*) 604; self-
denial &c. (*temperance*) 953.

well-doing; good actions, good behavior; discharge -, fulfillment -, per-
formance- of duty; well-spent life; innocence &c. 946.

morals; ethics &c. (*duty*) 926; cardinal
virtues.

[SCIENCE OF VIRTUE] aretaics (*contrasted with* eudemonism); aretology.

V. BE VIRTUOUS &c. *adj.;* practice vir-

945. Vice. — N. VICE; evildoing,
evil courses; wrongdoing; wickedness,
viciousness &c. *adj.;* hardness of heart;
iniquity, peccability, demerit; sin, Adam,
old Adam, offending Adam.

immorality, impropriety, indecorum,
scandal, laxity, looseness of morals;
want of -principle - ballast; knavery,
&c. (*improbity*) 940; atrocity, brutality
&c. (*malevolence*) 907; obliquity, backsliding, infamy.

DEPRAVITY, demoralization, pravity,
pollution; corruption &c. (*debasement*)
659; profligacy; flagrancy, unnatural
desires, unnatural habits, Sadism, Lesbianism, sodomy; lust &c. 961.

tue &c. *n.;* do –, fulfill –, perform –, discharge- one's duty; redeem one's pledge &c. 926; act well, – one's part; fight the good fight; acquit oneself well; command –, master- one's passions; keep in the right path, keep on the straight and narrow way.

set an example, set a good example; be on one's -good, – best- behavior.

Adj. vɪʀᴛᴜᴏᴜs, good; innocent &c. 646; meritorious, deserving, worthy, desertful [*rare*], correct; dutiful, duteous; moral, right, righteous, right-minded; well-intentioned, creditable, laudable, commendable, praiseworthy; above praise, beyond all praise; excellent, admirable; sterling, pure, noble; whole-souled.

exemplary; matchless, peerless; saintly, saintlike; heaven-born, angelic, seraphic, godlike.

Adv. vɪʀᴛᴜᴏᴜsʟʏ &c. *adj.;* e merito [*L.*].

⁂ esse quam videri bonus malebat [Sallust]; *Schönheit vergeht Tugend besteht;* "virtue the greatest of all monarchies" [Swift]; *virtus laudatur et alget* [Juvenal]; *virtus vincit invidiam;* "every noble life leaves the fibre of it in the work of the world" [Ruskin]; "the nobleness That lovely spirits gather from distress" [Masefield]; "He had the russet-apple mind That betters as the weathers worsen" [*ibid.*]; "Virtue is not the absence of vices or the avoidance of moral dangers; virtue is a vivid and separate thing, like pain or a particular smell" [Chesterton].

lowest dregs of vice, sink of iniquity, Alsatian den; *gusto picaresco* [*L.*].

ᴄᴀɴɴɪʙᴀʟɪsᴍ, endocannibalism, endophagy; exocannibalism, exophagy; "long pig" [*humorous*].

ᴡᴇᴀᴋɴᴇss &c. *adj.;* infirmity, weakness of the flesh, frailty, imperfection, error; weak side; foible; failing, failure; crying sin, besetting sin; defect, deficiency; cloven foot.

fault, crime; criminality &c. (*guilt*) 947.

ʀᴇᴘʀᴏʙᴀᴛᴇ; sinner &c. 949.

[ʀᴇsᴏʀᴛs] brothel &c. 961; gambling house &c. 621; joint [*slang*], opium den.

V. ʙᴇ vɪᴄɪᴏᴜs &c. *adj.;* sin, commit sin, do amiss, err, transgress; misdemean –, forget –, misconduct- oneself; misdo [*rare*], misbehave; fall, lapse, slip, trip, offend, trespass; deviate from the -line of duty, – path of virtue &c. 944; take a wrong course, go astray; hug a sin, hug a fault; sow one's wild oats.

ʀᴇɴᴅᴇʀ vɪᴄɪᴏᴜs &c. *adj.;* demoralize, brutalize; corrupt &c. (*degrade*) 659.

Adj.[1] vɪᴄɪᴏᴜs; sinful; sinning &c. *v.;* wicked, iniquitous, immoral, unrighteous, wrong, criminal; unprincipled, lawless, disorderly, dissolute, profligate, scampish; worthless, desertless [*rare*], disgraceful, recreant, disreputable; demoralizing, degrading.

miscreated, misbegotten; demoralized, corrupt, depraved; Sadistic, degenerate.

evil-minded, evil-disposed; ill-conditioned; malevolent &c. 907; heartless, graceless, shameless, virtueless, abandoned, lost to virtue; unconscionable; sunk –, lost –, deep –, steeped- in iniquity.

ʙᴀsᴇ, sinister, scurvy, foul, gross, vile, black, grave, facinorous [*obs.*], felonious, nefarious, shameful, scandalous, infamous, villainous, of a deep dye, heinous; flagrant, flagitious, atrocious, incarnate, accursed.

ᴅɪᴀʙᴏʟɪᴄ *or* diabolical, Mephistophelian, satanic, hellish, infernal, stygian, fiendlike, hellborn, demoniacal, devilish, fiendish.

ɪɴᴄᴏʀʀɪɢɪʙʟᴇ, irreclaimable, obdurate, reprobate, past praying for; culpable, reprehensible &c. (*guilty*) 947.

ᴜɴᴊᴜsᴛɪꜰɪᴀʙʟᴇ, indefensible, inexcusable, inexpiable, unpardonable, irremissible.

ɪᴍᴘʀᴏᴘᴇʀ, unseemly, indecorous, indiscreet, *contra bonos mores* [*L.*], unworthy, blameworthy, reprehensible, uncommendable, discreditable; naughty, incorrect, unduteous, undutiful.

ᴡᴇᴀᴋ, frail, lax, infirm, imperfect; spineless, invertebrate [*both fig.*]; dotty [*slang*]. **Adv.** wrong; sinfully &c. *adj.;* without excuse.

Int. fie upon! it smells to heaven!

⁂ alitur vitium vivitque tegendo [Vergil]; *genus est mortis male vivere* [Ovid]; *mala mens malus animus* [Terence]; *nemo repente fuit turpissimus;* "the trail of the serpent is over them all" [Moore]; "to sanction vice and hunt decorum down" [Byron]; "wild oats make a bad autumn crop" [*Cynic's Calendar*].

---

[1] Most of these adjectives are applicable both to the act and to the agent.

946. Innocence. — N. INNOCENCE; guiltlessness &c. *adj.;* incorruption, impeccability, inerrability, inerrableness.

clean hands, clear conscience, *mens sibi conscia recti* [Vergil].

INNOCENT, new-born babe; lamb, dove.

V. BE INNOCENT &c. *adj.; nil conscire sibi nullâ pallescere culpâ* [Horace].

ACQUIT &c. 970; exculpate &c. *(vindicate)* 937.

Adj. INNOCENT, not guilty; unguilty; guiltless, faultless, sinless, stainless, bloodless, spotless; clear, immaculate; *rectus in curiâ* [L.]; unspotted, unblemished, unerring; undefiled &c. 939; unhardened, Saturnian; Arcadian &c. *(artless)* 703; paradisaic *or* paradisaical, paradisiac *or* paradisiacal.

inculpable, unculpable [*rare*], unblamed, unblamable, blameless, unfallen, inerrable, above suspicion, irreproachable, irreprovable [*rare*], irreprehensible; unexceptionable, unobjectionable, unimpeachable; salvable; venial &c. 937.

virtuous &c. 944; unreproved, unimpeached, unreproached.

HARMLESS, inoffensive, innoxious [*obs.*], innocuous; dovelike, lamblike; pure, harmless as doves; innocent as -a lamb, – the babe unborn; "more sinned against than sinning" [*Lear*].

Adv. INNOCENTLY &c. *adj.;* with clean hands; with a -clear, – safe- conscience.

.*.* *murus aëneus conscientia sana* [Horace]; "He's armed without that's innocent within" [Horace, *trans. by* Pope]; "plain and holy innocence" [*Tempest*].

947. Guilt. — N. GUILT, guiltiness, culpability, criminality, criminousness [*obs.*]; deviation from rectitude &c. *(improbity)* 940; sinfulness &c. *(vice)* 945; peccability.

misconduct, misbehavior, misdoing, misdeed; fault, sin, error, transgression; dereliction, delinquency.

INDISCRETION, lapse, slip, trip, *faux pas* [F.], peccadillo; flaw, blot, omission, failing, failure; blunder, break *or* bad break [*colloq., U. S.*].

OFFENSE, trespass; misdemeanor, tort [*law*], delict, *delictum* [L.]; misfeasance [*law*], misprision, misprision of treason *or* felony [*law*]; malfeasance [*law*], official misconduct, nonfeasance [*law*]; malefaction, malversation, corruption, malpractice; crime, felony, capital crime.

enormity, atrocity, outrage; unpardonable sin, deadly sin, mortal sin; "deed without a name" [*Macbeth*].

corpus delicti [L.], body of the crime, substantial facts, fundamental facts, damning evidence.

Adj. GUILTY, blamable, culpable, peccable, in fault, censurable, reprehensible, blameworthy.

OBJECTIONABLE, exceptionable, uncommendable, illaudable; weighed in the balance and found wanting.

Adv. IN THE VERY ACT, *in flagrante delicto* [L.], red-handed.

.*.* *cui prodest scelus is fecit* [Seneca]; *culpam pœna premit comes* [Horace]; "O would the deed were good!" [*Richard II*]; "responsibility prevents crimes" [Burke]; *se judice nemo nocens absolvitur* [Juvenal]; "so many laws argues so many sins" [*Paradise Lost*].

948. Good Man. [GOOD WOMAN.**] — N.** GOOD MAN, worthy.

model, paragon &c. *(perfection)* 650; good example; hero, demigod, seraph, angel; saint &c. *(piety)* 987; benefactor &c. 912; philanthropist &c. 910; Aristides; noble liver, pattern.

salt of the earth; one in ten thousand; a man among men, white man [*slang*]; brick [*slang*], trump [*slang*], rough diamond.

GOOD WOMAN, virgin, innocent; goddess, queen, Madonna, ministering angel, heaven's noblest gift; "a perfect woman, nobly planned" [Wordsworth].

.*.* *si sic omnes!* "how few Know their own good, or knowing it, pursue" [Dryden]; "How near to good is what is fair!" [Ben Jonson]; "Only the young die good" [*Cynic's Calendar*].

949. Bad Man. [BAD WOMAN.**] — N.** BAD MAN, wrongdoer, worker of iniquity; evildoer &c. 913; sinner, transgressor; the wicked &c. 945; bad example.

rascal, scoundrel, villain, miscreant, budmash [*India*], caitiff, wretch, reptile, viper, serpent, cockatrice, basilisk; tiger, monster; devil &c. *(demon)* 980; devil incarnate; demon in human shape, Nana Sahib; hellhound, rakehell.

roué [F.], rake; Sadist, one who has sold himself to the devil, fallen angel, *âme damnée* [F.], *vaurien* [F.], *mauvais sujet* [F.], loose fish [*colloq.*], rounder [*slang*]; lost sheep, black sheep; castaway, recreant, defaulter; prodigal &c. 818.

BAD WOMAN, jade, Jezebel, hell-cat, quean, wench, slut; adultress &c. 962.

ROUGH, rowdy, ugly customer, ruffian, bully, tough [colloq., U. S.], hoodlum &c. 886; Jonathan Wild; hangman; incendiary, fire bug [U. S.]; thief &c. 792; murderer &c. 361.

CULPRIT, delinquent, criminal, malefactor, misdemeanant; felon; convict, jailbird or gaolbird, ticket-of-leave man [Brit.]; outlaw.

RIFFRAFF, scum of the earth; blackguard, polisson [F.], loafer, sneak, rascalion or rascallion; cullion, mean wretch, varlet [archaic], kern [obs.], âme-de-boue [F.], drôle [F.]; cur, dog, hound, whelp, mongrel; losel [archaic or dial.], loon or lown [obs. or dial. variant], ronion or ronyon or runnion [obs. or rare]; outcast, vagabond, runagate; rogue &c. (knave) 941.

SCAMP, scapegrace, rip [colloq.], ne'er-do-well, good for nothing, reprobate, scalawag or scallawag [colloq.], skeesicks or skeesix [colloq., U. S.], sad dog [colloq.], limb [colloq.], rapscallion [all the words in this paragraph are commonly applied jocularly or lightly].

Int. sirrah!

⁎ Acherontis pabulum; gibier de potence; "We have done with Hope and Honour, we are lost to Love and Truth, We are dropping down the ladder rung by rung" [Kipling]; "Our towns of wasted honour, Our streets of lost delight" [ibid.].

950. Penitence. — N. PENITENCE, contrition, compunction, repentance, remorse; regret &c. 833.

self-reproach, self-reproof, self-accusation, self-condemnation, self-humiliation; stings –, pangs –, qualms –, prickings –, twinge –, twitch –, touch –, voice- of conscience; "compunctious visitings of nature" [Macbeth].

acknowledgment, confession &c. (disclosure) 529; apology &c. 952; recantation &c. 607; penance &c. 952; resipiscence [rare].

awakened conscience, deathbed repentance, locus pœnitentiæ [L.], stool of repentance, cutty stool [Scot.], mourners' bench [local, U. S.].

PENITENT, repentant [rare], Magdalen, prodigal son, returned prodigal, "a sadder and a wiser man" [Coleridge].

951. Impenitence. — N. IMPENITENCE, irrepentance, recusancy, recusance; lack of contrition.

hardness of heart, heart of stone, seared conscience, induration, obduracy; deaf ears.

V. BE IMPENITENT &c. adj.; steel the heart, harden the heart; turn away from the light; die game, die and make no sign.

Adj. IMPENITENT, uncontrite, obdurate, hard, hardened, seared, recusant, unrepentant; relentless, remorseless, graceless, shriftless.

lost, incorrigible, irreclaimable.

unreclaimed, unreformed; unrepented, unatoned.

⁎ "The good die first, And they whose hearts are dry as summer dust Burn to the socket" [Wordsworth].

V. REPENT, be sorry for; be penitent &c. adj.; rue; regret &c. 833; think better of; recant &c. 607; knock under &c. (submit) 725; plead guilty; sing –miserere, – de profundis [L.]; cry peccavi [L.]; say culpâ meâ [L.], own oneself in the wrong; acknowledge, confess &c. (disclose) 529; humble oneself; beg pardon &c. (apologize) 952; turn over a new leaf, put on the new man, turn from sin; repent in sackcloth and ashes &c. (do penance) 952; learn by experience.

RECLAIM, reform, regenerate, redeem, convert, amend, set straight again, make a new man of, restore self -respect.

Adj. PENITENT; repenting &c. v.; repentant, contrite, softened, melted, touched; conscience-smitten, conscience-stricken; self-accusing, self-convicted.

penitential, penitentiary; reclaimed; not hardened: unhardened.

Adv. meâ culpâ [L.]; de profundis [L.].

⁎ peccavi; erubuit; salva res est [Terence]; "Vous l'avez voulu, George Dandin" [Molière]; "and wet his grave with my repentant tears" [Richard III]; "Indeed, indeed, Repentance oft before I swore — but was I sober when I swore?" [Omar Khayyám — Fitzgerald]; "Amid the roses, fierce Repentance rears her snaky crest" [Thomson]; "he who is penitent is almost innocent" [Seneca].

952. Atonement. — N. ATONEMENT, reparation; compromise, composition; compensation &c. 30; quittance, quits [*rare*], expiation, redemption, reclamation, conciliation, propitiation; indemnification, redress.

AMENDS, apology, *amende honorable* [*F*.], satisfaction; peace -, sin -, burnt- offering; scapegoat, sacrifice.

PENANCE, fasting, maceration, sackcloth and ashes, white sheet, shrift, flagellation, lustration; purgation, purgatory.

V. ATONE, atone for; expiate; propitiate; make amends, make good; reclaim, redeem, repair, ransom, absolve, purge, shrive, do penance, stand in a white sheet, repent in sackcloth and ashes.

set one's house in order, wipe off old scores, make matters up; pay the forfeit, pay the penalty.

APOLOGIZE, express regret, beg pardon, *faire l'amende honorable* [*F*.], give satisfaction; get -, fall- down on one's knees, - marrowbones [*slang or jocular*].

Adj. PROPITIATORY, expiatory, sacrific, sacrificial, sacrificatory [*rare*]; piacular, piaculous [*rare*].

* * "when the scourge Inexorable, and the torturing hour Calls us to penance" [*Paradise Lost*].

4. MORAL PRACTICE

953. Temperance. — N. TEMPERANCE, moderation, sobriety, soberness.

forbearance, abnegation; self-denial, self-restraint, self-control &c. (*resolution*) 604.

ABSTINENCE, abstemiousness, asceticism; Encratism, prohibition; frugality; vegetarianism, teetotalism, total abstinence; system of -Pythagoras, - Cornaro; Pythagorism,˙ Stoicism.

ABSTAINER, Pythagorean, gymnosophist; nephalist, teetotaler &c. 958; Encratite, vegetarian, fruitarian, hydropot [*rare*]; ascetic &c. 995.

V. BE TEMPERATE &c. *adj.*; abstain, forbear, refrain, deny oneself, spare; know when one has had enough; take the pledge; prohibit; control the -old Adam, - carnal man, - fleshly lusts; refrain from indulgence, look not upon the wine when it is red.

Adj. TEMPERATE, moderate, sober, frugal, sparing, abstemious, abstinent; within compass; measured &c. (*sufficient*) 639.

Pythagorean; vegetarian, fruitarian; teetotal.

₊ *appetitus rationi obediant* [Cic.]; *l'abstenir pour jouir c'est l épicurisme de la raison* [Rousseau]; *trahit sua quemque voluptas* [Vergil]; "feed on pulse, Drink the clear stream, and nothing wear but frieze" [Milton]; "holy dictate of spare Temperance" [*ibid.*]; "At rich men's tables eaten bread and pulse" [Emerson].

954. Intemperance. — N. INTEMPERANCE, sensuality, rakery [*rare*], animalism, carnality; tragalism; pleasure; effiminacy, silkiness; luxury, luxuriousness; lap of -pleasure, - luxury; free-living.

indulgence; high living, inabstinence, self-indulgence; voluptuousness &c. *adj.*; epicurism, epicureanism, sybaritism.

dissipation; licentiousness &c. *adj.*; debauchery; crapulence.

REVEL, revels, revelry, orgy; drunkenness &c. 959; debauch, carousal, jollification [*colloq.*], high old time [*colloq.*], drinking bout, wassail, saturnalia, excess, too much.

DRUG HABIT; Circean cup; bhang, hashish, opium, hop [*slang*], dope [*slang*], cocaine; drug fiend, dope fiend [*slang*].

V. BE INTEMPERATE &c. *adj.*; indulge, exceed; live -well, - high, - on the fat of the land; eat drink and be merry, look upon the wine when it is red, dine not wisely but too well; give free rein to indulgence &c. *n.*; wallow in voluptuousness &c. *n.*; plunge into dissipation; sensualize, brutify, carnalize.

revel, rake, live hard, run riot, sow one's wild oats; slake one's -appetite, - thirst; swill; pamper.

Adj. INTEMPERATE, inabstinent, excessive; sensual, self-indulgent; voluptuous, licentious, wild, dissolute, rakish, fast, debauched; orgiastic, Corybantic,

Paphian.

BRUTISH, crapulous, swinish, piggish, hoggish, beastlike, theroid [*med.*].

LUXURIOUS, Epicurean, Sybaritical; bred –, nursed- in the lap of luxury; indulged, pampered; full fed, high fed.

INTOXICATED, drunk &c. 959.

*** "being full of supper and distempering draughts" [*Othello*]; "swinish gluttony Ne'er looks to Heaven amidst his gorgeous feast" [Milton]; "lickerish baits, fit to ensnare a brute" [*ibid.*]; "And damn'd be him that first cries 'Hold, enough!'" [*Macbeth*].

954a. Sensualist. — N. SENSUALIST, Sybarite, voluptuary, Sardanapalus, man of pleasure, carpet knight; epicure, epicurean, *gourmet* [*F.*]; gourmand; glutton &c. 957; pig, hog; votary –, swine- of Epicurus; Heliogabalus; free liver, hard liver; libertine &c. 962; hedonist; tragalist.

*** "the sons Of Belial, flown with insolence and wine" [Milton]; "Serenely full, the epicure would say, Fate cannot harm me — I have dined to-day" [Sydney Smith]; "Ah, make the most of what we yet may spend, Before we too into the Dust descend" [Omar Khayyám — Fitzgerald].

955. Asceticism. — N. ASCETICISM, puritanism, sabbatarianism; cynicism, austerity; total abstinence; nephalism; Yoga.

mortification, maceration, sackcloth and ashes, flagellation; penance &c. 952; fasting &c. 956; martyrdom.

ASCETIC, anchoret *or* anchorite, *Heautontimorumenos* [*Gr.*]; hermit &c. (*recluse*) 893; puritan, sabbatarian, cynic; bhikshu, sannyasi *or* sanyasi, yogi [*all Hindu*]; dervish, fakir [*both Moham.*]; martyr.

Adj. ASCETIC, austere, puritanical; cynical; over-religious; acerb, acerbic.

*** "clothed with camel's hair, and with a girdle of skin about his loins; and he did eat locusts and wild honey" [*Bible*].

956. Fasting. — N. FASTING; xerophagy; famishment, starvation.

FAST, *jour maigre* [*F.*]; fast day, banyan day; Lent, quadragesima; Ramadan *or* Ramazan [*Moham.*]; spare –, meager- diet; lenten -diet, – entertainment; *soupe maigre* [*F.*], short commons, Barmecide feast; short rations; punishment of Tantalus.

V. FAST, starve, clem [*obs.*], famish, perish with hunger; dine with Duke Humphrey; make two bites of a cherry; "keep the larder lean."

Adj. FASTING &c. *v.*; lenten, quadragesimal; unfed; starved &c. *v.*; half-starved; hungry &c. 865.

*** "Spare Fast, that oft with gods doth diet" [Milton].

957. Gluttony. — N. GLUTTONY; greed; greediness &c. *adj.*; voracity.

epicurism, gastronomy; good –, high-living; edacity, gulosity [*rare*], crapulence; guttling, guzzle [*rare*], guzzling; pantophagy.

FEAST &c. (*food*) 298; good cheer, blow out [*slang*]; *batterie de cuisine* [*F.*].

GLUTTON, gormandizer, cormorant, hog &c. (*sensualist*) 954a; guttler, pantophagist; belly-god, Apicius, gastronome.

EPICURE, *bon vivant* [*F.*], gourmand [*obs. as* glutton], *gourmet* [*F.*].

V. GORMANDIZE, gorge; overgorge oneself, overeat oneself, glut, satiate, engorge, eat one's fill, cram, stuff, guttle, guzzle, bolt, devour, gobble up; gulp &c. (*swallow food*) 298; raven, eat out of house and home; have the stomach of an ostrich; play a good knife and fork &c. (*appetite*) 865; have a capacious -gorge, – maw.

pamper [*obs. as* glut], indulge.

Adj. GLUTTONOUS, greedy; gormandizing &c. *v.*; edacious, omnivorous, pantophagic, pantophagous, voracious, devouring, all-devouring, crapulent, swinish.

pampered [*obs. as* fed to excess]; overfed, overgorged, overindulged.

*** *jejunus raro stomachus vulgaria temnit* [Horace]; "His belly was upblown with luxury, And eke with fatness swollen were his eyne" [Spenser].

958. Sobriety. — N. SOBRIETY; teetotalism, nephalism.

WATER-DRINKER; hydropot [rare], prohibitionist; teetotaler or teetotaller, abstainer, nephalist, Good Templar, band of hope, W. C. T. U. (Women's Christian Temperance Union).

V. take the pledge.

Adj. SOBER, - as a judge; temperate, moderate.

. "Honest water, which ne'er left man in the mire" [Timon of Athens]; "a cup of cold Adam from the next purling spring" [Tom Brown]: "A Rechabite poor Will must live, And drink of Adam's ale" [Prior].

959. Drunkenness. — N. DRUNKEN-NESS &c. adj.; intemperance; drinking &c. v.; inebriety, inebriation, ebriety [rare], ebriosity [rare], insobriety, intoxication; temulence [rare], bibacity, wine-bibbing; compotation, potation; deep potations, bacchanals, bacchanalia, bacchanalianism, libations; bender [siang, U. S.].

alcoholism, oinomania, dipsomania; delirium tremens, D. T.'s [colloq.]; mania a potu [L.].

DRINK, alcoholic drinks, alcohol, blue ruin [slang], booze or bouse [colloq.], "the luscious liquor" [Milton]; grog, port

wine, punch; punchbowl, cup, rosy wine, flowing bowl; drop, - too much; dram; beer &c. (beverage) 298; aguardiente [Sp.]; apple-brandy, apple-jack; brandy, brandy-smash [U. S.]; chain lightning [slang], champagne, cocktail; gin, gin-sling; highball [U. S.], peg [slang, orig. India]; burra (or bara) peg, chota peg [both India]; rum, schnapps [U. S.], sherry, xeres, sling [U. S.], usquebaugh, whisky or whiskey, rye; stirrup cup, parting cup, doch-an-dorrach or doch-an-dorris [Scot.].

ILLICIT DISTILLING; moonshining, moonshine or moonshine whisky [dial. Eng. & colloq., U. S.], hooch [slang], home-brew; moonshiner [dial. Eng. & colloq., U. S.]; bootlegger [slang, U. S.].

DRUNKARD, sot, toper, tippler, bibber, winebibber; hard -, gin -, dram- drinker; soaker [slang], sponge [slang], tun [jocose], love-pot, tosspot, guzzler, guzzle [rare], boozer or bouser [colloq.], bum [slang, U. S.], tavern haunter, thirsty soul, reveler, carouser, Bacchanal, Bacchanalian: Bacchæ, bacchante, mænad; devotee to Bacchus.

V. GET or BE DRUNK &c. adj.; see double; take a -drop, - glass- too much; drink, tipple, tope [colloq.], booze or bouse [colloq.], guzzle, swill [slang], soak [slang], sot [rare], bum [slang, U. S.], besot, have a jag on [slang], lush [slang], bib [obs. or dial.], swig [dial. or colloq.], carouse; sacrifice at the shrine of Bacchus; take to drinking; drink -hard, - deep, - like a fish; have one's swill [slang], drain the cup, splice the main brace [slang], take a hair of the dog that bit you.

liquor, liquor up [both slang], wet one's -whistle, - clay, - swallow [colloq. or humorous]; wet the red lane [humorous]; raise the elbow, raise the little finger, hit the booze [slang], take a whet; crack a -, pass the- bottle; toss off &c. (drink up) 298; go to the -alehouse, - public house, - saloon.

make one drunk &c. adj.; inebriate, fuddle [colloq.], befuddle, fuzzle [obs.], get into one's head.

SELL ILLICITLY, bootleg [slang, U. S.].

Adj. DRUNK, tipsy, intoxicated, bibacious, inebrious, inebriate, inebriated; in one's cups; in a state of intoxication &c. n.; temulent, temulentive [both rare]; fuddled [colloq.], mellow, cut [slang], boozy or bousy [colloq.], full [vulgar], fou [Scot.], lit up]slang], glorious [humorous], fresh [slang], merry, elevated; flush, flushed, flustered, disguised [archaic], groggy [colloq.], beery; top-heavy; pot-valiant, potulent [obs.], squiffy [slang]; overcome, overtaken [obs.], whittled [obs.]; screwed, tight, primed, corned, raddled, sewed up, lushy [all slang], muzzy [colloq.], nappy [rare], muddled, obfuscated, maudlin; crapulous, blind drunk, dead drunk.[1]

inter pocula [L.], in liquor, the worse for liquor; having had a drop too much, half-seas over [slang], three sheets in the wind [sailors' slang], under the table.

---

[1] More than three hundred slang expressions coming under this category are given in Farmer and Henley's Dictionary of Slang and Colloquial English. C. O. S. M.

drunk as -a piper, – a fiddler, – a lord, – Chloe, – an owl, – David's sow, – a wheelbarrow [*all colloq.*].

DRUNKEN, bibacious, sottish; given –, addicted- to -drink, – the bottle; toping &c. *v.;* primed, – on the hip; heeled [*slang*].

₊ *nunc est bibendum;* "Bacchus ever fair and young" [Dryden]; "drink down all unkindness" [*Merry Wives*]; "O God, that men should put an enemy in their mouths to steal away their brains!" [*Othello*]; "Fetch me a quart of sack; put a toast in 't" *Merry Wives*]; "From Sabine jar bring forth the sparkling wine" [Horace]; "Drain we the cup. Friend, art afraid?" [Thackeray]; "What man dare, I dare!" [*Macbeth*]; "so gloz'd the tempter!" [Milton]; "Stands Scotland where it did?" [*Macbeth*]; "Once more unto the breach, dear friends, once more!" [*Henry V*]; "His devious course uncertain, seeking home" [Cowper].

960. Purity. — N. PURITY; decency, decorum, delicacy; continence, chastity, honesty, virtue, modesty, shame; pudicity, pucelage [*rare*], virginity.

virgin, vestal, prude; Lucretia, Diana, Athena Parthenos; Joseph, Hippolytus.

Adj. PURE, undefiled, modest, delicate, decent, decorous; *virginibus puerisque* [*L.*]; chaste, continent, virtuous, honest, Platonic.

₊ "as chaste as unsunn'd snow" [*Cymbeline*]; "a soul as white as heaven" [Beaumont and Fletcher]; "the sun-clad power of Chastity" [Milton]; "to the pure all things are pure" [Shelley].

961. Impurity. — N. IMPURITY; uncleanness &c. (*filth*) 653; immodesty; grossness &c. *adj.;* indelicacy, indecency, impudicity, obscenity, ribaldry, smut, bawdry, *double entente*, *équivoque* [*F.*]; pornography.

incontinence, debauchery, libertinism, libertinage, fornication, wenching, venery, dissipation.

concupiscence, lust, carnality, flesh, salacity; pruriency, lechery, lasciviousness, lewdness, lasciviency [*obs.*], lubricity; Sadism, Sapphism, Lesbianism, nymphomania, aphrodisia, satyriasis.

SEDUCTION; defloration, defilement, abuse, violation, stupration, rape; incest.

SOCIAL EVIL, harlotry, whoredom, concubinage, cuckoldom, adultery, advoutry [*obs.*], crim. con.; free-love.

INTRIGUE, amour, amourette, *liaison* [*F.*], *faux pas* [*F.*], entanglement; gallantry. [RESORTS] brothel, bagnio, stew, bawdyhouse, lupanar, house of ill fame, bordel [*obs.*]; Yoshiwara [*Jap.*], red-light district.

HAREM, seraglio, zenana [*India*].

V. BE IMPURE &c. *adj.;* debauch, defile, seduce; prostitute; abuse, violate, rape, stuprate [*rare*], deflower; commit adultery &c. *n.;* intrigue.

Adj. IMPURE; unclean &c. (*dirty*) 653; not to be mentioned to ears polite; immodest, shameless, indecorous, indelicate, indecent, Fescennine; loose, *risqué* [*F.*], coarse, gross, broad, free, equivocal, smutty, fulsome, ribald, obscene, bawdy, pornographic.

concupiscent, prurient, lickerish, rampant, lustful; carnal, carnal-minded; lewd, lascivious, lecherous, libidinous, erotic, ruttish, must *or* musty [*said of elephants*]; salacious, Paphian, voluptuous; goatish, beastly, bestial, incestuous.

UNCHASTE, light, wanton, licentious, adulterous, debauched, dissolute; of loose character, of easy virtue; frail, gay, riggish [*obs.*], incontinent, meretricious, rakish, gallant, dissipated; no better than she should be; on the town, on the streets, on the *pavé* [*F.*], on the loose [*colloq.*].

962. Libertine. — N. LIBERTINE; voluptuary &c. 954a; rake, debauchee, loose fish [*colloq.*], rip [*colloq.*], rakehell, fast man; intrigant, gallant, seducer, fornicator, lecher, satyr, goat, whoremonger, *paillard* [*F.*], advocater [*obs.*], adulterer, gay deceiver, Lothario, Don Juan, Bluebeard; chartered libertine.

ADULTRESS, advoutress [*obs.*], courtesan, prostitute, strumpet, harlot, whore, punk [*obsoles.*], *fille de joie* [*F.*], woman, woman of the town, streetwalker, Cyprian, miss [*obs.*], piece [*slang*], demirep, wench, trollop, trull, baggage, hussy, drab, bitch [*low*], jade, skit [*obs.*], rig [*obs.*], quean, mopsy [*dial. Eng.*], slut, minx, harridan; unfortunate, – female, – woman; woman -of easy virtue &c. (*unchaste*)

961; wanton, fornicatress; *lorette* [F.], *cocotte* [F.], *petite dame* [F.], grisette; demi-mondaine; chippy [*slang*, *U. S.*]; Sapphist; white slave.

Jezebel, Messalina, Delilah, Thais, Phryne, Aspasia, Lais.

demimonde, erring sisters, fallen women, frail sisterhood.

MISTRESS, concubine, kept woman, doxy, *chère amie* [F.]; *bona roba* [It.]; spiritual wife.

PROCURER, pimp, pander *or* pandar, bawd, *conciliatrix* [L.], procuress, mackerel [*archaic*], wittol [*obs.*].

.*. "she may be a good sort but she is a bad lot" [Shaw]; "Ah, take the Cash and let the Credit go, Nor heed the rumble of a distant drum" [Omar Khayyám — Fitzgerald].

5. INSTITUTIONS

963. Legality. — N. LEGALITY, legitimacy, legitimateness; legitimatization, legitimization.

LAW, code, *corpus juris* [L.], constitution, pandect, charter, act, enactment, statute, rule; canon &c. (*precept*) 697; ordinance, institution, regulation; by-law *or* bye-law; rescript, decree &c. (*order*) 741; ordonnance; standing order; plebiscite &c. (*choice*) 609; legislature.

legal process; form, formula, formality, rite, arm of the law; *habeas corpus* [L.]; *fieri facias* [L.].

equity, common law; *lex scripta* [L.]; *lex non scripta* [L.], unwritten law; law of nations, *droit des gens* [F.], international law, *jus gentium* [L.]; *jus civile* [L.]; civil –, canon –, crown –, criminal –, statute –, ecclesiastical- law; *lex mercatoria* [L.].

constitutionalism, constitutionality; justice &c. 922.

[SCIENCE OF LAW] jurisprudence, nomology; legislation, codification, nomography.

V. LEGALIZE, legitimate, legitimize, legitimatize; enact, ordain; decree &c. (*order*) 741; pass a law, legislate; codify, formulate, formalize, regularize, authorize.

Adj. LEGAL, legitimate; according to law; vested, constitutional, chartered, legalized; lawful &c. (*permitted*) 760; statutable, statutory; legislatorial, legislative; judicial, juridical; nomistic, nomothetical.

Adv. LEGALLY &c. *adj.;* in the eye of the law; *de jure* [L.].

.*. *ignorantia legis neminem excusat;* "where law ends tyranny begins" [Earl of Chatham]; "the majesty and power of law and justice" "the gladsome light of jurisprudence" [Coke]; "We must not make a scarecrow of the law" [M. for M.]; "the lawless science of our law" [Tennyson].

964. [ABSENCE OR VIOLATION OF LAW.] **Illegality. — N.** LAWLESSNESS; illicitness; breach –, violation- of law; disobedience &c. 742; unconformity &c. 83; arbitrariness &c. *adj.;* antinomy, violence, brute force, despotism, tyranny, outlawry.

mob –, lynch –, club –, Lydford –, martial –, drumhead- law; *coup d'état* [F.]; *le droit du plus fort* [F.]; *argumentum baculinum* [L.].

ILLEGALITY, informality, unlawfulness, illegitimacy, bar sinister.

trover and conversion; smuggling, bootlegging [*slang*, *U. S.*], illicit distilling &c. 959; poaching; simony.

V. VIOLATE THE LAW, offend against the law, set the law at defiance, ride roughshod over, drive a coach and six through a statute; make the law a dead letter, take the law into one's own hands.

smuggle, run, poach, bootleg [*slang*, *U. S.*].

Adj. ILLEGAL; prohibited &c. 761; not allowed, unlawful, illegitimate, illicit, contraband, actionable.

unchartered, unconstitutional; unwarranted, unwarrantable, unauthorized; informal, unofficial, injudicial [*rare*], extra-judicial.

LAWLESS, arbitrary, despotic, despotical; summary, irresponsible; unanswerable, unaccountable.

null and void; a dead letter.

Adv. ILLEGALLY &c. *adj.;* with a high hand, in violation of law.

.*. "Bleed, bleed, poor country! Great Tyranny! lay thou thy basis sure, For goodness dares not check thee!" [*Macbeth*].

[*II Henry IV*]; "The Law, our kingdom's golden chaine" [Dekker]; "there is a higher law than the Constitution" [Seward]; "the

965. Jurisdiction. [EXECUTIVE.] — **N.** JURISDICTION, judicature, administration of justice; soc, soke [*both A. S. & early Eng. law*]; executive, commission of the peace; magistracy &c. (*authority*) 737; judge &c. 967; tribunal &c. 966.

city government, municipal government, commission government, Oregon plan [*U. S.*]; municipality, corporation, bailiwick, shrievalty; police, police force; constabulary, Bumbledom.

EXECUTIVE OFFICER, officer, commissioner, lord lieutenant [*Brit.*], collector [*India*]; city manager, mayor, alderman, councilor *or* councillor, selectman; bailiff, tipstaff, bumbailiff [*Eng.*], catchpole *or* catchpoll, beadle; sheriff, shrieve [*obs.*], bailie [*Scot.*], constable; policeman, police constable, police sergeant, patrolman &c. 664; *sbirro* [*It.*], alguazil, *gendarme* [*F.*], kavass [*Turk.*], lictor, mace bearer, *huissier* [*F.*], tithingman; excise man, gauger *or* gager, customhouse officer, *douanier* [*F.*]; press gang *or* pressgang.

coroner, ædile *or* edile; reeve, portreeve [*early Eng. hist.*], paritor [*obs.*], *posse comitatus* [*L.*].

BUREAU, cutcherry [*India*], department, portfolio, secretariat.

V. JUDGE, sit in judgment; have jurisdiction over.

Adj. EXECUTIVE, administrative, judicative, municipal; inquisitorial, causidical; judicatory, judiciary, judicial, juridical.

Adv. *coram judice* [*L.*].

** "a dog's obeyed in office" [*King Lear*]; "Ill can he rule the great that cannot rule th' small" [Spenser].

966. Tribunal. — **N.** TRIBUNAL, court, curia, board, bench, judicature, judicatory; court of -justice, – law, – arbitration; inquisition; guild; durbar [*India*], divan [*Oriental*], Areopagus.

justice –, judgment –, mercy- seat; woolsack; bar, bar of justice; dock; forum, hustings, bureau, drumhead; jury-box; witness box, witness stand.

senate-house, town hall, theater *or* theatre; House of Commons, House of Lords; statehouse [*U. S.*], townhouse, courthouse.

[BRITISH COURTS], sessions; petty –, quarter –, special –, general- sessions [*Eng. law*]; assizes; eyre, justices in eyre, wardmote, burghmote, barmote, courtleet, courtbaron, court of piepoudre [*all old Eng. law*]; superior courts of Westminster; court of -record, – oyer and terminer, – assize, – appeal, – error; High court of -Judicature, – Appeal; Judicial Committee of the Privy Council; Star Chamber; Court of -Chancery, – King's *or* Queen's Bench, – Exchequer, – Common Pleas, – Probate, – Admiralty; Lords Justices' –, Rolls –, Vice Chancellor's –, Stannary –, Divorce –, Palatine –, county –, police- court; Court of Criminal Appeal; Court of Small Causes [*India*]; court of common council; board of green cloth.

[UNITED STATES COURTS] United States -Supreme Court, – District Court, – Circuit Court of Appeal; Federal Court of Claims, Court of Private Land Claims; Supreme Court, court of sessions, criminal court, police court, juvenile court.

COURT-MARTIAL (*pl.* courts-martial), drumhead court-martial.

ECCLESIASTICAL COURT, Rota *or* Rota Romana [*R. C. Ch.*]; Court of Arches [*Eng.*]. Papal Court, Curia.

Adj. JUDICIAL &c. 965; appellate; curial.

** *die Weltgeschichte ist das Weltgericht;* "Whoever fights, whoever fails, Justice conquers evermore" [Emerson]; "Justice discards party, friendship, kindred, and is therefore always represented as blind" [Addison]; "We have strict statutes and most biting laws" [*Measure for Measure*].

967. Judge. — **N.** JUDGE, justice; justiciar [*Eng. & Scot. hist.*]; justiciary [*Eng. & Scot. hist.*]; chancellor; justice –, judge- of assize; recorder, common serjeant; puisne –, assistant –, county court- judge; conservator –, justice- of the peace; J. P.; "the Great Unpaid" [*Eng.*]; court &c. (*tribunal*) 966; deemster [*Isle of Man & archaic*], moderator, bencher [*archaic*], jurat, magistrate, police magistrate, beak [*slang*]; his worship, his honor, his lordship; the court.

Lord Chancellor, Lord Justice; Master of the Rolls, Vice Chancellor; Lord Chief ¬Justice, – Baron; Chief Justice; Mr. Justice; Baron, – of the Exchequer.

assessor; arbiter, arbitrator, doomsman *or* domesman [*obs.*], umpire, referee, referendary [*rare*]; revising barrister [*Eng.*], receiver, official receiver; censor &c. (*critic*) 480; barmaster [*Eng.*].

archon, tribune, prætor, ephor, syndic, podesta [*It.*]; mollah, ulema, hakim, mufti, cadi *or* kadi [*all Moham.*]; alcalde [*Sp.*]; Rhadamanthus, Minos, Solomon.

jury, grand jury, petty jury, inquest, panel, country; twelve men in a box.

juror, juryman, talesman; grand-juror, grand-juryman, recognitor; petty-juror, petty-juryman.

litigant &c. (*accusation*) 938.

V. adjudge &c. (*determine*) 480; try a case, try a prisoner.

Adj. judicial &c. 965.

*** "a Daniel come to judgment" [*Merchant of Venice*]; "The law: it has honored us; may we honor it" [Daniel Webster].

968. Lawyer. — N. lawyer, jurist, legist, pundit [*India*], civilian, publicist, jurisconsult, legal adviser, advocate; barrister, barrister-at-law; counsel, counselor *or* counsellor, King's *or* Queen's counsel; K. C.; Q. C.; silk *or* silk gown; junior counsel, stuff *or* stuff gown; leader, serjeant-at-law, bencher, pleader, special pleader; tubman [*Eng. law*], judge &c. 967.

solicitor, attorney, vakil *or* vakeel [*India*], proctor; equity draftsman, conveyancer, notary, – public; scrivener, cursitor [*Eng. law*]; writer, – to the signet; S.S.C.; limb of the law; pettifogger, shyster [*U. S.*].

bar, legal profession, gentlemen of the long robe; junior –, outer –, inner- bar; Inns of Court [*Eng.*].

V. practice law; practice at (*or* within) the bar, plead; call to (*or* within) the bar, be called to (*or* within) the bar; admitted to the bar, take silk.

disbar, disbench [*Eng. law*], degrade.

Adj. learned in the law; at the bar; forensic.

*** *banco regis;* "Litigious terms, fat contentions, and flowing fees" [Milton]; "Oh 'tis a blessed thing to have rich clients" [Beaumont and Fletcher]; "with promise of high pay and great rewards" [*III Henry VI*]; "The first thing we do, let's kill all the lawyers" [*II Henry VI*].

969. Lawsuit. — N. lawsuit, suit, action, cause; litigation; suit in law; dispute &c. 713.

writ, summons, subpœna, citation, latitat [*Eng. law*]; *nisi prius, venire, venire facias, habeas corpus* [*all L.*].

arraignment, prosecution, impeachment; accusation &c. 938; presentment, true bill, indictment.

arrest, apprehension, committal, commitment; imprisonment &c. (*restraint*) 751.

pleadings; declaration, bill, claim; *procès-verbal* [*F.*], bill of right, information, *corpus delicti* [*L.*]; affidavit, state of facts, libel; answer, replication, plea, demurrer, rebutter, rejoinder: surrebutter, surrejoinder.

suitor, libelant *or* libellant, party to a suit; litigant &c. 938.

hearing, trial; judgment, sentence, finding, verdict &c. 480; appeal, – motion; writ of error; certiorari.

case, decision, precedent; decided case, reports.

V. go to law, appeal to the law; bring to -justice, – trial, – the bar; put on trial, pull up; accuse &c. 938; prefer *or* file a claim &c. *n.;* take the law of [*colloq.*], inform against.

cite, summon, summons, serve with a writ, arraign, sue, prosecute, bring an action against, indict, impeach, attach, distrain, commit; apprehend, arrest; give in charge &c. (*restrain*) 751.

empanel a jury, challenge the jurors; implead, join issue; close the pleadings; set down for hearing.

TRY, hear a cause; sit in judgment; adjudicate &c. 480.

Adj. LITIGIOUS &c. (*quarrelsome*) 713; *qui tam, coram judice, sub judice* [*all L.*].

Adv. *pendente lite* [*L.*].

. *adhuc sub judice lis est; accedas ad curiam; transeat in exemplum;* "these nice sharp quillets of the law "[*I Henry VI*]; "we are for law; he dies" [*Timon of Athens*]; "No man e'er felt the halter draw, With good opinion of the law" [Trumbull]; "Strive mightily, but eat and drink as friends" [*Taming of the Shrew*].

970. Acquittal. — N. ACQUITTAL, acquittment [*obs.*]; exculpation, acquittance, clearance, exoneration; discharge &c. (*release*) 750; *quietus* [*L.*], absolution, compurgation, reprieve, respite; pardon &c. (*forgiveness*) 918.

[EXEMPTION FROM PUNISHMENT] impunity, immunity.

V. ACQUIT, exculpate, exonerate, clear; absolve, whitewash, assoil [*archaic*], assoilzie [*Scot.*]; discharge, release; liberate &c. 750.

reprieve, respite; pardon &c. (*forgive*) 918; let off, let off scot-free.

Adj. ACQUITTED &c. *v.;* uncondemned, unpunished, unchastised; recommended to mercy.

. *nemo bis punitur pro eodem delicto;* "And earthly power doth then show likest God's When mercy seasons justice" [*M. of V.*].

971. Condemnation. — N. CONDEMNATION, conviction, judgment, penalty, sentence; proscription, damnation; death warrant.

attainder, attainture, attaintment.

V. CONDEMN, convict, cast [*obs. or dial.*], bring home to, find guilty, damn, doom, sign the death warrant, sentence, pass sentence on, attaint, confiscate, proscribe, sequestrate; nonsuit.

disapprove &c. 932; accuse &c. 938.

stand condemned, be convicted.

Adj. CONDEMNATORY, damnatory; condemned &c. *v.;* nonsuited &c. (*failure*) 732; self-convicted.

. *mutato nomine de te fabula narratur;* "unrespited, unpitied, unreprieved" [*P. L.*]; "Beyond the infinite and boundless reach Of mercy" [*King John*]; "every crime destroys more Edens than our own" [Hawthorne].

972. Punishment. — N. PUNISHMENT, punition, chastisement, chastening, correction, castigation; discipline, infliction, trial; judgment; penalty &c. 974; retribution; thunderbolt, Nemesis, Eumenides, the Furies; requital &c. (*reward*) 973; retributive justice; penology.

[FORMS OF PUNISHMENT] lash, scaffold &c. (*instrument of punishment*) 975; imprisonment &c. (*restraint*) 751; transportation, banishment, expulsion, exile, involuntary exile, ostracism; penal servitude, hard labor; galleys &c. 975; beating &c. *v.;* flagellation, fustigation, cudgeling, gantlet, strappado, estrapade, bastinado, *argumentum baculinum* [*L.*], stick law, rap on the knuckles, box on the ear; blow &c. (*impulse*) 276; stripe, cuff, kick, buffet, pummel; slap, – in the face; wipe [*dial. or slang*], douse or dowse [*rare*]; torture, rack; rail-riding, scarpines; picket [*obs.*], picketing; dragonnade.

CAPITAL PUNISHMENT, execution; hanging, shooting &c. *v.;* electrocution, decapitation, decollation, dismemberment; strangling, strangulation, garrote or garrotte; crucifixion, impalement; martyrdom, *auto-da-fé* (*pl. autos-da-fé*) [*Pg.*], *auto-de-fe* [*Sp.*], *noyade* [*F.*], harakiri [*Jap.*], seppuku [*Jap.*], happy dispatch [*jocular*], lethal chamber, hemlock.

V. PUNISH, chastise, chasten, castigate, correct, inflict punishment, administer correction, deal retributive justice; tar and feather; masthead, keelhaul.

visit upon, pay; pay out [*colloq.*], serve out [*colloq.*], settle, settle with, do for [*colloq.*], get even with, get one's own back [*slang*], make short work of, give a lesson to, serve one right, make an example of; have a rod in pickle for; give it to, give it one [*both colloq.*].

STRIKE &c. 276; deal a blow to, administer the lash, smite; slap, – the face; smack, cuff, box the ears, spank, thwack, thump, beat, lay on, swinge, buffet; thresh, thrash, pummel, drub, leather [*colloq. or slang*], trounce, baste, belabor; lace, – one's jacket; dress, dress down, give a dressing, trim [*colloq.*], warm [*colloq. & dial.*], warm one's jacket [*colloq.*], wipe [*dial. or slang*], tund [*obs.*], cob [*dial., Eng.*], bang, strap, comb [*humorous*], lick, larrup [*both colloq.*], wallop [*Scot., dial. Eng. &*

colloq., U. S]., cowhide, lambaste [*slang*], lash, whop [*obs.*], flog, scourge, whip, birch, cane, give the stick, switch, flagellate, horsewhip, bastinado, towel [*slang or dial. Eng.*], rub down with an oaken towel [*slang*], riboast [*slang*], dust one's jacket [*colloq. or slang*], fustigate, pitch into [*colloq.*], lay about one, beat black and blue; beat to a -mummy, – jelly; give a black eye; hit on the head, crack on the bean [*slang*], sandbag, blackjack, put away [*slang*]; pelt, stone, lapidate.

EXECUTE; bring to the -block, – gallows; behead, decapitate, decollate, guillotine; hang, turn off [*slang*], gibbet, bowstring, dismember, hang draw and quarter; shoot; burn; break on the wheel, crucify; impale *or* empale, flay; lynch; electrocute.

TORTURE, agonize, rack, put on (*or* to) the rack, martyr, martyrize, picket [*obs. or hist.*]; prolong the agony, kill by inches.

BANISH, exile, transport, deport, expel, ostracize; rusticate; drum out; dismiss, disbar, disbench [*Eng. law*]; strike off the roll, unfrock; post.

SUFFER, suffer for, suffer punishment; be flogged, be hanged &c.; come to the gallows, dance upon nothing [*ironical*], die in one's shoes; be rightly served.

Adj. PUNISHING &c. *v.;* penal, punitory, punitive, inflictive, castigatory; punished &c. *v.*

Int. *à la lanterne!* [*F.*].

⁎⁎ *culpam pœna premit comes* [Horace]; "eating the bitter bread of banishment" [*Richard II*]; *gravis ira regum est semper* [Seneca]; *sera tamen tacitis pœna venit pedibus* [Tibullus]; *suo sibi gladio hunc jugulo* [Terence]; "Thou shalt be whipp'd with wire, and stewed in brine, Smarting in ling'ring pickle" [*Antony and Cleopatra*]; "back to thy punishment, False fugitive, and to thy speed add wings" [*Paradise Lost*].

973. Reward. — N. REWARD, recompense, remuneration, prize, meed, guerdon, reguerdon [*obs.*]; price; indemnity, indemnification; quittance, compensation, reparation, redress, retribution, reckoning, acknowledgment, requital, amends, sop; atonement; consideration, return, *quid pro quo* [*L.*]; salvage.

perquisite, perks [*slang*]; vail &c. (*donation*) 784; *douceur* [*F.*], tip; bribe, bait &c. 784; hush-money, smart-money, blackmail; carcelage [*obs.*]; solatium.

ALLOWANCE, salary, stipend, wages; pay, payment; emolument; tribute; batta [*India*], shot, scot; premium, fee, honorarium; hire; dasturi *or* dustoori [*India*]; mileage.

crown &c. (*decoration of honor*) 877.

V. REWARD, recompense, repay, requite; remunerate, munerate [*obs.*]; compensate; fee, tip, bribe; pay one's footing &c. (*pay*) 807; make amends, indemnify, atone; satisfy, acknowledge.

get for one's pains, reap the fruits of.

Adj. remunerative, remuneratory [*rare*], munerary [*obs.*], compensatory, retributive, reparatory [*rare*], reparative.

⁎⁎ *fideli certa merces; honor virtutis præmium* [Cicero]; *tibi seris tibi metis;* "Besides commends and courteous breath, Gifts of rich value" [*M. of V.*]; "'Tis deeds must win the prize" [*Taming of the Shrew*]; "A Muezzin from the Tower of Darkness cries, 'Fools, your Reward is neither Here nor There'" [Omar Khayyám — Fitzgerald]; "God shall repay: I am safer so" [Browning].

974. Penalty. — N. PENALTY; retribution &c. (*punishment*) 972; pain, pains and penalties; wergild *or* weregild [*hist.*], bloodwite *or* bloodwit [*early Eng. law*]; *peine forte et dure* [*F.*]; penance &c. (*atonement*) 952; the devil to pay.

fine, mulct, amercement, sconce [*Oxford Univ., Eng.*], forfeit, forfeiture, escheat, damages, deodand, sequestration, confiscation, præmunire *or* premunire; doomage [*U. S.*].

V. PENALIZE, fine, mulct, amerce, sconce, confiscate, sequestrate, sequester, escheat, estreat, forfeit.

⁎⁎ "some of us will smart for it" [*Much Ado*]; "I crave the law, The penalty and forfeit of my bond" [*Merchant of Venice*].

975. [INSTRUMENT OF PUNISHMENT.] Scourge. — N. SCOURGE, whip, lash, strap, thong, cowhide, knout, cat, cat-o'-nine-tails; rope's end; *azote* [*Sp. Am.*], black-snake, bullwhack [*U. S.*], kurbash [*Turk.*], chabuk [*Hind.*], quirt, rawhide, sjambok [*S. Africa*].

ROD, cane, stick, rattan *or* ratan, birch, birch rod; rod in pickle; switch, ferule, cudgel, truncheon.

[VARIOUS INSTRUMENTS] pillory, stocks, whipping post; cucking stool, ducking stool, brank, trebuchet *or* trebucket; triangle, wooden horse, maiden; thumbscrew, boot, rack, wheel, iron heel; treadmill, crank, galleys; bed of Procrustes.

scaffold; block, ax, guillotine; stake; cross, gallows, gibbet, tree, drop; noose, rope, halter, bowstring; death chair, electric chair; *mecate* [*Sp.*].

PRISON, house of correction &c. 752; jailer *or* gaoler.

EXECUTIONER; electrocutioner; lyncher, garroter *or* garrotter, torturer; headsman, hangman, topsman *or* topping cove [*slang*], Jack Ketch.

MALEFACTOR, criminal, culprit, felon, evildoer, misdemeanant; victim, gallowsbird [*slang*], Jack Ketch's pippin [*old slang*].

** "Be ready, gods, with all your thunderbolts; Dash him to pieces" [*Julius Cæsar*]; "Nature knows best, and she says, *roar!*" [Edgeworth]; "whoso sheddeth man's blood, by man shall his blood be shed" [*Bible*].

Section V. RELIGIOUS AFFECTIONS

1. Superhuman Beings and Regions

976. Deity. — **N.** DEITY, Divinity, Godhead, Godship, Omnipotence, Omniscience, Providence.

[QUALITY OF BEING DIVINE] divineness, divinity.

GOD, Lord, Jehovah, The King of Kings, The Lord of Lords, The Almighty, The Supreme Being, The Eternal Being, The Absolute Being, The First Cause; I AM, The All-Father, *Ens Entium* [*L.*], Author of all things, Creator of all things, Author of our being; Cosmoplast, Demiurge; The Infinite, The Eternal; The All-powerful, The Omnipotent, The All-wise, The All-merciful, The All-holy, The All-knowing, The Omniscient.

Deus [*L.*], *Theos* [*Gr.* Θεός], *Dieu* [*F.*], *Gott* [*Ger.*], *Dio* [*It.*], *Dios* [*Sp.*], *Deos* [*Pg.*], *Gud* [*Nor., Sw., & Dan.*], *God* [*Du.*], *Bog'* [*Russ.*], *Brahmă* [*Skr.*], *Deva* [*Skr.*], *Khuda* [*Hind.*], *Allah Ar.*], *Kami* [*Jap.*], *Ten-shu* [*Jap., Christian*].

[ATTRIBUTES AND PERFECTIONS] infinite -power, – wisdom, – goodness, – justice, – truth, – love, – mercy; omnipotence, omniscience, omnipresence; unity, immutability, holiness, glory, light, majesty, sovereignty; infinity, eternity &c. (*perpetuity*) 112.

THE TRINITY, The Holy Trinity, The Trinity in Unity, The Triune God, Triunity, Threefold Unity, "Three in One and One in Three."

I. GOD THE FATHER, The Maker, The Creator, The Preserver.

[FUNCTIONS] creation, preservation, divine government, Theocracy, Thearchy; Providence; ways –, dealings –, dispensations –, visitations- of Providence.

II. GOD THE SON, Jesus Christ; The Messiah, The Anointed, The Saviour, The Redeemer, The Mediator, The Intercessor, The Advocate, The Judge; The Son of God, The Son of Man, The Son of David; The Only-Begotten, The Lamb of God, The Word, Logos; The Man of Sorrows, Jesus of Nazareth, King of the Jews, The Son of Mary, The Risen, Immanuel, Emmanuel, The King of Kings and Lord of Lords, The King of Glory, The Prince of Peace, The Good Shepherd, The Way, The Door, The Truth, The Life, The Bread of Life, The Light of the World, The Vine, The True Vine; The Lord our Righteousness, The Sun of Righteousness.

The Incarnation, The Hypostatic Union, The Word made Flesh.

[FUNCTIONS] salvation, redemption, atonement, propitiation, mediation, intercession, judgment; soteriology.

III. GOD THE HOLY GHOST, The Holy Spirit, Paraclete, The Comforter, The Consoler, The Intercessor, The Spirit of God, The Spirit of Truth, The Dove.

[FUNCTIONS] inspiration, unction, regeneration, sanctification, consolation, grace.

[THE DEITY IN OTHER RELIGIONS] BRAHMANISM *or* HINDUISM: Brahm *or* Brahmă (*neuter*), the Supreme Soul *or* Essence of the Universe; Trimurti *or* Hindu trinity *or* Hindu triad: (1) Prahmā (*masc.*), the Creator; (2) Vishnu, the Preserver; (3) Siva *or* Shiva, the Destroyer and Regenerator. For other Hindu deities see 979.

BUDDHISM: the Protestantism of the East; Buddha, the Blessed One, the Teacher, the Lord Buddha.

ZOROASTRIANISM: Zerâna-Akerana, the Infinite Being; Ahuramazda *or* Ormazd, the Creator, the Lord of Wisdom, the Wise Lord, the Wise One, the King of Light, the Guardian of Mankind (*opposed by* Ahriman, the King of Darkness).

MOHAMMEDANISM *or* ISLAM: Allah.

V. CREATE, fashion, make, form, mold *or* mould, manifest.

PRESERVE, uphold, keep, perpetuate, immortalize.

ATONE, redeem, save, propitiate, expiate; intercede, mediate.

PREDESTINATE, predestine, foreordain, preordain; elect, call, ordain.

BLESS, sanctify, hallow, justify, absolve, glorify.

Adj. ALMIGHTY, all-powerful, omnipotent; omnipresent, all-wise, all-seeing, all-knowing, omniscient, supreme.

DIVINE, heavenly, celestial; holy, hallowed, sacred, sacrosanct.

SUPERNATURAL, superhuman, hyperphysical, superphysical, spiritual, ghostly, supramundane, supersensuous, supersensitive, supersensual, supernormal, unearthly.
theistic; theocratic; deistic; anointed; soterial.

Adv. UNDER GOD, by God's will, by God's help, *Deo volente* [*L.*], D. V., God willing; in Jesus' name, in His name, in His fear, to His glory; *jure divino* [*L.*], by divine right.

.•. *Domine dirige nos; en Dieu est ma fiance; et sceleratis sol oritur* [Seneca]; "He mounts the storm and walks upon the wind" [Pope]; "Thou great First Cause, least understood" [Pope]; *sans Dieu rien*; "naught but God Can satisfy the soul" [Bailey]; "God's in His Heaven — All's right with the world!" [Browning]; "The Somewhat which we name but cannot know" [William Watson]; "If there were no God, it would be necessary to invent him" [Voltaire].

---

977. [BENEFICENT SPIRITS.] **Angel.** —
N. ANGEL, archangel, Messenger of God, guardian angel, ministering spirits, invisible helpers, Choir Invisible, heavenly host, host of heaven, sons of God; morning star; saint.

[CELESTIAL HIERARCHY OF PSEUDO-DIONYSIUS] (1) Seraphim (*sing.* seraph, *E. pl.* seraphs), Cherubim (*sing.* cherub, *E. pl.* cherubs; cherubim *or* cherubin *are often treated as sing.*), Thrones; (2) Dominions, Virtues, Powers; (3) Principalities, Archangels, Angels.

Michael, Gabriel, Raphael, Uriel, Chamuel, Jophiel, Zadkiel; Abdiel, Azrael.

MADONNA, Our Lady, *Notre Dame* [*F.*], Holy Mary, The Virgin, The Blessed Virgin, The Virgin Mary; *Dei Mater* [*L.*]. Mother of God; *Regina Cœli* [*L.*], Queen of Heaven; *Regina Angelorum* [*L.*], Queen of Angels; *Stella Maris* [*L.*], Star of the Sea; *Mater Dolorosa* [*L.*]; Zion's Lily; *Alma Mater Redemptoris*, *Virgo Gloriosa*, *Virgo Sponsa Dei*, *Virgo Potens*, *Virgo Veneranda*, *Virgo Prædicanda*, *Virgo Clemens*, *Virgo Sapientissima*, *Sanc'a Virgo Virginum* [all *L.*]; *La Vergine Gloriosa* [*It.*]; *La Grande Vierge* [*F.*].

Adj. ANGELIC, seraphic, cherubic, archangelic.

.•. "are they not all ministering spirits?" [*Bible*]; "And flights of angels sing thee to thy rest!" [*Hamlet*]; "Millions of spiritual creatures walk the earth Unseen, both when we wake and when we sleep" [*P. L.*]; "*Ave, maris stella, Dei Mater Alma, Atque semper Virgo, Felix cæli porta*" [*hymn*].

978. [MALEFICENT SPIRITS.] **Satan.** —
N. SATAN, the Devil, Lucifer, Belial, Beëlzebub, Eblis [*Ar.*], Ahriman [*Zoroastrianism*], Mephistopheles, Mephisto, Shaitan [*Hind.*], Samael, Asmodeus, Satanas [*archaic*], Abaddon [*Heb.*], Apollyon, *le Diable* [*F.*], Deil [*Scot.*], Teufel [*Ger.*], *Diabolus* [*L.*].

his Satanic Majesty, the Prince of the Devils, the Prince of Darkness, the Prince of this world, the Prince of the power of the air; the Tempter, the Adversary, the Evil One, the Evil Spirit, the Archenemy, the Archfiend, the Foul Fiend, the Devil Incarnate, the Father of Lies, the Author of Evil, the Father of Evil, the Old Serpent, the Wicked One, the Common Enemy, the angel of the bottomless pit.[1]

FALLEN ANGELS, unclean spirits, devils; the rulers of darkness, the powers of darkness; inhabitants of Pandemonium; demon &c. 980.

Moloch, Mammon, Azazel [*Milton*]; Belial [*P. L.*], Beëlzebub [*in P. L., the fallen angel next to Satan*], Loki [*Norse myth.*].

DIABOLISM, devil worship, devil lore, diablerie *or* diablery, diabolology *or* diabology, Satanism, devilism; devilship, devildom; demonry, demonism, demonology, Manichæism *or* Manicheism; Black Mass, Black Magic, demonolatry, demonomagy; witchcraft &c. (*sorcery*) 992; the cloven hoof; hoofs and horns; demonomy.

DIABOLIST, demonologist, demonol-

---

[1] The slang expressions "the Deuce, the Dickens, the Old Gentleman, Old Nick, Old Scratch, Old Horny, Old Harry, Old Gooseberry," have not been inserted in the text.

oger, demonolater, demonist, demonographer [rare], demonomist; Manichæan or Manichean.

V. DIABOLIZE [rare], demonize; bewitch, bedevil &c. (sorcery) 992; possess, obsess.

Adj. SATANIC, diabolic or diabolical, devilish, demoniac or demoniacal, infernal, hellborn.

∗∗∗ "Satan exalted sat, by merit raised To that bad eminence"[P. L.]; "from morn To noon he fell, from noon to dewy eve" [P. L.]; "The prince of darkness is a gentleman" [King Lear]; "The Devil, my friends, is a woman just now, 'Tis a woman that reigns in Hell" [Owen Meredith]; "Get thee behind me, Satan" [Bible].

979. Mythic and pagan deities. —

N. GOD, goddess; deus [L.], dea [L.]; deva (fem. devi) ["the shining ones," Skr.]; heathen gods and goddesses; pantheon; theogony.

[GREEK AND LATIN] Zeus, Jupiter or Jove (King); Apollon, Apollo (the sun); Ares, Mars (war); Hermes, Mercury (messenger); Poseidon, Neptune (ocean); Hephaistos, Vulcan (smith); Dionysus, Bacchus (wine); Pluton or Hades [Gr.], Pluto or Dis [L.] (King of the lower world); Kronos, Saturn (time); Eros, Cupid (love); Pan, Faunus (flocks, herds, forests, and wild life).

Hera, Juno (Queen); Demeter, Ceres (fruitfulness); Persephone, Proserpina or Proserpine (Queen of the lower world); Artemis, Diana (the moon and hunting); Athena, Minerva (wisdom); Aphrodite, Venus (love and beauty); Hestia, Vesta (the hearth); Rhea or Cybele ("Mother of the gods," identified with Ops, wife of Saturn); Gæa or Ge, Tellus (earth goddess, mother of the Titans).

[NORSE] Ymir (primeval giant), Reimthursen (frost giants), Bori (fashioner of the world), Bor (father of Odin), Odin or Woden (the All-father, =Zeus); the Æsir or Asas; Thor (the Thunderer), Balder or Baldr (=Apollo), Freyr (fruitfulness), Tyr or Tyrr (war), Bragi (poetry and eloquence), Höder or Höðr (blind god of the winter), Heimdall (warder of Asgard), Vidar (=Pan), Uller or Ullr (the chase), Forseti (peacemaker), Vali (knowledge and eternal light), Loki (evil).

the Vanir or Vans: Njorth or Njord (the winds and the sea), Frey or Freyr (prosperity and love), Freya or Freyja (goddess of love and beauty, =Venus).

Frigg or Frigga (wife of Odin), Hel (goddess of death, = Persephone), Sif (wife of Thor), Nanna (wife of Balder), Idun (goddess of spring, wife of Bragi), Sigyn (wife of Loki).

[HINDU] VEDIC GODS: Dyaus (the Heaven), Indra (cloud-compeller), Varuna (the sky, also the waters), Surya (the sun, =Gr. Helios), Savitar ("the Inciter," a sun god), Soma (the sus ainer), Agni (fire), Vavu (the winds), the Marutas (storm gods), Ushas ("the Dawn," goddess of wisdom).

BRAHMANIC GODS: Brahmâ, Vishnu, Siva or Shiva &c. (Brahmanism) 976; avatars of

434

980. Evil Spirits. — N. demon, fiend,

devil &c. (Satan) 978; evil genius, familiar, familiar spirit; bad -, unclean-spirit; cacodæmon or cacodemon, incubus, succubus and succuba; dæva or deev, bad peri, afreet, lamia, barghest or barguest; ogre, ogress, ghoul, vampire, harpy; Fury, the Furies, the Erinyes, the Eumenides; Titan; Friar Rush.

imp, bad fairy, sprite, jinni or jinnee (pl. jin), genius (pl. genii), flibberti-gibbet, ouphe, dwarf, troll, urchin, Cluricaune.

changeling, elf-child, auf, oaf; werewolf, loup-garou [F.]; satyr.

ELEMENTAL, sylph, gnome, salamander, nymph [Rosicrucian].

SIREN, nixie, undine, Lorelei.

BUGBEAR, bugaboo, bogy or bogey or bogie, bug [obs.], poker [rare], goblin, hobgoblin, boggart or boggard.

DEMONOLOGY, demonry &c. (diabolism) 978.

Adj. demoniac, demoniacal, fiendish, fiendlike, evil, ghoulish; pokerish [colloq., U. S.], bewitched.

∗∗∗ "For we wrestle not against flesh and blood, but against principalities, against powers, against the rulers of the darkness of this world" [Bible]; "to another [is given] discerning of spirits" [Bible]; "Whence and what art thou, execrable shape?" [Paradise Lost].

980a. Specter. — N. SPECTER or

spectre, ghost, revenant, apparition, spirit, sprite, shade, shadow, wraith, spook [now humorous], phantom, phantasm, fantasm [rare], idolum; materialization [Spiritualism], ectoplasmic manifestation; double, etheric body, etheric self, aura, auric egg, astral body, mayavi rupa, ego [all Theos. and Occultism]; vision, theophany.

banshee, White Lady, the White Ladies of Normandy, the White Lady of Avenel [Scott]; lemures, larva or larve [Roman relig.].

Vishnu: (1) Matsya, the fish; (2) Karma, the turtle; (3) Varah, the boar; (4) Narsinh, man-lion; (5) Vaman, the dwarf; (6) Parshuram, a Brahman; (7) Rama; (8) Krishna; (9) Buddha; (10) Kalki; Jagannath *or* Juggernaut (*Krishna*); Ganesha *or* Ganpati (*wisdom*), Hanuman (*monkey god*), Yama (*judge of the dead*).

Sarasvati (*sakti or wife of Brahmâ; goddess of poetry, wisdom, and fine art*), Lakshmi (*wife of Vishnu; goddess of wealth and prosperity*), Durga *or* Kali (*wife of Siva, conceived as a malignant deity*); Devi ("the goddess") *or* Uma ("light") *or* Gauri ("the brilliant") *or* Parvati ("the mountaineer," *wife of Siva, conceived as a beneficent deity*).

[EGYPTIAN] Ra *or* Amun-Ra (*the sun god*), Neph *or* Nef (*spirit or breath*), Pthah (*demiurge*), Khem (*reproduction*), Mut *or* Maut (= *Gr. Demeter*), Osiris (*judge of the dead*), Isis (*wife of Osiris*), Horus (*the morning sun; son of Osiris and Isis*), Anubis (*jackal-god, brother of Horus, a conductor of the dead*), Nephthys (*sister of Isis*), Set (*evil deity, brother of Osiris*), Thoth (*clerk of the under world*), Bast *or* Bubastis (*a goddess with head of a cat*), the Sphinx (*wisdom*).

[VARIOUS] Baal (*Heb. pl.* Baalim) [*Semitic*]; Astarte *or* Ashtoreth (*goddess of fertility and love*) [*Phœnician*]; Bel [*Babylonian*]; The Great Spirit [*N. Amer Indian*]; Mumbo Jumbo [*Sudanese Negroes, an idol or bugaboo*].

NYMPH, dryad, hamadryad, alseid, wood nymph; naiad, fresh-water nymph; oread, mountain nymph; nereid, sea nymph; limoniad *or* leimoniad, meadow nymph *or* flower nymph; Oceanid, ocean nymph; napæa, glen nymph; potamid, river nymph; Pleiades *or* Atlantides, Hyades, Dodonides.

FAIRY, fay, sprite *or* spright [*archaic*]; nix (*fem.* nixie), water sprite; the Good Folk, brownie *or* browny, pixy, elf (*pl.* elves), banshee *or* banshie; the Fates *or* Mœræ, *Clotho* (Spinner), *Lachesis* (Disposer of Lots), *Atropos* (Inflexible One); gnome, kelpie; faun; peri, nis, kobold, sylph, sylphid; undine, sea maid, sea nymph, mermaid (*masc.* merman); Mab, Oberon, Titania, Ariel; Puck, Robin Goodfellow, Hobgoblin; Leprechaun; denizens of the air; afreet &c. (*bad spirit*) 980.

FAMILIAR SPIRIT, familiar, genius, guide, good genius, tutelary genius, daimon, demon *or* dæmon, guardian.

MYTHOLOGY, mythical lore, heathen mythology, folklore, fairyism, fairy mythology.

Adj. MYTHICAL, mythic, mythological, fabulous, legendary &c. 515.

FAIRYLIKE, sylphlike, sylphine, sylphish, sylphidine; elfin, elflike, elfish, nymph-like.

• "Where'er he moves, the goddess shone before" [Homer — *Pope's trans.*]; "speak of the gods as they are" [Bias]; "You moonshine revelers and shades of night" [*Merry Wives*] "Where the bee sucks, there suck I; In a cowslip's bell I lie" [*Tempest*]; "Aërial spirits, by great Jove designed To be on earth the guardians of mankind" [Hesiod].

WILL-O'-THE-WISP, Friar's lantern &c. 423.

Adj. SPECTRAL, ghostly, ghostlike, spiritual, wraithlike, weird, uncanny, eerie *or* eery, spooky *or* spookish [*colloq.*], haunted; unearthly, supernatural.

• "Is not this something more than fantasy!" [*Hamlet*]; "But soft! behold! lo! where it comes again" [*ibid.*]; "Of calling shapes, and beck'ning shadows dire" [Milton].

---

981. Heaven. — N. HEAVEN; kingdom of -heaven, – God; heavenly kingdom; heaven of heavens, God's throne, throne of God, presence of God; inheritance of the saints in light.

Paradise, Eden, Zion, Holy City, New Jerusalem, Heavenly City, City Celestial, abode of the blessed; celestial bliss, eternal bliss, unending bliss, glory, never-ending day.

[MYTHOLOGICAL HEAVEN OR PARADISE] Olympus; Elysium, Elysian fields, Islands (*or* Isles) of the Blessed, Happy Isles, Fortunate Isles, Arcadia, bowers

982. Hell. — N. HELL, bottomless pit, place of torment; habitation of fallen angels; Pandemonium, Abaddon, Domdaniel; *jahannan* [*Hind.*], Sheol.

hell fire; everlasting -fire, – torment; lake of fire and brimstone; fire that is never quenched, worm that never dies.

purgatory, limbo, gehenna, abyss, Tophet.

[MYTHOLOGICAL HELL] Tartarus, Hades, Avernus, Styx, Stygian creek, pit of Acheron, Cocytus; infernal regions, inferno, shades below, realms of Pluto.

of bliss, garden of the Hesperides, third heaven, seventh heaven; Valhalla *or* Walhalla [*Scandinavian*]; Nirvana [*Buddhist*]; happy hunting grounds [*N. Amer. Indian*]; *Alfardaws, Assama; Falak al aflak*, ("the highest heaven") [*Mohammedan*].

FUTURE STATE, life after death, eternal home, resurrection, translation; resuscitation &c. 660; apotheosis, deification.

[THEOSOPHY] Devachan *or* Devaloka, the land of the Gods.

Pluto, Rhadamanthus, Erebus, Charon, Cerberus; Persephone, Proserpina *or* Proserpine; Minos, Osiris.

RIVERS OF HELL: Styx, Acheron, Cocytus, Phlegethon, Lethe.

Adj. HELLISH, infernal, stygian.

..* *dies iræ dies illa;* "the hue of dungeons and the scowl of night" [*L. L. L.*]; "Hell the Shadow from a Soul on fire Cast on the Darkness" [Omar Khayyám — Fitzgerald].

Adj. HEAVENLY, celestial, supernal, unearthly, from on high, paradisaic *or* paradisaical, paradisiac *or* paradisiacal, beatific, elysian, Olympian, Arcadian.

..* "looks through Nature up to Nature's God" [Pope]; "the great world's altar stairs, That slope through darkness up to God" [Tennyson]; "the treasury of everlasting joy" [*Henry VI*]; *vigeur de dessus;* "Heav'n but the Vision of fulfil'd desire" [Omar Khayyám — Fitzgerald]; "that bright kingdom where the souls who strove Live now forever, helping living men" [Masefield]; "that goal That lies beyond the purchase of the world" [Presland].

2. RELIGIOUS DOCTRINES

983. [RELIGIOUS KNOWLEDGE.] **Theology. — N.** THEOLOGY (natural and revealed), theosophy, divine wisdom, divinity, hagiology, hagiography, hierography; Caucasian mystery; monotheism, theism, religion; religious -persuasion, – sect, – denomination, – affiliation; creed &c. (*belief*) 484; articles –, declaration –, profession –, confession- of faith.

THEOLOGIAN, theologue [*now rare*], scholastic, divine, schoolman, canonist, theologist [*now rare*], theologus; monotheist, theist; Homoousian (*opp. to* Homoiousian); the Fathers.

Adj. THEOLOGICAL, religious, divine, canonical; denominational; sectarian &c. 984.

983a. Orthodoxy. — N. ORTHODOXY; strictness, soundness, religious truth, true faith; truth &c. 494; soundness of doctrine.

Christianity, Christianism; Catholicism, Catholicity; "the faith once delivered to the saints"; hyperorthodoxy &c. 984.

THE CHURCH, Holy Church, Church Militant, Church Triumphant; Catholic –, Universal –, Apostolic –, Established-Church; the Bride of the Lamb; temple of the Holy Ghost; Church –, body –, members –, disciples –, followers- of Christ; Christians.

true believer; textualist, textuary; canonist &c. (*theologian*) 983; the Orthodox; Christian community; Christendom, collective body of Christians.

CANONS &c. (*belief*) 484; thirty-nine articles; Apostles' –, Nicene –, Athanasian- Creed; Church Catechism.

Adj. ORTHODOX, sound, strict, faithful, catholic, schismless, Christian, evangelical, scriptural, literal, divine, mono-

984. Heterodoxy. [SECTARIANISM.] — **N.** HETERODOXY; error &c. 495; false doctrine, heresy, schism, schismaticism, schismaticalness; recusancy, backsliding, apostasy; materialism, hylotheism; atheism &c. (*irreligion*) 989.

anthropomorphism, anthropopathism, anthropopathy; idolatry &c. 991; superstition &c. (*credulity*) 486.

BIGOTRY &c. (*obstinacy*) 606; fanaticism, iconoclasm; hyperorthodoxy, precisianism; bibliolatry, hagiolatry; sabbatarianism, puritanism.

SECTARIANISM, sectarism [*obs.*], nonconformity; dissent &c. 489; secularism; syncretism; religious sects, the clash of creeds.

protestantism, Arianism, Adventism, Jansenism, Stundism, Erastianism, Calvinism, Quakerism, Methodism, Anabaptism, Puseyism, tractarianism, ritualism, Origenism, Sabellianism, Socinianism, Gnosticism, Mormonism, Second Adventism, materialism, positivism, latitudinarianism, ethicism,

theistic, theistic; true &c. 494; true blue.

₊ of the true faith; "Ever the fiery Pentecost Girds with one flame the countless host" [Emerson]; "Odinism was valor; Christianism was humility, another kind of valor" [Carlyle]; "prove their doctrine orthodox By apostolic blows and knocks" [Butler]; "orthodoxy is my doxy; heterodoxy another man's doxy" [Warburton]; "orthodoxy is the Bourbon of the world of thought; it learns not, neither can it forget" [Huxley]; "The Church . . . the world-tree of the nations for so long!" [Carlyle].

deism, higher pantheism, henotheism; monism, philosophical unitarianism &c.; the isms.

Anglicanism; High –, Low –, Broad –, Free- Church; ultramontanism; monasticism, monkery; Catholicism, Romanism, popery, papism, papistry, papacy, Maryolatry [usually opprobrious], Scarlet Woman, Church of Rome; Greek Church. [Generally speaking, each sect is orthodox to itself and heterodox to others.]

Judaism; Mohammedanism, Islam, Islamism.

Theosophy, New Thought, ethical culture, mental science, mental healing; Christian Science, Eddyism; Spiritualism, Spiritism, occultism; Swedenborgianism.

PAGANISM, heathenism, heathendom; mythology; animism, polytheism, ditheism, tritheism, pantheism; dualism.

Gentilism, Babism, Sufiism, Neoplatonism, Brahmanism, Hinduism, Vedantism, Buddhism, Lamaism; Sikhism, Jainism; Confucianism, Taoism; Shintoism, Sabæanism or Sabeanism or Sabeism.

PAGAN, heathen, paynim; giaour [Turk.], Gheber or Ghebre, kafir, non-Mohammedan; gentile; pantheist, polytheist, animist.

MISBELIEVER, heretic, apostate; backslider; antichrist; idolater; skeptic &c. 989.

BIGOT &c. (obstinacy) 606; fanatic, abdal, dervish, iconoclast.

SECTARIAN, sectary, sectarist [rare], schismatic; seceder, separatist, recusant, dissenter, nonconformist, nonjuror.

Huguenot, Protestant, Episcopalian; Trinitarian; latitudinarian; limitarian; orthodox dissenter, Puritan, Unitarian, Congregationalist, Independent; Presbyterian; Lutheran, Ubiquitarian, Calvinist, Methodist, Wesleyan; Anabaptist, Baptist; Mormon, Latter-day Saint; Irvingite, Sandemanian, Glassite, Erastian, Sublapsarian, Supralapsarian; Gentoo, Antinomian, Swedenborgian; Adventist, Second Adventist, Bible Christian, Bryanite, Brownian, Dunker, Ebionite, Eusebian; Faith Curer, Faith Curist, Faith Healer, Mental Healer, Christian Scientist; Familist, Jovinianist, Libadist, Restitutionist, Quaker, Shaker, Quietist, Stundist, Tunker &c.

Catholic, Roman Catholic, Romanist, Papist, ultramontane; Anglican, Oxford School; tractarian, Puseyite, ritualist; High Churchman.

Jew, Hebrew, Rabbinist; Mohammedan, Mussulman, Moslem, Islamite, Osmanli, Motazilite, Shiah, Sunni, Wahabi; Brahman or Brahmin; Brahmo; Vedantist, Jain or Jaina, Sikh, Parsi or Parsee, fire worshiper, Zoroastrian [erron. called fire worshiper]; Sufi, Babist, Buddhist; Confucianist, Taoist, Shintoist; Magi, Gymnosophist, Sabian, henotheist, Gnostic, Sadducee, Rosicrucian, Mystic, Occultist, Theosophist, Spiritualist, Spiritist &c.

MATERIALIST, hylotheist; positivist, deist, agnostic, atheist &c. 989.

Adj. HETERODOX, heretical, unorthodox, unscriptural, uncanonical, unchristian, antiscriptural, apocryphal; antichristian; schismatic, recusant, iconoclastic; sectarian, dissenting, dissident [now rare]; Protestant &c. n.; secular &c. (lay) 997; deistic, agnostic, atheistic; skeptical &c. 989.

bigoted &c. (prejudiced) 481, (obstinate) 606; superstitious &c. (credulous) 486; fanatical; idolatrous &c. 991; visionary &c. (imaginative) 515.

Judaical; Mohammedan, Islamic or Islamitic, Moslem; Brahmanic or Brahmanical, Brahminic or Brahminical; Buddhist &c. n.

Popish, papish, papistic or papistical, Romish.

PAGAN, heathen, heathenish, ethnic, ethnical; gentile, paynim; polytheistic, pantheistic, animistic.

₊ "slave to no sect" [Pope]; *superstitione tollendâ religio non tollitur* [Cicero]; "our wishes ought not to determine what we shall accept as truth" [H. C. Örsted]; "Whatever creed be taught or land be trod, Man's conscience is the oracle of God" [Byron]; "A Pagan suckled in some creed outworn" [Wordsworth]; "There lives more faith in honest doubt Believe me, than in half the creeds" [Tennyson]; "The religion of Christ is peace and good-will, that of Christendom war and ill-will" [Landor]; "Now join your hands, and with your hands your hearts" [*III Henry VI*]; "With malice toward none, with charity for all, with firmness in the right, as God gives us to see the right" [Lincoln].

985. Revelation. [BIBLICAL.] — **N.** REVELATION, inspiration, *afflatus* [*L.*]; theophany, theopneusty.

THE BIBLE, the Book, the Book of Books, the Good Book, the Word, the Word of God, Scripture, the Scriptures, Holy Writ, Holy Scriptures, inspired writings, Gospel.

OLD TESTAMENT, Septuagint, Vulgate, Pentateuch; Octateuch; the Law, the Jewish Law; the Prophets; major –, minor– Prophets; Hagiographa, Hierographa; Apocrypha.

NEW TESTAMENT; Gospels, Evangelists, Synoptic Gospels, Acts, Epistles, Apocalypse, Revelation; Good Tidings, Glad Tidings.

[HEBREW] Talmud, Mishna, Gemara; Masora *or* Masorah.

INSPIRED WRITERS, inspired penmen; prophet &c. (*seer*) 513; evangelist, apostle, disciple, saint; the Fathers, the Apostolic Fathers; Holy Men of old.

Adj. SCRIPTURAL, biblical, sacred, prophetic; evangelical, evangelistic, apostolic, apostolical; inspired, theopneustic, theopneusted [*rare*], apocalyptic, revealed; ecclesiastical, canonical, textuary; Talmudic.

₊ "Out from the heart of nature rolled The burdens of the Bible old" [Emerson]; "The word unto the prophet spoken Was writ on tables yet unbroken" [*ibid.*]; "Within that awful volume lies The mystery of mysteries!" [Scott]; "A glory gilds the sacred page, Majestic like the sun, It gives a light to every age, It gives but borrows none" [Cowper].

986. Sacred Writings. [NON-BIBLICAL.] — **N.** The Vedas (Rig-Veda, Yajur-Veda, Sama-Veda, Atharva-Veda), the Upanishads, the Puranas, Sutras, Sastra *or* Shastra, Tantra, Bhagavad Gita [*all Brahmanic*]; Zendavesta, Avesta [*Zoroastrian*]; The Koran *or* Alcoran [*Mohammedan*]; Tripitaka, Dhammapada [*Buddhist*]; Granth, Adigranth [*Sikh*]; the Agamas [*Jain*]; the Kings [*Chinese*]; the Eddas [*Scandinavia*].

Arcana Coelestia &c. [*Swedenborgian*]; Book of Mormon; "Science and Health with Key to the Scriptures" [*Christian Science*].

[NON-BIBLICAL PROPHETS AND RELIGIOUS FOUNDERS] Gautama (Buddha); Zoroaster, Confucius, Lao-tse [*Taoism*], Mohammed, Nanak Shah [*Sikhism*], Vaddhamana, "Maha-vira" [*Jainism*], Mirza Ali Mohammed, "Bab-ud-Din" (*Per.* "Gate of the Faith") [*Babism*], Ram Mohun Roy [*Brahmo-Samaj*].

Swedenborg, Joseph Smith [*Mormonism*], Mary Baker Eddy [*Christian Science*].

₊ "In Faith and Hope the world will disagree, But all mankind's concern is Charity" [Pope]; "There is only one religion, though there are a hundred versions of it" [Shaw].

---

3. RELIGIOUS SENTIMENTS

987. Piety. — **N.** PIETY, religion, theism, faith; religiousness, religiosity, holiness &c. *adj.;* saintship; religionism; sanctimony &c. (*assumed piety*) 988; reverence &c. (*respect*) 928; humility, veneration, devotion; prostration &c. (*worship*) 990; grace, unction, edification; sanctity, sanctitude [*rare*]; consecration.

988. Impiety. — **N.** IMPIETY; sin &c. 945; irreverence; profaneness &c. *adj.,* profanity, profanation; blasphemy, desecration, sacrilege; scoffing &c. *v.*

[ASSUMED PIETY] hypocrisy &c. (*falsehood*) 544; pietism, cant, pious fraud; lip-devotion, lip-service, lip-reverence; misdevotion, formalism, austerity; sanctimony, sanctimoniousness &c. *adj.;*

spiritual existence, odor of sanctity, beauty of holiness.

theopathy, beatification, adoption, regeneration, conversion, justification, theodicy, sanctification, salvation, inspiration, bread of life; Body and Blood of Christ.

BELIEVER, convert, theist, Christian, devotee, pietist, Saint.

the -good, – righteous, – just, – believing, – elect; the children of -God, – Our Father, – the kingdom, – light.

V. BE PIOUS &c. *adj.;* have faith &c. *n.;* believe, receive Christ; venerate, adore, worship, perform the acts of devotion; revere &c. 928; be converted &c.; experience the divine illumination [*Mysticism*]; be at one with God, be on God's side, stand up for Jesus, fight the good fight, keep the faith, let one's light shine.

REGENERATE, convert, edify, sanctify, hallow, keep holy, beatify, inspire, consecrate, enshrine.

Adj. PIOUS, religious, devout, devoted, reverent, godly, heavenly-minded, humble, pure, pure in heart, holy, spiritual, pietistic, saintly, saintlike; seraphic, sacred, solemn.

believing, faithful, Christian, Catholic.

REGENERATED; inspired, consecrated, converted, unearthly, not of the earth, in the world not of it.

elected, adopted, justified, sanctified.

*** *ne vile fano;* "pure-eyed Faith . . .; thou hovering angel girt with golden wings" [Milton]; "To me religion is life before God and in God" [Amiel]; "See God's world through the rags of this" [Masefield].

pharisaism, precisianism; sabbatism, sabbatarianism; *odium theologicum* [*L.*], sacerdotalism; bigotry &c. (*obstinacy*) 606, (*prejudice*) 481; blue laws.

APOSTASY, recusancy, hardening, backsliding, declension, perversion, reprobation.

HYPOCRITE &c. (*dissembler*) 548; "Scribes and Pharisees" [*Bible*]; *Rawana-sannyasi* [*Hind.*]; Tartufe, Mawworm, Holy Willie [*Burns*].

BIGOT, saint [*ironical*]; Pharisee, sabbatarian, formalist, methodist, puritan, pietist, precisian, religionist, devotee, ranter, fanatic; juramentado [*Moro*].

SINNER &c. 949; scoffer, blasphemer, sacrilegist [*rare*], sabbath breaker; worldling.

the wicked, the evil, the unjust, the reprobate; sons of -men, – Belial, – the wicked one; children of -the devil, – darkness.

V. BE IMPIOUS &c. *adj.;* profane, desecrate, blaspheme, revile, scoff; swear &c. (*malediction*) 908; commit sacrilege.

DISSEMBLE, simulate, play the hypocrite, hypocrify [*obs.*], hypocrize [*rare*], snuffle, talk through the nose, talk nasally, hold up the hands in horror, turn up the whites of the eyes; sing psalms for a pretense, make long prayers.

Adj. IMPIOUS; irreligious &c. 989; desecrating &c. *v.;* profane, irreverent, sacrilegious, blasphemous.

unhallowed, unsanctified, unregenerate; hardened, perverted, reprobate.

HYPOCRITICAL &c. (*false*) 544; canting, pietistical, sanctimonious, unctuous, pharisaical, overrighteous, righteous over much.

BIGOTED, fanatical, hidebound, narrow, illiberal, prejudiced, little; provincial, parochial, insular; priest-ridden.

Adv. under the -mask, – cloak, – pretense, – form, – guise- of religion; in blasphemy.

*** *giovane santo diavolo vecchio;* "Oh, for a *forty-parson power* to chant Thy praise, Hypocrisy!" [Byron]; "But all was false and hollow; though his tongue Dropped manna" [*P. L.*]; "O serpent heart, hid with a flowering face!" [*Romeo and Juliet*]; "Saint abroad, and a devil at home" [Bunyan].

989. Irreligion. — N. IRRELIGION, indevotion, impiety; ungodliness &c. *adj.;* laxity, apathy, indifference; quietism, passiveness, passivity.

SKEPTICISM, doubt; unbelief, disbelief, incredulity, incredulousness &c. *adj.;* want of -faith, – belief; pyrrhonism; doubt &c. 485; agnosticism, freethinking; deism; hylotheism; materialism, rationalism, positivism; nihilism.

INFIDELITY, antichristianity, antichristianism, atheism.

UNBELIEVER, infidel, atheist, antichristian; *giaour* [*Turk.*], heretic, miscreant [*archaic*], heathen, alien, gentile, Nazarene; *esprit fort* [*F.*], freethinker, skeptic, pyrrhonist, deist, latitudinarian, rationalist; materialist, positivist, nihilist, agnostic, somatist, theophobist.

V. BE IRRELIGIOUS &c. *adj.;* disbelieve, lack faith; doubt, question &c. 485.

dechristianize, antichristianize [*rare*]; serve Mammon, contend against the light, love darkness rather than light, deny the truth.

Adj. IRRELIGIOUS; indevout, undevout, devoutless, godless, graceless, ungodly; unholy, unsanctified, unhallowed; atheistic, without God.

SKEPTICAL, freethinking, unbelieving, unconverted; incredulous, faithless, lacking faith; deistic, deistical; antichristian, unchristian.

WORLDLY, mundane, earthly, carnal; worldly &c. worldly-minded, unspiritual.

Adv. IRRELIGIOUSLY &c. *adj.*

⁎ "Unbelief is blind" [Milton]; "the fool hath said in his heart, There is no God" [*Bible*]; "no one is so much alone in the world as a denier of God" [Richter].

4. ACTS OF RELIGION

990. Worship. — N. WORSHIP, adoration, devotion, cult, aspiration, homage, service, humiliation; kneeling, genuflection, prostration; latria, dulia, hyperdulia.

PRAYER, invocation, supplication, rogation, intercession, orison, holy breathing, petition &c. (*request*) 765; collect, litany, Lord's prayer, paternoster; *Ave Maria* [*L.*]; Hail, Mary; rosary, bead-roll.

revival; anxious –, revival –, camp- meeting.

THANKSGIVING; giving –, returning- thanks; grace, praise, glorification, pæan, benediction, doxology, hosanna, hallelujah *or* halleluiah, alleluia *or* alleluiah; *Te Deum, non nobis Domine, nunc dimittis; O Salutaris* [*all L.*]; Sanctus, *Agnus Dei* [*L.*], *Kyrie Eleison* [*Gr.*], *Gloria* [*L.*], The Annunciation, Tersanctus, Trisagion.

psalm, psalmody; hymn, plain song, chant, chaunt [*archaic*], response, anthem, motet, antiphon, antiphony.

OBLATION, sacrifice, incense, libation, offering; burnt –, heave –, thank –, votive-offering; offertory, collection.

DISCIPLINE, self-discipline, self-examination, self-denial; fasting, penance, confession.

DIVINE SERVICE, office, duty; exercises; morning prayer; Mass, matins, nones, complin *or* compline, evensong, vespers, vigils, lauds; undersong, tierce; holyday &c. (*rites*) 998.

PRAYER BOOK, missal, breviary, Virginal; ritual &c. 998.

WORSHIPER, congregation, communicant, celebrant.

V. WORSHIP, lift up the heart, aspire; revere &c. 928; adore, do service, pay homage; humble oneself, kneel; bow –, bend- the knee; throw oneself on one's knees, fall down, fall on one's knees; prostrate oneself, bow down and worship; beat the breast.

intone, chant, deacon *or* deacon off [*colloq., U. S.*], lead the choir, sing.

PRAY, invoke, supplicate; put –, offer- up -prayers, – petitions; beseech &c. (*ask*) 765; say one's prayers, tell one's beads, recite the rosary.

GIVE THANKS, return thanks, say grace, bless, praise, laud, glorify, magnify, sing praises; give benediction.

propitiate, offer sacrifice, fast, deny oneself; vow, offer vows, give alms.

ATTEND SERVICE, attend Mass, go to church, attend divine service; communicate &c. (*rite*) 998; work out one's salvation.

Adj. WORSHIPING &c. *v.;* devout, devotional, reverent, pure, solemn; fervid &c. (*heartfelt*) 821.

Int. HALLELUJAH *or* halleluiah! alleluia *or* alleluiah! hosanna! glory be to God! *sursum corda* [*L.*], *Deo gratias* [*L.*].

O Lord! pray God that! God -grant, – bless, – save, – forbid!

⁎ "making their lives a prayer" [Whittier]; *ora et labora;* "prayer ardent opens heaven" [Young]; "Be comforted, thou wouldst not seek Me if thou hadst not already found Me" [Pascal]; "what greater calamity can fall upon a nation than the loss of worship" [Emerson].

991. Idolatry. — N. IDOLATRY, idolatrousness, idololatry, idolism, idolodoulia, demonism, demonolatry, demonology; idol –, chthonian –, demon –, devil –, fire-worship; zoölatry, fetishism *or* fetichism; ecclesiolatry, heliolatry, bibliolatry, hierolatry [*rare*].

idolization, deification, apotheosis, canonization; hero worship.

SACRIFICE, idolothyte, hecatomb, holocaust; human sacrifices, immolation, mactation, infanticide, self-immolation, suttee.

IDOL, golden calf, graven image, fetish *or* fetich, eidolon, *thakur* [*Hind.*], joss [*Chinese*], *lares et penates* [*L.*]; god (*or* goddess) of one's idolatry; Baal, Moloch, Dagon, Juggernaut.

IDOLATER, idolatress, demonolater *or* demonolator, chthonian, fetishist *or* fetichist: idolatrizer, idolizer, idolant [*obs.*], idolaster [*obs.*]; ecclesiolater, heliolater, zoölater, bibliolater.

V. IDOLATRIZE, idolize; *adorer le veau d'or* [*F.*]; worship -idols, – pictures, – relics; apotheosize, worship, put on a pedestal, prostrate oneself before; make sacrifice to, immolate before; deify, canonize.

Adj. IDOLATROUS, idololatric [*rare*], idolatric [*rare*], idolistic, chthonian, demonolatrous, fetishic [*rare*], fetishistic *or* fetichistic, idolothyte; worshiping *or* worshipping, prone before, prostrate before, in the dust before, at the feet of; heliolatrous, zoölatrous.

. "the idol is the measure of the worshipper" [Lowell]; "he who offers God a second place offers him no place" [Ruskin]; "condemnable idolatry is insincere idolatry — a human soul clinging spasmodically to an Ark of the Covenant, which it half feels is now a phantasm" [Carlyle].

992. Sorcery. — N. SORCERY; occult -art, – sciences; magic, black magic, the black art, necromancy, theurgy, thaumaturgy; demonology, demonomy [*obs.*], demonomancy, demonship; diablerie, bedevilment, witchcraft, witchery; fetishism *or* fetichism; ghost dance, hoodoo, voodoo, voodooism; fire worship, heliolatry; obi *or* obiism, shamanism, vampirism; conjuration, incantation, bewitchment, glamour, enchantment; obsession, possession; exorcism.

divination &c. (*prediction*) 511; sortilege, ordeal, *sortes Vergilianæ;* hocuspocus &c. (*deception*) 545.

V. PRACTICE SORCERY &c. *n.;* cast a nativity, cast a horoscope, conjure, exorcise *or* exorcize [*rare in the sense of* conjure], charm, enchant, bewitch, bedevil, overlook, look on with the evil eye, witch, voodoo, hoodoo [*colloq.*]; entrance, fascinate &c. (*influence*) 615; taboo *or* tabu; wave a wand; rub the -ring, – lamp; cast a spell; call up spirits; raise spirits from the dead; raise ghosts, lay ghosts; command jinn *or* genii.

Adj. MAGIC, magical; witching, weird, cabalistic, talismanic, phylacteric, incantatory; charmed &c. *v.;* Circean; voodoo.

992a. Psychical Research. — N. PSYCHICAL RESEARCH, psychical (*or* psychic) investigation; abnormal psychology; abnormal –, supernormal –, mediumistic-phenomena; mysticism; psychophysics; "psychologist's fallacy" [William James].

THE SUBCONSCIOUS, the subconscious self, the subliminal self, the higher self: ego &c. 980*a*; subconsciousness, subliminal consciousness; dual personality, mental duality, secondary consciousness, intuition; multiple personality, mental dissociation, dissociation of personality, functional disintegration; impersonation, obsession, possession.

PSYCHOTHERAPY, psychotherapeutics, psychanalysis; hysteria, neurasthenia, psychasthenia; over-stimulation; dreams, visions, apparitions, hallucinations, veridical hallucinations; Freud's theory.

MESMERISM, animal magnetism; od, odyl *or* odylic force [*obsoles.*], electrobiology; mesmeric trance; hypnotism; hypnosis, hypnoidal state.

[PHENOMENA] TELEPATHY, thought transference, thought transmission, telepathic transmission; "malicious animal magnetism" *or* "M. A. P."; telepathic dreams; second sight, clairvoyance, clairaudience, psychometry.

PREMONITIONS, previsions, telepathic hallucinations; premonitory apparition, fetch, wraith, double; symbolic hallucinations; death lights, ominous dreams, ominous animals.

AUTOMATISM, automatic writing, planchette, ouija board, trance writing, spirit writing, psychography; trance speaking, inspirational speaking.

CRYSTAL GAZING, crystallomancy, crystal vision; hydromancy, lecanomancy, catoptromancy, onychomancy.

SPIRITUALISM, spiritism, spirit rapping, "Rochester knockings," table-turning, Poltergeist; spirit manifestations; ghost, specter &c. 980a; haunted houses; trance, spirit control, spirit possession; mediumistic communications; séance; materialization.

[THEOSOPHY AND OCCULTISM] astral body &c. 980a, kamarupa [Skr.], desire body; etheric body, linga sharira [Skr.]; dense body, sthula sharira [Skr.]; mental body; causal body; bliss body, Buddhic body.

SEVEN PRINCIPLES OF MAN: (1) spirit or atma [Skr.], (2) spiritual mind, (3) intellect, (4) instinctive mind, (5) prana or vital force, (6) astral body, (7) physical body [Yogi philosophy].

MEDIUM, ecstatica [rare], seer, clairvoyant, clairaudient, telepathist; guide, control; mesmerist, hypnotist.

V. PSYCHOLOGIZE; investigate the -abnormal, - suprarational, - supernormal, - the subconscious, - the subliminal; search beyond the threshold, traverse the borderland, know oneself.

MESMERIZE, magnetize, hypnotize, place under control, subject to suggestion, place in a trance, induce hypnosis.

HOLD A SÉANCE, call up spirits, summon familiar spirits, "call spirits from the vasty deep" [I Henry IV]; hold spirit communications; materialize.

Adj. PSYCHICAL, psychic, psychal [rare], psychological; spiritistic, spiritualistic, spiritual; subconscious, "coconscious" [Morton Prince], subliminal (opp. to supraliminal); supernormal, abnormal, suprarational; mystic or mystical.

mediumistic, clairvoyant, clairaudient, telepathic; psychometric; hypnoidal, hypnagogic.

₊ "There exists in nature, in myriad activity, a *psychic element* the essential nature of which is still hidden to us" [Flammarion]; "There are more things in heaven and earth, Horatio, Than are dreamt of in your philosophy" [Hamlet]; "I give you an eye divine" [Bhagavad Gita]; "But often, in the world's most crowded streets, But often, in the din of strife. There rises an unspeakable desire After the knowledge of our buried life" [Arnold].

993. Spell. — N. SPELL, charm, incantation, exorcism, weird [obs. or Scot.], cabala or cabbala, exsufflation [obs.], cantrip or cantraip or contrap [chiefly Scot.], runes, abracadabra, open sesame, or open-sesame, hocus-pocus, counter-charm, Ephesian letters, bell book and candle, Mumbo Jumbo, evil eye.

talisman, amulet, madstone [U. S.], periapt, telesm [archaic], phylactery, philter or philtre, fetish or fetich, manito or manitou or manitu; furcula, furculum, wishbone, merrythought; mascot or mascotte, rabbit's foot, hoodoo [colloq.], jinx [slang], scarabæus or scarab; Om or Aum, Om mani padme hum [Buddhist]; sudarium, veronica, triskelion; swastika, fylfot, gammadion.

WAND, caduceus, rod, divining rod, witch hazel, Aaron's rod.

[MAGIC WISH-GIVERS] Aladdin's lamp, Aladdin's casket, magic casket, magic ring, magic belt, magic spectacles, wishing cap, Fortunatus's cap; seven-league boots; cap of darkness, Tarnkappe, Tarnhelm.

[FAIRY LORE] fairy ring, fairy circle, fairy round; fernseed, rowan tree, quicken tree [dial. Eng.].

994. Sorcerer. — N. SORCERER, magician, wizard, warlock, necromancer, conjuror, prestidigitator, prestidigitateur [F.], charmer, exorcist, voodoo, thaumaturge, thaumaturgist, theurgist, mage [poetic], Magi (sing. Magus); diviner, dowser.

sorceress, witch, hag.

medicine man *or* medicine, witch doctor, shaman, shamanist.

VAMPIRE, lamia, ghoul; siren, harpy; incubus &c. 980.

ASTROLOGER, figure caster [*obs.*], figure flinger [*obs.*]; soothsayer &c. 513.

Katerfelto, Cagliostro, Merlin, Comus; Circe, weird sisters, Grææ *or* Graiæ, witch of Endor.

. "You secret, black, and midnight hags!" [*Macbeth*]; "Aroint thee, witch, aroint thee!" [*ibid.*].

5. RELIGIOUS INSTITUTIONS

995. Churchdom. — N. CHURCHDOM; church, ministry, apostleship, priesthood, prelacy, hierarchy, church government, pale of the church, christendom.

clericalism, sacerdotalism, episcopalianism, ultramontanism; ecclesiology; theocracy; priestcraft, *odium theologicum* [*L.*]; religious sects &c. 984.

MONASTICISM, monkhood, monachism; celibacy.

[ECCLESIASTICAL OFFICES AND DIGNITIES] cardinalate, cardinalship; primacy, archbishopric, archiepiscopacy; prelacy, bishopric, bishopdom, episcopate, episcopacy, see, diocese; deanery, stall; canonry, canonicate; prebend, prebendaryship, prebendal stall; benefice, incumbency, glebe, advowson, living, cure, charge, cure of souls; rectorship, vicariate, vicarship; pastorate, pastorship, pastoral charge; deaconry, deaconship; curacy; chaplaincy, chaplainship, chaplainry *or* chaplanry [*Scot.*]; abbacy, presbytery.

HOLY ORDERS, ordination, institution, consecration, induction, reading in [*Eng.*], preferment, translation, presentation.

PAPACY, pontificate, popedom, See of Rome, the Vatican, the apostolic see.

COUNCIL &c. 696; conclave, college of cardinals, convocation, conference [*Meth.*], session, synod, consistory, chapter, vestry, presbytery, standing committee; sanhedrim, *congé d'élire* [*F.*].

ECCLESIASTICAL COURTS, consistorial court, court of Arches.

V. CALL, ordain, induct, prefer [*rare*], translate, consecrate, present, elect, bestow take orders, take the veil, take vows.

Adj. ECCLESIASTICAL, ecclesiological; clerical, sacerdotal, priestly, prelatical, pastoral, ministerial, capitular, theocratic; hierarchical, archiepiscopal; episcopal, episcopalian; canonical; monastic, monachal, monkish; abbatial, abbatical; Anglican; Aaronic, levitical, pontifical, papal, apostolic; ultramontane; priestridden.

996. Clergy. — N. CLERGY, clericals, ministry, priesthood, presbytery, the cloth, the pulpit, the desk.

CLERGYMAN, divine, ecclesiastic, churchman, priest, presbyter, hierophant, pastor, shepherd, minister, clerk in holy orders, parson, sky pilot [*slang*]; father, – in Christ; padre, *abbé* [*F.*], *curé* [*F.*]; reverend; black coat; confessor.

997. Laity. — N. LAITY, flock, fold, congregation, assembly, brethren, people; society [*U. S.*]; class [*Meth.*].

LAYMAN, civilian [*obs.*], laic, parishioner, catechumen; secularist.

V. LAICIZE, secularize.

Adj. SECULAR, lay, laic *or* laical, congregational, civil, temporal, profane.

[DIGNITARIES OF THE CHURCH] ecclesiarch, sacrist, hierarch; patriarch [*Eastern Ch.*]; Abba Salamah, Abuna [*Abyssinian Ch.*]; eminence, reverence, primate, metropolitan, archbishop, bishop, angel [*as in the Cath. Apostolic Ch.*], prelate, diocesan, suffragan, bishop coadjutor, dean, subdean, archdeacon, prebendary, canon, rural dean, rector, vicar, perpetual curate, residentiary, beneficiary, incumbent, chaplain, curate; elder, deacon, deaconess; preacher, reader, Bible reader, lay reader, lecturer; capitular; missionary, propagandist, Jesuit, revivalist, field preacher, colporteur.

churchwarden, deacon, questman [*hist.*], sidesman; clerk, precentor, choir; almoner, *suisse* [*F.*], verger, beadle, sexton, sacristan; acolyte, thurifer, censorbearer; chorister, choir boy, member of the choir; soloist, quartet *or* quartette; organist.

[ROMAN CATHOLIC PRIESTHOOD] Pope, Holy Father, papa [*obs. or rare*], pontiff, high priest, cardinal; archbishop, bishop, bishop coadjutor; canon-regular, canon-secular, confessor, penitentiary, Grand Penitentiary, spiritual director.

RELIGIOUS, monastic, cenobite, conventual, abbot, prior, monk, friar, lay brother, beadsman *or* bedesman, mendicant, pilgrim, palmer; Jesuit, Franciscan, Friars minor, Minorites; Observant, Capuchin, Dominican, Carmelite; Augustinian; Gilbertine; Austin-, Black-, White-, Gray-, Crossed-, Crutched- Friars; Bonhomme, Carthusian, Benedictine, Cistercian, Trappist, Cluniac, Premonstratensian, Maturine; Templar, Hospitaler; Bernardine, Lorettine, pillarist, stylite; caloyer, hieromonach [*both Eastern Ch.*].

NUN, sister, *religieuse* [*F.*]; priestess, abbess, prioress, canoness; mother superior, superioress, the reverend mother; novice, postulant.

[JEWISH DISPENSATION] prophet, priest, high priest, Levite; Rabbi, Rabbin, scribe.

[MOHAMMEDAN] imam *or* imaum, kahin, kasis, sheik; mullah, murshid, mufti; hadji *or* haji, muezzin [*all Ar.*]; dervish *or* darvesh [*Pers.*], abdal (*pl.* abdali) [*Pers.*], fakir *or* faquir [*Ar.*], beshara [*Hind.*], bashara [*Hind.*], santon [*Turkey*].

[HINDU] Brahman *or* Brahmin, pujari, purohit [*family priest*]; pundit *or* pandit, guru; yogi, sannyasi *or* sanyasi; bhikshu, bhikhari, vairagi *or* bairagi, Ramwat, Ramanandi [*all Hind.*].

[BUDDHIST] poonghie *or* poonghee [*Burma*], talapoin [*Ceylon & Indo-China*], bonze; lama, Grand Lama *or* Dalai Lama [*Tibet*].

[VARIOUS] druid, druidess [*ancient Celts*]; flamen [*Rom. relig. and ancient Britain*]; hierus, hierophant [*Gr. relig.*]; daduchus *or* dadouchos, mystæ, epoptæ [*Eleusinian Mysteries*].

V. take orders &c. 995.

Adj. ORDAINED, in orders, in holy orders, called to the ministry; the Reverend, the very Reverend, the Right Reverend.

. "O most gentle pulpiter! what tedious homily of love have you wearied your parishioners withal!" *As You Like It*]; "The shepherd seeks the sheep and not the sheep the shepherd" [*M. for M.*]; "To have a thin stipend, and an everlasting parish, Lord, what a torment 'tis!" [*Beaumont and Fletcher*]; "Wait till you hear me from the pulpit, there you cannot answer me!" [Bishop Gilbert Haven].

998. Rite. — N. RITE, ceremony, ceremonial, ordinance, observance, function, duty; form, formulary; solemnity, sacrament; incantation &c. (*spell*) 993; service, ministry, ministration; liturgics.

SERMON, preaching, preachment, predication [*obs. or Scot.*], exhortation, religious harangue, homily, lecture, discourse, pastoral.

[SEVEN SACRAMENTS] BAPTISM, immersion, christening, chrism; baptismal regeneration; font.

CONFIRMATION, imposition of hands, laying on of hands.

EUCHARIST, Lord's supper, communion; the sacrament, the holy sacrament; consecrated elements, bread and wine; intinction; celebration, high celebration; *missa cantata* [*L.*]; *asperges* [*L.*]; offertory; introit; consecration; consubstantiation, impanation, subpanation, transubstantiation; real presence; elements; Mass; high -, low -, dry- mass; hunter's (*or* hunting) mass [*obs.*].

PENANCE &c. (*atonem nt*) 952; flagellation, maceration, fasting, sackcloth and ashes. EXTREME UNCTION, last rites, viaticum.

HOLY ORDERS, ordination &c. (*churchdom*) 995.

MATRIMONY, marriage, wedlock &c. 903.

WORSHIP &c. 990; invocation of saints, canonization, transfiguration, auricular confession, the confessional; absolution; reciting the rosary, telling of beads; processional; thurification, incense, holy water, aspersion.

circumcision; purification; visitation of the sick; burial &c. 363.

[SACRED ARTICLES] relics, rosary, beads, reliquary, host, cross, rood, crucifix; pyx, pix [*obs.*]; pax, *Agnus Dei* [*L.*], censer, thurible, incensory, patera; urceus, urceole; prayer wheel, prayer machine; Sangraal *or* Sangrael, Holy Grail.

RITUAL, rubric, canon, ordinal, missal, breviary, Mass book, beadroll; farse; liturgy, prayer book, Book of Common Prayer, *Pietà* [*It.*], euchologion *or* euchology [*Eastern Ch.*], litany, lectionary.

psalter, psalm book, hymn book, hymnal; hymnology, psalmody.

ritualism, ceremonialism; sabbatism, sabbatarianism; ritualist, sabbatarian.

HOLYDAY, feast, fast; Sabbath, Passover, Pentecost; Advent, Christmas, Epiphany, Lent; Passion Week, Holy Week; Good Friday, Easter; Ascension Day, Holy Thursday; Whitsuntide, Whitsunday *or* Whit-Sunday [*erroneously*, Whitsun Day]; Trinity Sunday, Corpus Christi; All Saints *or* All Saints' Day, All Souls' Day; love feast, agape; Candlemas *or* Candlemas Day; Lammas, Lammas Day, Lammastide; Michaelmas, Martinmas.

V. PERFORM SERVICE, do duty, minister, officiate; baptize, dip, sprinkle; confirm, lay hands on; give –, administer –, take –, receive –, attend –, partake of– the –sacrament, – communion, – Holy Eucharist; communicate; celebrate Mass, celebrate; administer –, receive– extreme unction; anele [*o s.*], shrive, absolve; administer –, receive– absolution; confess, make confession; do –, perform –, receive –, inflict-penance; tell one's beads; genuflect; make the sign of the Cross.

EXCOMMUNICATE, ban with bell book and candle.

PREACH, sermonize, predicate, lecture, address the congregation.

Adj. RITUAL, ritualistic, ceremonial; liturgic *or* liturgical; baptismal, eucharistical; paschal.

*** "what art thou, thou idol ceremony?" [*Henry V*].

999. Canonicals. — N. CANONICALS, vestments; robe, gown, Geneva gown, frock, pallium, surplice, cotta, cassock; communion cloth, eileton [*Eastern Ch.*], corporal [*Western Ch.*]; scapular *or* scapulary, cope, mozetta *or* mozzetta, amice, scarf, fanon *or* fannel, bands, chasuble, tunicle, dalmatic, alb *or* alba, stole; tonsure, cowl, hood, capuche, calotte; vagas *or* vakas *or* vakass; apron, lawn sleeves, pontificals, pall; miter *or* mitre, tiara, triple crown; shovel –, cardinal's– hat; biretta *or* berretta; crosier *or* crozier, cross staff, pastoral staff; Sanctus bell, sacring bell; seven-branched candlestick; monstrance; censer &c. 998; costume &c. 225.

1000. Temple. — N. TEMPLE, place of worship; house of God, house of prayer; cathedral, minster, church, kirk [*Scot. & dial. Eng.*], chapel, meeting-house, bethel, ebenezer [*Eng.*], conventicle, basilica, fane, holy place, chantry, oratory.

synagogue, tabernacle; mosque, masjid [*Moham.*]; dewal, kan-pati [*both Hindu*], girja [*Hind., Christian*]; pagoda, pagod [*archaic*], kiack [*Buddhist*]; Chinese temple, joss house [*colloq.*]; pantheon.

SHRINE, dagoba [*India*]; tope, stupa [*Buddhist*], Marabout [*Moham.*].

[INTERIOR] altar, sanctuary, Holy of Holies, *sanctum sanctorum* [*L.*], sacristy; sacrarium; communion –, holy –, Lord's– table; table of the Lord; pyx; baptistery, font; piscina; stoup; holy-water stoup, holy-water basin; ambry, aumbry [*archaic*]; sedile; reredos; rood screen, rood beam, chapel screen, jube; rood loft.

chancel, apse, choir, quire [*archaic*], nave, triforium, blindstory, aisle, transept, crypt, porch, cloisters; churchyard, golgotha; calvary, Easter sepulcher; stall, pew, seat, seating; pulpit, ambo, lectern, reading desk; confessional; prothesis, table (*or* altar) of prothesis, chapel of prothesis [*Eastern Ch.*]; credence, baldachin *or* baldaquin; belfry; vestry, chapter house; presbytery; diaconicon *or* diaconicum; mourners' bench, mourners' seat; anxious bench, anxious seat, penitent form.

MONASTERY, priory, abbey, friary, convent, nunnery, cloister.

PARSONAGE, rectory, vicarage, manse, deanery, clergy house; glebe; Vatican; bishop's palace; Lambeth.

Adj. CHURCHLY, claustral, cloistered, monastic, monasterial, monachal, conventual; cruciform.

*** *ne vile fano;* "there's nothing ill can dwell in such a temple" [*Tempest*]; "The hand that rounded Peter's dome And groined the aisles of Christian Rome Wrought in a sad sincerity; Himself from God he could not free; He builded better than he knew; — The conscious stone to beauty grew" [Emerson]; "Whilst love and terror laid the tiles" [*ibid.*].

INDEX GUIDE

IMPORTANT NOTE

The numbers following all references in this Index Guide refer to the *section numbers* in the text, and *not* to pages. Thus "Aaronic 995" refers to *section* 995, "Churchdom," under which the citation will be found. For further ease of reference, the *section* numbers will be found in bold type at the *top* of every page.

INDEX GUIDE

The numbers refer to the headings under which the words or phrases occur. **When the same** word or phrase can be used in various senses, the several headings under which it, or its synonyms, will be found are indicated by *Italics*. These words in Italics are not intended to explain the meaning of the word or phrase to which they are annexed, but only to assist in the required reference.

Italicized references within parentheses are merely suggestive, the parentheses indicating that the term itself is not included in the list referred to.

When the word given in the Index Guide is itself the title or heading of a category, the reference number is printed in bold-face type, thus: **abode 189**.

To keep the Index Guide — necessarily very large — from becoming unwieldy, a considerable number of obsolete, rare, foreign, dialectic, and slang terms has been omitted; for such words, while useful in the text, are not the ones for which synonyms would ordinarily be sought.

Derivatives likewise have been sparingly admitted, since the allied or basic term will serve as a key to the various derived forms; thus, *cold* is given, but not *coldness* and *coldly*. By such means, unnecessary duplication is avoided.

A

around 227
- it and about 573
- to 121
- to be 152
be - *busy with* 625
  active 682
beat - 629
come - 658
get - *public* 531
  recover 660
go - *turn* 311
going - *news* 532
put - *turn round* 283
round - 311
set - 676
turn - *invert* 218
what it is - 454
what one is - 625
above 206
- all *superior* 33
  important 642
- board *manifest* 525
  artless 703
  fair 939
- comprehension 519
- ground *alive* 359
- par *great* 31
  good 648
- praise 944
- price 814
- stairs 206
- suspicion 946
- the mark 33
- water *safe* 664
above-mentioned
  preceding 62
  repeated 104
  prior 116
abra 198
abracadabra 993
abrade [*see* abrasion]
Abraham,
  sham - 544
abrasion *paring* 38
  filing 330, 331
abrasive 331
abreast 216, 236
abregé 596
abreption 789
abridge *lessen* 36
  shorten 201
- *in writing* 572, 596
abridger 201
abridgment
  compendium 596
abroach 673
abroad *extraneous* 57
  distant 196
  uncertain 475
  astir 673
get - *public* 531
abrogation 756
abrupt *sudden* 113
  violent 173
  steep 217
  unexpected 508
  style 579
abruption 44
abscess 655
abscind 44
abscissa 466

abscission
  retrenchment 38
  division 44
abscond 623
absconder 808
absence
  nonpresence 187
- d'esprit 452
- of choice 609a
- of influence 175a
- of intellect 450a
- of mind 458
- of motive 615a
absent [*see* absence]
absentee 187
absent-minded 458
absinthe 435
absolute *not relative* 1
  great 31
  complete 52
  certain 474
  affirmative 535
  authoritative 737
  severe 739
  free 748
  unalienable 924
- establishment 478
- interest *property* 980
make - *confirm* 467
  adjudge 480
Absolute, the 450
absolution 918
absolutism 739
absolve *liberate* 750
  forgive 918
  exempt 927a
  shrive 952, 998
  acquit 970
absonant
  discordant 414
  unreasonable 477
absorb *combine* 48
  take in 296
  consume 677
- the mind
  attention 457
  inattention 458
- the soul 824
absorbed 451
absorbent 296 [*see*
  absorb]
absorbing *exigent* 630
  impressive 821
absorption 296
absquatulate 623
abstain *refrain* 623
  disuse 678
  temperance 953
- from action 681
- from voting 609a
abstainer 953, 958
abstemious 953
abstention 623
absterge 652
abstersive 662
abstinence [*see*
  abstain]
  total - 953, 955
abstract *separate* 44
  abridge 596
  take 789

  steal 791
- idea 453
- oneself
  inattention 458
- thought 451
  attention 457
in the - *apart* 44
  alone 87
abstracted
  inattentive 458
abstraction [*see*
  abstract]
abstruse 519
absurd [*see* absurdity]
- statement 546
absurdity
  impossible 471
  nonsense **497**
  ridiculous 853
abulia 605
Abuna 996
abundance 639
  poor in - 832
abundant *great* 31
  enough 639
abuse *deceive* 545
  illtreat 649
  misuse 679
  insolence 885
  malediction 908
  threat 909
  upbraid 932
  violate 961
- of language 563
- of terms 523
abusive
  discourteous 895
  defamatory 934, 936
abut *adjoin* 197
  touch 199
  rest on 215
abutment *defense* 717
abutter 199
aby *remain* 141
  endure 821, 826
abysm 198
abysmal *deep* 208
abyss *space* 180
  interval 198
  depth 208
  pitfall 667
  hell 982
acacia 367
academic *theory* 514
  teaching 537, 542
academical *style* 578
academician 492
  Royal - 559
academy 542
acanaceous 253
acanthophorous 253
acanthus 847
acariâtre 901
acarpous 169
acatalectic 597
acatastasia 139
acaudal 38
acaudate 38
accede *assent* 488
  submit 725
  consent 762

accelerate *early* 132
  stimulate 173
  velocity 274
  hasten 684
accension 384
accent *sound* 402
  tone of voice 580
  rhythm 597
accentuate 642
accentuated 581
accentuation 580
accept *assent* 488
  consent 762
  receive 785
  take 789
accepta 810
acceptable
  expedient 646
  agreeable 829
acceptance *security* 771
acceptation
  meaning 516
  interpretation 522
acception 522
access *approach* 286
  easy of - 705
  means of - 627
accessible *possible* 470
  easy 705
accession *increase* 35
  addition 37
- to office 737, 755
  consent 762
accessory *extrinsic* 6
  additive 37
  adjunct 39
  accompanying 88
  aid 707
  auxiliary 711
acciaccatura 413
accidence 567
accident *event* 151
  chance 156
  disaster 619
  misfortune 735
- of an accident 156
  fatal - 361
accidental *extrinsic* 6
  irrelative 10
  occasional 134
  fortuitous 156
  undesigned 621
accidentalism 156
Accipitres 739
acclamation *assent* 488
  approbation 931
  acclamatory 931
acclimatize
  domesticate 370
  inure 613
acclivity 217
accloy 641
accolade 894
accommodate *suit* 23
  adjust 27
  aid 707
  reconcile 723
  give 784
  lend 787
- oneself to
  conform 82

accommodating
kind 906
accommodation [*see* accommodate]
space 180
-train 272
accompaniment
adjunct 39
coexistence **88**
musical 415
accompanist 416
accompany *add* 37
coexist 88
concur 120
music 416
escort 664
accomplice 711
accomplish *execute* 161
complete 729
succeed 731
accomplishment
learning 490
talent 698
accompts 811
accord *uniform* 16
agree 23
music 413
assent 488
concord 714
grant 760
give 784
of one's own - 600, 602
accordance 23
according
-as *qualification* 469
-to *evidence* 467
-to circumstances 8
-to Gunter 82
-to law 963
-to rule
conformably 82
accordingly
logically 476
accordion 417
accordionist 416
accost 586
accouchement 161
accoucheur
minister 631
doctor 662
accoucheuse 662
account *list* 86
adjudge 480
description 594
credit 805
money - 811
fame 873
approbation 931
-as *deem* 484
-for *attribution* 155
interpret 522
-with *trade* 794
pay 807
call to -
censure 932
find one's - in
useful 644
success 731
make no - of
undervalue 483

despise 930
not - for
unintelligible 519
on - of *cause* 155
motive 615
behalf 707
on no - 536
send to one's -
kill 361
small - 643
take into -
attend to 457
qualify 469
to one's -
property 780
turn to -
improve 658
use 677
success 731
gain 775
accountable *liable* 177
debit 811
duty 926
accountant
treasurer 801
auditor 811
-general 801
accounting 811
accounts **811**
accouple 43
accouter 717
accouterment
dress 225
appliance 633
equipment 673
accoy 174
accredit
commission 755, 759
money 805
honor 873
accredited *believed* 484
recognized 613
- to 755, 759
accretion *increase* 35
coherence 46
accrimination 938
accroach 789
accrue *add* 37
result 154
acquire 775
be received 785, 810
accruement 775
accubation 213
accueil 894
accultural 658
acculturation 658
accumbent 213
accumulate *collect* 72
store 636
redundance 641
accumulation
[*see* accumulate]
increase 35
accurate 494
-knowledge 490
accurse 908
accursed
disastrous 649
undone 828
vicious 945
accusation **938**

accuse *disapprove* 932
charge 938
lawsuit 969
accustom *habit* 613
accustomary 613
ace *small quantity* 32
unit 87
aviator 269a
cards 840
within an - 197
aceldama *kill* 361
arena 728
acephalous 59
acequiador 350
acerb 397
acerbate *embitter* 659
aggravate 835
acerbic 955
acerbity *acrimony* 395
sourness 397
rudeness 895
spleen 900, 901
malevolence 907
acervate 72
acervatim 72, 102, 641
acescence 397
acetic 397
-acid 397
acetify 397
acetosity 397
acetous 397
acetum 397
achar 393
acharne 900
Achates, fidus -
friend 890
faithful 939
ache *cold* 383
physical 378
mental 828
Acheron
pit of - 982
achievable 470
achieve *end* 67
produce 161
do 680
accomplish 729
achievement
hatchment 550
sign 551
feat 861
Achillean 900
Achilles
- absent 187
heel of -
vulnerable 665
aching 383
achromatism **429**
achromatization 429
acicular 253
acid 397
acidify 397
aciform 253
acinaciform 253
acknowledge
answer 462
assent 488
disclose 529
avow 535
consent 762
observe 772

pay 807
thank 916
repent 950
reward 973
- the corn 529
acknowledged
custom 613
acme 210
- of perfection 650
acology 662
acolyte 996
acomia 846
aconite 663
acoumetry 602
acoustic 402, 418
- organs 418
acoustician 402
acoustics *sound* 402
hearing 418
acquaint
- oneself with 539
- with 527
acquaintance
knowledge 490
information 527
friend 890
make - with 888
acquest 780
acquiesce *assent* 488
willing 488
consent 762
tolerate 826
acquiescence
assent 488
submission 725
observance 772
acquire *develop* 161
get 775
receive 785
- a habit 613
- learning 539
acquirement
knowledge 490
learning 539
talent 698
receipt 810
acquisition
knowledge 490
gain **775**
acquisitive 775
acquit *liberate* 750
accounts 811
exempt 927a
vindicate 937
innocent 946
absolve 970
acquit oneself
behave 692
- of a debt 807
- of a duty 926
- of an obligation 772
acquittal **970**
acquittance *receipt* 771
acreage 180
acres *space* 180
land 342
property 780
Acres, Bob
coward 862
acrid *pungent* 392
unsavory 395

451

acridity *causticity* 171
  pungency 392
  unsavoriness 395
acrimony *physical* 171
  discourtesy 895
  hatred 898
  anger 900
  irascibility 901
  malevolence 907
acritude 395
acroama 490
acroamatic 490, 519
acrobat *strength* 159
  actor 599
  proficient 700
  mountebank 844
acrobatism 159
acropolis 666
acrospire 167
across *transverse* 219
  opposite 708
acrostic *letter* 561
  wit 842
act *imitate* 19
  physical 170
  - *of a play* 599
  personate 599
  voluntary 680
  statute 697
  - a part *feign* 544
  - one's part
    business 625
    duty 926
  - upon *physical* 170
    mental 615
    take steps 680
  - up to 772
  - well one's part 944
  - without authority
    738
  in the - *doing* 680
    guilt 947
acting *deputy* 759
actinic 420
actinology 420
actinometer 445
action *physical* 170
  voluntary **680**
  battle 720
  law 969
  line of - 692
  mix with - 170
  put in - 677
  suit the - to the word
    550, 599
  thick of the - 682
actionable 964
activate 171
active *physical* 171
  voluntary 682
  - service 722
  - thought 457
activity 682
actor *impostor* 548
  player 599
  agent 690
  affectation 855
Acts *record* 551
  Apostolic 985
actual *existing* 1
  present 118
  452

  real 494
  (identical 13)
actuality [*see* actual]
actualize 220
actuary 85, 811
actuate *influence* 175
  incite 615
acuity 253
aculeated 253
acumen 498
acuminated 253
acupuncture 260
acute *energetic* 171
  physically violent 173
  pointed 253
  physically   sensible
    375
  musical tone 410
  discriminative 465
  perspicacious 498
  cunning 702
  strong feeling 821
  morally painful 830
  - angle 244
  - ear 418
  - note 410
acutely 31
acuteness 465
A. D. 106
adactylism 848
adaga 727
adage 496
adagio *music* 415
  slow 275
Adam *sin* 945
adamant *strong* 159
  hard 323
Adam's ale 337
Adam's needle 253
adapt *agree* 23
  equalize 27
  - oneself to
    conform 82
adaptable
  conformable 82
  useful 644
adaptation [*see* adapt]
add *increase* 35
  join 37
  numerically 85
  accounts 811
addendum 39
adder 366, 913
  deafness 419
addict *habit* 613
adding machine 85
additament 39
addition [*see* add]
  adjunction **37**
  thing added 39
  arithmetical 85
addle *barren* 169
  incomplete 730
  abortive 732
  - the wits
    bewilder 475
    craze 503
addle-head 501
addle-headed 499
address *compose* 54
  residence 189

  direction 550
  speak to 586
  skill 698
  request 765
addressee 188
addresses
  courtship 902
adduce *bring to* 288
  evidence 467
adduct 288
adeem 789
adelomorphous 83
ademption 789
adenology 329
  intellectual 450
  proficient 698, 700
adept
adequate *power* 157
  sufficient 639
  for a purpose 644
  content 831
adespotic 738
adhere *stick* 46
  - to *persevere* 604a
    habit 613
  - to a duty 926
  - to an obligation 772
adherent 65, 711
adhesive *sticking* 46
  tenacious 327
  sticky 352
adhibit 677
adhortation 695
adiaphanous 426
adiathermancy 382
adieu *departure* 293
  loss 776
adipocere 356
adipose 355
adit *orifice* 260
  conduit 350
  passage 627
adjacent 197
adjection 37
adjective 39
  - jerker 593
adjoin *near* 197
  contact 199
adjourn *postpone* 133
  neglect 460
adjudge 480
adjudicate 480
adjunct *addition* 37
  thing added **39**
  accompaniment 88
  aid 707
  auxiliary 711
adjuration
  affirmation 535
  negation 536
adjure *request* 765
  promise 768
adjust *adapt* 23
  equalize 27
  regulate 58
  prepare 673
  settle 723
  - differences 774
adjustment 762, 774
adjutant *auxiliary* 711
  military 745

adjuvant *helping* 707
  auxiliary 711
admeasurement 466
administer *utilize* 677
  conduct 693
  exercise authority 737
  distribute 786
  - correction 972
  - oath 768
  - sacrament 998
  - to *aid* 707
  give 784
**administration of
  justice** 965
administrative
  official 737
  judicial 965
admirable *excellent* 648
  virtuous 944
admiral 745
Admiralty, court of -
  966
admiration *wonder* 870
  love 897
  respect 928
  approval 931
admirer 897
admissible *relevant* 23
  receivable 296
  tolerable 651
  - in society 852
admission [*see* admit]
admit *composition* 54
  include 76
  let in 296
  assent 488
  acknowledge 529
  permit 760
  concede 762
  accept 785
  - exceptions 469
  - of 470
admitted
  customary 613
  - maxim &c. 496
admixture 41
admonish *warn* 668
  advise 695
  reprove 932
admonitory 616
ado *activity* 682
  exertion 686
  difficulty 704
  make much - about
    important 642
  much - about nothing
    overestimate 482
    unimportant 643
    unskillful 699
adobe 635
adolescence **131**
Adonis 845
adonize 847
adopt *naturalize* 184
  choose 609
  appropriate 788
  - a cause *aid* 707
  - a course 692
  - an opinion 484
adoption *religious* 987
adore *love* 897

worship 990
adorn 847
adown 207
adrift *unrelated* 10
  disjoined 44
  dispersed 73
  uncertain 475
  unapt 699
  liberated 750
  go - *deviate* 279
  turn - *disperse* 73
  liberate 750
  dismiss 756
adroit 698
adscititious *extrinsic* 6
  added 37
  redundant 641
adulation 933
adulator 935
Adullam, cave of -
  desertion 624
  discontent 832
adult 131
adulterate *mix* 41
  deteriorate 659
adulterated *sham* 545
adulterer 962
adultery 961
adulthood 131
adultism 131
adumbrate
  darkness 421
  allegorize 521
  represent 554
adumbration
  semblance 21
  darkness 421
  allusion 526
aduncate 245
aduncity 244
adust *arid* 340
  heated 384
  brown 433
adustion 384
advance *increase* 35
  course 109
  progress 282
  assert 535
  improve 658
  aid 707
  succeed 731
  lend 787
  - against 716
  - agent 599
  - guard 234
  - of learning &c. 490
  - upon 303
  in - *precedence* 62
  front 234
  precession 280
  in - of
  superior 33
  in - of one's age 498
advanced 282
  - in life 128
  - work 717
advancement [*see*
  advance]
  infringement 303
advances, make -
  offer 763

social 892
advantage
  superiority 33
  increase 35
  influence 175
  benefit 618
  expedience 646
  - over *success* 731
  dressed to - 847
  find one's - in 644
  gain an - 775
  mechanical - 633
  set off to - 658
  take - of *use* 677
  make the most of
  698
advantageous
  beneficial 648
  profitable 775
advene 37
Advent 998
advent *futurity* 121
  event 151
  approach 286
  arrival 292
Adventist 984
adventitious
  extrinsic 6
  casual 156
adventive 156
adventure *event* 151
  chance 156
  pursuit 622
  danger 665
  trial 675
  undertaking 676
adventurer
  traveler 268
  experimenter 463
  deceiver 548
  gambler 621
  rash 863
  ignoble 876
adventures
  history 594
adventuress 548
adventurous
  undertaking 676
  bold 861
  rash 863
adversaria 551
adversary 710
Adversary, the - 978
adverse *contrary* 14
  opposed 708
  unprosperous 735
  disliking 867
  - party 710
adversity 735
advert 457
advertent 457
advertise 531
advice *notice* 527
  news 532
  counsel 695
  good - 695
advisable 646
advise *predict* 511
  inform 527
  counsel 695
  - with one's pillow 451

advised *predetermined*
  611
  intended 620
  better - 658
advisement *advice* 695
  [*see* advise]
  under - 453
adviser *teacher* 540
  counselor 695
advisory 527
advocacy
  approbation 931
advocate
  interpreter 524
  prompt 615
  recommend 695
  aid 707
  auxiliary 711
  friend 890, 914
  vindicate 937
  counselor 968
Advocate, the -
  Saviour 976
advocation *plea* 617
advoutress 962
advoutry 961
advowson 995
adynamic 160
adytum *room* 191
  prediction 511
  secret place 530
ædile 965
ægis 717
Æolian 349
  - harp 417
Æolus 349
æon 109, 110
aërate 334, 353
aëration 334
aërial *elevated* 206
  navigation 267, 273
  gas 334
  air 338
  - mail 534
  - mail-carrier 271
  - navigator 269
  - perspective 428
  - railway 840
aerie 189
aëriferous 334
aërification 334
aëriform 334
aërify 334
aëro 273
aëroboat 273
aërobus 273
aërodonetics 267
aërodrome 273
aërodynamics
  navigation 267
  gas 334
  wind 349
aërography 334, 349
aëro-hydroplane 273
aërolite 318
aërology *gaseity* 334
  air 338
  wind 349
aëromancy 511
aëromechanic 267, 334
aërometer 338

aërometric 338
aëronat 273
aëronaut 269a
aëronautic 273
  [*see* aëronautics]
aëronautics
  navigation 267
  air 338
aëroplane 273
  combatant 726
  by - 684
aëroplanist 269
aëroscope 338
aëroscopy 334
aërosphere 338
aërostat *balloon* 273
aërostatics 267 334
aërostation 338
aërotherapy 662
aëroyacht 273
aëry *gaseous* 334
  atmospheric 338
Æsculapius 662
Æsop 846
æsthetic *sensibility* 375
  beauty 845
  taste 850
æstival 125
æstivation 384
ætiology *causes* 155
  life 359
  knowledge 490
  disease 655
afar 196
afeard 860
affable
  condescending 879
  courteous 894
affair *event* 151
  topic 454
  business 625
  battle 720
  - of honor 720
affaires, chargé d' -
  758
affect *relate to* 9
  tend to 176
  qualify 469
  feign 544
  touch 824
  desire 865
  love 897
affectation 855
affected 583
  - manner 880
affected with
  feeling 821
  disease 655
affectibility 822
affecting *pathetic* 830
affection *feeling* 821
  love 897
affectionate 821, 897
affections 820
affettuoso *music* 415
affiance *promise* 768
  trust 858
affianced *love* 897
  marriage 903
affiche 531
affidation 769

affidavit
  affirmation 535
  record 551
  lawsuit 969
affiliation *relation* 9
  kindred 11
  attribution 155
affinal 11
affinitive 9
affinity *relation* 9
  similarity 17
affirmant 488
affirmation *evidence*
  467
  assent 488
  assert **535**
affirmative 535
affix *add* 37
  sequel 39
  fasten 43
  precedence 62
  letter 561
afflation 349
afflatus *wind* 349
  inspiration 985
afflict 830
  - *with illness* 655
affliction *pain* 828
  infliction 830
  adversity 735
affluence
  sufficiency 639
  prosperity 734
  wealth 803
affluent *river* 348
afflux 286
afford *supply* 784
  wealth 803
  yield 810
  sell for 812
  - *aid &c.* 707
affranchise
  make free of 748
  liberate 750
affray 720
affriction 331
affright 860
affront *molest* 830
  provocation 900
  insult 929
  - *danger* 861
affuse 337
affusion 73
afield 186
afire 382
afloat *extant* 1
  unstable 149
  going on 151
  ship 273
  navigation 267
  ocean 341
  news 532
  preparing 673
  keep oneself - 734
  set - *publish* 531
afoot *on hand* 625
  ready 673
  astir 682
afore 116
aforegoing 116
aforehand 116
454

afore-mentioned 62,
  116
aforesaid *preceding* 62
  repeated 104
  prior 116
aforesighted 116
aforethought 116, 611,
  907
aforetime 116
a fortiori
  superiority 33
  evidence 467
  reasoning 476
afraid 860
  - *to say uncertain* 4
  be - irresolute 605
afreet 980
afresh *repeated* 104
  new 123
African 431
Afric *heat* 382
Afrikander 57
aft 235
after *in order* 63
  in time 117
  too late 135
  rear 235
  pursuit 622
  - *all for all that* 30
  qualification 469
  on the whole 476
  - *time* 133
  be - intention 620
  pursuit 622
  go - follow 281
after acceptation 516
after-age 124
afterbirth 63
afterburden 63
afterclap 63, 154, 509
aftercome 65, 154
aftercrop 63, 154, 168
afterdamp 663
afterdinner 117
afterglow *decrement* 40a
  sequence 63
  light 420
aftergrass 63
aftergrowth 65, 154
afterlife 152
aftermath *sequence* 63
  effect 154
  fertile 168
  profit 775
afternoon 126
  - *farmer* 683
afterpain 63
after-part *sequel* 65
  rear 235
afterpiece 63, 599
aftertaste 63, 390
afterthought
  thought 451
  memory 505
  change of mind 607
aftertime 121, 133
afterwards 117
aga 745
again *duplicate* 90
  repeated 104
  - *and again* 136

come - *periodic* 138
against
  counteraction 179
  anteposition 237
  voluntary opposition
  708
  - *one's* expectation
  508
  - *one's will* 744
  - *one's wishes* 603
  - *the grain difficult*
  704
  painful 830
  dislike 867
  - *the stream* 704
  - *the time when* 510
  go - 708
agalloch 400
agamist 904
agape *opening* 260
  curious 455
  expectant 507
  wonder 870
agape *love feast* 998
Agapemone
  pleasure 827
  love 897
agate 847
age *time* 106
  period 108
  course 109
  long time 110
  present time 118
  oldness 124
  advanced life **128**
  from age to - 112
  of - 131
agency *physical* **170**
  instrumentality 631
  means 632
  employment 677
  voluntary action 680
  direction 693
  commission 755
agenda 625
  list of - 626
agent *physical* 153
  worker 686
  voluntary **690**
  consignee 758
  - *provocateur* 615
agentship 755
ages: - *ago* 122
  for - 110
agglomerate
  cohere 46
  assemble 72
agglutinate 46, 48
aggrandize
  in degree 35
  in bulk 194
  honor 873
aggravate
  increase 35
  vehemence 173
  exaggerate 549
  render worse 659
  distress 835
  exasperate 900
aggravating
  painful 830

aggravation **835**
aggregate
  whole 50
  collect 72
  number 84
aggregation 46
aggression 716
aggrieve *injure* 649
  distress 830
aggroup 72
aghast
  disappointed 509
  fear 860
  wonder 870
agile *swift* 274
  active 682
agio 813
agiotage 794
agitate *move* 315
  inquire 461
  activity 682
  excite the feelings 824
  - *a question* 476
agitation [see agitate]
  changeableness 149
  energy 171
  motion **315**
  in - *preparing* 673
agitator
  leader 694
aglet 554
aglow *warm* 382
  shine 420
agnate 11
agnition 762
agnomen 564
agnostic 487
agnosticism 451, 989
agnus Dei 998
ago 122
agog *expectant* 507
  desire 865
  wonder 870
  (*envious* 455)
agoing 682
  set - 707
agone 122
agonism 720
agonistic 159
agonize 972
agonizing
  thrilling 824
  painful 830
agony
  physical 378
  mental 828
  - *of death* 360
  - *of excitement* 825
agora 182
agoraphobia 860
agostadero 344
agrarian 371
agree *accord* 23
  concur 178
  assent 488
  concord 714
  consent 762
  compact 769
  compromise 774
  - *in opinion* 488
  - *with salubrity* 656

agreeable
  consistent 82
  physically 377
  consenting 762
  mentally 829
agreeably to
  conformably 82
agreement 23   [*see*
    agree]
  compact 769
agrestic 189, 371
agriculture 342, **371**
agriculturist 342
agronomics 342, 371
agronomist 371
agronomy 342, 371
aground *fixed* 150
  in difficulty 704
  failure 732
agua 337
aguardiente 959
ague 655
ague fit 860
agueweed 662
aguish *cold* 383
aha! *rejoicing* 838
ahead *in front* 234
  procession 280
  go - *progression* 282
Ahriman 978
aid *help* **707**
  charity 906
  - to memory 505
  by the - of
    instrument 631
    means 632
aidance 707
aid-de-camp
  auxiliary 711
  officer 745
aider [*see* aid]
aidless 160
aigrette 847
aiguille 253
aigulet 847
ail *sick* 655
  pain 828
aileron 267, 273
ailment 655
aim *direction* 278
  purpose 620
  essay 675
  - a blow at 716
  - high 305
aimable 278
aimless *without design*
  59, 621
  without motive 615a
air *unsubstantial* 4
  broach 66
  lightness 320
  gas 334
  atmospheric **338**
  wind 349
  tune 415
  appearance 448
  refresh 689
  fashionable 852
  fill the - 404
  fine - *salubrity* 656
  take - 531

air balloon 273
air bladder 334
air bubble 250
aircraft 273
air cruiser 273
air-drawn 515
air engine 633
air gun 727
air hole 260, 351
airing 266
air line 278
airman 269
airmanship 267, 698
air pipe 349, **351**
airplane 273
air pump 349
airs *affectation* 855
  pride 878
  vanity 880
  arrogance 885
air shaft 351
airship 273
air-tight 261
air tube 351
airward 206
airway 351
airwoman 269a
airworthy 273, 664
airy [*see* air]
  windy 349
  unimportant 643
  gay 836
  - hopes 858, 859
  - tongues 532
aisle *passage* 260
  way 627
  in a church 1000
ait 346
aitchbone 235
ajar *open* 260
  discordant 713
ajee 217
ajutage *opening* 260
  pipe 350
akimbo *angular* 244
  stand - 715
akin *related* 11
  similar 17
alabaster *white* 430
alack! 839
alacran 913
alacrity *willing* 602
  active 682
  cheerful 836
Aladdin's lamp 993
alameda 189
alar 39
alarm *warning* 668
  notice of danger **669**
  fear 860
  cause for - 665
  give an - *indicate* 550
alarmist 862
alarum *loudness* 404
  indication 550
  notice of danger 669
alas! 839
alate 39
alb 999
alba 999
Albany beef 298

Albany hemp 663
albata 430, 545
albatross 366
albeit 30
alberca 343
albescence 430
albication 430
albification 430
albinism 430
albino 443
albinoism 430
Alborah 271
album *book* 593
  compendium 596
albumen
  semiliquid 352
  protein 161, 357
albumin 357
albuminoid 357
Alcaic 597
alcaid 745
alcalde 745, 967
alchemy 144
alcohol 959
alcoholism 959
Alcoran 986
alcove *bower* 191
  hollow 252
Aldebaran 423
alder 367
alderman 745
Alderney 366
ale 298
Alecto 173
alectromancy 511
alehouse 189
  go to the - 959
alembic *conversion* 144
  vessel 191
  furnace 386
  laboratory 691
alert *watchful* 459
  active 682
alerte 669
alertness 457
aleuromancy 511
Alexandrian school 451
Alexandrine
  ornate style 577
  verse 597
  (*length* 200)
alexandrite 847
alexipharmic 662
alexiteric 662
alfalfa 367
alfilaria 367
alfresco 220
algæ 367, 369
algebra 85
algebraist 85
algid 383
algidity 383
algology 369
algorism 85
algorithm 85
alguazil 965
alias 18, 565
alibi 187
alien *irrelevant* 10
  foreign 57
  transfer 783

  gentile 989
alienable 783
alienage 57
alienate *disjoin* 44
  transfer 783
  estrange 889
  set against 898
alienation
  mental - 503
aliéné 503
alienism 57
alight *stop* 265
  arrive 292
  descend 306
  on fire 382
align *horizontal* 213
  direction 278
aligned 216
alike 17
aliment *food* 298
  (*materials* 635)
alimentary
  regimen 662
alimentation *aid* 707
alimony *property* 780
  provision 803
  income 810
aliquot *part* 51
  number 84
alive *living* 359
  sentient 375
  intelligent 498
  active 682
  cheerful 836
  - to *attention* 457
  cognizant 490
  informed 527
  able 698
  sensible 822
  - to impressions 375
  - with 102
  keep - *continue* 143
aljibar 636
alkahest 335
alkali 344
all *whole* 50
  complete 52
  generality 78
  - aboard 293
  - absorbing 642
  - agog 865
  - along 106
  - along of 154
  - at once 113
  - but 32
  - colors 440
  - considered
    thought 451
    judgment 480
  - day long 110
  - ears 418
  - eyes and ears 457
  - fours *easy* 705
    cards 840
  - hail! *welcome* 292
  honor to 873
  celebration 883
  courtesy 894
  - hands *everybody* 78
  - in 688
  - in all 50

- in good time 152
- in one's power 686
- manner of *different* 15
multiform 81
- one *equal* 27
indifferent 866
- out *completely* 52
error 495
- over *end* 67
universal 78
destruction 162
space 180
- powerful
mighty 159
God 976
completely 52
truly 494
- right! 922
- sorts *diverse* 16a
mixed 41
multiform 81
- talk 4
- the better 831
- the go 852
- the rage 852
- the time 106
- things to all men 894
- ways *distortion* 243
deviation 279
at - events *compensation* 30
qualification 469
true 494
resolve 604
at - points 52
at - times 136
in - ages 112
in - directions 278
in - quarters 180
on - hands 488
on - sides 227
Allah 976
allay *moderate* 174
pacify 723
relieve 834
- excitability 826
all-destroying 162
all-devouring 162
allective 615
allege *evidence* 467
assert 535
plea 617
allegiance
obedience 743
duty 926
allegorization 521
allegory
similitude 464
metaphor 521
allegresse 836
allegro *music* 415
cheerful 836
alleluia 990
all-embracing 56
all-engulfing 162
alleviate *moderate* 174
relieve 834
alley *court* 189
passage 260
way 627

Alhallowmas 138
alliance *relation* 9
kindred 11
physical coöperation 178
voluntary coöperation 709
party 712
union 714
allied 48
- to *like* 17
alligation 43
alligator 366, 913
- pear 298
alliteration
similarity 17
repetition 104
style in writing 577
all-knowing 976
allness 52
allocation 60, 786
allocution **586**
allodium *free* 748
property 780
allopathy 662
alloquy 586
allot *arrange* 60
distribute 786
due 924
allow *assent* 488
admit 529
permit 760
consent 762
give 784
allowable
permitted 760
due 924
allowance
qualification 469
gift 784
allotment 786
discount 813
salary 973
make - for *forgive* 918
vindicate 937
with grains of - 485
alloy *mixture* 41
combine 48
solution 335
debase 659
all-possessed 503
All Saints' Day 138
all-searching 461
all-seeing 976
all-sided 52
All Souls' Day 138
allspice 393
all-star 599
all-sufficient 159
allude *hint* 514
mean 516
refer to 521
latent 526
inform 527
allure *move* 615
create desire 865
alluring
pleasurable 829
allusion 516
allusive 9
alluvial *level* 213

land 342
plain 344
alluvion 270, 348
alluvium *deposit* 40
land 342
soil 653
all-wise 976
ally *combine* 48
auxiliary 711
friend 890
Alma Mater 542
almanac
chronometry 114
record 86, 551
- de Gotha 86
almighty 157
Almighty, the - 976
almond 298
almoner *giver* 784
treasurer 801
church officer 996
almonry 801
almost *nearly* 32
not quite 651
- all 50
- immediately 132
alms *gift* 784
benevolence 906
worship 990
almshouse 189, 666
almsman 785
Alnaschar's dream
imagination 515
hope 858
alod 748
aloes 395
aloes wood 400
aloft 206
alogy 497
alone *single* 87
unaided 706
let - *not use* 678
not restrain 748
never less - 893
along 200
- with *added* 37
together 88
by means of 631
get - *progress* 282
go - *depart* 293
go - with *concur* 178
assent 488
coöperate 709
alongside *near* 197
parallel 216
laterally 236
aloof *distant* 196
high 206
secluded 893
stand - *inaction* 681
refuse 764
cautious 864
aloofness 893
alopecia 226
aloud 404
think - *soliloquy* 589
naiveté 703
Alp 206
alpenstock 215
Alpha 66
- and Omega 50

alphabet
beginning 66
letters 561
alphabetarian 541
alphabetize 60
alphitomancy 511
alpine *high* 206
Alpine Club
traveler 268
ascent 305
already
antecedently 116
even now 118
past time 122
Alsatia *thieving* 791
Alsatian *den* 945
also 37
altar *marriage* 903
church 1000
alter 140
emasculate 158
- one's course 279
- the case 468
alterable 149
alterant 662
alteration
correlation 12
difference 15
alterative
remedy 662
altercation 713
altered *worn* 688
- for the worse 659
alter ego *similar* 17
auxiliary 711
deputy 759
friend 890
alternacy 138
alternate
reciprocal 12
vary 20a
sequence 63
discontinuous 70
periodic 138
substitute 147, 634
changeable 149
oscillate 314
alternation 148
alternative
substitute 147
choice 609
plan 626
although
compensation 30
counteraction 179
unless 469
(*opposition* 708)
altiloquence 577
altimeter 206
altimetry *height* 206
angle 244
measurement 466
altitude *height* 206
- and azimuth 466
alto 410, 415
hill 206
altogether
collectively 50
entirely 52
the - 50, 226
alto - rilievo

convex 250
sculpture 557
altruism 910, 942
altruist 906
alum 397
alumina 324
alumnus 541
alveary 370, 691
alveolate 252
alveolus 252
always *uniformly* 16
generally 78
during 106
perpetually 112
habitually 613
a. m. 125
amadou 388
amah 746, 753
amain *violence* 173
haste 684
amalgam, -ate
mixture 41
compound 48
amanuensis
recorder 553
secretary 590
amaranthine 112
amaritude 395
amass *whole* 50
collect 72
store 636
amassment 72
amateur
willingness 602
taste 850
votary 865
amateurish 643
amatory 897
amaurosis 442
amaze 870
amazement 508
amazingly 31
Amazon
warrior 726
courage 861
ambage
convolution 248
circumlocution 573
circuit 629
ambagious
winding 248
diffuse 573
ambassador
interpreter 524
messenger 534
representative 758
deputy 759
amber 356a
- *color* 436
ambergris 356a
ambidexter
right and left 238
fickle 607
clever 698
ambient 227
ambiguous
uncertain 475
unintelligible 519
equivocal 520
obscure 571
ambilevous 239

ambilogy 520
ambiloquy 520
ambit 230, 311
ambition
intention 620
desire 865
ambitious
[*see* ambition]
amble *pace* 266
slowness 275
ambo *school* 542
pulpit 1000
alike 17
friends 890
bad men 949
ambrosia 298
ambrosial *savory* 394
fragrant 400
ambulance
vehicle 272
hospital 662
ambulation 266
ambuscade 530
ambush *shade* 424
hiding **530**
pitfall 667
lie in - 528
ambustion 384
âme damnée
catspaw 711
servant 746
servile 886
bad man 949
ameer 875
ameliorate 658
amen *assent* 488
submission 725
content 831
amenable *liable* 177
docile 602
answerable 926
amend *improve* 658
repent 950
amendatory 30
amendment 658
18th - 761
amends
compensation 30
atonement 952
reward 973
amenity *pleasing* 829
courtesy 894
amentia 503
amerce 974
American 188
- *organ* 417
- *plan* 298
Americanism 563
Americanize 563
amethyst *purple* 437
jewel 847
amethystine 437
amiable *pleasing* 829
courteous 894
loving 897
kind 906
amianthoid 385
amianthus 385
amicable *assisting* 707
friendly 888
amice 999

amidships 68
amidst *mixed with* 41
between 228
amiss 619
come - *disagree* 24
mistime 135
inexpedient 647
do - 945
go - 732
nothing comes - 823
take - *dislike* 867
resent 900
amity *concord* 714
peace 721
friendship 888
ammeter 157, 272
ammonia 334, 387
ammonite 248
ammunition
materials 635
war 727
amnesia 506
amnesty
pacification 723
forgiveness 506, 918
amœba 193, 357
amœbæic 597
amœbean 63
amœbic 193
amœbiform 81
amœboid 193
amole 356
among *mixed with* 41
between 228
amorist 897
amoroso 599
amorous 897
- *glances* 902
amorphism **241**
amorphous *irregular* 83
formless 241
amortization 784
amotion 270
amount *quantity* 25
degree 26
sum of money 800
price 812
- to *equal* 27
number 85
gross - 50
amour *love* 897
intrigue 961
- *propre* 880
amourette 897
amphibians 368
amphibious 83
amphibology 520
Amphictyonic council
696
amphigory 497, 853
amphitheater
prospect 441
school 542
theater 599
arena 728
Amphitryon 890
amphora 191
ample *much* 31
spacious 180
large 192
broad 202

copious 639
content 831
amplify *expand* 194
exaggerate 549
diffuse style 573
amplitude
quantity 25
degree 26
size 192
breadth 202
enough 639
amputate 38
amuck
run - *kill* 361
attack 716
excite 825
amulet *talisman* 747
charm 993
amuse *please* 298
divert 840
amusement **840**
place of - 840
amylaceous 352
an *if* 514
ana 594, 596
Anabaptist 984
anachronism
false time **115**
inopportune 135
error 495
anachronize 115
anacoluthon 70
anaconda 913
anacreontic 597
anacrusis 597
anæmia 160
anæmic 429
anæsthesia
insensibility 376
numbness 381
inactivity 683
anæsthetist 662
anæsthetize 376, 662
anaglyph
representation 554
sculpture 557
anagoge
metaphor 521
latency 526
anagram
double sense 520
secret 533
letter 561
wit 842
play - 561
anagrammatism 520,
533
anagrammatize 520
analecta 596
analeptic 662
analgesia 823
analogy *relation* 9
similarity 17
analysis
decomposition 49
arrangement 60
algebra 85
inquiry 461
experiment 463
reasoning 476
grammar 567

compendium 596
analyst
 investigator 461
 experimenter 463
analytical [*see* analysis]
analyze *grammar* 567
 describe 594
 [*see* analysis]
anamorphoscope 555
anamorphosis
 distortion 243
 optical 443
 misrepresentation
 555
anapest 597
anaphrodisia 174, 866
anarch 710
anarchist
 opponent 710
 insurgent 742
 enemy 891
 evil doer 913
anarchy *disorder* 59
 social 738
anastatic printing 558
anastomosis
 junction 43
 crossing 219
anastomotic 219
anastrophe 218
anathema 908
anathematize *curse* 908
 censure 932
 detract 934
anatomize *dissect* 44
 investigate 461
anatomy
 dissection 44
 leanness 203
 texture 329
 science 357
 comparative - 368
anatripsis 331
anatriptic 331
ancestor 69, 166
ancestral
 bygone 122
 old 124
 aged 128
ancestry 69, 166
anchor *connection* 45
 stop 265
 safeguard 666
 check 706
 hope 858
 at - *fixed* 150
 stationed 184
 safe 664
 cast - *settle* 184
 arrive 292
 sheet - *means* 632
anchorage
 location 184
 roadstead 189
 refuge 666
anchored *fixed* 150
anchoretic 893
anchorite *recluse* 893
 ascetic 955
ancien régime 875
ancient *old* 124
458

flag 550
- *mariner* 269
- *times* 122
ancientness 122
ancillary 707
ancon 342
and *addition* 37
 accompaniment 88
andante 415
andiron 386
androgynous 83
androlepsia 789
androtomy 372
anecdote 594
anecdotist 594
anele 998
anemograph 349
anemography 349
anemology 349
 anemometer
 wind 349
 measure 466
 record 551
anemometrograph 349
anemometry 349
anemone 845
anemoscope 349
anent 9
aneroid 338, 340
anew *again* 104
 newly 123
anfractuosity 248
angel *messenger* 534
 backer 599, 711
 object of love 897
 good person 948
 supernatural being
 977
 bishop 996
- of death 360
 fallen - *bad man* 949
 devil 978
 guardian - *safety* 664
 auxiliary 711
 benefactor 912
angelic 944
angelus 550
anger 900
angina pectoris 655
angiology 329
angle 244
 point of view 448
 try 463
 at an - 217
angle rafter 215
Anglican *sectarian*
 984
 ecclesiastical 995
Anglicanism 984
Anglice 563
Anglicism 563
angling 622
Anglophobia 898
angry [*see* anger]
anguiform 248
anguilliform
 filament 205
 serpentine 248
anguilloid 248
anguillous 248
anguine 366

anguish *physical* 378
 moral 828
angular 244
- *velocity* 264
angularity 244
angustation 203
anhedonia 828, 837
anhelation 688
anhydrate 340, 670
anhydration 340
anhydric 340
anhydrous 340
anility *age* 128
 imbecility 499
anima 359
- *bruta* 359
- *divina* 359
- *mundi* 359
animadvert
 attend to 457
 reprehend 932
animal 366
- *cries* 412
- *economy* 359
- *gratification* 377
- *life* 364
- *magnetism* 992a
- *physiology* 368
- *spirits* 836
 female - 364
animalcular 193
animalcule
 minute 193
 animal 366
animalism
 animality 364
 sensuality 954
animality 364
animalization 364
animastic 450
animate *induce* 615
 excite 824
 enliven 836
animation *life* 359
 animality 364
 activity 682
 vivacity 836
 suspended - 823
animative 359
animism 317, 984
animist 317
animosity *dislike* 867
 enmity 889
 hatred 898
 anger 900
animus
 willingness 602
 intention 620
 desire 865
ankle 244
- deep *deep* 208
 shallow 209
anklet 847
ankus 615
ankylosis 150
annalist
 chronologist 115
 recorder 553
annals *chronology* 114
 record 551
 account 594

annatto 434
anneal 673
annex *add* 37, 39
 join 43
annexationist 43
annexe 39
annihilate *extinguish* 2
 destroy 162
anniversary 138, 883
anno 106
annotation
 explanation 522
 note 550
annotator *scholar* 492
 interpreter 524
 commentator 595
annotto 434
announce *herald* 116
 predict 511
 inform 527
 publish 531
 assert 535
announcement
 [*see* announce]
annoy *molest* 649, 907
 disquiet 830
annoyance 828
 source of - 830
annual *periodic* 138
 plant 367
 book 593
annuity 810
annul *destroy* 162
 abolish 756
annular 247
annularity 249
annulet 247
annunciate *inform* 527
 (*publish* 531)
Annunciation, the - 990
annunciative 527
annunciator 527
annunciatory 531
anodyne *lenitive* 174
 remedial 662
 relief 834
anoint *coat* 223
 lubricate 332
 oil 355
Anointed, the 976
anointment
 lubrication 332
 oil 355
anomalous 241
anomaly *disorder* 59
 irregularity 83
anon 132
anonymous 565
anopsia 442
anorexy 866
another *different* 15
 repetition 104
- *time* 119
answer
 to an inquiry **462**
 confute 479
 solution 522
 succeed 731
 pecuniary profit 775
 pleadings 969
- *for* *deputy* 759

promise 768
go bail 806
- one's turn 644
- the helm 743
- the purpose 731
- to *correspond* 9
require an - 461
answerable
  agreeing 23
  liable 177
  bail 806
  duty 926
  censurable 392
ant 366, 690
Antæus *strength* 159
  size 192
antagonism
  difference 14
  physical 179
  voluntary 708
  enmity 889
antagonist 710
antagonistic 24
antaphrodisiac 866
antarctic 237, 383
ante 621
  expend 809
- up 809
antecedence
  in order 62
  in time 116
antecedent 64
antechamber 191
antedate 115
antediluvian 124
antelope 274, 360
antemundane 124
antenna 379
antepast 510
anteposition 62
anterior
  in order 62
  in time 116
  in place 234
- to *reason* 477
anteroom 191
antevert 706
anthelion 423
anthelmintic 662
anthem 990
anthemion 847
antherozoid 357
anthology *writing* 590
  book 593
  collection 596
  poem 597
  store 636
anthracite 388
anthrax 655
anthropod 193
anthropogeny 372
anthropoid 372
anthropology
  zoölogy 368
  mankind 372
anthropomancy 511
anthropomorphism 984
anthropophagus 913
anthroposcopy 511
anthroposophy 372
anthropotomy 372

antic 840
antichristian
  heterodox 984
  irreligious 989
antichronism 115
anticipant 120
anticipate
  anachronism 115
  priority 116
  future 121
  early 132
  expect 507
  foresee 510
  prepare 673
  hope 858
  caution 864
anticipation 120
  [*see* anticipate]
anticlimax
  decrease 36
  bathos 497, 853
anticlinal 217
anticyclone 265
antidote 662
antigropelos 225
antifebrile 662
antilogarithm 84
antilogy 477
antiluetic 662
antimacassar 223
antimony 663
Antinomian 984
antinomy 964
Antinous 845
antiorgastic 174
antiparallel 217
antipathy
  contrariety 14
  dislike 867
  hate 898
antiphon *music* 415
  answer 462
  worship 990
antiphonal 462
antiphrasis 563
antipodes
  difference 14
  distance 196
  contraposition 237
antipoison 662
antiquary
  past times 122
  scholar 492
  historian 553
antiquated *aged* 128
  (*out of fashion* 851)
antique 124
antiquity 122
antiscriptural 984
antiseptic 662
antisocial 911
antispasmodic 174, 662
antispast 597
antistrophe 597
antithesis *contrast* 14
  difference 15
  contraposition 237
  style 577
antithesize 14
antitype 22
antler 253

antonomasia
  metaphor 521
  nomenclature 564
antrum 252
anvil *conversion* 144
  support 215
  on the -
  intended 620
  in hand 625, 730
  preparing 673
anxiety *solicitude* 459
  pain 828
  fear 860
  desire 865
anxious [*see* anxiety]
  - bench 1000
  - expectation 507
  - meeting 1000
  - seat 1000
any *some* 25
  part 51
  no choice 609a
  at - rate *certain* 474
  true 494
  at all hazards 604
anybody 78
anyhow *careless* 460
  in some way 627
aorist 109, 119
aorta 350
apace *early* 132
  swift 274
Apache 913
apache *assassin* 361
aparejo 215
apart *irrelative* 10
  separate 44
  singleness 87
  soliloquy 589
  set - 636
  wide - 196
apartment 191
  - house 189
  -s to let
  imbecile 450a, 499
apathetic 275
apathy *incuriosity* 456
  insensibility 823
  irreligion 989
ape *monkey* 366
  imitate 19
aperient 652, 662
apéritif 394
aperture 260
apery 19
apex *height* 206
  summit 210
aphelion 196
aphid 366, 659
Aphis 659
aphonic 403, 581
aphonia 581
aphorism 496
aphrodisia 173, 961
aphrodisiac 865
Aphrodite 845
apiarism 370
apiarist 370
apiary 370
apical 210
apiculate 253

apiculture 370
apiece 79
apish 19, 499
apishamore 223
aplomb *stability* 15C
  verticality 212
  self-possession 498
  resolution 604
Apocalypse 985
Apocrypha 985
apocryphal
  uncertain 475
  erroneous 495
  heterodox 984
apodeictic 478
apodeixis 478
apodosis 67
apograph 21
apolaustic 377
Apollo *sun* 318
  music 416
  luminary 423
  beauty 845
  - Musagetes 416
  magnus - *sage* 500
  adviser 695
apologue *metaphor* 521
  teaching 537
  description 594
apology *substitution* 147
  excuse 617
  vindication 937
  penitence 950
  atonement 952
apophthegm 496
apophysis 250
apoplexy 158
aporia 475
apostasy
  recantation 607
  dishonor 940
  heterodoxy 984
  impiety 988
apostate *convert* 144
  turncoat 607
  seceder 742
  heretic 984
  (*recreant* 941)
apostatize 607
apostle *teacher* 540
  disciple 541
  inspired 985
  -'s creed 983a
apostolic 985
  - church 983a
  - see 995
apostrophe
  typography 550
  address 586
  soliloquy 589
  appeal 765
apostrophize 765
apothecary 662
  -'s weight 319
apothegm 496
apotheosis
  resuscitation 163
  heaven 981
  hero worship 991
apozem *liquefy* 335
  fuse 384

459

curve 245
gateway 260
Arcadia
  pleasure 827
  paradise 981
Arcadian
  pastoral 371
  artless 703
  innocent 946
arcanum 533
arch *great* 31
  support 215
  curve 245
  convex 250
  concave 252
  clever 498
  cunning 702
  triumphal -
   trophy 733
  celebration 883
archæologist
  antiquary 122
  scholar 492
archæology 122
archaic *old* 124
archaism *past times* 122
  obsolete phrase 563
archangel 977
archbishop 996
archbishopric 995
archdeacon 996
archduchy 181
archduke 745
archdukedom 180
archebiosis 161
arched roof 245
archenemy, the - 978
archer 726, 840
archery 840
Arches, court of -
  tribunal 966
  churchdom 995
archetypal 20
archetype 22, 453
Archeus 359
archfiend 978
archiater 695
archiepiscopal 995
archigenesis 161, 357
archipelago 346
architect
  constructor 164
  agent 690
architectonic 161
architecture
  arrangement 60
  construction 161
  fabric 329
  ornament 847
architrave 210
archive 551
archlute 417
archon *ruler* 745
  deputy 759
  judge 967
archtraitor 941
archlike 245
arctic *northern* 237
  cold 383
arctics 225
arcuation 245

ardent *fiery* 382
  eager 682
  feeling 821
  loving 897
  - expectation 507
  - imagination 515
ardor *vigor* 574
  activity 682
  feeling 821
  desire 865
arduous 704
area 181, 182
arefaction 340
arefy 340
arena *space* 180
  region 181
  field of view 441
  field of battle **728**
arenaceous 330
arenosity 330
areola 247
areolar 219
areometer 321
Areopagus 966
ares 180
arescent 340
aretaics 944
arête 253
aretology 926, 944
Argand lamp 423
argent 430
argentine 430
argil 324
argillaceous 324
argol 653
argosy 273
argot 563
argue *evidence* 467
  reason 476
  indicate 550
argufy 476
argument *topic* 454
  discussion 476
  meaning 516
  have the best of an -
   478
Argus-eyed *sight* 441
  vigilant 459
argute 498
aria *composition* 54
  music 415
Arianism 984
arid *unproductive* 169
  dry 340
  uninteresting 841
Ariel *courier* 268
  swift 274
  messenger 534
  spirit 979
arietation 276
arietta 415
aright *well* 618
  (*skillful* 698)
ariolation 511
ariose 413, 415
arise *exist* 1
  begin 66
  happen 151
  mount 305
  appear 446
  - from 154

aristate 253
aristocracy *power* 737
  nobility 875
aristocrat 875
aristocratic 852
Aristotelian 476
Aristotelianism 451
arithmancy 511
arithmetic 85
ark *abode* 189
  asylum 666
  boat 273
arm *part* 51
  power 157
  instrument 633
  provide 637
  prepare 673
  war 722
  weapon 727
  - in arm
   together 88
   friends 888
   sociable 892
  - of the law 963
  - of the sea 343
  make a long - 200
armada 726
armadillo 366
Armageddon 361, 720
armament
  preparation 673
  arms 727
armchair 215
armed *defence* 717
  - at all points 673
  - force 664, 726
armet 717
armful 25
armiger 875
armigerous 722
armillary sphere 466
armipotent 157
armistice *cessation* 142
  deliverance 672
  pacification 723
armless 158
armlet *ring* 247
  gulf 343
armor *defense* 717
  arms 727
  buckle on one's - 673
armorial 550
armor-plated 223
armory *assembly* 189
  store 636
  workshop 691
arms **727** [*see* arm]
  heraldry 550
  war 722
  honors 877
  clash of - 720
  deeds of - 720
  in - *infant* 129
  under - 722
  up in - *active* 682
  discord 713
  resistance 719
  resentment 900
  enmity 889
arm's length
  at - 19²

keep at -
  repel 289
  defense 717
  enmity 889
  seclusion 893
  discourtesy 895
Armstrong gun 727
army *collection* 72
  multitude 102
  troops 726
  - list 86
arnica 662
aroint *begone* 297
  malediction 908
aroma 400
aromatize 400
around 227
  lie - 220
arouse *move* 615
  excite 824
  - oneself 682
arpeggio 413
arpent 180, 200
arquebus 727
arquebusade 662
arraign *accuse* 938
  indict 969
arrange
  set in order 60
  organize 357
  plan 626
  compromise 774
  (*prepare* 673)
  - in a series 69
  - itself 58
  - matters
   pacify 723
  - music 416
  - under 76
arrangement
  [*see* arrange]
  painting 556
  temporary - 111
arrant *identical* 31
  manifest 525
  notorious 531
  bad 649
  disreputable 874
  base 940
arras 847
arrastra 330
array *order* 58
  arrangement 60
  series 69
  assemblage 72
  multitude 102
  dress 225
  prepare 673
  adorn 847
  ostentation 882
  battle - 722
arrear, in -
  incomplete 53
  nonpayment 808
arrears *debt* 806
arrest *stop* 142
  restrain 751
  in law 963
  - the attention 457
arrière pensée
  afterthought 65

461

mental reservation
528
motive 615
set purpose 620
arriero 694
arrish 168
arrival 292
arrive *happen* 151
reach 292
complete 729
(*stop* 142)
- at a conclusion 480
- at an understanding
488
- at the truth 480*a*
arroba 319
arrogance
[*see* arrogant]
arrogant *severe* 739
proud 878
insolent 885
arrogate *assume* 885
claim 924
- to oneself
undue 925
arrondissement 181
arrosion 331
arrow *swift* 274
missile 284
arms 727
arrowhead *form* 253
writing 590
arrow-shaped 253
arroyo 350
arsenal *store* 636
workshop 691
(*arms* 727)
arsenic 663
arsenious oxide 663
arson 384
art *representation* 554
business 625
skill 698
cunning 702
(*deception* 545)
- gallery 556
- museum 556
- school 542
fine - 850
perfection of - 650
work of -
beauty 845
ornament 847
arteriosclerosis 655
artery *conduit* 350
channel 627
artesian well 343
artful *deceitful* 544
cunning 702
- dodge 545, 702
arthritis 655
arthropoda 368
artichoke 298
article *thing* 3
part 51
matter 316
chapter 593
review 595
goods 798
articled clerk 541
articles

- of agreement 770
- of faith
belief 484
theology 983
thirty-nine - 983*a*
articulates 368
articulation
junction 43
speech 580
articulo, in -
transient 111
dying 360
artifice *plan* 626
cunning 702
(*deception* 545)
artificer 690
artificial
fictitious 545
cunning 702
affected 855
- language 579
- light 420
artillery
explosion 404
arms 727
- of words 562
artilleryman 726
artisan 690
artist *painter* &c. **559**
contriver 626
agent 690
artiste *music* 416
drama 599
artistic *skillful* 698
beautiful 845
taste 850
- language 578
artistry 569
Artium - Baccalaureus
492
- Magister 492
artless 703
artlessness
natural **703**
(*veracious* 543)
arundinaceous 253
aruspex 513
aruspicy 511
as *motive* 615
- broad as long 27
- can be 52
- good as 27
- if *similar* 17
suppose 514
- it may be
circumstance 8
event 151
chance 156
- it were *similar* 17
metaphor 521
- little as may be 32
- much again 90
- soon as 120
- they say
proverb 496
news 532
- things are 7
- things go *event* 151
habit 613
- to 9
- usual 82

- you were 283
- well as 37
asafetida 395, 401
asbestic 385
asbestos 385
ascend *be great* 31
increase 35
rise 305
improve 658
ascendancy
power 157
influence 175
success 731
ascendant
in the -
influence 175
important 642
success 731
authority 737
repute 873
lord of the - 745
one's star in the -
prosperity 734
ascension
[*see* ascend]
calefaction 384
Ascension Day 998
ascent [*see* ascend]
gradient 217
rise **305**
glory 873
ascertain *fix* 150
determine 480
ascertained
certain 474
known 490
ascertainment 480*a*
ascetic 955
asceticism 953, **955**
ascititious
intrinsic 6
additional 37
supplementary 52
ascribe 155
ascription [*see* ascribe]
aseptic 662
ash 367, 384
- blond 429
- colored 432
ashamed 879, 881
ash cake 298
ashen 429
ashes *corpse* 362
dirt 653
lay in - 162
pale as -
colorless 429
fear 860
ashore 342
go - *arrive* 292
Ash Wednesday 138
ashy 429
Asian mystery 533
aside *laterally* 236
whisper 405
private 528
- from the purpose 10
say - 589
set - *displace* 185
neglect 460
negative 536

reject 610
disuse 678
abrogate 756
discard 782
step - 279
asinine *ass* 271
fool 499
ask *inquire* 461
request 765
for sale 794
price 812
(*invoke* 990)
- leave 760
askance 217
eye - *fear* 860
look - *vision* 441, 443
dissent 489
dislike 867
disapproval 932
asked in church 903
askew *oblique* 217
distorted 243
asking [*see* ask]
aslant 217
asleep 683
aslope 217
Asmodeus 978
asomatous 317
asp *animal* 366
evil doer 913
asparagus 298, **367**
Aspasia 962
aspect *feature* 5
state 7
situation 183
appearance 448
aspen leaf
shake like an -
motion 315
fear 860
asperges 998
aspergillum 337
asperity
roughness 256
discourtesy 895
anger 900
irascibility 901
asperse 934
aspersion
nonassemblage 73
cleanness 652
malediction 908
rite 998
asphalt *smooth* 255
resin 356*a*
asphodel 845
asphyxia 360
asphyxiate 361
aspirant *candidate* 767
desire 865
aspirate 402, 580
aspirated 681
aspire *rise* 305
project 620
hope 858
desire 865
worship 990
asportation 270
asquint 217
ass *beast of burden* 271
fool 501

- 's bridge
  unintelligible 519
  cheat 548
  bungler 701
  make an - of
  delude 545
assafetida 401
assagai 727
assail *attack* 716
  pain 830
assailant *opponent* 710
  attacker 726·
assassin, -ate 361
assault 716
  take by - 789
assay 463
assayer 463
assemblage 72
assembly *council* 696
  society 892
  religious 997
assemblyman 696
assembly room 189,
  588
assent *belief* 484
  agree **488**
  willing 602
  consent 762
  content 831
assert *affirm* 535
  claim as a right 924
assess *measure* 466
  determine 480
  tax 812
assessor *judge* 967
assets *property* 780
  money 800
  accounts 811
asseverate 535
assiduous 682
assign *commission* 755
  transfer 783
  give 784
  allot 786
  - a duty 926
  - as cause 155·
  - dower 784
  - places 60
assignable 270
assignat 800
assignation *tryst* 892
  place of - 74
assignee *transfer* 270
  donee 785
assignment 155
assimilate *uniform* 16
  resemble 17
  imitate 19
  agree 23
  transmute 144
assimilation 161
assist 707
assistant 711
assize *measure* 466
  tribunal 966
  justice of - 967
associate *mix* 41
  unite 43
  combine 48
  collect 72
  accompany 88

  colleague 690
  auxiliary 711
  friend 890
  - professorship 542
  - with
  sociality 892
association
  [*see* associate]
  relation 9
  coöperation 709
  partnership 712
  friendship 888
  - of ideas
  intellect 450
  thought 451
  intuition 477
  hint 514
associational psycholo-
  gy 457
assoil *acquit* 970
  (*liberate* 750)
assoilzie 970
assonance *agreement* 23
  music 413
  poetry 597
assort *arrange* 60
assortment
  collection 72
  class 75
assuage *moderate* 174
  relieve 834
  (- *morally* 826)
assuasive 174, 834
assuetude 613
assume *believe* 484
  suppose 514
  falsehood 544
  take 789
  insolent 885
  right 924
  - a character 554
  - a form 144
  - authority 737
  - command 741
  - the offensive 716
assumed
  - name 565
  - position 514
assuming *insolent* 885
assumption [*see* assume]
  severity 739
  hope 858
  insolence 885
  seizure 925
assurance
  speculation 156
  certainty 474
  belief 484
  confidence 507
  assertion 535
  promise 768
  security 771
  hope 858
  vanity 880
  insolence 885
  make - double sure
  safe 664
  caution 864
assure *render certain*
  474
  believe 484

  certify 535
  promise 768
  secure 771
  give hope 858
assured *self -satisfied*
  880
assuredly *assent* 488
astatic 320
asteism 856
asterisk 550
astern 235
  fall - 283
asteroid 318
asthenia 160
astigmatism 443
astir *ready* 673
  active 682
  set - 824
astonish 870
astonishing *great* 31
astonishment 508, 870
astound *be unexpected*
  508
  excite 824
  fear 860
  surprise 870
astraddle 215
astragal 847
astral 318
  - body 317, 992*a*
  - influence 601
  - plane 317
astray *at fault* 475
  error 495
  go - *deviate* 279
  sin 945
astriction 43, 195
astride 215
astringent 195, 397
astrolabe 466
astrology 511, 522
astronomy 318
astute *wise* 498
  cunning 702
asunder *separate* 44
  distant 196
  as poles - 237
asylum *hospital* 662
  retreat 666
  defense 717
asymptote 290
ataghan 727
atajo 72
atavism 145
atelier *studio* 556
  workshop 691
athanasia 112
Athanasian creed 983*a*
athanor 386
atheism 989
atheist 984
atheling 875
athermancy 382
athirst 865
athlete *strong* 159
  combatant 726
athletic *strong* 159
  school 542
  laborious 686
  gymnastic 720
  - sports

  contest 720
  games 840
athletics 720, 840
athwart *oblique* 217
  crossing 219
  opposing 708
Atkins, Tommy - 726
Atlantean *great* 31
  strong 159
  supporting 215
Atlantis 515
at large 750
atlas *arrangement* 60
  list 86
  maps 554
  store 636
Atlas *strength* 159
  support 215
atmosphere
  circumambience 227
  air 338
  painting 556
atmospheric blue 438
atole 298
atoll 346
atom *small in degree*
  32
  small in size 193
atomism 451
atomize 336
atomizer 336, 400
atoms
  crush to - 162
atomy 193, 203
atonement
  restitution 790
  expiation **952**
  amends 973
  religious 976
atonic 158
atony 158, 160
atrabilious 837
atramentous 431
atrium 191   ◄
atrocity *malevolence* 907
  vice 945
  guilt 947
atrophy *shrinking* 195
  disease 655
  decay 659
attach *add* 37
  join 43
  love 897
  legal 969
  - importance to 642
attaché *employé* 746
  diplomatic 758
attachment [*see* attach]
  dispossession 789
attack *voice* 580
  disease 655
  assault **716**
attaghan 727
attain *arrive* 292
  succeed 731
  - majority 131
attainable
  possible 470
  (*easy* 705)
attainder *taint* 651
  at law 971

B

center 222
grit 604
persevere 604a
soul 820
-game to the - 604
backcap 934
back door 627
backdown 725
backer 711
backfriend 891
backgammon 840
background
  distance 196
  rear 235
in the - *latent* 526
  ignoble 874
keep in the - *hide* 528
  modest 881
  seclusion 893
throw into the - 460
backhanded 217, 629
backlash 277
backlog 386, 388
backplate 717
backset
  agriculture 371
  reverse 735
backsettler 188
backside 235
backslider *turncoat* 607
  shirker 623
  apostate 984
backsliding
  regression 283
  tergiversation 607
  relapse 661
  vice 945
  heterodox 984
  impiety 988
backstairs *ambush* 530
  way 627
- *influence* 702
backward *tardy* 133
  rear 235
  regression 283
  unwilling 603
  unprogressive 659
backwardation 813
backwards 283
- and forwards
  interchange 148
  oscillation 314
  bend - 325
backwater *cessation* 142
  slowness 275
  regression 283
backwoods 233
backwoodsman
  inhabitant 188
  agriculture 371
bacon 298
  save one's -
  safety 644
  escape 671
Baconian method 461
bacteria 193, 369
bactericide 662
bacteriologist 357
bad 649
  unclean 653
  wrong 923

-blood *hate* 898
  malevolence 907
- break 947
- business 859
- case 477
- chance 473
- debt 806
- fairy 980
- faith 940
- grace 895
- habit 613
- hand 701
- humor
  discontent 832
  dejection 837
  anger 900
  sullen 901a
- intent 907
- job *evil* 619
  botch 699
  hopeless 859
- joke 851
- language 908
- luck &c. 735
- man **949**
- name 932, 934
- repute 874
- smell 401
- spirit 980
- spirits 837
- taste 851
- temper
  discourtesy 895
  resentment 900
  irascibility 901
  sullenness 901a
- time of it 828
- turn *evil* 619
  malevolence 907
- woman 949
from - to worse
  aggravation 835
go - *decay* 853
  deteriorate 659
in a - way
  disease 655
  worse 659
  danger 665
  adversity 735
in - odor 889
not a - idea 498
on - terms
  discord 713
  enmity 889
put a - construction
  on 523
take in - part
  discontent 832
  anger 900
view in a - light 934
badaud 501
badge 550
- of authority 747
- of infamy 874
- of slavery 746
badger 830
  stealing 791, 792
- dog 366
- game 791
badinage *wit* 842
  ridicule 856

badli 634, 759
badly off *adversity* 735
  poor 804
badness **649**
Baedeker 266
baffle *hinder* 706
  defeat 731
- description
  unconformable 83
  wonder 870
baft 235
bag *put up* 184
  receptacle 191
  protrude 250
  acquire 775
  take 789
  steal 791
- and baggage 780
bagatelle *trifle* 643
  pastime 840
baggage
  endearment 129
  transference 270
  *materi?l*3 635
  property 780
  hussy 962
- car 272
baggala 273
baggy 47
bagman 758, 767
bagnio 961
bagpipes 410, 417
bahl 497, 930
bail *receptacle* 191
  transference 270
  security 771
- one's own boat 692
- up 791
go - 806
leg - 623
bailiff *director* 694
  servant 746
  factor 758
  officer 965
bailiwick *region* 181
  jurisdiction 965
Bairam 138, 840
bairn 129, 167
bait *fulcrum* 215
  draw 288
  food 298
  trap 545
  lure 615
  refresh 689
  attack 716
  bribe 784
  harass 830
  reward 973
swallow the - 547
bake 384
baked beans 298
bakehouse 386
baker's dozen 98
baking heat 382
bakshish 784
bal 840
balais 847
balaklava helmet 225
balance *equal* 27
  mean 29
  compensate 30

  remainder 40
  numeration 85
  weigh 319
  compare 464
  measurement 466
  intelligence 498
  elegance 578
  hesitate 605
  money 800
  accounts 811
- accounts with
  pay 807
in the - 475
off one's -
  irresolute 605
  fail 732
the mind losing its -
  503
balanced *stable* 150
  symmetrical 242
  graceful 578
balbucinate 583
balbutiate 583
balcony 250
  theater 599
bald *bare* 226
  style 575
  uninteresting 841
  ugly 846
  plain 849
baldachin 223, 1000
balderdash 497, 517
baldness [see bald]
baldric *belt* 230
  ring 247
bale *bundle* 72
  load 190
  evil 619
- out 297
baleen 325
balefire 423, 550
baleful 649
balista 727
balister 727
balistraria 717
balize 550
balk *deviate* 279
  disappoint 509
  deceive 545
  hinder 706
balky 283, 606
ball *globe* 249
  missile 284
  shot 727
  dance 840
  party 892
- at one's feet
  success 731
  power 737
keep up the -
  continue 143
  active 682
ballad *song* 415
  poem 597
- monger 597
ballast
  compensation 30
  weight 319
  wisdom 498
  safety 666
without - *rash* **863**

vicious 945
ballet *drama* 599
　dance 840
ballet dancer 599
ballista 727
ballistics *projectiles* 284
　war 722
　arms 727
balloon 273, 325
balloonery 267
ballooning 267
balloonist 269
ballot 535, 609
　- box stuffing 545
ball player 840
ballproof 717
ballroom 840
balm *moderate* 174
　lubrication 332
　fragrance 400
　remedy 662
　relief 834
Balmoral *boot* 225
balmy *sleep* 683
balneal 337
balourdise 699
balsam 400, 662
balsamic
　salubrious 834
balustrade *support* 215
　inclosure 232
bam 544
bambino 129
bamboo 367
bamboozle 545
ban *prohibit* 761
　denounce 908
　- with bell, book, and
　candle 998
　under the - 906
banana 298, 369
banco regis 968
band *ligature* 45
　assemblage 72
　filament 205
　belt 230
　ring 247
　music 415, 416, 417
　party 712
　shackle 752
　- of hope 958
　-s *canonicals* 999
　- together 709
　- with 720
bandage *tie* 43
　ligature 45
　support 215
　cover 223
　remedy 662
　restraint 752
　the eyes -d 442
bandbox 191
banded together
　concurring 178
　party 712
banderole 550
bandit *slayer* 361
　brigand 792
bandmaster 416
bandobast
　[see bundobust]

bandog *animal* 366
　safeguard 664
　warning 668
bandolier 636
bandrol 550
bandurria 417
bandy *exchange* 148
　agitate 315
　- about
　publish 531
　- legged 243
　- words *discuss* 476
　converse 588
bane *evil* 619
　source of evil **663**
baneful 649
banewort 663
bang *impel* 276
　sound 406
　beat 972
banish *eject* 297
　seclude 893
　punish 972
　(*exclude* 55)
banister 215
banjo 417
bank *acclivity* 217
　side of lake 342
　store 636
　sand 667
　fence 717
　money 802
　- examiner 811
　- holiday 840
　- of Elegance 800
　- up 670
　sea - 342
banker
　man of means 639
　merchant 797
　treasurer 801
　card game 840
bank note 800
bankrupt 640
　- of life 683
bankruptcy *failure* 732
　nonpayment 808
banlieue *near* 197
　circumjacent 227
banner 550
　enlist under the -s of
　707
　raise one's - 722
banneret 875
banns
　forbid the - 761
　publish the -
　ask 765
　marriage 903
banquet *meal* 298
　pleasure 377
　feast 840
banquette 717
banshee 979, 980*a*
bant 38
bantam cock 887
banter *wit* 842
　ridicule 856
banterer 844
bantling *child* 129
　scion 167

banyan *tree* 367
　stint 640
　fast 956
baptize 564, 998
baptism *name* 564
　rite 998
Baptist 984
baptistery 1000
bar *except* 38
　fastening 45
　exclude 55
　hotel 189
　line 200
　support 215
　inclosure 232
　close 261
　music 413
　hindrance 706
　insignia 747
　prison 752
　prohibit 761
　tribunal 966
　legal profession 968
　- room 189
　- sinister *flaw* 651
　disrepute 874
　illegal 964
　- tender 746
baragouin 517
bara hazri 298
bara khana 298
bara sahib 642, 745
barb *spike* 253
　nag 271
　velocity 274
　- the dart *pain* 830
Barbados tar 356
barbarian *alien* 57
　inelegance 579
　uncivilized 876
　evildoer 913
barbaric *extraneous* 57
　vulgar 851
　rude 876
barbarism *neology* 563
　solecism 568
　bad style 579
　vulgarity 851
　discourtesy 895
barbarous
　unformed 241
　neologic 563
　plebeian 876
　maleficent 907
barbate 205, 253
barbecue
　repast 298, 892
　cook 673
barbed 225
　- wire entanglements
　717
barbel 205
barber *wind* 349
barbican 206, 717
barbouillage 590
bard *musician* 416
　poet 597
barded 225
bare *mere* 32
　nude 226
　manifest 525

disclose 529
　scanty 640
　- possibility 473
　- supposition 514
bareback 226
barebone 203
barefaced 885
barefoot 226
　poor 804
bareheaded *respect* 928
bargain *compact* 769
　barter 794
　cheap 815
　- and sale *transfer of
　property* 783
　- for 507
　into the - 37
barge 273
bargee 269
barghest 980
barf 383
baritone 408
barium sulphate 430
bark *rind* 223
　flay 226
　ship 273
　yelp 406, 412
　- at *threaten* 909
　censure 932
　- up the wrong tree
　699
　- worse than bite 885
　more - than bite 908
barkbound 751
barkeep 746
barkeeper 746
barkentine 273
barker *guide* 524
　tout 758
　petitioner 767
barley 367
barleycorn *little* 193
Barleycorn, Sir John -
　298
barm *leaven* 320
　bubbles 353
barmaster 967
Barmecide feast 956
barmote 966
barn 189, 370, 636
barnacles 368, 445
barndoor fowl 366
barney 545, 713
barograph 338
barometer *air* 338
　measure 466
　consult the - 463
baron *peer* 875
　husband 903
　- of the Exchequer
　967
　court - 966
baronage 875
baronet 875
baronial 878
baroque 853
baroscope 338
barouche 272
barque 273
barrack
　encampment 184

abode 189
shed 223
jibe 929
defence 717
barracker 936
barracoon 717
barrage *loudness* 404
drumming 407
attack 716
barranco 198
barrator 941
barratrous 940
barratry 940
barred *crossed* 219
striped 440
barrel *vessel* 191
cylinder 249
– *organ* 417
barrel house 189
barren 169
barricade *fence* 232
obstacle 706
defense 717
prison 752
barrier [*see* barricade]
barring *save* 38
excluding 55
except 83
– *out resist* 719
disobey 742
barrister 968
revising – 967
barrow *mound* 206
vehicle 272
grave 363
barter *reciprocate* 12
interchange 148
commerce **794**
barway 294
barytone 408
bas bleu *scholar* 492
affectation 855
base *low* 207
lowest part **211**
support 215
evil 649
menial 746
cowardly 862
shameful 874
servile 886
dishonorable 940
vicious 945
– *coin* 800
– *note* 408
– *of operations*
plan 626
attack 716
baseball 840
baseboard 211
baseborn 876
based on *ground of*
belief 467
baselard 727
baseless *unreal* 2
unsubstantial 4
basement *cellar* 191
lowest part 207, 211
baseness [*see* base]
inferiority 34
bashaw *tyrant* 739
ruler 745

468

bashful 881
bashfulness 881
bashi-bazouk 726
basilica 1000
basilisk
unconformity 83
sight 441
cannon 737
serpent 366, 949
basin *dock* 189
vessel 191, 211
hollow 252
plain 344
basis *lowest part* 211
support 215
preparation 673
bask *physical enjoyment*
377
warmth 382
prosperity 734
moral enjoyment 827
– *in the sun* 384
basket 191
– *of* 190
basket ball 840
bas-relief *convex* 250
sculpture 557
bass *music* 415
– *clarinet* 417
– *note* 408
– *tuba* 417
– *viol* 417
basset 446
basset horn 417
bassinet *cradle* 191
helmet 717
bassoon 417
basso profondo 408
basso-rilievo
convex 250
sculpture 557
bastard *spurious* 545
nameless 565
illegitimate 925
baste *beat* 276
punish 972
Bastille 752
bastinado 972
bastion 717
bat *strike* 276
club 727
spree 840
batch *quantity* 25
collection 72
bate *diminish* 36
subtract 38
reduce price 813
bateau 273
bated breath
with – *faint sound* 405
expecting 507
hiding 528
whisper 581
humble 879
bath 337, 652
– *s remedy* 662
warm – 386
Bath chair 272
bathe *immerse* 300
plunge 310
water 337

bathhouse 652
bathometer 208, 341, 466
bathos *anticlimax* 497
(*ridiculous* 853)
bathroom 191, 652
bathybic 341
bathycolpian 208
bathymeter 208
bathymetry 208
bathypelagic 208
bathysmal 208
batik 556
bating 55
batman 637
baton *support* 215
scepter 747
batophobia 206, 860, 867
batrachians 368
batta 973
battalia 726
battalion 726
batten 298
– *on* 886
batter *destroy* 162
beat 276
pulpiness 354
battered
worse for wear 659
tired 688
battering-ram 276
battering train 727
battery *artillery* 726
guns 727
floating – 726
plant a – 716
battle *killing* 361
contention 720
warfare 722
– *array order* 60
prepare 673
war 722
– *ax* 727
– *cruiser* 273
– *cry sign* 550
war 722
– *field arena* 728
– *ground discord* 713
– *with oppose* 708
half the – 642
win the – 731
battled 722
battledore 325
– *and shuttlecock*
interchange 148
game 840
battlement
embrasure 257
defense 717
battleship 664, 726
battologize 573
battology *repeat* 104
diffuse style 573
battue *kill* 361
pursuit 622
attack 716
bauble *trifle* 643
toy 840
bavardage
unmeaning 517

chatter 584
bavin 388
bawarchi-khana 191
bawcock 892
bawd 962
bawdy,-house 961
bawl 411
bawn 189
bay *concave* 252
gulf 343
cry 412
brown 433
at – *danger* 665
difficulty 604
defense 717, 719
– *leaf* 400
– *the moon*
useless 645
bring to – 716
bayadere 840
Bayard 271
bayard *bay* 433
bayberry 400
– *candle* 423
baygall 345
bayonet *kill* 361
attack 716
weapon 727
at the point of the –
war 722
severity 739
coercion 744
crossed – *s* 708
bayou 343
bay rum 400
bays *trophy* 733
crown 877
bay salt 336
bay window 245, 260
bazaar 799
B. C. 106
be 1
– *alive with* 102
– *all and end all*
whole 50
intention 620
importance 642
– *all up with* 162
– *off depart* 293
eject 297
retract 773
– *it so* 488
– *that as it may* 30
beach 342
beach comber 268, 348
beacon *sign* 550
warning 668
(*light* 423)
– *fire* 423, 550
bead 249, 847
beading 847
beadle *janitor* 263
law officer 965
church 996
beadledom 737
beadroll *list* 86
prayers 990
ritual 998
beads 847
tell one's – 990, 998

beadsman *servant* 746
　clergy 996
beagle 366
beak *face* 234
　nose 250
　magistrate 967
beaked 245
beaker 191
beam *support* 215
　quarter 236
　weigh 319
　light 420
　measurement 466
　on - ends
　powerless 158
　horizontal 213
　side 236
　fail 732
　wonder 870
beaming *beautiful* 845
beanfeast 840
beans 298
bear *produce* 161
　sustain 215
　carry 270
　animal 366
　admit of 470
　stock exchange 797
　suffer 821
　endure 826
　- a hand 680
　- a sense 516
　- away 789
　- away the bell
　best 648
　success 731
　- company 88
　- date 114
　- down *violent* 173
　insolent 885
　- down upon 716
　- false witness 544
　- fruit *produce* 161
　useful 644
　success 731
　prosper 734
　- hard upon 649
　- harmless 717
　- ill 825
　- off *deviate* 279
　- on 215
　- oneself 692
　- out *evidence* 467
　vindicate 937
　- pain 828
　- the brunt
　difficult 704
　defense 717
　- the burden 625
　- the cross 828
　- the palm *supreme* 33
　- through 707
　- up *approach* 286
　persevere 604a
　relieve 834
　cheerful 836
　- up against *resist* 719
　brave 861
　- upon *relevant* 9, 23
　influence 175
　- with *tolerate* 740

permit 760
　take coolly 826
　forgive 918
bring to - 677
more than flesh and
　blood can - 824
unable to -
　excited 825
　dislike 867
bear *savage* 907
　surly 895
　- garden *disorder* 59
　discord 713
　arena 728
　- leader 540
　- pit 370
　- skin *cap* 225
　helmet 717
bearable 651
beard *hair* 205
　prickles 253
　rough 256
　defy 715
　brave 861
　insolence 885
　pluck by the -
　disrespect 929
bearded *hairy* 256
beardless 127, 226
bearer 271
　funeral 363
　servant 746
bear grass 253
bearing *relation* 9
　support 215
　direction 278
　meaning 516
　demeanor 692
　- rein 706, 752
bearings
　circumstances 8
　situation 183
bearish 895
beast *animal* 366
　unclean 653
　discourteous 895
　- of burden
　carrier 271
　laborer 690
beastlike *unclean* 653
beastly *unclean* 653
　impure 961
beat *be superior* 33
　periodic 138
　region 181
　impulse 276
　surpass 303
　oscillate 314
　agitation 315
　crush 330
　sound 407
　verse 597
　line of pursuit 625
　path 627
　overcome 731
　sponger 886
　strike 972
　- about *circuit* 629
　- about the bush
　try for 463
　evade the point 477

prevaricate 544
　diffuse style 573
　- against 708
　- a retreat *retire* 283
　avoid 623
　submit 725
　- down *destroy* 162
　cheapen 794, 815, 819
　insolent 885
　- hollow 33
　- into *teach* 537
　- of drum *music* 416
　publish 531
　alarm 669
　war 722
　command 741
　pomp 882
　- off 717
　- one's breast 839
　- the air 645
　- the Dutch 508
　- time *clock* 114
　music 416
　- up *churn* 352
　- up against
　oppose 708
　- up for *cater* 637
　- up for recruits
　prepare 673
　aid 707
　- up one's quarters
　seek 461
　visit 892
beaten track
　habit 613
　way 627
　leave the - 83
　tread the - 82
beatific
　pleasing 827, 829
　heavenly 981
beatification *piety* 987
beating high
　the heart - 824
beau *man* 373
　fop 854
　admirer 897
　- catcher 256
　- idéal *perfect* 650
　beauty 845
　- monde
　fashion 852
　(*nobility* 875)
beautiful 845
beautify 845, 847
beautiless 846
beauty 845
　- of a lovely woman
　374
beaver *covering* 223
　hat 225
　animal 366
　- dam 706
becalm 265
because *cause* 153
　attribution 155
　answer 462
　reasoning 476
　motive 615
bechance 151
becharm 829

bêche de mer 298
beck *rill* 348
　sign 550
　mandate 741
　at one's - *aid* 707
　obey 743
beckon *sign* 550
　motive 615
　call 741
becloud *befog* 353
　dark 421
　dim 422
　hide 528
become
　change to 144
　accord with 23
　behove 926
　- of 151
becoming
　accordant 23
　proper 646
　beautiful 845, 847
　due 924
becripple 158
bed *lodgment* 191
　layer 204
　base 211
　support 215
　for animals 370
　garden 371
　marriage 903
　- bugs 366
　- maker 746
　- of down *repose* 687
　- of Procrustes 975
　- of roses *pleasure* 377
　prosperity 734
　brought to - 161
　death - 360
　go to - *quiet* 265
　sleep 683
　keep one's - *ill* 655
bedarken 421
bedaub *cover* 223
　dirt 653
　(*deface* 846)
bedazzle 420
bedding 215
bedeck 847
bedesman
　[see beadsman]
bedevil *derange* 61
　diabolize 978
　sorcery 992
bedew 339
bedfellow 890
bedgown 225
bedight 225, 847
bedim 421, 422
bedizen *invest* 225
　ornament 847
　vulgar 851
Bedlam
　- broke loose 59
　candidate for - 504
bedog 63
Bedouin 792
bedridden 655
bed rock 211
bedroom 191
bedstead 215

bedtime 126
bedwarf 195
bee 690
  gathering 892
  - in a bottle 407
  - in one's bonnet 503
  busy - 682
  swarm like -s 102
beech *tree* 367
beef 298
beefeater 263, 726
beefheaded 499
beehive *convexity* 250
  for bees 370
  workshop 691
bee line 278
Beelzebub 978
beënt 1
beer 298
beery 959
beeswax 352
beetle *overhang* 206
  project 250
  insect 366
  deafness 419
  - head 501
  blind as a - 442
  Colorado - 913
beetling 214
beet root 298
beets 298
beet sugar 396
befall 151
befit *agree* 23
  expedient 646
  due 924, 926
befog *becloud* 353
  conceal 528
befool *mad* 503
  deceive 545
befooled
  victimized 732
before *in order* 62
  in time 116
  presence 186
  in space 234
  precession 280
  preference 609
  - Christ 106
  - everything 153
  - long 132
  - mentioned 62, 116
  - now 122
  - one's eyes
  visible 446
  manifest 525
  - one's time 132
  - the house 454
  set - one 525
beforehand *prior* 116
  early 132
  foresight 510
  resolve - 611
befoul 653
befriend *aid* 707
  friendship 888
befuddle 959
beg *Turkish title* 745
beg *ask* 765
  - leave 760
  - one's bread 765

  poor 804
  - one's life 914
  - pardon 952
  - the question 477
beget 161
begetter 164, 166
beggar *idler* 683
  petitioner 767
  poor 804
  degrade 874
  low person 876
  - description
  unconformable 83
  nomenclature 564
  wonderful 870
  - my neighbor 840
  - on horseback 885
  -s mounted 885
  sturdy - 792
beggared
  bankrupt 808
beggar's-lice 253
beggarly *mean* 643
  vile 874
  vulgar 876
  servile 886
  - account of empty
  boxes
  insufficient 640
  poor 804
begging
  - letter 765
  go a - *too much* 641
  useless 645
  offered 763
  free 748
begilt 847
begin 66
  - again 104
beginner 541
beginning 66
  still ending and - 140
begird 227, 229
beglerbeg 745
begone *depart* 293
  ejection 297
  abrogate 756
  (disappear 440)
  - dull care 836
begrease 653
begrime 653
begrudge
  unwilling 603
  refuse 764
  stingy 819
  envy 921
beguile *mislead* 495
  deceive 545
  reconcile 831
  - the time
  inaction 681
  amusement 840
  to - many 615
begum 745, 875
behalf *advantage* 618
  aid 707
  in - of 759
behave oneself
  conduct 692
  fashion 852
  courtesy 894

behavior 692
  one's good -
  polite 894
  virtuous 944
behead *kill* 361
  execute 972
behemoth 192
behest 741
behind *in order* 63
  in space 235
  sequence 281
  - bars 754
  - one's back
  missing 187
  - the age *old* 124
  ignorant 491
  - the scenes
  cause 153
  unseen 447
  cognizant 490
  latent 526
  hidden 528
  playhouse 599
  - the veil 528
  - time 115, 133
behindhand *late* 133
  shortcoming 304
  adversity 735
  insolvent 808
behold *see* 441
  look 457
beholden *grateful* 916
  obligatory 926
beholder 444
behoof 618
behoove 926
being *abstract* 1
  concrete 3
  created - 366
  human - 372
  time - 106
Bel 979
belabor *buffet* 276
  thump 972
belated *late* 133
  ignorant 491
belaud 931
belay *join* 43
  restrain 706
belch *eject* 297
  emit gas 349
beldam
  grandmother 130
  hag 173, 913
belduque 253
beleaguer, 227, 716
belfry 206, 1000
Belial 978
  sons of - 988
belie *deny* 536
  falsify 544
  contradict 708
belief *credence* **484**
  religious creed 983
  easy of - 472
  hug a - 606
believe [*see* belief]
  suppose 514
  - who may 485
  not - one's senses 870
  reason to - 472

believer *religious* 987
  true - 983*a*
belike 472
belittle *decrease* 36
  underestimate 483
  detract 934
belittling *envy* 921
bell *time* 106
  sound 417
  sign 550
  alarm - 669
  bear away the -
  goodness 648
  success 731
  repute 873
  - book, and candle
  swear 535
  curse 908
  spell 993
  rite 998
  - boy 746
  - mare 64
  - note 408
  - pepper 393
  - the cat 861
  cracked - 408*a*
  passing - 363
  peal of -s 407
belladonna 663
belle 374, 854
belles-lettres 560
bellicose
  contentious 720
  warlike 722
bellied 250
belligerent
  contentious 720
  warlike 722
  combatant 726
belling 412
bellman 534
Bellona 722
bellow *loud* 404
  cry 411
  animal cry 412
  wail 839
bellows *wind* 349
  lungs 580
bell-shaped
  globose 249
  concave 252
bellwether
  go first 64
  direct 694
belly *inside* 221
  convex 250
  - god 957
bellyful *complete* 52
  enough 639
belomancy 511
belong to *related* 9
  component 56
  included 76
  attribute 157
  property 777, 780
  duty 926
beloved 897
below 207
  - its full strength 651
  - par *inferior* 34
  at a low ebb 207

contempt 643
bad 649
indifferent 651
discount 813
ignoble 876
- stairs 207
- the mark 32
here - 318
belt *inclose* 227
outline 230
ring 247
strait 343
swimming - 666
belvedere 441
bemask 528
bemingle 41
bemire 653
bemoan 839
bemused 458
bench *support* 215
council 696
tribunal 966
Bench, King's - 752
bencher 967, 968
bend *oblique* 217
angle 244
curve 245
incline 278
deviate 279
depression 308
circuit 311
give 324
submit 725
- backward 235
- one's course 278
- one's looks upon 441
- one's steps 622
- over 250
- sinister 874
- the bow 686
- the brows 932
- the knee
bow down 308
submit 725
humble 879
servile 886
courtesy 894
respect 928
worship 990
- the mind 457
- to tend 176
- to one's will 737
- to rules &c. 82
- towards 278
bender 959
beneath 207
- contempt 643
- notice 643
- one 940
Benedick 903
Benedictine 996
benediction
gratitude 916
approval 931
worship 990
nuptial - 903
benefaction 784
benefactor 816, **912**
benefice 995
beneficent 906
beneficial *good* 648

(*useful* 644)
- interest 780
beneficiary
possessor 779
receive 785
clergy 996
benefit *profit* 618
use 644, 677
do good 648
aid 707
acquisition 775
property 780
benevolence 906
(*improve* 658)
- s forgot 917
reap the - of 731
benevolence *tax* 812
love 897
kindness **906**
universal 910
Bengal heat 382
benighted *dark* 421
ignorant 491
benightedness 442
benign 656
benignant 906
benison 931
Benjamin's mess
greater 33
chief part 50
bent *tendency* 176
framework 232
angle 244
grass 367
turn of mind 820
desire 865
- on *willing* 602
resolved 604
intention 620
desirous 865
fool to the top of
one's - 856
benthal 208
Benthamite 910
benthopelagic 208
benthos 208, 366, 367
ben trovato
likely 472
imagination 515
untruth 546
wit 842
benumb *insensible* 376
cold 385
deaden affections 823
benzine 356, 652
benzoin 662
benzolin 652
beplaster 933
bepraise 931
bequeath 784
bequeathable 270
bequest *gift* 270, 784
(*acquisition* 775)
berate 527, 932
berceuse 415
bereavement
death 360
loss 776
take away 789
bereft *poor* 804
- of life 360

- of reason 503
berg *iceberg* 383
bergamot 400
Bergsonism 451
beriberi 655
Berkeleyism 451
berlin 272
berloque 407
Bernardine 996
bersagliere 726
berserk 173
berth *lodging* 189
bed 215
office 625
Bertillon system 550
beryl *green* 435
jewel 847
beseech *request* 765
pray 900
beseem 926
beset *surround* 227
follow 281
attack 716
entreat 765
annoy 830
fear 860
- with difficulties 704
besetting *general* 78
habit 613
- sin 945
beshrew 908
beside *except* 83
near 197
alongside 236
- oneself *mad* 503
excited 824
- the mark
irrelevant 10
error 495
besides 37
besiege *surround* 227
attack 716
solicit 765
fear 860
bésique 840
beslaver 933
beslime 653
beslubber 933
besmear *cover* 223
dirt 653
besnow 430
besom 652
besot 959
besotted 481
bespangle 847
bespangled 318
bespatter *dirt* 653
disapprove 932
flatter 933
detract 934
bespeak *early* 132
evidence 467
indicate 516
engage 755
ask for 765
bespeckle 440
bespot 440
besprinkle *mix* 41
variegate 440
best *good* 648
perfect 650

all for the -
good 618
prosper 734
content 831
hope 858
bad is the - 649
- bib and tucker
prepared 673
ornament 847
ostentation 882
- ever 646
- intentions 906
- man *marriage* 903
- part *great* 31
nearly all 50
- room 191
- seller 931
do one's - *care* 459
try 675
activity 682
exertion 686
have the - of it 731
make the - of it
overestimate 482
use 677
submit 725
compromise 774
take easily 826
hope 858
make the - of one's
time 684
to the - of one's belief
484
bestead 644
bestial 961
bestir oneself
activity 682
haste 684
exertion 686
bestow *give* 784
a benefice 995
- one's hand 903
- thought 451
bestraddle 215
bestrew 73
bestride *mount* 206
ride 215
bet 621
betacism 560
betake oneself to
journey 266
business 625
use 677
bête noire *fear* 860
hate 898
bethel 1000
bethink *think* 451
remember 505
bethrall
subjection 749
restraint 751
betide 151
betimes 132
bêtise 497
betoken *evidence* 467
predict 511
indicate 550
betongue 932
betray *disclose* 529
deceive 545
dishonor 940

471

- itself *visible* 446
betrayer 941
betrim 673
betroth *promise* 768
  marriage 903
betrothal 902
  [*see* betroth]
betrothed 897
better *good* 648
  improve 658
- half 903
- sort
  beau monde 875
for - for worse
  choice 609
  marriage 903
get - *health* 654
  improve 658
  refreshment 689
  restoration 660
get the - of 731
seen - days
  deteriorate 659
  adversity 735
  poor 804
think - of
  correct 658
  repent 950
betting house 621
betty 374
between 228
- cup and lip 111
- ourselves 528
- the lines 526
- two fires 665
far - 198
lie - 228
betwixt 228
bevel 217
bever 298
beverage 298
bevue 732
bevy *assemblage* 72
  multitude 102
bewail *regret* 833
  lament 839
beware 668
bewilder *put out* 458
  uncertain 475
  astonish 870
bewildered 495, 523
bewitch *fascinate* 615
  please 829
  excite love 897
  diabolize 978
  hoodoo 992
bey 745
beyond *superior* 33
  distance 196
- compare 31, 33
- control 471
- expression 31
- hope 731, 734
- measure 641
- mortal ken 528
- one's depth
  deep 208
  unintelligible 519
- one's grasp 471
- possibility 471
- praise *perfect* 650
472

approbation 931
  virtue 944
- price 814
- question 474
- range 196
- reason 471
- remedy 859
- seas 57
- the grave 528
- the mark
  transcursion 303
  redundance 641
- the veil 528
- the verge 180
go - 303
bezel 217
bezonian 876
bhang 663, 954
bhangi 652
bhikshu 955
bias *influence* 175
  tendency 176
  slope 217
  prepossession 481
  disposition 820
  (*motive* 615)
bib *pinafore* 225
  drink 959
  cleanness 652
bibber *weep* 839
  tope 959
bibble-babble 584
Bible 985
- Christian 984
- oath 535
biblioclasm 162
biblioclast 165
bibliognost 593
bibliographer 593
bibliography 593
bibliolatry *learning* 490
  heterodoxy 984
  idolatry 991
bibliologist 593
bibliomancy 511
bibliomania 490
bibliomaniac 492
bibliopegist 593
bibliophile 492, 593
bibliopole 593
bibliotheca 593
bibulous 298
bice 435, 438
bicentenary, 98, 138, 883
bicentennial 98, 138, 883
bicephalous 90
bichhona 215
bichloride of mercury 663
bicipital 90
bicker *flutter* 315
  quarrel 713
  (*contend* 720)
bickering 24
bicolor 440
biconjugate 91
bicorn 245
bicuspid 91
bicycle 266, 272

bid *order* 741
  offer 763
- a long farewell 624
- defiance 715
- fair *tend* 176
  probable 472
  promise 511
  hope 858
- for *intend* 620
  offer 763
  request 765
  bargain 794
- the banns 903
bidder 767
bidding *command* 741
biddy 746
bide *wait* 133
  remain 141
  take coolly 826
- one's time 133
  watch 507
  inactive 681
bidental 90
bidet 271
biduous 89
biennial *periodic* 138
  plant 367
  celebration 883
bienséance *polish* 852
  manners 894
bier 363
bifacial 90
bifarious 90
bifid 91
bifold 90
biform *double* 90
  (*two* 89)
bifurcate *bisect* 91
  angle 244
big *in degree* 31
  in size 192
  wide 194
- bug 875
- gun 875
- sounding
  loud 404
  words 577
  affected 855
- with 161
- with the fate of 511
look - *defy* 715
  proud 878
  insolent 885
talk - 885
  threat 909
bigamist 903
bigamy 903
biggin 191
bighead 655
bight 343
bigot *positive* 474
  prejudice 481
  obstinate 606
  heterodox 984
  impious 988
bigwig 875
bijou *goodness* 648
  beauty 845
  ornament 847
bijouterie 847
bike 272

bilabiate 90
bilander 273
bilateral *two* 90
  side 236
bilbao 727
bilboes 752
  put into - 751
bile 900
bilge *base* 211
  convex 250
  yawn 260
- water 653
biliary calculus 655
bilingual 560
bilious 837
bilk *disappoint* 509
  cheat 545
  steal 791
bill *list* 86
  hatchet 253
  placard 531
  ticket 550
  paper 593
  plan 626
  weapon 727
  money order 800
  money account 811
  charge 812
  in law 969
- and coo 902
- of exchange
  security 771
- of fare *food* 298
  plan 626
- of indictment 938
- of sale 771
- s of mortality 360
true - 969
billet *locate* 184
  apportion 786
billet *ticket* 550
  epistle 592
  business 625
- doux 902
billhook 253
billiard - ball
  round 249
- room 191
- table *flat* 213
billiards 840
billingsgate
  slang 563
  curse 908
  (*censure* 932)
billion 98, 102
billow *sea* 348
billows *ocean* 341
billy *kettle* 191
  club 727
billycock 225
billy goat 373
bimonthly 138
bin 191
bina 417
binary 89
binate 89
bind *connect* 43
  cover 223
  compel 744
  condition 770
  obligation 926

brave 861
- push *essay* 675
- relief *visible* 446
- stroke *plan* 626
  success 731
  make - with
  discourtesy 895
  show a - front
  defy 715
  brave 861
bold face *type* 591
boldfaced *insolent* 885
  printing 591
bole 50
bolero 840
boldness [*see* bold]
bolshevism 146, 742
bolshevist 146, 712
bolster *support* 215
  repair 658
  aid 707
- up *vindicate* 937
bolt *sift* 42, 652
  fasten 43
  fastening 45
  close 261
  move rapidly 274
  propel 284
  run away 370, 623
  safety 664
  escape 671
  hindrance 706
  shaft 727
  shackle 752
- food *swallow* 298
  gormandize 957
- in 751
- out of the blue 508
- the door 761
- upright 212
bolthead 191
bolus *mouthful* 298
  remedy 662
bomb 404, 406, 727
- explosion 361
- vessel 726
bombard 716
  circularize 592
bombardier 726
bombardon 417
bombast
  overestimation 482
  absurdity 497
  unmeaning 517
  magniloquence 577
  ridiculous 853
  boasting 884
  (*exaggeration* 549)
bombastic
  [*see* bombast]
bomber 269a
bombilation 404, 407
bombinate 407
bombing cruiser 273
bombproof 664
bon: - diable 844
- enfant *social* 892
  kindly 906
- mot 842
- ton 852
- vivant 957
476

voyage 267
bona fides
  veracity 543
  probity 939
bonanza *extra* 641
  wealth 803
bonbon 396
bond *tie* 45
  servile 746
  compact 769
  security 771
  money 800
  right 924
- of union 9, 45
bondage 749
bonded together 712
bonds [*see* bond]
  fetters 752
  securities 802
- of harmony 714
  in - *service* 746
bondsman 746
bone *dense* 321
  hard 323
  strength 159
- of contention 713, 720
- to pick *difficulty* 704
  discord 713
  bred in the - 5
  one - and one flesh 903
bonehouse 363
bones [*see* bone]
  corpse 362
  music 417
  break no - 648
  make no - *willing* 602
bonesetter 662
bonfire 382
  festivity 840
  celebration 883
  make a - of 384
bonhomie *candor* 703
  kindness 906
bonhomme 996
Boniface 890
bonne *servant* 746
  nurse 753
- bouche *treat* 377
  savory 394
  saving 636
  pleasant 829
bonnet 225
- rouge 742
bonny *cheerful* 836
  pretty 845
bonnyclabber 321
bonus *extra* 641
  gift 784
  money 810
bony 323
bonze 996
booby 501
boodle 784
boof 860
book *part* 51
  register 86
  record 551
  volume **593**
  libretto 599
  enter accounts 811

at one's-s 539
- collector 593
- learning 490
- madness 490
- of fate 601
- of poems 590
  bring to -
  evidence 467
  account 811
  reprove 932
  mind one's - 539
  school - 542
  without -
  by heart 505
bookbinder 593
bookbinding 593
bookcase 191
booked *dying* 360
bookish 490
bookkeeper 553
bookkeeping 811
bookless *unlearned* 493
bookmaker 156
bookmaking 156
bookseller 593
bookshop 593
bookstore 593
bookworm 492, 593
booly 268
boom *support* 215
  sail 267
  rush 274
  impulse 276
  sound 404
  roll 407
  obstacle 706
  defense 717
boomerang *recoil* 277
  weapon 727
boon 784
  beg a - 765
- companion 890
boor *clown* 876
boorish *ridiculous* 851
  uncourteous 895
boost *impulse* 276
  praise 931
booster 935
boot *box* 191
  dress 225
  advantage 618
  punishment 975
  to - *added* 37
booted and spurred 673
bootee 225
booth *stall* 189
  shop 799
bootikin 225
bootleg *drunkenness* 959
bootlegging 964
bootless *useless* 645
  failing 732
boots *dress* 225
  servant 746
  what - it 643
booty 35, **793**
booze 959
bo-peep *peep* 441
  hide 528

bordel 961
border *contiguity* 199
  edge 231
  flank 236
  flower bed 371
  ornament 847
- upon 197, 199
borderer 197
bordering 233
- upon 197
bore *diameter* 202
  hole 260
  tide 348
  tidal wave 667
  trouble 828
  plague 830
  weary 841
Boreal *Northern* 237
  cold 383
borean 349
Boreas 349
boredom 841
borer 262
boresome 275
born 359
- so 5
- to other things 865
- under a lucky star 734
- under an evil star 735
borne 826
- down *failure* 732
  defection 837
borné 499
borough 189
  rotten - 893
borrow *imitate* 19
  receive 788
borrowed plumes
  deception 545
borrower 806
borrowing 788
boscage 367
bosh *absurdity* 497
  unmeaning 517
  untrue 546
  trifling 643
bosk 367
bosky 367
bosom *breast* 221
  mind 450
  affections 820
- friend 890
- of one's family 221
  in the - of 229
boss *knob* 250
  will 600
  politician 694
  rule 737
  master 745
bossiness 600
bossism 693
boston 840
Boston bag 191
botanic 369
- garden 369, 371
botanomancy 511
botany 367, **369**
botch *disorder* 59
  mend 660

unskillful 699
difficulty 704
fail 732
both 89
bother
　uncertainty 475
　bustle 682
　difficulty 704
　trouble 828
　harass 830
botheration 828
bothy 189
bottle receptacle 191
　preserve 670
bee in a - 407
- green 435
- holder
　auxiliary 177
　mediator 724
- up remember 505
　hide 528
　restrain 751
crack a - 298
pass the - 959
smelling - 400
bottom lowest part 211
　support 215
　rear 235
　combe 252
　ship 273
　pluck 604a
　courage 861
at - 5
at the - of
　cause 153
- dollar 67, 800
- upwards 218
from the - of one's
　heart veracity 543
feeling 821
go to the - 310
probe to the - 461
bottomless 208
- pit 982
bottoms 345
bouderie 901a
boudoir 191
- cap 225
bouge 250
bough part 51
　curve 245
　tree 367
boughpot 400
bought flexure 245
bougie 423
bouilli 298
boulder 249
boulevards 227
bouleversement
　revolution 146
　destruction 162
　excite 824
bounce eject 297
　jump 309
　lie 546
　dismiss 756
　boast 884
　insolence 885
- upon arrive 292
　surprise 508
bouncer ejection 297

bouncing large 192
bound
　circumscribe 229, 233
　swift 274
　leap 309
　certain 474
- back recoil 277
- by 926
- for direction 278
　destination 620
- to promise 768
　responsible 926
I'll be - 535
boundary 233
bounden duty 926
boundless infinite 105
　space 180
bounds 233
　outline 230
- of modesty 881
- of possibility 470
keep within -
　moderation 174
　shortcoming 304
　restrain 751
　prohibit 761
bountiful liberal 816
　benevolent 906
bounty aid 707
　gift 784
bouquet fragrant 400
　beauty 847
bourdon staff 215
　melody 413
　drone 415
bourgeois medium 29
　type 591
　commoner 876
bourgeon 161, 194
bourn 233, 292
bourse 799
bouse 959
bout turn 138
　job 680
　fight 720
　prank 840
drinking - 954
boutade absurdity 497
　caprice 608
boutonnière 400
bovine ox 366
　beef-witted 499
bow fore part 234
　curve 245
　projection 250
　stoop 308
　fiddlestick 417
　weapon 727
　ornament 847
　servility 886
　reverence 894
　respect 928
bend the - 686
- down worship 990
- out 297
- submission 725
- window 245, 260
Bow bells 876
bowed down
　lament 837
　humble 879

boweless 914a
bowels inside 221
　conduit 350
- full of wrath 722
- of compassion 914
- of the earth 208
bower abode 189
　alcove 191
　cards 840
-s of bliss 981
bowery 424
bowie knife 253, 727
bowl vessel 191
　rotate 312
- along walk 266
　swift 274
flowing - 959
bowlder - 249
bow-legged 243
bowler hat 225
bowling green
　level 213
bowls 840
bowman 726
bowshot 197
bowsprit 234
bowstring
　execution 972, 975
bowwow 412
box house 189
　chest 191
　theater 599
　fight 720
- car 272
- pleat 258
- the compass
　direction 278
　rotation 312
　change of mind 607
- the ear anger 900
　strike 972
- up 751
horse - 272
in a - 704
musical - 417
wrong - error 495
　unskillful 699
　dilemma 704
boxer 726
boy 129
　servant 746
boyage 127
boyar 875
boycott eject 297
　resist 719
　seclude 893
　disapprove 893
boyhood 127
boylike 129
brabble discord 713
　contest 720
brabbler 901
brace tie 43
　fasten 45
　two 89
　strengthen 159
　support 215
　music 413
　typography 550
　refresh 689
- game 545

bracelet circle 247
　ornament 847
bracer 392, 662
brachial 633
brachygraphy 590
bracing salubrious 656
bracken 367
bracket tie 43, 45
　couple 89
　support 215
-s typography 550
brackish 392
bract 367
brad 45
bradawl 262
Bradshaw 266
brae 206
brag cards 840
　boast 884
braggadocio 482, 884
braggart 482, 884
Brahma 976
Brahman religion 984
　priest 996
Brahmanism 976
Brahmi 590
Brahmo 984
braid tie 43
　ligature 45
　net 219
　variegate 440
Braille 442
brain kill 361
　intellect 450
　skill 498
rack one's -s 451, 515
suck one's -s 461
brainless 499
brainpan 450
brainsick 458
brain storm 503
brainwork 451
brainy 450, 498
brake slowness 275
　copse 367
　check 706
　curb 752
apply the - slower 275
　hinder 706
put the -s on 265
　[see also break]
bramble thorn 253
　bane 663
bran 330
brancard 272
branch member 51
　posterity 167
　ramify 244
　stream 348
　tree 367
- off bifurcate 91
　diverge 291
- out ramify 91
　diffuse style 573
branchiæ 349
branching ramous 242
brand burn 384
　fuel 388
　torch 423
　mark 550
　sword 727

477

disrepute 874
censure 932
stigmatize 934
- new 123
- of discord 713
- with reproach 938
brandish
  oscillate 314
  flourish 315
  display 882
brandy smash 959
brangle 713
brangler 710
brank 975
brash *brittle* 328
  downpour 348
  sickness 655
brashness 885
brasier 386
brass *alloy* 41
  music 416
  insolence 885
  bold as - 861
  - band 416, 417
  - colored 439
  - farthing 643
brassard 550
brassière 225
brat 129, 167
brattice 224, 228
bravado 884
brave *healthy* 654
  defy 234, 715
  warrior 726
  bear 821, 826
  courage 861
bravery [see brave]
bravo *assassin* 361
  desperado 863
  applause 931
bravura 415, 416
brawl *cry* 411
  discord 713
  revel 840
brawler *disputant* 710
  rioter 742
  blusterer 887
brawny *strong* 159
  stout 192
bray *grind* 330
  cry 412
Bray, Vicar of -
  tergiversation 607
  servility 886
braze 43
brazen *unreserved* 525
  insolent 885
brazier 191
Brazil tea 298
breach *crack* 44
  gap 198
  quarrel 713
  violation 925
  - of faith 940
  - of law
    unconformity 83
    illegal 964
  - of the peace 713
  custom honored in
    the - 614
breachy 198
478

unruly 742
bread 298
  beg - 765
  selfish 943
  - of idleness 683
  - of life *Christ* 976
    piety 987
  - upon the waters 484
breadbasket 191
breadfruit 298
breadstuffs 298
breadth 202
  chiaroscuro 420
break *fracture* 44
  discontinuity 70
  change 140
  gap 198
  carriage 272
  deviate 279
  crumble 328
  train animals 370
  disclose 529
  discord 713
  cashier 756
  violate 773, 927
  bankrupt 808
  faux pas 947
  - a habit 614
  - a lance *attack* 716
    battle 722
  - a law 83
  - away *depart* 293
    avoid 623
  - bread 298
  - bulk 297
  - camp 293
  - down *destroy* 162
    fall short 304
    decay 659
    fail 732
  - for taller timber 666
  - forth 295
  - ground *begin* 66
    depart 293
  - in *ingress* 294
    domesticate 370
    teach 537
    tame 749
  - in upon *derange* 61
    inopportune 135
    hinder 706
  - jail 671
  - loose *escape* 671
    get free 750
  - no bones 648
  - of 660
  - of day *morning* 125
    twilight 422
  - off *cease* 70, 142
    relinquish 624
    abrogate 756
  - one's neck
    powerless 158
    die 360
  - on the wheel
    physical pain 378
    mental pain 830
    punishment 972
  - open 173
  - out *begin* 66
    violent 173

disease 655
  excited 825
  - Priscian's head 568
  - prison 750
  - short 328
  - silence 582
  - the heart *pain* 828,
    830
    dejection 837
  - the ice 888
  - the neck of *task* 676
    success 731
  - the peace *violence*
    173
    contest 720
  - the ranks 61
  - the teeth
    hard words 579
  - the thread 70
  - through a custom
    614
  - through the clouds
    visible 446
    disclose 529
  - up *disjoin* 44
    decompose 49
    end 67
    revolution 146
    destroy 162
  - up of the system
    death 360
    disease 655
  - with 713
  - with the past 146
  - word *deceive* 545
    improbity 940
breakable 328
breakbone fever 655
breakdown 840
breaker *of horses* 268
  wave 348
breakers *surf* 348
  shallow 667
  - ahead 665
  surrounded by - 704
breakfast 298
breakneck
  precipice 217
  rash 863
breakwater *refuge* 666
  obstruction 706
breast *interior* 221
  confront 234
  convex 250
  meat 298
  mind 450
  oppose 708
  soul 820
  at the - 129
  - high 206
  - the current 719
  in the - of 620
breastplate 717
breastwork 717
breath *instant* 113
  breeze 349
  life 359
  animality 364
  faint sound 405
  - of accusation 938
  hold - *quiet* 265

expect 507
wonder 870
in the same - 120
not a - of air *quiet* 265
  hot 382
out of - 688
shortness of - 688
take away one's -
  unexpected 508
  fear 860
  wonder 870
take - *rest* 265
  refresh 689
with bated - 581
breathe *exist* 1
  blow 349
  live 359
  faint sound 405
  evince 467
  mean 516
  inform 527
  disclose 529
  utter 580
  speak 582
  refresh 689
  - freely *pleasure* 827
    relief 834
  - one's last 360
  - the vital air 359
  not - a word 528
breathing *time* 106
  air 349
  - time *repose* 687
    truce 723
breathing-hole 351
breathless
  voiceless 581
  out of breath 688
  feeling 821
  fear 860
  eager 865
  wonder 870
  - attention 457
  - expectation 507
  - impatience 865
  - speed 684
breech *invest* 225
  rear 235
breeches 225
  - maker 225
  - pocket
    money 800, 802
  wear the - 737
breechloader 727
breed *race* 11
  kind 75
  multiply 161
  progeny 167
  animals 370
  rear 537
  (prepare 673)
breeding
  production 161
  style 852
  politeness 894
  - place 153
breeze *wind* 349
  discord 713
breezy 836
brethren 997
breve 413

brevet *warrant* 741
  commission 755
  permit 760
  - rank 873
breviary 990, 998
brevier 591
brevipennate 193
brevity *short* 201
  concise 572
brew *mix* 41
  prepare 673
brewing
  impending 152
Briarean 102, 159
Briareus 159, 192
bribe *equivalent* 30
  tempt 615
  offer 763
  gift 784
  buy 795
  reward 809, 973
bribery [*see* bribe]
bric-a-brac 847
brick *hard* 323
  pottery 384
  material 635
  trump 939, 948
  - color 434
  - over 386
  - red 434
  make -s without straw
    471
brickbat 727
brickkiln 386
bricklayer 690
bricky 434
bridal 903
bride 903
bridegroom 903
bridesmaid 890, 903
bridesman 903
bridewell 752
bridge
  intermedium 45
  way 627
  card game 840
  - of death 360
  - over *join* 43
  facilitate 705
  make peace 723
  compromise 774
bridle *depart* 293
  restrain 751
  rein 752
  - one's tongue
  silent 585
  cautious 864
  - road 627
  - up 900
brief *time* 111
  space 201
  concise 572
  compendium 596
  - case 191
  hold a - for 759
briefly *anon* 132
brier *sharp* 253
  bane 663
brig 273
brigade *arrange* 60
  military 726

brigadier 745
brigand 792
brigandage 791
brigandine 717
brigantine 273
bright *shine* 420
  color 428
  intelligent 498
  cheery 836
  beauty 845
  glory 873
  - colored 428
  - days 734
  - prospect 858
  - side 829
  - thought *sharp* 498
  good stroke 626
  wit 842
  look at the - side
  cheer 836
  hope 858
brighten up
  furbish 658
bright-eyed 845
brigue *party* 712
  contention 720
brilliant *shining* 420
  music 416
  good 648
  witty 842
  beautiful 845
  gem 847
  glorious 873
  be - *intellectual* 498
  - idea 842
brim 231
  - over 641
brimful 52
brimstone 388
brindled 440
brine *sea* 341
  salt 392
bring 270
  - about *cause* 153
  achieve 729
  - back 790
  - back to the memory
    505
  - forth *produce* 161
  extract 301
  - forward
  evidence 467
  manifest 525
  teach 537
  improve 658
  - gray hairs to the
    grave
  adversity 735
  pain 830
  - grist to the mill 644
  - home 775
  - home to 155
  - in *receive* 296
  income 810
  price 812
  - in a verdict 480
  - in its train 88
  - in question 461
  - into being 161
  - into play 677
  - low 874

  - off 672
  - out *discover* 480a
  manifest 525
  publish 591
  - over *persuade* 484
  - round *persuade* 615
  restore 660
  - to *convert* 144
  halt 265
  - to a crisis 604
  - to a point 74
  - to bear 470
  - to bear upon
  relation 9
  action 170
  - together *assemble* 72
  - to life 359
  - to light 480a
  - to maturity
  prepare 673
  complete 729
  - to mind 505
  - to perfection 677
  - to terms 723
  - to trial 969
  - under one's notice
    457
  - up *develop* 161
  vomit 297
  train 370
  educate 537
  - up the rear 235
  - word 527
brink 231
  - of the grave 360
  on the - *almost* 32
  coming 121
  near 197
briny 392
  - deep 341
brio *music* 415
briquette 388
brisk *prompt* 111
  energetic 171
  active 682
  cheery 836
bristle 253
  - up *stick up* 250
  angry 900
  - with *plenty* 639
  too much 641
  - with arms 722
bristling *thorny* 253
  discourtesy 895
bristly *rough* 256
Britannia metal 545
Briticism 563
British 188
  - courts 966
  - lion 604
Britisher 188
Briton 188
  true - 939
brittle 328
brittleness **328**
britzka 272
broach *begin* 66
  found 153
  perforate 262
  tap 297
  publish 531

  assert 535
broad *general* 78
  space 202
  lake 343
  emphatic 535
  indelicate 961
  - accent 580
  - arrow 550
  - awake *vigilant* 459
  brisk 682
  - daylight *light* 420
  manifest 525
  - farce 842
  - gauge 466
  - grin 838
  - highway 627
  - hint 527
  - meaning 516
broadcast *disperse* 73,
  291
  publish 531
  news 532
  sow - 818
broadcloth 219, 635
broaden 78
broadhearted 906
broadhorn 273
broadsheet 531, 593
broad-shouldered 159
broadside *lateral* 236
  publication 531
  cannonade 716
broadsword 727
Brobdingnagian 159,
  192
brocade 847
brocatelle 847
brochure 593
broder 549
brogan 225
brogue *boot* 225
  dialect 560, 563
broidery 847
broil *heat* 382
  fry 384
  fray 713, 720
broiler *fowl* 298
broken *divided* 51
  discontinuous 70
  weak 160
  of horses 370
  - color 428
  - down *decrepit* 659
  failing 732
  dejected 837
  - English 563
  - fortune
  adversity 735
  poverty 804
  - heart *pain* 828
  dejected 837
  hopeless 859
  - meat 645
  - reed 665
  - voice 581, 583
  - winded *disease* 655
  fatigue 688
broker *agent* 758
  merchant 797
brokerage *pay* 812
brokery 794

bromide
  conventionalist 82
bromidium 496
bronchia 351
broncho 271
- buster 370
bronchocele 655
bronze *brown* 433
  sculpture 557
brooch 847
brood *multitude* 102
  family 167
  hatch 370
- over *think* 451
  mope 837
brooding *preparing* 673
brook *stream* 348
  bear 826
broom *undergrowth* 367
  sweep 652
broomstick 491
broth 298
brothel 945, 961
brother *kin* 11
  similar 17
  equal 27
- Jonathan 188
brotherhood 712
brotherly
  friendship 888
  love 897
  benevolence 906
brougham 272
brought to bed 161
brouillerie 713
brouillon 626
brow *top* 210
  edge 231
  front 234
browbeat
  intimidate 860
  swagger 885
  disrespect 929
-en *humbled* 879
brown 433
- Bess 727
- ocher 433
- stone 635
- stone house 189, 831
- study *thought* 451
  inattention 458
  imagination 515
Brownian 984
brownie 979
brownness 433
browse 298
bruin 895
bruise *powder* 330
  hurt 619
  injure 649
bruised *blemished* 848
bruiser 726
bruit 531, 532
brumal 383
brummagem 545
brunch 572
brunette 433
Brunswick black 356a
brunt *beginning* 66
  impulse 276
  bear the -

  difficulty 704
  defense 717
  endure 821, 826
  (*resist* 719)
brush *tail* 235
  rough 256
  rapid motion 274
  groom 370
  touch 379
  clean 652
  fight 720
- away *reject* 297
  abrogate 756
- up *clean* 652
  furbish 658
  prepare 673
paint - 556
brushwood 367, 388
brusque *violent* 173
  haste 684
  discourtesy 895
Brussels sprouts 298
brustle 407
brutal *vulgar* 851
  rude 895
  savage 907
brutalize
  [see *brutal*]
  corrupt 659
  deaden 823
  vice 945
brute *animal* 366
  rude 895
  maleficent 913
- force *strength* 159
  violence 173
  animal 450a
  severe 739
  compulsion 744
  lawless 964
- matter *matter* 316
  inorganic 358
brutify 954
brutish [see *brute*]
  vulgar 851
  ignoble 876
  intemperate 954
Bryanite 984
bryophites 369
bubble
  unsubstantial 4
  transient 111
  little 193
  light 320
  water 348
  air 353
  error 495
  deceit 545
  trifle 643
- burst
  fall short 304
  disappoint 509
  fail 732
- reputation 873
- up *agitation* 315
bubbling 353
bubo 250
bubonic plague 655
buccaneer 791, 792
Bucephalus 271
buck *confront* 234

  leap 309
  stag 366
  male 373
  negro 431
  wash 652
  fop 854
- basket 191
- fever 825
- jump 309
- nigger 431
bucket *receptacle* 191
  load 270
- shop 621
  kick the - 360
bucking *attack* 716
buckle *tie* 43
  fastening 45
  distort 243
  curl 248
- oneself 604
- on one's armor 673
- to *resolution* 604
  exertion 686
- with *grapple* 720
buckler 717
buckram
  affectation 855
  pride 878
men in - 549
buckwheat 367
bucolic
  pastoral 370, 371
  poem 597
bud *beginning* 66
  germ 153
  expand 194
  graft 300
  blossom 367
- from 154
Buddha 976, 986
Buddhism 976, 984
Buddhist 984
- priests 996
- temple 1000
budding *young* 127
  expansion 194
buddy *chum* 890
budge 264
budget *heap* 72
  bag 191
  store 636
  finance 811
- of news 532
budmash 949
buff *skin* 223
  color 436
native - 226
buffalo 366
- bug 366
- robe 223
- wallow 343
buffer *hindrance* 706
  defense 717
buffet *strike* 276
  agitate 315
  evil 619
  bad 649
  affront 900
  smite 972
- the waves
  difficulty 704

  opposition 708
buffet *bar* 189
  cupboard 191
buffle-headed 499
buffo 599
buffoon *actor* 599
  humorist 844
  butt 857
buffoonery
  amusement 840
  humor 842
bug *littleness* 193
  insect 366, 653
bugaboo *alarm* 669
  fear 860
bugbear *imaginary* 515
  alarm 669
  fear 860, 980
buggy 272
bugle *instrument* 417
  war cry 722
- call *sign* 550
  command 741
bugles *ornament* 847
build *construct* 161
  form 240
- a campfire 384
- up *compose* 54
- upon *belief* 484
- upon a rock 150
builder 626, 690
building material 635
buildings 189
built on *basis* 211
bulb *knob* 249
  projection 250
bulbul 416
bulge 250
bulk *be great* 31
  whole 50
  size 192
bulkhead *covering* 223
  interjacence 228
  safety 664
  hindrance 706
bulky 31
bull *animal* 366
  male 373
  error 495
  absurdity 497
  solecism 568
  detective 664
  ordinance 741
  stock exchange 797
- in a china shop 59
take the - by the horns
  resolution 604
  courage 861
Bull, John - 188
bulla 250
bull calf 501
bulldog *animal* 327, 366
  pluck 604, 604a
  courage 861
bulldoze 860, 885
bulldozer 887
bullet *ball* 249
  arms 727
  (*missile* 284)
- proof 717

bulletin *list* 86
  news 532
  record 551
  letter 592
  - board 551
bullfight 720
bullhead 501
bullion 800
bull's-eye *center* 222
  lantern 423
  aim 620
bullwhack 975
bullwhacker 370
bully *boat* 273
  first-rate 648
  fighter 726
  jovial 836
  frighten 860
  rashness 863
  bluster 885
  blusterer 887
  resent 900
  threaten 909
  evildoer 913
  bad man 949
  - for you 931
bullyrag 830
bulrush *worthless* 643
bulwark 717
bum *idler* 683
  spree 840
  beggar 876
  drink 959
bumbailiff 965
Bumbledom
  authority 737
  jurisdiction 965
bumboat 273
bummer 683
bump *projection* 250
  thump 276
bumper 52
bumpkin 876
bumptious *proud* 878
  insolent 885
bun 298
bunch *collection* 72
  protuberance 250
bunch-backed 243
buncombe *lie* 544
  bombast 577
  boast 884
  flattery 933
Bund 712
bund *quay* 666
bunder 292, 666
bunderboat 273
bundle *packet* 72
  go 266
  start 284
  - along 274
  - off 234
  - on *hurry* 274
  haste 684
  - out 297
bundobust 60, 769
bung 263, 351
  - up 261
bungalow 189
bunghole 351
bungle 699

bungler **701**˙
bunk *reside* 186
  support 215
bunker 181
bunkie *bedfellow* 890
bunko 545,791
  - game 545
  - steerer 548
bunkoman 792
bunkum [*see* buncombe]
bunt 276
bunting 550
buoy *raise* 307
  float 320
  refuge 666
  hope 858
buoyant *floating* 305
  light 320
  elastic 325
  prosperous 734
  cheerful 836
  hopeful 858
bur *clinging* 46
  rough 256
  in engraving 558
burden *lading* 190
  weight 319
  melody 413
  music 415
  poetry 597
  too much 641
  clog 706
  oppress 828
  care 830
  - of a song
  repetition 104
  - the memory 505
burdensome
  [*see* burden]
  hurtful 649
  laborious 686
  cumbrous 830
bureau *chest* 191
  office 691
  shop 799
  tribunal 966
  department 965
bureaucracy 737
bureaucrat 694
bureaucratic 737
burgee 550
burgeon 161, 194
burgess 188
burgh 189
burgher 188
burghmote 966
burglar 792
  - alarm 550, 669
burglary 791
burgomaster 745
burgrave 745
burial 363
buried *deep* 208
  imbedded 229
  hidden 528
  - in a napkin 460
  - in oblivion 506
burin 558
burke 361
burlesque
  imitation 19

  travesty 21, 555
  absurdity 497
  drama 599
  comic 853
  ridicule 856
burletta 599
burly 192
burn *near* 197
  rivulet 348
  hot 382
  consume 384
  neglect 460
  near the truth 480a
  excited 825
  blemish 848
  love 897
  punish 972
  - daylight 683
  - in 384
  - one's fingers 699
  - out 385
  - the candle at both
    ends
  waste 638
  exertion 686
  prodigal 818
  - to 865
  - up the road 266
burner 423
burning [*see* burn]
  of a corpse 363
  passion 821
  angry 900
  - ghât 363, 384
  - glass 445
  - pain 378
  - shame 874
  - with curiosity 455
burnish *polish* 255
  shine 420
  beautify 845
burnoose 225
burnt [*see* burn]
  red 434
  - offering *atone* 952
  worship 990
  - orange 434
burr 253, 410
burra sahib 642, 745
burro 271
burrow *lodge* 184
  excavate 252
bursar 801
bursary 802
bursat 348
burst *disjoin* 44
  instantaneous 113
  explosion 173
  brittle 328
  sound 406
  paroxysm 825
  bubble -
  disclosure 529
  all over 729
  - away 623
  - forth *begin* 66
  expand 194
  be seen 446
  - in 294
  - into a flame 825
  - into tears 839

  - of anger 900
  - of eloquence 582
  - of envy 921
  - of laughter 838
  - out *violence* 173
  egress 295
  - upon *arrive* 292
  unexpected 508
  - with grief 839
  ready to -
  replete 641
  excited 824
burthen [*see* burden]
bury *inclose* 229
  inter 363
  conceal 528
  - one's talent 528
  - the hatchet 723
busby 225
bush *branch* 51
  lining 224
  jungle 344
  shrub 367
  beat about the - 629
  in the - 344
bushed 475, 688
bushel *much* 31
  multitude 102
  receptacle 191
  size 192
  hid under a - 460
  not hide light under a
    - 878
bushfighting 720
bushing 224
Bushman 431
bushranger 792
bushwhacker
  scythe 253
  guerrilla 726
  free lance 748
bushy 256
business *event* 151
  topic 454
  occupation **625**
  commerce 794
  full of - 682
  man of -
  proficient 700
  consignee 758
  mind one's -
  incurious 456
  attentive 457
  careful 459
  send about one's - 297
  stage - 599
businesslike
  orderly 58
  business 625
  active 682
  practical 692
  skillful 698
buskin *dress* 225
  drama 599
buss *boat* 273
  courtesy 894
  endearment 902
bust 554
  spree 840
bustee 189
bustle *energy* 171

dress 225
agitation 315
activity 682
haste 684
difficulty 704
bustling [see bustle]
eventful 151
busy 682
idly - 638, 683
busybody curiosity 455
  newsmonger 532
  activity 682
but on the other hand 30
  except 83
  limit 233
  qualifying 469
  - now 118
butcha 129, 167
butcher kill 361
  evildoer 913
butchered 53
butler 746
butt cask 191
  push 276
  aim 620
  attack 716
  laughingstock 857
  - end 67
  - in 294
butte 206
butter 356
  flattery 933
  - bread on both sides 641

- not melt in mouth 894
buttercup 845
buttered side
  know - skill 698
  selfish 943
  not know - 699
butter-fingers 701
butterfly insect 366
  variegated 440
  fickle 605
  beauty 845
  gaudy 882
  break - on wheel
  waste 638
  spite 907
butterscotch 396
buttery 636
Buttinsky 294
buttock 235
button fasten 43
  fastening 45
  little 193
  hanging 214
  knob 250
  trifle 643
  - up close 261
  restrain 751
  - up one's pockets 808
  take by the - 586
buttoned-up
  reserved 528
buttonhole flower 400
  bore 841

buttonholer 841
buttons page 746
button-top useless 645
buttress strength 159
  support 215
  defense 717
butyraceous 355
buxom 836
buy 795
  - and sell 794
  - a pig in a poke 621
buzz hiss 409
  insect cry 412
  publish 531
  news 532
  - saw 44
buzzard bird 366
  fool 501
  between hawk and -
  agitation 315
  worry 828
  blind as a - 442
  - dollar 800
by alongside 236
  instrumental 631
  sequestered 893
  - and by 121, 132
  - itself 87
  - means of 632
  - my troth &c. 535
  - no means 32
  - telegraph 532
  - the by 134
  - the card 82

- the hour &c.
  hire 788
- the way à propos 9
  beside the purpose 10
  parenthetical 134
- wireless 532
go - pass 303
have - one
  provide 637
  possess 777
bye departure 293
by-end 615
bygone past 122
  forgotten 506
  let -s be bygones 918
bylaw 963
byname 565
by-pass 287
bypast 122
bypath 279
byplay hint 527
  gesture 550
by-purpose 615
byre 189, 370, 636
byroad 278, 627
by-room 191
byssus 256
bystander near 197
  spectator 444
byway 627
byword maxim 496
  cant term 563, 564
  reproach 874
  contempt 930

C

cab 272
cabal plan 626
  confederacy 712
cabala latency 526
  spell 993
cabalism 526
cabalistic hidden 528
  sorcery 992
cabane 273
cabaret 189
cabasset 717
cabbage 298, 791
cabestro 45
cabin room 189
  receptacle 191
cabined 751
cabinet receptacle 191
  workshop 691
  council 696
  - picture 556
cable link 45
  dispatch 527
  news 531, 532
  telegraph 534
  by - 684
  - code 528
  slip - 623
  telegraphic - 534
cabled telegraphic 531
cabman traveler 268
  director 694
caboose 386

cabriolet 272
cacation 299
cachalot 192
cache 636
cachet 550
  lettre de - 751
cachexia weakness 160
  disease 655
cachinnation 838
cacique 745
cackle of geese 412
  chatter 584
  talk 588
  laugh 838
cacodemon 980
cacoëpy 410, 583
cacoëthes habit 613
  itch 865
  - loquendi 584
  - scribendi 590
cacographer 579
cacographic 579
cacography 590
cacology 579, 583
caconym 563
cacophonous
  [see cacophony]
cacophony stridor 410
  discord 414
  style 579
Cacus, den of - 791
cad servant 746

  vulgar 851
  plebeian 876
cadastral survey 466
cadastration 466
cadastre list 86
  measurement 466
cadaverous corpse 362
  pale 429
  hideous 846
caddy 191
cadeau 784
cadence pace 264
  fall 306
  sound 402
  music 415
cadenza 415
cadet junior 129
  soldier 726
  officer 745
  - blue 438
cadge 765
cadger beggar 767
  huckster 797
cadi 967
cadmium 439
caduceus insignia 747
  wand 215, 993
caducity fugacity 111
  age 128
  impotence 158
  decay 659
caducous 111

cæcal 261
cæcum 221, 350
Cæsar 745
cæsura disjunction 44
  discontinuity 70
  cessation 142
  interval 198
café 189
caftan 225
cafuzo 41
cage receptacle 191
  restrain 751
  prison 752
Cagliostro impostor 548
  sorcerer 994
cahoot 712
cahot 250, 315
cahotage disorder 59
  agitation 315
Cain 361
caique 273
cairn grave 363
  sign 550
caisson 191, 252
caitiff churl 876
  ruffian 913
  villain 949
cajole flatter 933
  [see cajolery]
cajolery
  imposition 544, 545
  persuasion 615

specification 527
grammar 567
affair 625
patient 655
lawsuit 969
be the -*exist* 1
true 494
- in point *agree* 23
conform 82
in - *circumstance* 8
event 151
supposition 514
in good - *healthy* 654
prosperous 734
make out a -
evidence 467
right 924
caseate 321
caseation 321
caseharden
strengthen 159
habituate 613
casehardened
callous 376, 823
obstinate 606
casein 321
casemate *barrack* 189
defense 717
casement 260
casern 189
cash *money* 800
pay 807
- *account* 811
- down 810
- on delivery 810
- register 85, 551, 802
in - 803
cashbook 551, 811
cashbox 802
cashier *dismiss* 756
treasurer 801
cashmere 635
casing 223
casino 712
cask 191
casket *box* 191
coffin 363
casque *helmet* 717
casquetel 717
Cassandra
prophet 513
warning 668
cassino 840
Cassiopeia's Chair 318
cassock 999
cast *mold* 21
small quantity 32
add 37
rôle 51
spread 73
tendency 176
exuviæ 223
form 240
throw 284
tinge 428
aspect 448
plan 626
staff 712
give 784
allot 786
condemn 971

- about for 463
- accounts 811
- adrift *disperse* 73
eject 297
liberate 750
dismiss 756
- a gloom 837
- a nativity
predict 511
sorcery 992
- anchor *stop* 265
arrive 292
- a shade 421
- aside 460
- a slur *discredit* 874
accuse 938
- a spell 992
- aspersions 934
- away *reject* 610
waste 638
lost 732
- away *care* 836
- behind one
forget 506
refuse 764
relinquish 782
- dishonor upon 874
- down 308
dejected 837
- eyes on 441
- in one's lot with 609
- in the eye 443
- in the same mold 17
- in the teeth 938
- iron *metal* 323
resolute 604
- lots 621
- luster upon 420
- of countenance 448
- of mind 820
- of the dice 156
- off *divest* 226
dismiss 756
relinquish 782
- off a habit 614
- off clothes 645
- off skin 223
- off trammels 750
- one's net 463
- out 610
- overboard
disuse 678
- reflection upon 932
- the eyes back 122
- the eyes over 457
- the parts 60
- the skin 226
- to the dogs 162
- up *add* 85
happen 151
eject 297
give one a - 707
set on a - 621
castaneous 433
castanet 417
castaway *exile* 893
reprobate 949
(impious 988)
caste *class* 75
party 712
rank 873

- mark 550
lose - 940
castellan *servant* 746
keeper 753
castellated 717
caster *cruet* 191
wheel 312
castigate *reprove* 932
punish 972
castigator 936
casting - vote 480
- weight 28, 30
castle *at chess* 148
abode 189
refuge 666
defense 717
- builder 515
- in the air
inattention 458
impossible 471
imagination 515
hope 858
castor *hat* 225
Castor and Pollux
twins 89
luminary 423
friends 890
castrametation
building 189
war 722
castrate *subduct* 38
impotent 158
casual *incidental* 6
chance 156
uncertain 475
nonobservant 773
casualty *event* 151
killed 361
evil 619
misfortune 735
casuist 476
casuistic 477
casuistry
sophistry 477
falsehood 544
duty 926
casus belli
quarrel 713
irritation 824, 900
cat *boat* 273
nine lives 359
animal 366
keen sight 441
fall on one's feet 734
cross 901
as the - jumps
event 151
- and dog life 713
- in pattens 652
gib -, tom - *male* 373
let - out of bag 529
see how the - jumps
foresight 510
fickleness 607
caution 864
catabasis 36
catacaustic 245
catachresis
metaphor 521
misinterpretation 523
cataclasm 44

cataclysm
convulsion 146
destruction 162
deluge 348
(redundance 641)
catacomb 363
catacoustics 402
catafalque 363
catalectic 597
catalepsy 265, 683
catalo 41
catalogue *arrange* 60
list 86
- raisonné 551
catalysis 49
catamaran
vessel 273
fighter 726
catamenia 138
catamount 913
cataphonics 402
cataplasm 662
catapult
propulsion 284
weapon 727
cataract *waterfall* 348
blindness 442, 443
catarrh 299
catastrophe
dénouement 154
disaster 619
finish 729
misfortune 735
end 67
catastrophic
revolutionary 146
[*see* catastrophe]
catboat 273
catcall *whistle* 417
disapproval 932
catch *imitate* 19
fastening 45
song 415
detect 480a
gather the meaning
518
cheat 545
receive 785
take 789
by -es 70
- a disease 655
- a glimpse of 441
- a likeness 554
- an idea 498
- a sound 418
- at *willing* 602
desire 865
- a Tartar *dupe* 547
retaliate 718
- at straws
overrate 482
credulous 486
unskillful 699
rash 863
- by surprise 508
- drain 191
- fire 384
- in a trap 545
- one's death 360
- the attention 457
- the breath 349

long time 110
cephalalgia 378
ceramic 384
- ware 557
ceramics 557
cerate 355, 662
Cerberus *janitor* 263
  custodian 664
sop for - 615
cereal 298, 367
cereals 369
cerebral *phonetic* 561
cerebrate 451
cerebration 451
cerebrum 450
cerecloth 223, 363
cerement *covering* 223
  wax 356
  burial 363
ceremonious 928
ceremony *parade* 882
  courtesy 894
  rite 998
cerise 434
cerograph 558
cerography
  engraving 558
  writing 590
ceromancy 511
ceroplastic 557
certain *special* 79
  indefinite number 100
  sure 474
  belief 484
  true 494
make - of 480a
of a - *age* 128
to a - *degree* 32
certainly *yes* 488
certainty **474**
certes *surely* 474
  yes 488
certificate
  evidence 467
  record 551
  security 771
certify *evince* 467
  affirm 535
certiorari 969
certitude 474
cerulean 438
cerulescent 438
ceruse 430
cespitose 367
cess *tax* 812
cessation **142**
cession *surrender* 725
  of property 782
  gift 784
cesspool 653
cest 247
cestus *ligature* 45
  girdle 247
chabuk 975
chafe *physical pain* 378
  warm 384
  irritate 825
  mental pain 828, 830
  discontent 832
  incense 900
chaff *trash* 643

  rubbish 645
  ridicule 856
  vulgar 876
not to be caught with-
  clever 698
  cunning 702
winnow - from wheat
  609
chaffer 794
chafing-dish 386
chagrin 828
chain *fasten* 43
  vinculum 45
  series 69
  measure 200
  interlinking 219
  imprison 752
  ornament 847
adamantine -s 360
- lightning 423
  drink 959
-s *fireplace* 386
drag a - 749
drag a lengthened -
  686
in -s *prisoner* 754
chain shot 727
chair *support* 215
  vehicle 272
  professorship 542
  throne 747
  celebration 883
  president 694
- car 272
in the - 693
chairman 694
chaise 272
chalcedony 847
chalcography 558
chalet 189
chalice 191
chalk *earth* 342
  white 430
  mark 550
  drawing 556
- out *plan* 626
- talk 537, 584
- talker 540
not know - from
  cheese 491
chalky 430
challenge
  question 461
  doubt 485
  claim 924
  defy 715
  accuse 938
- comparison 648
- the jurors 969
chalybeate 662
chamber *room* 191
  council 696
  mart 799
- concert 415
- fellow 890
- music 415
sick - 655
chamberlain 746
chambermaid 746
chameleon *lizard* 366
  changeable 149

  variegated 440
chamfer 259
chamois
  smoothness 255
  leap 306
  animal 366
champ 298
- the bit *disobedient*
  742
  chafe 825
  angry 900
champagne 959
champaign 344
champain 874
champak 400
champion *best* 648
  auxiliary 711
  defense 717
  combatant 726
  victor 731
  representative 759
  pity 914
championship 707
champlevé 847
chance
  absence of cause **156**
  liability 177
  absence of aim **621**
as - would have it 152
be one's - 151
-s against one *danger*
  665
game of - 840
great - 472
small - 473
stand a - *liable* 177
  possible 470
take one's - 675
chanceable 156
chanceful 156
chancel 1000
chancellor *judge* 664,
  967
  president 745
  deputy 759
- of the exchequer 801
chancery
- suit *delay* 133
court of - 966
chandelier 214, 423
chandler 797
change *alteration* **140**
  interchange 148
  mart 799
  small coin 800
- about 149
- color 821
- for 147
- hands 783
- of mind 607
- of opinion 485
- of place 264
radical - 146
sudden - 146
changeable 149
changeableness
  mutable **149**
  irresolute 605
changeful 607
changeling
  substitute 147

  fool 501
changer 797
channel *base* 211
  furrow 259
  opening 260
  conduit 350
  artery 627
chant *song* 415
  sing 416
  worship 990
chanter 416
chanticleer 366
chantress 416
chantry 1000
chaomancy 511
chaos 59
chap *crack* 198
  jaw 231
  fellow 373
chaparajos 225
chaparral 367
chap book 593
chapeau 225
chapel 189, 1000
chaperon
  accompany 88
  guard 459
  safety 664
chapfallen 837, 878
chaplain 996
chaplaincy 995
chaplet *circle* 247
  fragrance 400
  favor 550
  trophy 733
  ornament 847
chapman 797
chaps *chaparajos* 225
chapter *partition* 44
  part 51
  topic 454
  book 593
  council 696
  church 995
- and verse
  evidence 467
  exact 494
- of accidents 156, 621
chapter house 1000
chaqueta 225
char 384
char-à-bancs 272
character *nature* 5
  state 7
  class 75
  oddity 83
  letter 561
  drama 599
  disposition 820
characteristic
  intrinsic 5
  special 79
  mark 550
characterize *name* 564
  describe 594
characterized 820
charade *riddle* 533
  drama 599
charcoal *fuel* 384, 388
  black 431
  drawing 556

charge *fill* 52
  contents 190
  business 625
  mandate 630
  direction 693
  advice 695
  precept 697
  attack 716
  order 741
  custody 751
  commission 755
  bargain for 794
  price 812
  accusation 938
  churchdom 995
  - d *with*
  possessed of 777
  - on *attribute* 155
  in - *prisoner* 754
  justifiable - 937
  take - of *safe* 664
  take in - 751
chargeable *debt* 806
  - on *duty* 926
chargé d'affaires 758
charger *carrier* 271
  fighter 726
chargeship 625
chariot 272
  drag at one's - wheels
    749
charioteer
  driver 268
  pilot 694
charitable [*see* charity]
charity *give* 784
  liberal 816
  benefi:ent 906
  pity 914
  - that begins at home
    943
  cold as - *insensible* 823
charivari *loud* 404
  clatter 407
  discord 414
charlatan
  ignoramus 493
  impostor 548
  mountebank 844
  boaster 884
charlatanism
  ignorance 491
  falsehood 544
  affectation 855
Charles's wain 318
Charley 753
charm *draw* 288
  motive 615
  talisman 747
  please 829
  beauty 845
  love 897
  attraction 928
  conjure 992
  spell 993
  bear a -d life
  safe 664
  prosperous 734
charmer *sorcerer* 994
  voice of the -
  flattery 933

charming *taste* 850
  [*see* charm]
charnel house 363
chart *inform* 527
  represent 554
charter
  commission 755
  permit 760
  compact 769
  security 771
  privilege 924
chartered *legal* 963
  - accountant 811
  - libertine 962
chartulary 86
charwoman
  worker 690
  servant 746
chary *economical* 817
  stingy 819
  cautious 864
Charybdis
  whirlpool 312, 346
  danger 665
chase *emboss* 250
  drive away 289
  killing 361
  forest 367
  pursue 622
  ornament 847
  wild goose - 645
chaser 559
chasm *interval* 198
  opening 260
  gully 350
  abyss 667
  (*discontinuity* 70)
chassepot 727
chasser 297
  - *balancer* 605
chasseur 726
chassis 272
chaste *shapely* 242
  language 576, 578
  simple 849
  good taste 850
  pure 960
chasten *moderate* 174
  punish 972
chastened
  subdued spirit 826
chasteness [*see* chaste]
chastise *censure* 932
  punish 972
  - with scorpions 739
chastity 960
chasuble 999
chat 588
château 189
châtelaine 847
chatoyant 440
chattels *furniture* 633
  property 780
chatter 412, 584
chatterbox 584
chattering of teeth
  cold 383
chatti 191
chatty *talkative* 584
  sociable 892
chauffeur 268, 271, 694

chauki 752
chaunt [*see* chant]
chaussé 225
Chautauqua 537
chauvinism 884, 885
chauvinist 885
chawbacon 876
cheap *worthless* 643
  low price 815
  hold - 930
cheapen *haggle* 794
  begrudge 819
cheapness 815
cheat *deceive* 545
  deceiver 548
check *numerical* 85
  cessation 142
  moderate 174
  counteract 179
  slacken 275
  plaid 440
  experiment 463
  measure 466
  evidence 468
  ticket 550
  dissuade 616
  hinder 706
  misfortune 735
  restrain 751
  money order 800
  - in full career 142
  - oneself 829
  - the growth 201
checkered
  diversified 16a
  changeable 149
  variegated 440
checkers 440
  game 840
checkmate
  deadlock 142
  success 731
  failure 732
checkrein 706
checkroll 86
checkstring
  pull the - 142
cheek *side* 236
  - by jowl *with* 88
  near 197
cheeks *dual* 89
cheep 412
cheer *repast* 298
  cry 411
  aid 707
  pleasure 827
  relief 834
  mirth 836
  rejoicing 838
  amusement 840
  courage 861
  exult 884
  sociality 892
  welcome 894
  applaud 931
  (*please* 829)
  good - *hope* 858
  high living 957
cheerful 836
  - *giver* 816
cheerfulness 836

cheering 602
cheerless
  unpleasing 830
  dejected 837
cheese 298
cheesecake 298
cheeseparings
  remains 40
  dirt 653
  parsimony 819
cheetah 440
chef de cuisine
  proficient 700
  servant 746
chef-d'œuvre
  masterpiece 648
  master stroke 698
cheiromancy 522
chela 541
chemical 144
chemise 225
chemisette 225
chemistry 144
  organic - 357
cheque 800
chequer 440
  - roll 86
cherish *aid* 707
  love 897
  endearment 902
  - a belief 484
  - an idea &c. 451
  - feelings &c. 821
cheroot 392
cherry 298, 434
  two bites of a -
  overrate 482
  roundabout 629
  clumsy 699
cherry-cheeked 845
cherry-colored 434
chersonese 342
cherub 167,977
Cherubim 977
Cheshire cat 838
chess 840
chessboard 440
chest *box* 191
  money coffer 802
chestnut
  stale joke 105, 532
  fruit 367
  red 434
chestnut-color 433
cheval-de-bataille
  plea 617
  plan 626
cheval glass 445
chevalier 875
  -d'industrie 792
chevaux de frise
  spikes 253
  defense 717
chevron *obliquity* 217
  rank 550, 747, 877
chevronné 754
chew 298
  tobacco 392
  - the cud 451
chiaroscuro *light* 420
  gray 432

property 780
right 924
lawsuit 969
- the attention 457
claimant petitioner 767
right 924
clairaudience 450, 992a
clairaudient 450
clair-obscur 420, 421
clairvoyance 450, 992a
clairvoyant 450, 513, 992a
clam 298
clamant 411
clambake 840
clamber 305
clammy 352
clamor cry 411
wail 839
- against 932
- for 765
clamorous
[see clamor]
loud 404
excitable 825
clamp fasten 43
fastening 45
clan race 11
class 75
family 166
party 712
clandestine 528
clang 404
clangor 404, 508
clank 410
clannishness 481
clanship 709
clap shut 261
explosion 406
applaud 931
- on the back 931
- on the shoulder 615
- the hands rejoice 838
- together 43
- up imprison 751
thunder - prodigy 872
clapboard 223, 635
clapperclaw
contention 720
censure 932
claptrap absurdity 497
pretense 546
display 882
claque 72
claquer 935
clarence 272
claret 298
- color 434
clarify 652
clarinet 417
clarion music 417
war 722
clarity clearness 518
elegance 578
clash disagree 24
cross 179
concussion 276
sound 406
oppose 708
discord 713
- of arms 720
492

clashing
contrariety 14
wrangle 24
clasp fasten 43
fastening 45
stick 46
come close 197
belt 230
embrace 902
class arrange 60
category 75
learners 541
school 542
party 712
laity 997
- fellow 890
classfellow 890
classic old 124
symmetry 242
music 415
classical
elegant writing 578
taste 850
- education 537
classicism 578
classicist 578
classics 560
classification 60
classify 60
classis 696
classman 873
associate 890
classmate 492, 541, 890
class room 542
clatter noise 404
rattle 407
claudication
slowness 275
failure 732
clause part 51
passage 593
condition 770
claustral 1000
claustrophobia 860
clavate 250
clavichord 417
clavier 417
claviform 250
clavis opening 260
interpretation 522
claw tenacity 327
hook 781
grasp 789
- back 935
clawhammer coat 225
clay soft 324
earth 342
corpse 362
material 635
clay-cold 383
clayey 324
claymore 727
clean entirely 52
perfect 650
unstained 652
- bill of health 654
- breast
disclose 529
- cut 494
- forgotten 506

- hand
proficient 700
- out empty 297
- sweep
revolution 146
destruction 162
with - hands
honesty 939
innocence 946
cleanly 652
cleanness 652
cleanse 652
cleansing 652
clean-up 35
clear simple 42
leap 309
sound 413
light 420
transparent 425
visible 446
certain 474
intelligible 518
manifest 525
distinct 535
perspicuous 570
easy 705
liberate 750
profit 775
vindicate 937
innocent 946
acquit 970
- articulation 580
- as day 474
- conscience 946
- for action
prepare 673
- grit 604
- of distant 196
- off pay 807
- out empty 297
clean 652
- sky hope 858
- stage
occasion 134
easy 705
right 922
- the course 302
- the ground
facilitate 705
- the skirts of 937
- the throat 297
- up light 420
intelligible 518
interpret 522
coast - 664
get - off 671
keep - of 623
clearance 970
clear-cut true 494
plain 518
clear-eyed 441
clear-headed 498
clear-sighted vision 441
shrewd 498
clearing 181, 184
clearness [see clear]
clear-thinking 498
cleavage cutting 44
structure 329
cleave sunder 44
adhere 46

bisect 91
cleaver 253
cledge 342
clef 413
cleft disjoined 44
bisected 91
chink 198
in a - stick
difficulty 704
clem 956
clement lenient 740
long-suffering 826
compassionate 914
clench compact 769
retain 781
take 789
clepe 564
clepsydra 114
clerestory 191
clergy 996
- list 86
clerical 995, 996
- error 495
- staff 746
clericalism 995
clerk scholar 492
recorder 553
writer 590
helper 711
servant 746
agent 758
clergy 996
articled - 541
- of works 694
clerkship
commission 755
cleromancy 511
clever intelligent 498
skillful 698
witty 842
too - by half 702
clew ball 249
inquiry 461
answer 462
interpretation 522
indication 550
seek a - 461
click 406
client follower 65
dependent 711, 746
customer 795
clientele 795
clientship
subjection 749
cliff height 206
vertical 212
steep 217
climacteric 128
climate region 181
weather 338
fine - 656
climatology 338
climatometer 338
climax supremacy 33
summit 210
turning point 283
climb 305
fain would I - 860
thou -ing sorrow 828
clime 181
clinal 217

clinch *fasten* 43
close 261
certify 474
pun 563
complete 729
clutch 781
snatch 789
- an argument 479
- the fist at 909
clincher 479
cling *adhere* 46
- to *near* 197
willing 602
persevere 604a
habit 613
observe 772
desire 865
love 897
- to *hope* 858
- to one another 709
clinic *disease* 655
remedy 662
clink *resonance* 408
stridor 410
clinker *brick* 384
dirt 653
clinometer
oblique 217
angle 244
(*measurement* 466)
clinquant
ornament 847
vulgar 851
Clio 594
clip *shorten* 201
pace 264
blow 276
- one's words 583
- the wings
powerless 158
slow 275
useless 645
hinder 706
prohibit 761
(*prune* 38)
(*contract* 195)
clipper 273
clipping *small piece* 51
clique *class* 75
conclave 696
party 712
(*sociality* 892)
cliquish 712
clivers 253
cloaca *conduit* 350
foul 653
Cloacina 653
cloak *dress* 225
conceal 528
disguise 530
(*pretense* 546)
clock 114
clockwise 312
clockwork 633
by - *uniform* 16
order 58
regular 80
clod *lump* 192
earth 342
fool 501
bungler 701

clodhopper 876
clodpated *stupid* 499
clog *shoe* 225
hinder 706
cloisonné 557, 847
cloister *arcade* 189
passage 627
restraint 751
seclusion 893
convent 1000
(*seclusion* 893)
close *similar* 17
copy 21
tight 43
end 67
field 181
court 189
near 197
narrow 203
shut 261
dense 321
warm 382
hidden 528
concise 572
taciturn 585
complete 729
conclude 769
stingy 819
- at hand
to-morrow 121
imminent 152
near 197
- call 671
- formation 716
- in upon
converge 290
- inquiry 461
- one's eyes to
not attend 458
set at naught 773
- one's ranks 673
- prisoner 754
- quarters 197
approach 286
attack 716
battle 722
- study *thought* 451
attention 457
- the door upon
restrain 751
- the ears 419
- the eyes *die* 360
not see 442
- the hand *refuse* 764
- with *cohere* 46
assent 488
attack 716
contend 720
consent 762
compact 769
keep - *hide* 528
retain 781
closely [*see* close]
- packed 72
closet *receptacle* 191
ambush 530
closeted with
conference 588
advice 695
closure 261
stopping 142

clot *solidify* 321
earth 342
hindrance 706
(*cohere* 46)
cloth *vocation* 625
napkin 652
clergy 996
clothe 225
clothes 225
- basket 191
- horse 215
- press 191
grave - 363
clothier 225
clothing 225
clotpoll 501
clotted 352
- cream 321, 354
cloture 142
cloud *assemblage* 72
multitude 102
wind 349
mist **353**
darken 421
dim 422
shade 424
semitransparency 427
screen 520
break through the -s
446
- capt 206
- of dust 330
- of skirmishers 726
- of smoke 333
- of words 573
- over 421, 422
-s gathering *dark* 421
danger 665
warning 668
- topped 206
drop from the -s 508
in a - *uncertain* 475
hidden 528
in the -s *lofty* 206
inattentive 458
dreaming 515
under a -
insane 503
adversity 735
disrepute 874
secluded 893
censured 932
accused 938
cloud-built 4
cloudburst 348
clouded *variegated* 440
dejected 837
hopeless 859
- perception 499
cloudland 515
cloudless *light* 420
happy 827
cloudy *dim* 422
opaque 426
clough 206
clove 198
cloven 91
cloven foot *mark* 550
malevolence 907
vice 945
Satan 978

see the - 480a
show the - 907
clover *grass* 367
luxury 377
prosperity 734
comfort 827
in - 377, 827
clown *pantomime* 599
buffoon 844
vulgar 851
rustic 876
cloy *pall* 376
redundance 641
satiety 869
cloying 396
cloyment 869
club *combine* 48
place of meeting 74
house 189
association 712
weapon 727
sociality 892
- law
compulsion 744
lawless 964
- together
coöperate 709
clubbability 892
clubbable 712
club-footed 243
clubman 852
club-shaped 250
clubwoman 852
cluck 412
clue [*see* clew]
clump *assemblage* 72
projecting mass 250
- of trees 367
clumsiness
[*see* clumsy]
clumsy *unfit* 647
awkward 699
ugly 846
Cluniac 996
cluricaune 980
cluster 72
clutch *automobile* 272
retain 781
seize 789
clutches 737
in the - of 749
clutter *be loud* 404
roll 407
clypeate 245
clypeiform 245
clyster 300
coacervation 72
coach *carriage* 272
teach 537
tutor 540, 673
- road 627
- up 539
drive a - and six
through 964
coach house 191
coachman *travel* 268
pilot 694
coaction
concurrence 178
coöperation 709
compulsion **744**

compurgation
  evidence 467
  acquittal 970
compurgator 467
computable 85
compute 37, 85
computation
  addition 37
  accounts 811
comrade 890
comradeship 892
con *think* 451
  get by heart 505
  learn 539
conation *agency* 170
  tendency 176
  will 600
conative 170, 176
conatus 176
concamerate 245
concatenation
  junction 43
  continuity 69
  - of circumstances 621
concave 252
  - *mirror* 555
concavity **252**
conceal *invisible* 447
  hide 528
  cunning 702
concealment **528**
concede *assent* 488
  admit 529
  permit 760
  consent 762
  give 784
conceit *idea* 453
  overestimation 482
  folly 499
  supposition 514
  imagination 515
  wit 842
  affectation 855
  vanity 880
conceited *dogmatic* 481
conceivable 470
conceive *begin* 66
  teem 168
  note 450
  believe 484
  understand 490
  imagine 515
  concent 413
concentrate
  assemble 72
  centrality 222
  converge 290
concentric 216, 222
concentricity 216
concentus 23, 413
conception
  [*see* conceive]
  intellect 450
  idea 453
  guiding - 453
concern *relation* 9
  event 151
  care 459
  business 625
  importance 642
  firm 797
498

  grief 828
  - oneself with 625
concerning *relative to* 9
  (*topic* 454)
concert *agreement* 23
  synchronous 120
  music 415
  act in - 709
  - hall 189
  - master 416
  - measures 626
  - piece 415
  in - *musical* 413
    concord 714
concertina 417
concerto 415
concert room 840
concession
  permission 760
  consent 762
  giving 784
  discount 813
concetto 842
conch 204, 215
concha 418
conchate 245
conchiform 245
conchoid 245
conchology 223
concierge 263, 753
conciliate *talk over* 615
  pacify 723
  satisfy 831
  courtesy 894
  atonement 952
conciliatory [*see* con-
ciliate]
  concord 714
  courteous 894
  forgiving 918
conciliatrix 962
concinnity *agreement* 23
  style 578
  beauty 845
concise 572
  taciturn 585
conciseness **572**
concision 201
conclave *assembly* 72
  council 696
  church 995
conclude *end* 67
  infer 480
  resolve 604
  complete 729
  compact 769
conclusion [*see* con-
clude]
  sequel 65
  eventuality 151
  effect 154
  judgment 480
  foregone - 611
  hasty - 481
  try -s 476
conclusive [*see* con-
clude]
  final 67
  answer 462
  evidential 467
  certain 474

  proof 478
  manifest 525
  - *reasoning* 476
concoct *lie* 544
  plan 626
  prepare 673
concomitant
  accompany 88
  same time 120
  concurrence 178
concord *agree* 23
  music **413**
  assent 488
  harmony **714**
  (*amity* 888)
concordance
  dictionary 562, 593,
  636
concordant 178
concordat 769
concours 720
concourse
  assemblage 72
  convergence 290
  - of atoms 621
concremation 384
concrete *mass* 46
  density 321
  hardness 323
  materials 635
concretion 46
concubinage 961
concubine 926
concupiscence
  desire 865
  impurity 961
concur *coexist* 120
  causation 178
  converge 290
  assent 488
  concert 709
concurrence *crisis* 43
  coagency **178**
  observance 772
concurrent 178, 216
concussion 276
condemn 971
condemnation
  censure 932
  conviction **971**
condemnatory 971
condensation
  brevity 201
  [*see* condense]
condense
  compress 195
  dense 321
condensed 572
condescend 879
condescension 879
condign 924
condiment **393**
condisciple 541
condition *state* 7
  modification 469
  supposition 514
  term 770
  repute 873
  rank 875
  in - *plump* 192
  in good - 648

  in perfect - 650
  on - 770
  physical - 316
conditional 8
conditions **770**
condolence 914, **915**
condone 918
condottiere
  traveler **268**
  fighter 726
conduce
  contribute 153
  tend 176
  concur 178
  avail 644
conducent 176
conducive 631
conduct *transfer* 270
  procedure **692**
  lead 693
  - an inquiry 461
  - to 278
safe - *passport* 631
  safety 664
conduction 264
conductivity 157
conductor *guard* 268
  conveyer 271
  music 416
  director 694
  lightning - 666
conduit **350**
conduplicate 89
condyle 250
cone *round* 249
  pointed 253
cone-shaped 253
conestoga **wagon**
  272
confab 588
confabulation 588
confection 396
  confectionery 396
confederacy
  coöperation 709
  party 712
confederate
  combine 48
  auxiliary 711
Confederates 712
confer *advise* 695
  give 784
  - benefit 648
  - power 157
  - privilege 760
  - right 924
  - with 588
conference [*see* con-
fer]
  council 696
  churchdom 995
conferva 367
confess *assent* 488
  avow 529
  penitence 950
  - and avoid 937
confession [*see* con-
fess]
  worship 990
  auricular - 998
  - of faith 983

CONFESSIONAL

CONSECUTIVELY

confessional
disclosure 529
rite 998
temple 1000
confessions
biography 594
confessor 996
confidant
auxiliary 711
maid 746
friend 890
confidante
servant 746
friend 890
confidence *trust* 484
expectation 507
deception 545
hope 858
courage 861
- man 548
- trick 545
in - 528
confident [*see* confidence]
affirm 535
confidential 528
confiding 703
configuration 240
confine *place* 182
circumscribe 229
border 231
limit 233
imprison 751
confined
narrow judgment 481
ill 655
confinement
childbed 161
confines of
on the - 197
confirm
corroborate 467
assent 488
consent 762
compact 769
rite 998
confirmation 535
confirmatory 480
confirmed 150
- habit 613
confirmist 488
confiscate *take* 789
condemn 971
penalty 974
confiture 298, 396
conflagration 384
conflation 54
conflexure 245
conflict
disagreement 24
opposition 708
discord 713
contention 720
warfare 722
conflicting
contrary 14
counteracting 179
- evidence 468
confluence
junction 43
convergence 290

river 348
confluent 290
conflux
assemblage 72
convergence 290
conform *assent* 488
conformable
agreeing 23
concurrent 178
conformation 240
conformity 82
concurrence 178
- to rule 494
confound *disorder* 61
destroy 162
not discriminate 465a
perplex 475
confute 479
defeat 731
astonish 870
curse 908
confounded *great* 31
bad 649
confraternity *party* 712
friendship 888
confrère *colleague* 711
friend 890
confrication 331
confront *face* 234
compare 464
oppose 708
resist 719
- danger 861
- witnesses 467
Confucius 986
confuse *derange* 61
perplex 458
obscure 519
not discriminate 465a
abash 879
confused *disorder* 59
invisible 447
uncertain 475
perplexed 523
style 571
harmoniously - 81
confusion [*see* confuse]
obscurity 571
- of tongues 560, 563
- of vision 443
- seize 908
- worse confounded 59
in - *excited* 825
confutation 479
confute 479
congé *departure* 293
abrogation 756
- d'elire 995
congeal *dense* 321
cold 385
congener *similar* 17
included 76
congeneric *similar* 17
congenerous 9, 17
congenial *agreeing* 23
concord 714
love 897
(*expedient* 646)
congenital 5
inborn 820

congenite 5
Congeries 72
congestion 641
conglaciation 385
conglobation 72
conglomerate *cohere* 46
assemblage 72
dense 321
conglutinate 46
congratulate 896
- oneself 838
congratulation 896
congregation
assemblage 72
worshipers 990
laity 997
congregational 995
Congregationalist 984
congress *assembly* 72
convergence 290
conference 588
council 696
congressional 696
- medal 551
congressman 696
congreve *fuel* 388
- rocket 727
congruence 23
congruous
agreeing 23
(*expedient* 646)
conical *round* 249
pointed 25
conifer 369
conjectural 514
conjecture 514
conjoin 43
conjoint 48
conjointly 37
conjugal 903
conjugate *combined* 48
words 562
grammar 567
- in all its tenses &c. 104
conjugation
junction 43
pair 89
phase 144
contiguity 199
grammar 567
conjunction
junction 43
contiguity 199
in - with 37
conjunctive 48
conjuncture
contingency 8
occasion 134
conjure *deceive* 545
entreat 765
sorcery 992
- up 506
- up a vision 515
name to - with 873
conjuror *deceiver* 548
sorcerer 994
connate *intrinsic* 5
related 9
kindred 11
cause 153

connation 11
connatural *related* 9
uniform 16
similar 17
connaturality 13
connature 13, 16
connect *relate* 9
link 43
connection *kin* 11
coherence 46
connective 45
conned, well - 490
connivance 760
connive *overlook* 460
coöperate 709
allow 760
connivent 286
connoisseur *critic* 480
scholar 492
taste 850
connoisseurship 850
connotate 550
connotation 516
connote *mean* 516
indicate 550
connubial 903
conoscente 850
conquer 731
conquered (*failure* 732)
conqueror 731
conquest 749
consanguinity 11
conscience
knowledge 490
moral sense 926
awakened - 950
clear - 946
in all - *great* 31
affirmation 535
qualms of - 603
stricken - 950
tender - 926
honor 939
conscientious 926
faithful 21
scrupulous 939
(*veracious* 543)
(*virtuous* 944)
conscious
intuitive 450
knowledge 490
- of disgrace 874
- of glory 873
consciousness 450
subliminal - 992a
conscript 726
conscription 744
consecrate *use* 677
dedicate 873
sanctify 987
holy orders 995
consecration *rite* 998
consectary 478
- reasoning 476
consecution 63
consecutive
following 63
continuous 69
posterior 117
- fifths 414
consecutively

499

slowly 275
consension 23
consensus 23, 488
consent *assent* 488
  compliance **762**
  with one - 178
consentaneity 23
consentaneous
  agreeing 23
  concurrent 178
  (*expedient* 646)
consequence *event* 151
  effect 154
  importance 642
  in - 478
  of no - 643
  take the -s 154
consequent 63
consequential
  deducible 478
  arrogant 878
consequently
  reasoning 476
  effect 154
conservation
  permanence 141
  storage 636
  preservation 670
conservatism 141, 670
conservative 141
  - policy 681
Conservatives 712
**conservator of the
  peace** 967
conservatory
  receptacle 191
  floriculture 371
  furnace 386
  store 636
conserve *sweet* 396
  store 637
consider *think* 451
  attend to 457
  examine 461
  adjudge 480
  believe 484
considerable
  in degree 31
  in size 192
  important 642
considerate *careful* 459
  judicious 498
consideration
  purchase money 147
  thought 451
  idea 453
  attention 457
  qualification 469
  inducement 615
  importance 642
  gift 784
  benevolence 906
  respect 928
  requital 973
  deserve - 642
  in - of
    compensation 30
    reasoning 476
  on - 658
  take into -
    thought 451
500

attention 457
  under - *topic* 454
  inquiry 461
  plan 626
considered [*see* con-
  sider]
  all things -
    judgment 480
    premeditation 611
    imperfection 651
consign *transfer* 270
  commission 755
  property 783
  give 784
  - to oblivion 506
  - to the flames 384
  - to the tomb 363
consignee 270, **758**
consigner 796
consignificative 522
consignment
  commission 755
  gift 784
  apportionment 786
consilience 178
consimilarity 17
consist - in 1
  - of 54
consistence
  density 321
consistency
  uniformity 16
  agreement 23
consistent 82
  -ly with 82
consistory *council* 696
  church 995
consociate 890, 892
consolation *relief* 834
  condole 915
  religious 976
console *table* 215
consolidate *unite* 46,
  48
  condense 321
Consols 802
consommé 298
consonance 16
consonant
  agreeing 23
  musical 413
  letter 561
  (*expedient* 646)
consort
  accompany 88
  associate 892
  spouse 903
  - with 23
consortium 23
consortship 892
conspection 441
conspectus 596
conspicuous *visible* 446
  famous 873
  - by his absence 187
conspiracy 626
  - of silence 460
conspirator 626
  traitor 941
conspire *concur* 178
  coöperate 709

constable *safety* 664
  governor 745
  officer 965
constancy 743
constant *uniform* 16
  continuous 69
  regular 80
  frequent 136
  periodic 138
  immutable 150
  exact 494
  persevering 604a
  faithful 939
  - flow 69
constellation *stars* 318
  luminary 423
  glory 873
consternation 860
constipate 321
constipation
  closure 261
  density 321
constituency 609
constituent 56, 609
constitute
  compose 54, 56
  produce 161
constituted by 1
constitution
  nature 5
  state 7
  composition 54
  structure 329
  charter 924
  law 963
  higher law than - 926
constitutional *walk* 266
  - government 737
constitutive 153
constrain *compel* 744
  restrain 751
  abash 881
constraint
  contraction 195
  [*see* constrain]
constrict 195
constriction 706
constringe 195
constringency 195
construct *compose* 54
  produce 161
  organize 357
construction
  production 161
  form 240
  structure 329
  meaning 522
  put a false - upon 523
constructive
  creative 161
  latent 526
  - evidence 467
constructor 164
construe 522
consubstantiation 998
consuetude 613
consul 758, 759
consular 759
consulship 737
consult *remedy* 662
  advise 695

- one's own wishes 943
- one's pillow 133
- the wishes of 707
consultant 662
consultation 695
consume *decay* 49
  destroy 162
  waste 638
  use 677
  time
  time 106
  inactivity 683
consumer *user* 677
consuming 830
consummate *great* 31
  complete 52
  be perfect 650
  completed 729
  - skill 698
consummation *end* 67
  completion 729
  - devoutly   to   be
    wished
  good 618
  desire 865
consumption
  [*see* consume]
  decrease 36
  shrinking 195
  disease 655
consumptive 655
contact *contiguity* 199
  touch 379
  come in -
  arrive 292
contagion *transfer* 270
  unhealthy 657
contagious 655, 657
contain
  be composed of 54
  include 76
contained in 1
container
  receptacle 191
contaminate *soil* 653
  spoil 659
contaminated
  diseased 655
contamination 653, 659
contango 813
contemn 930
contemper 48, 174
contemplate *view* 441
  intellect 450
  think 451
  expect 507
  purpose 620
contemplation
  [*see* contemplate]
contemporaneous 120
contemporary 120
contemporation 174
contempt **930**
  - of danger 861
contemptible
  unimportant 643
  dishonorable 940
contemptuous
  defiant 715
  disrespectful 929
  disdainful 930

contend *reason* 476
  assert 535
  fight 720
  - for *vindicate* 937
  - with difficulties 704
content *assenting* 488
  willing 602
  calm 826
  satisfied **831**
  to one's heart's -
  sufficient 639
  success 731
contention **720**
contentious 901
contents
  ingredients 56
  list 86
  components **190**
  book 593
  synopsis 596
conterminate *end* 67
  limit 233
conterminous 199
contesseration 72
contest 708, 720
contestant 710
context 591
contexture 329
  (*state* 7)
contiguity **199**
contiguous 197
continence 960
continent 342
continental *trifle* 643
continentals 225
contingency
  junction 43
  event 151
  uncertainty 475
  expectation 507
contingent
  extrinsic 6
  conditional 8
  casual 156
  liable 177
  possible 470
  uncertain 475
  supply 635
  aid 707
  allotted 786
  donation 809
  - duration **108a**
  - interest 780
continual
  perpetual 112
  frequent 136
continuance 117, **143**
continuation
  affix 37
  adjunct 39
  sequence 63
  sequel 65
  - school 542
continuations
  trousers 225
continue *exist* 1
  endure 106, 110
  persist 143
continued 69
  - existence 112
  - success 731

continuing 143
continuity 16, **69**
continuous 69
contortion
  distortion 243
  convolution 248
  (*ugliness* 846)
contortionist 599
contortuosity 243
contour *outline* 230
  appearance 448
  - line 550
contra 14
  per - 708
contraband
  deceitful 545
  prohibited 761
  illicit 964
contrabandist 792
contrabasso 417
contraclockwise 283
contract *shrink* 195
  narrow 203
  promise 768
  bargain 769
  (*decrease* 36)
  (*curtail* 201)
  - a debt 806
  - a habit 613
  - an obligation 768
contractible 195
contractility 195
  (*elasticity* 325)
contraction **195**
  shorthand 590
  compendium 596
contractive 36, 464
contractor 690
contractual 769
contradict
  contrary 14
  dissent 489
  deny 536
  oppose 708
contradiction
  difference 15
  answer 462
contradictoriness 15
contradictory
  evidence 468
  discordant 713
contradistinction 15
contrafagotto 417
contraindicant 616
contraindicate
  dissuade 616
  warning 668
contralto 408
contraposition
  inversion 218
  reversion **237**
contrapuntal 415
contrapuntist 413
contrariety **14**, 15, 708
contrariness 708
contrariwise 148, 708
contrary *opposite* 14
  antagonistic 179
  captious 608
  opposing 708
  - to expectation

  improbable 473
  unexpected 508
  - to reason 471
  quite the - 536
contrast
  contrariety 14
  difference 15
  comparison 464
contrastive 15
contrate wheel 247
contravallation 717
contravene
  contrary 14
  counteract 179
  counterevidence 468
  deny 536
  hinder 706
  oppose 708
contre-coup 277
contrectation 379
contretemps
  ill timed 135
  hindrance 706
  misfortune 735
contribute *cause* 153
  tend 176
  concur 178
  aid 707
  give 784
contribution 784
  lay under -
  take 789
  due 924
contributor
  correspondent 592
  giver 784
contributory *extra* 37
contrition *abrasion* 331
  penitence 950
contrivance 626
contrive *produce* 161
  plan 626
  - to *succeed in* 731
contriving
  cunning 702
control *power* 157
  influence 175
  aviation 273
  regulate 693
  authority 737
  restrain 751
  board of - 696
  get - of 175
  under -
  obedience 743
  subjection 749
controller 694
controversial
  discussion 476
  discordant 713
controversialist   476,
  726
controversy
  discussion 476
  interlocution 588
  contention 720
controvert *deny* 536
controvertible
  uncertain 475
  debatable 476
  untrue 495

contumacy
  obstinacy 606
  disobedience 742
contumely
  arrogance 885
  rudeness 895
  disrespect 929
  scorn 930
  reproach 932
contund 330
contuse 330
conundrum *pun* 520
  riddle 533
  wit 842
  (*problem* 461)
convalesce 654
convalescence 654, 660
convection 270
convene 72
convenience 685
conveniences 632
convenient 646
convent 1000
  - school 542
conventicle
  assembly 72
  council 696
  chapel 1000
convention
  assembly 72
  canon 80
  council 696
  law 697
  treaty of peace 723
  compact 769
  - of society 852
conventional
  customary 613
conventionalism 613
conventionality 82
conventionality 613
conventionalize 82
conventual *monk* 996
  convent 1000
converge 290
convergence **290**
convergent 286, 290
conversable *talk* 588
  sociable 892
conversant
  know 490
  skillful 698
conversation 588
conversational 588
  sociable 892
conversationist 588
conversazione
  interlocution 588
  social gathering 892
converse
  reverse 14, 237
  talk 588
  hold high - 539
conversely 148, 168
conversible 144
conversion **144**
  trover and - 964
convert *deny* 536
  change 140
  change to 144
  opinion 484
  tergiversation 607

keep in - *conform* 82
  induce 615
  encourage 861
  vindicate 937
keep one's - *brook* 826
  not laugh 837
out of - *abashed* 879
put out of - 874
stare out of - 885
counter *contrary* 14
  number 84
  table 215
  rear 235
  reverse 237
  token 550
  shopboard 799
  - to 708
lie nailed to the - 934
over the - *barter* 794
  buy 795
  sell 796
run - 179
counteract
  compensate 30
  physically 179
  hinder 706
  voluntarily 708
counteraction **179**
counterbalance 30
counterblast
  counteract 179
  answer 462
  retaliate 718
counterchange
  correlation 12
  interchange 148
countercharge 462
countercharm 993
countercheck
  mark 550
  hindrance 706
counterclaim 30
counterclockwise 283
countercurrent 312
counterevidence **468**
counterfeit *imitate* 19
  copy 21
  simulate 544
  sham 545
  untrue 546
  - *presentment* 21
counterfeiter 800
counterfoil 550
counterjumper 746
countermand 756
countermarch
  journey 266
  regression 283
  regression 283
countermark 550
countermine
  excavate 252
  intrigue 626
  oppose 708
  defense 717
countermotion 283
counterorder 756
counterpane 223
counterpart
  identity 13
  complement 14
504

match 17
  copy 21
  duplicate 90
  reverse 237
counterplot
  plan 626
  oppose 708
  retaliate 718
counterpoint 14, 413
counterpoise
  compensate 30
  weight 319
  hinder 706
  (*counteract* 179)
counterpoison 662
counterpoie 14
counterproject 718
counterprotest 468
counter-revolution 146
counterscarp 717
counterscript 21
countersign
  evidence 467
  assent 488
  mark 550
counterstatement 462
counterstroke 718
countervail
  outweigh 28
  compensate 30
  evidence 468
counterweigh 319
counterwork 708
countess 875
countinghouse 799
countless 105
countrified *rustic* 189
  vulgar 851
country *region* 181
  abode 189
  rural 371
  state 737
  jury 967
  - seat 189
  - town 189
love of - 910
country-dance 840
countryman
  commonalty 876
  friend 890
countryside 182
county 181
  - council 696
  - council school 542
  - court 966
coup *instantaneous* 113
  action 680
  - de grâce *end* 67
  deathblow 361
  completion 729
  pity 914
  punishment 972
  - de main
  violence 173
  action 680
  attack 716
  - de maître
  excellent 648
  skillful 698
  success 731
  - d'état

revolution 146
  plan 626
  action 680
  lawless 964
coupé 272
coupelet 272
couple *unite* 43
  fastening 45
  combine 48
  two 89
  - d with *added* 37
  accompanied 88
coupler 45
couplet 89, 597
coupon 800
courage **861**
  - oozing out 862
  moral - 604
courageous 861
courier *traveler* 268
  interpreter 524
  messenger 534
course *order* 58
  continuity 69
  time 106, **109**
  layer 204
  motion 264
  locomotion 266, 267
  direction 278
  dinner 298
  river 348
  habit 613
  pursuit 622
  way 627
  conduct 692
  arena 728
bend one's - 266
  - of action 692
  - of business 625
  - of events 151
  - of inquiry 461
  - of preparation 673
  - of study 537
  - of things 151
  - of time 121
  - runs smooth 734
follow as of - 478
hold a - 278
in due - 109, 134
in the - of
  during 106
keep one's -
  progress 282
  persevere 604a
let things take their-
  continue 143
  inaction 681
mark out a - 626
of - *conformity* 82
  effect 154
  certain 474
  assent 488
  necessity 601
  custom 613
  consent 762
  expect 871
run its - *end* 67
  complete 729
take a - 622
take its - 151
courser *horse* 271

swift 274
courses 138
coursing *kill* 361
  pursue 622
court *close* 181
  house 189
  hall 191
  invite 615
  pursue 622
  council 696
  retinue 746
  solicit 765
  gentility 852
  wish 865
  woo 902
  flatter 933
  tribunal 966
bring into - 467
  - card 626
  - of honor 939
friend at - 711
pay - to
  servile 886
  love 897, 902
  flatter 933
put out of - 731
courteous 894
courtesan 962
courtesy
  politeness **894**
show - *respect* 928
courthouse 189
courtier *servile* 886
  flatterer 935
  - like 933
courtly 852
courtship 902
courtyard 182
cousin 11
cove *cell* 191
  hollow 252
  bay 343
covenant *compact* 769
  condition 770
  security 771
covenantor 488
Coventry
  Earl of - *cards* 840
  send to - *eject* 297
  disrepute 874
  seclusion 893
cover *compensate* 30
  include 76
  superpose, lid 223
  dress 225
  stopper 263
  course 298
  hat h 370
  conceal 528
  retreat 530
  report 531
  keep clean 652
  keep safe 664
  preserve 670
  - up one's tracks 528
  - with dust 653
  under - *hidden* 528
  pretense 545
  safe 664
covercle 223
covering **223**

(*inactivity* 683)
- in 294
- into a corner 893
- into the good graces
  of 933
- out 529
- upon one 508
- with *multitude* 102
  redundance 641
creeper 367
creeping
  sensation 380
- thing 366
creepy 380
creese 727
cremation
  of corpses 363
  burning 384
crematorium 363
crematory 384
crème
- de la crème 648
- de menthe 435
- glacée 298
Cremona 417
crenate 257
crenelate 257
crenelle 257
crenulate 257
creole 57
crêpe de Chine 635
crepitant 406
crepitation 406
crepuscle *dawn* 125
  dusk 422
crepuscular 125
crescendo *increase* 35
  musical 415
crescent *increasing* 35
  street 189
  curve 245
- shaped 253
crescive 35
cress 298
cresset *signal* 550
  (*luminary* 423)
crest *climax* 33
  summit 210
  pointed 253
  tuft 256
  sign 550
  armorial 877
  pride 878
crestate 253
crestfallen
  dejected 837
  humble 879
cretaceous 430
crevasse 198, 667
crevice 198
crew *assemblage* 72
  inhabitants 188
  mariners 269
  party 712
crib *bed* 215
  translation 522, 539
  steal 791
cribbage 840
cribbed *confined* 751
cribble 260
cribriform 260
506

Crichton, Admirable -
  scholar 492
  perfect 650
  proficient 700
crick *pain* 378
cricket *insect* 366
  game 840
- ground *level* 213
cricketer 840
crier 534
  send round the - 531
crim. con. 961
crime *guilt* 947
criminal *vicious* 945
  culprit 949
  malefactor 975
  (- *conversation* 961)
- law 963
criminality 947
criminate 938
crimp *crinkle* 248
  notch 257
  brittle 328
  deception 545
  deceiver 548
  take 789
  steal 791
crimple 258
crimson *color* 434
  feeling 821
cringe *submit* 725
  servility 886
cringing *servile* 746
crinite 256
crinkle *angle* 244
  convolution 248
  ruffle 256
  fold 258
crinoid 368
crinoline 225
cripple *disable* 158
  weaken 160
  injure 659
crippled
  disease 655
crisis *conjuncture* 8
  contingency 43
  present time 118
  opportunity 134
  event 151
  strait 704
  bring to a - 604
  come to a - 729
crisp *rumpled* 248
  rough 256
  brittle 328
  style 572
Crispin 225
crisscross 219, 840
criterion *test* 463
  evidence 467
  indication 550
crithomancy 511
critic *judge* 480
  taste 850
  detractor 936
  and stand a - 480
critical *contingent* 8
  opportune 134
  discriminating 465
  judicious 480

important 642
  dangerous 665
  difficult 704
  censorious 932
  nothing if not - 480
criticism
  judgment 480
  dissertation 595
  disapprobation 932
  detraction 934
criticize
  discriminate 465
  judge 480
  disapprove 932
  detract 934
critique
  [*see* criticism]
  discrimination 465
critter 271
croak *cry* 412
  hoarseness 581
  stammer 583
  warning 668
  discontent 832
  lament 839
croaker 832, 837
Croat 726
crochet *obstinacy* 608
crock 191
crockery 384
crocodile 366, 913
crocodile tears 54
crocus *yellow* 436
Crœsus 803
croft 189, 232
cromlech 363
crone *veteran* 130
  fool 501
crony *friend* 890
  sociality 892
  favorite 899
crook *support* 215
  curve 245
  deviation 279
  thief 792
crooked *sloping* 217
  distorted 243
  angular 244
  deviating 279
  latent 526
  crafty 702
  ugly 846
  dishonorable 940
- path 704
- stick *discourtesy* 895
- temper 901
- ways 279
croon 405
crop *stomach* 191
  harvest 154
  shorten 201
  eat 298
  store 636
  gather 775
  take 789
- out *reproduce* 163
  visible 446
  disclose 529
- up *begin* 66
  take place 151
  reproduction 163

second - *fertile* 168
  profit 775
cropped *fragmentary* 51
cropper *fall* 306
croquet *game* 840
- ground *level* 213
croquette 298
crore 98
crosier 215, 999
cross *mix* 41
  support 215
  across 219
  pass 302
  interment 363
  oppose 708
  failure 732
  disaster 735
  refuse 764
  vex 830
  decoration 877
  fretful 901
  punishment 975
  rites 998
- and pile 621
- debt 30
- fire *interchange* 148
  difficulty 704
  opposition 708
  attack 716
- purposes
  contrary 14
  disorder 59
  error 495
  misinterpret 523
  unskillful 699
  difficulty 704
  opposition 708
  discord 713
- questions
  inquiry 461
  discord 713
  game 840
- sea 348
- swords 722
- the mind 451
- the path of 706
- the Rubicon 609
  fire - 722
  red - 662
crossbar 219
crossbarred 219
crossbow 727
crossbreed 41, 83
crosscut 628
crossed 219
- bayonet 708
- in love 898
cross-examine 461
cross-eye 443
cross-grained
  rough 256
  obstinate 606
  irascible 901
  sulky 901a
crosshatch 259
crossing 219
- the bar *death* 360
crosspatch 895
crossroad 627
crossruff 314
cross-shaped 219

crosswise 219
crotch 91, 244
crotchet
  music 413
  misjudgment 481
  caprice 608
crouch *lower* 207
  stoop 308
  fear 860
  servile 886
  - before 725
croup 235
croupier 694
crow *bird* 366
  cry 412
  black 431
  rejoice 838
  boast 884
  as the - flies 278
  - to pluck
    discord 713
    anger 900
    accuse 938
  pluck a - with 932
crowbar 633
crowd *assemblage* 72
  multitude 102
  close 197
  redundance 641
  the masses 876
  - is not company 892
  in the - *mixed* 41
  the madding - 893
crowded 72, 102, 197
  [see crowd]
crown *top* 210
  circle 247
  be perfect 650
  complete 729
  trophy 733
  scepter 747
  install 755
  jewel 847
  decoration 877
  reward 973
  - ed head 745
  - law 963
  - of sorrow 828
  - wheel 247
  - with laurel 873
  - with success 731
  to - all 33, 642
crowning [see crown]
  superior 33
  end 67
  - point 210
crown-post 215
crow's-foot *age* 128
crow's nest *nautical* 210
crozier 747
crucial
  crossing 219
  proof 478
  - test 463
cruciate
  cruciform 219
  physical pain 378
  mental pain 830
crucible *dish* 191
  conversion 144
  furnace 386

  experiment 463
  laboratory 691
  put into the - 163
cruciferous 219
crucifix 219, 998
crucifixion *anguish* 828
  [see *crucify*]
cruciform 219, 1000
crucify
  physical torture 378
  mental agony 830
  execution 972
crude *color* 428
  inelegant 579
  unprepared 674
cruel *painful* 830
  inhuman 907
  - as death 907
  - only to be kind 830
cruelly *much* 31
cruelty [see cruel]
cruet 191
cruise *navigation* 267
cruiser 726
cruller 298
crumb *small* 32
  bit 51
  powder 330
  (*part* 51)
  (*little* 193)
  - of comfort 834
crumble *decrease* 36
  weak 160
  destruction 162
  brittle 328
  pulverize 330
  spoil 659
  - into dust
    decompose 49
  - under one's feet 735
crumbling
  [see *crumble*]
  dangerous 665
crumbly 330
crumenal 800
crump *distorted* 243
  curved 245
crumple *ruffle* 256
  fold 258
  - up *destroy* 162
  crush 195
crunch *shatter* **44**
  chew 298
  pulverize 330
crupper 235
crusade 361, 722
cruse 191
crush *crowd* 72
  destroy 162
  compress 195
  shatter 328
  pulverize 330
  humble 879
  (*injure* 649)
  - one's hopes
    disappoint 509
    hopeless 859
  - under an iron heel 739
crushed *unhappy* 828
crush hat 225

crushing *vigorous* 574
  painful 830
crust 223
crustacean 366, 368
crusty *discourteous* 895
  sullen 901a
crutch *support* 215
  angle 244
crux *cross* 219
  difficulty 704
cry *stridor* 410
  human **411**
  animal 412
  publish 531, 532
  call 550
  voice 580
  vogue 613
  weep 839
  - aloud *implore* 765
  - and little wool
    overrate 482
    boast 884
    disappoint 509
  - before hurt 839
  - down 932, 934
  - for 865
  - for joy 838
  - for vengeance 923
  - out against
    dissuade 616
    censure 932
  - shame 932
  - to *beseech* 765
  - up 931
  - wolf *false* 544
    alarm 669
  - you mercy
    deprecate 766
    pity 914
    forgive 918
  far - to 196
    full - *loud* 404
  raise a - 550
crying [see cry]
  urgent 630
  - evil 619
  - shame 874
  - sin 945
crypt *cell* 191
  grave 363
  ambush 530
  altar 1000
cryptic *uncertain* 475
  concealed 528
  secret 533
cryptography
  unintelligibility 519
  hidden 528
  writing 590
crystal *hard* 323
  water 337
  transparent 425
  - gazing 992a
  - oil 356
  snow - 383
crystalline *dense* 321
  transparent 425
crystallinity 321
crystallization 321, 323
crystallize 321
crystallomancy 511

crystallose 396
cub *young* 129
  offspring 167
  vulgar 851
  clown 876
  unlicked - 241
cubby-hole 191, 530
cube *three dimensions*
  92, 93
  form 244
cubeb 393
cubicle 191
cubist 556
cubit 200
cucking stool 975
cuckold 905
cuckoldom 961
cuckoo *imitation* 19
  repetition 104
  bird 366
  sound 407
  cry 412
  songbird 416
cucullate 223
cucumber 298
  - green 435
cuddle 902
cuddy 271
cudgel *beat* 276
  weapon 727
  punish 975
  - one's brains
    think 451
    imagine 515
  take up the -s
    aid 707
    attack 716
    contention 720
cudgeling
  punishment 972
cue *humor* 5
  rôle 51, 625
  hint 527
  watchword 550
  plea 617
  take one's - from 695
cue rest 215
cuff *sleeve* 225
  blow 276
  punishment 972
cuirass 717
cuirassier 726
cuisine 298
culbute
  inversion 218
  fall 306
cul-de-lampe
  engraving 558
  ornament 847
cul-de-sac
  concave 252
  closed 261
  difficulty 704
culet 211
culinary 298
  - art 673
cull *dupe* 547
  choose 609
  take 789
cullender 260
cullibility 486

cullion 949
cully *deceive* 545
  dupe 547
culm 388
culminate
  maximum 33
  height 206
  top 210
  complete 729
culpability *vice* 945
  guilt 947
culprit 949, 975
cult 990
cultivate *till* 365, 371
  sharpen 375
  improve 658
  prepare 673
  aid 707
  courtesy 894
cultivated
  courteous 894
  - *taste* 850
cultivation [*see* culti-
  vate]
  knowledge 490
cultivator 371
cultural 537, 542
culture
  knowledge 490
  improvement 658
  taste 850
  courtesy 894
culverin 727
culvert 350
cumber *load* 319
  obstruct 706
cumbersome
  incommodious 647
  disagreeable 830
cumbrous 830
cummerbund 225
cumshaw 784
cumulative
  assembled 72
  evidential 467
  - *evidence* 467
  - *vote* 609
cumulous 353
cumulus 353
cunctation *delay* 133
  (*inactivity* 683)
cuneate 244
cuneiform 244
  - *character* 590
cunning *prepense* 611
  sagacious 698
  artful **702**
  · - *fellow* 700
cup *vessel* 191
  hollow 252
  beverage 298
  remedy 662
  tipple 959
between - and lip 111
bitter - 828
- of humiliation 879
- that cheers &c. 298
- too low 837
- tossing 621
dash the - from one's
  lips 509
508

in one's -s 959
cupbearer 746
cupboard 191
cupel 384
cupellation 336, 384
Cupid *beauty* 845
  love 897
cupidity *avarice* 819
  desire 865
cupola *height* 206
  dome 223, 250
cupping 662
cup-shaped 252
cur *dog* 366
  sneak 949
curable 658, 660, 662
curacy 995
curate 996
curative 660
curator 694, 758
curb *moderate* 174
  slacken 275
  dissuade 616
  chance 621
  check 706
  restrain 751
  shackle 752
  mart 799
  - bit 706
  - roof 244
curcuma paper 463
curd *density* 321
  pulp 354
  (*cohere* 46)
curdle *condense* 321
  make the blood - 830
curdled 352
cure *reinstate* 660
  remedy 662
  preserve 670
  benefice 995
curé 996
cure-all 662
cureless 859
curfew 126
curia 966
curio 847
curiosity
  unconformity 83
  inquiring **455**
  phenomenon 872
curious
  exceptional 83
  inquisitive 455
  true 494
  beautiful 845
  desirous 865
curiously *very* 31
curl *bend* 245
  convolution 248
  hair 256
  cockle up 258
  - cloud 353
  - paper 256
  - up one's lip 930
curling *game* 840
curling tongs 386
curly 248
curmudgeon
  miser 819
currants 298

currency
  publicity 531
  money 800
current *existing* **1**
  general 78
  present 118
  happening 151
  of water 348
  of air 349
  rife 531, 532
  language 560
  habit 613
  danger 667
  account - 811
  against the - 708
  - belief 488
  - of events 151
  - of ideas 451
  - of time 109
  go with the - 82
  pass - *believed* 484
  fashion 852
  stem the - 708
curricle 272
curricular 272
curriculum 537
currish 895
curry *rub* 331
  condiment 393
  - favour with
  love 897
  flatter 933
currycomb 370
curse *bane* 663
  adversity 735
  painful 830
  malediction 908
  (*evil* 619)
cursed *bad* 649
cursitor 968
cursive 573
cursory *transient* 111
  inattentive 458
  hasty 684
  take a - view of 457
  neglect 460
curst *sullen* 901a
curt *short* 201
  concise 572
  taciturn 585
curtail *retrench* 38
  shorten 201
  (*decrease* 36)
  (*deprive* 789)
  -ed of its fair propor-
   tions
  distorted 243
  ugly 846
curtailment *decrease* 36
  [*see* curtail]
curtain *shade* 424
  hide 528, 530
  theater 599
  fortification 717
  behind the -
  invisible 447
  inquiry 461
  knowledge 490
  close the - 528
  - lecture 932
  - raiser *drama* 66, 599

raise the - 529
rising of the - 448
curtal 201
curtate 201
curtsy *stoop* 308, 314
  submit 725
  polite 894
curule 474, 696
curvate 245
curvature **245**
curve 245
curved 245
curvet *leap* 309
  turn 311
  oscillate 314
  agitate 315
curvilinear 245
  - motion 311
cushat 366
cushion *pillow* 215
  soft 324
  relief 834
cusp *angle* 244
  sharp 253
cuspidor 191
cussed 901a
cussedness 606
custard pie 298
custodian 753
custody *safe* 664
  captive 751
  retention 781
  in - *prisoner* 754
  accused 938
  take into - 751
custom *old* 124
  habit 613
  barter 794
  sale 796
  tax 812
  fashion 852
  - honored in breach
   614
customary
  [*see* custom]
  regular 80
customer 795
customhouse 799
  - officer 965
custos 573
  - rotulorum 553
cut *geld* 38
  divide 44
  bit 51
  discontinuity 70
  absent 187
  interval 198
  curtail 201
  layer 204
  form 240
  notch 257
  blow 276
  depart 293
  eject 297
  reap 371
  physical pain 378
  cold 385
  neglect 460
  carve 557
  engraving 558
  road 627

D

daisy - pied 847
 fresh as a - 654
dak 534
 - bungalow 189
dalal 758
dale *valley* 252
dally *delay* 133
 irresolute 605
 inactive 683
 amuse 640
 fondle 902
dalmatic 999
Daltonism 443
dam *parent* 166
 close 261
 pond 343
 obstruct 706
damage *evil* 619
 injure, spoil 659
 loss 776
 price 812
damages 974
damascene 440
damask 434
dame *woman* 374
 teacher 540
 lady 875
damn *malediction* 908
 condemn 971
 - with faint praise
  932, 934
damnability 649
damnable 649
damnatory *evil* 649
 disapprove 932
 condemn 971
damnify *damage* 649
 spoil 659
Damocles
 sword of - 667
damoiseau 129
damoiselle 129
Damon and Pythias
 890
damp *moderate* 174
 moist 339
 cold 385
 dissuade 616
 hinder 706
 depress 837
 dull 843
 - the sound 408a
dampen 339
damper *cake* 298
 furnace 386
 faintness 405
damsel *youth* 129
 female 374
damson 437
Danaë 803
dance *jump* 309
 oscillate 314
 agitate 315
 rejoice 838
 sport 840
 - attendance
  waiting 133
 follow 281
 servant 746
 petition 765
 servility 886
510

- music 415
- steps 840
- the back step 283
- the war dance 715
- upon nothing 972
lead one a-
 run away 623
 circuit 629
 difficult 704
 practical joke 929
lead the - 175
dancer 840
dander 900
dandi 272
Dandie Dinmont 366
dandify 847
dandiprat 193
dandle 902
dandruff 653
dandy *litter* 266, 272
 ship 273
 fop 854
dandyism 855
danger 665
- past 664
- signal 669
in - *liable* 177
source of - 667
dangerous
 [*see* danger]
- classes 913
- illness 655
- person 667
dangle *hang* 214
 swing 314
 display 882
dangler 281
Daniel *sage* 500
 judge 967
- come to judgment
  480
dank 339
danseuse 599
Dan to Beersheba
 complete 52
 extent 180
dapper *little* 193
 elegant 845
dapple-gray 432
dappled 432, 440
Darby and Joan
 secluded 893
 married 903
dare *confront* 234
 defy 715
 face danger 861
- not 860
- say *probable* 472
 believe 484
 suppose 514
dare-devil *courage* 861
 rash 863
 bluster 887
daring *unreserved* 525
 courageous 861
- imagination 515
dark *obscure* 421
 dim 422
 color 428
 black 431
 blind 442

 invisible 447
 unintelligible 519
 latent 526
 joyless 837
 insidious 940
- ages 491
- amid the blaze of
  noon 442
- cloud 735
- lantern 423
in the - *ignorant* 491
keep - *hide* 528
leap in the -
 experiment 463
 chance 621
 rash 863
view with - eyes 932
darken *obscure* 422
 look black 821
- over 421
darkened 421
darkle 422
darkling 421
darkly
 see through a glass -
  443
darkness [*see* dark] 421
 children of - 988
- of meaning 571
 powers of - 978
darksomeness 421
darky 431
darling *beloved* 897
 favorite 599
darn 660
dart *swift* 274
 propel 284
 missile 727
- to and fro 684
dartre 655
Darwinian 357
Darwinism 357
dash 911
 small quantity 32
 mix 41
 start 146
 swift 276
 fling 284
 mark 550
 courage 861
cut a - *repute* 873
 display 882
- at *resolution* 604
 attack 716
- cup from lips 761
- down 308
- hopes
 disappoint 509
 fail 732
 dejected 837
 despair 859
- off *compose* 54
 paint 556
 write 590
 active 682
 haste 684
- of the pen 590
- on 274
dashboard 666
dashed [*see* dash]
 humbled 879

dasher 666
dashing
 fashionable 852
 brave 861
 ostentatious 882
dastard 862
dasturi 973
data *evidence* 467
 reasoning 476
 supposition 514
datal 114
date *time* 106
 chronology 114
 to this - 118
 up to - 123
dateless 124
datum [*see* data]
daub *cover* 223
 bad painting 555
 dirt 653
daubing 635
daughter 167
daunt 860
dauntless 858, 861
davenport 191, 215
dawdle *tardy* 133
 slow 275
 inactive 683
dawn *precursor* 64
 begin 66
 priority 116
 morning 125
 light 420
 dim 422
 glimpse 490
day *period* 108
 present time 118
 light 420
all - 110
all in -'s work 625
clear as -
 certain 474
 intelligible 518
 manifest 525
close of - 126
- after day
 diuturnal 110
 frequent 136
- after the fair 135
- after to-morrow 121
- and night
 frequent 136
- before yesterday 122
- by day
 repeatedly 104
 time 106
 periodic 138
- of judgment 121
- of rest 686
- one's own 731
-s gone by 122
-s numbered
 transient 111
 death 360
-s of week 138
decline of - 126
denizens of the - 366
happy as the - is long
 827, 836
have had its - 124
open as - 703

defensive alliance 712
defer *put off* 133
  neglect 460
  - to *assent* 488
  submit 725
  respect 928
deference
  submission 725
  obedience 743
  humility 879
  courtesy 894
  respect 928
deferment 460
defial 715
defiance **715**
  threat 909
  - of danger 861
  in - *opposition* 708
  set at - *disobey* 742
defiant 715
deficiency
  [see deficient]
  vice 945
  - of blood 160
deficient *inferior* 34
  incomplete 53
  shortcoming 304
  insufficient 640
  imperfect 651
deficit
  incompleteness 53
  debt 806
defigure 846
defile *interval* 198
  march 266
  dirt 653
  spoil 659
  shame 874
  impure 961
define *limit* 233
  explain 522
  name 564
definite *special* 79
  limited 233
  visible 446
  certain 474
  exact 494
  intelligible 518
  manifest 525
  perspicuous 570
definition
  interpretation 521
definitive *final* 67
  affirmative 535
  decided 604
deflagration 384
deflate 195
deflect *curve* 245
  deviate 279
deflower *spoil* 659
  violate 961
defluent 348
defluxion *egress* 295
  flowing 348
defœdation 653, 659
deform 241, 846
deformed 243
deforming 241
deformity
  distortion 243
  ugliness 846

blemish 848
defraud *cheat* 545
  swindle 791
defray 807
defrayment 807
deft *suitable* 23
  clever 698
defunct 360, 362
defy *confront* 234
  set at defiance 715
  disobey 742
  threaten 909
  - danger 861
dégagé *free* 748
  fashion 852
degeneracy 659
degenerate
  deteriorate 659
  vice 945
deglutition 298
degradation
  deterioration 659
  shame 874
  dishonor 940
degrade *disbar* 968
  [see degradation]
degree 26
  term 71
  honor 873
  by -s 26
  by slow -s 275
  in no - 107
  no - 4
degustation 390
dehisce 260
dehiscence 260
dehort *dissuade* 616
  advise 695
dehydrate 340, 670
dehydration 340, 670
deification 981
deify *honor* 873
  idolatry 991
deign *condescend* 762
  consent 879
deism
  heterodoxy 984
  irreligion 989
deistic 976, 989
Deity 976
  tutelary - 664
dejection
  excretion 299
  melancholy **837**
déjeûner 298
dejudication 480
dekko 457
delaceration 659
delaminate 204
delation 133, 938
delator 527, 938
delay 133, 460
dele 162, 552
delectable *savory* 394
  agreeable 829
delectation 827
delectus 552
delegate *transfer* 270
  interpreter 524
  messenger 534
  commission 755

consignee 758
  deputy 759
delegated *acting* 759
delegation 755
delete 162
deleterious
  pernicious 649
  unwholesome 657
deletion 552
deletory *destructive* 162
deliberate *slow* 275
  think 451
  attentive 457
  leisure 685
  advise 695
  cautious 864
deliberately
  [see deliberate]
  late 133
  with *premeditation* 611
deliberation
  [see deliberate]
delicacy *weak* 160
  slender 203
  dainty 298
  texture 329
  savory 394
  delicate ear 418
  exact 494
  scruple 603
  ill health 655
  difficult 704
  pleasing 829
  beauty 845
  taste 850
  fastidious 868
  honor 939
  pure 960
delicate [see delicacy]
  color 428
  brittle 328
delicatessen 394
délice 377
delicious *taste* 394
  pleasing 829
delict 947
delictum 947
delight *pleasure* 377, 827
  pleasing 829
Delilah 962
delimit 233
delineate *outline* 230
  represent 554
  describe 594
delineavit 556
delinquency 304, 947
delinquent 949
deliquation 335
deliquesce 36, 335
deliquescent 335, 348
deliquium
  paralysis 158
  fatigue 688
deliriant 663
delirifacient 663
delirious 503, 825
delirium *raving* 503
  passion 825
  - tremens 959

delitescence
  invisible 447
  latency 526
  seclusion 893
deliver *transfer* 270
  utter 580, 582
  remedy 662
  rescue 672
  liberate 750
  give 784
  relieve 834
  - as one's act and deed 467
  - a speech 582
  - judgment 480
  - the goods 729
deliverance **672**
delivery [see deliver]
  bring forth 161
dell 252
Delphic oracle
  prophetic 513
  equivocal 520
  latent 526
delta *triad* 92
  land 342
delude *error* 495
  deceive 545
deluge *crowd* 72
  water 337
  flood 348
  redundance 641
delusion [see delude
  insane 503
  self - *credulous* 486
delve *dig* 252
  till 371
  - into *inquire* 461
demagogue
  director 694
  malcontent **710**
  rebel 742
demagogy 737
demand
  inquire 461
  user 677
  order 741
  ask 765
  price 812
  claim 924
  in - *require* 630
  salable 795
  desire 865
  public - 677
demarcate 233
demarcation 233
dematerialize 317
demean oneself
  conduct 692
  humble 879
  dishonor 940
demeanor *aid* 448
  conduct 692
  fashion 852
demency 503
dement 61
dementate 503
démenti 536
dementia 503
demerit 945
demesne *abode* 189

property 780
demi- 91
demigod *hero* 861
  angel 948
  - Authority 737
demigration 266
demijohn 191
demi-jour 422
demimondaine 876
demimonde
  plebeian 876
  licentious 962
demirep 962
demise *death* 360
  transfer 783
  lease 787
demisemiquaver 413
demission 756
demitint 421
Demiurge 976
demiurgic 153
demivolt 309
demobilize 750
democracy *rule* 737
  commonalty 876
democratic 737
Democrats 712
Democritus 838
demoiselle 129
demolish 479
demolishment 162
demon *violent* 173
  bane 663
  familiar spirit 979
  devil 980
  - in human shape 913, 949
  - worship 991
demonetize 800
  wicked 945
demoniacal
  malevolent 907
  furious 824
demonist 978
demonize 978
demonology
  demons 980
  sorcery 992
demonophobia 898
demonry 980
demonstration
  number 85
  proof **478**
  manifest 525
  ostentation 882
  ocular - 441, 446
demonstrative
  manifest 525
  indicative 550
  vehement 825
demonstrator 524
demoralize
  unnerve 158
  spoil 659
  vicious 945
Demosthenes 582
demulcent *mild* 174
  soothing 662
demur *disbelieve* 485
  dissent 489
  unwilling 603
514

hesitate 605
demure *grave* 826
  sad 837
  affected 855
  modest 881
demurrage 133
demurrer 969
den *abode* 189
  study 191
  sty 653
  prison 752
  seclusion 893
  - of thieves 791
denary 98
denaturalize
  corrupt 659
denaturalized
  abnormal 83
dendriform 242, 367
dendroid 242
dendrology 369
dengue fever 655
denial *negation* 536
  refusal 764
  self - 953
denigrate 431
denization 748
denizen *inhabitant* 188
  freeman 748
  -s of the air 979
  -s of the day 366
denominate 566
denomination *class* 75
  name 564
  sect 712
  religious - 983
denominational
  dissent 489
  party 712
  theological 983
  - education 537
denominator 84
denotative 550
denote *specify* 79
  mean 516
  indicate 550
dénouement *end* 67
  result 154
  disclosure 529
  completion 729
denounce *curse* 908
  disapprove 932
  accuse 938
dense *crowded* 72
  close 321
  vegetation 365
  ignorant 493
density **321**
dent *hollow* 252
  notch 257
dental 561
dentate 257
denticulated
  sharp 253
  notched 257
denticulation 257
dentifrice 652
dentiphone 418
dentist 662
dentistry 662
denude 226

denuded *loss* 776
  - of *insufficient* 640
denunciation 909
  [see denounce]
deny *dissent* 489
  negative 536
  refuse 764
  - oneself *avoid* 623
  seclude 893
  temperate 953
  ascetic 990
deobstruct 705
deobstruent 652, 662
deodand 974
deodorant 399
deodorize 399
  clean 652
deodorizer 399
deontology 926
deoppilation 705
deorganization 61
deosculation 902
deoxidation 140
deoxidization 140
depart 293
  - from *differ* 15
  deviate 279
  relinquish 624
  - this life 360
departed
  nonexistent 2
department *class* 75
  region 181
  business 625
  bureau 965
  - store 799
departmental 737
departure 293
  new - 66
  point of - 293
depend *hang* 214
  contingent 475
  - on circumstances 475
  - upon
   be the effect of 154
   evidence 467
   trust 484
  to be -ed on
   certain 474
   reliable 484
   honorable 939
dependence 46
dependency
  relation 9
  property 777, 780
dependent *effect* 154
  liable 177
  hanging 214
  puppet 711
  servant 746
  subject 749
deperdition 776
dephlegmation 340
dephlegmatory 340
depict 545, 556
  describe 594
depiction [see depict]
depilation 226
depilatory 662
depilous 226

deplete 638
depletion 640
deplorable *bad* 649
  disastrous 735
  painful 830
deplore *regret* 833
  complain 839
  remorse 950
deploy 194
depone 535
deponent 467
depopulate *eject* 297
  desert 893
deport 972
deportation
  removal 270
  emigration 297
deportment 692
depose *evidence* 467
  declare 535
  dethrone 738, 756
deposit *place* 184
  transference 270
  precipitate 321
  store 636
  security 771
  payment 809
depositary 801
deposition
  [see depose, deposit]
  record 551
depository 636
depot *station* 266
  store 636
  shop 799
depotentiate 158
deprave *spoil* 659
depraved *bad* 649
  vicious 945
depravity 945
deprecation **766**
  pity 914
  disapprove 932
deprecative 881
deprecatory 766, 881
depreciate
  disrespect 929
  [see depreciation]
depreciation
  decrease 36
  underestimate 433
  discount 813
  cheap 815
  censure 932
  detraction 934
  accusation 938
depreciator 483
depredation 791
depredator 792
deprehension 789
depress
  [see depression]
depressing
  painful 830
depression
  lowness 207
  depth 208
  concavity 252
  dent 257
  furrow 259
  lowering **308**

detailed
circumstantial 8
details *minuti ε* 32
unimportant 643
detain 781
detect 480a
detective 527, 664
detent 45
detention 781
- camp 751
house of - 752
in house of - 938
deter *dissuade* 616
alarm 860
deterge *clean* 652
detergent 652, 662
deteriorate 659
deterioration 659
determinable 278
determinate
special 79
exact 474
conclusive 480
intended 620
determinative 67
determine *end* 67
define 79
cause 153
direction 278
satisfy 462
make sure 474
judge 480
discover 480a
resolve 604
determined
resolute 604
deterration 529
detersion 652
detersive 662
detest
dislike 876
hate 898
detestable 649
dethronement
anarchy 738
abrogation 756
detonate *explode* 173
sound 406
detonation 404, 406, 872
detortion *form* 243
meaning 523
détour *curve* 245
circuit 629
detract *subduct* 38
underrate 483
defame 934
slander 938
detraction 934
detractor 936
detrain 292
detriment *evil* 619
deterioration 659
detrimental 649
detrital 330
detrition 330
detritus *fragments* 51
transference 270
powder 330
detrude
cast out 297
516

cut down 308
detruncate 38
detrusion
[see detrude]
detrusive 308
deuce *two* 89
devil 978
- is in him 608
play the - 825
deuced *great* 31
painful 830
deus ex machina
aid 707
auxiliary 711
deuterogamy 903
deva 979
Devanagari 590
devastate *destroy* 162
havoc 659
depopulate 893
devastation 162
develop *increase* 35
produce 161
expand 194
evolve 313
development 194
devexity *bending* 217
curvature 245
deviate *vary* 20a
change 140
turn 279
diverge 291
circuit 629
- from 15
- from rectitude 940
- from virtue 945
deviation 279
deviatory 311
device *motto* 550
expedient 626
artifice 702
devil
seasoned food 392
evil doer 913
bad man 949
Satan 978
demon 980
- in one
headstrong 863
temper 901
- may care *rash* 863
indifferent 866
insolent 885
-'s tattoo 407
- take 908
- take the hindmost
run away 623
haste 684
cowardice 862
- to pay *disorder* 59
violence 173
evil 619
failure 732
penalty 974
- worship 978
fig't like -s 722
give the - his due
right 922
vindicate 937
fair 939
have a - 503

machinations of the - 619
play the - with
injure 659
malevolent 907
printer's - 591
devil-dog 269
devilish *great* 31
bad 649
malevolent 907
vicious 945
devious *curved* 245
deviating 279
circuitous 311
devisable 270
devise *imagine* 515
plan 626
bequeath 784
-d by the enemy 546
devisee
transference 270
possess 779
receive 785
deviser 164
devitalize 158
devoid *absent* 187
empty 640
not having 777a
devoir *courtesy* 894
respect 928
devolution 659, 783
devolve 783
- on 926
Devonshire cream 321
devote *destine* 601
employ 677
consecrate 873
- oneself to 604
- the mind to 457
- to destruction 908
devoted *habit* 613
ill-fated 735
obedient 743
undone 828
love 897
devotee *zealot* 682
sports 840
aspirant 865
pious 987
fanatic 988
devotion
[see devotee, devoted]
love 897
piety 987
worship 990
self - 942
devour *destroy* 162
eat 298
gluttony 957
devoured by
feeling 821
devouring element 382
devout 987, 990
devoutless 989
devoutly 821
dew 339
Dewali 138
dewan 745
dewy 339
- eve 126

dexter 238
dexterous 238, 698
dextrality 238
dextrorsal 238
dey 745
dhobi 652
dhoti 225
dhow 273
dhu 431
diablerie 992
diabolic *bad* 649
malevolent 907
wicked 945
satanic 978
diabolist 978
diabolology 978
diacaustic 245
diaconicum 1000
diacoustics 402
diacritical 15, 550
diadem 747, 847
diæresis 49, 550
diagnosis 465, 522, 655
diagnostic
distinguishable 15
special 79
experiment 463
discriminative 465
indication 550
(*intrinsic* 5)
diagnostics 655
diagonal 217
diagram 554
dial 114
measure 466
as the - to the sun
veracious 543
faithful 772
dialect 563
dialectic *argument* 476
language 56
dialogism 586
dialogue 588, 599
diameter 202
diametrical 237
- ly opposite
contrariety 14
contraposition 237
diamond
lozenge 244
goodness 648
ornament 847
- cut diamond
cunning 702
retaliation 718
- wedding 883
rough - 703
Diana *moon* 318
chaste 960
diapason 413
diaper 847
diaphanous 425
diaphonics 402
diaphoresis 299
diaphragm *middle* 68
partition 228
diapo{r}esis 475
diarrhea 290
diary *journal* 114
record 551
diaskenast 593

disconnected
divided 51
feeble 575
disconnection
irrelation 19
disjunction 44
discontinuity 70
disconsolate 837
discontent 832
discontinuance
cessation 142
relinquishment 624
discontinuity 70
discontinuous 70
discord
disagreement 24
of sound **414**
of color 428
dissension **713**
discordance
[see discord]
discount *decrease* 36
decrement 40a
money **813**
at a - *disrepute* 874
disapproved 932
discountenance
disfavor 706
refuse 764
discourage
dissuade 616
sadden 837
frighten 860
(*disfavor* 706)
discourse *teach* 537
speech 582
talk 588
dissert 595
sermon 998
discourtesy 895
discous 202
discover *perceive* 441
solve 462
find 480a
disclose 529
- itself *be seen* 446
discovery 480a
discredit *disbelief* 485
dishonor 874
discreditable
vicious 945
discreet *careful* 459
cautious 864
(*clever* 698)
discrepancy 20a, 471
discrepant
differing 15
disagreeing 24
discordant 713
discrepate 15
discrete *separate* 44
disjunctive 70
single 87
discretion *will* 600
choice 609
skill 698
caution 864
surrender at - 725;
years of - 131
discriminate
[see discrimination]

discrimination
difference 15
nice perception **465**
wisdom 498
taste 850
fastidiousness 868
disculpate 937
discumbency 213
discursion 266
discursive *moving* 264
migratory 266
wandering 279
- *faculties* 450
argumentative 476
diffuse style 573
conversable 588
disserting 595
discus 840
discuss *eat* 298
reflect 451
inquire 461
reason 476
dissert 595
discussion
[see discuss]
open to - 475
under - 461
discutient 73
disdain
indifference 866
fastidious 868
pride 878
insolence 885
contempt 930
disdainful
[see disdain]
disrespectful 929
disease 655
diseased 655
- *mind* 503
disembark 292, 342
disembarrass 705
disembodied 317
disembody
decompose 49
disperse 73
spiritualize 317
disembogue *emit* 295
eject 297
flow out 348
disembowel 297, 301, 361
disembroil 60
disenable 158
disenchant
discover 480a
dissuade 616
displease 830
disencumber 705
disendow 756
disengage *detach* 44
facilitate 705
liberate 750
disengaged *to let* 763
disentangle
separate 44
arrange 60
unroll 313
decipher 522
facilitate 705
liberate 750

disenthrall 750
disenthrone 756
disentitle 925
disespouse 905
disestablish
displace 185
abrogate 756
disesteem
disrespect 929
censure 932
disfavor *oppose* 708
hate 898
disrespect 929
view with - 932
disfigure *deface* 241
injure 659
deform 846
blemish 848
disfranchise 925
disfurnish 226
disgorge *emit* 297
flow out 348
restore 790
pay 807
disgrace *shame* 874
dishonor 940
sense of - 879
disgraceful
vice 945
disgruntle 509
disgruntled 509
disguise *conceal* 528
mask 530
falsify 544
untruth 546
disguised
[see disguise]
- *in drink* 959
disgust *taste* 395
offensive 830
weary 841
dislike 867
hatred 898
- *of life* 837
disgusting
[see disgust]
dish *destroy* 162
plate 191
scoop out 252
food 298
- *of tea* 892
dishabille
undress 225
unprepared 674
dishearten
dissuade 616
pain 830
discontent 832
deject 837
dished 732
disherison 789
dishevel *loose* 47
disorder 61
disperse 73
intermix 219
dishevelment 59
[see dishevel]
dishing 252
dishonest *false* 544
base 940
dishonor *disrepute* 874

disrespect 929
baseness 940
- bills 808
dishwater 653
disillusion 509
disinclination 867
disincline
dissuade 616
dislike 867
disinclined 603
disinfect *purify* 652
restore 660
disinfectant 388, 662
disingenuous *false* 544
dishonorable 940
disinherit 782, 783, 789
disinheritance 789
disintegrate
separate 44
decompose 49
pulverize 330
disintegration 49
disinter *exhume* 363
discover 480a
disinterested 942
disinvigorate 158
disjoin 44
disjointed *disorder* 59
powerless 158
feeble 575
disjointure 44
disjunction 44
disjunctive 70
disk [see disc]
diskindness 907
dislike 867
reluctance 603
hate 898
dislimb 44
dislocate *separate* 44
put out of joint 61
dislocated *disorder* 59
dislodge *displace* 185
eject 297
disloyal 940
dismal *depressing* 830
dejected 837
- *universal hiss* 930
dismantle *destroy* 162
divest 226
render useless 645
injure 659
disuse 678
dismask 529
dismast
render useless 645
injure 659
disuse 678
dismay 860
dismember
separate 44
disperse 73
execute 972
dismemberment 972
dismiss *discard* 678
liberate 750
abrogate 756
relinquish 782
punish 972
- from the mind **452, 458**

519

dissonant 15, 713
dissuade 616
dissuasion **616**
dissuitable 24
dissyllable 561
distain *dirty* 653
  ugly 846
distal 196
distance **196**
  overtake 282
  go beyond 303
  defeat 731
  angular - 244
  - of time
    long time 110
    past 122
  keep at a -
    discourtesy 895
  keep one's -
    avoid 623
    modest 881
    respect 928
  teach one his - 879
distant 196
distaste 867
distasteful 830
distemper *color* 428
  painting 556
  disease 655
distend 194
distended 192
distich 89, 597
distichous 91
distill *come out* 295
  extract 301
  evaporate 336
  drop 348
distillation 336
distinct *disjoined* 44
  audible 402
  visible 446
  intelligible 518
  manifest 525
  express 535
  articulate 580
distinction
  difference 15
  greatness 31
  discrimination 465
  elegance 578
  fame 873
  rank 875
  - without a difference
    27
  lacking - 465a
distinctive
  different 15
  savory 394
  - feature 79
distingué
  fashion 852
  repute 873
distinguisn
  perceive 441
  discriminate 465
  - by the name of 564
distinguishable 15
distinguished
  superior 33
  repute 873
distinguishing 15

distort
  [*see* distortion]
distortion
  obliquity 217
  twist **243**
  of vision 443
  misinterpret 523
  falsehood 544
  misrepresent 555
  ugly 846
  (*misjudge* 481)
distract 458
distracted *confused* 475
  insane 503
  excited 824
distraction *passion* 825
  love to - 897
distrain *take* 789
  appraise 812
  attach 969
distrait 458
distraught 475, 503
distress *distraint* 789
  poverty 804
  affliction 828
  cause pain 830
  signal of - 669
distribute *arrange* 60
  disperse 73
  type 591
  allot 786
distribution
  [*see* distribute]
distributor
  electrical 272
district *to partition* 44
  area 181
  - court 966
distrust *disbelief* 485
  fear 860
distrustful 487
disturb *derange* 61
  change 140
  displace 185
  agitate 315
  excite 824
  distress 828, 830
disturbance
  disorder 59
disunion
  disagreement 24
  separation 44
  disorder 59
  discord 713
disunite *separate* 44
  break with 713
disunity 24
disuse *desuetude* 614
  relinquish 624
  unemploy **678**
disused 124, 678
disvaluation 932
disvalue 932
ditch *inclosure* 232
  hollow 252
  trench 259
  water 343
  conduit 350
  defense 717
ditch water 653
ditheism 984

dithyramb
  poetry 597
dithyrambic *wild* 503
ditto *iden ity* 13
  repe ition 104
  say - to 488
ditty 415
  - bag 191
diurnal 138
diuturnal 110
diuturnity **110**'
divagate 279
divan *sofa* 215
  council 696
  throne 747
  tribunal 966
divaricate *differ* 15
  bifurcate 91
  fork 244
  diverge 291
divarication 16a
dive *resort* 189
  swim 267
  plunge 310
  - into *inquire* 461
divellicate 44
diverge
  [*see* divergence]
divergence
  nonuniformity 16a
  difference 15
  dissimilarity 18
  variation 20a
  disagreement 24
  deviation 279
  separation **291**
divers *different* 15
  multiform 81
  many 102
  - colored 440
diverse 15
diversiform 81
diversify
  [*see* diversity]
  vary 20a
  change 140
diversion *change* 140
  deviation 279
  pleasure 377
  amusement 840
diversity
  difference 15
  irregular 16a
  dissimilar 18
  multiform 81
  - of opinion 489
divert *turn* 279
  deceive 545
  amuse 840
  - the mind 452, 458
divertissement
  drama 599
  amusement 840
Dives 803
divest *denude* 226
  take 789
  - oneself of
    abrogate 756
    relinquish 782
divestment **226**
divide *separate* 44

  part 51
  arrange 60
  arithmetic 85
  bisect 91
  measure 466
  vote 609
  apportion 786
dividend *part* 51
  number 84
  portion 786
dividers 466
divination
  prediction 511
  sorcery 992
divine *predict* 511
  guess 514
  perfect 650
  of God 976, 983, 983a
  clergyman 996
  - right
    authority 737
    due 924
  - service 990
diviner 994
diving 267
  - bird 310
divining rod
  sign 550
  magic 993
Divinity *God* 976
  theology 983
divisible
  [*see* divide]
  number 84
division [*see* divide]
  part 51
  class 75
  arithmetic 85
  school 542
  election 609
  discord 713
  military 726
divisor 84
divorce
  separation 44
  relinquish 782
  matrimonial **905**
Divorce Court 966
divorcée 905
divulge 529
divulsion 44
diwan 745
dixi 535
Dixie's land 827
dizen 225, 847
dizzard 501
dizziness
  [*see* dizzy]
dizzy *dim-sighted* 443
  confused 458
  vertigo 503
  - height 206
  - round 312
do *fare* 7
  suit 23
  produce 161
  cheat 545
  act 680
  complete 729
  succeed 731
  I beg 765

all one can - 686
- as done by 906, 942
- a service *useful* 644
  aid 707
- as one pleases 748
- as others do 82
- away with
  destroy 162
  eject 297
  abrogate 756
- battle 722
- business 625
- for *destroy* 162
  kill 261
  conquer 731
  punish 972
- good 906
- harm 907
- honor 873
- into *translate* 522
- justice to 595
- like 19
- little 683
- no harm 648
- nothing 681
- nothing but 136
- one's bidding 743
- one's office 772
- over 223
- tell 508
- the work 686
- up 660
- without 678
- wrong 923
  have to - with 680, 692
  plenty to - 682
  thing to - 625
doch-an-dorrach 959
docile *of horses* 370
  learning 539
  willing 602
docimastic 463
docimasy 463
dock *diminish* 36
  cut off 38
  port 189
  shorten 201
  store 636
  tribunal 966
- walloper 269
docked *incomplete* 53
docket *list* 69, 86
  evidence 467
  note 550
  record 551
  schedule 611
  security 771
  on the - 454
dockyard 691
doctor *learned man* 492
  prevaricate 544
  improve 658
  restore 660
  remedy 662
  after death the - 135
- accounts 811
  when -s disagree 475
doctorate 873
doctorship 873
    522

doctrinaire
  positive 474
  pedant 492
  theorist 514
  affectation 855
  blusterer 887
doctrinal 537
doctrine *tenet* 484
  knowledge 490
document 551
documentary 467
- evidence 467
dodder 160
dodecahedron 244
dodge *follow* 63
  change 140
  shift 264
  deviate 279
  oscillate 314
  pursue 461
  avoid 623
  stratagem 702
  (deceive 545)
doe *swift* 274
  deer 366
  female 374
doer *originator* 164
  agent 690
doff 226
- the cap 894
dog *follow* 63, 281
  animal 366
  male 373
  pursue 622
  wretch 949
  cast to the -s
  destroy 162
  reject 610
  disuse 678
  abrogate 756
  relinquish 782
- in manger 943
- in office 737
-s of war 722
  go to the -s
  destruction 162
  fail 732
  adversity 735
  poverty 804
  hair of - that bit you 959
dogcart 272
dog-cheap 815
dog days 382
doge 745
dogged *obstinate* 606
  valor 861
  sullen 901a
doggedness 606
  [see dogged]
dogger 273
doggerel *verse* 597
  ridiculous 851, 853
doggish 895
doghole 189
dog Latin 563
dogma *tenet* 484
  theology 983
dogmatic
  certain 474
  positive 481

assertion 535
  obstinate 606
dogmatism
  [*see* dogmatic]
dogmatist 887
dogmatization 474
dog's age 110
dog's-ear 258
dogsick 867
dog star 423
dogtrot 275
dog-weary 688
doily 852
doing
  up and - 682
  what one is - 625
doings *events* 151
  actions 680
  conduct 692
doit *trifle* 643
  coin 800
dokhma 363
dolce far niente 681
doldrums
  dejection 837
  sulks 901a
dole *mite* 32
  scant 640
  give 784
  allot 786
  parsimony 819
  grief 828
doleful 837
doll *small* 193
  image 554
dollar 800
- mark 550
dollish 129
dolor *physical* 378
  moral 828
dolorous 830
dolphin 341
dolt 501
doltish 499
domain *class* 75
  region 181
  property 780
dome *high* 206
  covering 223
  convex 250
Domesday book
  list 86
  record 551
domesman 967
domestic
  inhabitant 188
  home 189
  interior 221
  servant 746
  secluded 893
- animals 366
domesticate
  locate 184
  acclimatize 613
- animals 370
domesticize 370
domicile 189
domiciled
  inhabiting 186
domiciliary 188
- visit 461

dominant
  influence 175
  note in music 413
dominate *influence* 175
  rule 737
domination 175, 737, 939
domineer
  tyrannize 739
  insolence 885
Dominican 996
Dominie 540
dominion 181, 737
- rule 737
domino *dress* 225
  mask 530
  concealment 528
  game 840
don *put on* 225
  man 373
  scholar 492
  tutor 540
  noble 875
Doña 875
donate 784
donation
  compensation 30
  gift 784
- party 840
donative 784
done *finished* 729
- for *impotent* 158
  spoilt 659
  failure 732
- up *impotent* 158
  tired 688
  have - with *cease* 142
  relinquish 624
  disuse 678
  work - 729
donee 270, 785
donga 252
donjon
  defense 717
  prison 752
donkey *ass* 271
  fool 501
Donna 374
Donnybrook Fair
  disorder 59
  discord 713
donor 784
donship 875, 877
donzel 746
doodle 501
  music 416
doodlesack 410, 417
dooly 272
doom *end* 67
  fate 152
  destruction 162
  death 360
  judgment 480
  necessity 601
  assess 812
  sentence 971
- sealed *death* 360
  adversity 735
doomage 812, 974
doomed 735, 828
doomsday *end* 67

future 121
till - 112
door *entrance* 66
  cover 223
  brink 231
  barrier 232
  opening 260
  passage 627
  at one's - 197
  beg from door to - 765
  close the - upon 751
  death's - 360
  keep within -s 265
  lie at one's - 926
  open a - to
   liable 177
  open the - to
   receive 296
   facilitate 705
   permit 760
  show the - to
   eject 297
   discourtesy 895
   (*prohibit* 761)
doorkeeper 263
doormat 652
doorway 260
dope 465, 662
Dorado, El · 803
dormancy 172
dormant *inert* 172
  latent 526
  asleep 683
dormer 260
dormeuse 272
dormitive 841
dormitory 191
dormouse 683
dorp 189
dorsal 235
dorser 191
dorsigerous 215
dorsum *back* 235
  hump 250
dory 273
dose *quantity* 25
  part 51
  medicine 662
  apportion 786
dosser 191
dossil *cover* 223
  stopper 263
dot *small* 32
  point 180a
  place 182
  little 193
  variegate 440
  mark 550
dot *dowry* 784
dotage *age* 128
  imbecility 499
dotard *old* 130
  foolish 501
dotation 784
dote *drivel* 499, 503
  - upon 897
dotted 440
douanier 965
double *similar* 17
  increase 35
  duplex 90

substitute 147
fold 258
turn 283
finesse 702
specter 980a
wraith 992a
- acrostic *letters* 561
  wit 842
- a point 311
- eagle 800
- entry 811
- meaning 520
- quartet 415
- reef topsails 664
- sure 474
- the fist 909
- up
  render powerless 158
in quick time 274
march at the - 274
see - *dim sight* 443
  drunk 959
work - tides 686
double bass 417
double-dealer 607
double-dealing *lie* 544
  cunning 940
double-distilled 171
double-dyed 428
double-edged 171
double entente
  ambiguity 520
  impure 961
double-faced *lie* 544
  cunning 702
  dishonorable 940
double-handed 544
double-headed 90
double-hearted 940
double-minded 605
double-ripper 272
double-runner 272
double-shot 171
double-shotted 171
doublet 225
doublets 89
double-tongued
  lie 544
  cunning 702, 940
doubling 702
doubt *uncertain* 475
  disbelieve **485**
  skeptic 989
doubtful *uncertain* 475
  equivocal 520
  - meaning
   unintelligible 519
   (*equivocal* 520)
  more than - 473
doubtless *certain* 474
  belief 484
  assent 488
douceur *gift* 784
  reward 973
douche 337
dough *inelastic* 324
  pulp 354
  money 800
doughboy 726
doughface 605, 886
doughnut 298

doughty 159, 861
dour 739
douse *blow* 276, 972
  immerse 310
  splash 337
Dove *Holy Ghost* 976
dove *bird* 366
  innocent 946
  roar like sucking - 174
dove-color 432
dovecote 189
dovetail *agree* 23
  join 43
  intersect 219
  intervene 228
  angle 244
  insert 300
dowager *lady* 374
  widow 905
dowdy *dirty* 653
  vulgar 851
dower *property* 780
  bequest 784
  wealth 803
dowerless 804
down *upland* 180
  below 207
  sleep 306
  cast down 308
  light 320
  bear - upon 716
  bed of - *pleasure* 377
   repose 687
  be - upon *attack* 716
   severe 739
  come - 306
  - in price 815
  - in the mouth 837
  - on one's marrow-
   bones 886
  - on one's uppers 879
  get - 306
  go - *sink* 306
   calm 826
  go - like a stone 310
  money - 807
  take - *lower* 308
   rebuff 874
   humble 879
downcast
  descendent 306
  dejected 837
  - eyes 879
downcome 306
down-easter 188
downfall
  destruction 162
  fall 306
  earth 342
  failure 732
  misfortune 735
down-grade 306
down-hearted 837
downhill *sloping* 217
  descent 306
  go - *adversity* 735
downpour 348
down-reaching 208
downright *absolute* 31
  manifest 525
  sincere 703

downs *uplands* **180**
  heights 206
  wolds 344
down-trodden
  submission 725
  vanquished 732
  subject 749
  dejected 837
  disrepute 874
  contempt 930
downwards 306
downy *smooth* 255
  plumose 256
  soft 324
dowry *property* 780
  bequest 784
  provision 803
dowse 276
dowser 994
doxology 990
doxy 962
doyen 128, 130
doyley 652
doze 683
dozen 98
drab *color* 432
  slut 59, 653
  hussy 962
drabble 653
drachm 319
Draco *ruler* 694
  severe 739
draff 653
draft [*see also* draught]
  decrement 40a
  traction 285
  drawing 554, 556
  write 590
  abstract 596
  list 611
  plan 626
  physic 662
  combatant 726
  cheque 800, 805
  - off *displace* 185
  transfer 270
drafted man 726
draft-horse 271
drag *elapse* 109
  carriage 272
  crawl 275
  traction 285
  impediment 706
  - a chain *tedious* 110
  exertion 686
  subjection 749
  - along 106
  - anchor 706
  - into *implicate* 54
  compel 744
  - into open day 531
  continue 143
  - sail *check* 706
  - sheet 706
  - slow length
   long 200
   weary 841
  - through mire
   disrepute 874
   disrespect 929

duelist 726
duello 720
dueness 924
duenna *teacher* 540
  guardian 664
  keeper 753
dues 812
duet 415
duffer
  ignoramus 493
  bungler 701
  smuggler 792
dug 250
dugout *dwelling* 189
  trench 232
  boat 273
  safety 664
  defense 717
duke *ruler* 745
  noble 875
dukedom 877
dulcet *sweet* 396
  sound 405
  melodious 413
  agreeable 829
dulcify 174, 324, 396
dulcimer 417
dulcin 396
Dulcinea 897
dulcorate 396
dulia 990
dull *weak* 160
  unintelligent 32, 493
  inert 172
  moderate 174
  blunt 254
  slow 275
  insensible 376
  sound 405
  dim 422
  color 428
  colorless 429
  stolid 499
  style 575
  inactive 683
  unapt 699
  callous 823
  dejected 837
  weary 841
  prosing 843
  simple 849
  - of hearing 419
  - sight 443
dullard 501
dullish *blunt* 254
dullness 843
duly 924
dulse 367
duma 696
dumb *ignorant* 493
  voiceless 581
  - animal 366
  - friend 366
  - show 550

strike - *astonish* 870
  humble 879
dumb-waiter 307
dumdum bullet 727
dumfound
  disappoint 509
  silence 581
  astonish 870
  humble 879
dummy *substitute* 147
  impotent 158
  speechless 581
  printing 591
  inactive 683
  cards 840
dump *unload* 297
  music 415
  sale 796
  lament 839
  - cart 272
dumps *discontent* 832
  dejection 837
  sulk 901a
dumpy *little* 193
  short 201
  thick 202
dun *din* 422
  colorless 429
  gray 432
  importune 765
  creditor 805
dunce *ignoramus* 493
  fool 501
dunderhead 501
dune 206
dung 653
dungeon 752
dunghill *dirt* 653
  cowardly 862
  baseborn 876
  - cock 366
Dunker 984
duo 415
duodecimal 99
duodecimo *little* 193
  book 593
duodenal 221
duodenary 98
duodenum 221, 350
duologue
  interlocution 588
  drama 599
dupe *credulous* 486
  deceive 545
  deceived **547**
duplex 90
  - house 189
duplicate *copy* 21
  double 90
  repetition 104
  tally 550
  record 551
  redundant 641
  pawn 805

duplication
  imitation 19
  doubling **90**
  repetition 104
duplicature *fold* 258
duplicity *duality* 89
  falsehood 544
durability 141
durable *long time* 110
  permanent 141
  stable 150
durance 751
  in - 754
duration 106
  contingent - **108a**
durbar *conference* 588
  council 696
  tribunal 966
dure 106
duress *compulsion* 744
  restraint 751
Durga 979
Durham boat 273
during 106
  - pleasure &c. 108a
durity 323
durwan 263, 753
dusk *evening* 126
  half-light 422
dusky *dark* 421
  dim 422
  black 431
dust *levity* 320
  powder 330
  corpse 362
  trash 643
  dirt 653
  money 800
  come to - *die* 360
  - in the balance 643
  - one's jacket 972
  humbled in the - 879
  kick up a - 885
  level with the - 162
  lick the - *submit* 725
  fail 732
  make to bite the - 731
  throw - in the eyes
    blind 442
    deceive 545
    plead 617
  turn to -
    deorganized 358
    die 360
duster 652
dust hole 519
  fit for the -
    useless 645
    dirty 653
    spoilt 659
dustman
  cleaner 652
dustoor 613
dustoori 973

dust storm 330
dusty *powder* 330
  dirt 653
Dutch - auction 796
  - cap 225
  - courage 862
  - oven 386
  - treat 892
  high - 519
  it beats the - 508
Dutchman 57
  flying - 515
dutiable 812
dutiful 944
duty *business* 625
  work 686
  tax 812
  courtesy 894
  obligation **926**
  respect 928
  worship 990
  rite 998
  do one's - *virtue* 944
  on - 680, 682
duumvirate 737
Duval, Claude - 792
D. V. 470
dwarf *lessen* 36
  small 193
  elf 980
dwell *reside* 186
  abide 265
  - upon *descant* 573
dweller 188
dwelling *location* 184
  abode **189**
dwindle *lessen* 36
  shrink 195
  droop 655
dyad 193
dyadic 89
dye 428
  -d in the wool 709,
    820
dying 360
dyke [*see* dike]
dynamic 157
  - energy 157
dynamics 276
dynamitard 863
dynamite 727
dynamize 171
dynamo 157
dynamograph 276
dynamometer 276, 466
dynasty 737
dysentery 299
dysmerogenesis 161
dysmeromorph 357
dyspepsia 655
dyspeptic 655
dysphonia 581
dysphoria 149
dyspnœa 688

each 79
- in his turn 148
- other 12
- to each 786
eager *willing* 602
  active 682
  consenting 762
  ardent 821
  desirous 865
- expectation 507
eagle *bird* 366
  standard 550
  insignia 747
  coin 800
- eye *sight* 441
  intelligence 498
- winged *swift* 274
eagre 348, 667
ean 161
ear *of corn* 154
  hearing 418
  all - 418
  come to one's -s 527
  sin in the - *loud* 404
  drum 407
- for music 416, 418
  have the - of
  belief 484
  friendship 888
  in at one - out at the
    other
  inattention 458
  forget 506
  lend an - *hear* 418
  attend 457
  make the -s tingle
  anger 900
  meet the - 418
  nice - 418
  no - 419
  not for -s polite 961
  offend the - 410
  prick up the -s
  attention 457
  expectation 507
  pull about one's -s
    308
  quick - 418
  reach one's -s 527
  ring in the - 408
  set by the -s
  discord 713
  hate 898
  resentment 900
  split the -s 404
  together by the -s
  discord 713
  up to one's -s
  redundance 641
  active 682
  willing - 602
  word in the - 586
earache 378
eardrop 214
eardrum 418
eared 419
earl 875
earldom 877
earless 419
earliness **132**
early 132

get up - 682
earmark 550
ear muffs 384
earn 775
earnest *willing* 602
  determined 604
  emphatic 642
  pledge 771
  pay in advance 809
  eager 821
  serious 837
  in - *affirmation* 535
  veracious 543
  strenuous 682
earnings 775
ear-piercing 410
earring 847
earshot 197
  out of - 405
ear-splitting 402, 404
earth *ground* 211
  world 318
  land 342
  corpse 362
- flax 385
  what on - *inquiry* 461
  wonder 870
earthenware *baked* 384
  sculpture 557
earthling 372
earthly 318
earthly-minded
  selfish 943
  irreligious 989
earthquake
  revolution 146
  violence 173
earthwork 717
ear-witness 467
ease *abate* 36
  bodily 377
  style 578
  leisure 685
  facility 705
  mental 827
  content 831
  at one's -
  prosperous 734
- off *deviate* 297
- one of *take* 789
  mind at -
  cheerful 836
  set at - *relief* 834
  take one's - 687
easel *support* 215
  painting 556
- picture 556
easement
  property 780
  relief 834
easily [*see easy*]
- accomplished 705
- affected 375
- deceived 486
- persuaded 602
  let one down - 918
east *side* 236
  direction 278
Easter *period* 138
  rite 998
- Monday

  holiday 840
- offering *gift* 784
- sepulcher 1000
eastern 236
Easterner 57
easting 196
eastward 236
easy *gentle* 275
  style 578
  facile 705
- ascent 217
- chair *support* 215
  repose 687
- circumstances 803
- of belief 472
- sail *moderate* 174
  slow 275
- temper 894
- terms 705
- to understand 518
- virtue 961
  make one self - about
    484
  take it - *inactive* 683
  inexcitable 826
easy-going
  willing 602
  irresolute 605
  lenient 740
  inexcitable 826
  contented 831
  indifferent 866
eat *food* 298
  tolerate 826
- dirt 725
- heartily 298
- off the same trencher
    892
- one's fill *enough* 639
  gorge 957
- one's words 607
- out of house and
    home *take* 789
  prodigal 818
  gluttony 957
eatable 298
eatables 298
eaten up with 820
eating 298
eating house 189
eau de Cologne 400
eau sucrée 396
eaves 250
eavesdropper
  curiosity 455
  informer 527
eavesdropping
  hearing 418
  news 532
ebb *decrease* 36
  contract 195
  regress 283
  recession 287
  tide 348
  waste 638
  spoil 659
- and flow 314
- of life 360
  low - 36 *low* 207
  depression 308
  insufficient 640

ebb tide *decrease* 36
  low 207
  dry 340
ebenezer 1000
Ebionite 984
Eblis 978
ebon 431
ebony 431
éboulement 162, **716**
ebriety 959
ebullience
  [*see ebullient*]
  calefaction 384
ebullient *violent* 173
  hot 382
  excited 824
ebulliometer 384
ebullioscope 384
ebullition *energy* 171
  violence 173
  agitation 315
  heating 384
  excitation 825
  anger 900
eburin 430
écarté 840
ecbatic 155
eccentric *irregular* **83**
  exterior 220
  foolish 499
  crazed 503
  capricious 608
ecchymosis 299
ecclesiarch 996
ecclesiastic
  church 995
  clergy 996
ecclesiastical
  canonical 985
  temple 1000
- law 963
ecclesiolatry 991
ecco 457
eccrinology 299
ecdemic 220
ecderon 223
échafaudage 673
echelon *arrange* 60
  oblique motion 279
  attack 716
echinate 253
echinodermata 368
echo *similarity* 17
  imitate 19
  copy 21
  repeat 104
  recoil 277
  resonance 408
  answer 462
  assent 488
  applaud to the - **931**
echoes awaken - 404
echoless 403
éclat 873
eclectic *teaching* 537
  choice 609
eclecticism 451, 662
eclipse *surpass* 33
  disappearance 449
  hide 528
  outshine 873, 874

partial - *dim* 422
total - *dark* 421
under an - *invisible*
447
out of repute 874
ecliptic 318
eclogue 597
ecology 357
economic 692
- pressure 751
economical 817
economics 692
economize 817
economy *order* 58
preservation 670
conduct 692
frugality **817**
(*plan* 626)
animal - 359
ecphonesis 580
ecrhythmic 139
ecrhythmus 139
écru 426, 433
ecstasis 683
ecstasy *frenzy* 515
transport 821
rapture 827
ecstatic 829
ecstatica 992a
ecteron 223
ectoderm 223
ectogenous 161
ectropic 218
ectype 21
ecumenical 78
edacity 957
Edda 986
eddish 168
Eddy, Mary Baker -
986
eddy *whirlpool* 348
current 312
danger 667
Eden *heaven* 827
(*pleasure* 827)
edentate 254
edge *energy* 171
height 206
brink **231**
deviate 279
cutting - 253
- in 228
- of hunger 865
- one's way 282
set on - 256
take the - off 174
edge tools 253
play with - 863
edgewise 217
edging *obliquity* 217
border 231
ornament 847
edible 298
edict 531, 741
edification
building 161
teaching 537
learning 539
piety 987
edifice 161
edifying *good* 648
528

edile 965
edit *publication* 531
compile 596
revise 658
(*printing* 591)
edition 531
new - 658
editor *recorder* 553
book 593
commentator 595
editorial 595
edomorphic 221
educate *teach* 537
(*prepare* 673)
educated 490
education *teaching* 537
knowledge 490
man of - 492
educational 537
school 542
educe *extract* 301
discover 480a
educt 40
eduction 40a
edulcorate
sweeten 396
clean 652
eel *convolutions* 248
fish 298
- spear 727
wriggle like an - 315
efface *destroy* 162
disappear 449
obliterate 552
- from the memory
506
effect *consequence* **154**
complete 729
carry into - 692
in - 5
take - 731
to that - 516
with crushing - 162
effective
substantial 3
capable 157
influential 175
useful 644
practical 646
effects *property* 780
goods 798
effectual
influential 175
success 731
effectually 52
effectuate 729
effeminacy
[see effeminate]
effeminate *weak* 160
womanlike 374
timorous 862
sensual 954
effeminize 158
effendi 875
effervesce *energy* 171
violence 173
agitate 315
bubble 353
excited 825
effervescent
[see effervesce]

aërated 338
effete *old* 128
weak 160
useless 645
spoiled 659
efficacious
[see efficient]
efficient *power* 157
agency 170
reliable 632
utility 644
skill 698
effigy *copy* 21
representation 554
efflation 349
efflorescence 330
effluence *egress* 295
flow 348
effluent 295
effluvious 398
effluvium *vapor* 334
odor 398
efflux *egress* 295
(*flow* 348)
efformation 240
effort 686
effrontery 885
effulgence 420
effuse
pour out 295, 297
excrete 299
speech 582
effusion [see effuse]
loquacity 584
- of blood 361
effusive 295
eft 366
eftsoon 113, 117, 132
egad 535
egest 297
egesta 299
egestion 297
egestive 297
egg *beginning* 66
cause 153
food 298
- and dart
ornament 847
- on 615
too many -s in one
basket
unskillful 699
(*imprudent* 863)
walk among -s 704
eggplant 298
egg-shaped 247, 249
eggshell 223
ego *intrinsic* 5
immaterial 317
astral body 980a
non - 6
egohood 5
egoism 880
egoist 880
egotism
overestimation 482
vanity 880
cynicism 911
selfishness 943
egotist 482
egotistical [see egotism]

narrow 481
egregious
exceptional 83
absurd 497
exaggerated 549
important 642
egregiously *greatly* 31
supremely 33
egress **295**
egurgitate 295
Egyptian
- darkness 421
- deities 979
eiderdown 223, 324
eidoloclast 165
e.dolon 453, 991
eidouranion 318
eight *number* 98
boat 273
representative 759
eighty 98
eileton 999
Einstein theory 451
eisegesis 523
eisteddfod 72
either *choice* 609
happy with - 605
ejaculate *propel* 284
utter 580
eject 297
ejecta 299
ejection *displace* 185
emit **297**
excretion 299
ejective 297, 299
ejector 349
eke *also* 37
- out *complete* 52
spin out 110
ekka 272
elaborate *improve* 658
prepare 673
laborious 686
work out 729
elaboration
[see elaborate]
elaine 356
élan 276
elapse *flow* 109
pass 122
elastic
[see elasticity]
- fluid 334
elasticity *power* 157
strength 159
energy 171
spring **325**
elate *cheer* 836
rejoice 838
hope 858
vain 880
boast 884
elbow *angle* 244
projection 250
push 276
at one's - *near* 197
advice 695
- one's way
progress 282
pursuit 622
active 682

out at -s *undress* 226
  poor 804
  disrepute 874
elbowchair 215
elbow grease 331
elbowroom *space* 180
  freedom 748
eld 122, 124, 128
elder *older* 124
  aged 128
  veteran 130
  clergy 996
eldern 124, 128
El Dorado 803
Eleatic school 451
elect *choose* 609
  good 648
  predestinate 976
  pious 987
  churchdom 995
election *numerical* 84
  necessity 601
electioneering 609
elective franchise 609
elector 609, 745
electorate 737
  constituency 609
electric *carrier* 271
  vehicle 272
  trolley 273
  swift 274
  sensation 821
  excitable 825
  - bath 386
  - blue 438
  - car 273
  - chair 975
  - fan 349
  - light 423
  - stove 386
  - torch 423
electrician 690
electricity 157, 388
electrification 157
electrify *locomotion* 236
  unexpected 508
  excite 824
  astonish 870
electrobiology 992
electrocute 361, 972
electrocution 361, 972
electrocutioner 975
electrodynamics 157
electrodynamometer 157
electrokinetics 157
electrolier 423
electrolysis 49, 662
electrolyze 49, 662
electromagnetism 157
electrometer 157
electrometric 157
electromotion 157
electromotive force 157
electron 32
electrophorus 157
electroscope 157
electrostatics 157
electrotype 21, 550, 591

electuary 662
eleemosynary 784
Elegance, Bank of - 800
elegance *in style* 578
  beauty 845
  taste 850
elegy *interment* 363
  poetry 597
  lament 839
element
  substantiality 3
  component 56
  beginning 66
  cause 153
  matter 316
  devouring - 382
  in one's - *facility* 705
  content 831
  out of its - 185
elemental *simple* 42
  Rosicrucian 980
elementary *simple* 42
  - education 537
elements
  Eucharist 998
elench 477
elephant *large* 192
  carrier 271
  animal 366
  white - *bane* 663
elephantiasis 655
elephantine *huge* 192
  dull 843
eleutherian 748
elevated *tipsy* 959
elevation *height* 206
  vertical 212
  raising **307**
  plan 554
  loftiness 574
  repute 873
  angular - 244
  - of mind 942
  - of style 574
  improvement 658
  glory 873
elevator *ascent* 305
  descent 306
  elevation 307
eleven 98
  representative 759
eleventh hour
  evening 126
  late 133
  opportune 134
elf *infant* 129
  little 193
  fairy 979
elicit *cause* 153
  draw out 301
  discover 480a
  manifest 525
eligible 646
eliminant 299
eliminate *subduct* 38
  simplify 42
  exclude 55
  weed 103
  extract 301
eliminative 299, 350

elision *separation* 44
  shortening 201
élite *best* 648
  distinguished 873
  aristocrat 875
elixation 384
elixir 5, 662
  find the - of life 471
elk 366
ell 200
  take an - *take* 789;
  insolence 885
  wrong 923
  undue 925
  selfish 943
ellipse 247
ellipsis *shorten* 201
  typography 550
  style 572
ellipsoid 247, 249
elliptic 247
elm *tree* 367
elocation *displace* 185
  transfer 270
elocution 582
elocutionist 582
elongate 200
elongation
  distance 196
  lengthening 200
elopement *avoid* 623
  escape 671
eloquence *style* 569
  speech 582
  action is - 582
  to try thy - 582
else 37
elsewhere 187
elsewise 18
elucidate 82, 522
elucidative 522
elude *sophistry* 477
  avoid 623
  escape 671
  succeed 731
  palter 773
elusive [*see* elude]
  deceptive 545
elusory *untrue* 546
elutriate 652
elysian *delightful* 829
  heavenly 981
Elysium *bliss* 827
  paradise 981
elytron 223
emaciated *lean* 203
  starved 640
emaciation
  shrinking 195
  thinness 203
  disease 655
emanant 295
emanate *follow* 117
  go out of 295
  excrete 299
  - from 544
emanation *egress* 295
  vapor 353
  odor 398
emancipate
  deliver 672

  facilitate 705
  free 748, 750
emasculate
  castrate 38
  impotent 158
  (*weaken* 160)
embalm *interment* 363
  perfume 400
  preserve 670
  - in the memory 505
embankment
  esplanade 189
  refuge 666
  fence 717
  (*inclosure* 232)
embargo
  stoppage 265
  prohibition 761
  seclusion 893
embark *transfer* 270
  depart 293
  invest 787
  - in *begin* 66
  engage in 676
embarras
  - de choix 609
  - de richesses
  redundance 641
  wealth 803
embarrass
  render difficult 704
  hinder 706
embarrassed *poor* 804
  in debt 806
embarrassing
  uncertain 475
embarrassment
  [*see* embarrass]
embase 659
embassy *errand* 532
  commission 755
  consignee 758
embattled *arranged* 60
  leagued 712
  war array 722
embay 229
embed *locate* 184
  base 215
embellish 847
embers 384
embezzle 791
embitter
  deteriorate 659
  aggravate 835
  acerbate 900
emblazon *color* 428
  ornament 847
  display 882
emblem 550
  - of authority 747
embodied 316
embody *join* 43
  combine 48
  form a whole 50
  compose 54
  include 76
  materialize 316
embogue 297
embolden *hope* 858
  encourage 861
embolic 261

529

embolism
  interjacence 228
  closure 261
  insertion 300
  hindrance 706
embolus 261, 706
embonpoint 192
embosomed *lodged* 184
  interjacent 228
  circumscribed 229
emboss *convex* 250
  ornament 847
embouchure 260
embow 245
embowel 297
embrace
  compose 54
  include 76
  inclose 227
  choose 609
  take 789
  friendship 888
  sociality 892
  courtesy 894
  endearment 902
  - an offer 762
embrangle *derange* 61
embranglement
  discord 713
embrasure *notch* 257
  opening 260
embrocate 370
embrocation 662
embroider
  variegate 440
  lie 544
  exaggerage 549
  ornament 847
embroidery
  adjunct 39
  exaggeration 549
embroil *derange* 61
  discord 713
embroilment
  disorder 59
embrown 433
embryo *beginning* 66
  cause 153
  in - *destined* 152
  preparing 673
embryologist 357
embryology 357, 359, 368
embryonic *little* 193
  immature 674
emendation 658
emerald *green* 435
  jewel 847
emerge 295
emergency
  circumstance 8
  junction 43
  occasion 134
  event 151
  difficulty 704
emergent 295
emeritus *sage* 500
  respected 928
emersion 295
emery *sharpener* 253
  - paper *smooth* 255
  530

emesis 297
emetic 297, 662
émeute 742
emication 420
emigrant *stranger* 57
  traveler 268
emigrate *remove* 266
  egress 295
emigration
  [see emigrate]
eminence *height* 206
  fame 873
  church dignitary 996
eminently 33
emir *master* 745
  noble 875
emissary
  messenger 534
  consignee 758
emission 297
emissive 297
emit *eject* 297
  publish 531
  voice 580
  - vapor 336
Emmanuel 976
emmeleia 413
emmet 193
emollient 662
emolument
  acquisition 775
  receipt 810
  remuneration 973
emotion 821
emotional 821
  - appeal 824
empale *transfix* 260
  execute 972
empanel *list* 86, 611
  jury 969
empennage 273
emperor 745
  positiveness 535
emphasis *accent* 580
emphasize 535
emphatic
  positive assertion 535
  important 642
emphatically *much* 31
empierce 260
empire *region* 181
  dominion 737
  domain 780
emprema 476
empiric 548
empirical
  experiment 463
  essay 675
empiricism 451, 463
emplastrum 662
employ *business* 625
  use 677
  servitude 749
  commission 755
  - one's capital in 794
  - oneself 680
  - one's time in 625
  in one's - 746
employee *servant* 746
  agent 758
employer 795

employment
  [see employ]
  action 680
empoison 659
emporium 799
empower *power* 157
  commission 755
  delegate 759
  permit 760
empress 745, 877
emprise 676
emptiness
  [see empty]
emption 795
emptor 795
  caveat - 769
emptorial 795
empty *clear* 185
  vacant 187
  deflate 195
  drain 297
  ignorant 491
  waste 638
  deficient 640
  useless 645
  beggarly account of -
  boxes *poverty* 804
  - encomium 894
  - one's glass 298
  - purse 804
  - sound 517
  - stomach 865
  - title *name* 564
  undue 925
  - words 546
empty-handed 640
empty-headed 491
empurple 434, 437
empyrean *sky* 318
  blissful 829
empyreuma 401
empyrosis 384
emu 366
emulate *imitate* 19
  goodness 648
  rival 708
  compete 720
  glory 873
emulsify 352
emulsion 352
emunctory 295, 350
en - bloc 50
  - masse 50
  - passant
  parenthetical 10
  transient 111
  à propos 134
  - rapport 9
  - règle *order* 58
  conformity 82
  - route *journey* 266
  progress 282
enable 157
enact *drama* 599
  action 680
  conduct 692
  complete 729
  order 741
  law 963
enallage *metaphor* 521
  (*substitute* 147)

enamel *coating* 223
  painting 556
  porcelain 557
  ornament 847
enameler 559
enamor 897
enanthema 655
encage 751
encamp *locate* 184
  abode 189
encase 223
encaustic painting 556
enceinte *with child* 161
  region 181
  inclosure 232
enchafe 830
enchain *restrain* 751
  (*join* 43)
enchant *please* 829
enchanted *pleased* 827
enchanting
  beautiful 845
  love 897
enchantment
  sorcery 992
enchase 43, 223, 259
enchymatous 194
enchyridion 593
encincture 227, 229
encircle *include* 76
  surround 227
  go round 311
  revolve 312
enclave *close* 181
  boundary 233
enclose [see inclose]
enclosure
  [see inclosure]
enclothe 225
encomiast 935
encomium 931
encompass 227
  - with gloom 422
encore *again* 104
  approbation 931
encounter
  undergo 151
  clash 276
  meet 292
  withstand 708
  contest 720
  - danger 665
  - risk 621
encourage
  animate 615
  aid 707
  comfort 834
  hope 858
  embolden 861
Encratism 953
Encratite 953
encroach
  transcursion 303
  do wrong 923
  infringe 925
  - upon 927
encrust 223
encuirassed 223
encumber
  difficulty 704
  hindrance 706

encumbrance
  [see encumber]
encyclical 531
encyclopedia
  knowledge 490
  book 542, 593
  store 636
encyclopedical
  general 78
  - knowledge 490
encysted 229
end termination **67**
  effect 154
  object 620
  at an - 142
  come to its - 729
  - in smoke 732
  - of life 360
  - of one's tether
  sophistry 477
  ignorant 491
  insufficient 640
  difficult 704
  - one's days 360
  -s of the earth 196
  - to end space 180
  touching 199
  length 200
  on - 212
  one's journey's - 292
  put an - to destroy 162
  kill 361
end-all 67
endamage 649
endanger 665
endear 897
endearment **902**
endeavor pursue 622
  attempt 675
  - after 620
  use one's best - 686
endemic special 79
  interior 221
  disease 655
er.denizen 184
endermic 223
enderon 223
endimanche
  adorned 847
  display 882
endive 298
endless
  multitudinous 102
  infinite 105
  lasting 110
  perpetual 112
endlong 200
endogenous 567
endome 223
endophagy 945
endorse [see indorse]
endorsement
  [see indorsement]
endosmose 302
endow confer power 157
endowed with
  possessed of 777
endowment
  intrinsic 5
  power 157
  talent 698

gift 784
endrogynous 83
endue 157
endurable 110
endurance
  [see endure]
  perseverance 604a
  patience 831
endure exist 1
  time 106
  last 110
  continue 141, 143
  undergo 151
  feel 821
  submit to 826
  - for ever 112
  - pain 828
  unable to - 867
enduring
  remembered 506
endways 200
endwise 200, 212
enema 300, 337
enemy time 841
  foe 891
  - to society 891
  the common - 978
  thing devised by the
    - 546
energetic [see energy]
  undertaking 676
energize 157
energumen 504
energy power 157
  strength 159
  physical **171**
  resolution 604
  activity 682
  passion 820
enervate paralyze 158
  weaken 160
enervated 575
enervation 160, 575
enface 590
enfant
  - gâté prosperity 734
  satiety 869
  favorite 899
  - perdu hopeless 859
  reckless 863
  - terrible artless 703
  object of fear 860
enfeeble 160
enfeebled worn out 688
enfeoffment 783
Enfield rifle 727
enfilade lengthwise 200
  pierce 260
  pass through 302
enfold 229
enforce urge 615
  advise 695
  compel 744
  require 924
enfranchise free 748
  liberate 750
  permit 760
enfranchised
  privileged 924
engage bespeak 132
  induce 615

undertake 676
  do battle 722
  commission 755
  promise 768
  compact 769
  - the attention 457
  - with 720
  I'll - affirmation 535
engaged marriage 903
  be - mistime 135
  - in attention 457
engagement
  business 625
  battle 720
  endearment 902
engaging
  pleasing 829
  amiable 897
engarrison 717
engender 161
engild 439
engine 633
engine driver 268
engineer
  engine driver 268
  mechanician 690
  military 726
engineering 633
engird 227
English native 188
  broken - 563
  - horn 417
  - philosphy 451
  king's - 560
  murder the king's -
    568
  plain - intelligible 518
  interpreted 522
  style 576
Englishman 188
engobe 223
engorge swallow 296
  gluttony 957
engorgement
  swallowing 296
  too much 641
engrail 256
engrave furrow 259
  mark 550
  - in the memory 505
engraver 559
engraving **558**
engross write 590
  possess 777
  - the thoughts
  thought 451
  attention 457
engulf destroy 162
  swallow up 296
  plunge 310
enhance increase 35
  improve 658
enhancement 35
enharmonic 413
enigma question 461
  unintelligibility 519
  secret 533
enigmatic
  uncertain 475
  obscure 519
  (hidden 528)

enigmatical 520
enjoin 600
  advise 695
  command 741
  prescribe 926
enjoy physically 377
  possess 777
  morally 827
  - a state 7
  - health 654
enjoyment [see enjoy]
enkindle heat 384
  excite 824
  (induce 615)
enlarge increase 35
  swell 194
  in writing 573
  liberate 750
  - the mind 537
enlarged views 498
enlighten
  illumine 420
  inform 527
  teach 537
enlightened
  knowledge 490
enlist engage 615
  war 722
  commission 755
  - into the service 677
  - under the banners
    of 707
enlisted man 726
enliven delight 829
  inspirit 834
  cheer 836
  amuse 840
enmesh 545, 704
enmity **889**
ennead 98
enneahedral 98
enneastyle 98
ennoble 873
ennui 841
enormity crime 947
enormous great 31
  bid 192
  - number 102
enough much 31
  no more! 142
  sufficient 639
  moderately 651
  satiety 869
  - and to spare 639
  - in all conscience 641
  - to drive one mad
    830
  know when one has
    had - 953
enrage provoke 830
  aggravate 835
  incense 900
enragé 865
enrapture excite 824
  beatify 829
  love 897
enraptured 827
enravish
  beatify 829
enravished 827
enravishment 824

epitaph 363, 550
epithalamium 903
epithelium 223
epithem 662
epithet 564
epitome *miniature* 193
  short 201
  concise 572
  compendium 596
epitomist 201
epitomization 201
epitomizer 201
epizoötic 655, 657
epoch *time* 106
  period 108
  instant 113
  date 114
  present time 118
epochal 108
epode 597
eponym 564
epopœa 597
Epsom salts 662
epulation 298
epulotic 662
epuration 652
equable *uniform* 16
  equitable 922
equal *even* 27
  be parallel 216
  equitable 922
  - chance 156
  - times 120
  - to *power* 157
equality 27
  identity 13
equalize 213
equanimity 826
equate 27
  compensate 30
equation 37, 85
equator *middle* 68
  world 318, 550
equatorial 68
equerry 746
equestrian 268
equestrienne 268
equibalanced 27
equidistant 68, 216
equilibration 27
equilibrium 27
equine *carrier* 271
  horse 366
equinox *spring* 125
  autumn 126
equip *dress* 225
  prepare 673
equipage *vehicle* 272
  instruments 633
  display 882
equiparable 9
equiparant 9, 27
equiparate 27
equipment *gear* 633
  [*see* equip]
equipoise 27
equipollence 27
equiponderant 27
equitable *wise* 498
  just 922
  due 924

honorable 939
- interest 780
equitation 266
equity *right* 922
  honor 939
  law 963
  - draftsman 968
  in - 922
equivalent
  correlated 12
  identical 13
  equal 27
  compensation 30
  substitute 147
  translation 522
equivocalness
  dubious 475
  double meaning **520**
  impure 961
equivocate
  sophistry 477
  palter 520
  lie 544
equivocation
  [*see* equivocate]
  quirk 481
  without - 543
équivoque
  double meaning 520
  impure 961
era *time* 106
  period 108
  date 114
  - of indiction 108
eradicate *destroy* 162
  eject 297
  extract 301
eradication 103
erase *destroy* 162
  rub out 331
  obliterate 552
Erastian 984
erasure [*see* erase]
Erato 416
ere 116
  - long 132
  - now 116
  past 122
  - then 116
Erebus *dark* 421
  hell 982
erect *build* 161
  vertical 212
  - straight 246
  raise 307
  - the scaffolding 673
  with head - 878
erection *building* 161
  elevation 307
eremite 893
erewhile 116, 122, 132
ergo 476
ergophobia 683
ergotism 480, 489
e:gotize 485
Erinyes 173
eriometer 445
eristic 476
ermine *covering* 223
  badge of authority 747
  ornament 847

erode 36, 659
erosion [*see* erode]
erotic *amorous* 897
  impure 961
err - *in opinion* 495
  - *morally* 945
  to - *is human* 495
errand *message* 532
  business 625
  commission 755
errand boy 534
errant 279
erratic *irregular* 139
  changeable 149
  wandering 279
  capricious 608
erratum 495
errhine 349
erroneous 495
error *fallacy* **495**
  vice 945
  guilt 947
  court of - 966
  writ of - 969
erst 66, 122
erstwhile 122
erubescence 434
eructate 297
eructation 297, 349
erudite 490, 500, 539
erudition
  knowledge 490
  learning 539
erumpent 295
eruption *revolution* 146
  violence 173
  egress 295
  ejection 297
  explosion 406
  disease 655
  volcanic - 872
eruptive
  [*see* eruption]
eruptivity 297
erysipelas 655
erythroblast 357
escalade *mounting* 305
  at!ack 716
escalator 305, 307
escalop 248
escamoter 545
escapade *absurdity* 497
  freak 608
  prank 840
escape *flight* **671**
  liberate 750
  evade 927
  - notice &c.
  invisible 447
  inattention 458
  latent 526
  - the lips a
  disclosure 529
  speech 582
  - the memory 506
  means of - 664, 666
escarp *fortification* 717
escarpment
  stratum 204
  height 206
  oblique 217

eschar 204
escharotic
  caustic 171
  pungent 392
eschatology 67
escheat 145, 974
eschew *avoid*
  dislike 867
esclandre 828, 830
escopet 727
escort *accompany* 88
  safeguard 664
  keeper 753
escritoire 191
esculent 298
escutcheon 550, 551
esophagus 350
esoteric *private* 79
  unintelligible 519
  concealed 528
esotericism 528
espalier 232
especial 79
especially *more* 33
Esperanto 560, 563
espial 441
espionage *looking* 441
  inquiry 461
esplanade *houses* 189
  flat 213 (*plain* 344)
espousals 903
espouse *choose* 609
  marriage 903
  - a cause *aid* 707
  coöperate 709
esprit *shrewdness* **498**
  wit 842
  bel - 844
  - de corps
  bias 481
  coöperation 709
  sociality 892
  (*party* 712)
  - fort *thinker* 500
  irreligious 989
espy 441
esquire *rank* 875
  title 877
essay *experiment* **463**
  writing 590
  dissertation 595
  endeavor **675**
essayist
  author 593, 595
esse 1
essence *being* 1
  nature 5
  scent 398
  meaning 516
  (*important part* **642**)
essential
  real 1
  intrinsic 5
  great 31
  required 630
  important 642
  - nature 3
essentially
  substantially 3
establish *settle* 150
  create 161

place 184
evidence 467
demonstrate 478
- equilibrium 27
established
permanent 141
habit 613
- church 983a
establishment
party 712
shop 799
estafette 268, 534
estaminet 189
estate condition 7
kind 75
property 780
come to man's - 131
esteem believe 484
approve 931
in high - 928
estimable 648
estimate number 85
measure 466
adjudge 480
information 527
- too highly 482
estimation
[see esteem, estimate]
estival 382
estop 706
estrade 213
estrange disjoin 44
alienate 889
hate 898
estranged secluded 893
estrapade attack 716
punishment 972
estreat 974
estuary 343
estuation 384
esurient 865
et cætera add 37
include 76
plural 100
état major 745
etch furrow 259
engraving 558
etching 54, 558
Eternal, The - 976
eternal 112
- home 981
- rest 360
into the - secret 528
eternalize 112
eterne 112
eternity 112
an - 110
launch into - 360, 361
palace of - 543
ether space 180
lightness 320⁻
rarity 322
vapor 334
anæsthetic 376
ethereal 4
etheric body 980a
etheric double 317
ethical 926
- culture 984
ethicism 984
534

ethics 926
Ethiop black 431
Ethiopian 431
-'s skin
unchangeable 150
ethnic 984
ethnology 372
ethology 926
etiolate bleach 429
whiten 430
etiology
[see ætiology]
etiquette custom 613
fashion 852
ceremony 882
etymologist 492, 562
etymologize 562
etymology 562
etymon origin 153
verbal 562
Eucharist 998
euchology 998
euchre 840
defeat 731
eucrasy 41
eudæmonism 910, 944
eudæmonist 910
eudiometer air 338
salubrity 656
eudiometry 338
eugenics 658
eulogist 935
eulogize 482
eulogy 733, 931
Eumenides
violence 173
fury 900
evildoers 913
revenge 919
eumerogenesis 161
eunuch 158
eunuchize 158
eupepsia 654
euphemism
metaphor 521
affirmation 535
phrase 566
style 577, 578
flattery 933
euphemist
man of taste 850
flatterer 935
euphonium 417
euphony melody 413
elegant style 578
euphoria 654
Euphrosyne 836
euphuism
metaphor 521
elegant style 577
affected style 579
affectation 855
euphuize 855
Eurasian 41
eureka! answer 462
discovery 480a
Euripus 343
European plan 298
eurythmic 542
eurythmics 242, 537
eurythmy 242

Eusebian 984
Eustachian tube 418
Euterpe 416
euthanasia 360
eutrophy 707
evacuate quit 293
excrete 295
emit 297
evacuation 299
evade sophistry 477
avoid 623
not observe 773
exempt 927
evagation 279
evanescent small 32
transient 111
little 193
disappearing 449
evangelical 983a, 985
Evangelists 985
evanid 160
evaporable 334
evaporate
unsubstantial 4
transient 111
vaporize 336
dry up 340
evaporation
vaporization 336
dryness 340
cloud 353
preserviug 670
evaporator 336
evasion sophistry 477
quirk 481
concealment 528
falsehood 544
untruth 546
avoidance 623
escape 671
cunning 702
nonobservance 773
dereliction 927
evasive [seeevasion]
eve 126
on the - of
transient 111
prior 116
future 121
evection 61
even uniform 16
equal 27
still more 33
level 213
parallel 216
straight 246
flat 251
smooth 255
although 469
neutral 628
in spite of 708
be - with retaliate 718
pay 807
- course 628
- now 118
- off 27
- so for all that 30
yes 488
- temper 826
- tenor uniform 16
order 58

regularity 80
- terms 922
pursue the - tenor
continue 143
avoid 623
business 625
even-handed just 922
honorable 939
evening 126
- dress 225
- star 423
shades of - 422
evenness [see even]
symmetry 242
evensong 126, 990
event 151
bout 720
in the - of
circumstance 8
eventuality 151
destiny 152
supposition 514
justified by the - 937
eventful 151
remarkable 642
stirring 682
eventide 126
eventual future 121
eventuality 151
eventually effect 154
eventuate 151
ever invariable 16
perpetually 112
- and anon 136
- changing 149
- recurring 104
- so little 32
- so long 110
- so many 102
everduring 112
evergreen
continuous 69
lasting 110
always 112
fresh 123
plant 367, 369
everlasting
perpetual 112
destined 152
- fire 982
- life 152
evermore 112
eversible 140
eversion 140, 218
evert 140, 218
every general 78
periodic 138
at - turn 186
- day conformity 82
frequent 136
habit 613
- description 81
- hand against one
891
- inch 50
- other 138
- whit 52
in - mouth assent 488
news 532
repute 873
in - quarter 180

ın - respect 194
on - side 22
everybody 78
every one 78
 - his due 922
 - in his turn 148
everywhere *space* 180
 presence 186
evict 297
evidence 467
 manifestation 525
 disclosure 529
 ocular - 446
evident *visible* 446
 certain 474
 manifest 525
evidential 467
evil *harm* **619**
 badness 649
 demoniac 980
 impious 988
 - day *adversity* 735
 - eye *vision* 441
 malevolence 907
 disapprobation 932
 spell 993
 - favored 846
 - fortune 735
 - genius 980
 - hour 135
 - one 978
 - plight 735
 - spirits **980**
 - star 649
 prepare for - 673
 through - report &c.
  604a
evildoer **913**, 975
evildoing 945
evil-minded
 malevolent 907
 vicious 945
evil speaking
 malediction 908
 censure 932
 detraction 934
evince *show* 467
 prove 478
 disclose 529
evirate 158
eviscerate *eject* 297
 extract 301
eviscerated 4
eviternal 112
evoke *cause* 153
 call upon 765
 excite 824
evolution
 numerical 85
 production 161
 motion 264
 circuition 311
 turning out **313**
 organization 357
 training 673
 action 680
 military -s 722
evolutionary 264, 313
evolve *discover* 480a
evolved from 154
 [*and see* evolution]

evolvement 313
evulgate 531
evulsion 301
evviva! 931
ewe *sheep* 366
 female 374
ewer 191
ex - animo 602
 - dono 784
 - more 613
 - officio *officer* 694
 authority 737
 duty 924
 - parte 467
 - post facto 122, 133
 - tempore *instant* 113
 occasion 134
 - voto 768
exacerbate
 increase 35
 exasperate 173
 pervert 659
 aggravate 835
exact *similar* 17
 copy 21
 true 494
 literal 516
 style 572
 require 741
 tax 812
 insolence 885
 claim 924, 926
 - meaning 516
 - memory 505
 - observance 772
 - truth 494
exacting *severe* 739
 discontented 832
 grasping 865
exaction [*see* exact]
 undue 925
exactly *literally* 19
 just so 488
exactness [*see* exact]
exaggeration
 increase 35
 expand 194
 overestimate 482
 magnify **549**
 misrepresent 555
exalt *increase* 35
 elevate 307
 extol 931
 (*boast* 884)
 - one's horn 873
exalté 504
exalted *high* 206
 repute 873
 noble 875
 magnanimous 942
examination
 [*see* examine]
 evidence 467
 on - 463
 undergo - 461
examine
 attend to 457
 inquire 461
 - the books
 accounts 811
example *pattern* 22

 instance 82
 bad - 949
 good - 948
 make an - of 974
 set a good - 944
exanimate *dead* 360
 supine 683
exanthema 655
exarch 745
exasperate
 exacerbate 173
 aggravate 835
 enrage 900
excavate 252
excavation 252
execation 442
exceed *surpass* 33
 remain 40
 transgress 303
 intemperance 954
exceedingly (*greatly* 31)
excel *surpass* 33
 - in *skillful* 698
excellence
 goodness 648
 virtue 944
excellency *title* 877
excelsior 305
except *subduct* 38
 exclude 55
 reject 610
exception
 unconformity 83
 qualification 469
 exemption 777a
 disapproval 932
 take - *qualify* 469
 resent 900
exceptionable *bad* 649
 guilty 947
exceptional
 unimitated 20
 extraneous 57
 unconformable 83
 in an - degree 31
exceptions 901, 901a
excern 297
excerpt 551, 609
excerpta *parts* 51
 compendium 596
 selections 609
excerption 609
excess *remainder* 40
 redundance 641
 intemperance 954
excessive *great* 31
exchange
 reciprocity 12
 interchange 148
 saloon 189
 transfer 783
 barter 794
 mart 799
 bill of - 771
 - blows &c.
 retaliation 718
 battle 720
Exchequer 802
 Baron of - 967
 Court of - 966
 - bill 800

excise 812
exciseman 965
excision 38
excitability
 excitement **825**
 irascibility 901
excitant 171
excitation **824**
excitative 171
excite *energy* 171
 violence 173
 impassion 824
 - an impression **375**
 - attention 457
 - desire 865
 - hope 811
 - love 897
excited 173
 - fancy 515
excitement 824, 825
 anger 900
exclaim 411
 - against 932
exclamation
 typography 550
 utterance 580
exclude *sift* 42
 leave out 55
 reject 610
 prohibit 761
 banish 893
exclusion **55, 57**
exclusive *simple* 4.?
 omitting 55
 special 79
 irregular 83
 forbidding 761
 - of 38
 - possession 777
 - thought 457
excogitate
 ruminate 450
 thought 451
 imagination 515
excommunicate
 banish 893
 curse 908
 rite 998
 (*exclude* 55)
excoriate 226
excrement
 excretion 299
 dirt 653
excrescence
 projection 250
 blemish 848
excreta *excretion* 299
 dirt 653
excretion 297, **299**
excretory 295, 299, 350
excruciating
 physical pain 378
 mental pain 830
exculpate *forgive* 918
 vindicate 937
 acquit 970
excursion 266, 311
excursionist 268
excursive
 deviating 279
 - *style* 573

535

explorer 268
explosion
  [*see* explode]
  revolution 146
  violence 173
  loudness 404
  sound 406
  anger 900
explosive 727
  dangerous 665
exponent *numerical* 84
  interpreter 524
  informant 527
  index 550
export 295
expose *denude* 226
  confute 479
  disclose 529
  censure 932
  - oneself
  disreputable 874
  - to danger 665
  - to view *visible* 446
  manifest 525
exposé *confutation* 479
  disclosure 529
  description 594
exposed *bare* 226
  - to *liable* 177
exposition
  [*see* expose]
  explanation 522
  indication 550
  drama 599
  exhibition 882
expositor
  interpreter 524
  teacher 540
expository
  explaining 522
  informing 527
  disclosed 529
  disserting 595
expostulate
  dissuade 616
  advise 695
  deprecate 766
  reprehend 932
exposure
  [*see* expose]
  appearance 448
  - to weather 338
expound *interpret* 522
  teach 537
expounder 524
express *carrier* 268,
  271
  rapid 274
  squeeze out 301
  mean 516
  declare 525
  inform 527
  language 560
  intentional 620
  transit 627
  haste 684
  - by words 566
  - car 272
  - regret 952
  - sympathy for 915
  - train 272

expressed 566
  well - 578
expression
  [*see* express]
  musical - 416
  aspect 448
  nomenclature 564
  phrase 566
  mode of - 569
  new fangled - 563
expressive
  meaning 516
  sensibility 822
expressman 271
exprobation
  censure 932
  accusation 938
expropriation 782
expugnable 665
expugnation
  success 731
  (*taking* 789)
expuition 297
expulsion [*see* expel]
  exclusion 55
expunge *destroy* 162
  efface 552
expurgate 652
exquisite *savory* 394
  excellent 648
  pleasurable 829
  beautiful 845
  fop 854
exquisitely *very* 31
exradio 420
exsiccate 340
exspuition 297
exsudation 299
exsufflation 993
extant 1
extasy [*see* ecstasy]
extemporaneous
  [*see* extempore]
  transient 111
extempore
  instant 113
  early 132
  occasion 134
  offhand 612
  unprepared 674
extemporize 612
extemporizer 612
extend *expand* 194
  prolong 200
  (*increase* 35)
  - to 196
extended
  spacious 180
  long 200
  broad 202
extendibility 324
extensibility 324, 325
extensile 324
extension
  [*see* extend]
  increase 35
  continuance 143
  space 180
  - of time 110
extensive *great* 31
  wide 180

- knowledge 490
extent *degree* 26
  space 180
  length 200
extenuate
  decrease 36
  weaken 160
  excuse 937
extenuated 203
extenuating 937
  - circumstances
  qualification 469
  excuse 937
extenuatory 469
exterior 57, 220
exteriority 220
exterminate 162
extermination 301
exterminator 165
extern 220
external 220
  - evidence 467
  - senses 375
externalize 220
exterritorial 220
extinct *inexistent* 2
  past 122
  old 124
  destroyed 162
  darkness 421
extincteur 385
extinction
  obliteration 552
  - of life 360
extinguish
  destroy 162
  blow out 385
  darken 421
extinguisher 165
  put an - upon
  hinder 706
  defeat 731
extinguishment 2
extirpate 2, 301
extispicious 511
extispicy 511
extol
  overestimate 482
  praise 931
extort *extract* 301
  compel 744
  despoil 789
extorted *dissent* 489
extortion *dearness* 814
  rapacity 819
extortionate *severe* 739
  dear 814
  rapacious 819
  grasping 865
extortioner 789, 819
extra *additional* 37
  supernumerary 641
  ab - 220
extract *take out* 301
  record 551
  quotation 596
  remedy 662
extraction **301**
  paternity 166
  - of roots 85
extractor 301

extradition
  deportation 270
  expulsion 297
extrados 220
extrajudicial 964
extralimitary 220
extramundane 220, 31?
extramural 220
extraneous *extrinsic* 6
  not related 10
  foreign 57
  exterior 220
extraneousness **57**
extraordinary *great* 31
  exceptional 83
extraregarding 220
extraterrene 220
extraterrestrial 220
extraterritorial 220
extravagance
  [*see* extravagant]
extravagant
  inordinate 31
  violent 173
  absurd 497
  foolish 499
  fanciful 515
  exaggerated 549
  excessive 641
  high-priced 814
  prodigal 818
  vulgar 851
  ridiculous 853
extravaganza
  fanciful 515
  misrepresentation
  555
  drama 599
extravagation 303
extravasate *egress* 29**5**
  ejection 297
extreme
  inordinate 31
  end 67
  - unction 998
extremist 710
extremity *end* 67
  adversity 735
  tribulation 828
  at the last - 665
  drive matters to an -
  604
extricate *take out* 301
  deliver 672
  facilitate 705
  liberate 750
extrinsicality 6
extrinsic *evidence* 467
extrusion *eject* 297
  excrete 299
extrusive 297
exuberant
  - *style* 573
  redundant 639
exudation *egress* 295
  excretion 299
exudative 295
exude 295
exulcerate 659
exult *rejoice* 838
  boast 884

exultant *hopeful* 858
exulting *cheerful* 836
exunge 356
exuviæ 223, 653
  (*remains* 40)
exuvial 226
exuv.ate 226
eye *circle* 247
  opening 260
  organ of sight 441
  appear to one's - 446
  before one's -s
    front 234
    visible 446
    manifest 525
  cast the -s on
    see 441
  cast the -s over
    attend to 457
  catch the - 457
  close the -s
    blind 442

    death 360
    sleep 683
  dry -s 823
  - askance 860
  - disease 655
  - glistening 824
  - like Mars 441
  - of a needle 260
  - of the master 693
  -s draw straws 683
  -s of a lynx 459
  -s open
    attention 457
    care 459
    intention 620
  -s opened
    disclosure 529
  -s out 442
  fix the -s on 457
  have an - to
    attention 457
    intention 620

    desire 865
  have one's -s about
    one 459
  in one's - *visible* 446
    expectant 507
  in the - of the law
    963
  in the -s of
    appearance 448
    belief 484
  keep an - upon 459
  look with one's own -s
    459
  mind's - 515
  open the -s to 480a
  set one's -s upon 865
  shut one's -s to
    inattention 458
    permit 760
  to the -s 448
  under the -s of 186
  up to one's -s 641

  with moistened -s **839**
  with open -s 870
eyeglass 445
eyelashes 256
eyeless 442
eyelet 260
eye opener **508**
eyesight 441
eyesore *ugly* 846
  blemish 848
eyeteeth
  have cut one's -
    adolescence 131
    skill 698
    cunning 702
eyewater 662
eyewitness
  spectator 444
  evidence 467
eyot 346
eyre 966
eyrie 189

F

Fabian policy
  delay 133
  inaction 681
  caution 864
fable *error* 495
  metaphor 521
  fiction 546
  description 594
fabric *state* 7
  effect 154
  texture 329
  -s 635
fabricate *compose* 54
  form 56
  make 161
  invent 515
  falsify 544
fabrication *lie* 546
fabulist 594
fabulous
  enormous 31
  imaginary 515
  untrue 546
  exaggerated 549
  descriptive 594
  mythical 979
faburden 413
façade 234
face *exterior* 220
  covering 223
  line 224
  front 234
  aspect 448
  oppose 708
  resist 719
  impudence 885
  change the - of 146
  - about 279
  - of the country 344
  - of the thing
    appearance 448
  - the music 861
  - to face *front* 234
    contraposition 237

    manifest 525
  fly in the - of
    disobey 742
  in the - of
    presence 186
    opposite 708
  look in the - *see* 441
    proud 878
  make -s *distort* 243
    ugly 846
    disrespect 929
  not show -
    disreputable 874
    bashful 879
  on the - of
    manifest 525
  on the - of the earth
    space 180
    world 318
  put a good - upon
    sham 545
    calm 826
    cheerful 836
    hope 858
    pride 878
    display 882
    vindicate 937
  set one's - against 708
  show - *present* 186
    visible 446
  to one's - 525
  wry - 378
face cloth
  cleanness 652
face guard 717
facet 220
facetiæ 842
facetious 842
facia 234
facile *willing* 602
  irresolute 605
  easy 705
facile princeps 33
facilitate 705

facility *skill* 698
  easy **705**
facing *covering* 223
  lining 224
facinorous 945
façon de parler
  figure of speech 521
  exaggeration 549
facsimile *copy* 21
  duplication 90
  representation 554
fact *existence* 1
  event 151
  certainty 474
  truth 494
  in - 535
faction *company* 72
  party 712
  feud 713
factious 24, 713
factit.ous 545, 546
factor *numerical* 84
  agent 690
  director 694
  consignee 758
  (*merchant* 797)
factory 691
factotum *agent* 690
  manager 694
  employé 758
facts *evidence* 467
  summary of - 594
factual 1
facula 420
faculties 450
  in possession of one's
    - 502
faculty *power* 157
  profession 625
  skill 698
facundity 582
fad *bias* 481
  caprice 608
faddle 683

fade *vanish* 4
  transient 111
  become old 124
  droop 160
  grow dim 422
  lose color 429
  disappear 449
  spoil 659
  - away *cease* 142
    disappear 449
  - from the memory
    506
  - out 129
fadeless 873
fadge 23
fæces [*see* feces]
fag *labor* 686
  fatigue 688
  drudge 690
  - end *remainder* 40
    end 67
fagot *bundle* 72
  fuel 388
  - voter 4
faïence 557
fail *droop* 160, 655
  shortcoming 304
  be confuted 479
  not succeed 732
  not observe 773
  not pay 808
  dereliction 927
failing [*see* fail]
  incomplete 53
  insufficient 640
  vice 945
  guilt 947
  - heart 837
  - luck 735
  - memory 506
  - sight 443
  - strength 160
failure **732**
fain *willing* 602

compulsive 744
wish 865
fainéant 683
faint *small in degree* 32
  impotent 158
  weak 160
  sound 405
  dim 422
  color 429
  swoon 688
  damn with - praise
    930, 932, 934
  - heart *fear* 860
  cowardice 862
  wooing 902
faintness *sound* **405**
  [see faint]
fair *in degree* 31
  pale 429
  white 430
  wise 498
  important 643
  good 648
  moderate 651
  mart 799
  beautiful 845
  just 922
  honorable 939
  by -means or foul 631
  - chance 472
  - copy *copy* 21
  writing 590
  - field *occasion* 134
  freedom 748
  - game 857
  - name 873
  - play *922, 923*
  - question 461
  - sex 374
  - weather 734
  pleasurableness 829
  - weather sailor 701
  - wind 705
  - words 894
  in a - way
  tending 176
  probable 472
  convalescent 658
  prosperous 734
  hopeful 858
fairing 784
fairly
  intrinsically 5
  slightly 643
  get on - 736
fair-spoken
  courtesy 894
  flattery 933
fairway 267
fairy *fanciful* 515
  fay 979
  imp 980
  - lore 993
  - tale 594
  fabrication 546
fairyism 979
fairyland 515
fait accompli *certain* 474
  complete 729
'**aith** *belief* 484

hope 858
honor 939
piety 987
declaration of - 983
- cure 662
- curer 984
- healing 662
i' - 535
keep - with *observe* 772
plight - *promise* 768
love 902
true - *orthodox* 983a
want of -
  incredulity 487
  irreligious 989
faithful [see faith]
  like 17
  copy 21
  exact 494
  obedient 743
  - memory 505
  - to 772
faithless *false* 544
  dishonorable 940
  sceptical 989
fake *imitation* 19
  concoct 544
  swindle 545
  untruth 546
faker 548, 683, 797
fakir 804, 955, 996
falcade 309
falcate *pointed* 244
  carved 245
falchion 727
Falcidian law 780
falciform [see falcate]
falcon 792
falconet 727
faldstool 215
fall *autumn* 126
  happen 151
  perish 162
  slope 217
  regression 283
  descend 306
  die 360
  fail 732
  adversity 735
  vice 945
  - a cursing 908
  - a prey to
  defeated 732
  subject 749
  - asleep 683
  - astern *rear* 235
  regress 283
  - at one's feet 725
  - away 195
  - back *return* 283
  recede 287
  relapse 661
  - back upon *use* 677
  defense 717
  - dead *die* 360
  - down *collapse* 304
  worship 990
  - down before 928
  - flat on the ear 843
  - foul of *blow* 276
  hinder 706

oppose 708
discord 713
attack 716
contention 720
censure 932
- from one's high es-
  tate
  adversity 735
  disrepute 874
  - from the lips 582
  - in *order* 58
  continuity 69
  event 151
  - in love with 897
  - in price 815
  - in the way of 186
  - in with *agree* 23
  conform 82
  converge 290
  discover 480a
  concord 714
  consent 762
  - into *conversion* 144
  river 348
  - into a custom
  conform to 82
  - into a habit 613
  - into a passion 900
  - into a trap 547
  - into decay 659
  - into oblivion 506
  - into raptures 827
  - of day 125
  - off *decrease* 36
  deteriorate 659
  - off again 661
  - of snow 383
  - of the curtain 67
  - of the leaf 126
  - of the mercury 338
  - on one's knees
  submit 725
  servile 886
  gratitude 916
  worship 990
  - out *happen* 151
  quarrel 713
  enmity 889
  - short *inferior* 34
  contract 195
  shortcoming 304
  - through *fail* 732
  - to *eat* 298
  take in hand 676
  do battle 722
  - to dust 328
  - to one's lot
  event 151
  chance 156
  receive 785
  duty 926
  - to pieces
  disjunction 44
  destruction 162
  brittle 328
  - to the ground
  be *confuted* 479
  fail 732
  - to work 686
  - under *inclusion* 76
  subjection 749

- under one's notice
  457
- upon *discover* 480a
  unexpected 508
  devise 626
  attack 716
- upon the ear 418
have to - back upon
  provision 637
let - *lower* 308
  inform 527
water - 348
fallacy *sophistry* 477
  error 495
show the - of 497
fallen angel
  bad man 949
  Satan 978
fallible *uncertain* 475
  sophistical 477
falling
  - *action* 154
  - star *world* 318
  luminary 423
  - weather 348
fallow *unproductive* 169
  yellow 436
  unready 674
  inactive 681
false *sophistry* 477
  error 495
  untrue 544, 546
  spurious 925
  dishonorable 940
  - alarm 669
  - coloring
  misinterpretation 523
  falsehood 544
  - construction   523,
    544
  - doctrine 984
  - expectation 509
  - hearted 940
  - impression 495
  - light *vision* 443
  - money 800
  - ornament 851
  - plea *untruth* 546
  plea 617
  - position 704
  - pretenses *steal* 791
  - prophet
  disappoint 509
  (*pseudo-revelation*)
    986
  - reasoning 477
  - scent *error* 495
  mislead 538
  - shame 855
  - statement 546
  - step 732
  - teaching 538
  - witness *deceiver* 548
  detraction 934
falsehood **544,** 546
falsetto *squeak* 410
  music 415
  want of voice 581
falsification 555
falsify *error* 495
  falsehood 544, 546

field piece 727
field preacher 996
field work 717
fiend *ruffian* 913
  demon 980
fiendish 945
fiendlike
  malevolent 907
  wicked 945
  fiend 980
fierce *violent* 173
  passion 825
  daring 861
  angry 900
fieri facias 963
fiery *violent* 173
  hot 382
  strong feeling 821
  excitable 825
  angry 900
  irascible 901
  - cross *indication* 550
  alarm 669
  warfare 722
  - furnace 386
  - imagination 515
  - ordeal 828
fiesta 840
fife 410, 417
fifer 416
fifth 98, 99
fifty 98
  go - fifty 628
fig *food* 298
  unimportance 643
  - out 857
  - tree 367
  in the name of the
    prophet -s! 497
fight *contention* 720
  warfare 722
  - against destiny 606
  - it out 722
  - one's battles again
    594
  - one's way
  - shy *avoid* 623
  coward 862
  pursue 622
  active 682
  exertion 686
  - the good fight 944
  show - *defense* 717
  courage 861
fighter 726
fighting cock
  tenacity 604
  combatant 726
  courage 861
fighting man 726
figment 515
figurante 599
figurate number 84
figuration 240
figurative
  metaphorical 521
  representing 554
  - *style* 577
figure *number* 84
  form 240
  appearance 448

  metaphor 521
  indicate 550
  represent 554
  price 812
  ugly 846
cut a - *repute* 873
  display 882
  - to oneself 515
  - of speech 521
  exaggeration 549
poor - 874
figure flinger 994
figurehead *sign* 550
  representation 554
figurine 554
figuriste 559
filaceous 205
filament 205
filamentiferous 205
filamentous 256
filch 791
filcher 762
file *subduct* 38
  arrange 60
  row 69
  assemblage 72
  list 86
  reduce 195
  smooth 255
  pulverize 330
  record 551
  store 636
  soldiers 726
  - a claim 969
  - exceptions 469
  - leader 694
  - off *march* 266
  diverge 291
on - 551
file-fire 716
filgurate 420
filial 167
filiality 155
filiate 155
filiation
  consanguinity 11
  attribution 155
  posterity 167
filibeg 225
filibuster *delay* 133
  impede 706
  obstructionist 710
  plunder 791
  thief 792
filibusterer 707, 710
filibustering 791
filibusterous 708
filiciform 242
filicoid 242
filiform 205
filigree 219
filings 330
filius nullius 925
filius terræ 876
fill *complete* 52
  occupy 186
  contents 190
  stuff 224
  provision 637
  remedy 662
eat one's - 957

- an office
  business 625
  government 737
  -ed to overflowing 641
  - one's pocket 803
  - out *expand* 194
  - the bill 729
  - time 106
  - up *compensate* 30
  compose 54
  close 261
  restore 660
  - up the time
  inaction 681
  have one's -
  enough 639
  satiety 869
fille
  - de chambre 746
  - de joie 962
filled
  - to overflowing 641
fillet *band* 45
  filament 205
  circle 247
  indication 550
  ornament 847
filling *stuffing* 224
fillip *impulse* 276
  propulsion 284
  stimulus 615
  excite 824
filly 271
film *layer* 204
  opaque 426
  semitransparent 427
  - over the eyes
  dim sight 443
  ignorant 491
filmy *texture* 329
filter *percolate* 295
  clean 652
filth 653
filthy 653
filtrate 652
fimbria 256
fimbriated 256
fimetarious 653
fimicolous 653
fin 267
final *ending* 67
  completing 729
  commanding 741
  court of - appeal 474
  -cause 620
  - stroke 729
  - touch 729
  have the - word 153
finale *end* 67
  completion 729
finality 67, 729
finally *for good* 141
  eventually 151
  on the whole 476
finance *money* 800
  account 811
  minister of - 801
financier 639, 801
finch 366
find *eventuality* 151
  adjudge 480

  discover 480a
  acquire 775
  - a clue to 480a
  - credence 484
  - in *provide* 637
  - it in one's heart 602
  - means 632
  - one's account in 644
  - oneself *be* 1
  present 186
  - one s way 731
  - one's way into 294
  - out 480a
  - the cause of 522
  - the key of 522
  - the meaning 522
  - to one's cost 509
  - vent 671
fin-de-siècle 123
finding *judgment* 480
  lawsuit 959
  - store 799
fine *small* 32
  large 192
  thin 203
  rare 322
  not raining 340
  exact 494
  good 648
  beautiful 845
  adorned 847
  proud 878
  mulct 974
  - air 656
  - arts 554
  - by degrees 30
  - feather *strong* 159
  healthy 654
  - feeling 850
  - frenzy 515
  - gentleman *fop* 854
  proud 878
  - grain 329
  - lady 854, 878
  - powder 330
  - talking *overrate* 482
  boast 884
  - time of it 734
  - voice 580
  - writing 482, 577
  in - *end* 67
  after all 476
  one - morning 106
  some - morning 119
finedraw 660
fine-fingered 698
fineness [see fine]
finery *ornament* 847
  vulgarity 851
fine-spoken
  courtesy 894
  flattery 933
finespun *thin* 203
  sophistry 477
finesse *tact* 698
  artifice 702
  taste 850
  (*deception* 545)
finest
  the - *police* 664
finestill 336

fine-toned 413
finger *touch* 379
  hold 781
 - at one's -s' end
  near 197
  know 490
  remember 505
 - in the pie
  cause 153
  interfere 228
  act 680
  active 682
  coöperate 709
 - on the lips
  aphony 581
  taciturnity 585
 -'s breadth 203
 lay the - on
  point out 457
  discover 480a
 life a - 680
 not lift a - 681
 point the - at 457
 turn round one's little
  - 737
fingerling 193
finger post 550
finger print
 evidence 467
 dactylology 550
finger stall 223
fingle-fangle 643
finical *trifling* 643
 affected 855
 fastidious 868
finicality 457
finicking *trifling* 643
 affected 855
 fastidious 868
finis 67
finish *end* 67
 symmetry 242
 skill 698
 complete 729
finished *absolute* 31
 perfect 650
 skilled 698
finishing - stroke 361
 - touch 729
finite 32
finnan haddie 298
fiord 343
fir *tree* 367
 - balsam 400
fire *energy* 171
 eject 297
 heat 382
 make hot 384
 fuel 388
 shoot 406
 dismiss 756
 excite 834, 825
 between two -s 665
 catch - 384
  passion 820
 - and fury 900
 - and sword 162
 - at 716
 - a volley 716
 - off 284
 - of genius 498

 - the blood 824
 - up *excite* 825
  anger 900
go through - and water
 resolution 604
 perseverance 604a
 courage 861
 hell - 982
 on - 382
 open - *begin* 66
 play with - 863
 take - *excitable* 825
  angry 900
 under - *danger* 665
  war 722
fire alarm 550, 669
fire annihilator 385
firearms 727
fireball *fuel* 388
 arms 727
fire balloon 273
fire barrel 388
fire bell 669
firebox 386
firebrand *fuel* 388
 instigator 615
 dangerous man 667
 incendiary 913
fire brigade 385
fire bug 384, 913, 949
firecracker 406, 840
fire curtain *theater* 599
firedamp 663
fire department 385
firedog 386
firedrake 423
fire-eater *courage* 861
 fighter 726
 jingo 885
 blusterer 887
fire-eating *rashness* 863
 insolence 885
fire engine 385
fire escape 671
fire extinguisher 385
firefly 423
fireless cooker 386
fire light 422
firelock 727
fireman *stoker* 268
 extinguisher 385
fire-new 123
fireplace 386
fireproof 385
 safe 664
fireside 189
firewood 388
firework *fire* 382
 luminary 423
 amusement 840
fire worship 382, 991
fire worshipper 984
firing *fuel* 388
 explosion 406
firkin 191
firm *junction* 43
 stable 150
 hard 323
 resolute 604
 partnership 712
 merchant 797

 brave 861
 - belief 484
 - hold 781
 stand - 719
firman *decree* 741
 permit 760
firmness [*see* firm]
first 66
 at - *sight* 448
 come back to - *love*
  607
 - and foremost 66
 - and last 87
 - blow 716
 - blush *morning* 125
 vision 441
 appearance 448
 manifest 525
 - cause 976
 - come first served
  609a
 - fiddle
  importance 642
  proficient 700
  authority 737
 - impression 66
 - line 234
 - move 66
 - opportunity 132
 - stage 66
 - stone
  preparation 673
  attack 716
 - that comes 609a
 great - Cause 976
 in the - place 153
 of the - water
  best 648
  repute 873
 on the - summons 741
firstborn 124, 128
first-class *best* 648
first fruits 154
firstling *eldest* 128
 effect 154
first-rate
 important 642
 excellent 648
 man-of-war 726
firth 343
fisc 802
fiscal 800
fiscalize 800
fish *food* 298
 sport 361, 622
 animal 366
 zoölogy 368
 - for *seek* 461
  experiment 463
  desire 865
 - for compliments 880
 - fry 840
 - glue 352
 - hatchery 370, 636
 - in the air 645
 - in troubled waters
  difficult 704
  discord 713
 - out *inquire* 461
  discover 480a
 - out of water

 disagree 24
 unconformable 83
 displaced 185
 bungler 701
 - story 546, 549
 - up *raise* 307
 find 480a
food for -es 362
 other - to fry
 ill-timed 135
 busy 682
 queer - 857
fisherman 361¡
fishery 370
fishing *kill* 361
 pursue 622
fishing boat 273
fishmonger 637
fish pond *pool* 343
 pisciculture 370
fish-tail 267
fishy transaction 940
fisk *run* 266
 speed 274
fissile 328
fission 44
fissure *break* 44
 chink 198
fist *handwriting* 590
 grip 781
 shake the - *defy* 715
 threat 909
fisticuffs 720
fistula 260
fit *state* 7
 agreeing 23
 equal 27
 paroxysm 173
 agitation 315
 caprice 608
 expedient 646
 disease 655
 excitement 825
 anger 900
 right 922
 due 924
 duty 926
 by -s and starts
 irregular 59
 discontinuous 70
 agitated 315
 capricious 608
 haste 684
 - for 698, 924
 - of abstraction 458
 - of crying 839
 - out *dress* 225
  prepare 673
 - to be seen 845
 in -s 315
 think - 600
fitchet 401
fitchew 401
fitful *irregular* 139
 changeable 149
 capricious 608
fittings 633
five 98
 division by - 99
 - act play 599
 - and twenty 98

affections 820
gain - 194
ills that - is heir to
　evil 619
　disease 655
in the - 359
make the - creep
　pain 830
　fear 860
one - 903
way of all - 360
weakness of the - 945
flesh color 434
fleshly 316
fleshpots 298
fleshy *of fruit* 354
fleur-de-lis 847
fleuron 847
flexible *pliant* 324
　easy 705
flexion *curvature* 245
　fold 258
　deviation 279
flexuosity 248
flexuous 248, 348
flexure *curve* 245
　fold 258
flibbertigibber 980
flicker *changing* 149
　waver 314
　flutter 315
　light 420
　dim 422
flickering
　irregular 139
flies *insects* 366
　theater 599
flight *flock* 102
　volitation 267
　swiftness 274
　departure 293
　avoidance 623
　escape 671
- of fancy 515
- of stairs *ascent* 305
　way 627
- of time 109
put to - *propel* 284
　repel 717
　vanquish 731
flighty *inattentive* 458
　mad 503
　fanciful 515
flimflam *lie* 544
　caprice 608
flimsy *copy* 21
　weak 160
　rarity 322
　soft 324
　sophistical 477
　trifling 643
flinch *swerve* 607
　avoid 623
　fear 860
　cowardice 862
fling *propel* 284
　jig 840
　jeer 929
- aside 782
- away *reject* 610
　waste 638

548

　relinquish 782
- down 308
- to the winds
　destroy 162
　not observe 773
have a - at
　attack 716
　resent 900
　disrespect 929
　censure 932
have one's -
　active 682
　laxity 738
　freedom 748
　amusement 840
flint *hard* 323
flint-hearted 907
flip *beverage* 298
flippant *fluent* 584
　pert 885
　discourteous 895
flipper *paddle* 267
flirt *propel* 284
　changer 607
　coquette 854, 902
　love 897
　endearment 902
- a fan *affectation* 855
flirtation 902
flit *elapse* 109
　changeable 149
　move 264
　travel 266
　swift 274
　depart 293
　run away 623
flitter *small part* 32
　changeable 149
　flutter 315
flitting
　evanescent 111
flivver 272
float *establish* 150
　navigate 267
　boat 273
　buoy up 305
　lightness 320
before the -s
　on the stage 599
- before the eyes 446
- in the mind
　thought 451
　imagination 515
- on the air 405
floater *schemer* 702
floating [*see* float]
　rumored 532
- anchor 706
- battery 726
- capital 805
- debt 806
- hotel 273
floccillation 315
flocculence 324
flocculent *woolly* 256
　soft 324
　pulverulent 330
flock *assemblage* 72
　multitude 102
　laity 997
-s and herds 366

- together 72
floe *ice* 383
flog 684, 972
flood *much* 31
　crowd 72
　water 337
　river 348
　abundance 639
　redundance 641
　prosperity 734
- of light 420
- of tears 839
stem the - 708
floodgate *limit* 233
　egress 295
　conduit 350
open the -s
　eject 297
　permit 760
flood mark 466
flood tide *increase* 35
　complete 52
　height 206
　advance 282
　water 337
floor *level* 204
　base 211
　horizontal 213
　support 215
　overthrow 731
ground - 191
flop 315
flora 369
floral 367
floret 367
floriculture 371
florid *music* 416
　color 428
　red 434
- *style* 577
　health 654
florist 371
floss 256
flotation [*see* float]
flotilla *ships* 273
　navy 726
flotsam and jetsam 73
flounce *trimming* 231
　jump 309
　agitation 315
　(*move quickly* 274)
flounder *change* 149
　toss 315
　uncertain 475
　bungle 699
　difficulty 704
　fail 732
　(*blunder* 495)
flour 330
flourish
　brandish 314, 315
　vegetate 365, 367
　exaggerate 549
　language 577
　speech 582
　gain 618
　healthy 654
　prosperous 734
　ornament 847
　repute 873
　display 882

　boast 884
　(*succeed* 731)
- of trumpets *loud* 404
　publish 531
　ostentation 882
　celebrate 883
　boast 884
flourishing
　[*see* flourish]
　cheerful 836
flout *disrespect* 929
　contempt 930
　(*ridicule* 856)
flow *course* 109
　hang 214
　motion 264
　stream 348
　murmur 405
　abundance 639
- from *result* 154
- in 294
- into *river* 348
- of ideas 451
- of soul
　conversation 588
　affections 820
　cheerful 836
　social 892
- of time 109
- of words 582, 584
- out 295
- over 641
- with the tide 705
flower *essence* 5
　produce 161
　plant 367
　prosper 734
　beauty 845
　ornament 847
　repute 873
- of age 131
- of flock 648
- of life 127
- painting 556, 559
full many a - 447
floweret 367
flowering plant 367
flowerlike *beauty* 845
flowers *anthology* 596
- of rhetoric 577
flowery *ornamental* 847
be - *exaggerate* 549
flowing [*see* flow]
- periods 578
fluctuate *change* 149
　oscillate 314
　irresolute 605
flue *opening* 260
　air-pipe 351
　down 320
　dust 653
fluent *differential* 84
　fluid 333
　stream 348
- language 578
　speech 584
fluff 256, 320
fluffy 256
flugelman 694
fluid 333
- in motion 347

- one's good opinion
  932
forfeiture
  disfranchisement 925
forfend *hinder* 706
  defend 717
forgather 72
forge *imitate* 19
  produce 161
  furnace 368
  trump up 544
  foundry 691
  - ahead 282
  - fetters 751
forged *false* 546
forger *maker* 690
  thief 792
  counterfeiter 800
forgery *deception* 545
forget 506
  - benefits 917
  - injury 918
  - oneself 945
  hand - cunning 699
forgetful 506
forgive 918
forgiveness 918
forgo [see forego]
forgotten *past* 122
  ingratitude 917
  - by the world 893
fork *bifid* 91
  pointed 244
  - lightning 423
  - out *give* 784
  pay 807
  expenditure 809
forking 291
forlay 706
forlorn *dejected* 837
  hopeless 859
  deserted 893
  - hope *danger* 665
  hopelessness 859
  rashness 863
form *state* 7
  likeness 21
  make up 54
  order 58
  arrange 60
  convert 144
  produce 161
  bench 215
  shape **240**
  organization 357
  educate 537
  pupils 541
  school 542
  manner 627
  beauty 845
  fashion 852
  etiquette 882
  law 963
  create 976
  rite 998
  - a party 712
  - a resolution 604
  - part of 56
formal [see form]
  regular 82
  definitive 535

  style **579**
  severe 739
  taste 850
  affected 855
  stately 882
  - speech 582
formalism 739, 988
formalist 82, 988
formality [see formal]
  ceremony 852
  affectation 855
  law 963
formalize 963
formation
  composition 54
  production 161
  shape 240
formative *causal* 153
  form 240
  - notion 453
formed [see form]
  attempered 820
former *in order* 62
  prior in time 116
  past 122
formerly 66, 119
formication 380
formidable
  difficult 704
  terrible 860
formless 241
formula *rule* 80
  arithmetic 84
  maxim 496
  precept 697
  law 963
formulary 998
formulate 590
fornication 961
fornicator 962
forsake 624
forsaken 898
forsooth 535
forswear *deny* 536
  lie 544
  tergiversation 607
  refuse 764
  transgress 927
  improbity 940
fort *refuge* 666
  defense 717
fortalice 717
forte 698
forth 282
  come - *egress* 295
  visible 446
  go - *depart* 293
forthcoming
  destiny 152
  preparing 673
forthright 113, 132
forthwith 132, 507
fortification
  defense 717
fortify
  strengthen 159
fortitude
  endurance 826
  courage 861
fortnightly 138
fortress *refuge* 666

  defense 717
  prison 752
fortuitous
  adventitious 6
  chance 156
  undesigned 621
  - combination of cir-
    cumstances 621
  - concourse of atoms
    59
fortuity 156
fortunate
  opportune 134
  successful 731
  prosperous 734
Fortunatus's - cap
  wish 865
  spell 993
  - purse 803
fortune *chance* 156
  fate 601
  wealth 803
  be one's - 151
  evil - 735
  -s *narrative* 594
  good - 734
  make one's -
    succeed 731
  wealth 803
  tempt - *hazard* 621
  essay 675
  trick of - 509
  try one's - 675
  wheel of - 601
fortune hunter
  servile 886
  selfish 943
fortuneless 804
fortune teller 513
fortune telling 51
forty 98
  - winks 683
Forty-Niner 463
forum *place* 182
  school 542
  tribunal 966
forward *early* 132
  front 234
  transmit 270
  advance 282
  interjection 286
  willing 602
  improve 658
  active 682
  help 707
  vain 880
  insolent 885
  uncourteous 895
  bend - 234
  come - *in sight* 446
  offer 763
  display 882
  - in *knowledge* 490
  move - 282
  press - *haste* 684
  put - *aid* 707
  offer 763
  put oneself - 88
  set - 676
foss 348
fosse *inclosure* 232

  ditch 259
  defense 717
  (*interval* 198)
fossil *remains* 40
  ancient 124
  hard 323
  organic 357
  dry bones 362
fossilization 357
fossilize 357
foster *aid* 707
  excite 824
  caress 902
  - a belief 484
fou 959
foul *collide* 276
  bad 649
  dirty 653
  ugly 846
  base 940
  vicious 945
  fall - of *oppose* 708
  quarrel 713
  attack 716
  fight 720
  censure 932
  - fiend 978
  - invective 908
  - language
    malediction 908
  - odor 401
  - play *evil* 619
  cunning 702
  wrong 923
  improbity 940
  run - of *impede* 706
foul-mouthed
  uncourteous 895
foulness [see foul]
foul-spoken
  detraction 934
foumart 401
found *cause* 153
  support 215
foundation
  stability 150
  base 211
  support 215
  lay the -s 673
  sandy - 667
  shake to its -s 315
founded
  - on *base* 211
  evidence 467
  well - 472
founder
  originator 164
  sink 310
  projector 626
  fail 732
  religious -s 986
foundling *trover* 775
  derelict 782
  outcast 893
foundry 691
fount *type* 591
fountain *source* 153
  river 348
  store 636
  - pen 590
fountainhead 210

549

four 95
- in hand 272
- score &c. 98
- times 96
from the - winds 278
on all -s *identity* 13
  agreement 23
  horizontal 213
  easy 705
  prosperous 734
  humble 879
four-flush 545, 884
fourfold 96
Four Hundred 852, 875
Fourierism 910
four-oar 273
four-poster 215
fourragère 877
foursquare 244
fourth 96, 97
  musical 413
Fourth Estate 531
four-wheeler 272
fowl 298, 366
fowling piece 727
fox *animal* 366
  cunning 702
  - chase 622
  - hunting 622
foxhound 366
foxy *brown* 433
fox terrier 366
fox trot *dance* 840
fracas *disorder* 59
  noise 404
  discord 713
  contention 720
fraction *part* 51
  numerical 84
  less than one **100a**
Foxy Quiller 804
fractional 100a
  - currency 800
fractious 901
fracture
  disjunction 44
  discontinuity 70
  fissure 198
fragile *weak* 160
  brittle 328
fragment *small* 32
  part 51
  little 193
  extract 596
fragmentary 100a
fragrance **400**
fragrant 400
  - weed 392
frail *weak* 160
  brittle 328
  irresolute 605
  imperfect 651
  failing 945
  impure 961
  - sisterhood 962
frailty [*see* frail]
frame *intrinsicality* 5
  condition 7
  make 161
  support 215
  border 231

form 240
  substance 316
  structure 329
  contrive 626
  - of mind
  inclination 602
  disposition 820
have -d and glazed 822
frame house 189
framework *support* 215
  structure 329
franchise *freedom* 748
  right 924
  exemption 927a
Franciscan 996
franc-tireur 726
frangible 328
frank *open* 525
  sincere 543
  artless 703
  honorable 939
  - as rain 703
frankalmoigne 748
Frankenstein 913
Frankfurter 298
frankincense 400
frantic *violent* 173
  delirious 503
  excited 824
fraternal *brother* 11
  leagued 712
  concord 714
  friendly 888
  (*benevolent* 906)
  - order 711
fraternity *brothers* 11
  party 712
  friends 888
fraternize
  combine 48
  coöperate 709
  agree 714
  sympathize 888
  associate 892
fratricide 361
Frau 374
fraud *falsehood* 544
  deception 545
  impostor 548
  dishonor 940
pious - 988
fraudulent
  [*see* fraud]
  untruth 546
fraught *full* 52
  pregnant 161
  possessing 777
  (*sufficient* 639)
  - with danger 665
fray *rub* 331
  battle 720
in the thick of the - 722
frayed *worn* 659
freak 608
  - of nature 83
freckle 848
freckled 440, 848
fredaine 840
free *detached* 44, 47

unconditional 52
deliver 672
unobstructed 705
liberate 748, 750
expending 809
gratis 815
liberal 816
insolent 885
exempt 927a
impure 961
- and easy
  cheerful 836
  vain 880
  insolent 885
  friendly 888
  sociable 892
- companion 726
- fight 720
- from *simple* 42
- from imperfection 650
- gift 784
- giver 816
- lance 726, 748
- land 748
- liver 954a
- living 954
- love 897, 961
- lunch 815
- play 170, 748
- quarters *cheap* 815
  hospitality 892
- space 180
- stage 748
- trade *commerce* 794
- translation 522
- will 600
make - of 748
make - with
  frank 703
  take 789
  sociable 892
  uncourteous 895
freebooter 792
freeborn 748
free-burning 388
freedman 748
freedom **748**
free-handed 816
freehold 780
freely *willingly* 602
freeman 748
Freemason 711
freemasonry
  unintelligible 519
  secret 528
  sign 550
  coöperation 709
  party 712
free-spoken 703
freestone 635
freethinker 487, 748, 989
free thought 487
free trader 748
freeze 376, 385
  - the blood 830
freezing 383
  - machine 387
  - mixture 387
freight *lade* 184

cargo 190
  transfer 270
  - train 272
  - yard 636
freightage 270, 812
freighter *carrier* 271
  vessel 273
French 188
  - beans 298
  - gray 432
  - horn 417
  - leave *avoid* 623
  freedom 748
  - philosophy 451
  - polish 847
  peddler's - 563
Frenchman 188
frenetic 503
frenzy *madness* 503
  imagination 515
  excitement 825
frequency **136**
frequent
  in number 104
  in time 136
  in space 186
  habitual 613
frequenter 613
fresco *cold* 383
  painting 556
al - *out of doors* 220
  in the air 338
fresh *extra* 37
  new 123
  flood 348
  cold 383
  color 428
  remembered 505
  novice 541
  unaccustomed 614
  good 648
  healthy 654
  pert 885
  tipsy 959
  - breeze 349
  - color 434
  - news 532
freshen 689
freshet 348
freshman 492, 541
freshness [*see* fresh]
fresh-water
  - college 542
  - sailor 701
fret *suffer* 378
  grieve 828
  gall 830
  discontent 832
  sad 837
  ornament 847
  irritate 900
  - and fume 828
fretful 901
fretwork 219
Freud's theory 992a
friable *brittle* 328
  pulverulent 330
friandice 868
friar 996
  Black -s 996
  - Rush 980

-'s balsam 662
-'s lantern 423
friary 1000
fribble *slur over* 460
  trifle 643
  dawdle 683
  fop 854
fricassee 298
frication 331
friction *force* 157
  obstacle 179
  rubbing **331**
  on - wheels 705
fried - brains 298
  - eggs 298
  - sole 298
friend *auxiliary* 711
  wellwisher **890**
  sympathizer 914
  be -s 888
  - at court 631
  next - 759
  see one's -s 892
friendless 893
friendliness 888
friendly *amicable* 714
friendship 888
frieze 210, 329
frigate *man-of-war* 726
  (*ship* 273)
fright *cards* 840
  alarm 860
frighten 860
frightful *dreadful* 830
  ugly 846
frightfully *much* 31
frigid *cold* 383
  - *style* 575
  callous 823
  indifferent 866
frigidarium 387
frigorific 385
frill *border* 231
  convolution 248
frills 577
  - of style 577
fringe *border* 231
  lace 256
  exaggeration 549
  ornament 847
trippery *trifle* 643
  ornament 847
  finery 851
  ridiculous 853
  ostentation 882
  (*dress* 225)
friseur 225
frisk *prance* 266
  leap 309
  absurdity 497
  gay 836
  amusement 840
frisky *brisk* 682
  in spirits 836
frith *chasm* 198
  strait 343
  forest 367
fritiniancy 412
fritter *small* 32
  - away *lessen* 36
  waste 638

(*misuse* 679)
  - away time 683
frivolity [*see* frivolous]
frivolous *unreasonable*
    477
  foolish 499
  capricious 608
  trivial 643
friz *curl* 245, 248
  fold 258
frock *dress* 225
  canonicals 999
  - *coat* 225
frog *leaper* 309
  ornament 847
frolic 840
frolicsome 836
from *motive* 615
  - day to day 106, 138
  - end to end 52
  - that time 117
  - this cause 155
  - time   immemorial
      122
  - time to time 136
frond 367
fronder *censure* 932
frondeur *disobey* 742
  detract 936
front *first* 66
  wig 225
  fore part **234**
  resist 719
  insolence 885
  bring to the -
    manifest 525
  come to the -
    surpass 303
  important 642
  repute 873
  - danger 861
  - of the house 599
  - rank 234
  - to front 708
  in - 280
  in the - rank
    important 642
    repute 873
  present a - 719
frontage 234
frontal 220
frontier *vicinity* 199
  limit 233
fronting *opposite* 237
frontispiece 64
frost *cold* 383
  semitransparent 427
  whiten 430
  - over 427
frost-bite 383
frosted 427, 430
  - glass 427
frost smoke 353
frostwork 847
froth *bubble* 353
  trifle 643
  dirt 653
  - up *angry* 900
frothy 353
  - *style* 573, 577
  irresolute 605

frounce 258
frow 374
froward 901*a*
frown *lower* 837
  scowl 839
  discourteous 895
  angry 900
  sulky 901*a*
  disapprove 932
  - down *abash* 879
  -s of fortune 735
frowzy 401
frozen 383, 385
fructiferous 168
fructify *produce* 161
  be *productive* 168
  improve 658
  prosper 734
fructuous 168
frugal *economical* 817
  temperate 953
fruit *result* 154
  produce 161
  profit 775
  forbidden - 615
  - tree 367
  reap the -s
    succeed 731
    reward 973
fruitarian 953
fruit-bearing 168
fruitful 168
fruition 161, 827
fruitless
  unproductive 169
  useless 645
  failure 732
frumenty 298
frump *vulgar* 851
  unmannerly 895
frumpish *sulky* 901*a*
frustrate
  counteract 179
  prevent 706
  (*defeat* 731)
frustrated 732
frustum 51
fry *shoal* 102
  child 129
  heat 384
  small -
    unimportant 643
    commonalty 876
frying pan 386
  out of - into fire
    worse 659
    clumsy 699
    failure 732
    misfortune 735
    aggravation 835
fuchsine 434
fucoid 367
fuddled 959
fudge *unmeaning* 517
  trivial 643
  (*nonsense* 497)
fuel *combustible* **388**
  materials 635
  add - to the flame
    increase 35
    heat 384

  aggravate 835
  anger 900
fugacious 111
fugitive *transient* 111
  emigrant 268
  avoiding 623
  (*escape* 671)
  - writings 596
fugleman *pattern* 22
  director 694
fugue 415
fulciment 215
fulcrum *support* 215
  mechanical   power
      633
  (*leverage* 175)
fulfill *complete* 729
  - a duty 926
  - an obligation 772
fulgent 420
fulgurant 420
fulgurite 260
fuliginosity 426
fuliginous *dim* 422
  opaque 426
  black 431
full *circumstantial* 8
  much 31
  complete 52
  large 192
  loud 404
  abundant 639
  cleanse 652
  - age 131
  - bloom *health* 654
  beauty 845
  - colored 428
  - cry *aloud* 404
  bark 412
  pursuit 622
  - dress *dress* 225
  ornament 847
  fashion 852
  show 882
  - drive 274
  - feather
    prepared 673
  - force 159
  - gallop 274
  - heart 820
  - house *cards* 840
  - many 102
  - measure 639
  - of business 682
  - of incident 151
  - of meaning 516
  - of people 186
  - of point 842
  - of whims 608
  - play *facility* 705
  freedom 748
  - scope 748
  - score 415
  - size 192
  - speed 274
  - steam ahead 282
  - stop *cease* 142
  rest 265
  - swing *strong* 159
  active 682
  successful 731

free 748
- tide 348
- tilt *active* 682
    haste 684
- view 446
hands - *active* 682
receipt in - 807
full-blown
    expanded 194
    glorious 873
full-blooded 641
full-fed 954
full-flavored 392
full-grown
    adolescent 131
    large 192
    (*expanded* 194)
full-handed
    liberal 816
    prodigal 818
full-length 556
full-mouthed 411, 412
fullness [*see* full]
    in the - of time 109
full-toned 413
fully 31
fulminate *violent* 173
    propel 284
    loud 404
    malediction 908
    threat 909
- against *accuse* 932
fulsome *nauseous* 395
    fetid 401
    bad 649
    abhorrent 867
    adulatory 933
    impure 961
fulvescent 436
fulvid 436
fulvous 436
fumble *derange* 61
    handle 379
    grope 463
    awkward 699
fumbler 701
fume *violent* 173
    exhalation 334, 336
    air pipe 351
    heat 382
    odor 398
    excitement 824
    be *impatient* 825
    anger 900
    -s of fancy 515
    in a - *discontented* 832
fumid 426
fumigate *vaporize* 336
    cleanse 652
fumigator 388
fun *amusement* 840

humor 842
make - of 856
funambulist 700
function *algebra* 84
    office 170
    business 625
    utility 644
    pomp 882
    duty 926
functionary
    director 694
    consignee 758
fund *store* 636
    invest 787
    (*abundance* 639)
    sinking - 802
fundament 235
fundamental
    intrinsic 5
    base 211
    support 215
- *bass* 413
- *note* 413
fundamentally *very* 31
funds 800
    in - 803
    public - 802
funebrial 363
funeral *procession* 69
    interment 363
- director 363
- pace 275
- pyre 423
- ring 363
funerary 363
funereal *interment* 363
    dismal 837
fungate 365
fungi 369
fungiform 249
fungoid 369
fungologist 369
fungology 369
fungosity
    projection 250
fungous 367, 369
fungus *projection* 250
    vegetable 367
    fetor 401
    bane 663
funicle 205
funk *fear* 860
    cowardice 862
funnel *opening* 260
    conduit 350
    air pipe 351
funnel-shaped 252
funny *odd* 83
    boat 273
    humorous 842
    comic 853

fur *covering* 223
    hair 256
    warm 384
    dirt 653
furacious 791
furbelow 231
furbish *improve* 658
    prepare 673
    adorn 847
furcate 244
furcation 91
furcula 993
furcular 91, 244
furculum 91, 244
furfur 653
furfuraceous 330
Furies *anger* 900
    evildoers 913
furiosity 173
furious *violent* 173
    haste 684
    passion 825
    anger 900
furiously *much* 31
furl 312
furlong 200
furlough 760
furnace 386
    workshop 691
    like a - *hot* 382
    sighing like -
    lament 839
    in *love* 902
furnish *provide* 637
    prepare 673
    give 784
- a handle 617
- aid 707
- its quota 784
furniture 633
    (*property* 780)
furor *insanity* 503
    emotion 820, 821
    passion 825
    desire 865
- scribendi 592, 594
furore [*see* furor]
furrow 259
Fürst 745
further *extra* 37
    distant 196
    aid 707
    go - and fare worse
    worse 659
    bungle 699
    not let it go - 528
furthermore 37
furtive *clandestine* 528
    stealing 791
    (*false* 544)
furuncle 250

fury *violence* 173
    excitation 825
    anger 900
    demon 980
    filled with - 825
furze 367
fuscous 433
fuse *join* 43
    combine 48
    heat 382, 384
    torch 388
    (*melt* 335)
fuselage 273
fusel oil 356
fusiform *pointed* 253
fusil 727
fusileer 716, 726
fusilier 716, 726
fusillade *killing* 361
    attack 716
fusion *union* 48
    heat 384
    coöperation 709
fuss *agitation* 315
    activity 682
    haste 684
    difficulty 704
    excitement 825
    ostentation 882
    make a - about
    importance 642
    lament 839
    disapprove 932
fussy *circumstantial* 8
    crotchety 481
    bustling 682
    excitable 825
fustee 41
fustian *texture* 329
    absurd 497
    unmeaning 517
- *style* 577, 579
    ridiculous 853
fustic 436
fustigate 972
fusty *old* 124
    fetid 401
    dirty 653
futile 645
futility 499, 645
future 121
    expected 507
    eye to the - 510
- possession 777
- state *destiny* 152
    heaven 981
    in the - 152
futurist 556
futurity 121
fuzzle 959
fuzzy 447
fylfot 993

gab 584
  gift of the - 582
gabardine 225
gabble 583, 584
gabelle 812
gaberlunzie 876
gable *side* 236, - *end* 67
gad 266
gadabout 268
gadget 626
gaff 727
gaffer *old* 130
  man 373
  clown 876
gag *silence* 403
  render mute 581
  dramatic 599
  muzzle 751
  imprison 752
  (*taciturnity* 585)
gage *measure* 466
  security 771
  throw down the - 715
gage d'amour 768
gaggle 412
gaieté de cœur 836
gaillard 844
gain *increase* 35
  advantage 618
  acquisition 775
  - a point 731
  - a victory 731
  - credit 931
  - ground *progress* 282
  improve 658
  - head 175
  - laurels 873
  - learning 539
  - one's ends 731
  - over 615
  - private ends 943
  - strength 35
  - the confidence of 484
  - the start *priority* 116
  early 132
  - time *protract* 110
  early 132
  late 133
  - upon *approach* 286
  pass 303
  become a habit 613
gainful *useful* 644
gainless 646
gainsay 536
gairish [*see* garish]
gait *walk* 264
  manner 627
gaiter 225
gala *festival* 840
  display 882
  - day 687
galactic circle 318
galantuomo 939
galavant 902
galaxy *assemblage* 72
  multitude 102
  stars 318
  luminary 423
  glory 873
gale 349

galeiform 245
Galen 662
galimatias 497
galiongee 269
galiot 273
gall *hurt* 378
  bitter 395
  annoy 830
  insolence 885
  anger 900
  malevolence 907
  dip the pen in - 934
gallant *brave* 861
  courteous 894
  love 897
  licentious 961, 962
gallantry [*see* gallant]
  dalliance 902
gallanty-show
  spectacle 448
  amusement 840
galleon 273
gallery *room* 191
  passage 260
  spectators 444
  auditory 599
  museum 636
  picture - 556
galley *ship* 273
  furnace 386
  printing 591
  punishment 972, 975
  - proof 591
  work like a - slave 686
galliass 273
Gallic 188
Gallicism 563
Gallicize 562
galligaskin 225
gallimaufry 41
gallinaceous 366
gallipot 191
gallivant 902
galloon 847
gallop *pass away* 111
  ride 266, 370
  scamper 274
galloping *fast* 274
  - *consumption* 655
galloway 271
gallows *kill* 361
  punishment 975
  come to the - 972
gallstone 655
galoot 701
galopade 840
galore 102, 639
galvanic *power* 157
  excitable 825
galvanism *force* 157
galvanize 157, 824
galvanometer 157, 466
galvanoscope 157
gamache 225
gambade *leap* 309
  prank 840
gambado *gaiter* 225
  leap 309
gambit 66
gamble *chance* 156, 621
gambler 463, 840

gambling
  chance (156) 621
  sport 840
  rashness 863
gambling house 621, 945
gamboge 436
gambol 309, 840
gambrel roof 244
game *food* 298
  animal 366
  savory 394
  resolute 604
  persevering 604a
  aim 620
  gamble 621
  pursuit 622
  tactics 692
  amusement 840
  laughingstock 857
  brave 861
  - at which two can play 718
  - in one's hands *easy* 705
  succeed 731
  command 737
  - to the last 604a
  - up 732
  make - of *deceive* 545
  ridicule 856
  disrespect 929
  play the - of *coöperate* 709
gamecock *fighter* 726
  tenacity 604
  pluck 861
gamekeeper 370, 753
gamesome 836
gamester *chance* 621
  play 840
  rash 863
gametal 163
gametangium 357
gamete 357
gamic 161
gamin 876
gaming [*see* game]
gaming house 621
gammadion 621, 993
gammer *old* 130
  woman 374
gammon
  false 544, 545
  untruth 546
gamey 392
gamut 413
gander 373
gang *assemblage* 72
  go 264
  party 712
ganger 694
gangrene 655
gangway *opening* 260
  way 627
ganja 663
gantlet 972
  run the -
  resolution 604
  dare 861
gaol 752

  - delivery 672
gaoler *keeper* 753
  punishment 975
gap *discontinuity* 70
  chasm 198
  stand in the - 717
gape *open* 260
  curiosity 455
  wonder 870
  - for *desire* 865
gaping [*see* gape]
  expectant 507
gar 161
garage 191, 272
garb 225
  under the - of 545
garbage 653
garble *take from* 38
  exclude 55
  misinterpret 523
  falsify 544
  - accounts 811
garbled
  incomplete 53
garde - nationale 726
  - royale 726
garden *grounds* 189
  horticulture 371
  source of supply 636
  beautiful 845
  botanic - 371
  zoölogical - 370
gardener 371
gardens *street* 189
gare 266
gargle 337
gargoyle 350
garish *light* 420
  color 428
  ornament 847
  gay 845
  tawdry 851
  display 882
gari-wala 268
garland *circle* 247
  fragrance 400
  sign 550
  poetry 597
  trophy 733
  ornament 847
  decoration 877
garlic *condiment* 393
  fetid 401
garment 225
garner *store* 636
  (*collect* 72)
garnet 434, 847
garnish *addition* 39
  prepare 673
  fee 809
  ornament 847
garnishee 758
garniture *dress* 225
garran 271
garret *room* 191
  top 210
garrison *occupant* 188
  safety 664
  defense 717
  soldiers 726
garron 271

garrote
render powerless 158
kill 361
punishment 972
garrulity 584
garter *fastening* 45
decoration 877
- *blue* 438
garth 181
gas *gaseity* 334
fuel 388
light 420
bombast 884
- *bomb* 727
- *meter* 334
- *stove* 386
gasconade 884
gaseity 334
gaseous
unsubstantial 4
of gas 324
vaporous 336
gash *cut* 44
interval 198
wound 619
gasification 334, 336
gasiform 334
gasify 334
gaskins 225
gaslight 423
gasoline 272, 356
gasometer 636
gasp *blow* 349
droop 655
poison 663
fatigue 688
at the last - 360
- *for desire* 865
gassy 349
gastric 191, 298
gastriloquism 580
gastromancy 511
gastronomy 298, 957
gastroscope 445
gate *beginning* 66
inclosure 232
mouth 260
barrier 706
- *way way* 627
water - 350
gâteau 298
gatekeeper 263
Gath, tell it not in -
conceal 528
disapprove 932
gather
collect 72
expand 194
fold 258
conclude 480
acquire 775
take 789
- *breath* 689
- *flesh* 194
- *from one*
information 527
- *fruits* 731
- *grapes from thorns* 471
gathered
- *to one's fathers* 360

554

gathering
assemblage 72
abscess 655
- *clouds dark* 421
shade 424
omen 512
danger 665
warning 668
adversity 735
gathering place 74
Gatling gun 727
gauche *clumsy* 699
gaucherie 699
vulgarity 851
gaud *ornament* 847
gaudery *vanity* 880
gaudy *color* 428
vulgar 851
showy 882
gauge 466
rain - 348
wind - 349
gauger 965
gaunt *bulky* 192
lean 203
ugly 846
gauntlet *glove* 225
armor 717
fling down the - 715
take up the - 720
Gautama 986
gauze *shade* 424
semitransparent 427
gavel *worth* 812
sheaf 72
gavelkind 778
gavelock 633
gavot 840
gawk 501
gawky *awkward* 699
ugly 846
(ridiculous 853)
gay *color* 428
cheerful 836
adorned 847
showy 882
dissipated 961
- *deceiver* 962
- *world* 852
gayety [*see gay*] 836
gaze 441
gazebo 441
gazelle *swift* 274
animal 366
gazer *spectator* 444
gazette
publication 531
record 551
in the -
bankrupt 808
gazetteer *list* 86
information 527
record 551
gazingstock
ridiculous 857
wondrous 872
geanticline 245
gear *clothes* 225
automobile 272
cogwheel 312
harness 633

in - 673
out of - *disjoin* 44
derange 61
useless 645
unprepared 674
gearwheel 312
gehenna 982
Geist 982
gelatin 352
gelatinize 352
gelatinous 352
geld *subduct* 38
impotence 158
gelding *horse* 271
male 373
gelid 383
gelidity 383
gelignite 727
geloscopy 511
gem *excellence* 648
ornament 847
(perfect 650)
geminate 90
gemination 161
Gemini *twins* 89
O -! 870
gemma 153
gemmation 194
gemmule 153
gemot 72
gendarme *safety* 664
soldier 726
police 965
gender 75
genealogy *line* 69
paternity 166
general *whole* 50
generic 78
habitual 613
servant 690, 746
officer 745
- *breaking up* 655
- *conception* 25
- *favorite* 899
- *information* 490
- *meaning* 516
- *public* 372
- *run* 613
the - *commonalty* 876
things in - 151
generalissimo 745
generality *mean* 29
universal 78
generalize 476
generally 16
- *speaking* 613
generalship *tactics* 692
warfare 722
generate *produce* 161
productive 168
generation
consanguinity 11
period 108
production 161
mankind 372
rising - 167
spontaneous - 161
wise in one's - 498
generative 153, 161
generator *producer* 164
of automobile 272

generic 78
generosity *greatness* 31
giving 784
liberality 816
benevolence 906
disinterestedness 942
generous
[*see generosity*]
genesis *beginning* 66
production 161
genet 271
Genethliacs 511
genetic 5, 161
genetous 5
Geneva *gown* 999
genial *productive* 161
sensuous 377
warm 382
willing 602
delightful 829
(renascent 163)
geniality [*see genial*]
cheerfulness 836
geniculated 244
genital 161
genitor 166
geniture 161
genius *intellect* 450
talent 498
poet 597
skill 698
proficient 700
familiar spirit 979
evil- 980
- *borrows nobly* 19
- *for* 698
- *loci* 664
- *of a language* 560
good - friend 898
benefactor 912
spirit 979
man of - 492
tutelary - 711
genre *painting* 556
gens 712
gent *vulgar* 851
commonalty 876
genteel *fashion* 852
rank 875
(polite 894)
- *comedy* 599
gentile *heterodox* 984
without religion 989
gentilhomme 939
gentility *fashion* 852
rank 875
politeness 894
gentium, jus - 963
gentle *moderate* 174
slow 275
train 370
faint sound 405
lenient 740
meek 826
cool down 826
courteous 894
- *blood* 875
- *breeding* 894
- *hint* 527
- *slope* 217
gentlefolk 875

gentleman *male* 373
  squire 875
  man of honor 939
  - 's *agreement* 23, 709
  the old - 978
  walking - 599
gentlemanly
  fashionable 852
gentleness [*see* gentle]
Gentoo 984
gentry 875
  landed - 779
genuflexion *bowing* 308
  submission 725
  servility 886
  courtesy 894
  respect 928
  worship 990
genuine *true* 494
  good 648
genus 75
geodesic 318, 342
geodesist 85, 318, 342
geodesy 342, 466
geognost 342
geognosy 342
geogony 342
geographer 318, 342
geography 183, 342
geoid 249
geologist 342
geology 342, 358
geomancer 513
geomancy 511
geometrician 85
geometry 466
geophilous 342
geoponics 342, 371
georama 448
georgics 342, 371
geosyncline 245
germ *cause* 153
  littleness 193
  plan 626
  - cell 357
  - plasm 357
German *dance* 840
  - band 416
  - philosophy 451
  - silver 430, 545
  - tinder 388
germane *relevant* 23
  (*related* 9)
germicide 662
germinal 153
  - matter 357
germinate 194, 365
  - from 154
germination 161
gerocomy 128
gerontic 128
gerrymander 702
gest 680
geste 515
gestation
  propagation 161
  carriage 270
  maturation 673
gesticulate 550
gesture *hint* 527
  indication 550

get *become* 144
  beget 161
  acquire 775
  - ahead 35
  - ahead of 33
  - along 282
  - along with you
  ejection 297
  dismissal 756
  - a sight of *see* 441
  comprehend 490
  - at 480a
  - away 287
  - back *retire* 283
  regain 775
  - better 658
  - by heart 505
  - down *swallow* 298
  descend 306
  - for one's pains 973
  - home 292
  - in *collect* 72
  gather 775
  - into harness 673
  - into the way of 613
  - into trouble 732
  - loose 44
  - near 286
  - off *depart* 293
  escape 671
  - on *advance* 282
  prosper 734
  - out *eject* 297
  extract 301
  publish 531
  - over *recover from* 660
  succeed 731
  be content 831
  - over the ground 274
  - ready 673
  - rid of 42, 672
  - the best of 731
  - the gist of 457
  - there 731
  - the wrong pig by
    the tail 699, 732
  - through *end* 67
  transact 692
  complete 729
  expend 809
  - to *extend to* 196
  arrive 292
  - together 72
  - up *ascend* 305
  raise 307
  learn 539
  fabricate 544
  prepare 673
  rise early 682
  foment 824
  - you gone 297
gettings 35
get-up *form* 240
gewgaw *rifle* 643
  ornament 847
  vulgar 851
geyser 382, 384
gharri 272
  - wallah 268
ghastly *pale* 429
  hideous 846

  frightful 860
ghaut 203
ghazal 597
ghee 356
ghetto 189
ghost *shade* 362
  fallacy of vision 443
  soul 450
  writer 593
  apparition 980a
  - dance 992
  - of a chance 473
  give up the - 360
  pale as a -
  colorless 429
  fear 860
Ghost, Holy - 976
ghostlike *ugly* 846
ghostly *intellectual* 450
  supernatural 976,
    980a
ghoul *evildoer* 913
  demon 980
ghurry 108, 114
ghyll 348
giant *large* 192
  tall 206
  - refreshed *strong* 159
  refreshed 689
  - 's strides
  distance 196
  swift 274
giaour *heterodox* 984
  irreligion 989
gibber *stammer* 583
gibberish *absurdity* 497
  nonsense 517
  neology 563
gibbet *stigmatize* 932
  execute 972
  gallows 975
gibble-gabble 584
gibbous *globose* 249
  convex 250
gib-cat *male* 373
gibe *disrespect* 929
  (*ridicule* 856)
giddy *inattentive* 458
  vertiginous 503
  irresolute 605
  capricious 608
  bungling 699
giddy-head 501
giddy-headed 458
giddy-paced 315
gift *compensation* 30
  power 157
  transference 270
  talent 698
  given 784
  expenditure 809
  - of the gab 582
  look a - horse in the
    mouth
  fastidious 868
  ungrateful 917
gifted 698
gig 273
gigantic *strong* 159
  large 192
  tall 206

giggle 838
Gilbertine 996
gild *coat* 223
  yellow 436
  color 439
  ornament 847
  -ed rooster 875
  - refined gold 641
  - the pill *deceive* 545
  tempt 615
  please 829
  flatter 933
gilding [*see* gild]
Gilead, balm in -
  relief 834
  hope 858
gill *ravine* 252
  brook 348
  -s *respiration* 349
gillie 746
gilt 436, 847
gilt-edged
  excellent 648
  - securities 802
gimbals 312
gimcrack *weak* 160
  brittle 328
  trifling 643
  ornament 847
  ridiculous 853
  (*useless* 645)
gimlet 262
gimp *clean* 652
  pretty 845
gin *trap* 545
  instrument 633
  intoxicating 959
ginger 171
gingerbread
  weak 160
  vulgar 851
  (*ornament* 847)
gingerly
  moderately 174
  carefully 459
  cautiously 864
  (*slowly* 275)
gingham 635
gingle 408
gin palace 189
gipsy *wanderer* 268
  cheat 548
  wag 844
  - lingo 563
giraffe 206, 366
girandole 423
girasol 847
gird *bind* 43
  strengthen 159
  surround 227
  jeer 929
  - up one's loins
  brace 159
  prepare 673
girder *bond* 45
  beam 215
girdle *bond* 45
  circumference 230
  circle 247
  put a - round **about**
    the earth 274, 311

girl *young* 129
female 374
servant 746
girl bachelor 904
girleen 129
girlhood 127
girlish 374
girllike 129
girt 229
girth *bond* 45
circumference 230
gisarme 727
gist *essence* 5
meaning 516
important 642
gite 265
gittern 417
give *yield* 324
melt 382
bestow 784
discount 813
- a horse his head 748
- and take
compensation 30
interchange 148
retaliation 718
compromise 774
barter 794
equity 922
honor 939
- attention 418
- a turn to 140
- away 782, 784
in marriage 903
- back 790
- birth to 161
- chase 622
- consent 762
- cry 411
- ear 418
- expression to 566
- forth 531
- in *submit* 725
- in charge
restrain 751
- in custody 751
- in to *consent* 762
- it one *censure* 932
punish 972
- light 420
- notice *inform* 527
warn 668
- one credit for 484
- one the slip 671
- one to understand
527
- out *emit* 297
publish 531
bestow 784
- over *cease* 142
relinquish 624
lose hope 859
- place to
substitute 147
avoid 623
- play to the imagina-
tion 515
- points to 27
- quarter 740
- rise to 153
-- security 771

- the go-by 623
- the lie 536
- the mind to 457
- the once-over 461
- tongue 531
- up
not understand 519
reject 610
relinquish 624
submit 725
resign 757
surrender 782
restore 790
hopeless 859
- up the ghost 360
- way *weak* 160
brittle 328
submit 725
pine 828
despond 837
modest 881
given [see give]
circumstances 8
supposition 514
received 785
- over *dying* 360
- time 143
- to 613
- up 360
giver 784
giving **784**
stick in one's - 900
gizzard 191
glabrate 226
glabrous 226, 255
glacial 383
glaciarum 840
glaciate 385
glaciation 383
glacier 383
glacis 217, 717
glad *pleased* 827
pleasing 829
- rags 225
- tidings 532
would be - of 865
gladden 834, 836
glade *hollow* 252
opening 260
shade 424
gladiate 253
gladiator 726
gladiatorial 713, 720
- combat 361
gladsome 827, 829
glair 352
glaive 727
glamour 992
glance *touch* 379
look 441
sign 550
- at *take notice of* 457
allude to 527
censure 932
- off *deviate* 279
diverge 291
- coal 388
see at a - 498
gland 221
- cell 221
glanders 655

glandule 221
glare *light* 420
stare 441
imperfect vision 443
visible 446
glaring [see glare]
great 31
color 428
visible 446
manifest 525
glass *vessel* 191
smooth 255
brittle 328
transparent 425
lens 445
- of fashion 852
- too much 959
live in a - house
brittle 328
visible 446
danger 665
musical -es 47
see through a - darkly
491
glass-coach 272
Glassite 984
glassy [see glass]
shining 420
colorless 429
glaucous 435
glave 727
glaver 933
glaze 255
ice 383
gleam *small* 32
light 420
visibility 446
glean *choose* 609
acquire 775
glebe *land* 342
ecclesiastical 995
church 1000
glee *music* 415
satisfaction 827
merriment 836
gleek 929
glen 252
glib *voluble* 584
facile 705
glide *lapse* 109
move 264
travel 266
aviation 267
(*slow* 275)
- into *conversion* 144
glimmer *light* 420
dim 422
visible 446
slight knowledge 490,
491
glimpse *sight* 441
knowledge 490
glint 420, 441
glissade 306
glisten 420
glitter *shine* 420
be visible 446
illustrious 882
glittering
ornament 847
display 882

gloaming 126, **422**
gloar *look* 441
wonder 870
gloat - on
look 441
- over *pleasure* 377
look 441
delight 827
globated 249
globe *sphere* 249
world 318
on the face of the -
318
globe-trotter 268
globe-trotting 441
globoid 249
globularity 249
globule *small* 32
spherule 249
glochidiate 253
glomeration 72
gloom *darkness* 421
dimness 422
sadness 837
gloomy *dark* 421
sad 837
- horizon 859
gloriation 884
glorification
[see glorify]
glorify *honor* 873
approve 931
worship 990
glorious
illustrious 873
tipsy 959
glory *light* 420
honor 873
heaven 981
- be to God 990
- dies not 873
- in 878
King of - 976
gloss *smooth* 255
sheen 420
interpretation 522
falsehood 546
plea 617
beauty 845
- of novelty 123
- over *neglect* 460
sophistry 477
falsehood 544
plead 615
vindicate 937
glossarist 524
glossary *list* 86
dictionary 562
(*interpretation* 522)
glossographer 492
glossologist 492
glossology 560, 562
glossy [see gloss]
glottology 560, 562
glout 901a
glove 225
take up the - 720
throw down the - 715
glover 225
glow *warm* 382
shine 420

GLOWER

color 428
visibility 446
style 574
passion 821
glower *glare* 443
  discourteous 895
  sullen 901a
glowing [see glow]
  red 434
  orange 439
  excited 824
  beautiful 845
  - terms 574
glowworm 423
gloze *flutter* 933
  vindicate 937
glucose 396
glue *cement* 45
  cementing 46
  semiliquid 352
glum *discontented* 832
  dejected 837
  sulky 901a
glume 223
glut *wedge* 633
  redundance 641
  satiety 869
glutinous 327, 352
glutinousness 327
glutton 954a, 957
gluttony 957
  (desire 865)
glycerine
  lubrication 332
  oil 356
glyph 557
glyphography 558
glyptography 558
glyptotheca 557
glyster 300
gnarl *kink* 59
  distort 243
  convexity 250
  anger 900
  threat 909
gnarled *twisted* 59
  rough 256
  dense 321
gnarly 256
gnash one's teeth
  lament 839
  angry 900
gnat *little* 193
  strain at a - &c.
  caprice 608
gnaw *eat* 298
  rub 331
  injure 659
gnawing
  - grief 828, 830
  - pain 378
gnome 496, 980
gnomic 496
gnomon 114
Gnostic 984
Gnosticism 451
gnu 366
go *cease to exist* 2
  energy 171, 682
  move 264
  recede 287

depart 293
jade 429
disappear 449
fashion 852
as things - 613
come and - 314
give the - by to
neglect 460
deceive 545
avoid 623
not observe 773
- about
turn round 311
published 531
undertake 676
- about your business
ejection 297
dismissal 756
- across 302
- after *in time* 117
in motion 281
- against 708
- ahead *precede* 280
advance 282
active 682
- all lengths 604a
complete 52
resolve 604
exertion 686
- aloft 305
- astray 495
- away 293
- back 283
- back on 624
- bad 659
- bail 771
- before 280
- beyond 303
- by *conform to* 82
elapse 109
past 122
outrun 303
subterfuge 702
- by the board 158
- by the name of 564
- cahoots 712
- deep into 461
- down *sink* 306
decline 659
- down with
believed 484
tolerated 826
content 831
- farther and fare
  worse 659
- for nothing
sophistry 477
unimportant 643
- forth *depart* 293
publish 531
- from one's word 773
- halves 91
- hand in hand
accompany 88
same time 120
- hard 704
- in 294
- in for *resolution* 604
pursuit 622
- into *ingress* 294
inquire 461

dissert 595
- mad 503
- near 286
- no further
keep secret 528
- off *explode* 173
depart 293
die 360
wither 659
marry 903
- on *time* 106
continue 143
advance 282
- on for ever 112
- on ill 735
- on the stump 582
- out *cease* 142
egress 295
extinct 385
- out of one's head
  506
- over *passage* 302
explore 461
apostate 607
faithless 940
- round 311
- shares 778
- the limit 52, 604
- through
meet with 151
pass 302
explore 461
perform 599
conduct 692
complete 729
endure 826
- through fire and
  water 604a
- to *extend* 196
travel 266
direction 278
remonstrance 695
- to glory 162, 360
- to pieces 162
- to sleep 683
- to war 722
- under 162
- up 305
- West *die* 360
- with *assent* 488
concord 714
- with the stream
conform 82
servile 886
goad *for oxen* 370
motive 615
quicken 684
go-ahead 171, 682
goal *end* 67
reach 292
object 620
reach the -
complete 729
goat *jumper* 309
lecher 962
he - *male* 373
goatee 256
goatish 961
gob *sailor* 269
jaws 298
gobang 840

GOING

gobbet *small piece* 32
  food 298
gobble *cry* 412
  gormandize 957
  eat 298
gobemouche *fool* 501
  dupe 547
go-between
  interjacent 226
  instrumental 631
  mediate 724
  agent 758
goblet 191
goblin 980
  (bugbear 860)
gocart 272
GOD 976
  for -'s sake 765
  - bless me! 870
  - bless you
  farewell 293
  - forbid 766
  - forsaken 196
  - grant 990
  - knows 491
  -'s acre 363
  -'s grace 906
  -'s love 906
  -'s own country 189
  -'s will 601
  - willing 470
  house of - 1000
  kingdom of - 981
  sons of - 977
  to - be true 772
god 979
  household -s 189
  the -s *gallery* 444, 599
  tutelary - 664
godchild 771
goddess *love* 897
  good woman 948
  heathen 979
  she moves a - 374
godfather 771
Godhead 976
godlike 987
godly 944
godmother 771
godown 636
godsend *good* 618
  prosperity 734
Godspeed *farewell* 293
  hope 858
  courtesy 894
  benevolence 906
  approbation 931
goer *horse* 271
goes [see go]
  as one - 270
  here - 676
goggle 441
goggle-eyed 443
goggles 445
going [see go]
  general 78
  rumor 532
  - on *incomplete* 53, 730
  current 151
  transacting 625
  - to happen 152

557

goiter 655
Golconda 803
gold *yellow* 436
  orange 439
  money 800
  all is not - 486
  - brick 545, 702
  - mohur 800
  worth its weight in -
    648
  write in letters of -
    642
golden [*see* gold]
  - age *prosperity* 734
  pleasure 827
  - apple 615
  - calf *wealth* 803
  idolatry 991
  - dream
  imagination 515
  hope 858
  - mean
  moderation 174
  mid-course 628
  - opinions 931
  - opportunity 134
  - rule *precept* 697
  - season of life 127
  - wedding 883
  music's - tongue 415
golf 840
Golgotha *burial* 363
  churchyard 1000
Goliath *strength* 159
  size 192
gomashta 758
gondola 273
gondolier 269
gone [*see* go]
  past 122
  absent 187
  dead 360
  hopeless 859
  - bad 653
  - by *antiquated* 124
  - case 859
  - coon 859
  - out of one's recollec-
    tion 506
  - where the woodbine
    twineth 771
goneness 688
goner 859
gonfalon 550
gong 417
goniometer *angle* 244
  measure 466
gonorrhea 655
good *complete* 52
  palatable 394
  assent 488
  benefit **618**
  beneficial 648
  right 922
  virtuous 944
  pious 987
  as - as 197
  be - enough 765
  be so - as 765
  do - 906
  for - *diuturnal* 110
  558

  permanent 141
  - actions 944
  - as one's word
  veracity 543
  observance 772
  probity 939
  - at 698
  - at the price 815
  - auspices 858
  - behavior
  contingent 108a
  duty 926
  virtue 944
  - bye 293
  - chance 472
  - cheer *food* 298
  cheerful 826
  - circumstances 803
  - condition 192
  - day *arrival* 292
  departure 293
  courtesy 894
  - effect *goodness* 648
  beauty 845
  - enough
  not perfect 651
  - fellow 892
  - fight *war* 722
  virtue 944
  - for *useful* 644
  salubrious 656
  - fortune 734
  - Friday 138, 998
  - genius *friend* 890
  benefactor 912
  god 979
  - hand 700
  - humor *concord* 714
  cheerfulness 836
  amuse 840
  courtesy 894
  kindly 906
  - intention 906
  - judgment 498
  - lack! 870
  - living *food* 298
  gluttony 957
  - look out 459
  - looks 845
  - luck 734
  - man *man* 373
  husband 903
  worthy **948**
  - manners 894
  - morrow 292
  - name 873
  - nature 906
  - offices
  mediation 724
  kind 906
  - old time 122
  - omen 858
  - opinion 931
  - pennyworth 815
  - repute 873
  - sense 498
  - society 852
  - taste 850
  - tasting 394
  - temper 894
  - thing 648

  - time *early* 132
  opportune 134
  prosperous 734
  - turn *kindness* 906
  - understanding 714
  - wife *woman* 374
  spouse 903
  - will *willingness* 602
  benevolence 906
  - woman 948
  - word *approval* 931
  vindication 927
  - works 906
  in - case 192
  in - odor *repute* 873
  approbation 931
  in one's - books 888
  in one's - graces 888
  make - *evidence* 467
  provide 637
  restore 660
  complete 729
  substantiate 924
  vindicate 937
  atone for 952
  put a - face upon
  cheerful 836
  proud 878
  so far so - 931
  take in - part
  pleased 827
  courteous 894
  kind 906
  think - 931
  to - purpose 731
  to the - 780
  turn to - account 731
  what's the - 645
good-for-nothing
  impotence 158
  useless 645
good-looking 845
goodly *great* 31
  large 192
  handsome 845
good-natured 906
goodness
  [*see* good] **648**
  virtue 944
  - gracious! 870
  - of heart 906
  have the - *request* 765
goods *effects* 780
  merchandise 798
Goodwin sands 667
goody 374
goose *bird* 298, 366
  hiss 409
  game of - 840
  giddy as a - 458
  - egg *zero* 101
  - flesh 383
  - grass 253
  kill the - with golden
    eggs
  bungler 699
  prodigal 818
gooseberry *fruit* 298
  yarn 549
  - eyes 441, 443
  old - 978

goosecap 501
goosequill 590
goose-skin 383
Gordian knot
  tangled 59
  difficulty 704
  (*problem* 461)
gore *gusset* 43
  stab 260
  blood 361
gorge *ravine* 198, 350
  fill 641
  satiety 869
  gluttony 957
  (*eat* 298)
  - the hook 602
  raise one's - 900
gorge-de-pigeon   432,
    440
gorgeous *color* 428
  beauty 845
  ornament 847
Gorgon 860
gorilla 366, 913
gormandize *eat* 298
  gluttony 957
gorse 367
gory *murderous* 361
  red 434
  unclean 653
gospel *certainty* 474
  doctrine 484
  truth 494
  take for - 484
Gospels 985
gossamer *filament* 205
  light 320
  texture 329
gossamery
  unsubstantial 4
  weak 160
  light 320
gossip *news* 532
  babbler 584
  conversation 588
gossoon 876
Goth *vulgar* 851
  barbarian 876
gothamite 501
Gotham, wise men of
  501
gothic *amorphous* 241
Gothicism 851
gouache 556
gouge *concave* 252
  perforator 262
goulash 298
gourmand
  sensualist 954a
  glutton 957
gourmet
  fastidious 868
  sybarite 954a
gout 378
goût 390
govern *direct* 693
  authority 737
governess 540
government
  [*see* govern]
  ruling power **745**

divine - 976
- bonds 802
- mark 550
-s *authority* 737
- school 542
petticoat - 699
governor *father* 166
  tutor 540
  director 694
  ruler 745
  keeper 753
-'s message 695
gowk 501
gown *dress* 225
  canonicals 999
gownsman 492
grab *take* 789
  miser 819
grabble 379
grace *style* 578
  permission 760
  concession 784
  elegance 845
  polish 850
  title 877
  pity 914
  forgiveness 918
  honor 939
  piety 987
  worship 990
act of - 784
God's - 906
- before meat 916
heart of - 861
in one's good -s 888
say - 990
submit with a good -
  826
with a bad - 603
with a good -
  willing 602
  courteous 894
graceful *elegant* 578
  beautiful 845
  tasteful 850
graceless *inelegant* 579
  ugly 846
  vicious 945
  impenitent 951
  irreligious 989
Graces 845
gracile 203
gracious *willing* 602
  courteous 894
  kind 906
good - 870
gradatim *in order* 58
  continuous 69
  slow 275
gradation *degree* 26
  order 58
  continuity 69
gradatory 26
grade *degree* 26
  classify 60
  term 71
  obliquity 217
  ascent 305
  class 541, (75)
at - 219
- crossing 219

gradient 217, 305
gradual *degree* 26
  continuous 69
  slow 275
graduate *adjust* 23
  degree 26
  divide 44
  arrange 60
  series 69
  measure 466
  scholar 492
  teaching 537
  rank 873
- school 542
graduated scale 466
graduation *class* 541
  rank 873
gradus 86, 562
Græcist 492
graft *join* 43
  locate 184
  insert 300
- *a plant* 371
  teach 537
  bribe 784
  improbity 940
grain *essence* 5
  small 32
  tendency 176
  little 193
  rough 256
  weight 319
  texture 329
  powder 330
  paint 428
  temper 820
  ornament 847
against the-
  rough 256
  unwilling 603
  opposing 708
- elevator 636
- oil 356
-s of allowance
  qualification 469
  doubt 485
in the - 820
like -s of sand
  incoherent 47
grallatory 267
gramercy 916
gram-fed 192
graminivorous 298
grammar
  beginning 66
  teaching 537
  school 542
  language 567
bad - 568
  comparative - 560
- school 537
grammarian 492
grammatical 567
- blunder 568
grammatism 561
gramophone 417, 418,
  551
granary 636
grand *august* 31
  vigor 574
  important 642

  handsome 845
  glorious 873
  ostentatious 882
- climacteric 128
- doings 882
- juror 967
- manner *solecism* 568
- piano 417
- seignior 745
- style 556, 568
- tour 266
- Turk 745
- vizier 694
grandam 130
grandchildren 167
grandee 875
grandeur *greatness* 31
  vigor 574
  repute 873
grandfather
  veteran 130
  paternity 166
grandiloquent 577
grandiose 482, 577
grandmother
  maternal 166
  simple 501
teach - 538
grandness [see grand]
grandsire *veteran* 130
  paternity 166
grandstand 444
grange 189
granger 371
granite 323, 635
granivorous 298
  qualification 469
  unbelief 485
granny 130
granolithic pavement
  255
grant *admit* 529
  permit 760
  consent 762
  confer 784
God - 990
- a lease 771
- in-aid school 542
granted 488
take for - *believe* 484
  suppose 514
grantee
  transference 270
  possessor 779
  receiver 785
grantor 784
granular 330
granulate 330
granulated 330
- sugar 386
granule 32
grapefruit 298
grapes 298
sour -
  unattainable 471
  falsehood 544
  excuse 617
grapeshot *attack* 716
  arms 727
graphic *intelligible* 518
  painting 556

  vigorous 574
  descriptive 594
graphology 590
graphomania 590
graphomaniac 590
graphometer 244
graphophone 417
graphotype 558
grapnel 666
grapple *fasten* 43
  clutch 789
- with
- a question 461
- difficulties 704
  oppose 708
  resist 719
  contention 720
grappling iron
  fastening 45
  safety 666
grasp *comprehend* 518
  power 737
  retain 781
  seize 789
- at 865
- of intellect 498
in one's - 737
  possess 777
tight - *severe* 739
grasping *miserly* 819
  covetous 856
grass *fell* 213
  vegetation 367
- widow 905
let the - grow under
  one's feet
  neglect 460
  inactive 683
not let the - &c.
  active 682
grasshopper 309, 366
grassland 367
grassplot 371
grassy 367
grate *arrangement* 60
  rub 330
  physical pain 378
  stove 386
- on the ear
  harsh sound 410
- on the feelings 830
grated *barred* 219
grateful
  physically pleasant
    377
  agreeable 829
  thankful 916
grater 330
gratification
  animal - 377
  moral - 827
gratify *permit* 760
  please 829
gratifying 377, 829
grating [see grate]
  lattice 219
  stridor 410
gratis 815
gratitude 916
gratuitous
  inconsequent 477

grope *feel* 379
  experiment 463
  try 675
  (*inquire* 461)
  - in the dark
  blind 442
  difficult 704
gross *great* 31
  whole 50
  number 98
  ugly 846
  vulgar 851
  vicious 945
  impure 961
  - *credulity* 486
  - receipts 810
grossièreté 895
grossness [*see* gross]
grot [*see* grotto]
grotesque *odd* 83
  distorted 243
  - *style* 579
  ridiculous 853
grotto *alcove* 191
  hollow 252
grouch *sullen* 901a
ground
  cause 153
  region 181
  situation 183
  base 211
  fell 213
  support 215
  coating 223
  land 342
  plain 344
  evidence 467
  teach 537
  motive 615
  plea 617
  above - 359
  down to the - 52
  dress the - 371
  fall to the - 732
  get over the - 274
  go over the - 302
  - bait 784
  - cut from under one
    732
  - floor *chamber* 191
  low 207
  base 211
  - hog day 138
  - of quarrel 713
  - on *attribute* 155
  - plan 554
  - sliding from under
    one
    danger 665
  - swell
  agitation 315
  waves 348
  level with the - 162
  maintain one's -
  persevere 604a
  play - 840
  prepare the - 673
  stand one's -
  defend 717
  resist 719
grounded *stranded* 732

- on *basis* 211
  evidence 467
  well - 490
groundless
  unsubstantial 4
  illogical 477
  erroneous 495
groundling 876
grounds *dregs* 653
groundwork
  substantiality 3
  precursor 64
  cause 153
  basis 211
  support 215
  preparation 673
group *marshal* 60
  cluster 72
grouse 298, 366
grout *vinculum* 45
  sullen 901a
grouty 901a
grove *group* 72
  street 189
  glade 252
  wood 367
grovel *below* 207
  move slowly 275
  cringe 886
  base 940
grow *increase* 35
  become 144
  expand 194
  vegetation 365, 367
  - from *effect* 154
  - into 144
  - less 195
  - like a weed 365
  - old gracefully 128
  - rank 365
  - taller 206
  - together 46
  - up 194
  - upon one 613
grower 164
growl *blow* 349
  cry 412
  complain 839
  discourtesy 895
  anger 900
  threat 909
growler *cab* 272
  discontented 832
  sulky 901a
grown up 131
growth [*see* grow]
  development 161
  - *in size* 194
  tumor 250
  vegetation 367
groyne 706
grub *small animal* 193
  food 298
  - up *eradicate* 301
  discover 480a
grudge *unwilling* 603
  refuse 764
  stingy 819
  hate 898
  anger 900
  envy 921

  bear a - 907
  owe a - 898
grudging
  unwilling 603
  envious 921
  - praise 932
gruel 298, 352
gruesome 846
gruff *harsh sound* 410
  discourteous 895
  (*morose* 901a)
grum *harsh sound* 410
  morose 901a
grumble *cry* 411
  complain 832, 839
grume 321, 354
grumose 321
grumous *dense* 321
  pulpy 354
grumpy 901a
Grundy, Mrs. 852
grunt *animal sound* 412
  complain 839
G string *loincloth* 225
guano 653
guarantee
  promise 768
  security 771
guaranty 771
guard *stopper* 263
  traveling 268
  safety rail 664
  defense 717
  soldier 726
  sentry 753
  advanced - 668
  - against *prepare* 673
  defense 717
  - ship *protection* 664
  man-of-war 726
  mount - *care* 459
  safety 664
  off one's -
  inexpectant 508
  on one's - *careful* 459
  cautious 864
  rear - 668
  throw off one's -
  cunning 702
guarded
  conditions 770
guardian *safety* 664
  defense 717
  keeper 753
  - angel *helper* 711
  benefactor 912
  spirit 977
guardianship 664, 717
guardless 665
guardroom 752
guardsman 726
gubernation 693
gubernatorial 693, 737
gudgeon 547
guerdon 973
guerrilla 722, 726
guess 514
guesswork 514
guest 890
  the parting - 892
guffaw 838

guggle *gush* 348
  bubble 353
  resound 408
  cry 412
guidable 278
guidance [*see* guide]
guide *model* 22
  - *a horse* 370
  teach 537
  teacher 540
  indicate 550
  direct 693
  director 694
  advise 695
  familiar spirit 979
  - philosopher and
    friend 695
guidebook 527
guided by, be -
  conform 82
guideless 665
guidepost 550
guiding star 693
guidon 550
guild *society* 712
  tribunal 966
guildhall 799
guile *deceit* 544, 545
  cunning 702
guileless
  veracious 543
  artless 703
guillemets 550
guillotine
  decapitate 361, 972
  ax 975
guilt **947**
  (*vice* 945)
guiltless 946
guilty 947
  find - 971
  plead - 950
guimpe 225
guinea 800
guisard 599
guise *state* 7
  dress 225
  appearance 448
  plea 617
  mode 627
  conduct, 692
guiser 599
guitar 417
gulch 198, 350
gules 434
gulf *interval* 198
  deep 208
  lake **343**
gulfy 312
gull *bird* 366
  deceive 545
  dupe 547
gullet *throat* 260, 350
gullible 486
gully *gorge* 198
  hollow 252
  evening 260
  conduit 350
gulosity 957
gulp *swallow* 296
  take food 298

- down
  credulity 486
  submit 725
gum *fastening* 45
  fasten 46
  resin 356a
  cheat 545
  - elastic 325
  - game 545
gumbo 298
gumminess 327
gummosity 352
gummous 352, 356a
gummy
  tenacious 327
  semiliquid 352
  resinous 356a
gumption 498
gumshoe
  be concealed 528
gun *report* 406
  weapon 284, 727
  blow great -s 349
  -s *loudness* 404
  sure as a - 474
guna 561
gunate 561
gunboat 726
guncotton 727
gunflint 727
gunman 361, 726, 913
gunner 284, 726
gunnery 284, 722, 727

gunpowder *warfare* 722
  ammunition 727
  not invent - 665
  sit on barrel of - 501
gunshot 197
gurge *eddy* 312
  torrent 348
gurgle *flow* 348
  bubble 353
  faint sound 405
  resonance 408
gurgoyle 350
guru *scholar* 492
  teacher 540
  holy man 996
gurry 653
gush *flow out* 295
  flood 348
  overestimation 482
  loquacity 584
  ardor 821
gushing *egress* 295
  emotional 821
  impressible 822
gusset 43
gust *wind* 349
  physical taste 390
  passion 825
  moral taste 850
gustable 298
gustation 390
gustative 390
gustful 390, 394

gustless 391
gusto [see gust]
  physical pleasure 377
  emotion 821
gusty 349
gut *destroy* 162
  opening 260
  strait 343
  eviscerate 297
  sack 789
  steal 791
guts *inside* 221
gutta 442
- serena 442
gutter *groove* 259
  conduit 350
guttle 957
guttural
  letter 561
  inarticulate 583
guy *vinculum* 45
  tether 752
  grotesque 853
guzzle *gluttony* 957
  drunkenness 959
guzzler 959
gybe 279
gymkhana 720
gymnasium
  hall 189
  school 542
  arena 728
gymnast *strong* 159

gymnastic *strong* 159
  school 542
  athletic 720
gymnastics
  training 537
  exercise 686
  contention 720
  sport 840
gymnosophist
  abstainer 953
  sectarian 984
gynæceum 374
gynæcic 374
gynandrous 83
gynarchy 737
gynecocracy 737
gynecology 662
gyneolatry 897
gynephobia 898
gyniatrics 662
gynics 374
gyp 746
gypsy 268
gyral 312
gyrate 312
gyrocar 312
gyromancy 511
gyroplane 312
gyroscope 312
gyrostat 312
gyrostatics 312
gysart 599
gyve 311, 752

H

habeas corpus 963
haberdasher 225, 797
habergeon 717
habiliment 225
habilitation 698
habit *essence* 5
  coat 225
  custom **613**
  - of mind 820
  -s of business 682
  want of - 614
habitant 188, 371
habitat 189
habitation 189
habit maker 225
habitual *orderly* 58
  normal 80
  ordinary 82
  customary 613
habituate *train* 537
  accustom 613
habituation 82, 613
habitude *state* 7
  habit 613
habitué 613
hachure 550
hacienda *abode* 189
  property 780
hack *cut* 44
  shorten 201
  horse 271
  vehicle 272
  writer 593

worker 690
- writer 534
  literary - 593
hackamore 752
hackbut 727
hackee 274
hackery 272
hackle 44
  comb 253, 652
hackman 268
hackney coach 272
hackneyed *known* 490
  trite 496
  habitual 613
haddock 298
Hades 982
hadji *traveler* 268
  priest 996
hæmatobious 5, 161
hæmatose 641
hæmorrhage
  [see hemorrhage]
haft 633
hag *ugly* 846
  wretch 913
  witch 994
haggard *insane* 503
  tired 688
  wild 824
  ugly 846
haggis 298
haggle *cut* 44
  chaffer 794

hagiographa 985
hagiology 983
hagioscope 260
ha-ha *ditch* 198
  defense 717
haik 225
hail *welcome* 292
  ice 383
  call 586
  rejoicing 838
  honor to 873
  celebration 883
  courtesy 894
  salute 928
  approve 931
  - fellow well met
  friendship 888
  sociality 892
  - from 293
hailstone 383
hair *small* 32
  filament 205
  roughness 256
  - breadth escape
  danger 665
  escape 671
  -'s breadth *near* 197
  narrow 203
  -s on the head
  multitude 102
  make one's - stand
    on end
  distressing 830

fear 860
  wonder 870
  to a - 494
hairdresser 225
hairif 253
hairless 226
hair-splitting 480
hairy *rough* 256
hajj 266
hakim *safety* 664
  master 745
  judge 967
halberd 727
halberdier 726
halcyon *calm* 174
  peace 721
  prosperous 734
  joyful 827, 829
  cheerful 836
  - birds *omen* 512
hale 654
half 91
  - a dozen *six* 98
  several 102
  - a gale 349
  - a hundred 98
  - and half *equal* 27
  mixed 41
  incomplete 53
  - distance 68
  - light 422
  - mast 669
  - masted flag **550**

- to one's name
 name 564
 honor 877
make a - of 677
handmaid
 instrumentality 631
 auxiliary 711
 servant 746
hand mirror 445
hand post 550
handsel *begin* 66
 security 771
 gift 784
 pay 809
handsome *liberal* 816
 beautiful 845
 disinterested 942
 - fortune 803
 - is that handsome
 does 816
handspike 633
handstaff 727
handwriting
 evidence 467
 signature 550
 autograph 590
 - on the wall
 warning 668
handy *near* 197
 useful 644
 ready 673
 dexterous 698
hang *lateness* 133
 pendency 214
 kill 361
 curse 908
 execute 972
 - about 133, 197
 - back 133, 623
 - by a thread 665
 - down the head 837
 - fire *late* 133
 cease 142
 unproductive 169
 inert 172
 slow 275
 reluctance 603
 inactive 683
 not finish 730
 fail 732
 refuse 764
 - in doubt 485
 - in suspense 605
 - in the balance 133
 - it! *regret* 833
 contempt 930
 - on *accompany* 88
 - on hand 641
 - on the sleeve of
 servant 746
 servility 886
 flattery 933
 - out *display* 882
 - out a light 420
 - out a signal 550
 - out one's shingle 184
 - over *destiny* 152
 height 206
 project 250
 (futurity 121)
 - over the head 152
564

- together *joined* 43
 cohere 46
 concur 178
 coöperate 709
 - up *delay* 133
 - up the fiddle 67
 - upon *effect* 154
 dependency 749
 - upon the lips of 418
hangar 191, 273
hang-dog look 901a
hanger *weapon* 727
hanger-on
 accompaniment 88
 servant 746
 servile 886
 pothooks and -s 590
hanging [see hang]
 oblique 217
 elevated 307
 ornament 847
 - look 846
hangman *evildoer* 913
 bad man 949
 executioner 975
hangnail 214
hank *tie* 45
hanker 865
Hansard 551
hansom 272
hap 156
haphazard
 chance 156, 621
hapless
 unfortunate 735
 (miserable 828)
 (hopeless 859)
haplography 495
haply *possibly* 470
 (by chance 156)
happen 151
 - as it may
 chance 621
 - what may
 certain 474
 reckless 863
happening 151
happiness
 [see happy]
 the greatest - of the
 greatest number
 910
happy *fit* 23
 opportune 134
 style 578
 glad 827
 cheerful 836
 - as a clam 827
 - dispatch 972
 - go lucky 674
 - hunting grounds 981
 - release 360
 - returns of the day
 896
 - thought 842
 - valley 515, 827
 imagination 515
 delight 827
harakiri 361, 972
harangue *teaching* 537
 speech 582

 allocution 586
harass *fatigue* 688
 vex 830
 worry 907
harbinger *precursor* 64
 omen 512
 informant 527
harbor *abode* 189
 haven 292
 refuge 666
 cherish 821
 - a design 620
 - an idea 451
 - revenge 919
 natural - 343
harborless 185, 665
hard *strong* 159
 dense 323
 physically insensible
 376
 sour 397
 difficult 704
 severe 739
 morally insensible
 823
 grievous 830
 impenitent 951
 blow - 349
 go - *difficult* 704
 failure 732
 adversity 735
 pain 828
 - a-lee 273
 - and fast rule 80
 - a-port 273
 - at it 682
 - at work 682
 - bargain 819
 - by 197
 - case 735
 - cash 800
 - earned 704
 - fought 704
 - frost 383
 - heart
 malevolent 907
 vicious 945
 impenitent 951
 - hit 732
 - knocks 720
 - life 735
 - lines *adversity* 735
 severity 739
 - liver 954a
 - lot 735
 - master 739
 - measure 739
 - names 932
 - necessity 601
 - nut to crack 704
 - of belief 487
 - of hearing 419
 - pressed *haste* 684
 difficulty 704
 hindrance 706
 - put to it 704
 - set 704
 - tack 298
 - task 703
 - time 704
 - to believe 485

- to please 868
 - up *difficulty* 704
 poor 804
 - upon *nearness* 197
 attack 715
 severe 739
 censure 932
 - winter 383
 - words *obscure* 571
 rude 895
 censure 932
 - work 686
 hit - 276
 look - at 441
 not be too - upon 918
 strike - *energy* 171
 impulse 276
 try - 675
 work - 686
harden [see hard]
 strengthen 159
 accustom 613
 - the heart
 insensible 823
 enmity 889
 impenitence 951
hardened *impious* 988
 - front *insolent* 885
hardening *habit* 613
hard-favored 846
hard-featured 846
hard-fisted 819
hard-handed 739
hard-headed 498, 871
hard-hitting 518
hardihood
 courage 861
 insolence 885
hardiness [see hardy]
hardly *scarcely* 32
 deal - with 739
 - any *few* 103
 - anything *small* 32
 unimportant 643
 - ever 137
hard-mouthed 606
hardness 323
hardpan 211
hard-shell 739
hardship 735
hard-visaged 846
hardware 323
hardy *strong* 159
 healthy 654
 brave 861
hare 274, 298
 hold with the - and
 run with the
 hounds
 fickle 607
 servile 886
harebrained *giddy* 458
 rash 863
 (foolish 499)
 (mad 503)
harelip 243, 848
harem *household* 189
 woman 374
 marriage 903
 impurity 961
haricot 298

hariff 253
hariolation 511
hark *hear* 418
  attention 457
  - back 283
harl 205
harlequin
  changeable 149
  nimble 274
  motley 440
  pantomimic 599
  humorist 844
harlequinade 599
harlot 962
harlotry 961
harm *evil* 619
  badness 649
  malevolence 907
harmattan 349
harmful 619
harmless
  impotent 158
  good 648
  perfect 650
  salubrious 656
  safe 664
  innocent 946
  bear - 717
harmonica 417
harmonics 413
harmoniphon 417
harmonist 413
harmonious
  [see harmony]
  concurring 178
harmonium 417
harmonization 413
harmonize *arrange* 60
  conform 82
  concur 178
  music 416
harmony
  agreement 23
  order 58
  music 413
  color 428
  concord 714
  peace 721
  friendship 888
  want of - 414
harness *fasten* 43
  fastening 45
  accouterment 225
  - a horse 370
  instrument 633
  prepare 673
  restraint 752
  - up 293
  in - *prepared* 673
  in action 680
  active 682
  subjection 749
harp *repeat* 104
  musical instrument 417
  weary 841
Harpagon 819
harper 416
harpoon 727
harpsichord 417
harpy *relentless* 739

  thief 792
  miser 819
  evildoer 913
  demon 980
harquebus 727
ha-ridan *hag* 846
  trollop 962
harrier 366
harrow *agriculture* 371
  - up the soul 860
  under the - 378
harrowing 830
harry *pain* 830
  attack 716
  persecute 907
Harry, old - 978
harsh *acrid* 171
  sound 410
  style 579
  discordant 713
  severe 739
  disagreeable 830
  morose 895
  malevolent 907
  - voice 581
harshness [see harsh]
hart *deer* 366
  male 373
hartshorn 392
harum-scarum
  disorder 59
  inattentive 458
haruspice 513
haruspicy 511
harvest
  evening 126
  effect 154
  profit 618
  store 636
  acquisition 775
  get in the -
  complete 729
  succeed 731
  - home *celebration* 883
  - time *exertion* 686
has been 122
hash *mix* 41
  cut 44
  confusion 59
  food 298
  make - 699
hashed 53
hashish 663, 954
hasp *fasten* 43
  fastening 45
  safety 664
hassock 215
hastate 253
haste *velocity* 274
  activity 682
  hurry **684**
hasten *promote* 707
hasty *transient* 113
  hurried 684
  impatient 825
  irritable 901
hasty pudding 298
hat 225
  cardinal's - 999
  - in hand 886
  send round the - 765

shovel - 999
hatch *produce* 161
  gate 232
  opening 260
  incubate 370
  fabricate 544
  shading 556
  plan 626
  prepare 673
  - a plot 626
hatchel 253
hatches, under -
  restraint 751
  prisoner 754
  poor 804
hatchet *cutting* 253
  dig up the - 722
  throw the helve after
    the - 818
hatchet-faced 203
hatchet man 361
hatchment *funeral* 363
  arms 550
  record 551
hatchway 260
hate *dislike* 867
  hatred **898**
hateful *noxious* 649
  painful 830
hatrack 215
hatred [see hate]
  object of - 898
hatter 225
hatti-sherif 741
hattock 72
hauberk 717
haugh 344
haughty *proud* 878
  insolent 885
  contemptuous 930
haul *drag* 285
  catch of fish &c. 789
  - down one's flag 725
haunch 236
haunt *focus* 74
  presence 186
  abode 189
  alarm 860
  persecute 907
  - the memory
  remember 505
  trouble 830
haunted 980a
hautboy 417
hauteur 878
haut monde 875
Havana *cigar* 392
have *confute* 479
  ken 490
  possess 777
  - a high opinion of 928
  - a jag on 959
  - an ax to grind 702
  - at 716
  - done! 142
  - for one's own 780
  - in store *destiny* 152
  provision 637
  - it *discover* 480a
  believe 484
  - it your own way

  submission 725
  - no choice 609a
  - no end 112
  - nothing to do with
    10
  - one's rights 924
  - one know 527
  - other fish to fry 135
  - rather 609
  - some knowledge of
    490
  - the advantage
  unequal 28
  superior 33
  - the start 116
  - to 620
  - to do with 9
  - up 638
haven *arrival* 292
  refuge 666
haversack 191
havildar 745
havoc *destruction* 162
  cry - *war* 722
  play - *spoil* 659
haw 583
hawk *spit* 297
  bird 366
  stammer 583
  swindler 792
  between - and buz-
    zard
  agitation 315
  worry 828
  eye of a - 498
  - about *publish* 531
  offer 763
  sell 796
  - at 716
  know a - from a hand
    saw
  discriminate 465
  skill 698
hawker 797
hawk-eyed 441
hawking *chase* 622
hawser 45
haycock 72
hay fever 655
hay-seed 876
hayward 753
hazard *chance* 156, 621
  danger 665
  all is on the - 349
  at all -s 604
  - a conjecture 514
  - a proposition 477
haze *mist* 353
  uncertainty 475
  joke 856
  in a - *hidden* 528
hazel 433
hazy 427
he 373
head *precedence* 62
  beginning 66
  class 75
  summit 210
  coiffure 225
  lead 280
  froth 353

heartfelt *emotion* 821
  pleasure 829
hearth *home* 189
  fireplace 386
heartily [*see* hearty]
heartless
  insensible 823
  vicious 945
heartquake 860
heartrending 830
heart-robbing 829
heart's-ease 831
heartshaped 245
heartsick
  dejection 837
  dislike 867
  satiety 869
heart-sickening 830
heart-sinking 860
heartsome 858
heart-stirring 824
heartstricken 828
heartstrings, tear the -
  830
heartswelling
  excitation 824
  resentment 900
hearty *willing* 602
  healthy 654
  feeling 821
  cheerful 836
  friendly 888
  social 892
  - laugh 838
  - meal 298
  - reception 892
heat *warmth* 382
  make hot 384
  contest 720
  excitement 824, 825
  desire 865
  dead - 27
  - of passion 900
heated *hot* 382
  quarrelsome 713
  - imagination 515
heat engine 633
heater 386
heath *moor* 344
  plant 367
heathen *pagan* 984
  irreligious 989
  - mythology 979
heathendom 984
heathenish
  vulgar 851
heather *moor* 344
  plant 367
heaume 717
heautontimoreumenos
  croaker 837
  ascetic 955
heave *raise* 307
  emotion 821
  - a sigh 839
  - in sight 446
  - the lead *depth* 208
  measure 466
  - to 265
heaven *bliss* 827
  paradise 981

call - to witness 535
for -'s sake 765
- be praised
  rejoicing 838
  gratitude 916
- forfend! 766
- knows *uncertain* 475
  ignorant 491
in the face of - 525
light of - 420
the -s 180, 318
move - and earth 686
will of - 601
heaven-born *wise* 498
  repute 873
  virtue 944
heaven-directed 498
heaven-kissing 206
heavenly *celestial* 318
  rapturous 829
  divine 976
  of heaven 981
  - bodies 318
  - host 977
  - kingdom 981
heavenly-minded 987
heavenward 305
heave offering 990
heaves 655
heavy *great* 31
  inert 172
  weighty 319
  stupid 499
  actor 599
  sleepy 683
  dull 843
  brutish 851
  - affliction 828
  - cost 814
  - dragoon 726
  - father 599
  - gun 727
  - hand *clumsy* 699
  severe 739
  - heart *loth* 603
  pain 828
  dejection 837
  - hours 841
  - news 830
  - on hand 641
  - on the mind 837
  - sea *agitation* 315
  waves 348
  - sleep 683
  - wet 298
heavy-footed *dull* 843
heavy-laden
  hindrance 706
  unhappy 828
hebdomadal 138
Hebe 845
hebetate 823, 826
hebetic 127
hebetude *imbecile* 499
  insensible 823
  inexcitable 826
hebetudinous 499
Hebraist 492
Hebrew
  unintelligible 519
  Jew 984

hecatomb *number* 98
  sacrifice 991
heckle *comb* 253, 652
  harry 830
hectic *hot* 382
  red 434
  flush 821
  - fever 821
  - flush 821
Hector *brave* 861
  rash 863
  bully 887
hector *domineer* 885
  resent 900
heddle 633
hedge *compensate* 30
  circumjacence 227
  inclosure 232
  - in *circumscribe* 229
  hinder 706
  conditions 770
hedgehog 253
hedgerow 232
hedonic 827, 836
hedonism 377, 451, 827
hedonist 954a
hedonistic 377
heed *attend* 457
  care 459
  beware 668
  caution 864
heedful 457
heedless
  inattentive 458
  neglectful 460
  forgetful 506
  rash 863
heel *follow* 63
  support 215
  lean 217
  tag 235
  deviate 279
  go round 311
  - of Achilles 665
  iron - 975
  turn on one's -
  go back 283
  go round 311
  avoid 623
heeler 886
heelpiece *sequel* 65
  back 235
  repair 660
heeltap *remainder* 40
  dress 653
heels *lowness* 207
  at the - of
  near 197
  behind 235
  cool one's - 681
  follow on the - of 281
  - over head
  inverted 218
  hasty 684
  rash 863
  laid by the - 751
  lay by the - 789
  show a light pair of -
  623
  take to one's - 623
  tread on the - of

near 197
  follow 281
  approach 286
heft *weight* 319
  handle 633
  exertion 686
hefty *laborious* 686
Hegelianism 451
hegemonic 33
hegemony
  influence 175
  direction 693
  authority 737
hegira 293
heifer 366
heigho! 839
height *degree* 26
  altitude 206
  summit 210
  at its - *great* 31
  supreme 33
  draw oneself up to his
  full - 307
heighten
  increase 35
  elevate 307
  exaggerate 549
  aggravate 835
heinous 945
heir *futurity* 121
  posterity 167
  inheritor 779
heirloom 780
heirship 777
heliacal 318
helical 248
Helicon 597
Heliogabalus 954a
heliograph
  signal 550
  picture 554
heliography
  light 420
  painting 556
heliolater 382
heliolatry 382, 991
heliology 420
heliometer 420
heliometry 420
heliophagous 420
Helios 318, 423
helioscope 445
heliotherapy 420, 662
heliotrope *purple* 437
  ornament 847
heliotype 437, 554, 558
helix 248
hell *abyss* 208
  gaming house 621
  gehenna 982
  - broke loose 59
  - upon earth
  misfortune 735
  pain 828
  - within 926
hellborn *vicious* 945
  satanic 978
hellebore 663
hell-cat 949
Hellenist 492
hellhag 913

hellhound
  evildoer 913
  bad man 949
hellish malevolent 907
  vicious 945
  hell 982
  (bad 649)
helm handle 633
  scepter 747
  (authority 737)
  answer the - 743
  at the - 693
  obey the - 705
  take the - 693
helmet hat 225
  armor 717
helminth 663
helminthagogue 662
helminthology 368
helmsman 269, 694
helot 746
help benefit 618
  utility 644
  remedy 662
  aid 707
  servant 746
  give 784
  - oneself to 789
  it can't be -ed
  submission 725
  never mind 823
  content 831
  God - you 914
  so - me God 535
helper 711
helpful 746
helpless
  incapable 158
  exposed 665
helpmate
  auxiliary 711
  wife 903
helpmeet 903
helter-skelter
  disorder 59
  haste 684
hem edge 231
  fold 258
  indeed! 870
  - in inclose 229
  restrain 751
  kiss the - of one's gar-
    ment 886
hemeralopia 443
hemi- 91
hemiplegia 376
hemisphere 181
hemispheric 250
hemlock herb 367
  unsavoriness 395
  bane 663
  punishment 972
hemorrhage 299
hemorrhoids 655
hemp
  filament 205
  poison 663
hen bird 366
  female 374
  source of supply 636
  - party 892
    568

  - with one chicken
    busy 682
henbane 663
hence arising from 155
  departure 293
  deduction 476
henceforth 121
henchman 746
hencoop 370
hen-headed 458
hen-hearted 862
henhussy 374, 501
henna 433, 439
henotheism 984
henpecked
  obedient 743
  subject 749
hepatize 641
heptad 98, 193
heptagon 98, 244
heptahedral 98
heptamerous 98
heptangular 98
herald precursor 64
  precede 116
  precession 280
  predict 511
  informant 527
  proclaim 531
  messenger 534
heraldry 550
herb 367
herbaceous 367
herbage 367
herbal 369
Herbartianism 451
herbivore 298
herbivorous 298
herborize 369
herculean great 31
  strong 159
  exertion 686
  difficult 704
Hercules strength 159
  size 192
  support 215
  pillars of - limit 233
  mark 550
herd assemblage 72
  multitude 102
herder 370
herdsman 746
here situation 183
  presence 186
  arrival 292
  come -! 286
  - and there
  dispersed 73
  few 103
  place 182, 183
  - below 318
  - goes 676
  - there and every-
    where
  diversity 16a
  space 180
  omnipresence 186
  - to-day and gone to-
    morrow 111
hereabouts site 183
  near 197

hereafter 121
  destiny 152
hereby 631
hereditament 780
hereditary
  intrinsic 5
  derivative 154, 167
  property 780
heredity 154, 167
herein 221
heresy error 495
  religious 984
heretic 489, 984
heretical 495, 984
heretofore 122
hereupon 106
herewith
  accompanying 88
  means 632
heritage futurity 121
  possession 777
  property 780
heritor 779
hermaphrodite 83
  - brig 273
hermeneutics 522
Hermes 582
hermetically 261
hermit recluse 893
  ascetic 955
hermitage house 189
  cell 191
  seclusion 893
hermitize 893
hernia 655
hero brave 861
  glory 873
  good man 948
  - worship
  approbation 931
  idolatry 991
Herod, out-Herod-
  549
heroic [see hero]
  magnanimous 942
  mock - 853
heroics 884
heroism 861
heron 366
herpes 655
herpetology 368
herring fish 298
  pungent 392
  - pond 341
  trail of a red - 615,
    706
herring-gutted 203
hesitate uncertain 475
  skeptical 485
  stammer 583
  reluctant 603
  irresolute 605
  fearful 860
Hesperian 236
Hesperides
  garden of the - 981
Hesperus 423
Hessian 726, 819
Hessian boot 225
hest 741
heterarchy 737

heteroclite 83, 139
heterodox 487, 489
heterodoxy 984
heterogamy 161, 357
heterogeneity 15, 16a
heterogeneous
  unrelated 10
  different 15
  mixed 41
  multiform 81
  exceptional 83
heterogenesis 161
heteromorphism 16a
heteronomy 737
heteropathy 662
heterotopy 185
hetman 745
hew cut 44
  shorten 201
  fashion 240
  - down 213, 308
hewers of wood
  workers 690
  commonalty 876
hexad 98, 193
hexaglot 560
hexagon 98, 244
hexahedral 98
hexahedron 98, 244
hexameter 98, 597
hexangular 98
hexastyle 98
heyday
  exultation 836, 838
  festivity 840
  wonder 870
  - of the blood 820
  - of youth 127
hiation 260
hiatus interval 198
  (discontinuity 70)
hibernal 383
hibernate 683
Hibernian 188
Hibernicism
  absurdity 497
  neology 563
hiccup 349
hickory shirt 225
hid
  - under a bushel 460
hidalgo 875
hidden 528
  - meaning 526
hide skin 223
  conceal 528
  - and seek
  deception 545
  avoid 623
  game 840
  - diminished head
  inferior 34
  decrease 36
  humility 879
  - one's face
  modesty 881
hidebound
  strait-laced 751
  stingy 819
  bigoted 988
hideous 846

within 221
at ease 705
social gathering 892
at - in *knowledge* 490
skill 698
at - with
friendship 888
be at - *to visitors* 892
bring - to *evidence* 467
belief 484
accuse 938
condemn 971
come - 292
drive - 729
eternal - 98
feel at - *freedom* 748
pleasure 827
content 831
from - 187
get - 292
go from - 293
go - 283
- rule 737
- stroke 170
- thrust
attack 716
censure 932
look at -
accusation 938
make oneself at -
free 748
sociable 892
not be at - 764
stay at - 265
strike - *energy* 171
attack 716
1ome-bred 851
1ome-felt 821, 824
1ome-grown 367
1omeless
unhoused 185
banished 893
1omelike 849
1omeliness 851
[see homely]
1omely *language* 576
unadorned 849
common 851, 876
1omeopathic
small 32
little 193
1omeopathy 662
1omesick 833
homespun *simple* 42
texture 219, 329, 635
homestall 189
homestead 189
homeward bound 292
homicide 361
homiletical 537
homily *teaching* 537
advice 595
sermon 998
1ominy 298
1omish 849
homme de cour 886
homocentric 68
1omogeneity *relation* 9
identity 13
uniformity 16
simplicity 42

homogenesis 161
homoiousia 17
homoiousian 983
homologate 23
homologue 714
homology *relation* 9
uniformity 16
equality 27
concord 714
homonym
equivocal 520
vocal sound 580
homonymy 520
homoousia 13
homoousian 983
homophonic 402
homophony 402, 413
homunculus 193
hone 253
honest *veracious* 543
honorable 939
pure 960
- meaning 516
- truth 494
turn an - penny 775
honey *sweet* 396
favorite 899
- sweet 396
milk and - 734
honeybee 366
honeycomb
concave 252
opening 260
deterioration 659
honeyed - phrases 894
- words
allurement 615
flattery 933
honeymoon
pleasure 827
endearment 902
marriage 903
honey-mouthed
courteous 894
flatter 933
honor *demesne* 780
glory 873
title 877
respect 928
approbation 931
probity 939
affair of - 720
do - to 883
do the -s
sociality 892
courtesy 894
respect 928
his - *judge* 967
- a bill 807
- be to 873
- bright *veracity* 543
probity 939
in - of 883
man of - 939
upon my - 535
word of - 768
honorable
[see honor]
reliable 632
honorarium *gift* 784
reward 973

honorary 815
honored 500
[see honor]
hooch 298
hood *cap* 225
automobile 272
distinction 550
cowl 999
hooded 223
hoodlum 887, 913
hoodoo *chance* 621
bane 649
sorcery 992
hoodooed 735
hoodwink *ignore* 491
blind 442
hide 528
deceive 545
hoof 211
hook *fasten* 43
fastening 45
hang 214
curve 245
deceive 545
retain 781
take 789
by - or by crook 631
hooked 244, 245
hooker *ship* 273
hookey, blind - 840
hooklike 245
hook-shaped 245
hooligan 887, 913
hoop *circle* 247
cry 411
hoot *cry* 411, 412
deride 929
contempt 930
censure 932
hop *leap* 309
dance 840
- skip and jump
leap 309
agitation 315
haste 684
game 840
- the twig 360
hope 858
band of - 958
beyond all - 734
dash one's -s 837
excite - 511
foster - 858
- against hope 858
- deferred
dejection 837
lamentation 859
- for *expect* 507
desire 865
- for the best 858
well grounded - 472
hopeful *infant* 129
probable 472
hope 858
hopelessness 471, 859
hop garden 371
hop-o'-my-thumb 193
hopper 191
hopple 751
hopples 752
hopscotch 840

horary 108
horde *assemblage* 72
party 712
commonalty 876
horehound 400
ho.izon *distance* 196
view 441
expectation 507
(future 121)
gloomy - 859
horizontality 213
horizontally 213, 251
horn *receptacle* 191
pommel 215, 249
sharp 253
music 417
draw in one's -s
recant 607
submit 725
humility 879
exalt one's - 873
- in 294
- of plenty 639
-s of a dilemma
reasoning 476
difficulty 704
wear the -s 905
hornbook 542
horned 245
hornet *evildoer* 913
-'s nest *pitfall* 667
difficulty 704
adversity 735
painful 830
resentment 900
censure 932
hornpipe 840
horn-shaped 253
hornwork 717
horny 323
Horny, old - 978
horologer 114
horology 114
horoscope 511
horrible *great* 31
noxious 649
dire 830
ugly 846
fearful 860
horrid [see horrible]
vulgar 851
horrific [see horrible]
horrified
pain 828
fear 860
horrify *pain* 830
terrify 860
horripilation 383
horrisonous 410
horror *fear* 860
dislike 867
view with - 898
horrors *dejection* 837
cup full of - 828
horror-stricken 828
hors de combat
impotent 158
useless 645
tired out 688
put - 731
hors d'œuvre 298, 394

I

ileum 221, 350
ilk 13
ill *evil* 619
  badness 649
  sick 655
  as - luck would have
   it 135
  bird of - omen 668
  do an - office to 907
  go on - *fail* 732
   adversity 735
  house of - fame 961
  - at ease *pain* 828
   dejection 837
  - betide 908
  - blood *hate* 898
   malevolence 907
  - humor *anger* 900
   sullenness 901a
  - luck 735
  - name 874
  - off *insufficient* 640
   adversity 735
   poor 804
  - repute 874
  -s that flesh is heir to
   evil 619
   disease 655
  - temper 900
  - turn *evil* 619
   affront 900
   spiteful 907
  - usage 907
  - will 907, 921
  - wind *bad* 649
   hindrance 706
   adversity 735
  look - 846
  take - *discontent* 832
   anger 900
ill-adapted 24
ill-advised *foolish* 499
  inexpedient 647
  unskillful 699
ill-affected 901a
illapse *conversion* 144
  ingress 294
illaqueate 545
ill-assorted 24
illation 480
illaudible 947
ill-behaved 895
ill-boding 512
ill-bred *vulgar* 851
  rude 895
ill-conditioned *bad* 649
  difficult 704
  discourteous 895
  malevolent 907
  vicious 945
ill-conducted
  unskillful 699
ill-contrived
  inexpedient 647
  bad 649
  unskillful 699
  malevolent 907
ill-defined 447
ill-devised *foolish* 499
  unskillful 699
ill-digested 674

ill-disposed *bad* 649
  sullen 901a
  spiteful 907
illegality 964
illegible 519
  render - 552
  - hand 590
illegitimate
  deceitful 545
  undue 925
  illegal 964
ill-fated 135, 735
ill-favored 395
ill-furnished 640
illiberal
  narrow-minded 481
  stingy 819
  uncourteous 895
  selfish 943
  bigoted 988
illicit *undue* 925
  illegal 964
ill-imagined
  foolish 499
  unskillful 699
illimited 105
ill-intentioned 907
illiteracy 491
illiterate 491, 493
ill-judged *foolish* 499
  unskillful 699
ill-judging 481
ill-made *distorted* 243
  ugly 846
ill-mannered
  vulgar 851
  rude 895
ill-marked *invisible* 447
ill-natured 907
illogical
  sophistical 477
  erroneous 495
ill-omened
  untoward 135
  danger 605
  adverse 735
  hopeless 859
ill-proportioned 243
ill-provided 640
ill-qualified 699
ill-requited 917
ill-rewarded 917
ill-shaped *ugly* 846
ill-spent 646
ill-starred 135, 735
ill-tempered 901
ill-timed 135
illtreat *bad* 649
  severe 739
  malevolent 907
illuminant 388, 420
illuminate
  enlighten 420
  color 428
  comment 595
  ornament 847
illuminati 492
illumination
  [see illuminate]
  book illustration 558
  celebration 883

illumine *lighten* 420
  excite 824
ill-use 907
ill-used 828
illusion
  fallacy of vision 443
  error 495
illusive [see illusive]
illusive
  unsubstantial 4
  sophistical 477
  erroneous 495
  deceitful 545, 546
illusory [see illusive]
illustrate
  exemplify 82
  interpret 522
  represent 554
  engravings 558
  ornament 847
illustrious 873
image *likeness* 17
  appearance 448
  idea 453
  metaphor 521
  representation 554
  graven - *idol* 991
  - in the mind 453
imagery *fancy* 515
  metaphor 521
  representation 554
imaginable 470
imaginary
  non-existing 2
  fancied 515
  - *quantity* 84
imagination 515
imaginative 515
imaum *prince* 745
  priest 996
imbecile *incapable* 158
  ignorant 493
  foolish 499
  fool 501
imbecility
  impotence 158
  folly **499**
  unmeaningness 517
imbed *locate* 184
  base 215
  insert 300
imbedded 229
imbibe 296
  - *learning* 539
imbibitory 296
imbrangle 61
imbricate 223
imbrication 223
imbroglio *disorder* 59
  difficulty 704
  discord 713
imbrue *impregnate* 300
  moisten 339
  - one's hands in blood
   killing 361
   war 722
  - the soul 824
imbue *mix* 41
  impregnate 300
  moisten 339
  tinge 428
  teach 537

imbued
  combination 48
  affections 820
  - with *belief* 484
  habit 613
  feeling 821
imburse 803
imitate *copy* 19
  appropriate 788
imitation *copying* **19**
  copy 21
  representation 554
  misrepresentation
   555
imitative *imitating* 19
  music 415
imitator 19
immaculate
  perfect 650, 847
  clean 652
  innocent 946
  (*excellent* 648)
immanence 5
immanent 5, 132
Immanity 907
immanuel 976
immaterial
  unsubstantial 4
immaterialist 317
immateriality
  spiritual **317**
  trifling 643
immaterialize 317
immature *new* 123
  unprepared 674
immeasurable
  great 31
  infinite 105
immediate
  continuous 69
immediately
  instantly 113
  early 132
immedicable 859
immelodious 414
immemorial 124
  from time - 122
  - usage 613
immense *great* 31
  infinite 105
  - *size* 192
immensity
  infinity 105
  size 192
immerge *introduce* 300
  dip 337
immerse *insert* 300
  submerge 310
  dip 337
immersed in 229
immersion
  [see immerse]
  baptism 998
immesh 545
immethodical 59, 139
immigrant *alien* 57
  traveler 268
  entering 294
immigration
  migration 266
  entrance 294

imminent
  destined 152
  approaching 286
immiscible 47
immission 296
immitigable
  violence 173
  hopeless 859
  revenge 919
immix 41
immixture 41
immobility
  immutability 150
  quiescence 265
  (*resolution* 604)
immoderately 31
immodest 961
immolation
  killing 361
  giving 784
  sacrifice 991
immoral *wrong* 923
  vicious 945
immortal
  diuturnal 110
  perpetual 112
  glorious 873
  celebrated 883
  her - *part* 112
immortalize
  perpetuate 112
  preserve 976
immotile 265
immovable
  stable 150
  quiescent 265
  obstinate 606
  (*resolved* 604)
immundicity 653
immune *innocuous* 656
  [*see* immunity]
immunity
  freedom 748
  exemption 777a
  right 924
  exemption 927a
  acquittal 970
immure *imprison* 751
  (*inclose* 229)
immutable *stable* 150
  deity 976
imo pectore, ab - 821
imp *child* 167
  demon 980
  (*evildoer* 913)
  (*bad man* 949)
impact *contact* 43
  impulse 276
  insertion 300
  touch 379
impair 659
impairment 659
impale *transfix* 260
  execute 972
impalpable
  small 193
  powder 330
  intangible 381
impanation 998
imparadise 829
imparity 28
576

impart *inform* 527
  give 784
impartial
  judicious 498
  neutral 628
  just 922
  honorable 939
  - *opinion* 484
impassable
  closed 261
  impossible 471
  (*difficult* 704)
impasse 7
impassible 823
impassion 824
impassionable 822
impassioned
  - *language* 574
  sentimental 822
  excited 825
impassive 823
impatient 825
  - *of control* 742
impawn 771
impeach *censure* 932
  accuse 938
  go to law 969
impeachment 738
  [*see* impeach]
  soft - 902
impeccability
  faultless 650
  innocent 946
impecunious 804
impede 179, 706
impediment 706
  - *in speech* 583
impedimenta
  instrument 633
  luggage 780
impel *push* 276
  induce 615
impend *future* 121
  destiny 152
  overhang 206
impending 132
  [*see* impend]
impenetrable
  closed 261
  solid 321
  unintelligible 519
  latent 526
  (*hidden* 528)
impenitence 951
imperative
  require 630
  command 737
  severe 739
  commanding 741
  duty 926
imperator 745
imperceptible
  small 32
  minute 193
  slow 275
  invisible 447
  latent 526
impercipient 376
imperdible 664
imperfect
  incomplete 53

  failing 651
  vicious 945
  - *vision* 143
imperfection 651
  inferiority 34
  vice 945
imperfectly 32
imperforate 261
imperial *trunk* 191
  beard 256
  authority 737
imperil 665
imperious
  command 737
  proud 878
  arrogant 885
  - *necessity* 601
imperishable
  eternal 112
  stable 150
  glorious 873
impermanent
  transient 111
  (*changeable* 149)
impermeable
  closed 261
  dense 321
impersonal
  general 78
  neuter 316
impersonate 554
imperspicuity 519
impersuasible 606
impertinent
  irrelevant 10
  insolent 885
  (*disagreeing* 24)
  (*inexpedient* 647)
imperturbable
  inexcitable 826
  contented 831
  unamazed 871
impervious *closed* 261
  impossible 471
  insensible 823
  - *to light* 426
  - *to reason* 606
impetiginous 653
impetrate 765
impetuosity
  [*see* impetuous]
impetuous
  boisterous 173
  hasty 684
  excitable 825
  rash 863
  eager 865
impetus 276
impiety 988, 989
impignorate 787
impinge 276
impious 988
impish 980
implacable *hatred* 898
  unforgiving 919
  (*wrath* 900)
implant *insert* 296, 300
  teach 537
implanted
  ingrained 5
  adventitious 6

  - *by nature* 820
implausible 473
implead 969
implement 633
impletion 52
implex 41
implicate
  involve 54, 526
  accuse 938
implicated
  related 9
  component 56
implication *disorder* 59
  meaning 516
  metaphor 521
  latency 526
implicit 526
  - *belief* 484
implied [*see* imply]
implore 765
imply *evidence* 467
  mean 516
  involve 526
  (*metaphor* 521)
impolicy 699
impolite 895
imponderable 4, 320
imporous *closed* 261
  dense 321
import *put between* 228
  ingress 294
  take in 296
  insert 300
  mean 516
  involve 526
  be of consequence 642
importance
  greatness 31
  consequence **642**
  attach - to 642
  attach too much - to
  482
  of no - 643
important 642
importune *ask* 765
  pester 830
impose *print* 591
  order 741
  awe 928
  - *upon credulity* 486
  deceive 545
  be unjust 923
imposing
  important 642
  exciting 824
  glorious 873
imposition
  [*see* impose]
  undue 925
  - *of hands* 998
impossibilities
  seek after - 645
impossibility **471**
impossible 471
  deception 702
  refusal 764
  (*difficulty* 704)
  - *quantity*
  algebra 84
impost 812
impostor 548, 925

impostume 655
imposture 545
impotence **158**
impotent 732
- conclusion 732
- to rise 158
impound
   imprison 751
   (*inclose* 229)
impoverish
   weaken 160
   waste 638
   despoil 789
   render poor 804
impracticable
   impossible 471
   misjudging 481
   obstinate 606
   difficulty 704
impracticality 471
imprecation
   prayer 765
   curse 908
imprecatory 765, 908
impregnable
   strong 159
   safe 664
impregnate *mix* 41
   combine 48
   fecundate 161, 168
   insert 300
   teach 537
- with *cloy* 641
impresario 599
imprescriptible 924
impress *effect* 154
   cause sensation 375
   mark 550
   excite feeling 824
- upon the mind
   memory 505
   teach 537
impressed with
   belief 484
   feeling 821
impressibility 375
impressible
   motive 615
   sensibility 822
impression *effect* 154
   sensation 375
   idea 453
   belief 484
   publication 531
   mark 550
   engraving 558
   print 591
   emotion 321
   make an *act* 171
   thought 451
impressionable   375,
   822
impressive
   language 574
   important 642
   feeling 821, 824
imprimit 558
imprimus 66
imprint *publisher* 531
   indication 550
- in the memory 505

imprison
   circumscribe 229
   restrain 751
   punish 972
improbability **473**
improbate 932
improbity **940**
impromptu 612
improper
   incongruous 24
   foolish 499
   solecistic 568
   inexpedient 647
   wrong 923
   unmeet 925
   vicious 945
- *time* 135
impropriate
   possess 777
   take 789
impropriator 779
impropriety
   [*see* improper]
improve 658
- the occasion 134
- the shining hour 682
- upon 658
improvement **658**
improvident
   careless 460
   not preparing 674
   prodigal 818
   rash 863
improvisator 416, 582
improvisatore
   speech 582
   poetry 597
   impulse 612
improvise
   imagination 515
   extemporize 612
   unprepared 674
improviser 612
imprudent
   neglectful 460
   rash 863
   (*unwise* 699)
impudence
   insolence 885
   discourtesy 895
impudent *insolent* 885
   discourteous 895
impudicity **961**
impugn *deny* 536
   attack 716
   blame 932
impugnation 708
impugnment 708
impuisance 158
impulse *push* **276**
   sudden thought **612**
   motive 615
   blind - 601
   creature of - 612
   give an - to
   propel 284
   aid 707
impulsive
   [*see* impulse]
   intuitive 477
   unaccustomed 604

   excitable 825
   rash 863
impunctual 133
impunity *escape* 671
   acquittal 970
   with - *safely* 664
impurity
   inelegance 579
   foul 653
   licentious **961**
imputation *ascribe* 155
   slur 874
   accuse 938
in 221
go - 294
- a jiffy 113
- and out 314
- a rut 16
- as much as
   relation 9
   degree 26
- for *undertake* 676
   promise 768
-s and outs 182
in
- camera 528
- extenso *whole* 50
   diffuse 573
- loco 23
- medias res 68
- propriâ personâ 79,
   186
- re 9
- statu quo 141
- statu quo ante bel-
   lum 140
- toto 52
- transitu *transient*111
   transfer 270
inability
   want of power 158
   want of skill 699
- to discriminate 465*a*
inabstinent 954
inaccessible
   distant 196
   impossible 471
inaccordant 24
inaccurate *error* 495
   solecism 568
inacquiescent 24
inaction
   inertness 172
   not doing **681**
inactivity **683**
   inertness 172
inadequacy
   [*see* inadequate]
inadequate
   unequal 28
   powerless 158
   insufficient 640
   useless 645
   imperfect 651
   (*weak* 160)
inadmissible
   incongruous 24
   excluded 55
   extraneous 57
   inexpedient 647
inadvertence 458

inadvisable 647, 649
inaffable 895
inalienable
   retention 781
   right 924
inamorata 897
inane *void* 4
   incogitancy 452
   unmeaning 517
   insufficient 640
   trivial 643
   useless 645
inanimate 360
- *matter* 358
inanition 158
inanity [*see* inane]
inappetency
   insensibility 823
   indifference 866
inapplicable
   irrelation 10
   disagreement 24
inapposite
   irrelation 10
   disagreement 24
inappreciable
   in degree 32
   in size 193
   unimportant 643
inapprehensible
   stolid 499
   unintelligible 519
inappropriate
   unconsonant 24
   inexpedient 647
inapt *incongruous* 24
   impotent 158
   useless 645
   inexpedient 647
   unskillful 699
inarticulate 581, 583
inartificial 703
inartistic 846
inasmuch *whereas* 9
   however 26
   because 476
inattention **458**
inattentive 419, 458
inaudible *silence* 403
   faint sound 405
   deaf 419
   voiceless 581
inaugural
   precursor 64
inaugurate *begin* 66
   install 755
   celebrate 883
inauguratory 66
inauspicious
   untimely 135
   untoward 649
   adverse 735
   hopeless 859
inbeing 5
inborn *intrinsic* 5
   affections 820
   (*habit* 613)
- *proclivity* 601
inbound 294
inbred [*see* inborn]
inca 745

incage 751
incalculable *much* 31
  infinite 105
incalescence 382
incandescence 382
incantation
  invocation 765
  spell 993
incantatory 992
incapable
  impotent 158
  (*weak* 160)
incapacious 203
incapacitate 158
incapacity
  impotence 158
  ignorance 491
  stupidity 499
  (*weakness* 160)
incarcerate
  imprison 751
  (*surround* 229)
incarnadine 434
incarnate
  intrinsic 5
  materiality 316
  to incorporate 364
  vicious 945
devil - *bad man* 949
Satan 978
incarnation 316, 976
incase *cover* 223
  surround 229
incautious *rash* 863
  (*neglect* 460)
incendiary *destroy* 162
  burn 384
  influence 615
  pitfall 667
  malevolent 907
  evildoer 913
  bad man 949
incensation 400
incense *fuel* 388
  fragrant 400
  hate 898
  anger 900
  flatter 933
  worship 990
  rite 998
  - *breathing* 400
  - *burner* 400
incension *burning* 384
incensorium 400
incentive 615
incept 66, 537
inception 66
inceptive *beginning* 66
  causal 153
  generative 168
inceptor 541
incertitude 475
incessant *repeated* 104
  ceaseless 112
  frequent 136
incest 961
inch *small* 32
  length 200
  move slowly 275
  measure 466
by - es 275
578

give an - and take an
  ell 789
- by inch
  by degrees 26
  in parts 51
  slowly 275
not see an - beyond
  one's nose 699
not yield an - 606
to an - 494
inchoation
  beginning 66
  preparation 673
incide 44
incidence 278
incident 151
  full of - 151
incidental *extrinsic* 6
  circumstance 8
  irrelative 10
  occurring 151
  casual 156
  liable 177
  chance 621
  - *music* 415
incinerate 384
incinerator 384
incipience 66
incircumspect 460
incise *cut* 44
  furrow 259
incision *cut* 44
  furrow 259
incisive *energy* 171
  vigor 574
  feeling 821
incite *exasperate* 173
  urge 615
incitement [*see* incite]
incivility 895
incivism 911
inclasp 229
inclement *violent* 173
  cold 383
  severe 739
  pitiless 914a
inclination [*see* incline]
  descent 306
  will 600
  affection 820
  desire 865
  love 897
incline *tendency* 179
  slope 217
  direction 278
  willing 602
  induce 615
  - *an ear to* 457
inclined *oblique* 217
  intended 620
  - *plane* 633
inclose
  place within 221
  surround 227
  hem in 229
inclosure *region* 181
  envelope **232**
  fence 752
include
  composition 54
  - *in a class* 76

inclusion 76
inclusive *additive* 37
  component 56
  class 76
inclusory 56
incogitance **452**
incognito 528
incognizable 519
incoherence
  physical **47**
  mental 503
incombustible 385
income *means* 632
  profit 775
  property 780
  wealth 803
  receipt 810
incomer
  immigrant 294
incoming *ingress* 294
  receipt 810
incommensurable
  irrelation 10
  (*disagreeing* 24)
  - *quantity* 84, 85
incommode *hinder* 706
  (*trouble* 830)
  (*incommodious* 647)
incommodious 647
incommunicable
  unmeaning 517
  unintelligible 519
  retention 781
incommutable 150
incomparable
  superior 33
  (*good* 648)
incompassionate 914a
incompatibility 15
incompatible 24
incompetence
  inability 158
  incapacity 499
  unskillful 699
incomplete
  fractional 51
  not complete 53, 730
incompleteness **53**
  noncompletion 730
incomplex 42
incompliance 764
incomprehensible
  infinite 105
  unintelligible 519
incomprehension 491
incompressible 321
inconceivable
  unthought of 452
  impossible 471
  improbable 473
  incredible 485
  unintelligible 519
  wonder 870
inconceptible 519
inconcinnity
  disagreement 24
  ugliness 846
inconclusive 477
inconcoction 674
incondite 851
inconformity 15

incongruous
  differing 15
  disagreeing 24
  faulty 568
  discordant 713
inconnection
  irrelation 10
  disjunction 44
inconsequence
  irrelation 10
inconsequential
  illogical 477
inconsiderable
  small 32
  fractional 100a
  unimportant 643
inconsiderate
  thoughtless 452
  inattentive 458
  neglectful 460
  foolish 699
inconsistent
  contrary 14
  disagreeing 24
  illogical 477
  absurd 497
  foolish 499
  discordant 713
  capricious 608
inconsolable 837
inconsonant
  disagreeing 24
  fitful 149
inconspicuous 447
inconstant 149
incontestable
  strong 159
  certain 474
incontiguous 196
incontinent 961
incontinently 132
incontrollable 173
incontrovertible
  certain 474
  (*stable* 150)
inconvenience 647
  put to - 706
inconvenient 135, 647
inconversable
  taciturn 585
  unsociable 893
inconvertible
  continuing 143
  (*stable* 150)
inconvincible 487
incorporality 317
incorporate *combine* 48
  include 76
  materialize 316
  immaterial 317
  animality 364
incorporation
  [*see* incorporate]
incorporeal 317
  - *hereditaments* 780
incorrect *illogical* 477
  erroneous 495
  solecism 568
  vicious 945
incorrigible
  obstinate 606

hopeless 859
vicious 945
impenitent 951
incorruptible
honorable 939
incorruption
probity 939
innocence 946
(*health* 654)
incrassate
increase 194
density 321
- *fluids* 352
(*thick* 202)
increase
- *in degree* **35**
- *in number* 102
- *in size* 194
incredible *great* 31
impossible 471
improbable 473
doubtful 485
wonderful 870
incredulity
unbelief **487**
religious - 989
increment *increase* 35
addition 37
adjunct 39
expansion 194
increpation 932
incriminate 938
incrust *coat* 223
line 224
incubate 370
incubation 673
incubus *hindrance* 706
pain 828
demon 980
inculcate 537
inculcated 6
inculpable 946
inculpate 938
inculture 674
incumbency
business 625
churchdom 995
incumbent
inhabitant 188
high 206
weight 319
duty 926
clergyman 996
incumber 706
incumbered 806
incumbrance 706
incunabula 66, 127
incur 177
- *a debt* 806
- *a loss* 776
- *blame* 932
- *danger* 665
- *disgrace* 874
- *the risk* 621
incurable *ingrained* 5
disease 655
hopeless 859
incuriosity **456**
incursion
ingress 294
attack 716

incurvation 245
incus 418
indagation 461
indebted *owing* 806
gratitude 916
duty 926
indecent 961
indeciduous 150
indecipherable 519
indecision 605
indecisive 475
indeclinable 150
indecorous *vulgar* 851
vicious 945
impure 961
indeed *existing* 1
very 31
assent 488
truly 494
assertion 535
wonder 870
indefatigable
persevering 604a
active 682
indefeasible *stable* 150
certainty 474
necessity 601
due 924
indefectible 650
indefensible
powerless 158
submission 725
accusable 938
wrong 945
indeficient 650
indefinite *great* 31
every 78
infinite 105
aoristic 119
misty 447
uncertain 475
inexact 495
vague 519
indeliberate 612
indelible *stable* 150
memory 505
mark 550
feeling 821
indelicate 961
indemnification 790,
952
indemnificatory 30
indemnity
compensation 30
forgiveness 918
reward 973
deed of - 771
indent *list* 86
scallop 248
indentation 252, 257
indenture *compact* 769
security 771
(*evidence* 467)
(*record* 551)
independence
irrelation 10
freedom 748
wealth 803
Independence   Day
138, 840
Independent 984

independent
[*see* independence]
indescribable
great 31
wonderful 870
indesinent 112
indestructible 150
indeterminate
chance 156
uncertain 475
equivocal 520
irresolute 605
indevotion 989
index *arrangement* 60
exponent 84
list 86
sign 550
words 562
index   expurgatorius
761
indexterity 699
Indian
- *file* 69
- *gift* 794
- *giver* 702
- *rubber* 325
- *ruling chiefs* 875
- *sage* 662
- *summer* 126
- *weed* 392
indicate *specify* 79
direct attention to 457
mean 516
mark 550
indication 75, **550**
indicative
evidence 467
indicating 550
indicatory 550
indicolite 438
indict *accuse* 938
arraign 969
indiction 108, 531
indifference
incuriosity 456
unwillingness 603
no choice 609a
insensibility 823
unconcern **866**
irreligion 989
matter of - 643
indifferent
[*see* indifference]
unimportant 643
bad 649
indigence
insufficiency 640
poverty 804
indigene 188
indigenous
intrinsic 5
inhabitant 188
indigested 674
indigestible 657
indigestion 655, 657
indigitate 457
indign 940
indignation 900
- *meeting* 832
iron - 722
indignity *affront* 900

insult 929
indigo 438
indiligence 683
indirect *oblique* 217
devious 279
latent 526
circuitous 629
indiscernible 447
indiscerptible *whole* 50
unity 87
dense 321
indiscoverable 526
indiscreet *rash* 863
blamable 945
(*neglectful* 460)
(*unskillful* 699)
indiscrete 48
indiscretion *guilt* 947
[*see* indiscreet]
indiscriminate
mixed 41
unarranged 59
multiform 81
casual 621
indiscrimination **465a**
indispensable 630
indispose
dissuade 616
indisposed
unwilling 603
sick 655
- *to believe* 487
indisputable 474
indissoluble
joined 43
whole 50
stable 150
dense 321
indissolvable
[*see* indissoluble]
indistinct *dim* 447
(*vague* 519)
indistinction 465a
indistinguishable
identical 13
invisible 447
indiscriminate 465**a**
indisturbance
quiescence 265
inexcitation 826
indite 54, 590
individual *whole* 50
special 79
unity 87
person 372
individuality
speciality 79
unity 87
individualize 79
indivisible *whole* 50
dense 321
indocility
incapacity 158
obstinacy 606
indoctrinate 537
indolence 683, 927
indomitable *strong* 159
determined 604
persevering 604a
resisting 719
courage 861

inofficious 907
inoperative
  powerless 158
  unproductive 169
  useless 645
inopportune
  untimely 135
  inexpedient 647
inordinate great 31
  excessive 641
inorganic 358
inorganization **358**
inornate 849
inosculate join 43
  combined 48
  intersect 219
  convoluted 248
inquest 461, 967
inquietude
  changeable 149
  uneasy 828
  discontent 832
  apprehension 860
  (motion 264)
inquinate 659
inquire 461
  - into 595
inquirer 461, 541
inquiring 461
  - mind 455
inquiry **461**
inquisition
  inquiry 461
  severity 739
  tribunal 966
inquisitive 455
inquisitorial
  prying 455
  inquiry 461
  severe 739
  jurisdiction 965
inroad ingress 294
  trespass 303
  devastation 659
  invasion 716
insalubrity **657**
insanity 61, **503**
insatiable 865
inscribe write 590
  blazon 873
inscription
  [see inscribe]
  interment 363
  record 551
inscroll 551
inscrutable 519
insculpture 557
insculptured 558
insecable junction 43
  unity 87
insect 366, 368
  minute 193
  injurious -s 913
  - cry 412
insecure danger 665
  (uncertain 475)
insensate
  foolish 499
  insane 503
insensibility slow 275
  physical **376**

moral **823**
  - of benefits 917
  - to the past 506
insensible numb 381
  [see insensibility]
inseparable
  junction 43
  coherence 46
insert locate 184
  interpose 228
  enter 294
  put in 300
  record 551
  - itself 300
insertion **300**
  ornament 847
inservient 645
insessorial 206
inseverable
  junction 43
  unity 87
inside 221
  - out 218
  - part music 415
  turn - out 529
insidious deceitful 545
  cunning 702
  dishonorable 940
insight 490, 868
insignia 550
  - of authority 747
insignificant
  unmeaning 517
  unimportant 643
insincere 544, 855
insinuate intervene 228
  ingress 294
  insert 300
  latency 526
  hint 527
  ingratiate 897
  blame 932
  (suppose 514)
  (mean 516)
insipid tasteless 391
  style 575
  trifling 643
insipidity
  tasteless **391**
  indifferent 866
insist argue 476
  command 741
  - upon affirm 535
  dwell on 573
  be determined 604
  contend 720
  compel 744
  conditions 770
  due 924
insistence [see insist]
  influence 615
insnare 545
insobriety 959
insolation 340, 382, 384
insolence **885**
insolent defiant 715
  arrogant 885
  disrespectful 929
insoluble dense 321
  unintelligible 519
insolvable 519

insolvent poverty 804
  debt 806
  nonpayment 808
insomnium 682
insouciance
  thoughtlessness 458
  supineness 823
  indifference 866
inspan 293
inspect look 441
  attend to 457
inspector
  inquisitor 461
  judge 480
  director 694
inspiration
  breathing 349
  wisdom 498
  imagination 515
  impulse 612
  motive 615
  feeling 821
  Deity 976
  revelation 985
  religious - 987
inspirator 349
inspire breathe 349
  prompt 615
  improvement 658
  animate 824
  cheer 836
  - courage 861
  - hope 858
  - respect 928
inspired 615
  - writers 985
inspirit incite 615
  animate 824
  cheer 834
  hope 858
  encourage 861
inspiriting hopeful 858
inspissate dense 321
  semiliquid 352
instability 149, 605
install locate 184
  commission 755
  celebrate 883
installment portion 51
  payment 807, 809
instance example 82
  motive 615
  solicitation 765
instant moment 113
  present 118
  destiny 152
  required 630
  importance 642
  active 682
  lose not an - 684
  on the - 132
instantaneity **113**
instanter 113, 132
instate 883
instauration 660
instead 147
instigate 615
instigator 615
instill imbue 41
  introduce 296
  insert 300

teach 537
instinct intellect 450
  intuition 477
  impulse 601
  brute - 450a
  - with motive 615
  possession 777
instinctive inborn 5
institute begin 66
  cause 153
  produce 161
  academy 542
  society 712
  - an inquiry 461
institution
  academy 542
  society 712
  political - 963
  church 995
institutional 712
institutor 540
instruct teach 537
  advise 695
  precept 697
  order 741
instructed 490
instruction
  [see instruct]
instructional 537
instructive 537
instructor 540
instructorship 542
instrument
  implement **633**
  security 771
  musical - 417
  optical - 445
instrumental 631
  - music 415
instrumentalist 416
instrumentality **631**
instrumentation 54, 60
insubordinate 742
insubstantial
  inexistent 2
  unsubstantial 4
  immaterial 317
  - pageant 853
insubstantiality
  disappearance 449
  [see insubstantial]
insufferable
  painful 830
  dislike 867
insufficiency **640**
insufflation 349
insular unrelated 10
  detached 44
  single 87
  region 181
  island 346
  narrow 481
  bigoted 988
insulate 44, 346
insulse stupid 499
  dull 843
insult insolence 885
  rudeness 895
  offense 900
  disrespect 929
insulting 898

582

insuperable 471
- obstac[e 706
insupportable 725, 830
insuppressible 173
insurance 768, 771
insure *make sure* 474
  obtain security 771
insurer
  underwriter 758
insurgent 146, 742
insurmountable 471
insurrection
  resistance 719
  disobedience 742
insurrectionary 146
insusceptible 823
- of change 150
intact *permanent* 141
  perfect 650
  preserved 670
intactness
  completeness 52
  [see intact]
intaglio *mold* 22
  concave 252
  sculpture 557
intake *automobile* 272
intangible *little* 193
  numb 381
integer *whole* 50
  number 84
  unity 87
integral 50
- calculus 85
- part 56
integrant 56
integrate
  consolidate 50
  (*complete* 52)
integrity *whole* 50
  completeness 52
  probity 939
  virtue 944
integument 223
intellect **450**
  absence of - **450a**
  exercise of the - 451
intellection 450, 451
intellectual 450
- force 574
- powers 450
intelligence *mind* 450
  capacity **498**
  news 532
intelligencer 527
intelligent **498**
intelligential 527
intelligibility **518**
  (*perspicuity* 570)
intelligible 518
intemperance **954**
  drunkenness 959
intempestive 115, 135
intempestivity **135**
intend 620
intendant 694
intended *will* 600
  predetermined 611
intense *great* 31
  energetic 171
- color 428

- thought 457
intensify *increase* 35
  stimulate 171
intensity *degree* 26
  greatness 31
  energy 171
intensive 35
intent *attention* 457
  well 600
  design 620
  active 682
- upon *desire* 865
  resolved 604
to all -s and purposes
  27, 52
intention **620**
  bad - 607
  good - 906
inter 363
interact 12
interaction
  working 170
  (*intermedium* 228)
interactive 148
interagent 228, 631
intercalate 228
intercalation 228, 300
intercede
  be concordant 714
  mediate 724, 976
  deprecate 766
interceder 714
intercept
  hinder 706
  take 789
intercession
  [see intercede]
  worship 990
Intercessor 976
intercessor 714
interchange **148**
  barter 794
- visits &c. 892
interchangeable 12
intercipient 706
interclude 706
intercollegiate 148
intercolumnar 228
intercommunication
  527
intercommunion 892
interconnection 9, 12
intercostal 228
intercourse
  friendship 888
  sociality 892
  verbal - 582, 588
intercross 219
intercurrence
  interchange 148
  interjacence 228
  passage 302
interdenominational
  148
interdependence 12
interdict 761
interdigitate
  intersect 219
  intervene 228
interest *concern* 9
  influence 175

  curiosity 455
  advantage 618
  importance 642
  property 780
  debt 806
  excite 824
  please 829
  amuse 840
  devoid of - 841
  feel an - in 906
- bearing 810
  make - for 707
  not know one's own -
    699
  place out at -
  lend 787
  economy 817
  take an - in
  curiosity 455
  love 897
  take no - in
  insensibility 823
  indifference 866
  want of - 866
interested *selfish* 943
interesting *lovable* 897
interfacial 228
interfere *disagree* 24
  counteract 179
  intervene 228
  activity 682
  thwart 706
  mediate 724
interferometer 193
interfuse 48
interfusion 41
intergrowth 228
interim *time* 106
  short time 111
interior 221
  painting 556
interiority **221**
interjacence
  middle 68
  coming between **228**
interject *interpose* 228
  insert 300
interlace *join* 43
  combine 48
  twine 219
interlacement 41
interlard *mix* 41
  combine 48
  interpolate 228
interleave 228
interline
  interpolate 288
  write 590
interlineal 228
interlineation 37, 300
interlink *join* 43
  twine 219
interlobular 228
interlocation 228
interlocular 228
interlocution **588**
interlocutor 582
interloper
  extraneous 57
  intervene 228
  obstruct 706

interlude *time* 106
  dramatic 599
intermarriage 903
intermarry 903
intermaxillary 228
intermeddle
  interfere 682
  hinder 706
intermeddling 724
intermedial 228, 631
intermediary 534, 631
intermediate
  mean 29
  middle 68
  intervening 228
  ministerial 631
- time 106
intermediation
  agency 170
intermedium *mean* 29
  link 45
  intervention 228
  instrument 631
  (*means* 632)
interment **363**
  insertion 300
intermigration 266
interminable
  infinite 105
  eternal 112
  long 200
intermingle 41
intermission *time* 106
  discontinuance 142
intermit *interrupt* 70
  recur 138
  discontinue 142
intermittence *time* 106
  periodicity 138
intermittent 138
intermix 41, 48
intermolecular 228
intermundane 228
intermutation 148
intern 221
internal *intrinsic* 5
  interior 221
- evidence 467
internasal 228'
international
  reciprocal 12
  interchange 148
  sociality 892
- law 963
interne 662
internecine 361
- war 722
interneural 228
internodal 228
internuncio
  messenger 534
  diplomatist 758
interoceanic 228
interosseal 228
interpel 142
interpellation
  inquiry 461
  address 586
  summons 471
  command 741
  appeal 765

interpenetration
  interjacence 228
  ingress 294
  passage 302
interplanetary 228
interpolar 228
interpolation
  analytical 85
  interpose 228
  insertion 300
interpose
  intervene 228
  act 682
  hinder 706
  mediate 724
interposit 799
interposition
  [*see* interpose]
interpret 522, 595
interpretation 516, **522**
  (*answer* 462)
interpreter **524**
interradial 228
interregnum
  intermission 106
  transient 111
  discontinuance 142
  interval 198
  inaction 681
  laxity 738
  (*discontinuity* 70)
interrelation 9, 12
interrenal 228
interrogate 461
interrogation 461
  typography 550
interrupt
  discontinuity 70
  cessation 142
  hinder 706
interruption
  derangement 61
  interval 198
interscapular 228
interscholastic 148
intersect 219
intersection 198, 219
interseptal 228
interspace *interval* 198
  interior 221
intersperse *diffuse* 73
  interpose 228
  (*music* 41)
interstate 148
interstellar 228
interstice 198
interstitial *internal* 221
  interjacent 228
intertanglement 41
intertexture
  mixture 41
  intersection 219
  tissue 329
intertribal 148
intertwine *unite* 43
  cross 219
intertwist 43, 219
interurban 148
interval *degree* 26
  - of time 106
  - of space **198**
  584

  - in music 413
  at -s
    discontinuously 70
  at regular -s 138
intervalvular 228
intervascular 228
intervene
  - in order 70
  - in time 106
  - in space 228
  be instrumental 631
  mediate 724
  (*agent* 758)
intervener 228
interventricular 228
intervert *change* 140
  deviate 279
intervertebral 228
interview
  conference 588
  society 892
interviewer 553, 554
intervolved 43
interweave *join* 43
  cross 219
  interjacence 228
interwork 148
interworking 170
intestate 552
intestine 221, 350
inthrall *subjection* 749
  restraint 751
intimacy 888
intimate *special* 79
  close 197
  tell 527
  friendly 888
  friend 890
intimately *joined* 43
intimation 527
intimidate *frighten* 860
  insolence 885
  threat 909
intinction 998
into go - 294
  put - 300
  run - 300
intolerable 830
intolerance
  prejudice 481
  obstinacy 606
  impatience 825
  insolence 885
  malevolence 907
intolerant 489
intomb 363
intonation *sound* 402
  musical 413
  voice 580
intone *sing* 416
  worship 990
intort 248
intoxicant *bane* 663
intoxicated 959
intoxication
  excitement 824, 825
  inebriation 959
intracanal 221
intracellular 221
intractable
  obstinate 606

  difficult 704
  sullen 901a
intrados 221
intralobular 221
intramarginal 221
intramolecular 221
intramundane 221
intramural 221
intransient 110
intransigence 604
intransigent 604
intransitive 110
intransmutable
  diuturnal 110
  stable 150
intraocular 221
intrap 545
intraregarding 221
intraseptal 221
intratelluric 221
intrauterine 221
intravascular 221
intravenous 221
intraventricular 221
intrench *safety* 664
  defend 717
  - on 303
intrepid 861
intricacy 533
intricate *confused* 59
  convoluted 248
  difficult 704
intrigant
  meddlesome 682
  cunning 702
  libertine 962
intrigue *plot* 626
  activity 682
  cunning 702
  licentiousness 961
intriguer *activity* 682
  cunning 702
intrinsic 5
  forming 56
  - evidence 467
  - habit 613
  - truth 494
intrinsicality **5**
introception 296
introduce *lead* 62
  interpose 228
  precede 280
  insert 300
  - new blood 140
  - new conditions 469
  - to 888
introducer 164
introduction
  [*see* introduce]
  preface 64
  reception 296
  drama 599
  friendship 888
  courtesy 894
introductory
  precursor 64
  beginning 66
  priority 116
  receptive 296
introgression 294
introit 296, 998

intromissive 296
intromit *receive* 296
intromittent 296
introspection
  look into 441
  attend to 457
introspective 451
introvert 218
intrude *interfere* 24
  inopportune 135
  intervene 228
  enter 294
  trespass 303
intruder 57 ¶
intrusion [*see* intrude]
intrusive 706
intrusiveness 682
intrust *commit* 755
  lend 787
intuition *mind* 450
  unreasoning **477**
  knowledge 490
  subconsciousness
    992a
intumescence
  swell 194
  convex 250
intussuscept 14, 218
intwine *join* 43
  twist 248
inunction 223
inundate *effusion* 337
  flow 348
  redundance 641
inurbanity 895
inure *habituate* 613
  train 673
inured *insensible* 823
inurn 363
inusitate 20
inusitation 614
inutility **645**
invade *ingress* 294
  trespass 303
  attack 713
invaginate 14, 218
invagination 218, 357
invalid *powerless* 158
  illogical 477
  diseased 655
  undue 925
invalidate *disable* 158
  weaken 160
  confute 479
invalidity *disease* 655
invaluable 644, 648
invariable *intrinsic* 5
  uniform 16
  conformable 82
  stable 150
invasion
  ingress 294
  attack 716
invective 932
inveigh 932
inveigle *deceive* 545
  seduce 615
invent *imagine* 515
  lie 544
  devise 626
invented *untrue* 546

invention [see invent]
  composition 54
inventive skillful 698
inventor 164
inventory 86
inverse contrary 14
  upside down 218
inversion
  derangement 61
  change 140
  of position 218
  contraposition 237
  reversion 145
  language 577
invertebracy 158
invertebrate
  impotent 158
  frail 945
invest impower 157
  clothe 225
  surround 227
  besiege 716
  commission 755
  give 784
  lend 787
  expend 809
  - in locate 184
  purchase 795
  - money 817
  - with ascribe 155
investigate 461
investiture
  appointment 755
investment
  clothing 225
  [see invest]
  make -s 673
investor 784
inveterate old 124
  established 150
  inborn 820
  - belief 484
  - habit 613
invidious painful 830
  hatred 898
  spite 907
  envy 921
invigilation 459
invigorate
  strengthen 159
  improve 658
  inspirit 834
invigorating
  healthy 656
invincible 159
inviolable secret 528
  right 924
  honor 939
inviolate permanent 141
  secret 528
  honorable 939
invious closed 261
  pathless 704
invisibility 447
invisible small 193
  not to be seen 447
  concealed 526
  - government 526
  - helpers 977
invitation [see invite]
invitatory 765

invite induce 615
  offer 763
  ask 765
  - the attention 457
inviting [see invite]
  pleasing 829
invocation [see invoke]
invocative 765
invoice 86
invoke address 586
  implore 765
  pray 990
  - curses 908
  - saints 998
involucrum 223
involuntary
  necessary 601
  unwilling 603
  - servitude 749
involution [see involve]
  algebra 85
involve include 54
  derange 61
  wrap 225
  evince 467
  mean 516
  latency 526
involved disorder 59
  convoluted 248
  secret 533
  obscure style 571
  in debt 806
involvement 61, 704
invulnerable 664
inward intrinsic 5
  inside 221
  incoming 294
  - monitor 926
inweave 219, 300
inwrap 225
inwrought 5
Ionian school 451
Ionic 597
iota small 32
  trifle 643
  (minute 193)
I O U security 771
  money 800
ipecacuanha 662
ipse dixit
  certainty 474
  affirmation 535
ipso facto 1
irascibility 901
irate 900
ire 900
iridescent 440
iridosmine 323
Iris traveler 268
  messenger 534
iris rainbow 440
  eye 441
irisated 440
irisation 440
Irish 188
  - green 435
Irishism 497
Irishman 188
irk 688, 830
irksome
  tiresome 688

difficult 704
  painful 830
  weary 841
iron strength 159
  smooth 255
  hard 323
  resolution 604
  - age adversity 735
  pain 828
  - cross 551, 733
  - entering into the
    soul 828, 830
  - gray 432
  - grip 159
  - gripe 781
  - heel 739
  - necessity 601
  - rule 739
  - sway 739
  - will 604
  rule with a rod of -
    739
iron-bound coast
  land 342
  danger 667
ironclad covering 223
  defense 717
  man of war 726
iron-handed 739
iron-hearted 861
ironic [see irony]
iron mold 434
irons 752
  fire - 386
  - in the fire
    business 625
    redundance 641
    active 682
    unskillful 699
  put in - 751
irony
  figure of speech 521
  untruth 546
  ridicule 856
irradiate 420
irrational number 84
  illogical 477
  silly 499
irreclaimable
  hopeless 859
  vicious 945
  impenitent 951
irreconcilable
  unrelated 10
  discordant 24
  unwilling 603
  intransigent 604
  opponent 710
  enmity 889
irrecoverable past 122
  hopeless 859
  (lost 776)
irredeemable
  hopeless 859
  (lost 776)
irreducible
  discordant 24
  out of order 59
  unchangeable 150
irrefragable 478
irrefutable certain 474

proved 478
irregular diverse 16a
  out of order 59
  multiform 81
  against rule 83
  - in recurrence 139
  distorted 243
  guerrilla 722
  combatant 726
irregularity 139
irrelation 10
irrelevant unrelated 10
  unaccordant 24
  sophistical 477
  unimportant 643
irreligion 989
irremediable bad 649
  hopeless 859
  (spoiled 659)
  (lost 776)
irremissible 945
irremovable 141, 150
irreparable
  hopeless 859
  (bad 649)
  (spoiled 659)
  (lost 776)
irrepentance 951
irreprehensible 946
irrepressible
  violent 173
  free 748
  excitable 825
irreproachable 946
irreprovable 946
irresilient 326
irresistible strong 159
  demonstration 478
  necessary 601
  impulsive 615
irresoluble 150
irresolution 605
irresolvable 87
irresolvedly 605
irrespective 10
irresponsible
  vacillating 605
  exempt 927a
  arbitrary 964
irretrievable stable 150
  lost 776
  hopeless 859
irrevealable 528
irreverence
  disrespect 929
  impiety 988
irreversible
  stable 150
  resolute 604
  hopeless 859
  (past 122)
irrevocable stable 150
  necessary 601
  resolute 604
  hopeless 859
irrigate 337
irriguous 339
irrision ridicule 856
  disrespect 929
irritable excitable 825
  irascible 901

irritate *violent* 173
  excite 824
  pain 830
  provoke 898
  incense 900
irritating
  [see irritate]
  stringent 171
irritation
  [see irritate]
  pain 828
  source of - 830
irruption *ingress* 294
  invasion 716
Irvingite 984
is - to be 152
  that - 118
ischiagra 378
ischialgia 378
Ishmael 83
isinglass 352
Isis 979
Islam 976
Islamism 984
island 44, **346**
islander 188

isle 346
isobar 338, 550
isobath 27
isocheimal 383
isochronal 27, 114
isochronize 120
isochronous 114, 120
isogamy 17, 161, 357
isolate *detach* 44
  seclude 893
isolated
  unrelated 10
  single 87
isomorph 240
isomorphism 240
isonomy 27
isoperimetric 27
isopiestic line 338, 550
isopolity 27
isotherm 550
isothermal 382
isotonic 413
isotropy 27
issue *distribute* 73
  focus 74
  event 151

effect 154
  posterity 167
  depart 293
  egress 295
  stream 348, 349
  inquiry 461
  publication 531
  book 593
  ulcer 655
  dénouement 729
  money 800
  at - *discussion* 476
  dissent 489
  negation 536
  opposition 708
  discord 713
  contention 720
  in - 461
  - a command 741
  join - *lawsuit* 969
issueless 169
isthmus
  connection 45
  narrow 203
  land 342
it *importance* 642

italics *mark* 550
  printing 591
  put in -
  importance 642
itch *titillation* 380
  disease 655
  desire 865
itching 380
  - palm 819
item *addition* 37, 39
  part 51
  speciality 79
  integer 87
itemize, 79, 594
iterance 104
iteration 104
itinerant
  moving 266
  traveler 268
itinerary
  journey 266
  guidebook 527
ivory 430
ivy
  cling like - 46
Ixion 312

J

jab 276
jabber *unmeaning* 517
  stammer 583
  chatter 584
jacal 189
jacent 213
jacet, hic - 363
jacinth 847
jack *rotation* 312
  ensign 550
  cards 840
Jack *sailor* 269
  - at a pinch 711
  - Cade 742
  - in office *director* 694
  bully 887
  - Ketch 975
  - of all trades 700
  - o' lantern 423
  - Pudding *actor* 599
  humorist 844
  - tar 269
jack-a-dandy
  buffoon 844
  fop 854
jackal *auxiliary* 711
  sycophant 886
jackanapes *fop* 854
  blusterer 887
jackass 271
jack boot 225
jackeroo 57
jacket 225
  cork - 666
jackleg 792
jackpot 775, 840
jackstones 840
Jacobin 710
Jacob's ladder 305
Jacquerie *tumult* 719
586

jactation 315
jactitation *tossing* 315
  boasting 884
jaculation 284
jade *horse* 271
  worn-out 659
  fatigue 688
  low woman 876
  scamp 949
  drab 962
jadu 621, 649
jag 257
  burden 190
  dent 257
jäger 726
jagged 244, 256
jaguar 440, 913
jail 752
jailbird *prisoner* 754
  bad man 949
jailer *keeper* 753
  punisher 975
jakes 653
jalousie 351, 424
jam *squeeze* 43
  pulp 354
  sweet 298, 396
  - in *interpose* 228
Jamaica
  - bayberry 400
  - pepper 393
jamb 215
jamboree 840
jammed in
  restraint 751
jampan 272
jane *woman* 374
jangle *harsh sound* 410
  quarrel 713
janissary 726

janitor 263
Jansenist 984
janty [see jaunty]
January 138
Janus *deceiver* 607
  tergiversation 607
  close the temple of -
  723
Janus-faced 544
japan *coat* 223
  resin 356a
  ornament 847
jaquima 752
jar *clash* 24
  vessel 191
  agitation 315
  stridor 410
  discord 713
  - upon the feelings 830
jardinière 191
jargon *absurdity* 497
  no meaning 517
  unintelligible 519
  neology 563
jarring 24, 414
jasper 435, 847
jaundice 436
jaundiced *yellow* 436
  prejudiced 481
  dejected 837
  jealous 920
  view with - eyes
  disapprove 932
jaunt 266
jaunting car 272
jaunty *gay* 836
  pretty 845
  stylish 852
  showy 882
  insolent 885

javelin 727
jaw *chatter* 584
  scold 932
jaw-fallen 837
jaws *mouth* 231
  eating 298
  - of death 360
jay 584
  dupe 547
jazz *music* 415
  dance 840
  - band 416
jealous 920
  - of honor 939
jealousy **920**
  suspicion 485
jeer *flout* 929
  (*joke* 842)
  (*banter* 856)
Jehovah 976
Jehu *traveler* 268
  director 694
jejune *incomplete* 53
  unproductive 169
  insipid 391
  style 575
  scanty 640
  wearying 841
  dull 843
jejunum 221, 350
jell 352
jellify 352
jelly 352
  beat to a - 972
jellyfish 368
jemadar 745
jemmy *lever* 633
  dandy 854
jennet 271
jenny 633

jeopardy 665
jerboa 309
jereed 727
jeremiad *lament* 839
  invective 932
  (*accusation* 938)
Jericho, send to - 297
jerk *start* 146
  throw 284
  pull 285
  agitate 315
jerkin 225
jerks, by - 70
  the - 315
jerky 315
jerry *deceived* 545
jerry-build 545
jerry-building 545
jerry-built 160, 545
Jerry Sneak
  coward 862
  knave 941
Jersey *cow* 366
jersey *clothing* 225
jessamy *affectation* 855
jest *trifle* 643
  wit 842
jest book 842
jester 844
jesting stock 857
Jesuit *deceiver* 548
  priest 996
jesuitical
  sophistical 477
  deceitful 544
Jesus 976
jet *stream* 348
  - black 431
jetsam 782
jettison 782
jetty *projection* 250
  harbor 666
jeu - de mots 842
  - d'esprit 842
  - de theatre 599
Jew. In the original
  edition Roget includ-
  ed the word Jew in
  several groups of syn-
  onyms. In this print-
  ing all uncompliment-
  ary racial allusions
  have been omitted.
jewel *gem* 648
  ornament 847
  favorite 899
  -s five words long 648
jewelry 847
  false - 545
jew's-harp 417
Jezebel *wicked* 913
  wretch 949
  courtesan 962
jhil 345
jhilmil 351
jib *reverse* 140
  front 234
  recoil 276
  regression 283
  cut of one's -
    form 240

appearance 448
jibe *concur* 178
jiffy 113
jig *dance* 840
  (*music* 415)
jigger 215, 272
jilt *disappoint* 509
  deceive 545
  deceiver 548
  dishonor 940
jilted 898
jimp 845
jingal 727
jingle 408
jingo *boaster* 884
  insolence 885
  blusterer 887
jingoism 884, 885
jinks, high - 840
jinn 980
jinrikisha 266, 272
jitney 272
jiujitsu 720
jiva 157
job *business* 625
  action 680
  unfair 940
  tough - 704
Job
  -'s comforter
  dejection 837
  hopeless 859
  patience of - 826
  poor as - 804
jobation 932
jobber *deceiver* 548
  tactician 700
  merchant 797
  trickster 943
jobbernowl 501
jobbery *cunning* 702
  improbity 940
jobbing *barter* 794
jockey *rider* 268
  deceive 545
  servant 746
jocose *gay* 836
  witty 842
jocoseness *fun* 840
jocular *gay* 636
  droll 842
jocund *gay* 836
  sportive 840
Joe Miller *wit* 842
  humorist 844
jog *push* 276
  shake 315
  - on *continue* 143
  trudge 266
  slow 275
  advance 282
  mediocrity 736
  - the memory 505
jogger *memory aid* 505
joggle 315
jog-trot *uniformity* 16
  trudge 266
  slow 275
  habit 613
John Doe and Richard
  Roe 4

Johnsonian 577
join *connect* 43
  assemble 72
  contiguous 199
  arrive 272
  party 712
  sociality 892
  marry 903
  - battle 722
  - forces 708
  - hands 708
  - in 778
  - in the chorus 488
  - issue *discuss* 476
  deny 536
  quarrel 713
  contend 720
  lawsuit 969
  - the choir invisible
    360
  - the majority 360
  - with 709
joining *meeting* 292
joint *junction* 43
  part 51
  accompanying 88
  concurrent 178
  meat 298
  low resort 621, 945
  - concern 712
joint stock
  coöperation 709
  participation 778
joint tenancy 778
jointure 780
joist 215
joke *absurdity* 497
  trifle 643
  wit 842
  ridicule 856
  in - 842
  mere - 643
  no - *existing* 1
  important 642
  practical -
  deception 545
  ridicule 856
  disrespect 929
  take a - 498
joker 844
  cards 840
joking apart
  affirmation 535
  resolution 604
jole 236
jollification
  amusement 840
  intemperance 954
jollity
  amusement 840
  sociality 892
jolly *plump* 192
  marine 269
  gay 836
  flattery 933
  - boat 273
  - fellow 892
jolt *impulse* 276
  agitation 315
jolthead 501
Jonah 621, 649

Jones
  Davy -'s locker 360
  Paul - 792
jongleur 597
jonquil 436
Jordan 360
jornada 200
jorum 191
Joseph 960
  -'s coat 440
joss 991
joss-house 1000
joss-stick 388
jostle *rush* 276
  jog 315
  clash 713
  contend 720
  (*disagree* 24)
jot *small* 32
  unimportant 643
jotting
  indication 550
  record 551
jounce 315
journal *annals* 114
  newspaper 531
  record 551
  magazine 593
  narrative 594
  accounts 811
journalism 551
journalist *recorder* 553
  representation 554
  author 593
journey 266
  -'s end 292
journeyman
  artisan 690
  servant 746
joust 720
Jove 979
  sub - *out of doors* 220
  air 338
jovial *gay* 836
  amusement 840
  social 892
Jovinianist 984
jowl 236
joy 827
  give one - 896
  - rider 274
joyful 836
joyless *painful* 830
  sad 837
J. P. 967
Juan, Don - 962
jubbah 225
jube 1000
jubilant *gay* 836
  rejoicing 838
  celebrating 883
  boastful 884
jubilate 884
jubilee *anniversary* 138
  celebration 883
jucundity 829
Judaism 984
Judas *deceiver* 548
  knave 941
  - kiss *hypocrisy* 544
  base 940

judge *intellect* 450
  decide 480
  interpreter 524
  justice 664
  master 745
  taste 850
  magistrate **967**
  - in a lump 465a
Judge *deity* 976
Judgment, Day of - 67
judgment *intellect* 450
  discrimination 465
  decision **480**
  wisdom 498
  condemnation 971
  sentence 972
judgment seat 966
judication 480
judicatory 965, 966
judicature 965, 966
judicial 965
  - astrology 511
  - murder 361
  - separation 905
judiciary 664
judicious 498
jug 191
juggernaut *kill* 361
  god 979
  idolatry 991
juggle *deceive* 545
  cunning 702
juggler 548
jugglery 545
jugulate 361
juice **333**
juiceless 340
juicy 339
jujube 396
julep 396

julienne *soup* 298
jumble *mixture* 41
  confusion 59
  derange 61
  indiscrimination
    465a
Jumbo 192
jument 271
jump
  sudden change 146
  leap 309
  neglect 460
  at one - 113
  - about 315
  - at *willing* 602
  pursue 622
  hasten 684
  consent 762
  seize 789
  desire 865
  - over 460
  - to a conclusion
  misjudge 481
  credulous 486
  - up 307, 309
jumper *clothing* 225
  vehicle 272
junction **43**
juncture
  circumstance 8
  junction 43
  period 134
jungle *disorder* 59
  vegetation 367
jungly 365
junior *secondary* 34
  youth 127
  student 492
juniority 34
juniper 367

junk 273
  lumber 645
junket *dish* 298
  merrymaking 840
Juno 920
junta 696
junto 712
jupe 225
jupiter 979
juramentado 988
jurat 967
juridical 965
jurisconsult 968
jurisdiction **965**
  authority 737
jurisprudence 963
jurist 968
juror 967
jury 967
  impanel a - 969
  - box 966
  - mast
  substitute 147
  refuge 666
juryman 967
jussive 567, 741
just *accurate* 494
  right 922
  equitable 939
  pious 987
  - as *similar* 17
  same time 120
  - do 639
  - in time 134
  - now 118
  - out 123
  - reasoning 476
  - so 488
  - then 113
  - the thing

  agreement 23
  exact 494
just *tilt* 720
juste milieu
  middle 68
  moderation 174
  mid-course 628
justice *judge* 664
  right 922
  honor 939
  magistrate 967
  administration   of
    965
  bring to - 969
  court of - 966
  do - to *eat* 298
  duty 926
  praise 931
  vindicate 937
  - seat 966
  not do - to 483
  retributive - 972
justiciary 967
justifiable *right* 922
  vindication 937
justification
  printing 591
  vindication 937
  religious 987
justle *push* 276
  contend 720
jut 214
jute 205
jut out 250
jutting over 214
jutty 250
juvenescent 127
juvenile *youth* 127
  actor 599
juxtaposition 199

K

Kaa 366
kachcha 674
kadi 967
kaffiyeh 225
kahin 996
kail 840
kaiser 745
kal 121
kala jagah 189
kala pani 341
kaleidophon 445
kaleidoscope 149, 428,
  445
Kali 979
kalpa 106, 109
kangaroo 309, 366
Kantianism 451
kantikoy 840
karma 922
karoo 169
karyaster 357
karyoplasmic 357
karyosome 357
kassis 996
Katerfelto 994
kavass 965

kayak 273
K. C. 968
keck 297
keddah 261
kedge *navigate* 267
  anchor 666
keel 211
  - upwards 218
keel boat 273
keelhaul 972
keen *energetic* 171
  sharp 253
  sensible 375
  cold 383
  intelligent 498
  poignant 821
  lament 550, 839
  eager 865
  - blast 349
keener
  mourner 363, 839
  schemer 702
keen-eyed 441
keenness [*see* keen]
  fastidiousness 868
keen-sighted 498

keen-witted 842, 498
keep *do often* 136
  persist 141
  continue 143
  food 298
  store 636
  provision 637
  refuge 666
  preserve 670
  citadel 717
  custody 751
  prison 752
  observe 772
  retain 781
  celebrate 883
  preserve 976
  - accounts 811
  - a good look out for
    507
  - alive *life* 359
  preserve 670
  - aloof *absence* 187
  distance 196
  avoidance 623
  - an account with 805
  - an eye upon 459

  - apart 44
  - a secret 528
  - a shop 625
  - a stiff upper lip 836
  - away 187
  - back *late* 133
  conceal 528
  dissuade 616
  not use 678
  restrain 751
  retain 781
  - body and soul to-
    gether *life* 359
  health 654
  - close 781
  - company 88
  - firm 150
  - from *conceal* 528
  refrain 623
  not do 681
  restrain 751
  - going *continue* **143**
  move 264
  - hold 150
  - holy 987
  - house 184

kitten *young* 129
   bring forth 161
   playful as a - 836, 840
kittereen 272
kitty *profit* 775
kleptomania
   insanity 502
   stealing 791
   desire 865
kleptomaniac 504
knack 698
   get into the - 613
knag 706
knap 306
knapsack 191
knarl 59
knave *deceiver* 548
   cards 840
   rogue **941**
knavery *deception* 545
   cunning 702
   improbity 940
   vice 945
knead *mix* 41
   mold 240
   soften 324
   touch 379
knee *angle* 244
   bend the - *stoop* 308
   submission 725
   down on one's -s
   humble 879
   fall on one's -s
   beg 765
   atone 952
   on one's -s *beg* 765
   respect 928
   on the -s of the gods
   152
knee-deep 208, 209
kneel *stoop* 308
   submit 725
   beg 765
   servility 886
   courtesy 894
   ask *mercy* 914
   respect 928
   worship 990
knell 363
   strike the death - 361

knickerbockers 225
knickers 225
knickknack 643, 847
knife 253
   - pleat 248
   play a good - and fork
   eat 298
   appetite 865
knight 875
   - errant *defender* 717
   rash 863
   philanthropist 910
   - marshal 745
   - of the road 460
   - service 777
   -'s move 279
   - Templar 712
knighthood 877
knit 43
   - the brow
   discontent 832
   anger 900
   disapprobation 932
   well - 159
knob *pendency* 214
   ball 249
   protuberance 250
knobby 206, 250
knock *blow* 276
   sound 406
   dispraise 932
   (*punish* 972)
   hard -s 720
   - at the door
   death 360
   request 765
   - down *destroy* 162
   lay flat 213
   lower 308
   injure 659
   dishearten 837
   - off *complete* 729
   - one's head against
   699
   - on the head *kill* 361
   - out 162
   - out blow 162
   - over 162
   - under 725
   - up 688

knock-down argument
   479
knocked
   - on the head
   failure 732
   - to atoms 162
knocker *instrument* 633
   detractor 936
knock-kneed 243, 244
knock-out 67
   - drops 649
knoll 206
knot *ligature* 45
   entanglement 59
   group 72
   length 200
   intersection 219
   distortion 243
   round 249
   convexity 250
   dense 321
   difficulty 704
   hindrance 706
   junto 712
   ornament 847
   tie the nuptial - 903
   true lover's - *love* 897
   endearment 902
knotted *rough* 256
knout 975
know *believe* 484
   knowledge 490
   friendly 888
   associate 892
   I'd have you -
   attend 457
   assertion 535
   I - better 536
   - by heart 505
   - for certain 484
   - no bounds *great* 31
   infinite 105
   redundance 641
   - nothing of 491
   - one's own mind 604
   - what one is about
   698
   - what's what 698
   - which is which 465
   not that one -s 491

knowing 702
knowingly 620
knowledge **490**
   [*see* know]
   acquire - 539
   come to one's - 527
   - of the world 698
   practical - 698
known 490
   become - 529
   - as 564
   - by 550
   make - *inform* 527
   publish 531
   well - 490
   habitual 613
knuckle 244
   - down 725
knuckle-duster 727
knur 250
knurl 250, 256
knurly 256
knurr and spell 840
kobold 979
kodak 445
Koh-i-noor 650
koniology 330
kooshti 720
Koran 986
kos 200
kosmos 318
kotow *bow* 308
   submission 725
   courtesy 894
   respect 928
kraal 189
kraken 83
kriegspiel 722
kris 727
Krishna 979
krupp 727
kucha 160, 321
kudos 931
Kuklux 712
Kultur 885
kurbash 975
kutcherry 802, 965
kyanization 670
kyanize 670
kyle 343

L

laager 717
labarum 550
labefy 659
label 550
labent 306
labial *lip* 231
   phonetic 561
labor *parturition* 161
   work 680
   exertion 686
   hard - *punishment* 972
   - for 620
   - in one's vocation
   625
   - in vain *fall short* 304
   useless 645
   590

   - of love *willing* 602
   amusement 840
   disinterested 942
   - under *state* 7
   disease 655
   difficulty 704
   feeling 821
   affliction 828
   mountain in - 638
laboratory 691
Labor Day 138, 840
labored
   style 579
   prepared 673
   - study 457
laborer 686, 690

laboring 686
   - man 690
   - oar 686
laborious *active* 682
   exertion 686
   difficult 704
labor-saving 633
labyrinth *disorder* 59
   convolution 248
   internal ear 418
   secret 533
   (*difficulty* 704)
labyrinthine 533
lac *number* 98
   resin 356a
   - of rupees 800

lace *stitch* 43
   netting 219
   ornament 847
   - one's jacket 972
lacerable 328
lacerate 44, 378
   - the heart 830
laches *neglect* 460
   nonobservance 773
lachrymation 839
lachrymose 837
   - gas 663
laciniate 256
lack *incompleteness* 53
   require 630
   insufficient 640

destitute 804
want 865
- faith 989
- of contrition 951
- preparation 674
- wit 501
lackadaisical
  inactive 683
  melancholy 837
  indifferent 866
lackadaisy!
  lament 839
  wonder 870
lackaday 839
lackbrain 499, 501
lacker [*see* lacquer]
lackey 746
lackluster 422, 429
laconic 572, 585
laconicism 572
laconize 572
lacquer
  covering 223
  resin 356a
  adorn 847
lacrosse 840
lacteal 352
lactescence 352, 430
lacuna *gap* 198
  pit 252
lacustrine 343
- dwelling 189
lad 129
ladder *ascent* 305
  way 627
  kick down the - 604
laddie 129
lade *load* 184
  transfer 185, 270
  contents 190
- out 297
laden 52
  heavy - 828
- with 777
lading *contents* 190
  property 780
  bill of - *list* 86
ladino 41, 271
ladle *receptacle* 191
  transfer 270
  vehicle 272
lady *woman* 374
  rank 875
  wife 903
- help 746
Lady day 138
ladylike *womanly* 374
  fashionable 852
  (*courteous* 894)
ladylove 897
lady's maid 746
lætificant 829
lag *linger* 275
  follow 281
  dawdle 683
lager-beer 298
laggard
  unwilling 603
  inactive 683
lagoon 343
lagniappe 784

laical 997
laicize 997
laid - by the heels 751
- low 160
- on one's back 158
- up 655
lair *den* 189
  sty 653
laird *master* 745
  proprietor 779
  nobility 875
Lais 962
laisser - aller, - faire
  permanence 141
  neglect 460
  inaction 681
  laxity 738
  freedom 748
  inexcitable 826
laity **997**
lake *water* **343**
  pink 434
- dwelling 189
- of fire and brim-
  stone 982
lakh 98
laky *red* 434
Lama *ruler* 745
  prince 996
Lamarckism 357
lamb *infant* 129
  food 298
  animal 366
  gentle 826
  innocent 946
  go out like a - 174
  lion lies down with-
  721
lamba-chauki 215
lambaste 972
lambency 379
lambent *touching* 379
- flame *heat* 382
  light 420
Lambeth 1000
lambkin 167, 223
Lamb of God 976
lame *incomplete* 53
  impotent 158
  weak 160
  imperfect 651
  disease 655
  injury 659
  failing 732
  (*bad* 649)
  (*lax* 738)
  help a - dog over a
  stile *aid* 707
  vindicate 937
- conclusion
  illogical 477
  failure 732
- duck 808
- excuse 617
lamellar 204
lamentable *bad* 649
  painful 830
  sad 837
lamentably *very* 31
lamentation **839**
  (*regret* 833)

lamenter 363
lamia *demon* 980
  sorcerer 994
lamina *part* 51
  layer 204
laminate 204
Lammas 998
lamp 423
- shells 368
  rub the - 992
  safety - 666
  smell of the -
  style 577
  prepared 673
lamplight 423
lamplighter
  quick 682
lampoon *censure* 932
  detraction 934
lampooner 936
lampreys 368
lanate 255, 256
lance *pierce* 260
  throw 284
  spear 727
  break a - with
  attack 716
  warfare 722
  couch one's - 720
- corporal 745
lanceolate 253
lancer 726
lancet *sharp* 253
  piercer 262
lanciform 253
lancinate
  bodily pain 378
  mental pain 830
land *arrive* 267, 292
  ground **342**
  estate 780
  how the - lies
  circumstances 8
  experiment 463
  foresight 510
  hug the - 286
  in the - of the living
  359
- flowing with milk
  and honey 168
  make the - 286
  on - 342
  see - 858
landamman 745
landau 272
landed *property* 780
- gentry 779
- estate 780
landgrave 745
landholder 779
landing place
  stage 215
  arrive 292
  refuge 666
landlady 779
landlocked 229
landloper 268
landlord *innkeeper* 637
  possessor 779
landlubber 268, 342,
  701

landmark *limit* 233
  measurement 466
  indication 550
landowner 779
landreeve 694
landscape *prospect* 448
- gardening
  agriculture 371
  beauty 845
- painter 559
- painting 556
landshark 792
landslide 306
landslip 306
landsman 268, 342
Landsturm 726
landsurveying 466
Landwehr 726
lane *street* 189
  opening 260
  way 627
langrage shot 727
langrel 727
langsyne 122
language **560**
  command of - 582
  strong -
  vigor 574
  malediction 908
languid *weak* 160
  inert 172
  slow 275
- *style* 575
  inactive 683
  torpid 823
languish *decrease* 36
  ill 655
  inactive 683
  repine 828
  affect 855
- for 865
languishing 160
languishment
  lament 839
languor [*see* languid]
laniate 162
lank *long* 200
lanky *thin* 203
  tall 200, 206
lantern *window* 260
  lamp 423
- jaws 203
- of Diogenes 461
  magic - 448
lanuginous 256
Laocoön 557
Laodicean 823
lap *flap* 39
  abode 189
  eager 204
  support 215
  interior 221
  wrap 225
  encompass 227, 229
  drink 298
  circuition 311
- of waves 405
- of luxury
  pleasure 377
  inactivity 683
  voluptuousness 954

lapdog *animal* 366
  servile 886
lapel 39, 258
lapidate *kill* 361
  attack 716
  punish 972
lapideous 323
lapidescence 323
lapidify 323, 357
lapis lazuli *blue* 438
  jewel 847
lappet 39
lapse *course* 109
  past 122
  conversion 144
  fall 306
  degeneracy 659
  relapse 661
  loss 776
  vice 945
  guilt 947
  - of memory 506
  - of time 109
lapsus linguæ
  mistake 495
  solecism 568
  stammering 583
larboard 239
larceny 791
larch 367
lard 355, 356
lardaceous 355
larder 636
  contents of the - 298
lares et penates
  home 189
  idols 991
large *quantity* 31
  size 192
  at - *diffuse* 573
  free 748
  liberated 750
  become - 194
  -number 102
  - type 642
large-hearted
  liberal 816
  benevolent 906
  disinterested 942
larger 194
largess 785
largest 784
largest portion 192
larghetto *slow* 275
  music 415
largiloquent
  verbose 573
largo *slow* 275
  music 415
lariat 45
larigo 45
lark *ascent* 305
  bird 366
  musician 416
  spree 840
  with the -
  morning 125
larmier 210
larrigan 225
larrikin 887, 913
larrup 972

592

larum *loud* 404
  alarm 669
larva 129, 193
larynx 351
lascar 269
lascivious 961
lash *tie together* 43
  violence 173
  whip 370
  incite 615
  censure 932
  punish 972
  scourge 975
  - into fury 900
  - the waves 645
  under the - *compelled*
    744
  subject 749
lashes *hair* 256
lass *girl* 129
  (*woman* 374)
lassitude *fatigue* 688
  weariness 841
lasso *tie* 45
  loop 247
last *abide* 1
  model 22
  - *in order* 67
  endure 106
  durable 110
  - *in time* 122
  continue 141
  at - 133
  at the - extremity 665
  breathe one's - 360
  die in the - ditch 604a
  game to the - 604a
  go to one's - home 360
  - but one &c. 67
  - finish 729
  - for ever 112
  - gasp 360
  - home 363
  - post 550
  - resort 666
  - shift 601
  - sleep 360
  - stage 67
  - straw 153
  - stroke 729
  - touch 729
  - word *affirmation* 535
    obstinacy 606
  - year &c. 122
  never hear the - of 104
  on - legs *weak* 160
    dying 360
    spoiled 659
    adversity 735
lastingness 141
latch *fasten* 43
  fastening 45
latchet 45
latchkey 631
latchstring
  find the - out 892
  have the - out 888
late *past* 122
  new 123
  tardy 133
  dead 360

  too - 135
lately *formerly* 122
  recently 123
latency 526
lateness 133
latent *inert* 172
  concealed 526
  influence 526
later 117
laterality 236
lateritious 434
latest 118
lateward 132, 133
lath 205, 635
  thin as a - 203
lathe *region* 181
  conversion 144
  machine 633
lather
  lubrication 332
  bubble 353
lathi 215
lathy 203
latifoliate 202
Latin - deities 979
  thieves' - 563
latitancy 528
latitat 969
latitude *extent* 180
  region 181
  breadth 202
  measurement 466
  map drawing 550
  freedom 748
  - and longitude
  situation 183
latitudinarian
  heterodox 984
  irreligious 989
latration 412
latria 990
latrine 653
latrocinium 791
latrociny 791
latter *sequent* 63
  past 122
Latter-day Saint 984
latterly 123
lattice *crossing* 219
  opening 160
  opening 260
laud *praise* 931
  worship 990
laudable 944
laudanum 174
laudation 883
laudator 935
laudatory 931
laugh 838
  - at *ridicule* 856
  sneer 929
  (*undervalue* 483)
  - in one's sleeve
  latent 526
  ridicule 856
  disrespect 929
  contempt 930
  - on the wrong side of
    one's mouth
  disappointed 509
  dejected 837

  in disrepute 874
  - to scorn *defy* 715
  despise 930
  make one - 853
  raise a - 840
laughable 853
laughing - gas 376
  no - matter 642
laughingstock 857
laughter
  [*see* laugh]
  - holding both his
    sides 838
laughter-loving 836
launch *begin* 66
  boat 273
  propel 284
  - forth 676
  - into 676
  - into eternity 360,
    361
  - out 573
  - out against 716
laundress
  washerwoman 652
  agent 690
  servant 746
laundry *room* 191
  heat 386
  clean 652
laundryman 652
laureate 875
  poet - 597
laurel *trophy* 733
  glory 873
  decoration 877
  (*reward* 973)
  repose on one's -s 265
lava *excretion* 299
  semiliquid 352
lavage 300
lavatory 386, 652
lave *water* 337
  clean 652
lavement 300
lavender *color* 437
laver la tête 932
lavish *profuse* 641
  give 784
  expend 809
  squander 818
  - of praise 931
law *regularity* 80
  statute 697
  permission 760
  legality 963
  court of - 966
  give the - 737
  go to - 969
  Jewish - 985
  - of the Medes and
    Persians 80
  lay down the -
  certainty 474
  affirm 535
  command 741
  learned in the -
  practice - 968 968
  set the - at defiance
    964
  so many -s 947

take the - into one's
  own hands
war 722
disobedience 742
lawless 964
take the - of 969
law-abiding 743
lawful *permitted* 760
  due 924
  legal 963
lawgiver *director* 694
  (*master* 745)
lawless *irregular* 83
  mutinous 742
  nonobservant 773
  vicious 945
  arbitrary 964
lawn *plain* 344
  sward 367
  agriculture 371
  fabric 635
  - *sleeves* 999
  - *tennis* 840
lawsuit 969
lawyer 968
lax *incoherent* 47
  soft 324
  error 495
  - *style* 575
  remiss 738
  nonobservant 773
  dishonorable 940
  licentious 945
  irreligious 989
laxative 652
  remedial 662
laxity **738**
laxness 738, 773
lay *arrangement* 60
  moderate 174
  place 184
  ley 344
  music 415
  poetry 597
  bet 621
  secular 997
  - about one *active* 682
  exertion 686
  attack 716
  content 720
  punish 972
  - apart *exclude* 55
  relinquish 782
  - aside *neglect* 460
  reject 610
  disuse 678
  give up 782
  - at one's feet 763
  - at the door of 155
  - bare 529
  - before 527
  - brother 996
  - by *store* 636
  provide 637
  sickness 655
  disuse 678
  - by the heels 162
  - claim to 924
  - down [*see below*]
  - eggs 161
  - figure

thing of naught 4
model 22
representation 554
- hands on *use* 677
take 789
rite 998
- heads together
advise 695
coöperate 709
- in *eat* 298
store 636
provide 637
- in ruins 162
- in the dust 162
- it on thick *cover* 223
too much 641
flatter 933
- on 972
- one's account for
  484
- oneself open to 177
- oneself out for 673
- one's finger upon
  480a
- one's head on the
  block 942
- on the table 133
- open *divest* 226
opening 260
show 525
disclose 529
- out *destroy* 162
horizontal 213
- *corpse* 363
plan 626
expend 809
- over 133
- siege to 716
- stress on 642
- the ax at the root
  of tree 162
- the first stone 66
- the flattering unc-
  tion to one's soul
content 831
relief 834
- the foundations
originate 153
prepare 673
- to *attribute* 155
rest 265
- together 43
- to one's charge 938
- train 626
- under hatches 751
- under restraint 751
- up *store* 636
sickness 655
disuse 678
- waste 162
lay down *locate* 184
horizontal 213
assert 535
renounce 757
relinquish 782
pay 807
- a plan 626
- one's arms
passification 723
submission 725
- one's life 360

- the law *certain* 474
assert 535
command 741
insolence 885
layer 204
layette 225
layman 997
laystall 653
lazar house 662
lazy *inactive* 683
  (*slow* 275)
lazzarone 683
lb. 319
lea *land* 342
  plain 344
leach 295, 335
leachy 335
lead *supremacy* 33
  in order 62
  influence 175
  tend 176
  soundings 208
  - *in motion* 280
  heavy 319
  induce 615
  direct 693
  authority 737
  heave the - 466
  - a dance
  run away 623
  circuit 629
  difficulty 704
  disrespect 929
  - a life 692
  - astray 495
  - by the nose 737
  - captive *subject* 749
  restraint 751
  - on 693
  - one to expect 511
  - the choir 990
  - the dance 280
  - the way
  precedence 62
  begin 66
  precession 280
  importance 642
  direction 693
  repute 873
  - to no end 645
  - to the altar 903
  red - 434
  take the -
  influence 175
  importance 642
  authority 737
leadable 298
leaden *dim* 422
  colorless 429
  gray 432
  inactive 683
leader *precursor* 64
  dissertation 595
  director 694
  counsel 968
  - writer 595
leaders *typography* 550
leadership 737
leading *beginning* 66
  important 642
  - article 595

- lady *actress* 599
- note *music* 413
- part 175
- question 461
- strings *childhood* 127
  child 129
  pupil 541
  subject 749
  restraint 751, 752
leads 223
leaf *part* 51
  layer 204
  plant 367
  - *of a book* 593
  - green 435
  turn over a new - 658
leafage 367
leafless 226
leaflet 531
leafy 256
league *combine* 48
  length 200
  coöperation 709
  party 712
leak *crack* 198
  dribble 295
  waste 638
  - out *disclosure* 529
  spring a-
  injury 659
leakage [*see* leak]
leaky *oozing* 295
  imperfect 651
lean *thin* 203
  oblique 217
  - on 215
  - to *shed* 191
  willing 602
  - towards *favor* 923
  - upon *belief* 484
  subjection 749
  hope 858
leaning *tendency* 176
  willingness 602
  desire 865
  friendship 888
  favoritism 923
lean-witted 499
leap *sudden change* 146
  ascent 305
  jump **309**
  by -s and bounds **274**
  - in the dark
  experiment 463
  uncertain 475
  chance 621
  rash 863
  - with joy 838
  make a - at 622
leapfrog 840
leaping 309
leap year 138
learn 539
  - by experience 950
  - by heart 505
learned 490, 539
  - man 492
learner 492, **541**
learning
  knowledge 490
  acquisition of - **539**

lease *property* 270, 780
  lending 787
  grant a - 771
  - and release 783
  take a new - of life 654
leasehold 780
leash *tie* 43
  three 92
  hold in - 751
least
  - *in quantity* 34
  - *in size* 193
  at the - 32
leather *skin* 223
  tough 327
  beat 972
  - or prunello 643
  nothing like - 481
leave *remainder* 40
  part company 44
  relinquish 624
  permission 760
  bequeath 784
  French - 623
  give me - to say 535
  - alone *inaction* 681
  freedom 748
  permit 760
  - a loophole 705
  - an inference 526
  - a place 293
  - in the lurch
  pass 303
  decisive 545
  - it to one 760
  - no trace
  disappear 449
  obliterate 552
  - off *cease* 142
  desuetude 614
  relinquish 624
  disuse 678
  - out 55
  - out of one's calcula-
    tion 460
  - the beaten track 83
  - to chance 621
  - to oneself 748
  - undecided 609a
  - undone 730
  - void *regret* 833
  - word 527
  take - *depart* 293
  freedom 748
leaven *component* 56
  cause 153
  lighten 320
  qualify 469
  deterioration 659
  bane 663
leavings *remainder* 40
  useless 645
lecher 962
lechery 961
lectern 1000
lection *special* 79
  interpretation 522
lectionary 998
lecture *teach* 537
  speak 582
  dissertation 595
594

censure 932
  sermon 998
  - room 542
lecturer *teacher* 540
  speaker 582
  preacher 996
lectureship 542
led - captain
  follower 746
  servile 886
  favorite 899
  - by the nose 749
ledge *height* 206
  horizontal 213
  shelf 215
  projection 250
ledger *list* 86
  record 551
  accounts 811
lee *front* 234
  side 236
leech *remedy* 662
  physician 695
Lee Enfield rifle 727
leef 829
leek 401
  eat the - *recant* 607
  submit 725
Lee-Metford rifle 727
leer *stare* 441
  dumb show 550
leery 702
lees 321, 653
lee shore
  danger 665, 667
leet, court - 966
lee wall 666
leeward 236
leeway *tardy* 133
  space 180
  navigation 267
  progression 282
  shortcoming 304
left *residuary* 40
  sinistral 239
  - alone 748
  - bower 840
  - in the lurch 732
  - to shift for oneself
    893
  over the - 545
  pay over the - shoul-
    der 808
left-handed *clumsy* 699
  - compliment 932
  - marriage 903
leg *support* 215
  walker 266
  food 298
  thief 792
  best - foremost 686
  fast as -s will carry
    274
  keep on one's -s 654
  last -s *spoiled* 659
  fatigue 688
  - bail 623
  light on one's -s 734
  make a - 894
  not a - to stand on
    illogical 477

  confuted 479
  failure 732
  off one's -s
    propulsion 284
  on one's -s
    upright 212
    elevation 307
    speaking 582
    in health 654
    active 682
    free 748
  set on one's -s 660
legacy *transference* 270
  property 780
  gift 784
legadero 45
legal *permitted* 760
  legitimate 924
  relating to law 963
  - adviser 968
  - estate 780
  - pledge 535
legality **963**
legalize 963
legate 534
legatee *transferee* 270
  possessor 779
  receiver 785
legation 755
legato 415
legend *record* 551
  description 594
legendary
  imaginary 515
  mythical 979
legerdemain
  change 146
  trick 545
  (*cunning* 702)
leggings 225
leghorn 225
legible 518
  - hand 590
legion *multitude* 102
  army 726
legionary 726
legisiation
  government 693
  legality 963
legislative
  - assembly 696
legislator 694
legislature 72, 696
legist 968
legitimate *true* 494
  permitted 760
  right 922
  due 924
  legal 963
legume 298, 367
legumin 321
leguminous 365, 367
Leibnitzianism 451
leiodermatous 255
leisure
  spare time **685**
  (*opportunity* 134)
  at one's - *late* 133
leisurely *slowly* 275
leman 897
lemma 476

lemon *fruit* 298
  sour 397
  color 436
  - pie 298
lemures 980
lend 787
  - a hand 680
  - aid 707
  - countenance 707
  - oneself to
    assent 488
    coöperate 709
  - on security 789
  - wings to 707
lender *creditor* 805
lending **787**
  - library 593
length **200**
  at - *in time* 133
  full - *portrait* 556
  go all -s
    resolution 604
    activity 682
    exertion 686
  go great -s 549
  - and breadth of 50
  - and breadth of the
    land
    space 180
    publication 531
  - of time 110
lengthen *increase* 35
  make long 200
  - out *diuturnity* 110
  late 133
lengthwise 200, 251
lengthy *long* 200
  diffuse 573
lenient *moderate* 174
  mild 740
  compassionate 914
lenify 174
lenitive
  moderating 174
  lubricant 332
  qualification 469
  remedy 662
  relieving 834
lenity **740**
lens 445
lens-shaped 245
Lent *fasting* 956
  rite 998
lenten 956
lenticular *curved* 245
  convex 250
lentiginous 330, 653
lentor *slowness* 275
  spissitude 352
  inactivity 683
  (*inertness* 172)
lentous 352
leonine verses 597
leopard *variegated* 440
  -'s spots
    unchanging 150
leper *outcast* 892
lepidote 330
Leprechaun 979
leprosy 655
lerret 273

- at one's door 926
- at the root of 153
- by 681
- down *flat* 213
  rest 687
- fallow 674
- hid 528
- in *be* 1
  give birth 161
- in ambush 528
- in a nutshell 32
- in one's power 157
- in wait for
  expect 507
  inaction 681
- on 215
- over *defer* 133
  destiny 152
- still 265
- to *quiescence* 265
  inaction 681
- under 177
- under a necessity
  601
white - 617
Liederkranz 416
Liedertafel 416
lief *pleasant* 829
as - *willing* 602
  choice 609
liege 745, 746
liegeman 746
lien *security* 771
  credit 805
lienteria 653
lieu 182
in - of 147
lieutenant *officer* 745
  deputy 759
  lord - 965
life *essence* 5
  events 151
  vitality **359**
  biography 594
  activity 682
  conduct 692
  cheerful 836
  animal - 364
  battle of - 682
  come to - 660
  infuse - into
    excite 824
  - and spirit 682
  - beyond the grave
    152
  - or death *need* 630
    important 642
    contention 720
  - to come 152
  put - into 359
  recall to - 660
  see - 840
  support - 359
  take away - 361
  tenant for - 779
Life, the 976
lifeblood *intrinsic* 5
  vital 359
lifeboat *boat* 273
  safety 666
life-giving 168
596

life guard 664, 726
lifeless *inert* 172
  dead 360
lifelike 17
lifelong 110
life preserver 666, 727
life saver 664
life-size 192
lifetime 108
life-weary 841
lift *raise* 307
  improvement 658
  aid 707
  - a finger 680
  - cattle 791
  - hand against 716
  - one's head 734
  - the mask 529
  - the voice *shout* 411
    speak 582
  - up the eyes 441
  - up the heart 990
lifting power 273
lift smoke 840
ligament 45
ligation 43
ligature 45
light *state* 7
  small 32
  window 260
  velocity 274
  arrive 292
  descend 306
  levity 320
  kindle 384
  match, illuminant
    388
  luminosity **420**
  luminary 423
  - *in color* 429
  white 430
  aspect 448
  knowledge 490
  interpretation 522
  unimportant 643
  easy 705
  gay 836
  loose 961
blue - *signal* 550
bring to -
  discover 480a
  manifest 525
  disclose 529
children of - 987
come to - 529
false -s 443
foot -s 599
half - 422
in one's own - 699
- and shade 420
- comedy 599
- fantastic toe 309
- heart 836
- horse 726
- infantry 726
- of heel 274
- of truth 543
- purse 804
- under a bushel
  hide 528
  not hide 878

modesty 881
- up *illumine* 420
  excite 824
  cheer 836
- upon one's feet 664
- upon *chance* 156
  arrive at 292
  discover 480a
  acquire 775
make - of
  underrate 483
  easy 705
  inexcitable 826
  despise 930
obstruct the - 426
see the - *life* 359
  publication 531
throw - upon 522
transmit - 425
lighten *make light* 320
  illume 420
  facilitate 705
lighter *boat* 273
lighterman 269
light-fingered 791, 792
light-footed *fleet* 274
  active 682
light-headed 149, 503
lighthouse 550
lightless 421
light-minded 605
lightning *velocity* 274
  flash 420
  spark 423
  omen 512
brief as the - 421
- express 272
- speed 274
Light of the World 976
lightsome
  luminous 420
  irresolute 605
  cheerful 836
lign-aloes 400
ligneous 367
lignite 388
lignography 558
ligulate 205, 245
like *similar* 17
  relish 394
  enjoy 827
  wish 865
  love 897
do what one -s 748
- a shot 274
- master like man 19
look - 448
likely 470, 472
  think - 507
  - to 176
likeness *copy* 21
  portrait 554
  bad - 555
likewise 37
likin 812
liking *willingness* 602
  desire 865
  love 897
have a - for 827
to one's - 829
lilac *color* 437

Liliputian 193
lilt *cheery* 836
  sing 416
lily *botany* 369
  white 430
  beauty 845
paint the - 641
lily-livered 862
lima beans 298
limæ labor *improve* 658
  toil 686
limature
  pulverulence 330
  friction 331
limb *member* 51
  instrument 633
  scamp 949
  - of the law 968
limber *fleet* 272
  pliable 324
limbo *prison* 751, 752
  pain 828
  purgatory 982
lime *fruit* 298, 367
  sour 397
  entrap 545
limekiln 386
limelight *luminary* 423
  publicity 531
  theater 599
limerick 497
limestone 635
limine, in - 66
limit *complete* 52
  end 67
  circumscribe 229
  boundary **233**
  qualify 469
  completion 729
  restrain 751
  prohibit 761
limitarian 984
limitation [*see* limit]
  estate 780, 783
limitative 8
limited
  - *in quantity* 32
  - *in size* 193
  - *train* 272
to a - extent
  imperfect 651
limitless 105
limn 554, 556
limner 559
limousine 272
limp *weak* 160
  slow 275
  supple 324
  fail 732
limpid 425, 570
limy 432
lin *lake* 343
  river 348
linaloa *fragrance* 400
lincture 662
linden 367
line *fastening* 45
  lineage 69
  continuous 69
  ancestors 166
  descendants 167

length 200
no breadth 203
string 205
lining 224
outline 230
straight 246
direction 278
music 26, 413
appearance 448
measure 466
mark 550
writing 590
verse 597
vocation 625
army and navy 726
between the -s 526
boundary - 233
draw the - 465
in a - continuous 69
straight 246
in a - with 278
- engraving 558
- of action 692
- of battle 69
- of battle ship 726
- of march 278
- of road 627
- of steamers 273
-s cue 51
read between the -s 522
sounding - 208
straight - 246
troops of the - 726
lineage kindred 11
series 69
ancestry 166
posterity 167
lineament outline 230
feature 240
appearance 448
mark 550
linear continuity 69
pedigree 166
length 200
linen 225, 635
linen draper 225
liner 273
lines fortification 717
reins 752
hard - adversity 735
severity 739
linger protract 110
delay 133
loiter 275, 291
- on time 106
lingo language 560
neology 563
linguacious 584
lingua franca 563
lingual language 560
speech 582
linguiform 245
linguist scholar 492
linguistics 560
lingulate 245
liniment ointment 356
remedy 662
lining 224
link relation 9
connect 43

connecting - 45
part 51
term 71
crossing 219
torch 423
missing - wanting 53
completing 729
linkboy 694
linked together
party 712
linn 343, 348
linoleum 223, 635
linotype 591
linseed oil 356
linsey-woolsey 41, 329
linstock 388
lint 223
lintel 215
lion animal 366
courage 861
prodigy 872
repute 873
come in like a - 173
heard -s roar 861
in the - 's den 665
- in the path 706
- lies down with the
lamb 721
-'s share more 33
chief part 50
too much 641
undue 925
lioness 374
lion-hearted 861
lionize curiosity 455
repute 873
lip beginning 66
edge 231
side 236
prominence 250
between cup and -
111
finger on the -s
silent 581
speechless 585
hang on the -s of 418
- homage flattery 933
- service falsehood 544
hypocrisy 988
- wisdom 499
open one's -s
speak 582
seal the -s 585
smack the - taste 390
savory 394
lipothymy 688
lipotype 187
lippitude 443
liquation 382
liquefaction 333, 335
- by heat 384
liquefy 382, 335
liquescence 335
liqueur drink 298, 392
sweet 396
liquid fluid 333
sound 405
letter 561
- diet 298
liquidate pay 807
assess 812

liquidator 801
liquidity 333
liquor potable 298
fluid 333
in - 959
- up 959
liquorish [see lickerish]
lisp 583
lissom 324
list arrange 69
catalogue 86
strip 205
leaning 217
fringe 231
hear 418
record 551
will 600
choose 609
schedule 611
arena 728
desire 865
enter the -s attack 716
contend 720
listed 440
listel 847
listen 418
be -ed to 175
- to 457
- to reason 498
listless inattentive 458
inactive 683
indifferent 866
litany worship 990
rite 998
literal imitated 19
exact 494
- meaning 516
manifest 525
letter 561
word 562
- meaning 516
- translation 522
literary 560
- hack 593
- man 492
- power 569
literati 492
literatim [see literal]
literature learning 490
language 560
lithagogue 662
lithe 324
lithic 323
lithify 323
lithograph 550, 558
lithoidal 358
lithology 358
lithomancy 511
lithotint 558
litigant litigious 713
combatant 726
accusation 938
litigation quarrel 713
contention 730
lawsuit 969
litigious 713
litotes 483
litter disorder 59
derange 61
multitude 102
brood 167

support 215
vehicle 266, 272
bedding for cattle 370
useless 645
littérateur scholar 492
author 593
Little - Bear 318
- Mary 191
little - in degree 32
- in size 193
darling 897
mean 940
bigoted 988
cost - 815
do - 683
- by little degree 26
slowly 275
- did one think 508
- name 565
- one 129
make - of 483
signify - 643
think - of 458
to - purpose
useless 645
failure 732
littleness 193
littoral 342
liturgics 998
liturgy 998
lituus 215
live exist 1
continue 141
dwell 186
life 359
glowing 382
activity 682
repute 873
- again 660
- and let live
inaction 681
freedom 748
inexcitability 826
- by one's wits 545
- circuit 157
- from hand to mouth
674
- hard 954
- in hope 858
- in the memory 505
- man 682
- matter 591
- on 298
- rail 157
- to explain 485
- to fight again 110
- upon nothing 819
- wire hustler 682
we - in deeds 680
livelihood 803
liveliness [see lively]
livelong 110
lively leap 309
keen 375
- style 574
active 682
acute 821
sensitive 822
sprightly 836
- imagination 515
- pace 274

liver *organ* 221
  hard - 954a
  white - 862
liver-colored 433
livery *suit* 225
  color 428
  badge 550
  decoration 877
  - *servant* 746
liveryman 748
livid *dark* 431
  gray 432
  purple 437
living *life* 359
  business 625
  benefice 995
  good - 957
  - *beings* 357
  - *room* 191
  - *soul* 372
  - *thing* 366
livraison 51, 593
livret 593
lixiviate 295, 335, 652
lixivium 335
lizard 366
  lounge - 683
llama 271
llano 180, 344, 367
Lloyd's register 86
lo! *attention* 457
  wonder 870
load *quantity* 31
  fill 52
  lade 184
  cargo 190
  weight 319
  store 636
  redundance 641
  hindrance 706
  adversity 735
  anxiety 828
  oppress 830
  - the *memory* 505
  - with 637
  - with reproaches 932
  prime and - 673
  take off a - of care 834
load line 466
loadstar [*see* lodestar]
loadstone
  attraction 288
  motive 615
  desire 865
loaf *mass* 192
  dawdle 683
  - *sugar* 396
loafer *stroller* 268
  inactive 683
  bad man 949
loafing *inaction* 681
loam 342
loan 787
loath *unwilling* 603
  dislike 867
loathe *dislike* 867
  hate 898
loathing [*see* loathe]
  weariness 841
loathsome
  unsavory 395
598

  painful 830
  dislike 867
loaves and fishes
  prosperity 734
  acquisition 775
  wealth 803
lobby *chamber* 191
  way 627
lobbyism 615
lobe *part* 51
  pendency 214
  - *of ear* 418
lobelia 434
lobiform 245
lob's pound, in - 751
lobster 298, 368
lobule 418
local 183
  - *board* 696
  - *habitation*
    location 184
    abode 189
locale 183
locality 182, 183
localize 184
locate 184
  be -d 183
location 182, **184**
loch 343
Lochaber ax 727
lock *fasten* 43
  fastening 45
  tuft 256
  canal 350
  hindrance 706
  prison 752
  dead - 265
  in the - up 938
  - *hospital* 662
  - stock and barrel 50
  - the stable door
    too late 135
    useless 645
    unskillful 699
  - up *hide* 528
    imprison 751
  - *weir* 350
  under - and key
    safe 664
    restraint 751
    prisoner 754
locker 191
locket 847
lockjaw 655
lockout *exclusion* 55
  insurrection 719
locksmith 690
lockup *prison* 752
locofoco 388
locomobile 266, 272
locomotion 264
  - by air 267
  - by land 266
  - by water 267
locomotive *travel* 266
  carriage 271
locos y ninos 450
locular 191
locum tenens
  substitute 147
  inhabitant 188

  deputy 759
locust *insect* 366
  prodigal 818
  evildoer 913
  swarm like -s 102
locution 566, 582
lode 636
lodestar *attraction* 288
  indication 550
  direction 693
lodestone
  [*see* loadstone]
lodge *place* 184
  presence 186
  dwelling 189
  - a *complaint* 938
lodgement 184
lodger *inhabitant* 188
  possessor 779
lodging 189
loft *garret* 191
  top 210
lofty *high* 206
  - *style* 574
  proud 878
  insolent 885
  magnanimous 942
log *length* 200
  velocity 274
  fuel 388
  measurement 466
  record 551
  - *book* 551
  - *canoe* 273
  - *house* 189
  - *line* 466
  heave the - 466
  sleep like a - 683
logan 314
loganberry 298
logarithm 84
logger 371
loggerhead 501
  at -s *discord* 713
  contention 720
  hate 898
logic 476
  - of facts 467
logician 476
logistics 85
logography 590
logogriph 533
logomachy
  discussion 476
  words 588
  dispute 720
logometer 85
logometric 84
Logos 976
logotype 591
logrolling 709
logy 843
loin *back* 235
  side 236
  gird up one's -s
  strong 159
  prepare 673
loin cloth 225
loiter *tardy* 133
  slow 275
  lag 281

  inactive 683
  (*temporize* 110)
Loki 978
loll *sprawl* 213
  recline 215
  inactive 683
lollipop 396
lollop 683
lolly 383
loma 206
lone 87
lonely 893
lonesome 893
long - *in time* 110
  - *in space* 200
  typography 550
  diffuse 573
  draw the - bow 549
  go to one's - account
    360
  - ago 122
  - and the short
    whole 50
    concise 572
  - but 800
  - clothes 129
  - drawn out 573
  - duration 110
  - expected 507
  - face *discontent* 832
    dejection 837
  - for 865
  - home *interment* 363
  - life to *glory* 873
    approval 931
  - odds *chance* 156
    improbability 473
    difficulty 704
  - pending 110
  - pull and strong pull
    285
  - range 196
  - robe 968
  - run *average* 29
    whole 50
    destiny 152
  - sea 348
  - since 122
  - time 110
  make a - arm
    exertion 686
    seize 789
  take a - breath
    refreshment 689
    relief 834
longanimity
  inexcitable 826
  forgiving 918
longboat 273
long chair 215
longevity
  diuturnal 110
  age 128
longevous 110
longhead
  wise man 500
long-headed *wise* 498
longiloquence 573
longing 865
longinquity 196
longish 200

longitude
  situation 183
  length 200
  measurement 466
  map drawing 550
longitudinal 200
long-limbed 200
long-lived 110
longness 200
longshoreman
  waterman 269
  preparer 673
  plebeian 876
long-sighted
  dim-sighted 443
  wise 498
  foresight 518
longsomeness 573
longspun 573
long-standing
  diuturnal 110
  old 124
long-suffering
  lenity 740
  inexcitable 826
  pity 914
longways 217
long-winded 573
loo 840
looby *fool* 501
  bungler 701
  clown 876
look *small degree* 32
  see 441
  appearance 448
  attend to 457
  - about *take care* 459
  seek 461
  - after *care* 459
  direction 693
  - ahead 510
  - another way 442
  - back 122
  - before one leaps 864
  - behind the scenes
    461
  - beyond 510
  - black *or* blue
  feeling 821
  discontent 832
  dejection 837
  - down upon 930
  - foolish 874
  - for *seek* 461
  expect 507
  - forwards *future* 121
  foresight 510
  - here 457
  - in the face
  sincerity 703
  courage 861
  pride 878
  - into *attend to* 457
  inquire 461
  - like *similarity* 17
  appearance 448
  - on 186
  - out *care* 459
  seek 461
  expect 507
  warning 668

  - over *examine* 461
  - round *seek* 461
  - sharp 682
  - through *seek* 461
  - to *care* 459
  duty 926
  - up *prosper* 734
  high price 814
  hope 858
  visit 892
  - upon as *adjudge* 480
  believe 484
  - up to *repute* 873
  respect 928
  approbation 931
looker-on 444
looking
  - before and after 441,
    673
  - forward to 507
looking-glass 445
lookout *view* 448
  intention 620
  business 625
  sentinel 668
loom *magnify* 31
  destiny 152
  dim 422
  dim sight 443
  come in sight 446
  instrument 633
  weave 691
  - large 525
  - of the land 342
loon *diving bird* 310
  fool 501
  clown 876
  rascal 949
loony 501
loop *curve* 245
  circle 247
  circuit 629
  looping the - 267
loophole *opening* 260
  vista 441
  plea 617
  device 626
  escape 671
  fortification 717
loose *detach* 44
  incoherent 47
  pendent 214
  desultory 279
  illogical 477
  vague 519
  - style 575
  lax 738
  free 748
  liberate 750
  debauched 961
  at a - end 685
  give a - to
  - *imagination* 515
  laxity 738
  permit 760
  indulgence 954
  let - 750
  - *character* 961
  - fish *bad man* 949
  libertine 962
  - morals 945

  - rein 738
  - suggestion 514
  - thread 495
  leave a - 460
  take up a - 664
  on the - 961
  screw - 713
loosen *make loose* 47
  let loose 750
looseness 573
loot *steal* 791
  booty 793
lop 201
  - and top 371
lopped *incomplete* 53
lopper 321
lop-sided 28
loquacious 562, 584
loquacity 562, 584
lorcha 273
Lord, lord *ruler* 745
  nobleman 875
  God 976
  - Chancellor 967
  - it over
  authority 737
  insolence 885
  - Justices 966, 967
  - lieutenant 965
  - of Lords 976
  - of creation 372
  - of the manor 779
  - of thy presence 745
  -'s day 687
  -'s prayer 990
  -'s supper 998
  -'s table 1000
  O - *worship* 990
  fhe - knows 491
lordling 875
lordly *repute* 873
  pride 878
Lord Mayor 745
  -'s show 883
lordship *authority* 737
  property 780
  title 877
  judge 967
lore 490, 539
lorette 962
Lorettine 996
lorgnette 445
loricated *clothed* 223
lorica 717
lorn 893
lorry 272
lose *forget* 506
  unintelligible 519
  fail 732
  loss 776
  - an opportunity 135
  - breath 688
  - caste *disrepute* 874
  dishonor 940
  - color 429
  - flesh 195
  - ground *slow* 275
  regression 283
  shortcoming 304
  - heart 837
  - hope 859

  - labor 732
  - no time *active* 682
  haste 684
  - one's balance 732
  - one's cunning 699
  - one's head
  bewildered 475
  - one's heart 897
  - one's life 360
  - oneself *uncertain* 475
  - one's reason 503
  - one's temper 900
  - one's way
  - sight of *blind* 442
  disappear 449
  neglect 460
  oblivion 506
  not complete 730
  - the clew
  uncertain 475
  unintelligible 519
  - the day 732
  - time 683
  wander 279
  unskillful 699
  difficulty 704
  no time to - 684
losel 893, 949
losing game
  failure 732
  misfortune 735
loss *decrement* 40a
  death 360
  evil 619
  deterioration 659
  privation 776
  at a - *uncertain* 475
  at a - for *desiring* 865
  - of fortune 804
  - of health 655
  - of life 360
  - of right 925
  - of strength 160
lost *nonexisting* 2
  absent 187
  invisible 449
  abstracted 458
  uncertain 475
  failure 732
  loss 776
  over-excited 824
  pain 828
  dejection 837
  impenitent 951
  - in admiration 931
  - in astonishment 870
  - in iniquity 945
  - in thought 458
  - labor 645
  - to shame
  insolent 885
  improbity 940
  bad man 949
  - to sight 449
  - to view 449
  - to virtue 945
lot *state* 7
  quantity 25
  group 72
  multitude 102
  necessity 601

599

chance 621
sufficient 639
allotment 786
be one's - 151
cast in one's - with
choose 609
coöperate 709
cast -s 621
fall to one's - 156
in -s 51
where one's - is cast 189
lota 191
loth [see loath]
Lothario lover 897
libertine 962
lotion liquid 337
clean 652
remedy 662
loto 840
lotto 156, 840
lottery chance 156
cards 840
put into a - 621
lotus-eater 683
loud noisy 404
unreserved 525
bad taste 851
loudness **404**
lough 343
lounge chamber 191
inactive 683
(quiet 275)
- lizard 683
loup garou 980
louse 653
lousiness 653
lousy 653
lout fool 501
clown 876
louver 349, 351
lovable 897
'ove desire 865
courtesy 894
affection **897**
favorite 899
abode of - 897
God's - 906
labor of -
willing 602
inexpensive 815
amusement 840
disinterested 942
- affair 897
- all trust a few 864
- of country 910
make - 902
no - lost 713
not for - or money
scarce 640
dear 814
love knot token 550
loveliness [see lovely]
lovelock 256
lovelorn 898
lovely beautiful 845
lovable 897
love making 902
love pot 959
lover [see love]
love-sick 897, 902
600

love story 897, 902
love token 897, 902
loving cup social 892
courteous 894
loving-kindness 906
low small 32
not high 207
- sound 405
moo 412
vulgar 851
disreputable 874
common 876
at a - ebb small 32
inferior 34
depressed 308
waste 638
deteriorated 659
bring - 308
in - automobile 275
- comedy 599
- condition 876
- estimation 929
- fellow 876
- green tent 363
- life 851
- note 408
- origin 876
- price 815
- spirits 837
- tide 207
- tone black 431
mutter 581
- water low 207
dry 340
insufficient 640
poor 804
lowborn 876
low-brow ignorance 491
lower inferior 34
decrease 36
hang 214
depress 207, 308
dark 421
dim 422
predict 511
sad 837
irate 900
sulky 901a
- case 591
- one's flag 725
- one's note 879
- orders 876
- quality 34
lowering hanging 214
ominous 668
hopeless 859
lowermost 207
lowlands 207
lowliness 879
lowly 879
low-minded
vulgar 876
base 940
lown fool 501
knave 949
lowness [see low] **207**
humility 879
loxic 217
loxodromic 217
loy 272
loyal obedient 743

observant 772
honorable 939
lozenge 244
L. s. d. 800
lubbard [see lubber]
lubber slow 683
bungler 701
lubberly huge 192
awkward 699
lubricant 332
lubricate oil 332, 355
smooth 255
lubrication smooth 255
oil **332**
lubricity slippery 255
lubrication 332
unctuous 355
impure 961
lubricous 332
lucent 420
lucid luminous 420
transparent 425
intelligible 518
rational 502
- style 570
- interval 502
lucidity [see lucid]
lucifer 388
Lucifer 306, 423, 978
lucimeter 445
luck chance 156, 621
prosperity 734
as - may have it 470
luckless 735
lucky occasion 134
successful 731
lucrative 775
lucre gain 775
wealth 803
Lucretia 960
luctation 720
lucubration 451, 590
luculent 420
lucus a non lucendo
dissimilar 18
misnomer 565
Luddites 712
ludibrous 840
ludicrous 853
luetic 655
luff 267
lug flap 39
pull 285
ear 418
luggage 270, 780
- van 272
lugger 273
lugubrious 837
lukewarm
temperate 382, 383
torpid 823
indifferent 866
lukewarmness
irresolution 605
[see lukewarm]
lull cessation 142
mitigate 174
silence 403
- by soft zephyrs 349
- to sleep 265
lullaby moderate 174

song 415
verses 597
inactivity 683
relief 834
lumbago 378
lumbar 235
lumber disorder 59
slow 275
store 636
useless 645
hindrance 706
lumbering unfit 647
ugly 846
lumber house
- of books 539
lumberjack 371
lumberman 371
lumber room 191
lumbriciform 249
luminary star 318
light **423**
sage 500
luminosity 420
luminous light 420
intelligible 518
lummox 501
lump whole 50
chief part 51
amass 72
mass 192
projection 250
weight 319
density 321
in the - 50
- of affection 855
- sugar 396
- sum 800
- together join 43
combine 48
assemble 72
lumper 690
lumpish [see lump]
ignorant 493
inactive 683
ugly 846
Luna 318
lunacy 503
lunar 318
- caustic 384
lunate 245
lunatic 503, 504
lunation 108
lunch 298
luncheon 298
lunge impulse 276
attack 716
lungi 225
lungs wind 349
loudness 404
shout 411
voice 580
luniform, &c. 245
lunkhead 501, 876
lupanar 961
lupine 789
lurch incline 217
sink 306
oscillation 314
failure 732
leave in the -
outstrip 303

deceive 545
  relinquish 624
left in the -
  defeated 732
lurcher *dog* 366
lure *draw* 288
  deceive 545
  entice 615
lurid *dark* 421
  dim 422
  reddish brown 433
lurk *unseen* 447
  latent 526
  hidden 528
lurking place 530
luscious *savory* 394
  grateful 829
lush *vegetation* 365
  drunkenness 959
lushy 959
lusk 683
lusory 840

lust *desire* 865
  concupiscence 961
  - quencher 866
luster *brightness* 420
  chandelier 423
  glory 873
lustily *loud* 404
  exertion 686
  cry out - 839
lustless 158
lustration
  purification 652
  atonement 952
lustrous *shining* 420
lustrum 108
lusty *strong* 159
  big 192
lute *cement* 45, 46
  guitar 417
luteolous 436
luteous 436
lutescent 436

Lutheran 984
lutose 653
luxation 44
luxuriant *fertile* 168
  rank 365
  sufficient 639
luxuriate 365
  - in *pleasure* 377
  delight 827
luxurious *pleasant* 377
  delightful 829
  intemperate 954
luxury *physical* - 377
  redundance 641
  enjoyment 827
  sensuality 954
  - of doing good 648
lycanthropy 503
lyceum 537, 542
lyddite 727
Lydford law 964
Lydian measure 415

lye 652
lying *decumbent* 213
  deceptive 544
  faithless 986
lymph *fluid* 333
  water 337
  transparent 425
lymphatic *slow* 275
  fluid 333, 337
  conduit 350
lynch 972
  - law 744, 964
lyncher 975
lynx 366
lynx-eyed *sight* 441
  careful 459
  intelligence 498
lyre 417
lyric *music* 415, 416
  - poetry 597
lyrist 597
lyssa 867

M

Mab 979
mabap 166
macadamize 255
macaroni 854
macaronic
  absurdity 497
  neology 563
  verses 597
macaroon 298
mace *weapon* 727
  scepter 747
mace bearer 965
macerate 337, 354
maceration
  saturation 337
  atonement 952
  asceticism 955
  rite 998
Macheath 792
Machiavel 702
Machiavellism
  falsehood 544
  cunning 702
  dishonesty 940
machicolation
  notch 257
  fortification 717
machination *plan* 626
  cunning 702
  -s of the devil 619
machinator 626
machine
  automobile 272
  instrument 633
  party 712
  be a mere - 749
machine gun 727
machinery 633
machinist
  theatrical - 599
  workman 690
macilent 203
mackerel 298
  mottled 440

procuress 962
  - sky 349, 353
mackinaw 225
mackintosh 225
mackle 591
macrobiotic 110
macrocolous 200
macrocosm 318
macrogamete 357
macrology 577
mactation 991
macula 848
maculate *unclean* 653
maculation
  variegation 440
  blemish 848
mad *insane* 503
  excited 824
  (violent 173)
drive one - 900
go - 825
  - after 865
  - with rage 900
madam 374, 877
madbrained 503
madcap
  violent 173
  lunatic 504
  excitable 825
  buffoon 844
  rash 863
madder *color* 434
made - man 734
  - to one's hand 673
madefaction 339
madid 339
madman **504**
madness [*see* mad]
Madonna *good* 948
  angel 977
  pious 987
madrigal *music* 415
  verses 597
madstone 993

Mæcenas *friend* 890
Maelstrom *whirl* 312
  water 348
  pitfall 667
maestro 415
maffick *exult* 884
magazine *record* 551
  book 593
  store 636
  - rifle 727
Magdalen 950
mage 994
magenta 434, 437
maggot *little* 193
  fancy 515
  caprice 608
  desire 865
maggoty
  fanciful 515
  capricious 608
  unclean 653
  - headed *excitable* 825
Magi *sage* 500
  sect 984
magic *influence* 175
  prediction 511
  sorcery 992
  - lantern
    instrument 445
    show 448
magician 548, 994
magilp 356a
magisterial *proud* 878
  insolent 885
magistery 330
magistracy
  authority 737
  jurisdiction 965
magistrate
  safety 664
  ruler 745
  justiciary 967
magistrature 737
magma 41

Magna Charta 769
magnanimity 942
magnate 875
magnet *attract* 288
  desire 865
magnetic *powerful* 157
magnetism *power* 157
  influence 175
  attraction 288
  motive 615
  animal - 992
magnetite 288
magnetize *power* 157
  influence 175
  attraction 288
  motive 615
  conjure 992
magneto
  automobile 272
magneto-electricity 157
magnetometer 157
magnetomotive 157
magnetoscope 157
magnificent *large* 192
  fine 845
  grand 882
  (magnanimous 942)
magnifico 875
magnifier 445
magnify *increase* 35
  enlarge 194
  overrate 549
  approve 931
  praise 990
magniloquent
  language 577
  boast 884
magnitude *quantity* 25
  greatness 31
  size 192
magnolia 367
magnum bonum 618
Magnus Apollo 500
magpie 584

malgre 179
malice *hate* 898
  spite 907,
  bear - *revenge* 919
  - prepense 907
malign *bad* 649
  malevolent 907
  detract 934
malignant 649, 901*a*,
  907
malignity 173, 907
malinger 544, 548, 655
malison 908
malkin *mop* 652
  slattern 653
mall *walk* 189
  opening 260
  club 276
malleable *soft* 324
  (*facile* 705)
mallet 276
malleus 418
malnutrition 655
malodor 401
malpractice 974
malt liquor 298
maltreat *injure* 649
  aggrieve 830
  molest 907
malversation
  rapacious 819
  guilt 947
mamelon 250
Mameluke 726
mamma 166
mammal 366, 368
mammalogy 368
mammiform 250
mammilla 250
Mammon 803
mammoth 192
man *adult* 131
  mankind 372
  male **373**
  prepare 673
  workman 690
  defend 717
  servant 746
  courage 861
  husband 903
make a - of *good* 648
  brave 861
  - among men 948
  - and a brother 372
  - and wife 903
  - at-arms 726
  - in office 745
  - in the street 876
  - of action 682, 686
  - of letters 271
  - of straw 545, 746
  -'s estate 131
one's - of business 758
Son of - 976
to a - 488
manacle *restraint* 751
  fetter 752
manage *influence* 175
  direct 693
  - to *succeed* 731
manageable *easy* 705

management
  conduct 692
  skill 698
manager *stage* - 599
  director 694
managery 693
man bird 269
mancipation 751
manciple 637
mandamus 741
mandarin 745
mandate
  requirement 630
  command 741
mandible 298
mandola 417
mandolin 417
mandragora 174
mandrel 312
manducation 298
mane 256
man-eater 361
manège *riding* 266
  equestration 370
manes 362
maneuver
  operation 680
  stratagem 702
  (*scheme* 626)
manful *strong* 159
  resolute 604
  brave 861
mange 380, 655
manger 191
mangle *separate* 44
  smooth 255
  injure 659
mangled 53
  [*see* mangle]
mango 298
mangosteen 298
mangy 380, 655
man hater 911
manhood 131, 861
mania *insanity* 503
  desire 865
  - a potu 959
maniac 504
Manichæism 451, 978
manichord 417
manicure 662
manie 865
manifest *list* 86
  visible 446
  obvious 525
  disclosure 529
  (*appear* 448)
  (*intelligible* 518)
manifestation **525**
manifesto 531
manifold *multiform* 81
  multitude 102
  automobile 272
  writing 590
  - *linguist* 492
manikin *dwarf* 193
  image 554
manipulate *handle* 379
  use 677
  conduct 692
manito 993

mankind **372**
manlike 131
manly *adolescent* 131
  strong 159
  male 373
  brave 861
  upright 939
manna *food* 396
  - in the wilderness
    aid 707
  pleasing 829
mannequin 554
manner *kind* 75
  style 569
  way 627
  conduct 692
by all - of means 536
by no - of means 602
in a - 32
to the - born 5
mannered 579
mannerism *special* 79
  unconformity 83
  affectation 855
  vanity 880
mannerly 894
manners *breeding* 852
  politeness 894
man-of-war
  ship 273, 664
  combatant 726
man-of-war's man 269
manor 780
  lord of the - 779
  - house 189
manorial 780
mansard 223
  - roof 244
manse 1000
mansion 189
manslaughter 361
mansuetude 894
mantelpiece 215
mantilla 225
mantle *spread* 194
  dress 225
  foam 353
  shade 424
  redden 434
  robes 747
  flush 821, 824
  anger 900
mantlet *cloak* 225
  defense 717
mantology 511
manual *guide* 527
  schoolbook **542**
  book 593
  advice 695
  - labor 686
manubial 793
manufactory 691
manufacture 161, 680
manufacturer 690
manu forti 604, 686,
  739
manumission 750
manumotor 272
manure *agriculture* 371
  dirt 653
  aid 707

manuscript 21, 590
many 102
  frequency 136
  for - a day 110
  - irons in the fire 682
  - men many minds
    489
  - times *repeated* 104
  frequent 136
  the - 876
many-colored 428, 440
manyplies 191
many-sided
  multiform 81
  sides 236
many-tongued 532
map *information* 527
  representation 554
  - of days outworn 236
  - out 626
maple 367
  - sugar 396
  - syrup 396
mar *deface* 241
  spoil 659
  botch 699
  obstruct 706
marabou 41
Marabout 1000
marah 395
maranatha 908
marasmus
  shrinking 195
  atrophy 655
  deterioration 659
Marathon race 274
maraud 791
marauder 792
marble *ball* 249
  hard 323
  sculpture 557
  tablet 590
  materials 635
  insensible 823
marble-constant 939
marbled 440
marble-hearted 907
marcescence 659
march *region* 181
  journey 266
  progression 282
  music 415
  dead - 363
  forced - 684
  - against 716
  - of events 151
  - off 293
  - of intellect
    knowledge 490
  improvement 658
  - of time 109
  - on a point 278
  - past 882
  - with 199
  on the - 264
  steal a - *advance* 280
  go beyond 303
  deceive 545
  active 682
  cunning 702
March, Ides of - 601

marches 233
marchioness 875
marchpane 298
marcid 203
marconigram 532
marcor 203
Mardi gras 840
mare *horse* 271
  female 374
marechal 745
mare's-nest 497, 546
mare's-tail *wind* 349
  cloud 353
margin *space* 180
  edge 231
  redundance 641
  latitude 748
marginate 231
margrave
  master 745
  nobility 875
mariage de conve-
  nance 903
marigraph 348
marinate 337
marine *fleet* 273
  sailor 269
  oceanic 341
  safety 664
  soldier 726
  -painter 559
  - painting 556
  tell it to the -s 497
mariner 269
Marinism 579
Mariolatry 991
marionette
  representation 554
  drama 599
marish 345
marital 903
maritime
  navigation 267
  ship 273
  oceanic 241
mark *degree* 26
  term 71
  take cognizance 450
  attend to 457
  measurement 466
  indication 550
  record 551
  writing 590
  object 620
  importance 642
  repute 873
  beyond the - 303
  leave one's - 873
  man of -
    repute 873
    rank 875
  - of Cain 550
  - off 551
  - of recognition 894
  - out *choose* 609
    plan 626
    command 741
  - time
    chronometry 114
    halt 265
    expectation 507

- with a red letter 883
- with a white stone
  931
near the - 197
overshoot the - 699
put a - upon 457
save the - 870
up to the -
  enough 639
  good 648
  skill 698
  due 924
wide of the -
  distant 196
  error 495
within the - 304
marked [*see* mark]
  great 31
  special 79
  affirmed 535
in a - degree 31
- down *cheap* 815
well - 446
marker *interment* 363
market *provision* 637
  consumer 677
  buy 795
  mart 799
  bring to - 796
  buy in the cheapest
    &c. - 794
  in the - *offered* 763
    barter 794
    sale 796
  - garden 371
  - overt *manifest* 525
  - place *street* 189
    mart 799
  - price 812
  public - 637
  rig the - 794
marketable 794, 796
marksman 700
marksmanship 698
marl 342
marmalade 396
marmoreal 430
marmot 683
maroon *brown* 433
  red 434
  fugitive 623
  abandon 782
  outlaw 893
marplot *bungler* 701
  obstacle 706
  malicious 913
marque, letters of -
  791
marquee 223
marquetry
  variegated 440
marquis 875
marquisate 877
marriable 131
marriage 903
  ill-assorted - 904
  - bell 836
  - broker 903
marriageable
  adolescent 131
  nubile 903

married
  903
- man 903
- woman 903
marrow *essence* 5
  interior 221
  central 222
  (*meaning* 516)
  (*importance* 642)
  chill to the - 385
marrowbones, on
  one's -
  submit 725
  beg 765
  humble 879
  servile 886
  atonement 952
marrowless 158
Marrubium 400
marry *combine* 48
  assertion 535
  wed 903
  - come up
  defiance 715
  anger 900
  censure 932
Mars 722
  - orange 439
marsh 345
  - gas 663
marshal *arrange* 60
  messenger 534
  auxiliary 711
  officer 745
Marshalsea 752
marshy 345
marsupial 191, 368
mart 799
martello tower 206, 717
martial 722
  court - 966
  - law *severe* 739
  compulsory 744
  illegal 964
  - music 415
martinet 739
martingale 752
Martinmas 998
martyr
  bodily pain 378
  mental pain 828
  ascetic 955
  punishment 972
  - to disease 655
martyrdom *killing* 361
  agony 378, 828
  unselfish 942
  punishment 972
marvel *wonder* 870
  prodigy 872
  - whether 514
marvelous *great* 31
  wonderful 870
deal in the - 549
Masaniello 742
mascot 621, 993
masculine *strong* 159
  male 373
mash *mix* 41
  disorder 59
  soft 324

  semiliquid 352
  pulpiness 354
masher 854
masjid 1000
mask *dress* 225
  shade 424
  concealment 528
  ambush 530
  deceit 545
  shield 717
  put on the - 544
masked *concealed* 528
  - battery 667
masker 599
masochism 659
mason 690
Masonic 712
Masorah 985
masque 599
masquerade
  dress 225
  concealment 528
  deception 545
  frolic 840
  - dress 530
masquerader 528
Mass *worship* 990
  Eucharist 998
  - book 998
mass *quantity* 25
  much 31
  whole 50
  heap 72
  size 192
  gravity 319
  density 321
  in the - 50
  - of society 876
massacre 361
massage 324, 331, 379,
  662
masses, the - 876
masseur 331, 662
massicot 436
massive *huge* 192
  heavy 319
  dense 321
mast 206
mastaba 363
master, Master
  boy 129
  influence 175
  man 373
  know 490
  understand 518
  learn 539
  teacher 540
  director 694
  proficient 698, 700
  succeed, conquer 731
  ruler 745
  possession 777
  possessor 779
  title 877
  eye of the - 693
  hard - 739
  - hand 700
  - key *open* 260
  instrument 631
  - mariner 269
  - mind *sage* 500

proficient 700
- of Arts 492
- of one's time 685
- of self 604
- of the position 731
- of the revels 840
- of the Rolls
  recorder 553
  judge 967
- of the situation
  success 731
  authority 737
- one's feelings 826
- one's passions 944
- passion 820
- spirit of the age
  sage 500
  repute 873
past - 700
masterdom 737
masterpiece *good* 648
  perfect 650
  skill 698
masterstroke *plan* 626
  masterpiece 650
  success 731
masterwork 698
mastery *success* 731
  authority 737
  get the - of 175
masthead
  punish 972
mastic *viscid* 352
  resin 356a
masticate 298, 354
mastiff 366
mastology 368
mat *support* 215
  woven 219
  roughness 256
  doormat 652
matador 361
match *similar* 17
  copy 19
  equal 27
  fuel 388
  retaliate 718
  contest 720
  marriage 903
matchless *unequal* 28
  supreme 33
  virtuous 944
  best 648
  (*perfect* 650)
matchlock 727
matchmaker
  marriage 903
mate *similar* 17
  equal 27
  duality 89
  auxiliary 711
  master 745
  friend 890
  wife 903
  check - 732
maté 298
mater, alma - 542
- *familias* 166
material *substance* 316
  stuff 635
  important 642

- *existence* 316
- for thought 454
- point 32
materialism *matter* 316
  heterodoxy 984
  irreligion 989
materiality
  substantiality 3
  matter **316**
  importance 642
materialization
  materiality 316
  manifestation 525
  spiritualism 992a
materialize 316, 446
materials **635**
materia medica 662
matériel 316, 633
maternal *parental* 166
  benevolent 906
- *love* 897
maternity 166
mathematical
  precise 494
- *point* 193
mathematician 85
mathematics 25
mathesis 25
matin 125
matinée 892
- *idol* 899
matins 125, 990
matrass 191
matriarch 166
matriarchy 737
matriculate 86
matriculation 539
matrimonial 903
- *agency* 903
matrimony *mixture* 41
  wedlock 903
matrix *mold* 22
  printing 591
  workshop 691
matron *woman* 374
  married 903
- of honor
  marriage 903
matronize 459, 693
matronly *age* 128
  adolescent 131
matross 726
matter *substance* 3
  copy 21
  material world 316
  topic 454
  meaning 516
  printing 591
  business 625
  importance 642
  pus 653
  in the - of 9
- in dispute 461
- in hand *topic* 454
  business 625
- nothing 643
- of course
  conformity 82
  certain 474
  habitual 613
- of fact *event* 151

  certainty **474**
  truth 494
- of indifference 866
- of no consequence 4
-s *affairs* 151
no - 460
the wreck of - 59
what - 643
what's the -
  curiosity 455
  inquiry 461
matter-of-fact
  prosaic 576
  artless 703
  dull 843
mattock 253
mattress 215
maturate 650, 673
maturative 662
mature *old* 124
  adolescent 131
  conversion 144
  scheme 626
  perfect 650
  improve 658
  prepare 673
  completing 729
- *thought* 451
Maturine 996
maturity
  [*see* mature]
  bring to - 729
matutinal
  morning 125
  (*early* 132)
matzo 298
maudlin *inactive* 683
  sentimental 822
  drunk 959
mauger 30, 179
maukin 652
maul *hammer* 276
  hurt 649
- and wedges 780
maund *basket* 191
  mumble 583
maunder
  diffuse style 573
  mumble 583
  loquacity 584
  lament 839
Maundy Tuesday 138
Mauser rifle 727
mausoleum 363
mauvais
- goût 851
- quart d'heure 828
- sujet 949
- ton 851
mauve 437
mavis 366, 416
maw 191
mawkish 391
mawworm
  deceiver 548
  sham piety 988
maxim 80, **496**
maximal 33
Maxim gun 727
maximum *supreme* 33
  summit 210

may be 470
  as it - 156
May Day 840
May fly 111
mayhap 470
mayor 745
maypole 206
May queen 847
mazard 298
maze *convolution* 248
  enigma 533
  difficulty 704
  (*ignorance* 491)
  in a - *uncertain* 475
mazed 503
mazurka 840
mazy 533
me 317
mead *plain* 344
  field 367
  sweet 396
meadow *plain* 344
- land 371
meager *small* 32
  incomplete 53
  thin 203
- *style* 575
  scanty 640
  poor 643
- *diet* 956
meal *repast* 298
  powder 330
mealy-mouthed
  falsehood 544
  servile 886
  flattering 933
mean *average* **29**
  small 32
  middle 68
  interjacent 228
  signify 516
  intend 620
  contemptible 643
  stingy 819
  shabby 874
  ignoble 876
  sneaking 886
  base 940
  selfish 943
  golden - 174
- nothing 517
- parentage 876
- wretch 949
  take the - 774
meander
  convolution 248
  deviate 279
  circuition 311
  river 348
  maze 533
meandering
  diffuse 573
meaning **516**
meaningless 517
meanness
  inferiority 34
  [*see* mean]
means *appliances* **632**
  property 780
  wealth 803
  by all - 602

mendicity 804
menial *servant* 746
  rustic 876
meniscal 245
meniscus 245, 445
menses 138, 299
menstrual 138
menstruum 335
mensuration 466
mental 450
  - acquisitiveness 455
  - calm 826
  - cultivation 539
  - excitement 824
  - healing 984
  - pabulum 454
  - philosophy 450
  - poise 498
  - reservation 528, 543
  - suffering 828
mentality 450
mentalize 451
mentation 451
menticulture 490, 658
mention 527
  above -ed 104
  not worth -ing 543
mentor *sage* 500
  teacher 540
  adviser 695
mentum 234
menu *list* 86
  food 298
Mephistopheles 978
Mephistophelian 945
mephitic *fetid* 401
  deleterious 654
mephitis 663
meracious 392
mercantile 794
mercatoria, lex - 963
mercature 794
mercenary *soldier* 726
  servant 746
  price 812
  parsimonious 819
  selfish 943
mercer 225
merchandise **798**
merchant **797**
merchantable 795
merchantman 273
merciful 914
merciless 914*a*
mercurial
  changeable 149
  mobile 264
  quick 274
  excitable 825
mercurous chloride 662
Mercury *traveler* 268
  quick 274
  messenger 534
  -'s rod 747
mercy *lenity* 740
  pity 914
  at the - of *liable* 177
  subject 749
  cry you - 766
  for -'s sake 765
  have no - 914*a*

- on us! 870
- seat 966
mere *simple* 32
  lake 343
  trifling 643
  buy for a - nothing
    815
- nothing *small* 32
  trifle 643
- pretext 617
- words 477
- wreck 659
merelles 840
meretricious
  false 495
  vulgar 851
  licentious 961
merge *combine* 48
  include 76
  insert 300
  plunge 337
- in 56
- into *become* 144
merged 228
merger 712
meridian *region* 181
  room 125
  summit 210
  light 420
  map drawing 550
- of life 131
meridional 125, 237
meringue 298
merit *goodness* 648
  due 924
  virtue 944
  make a - of 884
- notice 642
merito, e - 944
meritorious 931
mermaid *monster* 83
  ocean 341
  mythology 979
merman 341
meroblast 357
merogenesis 161
merriment
  cheerful 836
  amusement 840
merry *cheerful* 836
  drunk 959
  make - *sport* 840
  make - with *wit* 842
  ridicule 856
- and wise 842
- as the day is long
  836
- heart 836
  wish a - Christmas
    &c. 896
merry-andrew 844
merry-go-round 840
merrymaking *revel* 840
  sociality 892
merrythought 842, 993
mersion 337
mesa 344
mésalliance
  ill-assorted 24
  marriage 903
meseems 484

mesh *interstices* 198
  crossing 219
meshes *trap* 545
  difficulty 704
- of sophistry 477
mesial *middle* 68
  (central 222)
mesilla 344
mesmerism 992
mesmerist 992*a*
mesne 228
- lord 779
mesoblast 357
mess *mixture* 41
  disorder 59
  derangement 61
  meal 298
  difficulty 704
  portion 786
  make a - *unskillful* 699
  fail 732
message *dispatch* 527
  intelligence 532
  command 741
Messalina 962
messenger *traveler* 268
  cloud 353
  envoy **534**
  servant 746
- balloon 463
Messiah 976
messmate 890
messuage 189, 780
mestee 41
mestizo 41
metabatic 264
metabola 140
metabolism 140, 357
metabolize 140
metacenter 222
metachronism 115
metage 466
metagenesis 140
metagrammatism 561
metal 635
  Britannia - 545
metalepsis 521
metallic *harsh* 410
metallurgy 358
metamorphosis 140
metamorphotic 81
metaphor
  comparison 464
  figure 521
  (analogy 17)
metaphrase 522
metaphrast 524
metaphrastic 516
metaphysics 450
metaplasm 357
metasomatism 140
metastasis *change* 140
  inversion 218
  displacement 270
metathesis *change* 140
  inversion 218
  displacement 270
  metaphor 521
mete *measure* 466
  distribute 786
- out *give* 784

metempirical 519
metempsychosis 140
meteor
  heavenly body 318,
    353
  luminary 423
meteoric *transient* 111
  violent 173
  light 420
meteorite 318
meteorology 338, 353
meteoromancy 466
meter *length* 200
  measure 333, 466
  versification 597
methane 663
metheglin 396
methinks 484
method *order* 58
  way **627**
  want of - 59
methodical *arranged* 60
  regular 80, 138
  businesslike 692
Methodist 984
methodist *formalist*
  988
methodize 58, 60
Methuselah 130
  old as - 128
  since the days of -
    124
metic 57
meticulosity 457, 459,
  868
meticulous *exact* 494
  observant 772
  fastidious 868
métis 83
metogenesis 161
metonymy 521
metopic 234
metoposcopist 234, 448
metoposcopy
  front 234
  appearance 448
  interpret 522
metrical *measured* 466
  verse 597
metrocracy 737
metrology 466
metropolis 189, 222
metropolitan
  archbishop 996
mettle *energy* 171
  spirit 820
  courage 861
  man of - 861
  on one's -
  resolved 604
  put on one's -
  excite 824
  encourage 861
mettlesome
  energetic 171
  sensitive 822
  excitable 825
  brave 861
meum et tuum 777, 780
  disregard distinction
    between - 791

minded *willing* 602
  intending 620
mindful *attentive* 457
  memory 505
mindless
  inattentive 458
  imbecile 499
  forgetful 506
  insensible 823
mine *sap* 162
  hollow 252
  open 260
  snare 545
  intrigue 626
  store 636
  abundance 639
  damage 659
  intrench 664
  pitfall 667
  attack 716
  defense 717
dig a - *plan* 626
  prepare 673
- layer 726
- of wealth 803
spring a -
  unexpected 508
  attack 716
miner 252
sapper and - 726
mineral 358
- oil 356
mineralize 358
mineralogy 358
Minervâ invitâ
  unwilling 603
  difficult 704
Minerva press
  fustian 577
mingle 41
miniature *small* 32, 193
  portrait 556
- painter 559
Minié rifle 727
minikin 32, 193
minim *small* 32
  music 413
minimifidian 487
minimize 36, 483
minimum *small* 32
  inferior 34
minion 899
minister
  instrumentality 631
  remedy 662
  agent 690
  director 694
  aid 707
  deputy 759
  give 784
  clergy 996
  rites 998
- to *help* 746
ministerial
  clerical 995
ministering - angel 948
- spirit 977
ministration
  direction 693
  aid 707
  rite 998

ministry *direction* 693
  aid 707
  church 995
  clergy 996
  rite 998
minium 434
miniver 223
minnesinger 597
minnow 193
minor *inferior* 34
  infant 129
- key 413
- poet 597
Minorites 996
minority *few* 103
  youth 127
Minos 694
minotaur 83
minster 1000
minstrel *musician* 416
  poet 597
minstrelsy 415
mint *mold* 22
  fragrance 400
  workshop 691
  wealth 803
- julep 298
minuend 38
minuet *music* 415
  dance 840
minus *inexistent* 2
  less 34
  subtracted 38
  absent 187
  deficient 304
  loss 776
  in debt 806
  nonpayment 808
minusculæ 561
minute
  circumstantial 8
- *in degree* 32
  special 79
- *of time* 108
  instant 113
- *in size* 193
  record 551
  compendium 596
  (*unimportant* 643)
- account 594
- attention 457
to the - 132
minutemen 726
minuteness *care* 459
minutiæ *small* 32
  details 79
  unimportant 643
minx *girl* 129
  malapert 887
  wanton 962
miosis 483
mir 188
miracle *exceptional* 83
  prodigy 872
- play 599
miraculous
  wonderful 870
mirage 443
mire 653
mirror *imitate* 19
  reflector 445

  perfection 650
  glory 873
hold the - up to na-
  ture 554
hold up the - 525
  magic - 443
mirth 836
misacceptation 523
misadventure
  contretemps 135
  adversity 735
  (*evil* 619)
  (*failure* 732)
misadvised 699
misanthropy 911
misapply
  misinterpret 523
  misuse 679
  mismanage 699
misapprehend
  mistake 495
  misinterpret 523
misappropriate 679
misarrange 61
misbecome 925
misbegotten
  crooked 243
  vicious 945
misbehave *vulgar* 851
  vice 945
misbehavior
  discourtesy 895
  guilt 947
misbelief 485
misbeliever 487, 984
miscalculate
  misjudge 481
  err 495
  disappoint 509
miscall 565
miscarry 732
miscegenation 41, 903
miscellany
  mixture 41
  collection 72
  generality 78
  compendium 596
  poetry 597
mischance *evil* 619
  misfortune 735
  (*failure* 732)
mischief 619
do - 649
make - 649
mischief-maker
  evildoer 913
  knave 941
mischievous 649
miscible 41
miscite 544
miscompute
  misjudge 481
  mistake 495
misconceive
  mistake 495
  misinterpret 523
misconception 495, 523
misconduct
  bungling 699
  guilt 947
- oneself 945

misconjecture 481
misconstrue 523
miscorrect 538
miscount 495
miscreance 485
miscreant 487, 949
miscreated 945
misdate 115
misdeed 947
misdemean 945
misdemeanant 949, 975
misdemeanor 947
misdescribe 538
misdevotion 988
misdirect *misteach* 538
  unskillful 699
misdo 945
misdoing 947
misdoubt 485, 523
mise en scène
  appearance 448
  drama 599
  display 882
misemploy 679
miser 640, 819
miserable *small* 32
  contemptible 943
  unhappy 828
miserably *very* 31
misère 840
miserere *sing* - 950
misericordia Domini
  470
miserly 819
misery 828
put out of one's - 914
misesteem 481
misestimate
  misjudge 481
  (*mistake* 495)
misfeasance
  bungling 699
  guilt 947
misfire 732
misfortune
  adversity 735
  unhappiness 830
  (*evil* 619)
  (*failure* 732)
misgiving *doubt* 485
  fear 860
misgovern 699
misguide *error* 495
  misteaching 538
misguided 699
mishap *evil* 619
  failure 732
  misfortune 735
  painful 830
mishmash 59
Mishna 985
misinform 538
misinformed 491
misinstruct 538
misintelligence 538
misinterpretation **523**
misjoined 24
misjudgment
  sophistry 477
  misjudge **481**
  (*error* 495)

mislay *derange* 61
　lose 776
mislead *error* 495
　misteach 538
　deceive 545
mislike 867
mismanage 699
mismatch
　difference 15
　disagreement 24
misname 565
misnomer **565**
misogamist
　celibacy 904
　misanthropy 911
misogyny 904
mispersuasion 538
misplace *derange* 61
　displace 185
misplaced
　intrusive 24
　unconformable 83
　displaced 185
　(*disorder* 59)
misprint 495
misprision
　concealment 528
　guilt 947
　- of treason 742
misprize
　underrate 483
　disrespect 929
mispronounce 583
misproportion 241
misproportioned
　distortion 243
　ugly 846
misquote 544
misreckon
　misjudge 481
　mistake 495
misrelation 10
misrelish 867
misreport *err* 495
　falsify 544
misrepresent
　misinterpret 523
　misteach 538
　lie 544
misrepresentation 555
　untruth 546
misrule *misconduct* 699
　laxity 738
　Lord of - 701
miss *girl* 129
　neglect 460
　error 495
　unintelligible 519
　fail 732
　lose 776
　want 865
　courtesan 962
　- one's aim 732
　- one's way
　　uncertain 475
　　unskillful 699
　- stays 304
missa cantata 998
missal 990, 998
missay *neology* 563
　stammering 583

missend 699
misshapen
　shapeless 241
　distorted 243
　ugly 846
missile 727
missing *nonexistent* 2
　absent 187
　disappear 449
　- link *wanting* 53
　completing 729
mission *business* 625
　commission 755
missionary
　teacher 540
　clergyman 996
　- school 542
missive 592
misspell 523
misspend 818
misstate *mistake* 495
　misrepresent 523
　falsify 544
misstatement *error* 495
　untruth 546
　misrepresentation 555
mist *cloud* 353
　dark 424
　semitransparency 427
　(*dim* 422)
　in a - 528
　- before the eyes 443
　-s of error 495
　seen through a - 519
mistake *error* 495
　misconstrue 523
　mismanage 699
　failure 732
　lie under a - 495
misteaching **538**
mister 373
misterm 565
misthink 481
mistime 135
mistral 349
mistranslate 523
mistress *lady* 374
　master 745
　possessor 779
　love 897
　concubine 962
mistrust 485
misty [*see* mist]
　become - 427
misunderstand
　misinter,ret 523
misunderstanding
　disagreement 24
　error 495
　discord 713
misuse **679**
misventure 135
mite *bit* 32
　infant 129
　small 193
　arachnid 368
　dole 640
　money 800
miter *junction* 43
　angle 244
　crown 747, 999

mithai 396
mithridate 662
mitigate *abate* 174
　improve 658
　relieve 834
　(*calm* 826)
mitigation
　[*see* mitigate]
　qualification 469
　extenuation 937
mitosis *production* 161
mitraille 727
mitrailleuse 727
mitten 225, 384
mittimus 741
mix 41
　disorder 59
　- oneself up with
　　meddle 682
　　coöperate 709
mixed *confused* 523
　[*see* mix]
mixen 653
mixture **41**
　mere - *disorder* 59
mizzen 235
　- mast 235
mizzle 293, 348
mnemonics 505
mnemotecnhics 505
Mnemosyne 505
moan *faint sound* 405
　cry 411
　lament 839
moat *inclosure* 232
　ditch 259
　canal 350
　defense 717
mob *crowd* 72
　vulgar 876
　hustle 929
　scold 932
　king - 876
　- cap 225
　- law *authority* 738
　　compulsion 744
　　illegality 964
mobcap 225
mobile *inconstant* 149
　movable 264
　sensitive 822
mobility the - 876
mobilization 72, 264,
　722
mobilize 264
　- troops 722
mobocracy 738
moccasin 225
mock *imitate* 17, 19
　repeat 104
　erroneous 495
　deceptive 545
　chuckle 838
　ridicule 856
　desrespect 929
　- danger 861
　- modesty 855
　- sun 423
　- turtle soup 298
mockery [*see* mock]
　unsubstantial 4

　- delusion and snare
　　sophistry 477
　　deception 545
　solemn - 882
mocking bird 19
modal 6, 7, 8
mode *state* 7
　music 413
　habit 613
　method 627
　fashion 852
　- of expression 569
model *copy* 21
　prototype 22
　rule 80
　form 240
　representation 554
　sculpture 557
　perfection 650
　good man 948
　- after 19
　- condition 80
　new - 658
modeler 559
moderate *small* 32
　allay **174**
　slow 275
　neutral 628
　sufficient 639
　lenient 740
　cheap 815
　temperate 953
　- circumstances
　　mediocrity 736
moderately
　imperfect 651
moderation **174**
　inexcitability 826
　patience 831
　[*see* moderate]
moderato *music* 415
moderator
　moderation 174
　lamp 423
　director 694
　mediator 724
　judge 967
modern 123
　- philosophy 451
modernist 123
modernity 123
modernization 123
modest *small* 32
modesty *humility* **881**
　purity 960
　mock - 855
modicum *little* 32
　allotment 786
modification
　difference 15
　variation 20a
　change 140
　qualification 469
modillion 215
modiolus 215
modish 852
modiste 225
modulate 469
modulation *change* 140
　music 413
module 22

MODULUS

MOON

modulus 84
modus operandi 627, 692
modus vivendi 723
mofussil 181
mogul 745
Mohammed 986
Mohammedan 984
- priests 996
- temples 1000
Mohammedanism 976
Mohawk
  swaggerer 887
  evildoer 913
moider inattention 458
  uncertain 475
moiety 51, 91
moil plod 682
  exertion 686
moisture wet 337
  humid 339
moke 219
molar 250
molasses 352, 396
mold condition 7
  matrix 22
  convert 144
  form 240
  structure 329
  earth 342
  vegetation 367
  model 554
  carve 557
  decay 653
  remedy 662
  turn to account 677
  create 976
molded 820
- on 19
molder decay 653
  deteriorate 659
molding 847
moldy fetid 401
  unclean 653
  deteriorated 659
mole wound 206
  prominence 250
  refuge 666
  defense 717
  spot 848
molecular 32
molecule 193
mole-eyed 443
molehill little 193
  low 207
  trifling 643
molest trouble 830
molestation
  damage 649
  malevolence 907
mollah judge 967
mollescence 324
mollify allay 174
  soften 324
  (mental calm 826)
mollusca 368
mollusk 366, 368
mollycoddle 158, 372
Moloch slaughter 361
  demon 978
  heathen deity 991

molt 226
molten liquefied 384
  (heated 335)
molybdomancy 511
moment - of time 113
  importance 642
  for the - 111
  lose not a - 684
  not have a - 682
  on the spur of the - 612
momentous 151
momentum 276
Momus 838
monachal 1000
monachism 995
monad 87, 193
monarch 745
monarchical 737
monarchy 737
monastery 1000
monastic 995
monasticism 995
monde 852
monetary 800
- arithmetic 811
monetize 800
money 800
  wealth 803
  bad - 800
  command of - 803
  for one's - 609
  made of - 803
  make - 775
  - burning one's pocket 818
  - coming in 810
  - down 807
  - going out 809
  - market 800
  - matters 811
  - paid 809
  -'s worth useful 644
  price 812
  cheap 815
  raise - 788
  save - 817
  throw away one's - 818
money bag 802
money box 802
money broker 797
money changer
  merchant 797
  treasurer 801
moneyed 803
money-grubbing 775
moneyless 804
monger 797
mongoose 366
mongrel
  mixture 41
  anomalous 83
  dog 366
  base 949
moniliform 249
monism 984
monition
  information 527
  warning 668
  (advice 695)

monitor oracle 513
  pupil teacher 540, 541
  director 694
  adviser 695
  war ship 726
  inward - 926
  - building 189
monitory
  prediction 511
  dissuasion 616
  warning 668
monk 904, 996
monkery 984
monkey imitative 19
  support 215
  catapult 276
  animal 366
  ridiculous 857
  - trick absurdity 497
  sport 840
  - up 900
  play the - 499
monkeyshine 497
monkhood 995
monkish Latin 553
monochord 417
monochrome
  no color 429
  painting 556
monoclinous 83
monocracy 737
monoculous 443
monocycle 272
monodic 402
monodrame 599
monody poem 597
  lament 839
monogamist 903
monogamy 903
monogram cipher 533
  indication 550
  diagram 554
  letter 561
monograph
  writing 590
  description 594
monographer 598
monolith 551
monolithic 983a
monologist 582, 589
monologue
  soliloquy 589
  drama 599
monomachy 720
monomania
  insanity 503
  obstinacy 606
  excitability 825
monomaniac 504
monophonic 402
monoplane 273
monoplanist 269a
monopolist 751, 943
monopoly restraint 751
  possession 777
monospermous 87
monostich 572
monosyllable 561
monotheism 983
monotone 104

monotonous
  uniform 16
  equal 27
  repetition 104
  permanent 141
  - style 575
  weary 841
  dull 843
monotony
  [see monotonous]
monotype 591
Monroe Doctrine 748
monsoon 348, 349
monster exception 83
  large 192
  ugly 846
  prodigy 872
  evildoer 913
  ruffian 949
monstrance 191, 999
monstrosity
  [see monster]
  distortion 243
monstrous excessive 31
  exceptional 83
  huge 192
  ugly 846
  vulgar 851
  ridiculous 853
  wonderful 870
montagne Russe
  slope 217
  sport 840
mont de piété 787
monte 840
Montgolfier 273
month 108
monthly 138
- nurse 662
monticle 206
monticoline 206
monument tall 206
  tomb 363
  record 551
monumentalize 112
moo 412
mood nature 5
  state 7
  change 140
  tendency 176
  willingness 602
  temper 820
moodish rude 895
  irascible 901
  sullen 901a
moods and tenses
  difference 15
  variation 20a
moody furious 825
  sad 837
  sullen 901a
moolvi 492
moon period 108
  changes 149
  world 318
  bay the - 645
  jump over the - 309
  man in the - 515
  - blindness 443
  - glade 422
  - of green cheese

611

motor bus 272
motor car 272
motorcycle 266, 272
motorial 264
motorist 268
motorium 264
motorize 266
motorman 268, 694
motory 264
motte 367
mottled 440
motto *maxim* 496
 device 550
 phrase 566
mouchard 527
mould [*see* mold]
mound *large* 192
 hill 206
 defense 717
mount *greatness* 31
 increase 35
 hill 206
 ascend 305
 raise 307
 display 882
 - guard *care* 459
 safety 664
 - up to *money* 800
 price 812
mountain *large* 192
 hill 206
 weight 319
 make -s of molehills
 482
 - brought forth mouse
 disappoint 509
 - flax 385
mountaineer 268
mountainous 206
mountebank
 quack 548
 drama 599
 buffoon 844
mounted rifles 726
mourn *grieve* 828
 lament 839
mourner 839
mourners' bench 1000
mournful *afflicting* 830
 sad 837
 lamentable 839
mourning *dress* 225
 in - *black* 431
 lament 839
mouse *little* 193
 animal 366
 search 461
 mountain brought
 forth - 509
 - over 451, 461
 not a - stirring 265
mouse-colored 432
mousehole 260
mouser 366
mouse trap 545
mousseux 353
mouth *entrance* 66
 receptacle 191
 brink 231
 opening 260
 eat 298

estuary 343
 drawl 583
 down in the - 879
 make -s 929
 - honor *falsehood* 544
 show 882
 flattery 933, 940
 - wash 652
 - watering 865
 open one's - 582
 pass from - to mouth
 531
 stop one's - 581
 word of - 582
mouthful *quantity* 25
 small 32
 food 298
mouthpiece
 speaker 534
 information 527
 speech 582
mouthy *style* 577
moutonné 250
movable *motion* 26
 transference 270
movables 780
move *begin* 66
 motion 264
 propose 514
 induce 615
 undertake 676
 act 680
 offer 763
 excite 824
 good - 626
 - back 287
 - forward 282
 - from 287
 - heaven and earth
 686
 - in a groove 82
 - off 293
 - on *progress* 282
 activity 682
 - out of 295
 - quickly 274
 - slowly 275
 - to 894
 on the - 293
moved with 821
moveless 265
movement
 motion 264
 music 415
 action 680
 activity 682
mover 164
movies
 theater 448, 599, 840
moving 185
 keep - 682
 - pictures 448, 599
 - picture machine 445
mow *shorten* 201
 smooth 255
 agriculture 371
 store 636
 - down *destroy* 162
 level 213
moxa 384
mozetta 999

M. P. 696
Mr. *man* 373
 gentleman 877
Mrs. 374
M. S. 590
much 31
 make - of
 important 642
 friends 888
 love 897
 endearment 902
 approval 931
 - ado *exertion* 686
 difficulty 704
 - ado about nothing
 overestimate 482
 exaggerate 549
 unimportant 643
 unskillful 699
 - cry and little wool
 884
 - speaking 584
 - the same *identity* 13
 similarity 17
 equality 27
 not say - for 932
 think - of *respect* 928
 approbation 931
muchness 31
mucid *semiliquid* 352
 unclean 653
mucilage 352
muck 653
muckle 31
muckrake 934
muckraker 936
muckworm *miser* 819
 lowborn 876
mucor 653
mucosity 352
mucous 352
mucronate 253
mucronulate 253
muculent 352
mucus 352
mud *marsh* 345
 semiliquid 352
 dirt 653
 clear as - 519
 stick in the - 704
muddle *disorder* 59
 derange 61
 inattention 458
 render uncertain 475
 absurd 497
 difficulty 704
 blunder 732
 - away 638
 - one's brains 475
muddled 730, 959
muddle-headed 499
muddy *moist* 339
 dim 422
 opaque 426
 color 429
mudguard 666
mud lark *dirty* 653
 commonalty 876
muezzin 996
muff *incapable* 158
 dress 225

effeminacy 374
 warmth 384
bungle 699
bungler 701
muffer *bungler* 701
muffle *wrap* 225
 silent 403
 faint 405
 nonresonant 408a
 conceal 528
 voiceless 581
 stammer 583
muffled *faint* 405
 latent 526
 - drums *funeral* 363
 nonresonance 408a
muffler *dress* 225
 wrap 384
 silencer 405, 408a
mufti *undress* 225
 judge 967
 priest 996
mug *cup* 191
 face 234
 pottery 384
mugger 913
muggy *moist* 339
mughouse 189
mugient 412
mugwump 607
Muharram 138
mulada 72
mulatto *mixture* 41
 exception 83
mulct *steal* 791
 fine 974
mule *mongrel* 83
 beast of burden 271
 obstinate 606
muleteer 694
muliebrity 374
mulish 606
mull *prominence* 250
 sweeten 396
 - over 451
mullah 492, 996
mulligatawny 298
mullion 215
multangular 244
multifarious
 irrelevant 10
 diverse 16a
 multiform 81
multifid *divided* 51
multifold 81, 102
multiformity 81
multigenerous 81
multilateral *sides* 236
 angles 244
multilocular 191
multiloquence
 speech 582
 loquacity 584
multinominal 102
multiparity 168
multiparous 168
multipartite 44
multiphase 81
multiple *product* 84
 numerous 102
multiplex 81

613

multiplicand 84
multiplication
  arithmetic 85
  multitude 102
  reproduction 163
  productiveness 168
multiplicator 84
multiplicity 102
multiplier 84
multiply
  [*see* multiplication]
multipotent 157
multisonous 404
multitude *number* **102**
  (*assemblage* 72)
  many-headed – 102
  the – 876
multum in parvo 596
multure 330
mum *mute* 581
  taciturn 585
mumble *chew* 298
  mutter 583
mumble peg 840
mumblety 840
Mumbo Jumbo
  god 979
  spell 993
mummer 599
mummery
  absurdity 497
  imposture 545
  masquerade 840
  parade 882
  (*ridicule* 856)
mummify 357, 363
mumming 840
mummy *dry* 340
  corpse 362
  brown 433
  beat to a – 972
mump *mutter* 583
  beg 765
mumper *beggar* 767
  pauper 804
mumpish *sad* 837
mumps *dejection* 837
  sullenness 901*a*
mumpsimus 495
munch 298
Munchausen 549
munchil 272
mundane *world* 318
  selfish 943
  irreligious 989
mundation 652
mundivagant 266
munerary 973
munerate 973
municipal 965
munificent 816
muniment
  evidence 467
  record 551
  defense 717
  security 771
munition
  materials 635
  defense 717

munshi
  learned man 493
  teacher 540
mural 717
murder 361
  – the King's English
    solecism 568
    stammering 583
  the – is out 529
murderer 361
muricated 253
murky *dark* 421
  opaque 426
  black 431
  gloomy 837
murmur *purl* 348
  sound 405
  voice 580
  complain 839
murmurer 832
murrain 655
Murray *travel* 266
  Lindley – 542
murrey 434
muscadine 400
muscle 159
muscular 159
muse 451
  [*see* musing]
Muse *poetry* 597
  historic – 594
  – of fire 597
  unlettered – 579
museology 72
Muses, the – 416
musette 417
museum
  collection 72
  store 636
mush *food* 298
mushroom
  unsubstantial 4
  new 123
  fungus 367
  upstart 734
  lowborn 876
  – anchor 706
  –s *food* 298
  fungi 369
  spring up like –s 163
music **415**
  – box 417
  – of the spheres
    order 58
    universe 318
  set to – 416
musical 413, 415. 416
  – ear *musician* 416
    hearing 418
  – instruments **417**
  – note 413
  – voice 580
musicale 415
music hall
  playhouse 599
  amusement 840
musician 416
musing *thought* 451
  – on other things 458

thick-eyed – 837
musk 400
musket 727
  shoulder a – 722
musketeer 726
musketry 727
musk ox 366
muskrat 400
musk root 400
muslin
  semitransparent 427
  fabric 635
musnud *support* 215
  council 696
  scepter 747
muss 59, 61
mussuk 191, 348
Mussulman 984
mussy 61, 653
must *necessity* 601
  mucor 653
  compulsion 744
mustache 256
mustang 271
mustard *pungent* 392
  condiment 393
  after meat – 135
mustard gas 663, 737
mustard seed 193
musteline 433
muster *collect* 72
  numeration 85
  schedule 611
  – courage 861
  not pass – 651
  pass – 639
muster roll *list* 86
  (*record* 551)
musty 961
  smelling 401
  foul 653
mutable
  changeable 149
  (*irresolute* 605)
mutation 140
mutatis mutandis
  correlation 12
  change 140
  interchange 148
mute *funeral* 363
  silent 403
  sordine 405, 408*a*,417
  letter 561
  speechless 581
  taciturn 585
  drama 599
  deaf – 419
  render – 581
mutescence 408*a*
mutilate *retrench* 38
  deform 241
  injure 659
mutilated
  incomplete 53
  imperfect 651
mutilation *evil* 619
mutineer 742
mutiny *revolution* 146
  disobedience 742

(*resistance* 719)
mutter *faint sound* 405
  imperfect speech 583
  grumble 839
  threaten 909
mutton 298
  – chop 298
muttonhead 501
mutton-headed 499
mutual *correlative* 12
  interchange 148
  – concession 774
  – understanding 23
muzzle *powerless* 158
  edge 231
  opening 260
  silence 403
  render speechless 581
  restrain 751
  gag 752
muzzle-loader 727
muzzy *confused* 458
  in liquor 959
myatism 560
mycologist 369
mycology 369
mynheer 877
myology 329
myomancy 511
myopia 443
myriad
  ten thousand 98
  multitude 102
myrmidon 726
myrrh 400
myrtle *tree* 367
  love 897
myself *I* 79
  immateriality 317
mysterious
  invisible 447
  uncertain 475
  obscure 519
  concealed 528
mystery
  [*see* mysterious]
  latency 526
  secret 533
  play 599
  craft 625
  into the supreme – 528
mystic *obscure* 519
  concealed 528
  psychic 992*a*
mysticism *thought* 451
  latency 526
  concealment 528
mystify *falsify* 477
  unintelligible 519
  hide 528
  misteach 538
  deceive 545
myth *fancy* 515
  untruth 546
mythic deities **979**
mythical *descriptive* 594
mythogenesis 515
mythology *gods* 979
  heathen 984

nab *deceive* 545
  seize 789
Nabob *master* 745
  wealthy 803
nacreous 440
nadir 211
nævose 440
nag *horse* 271
  quarrel 713
Nagari 590
naggy 901*a*
Naiad *ocean* 341
  mythology 979
naik 745
nail *fasten* 43
  fastening 45
  measure of length 200
  peg 214
  hard 323
  retain 781
  hit the right - on the
    head
  discover 480*a*
  skill 698
  on the - *present* 118
  pay 807
nailery 691
naïveté 703
naked *denuded* 226
  manifest 525
  - eye 441
  - fact 151
  - sword 727
  - truth 494
namby-pamby
  trifling 643
  affected 855
name *indication* 550
  appellation 564
  appoint 755
  celebrity 873
  assume a - 565
  call -s *disrespect* 929
  disapprobation 932
  fair - 873
  good - 873
  in the - of *aid* 707
  authority 737
  due 924
  - to conjure with 873
nameless
  anonymous 565
  obscure 874
namely *special* 79
  interpretation 522
namesake 564
nanny goat 374
nap *down* 256
  texture 329
  sleep 683
nape *back* 235
napha water 400
naphtha 356
napiform 245
napkin 652
  buried in a - 460
  lay up in a - 678
napless 226
napoleon *cards* 840
napping
  inattentive 458

inexpectant 508
  dull 843
  catch - 508
nappy *frothy* 353
  tipsy 959
Narcissus 845
narcosis 376, 381
narcotic
  unhealthy 657
  remedy 662
  (*bad* 649)
narcotization 381
narikin 123
Narraganset 271
narration 594
narrator 529
narrow *contract* 195
  thin 203
  qualify 469
  constrained 751
  bigoted 988
  - end of the wedge 66
  - escape 671
  - gauge 466
  - house 363
  - means 804
  - search 461
narrow-minded
  bigoted 481
  selfish 943
narrowness 203
narrows 343
narrow-souled 481
nasal 349
  - accent 583
nascent 66
nasty *unsavory* 395
  foul 653
  offensive 830
  cheap and - 815
natal *birth* 66
  indigenous 188
  - day 138
natation 267
natatorium 652
nathless 30
nation 372
  law of -s 963
national 372
  - guard 726
nationality *nation* 372
  patriotism 910
nationwide 78
native *inhabitant* 188
  indigenous 367
  artless 703
  - accent 580
  - land 189
  - soil 189
  - tendency 601
  - tongue 560
nativity *birth* 66
  cast a - *predict* 511
  sorcery 992
natty 845
natural *intrinsic* 5
  musical note 413
  true 494
  fool 501
  plain 576
  - style 578

spontaneous 621
  not prepared 674
  artless 703
  simplicity 849
  - affection 897
  - course of things 613
  - death *death* 360
  completion 729
  - gas 388
  - history 357
  - impulse 601
  - meaning 516
  - order of things 82
  - philosophy 316
  - state 80
  - theology 983
  - turn 820
naturalist 357
naturalistic 537
naturalization
  conformity 82
  conversion 144
  location 184
naturalize *habit* 613
naturalized
  inhabitant 188
naturally 154
nature *essence* 5
  rule 80
  tendency 176
  world 318
  reality 494
  artlessness 703
  affections 820
  animated - 357
  in - 's garb 226
  organized - 357
  second - 613
  state of - *naked* 226
  raw 674
naught *nothing* 4
  zero 101
  bring to - 732
  set at -
    make light of 483
    opposition 708
    disobey 742
    not observe 773
    disrespect 929
    contempt 930
naughty 945
naumachia 720
nausea *weariness* 841
  disgust 867
nauseate
  unsavory 395
  give pain 830
nauseous
  unsavory 395
  unpleasant 830
  disgusting 867
nautch 840
nautch girl 840
nautical 267, 273
  -almanac 86
nautilus 368
naval 267, 273
  - authorities 745
  - engagement 720
  - forces 627
  - school 542

navarch 745
nave *middle* 68
  center 222
  circularity 247
  church 1000
navel *middle* 68
  center 222
navicular 245
naviform 245
navigation 267
navigator 269
navvy *pioneer* 673
  laborer 690
navy *ships* 273
  fighters 664, 726
  - blue 438
  - list 86
nawab 745, 875
nay 536
  - rather 14
Nazarene 989
naze 250
ne plus ultra
  supreme 33
  complete 52
  distance 196
  summit 210
  limit 233
  perfection 650
  completion 729
neap *going down* 195
  low 207
  - tide 36
near *like* 17, 19
  - *in space* 197
  - *in time* 121
  soon 132
  impending 152
  approach 286
  stingy 819
  bring - 17
  come - 286
  draw - 197
  - at hand 132
  - one's end 360
  - run 32
  - side 239
  - sight 443
  - the mark 32
  - the truth 480*a*
  - upon 32
  sail - the wind
  skillful 698
  rash 863
nearly 32
  - all 50
nearness 9, **197**
nearsighted 443
neat *simple* 42
  order 58
  form 240
  in writing 572, 576,
    578
  clean 652
  spruce 845
  - 's foot oil 356
neat-handed 698
neatherd 370
neb 250
nebula *stars* 318
  mist 353

nebular *dim* 422
nebulous *misty* 353
  obscure 519
necessarian 601
necessaries 630
necessarily
  cause and effect 154
necessary
  [*see* necessity]
necessitarianism 601
necessitate 630
necessity *fate* 601
  predetermination 611
  requirement 630
  compulsion 744
  indigence 804
  need 865
 make a virtue of - 698
neck *contraction* 195
  narrow 203
 break one's - 360
 - and crop
  completely 52
  turn out - 297
 - and neck 27
 - of land 342
 - or nothing
  resolute 604
  rash 863
neckcloth 225
necklace *circle* 247
  ornament 847
necrology *obituary* 360
  biography 594
necromancer 548, 994
necromancy 511, 992
necropolis 363
necropsy 363
necroscopic 363
necrosis 655
nectar *savory* 394
  sweet 396
nectareous 394, 396
need *necessity* 601
  requirement 630
  insufficiency 640
  indigence 804
  desire 865
 friend in - 711
 in one's utmost - 735
needful *necessary* 601
  requisite 630
  money 800
 do the - *pay* 807
needle *sharp* 253
  perforator 262
  compass 693
  foliage 367
 as the - to the pole
  veracity 543
  observance 772
  honor 939
 - in a bottle of hay
  475
needle gun 727
needle-shaped 253
needless 641
needle-witted 498
needlewoman 690
needlework 847
ne'er 107
616

ne'er-do-well 949
nefarious 945
negation **536**, 764
negatory 764
negative *inexisting* 2
  contrary 14
  prototype 22
  quantity 84
  confute 479
  deny 536
  photograph 558
  refuse 764
 prove a - 468
neglect **460**
  disuse 678
  leave undone 730
  omit 773
  evade 927
  disrespect 929
 - of time 115
négligé 225
negligence 460
negligent 460
negotiable
  transferable 270
  mediatory 724
negotiate *leap* 309
  mediate 724
  bargain 769
  transfer 783
  traffic 794
negotiator
  go-between 724
  agent 758
negress 431
Negrillo 193, 431
Negrito 193, 431
negro *black* 431
  slave 746
negro head 392
negrophobia 898
negus 298
neif 781
neigh *cry* 412
  boast 884
neighbor *near* 197, 199
  friend 890
neighborhood 197, 227
neighborly *aid* 707
  friendly 888
  social 892
  courteous 894
neither 610
 - here nor there
  irrelevant 10
  absent 187
 - more nor less
  equal 27
  true 494
 - one thing nor an-
  other 83
nekton 366
nem. con. 488
Nemesis
  vengeance 919
  justice 922
  punishment 972
nenia 839
neo-criticism 451
neogamist 903
Neo-Hegelianism 451

Neo-Lamarckism 357
neologism 123
neologist 123
neology **563**
neophyte 144, 541
Neoplatonism 451, 984
neoteric 123
neo-voluntarism 451
nepenthe *remedy* 662
  cheer 836
nephalism 953, 955
nephelognosy 353
nephelometer 353
nephew 11
nephograph 353
nephology 353
nephoscope 353
nepotism *nephew* 11
  wrong 923
  dishonest 940
  selfish 943
Neptune 341
Nereid *ocean* 341
  mythology 979
nerve *strength* 159
  courage 861
 with exposed -s 378
nerveless *impotent* 158
  - *style* 575
  imperturbable 871
nervous *weak* 160
  style 574
  timid 860
  modest 881
nescience 491
ness 250
nest *cradle* 153
  lodging 189
 - of boxes 204
nest egg 636
nestle *lodge* 186
  safety 664
  endearment 902
nestling 129, 167
Nestor *veteran* 130
  sage 500
  advice 695
net *remainder* 40
  receptacle 191
  intersection 219
  inclosure 232
  snare 545
  difficulty 704
  gain 775
 - *profit gain* 775
  receipt 810
nether 207
nethermost 207, 211
netlike 219
netting 219
nettle *bane* 663
  sting 830
  incense 900
network *disorder* 59
  crossing 219
neural 235
neuralgia 378
neurasthenia 158, 655,
  992*a*
neurology 329
neurotic 662

neuter *matter* 316
  no choice 609*a*
 remain - *irresolute* 605
 stand - *indifferent* 866
neutral *mean* 29
  no choice 609*a*
  avoidance 623
  mid-course 628
  pacific 721
  indifferent 866
 - tint *colorless* 429
  gray 432
neutrality
  mid-course 628
  peace 721
  insensibility 823
  indifference 866
neutralize
  compensate 30
  counteract 179
nevée 383
never 107
 it will - do
  inexpedient 647
  prohibit 761
  discontent 832
  disapprobation 932
 - a one 4
 - dying 112
 - ending 112
 - fading *perpetual* 112
  glory 873
 - forget 916
 - hear the last of 841
 - indebted 807
 - mind *neglect* 460
  unimportant 643
  insensible 823
  indifferent 866
  contempt 930
 - more 107
 - otherwise 16
 - say die
  persevere 604*a*
  cheerful 836
  hope 858
 - so 31
 - tell me 489
 - thought of 621
 - tired *active* 682
 - tiring
  persevering 604*a*
 - to be forgotten 642
 - to return 122
 - was seen the like 83
neverness 107
nevertheless 30
ne vile fano 987, 1000
new *different* 18
  extra 37
  novel 123
  unaccustomed 614
 give - life to
  aid 707
  stimulate 824
 - birth 660
 - blood *change* 140
  improve 658
  excite 824
 - brooms
  desuetude 614

active 682
- chum 57
- conditions 469
- departure 66
- edition
  repetition 104
  reproduction 163
  imyrovement 658
- ethical movement 451
- ideas 537
- woman 374
put on the - man 950
turn over a - leaf
  change 140
  repent 950
view in a - light 658
newborn *new* 123
  infant 129
Newcastle, carry coals
  to - 641
newcomer 57, 294
New England Primer
  542
newfangled
  unfamiliar 83
  new 123
  change 140
  neology 563
newfashioned 123
new-fledged 129
Newfoundland dog 366
Newgate 572
new-gilt 847
uew-model
  convert 144
  revolutionize 146
  improve 658
newness **123**
news **532**
newsboy 534
newsmonger
  curious 455
  informant 527
  news 532
newsmongery 455
uewspaper
  publish 531
  record 551
- correspondent 758
- war 588
uewspaperman 554
newsy 532
newt 366
New Thought 984
New Year's Day 138
next *following* 63
  later 117
  future 121
  near 197
- friend 759
- of kin 11
- to nothing 32
- world 152
Niagara 348
niasis 501
niaiserie 517
uib *cut* 44
  end 67
  summit 210
  point 253

nibble *eat* 298
- at *censure* 932
- at the bait
  dupe 547
  willing 602
nice *savory* 394
  discriminative 465
  exact 494
  good 648
  pleasing 829
  fastidious 868
  honorable 939
  (*taste* 850)
- ear 418
- hand 700
- perception 465
- point 697, 704
nicely *completely* 52
Nicene Creed 983*a*
niceness [*see* nice]
nicety 494
niche *recess* 182
  receptacle 191
  angle 244
- in the temple of
  fame 873
nick *notch* 257
  deceive 545
  mark 550
- it 731
- of time 134
nickel 800
Nick, Old - 978
nicknack 643
nickname 564, 565
nicotine *pungent* 392
  poison 663
nictate 443
nictitate 443
nidget 862
nidification 189
nidor 398
nidorous 401
nidus *cradle* 153
  nest 189
niece 11
niggard
  insufficiency 640
  miser 819
  (*trifling* 643).
nigger 57, 431
niggerhead 392
niggle *mock* 929
niggling *trifling* 643
nigh 197
nighness 197
night 421
  labor day and - 686
- and day 136
- watchman 753
orb of - 318
nightcap 225
nightfall 126, 422
nightgown 225
nightingale 366, 416
nightmare
  bodily pain 378
  dream 515
  incubus 706
  mental pain 828
  alarm 860

nightshade 663
nightshirt 225
nighttide 126
nightwalker 268
nightwalking 266
nigrescence 431
nigricant 431
nigrification 431
nihilism 738, 989
nihilist 165, 913
nihilistic 738
nihility *inexistence* 2
  unsubstantiality 4
nil *inexistence* 2
  unsubstantiality 4
nill *unwilling* 603
  refuse 764
nilometer 348
nim 791
nimble *swift* 274
  active 682
  (*skillful* 698)
nimble-fingered 698
nimble-footed 274
nimble-witted
  intelligence 498
  wit 842
nimbus *cloud* 353
  halo 420
  glory 873
nimiety 641
Nimrod *slayer* 361
  hunter 622
nincompoop 501
nine 98
  team 759
- day's wonder
  transient 111
  unimportant 643
- lives 359
- men's morris 840
- points of the law 777
tuneful - *music* 416
  poetry 597
ninefold 98
ninepins 840
ninety 98
ninny 501
Niobe *all tears* 839
- of nations 828
nip *cut* 44
  destroy 162
  shorten 201
  dram 298
  freeze 385
  pungent 392
- in the bud
  kill 361
  hinder 706
- up 789
nipperkin 191
nippers 327, 781
nipple 250
Nirvana 2, 981
nis 979
nisi prius
  summons 741
  lawsuit 969
nisus 176
nitency 420
niter 392

nitric acid 384
nitrogen 663
nitroglycerin 727
nitrous oxide 376
niveous *white* 430
nix *nothing* 101
  absence 187
  fairy 979
nixie *fairy* 979
nizam 745
nizy 501
no *zero* 101
  dissent 489
  negation 536
  refusal 764
and - mistake 474
at - great distance 197
at - hand 32
at - time 107
have - business there
  83
have - end
  perpetual 112
in - degree 32
- chicken *aged* 128
  grown up 131
- choice *necessary* 601
  neutral 609*a*
- conjuror *fool* 501
  bungler 701
- consequence 643
- doubt *certain* 474
  assent 488
- end of *great* 31
  multitude 102
  length 200
- go *shortcoming* 304
  failure 732
- less 639
- longer 122
- man's land
  arena 728
- matter *neglect* 460
  unimportant 643
- more *inexistent* 2
  past 122
  dead 360
- more than 32
- object 643
- one 4
- one knows who 876
- other *same* 13
  one 87
- scholar 493
- sooner said than
  done
  instantaneous 113
  early 132
- stranger to 490
- such thing
  nonexistent 2
  unsubstantial 4
  contrary 14
  dissimilar 18
- thank you 764
- wonder 871
on - account 761
unable to say - 605
with - interval 199
Noah's ark *mixture* 41
  assemblage 72

nob 210
Nobel prize 733
nobilitate 873
nobility **875**
noble *great* 31
　important 642
　rank 873
　peer 875
　upright 939
　disinterested 942
　virtuous 944
　- liver 948
　- scorn 919
noblesse 875
noblesse oblige 875
nobody *unsubstantial* 4
　zero 101
　absence 187
　lowborn 876
　- home *want of intel-*
　　lect 450a
　- knows
　　ignorance 491
　- knows where
　　distance 196
　- present 187
　- would think 508
noctambulation 266
noctambulist 268
noctivagant *travel* 266
　dark 421
noctograph 442
nocturnal *night* 126
　dark 421
　black 431
nocturne 415
nocuous 649
nod *wag* 314
　assent 488
　signal 550
　sleep 683
　command 741
　bow 894
　(*hint* 527)
　- of approbation 931
　- of assent 488
nodding to its fall
　destruction 162
　descent 306
noddle *summit* 210
　head 450
noddy 501
node 250
nodose 256
nodosity *convex* 250
　rough 256
nodule 87, 250
noggin 191
noise *sound* 402
　loud 404
　make a - in the world
　　873
　- abroad 531
noiseless 403
noisome *fetid* 401
　bad 649
　unhealthy 657
noisy 404
nolition 603
nolleity 603
nolle prosequi 624

nomad 268
nomadic 266
nomadization 266
Nomancy 511
nom de guerre 565
nom de plume 565
nomenclature **564**
nominal
　unsubstantial 4
　word 562
　name 564
　- price 815
nomination
　naming 564
　appointment 755
nominee 758
nomistic 965
nomography 963
nomology 963
nomothetical 965
non - ens 2
　- esse 2
　- possimus
　　impossible 471
　　obstinate 606
　　refusal 764
　- sequitur 477
nonaddition 38
nonadmission 55
nonage 127
nonagenarian 130
nonappearance 447
nonary 98
nonassemblage **73**
nonattendance 187
nonbeing 2
non-Biblical
　- prophets 986
　- writings **986**
nonce 118
　for the -
　　present 118
　　occasion 134
nonchalance
　neglect 460
　insensibility 823
　indifference 866
noncohesive 47
noncoincidence 14
noncommissioned
　　officer 745 '
noncommittal 864
noncompletion **730**
noncompliance
　disobedience 742
　refusal 764
nonconductive 175a
nonconformity
　exception 83
　dissent 489
　sectarianism 984
nonconsent 489
noncontent 489
noncoöperation 927
nondescript 83
none 101
　- else 87
　- in the world 4
　- the worse 660
　- to spare 640
nonendurance 825

nonentity *inexistence* 2
　unsubstantial 4
　unimportant 643
nonessential *extrinsic* 6
　unimportant 643
nonesuch
　unconformity 83
　goodness 648
nonexistence **2**
nonexpectance 508
nonextension 180a
nonfeasance 947
nonfulfillment 730, 732
　- of one's hopes 509
nonidentical 18
nonillion 102
nonimitation **20**
noninclusion 55
noninterference
　inaction 681
　freedom 748
nonius 466
nonjuror *dissent* 489
　heterodox 984
nonny 501
nonobjective 317
nonobservance
　inattention 458
　desuetude 614
　infraction **773**
　dereliction 927
nonpareil 28, 648
nonpayment **808**
nonperformance
　noncompletion 730
　dereliction 927
nonpertinence 10
nonplus
　uncertain 475
　difficulty 704
　conquer 731
nonpreparation **674**
nonprevalence 614
nonresidence 187
nonresistance
　submission 725
　obedience 743
nonresonance **408a**
nonsense *absurdity* 497
　unmeaning 517
　trash 643
　talk - *folly* 499
　to varnish - 499
nonsubjective 316
nonsubsistence 2
nonsuccess 732
nonsuit *defeat* 731
　fail 732
　condemn 971
nonunderstanding 452
nonuniformity 16a
nonvocal 581
noodle 501
nook *place* 182
　receptacle 191
　corner 244
noölogy 450
noon *midday* 125
noonday *midday* 125
　light 420
　clear as -

intelligible 518
　manifest 525
nooning 125
noontide 420
nooscopic 450
noose *ligature* 45
　loop 247
　snare 545
　gallows 975
N or M 78
norm 697
normal *intrinsic* 5
　average 29
　orderly 58
　regular 80, 82
　perpendicular 212
　sane 502
　- condition *rule* 80
normalcy 80, 502
normality [*see* normal]
normalize 58
Norse mythology 979
North 278
　- and South 237
　- Pole 383
　- Star 550
northeaster 349
norther 349
northerly 237
northern 237
　- lights 423
　- star *constant* 939
northward 237
Northwest passage 311
nose *prominence* 250
　curiosity 455, 461
　smell 398
　lead by the -
　　induce 615
　　govern 737
　led by the - 749
　- out 461
　not see beyond one's -
　　misjudge 481
　　folly 499
　　unskillful 699
　put one's - out of
　　joint *defeat* 731
　　disrepute 874
　　(*supplant* 147)
　speak through the -
　　583
　thrust one's - in
　　interjacence 228
　　busy 682
　under one's -
　　present 186
　　near 197
　　manifest 525
　　defy 715
nose dive
　aëronautics 267
nosegay *fragrance* 400
　ornament 847
nosey *curious* 455
nosology 655
nostalgia 833
nostology 128
nostril 351
　breath of one's - s 359
　stink in the -s 401

nostrum
  contrivance 626
  remedy 662
not *negation* 536
  (*dissent* 489)
  it will - do 923
  - a bit 536
  - a few 102
  - a leg to stand on 158
  - a little 31
  - allowed 964
  - amiss *good* 618
    mediocre 651
    pretty 845
  - any 101
  - a particle 4
  - a pin to choose 27
  - a soul 101
  - at all 32
  - bad 651
  - bargain for 508
  - come up to 34
  - expect 508
  - fail 939
  - far from 197
  - fit to be seen 846
  - following 477
  - for the world
    unwilling 603
    refusal 764
  - grant 764
  - guilty 946
  - hardened 950
  - having *absent* 187
    exempt 777a
  - hear of 764
  - included 55
  - know what to make
    of 519
  - matter
    unimportant 643
  - mind *insensible* 823
    contempt 930
  - often 137
  - of the earth 987
  - one 101
  }- on speaking terms
    889
  - on your life 764
  - particular 831
  - pay 808
  - quite 32
  - reach 304
  - right 503
  - seldom 136
  - sorry 827
  - the thing 925
  - to be borne 830
  - to be despised 642
  - to be had
    impossible 471
    insufficient 640
  - to mention
    together with 37
  - to be put down 604
  - to be thought of
    incogitancy 452
    impossible 471
    refusal 764
    hopeless 859
    undue 925

  disapprobation 932
  - trouble oneself
    about 460
  - understand 519
  - vital
    unimportant 643
  - vote 609a
  - within previous ex-
    perience 137
  - wonder 871
  - worth *trifling* 643
    useless 645
  what is - 546
  what ought - 923
nota bene 457
notabilia 642
notabilities 875
notable *great* 31
  manifest 525
  important 642
  active 682
  distinguished 873
notables 875
notably 31
notary *recorder* 553
  lawyer 968
notation 85
notch *gully* 198
  nick **257**
  mark 550
note *music* 413
  take cognizance 450
  remark 457
  explanation 522
  sign 550
  record 551
  printing 591
  epistle 592
  minute 596
  money 800
  fame 873
  change one's - 607
  make a - of 551
  - of admiration 870
  - of alarm 669
  - of preparation 673
  of - 873
  take - of 457
notebook *record* 551
  compendium 569
  writing 590
noted *known* 490
  famous 873
noteworthy *great* 31
  exceptional 83
  important 642
nothing *nihility* 4
  zero 101
  trifle 643
  come to -
  fall short 304
  fail 732
  do - 681
  for - 815
  go for - 643
  good for - 646
  make - of
  underestimate 483
  fail 732
  - comes amiss 831
  - in it 4

  - loth 602
  - more to be said 478
  - of the kind *unlike* 18
    negation 536
  - on 226
  - to do 681
  - to do with 764
  - to go upon 471
  - to signify 643
  take - by 732
  think of - 930
  worse than - 808
nothingness 2
notice *intellect* 450
  observe 457
  review 480
  information 527
  warning 668
  bring into - 525
  deserve - 642
  give - *manifest* 525
  inform 527
  indicate 550
  - is hereby given
    publication 531
  - to quit 782
  short - 111
  take - of 450
  this is to give - 457
  worthy of - 642
noticeable 31
notification
  information 527
  (*publication* 531)
notion *idea* 453
  (*belief* 484)
  (*knowledge* 490)
  have no - of 489
notional *fanciful* 515
notionalist 514
notoriety
  publication 531
  fame 873
notorious *known* 490
  public 531
  famous 873
  infamous 874
Notre Dame 977
notturno 415
notwithstanding 30,
  179
nought
  unsubstantiality 4
  [*see* naught]
noun 564
nourish 707
nourishment *food* 298
  aid 707
nous 498
nousle 545
nouveau riche 123
novaculite 253
novation 140, 609
Nova Zembla 383
novel *dissimilar* 18
  new 123
  unknown 491
  tale 594
  (*romance* 515)
  (*fiction* 546)
novelist 594, 598

novelize 594
novena 98, 108
novenary 98
novice *ignoramus* 493
  learner 541
  bungler 701
  religious 996
novitiate *learning* 539
  training 673
novocain 376
novus homo
  stranger 57
  upstart 876
now 118
  - and then 136
  - or never 134
noways 32, 536
nowhere 187
nowise *small* 32
  negation 536
noxious *bad* 649
  unhealthy 657
noyade 361
  kill 361
  punish 972
nozzle *projection* 250
  opening 260
  for water 337
  air pipe 351
nuance *difference* 15
  discrimination 465
nubiferous 353, 426
nubilation 426
nubile *adolescent* 131
  marriage 903
nubilous 426
nuclear 222
nucleolus 357
nucleus *middle* 68
  cause 153
  center 222
  kernel 642
nudation 226
nude 226
nudge 550
nudity 226, 849
nugacity *absurdity* 497
  folly 499
  inutility 645
nugatory
  powerless 158
  useless 645
nuggar 273
nugget *mass* 192
  money 800
nuisance *evil* 619
  annoyance 830
null *inexistent* 2
  unsubstantial 4
  absent 187
  declare - and void
  abrogation 756
  nonobservance 773
  - and void
  powerless 158
  unproductive 169
  illegal 964
  (*inexistence* 2)
nullah 198, 252
nullibiety 187
nullicity 187
nullifidian 487

nullify *inexistence* 2
  compensate 30
  destroy 162
  abrogate 756
  not observe 773
  not pay 808
nullity *inexistence* 2
  unsubstantiality 4
numb *physically insensible* 376, 381
  morally insensible 823
number *part* 51
  abstract - 84
  count 85
  plural 100
  - of a magazine &c. 593
  -among 76
  -of times 104
  take care of - one 943
numbered, days -
  kill 361
  necessity 601
  hopeless 859
  - with the dead 360
numberless 105
numbers *many* 102

verse 597
numbness 381
numdah 223
numerable 85
numeral 84, 85
numeration 85
numerator 84
numerical 85
numerous 102
numismatics 800
nummary 800
numps 501
numskull 493, 501
nun 904, 996
nunc dimittis 990
nuncio *messenger* 534
  diplomatist 758
nuncupation
  naming 564
nuncupative 527, 582
nuncupatory
  informing 527
nundination 794
nunnation 560
nunnery 1000
nuptial 903
  - knot 903

nuptials 903
nurse *remedy* 662
  preserve 670
  help 707
  servant 746
  custodian 753
  put to - 537
nursery *infancy* 127
  nest 153
  room 191
  garden 371
  school 542
  plants 691
  - rhymes 597
  - tale *fiction* 546
  narrative 594
nursling 129
nurture *feed* 298
  educate 537
  prepare 673
  aid 707
  - a belief 484
  - an idea 451
nut 298
  madman 504
  - to crack
  riddle 533

  difficulty 704
  - oil 365
nutation 314
nut-brown 433
nutmeg 393
  - grater 330
nuts *good* 618
  pleasing 829
nutshell *small* 32
  lie in a -
  little 193
  compendium 596
nutriment 298
nutrition 707
nutritious *food* 298
  healthy 656
  remedy 662
nux vomica 663
nuzzle 902
nyctalopia 443
nymph *child* 129
  woman 374
  mythology 979
  elemental 980
  sea - 341
nympha 129
nystagmus 443

O

O! *wonder* 870
  discontent 932
  - for *desire* 865
oaf *fool* 501
oak *strong* 159
  tree 367, 369
  heart of - *hard* 323
  brave 861
oakleaf *insignia* 747
oakum 205
oar *paddle* 267
  oarsman 269
  instrument 633
  laboring - 686
  lie upon one's -s 681
  ply the - *navigate* 267
  exert 686
  pull an - 680
  put in an -
  interpose 228
  busy 682
  rest on one's -
  cease 142
  quiescence 265
  repose 687
  stroke - 693
oar-shaped 245
oarsman 269
oasis *separate* 44
  land 342
oath *assertion* 535
  bad language 908
  - helper 467
  rap out -s 885
  upon - 768
oatmeal 298
oats 367
obbligato
  accompaniment 88

  music 415
obconic 245
obduction 223
obdurate
  obstinate 606
  severe 739
  malevolent 907
  graceless 945
  impenitent 951
obedience 743
obeisance *bow* 308
  submission 725
  courtesy 894
  reverence 928
obelisk *tall* 206
  monument 551
Oberon 979
obese 194
obesity 192
obey 743
  be subject to 749
  - a call 615
  - rules 82
  - the helm 705
obfuscate *dark* 421
  opaque 426
obfuscated *drunk* 959
obi 992
obiism 992
obit *death* 360
  interment 363
  post - 360, 363
obiter dictum
  irrelevant 10
  occasion 134
  interjacent 228
obituary *death* 360
  biography 594
object *thing* 3

  matter 316
  intention 620
  ugly 846
  disapprove 932
  be an -
  important 642
  - lesson 82
  - to *dislike* 867
objectify 220
objection
  hindrance 706
  disapproval 932
  no - 762
objectionable
  inexpedient 647
  wrong 923
  guilty 947
objective
  extrinsic 6
  material 316
objectize 220
objurgate 932
oblate 201
  - spheroid 249
oblation *gift* 784
  religious - 990
  (*offer* 763)
oblectation 827
obligation
  necessity 601
  promise 768
  conditions 770
  debt 806
  confer an -
  good 648
  feeling of - 916
  under an -
  gratitude 916
  duty 926

oblige *benefit* 707
  compel 744
  duty 926
obliged *grateful* 916
  duty 926
  be - 601
obligee 800
obliging *helping* 707
  courteous 894
  kind 906
obliquation 279
obliquity *slope* 217
  vice 945
  - of judgment 481
  - of vision 443
obliterate 2, 162
  - of the past 506
obliteration 552
  - of the past 506
oblivion 506
  inexistence 2
  forgiveness 918
  - of benefits 917
  - of time 115
  redeem from - 505
oblivious 506
oblong 200
  - spheroid 249
obloquy
  disrepute 874
  disapprobation 932
  detraction 934
obmutescence
  voiceless 581
  taciturn 585
obnoxious
  pernicious 649
  unpleasing 830
  hateful 898
  - to *liable* 177

œnomancy 511
o'er [see over]
œstrus 865
œuvres 161
of - all things 33
 - a piece *uniform* 16
 similar 17
 agreeing 23
 - course
 conformity 82
 effect 154
 - late 123
 - no effect 169
 - old 122
 - one mind 23
off 196
be - 623
keep - 623
make - with 791
move - 287
 - and on
 periodical 138
 changeable 149
 irresolute 605
 - one's balance 605
 - one's guard
 neglect 260
 inexpectant 508
 - one's hands 776
 - one's head 503
 - one's legs
 carry one - 284
 dance one - 309
 - one's mind 452
 - side 238
 - the track 475
 - with you 297
sheer - 287
stand - 287
start - 293
take - one's hands 785
throw - one's center 874
throw - the scent
 uncertain 475
 avoid 623
offal 653
offend *pain* 830
 vice 945
 - against the law 964
offender
 - never pardons 918
offense *attack* 716
 anger 900
 guilt 947
offensive *unsavory* 395
 fetid 401
 foul 653
 aggressive 716
 displeasing 830
 distasteful 867
 obnoxious 898
 - and defensive alliance 712
 - to ears polite 579
offer *volunteer* 602
 proposal **763**
 give 784
 - a choice 609
 - for sale 796
 - of marriage 902
622

 - oneself 763
 - sacrifice 990
 - the alternative 609
 - up prayers 990
offering *gift* 784
burnt - 990
sin - 952
offertory *gift* 784
 worship 990
 rite 998
offhand *soon* 132
 inattentive 458
 careless 460
 spontaneous 612
 (*unprepared* 674)
office *doing* 170
 room 191
 business 625
 mart 799
 worship 990
do an ill - 907
do one's - 772
good -s
 mediate 724
 kind 906
hold - 693
kind -s 906
man in - 694
 - force 746
 - holder 694
officer *director* 694
 soldier 726
 commander 745
 constable 965
offices *kitchen &c.* 191
official *certain* 474
 true 494
 business 625
 man in office 694
 authoritative 737
 master 745
 servant 746
 - receiver 967
officialism 739
officiate *business* 625
 instrumentality 631
 act 680
 conduct 692
 religious 998
officious 682
offing *distance* 196
 ocean 341
offprint 21
offsaddle 292
offscourings *useless* 645
 dirt 653
offscum 653
offset
 compensation 30
 offspring 167
 counteract 179
 printing 591
offshoot *adjunct* 39
 part 51
 effect 154
 offspring 167
offspring *posterity* 167
offtake 40a
offuscate *dark* 421
 opaque 426
often *repeated* 104

 frequent 136
 most - 613
Ogham 590
ogle *look* 441
 desire 865
 rude 895
 endearment 902
ogre *bugbear* 860
 evildoer 913
 demon 980
oil *lubricate* 332
 grease 355, **356**
 fuel 388
 - on the troubled waters 174
 - stove 386
pour - on *relieve* 834
oilcloth 223, 635
oil painting 556
oilskins 225
oily *smooth* 255
 greasy 355
 servile 886
 courteous 894
 flattery 933
oinomania 959
ointment
 lubrication 332
 grease 356
 remedy 662
old 124
die of - *age* 729
of - 122
 - age 128
 - bachelor 904
 - clothes 225
 - fogy *fool* 501
 laughingstock 857
 - glory 550
 - gold 439
 - joke 842
 - maid *cards* 840
 spinster 374, 904
 - man *veteran* 130
 husband 903
 - man of the sea 706
 - Nick 978
 - school
 antiquated 124
 obstinate 606
 habit 613
 - soldier 392
 - song *repetition* 104
 trifle 643
 cheap 815
 - stager *veteran* 130
 proficient 700
 - story *repetition* 104
 stale news 532
 love 897
 - stuff *repetition* 104
 - times 122
 - woman *fool* 501
 effeminacy 374
 wife 903
 - womanish 499
 - world 124
one's - way 613
pay off - scores 718
older 128
old-fangled 124

old-fashioned 124
oldness **124**
oldster 130
oldwife 130
oleagine 356
oleaginous 355
olein 356
olfactible 398
olfactory 398
 - organ 250
olibanum 400
olid 401
oligarch 745
oligarchy 737
olio 41
olivaceous 435
olive 367
olive branch
 infant 129
 offspring 167
 pacification 723
olive drab 225
olive green 435
olivine 435
olla podrida 41
Olympus 981
Om 993
omasum 191
omber 840
ombrometer 348
omega *end* 67
omelet 298
omen **512**
ominate 511
ominous
 predicting 511
 danger 665
 warning 668
 adverse 735
 hopeless 859
omission
 incomplete 53
 exclusion 55
 neglect 460
 failure 732
 nonobservance 773
 guilt 947
omit [see omission]
omitted *inexistent* 2
 absent 187
omnibus 272
omnifarious 81
omnific 168
omniform 81
omnigenous 81
omnipotence *power* 157
 God 976
omnipresence
 presence 186
 God 976
omniscience
 knowledge 490
 God 976
omnium-gatherum
 mixture 41
 confusion 59
 assemblage 72
omnivorous *eating* 298
 desire 865
 gluttony 957
omophagic 298

opera-hat 225
operant 170
operate *cause* 153
  produce 161
  act 170
  remedy 662
  work 680
  - upon *motive* 615
operation
  [see operate]
  arithmetical - 85
  in - 680
  put in - 677
  surgical - 662
operative *acting* 170
  doing 680
  workman 690
operator *surgeon* 662
  doer 690
operculated 261
operculum 223, 261
operetta 415
operose *toilsome* 686
  difficult 704
ophicleide 417
ophidian 366
ophiology 368
ophiomancy 511
ophite 440
ophthalmia 443
ophthalmic 441
opiate 174, 841
opine 484
opiniative 481
opiniator 606
opiniatre 481
opinion 484
  give an - 480
  have too high an - of
    oneself 880
  popular - 488
  system of -s 484
  wedded to an - 606
opinionate
  narrow-minded 481
  obstinate 606
opinionated 474, 606
  self - 880
opinionative 474
opinioned *narrow* 481
opinionist
  positive 474
  obstinate 606
opitulation 707
opium *soothe* 174
  deaden sense 376
  narcotic 662
  intemperance 954
  - den 945
opium eater 683
opossum 366
oppidan 188, 189
oppilation 706
opponent
  antagonist **710**
  enemy 891
opportune
  well timed 134
  expedient 646
opportunism 646
opportunist 605

624

opportunity 134, 646
  lose an - 135
oppose *contrary* 14
  counteract 179
  front 234
  evidence 468
  clash 708
opposed [see oppose]
  unwilling 603
opposite
  contrary 14
  - scale 30
  - side 237
opposition 706, **708**
  [see oppose]
  the - 710
oppositionist 710
oppress *molest* 649
  severe 739
  malevolence 907
oppressive *hot* 382
  painful 830
oppressor *tyrant* 739
  evildoer 913
opprobrium 874
oppugnance 719
oppugnant 708, 710,
  719
oppugnation
  opposition 708
  resistance 719
opsimathy 537
optative 865
optic 420
optical 441
  - devices 441
  - instruments **445**
optician 445
optics *light* 420
  sight 441
  optical instruments
    445
optimacy 875
optimates 875
optimism
  overestimation 482
  hopeful 858
optimist 482, 935
optimize 482, 549
option 609
optional 600
optometer 445
optometry 445
opulence 803
opus *composition* 54
  production 161
  music 413
opuscule 593
or *yellow* 436
  alternative 609
oracle *sage* 500
  prediction 511
  prophet **513**
Oracle, Sir -
  positive 474
  vanity 880
  blusterer 887
oracular *answer* 462
  ambiguous 475
  wise 498, 500
  prediction 511

oral *evidence* 467
  declaratory 527
  voice 580
  speech 582
  - communication 588
  - evidence 467
orange *fruit* 298
  round 249
  color **439**
orangery 371
oration 582
  funeral - 363
orator 582
oratorical 582
oratorio 415
oratory *speaking* 582
  place of prayer 1000
orb *region* 181
  circle 247
  luminary 423
  eye 441
  sphere of action 625
  - of day *sun* 318
  luminary 423
  - of night 318
orbicular 247
orbiculation 249
orbit *circle* 247
  heavens 318
  path 627
orchard 371, 636, 691
orchestra *music* 415
  musicians 416
  instruments 417
  theater 599
orchestral 415
  - score 415
orchestrate 413, 416
orchestration 60, 413
orchestrion 417
orchid 369
orchotomy 158
ordain *command* 741
  commission 755
  due 924
  legal 963
  God 976
  church 995
ordained *due* 924
  clergy 996
ordeal
  experiment 463
  trouble 828
  sorcery 992
  - of battle 722
order *regularity* **58**
  class 75
  requirement 630
  direct 693
  command 741
  money 800
  rank 873
  quality 875
  decoration 877
  law 963
  at one's - 743
  call to - 932
  in - 620
  in working - 673
  keep in - 693
  money - 800

  - of the day
    conformtiy 82
    events 151
    habit 613
    plan 636
    command 741
  - of your going 684
  out of - 651
  pass to the - of the
    day 624
  put in - 60
  recur in regular - 138
  set in - 60
  set one's house in -
    673
  standing - 613
  under -s 749
orderless 59
orderly
  regular 58, 80
  arrange 60
  conformable 82
  servant 746
  - of succession 63
  - of things 80
orders, holy - 995
  in - 996
ordinal 998
ordinance
  command 741
  law 963
  rite 998
ordinary *usual* 82
  meal 298
  habitual 613
  imperfect 651
  mediocre 736
  ugly 846
  simple 849
  in - *store* 636
  - condition
    rule 80
  - course of things 613
ordinate 466
ordination
  arrangement 60
  measurement 466
  command 741
  commission 755
  church 995
  rite 998
ordnance 727
ordonnance 963
ordure 653
ore 635
oread 979
orectic 865
organ *music* 417
  voice 580
  instrument 633
  - of the soul 580
  - point 408, 413
organic *state* 7
  structural 329
  protoplastic 357
  - change 146
  - chemistry 357
  - remains 357
  dead 362
organism 329, 366
organist 416, 996

organization
arrangement 60
production 161
structure 329
animated nature **357**
organize *arrange* 60
produce 161
animated nature 357
plan 626
(*prepare* 673)
organized
[*see* organize]
- *hypocrisy* 544
- *massacre* 361
- *murder* 361
organizer 626
organography 329
organology 329
organotherapy 662
orgasm 173
orgiastic 954
orgies 954
oriel *recess* 191
corner 244
window 260
chapel 1000
Orient *East* 236
sunrise 420
Oriental 236
- *philosophy* 451
orientate 236
orifice *beginning* 66
opening 260
oriflamme 550
Origenism 984
origin *beginning* 66
cause 153
derive its - 154
original *dissimilar* 18
not imitated 20
model 22
individual 79
exceptional 83
cause 153
invented 515
unaccustomed 614
laughingstock 857
return to - state 660
originality *will* 600
want of - 843
originate *begin* 66
cause 153
invent 515
- in 154
originative 153, 168
originator 164
Orion's belt 318
orismology *word* 562
name 564
orison *request* 765
worship 990
ormolu *sham* 545
ornament 847
Ormazd 976
ornament
in writing **577**
adornment **847**
glory 873
excess of - 851
ornamental art 847
painting 556

ornamentation 847
ornate
- *writing* 577
ornamental 847
orniscopy 511
ornithology 368
ornithomancy 511
orotund 577
orotundity 249, 577
Orpheus 416
orpiment 436
orrery 318
orthodox
conformable 82
- *religion,* 983a
- *dissenter* 984
orthodoxy **983a**
orthoepist 562
ortho.py 562, 580
orthogonal 212
orthography 561
orthology 494
orthometry
measurement 466
prosody 597
orthopedist 662
orthopraxy 662
orts *remnants* 40
useless 645
(*trifles* 643)
oryctology
minerals 358
organic remains 368
O Salutaris 990
oscillation *change* 149
motion **314**
center of - 222
oscitancy
opening 260
sleepy 683
osculation *contact* 199
touch 379
endearment 902
osculature 43
Osiris 979
Osmanli 984
osmiridium 323
osmosis 302
Ossa on Pelion
heap 72
weight 319
osseous 323
ossify 323
ossuary 363
ostensible
appearance 448
probable 472
manifest 525
plea 617
ostentation 847, **882**
ostentatious 845, 882
osteology 329
osteopathy 662
ostiary *mouth* 260
doorkeeper 263
estuary 343
ostium 260
ostler 746
ostracism [*see* ostracize]
ostracize *exclude* 55
eject 297

banish 893
censure 932
punish 972
ostrich 274, 366
stomach of an - 957
otalgia 378
other *different* 15
extra 37
do unto -s as we
would men should
do unto us 942
enter into the feelings
of -s 906
every - 138
in - words 522
just the - way 14
- extreme 14
- self *friend* 890
- side of the shield 468
- than 18
- things to do 683
- time 119
the - day 123
otherwise 18
otic 418
otiose 169, 683
otiosity 683
otography 418
otologist 418
otology 418
otopathy 418
otoplasty 418
otorrhea 418
otoscope 418
otoscopy 418
ottar, otto [*see* attar]
otter hound 366
ottoman 215
oubliette *ambush* 530
prison 752
ough! 874
ought - to be 922
- to be done 926
ouija board 992a
ounce *weight* 319
ouphe 980
Our Lady 977
ourselves 372
oust *eject* 297
dismiss 756
deprive 789
out *exterior* 220
in error 495
come - 446
go - *egress* 295
cool 385
- and out 52
- at elbows **874**
- at heels 804
- in one's reckoning
495
- of [*see below*]
- upon it
malediction 908
censure 932
- with it *disclose* 529
obliterate 552
play - 729
send - 297
time - of joint 735
waters - 337

outbalance
compensate 30
superiority 33
outbid 794
outbound 295
outbrave 885
out-brazen 234, 885
outbreak *beginning* 66
violence 173
egress 295
discord 713
attack 716
revolt 742
passion 825
outburst *violence* 173
egress 295
revolt 825
outcast
unconformable 83
Pariah 876
secluded 893
bad man 949
outcome *effect* 154
egress 295
produce 775
outcry *noise* 404, 411
auction 796
complaint 839
censure 932
outdo *superior* 33
transcursion 303
activity 682
conquer 731
outdoor 220
outdoors 338
outer 220
outermost 220
outface 885
outfit *clothes* 225
equipment 673
outflank *flank* 236
defeat 731
outflow 295
outgate 295
outgeneral 731
outgo 303
outgoing 295
outgoings 809
outgrow 194
outgrowth 65, 154
out-Herod
superior 33
bluster 174
(*exaggerate* 549)
outhouse 191
outing 266
outjump
transcursion 303
repute 873
outlandish *foreign* 10
extraneous 57
irregular 83
barbarous 851
ridiculous 853
outlast 110
outlaw *irregular* 83
secluded 893
reprobate 949
outlawry 964
outlay 809
outleap 303

outlet *opening* 260
  egress 295
outlie 196
outline *contour* **230**
  form 240
  features 448
  sketch 554
  painting 556
  plan 626
outlines *rudiments* 66
  principles 596
outlive *survive* 110
  continue 141
outlook *view* 448
  outstare 885
outlying *remaining* 40
  exterior 220
outmaneuver *trick* 545
  defeat 731
outmarch 274
outnumber 102
out of *motive* 615
  insufficient 640
  get - the way 623
  get well - 671
  go - one's way 629
  - all proportion 31
  - breath 688
  - cash 804
  - character 24
  - conceit with 867
  - countenance
   disrepute 874
   humbled 879
  - danger 664
  - date
   anachronism 115
   old 124
   ill-timed 135
  - doors 220, 338
  - earshot 419
  - employ 681
  - favor 867
  - focus 447
  - gear *disorder* 59
   powerless 158
   unprepared 674
  - hand *soon* 132
   completed 729
  - harness 748
  - health 655
  - hearing *distant* 196
   not hear 419
  - humor
   discontent 832
   anger 900
  - joint *disorder* 59
   impotent 158
   evil 619
  - kilter 59
  - luck 735
  - one's depth
   deep 208
   shortcoming 304
   difficult 704
   rash 863
  - one's mind 503
  - one's power 471
  - one's reckoning
   uncertain 475
   error 495
626

  inexpectation 508
  disappointment 509
  - one's teens 131
  - one's wits 824
  - order *disorder* 59
  unconformity 83
  imperfect 651
  - patience 825
  - place *disorder* 59
  unconformable 83
  displaced 185
  inexpedient 647
  - pocket *loss* 776
  poverty 804
  debt 806
  - print 552
  - range 196
  - reach *distant* 196
  impossible 471
  - repair 659
  - repute 874
  - season 135
  - shape 243
  - sight *completeness* 52
  - sorts *disorder* 59
  dejection 837
  - spirits 837
  - the common 83
  - the perpendicular 217
  - the question
  impossible 471
  dissent 489
  rejection 610
  hopeless 859
  refusal 764
  undue 925
  - the sphere of 196
  - the way *irrelevant* 10
  unimitated 20
  exceptional 83
  absent 187
  distant 196
  ridiculous 853
  secluded 893
  - the world *dead* 360
  secluded 893
  - time *unmusical* 414
  imperfect 651
  spoiled 659
  discord 713
  - work 681
  put - sight
   invisible 447
   neglect 460
   conceal 528
  turn - doors 297
outogeny 357
outpost *distant* 196
  circumjacent 227
  front 234
outpouring
  egress 295
  information 527
  abundance 639
output *egress* 295
  produce 775
outrage *violence* 173
  evil 619
  badness 649
  injury to 659

  resentment 900
  malevolence 907
  disrespect 929
  guilt 947
outrageous
  excessive 31
  violent 173
  scandalous 874
outrank 33, 62
outré *exceptional* 83
  exaggerate 549
  ridiculous 853
outreach *distance* 196
  deception 545
outreckon 482
outre mer 196
outride 303
outrider 64
outrigger *support* 215
  boat 273
outright 52
outrival *superior* 33
  surpass 303
  fame 873
outrun 303
  - the constable
  debt 806
  prodigal 818
outscourings 653
outset *beginning* 66
  departure 293
outshine *glory* 873
  eclipse 874
outside *extraneous* 57
  exterior 220
  appearance 448
  clean the - of the platter
  ostentation 882
  mere - 544
  - car 272
outsider 57, 893
outskirts *distant* 196
  environs 227
outspan 292
outspeak 582
outspoken *say* 582
  artless 703
  be - *censure* 932
outspread 202
outstanding
  remaining 40
  outside 220
  - accounts 811
  - debt 806
outstare 885
outstart 66
outstep 303
outstretched 202
  with - arms 894
outstrip 303
outtalk 584
outvie *contend* 720
  shine 873
outvote 731
outward 220
  - bound 293, 295
outwear 677
outweigh *exceed* 33
  predominate 175
  (unequal 28)

outwit *deceive* 545
  defeat 731
outwork *defense* 717
outworn 124
oval 247, 249
ovarian 353
ovary 357
ovate 247, 249
ovation *procession* 69
  triumph 883
  (trophy 733)
oven 386
  like an - *hot* 382
over *more* 33
  remainder 40
  end 67
  past 122
  high 206
  too much 641
  all - *completed* 729
  all - with
   destroyed 162
   dead 360
   failure 732
   adversity 735
  danger - 664
  fight one's battles - again 594
  get - 660
  hand - 783
  make - 784
  - again
   repeatedly 104
  - against 237
  - all 200
  - and above
   superior 33
   added 37
   remainder 40
   redundance 641
  - head and ears
   complete 52
   height 206
   feeling 821
  - the border 196
  - the hills and *far away* 196
  - the mark 33
  - the way 237
  set - 755
  turn - 218
overabound 641
overact *bustle* 682
  affect 855
overall 225
overanxiety 865
overarch 223
overawe *sway* 737
  intimidate 860
  respect 928
overbalance *unequal* 28
  compensation 30
  superior 33
overbear *influence* 175
overbearing 885
overboard *throw* -
  eject 297
  reject 610
  disuse 678
  abrogate 756
  relinquish 782

overborne *failure* 732
  subjection 749
overburden
  redundant 641
  bad 649
  fatigue 688
overcast *cloudy* 353
  dark 421
  dim 422
overcautious 864
overcharge
  exaggerate 549
  style 577
  redundance 641
  dearness 814
overcloud 353
overcoat 225
overcolor 549
overcome
  counteract 179
  induce 615
  conquer 731
  sad 837
  disgraced 874
  tipsy 959
  - an obstacle 731
overconfident
  credulous 486
  rash 863
overcredulous 486
overcurious 455
overdate 115
overdistention 194
overdo *redundance* 641
  bustle 682
  affectation 855
overdone - *meat* 298
overdose 641
overdraw
  exaggerate 549
  misrepresent 555
  prodigal 818
overdrawn account
  808
overdrive *misuse* 679
overdue 115, 133
overeager 865
overeat oneself 957
overestimation 482
overfatigued 688
overfed 869, 957
overfeed 641
overflow *stream* 348
  redundance 641
  - with gratitude 916
overgo 303
overgorged *satiety* 869
  gluttony 957
overgrown *much* 31
  large 192
  expanded 194
overhang *high* 206
  pendency 214
overhanging *destiny* 152
  pendency 214
overhasty 901
overhaul *count* 85
  attend to 457
  inquire 461
  censure 932
overhead 206

overhear *hear* 418
  be informed 527
overjoyed 827
overjump 303
overlap *inwrap* 225
  go beyond 303
overlay *layer* 204
  cover 223
  exaggerate 549
  excess 641
  overdo 682
  hinder 706
  - with ornament
    writing 577
overleap 303
overliberal 818
overlie 223
overload *ornament* 577
  redundance 641
  hinder 706
overlook *slight* 458
  neglect 460
  superintend 693
  forgive 918
  disparage 929
  bewitch 992
overlooked 642
  not to be - 642
overlooker 694
overlord 745
overlying 206
overman 33
overmaster 731
overmastering 821
overmatch
  unequal 28
  superior 33
  strength 159
  conquer 731
overmeasure 641
overmodest 881
overmost 210
overmuch 641
overnight 122
overofficious 682
overpaid 816
overpass
  exceed 33
  transgress 303
overpersuade 615
overplus *remainder* 40
  excess 641
overpoise 179
overpower
  counteract 179
  subdue 731
  emotion 824
overpowering
  strong 159
overpraise
  overrate 482
  exaggerate 549
  flatter 933
overprize 482
overrate 482
overreach *pass* 303
  deceive 545
  baffle 545
overreckon 482
overrefinement 477
over-religious 955

override *superior* 33
  influence 175
  pass 303
  hinder 706
  defeat 731
  authority 737
  severity 739
  abrogate 756
overrighteous 988
overrule *control* 737
  cancel 756
overruling
  important 642
overrun *presence* 186
  spread 194
  motion beyond **303**
  printing 591
  redundance 641
  despoil 659
overscrupulous 939
oversea 57, 341
overseas *cap* 225
oversee 693
overseer 694
oversensitive 822
overset *invert* 218
  level 308
  subvert 731
overshadow
  darken 353, 421
  repute 873
  disrepute 874
overshoot the mark
  go beyond 303
  exaggerate 549
  overdo 682
  clumsy 699
oversight
  inattention 458
  error 495
  superintendence 693
  failure 732
overskip 303
oversleep 683
overspent 688
overspread *disperse* 73
  be present 186
  cover 223
overstate 549, 555
overstep 303
overstock 641
overstrain *extol* 482
  fatigue 688
oversupply 641
overt 525
  - act 680
overtake 292
overtaken *tipsy* 959
overtask *misuse* 679
  fatigue 688
overtax 679, 688
overthrow
  revolution 146
  destroy 162
  level 308
  confute 479
  vanquish 751
overthrown
  vanquished 732
overthwart 708
overtired 688

overtone 413
overtop *surpass* 33
  height 206
  (perfection 650)
overtrustful 486
overture
  precursor 62, 64
  music 415
  offer 763
  request 765
overturn *revolution* 146
  destroy 162
  invert 218
  level 308
  confute 479
overvalue 482
overweening
  excess 641
  rash 863
  pride 878
  conceit 880
  insolence 885
overweigh *exceed* 33
  influence 175
  overrate 482
overwhelm *ruin* 162
  redundant 641
  thwart 706
  affect 824
overwhelmed
  defeated 732
  subjection 749
overwhelming
  strong 159
  wonderful 870
overwise 880
overwork *misuse* 679
  fatigue 688
overwrought
  exaggerated 549
  emotion 824
  affectation 855
overzealous 825
ovicell 357
oviform 249
ovo, in - 153
ovoid 247, 249
ovule 247
ovum 357
owe 806
  - it to oneself 926
owelty 27
owing *debt* 806
  attribution 155
owl *bird* 366
  fool 501
  -'s light 422
  -s to Athens 641
  screech - 412
own *assent* 488
  divulge 529
  possess 777
  property 780
  act on one's - respon-
    sibility 738
  after one's - heart 897
  at one's - risk 926
  come by one's - 775
  condemned out of
    one's - mouth 479
  hold one's - 737

look after one's - interest 943
look with one's - eyes 459
out of one's - head 600
- flesh and blood *consanguinity* 11

owner *possessor* 779
without an - 777*a*
ownership
property 780
ox *animal* 366
male 373
hot enough to roast an - 382

Oxford school 984
Oxford shoe 225
oxgoad 727
oxidation 357
oxreim 45
ox-tail soup 298
oxygen 359
oxygon 244

oyer and terminer, court of - 966
oyes 531
oyez! *hear* 418
pubivication 531
oyster 298
- plant 298
- stew 298

P

P
mind one's - 's and Q's
care 459
polite 894
duty 926
pabulum *food* 298
material 316
mental - 454
pace *walk* 264
journey 266
measure 466
keep - with
concur 178
velocity 274
- up and down 266
put through one's -s 525
show one's -s
ostentation 882
pace *permission* 760
- tanti nominis 928
pachydermatous
physically - 376
morally - 823
pacific 721
pacification **723**
pacifism 721
pacify *allay* 174
(*compose* 823)
(*forgive* 918)
pack *arrange* 60
assemblage 72
locate 184
squeeze 195
prepare 673
burden 706
- off *depart* 293
eject 297
- of nonsense 643
- up 229
send -ing 297
package
assemblage 72
packer 673
packet *assemblage* 72
ship 273
pack horse 271
pack saddle 215
pack thread 205
pact 769
Pactolus 803
pad *thicken* 194
line 224
horse 271
diffuseness 573
writing 590
padding *lining* 224
stopper 263

soft 324
diffuseness 573
paddle *walk* 266
row 267
oar 633
- one's own canoe
conduct 692
free 748
- steamer 273
paddock 232
Paddy *Irishman* 188
paddy *rice* 330
padishah 745
padlock *fastening* 45
fetter 752
put a - on one's lips 585
padre 996
padrone 745
pæan *rejoicing* 838
celebration 883
gratitude 916
approbation 931
worship 990
pagan 984
- deities **979**
paganism 984
page *numeration* 85
printing 591
book 593
attendant 746
pageant *spectacle* 448
amusement 840
show 882
pagination 85
pagoda 206, 1000
pagri 225
pah 717
pai 643
pail 191
paillard 962
paillasse 215
pain *physical* - **378**
moral - **828**
penalty 974
painfulness **830**
painfully *very* 31
painless 827
pains 686
get for one's - 973
- and penalties 974
take - 686
painstaking *active* 682
laborious 686
paint *coat* 223
color 428
deceive 545
delineate 55€

ornament 847
- the lily 641
- the town red 840
painter *rope* 45
artist 559
painting 54, **556**
painty 556
pair *similar* 17
combine 48
couple 89
- horses 272
- off *average* 29
marry 903
pair-oar 273
pairs *cards* 840
pajamas 225
pakka [*see* pucka]
paktong 545
pal *ally* 711
chum 890
palace **189**
bishop's - 1000
- car 272
Paladin *defense* 717
combatant 726
palæocrystic 124
palæology
[*see* paleology &c.]
palæstra *school* 542
arena 728
palæstral *strength* 159
school 542
contention 720
palæstric *exertion* 686
[*see* palæstral]
palang 215
palanquin 266, 272
palatable *savory* 394
pleasant 829
palatal *phonetic* 561
palate 390
tickle the - 394
palatial *palace* 189
ostentatious 882
palatinate 181
palatine 745
Palatine Court 966
palaver *unmeaning* 517
speech 582
loquacity 584
colloquy 588
council 696
pale *region* 181
inclosure 232
limit 233
dim 422
colorless 429
frightened 860

- its ineffectual fire
dim 422
out of repute 874
- of the church 995
turn - *lose color* 429
emotion 821
fear 860
pale-faced 429
paleanthropic 124
paleography *past* 122
philology 560
paleology *past* 122
language 160
paleontology 357, 368
paleozoic 124
paleozoölogy 357
palestra
[*see* palæstra &c.]
paletot 225
palette 556
palfrey 271
palimpsest 147, 528
palindrome
inversion 218
neology 563
paling *fence* 232
prison 752
palingenesis 163, 660
palinody 607
palisade *defense* 717
prison 752
-s *cliff* 212
palki 272
pall *mantle* 225
funeral 363
disgust 395
insignia 747
weary 841
dislike 867
satiety 869
canonicals 999
- bearer 363
palladium
safety 664
(*defense* 717)
pallet *support* 215
painter's - 556
palliament 225
palliate *moderate* 174
mind 658
relieve 834
extenuate 937
moderation 174
palliative 174
qualification 469
remedy 662
pallid 429
pallium 999

paraphrast 524
paraphrastic
  imitative 19
  interpretation 522
parasite *follower* 65
  puppet 711
  petitioner 767
  desire 865
  servile 886
  flatterer 935
parasitic
  servile 746, 886
  subjection 749
  grasping 789
parasol *covering* 223
  shade 424
parboil 384
parbuckle 633
Parcæ 601
parcel *divide* 44
  part 51
  group 72
  - out *arrange* 60
  allot 786
  part and - 66
parcels *property* 780
parch *dry* 340
  heat 382
  bake 384
parched 340
  - with thirst 865
parchment
  writing 590
  security 771
parcity 819
pardon 918
  beg - 952
  general - 506
  - me 489
pardonable 937
pare *cut* 38
  reduce 195
  peel 204
  divest 226
  (*scrape* 331)
  - down *shorten* 201
paregoric 662
parenchyma
  materiality 316
  structure 329
parent 166
parentage
  consanguinity 11
  paternity 166
parenthesis
  discontinuity 70
  inversion 218
  interjacence 228
  indication 550
  by way of -
    occasion 134
parenthetical
  irrelative 10
parget 223
pargeting 847
parhelion 423
pariah
  commonalty 876
  outcast 83, 893
parian *sculpture* 557
paries 236

parietal 236
parietes 224
paring [*see* pare]
  small 32
  (*part* 51)
paring-knife 253
parish 181
  bring to the - 804
  come upon the - 804
parishioner 997
paritor 965
parity 17, 27
park *house* 189
  vale 252
  plain 344
  trees 367
  artillery 727
  pleasure ground 840
  - paling 232
parlance 582
  in common - 576
parlementaire
  messenger 534
  flag of truce 723
parley *talk* 588
  mediation 724
parliament 696
parliamentary 696
  - securities 802
parlor 191
parlor car 272
parlor maid 746
parlous 665
Parnassus 597
parochial *regional* 181
  narrow 481
  bigoted 988
parody *imitation* 19
  copy 21
  absurdity 497
  misinterpret 523
  misrepresentation 555
  travesty 856
parole *speech* 582
  on - *restraint* 751
  prisoner 754
  promise 768
Parolles 887
paronomasia
  neology 563
  ornament 577
paronymous 9, 562
parotid 221
paroxysm *violence* 173
  agitation 315
  emotion 825
  anger 900
parquet 440, 599
parquetry 440
parricide 361
parrot *imitation* 19
  bird 366
  loquacity 584
  repeat like a - 505
parrotism 19
parry *confute* 479
  avert 623
  defend 717
parse *analysis* 461
  grammar 567

Parsi 382, 984
parsimony **819**
parsnip 298
parson 996
parsonage 1000
part *divide* 44
  portion **51**
  diverge 291
  music 413
  book 593
  rôle 599
  function 625
  duty 926
  act a - *action* 680
  bear - in 709
  component - 56
  for my - 79
  fractional - 100a
  in - *a little* 32
  on the - of 707
  - and parcel 56
  - by part 51
  - company
    disjunction 44
    avoid 623
    quarrel 713
  - of speech 567
  - song 415
  - with *relinquish* 782
    give 784
  play a - in
    influence 175
  principal - 642
  take an active - 682
  take a - in 680
  take no - in 623
  take - with
    coöperate 709
  take the - of 709
partake 778
  - of the sacrament 998
parterre *level* 213
  cultivation 371
  (*vegetation* 367)
parthenogenesis 161
partial *unequal* 28
  part 51
  special 79
  fractional 100a
  misjudging 481
  unjust 923
  - shadow 422
partiality
  preponderance 33
  desire 865
  friendship 888
  love 897
partially *a little* 32
  partly 51
partibility 44
particeps criminis
  doer 690
  auxiliary 711
participate
  coöperate 709
  share 778
  - in *be a doer* 680
participation **778**
participator *agent* 690
particle *small* 32
  grain 333

particular *item* 51
  event 151
  attentive 457
  careful 459
  exact 494
  capricious 608
  odd 851
  fastidious 868
  in - 79
  - account 594
  - estate 780
particularization 75
particularize
  special 79
  describe 594
particularly *very* 31
  more 33
particulars
  speciality 79
  description 594
parting 44
  - cup 959
Partington, Mrs. 471
parti pris 611
partisan *follower* 65
  auxiliary 711
  weapon 727
  friend 890
  sympathizer 914
partisanship
  warped judgment 481
  coöperation 709
  wrong 923
partition *divide* 44
  wall 228
  allot 786
partlet 366
partly 51
partner *companion* 88
  auxiliary 711
  sharer 778
  friend 890
  spouse 903
  sleeping - 683
partnership *party* 712
  join - with 709
partridge 298
parts *intellect* 450
  skill 698
  wisdom 498
parturient 161
parturition 161
party *assemblage* 72
  special 79
  person 372
  association **712**
  sociality 892
  - spirit *warped judgment* 481
  coöperation 709
  wrong 923
  - to *action* 680
  agent 690
  coöperate 709
  - to a suit 969
  - wall 228
party-colored 428, **440**
parvenu *new* 123
  successful 734
  vulgar 851
  lowborn 876

Peeping Tom 455
peep show *view* 448
  amusement 840
peer *equal* 27
  pry 441
  inquire 461
  lord 875
  - out 446
peerage 875
peerless *unequaled* 28
  supreme 33
  best 648
  glorious 873
  virtuous 944
  (*perfect* 650)
peevish *cross* 895
  irascible 901
peg *grade* 71
  hang 214
  project 250
  drink 959
  come down a - 306
  let down a - 308
  not stir a - *quiet* 265
  inaction 681
  - away *activity* 682
  - on *journey* 266
  - to hang on *plea* 617
Pegasus 271
pegology 348
pegomancy 511
pegs *legs* 266
pelagic 341
pelerine 225
pelf *gain* 775
  property 780
  money 803
pelican 366
pelisse 225
pellet 249
  paper - 643
pellicle *film* 204
  skin 223
pellmell 59, 825
pellucid 425, 570
peloric 242
pelt *skin* 223
  dress 225
  throw 276
  attack 716
  punish 972
peltate 245
peltry 223
pen *inclosure* 232
  write 590
  writer 593
  restrain 751
  imprison 752
  draw the - through 552
  - and ink 590
  - in hand 590
  ready - 569
  slip of the - *error* 495
  solecism 568
  stroke of the -
  write 590
  authority 737
  command 741
pena 206
penal 972

- *servitude* 972
- *settlement* 752
penalize 974
penalty 971, **974**
penance
  atonement 952
  penalty 974
  worship 990
penchant *willing* 602
  desire 865
  love 897
pencil *bundle* 72
  - *of light* 420
  write 590
pencil drawing 556
pencraft 590
pendant *match* 17
  pendency 214
  - world 318
pendency *time* 106
  hanging **214**
pendragon 745
pendulate 605
pendulous
  hanging 214
  oscillating 314
pendulum *hang* 214
  motion of a - 314
Penelope, work of -
  useless 645
  incomplete 730
peneplain 344
penetralia 221
penetrate *ingress* 294
  passage 302
  sagacity 498
  - the soul 824
penetrated with
  belief 484
  feeling 821
penetrating
  sagacious 498
  feeling 821
  - *glance* 441
penetration 465
penguin 310, 366
peninsula 342
penitence **950**
penitentiary 752
  confessor 996
penknife 253
penman 590
  inspired - 985
penmanship 590
pen name 565
pennant 550
penniless 804
  a - lass 804
pennon 550
penny 800
  cost a pretty - 814
  in for a - in for a pound 768
  no - no paternoster 812
  not have a - 804
  - ante 840
  - dreadful 594
  - trumpet 410
  - whistle 410, 417
turn a - 775

penny-a-liner
  envoy 534
  writer 593
penny-a-lining
  diffuse style 573
pennyweight 319
penny wise 819
  - and pound foolish
  caprice 608
  waste 638
  prodigal 818
pennyworth 812
penology 972
pensée, arrière - 528
penseroso 837
pensile 214
pension *income* 810
pensioner *learner* 541
  servant 746
  receiver 785
pensive
  thoughtful 451
  sad 837
penstock 350
pentad 193
pentagon 98, 244
pentahedron 244
pentameter 98, 597
pentangular 98
pentastyle 98
Pentateuch 985
Pentecost 998
Penthesilean 861
penthouse 191
pent up 751
  - in one's memory 505
penultimate 67
penumbra 421
penurious 819
penury *poverty* 804
  (*scantiness* 640)
peon 726
peonage 603
people
  consanguinity 11
  multitude 102
  location 184
  inhabit 186
  mankind 372
  subjects 746
  commonalty 876
  laity 997
pep 171, 682
  full of - 574
pepastic 662
pepper *pungent* 392
  condiment 393
  attack 716
  (*energy* 171)
pepper-and-salt
  gray 432
  variegated 440
peppercorn 643
  cheap 815
  - rent 815
peppery
  irascible 901
pepsin 320
peptic 662
per 631
  - contra

  contrariety 14
  counterevidence 468
  opposition 708
  - *saltum*
  discontinuous 70
  instantaneous 113
  - se 87
peradventure 470
peragrate 266
perambulate 266
perambulator
  measure of length 200
  vehicle 272
perambulatory 266
perceivable 446
perceive
  be sensible of 375
  see 441
  know 490
percentage
  number 84
  discount 813
perceptible 446
perception *idea* 453
  knowledge 490
perceptive 375, 465
perch *location* 184
  abide 186
  habitation 189
  height 206
  support 215
  - up 307
perchance
  by chance 156
  possibly 470
perching 206
percipience 450
percolate *ooze out* 295
  liquefaction 335
  water 337
  stream 348
  clean 652
percolator 191
percursory 458
percussion 276
  center of - 222
percussive 277
perdition
  destruction 162
  ruin 732
  loss 776
perdu 528
  enfant - *hopeless* 859
  rash 863
perdure 106
perdy 535
peregrination 266
peregrinator 268
peremptory
  assertion 535
  firm 604
  authoritative 737
  rigorous 739
  compulsory 744
  duty 926
  - denial 536
  - refusal 764
perennate 106
perennial
  continuous 69
  diuturnal 110

physique *strength* 159
  animality 364
phytivorous 298
phytobiology 369
phytology 369
phyton 369
phytopathologist 369
phytotomy 369
phytozoaria 193
pi 591
piacular 952
pianino 417
pianissimo 415
pianist 416
piano *gentle* 174
  slow 275
  music 415
  - player 417
  - score 415
pianoforte 417
piazza 182, 189, 191
pibroch *music* 415
  indication 550
  war 722
pica 591
picacho 206
picaroon 792
picayune 643
piccolo 410, 417
pick *ax* 253
  eat 298
  select 609
  best 648
  clean 652
  gain 775
  - a quarrel 713
  - holes *censure* 932, 934
  - one's steps 459
  - one's way 675
  - out *extract* 301
  select 609
  - the brains of 461
  - the lock 480a
  - to pieces *separate* 44
    destroy 162
    find fault 932
  - up *learn* 539
    get better 658
    gain 775
pickaninny 129
pickax 253
picked 648
  - men 700
pickeer 720
pickeerer 792
pickelhaube 717
picket *join* 43
  locate 184
  fence 229
  guard 668
  defense 717
  soldiers 726
  restrain 751
  imprison 752
  torture 972
pickings *gain* 775
  booty 793
pickle *condition* 7
  macerate 337
  pungent 392
  condiment 393

636

preserve 670
  difficulty 704
  have a rod in - 673
pickle-herring 844
pick-me-up 392, 662
pickpocket 792
  abuse like a - 932
pickthank *busy* 682
  servile 886
picnic *food* 298
  participation 778
  amusement 840
picot edge 257
picquet 840
pictorial *painting* 556
  beauty 845
picture *appearance* 448
  representation 554
  painting 556
  description 594
  - post card 592
  - to oneself 515
picture gallery 556
picturesque
  painting 556
  beauty 845
piddle *dawdle* 683
piddling 643
pidgin English 563
pie *food* 298
  sweet 396
  printing 591
piebald 440
piece *adjunct* 39
  bit 51
  change 140
  painting 556
  drama 599
  cannon 727
  coin 800
  courtesan 962
fall to -s 162
give a - of advice 695
in -s 330
make a - of work
  about 642
of a - 42
- of a good fortune
  618
- of music 415
- of news 532
- of work *discord* 713
- out 52
- together 43
pull to -s 162
pièce
  - de résistance 298
  - justificative 467
piecemeal 51
pied 440
pier 666
pierce *perforate* 260
  insert 300
  bodily pain 378
  chill 385
  hurt 649
  wound 659
  affect 824
  mental pain 830
  - the head 410
  - the heart 830

piercer 262
piercing *cold* 383
  loud 404
  shrill 410
  intelligent 498
  feeling 821
  - eye 441
  - pain 378
pier glass 445
Pierian spring 597
Pierides 416
pietas 998
pietism 988
pietist 987, 988
piety 987
pig *animal* 366
  sensual 954a
  - in a poke
    uncertain 475
    chance 621
    rash 863
  - together 72
pigeon *bird* 298, 366
  dupe 547
  steal 791
  gorge de - 440
pigeon-hearted 862
pigeonhole
  receptacle 191
  hole 260
  shelve 460
piggery 636
piggin 191
piggish 954
pig-headed *foolish* 499
  obstinate 606
pigment 428
pigmy [*see* pygmy]
pignoration 771
pig-sticking 361
pigsty 653
pigtail 214
Pigwiggen 193
pike *hill* 206
  sharp 253
  fish 366
  weapon 727
pikeman 726
pikestaff *tall* 206
  plain 525
pilaster
  support 215
  projection 250
  ornament 847
pile *heap* 72
  multitude 102
  edifice 161
  velvet 256
  store 636
  money 800
  (*house* 189)
  funeral - 363
  - on the agony 860
  - up *exaggeration* 549
    redundance 641
pile-driver 276
pile-dwelling 189
pileous 256
piles 655
pilfer *steal* 791
pilferer 792

pilgarlic *outcast* 893
pilgrim *traveler* 268
  palmer 996
pilgrimage *journey* 266
  undertaking 676
pill *sphere* 249
  medicine 662
  bore 841
  bitter - 735
pillage *injury* 659
  theft 791
pillager 792
pillar *stable* 150
  lofty 206
  support 215
  monument 551
  tablet 590
  from - to post
    transfer 270
    agitation 315
    irresolute 505
    circuit 629
  - of the state &c. 873
  -s of Hercules 550
pillarist 996
pillion 215
pillory 975
pillow *support* 215
  soft 324
  consult one's -
    temporize 133
    reflect 451
pillowcase 223
pilon 784
pilose 256
pilot *mariner* 269
  inform 527
  guide 693
  director 694
pilot balloon
  experiment 463
pilot boat 273
pilot bread 298
pilot jacket 225
Pilsener beer 298
pimento 393
pimp 962
pimple *tumor* 250
  blemish 848
pin *fasten* 43
  fastening 45
  locate 184
  sharp 253
  axis 312
  trifle 643
  might hear a - drop
    403
  not a - to choose
    equal 27
    no choice 609a
  - down *compulsion* 744
    restraint 751
  - oneself upon
    serve 746
    servile 886
  - one's faith upon **484**
  point of a - 193
pinacotheca 556
pinafore 225
pince-nez 445
pincers 781

pleasant
agreeable 829
amusing 840
witty 842
make things -
deceive 545
induce 615
please 829
flatter 933
pleasantry 840, 842
please 829
as you -
obedience 743
do what one -s 748
if you - *obedience* 743
consent 762
request 765
- oneself 943
pleasing 394, 829
pleasurableness 829
pleasure *physical* - **377**
will 600
moral - **827**
dissipation 954
at - 600
at one's - 737
during - 108a
give - 829
make toil of - 682
man of - 954a
take one's - 840
will and - 600
with - *willingly* 602
pleasure-giving 829
pleasure ground
demesne 189
amusement 840
pleat 219, 258
plebe 493, 541
plebeian 851, 876
plebiscite
judgment 480
choice 609
pledge *promise* 768
security 771
borrow 788
drink to 883, 894
hold in - 771
- oneself 768
- one's word 768
take the -
temperance 771
sobriety 958
pledget *lining* 224
stopper 263
remedy 662
Pleiades *cluster* 72
stars 318
plenary *full* 31
complete 52
plenipotent *power* 157
plenipotentiary
interpreter 524
consignee 758
deputy 759
plenitude 639
in the - of power 159
plenteous 168, 639
plenty *multitude* 102
sufficient 639
- to do 682

plenum *substance* 3
space 180
matter 316
pleonasm
repetition 104
diffuseness 573
redundance 641
plerophory 484
plethora 641
plexiform 219
plexure 219
plexus 219
pliable 324
pliant *soft* 324
irresolute 605
facile 705
servile 886
plicature 258
pliers *extractor* 301
holder 781
plight *state* 7
circumstance 8
promise 768
security 771
evil - 735
- one's faith 902
- one's troth 768, 902
plighted love *love* 897
endearment 902
Plimsoll mark 466
plinth *base* 211
rest 215
plod *journey* 266
slow 275
persevere 604a
work 682
plodder *worker* 686
plodding 604a, 682
dull 843
plot - *of ground* 181
plain 344
measure 466
plan 626
the - thickens
assemblage 72
events 682
plough [see plow]
plover 366
plow *furrow* 259
agriculture 371
- in 228
- one's way 266
- the ground
prepare 673
- the waves 267
plowable 371
plowboy 876
plowed *failure* 732
plowman 371
plowshare 253
pluck *music* 416
cheat 545
resolution 604
persevere 604a
take 789
steal 791
courage 861
- a crow with 932
- out 301
- up *reject* 610
- up courage 861

plucked 732
plucky 604
plug *close* 261
stopper 263
blow 276
deterioration 659
plugugly 913
plum *number* 98
money 800
- pudding 298
plumage 256
plumb *vertical* 212
straight 246
close 261
measure 466
plumber 690
plumb line 212
plum-colored 437
plume *feather* 256
ornament 847
borrowed -s 788
- oneself 878
plumigerous 256
plummet *depth* 208
verticality 212
plumose 256
plump
instantaneous 113
fat 192
tumble 306
plunge 310
unexpected 508
- down 306
- upon 292
plumper *expansion* 194
vote 609
plumpness
[see plump]
plumule 167
plunder *gain* 35
steal 791
booty 793
(*ravage* 659)
plunge *revolution* 146
insert 300
dive **310**
immerse 337
chance 621
hurry 684
- headlong 684
- in medias res
plain language 576
resolute 604
- into *adventure* 676
- into difficulties 704
- into dissipation 954
- into sorrow 830
plunged - in debt 806
- in grief 828
plunger
gambler 463, 621, 840
pluperfect 122
plurality 33, **100**
plus 37
plush 256
Pluto ʃ 82
realms of - 982
plutocracy 803
plutocrat 639
plutonic 382
Plutus 803

pluvial 348
pluviograph 348
pluviometer 348
pluviometry 348
ply *layer* 204
fold 258
use 677
exert 686
request 765
- a trade 794
- one's task 680
- one's trade 625
plytophagous 298
p. m. 126
pneuma 450
pneumatics 334, 338
pneumatogram 532
pneumatograph 662
pneumatology 334, 450
pneumatolytic 334
pneumatometer 334, 662
pneumatonomy 334
pneumatoscope 334
pneumatoscopic 317
pneumatotherapy 662
pneumometer 662
pneumonia 655
poach *steal* 791
illegality 964
poached eggs 298
poacher 792
poachy 345
pock 250
pocket *place* 184
pouch 191
diminutive 193
receive 785
take 789
money 800
treasury 802
brook 826
button up one's - 808
out of - *loss* 776
debt 806
- the affront
submit 725
forgive 918
touch the - 800
pocketbook 551
purse 802
pocket handkerchief 225
pocket money 800
pocket pistol *bottle* 191
pococurante
insensible 823
indifferent 866
pod *receptacle* 191
covering 223
podagra 378
podesta 967
poem 597
poesy 597
poet 597
poetaster *poet* 597
affectation 855
poetic *style* 574
- vigor 574
- prose 598
poetize 597

poeticize 597
poetry 597
pogrom 361
poignancy
  physical energy 171
  pungency 392
  feeling 821
poignant 378
  [*see* poignancy]
poignard
  [*see* poniard]
point *condition* 8
  degree 26
  small 32
  end 67
  term 71
  integer 87
  time 106
  poignancy 171
  no magnitude 180a
  place 182
  speck 193
  sharp 253
  topic 454
  mark 550
  vigor 574
  intention 620
  wit 842
  punctilio 939
  at the - of 197
  at the - of the bayo-
    net 173
  at the - of the sword
    violence 173
  severity 739
  compulsion 744
  come to the -
    special 79
    attention 457
    reasoning 476
    plain language 576
  culminating - 210
  disputed - 713
  from all -s 180
  full of - 574
  give -s to 27
  go straight to the - 278
  in - *relative* 9
    agreeing 23
    conformable 82
  in - of fact 1
  knotty - 704
  make a - of
    resolution 604
    contention 720
    compulsion 744
    conditions 770
    due 924
    honor 939
  on the - of
    transient 111
    future 121
  - a moral 537
  - an antithesis 578
  - at *direction* 278
    direct attention 457
    intend 620
    discourtesy 895
    disrespect 929
    censure 932
  - at issue 454
640

- in dispute 461
- of attack 716
- of convergence 74
- of death 360
- of etiquette 852
- of honor 939
- of land 250
- of the compass 278
- of view *view* 441
  aspect 448
- out *indicate* 79
  - *the reason* 155
  draw attention 457
  inform 527
- system 591
- the finger of scorn
  930
- to *attribute* 155
  direction 278
  probable 472
  predict 511
  mean 516
to the - *concise* 572
  material 642
point-blank
  direct 278
  plain language 576
  refusal 764
point champain 874
point d'appui 215
pointed *great* 31
  sharp 253
  affirmation 535
  marked 550
  concise 572
  language 574
pointedly
  intention 620
pointer *dog* 366
  discrimination 465
  indicator 550
pointless 254, 843
point-to-point race 720
poise *balance* 27
  weight 319
  measurement 466
  health 654
  inexcitability 826
poison *injure* 659
  bane 663
  - gas 663, 722, 727
poisoned 655
  commend the - chal-
    ice 544
poisonous 657, 665
poke *pocket* 191
  loiterer 275
  dawdle 683
pig in a -
  uncertain 475
  chance 621
  rash 863
  - at *thrust* 276
    attack 716
  - fun at 856
  - one's nose in 455,
    682
  - out *project* 250
  - the fire 384
poker 386
  cards 840

poker dice 621
pokerish 980
polacca 273
polacre 273
polar 210
  - coördinates 466
  - lights 423
Polaris 423
polariscope 445
polarity *duality* 89
  counteraction 179
  contraposition 237
pole *measure of length*
  200
  tall 206
  summit 210
  axis 222
  oar 267
  rotation 312
  from - to pole 180
  greasy - 840
  opposite -s 237
  - vault 309
poleax 727
polecat 401
polemic *discussion* 476
  discord 713
  contention 720
  combatant 726
polemoscope 445
polestar *attraction* 288
  luminary 423
  indication 550
  direction 693
  (*guide* 695)
police *regulate* 58
  guardian 965
  - court 966
  - dog 366
  - officer 664
  - magistrate 967
  - van 272
  - whistle 669
policeman
  safeguard 664
  jurisdiction 965
policy *plan* 626
  conduct 692
polish *smooth* 255
  rub 331
  furbish 658
  beauty 845
  ornament 847
  taste 850
  politeness 894
  - off *finish* 729
Polish bank 840
polished
  - *language* 578
  fashionable 852
  polite 894
polisson 949
polite 894
  offensive to ears - 579
  - literature 560
  - society 852
politeness 894
politic *wise* 498
  cunning 702
  cautious 864
  (*skillful* 698)

  body - *mankind* 372
  government 737
political economy 692
politician
  director 694
  proficient 700
politics 702
polity *conduct* 692
  state 737
  duty 926
polka 415, 840
poll *count* 85
  list 86
  vote 609
  schedule 611
pollard *little* 193
  short 201
  tree 367
polloi, hoi 876
poll tax 812
pollute *soil* 653
  corrupt 659
  disgrace 874
  (*dishonor* 940)
pollution *disease* 655
  vice 945
polo 840
Poltergeist 992a
poltroon 862
polyandry 903
polychord 417
polychromatic
  colored 428
  variegated 440
polychrome 440
  painting 556
polyclinic 655
polycoustics 402
polygamy 903
polygastric 191
polyglot
  translation 522
  language 560
polygon *buildings* 189
  figure 244
polygraphy 590
polylogy 573
polymorphic 81
polymorphism 357
Polyphemus 159, 192
polyphonism 580
polyphony 402
polypus 250
polyscope 445
polysyllable 561
polytheism 984
pomade 356
pomatum 356
Pomeranian 366
pommel *support* 215
  round 249
  beat 972
pomologist 369
pomology 369
Pomona 369
pomp 882
pompom 727
pomposity 878, 882
pompous *inflated* 482
  language 577
  pride 878

poncho 225
pond *lake* 343
  store 636
  fish - 370
ponder 451
ponderable *matter* 316
  weight 319
ponderation
  weighing 319
  judgment 480
ponderous *heavy* 319
  - *style* 574, 579
poniard 727
pons asinorum
  unintelligible 519
  difficulty 704
pontiff 996
pontifical 995
pontificals 999
pontificate 995
pontoon *vehicle* 272
  boat 273
  way 627
pony 271
  translation 522, 539
  - up *expend* 809
poodle 366
pooh, pooh!
  absurd 497
  unimportance 643
  contempt 930
pool *lake* 343
  coöperate 709
  prize 775
  billiards 840
  - room 621
  - shark 621
poonghie 996
poop 235
poor *incomplete* 53
  weak 160
  emaciated 203
  - *reasoning* 477
  - *style* 575
  insufficient 640
  trifling 643
  indigent 804
  unhappy 828
  cut a - *figure* 874
  - hand 701
  - head 499
  - in spirit 881
  - man 640, 804
  - thing 914
poorhouse 189
poorly 655
  - off 804
poorness [*see* poor]
  inferiority 34
poor-spirited 862
pop *bubble* 353
  noise 406
  concert 415
  unexpected 508
  - a question 461
  - at 716
  - in *ingress* 294
  insertion 300
  - off *die* 360
  - the question
  request 765

endearment 902
  - upon *arrive* 292
  discover 480a
pope *infallibility* 474
  priest 996
popedom 995
Pope Joan 840
popery 984
popgun *trifle* 643
popinjay 854
poplar *tall* 206
  tree 367
poppy *sedative* 174
poppy-cock 517
populace 876
popular *choosing* 609
  salable 795
  desirable 865
  celebrated 873
  favorite 897
  approved 931
  - concert 415
  - demand 677
  - opinion 488
popularize
  render intelligible 518
  facilitate 705
  make pleasant 829
population
  inhabitants 188
  mankind 372
populous
  crowded 72
  multitude 102
  presence 186
porcelain *baked* 384
  sculpture 557
porch *entrance* 66
  lobby 191
  mouth 231
  opening 260
  (*way* 627)
porcupine *prickly* 253
  touchy 901
pore *opening* 260
  egress 295
  conduit 350
  - over *look* 441
  apply the mind 457
  learn 539
porism *inquiry* 461
  judgment 480
pork 298
pornographic 961
porous *open* 260
  outgoing 295
  spongy 322
  liquescent 335
porpoise 192, 366
porraceous 435
porridge 298, 352
porringer 191
port *abode* 189
  sinistral 239
  gait 264
  arrival 292
  carriage 448
  harbor 666
  - admiral 745
  - fire 388
  - wine 959

portable *small* 193
  transferable 270
  light 320
portage 270
portal *entrance* 66
  mouth 231
  opening 260
  (*way* 627)
portamento 270
portative *small* 193
  transferable 270
  (*light* 320)
portcullis
  hindrance 706
  defense 717
portemonnaie 802
portend 511
portent 512
portentous
  prophetic 511
  fearful 860
porter *janitor* 263
  carrier 271
porterage 270
porterhouse steak 298
portfolio *case* 191
  book 593
  file 636
  direction 693
  authority 747
  jurisdiction 965
porthole 260
portico *entrance* 66
  room 191
portière 424
portion *part* 51
  allotment 786
  - out 786
portional 100a
portly 192
portmanteau 191
  - word 572
portrait 554
  - painter 559
  - painting 556
portraiture 554, 556
portray 554
portreeve *master* 745
  functionary 965
portress 263
posada 189
pose *situation* 183
  form 240
  inquiry 461
  puzzle 475
  difficulty 704
  affectation 855
  - as 554
poser 461
Poseidon 341
posited 184
position
  circumstances 8
  term 71
  situation 183
  proposition 514
  assertion 535
  - in society 873
positive *real* 1
  great 31
  strict 82

  certain 474
  narrow-minded 481
  belief 484
  unequivocal 518
  assertion 535
  obstinate 606
  absolute 739
  (*precise* 494)
Philosophie - 316
  - color 428
  - degree 31
  - fact 474
  - quantity 84
Positivism 451
positivism
  heterodoxy 984
  irreligion 989
posnet 191
posology 662
posse *collection* 72
  party 712
  in - 470
  - comitatus
  collection 72
  army 726
  authority 737
  jurisdiction 965
possess 777
  bedevil 978
  - a state 7
  - knowledge 490
  - oneself of 789
  - the mind 484
  - the soul 824
possessed 777
  - with a devil 503
possession **777**, 780
  sorcery 992
  come into - 775, **783**
  in one's - 777
  person in - 779
  put one in - of 527
  remain in - of the field
    731
possessor **779**
possibility *chance* 156
  liability 177
  may be **470**
  property 780
  - upon a possibility
    475
possible
  [*see* possibility]
post *fastening* 45
  list 86
  situation 183
  location 184
  support 215
  send 270
  swift 274
  publish 531
  mail 534
  beacon 550
  record 551
  employment 625
  accounts 811
  stigmatize 874
  punish 972
  at one's - *persist* 604a
  prepared 673
  on duty 926

practiced *skilled* 698
- eye 700
- hand 700
practitioner
  medical - 662
  doer 690
præcognita 467
prædial 3-12, 371
præmunire 742, 974
prænomen 564
prætor 967
pragmatic *narrow* 481
  teaching 537
  practical 646
- sanction 769
pragmatical
  pedantic 855
  vain 880
pragmatism
  philosophy 451
  expedience 646
  use 677
prahu 273
prairie *space* 180
  plain 344
  vegetation 367
- dog 366
- schooner 272
praise *thanks* 916
  commendation 931
  worship 990
praiseworthy
  commendable 931
  virtue 944
prance *move* 266
  leap 309
  dance 315
prank *caprice* 608
  amusement 840
  adorn 847
prate 584
prattle *talk* 582
  chatter 584
pravity 945
prawns 298
praxis *grammar* 567
  action 680
Praxiteles 559
pray *beg* 765
  worship 990
prayer *request* 765
  worship 990
  house of - 1000
- of Ajax 421
prayer book 990, 998
prayer wheel 998
preach *teach* 537
  allocution 586
  predication 998
- to the winds 645
- to the wise 538
preacher *teacher* 540
  speaker 582
  priest 996
preachment 998
preadamite *antique* 124
  veteran 130
preamble 62, 64
preapprehension 481
prebend 995
prebendary 996

precarious *transient* 111
  uncertain 475
  dangerous 665
precatory 765
precaution *care* 459
  expedient 626
  safety 664
  preparation 673
precede *superior* 33
- *in order* 62
- *in time* 116
- *in motion* 280
precedence 62
  rank 873
  [*see* precede]
precedent
  [*see* precede]
  prototype 22
  precursor 64
  priority 116
  habit 613
  legal decision 969
  follow -s 82
precentor *musician* 416
  leader 694
  priest 996
precept
  requirement 630
  maxim **697**
  order 641
  permit 760
preceptor 540
precession
- *in order* 62
- *in motion* **280**
précieuse *ridicule* 855
precinct *region* 181
  place 182
  environs 227
  boundary 233
precious *great* 31
  excellent 648
  expending 809
  valuable 814
  beloved 897
- metals 800
- stone *goodness* 648
  ornament 847
precipice *vertical* 212
  slope 217
  dangerous 667
  on the verge of a - 665
precipitancy *haste* 684
  rashness 863
precipitate *early* 132
  sink 308
  consolidate 321
  refuse 653
  haste 684
  rash 863
- oneself 306
precipitous 217
précis 596
precise *exact* 494
  severe 739
  taste 850
precisely *imitation* 19
  assent 488
precisian 739, 850
precisianism
  affectation 855

heterodoxy 984
  overreligious 988
preclude 706
preclusion 55
preclusive 55
precocious *early* 132
  immature 674
  pert 885
precognition
  forethought 490
  knowledge 510
precompose 56
preconception 481
preconcert
  predetermination 611
  plan 626
precursal 511
precurse 511
precursor
- *in order* 62, **64**
- *in time* 116
  (*predict* 511)
  (*presage* 512)
predacious 789, 791
predacity 789
predatory *taking* 789
  thieving 791
predecessor 64
predeliberation
  foresight 510
  predetermination 611
predella 215
predesigned 611
predestination *fate* 152
  necessity 601
  predetermination 611
  Deity 976
predetermination 601, **611**
predial *land* 342
  agriculture 371
  manorial 780
predicament *state* 7
  circumstances 8
  junction 43
  character 75
predicate *forecast* 507
  affirm 535
  preach 998
predict 511
prediction **511**
predilection *bias* 481
  affection 820
  desire 865
  (*love* 897)
predispose
  motive 615
  prepare 673
predisposed
  willing 602
predisposition
  tendency 176
  affection 820
predominance 157
  [*see* predominant]
predominant
  influence 175
  directing 693
  authority 737
predominate
  superior 33

preëminent *superior* 33
  celebrated 873
preëmption 795
preëngage *early* 132
preëngagement 768
preëstablish 626
preëxamine 461
preëxist *existence* 1
  priority 116
  (*past* 122)
preface *precedence* 62
  precursor 64
  book 593
prefect *learner* 541
  ruler 745
  deputy 759
- of studies 542
prefecture 737
prefer *choose* 609
- a claim 969
- a petition 765
preference 62
preferment
  improvement 658
  ecclesiastical - 995
prefigure
  prediction 511
  (*indication* 550)
prefix 62, 64
preglacial 124
pregnable 158]
pregnant *producing* 161
  productive 168
  predicting 511
- *style* 572
- *important* 642
- with meaning 516
prehensile 789
prehension 789
prehistoric 124
preinstruct 537
prejudge 481
prejudicate 481
prejudice *misjudge* 481
  evil 619
  detriment 659
prejudicial 649
prelacy 995
prelate 996
prelation 609
prelect *expound* 531
  teach 537
  speech 582
prelection 537, 582
prelector 540, 582
prelibation 510
preliminaries
- of peace 723
  settle - 673
preliminary
  preceding 62
  precursor 64
  reception 296
  (*prior* 116)
prelude *prefix* 62
  precursor 64
  beginning 66
  music 415
  (*priority* 116)
premature *early* 132
  unripe 674

643

premeditate
  predetermine 611
  intend 620
premices 154
premier *director* 694
  vicegerent 759
  - pas 66
premiership 693
premise *prefix* 62
  announce 511
premises *precursor* 64
  prior 116
  ground 182
  evidence 467
  logic 476
premium *debt* 806
  receipt 810
  reward 973
  at a - 814
premonish 668
premonition 668, 992*a*
premonitory
  prediction 511
  warning 668
Premonstratensian
  996
premonstration
  appearance 448
  prediction 511
  manifestation 525
premunire
  [*see* præmunire]
prenotion
  misjudgment 481
  foresight 510
prensation 789
prentice 541
prenticeship 539
preoccupancy
  possession 777
preoccupation
  inattention 458
preoption 609
preordain 611
  destiny 152
  necessity 601
  Deity 976
preparation **673**
  music 413
  instruction 537
  writing 590
  in course of - *plan* 626
preparatory *preceding*
  62
prepare 673
  - the way 705
prepared *predict* 507
  deft 698
preparedness 673
preparing *destined* 152
prepense
  spontaneous 600
  predetermined 611
  intended 620
  malice - 907
prepollence 157
preponderance
  superiority 33
  influence 175
  dominance 737
  (*importance* 642)
644

prepossessed
  obstinate 606
prepossessing 829
prepossession
  prejudice 481
  possession 777
preposterous *great* 31
  absurd 497
  imaginative 515
  exaggerated 549
  ridiculous 853
  undue 925
prepotency 157
Pre-Raphaelite 122,
  124
prerequire 630
prerequisite 630
preresolve 611
prerogative
  authority 737
  right 924
presage *predict* 511
  omen 512
presbyopia 443
presbyter 996
Presbyterian 984
presbytery 995, 996,
  1000
prescience 510
prescient 510, 511
prescious 511
prescribe *direct* 693
  advice 695
  order 741
  entitle 924
  enjoin 926
prescript *precept* 697
  decree 741
prescription
  remedy 662
prescriptive *old* 124
  unchanged 141
  habitual 613
  due 924
presence *in space* **186**
  appearance 448
  breeding 894
  in the - of *near* 197
  - chamber 191
  - of God 981
  - of mind *calm* 826
  cautious 864
  real - 998
  saving one's - 928
present
  - *in time* 118
  - *in space* 186
  offer 763
  give 784
  church preferment 995
  at - 118
  - a bold front 861
  - a front 719
  - arms *courtesy* 894
  respect 928
  - in spirit 187
  - itself *event* 151
  visible 446
  thought 451
  - oneself *presence* 186
  offer 763

  courtesy 894
  - time **118**
  instant 113
  - to the mind
  attention 457
  memory 505
  - to the view 448
  these -s *writing* 590
  epistle 592
presentable 845, 852
presentation
  [*see* present]
  celebration 883
  courtesy 894
presentiment
  instinct 477
  prejudgment 481
  foresight 510
presently 132
presentment
  information 527
  law proceeding 969
preservation
  continuance 141
  conservation **670**
  Divine attributes 976
preserve *sweets* 396
  provision 637
  [*see* preservation]
  - a middle course 628
preserver
  safeguard 664
preshow 511
preside
  - at the board
  direction 693
  - over *authority* 737
presidency 737
president
  director 694
  master 745
  -'s message 695
press *crowd* 72
  closet 191
  weight 319
  public - 531
  printing 591
  book 593
  move 615
  compel 744
  offer 763
  solicit 765
  go to - 591
  - agent's yarn 546
  - in 300
  - into the service
  use 677
  aid 707
  - of business 682
  - on *course* 109
  progression 282
  haste 684
  - one hard 716
  - out 301
  - proof 591
  - to the bosom 902
  under - of 744
  writer for the - 593
pressed, hard - 704
  - for time 684
pressgang 965

pressing *need* 630
  urgent 642
pressman 554
press room 591
pressure *power* 157
  influence 175
  weight 319
  urgency 642
  adversity 735
  center of - 222
  high - 824
presswork 591
Prester John 515
prestidigitation 545
prestidigitator 548
prestige *bias* 481
  authority 737
  fascination 865
  fame 873
prestigiation 545
prestissimo 415
presto *instantly* 113
  music 415
prestriction 442
presumable 472
presume
  probability 472
  misjudge 481
  believe 484
  suppose 514
  hope 858
  pride 878
presumption
  [*see* presume]
  probability 472
  expectation 607
  rashness 863
  arrogance 885
  unlawfulness 925
presumptive
  probable 472
  supposed 514
  due 924
  heir - 779
  - evidence
  evidence 467
  probability 472
presumptuous 885
presuppose
  misjudge 481
  suppose 514
presurmise *foresee* 510
  suppose 514
pretend *assert* 535
  simulate 544
  untruth 546
pretended 545
pretender *deceiver* 548
  braggart 884
  unentitled 925
pretending 544
pretense *imitation* 19
  falsehood 544
  untruth 546
  excuse 617
  ostentation 882
  boast 884
pretension
  ornament 577
  affectation 855
  due 924

pretentious
  inflated 482
  specious 846
  affected 855
  vain 880
  ostentatious 882
  boasting 884
  undue 925
preterience 111
preterit 122
preterition 122
preterlapsed 122
pretermit 460
preternatural 83
pretext *untruth* 546
  plea 617
pretty *much* 31
  imperfectly 651
  beautiful 845
  - fellow 501
  - good 651
  - kettle of fish, pass,
    &c.
  disorder 59
  difficulty 704
  - quarrel 720
  - well *much* 31
  little 32
  trifling 643
preux chevalier 939
prevail *exist* 1
  superior 33
  general 78
  influence 175
  habit 613
  succeed 731
  - upon 615
prevailing 78
  - taste 852
prevalence
  [*see* prevail]
prevaricate
  falsehood 544
  (*equivocate* 520)
prévenance 894
prevene 116
prevenient
  precedent 62
  early 132
prevent 706
prevention
  prejudice 481
  hindrance 706
  - of waste 817
preventive 55
previous
  - in time 116
  (- *in order* 62)
  move the - question
    624
  not within - experi-
    ence 137
prevision 510
prewarn 668
prey *food* 298
  quarry 620
  booty 793
  victim 828
  fall a - to
  be defeated 732
  subjection 749

- on the mind
  excite 824
  regret 833
  fear 860
- on the spirits 837
- to grief 828
- to melancholy 837
price *consideration* 147
  value 648
  money **812**
  at any - 604a
  beyond - 814
  cheap at the - 815
  have one's - 812
  of great - *good* 648
  dear 814
  reward 973
price current 812
priceless *valuable* 648
  dear 814
prick *sharp* 253
  hole 260
  sting 378
  sensation of touch 380
  incite 615
  mental suffering 830
  kick against the -s
  useless 645
  resistance 719
  - up one's ears *hear*
    418
  curiosity 455
  attention 457
  expect 507
prickle *sharp* 253
  sensation of touch 380
prickly 253
pride *ornament* 847
  loftiness **878**
  take a - in 878
prie-dieu 215
priest 904, 996
priestcraft 995
priestess 996
priesthood 995, 996
priest-ridden
  false piety 988
  churchdom 995
prig *steal* 791
  puppy 854
  affected 855
  blusterer 887
priggish *affected* 855
  vain 880
prim *taste* 850
  affected 855
  proud 878
prima donna
  actress 599
  important 642
  proficient 700
primacy
  superiority 33
  celebrity 873
  church 995
prima facie *sight* 441
  appearance 448
  probable 472
  - *meaning* 516
  manifest 525
primal 66

primary *initial* 66
  cause 153
  important 642
  - color 428
  - education 537
primate 996
primates 875
prime *initial* 66
  primeval 124
  early 132
  teach 537
  important 642
  excellent 648
  prepare 673
  in one's - 131
  - and load 673
  - cost *price* 812
  cheap 815
  - minister 694
  - mover 153, 164
  - number 84
  - of life *youth* 127
  adolescence 131
  - of the morning 125
primed *skilled* 698
  tipsy 959
primer *automobile* 272
  schoolbook 542
primeval 124
primices 154
primigenous 124
priming 556
primitive *old* 124
  cause 153
  - color 428
primogenial
  beginning 66
primogeniture *old* 124
  age 128
  posterity 167
  heritage 777
primordial *original* 20
  old 124
  cause 153
primordiate 124
primordium 153
primrose-colored 436
prince *perfection* 650
  master 745
  nobility 875
  - of darkness 978
Prince Albert coat 225
princely
  authoritative 737
  liberal 816
  famous 873
  noble 875
  generous 942
princess 745, 875
principal *important* 642
  director 694
  - part *great* 31
  whole 50
principality *region* 181
  property 780
principally 33
principia 66, 496
principle *intrinsic* 5
  rule 80
  cause 153
  element 316

  reasoning 476
  tenet 484
  maxim 496
  motive 615
  probity 939
  on - 615
  want of - 945
prink *adorn* 847
  show off 882
print *news* 532
  mark 550
  engraving 558
  letterpress 591
  out of - 552
printer 591
printing **591**
  - press 591
prior - *in order* 62
  - *in time* 116
  clergy 996
priority **116,** 234
priory 1000
prism *angularity* 244
  optical instrument 445
  see through a - 443
prismatic *color* 428
  variegated 440
prison **752**
  cast into - 751
  in - 751, 754
prisoner *restraint* 751
  captive **754**
  accused 938
  take - *restrain* 751
  seize 789
pristine 122
prithee 765
prittle-prattle 588
privacy *conceal* 528
  seclude 893
private *special* 79
  hidden 528
  secluded 893
  in - 528
  keep - 881
  - road 627
  - soldier 726
  talk to in - 586, 588
  to gain some - ends 943
privateer *combatant* 726
  robber 792
privateering 791
privately 881
privation *loss* 776
  poverty 804
privative 789
privilege *freedom* 748
  permission 760
  exemption 777a
  due 924
privity *relation* 9
  knowledge 490
privy *hidden* 528
  latrines 653
  - to 490
Privy Council
  tribunal 966
prize *good* 618
  masterpiece 650
  palm 733
  gain 775

prolegomena 64
prolepsis *precursor* 64
  anachronism 115
proletarian 876
proliferous 163, 168
prolific 168
proligerous 163
prolix 573
prolixity 573
prolocutor
  interpreter 524
  teacher 540
  speaker 582
prologue
  precursor 64
  drama 599
  what's past is- 122
prolong *protract* 110
  late 133
  continue 143
  lengthen 200
prolongation
  sequence 63
  protraction 110
  posterity 117
  continuance 143
prolusion 64
promenade *walk* 266
  display 882
Promethean 359
  -spark 359
prominence
  [*see* prominent]
prominent *convex* 250
  manifest 525
  important 642
  eminent 873
prominently *much* 31
  more 33
promiscuous *mixed* 41
  irregular 59
  indiscriminate 465a
  casual 621
promise *predict* 511
  engage **768**
  hope 858
  keep one's- 939
  keep - to ear and
    break to hope 545
  - of celestial worth
    511
  - oneself *expect* 507
  hope 858
promissory 768
  - note *security* 771
  money 800
promontory *height* 206
  projection 250
  land 342
promorphology 357
promote *improve* 658
  aid 707
promoter *planner* 626
promotion *class* 541
  improvement 658
prompt *early* 132
  remind 505
  tell 527
  induce 615
  active 682
  advise 695

  (*quick* 274)
  - book 505
  - memory 505
prompter *theater* 599
  tempter 615
  adviser 695
promptuary 636
promulgate 531
  - a decree 741
pronation and supina-
  tion 218
prone *horizontal* 213
proneness *tendency* 176
  disposition 820
prôner *ostentation* 882
  praise 931
pioneur 935
prong 91
pronounce *judge* 480
  assert 535
  voice 580
  speak 582
pronounced 31, 525
pronouncement 531,
  535
pronunciation 562, 580
pronunciative 535
proof *hard* 323
  insensible 376
  test 463
  demonstration 478
  indication 550
  printing 591
  draft 626
  ocular - 446
  - against *strong* 159
  resolute 604
  safe 664
  defense 717
  resistance 719
  insensible 823
proof reader 591
prop *support* 215
  help 707
propædeutic 537
propædeutics 537
propagable 168
propaganda
  teaching 537
  school 542
  preparation 673
propagandism 537
propagandist
  teacher 540
  priest 996
propagate *produce* 161
  be productive 168
  publish 531
  teach 537
propel 284
propeller 284, 312
propend 602
propendency
  predetermination 611
  inclination 820
propense 602
propension 820
propensity
  tendency 176
  willingness 602
  inclination 820

proper *special* 79
  expedient 646
  handsome 845
  due 924
  (*right* 922)
  in its - place 58
  - name 564
  - time 134
  show a - spirit 939
  the - thing *duty* 926
properties, theatrical -
  costume 225
  drama 599
property *power* 157
  possessions **780**
  wealth 803
property-man 599
prophasis 510
prophecy 511
prophet *oracle* 511
  seer 513
  preparer 673
  priest 996
  non-Biblical -s 986
prophetess 513
prophetic *predict* 511
  revelation 985
Prophets, the - 985
prophylactic
  healthful 656
  remedy 662
  preservative 670
  hindrance 706
prophylaxis 670
propinquity 197
propitiate *pacify* 723
  mediate 724
  calm 826
  content 831
  love 897
  pity 914
  forgive 918
  atone 952
  worship 990
propitiator 714, 724
propitious *timely* 134
  beneficial 648
  helping 707
  prosperous 734
  auspicious 858
proplasm 22
proportion *relation* 9
  mathematical 84
  sum 85
  symmetry 242
  elegance 578
  allotment 786
proportionate
  agreeing 23
proportions *space* 180
  size 192
proposal 765
  plan 626
propose *suggest* 514
  broach 535
  intend 620
  offer 763
  offer marriage 902
  - a question 461
proposition
  supposition 454

  reasoning 476
  project 626
  suggestion 514
  offer 763
  request 765
propound *suggest* 514
  broach 535
  - a question 461
proprietary 779
proprietor 779
proprietorship 780
propriety
  agreement 23
  elegance 578
  expedience 646
  fashion 852
  right 922
  duty 926
propugn *resist* 717
  vindicate 937
propugnaculum 717
propulsion **284**
propulsive 276, 284,
  633
propylon 66
prore 234
prorogue 133
proruption 295
prosaic *usual* 82
  slow 275
  - *style* 575
  dry 576
  dull 843
prosaism *prose* 598
prosal 598
proscenium *front* 234
  theater 599
proscribe *interdict* 761
  banish 893
  curse 908
  condemn 971
  (*exclude* 77)
prose *diffuse style* 573
  prate 584
  not verse **598**
  - run mad *ornate* 577
  poetical 597
  - *writer* 598
prosecute *pursue* 622
  act 680
  accuse 938
  arraign 969
  - an inquiry 461
prosecutor 938
proselyte
  conversion 144
  learner 541
  convert 607
proselytism 537
proser 841
prosody 597
prosopopœia 521
prospect *futurity* 121
  view 448
  probability 472
  expectation 507
  landscape painting
    556
  good - 858
  in - *intended* 620
prospector 463

psychopath 450
psychophysicist 450
psychophysics 450
psychotherapy 662, 992a
psychrometer 349
pteridophytes 369
ptisan 662
ptyalism 299
ptyalize 297
puberty 127
pubescent 131
public, general - 372
make - 531
- demand 677
- enemy 891
- good 644
- library 593
- mind 593
- opinion 488
- press 531
- school 542
- servant 644
- spirit 910
- welfare 910
purchasing - 677
publication
production 161
disclosure 529
promulgation **531**
book 593
public house 189
go to the - 959
publicist 554, 593, 968
publicity 531
publish 531
- the banns 765
publisher 593
puce 433, 437
pucelage *youth* 127
celibacy 904
purity 960
Puck 274, 979
play - 699
pucka *permanent* 141
solid 321
valid 494
ripe 673
pucker *contracted* 195
fold 258
anger 900
in a - *excited* 824
pudder *disorder* 59
pudding *food* 298
soft 324
pulpy 354
sweets 396
in - time 132
puddle 343
pudgy 201
pudicity 960
pue.ile *boyish* 129
foolish 499
feeble 575
trifling 643
puerperal 161
puff *inflate* 194
wind 349
tartlet 396
pant 688
boast 884

praise 931
flatter 933
- of smoke 330
- up *vanity* 880
puffed up *inflated* 482
pride 878
puffer 935
puffery 884
puffy 194
pug *short* 201
dog 366
footprint 551
puggaree 225
pugilism 720
pugilist 726
pugilistic 720
pugnacity
contentiousness 720
irascibility 901
puisné *young* 127
puissant *powerful* 157
strong 159
puke 297
pulchritude 845
pulcinella
actor 599
buffoon 844
pule *cry* 411, 412
weep 839
pull *superiority* 33
power 157
influence 175, 615, 631
row 267
draw 285
attraction 288
indicate 550
printing 591
a long and a strong -
coöperate 709
- about one's ears 308
- an oar 680
- by the sleeve 505
- different ways 713
- down *destroy* 162
lay low 308
- in 751
- out 301
- the check string 142
- the wires 693
- through
restoration 660
aid 707
- together 709
- to pieces *separate* 44
destroy 162
censure 932
detract 934
- towards*attract* 288
- up *stop* 142
rest 265
root out 301
reprimand 932
accuse 969
- upon the purse 814
strong - *exertion* 686
pulled down *weak* 160
fatigued 688
pullet 129
pulley 633
Pullman car 272

pullulate
produce 161, 168
multiply 168
grow 194
pulmonary 349
pulmonate 349
pulmonic 655
pulmotor 349, 662
pulp 354
pulpiness **354**
pulpit *rostrum* 542
clergy 996
church 1000
pulsate *periodic* 138
oscillate 314
agitate 315
pulsation *feeling* 821
pulse [*see* pulsate]
vegetable 367
feel the - *inquire* 461
test 463
pulsion 276
pultaceous 354
pulverable 330
pulverize 330, 358
pulverulence **330**
pulvil 400
puma 913
pummel [*see* pommel]
pump *shoe* 225
water supply 348
inflate 349
inquire 461
instrument 633
pumpkin 298
pump room *house* 189
remedy 662
pun *similarity* 17
absurdity 497
ambiguity 520
misinterpretation 523
neology 563
wit 842
punce 276
Punch *buffoon* 844
- and Judy 599
punch *mold* 22
perforate 260
perforator 262
nag 271
strike 276, 716
beverage 298
engrave 558
vigor 574
punchbowl *vessel* 191
hollow 252
tippling 959
puncheon 635
vessel 191
perforator 262
puncher 262
punchinello 599, 844
punctated 440
punctilio *fashion* 852
punctilious *exact* 494
severe 739
observant 772
ostentation 882
scrupulous 939
puncto 882
punctual *early* 132

periodical 138
exact 494
observance 772
scrupulous 939
punctuation 567
puncture 260
pundit *learned man* 492
sage 500
lawyer 968
pung 272
pungency **392**
physical energy 171
taste 392
pungent *pain* 378
taste 392
odor 398
vigor 574
feeling 821
punish 972
punishment **972**
punition 972
punitive 972
punk 962
fuel 388
punkah 349
punster 844
punt *row* 267
boat 273
punter 840
puny 193
pup *infant* 129
give birth 161
dog 366
pupa 129
pupil - *of the eye* 441
student 492
learner 541
pupilage *youth* 127
learning 539
pupillary 541
puppet *little* 193
dupe 547
effigy 554
auxiliary 711
tool 746
be the - of 749
make a - of 737
puppet show
drama 599
amusement 840
puppy *infant* 129
dog 366
fop 854
braggart 884
blusterer 887
puppyism 855
Purana 986
purblind
dim sight 443
weak judgment 481
purchase *support* 215
acquisition 775
buy **795**
purchase money 147
purchaser 147
purdah
screen for women 374
shade 424
ambush 530
pure *simple* 42
true 494

649

Q

put to the - 830
- at issue 461
questionable
  uncertain 475
  doubtful 485
  disreputable 874
  improbity 940
questioner 455
questionist 541
questionless
  certain 541
questor 801
queue 65, 214
quib 856
quibble *sophistry* 477
  quirk 481
  unmeaning 517
  equivocation 520
  falsehood 544
  wit 842
  verbal - *absurdity* 497
quick *transient* 111
  rapid 274
  alive 359
  intelligent 498
  active 682
  skillful 698
  feeling 821
  sensibility 822
  irascible 901
  cut to the - 824
  probe to the - 461
  - as thought 113
  - ear 418
  - eye 441
  - in response 375
  - succession 136
  - time 274
  sting to the -
    pain 830
    anger 900
  to the - *physically* 375
    mentally 822
  touch to the - 822, 824
quicken *work* 170
  violence 173
  come to life 359
  promote 707
  excite 824
quickening power 170
quickly *soon* 132
quicksand *danger* 667
  difficulty 704
  - of deceit 545

quick-scented 398
quickset hedge 232
quicksilver
  changeable 149
  energy 171
  motion 264
  velocity 274
quick-witted 842
quid *essence* 1
  pungency 392
quid pro quo
  compensa. - 30
  substitution 147
  interchange 148
  retaliation 718
  barter 794
  wit 842
  reward 973
quidam 372
quiddity
  essence 5
  quibble 477
  wit 842
quidnunc 455
quiescence 265
quiet *calm* 174
  rest 265
  silence 403
  dissuade 616
  leisure 685
  inexcitability 826
  all - on Potomac 721
  keep - 681
  - life 721
quietism
  quiescence 265
  insensibility 823
  inexcitability 826
  content 831
  irreligion 989
quietly *modest* 881
  get on - 736
quietude 826
quietus *death* 360
  failure 732
  acquittal 970
  give a - 361
  receive its - 756
quill 590
  my gray goose - 590
quill-driver 590
quillet 477
quilt *covering* 223
  variegated 440
quinary 98

quincunx 98
quinine 662
quinquefid 99
quinqueliteral 99
quinquennial 138
quinquennium 108
quinquepartite 99
quinquesect 99
quinquesection 99
quinsy 655
quint 98
quintain *aim* 620
  game 840
quintal 319
quintessence 5
quintet 98, 415
quintroon 41
quintuple 98
quintuplicate 98
quinze 840
quip *amusement* 840
  wit 842
  ridicule 856
  disrespect 929
quire *singers* 416
  paper 593
  church 1000
quirk
  sophistry 477
  misjudgment 481
  caprice 608
  amusement 840
  wit 842
quirt 975
quit *depart* 293
  relinquish 624
  pay 807
  - claim 927a
  - of *loss* 776
    relinquish 782
  - one's hold 782
  - scores 807
qui-tam 969
quitclaim 270, 927a
quite 52
  - another thing
    irrelevant 10
    unlike 18
  - the reverse 14
  - the thing 23
quits *equal* 27
  atonement 952
  be - with
    retaliation 718
    pay 807

quittance
  security 771
  payment 807
  forgiveness 918
  atonement 952
  reward 973
quitter *avoidance* 623
quiver *receptacle* 191
  oscillation 314
  agitation 315
  shiver 383
  store 636
  feeling 821
  sensibility 822
  fear 860
  in a - 921, 824
  - with rage 900
qui-vive 669
  on the - 459
Quixote, Don -
  mad 504
  rash 863
quixotic *fanciful* 515
  rash 863
quixotism 825
quiz *ridicule* 856
  laughingstock 857
quizzical *ridiculous* 853
quod *prison* 752
  in - 754
quodlibet *inquiry* 461
  sophism 477
  wit 842
quoits 840
quondam 122
quorum 696
quota *quantity* 25
  number 84
  contingent 786
  expenditure 809
  furnish its - 784
quotation
  imitation 19
  conformity 82
  evidence 467
  price 812
  - marks 550
quote 82
  evidence 467
quoth *affirmative* 535
  speech 582
quotidian 138
quotient 84
quotiety 25, 136
quotum 25

R

Ra 423
rabat 225
rabbet 43
Rabbi 996
Rabbinist 984
rabbit 298
  productive 168
rabble *assemblage* 72
  mob 876
rabid *insane* 502
  emotion 821
  652

  eager 865
  angry 900
rabies 503
raccoon 366
raccroc 156
race *relation* 111
  sequence 69
  kind 75
  lineage 166
  run 274
  stream 343, 348

  conduit 350
  pungency 392
  course 622
  business 625
  culture 658
  career 692
  opposition 708
  contention 720
  one's - is run 360
  run a - 720
  run in a - 680

  run one's - 729
race course 728
race horse
  horse 271
  swift 274
racer *vehicle* 272
rachidian 222
rachis 235
rachitis 655
racial 166
raciness 574

rack *receptacle* 191
  frame 215
  cloud 253
  physical pain 378
  purify 652
  anguish 828
  torture 830
  punish 972
  instrument of torture 975
  go to - and ruin 735
  on the - 507
  - one's brains
    thought 451
    imagination 515
  - rent 810
rackabones 659
racket *agitation* 315
  loud 404
  roll 407
  discord 414, 713
racket court 840
racketing *active* 682
  amusements 840
rackets 840
rackety *loud* 404
raconteur 594
racy *strong* 171
  pungent 392
  - *style* 574
  feeling 821
raddle *weave* 219
raddled *tipsy* 959
radial 291
radiance *light* 420
  beauty 845
radiant *diverging* 291
  beauty 845
  glorious 873
radiate 73, 291
radiated 242
radiation 242, 291
radiator 386
radical *essential* 5
  complete 52
  algebraic root 84
  cause 153
  important 642
  reformer 658
  - change 146
  - cure 662
  - reform 658
radically *greatly* 31
radication 153, 613
radicle 153
radiculose 367
radio 534
radioactive *energy* 171
  calefaction 384
  light 420
radiogram 532, 554
radiograph 421, 554, 556
radiography 556
radiology 420
radiometer *light* 420
  optical instrument 445
  measurement 466
radiometry 420
radiomicrometer 389

radiophone 527, 531, 534
radiophony 402
radioscopy 420
radiotelegraph 434
radiotelegraphic 431
radiotelegraphy 420
radiotelephone 534
radiotherapy 420, 662
radish 298
radium 384
  - emanation 420
radius *length* 200
  width 202
radix 84, 153
radoter 499
radoteur 501
raff *refuse* 653
  rabble 876
  (*miscreant* 949)
raffle 621
raft 273
rafter 215
rag *small* 32
  (*part* 51)
ragamuffin 876
rage *violence* 173
  influence 175
  excitement 824, 825
  fashion 852
  desire 865
  wrath 900
  the battle -s 722
ragged 226
ragout 298
rags *clothes* 225
  useless 645
  do to - 384
  tear to - 162
  worn to - 659
ragtag
  - and bobtail 876
ragtime *music* 415
  dance 840
raid *attack* 716
  pillage 791
rail *inclosure* 232
  prison 752
  - at 932
  - in *circumscribe* 229
  restrain 751
railing 232
raillery 856
rail-riding 972
railroad *travel* 266
  method 627
  expedite 684
railway 627
  - speed 274
  - station 266
raiment 225
rain *stream* 348
  sufficient 639
  - of blood *omen* 512
  - or shine *certain* 474
  at all hazards 604
rainbow 440
  omen 512
rain chart 348
rain gauge 348
rainless 340

rains *monsoon* 348
rainy 348
  provide against a -day
    prepare 673
    economy 817
  - day *adversity* 735
  - season 348
raise *increase* 35
  produce 161
  elevate 212, 307
  leaven 320
  excite 824
  - a cry 531
  - a dust 682
  - a hue and cry *against* 932
  - alarm 860
  - a laugh 840
  - anger 900
  - a question
    inquire 461
    doubt 485
  - a report 531
  - a siege 723
  - a storm 173
  - Cain 900
  - expectations 858
  - funds 775
  - hope 511
  - money 788
  - one's banner 722
  - one's head
    improve 658
    refresh 689
    prosperity 734
    repute 873
  - one's voice
    affirm 535
  - one's voice against 932
  - spirits from the dead 992
  - the finger 550
  - the mask 529
  - the spirits 836
  - the voice *shout* 441
  - the wind *gain* 775
    borrow 788
  - troops 722
  - up *vertical* 212
    excite 824
raised *convex* 250
raiser *producer* 164
raisins 298
raison d' être 620
rajah 745, 875
rajput 726
rake *drag* 285
  gardening 371
  clean 652
  profligate 949
  intemperance 954
  libertine 962
  - out 301
  - up *collect* 72
    extract 301
    recall 505
    excite 824
  - up evidence 467
rakehell 949, 962
raking fire 716

rakish *intemperate* 954
  licentious 961
rallentando 415
rally *arrange* 60
  improve 658
  restore 660
  ridicule 856
  encourage 861
  - round *order* 58
    coöperate 709
rallying cry
  indication 550
  encouragement 861
rallying point 74
ram *impulse* 276
  sheep 366
  male 373
  man-of-war 726
  milk the - 645
  - down *close* 261
  dense 321
  - in 300
Ramadan 138, 956
ramage 367
ramble *stroll* 266
  wander 279
  folly 499
  delirium 503
  digress 573
rambler 269
rambling
  irregularity 139
ramification *part* 51
  bisection 91
  posterity 167
  filament 205
  symmetry 242
  divergence 291
ramify *angularity* 244
  [*see* ramification]
rammer *plug* 263
  impeller 276
ramose 242
  (*rough* 256)
ramp *obliquity* 217
  climb 305
  leap 309
rampage 173
rampant *violent* 173
  prevalent 175
  vertical 212
  raised 307
  free 748
  vehement 825
  licentious 961
rampart 717
ramrod 263, 276
ramshackle 665
ranch 780
rancho 189
rancid *fetid* 401
  unclean 653
rancour *enmity* 889
  malevolence 907
  revenge 919
randan 273
randem *vehicle* 272
random *casual* 156
  uncertain 475
  aimless 621
  talk at - *sophistry* 477

653

iudge 480
credit 873
love 897
respect 928
approbation 931
have - to 457
merit - 642
pay - to *believe* 484
honor 873
- as 484
regardful *attentive* 457
careful 459
regardless
inattentive 458
insensible 823
regards *courtesy* 894
respect 928
regatta *contention* 720
amusement 840
regelate 385
regency 755
regenerate
reproduce 163
restore 660
penitence 950
piety 987
regeneration
conversion 144
divine function 976
baptismal - 998
regent *governor* 745
deputy 759
regicide 361
régime *circumstances* 8
conduct 692
authority 737
ancien - 875
regimen *diet* 298
remedy 662
regiment *assemblage* 72
army 726
regimentals 225
region **181**, 342
regional 181, 189
register *arrange* 60
list 86
chronicle 114
furnace 386
record 551
recorder 553
schedule 611
registrar 553
registration 551
registry 114
record 551
reglet 591
regnant *influence* 175
authority 737
regorge 790
regrade 283
regrate 777, 795
regrater 797
regress 287
regression **283**, 287
regret *sorrow* **833**
penitence 950
regretted, to be - 833
regrowth 163
reguerdon 973
regular *uniform* 16
complete 52

order 58
arrangement 60
rule 80
conformity 82
periodic 138
symmetric 242
habitual 613
by - *intervals* 58
- *return* 138
regularity
[*see* regular]
regularize *legal* 963
regulars 726
regulate *adjust* 23
order 58
arrange 60
direct 693
regulated by
conformity 82
regulation
precept 697
law 963
(*command* 741)
regulative principle 453
regurgitate *return* 283
flow 348
restore 790
rehabilitate
reconstruct 660
restore 790
rehearse *repeat* 104
try 463
describe 594
drama 599
prepare 673
Reichsrath 696
reign *influence* 175
government 737
- of terror *severity* 739
fear 860
- of violence 738
reimburse *restore* **790**
pay 807
rein *means of restraint* 752
(*moderate* 174)
(*counteract* 179)
- in *retard* 275
restrain 751
reindeer 271, 366
reinforce
[*see* reënforce]
reinforcement
[*see* reënforcement]
reinless 738
reins [*see* rein]
direction 693
give - to the imagination 515
give the - to
facilitate 705
lax 738
permit 760
hold the - 693
take the -
authority 737
reinstall 660
reinstate 660, 790
reinvest 790
reinvigorate 689

reiterate 104
reject *exclude* 55
eject 297
refuse 764
rejected *hateful* 898
rejection **610**
rejoice *exult* 838
amuse 840
- in 827
- in the name of 564
- the heart *gratify* 829
cheer 836
rejoicing **838**
rejoin *assemble* 72
arrive 292
rejoinder *answer* 462
law pleadings 969
rejoining *meeting* 292
rejuvenescence 660
rekindle *ignite* 384
excite 824
(*incite* 615)
relapse *turn back* 145
regression 283
fall back **661**
relate *narrate* 594
- to *refer* 9
related *kin* 11
relation **9**
kin 11
narrative 594
relationship 9
relative
comparative **464**
- *position* 9
relativism 451
relax *loose* 47
weaken 160
moderate 174
slacken speed 275
soften 324
inactive 683
repose 687
misrule 738
liberate 750
relent 914
- one's efforts 681
- the mind 452
relaxation [*see* relax]
amusement 840
dereliction 927
relaxed *weak* 160
relay *materials* 635
provision 637
release *death* 360
deliver 672
liberate 750
exempt 760
from engagement **768a**
security 771
exemption 777a
restore 790
repay 807
forgive 918
exempt 927a
discharge 970
deed of - 723
relegate *banish* 55
transfer 270
remove 297

relent *moderate* 174
soften 324
submit 725
pity 914
relentless *resolute* 604
severe 739
wrathful 900
malevolent 907
revenge 919
impenitent 951
relessee *possessor* 779
receiver 785
relevancy
pertinence 9
congruity 23
relevé 298
reliability [*see* reliable]
solvency 800
reliable *certain* 474
trustworthy 632
reliance *confidence* 484
expectation 507
hope 858
relic *remainder* 40
reminiscence 505
token 551
relics *corpse* 362
sacred 998
relict 905
relief *composition* 54
silhouette 230
prominence 250
aid 707
comfort **834**
bas - *convex* 250
sculpture 557
in strong - *visible* 443
manifest 525
relieve *improve* 658
aid 707
comfort 834
relievo *convex* 250
sculpture 557
religieuse 996
religion *theology* 983
piety 987
under the mask of 988
religionist 988
religious *celibacy* 904
honorable 939
theological 983
pious 987
over - 955
- education 537
- persuasion 983
- sects 984
relinquish 624, 782
- a purpose 624
recant 607
- hope 859
- life 360
- property 782
relinquishment **624, 782**
resignation 757
reliquary *box* 191
sacred 998
reliquiæ 362
relish *pleasure* 377
taste 390

condiment 393
savory 394
delight 827
desire 865
reluctent *light* 420
reluct 720
reluctance
　dissuasion 616
　unwilling 603
　dislike 867
reluctation 719
relume *ignite* 384
　light 420
rely *believe* 484
　hope 858
　(*expect* 507)
remain *abide* 1
　be left 40
　endure 106
　long time 110
　continue 141
　be present 186
　stand 265
　- firm 150
　- in one's mind 505
　- in possession of the
　　field 731
　- neuter 605
　- on one's hands 641
remainder 40
　estate 780
　in - *posterior* 117
remainder-man 779
remains *remainder* 40
　corpse 362
　vestige 551
　organic - 357
remand *defer* 133
　order 741
remanet 40
remark *observe* 457
　affirmation 535
　worthy of - 642
remarkable *great* 31
　exceptional 83
　important 642
remarry 993
remediable *restore* 660
　remedy 662
remedial 660, 662
remediless 859
remedy *restore* 660
　cure 662
remember 505
remembered 505, 506
remembrance 505
remembrances 894
rememoration 505
remiform 245
remigration
　regression 283
　arrival 292
　egress 295
remind *remember* 505
　recollect 506
　that -s me 134
reminder 505
reminiscence 505
remise 927*a*
remiss *neglectful* 460
　reluctant 603

shiftless 674
idle 683
lax 738
remission *cessation* 142
　moderation 174
　laxity 738
　forgiveness 918
　exemption 927*a*
remit [*see* remission]
　- one's efforts 681
remittance
　payment 807
remittent 138
remitter 790
remnant *remainder* 40
　reserve 632
remodel *convert* 144
　revolutionize 146
　improve 658
remollient 324
remonetize 800
remonstrance
　dissuasion 616
　deprecation 766
　censure 932
remora *cohere* 46
　hindrance 706
remorse 950
remorseless 919
remote *not related* 10
　distant 196
　- age 122
　- cause 153
　- future 121
　- region 196
remotion 270
removal [*see* remove]
remove *subduct* 38
　term 71
　displace 185
　transfer 270
　recede 287
　depart 293
　dinner 298
　extract 301
　school 541
　- the mask 529
removedness
　distance 196
remuda 72
remugient 412
remunerate *reward* 973
remunerative *useful* 644
　gain 775
　receipt 810
Renaissance 554
renaissance 660
renascent 163
rencounter *contact* 199
　meeting 292
　fight 720
rend 44
　- the air *loud* 404
　cry 411
　lament 839
　- the heartstrings 830
render *convert* 144
　interpret 522
　give 784
　restore 790
　- an account

inform 527
describe 594
- a service 644
rendezvous *assemble* 72
　focus 74
rendition
　interpretation 522
　restore 790
renegade *convert* 144
　traveler 268
　turncoat 607
　shirker 623
　disobey 742
　apostate 941
renew *twice* 90
　repeat 104
　reproduce 163
　recollect 505
　restore 660
　- one's strength 689
reniform 245
renitence
　counteraction 179
　hardness 323
　elasticity 325
　unwillingness 603
　resistance 719
renounce *disavow* 536
　recant 607
　relinquish 624
　resign 757
　- property 782
　repudiate 927
　(*deny* 536)
renovate *reproduce* 163
　restore 660
renovated *new* 123
renovation
　[*see* renovate]
renown 505, 873
renowned 31
renownless 874
rent *tear* 44
　fissure 198
　hire 788
　purchase 795
rentage 810
rental 810
renter 779
rent-free 815
rent roll *property* 780
　receipts 810
rents *houses* 189
renunciation
　[*see* renounce]
　refusal 764
　exemption 927*a*
reorganize *convert* 144
　improve 658
　restore 660
repair *mend* 658
　make good 660
　refresh 689
　out of - 659
　- to 266
reparation
　[*see* repair]
　restitution 790
　atonement 952
　reward 973
reparative 30

repartee *answer* 462
　wit 842
reparteeist 844
repartition 786
repass 314
repast 298
repay *pay* 807
　reward 973
repeal 756
repeat *imitate* 19
　duplication 90
　iterate 104
　reproduce 163
　affirm 535
　- by rote 505
repeated *frequent* 136
　iteration 104
repeater *watch* 114
　cunning 702
　firearm 727
repel *repulse* 289
　deter 616
　defend 717
　resist 719
　refuse 764
　give pain 830
　disincline 867
　banish 893
　excite hate 898
repellent [*see* repel]
repent 950
repentant
　my - tears 951
repercuss 277, 289
repercussion *recoil* 277
　(*counteraction* 179)
répertoire 599
repertory 599, 636
repetend
　arithmetical 84
　iteration 104
repetition *imitation* 19
　iteration **104**
　(*copy* 21)
　(*twice* 90)
repine *pain* 828
　discontent 832
　regret 833
　sad 837
　(*repent* 950)
replace *substitute* 147
　locate 184
　restore 660
replenish *complete* 52
　fill 637
repletion *filling* 639
　redundance 641
　satiety 869
replevin *security* 771
　recovery 775
　restore 790
replica 21, 90
replication *answer* 462
　law pleadings 969
reply *answer* 462
　vindicate 937
report *noise* 406
　judgment 480
　inform 527
　publish 531
　rumor 532

retrieve *restore* 660
  acquire 775
retriever *dog* 366
retroaction
  counteraction 179
  recoil 277
  regression 283
retroactive *past* 122
retrocession
  reversion 145
  regression 283
  recession 287
retroflexion 218
retrograde *contrary* 14
  moving back 283
  recession 287
  deteriorated 659
  relapsing 661
retrogression
  regression 283
  deterioration 659
  relapse 661
retrorse 145
retrospection *past* 122
  reversion 145
  thought 451
  memory 505
retroussé 201, 307
retroversion 218
retrude 289
return *list* 86
  repeat 104
  periodic 138
  reverse 145
  recoil 277
  regression 283
  arrival 292
  answer 462
  report 551
  relapse 661
  appoint 755
  profit 775
  restore 790
  proceeds 810
  reward 973
  in - *compensation* 30
  - thanks *gratitude* 916
   worship 990
  - the compliment
   interchange 148
   retaliate 718
  - to the original state
   660
reunion *junction* 43
réunion *assemblage* 72
  concord 714
  point de - 74
  social - 892
reveal 529
  - itself 446
reveille 550
revel *amuse* 840
  dissipation 954
  - in *enjoy* 377
revelation
  discovery 480a
  disclosure 529
  theological 985
Revelation 985
reveler 840
  drunkard 959
662

reveling
  disorder 59
  rejoicing 838
revelry 954
revenant 361, 980a
revendicate *claim* 741
  acquisition 775
  due 924
revenge 919
  breathe - *anger* 900
revenue 810
  means 632
  - cutter 273
reverberate *recoil* 277
  sound 408
reverbatory 386
revere *love* 897
  respect 928
  piety 987
revered *sage* 500
reverence *title* 877
  respect 928
  piety 987
  clergy 996
reverenced 500
reverend *title* 877
  clergy 996
  - sir 130
reverent *pious* 987
  worship 990
reverential
  respectful 928
reverie
  train of thought 451
  inattention 458
  imagination 515
reversal *inversion* 218
  revolution 607
  irresolute 605
reverse *contrary* 14
  return 145
  inversion 218
  - of a medal 235
  anteposition 237
  adversity 735
  abrogate 756
  cards 840
  - of the shield 468
reverseless 150
reversible
reversion [see reverse]
  posteriority 117
  return **145**
  possession 777
  property 780
  succession 783
  remitter 790
reversioner 779
reversis 840
revert *repeat* 104
  return 145
  turn back 283
  revest 790
  - to 457
revest 790
reviction 660
review *consider* 457
  inquiry 461
  judge 480
  recall 505
  dissertation 595

  compendium 596
  revise 658
  parade 882
reviewer 480, 595
revile *abuse* 932
  blaspheme 988
reviler 936
revise *copy* 21
  consider 457
  printing 591
  plan 626
  edit 658
revising barrister 967
revision 658
  under - 673
revisit 186
revival
  reproduction 163
  life 359
  restoration 660
  worship 990
revivalist 996
revive *reproduce* 163
  refresh 658
  resuscitate 660
  excite 824
revivify *reproduce* 163
  life 359
  resuscitate 660
revocable 605
revocation 536
revoke *recant* 607
  cancel 756
  (*deny* 536)
  (*refuse* 764)
revolt *contrariety* 14
  revolution 146
  resist 719
  disobey 742
  shock 830
  disapproval 932
  - against *hate* 898
  - at the idea
  dissent 489
revolting *painful* 830
revolution
  periodicity 138
  change **146**
  rotation 312
revolutionary 146, 742
revolutionize 140, 146
revolve
  [see revolution]
  - in the mind 451
revolver 727
revulsion *reversion* 145
  revolution 146
  inversion 218
  recoil 277
revulsive 276
revulsively 145
reward 30, **973**
reword 104
rewriting 21
Reynard *animal* 366
  cunning 702
rez de chaussée
  room 191
  low 207
rhabdology 85
rhabdomancy 511

rhadamanthus
  judge 967
  hell 982
rhamphoid 245
rhapsodical
  irregular 139
rhapsodist *fanatic* 504
  poet 597
rhapsodize 497
rhapsody
  discontinuity 70
  nonsense 497
  fancy 515
rheometer 157
rhetoric *speech* 582
  flowers of - 577
rheum *excretion* 299
  fluidity 333
rheumatism 378
rhino 800
rhinoceros 366
  - hide *physically insensible* 376
  morally insensible 823
rhipidate 194
rhizanthous 367
rhododendron 845
rhomb 244
rhomboid 244
rhubarb 298
rhumb 278
rhyme [see rime &c.]
rhythm *periodicity* 138
  melody 413
  elegance 578
  verse 597
rhythmic 413, 578
rhythmical
  - *style* 578
riant 836
rib *support* 215
  ridge 250
  wife 903
ribald *vulgar* 851
  disreputable 874
  impure 961
ribaldry 908
ribband [see ribbon]
ribbed *furrowed* 259
ribbon *tie* 45
  filament 205
  record 551
  decoration 877
ribbons *reins* 752
ribroast 972
rice 330, 367
ricebird 298
rich *savory* 394
  color 428
  language 577
  abundant 639
  wealthy 803
  beautiful 845
  ornament 847
  - gifts wax poor 907
  - man 639, 803
riches 803
richly *much* 31
  - deserve 924
rick *accumulation* 72

store 636
rickety *weak* 160
  ugly 846
  imperfect 651
rickrack 257
ricksha 272
ricochet 277
rid *deliver* 672
  get - of *eject* 297
  liberation 750
  loose 776
  relinquish 782
riddance 672, 776, 782
riddle *arrange* 60
  crossing 219
  sieve 260
  secret 533
  sift 652
  (*question* 461)
ride *get above* 206
  move 266
  - *a horse* 370
  - and tie
  periodicity 138
  journey 266
  - at anchor 265
  - full tilt at
  pursue 622
  attack 716
  - hard 274
  - in the whirlwind
  will 604
  rule 737
  - one's hobby 622
  - out the storm 664
  - roughshod
  violence 173
  severity 739
  insolence 885
  illegality 964
  - the waves 267
rider *affix* 37
  appendix 39
  equestrian 268
ridge *narrow* 203
  height 206
  prominence 250
ridicule 856
  disrespect 929
ridiculous *absurd* 497
  foolish 499
  trifling 643
  grotesque 853
ridiculousness 853
riding *district* 181
  journey 266
ridotto *gala* 840
  rout 892
rifacimento
  repetition 104
  resuscitation 660
rife *general* 78
  influence 175
riffle 348
riffraff *dirt* 653
  commonalty 876
  bad folk 949
rifle *musket* 406, 727
  plunder 791
  - grenade 727
rifled cannon 727

rifleman 726
rifler 792
rifles 726
rifle shooting 840
rift *separation* 44
  fissure 198
rig *dress* 225
  vehicle 272
  prepare 673
  frolic 840
  strumpet 962
  - the market 794
  run the - upon 929
rigadoon 840
rigging *ropes* 45
  gear 225
  instrument 633
riggish 961
right *dextral* 238
  straight 246
  true 494
  freedom 748
  property 780
  just **922**
  privilege 924
  duty 926
  honor 939
  virtuous 944
  bill of - 969
  by - 924
  have a - to 924
  hit the - nail on the
    head
  discover 480a
  skill 698
  in one's - mind
  wise 498
  sane 502
  in the - place 646
  keep the - path 944
  - about [*see below*]
  - ahead 234
  - and left *space* 180
  circumjacence 227
  lateral 236
  - angle 212
  - as a trevet 650
  - ascension 466
  - away 113, 143
  - bower 840
  divine - of kings
    737
  - establishment 478
  - hand [*see below*]
  - itself 660
  - line 246
  - man in the right
    place 23
  - owner 779
  - passage 279
  - thing to do 926
  - word in the right
    place 578
  set - *inform* 527
  disclose 529
  step in the - direction
    644
  that's - 931
right-about
  go to the -
  circuit 311

  tergiversation 607
  send to the - *eject* 297
  reject 610
  refuse 764
  to the - 283
  turn to the -
  inversion 218
  deviation 279
righteous *virtuous* 944
  - overmuch 988
  the - 987
Righteousness
  Lord our - 976
  Sun of - 976
rightful 922
  - owner 779
right hand *power* 157
  dextrality 238
  help 711
  not let the - know
    what the left is
    doing 528
  - of friendship 888
right-handed 238
right-minded
  sanity 502
  probity 939
  virtue 944
rights, put to -
  restore 660
  set to - *arrange* 60
  stand on one's - 748
rigid *regular* 82
  hard 328
  exact 494
  severe 739
  (*stubborn* 606)
rigmarole
  unmeaning 517
  (*absurd* 497)
rigor 383, 494, 739
  (*compulsion* 744)
  - mortis 360
rigorous *exact* 494
  severe 739
  revengeful 919
  - establishment 478
Rigsdag 696
riksdag 696
rile *annoy* 830
  hate 898
  anger 900
rilievo *convex* 250
  sculpture 557
rill 348
rim 231, 272
rime *chink* 198
  frost 383
rime *or* **rhyme** *simi-*
  larity 17
  melody 413
  poetry 597
  without - or reason
  absurd 497
  caprice 608
  motiveless 615a
rimeless *prose* 598
rimester 597
rimer 262
rimiform 259
rimose 198

rimple 258
rimulose 198
rind *covering* 223
  flay 226
rinderpest 655
ring *fastening* 45
  pendency 214
  circle 247
  loud 404
  resonance 408
  clique 712
  arena 728
  have the true - 494
  in a - fence
  circumscription 229
  inclosure 232
  - dove 366
  - in the ear 408
  - the changes
  repeat 104
  change 140
  changeable 149
  - the tocsin 669
  - untrue 546
  - with the praises of
    931
  rub the - 902
ring-dove 416
ringent 260
ringer *impostor* 548
ringleader *director* 694
  mutineer 742
ringlet *circling* 247
  hair 256
ringworm 655
rink 840
rinse 652
rinsings 653
riot *confusion* 59
  derangement 61
  violence 173
  discord 713
  resist 719
  mutiny 742
  - in *pleasure* 742
  run - *activity* 682
  excitement 825
  intemperance 954
rioter 742
riotous 173
rip *open* 260
  bad man 949
  libertine 962
  - open 260
  - up *tear* 44
  excite 824
riparian 342
ripe *of cheese* 298
  prepared 673
  - age *old* 128
  grown up 131
ripen *perfect* 650
  improve 658
  prepare 673
  complete 729
  - into 144
ripicolous 342
riposte 462
ripple *ruffle* 256
  shake 315
  water 348

murmur 405
riprap 215
rire, pour - 853
rise *grow* 35
  begin 66
  revolt 146, 742
  slope 217
  progress 282
  ascend 305
  stir 682
  - above 31, 206
  - again 660
  - from 154
  - in arms 722
  - in price 814
  - in the world 734
  - up *elevation* 307
risible *laughable* 838
  ridiculous 853
  (*wit* 842)
rising [*see* rise]
  - generation
  youth 127
  posterity 167
  - ground *height* 206
  slope 217
  - of the curtain
  beginning 66
  appearance 448
  worship the - sun 886
risk *chance* 621
  danger 665
  invest 787
  at all -s 604
  at any - 604
risqué 961
rite *law* 963
  religious **998**
  funeral - 363
ritornel 62, 64
ritornello 104
ritual *ostentation* 882
  worship 990
  rite 998
ritualism
  religious sect 984
rival *emulate* 648
  oppose 708
  opponent 710
  compete 720
  combatant 726
  outshine 873
rivalry *envy* 921
rive 44
rivel 258
river **348**
  - of death 360
  -s of hell 982
rivet *fasten* 43
  fastening 45
  - in the memory 505
  - the attention
  attend 457
  excite 824
  - the eyes upon 441
  - the yoke 739
riveted *firm* 150
rivulation 219, 248
rivulet 348
rivulose 248
rixation 713

664

riziform 249
road *street* 189
  direction 278
  way 627
  on the -
  transference 270
  progression 282
  approach 286
  on the high - to 278
  - to ruin
  destruction 162
  danger 665
  adversity 735
road book 266
road hog *traveler* 268
  selfishness 943
roads *lake* 343
roadstead *location* 184
  abode 189
  refuge 666
roadster 271, 272
roadway 627
roam 266
roan *horse* 271
  color 433
roanoke 800
roar *violence* 173
  blow violently 349
  sound 404, 407
  bellow 411, 412
  laugh 838
  weep 839
rcarer 887
roaring *great* 31
  - trade 731, 734
roast *heat* 384
  inquire 461
  ridicule 856
  rib - 972
  - and boiled 298
  - an ox 883
  - beef &c. 298
  rule the - 737
roasting *heat* 382
rob *juice* 352
  pulp 354
  plunder 791
  - Peter to pay Paul
  compensation 30
  steal 791
  wrong 923
robber 792
robbery 791
robe *covering* 223
  dress 225
  canonicals 999
  - s of state 747
robin 366
Robin Goodfellow 979
roborant 662
robust *strong* 159
  healthy 654
roc 83
Rochester knockings 992a
Rocinante 271
rock *firm* 150
  oscillate 314
  hard 323
  land 342
  safety 664

  danger 667
  attack 716
  money 800
  build on a - 156
  - ahead 665
  - bound coast 342
  - oil 356
  split upon a - 732
rockaway 272
rocket *rapid* 274
  rise 305
  light 423
  signal 550
  arms 727
  go up like a - and
    come down like
    the stick 732
rocking-stone 314
rocking-chair 215
rocky 323
rococo 847
rod *support* 215
  measure 466
  scourge 975
  divining 993
  kiss the - 725
  - in pickle
  prepared 673
  accusation 938
  punishment 972
  scourge 975
  - of empire 747
  sounding - 208
rodomontade
  overestimation 482
  unmeaning 517
  boast 884
  (*absurdity* 497)
roe *deer* 366
  female 374
rogation *request* 765
  worship 990
rogue *cheat* 548
  knave 941
  scamp 949
  -'s march 297
roguery 940
roguish *playful* 840
roil 653, 898
roister 885
roisterer 887
Roland for an Oliver
  retaliation 718
  barter 794
rôle *drama* 599
  business 625
  plan 626
  conduct 692
roll *list* 86
  fillet 205
  convolution 248
  rotundity 249
  make smooth 255
  move 264
  wind 311
  rotate 312
  rock 314
  flow 348
  sound 407
  record 551
  money 800

  - along 312
  - in *plenty* 639
  redundance 641
  - in riches 803
  - in the dust 731
  - into one 43
  - in wealth 803
  - of honor 86
  - on 109
  - on the ground 839
  - up 312
  - up in 225
  strike off the -
  abrogate 756
  punish 972
  (*degrade* 874)
roll call 85
roller *fillet* 45
  round 249
  clothing 255
  rotate 312
  - coaster 840
  - skates 266, 272
rollers *billows* 348
rollic 836
rollicker 838
rollicking
  frolicsome 836
  blustering 885
rolling 348
  - pin 249
  - stock 272
  - stones 149, 312
Rolls, Master of the -
  recorder 553
  judge 967
  - Court 966
romaine 298
roman 591
Roman Catholic 423,
  984
romance *absurdity* 497
  imagination 515
  untruth 546
  fable 594
romancer
  story-teller 594
Romanism 984
romantic
  imaginative 515
  descriptive 594
  sensitive 822
romanticism 515
Romany 563
Rome, Church of - 984
  do at - as the Romans
    do 82
romp *child* 129
  violent 173
  game 840
rondeau *music* 415
Röntgen ray 420
rood *length* 200
  cross 219, 998
rood loft 1000
roof *house* 189
  summit 210
  cover 223
  (*height* 206)
  (*summit* 210)
rookie 726

roofless 226
rook *steal* 791
  thief 792
rookery *nests* 189
  dirt 653
room *occasion* 134
  space 180
  presence 186
  chamber 191
  class 541
  classroom 542
  plea 617
  assembly - 840
  in the - of 147
  make - for
    opening 260
    respect 928
roomer 188
roommate 890
roomy 180
roorback 934
roost *abode* 189
  bed 215
rooster 366
root *algebraic* - 84
  cause 153
  place 184
  abide 186
  base 211
  etymon 562
  cut up - and branch
    162
  lie at the - of 642
  pluck up by the -s 301
  - and branch 52
  - for *applaud* 931
  - out *eject* 297
  extract 301
  discover 480a
  strike at the - of 716
  [take - *influence* 175
  locate 184
  habit 613
rooted *old* 124
  firm 150
  located 184
  habit 613
  (*permanent* 141)
  deep - 820
  - antipathy 867
  - belief 484
rooter *sports* 840
rope *fastening* 45
  cord 205
  freedom 748
  scourge 975
  give - enough 738
  - of sand
    incoherence 47
    weakness 160
    impossible 471
  -'s end 975
ropedancer 700
ropedancing 698
ropy 352
roquelaure 225
roric 339
rorid 339
rosâ, sub - 528
rosary 990, 998
roscid 339

Roscius 599
rose *pipe* 350
  fragrant 400
  red 434
  beauty 845
  bed of -s
    pleasure 377
    prosperity 734
  couleur de - *red* 434
    good 648
    prosperity 734
    hope 858
  under the - 528
  welcome as the - s in
    June *pleasing* 829
    sociality 892
roseate *red* 434
  hopeful 858
rose-colored *hope* 858
rosehead 350
rosette 847
rose water
  moderation 174
  flattery 933
  not made with - 704
Rosicrucian 984
rosin *rub* 331
  resin 356a
Rosinante 271
roster 69, 86
rostrate 245
rostriferous 245
rostrum *beak* 234
  pulpit 542
rosy 434
  - wine 959
rosy-cheeked 845
rot *decay* 49
  putrefy 653
  disease 655
  decay 659
rota *list* 86
  period 138
  court 966
rotation *periodicity* 138
  motion round 312
rote, by - 505
  know - 490
  learn - 539
roti 298
rotogravure 558
rotten *weak* 160
  bad 649
  foul 653
  decayed 659
  (*fetid* 401)
  - at the core
    deceptive 545
    diseased 655
  - borough 893
  - in state of Denmark
    702
rotund 249
rotunda 189
rotundity 249
roturier 876
roué 949
rouge 434
rouge et noir 621
rough *violent* 173
  shapeless 241

uneven 256
pungent 392
unsavory 395
sour 397
sound 410
raucous 581
unprepared 674
fighter 726
ugly 846
low fellow 876
bully 887
churlish 895
evildoer 913
bad man 949
in the - 241
- and tumble 59
- breathing 402
- copy *writing* 590
  unprepared 674
- diamond
  amorphism 241
  artless 703
  vulgar 851
  commonalty 876
  good man 948
- draft 590, 626
- guess 514
- it 686
- sea 348
- side of the tongue
  censure 932
- weather *violent* 173
  wind 349
roughcast *covering* 223
  shape 240
  roughness 256
  scheme 626
  unpolished 674
roughhew *form* 240
  prepare 673
rough-house 173
roughly *nearly* 197
roughness **256**
  blemish 848
  [*see* rough]
roughrider 268
roulade 415
rouleau *assemblage* 72
  cylinder 249
  money 800
roulette 621
round *series* 69
  revolution 138
  - of a ladder 215
  curve 245
  circle 247
  rotund 249
  music 415
  fight 720
  all - *circumjacent* 227
  bring - *restore* 660
  come - *periodic* 138
  recant 607
  persuade 615
  dizzy - 312
  get - 660
  go - 311
  go one's -s 266
  go the -
    publication 531
  go the same - 104

  in - *numbers*
    mean 29
    nearly 197
  make the - of 311
  - a corner 311
  - and round
    periodic 138
    rotation 312
  - assertion 535
  - game 840
  - like a horse in a mill
    613
  - number *number* 84
    multitude 102
  - of life 151
  - of pleasures
    pleasure 377
    amusement 840
  - of the ladder 71
  - of visits 892
  - pace 274
  - robin
    information 527
    petition 765
    censure 932
  - sum 800
  - terms 566
  - trot 274
  - up *cattle* 370
  run the - of *active* **682**
turn - *invert* 218
  retreat 283
  revolve 311
roundabout
  circumjacent 227
  deviation 279
  circuit 311
  amusement 840
  - phrases 573
  - way 629
rounded 247
  - periods 577, 578
roundelay 597
rounder 949
rounders 840
roundhouse 752
roundlet 247
round-shouldered 243
round-up 72
roup 796
rouse *stimulate* 615
  excite 824
  - oneself 682
rouser 83
rousing 171
roustabout 460, 690
rout *agitation* 315
  printing 591
  overcome 731
  discomfit 732
  rabble 876
  assembly 892
  put to the - 731
  - out 652
route 627
  en - 270
  en - for 282
routine *uniform* 16
  order 58
  rule 80
  periodic 138

custom 613
business 625
rove *travel* 266
deviate 279
rover *traveler* 268
pirate 792
roving commission 475
row *disorder* 59
series 69
violence 173
street 189
navigate 267
discord 713
- in the same boat 88
rowdy *rough* 726
vulgar 851
blusterer 887
bad man 949
rowel *sharp* 253
stimulus 615
rowen 168
rower 269
rowlock 215
royal 737
- road *way* 627
easy 705
Royal Academician
559
royalist 737
royalty 737
royne 298
ruade *impulse* 276
attack 716
rub *friction* 331
touch 379
massage 662
difficulty 704
adversity 735
painful 830
- down *lessen* 195
powder 330
- *a* horse 370
- down with an oaken
towel 972
- off 552
- off corners 82
- on *slow* 275
progress 282
inexcitable 826
- one's eyes 870
- one's hands 838
- on the raw 900
- out 552
- up 658
- up the memory 505
rubadub 407
rubber *eraser* 331
masseur 662
whist 840
rubberneck 444, 455
rubbers 225
rubbing 379
rubbish *unmeaning* 517
trifling 643
useless 645
rubble 645
rube 501, 876
rubefaction 434
rubeola 655
rubescence 434
Rubicon *limit* 233

pass the - *begin* 66
cross 303
choose 609
rubicose 434
rubicund 434
rubicundity 382, 434
rubiform 434
rubify 434
rubiginous 433
rubigo 653
rubious 434
rubric *precept* 697
liturgy 998
rubricate *redden* 434
ruby *red* 434
gem 648
ornament 847
ruck 258
ructation 297
rudder 273, 633, 693
rudderless 158
ruddle 434
ruddy *red* 434
beautiful 845
rude *violent* 173
shapeless 241
strident 410
ignorant 491
inelegant 579
ugly 846
vulgar 851
uncivilized 876
uncivil 895
disrespect 929
- health 654
- reproach 908
rudera 645
rudiment *beginning* 66
cause 153
rudimental *small* 193
immature 674
rudimentary *small* 193
learner 541
rudiments
knowledge 490
school 542
rue *bitter* 395
regret 833
repent 950
rueful *painful* 830
sad 837
ruff 225
ruffian *combatant* 726
maleficent 913
scoundrel 949
ruffianism 851, 907
ruffle *disorder* 59
derange 61
roughen 256
fold 258
feeling 821
excite 824, 825
pain 830
irritate 898
anger 900
rufous 433, 434
rufulous 434
rug *support* 215
covering 223
rugged *shapeless* 241
rough 256

difficult 704
ugly 846
churlish 895
rugose 256
rugulose 256
ruin *destruction* 162
evil 619
failure 732
adversity 735
poverty 804
(decay 659)
ruined *nonpayment* 808
hopeless 859
ruinous *painful* 830
ruins *remains* 40
rule *normal* 29
regularity **80**
influence 175
length 200
measure 466
decide 480
custom 613
precept 697
government 737
law 963
absence of - 699
as a - 613
by - 82
golden - 697
obey -s 82
- of three 85
- of thumb
experiment 463
unreasoning 477
essay 675
unskilled 699
ruler 737, 745
ruling passion
obstinacy 606
character 820
rum *queer* 853
drink 959
rumal 225
rumble 407
rumen 191
ruminate *chew* 298
think 450, 451
rummage 461
rummer 191
rumor *publicity* 531
report 532
rumored 531
publicly - 532
rump *remainder* 40
rear 235
beef 298
rumple *disorder* 59
derange 61
roughen 256
fold 258
rumpus *confusion* 59
violence 173
discord 713
(contention 720)
run *rule* 29
generality 78
repetition 104
time 106
course 109
continuance 143
eventuality 151

motion 264
speed 274
trend 278
cards 281
liquefy 335
flow 348
habit 613
demand 630
smuggle 791
contraband 964
have a - *fashion* 852
repute 873
have - of 748
he that -s may read
525
near - 197
race is - 729
- abreast 27
- a chance
probable 472
chance 621
- after *pursue* 622
in repute 873
- against *impact* 276
oppose 708
attack 716
- amuck *violent* 173
kill 361
attack 716
- a race *speed* 274
conduct 692
contend 720
- a rig 840
- a risk 665
- at 716
- a tilt at *attack* 716
contend 720
- away *avoid* 623
(escape 671)
- away with *take* 789
steal 791
- away with a notion
misjudge 481
credulous 486
- back 283
- counter 468
- counter to 708
- down *pursue* 622
bad 649
attack 716
depreciate 932
detract 934
- dry *waste* 638
insufficient 640
- foul of 276
- hard *danger* 665
difficult 704
success 731
- high *great* 31
violent 173
- in *introduce* 228
- in a race *act* 680
- in couples 17
- in the head
think 451
remember 505
- into *conversion* 144
insert 300
- into danger 665
- into debt 806
- its course *course* 109

S

bad 649
painful 830
dejected 837
- disappointment 509
- dog 949
- times 735
- work 699
sadden 830, 837
saddle *attribute* 155
support 215
meat 298
in the - 673
- blanket 223
- on *add* 37
join 43
- on the right horse
discovery 480a
skill 698
right 922
fair 939
- on the wrong horse
mistake 495
bungle 699
- with *add* 37
quarter on 184
clog 706
impose a duty 926
accuse 938
saddlebags 191
saddle-shaped 250
Sadducee 984
sadiron 253, 386
sadism 945, 961
sadist 949
sadness 837
in - *without joking* 535
safe *cupboard* 191
ambush 530
secure 664
treasury 802
caution 864
on the - side
cautious 864
- and sound
health 654
- bind, safe find 864
- conscience *duty* 926
innocent 946
safe-conduct 631
safe-keeping 670
safety 664
- bicycle 272
- first 864
- in valor 861
- match 388
- valve 666
saffron *color* 436
sag *oblique* 217
curve 245
saga 594
sagacious
intelligent 498
foresight 510
(skilful 698)
sagamore 745
sage *wise* 498
wise man **500**
adviser 695
- maxim 496
sagittary 83
sagittate 253

sagum 225
Sahara 169
sahib 373, 745, 875
saic 273
said *preceding* 62
repeated 104
prior 116
it is - 532
more easily - than
done 704
thou hast - 488
sail *navigate* 267
ship 273
set out 293
easy - 174
full - 274
press
press of - 274
- before the wind 734
- near the wind 698
- too near the wind 863
shorten - 275
take in - 174
take the wind out of
one's -s 706
too much - 863
under - 267
sailing, plain - 705
- vessel 273
sailor 269
fair weather - 701
saint *angel* 977
revelation 985
piety 987
false piety 988
- abroad 548
tutelary - 664
Saint
- Anthony's fire 655
- Bernard *dog* 366
- Elmo's fire 423, 872
- Martin's summer
126
- **Swithin, reign of** -
348
- Swithin's day 138
- Tib's eve 107
- Vitus's dance 315,
655
saintly *virtuous* 944
pious 987
Saint's day 138
Saint Simonianism 910
sake
for goodness'- 765
for the - of
motive 615
aid 707
salaam *obeisance* 725
courtesy 894
respect 928
salable 796
salacity 961
salad 41
- oil 356
salade 717
salamander
elemental 83, 980
furnace 386
salamandrine 384
sal ammoniac 392

salary 973
sale **796**
bill of - 771
for - *offer* 763
barter 794
salebrosity 256
salesman 758, 767, 797
salesmanship 796
salient *projecting* 250
sharp 253
manifest 525
important 642
- angle 244
- point 642
saline 392
saliva *excretion* 299
lubrication 332
salivant 297
salivate 297, 332
salle-à-manger 191
sallow *colorless* 429
yellow 436
sally *issue* 293
attack 716
wit 842
sally port *egress* 295
fortification 717
salmagundi 41
salmis 298
salmon *fish* 298
red 434
salmon-colored 434
salon 191
saloon 191
bar 189
salsify 298
salt *sailor* 269
pungent 392
condiment 393
importance 642
preserve 670
money 800
wit 842
below the - 876
- of the earth
goodness 648
goodman 948
- tax 812
- water 341
worth one's - 644
saltant 315
saltation 309
saltatory 315
saltimbanco 548
saltpeter *pungent* 392
gunpowder 727
salubrity **656**
salutary *healthful* 656
(remedial 662)
salutation [*see* salute]
salutatory 582, 587
salute *allocution* 586
celebration 883
courtesy 894
kiss 902
respect 928
salutiferous
[*see* salutary]
salvable 946
salvage *acquisition* 775
tax 812

discount 813
reward 973
salvation
preservation 670
deliverance 672
religious 976
piety 987
work out one's - 990
salve
lubrication 332, 355
remedy 662
relieve 834
salver 191
salvo *exception* 83
explosion 406
qualification 469
excuse 937
(condition 770)
- of artillery
celebration 883
sal-volatile 392
Samaol 978
Samaritan, good
benevolent 906
benefactor 912
sambar 366
sambo 41, 431
Sam Browne belt 747
same 13
all the - to 823
at the - time
compensatory 30
synchronous 120
go over the - ground
104
in the - boat 709
in the - breath
instantaneous 113
synchronous 120
of the - mind 488
on the - tack 709
sameness 16
samiel 349
samisen 417
samo 720
samovar 191
samp 298
sampan 273
sample 82
Samson 159
samurai 875
sanation
restoration 660
sanative
remedial 662
sanatorium 189, 662
sanctification 976
sanctify *authorize* 920
piety 987
sanctimony 988
sanction
permission 760
dueness 924
approbation 931
to - vice 945
sanctitude 987
sanctity 987
sanctuary *refuge* 666
altar 1000
claim - 666
sanctum *chamber* 191

- sanctorum
  abode 189
  privacy 893
  temple 1000
sanctus 900
- bell 550, 999
sand *powder* 330
  resolution 604
  built upon - 665
  sow the - 645
sandal 225
sandalwood 400
sandbag 727, 972
sandbagger 792
sand-blind 442
Sandemanian 984
sandpaper 255
sands *danger* 667
- on the seashore
  multitude 102
sand storm 330
sandstone 635
sandwich-wise 228
sandy *yellow* 436
  red 434
sane 502
sangar 717
sang-froid
  insensibility 823
  inexcitability 826
  presence of mind 864
sangraal 998
sanguinary 361
sanguine *red* 434
  hopeful 858
- expectation
  expect 507
  hope 858
- imagination 515
sanguineous 434
sanguisage 662
sanhedrim
  council 696
  churchdom 995
sanies 333
sanious 333
sanitarian 656
sanitarium 189, 656,
  662
sanitary 656
sanity *mental* **502**
  bodily - 654
sannyasi 804, 955, 996
sans 187
- cérémonie
  friendly 888
  social 892
- façon *simple* 849
  modest 881
  social 892
- pareil 33
- peur et sans re-
  proche
  perfect 650
  heroic 873
  honorable 939
- souci *insensible* 823
  pleasure 827
  content 831
sans-culotte *revel* 742
  commonalty 876

sans-culottic 146
sans-culottism 146
sans Dieu rien 976
Sanskrit 124
Sanskritist 492
santon *hermit* 893
  priest 996
sap *essence* 5
  destroy 162
  excavate 252
  juice 333
  damage 659
  attack 716
- the foundations 162,
  659
sap-headed 499
sapid 390
sapient 498
sapless *weak* 160
  dry 340
sapling 129, 367
saponaceous 355
saporific 390
sapper *excavator* 252
  soldier 726
sappers and miners
  preparers 673
Sapphic 597
sapphire *blue* 438
  gem 847
sapphism 961
sapphist 962
sappy *young* 127
  juicy 333
  foolish 499
saprogenic 653
saraband 840
sarcasm *disrespect* 929
  censure 932
  detraction 934
sarcastic *ridicule* 856
  discourteous 895
carcology 662
sarcoma 250
sarcophagus 363
sarculation 103
sard 847
Sardanapalus 954a
sardines 298
sardonic *censure* 932
  detraction 934
- grin *laughter* 838
  ridicule 856
  discontent 932
sardonyx 847
sargasso 367
Sargasso Sea 367
sark 225
sarmentum 51
sartorial 225
sash 247
sassafras 662
Sastra 986
Satan **978**
satanic *malevolent* 907
  vicious 945
  diabolic 978
satchel 191 ⸀
sate 869
satellite *companion* 88
  follower 281

heavenly body 318
  auxiliary 711
  servant 746
satiate 52, 376
satiety *sufficient* 639
  pleasant 829
  cloy **869**
  (*redundance* 641)
satin 219, 329, 635
  smoothness 255
satire *metaphor* 521
  poetry 597
  ridicule 856
  censure 932
satiric *untruth* 546
satirical 932
  detraction 934
satirist *poet* 597
  detractor 936
satirize 597
satisfaction
  [see satisfy]
  duel 720
  pleasure 827
  atonement 952
hail with - 931
satisfactorily 618
satisfactory
  [see satisfy]
  good 648
satisfy *answer* 462
  convince 484
  sufficient 639
  consent 762
  observance 772
  pay 807
  gratify 829
  content 831
  satiate 869
  reward 973
- an obligation 926
- oneself 484
satisfying 831
satrap *governor* 745
  (*deputy* 759)
satsuma 557
saturate *fill* 52
  moisten 339
  satiate 869
saturnalia *disorder* 59
  games 840
  intemperance 954
- of blood 361
Saturnian *pleasing* 829
  innocent 946
- age 734
Saturnia regna
  prosperity 734
  pleasure 827
saturnine 837
satyr *ugly* 846
  libertine 962
  demon 980
sauce *adjunct* 39
  mixture 41
  condiment 393
  abuse 908
pay - for all 807
what is - for the goose
  27
saucebox *blusterer* 887

saucepan 191
sauce piquante
  condiment 393
  pleasing 829
saucer 191
- eyes 441
saucy *insolent* 885
  flippant 895
sauerkraut 298
saunter *ramble* 266
  dawdle 275
sausage 298
sauvage 893
sauve qui peut
  run away 623
  alarm 669
  haste 684
  cowardice 862
savage *violent* 173
  vulgar 851
  brave 861
  boorish 876
  angry 900
  malevolent 907
  evildoer 913
savagery
  [see savage]
savanna 344, 367
savant *knowledge* 490
  learned man 492
  sage 500
save *subduct* 38
  exclude 55
  except 83
  store 636
  preserve 670
  deliver 672
  economize 817
God - 990
- and except 83
- money 817
- one's bacon 671
- the necessity 927a
- us 707
save-all 817
saving 817
- clause 469
- one's presence 928
savings *store* 636
  economy 817
savior *benefactor* 912
Saviour 976
savoir faire
  skill 698
  fashion 852
savoir vivre *skill* 698
  fashion 852
  sociality 892
savor 390
- of *resemble* 17
- of the reality 780
savoriness **394**
savorless 391
savory 390, 394
savvy 490, 498
saw *cut* 44
  jagged 257
  maxim 496
- the air *gesture* 550
sawder, soft -
  flattery 933

sawdust 330
sawney 501
saxhorn 417
Saxon
  style of language 576,
    578
say *nearly* 32
  turn 138
  assert 535
  express 560
  speak 582
  have one's - 535, 582
  not - I did it 938
  - by heart 505
  - no 489
  - nothing 585
  - one's prayers 990
  - to oneself 589
  - what comes upper-
    most 612
  that is to - 522
  what do you - to that
    870
  you don't - so 870
sayid 745
saying *maxim* 496
  assertion 535
sbirro 965
scab *apostate* 607
scabbard 191
  throw away the -
    resolution 604
  war 722
scabby 940
scabies 380, 655
scabrous 256
scaffold
  support 215
  preparation 673
  execution 975
  (way 627)
  (means 632)
scagliola 223, 545
scaithless
  [*see* scathless]
scalawag 949
scald *burn* 382, 384
  poet 597
scale *portion* 51
  series 69
  term 71
  slice 204
  skin 223
  mount 305
  weigh 319
  gamut 413
  measure 466
  printing 591
  hold the -s 480
  hold the -s even 922
  -s falling from the
    eyes *see* 441
  disclose 529
  -s of justice 922
  - the heights 305
  - the walls 716
  turn the-
    reversion 145
    influence 175
    counter evidence 468
    motive 615
  670

scalene 243
scaling ladder 305
scallion 298
scallop *convolution* 248
  notch 257
scalp 226
scalpel 253
scalp lock 256, 550
scaly 223
scamble 44
scamp *neglect* 460
  rascal 949
scamped *sham* 545
scamper *speed* 274
  - off 623
scampish 945
scan *see* 441
  attend to 457
  inquire 461
  know 490
  prosody 597
scandal *news* 532
  obloquy 934
scandalize 932
scandalmonger 532
scandalous
  disreputable 874
  vicious 945
scandent 305
scansion 597
scant *small* 32
  few 103
  little 193
  narrow 203
  insufficient 640
scantling *model* 22
  scrap 32
  dimensions 192
  (part 51)
scanty [*see* scant]
scape 671
scapegoat
  substitute 147
  atonement 952
scapegrace *reckless* 863
  rascal 949
scaphoid 245
scapin *cheat* 548
  knave 941
scapulary 999
scar *shore* 342
  record 551
  blemish 848
  he jests at -s 830
scarab 993
Scaramouch 844
scarce *incomplete* 53
  few 103
  infrequent 137
  insufficient 640
  make oneself -
    absent 187
    run away 623
scarcely 32
  - any 103
  - anything 643
  - ever 137
scarcity [*see* scarce]
scare 860
scarecrow *ugly* 846
  frighten 860

scarf *dress* 225
  canonicals 999
scarfskin 223
scarify *notch* 257
  torment 830
scarlatina 655
scarlet 434
  - Woman 984
scarp *oblique* 217
  defense 717
scarpines 972
scathe *badness* 649
  injury 659
  (evil 619)
  (bane 663)
scatheless *perfect* 650
  (secure 664)
  (saved 672)
scatter *derange* 61
  disperse 73
  diverge 291
  - to the winds
    destroy 162
    confute 479
scatter-brained
  inattentive 458
  insane 503
scatterling 268
scavenger 652
scene *appearance* 448
  painting 556
  drama 599
  excitement 825
  - of action 728
scene painter 559
scene painting 556
scenery 448, 599
sceneshifter 599
scenic 599, 882
scenography 54, 556
scent *smell* 398
  discovery 480a
  disbelieve 485
  knowledge 490
  sign 550
  trail 551
  get - of 527
  on the - 622
  on the right - 462
  put on a new - 279
  - from afar 510
  throw off the - 623
scent bag 400
scent bottle 400
scent container 400
scented 400
scentless 399
scepter 33, **747**
  sway the - 737
sceptic [*see* skeptic]
scepticism
  [*see* skepticism]
schatchen 903
schedule 86, 611
Schelling's philosophy
    451
schematism 60
schematist 626
scheme *draft* 554
  plan 626
schemer 626, 702

schenk beer 298
scherzo 415
schesis 7
schism *dissent* 489
  discord 713
  heterodoxy 984
schismless 983a
schistose 204
schnapps 959
schnorrer 804
scholar *erudite* **492**
  learner 541
  rank 873
scholarly 539
scholarship
  knowledge 490
  learning 539
  trophy 733, 873
scholastic
  knowledge 490
  teaching 537, 540
  learning 539
  school 542
  theology 983
Scholasticism 451
scholiast 492, 524
scholium *maxim* 496
  interpretation 522
school *herd* 72
  system of opinions
    484
  knowledge 490
  teaching 537
  academy **542**
  painting 556
  go to - 539
  - bag 191
  - days 127
  send to - 537
  - of art 542
  -s of painting 556
  -s of sculpture 557
schoolbook 542
schoolboy *lad* 129
  learner 541
  (tyro 193)
  a -'s tale 111
  familiar to every - 490
schoolfellow 541
schoolgirl 129, 541
schoolman *scholar* 492
  theologian 983
schoolmaster 540
  - abroad
  knowledge 490
  learning 537
schoolmistress 540
schoolroom 191, 542
schooner 273
  receptacle 191
Schopenhauer's
    philosophy 451
schrod 298
sciamachy 497
sciatica 378
science *knowledge* 490
  skill 698
  - of language 562
  - of virtue 944
scientific *exact* 494
  teaching 537

scientist *reasoner* 476
  learned man 492
scimitar 727
  - *shaped* 253
scintilla *small* 32, 193
  spark 420, 423
scintillate
  [*see* scintillation]
  intelligence 498
scintillation *heat* 382
  light 420
  wit 842
sciolism 491
sciolist 493
sciomancy 511
scion *part* 51
  child 129
  posterity 167
scission 44
scissors 253
  - and paste 609
scissure 198
sclerotics 195
scobs 330
scoff *ridicule* 856
  deride 929
  impiety 988
  - *at despise* 930
  censure 932
scold *berate* 527
  shrew 901
  malediction 908
  censure 932
  (*detractor* 936)
scolecoid 248
scollop *convolution* 248
  notch 257
sconce *top* 210
  candlestick 423
  brain 450
  defense 717
  mulct 974
scone 298
scoop *depression* 252
  perforator 262
scop 597
scope *degree* 26
  occasion 134
  extent 180
  meaning 516
  freedom 748
  (*intention* 620)
scorch 382, 384
scorcher 268, 274
scorching *violent* 173
score *compose* 54
  arrangement 60
  count 85
  list 86
  twenty 98
  indent 257
  furrow 259
  music 415
  berate 527
  mark 550
  credit 805
  debt 806
  accounts 811
  on the - of
  relation 9
  motive 615

- a success 731
- board 551
- sheet 551
scores *many* 102
scoriaceous 384
scoriæ *ash* 384
  dirt 653
  (*useless* 645)
scorify 384
scorn 930
scorpion *insect* 368
  painful 830
  evildoer 913
  (*bane* 663)
  chastise with -s 739
scorse 794
scot *reward* 973
scotch *notch* 257
  injure 659
  - the snake *maim* 158
  insufficient 640
  noncompletion 730
  - the wheel 706
Scotchman 188

scot-free *escape* 671
  free 748
  cheap 815
  exempt 927a
  escape -
  escape 671
  let off - 970
scotograph 554
scotomy 443
Scotsman 188
Scotticism 563
scoundrel 949
scour *run* 274
  rub 331
  clean 652
  - the country 266
  - the plain 274
scourge *bane* 663
  painful 830
  punish 972
  instrument of punishment **975**
  - of the human race 913
scourings 645
scout *vanguard* 234
  aviator 269a
  spectator 444
  feeler 463
  messenger 534
  reject 610
  patrol 664
  warning 668
  servant 746
  disrespect 929
  disdain 930
  (*looker* 444)
  (*underrate* 483)
  (*ridicule* 856)
scow 273
scowl *complain* 839
  frown 895
  anger 900
  sullen 901a
  disapprobation 932
  - of night 982

scrabble
  unmeaning 517
  scribble 590
scrag 203
scraggy *lean* 193
  amorphous 241
  rough 256
  (*ugly* 846)
scramble *confusion* 59
  climb 305
  pursue 622
  haste 684
  difficulty 704
  contend 720
  seize 789
scrambled eggs 298
scranch 330
scrannel 643
scrap *small* 32
  piece 51
  child 129
  (*minute* 193)
scrapbook 596
scrape *subduct* 38
  reduce 195
  pulverize 330
  abrade 331
  - *the fiddle* 416
  mezzotint 558
  clean 652
  difficulty 704
  mischance 732
  bow 894
  - *together*
  assemble 72
  acquire 775
scraper 652
scratch *groove* 259
  abrade 331
  unmeaning 517
  mark 550
  daub 555
  draw 556
  write 590
  hurt 619
  wound 649
  come to the -
  contention 720
  courage 861
  mere - 209
  old - 978
  - out 552
  - the head 461
  up to the - 861
  without a - 670
scrawl *unmeaning* 517
  write 590
scrawny 203
screak 411
scream *blow* 349
  cry 411
  wail 839
screaming 853
screech 411, 412
screed 86, 590
screen *sift* 60
  crossing 219
  sieve 260
  shade 424
  hide 528
  hider 530

  side scene 599
  sift 652
  safety 664
  shelter 666
  defense 717
  - from sight 442
screw *fasten* 43
  fastening 45
  distortion 243
  oar 267
  propeller 284
  rotation 312
  instrument 633
  miser 819
  put on the -
  severity 739
  compel 744
  -'loose *insane* 503
  imperfect 651
  unskillful 699
  hindrance 706
  attack 713
  - one's courage to the
  sticking place 861
  - up *fasten* 43
  strengthen 159
  prepare 673
  - up the eyes 443
screw-driver 633
screwed *drunk* 959
screw-shaped 248
screw steamer 273
scribble *compose* 54
  unmeaning 517
  write 590
scribbler 593
scribe *recorder* 553
  writer 590, 593
  priest 996
scrimmage *discord* 713
  contention 720
scrimp *short* 201
  insufficient 640
  stingy 819
scrip 191
script 590
scriptural
  orthodox 983a
Scripture *certain* 474
  revelation 985
scrivener *writer* 590
  lawyer 968
scrofula 655
scroll *list* 86
  record 551
scrub *short* 201
  rub 331
  bush 367
  clean 652
  dirty person 653
  commonalty 876
scrubby *small* 193
  trifling 643
  disreputable 874
  vulgar 876
  shabby 940
scruple
  small quantity 32
  weight 319
  doubt 485
  reluctance 603

probity 939
make no - of 602
scrupulous *careful* 459
  incredulous 487
  exact 494
  reluctant 603
  observant 772
  fastidious 868
  punctilious 939
scrutator 461
scrutinizer 461
scrutiny *attention* 457
  inquiry 461
scrutoire 191
scud *sail* 267
  speed 274
  shower 348
  cloud 353
  - under bare poles 704
scuffle 720
scull *row* 267
scullery 191
scullion 746
sculptor 559
sculpture *form* 240
  carving **557**
scum *foam* 353
  dirt 653
  - of the earth 949
  - of society 876
scupper 350
scurf 653
scurrility 908
scurrilous
  ridicule 856
  disrespect 929
  detraction 934
scurry *haste* 274, 684
  excitability 825
scurvy *insufficient* 640
  unimportant 643
  base 940
  wicked 945
scut 235
scutate 245
scutcheon
  standard 550
  honor 877
scutiform 245, 251
scuttle *destroy* 162
  receptacle 191
  speed 274, 684
  - along *haste* 684
scutum 717
Scylla and Charybdis
  between - *danger* 665
  difficulty 704
scyphiform 252
scythe 253
  - of Time 106
scytho *pointed* 244
  sharp 253
sea *multitude* 102
  ocean 341
  at - 341
  uncertain 475
  go to - 293
  heavy - 315
  - of doubt 475
  - of troubles
  difficulty 704
     672

adversity 735
sea anchor 706
seaboard 342
seacoast 342
  - gun 727
sea dog 269
sea duck 310
seafarer 269
seafaring 267, 273
sea fight 720
seagirt 346
seagoing 267, 341
sea green 435
sea king 791
seal *matrix* 22
  close 261
  animal 366
  evidence 467
  mark 550
  resolve 604
  complete 729
  authority 747
  compact 769
  security 771
  marriage 903
  break the - 529
  - brown 433
  - of secrecy 528
  - one's infamy 940
  - the doom of 162
  - the lips 585
  - up *restrain* 751
  under - 769
sealed 261
  hermetically - 261
  one's fate is - 601
  - book *ignorance* 491
  unintelligible 519
  secret 533
sealing 903
sealing wax 747
seals *insignia* 747
seam 43
sea-maid 979
seaman 269
seamanship
  conduct 692
  skill 698
seamark 550
seamless 50
sea mosses 368
seamstress 690
seamy side 651
séance *assemblage* 72
  manifestation 525
  council 696
  spiritualism 992a
seapiece 556
seaport 666
sear *dry* 340
  burn 384
  deaden 823
  - and yellow leaf
  age 128
  - ed conscience 951
search 455, 461
searching *severe* 739
  painful 830
searchless 519
searchlight 423, 550
seascape 448, 556

sea serpent 83
seashore 342
seasickness 655
seaside 342
sea slug 298
season *mix* 41
  time 106
  pungent 392
  accustom 613
  preserve 670
  prepare 673
seasonable *fit* 23
  early 132
  opportune 134
sea song 597
seasoning
  condiment 393
seat *place* 183
  locate 184
  abode 189
  support 215
  rump 235
  direction 693
  judgment - 966
  - of government 737
  - of war 728
seated 184
  firmly - 150
sea urchins 368
sea view 556
seawant 800
seaway 180
seaweed 367
seaworthy 273, 341,
664
sebaceous 355
secant 44, 219
secede *dissent* 489
  relinquish 624
  disobey 742
seceder
  heterodox 984
secern 299
Secessionist 742
seclude 893
seclusion **893**
second *duplication* 90
  - of time 108
  instant 113
  - in music 413, 415
  abet 707
  one's - self 17
  play or sing a - 416
  play - fiddle
  obey 743
  subject 749
  disrepute 874
  - best *imperfect* 651
  failure 732
  - childhood *age* 128
  imbecility 499
  - crop *fertile* 168
  profit 775
  - edition 104
  - nature 613
  - sight *foresight* 510
  clairvoyance 992a
  - thoughts *sequel* 65
  thought 451
  improvement 658
  - to none 33

- youth 660
secondary *inferior* 34
  following 63
  imperfect 651
  deputy 759
  - education 537
  - evidence 467
seconder 711
secondhand
  imitation 19
  old 124
  deteriorated 659
  received 785
secondly 90
second-rate 651
secrecy [*see* secret]
secret *key* 522
  latent 526
  hidden 528
  riddle **533**
  in the - 490
  keep a - *silent* 585
  - motive 615
  - passage 627
  - place 530
  - writing 590
secrétaire 191
secretariat 965
secretary *desk* 191
  recorder 553
  writer 590
  director 694
  auxiliary 711
  servant 746
  consignee 758
secrete 299
  conceal 528
secretion 299
secretive 528
secretory 299
sect 75
  religious - 983, 984
sectarian *dissent* 489
  ally 711
  heterodox 984
sectary 65
section *division* 44
  part 51
  class 75
  indication 550
  printing 591
  chapter 593
  troops 726
sector *part* 51
  circle 247
secular *centenary* 98
  periodic 138
  laity 997
  - education 537
secularism 984
secularization 756
secundines 63
secundum artem
  conformable 82
  skillful 698
secure *fasten* 43
  bespeak 132
  belief 484
  safe 664
  restrain 751
  engage 768

gain 775
confident 858
- an object
success 731
securities 805
security *safety* 664
pledge **771**
hope 858
lend on - 787
sedan 272
sedan chair 272
sedate *thoughtful* 451
calm 826
grave 837
sedative *calming* 174
remedy 662
sedentary 265
sedge 367
sedile 1000
sediment 321, 653
sedimentary
remainder 40
sedition 742
seditionist 891
seduce *entice* 615
love 897
debauch 961
seducer 962
seduction *pleasing* 829
desire 865
seductress 615
sedulous *active* 682
desirous 865
see *view* 441
look 457
believe 484
know 490
bishopric 995
- after 459
- at a glance 498
- daylight 480a
- double 959
- fit 600, 602
- justice done 922
- life *amusement* 840
- one's way
foresight 510
intelligible 518
skill 698
easy 705
- service 722
- sights 455
- the light *born* 359
published 531
- through   *discover*
480a
intelligence 498
- to *attention* 457
care 459
direction 693
we shall - 507
seed *small* 32
cause 153
posterity 167
grain 330
agriculture 371
run to - *age* 128
lose health 659
- plants 369
sow the - 673
seedling 129, 367

seed plot
productive 168
agriculture 371
seedtime of life 127
seedy *weak* 160
disease 655
deteriorated 659
exhausted 688
needy 804
seeing 441
- that
circumstance **8**
reasoning 476
seek *inquire* 461
pursue 622
offer 763
request 765
- safety 664
seek-sorrow 837
seel 217
seem 448
as it -s good to 600
seeming 488
seemingly 472
seemless *ugly* 846
undue 925
seemliness *duty* 926
seemly *expedient* 646
handsome 845
*due;*924
seep 295, 337
seepage 337
seer *veteran* 130
madman 504
oracle 511, 513
sorcerer 994
seesaw 12, 314
seethe *moisture* 339
hot 382
make hot 384
excitement 824
seething caldron 386
segar 392
segment 44, 51
segnitude 683
segregate
not related 10
separate 44
exclude 55
segregated
incoherent 47
seignior *master* 745
nobility 875
seigniory
authority 737
property 780
seine net 232
seisin [*see* seizin]
seismic 314
seismograph 314, 551
seismology 314
seismometer 276
seismoscope 314
seize *take* 789
rob 791
- an opportunity 134
- the present hour 134
seized with *disease* 655
feeling 821
seizin *possession* 777
property 780

seizure 315, 925
sejunction 44
seldom 137
select *specify* 79
choose 609
good 648
selection 75
selectman 965
Selene 318
self *identity* 13
speciality 79
- abasement 879
- accusing 950
- admiration 880
- annulling 497
- applause 880
- assertion 885
- called 565
- command
resolution 604
caution 864
(*temperance* 953)
- communing 451
- complacency
cheerful 836
vanity 880
- confidence 880
- conquest
resolution 604
(*temperance* 953)
- conscious 855
- consultation 451
- contradictory   471,
497
- control 604
- convicted 950
- conviction *belief* 484
penitent 950
condemned 971
- council 451
- deceit *error* 495
- deception
credulity 486
- defense 717
- delusion 486, 347
- denial
disinterested 942
temperance 953
penance 990
- depreciation 483
- determination   737,
748
- detraction 483
- discipline 990
- educated 490
- esteem 880
- evident *certain* 474
manifest 525
- examination 990
- existing 1
- government
authority 737
freedom 748
(*virtue* 944)
- help 698
- immolation 991
- importance 878
- indulgence
selfishness 943
intemperance 954
- instruction 539

- interest 943
- knowledge 881
- love 943
- luminous 423
- made 490
- opinionated 481
- opinioned
narrow-minded 481
(*foolish* 499)
(*obstinate* 606)
- possessed 852
- possession *sanity* 502
resolution 604
inexitability 826
caution 864
- praise 864
- preservation 717
- reliance
resolution 604
hope 858
courage 861
- reproach 950
- respect *pride* 878
- restraint 826, 953
- sacrifice 942
- satisfied 880
- seeker 943
- seeking 943
- starter   *automobile*
272
- styled 565
- sufficiency 893
- sufficient 880
- taught 490
- tormentor 837
- will 606
selfish 943
selfishness 943
selfsame 13
sell *absurdity* 497
deception 545
untruth 546
sale 796
- for 812
- off 796
- oneself 940
- one's life dearly
resist 719
fight 722
- out 796
seller 796
selliform 250
selling ability 796
selvedge 231
semaphore 550
sematic 668
semblance
similarity 17
imitation 19
copy 21
probability 471
wear the - of
appearance 448
semeiology 522, 655
semeiotics 550
semen 153
semester 108
semi - 91
semibarbarian 913
semibreve 413
semicircle 247

semicircular 245
semicolon 142
semidiaphanous 427
semifluid 352
semiliquidity **352**
semilunar 245
seminal *causing* 153
seminar 542
seminary 542
semination
  preparation 673
semiopaque 427
semipellucid 427
semiquaver 413
semitone 413
semitransparency **427**
sempervirid 110, 123
sempiternal 112
sempiternity 110, 112
sempstress
  dressmaker 225
  workwoman 690
senary 98
senate 72, 696
senate house 966
senator *counsel* 695
  councillor 696
senatorship 693
send *transfer* 270
  propel 284
 - about one's business
  289
 - adrift 597
 - a letter to 592
 - away *repel* 289
  eject 297
  refuse 764
 - for 741
 - forth *propel* 284
  publish 531
 - off 284
 - out *eject* 297
  commission 755
 - word 527
seneca-oil 356
senectitude 128
senescence 128
seneschal *director* 694
  master 745
  servant 746
seneschalship 737
senile 128, 158, 499
 - dementia 499
senior *age* 128
  student 492
  master 745
seniority *oldness* 124
  age 128
señor 877
sensation
  physical sensibility
  375
  emotion 821
  wonder 870
sensational
  language 574
  exciting 824
sensation drama 599
sensations of touch **380**
sense *wisdom* 498
  meaning 516

674

accept in a particular
 - 522
deep - 821
in no - 565
 - of duty 926
senseless
  insensible 376
  absurd 497
  foolish 499
  unmeaning 517
senses *external* - 375
  intellect 450
  sanity 502
sensibility
  physical - **375**
  moral **822**
sensible *material* 316
  wise 498
sensitive 375, 822
 - *plant* 822
sensorial 821
sensorium 450
sensual *pleasure* 377
  intemperate 954
sensualist 954*a*
sensualize 954
sensuous
  sensibility 375
  pleasure 377
  feeling 821
sentence *decision* 480
  maxim 496
  affirmation 535
  phrase 566
  lawsuit 969
  condemnation 971
  my - is for war 722
sententious
  concise 572
 - *language* 574, 577
  taciturn 585
sentient
 - *physically* 375
 - *morally* 821
sentiment *idea* 453
  (opinion 484)
  (maxim 496)
sentimental
  sensitive 822
  affected 855
sentinel *guard* 263
  guardian 664
  watch 668
  keeper 753
sentry 664, 668, 753
sepal 367
separable 44
separate *disjoin* 44
  exclude 55
  bisect 91
  diverge 291
  clean 652
  divorce 782, 905
 - into elements 49
 - maintenance 905
 - the chaff from the
  wheat
  discriminate 465
  select 609
separation
  [*see* separate]

separatist 489, 984
  disjunction 44
separative 49
sepia 433
seposition
  disjunction 44
  exclusion 55
sepoy 726
seppuku 972
sept *kin* 11
  class 75
  clan 166
septal 228
septenary 98
septennial 138
Septentrional 237
septet 415
septic 655, 657, 662
septicæmia 655
septicity 655
septimal 98
septuagenary 98
septuagesimal 98
Septuagint 985
septulum 228
septum 228
septuple 98
sepulcher 363
  whited - 545
sepulchral
  interment 363
  resonance 408
  stridor 410
  hoarse 581
sepulture 363
sequacious 63, 117
sequacity *soft* 324
  tenacity 327
sequel *following* **65**
 - *in time* 117
  sequence 281
  (addition 39)
sequela 63, 65
sequence
 - *in order* **63**
 - *in time* 117
  motion **281**
  logical - 476
sequent 63, 117
sequester *take* 789
  confiscate 974
  (hide 528)
sequestered
  secluded 893
sequestrate *seize* 789
  condemn 971
  confiscate 974
sérac 383
seraglio *abode* 189
  woman 374
  marriage 903
  impurity 961
seraph *saint* 948
  angel 977
seraphic *blissful* 829
  virtuous 944
  pious 987
Seraphim 977
seraphina 417
seraskier 745
sere [*see* sear]

 - and yellow leaf 128
serein *dew* 339
  rain 348
serenade *music* 415
  compliment 894
  endearment 902
serene *pellucid* 425
  calm 826
  content 831
 - *highness* 877
serf *slave* 746
  clown 876
serfdom 749
serge 635
sergeant 745
serial *continuous* 69
  periodic 138
  book 593
seriatim *in order* **58**
  continuously 69
  each to each 79
  slowly 275
series *continuity* 69
  number 84
serif 591
serio-comic 853
serious *great* 31
  resolved 604
  important 642
  dejected 837
seriously 535
serjeant
  common - 967
  -at-law 968
sermon *lesson* 537
  speech 582
  dissertation 595
  pastoral 998
  funeral - 363
sermonize 586
sermonizer 584
serosity *fluid* 333
serotherapy 662
serotine 133
serpent *tortuous* 248
  snake 366
  hiss 409
  wind instrument 417
  wise 498
  deceiver 548
  cunning 702
  evildoer 913
  knave 941
  demon 949
  great sea - 515
  the old - 978
serpentine 248
serrated *angular* 244
  notched 257
serried *crowded* 72
  dense 321
serum *lymph* 333
  water 337
servant *minister* 631
  agent 690
  help 711
  retainer **746**
 - of all work 690
serve *benefit* 618
  business 625
  utility 644

ended 67
account - 811
- opinion 484
- principle 496
- purpose 620
settlement [*see* settle]
  location 184
  colony 188
  dregs 653
  compact 769
  deed 771
  property 780
  strict - 781
settler 188
settlings 321
settlor 784
seven 98
  in - league boots 274
  wake the - sleepers
  404
Seven Seas 341
seventy 98
seventy-five *gun* 727
sever 44
severable 44
several *special* 79
  plural 100
  many 102
  - times 104
severalize 465
severally *divided* 44
  respectively 79
severalty 44
severe *energetic* 171
  symmetry 242
  exact 494
  - *style* 576
  harsh 739
  painful 830
  simple 849
  critical 932
severely *very* 31
severity **739**
  [*see* severe]
sew 43
sewage *excretion* 299
  filth 653
sewed up *drunk* 959
sewer *drain* 350
  cloaca 653
sewerage *drainage* 652
  filth 653
sewer gas 663
sewing silk 205
sex *kind* 75
  women 374
  fair - 374
sexagenarian 130
sexagenary 98, 99
sexagesimal 98
sextan 98
sextant *angle* 244
  circle 247
sextennial 138
sextet 98
  verse 597
sextodecimo 593
sexton *interment* 363
  clergy 996
sextuple 98
sexual congress 43

676

shabbiness
  [*see* shabby]
  inferiority 34
shabby *trifling* 643
  deteriorated 659
  stingy 819
  mean 874
  disgraceful 940
  (*bad* 649)
shabby genteel 851
shack 189
shackle *fastening* 45
  hinder 706
  restrain 751
  fetter 752
shad 298
shade *degree* 26
  small quantity 32
  manes 362
  darkness 421
  dimness 422
  shadow **424**
  color 428
  conceal 528
  screen 530
  paint 556
  ghost 980a
  distribution of - 421
  in the - *hidden* 528
  out of repute 874
  shadow of a - *small* 32
  dim 422
  throw all else into the
  - 642
  throw into the -
  surpass 303
  conceal 528
  glory 873
  thrown into the -
  inferior 34
  disrepute 874
  under the - of 664
  without a - of doubt
  474
shades
  - below 982
  - of death 360
  - of difference 15
  - of evening 422
  welcome ye - 424
shading 421
  - off 26
shadow
  unsubstantial 4
  copy 21
  small 32
  remains 40
  follow 63
  accompaniment 88
  thin 203
  pursue 235, 622
  sequence 281
  cloud 353, 422
  dark 421
  shade 424
  inquire 461
  dream 515
  ghost 980a
  disdains the - 878
  fight with a - 699
  follow as a - 281

may your - never be
less
  courtesy 894
  respect 928
  approbation 931
  partial - 422
  - forth *dim* 422
  predict 511
  metaphor 521
  represent 554
  - of coming events 511
  - of the tomb 363
  take the - for the sub-
  stance
  credulous 486
  mistake 495
  unskillful 699
  under the - of one's
  wing 664
  without a - of turn-
  ing 141
  worn to a - *thin* 203
  worse for wear 659
shadowy *inexistent* 2
  unsubstantial 4
  shady 424
  invisible 447
shaft *deep* 208
  frame 215
  pit 252, 260
  air pipe 351
  handle 633
  weapon 727
  (*missile* 284)
shaggy 256
shagreen 223
shah 745
shaitan 978
shake *totter* 149
  weak 160
  vibrate 314
  agitation 315
  shiver 383
  trill 407
  music 416
  dissuade 616
  shingle 635
  injure 659
  impress 821
  excited 824
  fear 860
  - hands
  pacification 723
  friendship 888
  courtesy 894
  forgive 918
  - off 297
  - off the yoke 750
  - one's faith 485
  - one's sides 838
  - the head *dissent* 489
  deny 536
  refuse 764
  disapprove 932
  - to pieces 162
  - up 315
shakedown *bed* 215
shaker 984
shakes, no great -
  trifling 643
  imperfect 651

shaking prairie 344
shako *hat* 225
  helmet 717
shaky *weak* 160
  in danger 665
  fearful 860
shallop 273
shallow
  unintelligent 32
  not deep 209
  ignorant 491
  ignoramus 493
  foolish 499
  trifling 643
  - *pretext* 617
  - *profundity* 855
shallow-brain
  fool 501
shallowness **209**
  [*see* shallow]
shallow-pated 499
shallows *danger* 667
sham *falsehood* 544
  deception 545
  untruth 546
  - *fight* 720
shaman 548, 994
shamanism 992
shamble *dawdle* 275
  stagger 315
shambles 361
shame *disrepute* 874
  wrong 923
  censure 932
  chastity 960
  cry - upon 932
  false - 855
  for - 874
  sense of - 879
  - the devil 939
  to one's - be it spoken
  874
shamefaced 881
shameful
  disgraceful 874
  profligate 945
shameless
  unreserved 525
  impudent 885
  profligate 945
  indecent 961
shamianah 223
shampoo 662
shamrock 92
shandrydan 272
shanghai 545
shank *support* 215
  printing 591
  instrument 633
shanks 266
  - 's mare 266
shanty 189
shape *state* 7
  harmonize 82
  form 240
  aspect 448
  (*state* 7)
  (*convert* 144)
  - one's course
  direction 278
  pursuit 622

conduct 692
- out a course
  plan 626
shapeless
  amorphous 241
  ugly 846
shapely *form* 240
  symmetrical 242
  comely 845
share *part* 51
  participate 778
  allotted portion 786
  - and share alike 778
  - one's sorrow 915
shareholder 778
shark *fish* 366, 368
  thief 792
  (*cheat* 548)
sharp *energetic* 171
  violent 173
  acute 253
  sensible 375
  pungent 392
  - *sound* 410
  musical tone 413
  intelligent 498
  active 682
  clever 698
  cunning 702
  feeling 821
  painful 830
  rude 895
  censorious 932
  look - *take care* 459
  be active 682
  - *appetite* 865
  - contest 720
  - ear 418
  - eye 441
  - fellow *active* 682
  proficient 700
  - frost 383
  - lookout
    vigilance 459
    expectation 507
  - pain 378
  - practice
    deception 545
    cunning 702
    severity 739
    improbity 940
sharpen [*see* sharp]
  excite 824
  - one's tools 673
  - one's wits 537
sharpener 253
sharper *thief* 792
  (*cheat* 548)
sharpness 253
  fastidiousness 868
sharp-set 865
sharpshooter 716, 726
sharpshooting 716
Shastra 986
shatter *disjoin* 44
  render powerless 158
  destroy 162
shatterbrained 503
shattered *weak* 160
  fatigued 688
shave *reduce* 195

shorten 201
layer 204
smooth 255
grate 330
lie 546
shaving *small* 32
  layer 204
  filament 205
  (*part* 51)
shawl 225, 384
shay 272
she 374
sheaf 72
shear *reduce* 195
  shorten 201
  - *sheep* 370
  take 789
shears 253
sheath *receptacle* 191
  envelope 223
sheathe *moderate* 174
  line 224
  clothe 225
  - the sword 723
sheathing 223, 224
shebeen 189
shed *scatter* 73
  building 189
  emit 297
  give 784
  - a luster on 873
  - blood 361
  - light upon 420
  - tears 839
sheen 420
sheep 366
sheep dog 366
sheepfold 232
sheepish 881
sheep's eyes
  desire 865
  modest 881
  endearment 902
sheer *mere* 32
  simple 42
  complete 52
  deviation 279
  - off *avoid* 623
  (*depart* 293)
sheet *layer* 204
  covering 223
  paper 593
  - of fire 382
  - of water 343
  white - *penance* 952
  winding - 363
sheet anchor
  safety 664, 666, 706
  hope 858
sheet lightning 423
sheet work 591
sheik *ruler* 745
  priest 996
shelf *support* 215
  rock 667
  on the - *powerless* 158
  disused 678
  inaction 681
shell *cover* 223
  coffin 363
  bomb 404, 727

bombard 716
warfare 722
- game 545
- out 807, 809
shellac 356*a*
shellback 269
shellfish 366
shellproof 664
shell-shaped 245
shell-shock 655
shelter *safety* 664
  refuge 666
  - oneself under plea
    of 617
sheltie 271
shelve *lateness* 133
  locate 184
  slope 217
  neglect 460
  disuse 678
shelved *unsalable* 796
shelving beach 217
shenanigan 842
shend 659
sheol 982
shepherd
  tender of sheep 370
  director 694
  pastor 996
Shepherd, the Good
  - 976
shepherd's dog 366
Sheppard, Jack - 792
sherbet 298
shereef *governor* 745
  noble 875
sheriff 664, 965
sherry 959
Shetland 271
Shiah 984
shibboleth 550
shield *heraldry* 550
  safety 664
  buckler 666
  defend 717
  scutcheon 877
  look only at one side
    of the - 481
  reverse of the -
    rear 235
    counter evidence 468
  under the - of 664
shield-shaped 245
shift *change* 140
  convert 144
  substitute 147
  changeable 149
  displace 185
  chemise 225
  more 264
  transfer 270
  deviate 279
  prevaricate 546
  plea 617
  cunning 702
  (*expedient* 626)
  last - 601
  left to - for oneself
    893
  make a - with
    substitute 147

use 677
put to one's -s
  difficulty 704
  poverty 804
  - for oneself
    conduct 692
    freedom 748
  - off *defer* 133
  - one's ground 607
  - one's quarters 264
  - the scene 140
  - to and fro 149
shifting [*see* shift]
  transient 111
  - sands 149
  - trust or use 783
shiftless
  unprepared 674
  inhabile 699
shifty 702
shikar 622
shillalah 727
shilling 800
  cut off with a - 789
  - shocker 594
shilly-shally 605
shimmer 420
shimmy *dance* 840
shin *climb* 305
shindig 840
shindy 720
shine *light* 420
  beauty 845
  glory 873
  - forth 873
  - in conversation 588
  - upon *illumine* 420
  aid 707
  take the - out of 874
shingle *covering* 223,
  635
  powder 330
  - house 189
shining [*see* shine]
  - light *sage* 500
shinny 840
shinplaster 800
shintiyan 225
shiny 420
ship *lade* 190
  transfer 270
  vessel **273**
  one's - coming in 803
  - of the line 726
  take - *sail* 267
  depart 293
ship biscuit 298
shipboard, on - 273
shipentine 273
shipload *much* 31
  cargo 190
  (*abundance* 639)
shipman 269
shipmate 890
shipment *contents* 190
  transfer 270
shippen 189
shipping 273
shipshape *order* 58
  conformity 82
  skill 698

shipwreck
  destruction 162, 361
  vanquish 731
  failure 732
shire 181
shirk *shuffle* 605
  avoid 623
  disobey 742
shirred eggs 298
shirt 225
shirt waist 225
Shiva 976
shivaree 414
shive *small piece* 32
  layer 204
shiver *small piece* 32
  divide 44
  destroy 162
  filament 205
  shake 315
  brittle 328
  cold 383
  fear 860
  go to -s 162
  - in one's shoes 860
shivery *brittle* 328
  powdery 330
shizoku 875
shoal *assemblage* 72
  multitude 102
  shallow 209
shoals *danger* 667
  surrounded by -
  difficulty 704
shock *sheaf* 72
  violence 173
  concussion 276
  agitation 315
  unexpected 508
  discord 713
  affect 821
  move 824
  pain 828
  give pain 830
  dislike 867
  scandalize 932
  (contest 720)
shocking *bad* 649
  painful 830
  ugly 846
  vulgar 851
  fearful 860
  disreputable 874
  hateful 898
  in a - temper 901*a*
shockingly *much* 31
shod 225
shoddy 645
shoe *support* 215
  dress 225
  hindrance 706
  stand in the -s of
  commission 755
  deputy 759
  where the - pinches
  badness 649
  difficulty 704
  opposition 708
  sensibility 822
  painful 830
shoemaker 225

shog 173
shoot *offspring* 167
  expand 194
  dart 274
  propel 284
  kill 361
  vegetable 367
  pain 378
  execute 972
  - ahead 282
  - ahead of 303
  - at 716
  - out beams 420
  - up *increase* 35
    prominent 250
    grow 365
    (ascend 305)
  teach the young idea
    to - 537
shooter *pistol* 727
shooting [*see* shoot]
  chase 622
  - pain 378
  - star *world* 318
  luminary 423
  omen 512
shooting coat 225
shooting iron 727
shop *buy* 795
  mart 799
  keep a - *business* 625
  trade 794
  shup up - *end* 67
  cease 142
  relinquish 624
  rest 687
  smell of the - 851
shopkeeper 797
shoplifter 792
shoplifting 791
shopman 797
shopmate 890
shopping 794, 795
shop-worn *cheap* 815
shore *support* 215
  border 231
  land 342
  buttress 717
  hug the - 286
  on - 342
  - up 215, 669, 670
shoreless 180
shorn *cut short* 21
  divided 51
  deprived 776
  - lamb 828
  - of its beams
  dim 422
  inglorious 874
short *not long* 201
  brittle 328
  typography 550
  concise 572
  uncivil 895
  at - notice
  transient 111
  early 132
  come - of, fall - of
  inferior 34
  shortcoming 304
  insufficient 640

  in - *concisely* 572
  compendium 596
  make - work of
  destroy 162
  active 682
  haste 684
  complete 729
  conquer 731
  punish 972
  - allowance 640
  - answer 895
  - bit *money* 800
  - breath 688
  - by 201
  - commons
  insufficiency 640
  fasting 956
  - cut *straight* 246
  mid-course 628
  - distance 197
  - life and merry 840
  - measure 53
  - of *small* 32
  inferior 34
  subtraction 38
  incomplete 53
  shortcoming 304
  insufficient 640
  - of cash 804
  - rations 956
  - sea 348
shortage 53
shortbread 298
shortcoming
  inequality 28
  inferiority 34
  motion short of **304**
  noncompletion 730
shorten 201
  - sail 275
shorthand 590
short-handed 651
shorthorn 366
short-lived 111
shortly *soon* 132, 507
shortness **201**
  for - sake 572
shorts 225
shortsighted
  myopic 443
  misjudging 481
  foolish 499
short-winded
  weak 160
  fatigue 688
short-witted 499
shot *missile* 284
  variegated 440
  guess 514
  war material 722, 727
  price 812
  reward 973
  bad - 701
  exchange -s 720
  good - 700
  have a - at 716
  like a - 113
  not have a - in one's
    locker 804
  off like a - 623
  random -

  experiment 463
  chance 621
  round - 727
  - in the locker 632
shot-free 815
shotgun 727
should be
  no better than she -
    961
  what - 922
shoulder *support* 215
  projection 250
  shove 276
  printing 591
  broad -ed 159
  cold - 289
  have on one's -s 625
  on the -s of *high* 206
  elevated 307
  instrumentality 631
  rest on the -s of 926
  - a musket 722
  - arms 673
  - to shoulder
  coöperate 709
  party 712
  - to the wheel
  resolution 604
  undertaking 676
  shrug the -s
    [*see* shrug]
  take upon one's -s 676
shoulder knot 847
shout *loud* 404
  cry 406, 411
  rejoice 838
  (voice 580)
shove 276
  give a - to *aid* 707
shovel *receptacle* 191
  transfer 270
  vehicle 272
  fire iron 386
  cleanness 652
  - away 297
shovel hat 999
show *occasion* 134
  visible 446
  appear 448
  draw attention 457
  evidence 467
  demonstrate 478
  manifest 525
  drama 599, 840
  ornament 847
  parade 882
  dumb - 550
  make a - 544
  mere - 544
  peep - 840
  - a light pair of heels
    623
  - cause 527
  - fight *defy* 715
  attack 716
  defend 717
  brave 861
  - forth 525
  - in front 303
  - itself 446
  - of *similarity* 17

probability 472
- off *display* 882
  boast 884
- one's cards 529
- one's colors 550
- one's face
  presence 186
  manifest 525
  disclose 529
- one's hand 529
- one's teeth 715
- up *visible* 446
  manifest 525
  ridicule 856
  degrade 874
  censure 932
  accuse 938
show-down 525
shower *assemblage* 72
  shower bath 337
  rain 348
- bath 337, 386
- down
  abundance 639
- down upon
  give 784
  liberal 816
showman 524
showy *color* 428
  ugliness 846
  ornament 847
  tawdry 851
  fashionable 852
  ostentatious 882
shrapnel 727
shred *small* 32
  filament 205
  (*part* 51)
shrew 901
shrewd *knowing* 490
  wise 498
  cunning 702
  (*clever* 698)
shriek 410, 411
shrievalty 965
shrieve 965
shrift *confession* 529
  absolution 952
shriftless 951
shrill *loud* 404, 410
  cry 411
shrimp 193, 298
shrine *receptacle* 191
  tomb 363
  temple 998, 1000
shrink *decrease* 36
  shrivel 195
  go back 283, 287
  unwilling 603
  avoid 623
  sensitive 822
- from *fear* 860
  dislike 867
  hate 898
shrive 952
shrivel *contract* 195
  fold 258
  (*decrease* 36)
shriveled *thin* 203
  (*small* 193)
shroud *covering* 223

invest 225
  funeral 363
  hide 528
  safety 664
  defend 717
-ed in mystery 519
shrub *plant* 367
  plantation 371
shrug *sign* 550
  (*hint* 527)
- the shoulders
  dissent 489
  submit 725
  discontent 832
  dislike 867
  contempt 930
  disapprobation 932
shrunk *little* 193
  shrink 195
shudder *cold* 383
  fear 860
  make one -
  painful 830
- at *aversion* 867
  hate 898
shuffle *mix* 41
  derange 61
  change 140
  interchange 148
  changeable 149
  move slowly 275
  agitate 315
  falsehood 544
  untruth 546
  irresolute 605
  recant 607
  improbity 940
  patience and - the
    cards 826
- off *run away* 623
- off this mortal coil
    360
- on 266
- the cards
  begin again 66
  change 140
  chance 621
  prepare 673
shuffler 548
shun *avoid* 623
  dislike 867
shunt *transfer* 270
  deviate 279
  remove 287
shunted *shelved* 460
shut 261
- in 751
- one's ears *deaf* 419
  not believe 487
- oneself up 893
- one's eyes to
  not attend to 458
  neglect 460
  not believe 487
  permit 760
  not observe 773
- out *exclude* 55
  prohibit 761
- the eyes 442
- the door 761
- the door in one's

  face 764
- the door upon 893
- the gates of mercy
    914a
- up *close* 261
  confute 479
  imprison 751
  (*inclose* 229)
- up shop *end* 67
  cease 142
  relinquish 624
  repose 687
shutter 424
shuttle *correlation* 12
  oscillate 314
  instrument 633
shuttlecock 605
shuttlewise 314
shy *deviate* 279
  draw back 283
  propel 284
  avoid 623
  fearful 860
  cowardly 862
  modest 881
fight - of 623
have a - at 716
- cock 862
- of *doubtful* 485
  unwilling 603
  cautious 864
  dislike 867
- of belief 487
Shylock 787
shyster 941, 968
Siamese twins 89
sib 11
Siberia 383
sibilation *hiss* 409
  disrespect 929
  disapprobation 932
sibyl *oracle* 513
  ugly 846
sibylline 511
- leaves 513
sic *imitation* 19
  exact 494
siccation 340
siccity 340
sick *ill* 655
  make one -
  painful 830
  aversion 867
- at heart 837
- of *weary* 841
  dislike 867
  satiated 869
  visitation of the - 998
sick chamber 655
sicken *nauseate* 395
  disease 655
  pain 830
  weary 841
  disgust 867
sickener *too much* 641
sickle *pointed* 244
  sharp 253
sickle-shaped 245
sickly *weak* 160
sickness 655
sick room 655

side *consanguinity* 11
  edge 231
  laterality 236
  party 712
at one's - 197
from - to side 314
look only at one - of
    the shield 481
on every - 227
on one - 243
on one's - 714
pass from one - to
    another 607
- by side
  accompaniment 88
  near 197
  laterality 236
  party 712
- issue 39
- with *aid* 707
  coöperate 709
  concord 714
take up a - 476
wrong - up 218
side arms 727
side blow 702
sideboard 191
side dish 298
side drum 417
sideling 237, 279
sidelong 236, 237, 279
side partner 891
sideration 318
sidereal 318
siderite 288
sideromancy 511
sidesaddle 215
side scene 599
sidesman 996
sidetrack 279, 287
sidewalk 627
sideways *oblique* 217
  lateral 236
side wind *oblique* 217
  circuit 629
  cunning 702
sidewinder 276
sidewipe 276
sidewise 237
sidle *oblique* 217
  lateral 236
  deviate 279
siege 716
lay - to 716
state of - 722
siege cap 717
siege gun 727
siege train 727
siesta 683
sieve *sort* 60
  crossing 219
  perforate 260
  sift 652
pour water into a -
  waste 638
  lavish 818
stop one hole in a -
    819
sift *simplify* 42
  sort 60
  inquire 461

discriminate 465
clean 652
- the chaff from the wheat 609
sifter 219
sigh 839
- for 865
sighing 839
- like furnace 902
sight *much* 31
multitude 102
vision 441
appearance 448
ugly 846
prodigy 872
at - *soon* 132
seeing 441
dim - 443
in - 446
in - of *near* 197
seen 441
keep in - 457
within - of shore 858
sightless *blind* 442
invisible 447
ugly 846
sightly 845
sight-reading
music 415
sights, see - 455
sight-seeing 441
sight-seer
spectator 444
curiosity 455
sight-singing 415
sigil *seal* 550
evidence 769
sigmoid 245, 248
sign *attest* 467
omen 512
indication 550
record 551
write 590
talisman 747
compact 769
prodigy 872
give - of 525
make no - 585
-s of the times
omen 512
warning 668
-s of the zodiac 318
signal *great* 31
eventful 151
sign 550
important 642
give the - 741
- of distress 669
signalize *indicate* 550
glory 873
celebrate 883
signally 31
signal light 423
signal post 550, 668
signature
mark, identification 550
writing 590
printing 591
compact 769
security 771
680

signboard 550
signet
mark, identification 550
sign of authority 747
compact 769
(evidence 467)
writer to the - 968
significant
[*see* signify]
evidence 467
importance 642
(clear 518)
signifies, what - 643
signify *forebode* 511
mean 516
inform 527
indication 550
signior 875
sign manual 550, 590
signor 877
sign painting 555
signpost 550
sike 348
Sikes, Bill - 792
silence *disable* 158
no sound **403**
confute 479
latency 526
concealment 528
aphony 581
taciturn 585
check 731
silencer 405, 408a
silent [*see* silence]
silhouette *outline* 230
appearance 448
portrait 556
siliquose 191
silk *texture* 219, 329, 635
smooth 255
soft 324
make a - purse out of a sow's ear 471
- gown *barrister* 968
silken 255
- *repose* 687
silkiness
voluptuousness 954
sill 215
silly *credulous* 486
imbecile 499
insane 503
silo 636
silt *dirt* 653
(remainder 40)
silvan 367
silver *bright* 420
white 430
gray 432
money 800
bait with a - hook 615
German - 545
- footed queen 318
- lining of the cloud 858
- wedding 883
silver-toned 413
silviculture 371
simagrée 855

simian 499
similarity **17**
- of form 240
simile *similarity* 17
comparison 464
metaphor 521
similitude *likeness* 17
copy 21
simious 499
simmer *agitation* 315
boil 382, 384
excitement 824
simmering 825
Simon, Simple - 547
Simon Pure
the real - 494
Simon Stylites 893
simony 964
simoon 349, 382
simous 243
simper *smile* 838
affectation 855
simple *mere* 32
unmixed 42
credulous 486
ignorant 493
silly 499
- *language* 576
instrumental 633
herb 662
artless 703
unadorned 849
- *duty* 926
- *meaning* 516
simple-hearted 543
simple-minded 849
simpleness **42**
Simple Simon 501, 547
simpleton 501
simplicity **849**
ignorance 491
[*see* simple]
simplify [*see* simple]
elucidate 518
simply *little* 32
singly 87
more - *interpreted* 522
simulate *resemble* 17
imitate 19
cheat 544
impiety 988
simultaneous 120
sin *vice* 945
guilt 947
Sinæan 188
sinapism 662
since *under the circumstances* 8
after 117
cause 155
reason 476
sincere *veracious* 543
ingenuous 703
feeling 821
sine 217
sine die *never* 107
defer 133
sine quâ non
required 630
important 642
condition 770

sinecure 681
no - 682
sinew 159
sinewless 158
sinews of war
money 800
sinewy 159
sinful 945
sing *blow* 349
bird cry 412
music 416
poetry 597
rejoice 838
- in the shrouds 349
- out 411
- praises *approve* 931
worship 990
- small 879
singe 382, 384
singer *musician* 416
poet 597
singing club 416
single *unmixed* 42
unit 87
secluded 893
unmarried 904
ride at - anchor 863
- combat 720
- entry 811
- file 69
- out 609
single-foot 275
single-handed *one* 87
easy 705
unassisted 706
single-minded 703
singleness [*see* single]
- of heart *artless* 703
probity 939
- of purpose
perseverance 604a
artless 703
single-seater 273
singlestick 720
singsong 16, 414
singular *special* 79
exceptional 83
one 87
singularly *very* 31
nonconformity 83
sinister *left* 239
bad 649
adverse 735
vicious 945
bar - *imperfect* 651
disrepute 874
sinistrality **239**
sinistrorsal 239
sinistrous
sullen 901a
sink *disappear* 4, 111
destroy 162
descend 306
lower 308
submerge 310
neglect 460
conceal 528
cloaca 653
fatigue 688
vanquish 731
fail 732

adversity 735
invest 787
pain 828
depressed 837
(decay 659)
- back 661
- in the mind
thought 451
memory 505
excite 824
- into oblivion 506
- into the grave 360
- money 809
- of corruption 653
- of iniquity 945
- or swim
certainty 474
perseverance 604a
sinking
heart - 837
- fund 802
sinless 946
sinned against
more - than sinning 946
sinner 949
Sinn Fein 742
Sinn Feiner 710, 712, 742
sin offering 952
sinologist 492
sinuous 217, 248
sinus 252
sip small 32
drink 298
siphon 348, 350
sippet 298
sir man 373
title 877
- Oracle 887
sircar 745
sirdar 745
sire 166
siren sea nymph 341
musician 416
musical instrument 417
seducing 615
warning 668
alarm 669
evildoer 913
evil spirit 980
sorcerer 994
- strains 415
song of the -s 615
sirene
musical instrument 417
siriasis 503
sirius 423
sirkar 745
sirloin 298
sirocco wind 349
heat 382
sirrah! 949
sirup 352, 396
siskin 366
sissy milksop 158
sister kin 11
likeness 17
nurse 662

celibacy 904
sisterhood party 712
friendship 888
frail - 962
sisterly 906
sisters, - three 601
weird - 994
Sisyphus task of -
useless 645
difficult 704
(not complete 730)
sit 308
hatch 370
- down settle 184
lie 213
stoop 308
- in judgment
adjudge 480
jurisdiction 965
lawsuit 969
- on 215
- on thorns
annoyance 828
fear 860
- up for 133
site 182, 183
sith circumstance 8
reason 476
sitting [see sit]
incubation 673
convocation 696
- up late 133
work 686
sitting room 191
situation
circumstances 8
place 183
location 184
business 625
out of a - 185
situs 183
sitz bath 386
Siva 976
six 98
- of one and half a dozen of the other 27
sixes and sevens
at - disorder 59
discord 713
six-shooter 727
sixty 98
sizar 746
size magnitude 31
glue 45
arrange 60
dimensions 192
viscid 352
- up 480
sizz 409
sizzle 409
sjambok 975
skald 597
skate locomotion 266
vehicle 272
deterioration 659
skating 840
skating rink 840
skean 727
skean dhu 727
skedaddle 274, 623

skeel 191
skeesicks 949
skein 219
tangled - 59
skeletal 203
skeleton remains 40
essential part 50
thin 203
support 215
corpse 362
plan 626
reduced to a - 659
- in the closet
bad 649
painful 830
skeptic
agnostic 485, 984
skepticism
thought 451
doubt 485
incredulity 487
irreligion 989
sketch delineate 230
form 240
represent 554
paint 556
describe 594
outline 626
sketcher 559
sketchy incomplete 53
feeble 575
unfinished 730
skew 217
skewbald 440
skewer 45
ski 225, 266, 272
skiagram 421, 554
skiagraph 421
skiagraphy shadow 421
representation 554, 556
skid support 215
hindrance 706
skies [see sky]
exalt to the - 873
praise to the - 933
skiff 273
skill 698
acquisition of - 539
game of - 840
skillet 191, 386
skillful 698
skim move 266
navigate 267
rapid 274
neglect 460
summarize 596
skimp 460
skin outside 220
tegument 223
peel 226
thief 792
mere - and bone 203
- a flint
impossible 471
parsimony 819
- game 545
- over 660
wet to the - 339
with a whole - 670
without - 822

skin-deep
shallow 32, 209
external 220
skinlike 223
skinned thick - 376
thin - 375
skinny thin 203
all skin 223
skip depart 293
jump 309
neglect 460
rejoice 838
(amusement 840)
skipjack
prosperous 734
lowborn 876
skipper
sea captain 269
captain 745
skippet 191
skippingly 70
skirmish 720
skirmisher 726
skirt appendix 39
pendent 214
dress 225
surrounding 227
edge 231
side 236
woman 374
hang upon the -s of 281
on the -s of near 197
skirt-dance 840
skirting 231
skit ridicule 856
detraction 934
prostitute 962
skittish capricious 608
excitable 825
timid 862
bashful 881
skittles 840
skive 204
skulk hide 528
cowardly 862
skull 450
skullcap 225
skunk 366, 401
skunk cabbage 401
skurry 684
sky summit 210
world 318
air 338
sky-aspiring 865
sky-blue 438
skylark 305
skylarking 840
skylight 260
sky line 196
skyrocket 305
skyscraper 210
skyward 210, 305
slab layer 204
support 215
flat 251
puddle 343
viscous 352
record 551
slabber slaver 297
unclean 653

slabsided 200, 203
slack *loose* 47
  weak 160
  inert 172
  slow 275
  cool 385
  coal 388
  unwilling 603
  insufficient 640
  unprepared 674
  inactive 683
  lax 738
  nonobservant 773
slacken *loosen* 47
  moderate 174
  neglect 460
  repose 687
  hinder 706
  one's pace 275
slacker 623, 927
slade 252
slag *embers* 384
  rubbish 645
  dirt 653
  (*remains* 40)
slake *quench* 174
  gratify 829
  satiate 869
  (*content* 831)
  - one's appetite
  intemperance 954
slam *shut* 261
  slap 276
  snap 406
  - the door in one's
    face *oppose* 708
  refuse 764
slammerkin 653
slammock 653
slander 934
slanderer 936
slang 563
slang-whanger 887
slangy 560
slant 217
slap *instantly* 113
  strike 276
  censure 932
  punish 972
  - in the face
  opposition 708
  attack 716
  anger 900
  disrespect 929
  disapprobation 932
  - the forehead 461
slap-bang 406
slap-dash 684
slap-stick 599
slash 44
slashing *style* 574
slate *list* 86
  writing tablet 590
  schedule 611
  plan 626
  - loose *mad* 503
slate-colored 432
slates *roof* 223
slattern *disorder* 59
  dirty 653
  bungler 701
682

vulgar 851
  (*negligent* 460)
slatternly [*see* slattern]
  unskillful 699
slaughter 361
slaughterhouse 361
slave *servant* 631, 746
  worker 686
  a - to 749
  - to no sect 984
  - trade 795
slaver *ship* 273
  slobber 297
  dirt 653
  flatter 933
slavery *toil* 686
  subjection 749
slavish *servile* 746, 886
  subject 749
slay 361
sleave 59
sleazy 160
sled 272
sledge 272
sledge hammer 276
  with a - *destroy* 162
  exertion 686
sleek *smooth* 255
  pretty 845
sleep *inactivity* 683
  balmy - 683
  last - 360
  not have a wink of -
    825
  put to - 376
  rock to - *smooth* 174
  send to - 841
  - at one's post 683
  - upon *defer* 133
  consider 451
  - with one eye open
    459
sleeper *support* 215
  wake the seven -s 404
sleeping car 272
sleeping partner 683
sleepless *active* 682
sleepwalker 268
sleepwalking 266
sleepy 683
sleet 383
sleeve *skein* 219
  dress 225
  hang on the - of 746
  in one's - *hidden* 528
  laugh in one's -
    latency 526
  rejoice 838
  hope 856
  wear one's heart upon
    one's - *manifest* 525
  artless 703
sleeveless *foolish* 499
  unreasonable 608
  - errand *useless* 645
  unskillful 699
sleigh 272
sleight *skill* 698
  - of hand *deception* 545
  (*interchange* 146)
slender *small* 32

thin 203
  trifling 643
  - means 804
sleuth 527
  - hound 913
slice *cut* 44
  piece 51
  layer 204
slick *smooth* 255
  smart 698
slicker 225
slide *elapse* 109
  smooth 255
  pass 264
  locomotion 266
  descend 306
  - back 661
  - in 228
  - into 144
slide valve 263
sliding *amusement* 840
sliding panel 545
sliding rule 85
slight *small* 32
  shallow 209
  rare 322
  neglect 460
  disparage 483
  feeble 575
  trifle 643
  dereliction 927
  disrespect 929
  contempt 930
slight-made 203
slily *surreptitiously* 544
  craftily 702
slim 203
  cunning 702
slime *viscous* 352
  dirt 653
sling *hang* 214
  project 284
  weapon 727
  drink 959
slink *hide* 528
  cowardice 862
  - away *avoid* 623
  disrepute 874
  (*escape* 671)
slinky 203
slip *small* 32
  elapse 109
  child 129
  strip 205
  descend 306
  error 495
  workshop 691
  fail 732
  false coin 800
  vice 945
  guilt 947
  give one the - 671
  let - *liberate* 750
  lose 776
  relinquish 782
  let - the dogs of war
    722
  - away 187, 623
  - cable 623
  - in (*or* - into) 294
  - of the pen 495, 568

- of the tongue
  solecism 568
  stammering 583
  - on 225
  - over *neglect* 460
  - the collar
  escape 671
  free oneself 750
  - the memory 506
  - through the fingers
  miss an opportunity
    135
  escape 671
  fail 732
  -'twixt cup and lip
    509
slipper 225
  hunt the - 840
slippery *transient* 111
  smooth 255
  greasy 355
  uncertain 475
  vacillating 607
  dangerous 665
  facile 705
  nonobservant 773
  faithless 940
  - ground 667
slipshod 575
slipslop *absurdity* 497
  solecism 568
  weak language 575
slit *divide* 44
  chink 198
  furrow 259
sliver 51
slobber *drivel* 297
  slop 337
  dirt 653
sloe *black* 431
slogan 722
sloop 273
  - of-war 726
slop *spill* 297
  water 337
  dirt 653
slope *oblique* 217
  run away 623
sloping 306
sloppy *moist* 339
  marsh 345
  style 575
slops *clothes* 225
slosh 337, 653
slot 260
sloth 683
slouch *low* 207
  oblique 217
  move slowly 275
  inactive 683
slouching *ugly* 846
slough *covering* 223
  divest 226
  quagmire 345
  dirt 653
  difficulty 704
  adversity 735
  (*remains* 40)
  - of Despond 859
sloughy 226
sloven *untidy* 59

bungler 701
  vehicle 272
slovenly *untidy* 59
  careless 460
  style 575
  dirty 653
  awkward 699
  vulgar 851
slow *tardy* 133
  inert 172
  moderate 174
  motion 275
  inactive 683
  wearisome 841
  dull 843
  be - to
    unwilling 603
    not finish 730
    refuse 764
  by - degrees 26
  march in - time 275
  - down 174
  - movement
    music 415
slow-burning 388
slow coach 701
slowness **275**
slowworm 419
sloyd 537
slubber *unclean* 653
  (inactive 683)
slubberdegullion 876
sludge 653
slug *slow* 275
  printing 591
  inaction 681
  inactivity 683
  bullet 727
  money 800
sluggard 275, 683
sluggish *inert* 172
  callous 823
sluice *limit* 233
  egress 295
  river 348
  conduit 350
  open the -s 297
slum 653
slumber 683
slummock 653
slump 304, 306
slung shot 727
slur *stigma* 874
  gloss over 937
  reproach 938
  - over *neglect* 460
  slight 483
  (exclude 55)
  (inattention 458)
  (conceal 528)
slush *marsh* 345
  semiliquid 352
  dirt 653
slut *untidy* 59
  dog 366
  dirty 653
  wench 876
  unchaste 962
  (neglect 460)
sly *shrewd* 498
  stealthy 528

cunning 702
  (false 544)
slyboots 702
smack
  small quantity 32
  mixture 41
  boat 273
  impulse 276
  taste 390
  courtesy 894
  kiss 902
  strike 972
  - of resemble 17
  - the lips
    pleasure 277
    taste 390
    savory 394
    rejoice 838
small - *in degree* 32
  - in size 193
  become - 195
  esteem of - account
    930
  feel - 879
  not think - beer of
    oneself 880
  of - account 643
  on a - scale 32, 193
  - arms 727
  - beer 643
  - bore 727
  - chance 473
  - coin 800
  - fry *littleness* 193
    unimportant 643
    commonalty 876
  - hours 125
  - matter 643
  - number 103
  - part 51
  - talk 588
  think no - beer of one-
    self 878
  think - beer of 930
smallclothes 225
smaller *in degree* 34
  in size 195
smallness **32**
smalls 225
smalt 438
smart *pain* 378
  active 682
  clever 698
  feel 821
  grief 828
  witty 842
  pretty 845
  ornamental 847
  - pace 274
  - saying 842
  - set 852
  - under 821
smarten 847
smart money 973
smash
  destruction 162
  failure 732
smasher 792
smatch 390
smatterer 493
smattering 491

smear *cover* 223
  grease 355
  soil 653
smeared 426
smell 398, 401
  bad - 401
  - a rat 485
  - of the lamp
    ornate style 577
    prepared 673
  - powder 722
smell-feast 886
smelling bottle 400
smelt *heat* 384
  prepare 673
smicker 838
smile *cheerful* 836
  rejoice 838
  raise a - 840
  - at 856
  - of contempt 930
  - of fortune 734
  - upon *aid* 707
    courtesy 894
    endearment 902
smirch *blacken* 431
  dirty 653
smirk 838
smite *maltreat* 649
  excite 824
  afflict 830
  punish 972
  (strike 276)
smith 690
smitten *love* 897
  - with *moved* 615
smock *clothing* 225
  wrinkle 258
smock-faced 862
smock frock 225
smoke *dust* 330
  vapor 336
  heat 382
  tobacco 392
  discover 480a
  suspect 485
  unimportant 643
  dirt 653
  end in -
    shortcoming 304
    failure 732
  - the calumet of peace
    723
smoke bomb 727
smoked glasses 424
smokejack 312
smoke screen 424
smokeshaft 351
smoker *concert* 892
smokestack 260, 351
smoke talk 584
smoking hot 382
smoking jacket 225
smoking room 191
smoky *opaque* 426
  dirty 653
smolder *inert* 172
  burn 382
  latent 526
smooth *uniform* 16
  calm 174

make level 213
  flat 251
  not rough 255
  easy 705
  - as glass 255
  - down 174
  - over 174
  - sailing 705
  - the bed of sickness
    aid 707
    benevolence 906
  the ruffled brow of
    care 834
  - the way
    facilitate 705
  - water *easy* 705
smooth bore 727
smoothly [see smooth]
  go on - *prosperous* 734
smoothness 255
smooth-tongued
  lie 544
  flatter 933
smother *repress* 174
  kill 361
  suppress 528
  stifle sound 581
  restrain 751
  (abide 826)
smudge *fuel* 388
  blackness 431
  dirt 653
  blemish 848
smug *affected* 855
smuggle *introduce* 228
  steal 791
  illegal 964
  (ingress 294)
smuggler 792
smut *black* 431
  dirt 653
  impurity 961
  (blemish 848)
smutch 431
smutty *black* 431
  impure 961
snack
  small quantity 32
  food 298
snacks, go - 778
snaffle 706, 752
snag *projection* 250
  sharp 253
  danger 667
  hindrance 706
snail *slow* 275
  mollusk 368
snake *coil* 248
  draw 285
  serpent 366
  hissing 409
  miscreant 913
  scotch the - 640
  - in the grass
    hidden 528
    deceiver 548
    bad 649
    source of danger 667
    evildoer 913
    knave 941
snakelike 248, 366

snakestone 248
snap *break* 44
  time 106
  shut 261
  eat 298
  brittle 328
  noise **406**
  impulse 612
  activity 682
  cheapness 815
  rude 895
  - at *seize* 789
  bite 830
  censure 932
  - of the fingers
  trifle 643
  - one's fingers at
  defy 715
  insolence 885
  despise 930
  - one up *censure* 932
  - the thread 70
  - up *seize* 789
snapdragon 840
snappish 901
snappy *news* 532
snap shot 554
snare *deception* 545
  (*source of danger*
  667)
snare drum 417
snarl *growl* 412
  discord 713
  rude 895
  angry 900
  threaten 909
snarled *confused* 523
snatch
  small quantity 32, 51
  seize 789
  by -es 70
  - at *pursue* 622
  seize 789
  - a verdict *deceive* 545
  cunning 702
  - from one's grasp 789
  - from the jaws of
  death 672
sneak *hide* 528
  coward 862
  servile 886
  base 940
  knave 941
  bad man 949
  - off, - out of 623
  - thief 792
sneakers *shoes* 225
sneer *disparage* 929
  contempt 930
  blame 932
sneeze *blow* 349
  snuffle 409
  not to be -d at 642
  - at *despise* 930
snick *small quantity* 32
  part 51
snicker *rejoicing* 838
  ridicule 856
snide 545
sniff *blow* 349
  odor 398

  discovery 480a
sniffle 349
snifting valve 664
snigger *laugh* 838
  ridicule 856
  disrespect 929
sniggle 545
snip *small quantity* 32
  cut 44
  tailor 225
snipe 298, 366
snippet 32
snip-snap 713
snivel *weep* 839
sniveling *servile* 886
snob *vulgar* 851
  plebeian 876
  servile 886
snobbishness
  flattery 933
snood *headdress* 225
  circle 247
snooze 683
snore *noise* 441
  sleep 683
snort 411, 412
snorter 83
snout 250
snow *ship* 273
  ice 383
  white 430
snow avalanche 383
snowball 72, 383
snow blindness 443
snow-bound 383
snowdrift 72
snowshoes 225, 266,
  272
snowslide 306, 383
snowslip 306, 383
snowstorm 383
snub *short* 201
  hinder 706
  cast a slur 874
  humiliate 879
  bluster 885
  censure 932
snub-nosed
  distortion 243
  (*ugly* 846)
snuff *blow* 349
  pungent 392
  odor 398
  go out like the - of a
  candle 360
  - out *destroy* 162
  dark 421
  - up *inhale* 296
  smell 398
  up to - *skillful* 698
  cunning 702
snuff-color 433
snuffle *blow* 349
  hiss 409
  stammer 583
  hypocrisy 988
snuffy 653
snug *closed* 261
  comfortable 377
  safe 664
  prepared 673

  content 831
  secluded 893
  keep - *conceal* 528
  seclude 893
  make all - *prepare* 673
snuggery 189
snuggle 902
snugness 827
so *similar* 17
  very 31
  therefore 476
  method 627
  - be it *assent* 488
  consent 762
  - far so good 618
  - let it be 681
  - much the better
  content 831
  rejoicing 838
  - much the worse
  discontent 832
  aggravation 835
  - to speak *similar* 17
  metaphor 521
soak *immerse* 300
  water 337
  moist 339
  drunkenness 959
  - up 340
soap *lubricate* 332
  oil 356
soapy *unctuous* 355
  service 886
  flattery 933
soar *great* 31
  height 206
  fly 267
  rise 305
  air 338
sob 839
sober *substantial* 3
  moderate 174
  wise 498
  sane 502
  plain 576
  grave 837
  temperate 953
  abstinent 958
  in - sadness
  affirmation 535
  - down 174, 502
  humility 879
  - senses 502
  - truth *fact* 494
sober-minded 502
  calm 826
  humble 879
soberness 953
sobriety **958**
sobriquet 565
soc *jurisdiction* 965
socage 777
so-called
  deception 545
  misnomer 565
sociable *carriage* 272
  sociality 892
social *mankind* 372
  sociable 892
  - circle 892
  - evil 961

  - gathering 892
  - science 910
  - service 602
  - smile 906
  - worker 602
socialism
  government 737
  participation 778
  philanthropy 910
Socialists 712
sociality **892**
society *mankind* 372
  party 712
  fashion 852
  sociality 892
  laity 997
  position in - 873
sociological 537
  - school 451
sociology 910
socinianism 984
socius criminis 711
sock *hosiery* 225
  drama 599
sockdolager 67, 479
socket *receptacle* 191
  concave 252
socle 215
Socratic method 461
Socratic school 451
sod 344
  beneath the - 363
sodality *party* 712
  friendship 888
  (*sociality* 892)
sodden *moist* 339
  boiled 384
sofa 215
soft *stop!* 142
  weak 160
  moderate 174
  smooth 255
  not hard 324
  moist 339
  marsh 345
  silence! 403
  - *sound* 405
  dulcet 413
  credulous 486
  silly 499
  lenient 740
  tender 822
  timid 862
  (*docile* 602)
  (*irresolute* 605)
  own the - *impeach-*
  ment 421
  - buzzing *slander* 934
  - music 415
  - pedal 405
  - sawder *plea* 617
  flattery 933
  - snap 681
  - soap *oil* 356
  flattery 933
  - thing 681
  - tongue, - words 894
soften [*see* soft]
  moderate 174
  relieve 834
  pity 914

palliate 937
  penitent 950
  - down 834
softening 324
  - of the brain 158
softer sex 374
soft-hearted 914
softling 160
softness **324**
  persuasibility 615
soft-spoken 894
soggy 339
soho *attention* 457
  parley 586
  hunting 622
soi-disant
  asserting 535
  misnomer 565
  vain 880
soil *region* 181
  land 342
  dirt 653
  deface 846
  (spoil 659)
  (blemish 848)
  till the -
  agriculture 371
  prepare 673
soilure 653
soirées 892
sojourn *dwell* 186
  abode 189
  (rest 265)
sojourner 188
soke 181
solace *relief* 834
  recreation 840
  - oneself with
  pleasure 827
solar 318
  - system 318
solatium 973
sola topi 225
soldan 745
solder *join* 43
  cement 45
  cohere 46
soldier 726
soldierlike *war* 722
  brave 861
sole *alone* 87
  base 211
  support 215
  fish 298
feme - 904
solecism
  ungrammatical **568**
  (sophistry 477)
solemn
  affirmation 535
  important 642
  grave 837
  glorious 873
  ostentatious 882
  commemoration 883
  religious 987
  worship 990
  - avowal 535
  - declaration 535
  - mockery 882
  - silence 403

solemnity *rite* 998
solemnization 883
sol-fa 416
solfeggio 415
solferino 434, 437
so!¹cit *induce* 615
  request 765
  desire 865
  - the attention 457
solicitor *agent* 758
  petitioner 767
  merchant 797
  lawyer 968
solicitous 765, 865
solicitude *care* 459
  pain 828
  anxiety 860
  desire 865
solid *complete* 52
  dense 321
  certain 474
  learned 490
  exact 494
  wise 498
  persevering 604a
  - in galleys 591
solidarity *party* 712
solidify 48, 321
solidity [see solid]
  solvency 800
solidungulate 366
soliloquist 589
soliloquy **589**
soliped 366
solitaire *game* 840
  hermit 893
solitary *alone* 87
  secluded 893
solitude 87, 893
solmization 415
solo 415
soloist 996
Solomon 498, 500
Solon 498, 500
soluble *fluid* 333
  liquefy 335
solus 87
solution *fluid* 333
  liquefaction 335
  music 413
  answer 462
  explanation 522
  - of continuity 70
solve *liquefy* 335
  discover 480a
  unriddle 522
solvency [see solvent]
solvent
  decomposition 49
  liquefier 335
  diluent 337
  sound 800
  moneyed 803
  payment 807
somatics 316
somatist 316, 989
somatologist 316
somatology 316
somber *dark* 421
  color 428
  black 431

gray 432
  sad 837
sombrero 225
some *indefinite quantity*
  25
  small quantity 32
  more than one 100
at - other time 119
in - degree *degree* 26
  small 32
in - place 182
- ten or a dozen 102
- time ago 122
- time or other 119
somebody
  person 372
  important 642
  distinguished 873
somehow 155
- or other *cause* 155
  instrument 631
somersault 218
something *thing* 3
  small degree 32
  matter 316
  - else 15
  - like 17
  - or other 475
sometimes 136
somewhat *a little* 32
  a trifle 643
somewhere 182
  - about 32
somnambulism
  walking 266
  trance 515
somnambulist
  walker 268
  dreamer 515
somnifacient 683
somniferous *sleepy* 683
  weary 841
somnolence 683
Somnus 683
son 167 [see sons *below*]
Son, God the - 976
sonant 402, 561
sonata 415
Sonderbund 769
song *music* 415
  poem 597
  death - *death* 360
  lament 839
  for a mere - 815
  love - 597
  no - no supper 812
  old - 643
song bird 416
song leader 416
songster 416
soniferous 402
sonification 402
sonnet 597
sonneteer 597
sonorescence 402
sonorous *sound* 402
  loud 404
  language 577
sons - of Belial 988
  - of God 977
  - of Martha 876

sontag 225
soon *transient* 111
  future 121
  early 132
  expected 507
  too - for 135
sooner - or later
  another time 119
  future 121
  - said than done 704
soot *black* 431
  dirt 653
sooth *prediction* 511
in good - 543
soothe *allay* 174
  relieve 834
  flatter 933
  (calm 826)
soothing
  faint sound 405
  - sirup 174
soothsay 511
soothsayer *oracle* 513
  magician 994
soothsaying 511
sootiness 421
sop *small quantity* 32
  food 298
  sodden 339
  fool 501
  inducement 615
  reward 973
  - in the pan 615
  - to Cerberus 458
soph *scholar* 492
  student 541
Sophism 451
sophism *bad logic* 477
  absurdity 497
sophist *scholar* 492
  dissembler 548
sophister 492
  student 541
sophistical 477
sophisticate *mix* 41
  debase 659
sophisticated
  spurious 545
sophistry **477**
sophomore 492, 541
soporific *sleepy* 683
  weary 841
soporose 683
soprano 410
sorcerer 548, **994**
sorcery 511, **992**
sordes 653
sordet 417
sordid *stingy* 819
  covetous 865
sordine 405, 408a, 417
sore *bodily pain* 378
  disease 655
  mental suffering 828,
    830
  discontent 832
  anger 900
  - place 822
  - subject 830, 900
sorely *very* 31
sorghum 396

with no - hand 639
spark *small* 32
  heat 382
  light 420
  luminary 423
  wag 844
  fop 854
  as the -s fly upwards
  habit 613
sparkle *bubble* 353
  glisten 420
sparkling *vigorous* 574
  excitement 824
  cheerful 836
  wit 842
  beauty 845
  with - eyes 827
spark plug 272
sparrow *bird* 366
  love 897
sparse 73, 103
sparseness 73, 103, 137
Spartacus 742
Spartan 739
spasm
  sudden change 146
  violence 173
  agitation 315
  pain 378
spasmodic
  discontinuous 70
  irregular 139
  changeable 149
  violent 173
  - cholera 655
spat
  production 161, 167
  quarrel 713
spathic 204
spats 225
spatter *dirt* 653
  (*damage* 659)
  (*defame* 634)
spatterdash 225
spatula *receptacle* 191
  vehicle 272
spavined 655
spawn
  offspring 161, 167
  productiveness 168
  dirt 653
spay 38, 158
speak *voice* 580
  speech 582
  - for 937
  - for itself
  intelligible 518
  manifest 525
  - ill of *censure* 932
  detract 934
  - low 581
  - of *meaning* 516
  publish 531
  speak 582
  (*describe* 594)
  - one fair 894
  - out *make*
  manifest 525
  artless 703
  artless 703
  - softly 581

- to 586
- up 411
- up for 937
- volumes 467
- well of 931
speaker
  interpreter 524
  soliloquy 589
  chairman 694
speaking 582
  much - 584
  on - terms 888
  - likeness 554
  - of 134
  way of - 521
speaking trumpet 418
spear *pierce* 260
  weapon 727
spearman 726
spear-shaped 253
special *particular* 79
  (*intrinsic* 5)
speciality 79
specialize 79, 662
special pleader 968
special pleading
  sophistry 477
specialty *compact* 769
  security 771
specie 800
species *kind* 75
  · *appearance* 448
  human - 372
specific *special* 79
  remedy 662
  - *gravity* 321
specification *class* 75
  description 594
specify *particularize* 79
  tell 527
  name 564
specimen 82
specious *probable* 472
  sophistical 477
  showy 846
  flattering 933
  pardonable 937
speck
  small quantity 32
  inextension 180a
  (*dot* 193)
  (*blemish* 848)
specked *imperfect* 651
speckle *variegate* 440
  blemish 848
spectacle
  appearance 448
  prodigy 872
  show 882
  drama 599
spectacles 441, 445
spectacular 599, 882
spectator 197, **444**
specter
  fallacy of vision 443
  ugly 846
  ghost 361, 980a, 992a
spectral *inexistence* 2
  unsubstantial 4
  uncanny 980a
spectrogram 554

spectroheliogram 554
spectroheliography 554
spectrometer 445
spectroscope *light* 420
  color 428
  optical instrument
  445
spectrum *color* 428
  variegation 440
  optical illusion 443
speculate *view* 441
  think 451
  suppose 514
  chance 621
  essay 675
  traffic 794
speculation
  experiment 463
  cards 840
speculative *thought* 451
  experiment 463
  supposition 514
  unsound 665 ˌ
speculator
  experiment 463
  theorist 514
  chance 621
speculum 445
  veluti in - 446
sped *completed* 729
speech 582
  figure of - 521
  parts of - 567
  - from the throne 695
  - of angels *music* 415
speechify 582
speechless 403, 581
speechmaker 582
speed *journey* 266
  velocity 274
  activity 682
  help 707
  succeed 731
  - mania 274
  - maniac 268
  - the parting guest
  293
  with breathless - 684
speedily *soon* 132
speedometer 200, 274,
  551
  automobile 272
speedway 626
speil *period* 106
  influence 175
  read 539
  letter 561
  necessity 601
  motive 615
  exertion 686
  charm **993**
  cast a - 992
  wonder 870
  - out *interpret* 522
spellbind 586
spellbound 601, 615
spelling 561
spence 636
spencer 225
spend *effuse* 297
  waste 638

  give 784
  purchase 795
  expend 809
  - freely 816
  - one's time in 625
  - time 106
  - time in 683
spendthrift 818
spent *weak* 160
  tired 688
sperm 153
spermaceti 356
spermary 357
spermatic 168
spermatize 168
spermatophytes 369
spermatozoön 357
sperm gland 357
spew 297
sphacelate 659
sphacelation 655
sphacelus 655
sphere *rank* 26
  space 180
  region 181
  ball 249
  world 318
  business 625
  - of influence 786
spheroid 249
spherule 249
sphery 318
sphinx *monster* 83
  oracle 513
  ambiguous 520
  riddle 533
spial 668
spice *small quantity* 32
  mixture 41
  pungent 392
  condiment 393
spiced *taste* 390
spicilegium
  assemblage 72
  allocution 596
spick and span 123
spiculate 253
spiculum 253
spicy *fragrant* 400
  exciting 824
spider *animal* 368:
  receptacle 191
  pan 386
spieler 548, 792
spigot 263
spike *sharp* 253
  pierce 260
  plug 263
  (*pass through* 302)
  - guns *powerless* 158
  useless 645
spikebit 262
spike team 92, 272
spile 263
  - hole 351
spill *filament* 205
  stopper 263
  shed 297
  splash 348
  match 388
  waste 638

lavish 818
  (misuse 679)
- and pelt 59
- blood 722
spin journey 266
  aviation 267
  rotate 312
- a long yarn
  exaggerate 549
- out protract 110
  late 133
  prolong 200
  diffuse style 573
spinach 298
spinal 222, 235
spindle 312
spindle-shanks 203
spindle-shaped 253
spindrift 353
spine 253
spinel 847
spineless weak 945
spinet copse 367
  harpsichord 417
spinney 367
spinosity
  unintelligible 519
  discourtesy 895
  sullenness 901a
spinous prickly 253
Spinozism 451
spinster 374, 904
spinuliferous 253
spiny 253
spiracle 260, 351
spiral 248, 311
spire height 206
  peak 253
  soar 305
spiriferous 248
spirit essence 5
  immateriality 317
  intellect 450
  meaning 516
  vigorous language 574
  stimulate 615
  activity 682
  affections 820
  courage 861
  ghost 361, 980
  evil - **980a**
  keep one's - up
    hope 858
- away 791
- control 992a
- of my dream 515
- of myrcia 400
- up induce 615
  excite 824
  unclean - 978
  with life and - 682
Spirit, the Holy - 976
spirited language 574
  active 682
  sensitive 822
  cheerful 836
  dashing 852
  brave 861
  generous 942
spiritism 317, 992a
spiritist 317, 450

spiritistic 317
spiritless
  insensible 823
  sad 837
  cowardly 862
spiritoso music 415
spirit rapping 992a
spirits drink 298
  cheer 836
spirit-stirring 824
spiritual
  immaterial 317
  psychical 450
  divine 976
  pious 987
- director 996
- existence 987
- wife 903, 962
spiritualism
  immateriality 317
  intellect 450
  heterodoxy 984
  psychical research
    992a
spiritualist 317
spiritualize 317
spirituel 842
spiroid 248
spirograph 662
spirometer 662
spirt eject 297
  stream 348
  haste 684
  exertion 686
spirtle disperse 73
  splash 348
spissitude dense 321
  viscid 352
spit pointed 253
  perforate 260
  eject 297, 299
  rain 348
- fire irascible 901
spite 907
  envy 921
  in - of disagreement 24
  counteraction 179
  opposition 708
  in - of one's teeth
    unwilling 603
spiteful
  malevolent 907
  hating 898
spittle 299
spittoon 191
splanchnic 221, 329
splanchnology 221, 329
splash affuse 337
  stream 348
  spatter 653
  parade 882
  make a - fame 873
  display 882
splashboard 666
splayfooted 243
spleen melancholy 837
  hatred 898
  anger 900
  sullen 901a
  harbor - 907
spleenless 906

splendiferous 851
splendor bright 420
  beautiful 845
  glorious 873
  display 882
splenetic sad 837
  morose 901a
splice join 43
  cross 219
  interjacent 228
  repair 660
- the main brace
  tipsy 959
spliced, be -
  marriage 903
splint 215, 662, 752
splinter small piece 32
  divide 44
  filament 205
  brittle 328
  (part 51)
split divide 44
  bisect 91
  brittle 328
  divulge 529
  quarrel 713
  fail 732
  laugh 838
- hairs
  discriminate 465
  sophistry 477
- one's sides 838
- the difference
  mean 29
  compromise 774
- the ears loud 404
  stridor 410
  deafness 419
- the lungs 411
- upon a rock 732
splurge 882
splutter energy 171
  spit 297
  stammer 583
  haste 684
spoil waste 638
  vitiate 659
  botch 699
  hinder 706
  lenity 740
  plunder 791
  booty 793
  satiate 869
  (bad 649)
-s of time 106
- sport 706
- trade 708
spoiled child
  satiated 869
  favorite 899
- of fortune 734
spoiler 792
spoke radius 200
  tooth 253
  obstruct 706
  put a - in one's wheel
  render powerless 158
  hinder 706
spokesman
  interpreter 524
  speaker 582

spoliate 791
spoliative 793
spondee 597
sponge stopper 263
  moisten 339
  dry 340
  pulpiness 354
  marine animal 368
  clean 652
  despoil 791
  drunkard 959
  apply the -
  obliterate 552
  nonpayment 808
- out 552
sponger 886
sponging-house 752
spongy porous 252
  soft 324
  squashy 345
sponsion 771
sponsor witness 467
  security 771
  be - for promise 768
  obligation 926
sponsorship 771
spontaneous
  voluntary 600
  willing 602
  impulsive 612
- generation 357
spontoon 727
spoof 545
spook 361, 980a
  fish 368
spool 312
spoon receptacle 191
  ladle 272
  bill and coo 902
  born with a silver -
    in one's mouth 734
spoondrift 353
Spoonerism 495
spoonful some 25
  small quantity 32
spoon-meat 298
spoony foolish 499
  lovesick 902
spoor 550
sporaceous 330
sporadic
  unassembled 73
  infrequent 137
  disease 655, 657
spore 330
sporogenous 161
sporophyte 357
sporous 330
sport killing 361
  chase 622
  amusement 840
  show off 882
  (enjoyment 827)
  in - pastime 840
  humor 842
- of fortune 735
- one's oak 893
  the - of 749
sporting killing 361
  contention 720
  amusement 840

- dog 366
sportive *gay* 836
  frolicsome 840
sportsman 361, 622, 840
sportswoman 840
sportulary 784, 785
sportule 784
sporule 330
sposh 653
spot *inextension* 180a
  place 182
  discover 480a
  mark 550
  dirt 653
  blemish 848
  blot 874
  (*decoloration* 429)
  (*sully* 846)
  (*disgrace* 940)
  on the - *instantly* 113
  present time 118
  soon 132
  in one's presence 186
spotless *perfect* 650
  clean 652
  innocent 946
  (*beautiful* 845)
spotlight 423, 550, 599
spotted *variegated* 440
  damaged 659
  ugly 846
spotter *aviator* 269a
spousal 903
spouse *companion* 88
  married 903
spouseless 904
spout *egress* 295
  flow out 348
  conduit 350
  speak 582
  act 599
  pawn 771
  (*lend* 787)
sprag 633
sprain *powerless* 158
  weak 160
sprat
  - to catch a herring
  barter 794
  - to catch a whale
  bungling 699
sprawl *length* 200
  horizontal 213
  descend 306
spray *sprig* 51
  atomizer 336
  foam 353
  foliage 367
  flowers 400
spread *enlarge* 35
  disperse 73
  universalize 78
  expanse 180
  expand 194
  diverge 291
  meal 298
  publish 531
  - abroad 531
  - a shade 421
  - canvas 267

- out 194
- sail 267
- the toils 545
spread-eagle 884
spree 840
sprig *branch* 51
  infant 129
sprightly
  cheerful 836
  witty 842
spring *early* 125
  source 153
  strength 159
  velocity 274
  recoil 277
  fly 293
  leap 309
  elasticity 325
  rivulet 348
  instrument 633
  store 636
  remedy 662
  - a leak *imperfect* 651
  damage 659
  - a mine *destroy* 162
  unexpected 508
  attack 716
  - a project 626
  - back 277
  - from 154
  - of life 131
  -s of action 615
  - tide *flood* 31, 35, 52
  high 206
  water 337
  wave 348
  (*abundance* 639)
  - to one's feet 307
  - up *begin* 66
  event 151
  grow 194
  ascend 305
  visible 446
  - upon 508, 789
spring balance 319
springe 545
Springfield rifle 727
spring gun 545, 667
springle 545
spring-net 545
springtide *youth* 127
springy 325
sprinkle *add* 37
  mix 41
  scatter 73
  wet 337, 348
  variegate 440
  baptize 998
sprinkler 337
sprinkling
  small quantity 32
sprint 274
sprit *sprout* 167
  support 215
sprite *good spirit* 979
  demon 980
sprout *grow* 35, 365
  offspring 167
  expand 194
  - from *result* 154

spruce *tree* 367
  neat 652
  beautiful 845
  - up 652, 847
sprue 653
sprung *imperfect* 651
  damaged 659
spry *active* 682
  cheerful 836
  (*skillful* 698)
spud 272
spume 353
spunk 861
spun out
  long time 110
  diffuse style 573
spur *pointed* 250
  sharp 253
  - a horse 370
  incite 615
  quicken 684
  on the - of the moment
  instantly 113
  now 118
  soon 132
  opportune 134
  impulse 612
  win -s *succeed* 731
  glory 873
spurious *erroneous* 495
  false 544
  deceptive 545
  illegitimate 925
spurn *reject* 610
  disdain 930
spurred 253
spurt *transient* 111
  swift 274
  gush 348
  impulse 612
  haste 684
  exertion 686
spurtle 73
sputum 299
sputter *emit* 297
  splash 348
  stammer 583
spy *see* 441
  spectator 444
  inquire 461
  informer 527
  emissary 534
  scout 664
  warning 668
spyglass 445
squab *large* 192
  short 201
  broad 202
  bench 215
  nestling 298
squabble 713
squad *assemblage* 72
  soldiers 726
squadron *fighters* 726
  (*crowd* 72)
  (*ships* 273)
squalid *dirty* 653
  unsightly 846
squall *violent* 173
  wind 349

  cry 411
  quarrel 713
squalor 653
squamate 223
squamiferous 223
squamous *layer* 204
  skin 223
squander *waste* 638
  misuse 679
  lose 776
  prodigal 818
squandering 776
squantum 840
square *congruous* 23
  compensate 30
  four 95
  place 182
  houses 189
  perpendicular 212
  form 244
  measure 466
  sparring 720
  justice 924
  honorable 939
  make all - 660
  on the - 939
  - accounts
  pay 807
  account 811
  put a - thing into a round hole 699
  - deal 922
  - inches 180
  - piano 417
  - the circle 471
  - up 556
  - with 23
  - yards 180
square-toes 857
squash *destroy* 162
  flatten 251
  blow 276
  fruit 298
  soft 324
  marsh 345
  semiliquid 352
  pulpiness 354
  hiss 409
  - pie 298
squashy 345, 352
squat *locate oneself* 184
  little 193
  short 201
  thick 202
  low 207
  sit 308
  (*ugly* 846)
squatter 188
squaw *woman* 374
  wife 903
squeak *human cry* 411
  animal cry 412
  disclosure 529
  (*weep* 839)
squeal [see squeak]
squealer 532, 941
squeamish
  unwilling 603
  sick 655
  fastidious 868
  (*censorious* 932)

squeeze *contract* 195
  condense 321
  embrace 894
  (*narrow* 203)
squeeze out
  extract 301
  give 784
squeezers 840
squelch 162, 251
squib *sound* 406
  lampoon 856
  detraction 934
squid 368
squidgy 201
squiffy 959
squint *look* 441
  defective sight 443
squirarchy 875
squire *aid* 707
  attendant 746
  gentry 875
squireen 875
squirm 315
squirrel *swift* 274
  animal 366
  nimble 682
squirt *eject* 297
  sport 348
stab *pierce* 260
  kill 361
  pain 378, 649
  injure 659
stability 16, **150**
  (*quiescence* 265)
  (*perseverance* 604a)
stabilize 150
stable *firm* 150
  house 189, 370
  store 636
  lock the - door when
    the steed is stolen
  too late 135
  useless 645
  bungling 699
 - companion 890
 - equilibrium 150
staccato 415
stack *assemblage* 72
  store 636
staddle 215
  infant 129
stadtholder 745
staff *support* 215
  music 413, 415
  signal 550
  council 696
  party 712
  weapon 727
  chief 745
  retinue 746
  (*directors* 694)
  (*hope* 858)
  pastoral - 999
 - officer 745
 - of honor 128
 - of life 298
 - of office 747
stag *deer* 366
  male 373
  defaulter 808
  sociality 892
    690

 - dance 840
 - party 892
 - the market 794
stage *degree* 26
  term 71
  time 106
  position 183
  layer 204
  platform 215
  forum 542
  drama 599
  arena 728
  come upon the - 446
  go off the - *depart* 293
  on the - *manifest* 525
  theatrical 599
 - business 599
 - direction 697
 - effect *display* 882
 - manager 599
 - name 565
 - play 599
 - player 599
 - whisper 580
stagecoach 272
stagecraft 599
stager *player* 599
  doer 690
  old - 130
stage-struck 599
stagger *slow* 275
  totter 314
  agitate 315
  unexpected 508
  dissuade 616
  feeling 821
  affect 824
  astonish 870
 - belief *doubt* 485
 - like a drunken man
  irresolute 605
staggers 315
Stagirite 850
stagnant *inert* 172
  quiescent 265
  unprogressive 659
stagnate 265
  (*persist* 141)
stagnation *inertness*172
  quiescence 265
  inaction 681
stagy *drama* 599
  affected 855
staid *wise* 498
  calm 826
  grave 837
stain *coating* 223
  color 428
  dirt 653
  spoil 659
  blemish 848
  disgrace 874
  (*deface* 846)
  (*dishonor* 940)
 - paper *writing* 590
stained, travel - 266
stainless *clean* 652
  honorable 939
  innocent 946
stair 305, 627
staircase 305

stairway 305, 306
stake *fastening* 45
  wager 621
  danger 665
  security 771
  property 780
  lay down 807
  execution 975
  at - *intended* 620
  in danger 665
stalactite 224
stalagmite 224
stale *old* 124
  insipid 391
  deteriorated 659
  (*undesired* 866)
 - flat and unprofit-
   able 645
 - news 532
stalemate 731, 732
stalk *support* 215
  walk 266
  chase 622
 - abroad *generality* 78
  proud 878
stalking 528
stalking-horse
  ambush 530
  plea 617
stall *lateness* 133
  cessation 142
  abode 189
  receptacle 191
  support 215
  theater 599
  mart 799
  churchdom 995
  cathedral 1000
  finger - 223
stallion *horse* 271
  male 373
stalwart *strong* 159
  large 192
  (*tall* 206)
stamina
  strength 159
  perseverance 604a
stammel 434
stammering **583**
stamp *character* 7
  prototype 22
  kind 75
  form 240
  mark 550
  engraving 558
  complete 729
  security 771
  (*record* 551)
 - in the memory 505
 - out *destroy* 162
  extinguish 385
 - the foot *anger* 900
stampede 860
stanch - *a flow* 348
  persevering 604a
  health 654
  reinstate 660
  honest 939
 - belief 484
stanchion 215
stanchless 825

stand *exist* 1
  rank 71
  time 106
  long time 110
  permanent 141
  support 215
  quiescence 265
  difficulty 704
  resistance 719
  brook 821
  patience 826
  brave 861
  at a - 681
  come to a - 704
  make a - *oppose* 708
  resist 719
 - a chance *possible* 470
  probable 472
 - aghast 870
 - aloof *avoidance* 623
  inaction 681
  refuse 764
 - at attention 507
 - at ease 458
 - by *near* 197
  aid 707
  defend 717
 - committed 754
 - fair for 472
 - fast 143, 265
 - fire 861
 - firm *stability* 10
  remain 265
  resist 719
 - first 66
 - for *indicate* 550
  deputy 759
  candidate 763
 - forth *visible* 446
 - in need of 630
 - in one's own light
   699
 - in the shoes of 147
 - in the way of 706
 - no nonsense 604
 - of arms 727
 - off *recede* 287
  avoid 623
 - on 215
 - one in 812
 - one in good stead 644
 - one's ground
  preserved 670
  resist 719
 - on one's rights 748
 - out *project* 250
  visible 446
  obstinate 606
 - over 133
 - siege 717
 - still *remain* 141
  stop 265
  difficulty 704
 - the brunt 717
 - the hazard of the die
   621
 - the proof 648
 - the test *true* 494
  good 648
 - to one's engagement
   772

from the - to the ri-
  diculous 853
Sublime Porte 745
subliminal 450
 - **consciousness** 450,
  992a
 - **self** 317
sublimity
  [*see* sublime]
sublineation 550
sublunary 318
submarine 208
 boat 726
 - *chaser* 726
submediant 413
submerge *destroy* 162
 immerse 300
 plunge 310
 steep 337
submergible 310
submersible 310, 726
submersion *depth* 208
 plunge 310
subministration 707
submission **725**
 obedience 643
 with - 928
submissive
 tractable 705
 enduring 826
 humble 879
 (*penitent* 950)
submit *propound* 514
 mediate 724
 yield 725
 - *to arbitration* 774
submittal 725
submonish 695
submultiple 84
subordinacy 34
subordinate
 inferior 34
 unimportant 643
 subject 749
subordination
 order 58
 (*obedience* 743)
suborn *induce* 615
 purchase 795
 (*bribe* 784)
subpanation 998
subpœna *command* 741
 lawsuit 969
subreption
 falsehood 544
 acquisition 775
subrogate 147
subscribe *assent* 488
 aid 707
 agree to 769
 give 784
subscriber
 [*see* subscribe]
subscript 37, 65
subscription *gift* 784
subsequent
 - *in order* 63
 - *in time* 117
 - *time* 121
subserviency
 servility 886

subservient
 instrumental 631
 aid 707
 servile 746
subside *decrease* 36
 sink 306
subsidiary
 extrinsic 6
 aid 707
 servant 746
 (*tending* 176)
subsidy *aid* 707
 gift 784
 pay 809
subsist *exist* 1
 continue 141, 106
 live 359
subsistence *food* 298
subsoil *interior* 221
 earth 342
substance *thing* 3
 intrinsicality 5
 quantity 25
 inside 221
 matter 316
 texture 329
 meaning 516
 important part 642
 wealth 803
 in - 596
 man of - 803
substantial *existing* 1
 hypostatic 3
 material 316
 dense 321
 true 494
 - *meaning* 516
substantialism 316
substantialist 316
substantiality **3**
substantialize 316
substantially
 intrinsically 5
 - *true* 494
substantiate
 materialize 316
 evidence 467
 make good 924
substantive
 existing 1
 substantial 3
substitute *change* 147
 means **634**
 deputy 759
substitution **147**
substratum
 substance 3
 layer 204
 base 211
 support 215
 interior 221
 materiality 316
substructure 211
subsultory 315
subsultus 315
subsume 76
subtend 237
subterfuge
 sophistry 477
 quirk 481
 lie 546

 pretense 617
 cunning 702
subterrane 252
subterranean 208
subtile *light* 320
 rare 322
 - *texture* 329
subtility 498
subtilize *rarefy* 322
 sophistry 477
subtilty 322
subtle *slight* 32
 light 320
 rarity 322
 texture 329
 color 428
 cunning 702
 - *point* 704
 - *reasoning* 476
subtlety
 sophistry 477
 wisdom 498
subtraction
 subduction 38
 arithmetic 85
 taking 789
subtrahend
 subtract 38
 number 84
subulate 253
suburb *town* 189
 near 197
 environs 227
subvention
 support 215
 aid 707
 gift 784
subversion
 revolution 146
subvert *destroy* 162
 invert 218
 depress 308
succedaneum 147
succeed *follow* 63
 posterior 117
 success 731
 transfer 783
 - *to acquire* 775
success **731**
succession
 sequence 63
 continuity 69
 repetition 104
 posteriority 117
 transfer 783
 in quick - 136
 in regular - 138
 - *of ideas* 451
 - *of time* 109
successless 732
successor *sequel* 65
 posterior 117
succinct 572
succor 707
succotash 298
succubus 980
succulent
 nutritive 298
 juicy 333
 semiliquid 352
 pulpy 354

succumb *fatigue* 688
 yield 725
 fail 732
 (*obey* 743)
succussion 315
such - *a one* 372
 - *as* 17
 - *being the case* 8
 - *like* 17
suchwise 8
suck *draw off* 297
 drink 298
 take 789
 - *in* 296
 - *the blood of* 789
sucker 260
 dupe 547
 servility 886
sucking pig 298
suckle 707
suckling *infant* 129
sucrose 386
suction *force* 157
 reception 296
sudarium 652, 993
sudary 652
sudation 299
sudatorium 386
sudatory 386
sudden *transient* 111
 instantaneous 113
 soon 132
 unexpected 508
 - *and quick in quarrel*
  901
 - *burst* 508
 - *death* 360
 - *thought* 612
sudorific 382
suds *froth* 353
 in the - *difficulty* 704
 dejected 837
sue *demand* 765
 go to law 969
suet 356
suffer
 physical pain 378
 disease 655
 allow 760
 feel 821
 endure 826
 moral pain 828
 - *for* 972
 - *punishment* 972
sufferance 826
 tenant on - 779
suffice 639
sufficiency **639**
sufficient *enough* 639
 economical 817
 satisfactory 831
suffix *adjunct* 39
 sequence 63
 sequel 65
 letter 561
sufflation 349
suffocate *kill* 361
 excess 641
suffocating *hot* 382
 fetid 401
suffocation *death* 361

suffragan 996
suffrage 609
   vote 535
suffragette 374
suffragist 609
suffusion *mixture* 41
   feeling 821
   blush 879
Sufi *religious sect* 984
Sufism 984
sugar 396
sugar loaf *pointed* 253
sugary 396
suggest *suppose* 514
   inform 527
   advise 695
  - itself *thought* 451
   fancy 515
  - a question 461
suggester *tempter* 615
suggestion *plan* 626
   advice 695
suggestive
   reminder 505
   significant 516
   descriptive 594
suicidal
   destructive 162
suicide *killing* 361
sui generis 20, 83
suigenetic 163
suisse *beadle* 964
Suisse point d'argent
   point de - 812
suit *accord* 23
   series 69
   class 75
   clothes 225
   expedient 646
   petition 765
   courtship 902
  do - and service 743
  follow - 19
  law - 969
  love - 897
  - in law 969
  - the action to the
    word 550
  - the occasion 646
suitable 23, 646
  - season 134
suit case 191
suite *sequel* 65
   series 69
   retinue 746
  - of rooms 191
suitor *petitioner* 767
   lover 897
   lawsuit 969
sulcated 259
sulcus 259
sulkiness [*see* sulky]
   discourtesy 895
sulky *carriage* 272
   obstinate 606
   discontented 832
   dejected 837
   sullen 901a
sulks 895
sullen *obstinate* 606
   gloomy 837
       698

   discourteous 895
   sulky 901a
sullenness **901a**
sully *dirty* 653
   dishonor 874
   (*deface* 846)
sulphite 83
sulphur 388
sulphur-colored 436
sultan 745
sultry 382
sum *add* 37
   number 84
   money 800
  - and substance
   meaning 516
   synopsis 596
   important part 642
  - total 800
  - up *reckon* 85
   discriminate 465
   description 594
   compendium 596
sumless 105
summarize 551, 596
summation 37, 85
summary *transient* 111
   early 132
   short 201
   concise 572
   compendious 596
   illegal 964
  - of facts 594
summer *season* 125
   support 215
   heat 382
  - lightning 423
  - school 542
summerhouse 191
summerset 218
summit *top* **210**
   (*superiority* 33)
summon *command* 741
   lawsuit 969
   (*accuse* 938)
  - up *memory* 505
   excite 824
  - up courage 861
summons *evidence* 467
   command 741
   lawsuit 969
sump *base* 211
   inlet 343
   slough 345
   cess 653
sumpter-horse 271
sumptuary
   money 800
   expenditure 809
sumptuous 882
sum total 50
sun *heavenly body* 318
   luminary 423
   glory 873
  as the - at noonday
   bright 420
   certain 474
   plain 525
  bask in the - 377
  farthing candle to the
   - 645

  going down of the -
   126
  - oneself 384
  under the - *space* 180
   world 318
Sun of Righteousness
   976
sunbeam 420
  -s from cucumbers
   471
sunburn 384
sunburnt 433
Sunday 138, 687
  - best *ornament* 847
   show 882
  - school 542
sunder 44
sundial 114
sun dog 423
sundown 126
sundowner 460, 876
sundry 102
sunflower 369
sunk [*see* sink]
   deep 208
  - fence 717
  - in iniquity 945
  - in oblivion 508
sunken rocks 667
sunless 421
sunlight 420
Sunni 984
sunny *warm* 382
   luminous 420
   cheerful 836
sunny side 829
  - of hedge 734
  view the - 858
sun painting 556
sunrise 125, 236
sunset 126, 236
  at - 133
  - glow 420
sunshade *cover* 223
   shade 424
sunshine *light* 420
   prosperity 734
   happy 827
   cheerful 836
sunshiny 382
sunstone 847
sunstroke *heat* 384
   madness 503
sun-up 125
sun worship 382
sunyasi [*see* sannyasi]
   retaliation 718
   punishment 972
sup *small quantity* 32
   feed 298
  - full of horrors 828
supawn 298
super *theatrical* 599
superable *possible* 470
   (*easy* 705)
superabound 641
   sufficiency 639
superadd 37
superannuated 128,
   158
superb 845

supercargo 694
supercherie 545
supercilious *proud* **878**
   insolent 885
   disrespectful 929
   scornful 930
superdreadnought 726
supereminence
   goodness 648
   repute 873
supererogation
   redundant 641
   useless 645
   (*activity* 682)
superexaltation 873
superexcellence 648
superfetation
   added 37
   productive 168
superficial *shallow* 209
   outside 220
   misjudging 481
   ignorant 491
  - extent 180
superficies 220
superfine 648
superfluitant 305
superfluity
   remainder 40
   redundance 641
superfluous
   remaining 40
   redundant 641
   useless 645
superhuman
   perfect 650
   godlike 976
superimpose 233
superimposed 206
superincumbent
   above 206
   heavy 319
superinduce
   change 140
   cause 153
   produce 161
superintend 693
superintendent 694
superior *greater* 33
  - in size 194
   high 206
   important 642
   good 648
   director 694
superiority **33**
superjunction 37
superlative 33
superman 33
supernal *height* 206
   summit 210
   heavenly 981
supernatant *high* 206
   ascent 305
supernatural *deity* 976
   spectral 980a
  - aid 707
supernaturalism 528
supernormal 20, **976**
supernumerary
   adjunct 39
   theatrical 599

- in hand *prepare* 673
  war 722
turn -s into plow-
  shares 723
sword-shaped 253
swordsman 726
Sybarite 954*a*
sybaritism 954
syce 268
sycophancy
  flattery 933
sycophant
  follower 65
  petitioner 767
  desirer 865
  servile 886
  flatterer 935
sycophantic 746
syenite *blue* 438
syllabicate 567
syllable 561
  breathe not a - 528
syllabus *list* 86
  compendium 596
syllepsis 567
syllogism 476
syllogistic 476
sylph 979, 980
sylvan 367
symbol
  mathematical - 84
  sign 550
symbolic *latent* 526
  indicative 550
symbolize *latency* 526
  indicate 550
  represent 554
symmetrical *regular* 80
  form 240

elegant 578
  [*see* symmetry]
symmetry
  equality 27
  order 58
  conformity 82
  centrality 222
  regular form **242**
  elegance 578
  beauty 845
  want of - 846
sympathetic
  [*see* sympathy]
  - ink 528
  - tear 906
sympathize
  [*see* sympathy]
sympathizer
  partisan 890
sympathy *concord* 714
  friendship 888
  love 897
  kindness 906
  pity 914
  condolence 915
symphonic 415
  - poem 415
symphonious 413
symphony
  overture 64
  music 415
  concord 714
symphysis 43
symposium
  meal 298
  festival 840
  (*drunken* 959)
symptom 550, 668
symptomatic 668

symptomatology   522,
  550, 655
synæresis 48, 54
synagogue 1000
synchronic 120
synchronism **120**
synchysis 218
synclinal 217
syncopate 195
syncopation 195, 415
syncope *impotence* 158
  contraction 195
  musical 413
  rhetoric 572
  fatigue 688
syncretic
  derangement 61
syncretism
  disagreement 24
  heterodoxy 984
syncretize 48
syndic *ruler* 745
  judge 967
syndicate
  directorate 542
  council 696
  league 712
synecdoche 521
synergism 709
synergy 178, 709
syngenic 5
synizesis 48, 54
synod *council* 696
  church 995
  (*assemblage* 72)
synonym
  meaning 516
  interpretation 522
  nomenclature 564

synonymize 516
synopsis
  arrangement 60
  list 86
  grammar 567
  compendium 596
synovia
  lubrication 332
  oil 356
synovial 332
syntactic 567
syntagma 60
syntax 567
syntectic 655
synthesis
  combination 48
  composition 54
  reasoning 476
synthetic 476
syringe *water* 337
  stream 348
syrinx 410
syrt 667
syrup [*see* sirup]
system *order* 58
  rule 80
  plan 626
  - of knowledge **490**
  - of opinions 484
systematic
  regular 80
systematize *order* 58
  arrange 60
  organize 357
  plan 626
systole 195
  - and diastole **138,**
  314
syzygy 199

T

T to a - 494
tab 39
tabard 225
tabasco 393
tabby *mottled* 440
  gossip 588
tabefaction 195
tabernacle *house* 189
  temple 1000
tabes 195
tabescent 195
tabetic 195, 203, 655
tabic 203
tabid *shrunk* 195
  thin 203
  disease 655
  deteriorated 659
table *arrangement* 60
  list 86
  defer 133
  layer 204
  support 215
  flat 251
  repast 298
  neglect 460
  writing 590
  on the - *preparing* 673

- of the Lord 1000
  turn the -s 218
  under the - *hidden* 528
  drunk 959
tableau *list* 86
  appearance 448
  painting 556
  theatrical 599
tablecloth 652
table d'hôte 298
table-land
  horizontal 213
  plain 344
tablespoon 191
tablet *layer* 204
  flat 251
  record 551
  writing 590
  -s of the memory 505
table talk *news* 532
  conversation 588
table-turning 992
tableware 191
tablier 225
tablinum 191
taboo *prohibited* 761
  magic 992

tabor 417
tabouret 215
tabret 417
tabular 60
tabula rasa
  inexistence 2
  absence 187
  ignorance 491
  obliterated 552
  facility 705
tabulate *arrange* 60
  series 69
  list 86
tabulation
  record 551
tace 403
tachygraphy 590
tacit *implied* 516
  latent 526
taciturnity 585
Tacitus
  concise style 572
tack *join* 43
  nails 45
  change course 140
  direction 278
  turn 279

way 627
  - to *add* 37
  wrong - 732
tackle *fastening* 45
  gear 633
  undertake 676
  manage 693
tacky 352
  dowdy 659
tact *touch* 379
  discrimination 465
  wisdom 498
  skill 698
  taste 850
  want of - 851
tactful [*see* tact]
  affable 894
tactician 700
tactics *conduct* 692
  warfare 722
  (*plan* 626)
  (*skill* 698)
tactile 379
taction 379
tactlessness 895
tactual 379
tadpole 129

701

not put one's - in a
  napkin 878
talesman 967
talionic 718
taliped 243
talisman
  insignia 747
  charm 993
talismanic 992
talk *unsubstantial* 4
  rumor 532
  speak 582
  conversation 588
  small - 588
  - against time
    time 106
    protract 110
    inaction 681
  - at random
    illogical 477
    loquacity 584
  - big *boast* 884
    insolent 885
    threat 909
  - glibly 584
  - nonsense 497
  - of *signify* 516
    publish 531
    intend 620
  - of the town
    gossip 588
    dame 873
  - oneself out of breath
    584
  - over *confer* 588
    persuade 615
  - together 588
  - to in private 586
  - to oneself 589
talkative 584
talkativeness 582, 584
talked of 873
talker 584, 588
talking, fine -
  overestimation 482
tall *great* 31
  high 206
  - talk 884
tallage 812
tallies 85
tallow 356
  - candle 423
tallow-faced 429
tally *agree* 23
  numeration 85
  list 86
  sign 550
  credit 805
  - with *conform* 82
tallyho 622
tallyman 797
talma 225
Talmud 985
talon 327
talons *authority* 737
  claws 781
talus 217
tamasha 892
tambourine 417
tame *inert* 172
  moderate 174, 826

domesticate 370
  teach 537
  feeble 575
  subjugate 749
  insensible 823
  calm 826
tameless *violent* 173
  malevolent 907
Tammany 712
tam-o'-shanter 225
tamper *mallet* 276
  - with *alter* 140
    seduce 615
    injure 659
    meddle 682
tampion 263
tam-tam 417
tan *color* 433
tandem *at length* 200
  vehicle 272
tang *taste* 390
  pungency 392
  bane 663
tangent 199, 379
  fly off at a -
    deviate 279
    diverge 291
    excitable 825
tangible *material* 316
  touch 379
  exact 494
  sufficient 639
  useful 644
tangle *derange* 61
  matted 219
tangled *disordered* 59
  confused 523
  weave a - web
    difficulty 704
tank *reservoir* 636
  (receptacle 191)
tankard 191
tannin 663
tantalize *balk* 509
  induce 615
  desire 865
tantalizing
  exciting 824
Tantalus
  torment of -
    expectation 507
    desire 865
tantamount *equal* 27
  synonymous 516
taniara 407
tanti 642
tantivy *speed* 274
tantra 986
tantrum 900
tap *open* 260
  plug 263
  hit 276
  let out 295, 297
  sound 406
  turn on the - 297
tape *string* 205
  (fastening 45)
taper *contract* 195
  narrow 203
  candle 423
  - to a point 253

tapestry
  painting 556
  ornament 847
tapir 366
tapis on the -
  event 151
  topic 454
  intention 620
  plan 626
taproot 153
tapster 746
tar *cover* 223
  sailor 269
  pitch 356a
  - and feather
    disrespect 929
    punish 972
tarantella 315
tarantism 315
tarboosh 225
tardigrade 275
tardiloquence 583
tardy *dilatory* 133
  slow 275
tare *discount* 40a
  - and tret 813
tares 645
target 620, 717
tariff 812
tarn 343
tarnish
  discoloration 429
  soil 653
  deface 848
  disgrace 874
  (damage 659)
tarpaulin 223
tarpon 298
tarradiddle 546
tarred 356a
tarriance 133
tarry *remain* 110
  later 133
  continue 141
  stay 265
  - for *expect* 507
tart *pastry* 298, 396
  acid 397
  rude 895
  irascible 901
tartan 440
tartane 273
Tartar *choleric* 901
  catch a - *dupe* 547
    unskillful 699
    retaliation 718
    (failure 732)
tartar *sourness* 397
  dirt 653
  - emetic 663
Tartarean 907
tartarize 397
Tartarus 982
Tartufe
  hypocrisy 544
  deceiver 548
  impiety 988
tartufish 544
tartufism 544
task *lesson* 537
  business 625

put to use 677
  fatigue 688
  command 741
  hard - 704
  set a - 741
  take to - 932
  - the memory 505
taskmaster 694
tassel 214, 847
tastable 390
taste *sapidity* **390**
  elegance 578
  experience 821
  good taste **850**
  man of - 850
  - good 394
  - of quality 5
  to one's - *savory* 394
    pleasant 829
    love 897
tasteful 850
tasteless *insipid* 391
  inelegant 579
tasty 390, 394, 850
tatter
  small quantity 32
tatterdemalion 876
tatters *garments* 225
  tear to - 162
Tattersall's 799
tattle 588
tattler
  newsmonger 532
  gossip 588
tattletale 532
tattoo
  drumming 407
  mottled 440
  summons 741
tau 219
taught [see teach]
  fastened 43
taunt *disrespect* 929
  reproach 938
  (ridicule 856)
tauromachy 720
taut 43
tautologize 104
tautology
  repetition 104
  diffuse style 573
tautophony 104
tavern 189
  - haunter 959
tawdry 851
tawed leather 327
tawny *brown* 433
  yellow 436
tax *inquire* 461
  employ 677
  fatigue 688
  command 741
  compel 744
  request 765
  accounts 811
  impost 812
  accuse 938
  - one's energies 686
  - the memory 505
taxable 812
taxation 812

taxi 272
taxicab 272
taxidermy 368
taxis 60
taxonomy 60
tazza 191
tea 298
teach 537
- one's grandmother
    redundant 641
    impertinent 885
teachable 539
teacher **540,** 673
teaching **537**
    false - 538
teacup, storm in a -
    overrate 482
    exaggerate 549
tea gown 225
teak 367
teal 298
team continuity 69
    assemblage 72
    conveyance 272
    crew 712
    representative 759
teamster 694
tea party 892
teapot 191
teapoy 215
tear weeping 839
    draw -s 830
    shed -s 839
    -s in one's eyes
        excited 824
        sad 837
tear separate 44
    violence 173
    move rapidly 274
    excite 825
    spree 840
    - asunder one's bonds
        750
    - away from 789
    - oneself away 623
    - one's hair 839
    - out 301
    - to pieces separate 44
        destroy 162
    - up destroy 162
tearful 839
tear gas 663, 727
tease annoy 830
    aggravate 835
    spite 907
teaser
    difficult 704
teasing 830
teat 250
tea-table talk 588
technical
    conformable 82
    workmanlike 698
    - education 537
    - knowledge 698
    - school 542
    - term 564
technicality
    special 79
    cant term 563
    formulary 697
704

technique
    painting 556
    skill 698
technology 698
techy 901
tectiform 223
tectology 357
ted 73
tedge 350
Te Deum 990
tedious 841
    while away the - hours
        681
tedium 841
tee 66
teem produce 161
    productive 168
    abound 639
    - with multitude 102
teemful 168
teeming crowd 72
teemless 169
teens 98
    in one's - 127, 129
teeter 314
teeth grinders 330
    holders 781
    armed to the -
        prepared 673
        defense 717
        warfare 722
    between the - 405
    cast in one's - 938
    chattering of -
        cold 383
    grind one's - 900
    have cut one's eye -
        698
    in one's -
        opposition 708
        compulsion 744
    in the - of
        difficulty 704
        opposition 708
    make one's - chatter
        cold 385
        fear 860
    run of one's - 815
    set one's - 604
    set the - on edge
        scrape 331
        saw 397
        stridor 410
        pain the feelings 830
    show one's - 900
teetotalism
    temperance 953
    sobriety 958
teetotum
    rotation 312
    toy 840
teg 366
tegumen 223
tegument 223
tehee 856
teichopsia 442
teinoscope 445
telamon 215
telegony 154
telegram 527, 531, 532
telegraph velocity 274

    inform 527
    messenger 534
    signal 550
    by - haste 684
telegraphic 531
telegraphone 527
telegraphy
    publication 531
telekinesis 264
telemeter 200
teleology 620
telepathic 450
telepathy 450, 992a
telephone 418
    inform 527
    messenger 534
telephony 402
telescope 441, 445, 572
    collide 276
telescopic 196
telesm 993
telethermometer 389
tell count 85
    influence 175
    evidence 467
    inform 527
    speak 582
    describe 594
    succeed 731
    let me - you 535
    - a lie 544
    - fortunes 511
    - how 155
    - its own tale 518
    - of 467
    - off 85
    - one plainly 527
    - one's beads 990, 998
    - tales disclose 529
    - the cause of 522
    - the truth 543
    who can - 475
teller treasurer 801
telling influential 175
    graphic 518
    important 642
    exciting 824
    with - effect
        energy 171
        influence 175
telltale news 532
    indicator 550
    knave 941
telluric 318
temerity 863
temper nature 5
    state 7
    moderate 174
    elasticity 323
    pliability 324
    qualify 469
    prepare 673
    affections 820
    irascibility 901
    command of - 826
    lose one's - 900
    out of - 901a
    - the wind to the
        shorn lamb 834
    trial of - 824
tempera 556

temperament nature 5
    tendency 176
    musical 413
    affections 820
temperance 174, **953**
temperate moderate 174
    mild 826
    abstemious 953
temperature 382
    increase of - 384
    reduction of - 385
tempest violence 173
    agitation 315
    wind 349
    exaggeration 549
    excitement 825
tempestivity 134
tempest-tossed
    excited 824
Templar 996
    good - 958
temple house 189
    side 236
    church **1000**
    - of the Holy Ghost
        983a
temporal transient 111
    chronological 114
    laical 997
    lords - and spiritual
        875
temporary 111
    - expedient 147
temporize protract 110
    defer 133
    cunning 702
    (occasion 134)
temporizer 943
tempt entice 615
    attempt 675
    desire 865
    - fortune hazard 621
        essay 675
    - Providence rash 863
        arrogate 885
    - the appetite 394
temptation
    - hath a music 615
tempter 615
    Satan 978
    voice of the - 615
temulence 959
ten 98
    - thousand 98
    - to one 472
tenable 664
tenacity coherence 46
    toughness **327**
    memory 505
    resolution 604
    perseverance 604a
    obstinacy 606
    retention 781
    avarice 819
    - of life 357
    - of purpose 604a
tenaculum 781
tenancy 777
tenant present 186
    occupier 188
    possessor 779

tenantless
  absence 187
  seclusion 893
tenax propositi
  determined 204
  honorable 939
tend *conduce* 176
  - *animals* 370
  minister 631
  aid 707
  serve 746
  - stock 370
  - towards
  direction 278
tendence 176, 749
tendency **176**
tender *slight* 32
  ship 273
  soft 324
  color 428
  war vessel 726
  offer 763
  susceptible 822
  affectionate 897
  benevolent 906
  compassionate 914
  - age 127
  - conscience *duty* 926
    (*honor* 939)
  - heart *susceptible* 822
  kind 906
  compassionate 914
  - mercies [ironical]
  badness 649
  severity 739
  cruelty 907
  - one's resignation 757
  - passion 897
  - to 707
tenderfoot 57, 541
tenderling 158
tendon 45
tendril *fastening* 45
  runner 51, 367
  infant 129
  filament 205
  convoluted 248
tenebrious 421
tenement *house* 189
  apartment 191
  property 780
  - of clay 362
tenet *belief* 484
  (*theology* 983)
tenez 142
tenfold 98
tennis 840
tenor *course* 7
  degree 26
  directions 278
  high note 410
  violin 417
  meaning 516
  (*musician* 416)
  pursue the noiseless -
    of one's way 881
  - horn 417
tenpins 840
ten pounder 727
tense *hard* 323
tensibility 325

tensile 325
tension *strength* 159
  length 200
ten-strike 731
tensure 200
tent *abode* 189
  covering 223
  pitch one's -
    locate 184
    arrive 292
tentacle 781
tentative *inquiry* 461
  experimental 463
  essaying 675
tented field 722
tenter-hook 214
  on -s 507
tenth 99
tenths *tithe* 812
tent pegging 840
tenuity *smallness* 32
  thinness 203
  rarity 322
tenuous [see tenuity]
  unsubstantial 4
tenure
  possession 777
  property 780
  due 924
tepee 189, 223
tepefaction 384
tepefy 384
tephramancy 511
tepid *warm* 382
  half cold 383
tepidarium 386
teratism 83
teratogenic 83
teratology
  unconformity 83
  distortion 243
  altiloquence 577
  boasting 884
tercentenary 98, 883
terceron 41
terebration
  opening 260
  (*passage through* 302)
tergal 235
tergiversate 140, 607
tergiversation
  regress 283
  change of mind **607**
tergum 235
term *end* 67
  place in series **71**
  period of time 106
  limit 233
  word 562
  name 564
  lease 780
termagant 901
terminable 233
terminal *end* 67
  limit 233
terminate *end* 67
  limit 233, 292
  journey 266
termination 67, 151
terminology 562
terminus *end* 67

  limit 233
  journey 266
  arrival 292
termite 366, 690
termless 105
terms [see term]
  circumstances 8
  reasoning 476
  pacification 723
  conditions 770
  bring to - 723
  come to - *assent* 488
  pacify 723
  submit 725
  consent 762
  compact 769
  couch in - 566
  in no measured - 574
  on friendly - 888
ternal 94
ternary 93
ternion 92
Terpsichore *music* 416
  dancing 840
terra cotta *baked* 384
  brown 433
  sculpture 557
terra firma *support* 215
  land 342
terra incognita 491
terrace *houses* 189
  level 213
terrain 181
terraqueous 318
terrene *world* 318
  land 342
terrestrial 318
terret 45
terre verte 435
terrible *vast* 31
  fearful 860
terribly *greatly* 31
terrier *list* 86
  auger 262
  dog 366
terrific *painful* 830
  fearful 860
terrify 860
terrine 191
territorial *land* 342
territory *region* 181
  property 780
terror 860
  King of -s 360
  reign of - *severity* 739
  pain 828
terrorism 860
  insolence 885
terrorist
  combatant 726
  intimidator 860
  coward 862
  blusterer 887
  evildoer 913
terrorize 860, 885
Tersanctus 900
terse 572
tertian *periodic* 138
tertiary 92, 93
tertium quid
  dissimilar 18

  mixture 41
  combination 48
  unconformable 83
terza 93
terzetto 415
tessellated
  variegated 440
  ornament 847
tessellation 440
tesseræ *mosaic* 440
  counters 550
test 463
testa 223
testaceology 223
testaceous 223
testament *security* 771
  (*record* 551)
Testament 985
testamur 467
testator 784
tester *bedstead* 215
  sixpence 800
testicle 357
testify *evidence* 467
  sign 550
testimonial 551
testimony 467
testy 901
tetanus 655
tetchy 901
tête-à-tête *two* 89
  near 197
  confer 588
tether *fasten* 43
  locate 184
  restrain 751
  means of restraint
    752
  go beyond the length
    of one's - 738
tethered *firm* 150
tetrachord 413
tetract 95
tetrad 95, 193
tetragon 95
tetragram 95
tetrahedral 253
tetrahedron 95, 244
tetrarch 745
tetter 655
Texas fever 655
text *prototype* 22
  topic 454
  meaning 516
  printing 591
  book 593
  libretto 599
textbook *school* 542
  synopsis 596
  (*teaching* 537)
  - committee 542
textile *woven* 219
  texture 329
textuary *orthodox* 983a
  revelation 985
texture *mixture* 41
  roughness 256
  fabric 329
  (*condition* 7)
Thais 962
Thalia 599

experiment 463
unreasoning 477
essay 675
- over 539
-s down! 361
under one's -
authority 737
subjection 749
thumb print
evidence 467
thumbscrew 975
thump *beat* 276
noise 406
nonresonance 408a
- *the piano* 416
punish 972
thumping *great* 31
big 192
thunder *violence* 173
noise 404
omen 512
prodigy 872
threaten 909
look black as -
discontented 832
angry 900
- against
malediction 908
censure 932
- at the top of one's
voice 411
- by 274
- forth 531
- of applause 931
-s of the Vatican 908
thunderbolt
weapon 727
prodigy 872
thunderburst 406
thunderclap *noise* 406
unexpected 508
prodigy 872
thunderhead 353
thundering *immense* 31
big 192
thunderstorm 173
thunderstruck 870
thundertube 260
thurible 400, 998
thurifer 400
thuriferous 400
thurification
fragrance 400
rite 998
thus *circumstance* 8
therefore 476
- *far little* 32
limit 233
thwack *beat* 276
punish 972
thwart *across* 219
wrong 649
obstruct 706
oppose 708
annoy 830
thwarted 732
thyroid 221
thyrsus 215
tiara *insignia* 747
jewelry 847
canonicals 999

tic douloureux 378
tick *oscillation* 314
insect 368
sound 407
mark 550
credit 805
go on - 806
- off *record* 551
ticket 550
plan 626
ticket of leave 760
- man *prisoner* 754
bad man 949
tickle *touch* 380
please 829
amuse 840
(*physical pleasure* 377)
- the fancy 829, 840
- the palate 394
- the palm *give* 784
pay 807
tickler *pungency* 392
tickling 380
ticklish *touch* 380
uncertain 475
dangerous 665
difficult 704
tidal wave 348, 667
tidbit *food* 298
gem 646
good 648
pleasing 829
tide *time* 106
ocean 341
wave 348
abundance 639
prosperity 734
against the - 708
drift with the -
facile 705
go with the -
conformity 82
high &c. - 348
stem the - 708
swim with the -
prosperity 734
- of eloquence 582
- of events 151
- of time 109
- over *time* 106
defer 133
safe 664
inaction 681
succeed 731
- race 348, 667
turn of the - 210
tidings 532
tidy *orderly* 58
arrange 60
covering 223
good 648
clean 652
pretty 845
tie *relation* 9
equality 27
fasten 43
fastening 45
neckcloth 225
security 771
obligation 926

nuptial - 903
ride and - 266
- down *hinder* 706
compel 744
restrain 751
- oneself *promise* 768
- the hands
render powerless 158
restrain 751
-s of blood 11
- up *restrain* 751
condition 770
entail 771
tiebeam 45
tied up *in debt* 806
tier *continuity* 69
layer 204
tierce *triality* 92
worship 990
carte and - 716
tiff *quarrel* 713
anger 900
tiffin 298
tigella 367
tiger *violent* 173
servant 746
cheer 838
courage 861
savage 907
evildoer 913
bad man 949
tight *fast* 43
closed 261
smart 845
drunk 959
keep a - hand on 751
on one's - ropes 878
- grasp 739
- hand 739
tighten 43
contract 195
tight-fisted 819
tights 225
tigress 374
tike 876
tilbury 272
tilde 550
tile *roof* 223
hat 225
- loose *insane* 503
tiler *sentinel* 263
till *up to the time* 106
coffer 191
cultivate 371
treasury 802
- doomsday 112
- now 122
- the soil *prepare* 673
tillable 371
tiller *instrument* 633
money-box 802
- of the soil
agriculture 342, 371
clown 876
tilmus 315
tilpah 223
tilt *slope* 217
cover 223
propel 284
fall 306
contention 720

full - *direct* 278
active 682
haste 684
ride full - at
pursue 622
attack 716
run a - at 716
- over 218
- up 307
- with 720
tilth 371
tilting 720
- at the ring 840
tilt-yard 728
timbal 417
timber *trees* 367
materials 635
timbre 413
timbrel 417
timbrology 550
time 106
adjust 58
instant 113
leisure 685
against - *haste* 684
at -s 136
course of - 109
employ one's - in 625
glass of - 106
in - *course* 109
early 132
destiny 152
measure - 114
no - *instantly* 113
soon 132
no - to lose *need* 630
haste 684
no - to spare 684
ravages of - 659
slow - 275
take - *slow* 275
inaction 681
inactive 683
there being -s when 136
- after time 104
- and again 104
- being 118
- clock 550, 551
- drawing on 121
- enough 132
- gone by 135
- hanging on one's hands
inaction 681
leisure 685
weariness 841
- has been 122
- immemorial 122
- is out of joint 106
- of day 113
- of life *duration* 106
now 118
age 128
- out of mind 122
- to come 121
- to spare 685
- up *transient* 111
occasion 134
- was 122
- wasted 106

true - 113
waste - 683
timeful 134
time-honored *old* 124
　repute 873
　respected 928
timekeeper 114
timeless 135
timely *early* 132
　opportune 134
timeous 134
timepiece 114
timepleaser 607, 943
times *present* 118
　events 151
　hard - 735
　many - 136
timeserver 607, 943
timeserving
　tergiversation 607
　cunning 702
　servility 886
　improbity 940
　selfishness 943
time-worn *old* 124
　age 128
　deteriorated 659
timid *fearful* 860
　cowardly 862
　humble 881
timidity [*see* timid]
　humility 879
timist 607
timocracy 803
Timon of Athens
　wealth 803
　seclusion 893
　misanthrope 911
timorous [*see* timid]
timothy 367
timpano 417
tin *preserve* 670
　money 800
　- oven 386
　- wedding 883
tinct 428
tinction 428
tinctorial 428
tincture
　small quantity 32
　mixture 41
　color 428
tinctured
　disposition 820
tinder *fuel* 388
　irascible 901
tine 253
tinge *small quantity* 32
　mix 41
　color 428
tingent 428
tingible 428
tingle *pain* 378
　touch 380
　emotion 821
　make the ears - 900
tink 408
tinker *repair* 660
　(*improve* 658)
tinkle *faint sound* 405
　resonance 408

tinkling cymbal 517
tinned goods 670
tinnient 408
tinsel *glitter* 420
　sham 545
　ornament 847
　frippery 851
tint 428
tintamarre 404
tintinnabulary 408
tintinnabulation 408
tiny 193
tip *end* 67
　summit 210
　cover 223
　discrimination 465
　give 784
　(*pay* 807)
　on - toe *high* 206
　expect 507
　- off 465
　- the wink 550
tipcat 840
tippet 214, 225
tipple *drink* 298
　tope 959
tippler 959
tippybob 803
tipstaff 965
tipsy 959
tiptop *summit* 210
　good 648
tirade *speech* 582
　censure 932
tirailleur 726
tire *invest* 225
　automobile 272
　fatigue 688
　worry 830
　weary 841
tiresome [*see* tire]
tisane 662
Tisiphone 173
tissue *whole* 50
　assemblage 72
　matted 219
　texture 329
tit *small* 193
　pony 271
Titan *strength* 159
　size 192
　sun god 423
　demon 980
Titaness 192
Titanic 159
titanic 31, 192
titbit *savory* 394
　pleasing 829
tit for tat 718
tithe *tenth* 99
　tax 812
tithing 181
tithingman 965
Titian red 434
titillate *amuse* 840
　provoke desire 865
titillation *pleasure* 377
　touch 380
titivate 847·
title *indication* 550
　name 564

book 593
　authority 747
　right to property 780
　distinction **877**
　right 924
titled 875
title deed 771
title-page 66
titter 838
tittle *small quantity* 32
　inextension 180a
　to a - 494
tittle-tattle *news* 532
　small talk 588
titubancy 583
titubate *fall* 306
　fail 732
titular *word* 562
　nomenclature 564
tivoli 840
tmesis 218
T.N.T. 727
to *direction* 278
　lie - 681
　- a certain degree 32
　- a great extent 31
　- all intents and pur-
　　poses
　equally 27
　whole 52
　- a man 78
　- and fro 12, 148, 314
　- a small extent 32
　- be sure 488
　- come *future* 121
　destiny 152
　- crown all 33, 642
　- do 59
　- some extent 26
　- the credit of 805
　- the end of the chap-
　　ter 52
　- the end of time 112
　- the full 52
　- the letter 19
　- the point 23
　- the purpose 23
　- this day 118
　- wit 79
toad *hateful* 649
　ugly 846
　- under a harrow 378
toadeater *servile* 886
　sycophant 935
toadeating *flattery* 933·
toadstool 367
toadying 886
toadyism 933
toast *roast* 384
　celebrate 883
　- brown 433
toaster 386
tobacco 392
toboggan 272
tobogganing 840
toby 191
toccata 415
tocogony 161
tocology 161, 662
tocsin 669
tod 319

to-day 118
toddle *walk* 266
　limp 275
toddy 298
toe 211
　on the light fantastic -
　jump 309
　dance 840
toes turn up the -
　die 360
toft 189, 780
toga *coat* 225
　robes 747
　assume the　-　**virilis**
　131
together
　accompanying 88
　same time 120
　come - 290
　get - 72
　hang - 709
　lay heads - 695
　- with *added to* 37
　accompanied by 88
toggery 225
toil *activity* 682
　exertion 686
　- of a pleasure 682
　-s *trap* 545
　(*danger* 667)
　(*wile* 702)
toilet 225
　- water 400
toilette 225
　en grande - 847
toilsome 686
　difficult 704
toilworn 688
token 550
　give - *manifest* 525
　- of remembrance 505
tolderolloll 838
Toledo 727
tolerable *a little* 32
　trifling 643
　not perfect 651
　passable 845
toleration *laxity* 738
　lenity 740
　permission 760
　feeling 821
　calmness 826
　benevolence 906
toll *sound* 407
　tax 812
　- the knell 363
tollbooth *prison* 752
　market 799
tom *male* 373
tomahawk 727
tomato 298
tomb 363
　lay in the - 363
　- of the Capulets **506**
tombola 156
tomboy 129, 851
tombstone 363
tomcat 373
tome 593
tomentose 256
tomfool 501

709

tomfoolery
absurdity 497
amusement 840
wit 842
ostentation 882
Tommy Atkins 726
tomnoddy 501
Tom o' Bedlam 504
to-morrow 121
- and to-morrow
repetition 104
course of time 109
tompion 263
tomtit 193
Tom Thumb 193
tom-tom *music* 417
military 722
ton *weight* 319
fashion 852
tonality *music* 413
light and shade 420
tone *state* 7
strength 159
tendency 176
sound 402
music 413
color 428
painting 556
method 627
disposition 820
give a - to 852
- down *moderate* 174
darken 421
discolor 429
- of voice 580
- poem 415
tong 712
tonga 272
tongs *fire irons* 386
retention 781
tongue *projection* 250
food 298
touch 379
taste 390
language 560
bite the - 392
bridle one's - 585
give - 404, 580
have a - in one's head 582
hold one's - 403
keep one's - between one's teeth 585
on the tip of one's -
near 197
forget 506
latent 526
speech 582
slip of the - *error* 495
solecism 568
stammering 583
- cleave to the roof of one's mouth 870
- of land 342
- running loose 584
wag the - 582
tongue-lash *berate* 932
tongueless 581
tongue-shaped 245
tongue-tied 581
tonic *musical note* 413

phonetic 561
healthy 656
medicine 662
tonicity *strength* 159
tonic sol-fa 415
tonjon 272
tonnage 192
tonneau 272
tonsillitis 655
tonsils 351
tonsure 550, 999
tonsured 226
tontine 810
tony 501
Tony Lumpkin 876
too *also* 37
excess 641
in a - great degree 31
- bad *disreputable* 874
wrong 923
censure 932
- far 641
- hot to hold one 830
- late 133
- late for 135
- little 640
- many 641
- much [*see below*]
- soon 132
- soon for 135
true *regret* 833
lamentation 839
too much
redundance 641
intemperance 954
have - of 869
make - of 482
- for 471
- of a good thing 869
tool *instrument* 633
steer 693
cat's-paw 711
servile 886
edge - 253
mere - 690
tooling 847
toot 406, 416
tooth *fastening* 45
projection 250
sharp 253
roughness 256
notch 257
texture 329
taste 390
sweet - *desire* 865
fastidious 868
- and nail *violence* 173
exertion 686
attack 716
- of time 106, 551
- paste 652
- powder 652
toothache 378
toothed 253
toothful 392
toothless 254
tooth-shaped 253
toothsome 394
tootle 407, 416
top *supreme* 33
summit 210

roof 223
automobile 272
spin 312
at the - of one's speed 274
at the - of one's voice
loud 404
shout 411
at the - of the tree 873
fool to the - of one's bent 545
from - to toe 200
sleep like a - 683
- of the ladder 873
- to bottom
completely 52
toparchy 737
topaz *yellow* 436
jewel 847
top-boot 225
tope *tomb* 363
trees 367
drink 959
temple 1000
topek 189
toper 959
topfull 52
top-gallant mast
height 206
summit 210
top-heavy
unbalanced 28
inverted 218
dangerous 665
tipsy 959
Tophet 982
topiary 847
topic 454
- of the day 532
topical 183
toploftiness 878, 885
topmast 206
topmost 210
topographer 466
topography 183, 466, 550
topple *unbalanced* 28
perish 162
decay 659
- down *fall* 306
- over 28, 306
topsail schooner 273
top sawyer
important 642
proficient 700
top-sergeant 745
topsy-turvy 59, 218
tor 206
torch *fuel* 388
luminary 423
apply the - 824
light the - of war 722
- of Hymen 903
Tories 712
torment *physical* 378
moral 828, 830
place of - 982
tormina 378
torminous 378
torn [*see tear*]

discord 713
tornado *whirl* 312
wind 349
(*violence* 173)
torose 250
torpedinous 823
torpedo *vehicle* 272
detonator 406
weapon 727
evildoer 913
torpedo boat 726
torpescent 683
torpid *inert* 172
inactive 683
insensible 823
torpor [*see torpid*]
torpids 720
torporific 823
torque 847
torrefy 340, 384
torrent *violence* 173
rapid 274
flow 348
rain in -s 348
torrid 382
torsion 248
torso 50
tort 925, 947
torticollis 378
tortile 248
tortious 925
tortive 248
tortoise 275
tortoise-shell 440
tortuous *twisted* 248
concealed 528
dishonorable 940
torture *physical* 378
moral 828, 830
cruelty 907
punishment 972
- a question 476
torturer 975
torturous 378
torvity 901*a*
toss *derange* 61
throw 284
oscillate 314
agitate 315
- in a blanket 929
- off *drink* 298
- on one's pillow 825
- overboard 610
- the head *pride* 878
insolence 885
contempt 930
- up 156, 621
tosspot 959
tot *child* 129, 167
- up 811
total *add* 37
whole 50
number 84, 85
- abstinence
temperate 953
ascetic 955
- eclipse 421
sum - 800
totality 52
totalizator 551, 621
totally 52

- upon *badness* 649
  severity 739
tramway 627
trance *dream* 515
  sleep 683
  lethargy 823
tranquil *calm* 174
  quiet 265
  peaceful 721
  - mind 826
tranquillize
  moderate 174
  pacify 723
  soothe 826
transact *act* 680
  conduct 692
  - business 625
  - business with 794
transaction
  event 151
  action 680
  -s of *record* 551
transalpine 196
transanimation 140
transatlantic 196
transcalency 384
transcend *great* 31
  superior 33
  go beyond 303
transcendency 641
transcendent
  unequal 28
  superior 33
  glorious 873
  (*perfect* 650)
transcendental
  intellectual 450
  unintelligible 519
transcendentalism 450,
  451
transcolate
  exude 295
  (*stream* 348)
transcribe *copy* 19
  manifest 525
  write 590
transcript *copy* 21
  writing 590
transcursion 303
transept *church* 1000
transeunt 111
transfer *copy* 21
  displace 185
  - of *things* 270
  - of *property* **783**
transferable 270, 783
transferee 270
transference **270**
transfiguration
  change 140
  divine - 908
transfix 260
transfixed *firm* 150
transforation 260
transform 140
transformation scene
  599
transfuse *mix* 41
  transfer 270
  remedy 662
  - the sense of 522
  712

transgress
  go beyond 303
  infringe 773
  violate 927
  sin 945
transgression *guilt* 947
transgressor 949
transience **111**
transient *time* 109, 111
  changeable 149
  traveler 268
transilience
  revolution 146
  transcursion 303
transit *conversion* 144
  angularity 244
  motion 264
  transference 270
  measurement 466
transition 144, 270
transitional *change* 140
transitory 111
translate *interpret* 522
  manifest 525
  word 562
  promote 995
translation
  transference 270
  crib 539
  word 562
  resurrection 981
translator 524
transliterate 561
translocate 185
translocation 270
translucence 425
translumination 425
transmarine 196
transmigration
  change 140
  conversion 144
transmission
  moving 270
  automobile 272
  passage 302
  - of *property* 783
transmit 270, 302
  transfer 783
  - light 425
transmogrify 140
transmorphism 140
transmutation
  change 140
  conversion 144
transom 215, 349
transparency **425**
transparent
  transmitting light 425
  obvious 518
transpicuous
  transmitting light 425
  obvious 518
transpierce 260
transpire *evaporate* 336
  appear 525
  be disclosed 529
transplace 270
transplant 270, 371
transplendent 420
transpontine 196
transport *transfer* 270

ship 273
  war vessel 726
  excitement 825
  delight 827
  please 829
  punish 972
  (*emotion* 821, 824)
  - of *love* 897
transportation 144
transported
  overjoyed 827
transposal 148, 218
transpose *invert* 14, 218
  exchange 148
  displace 185
  transfer 270
  - *music* 413
transshape 140
transshipment 185
transubstantiation
  change 140
  sacrament 998
transudatory 295
transude *ooze* 295
  pass 302
  (*stream* 348)
transume *change* 140
transumption
  transfer 270
transverse *change* 140
  oblique 217
  crossing 219
tranter 271
trap *closure* 261
  gig 272
  snare 545
  stage - 599
  pitfall 667
  fall into a - *dupe* 547
  clumsy 699
  lay a - for 545
trapan 545
trapdoor *opening* 260
  snare 545
  pitfall 667
trapes 701
trappings *adjunct* 39
  clothes 225
  equipment 633
  ornament 847
Trappist 996
traps *clothes* 225
  baggage 780
trash *unmeaning* 517
  trifling 643
  useless 645
  riffraff 876
trashy - *style* 575
traulism 583
traumatic 662
travail *childbirth* 161
  labor 686
trave 215
travel 266
  - out of the record 10,
    477
traveler **268**
  bagman 758
  tricks upon -s
  deception 545
  cunning 702

-'s tale *untruth* 546
  exaggeration 549
traveling 266
  - bag 191
  - salesman 758
traverse *contravene* 179
  move 266
  pass 302
  negative 536
  obstruct 706
travestie *copy* 21
  ridicule 856
travesty *imitate* 19
  misinterpret 523
  burlesque 555
  ridicule 856
travis 215
trawl 285, 463
trawler 273
tray 191
treacherous 907, 940
  - memory 506
treachery
  deception 545
  dishonesty 940
treacle *thick* 352
  sweet 396
tread *motion* 264
  walk 266
  - a path *journey* 266
  pursuit 622
  - down *harsh* 739
  humble 879
  - in the steps of 19
  - on the heels of 281
  - the beaten track
  conformity 82
  habit 613
  - the boards 599
  - the stage 599
  - under foot
  destroy 162
  subjection 749
  disrepute 874
  insolence 885
  contempt 930
  - upon *persecute* 649
treadle 633
treadmill 312, 975
treason *revolt* 742
  treachery 940
treasure *store* 636
  goodness 648
  money 800
  - trove 618
  - up in the memory
    505
treasurer **801**
treasury **802**
treat
  physical pleasure 377
  manage 692
  bargain 769
  delight 827, 829
  amusement 840
  - of 595
  - oneself to 827
  - well 906
treatise 593, 595
treatment
  painting 556

conduct 692
ill - 649
medical - 662
treaty 769
treble *three* 93
  shrill 410
  (*music* 413)
  childish - 581
trebucket 727, 975
trecento 114, 554
tree *pedigree* 69, 166
  plant 367
  gallows 975
  as the - falls 151
  top of the - 210
  - of knowledge 493
  up a - 704
treelike 367
treenail 45
trefoil 92
trek 266
trekker 268
trellis 219
tremble *fluctuate* 149
  weakness 160
  shake 315
  cold 383
  emotion 821
  fear 860
  make one - 860
trembling
  - in the balance
  uncertain 475
  danger 665
  - prairie 344
  - to its fall
  destruction 160
tremellose 352
tremendous
  painful 830
  fearful 860
tremendously 31
tremor *agitation* 315
  emotion 821
  fearful 860
tremulous *agitated* 315
  - *voice* 583
  irresolute 605
  fear 860
trench *dike* 232
  furrow 259
  defense 717
  open the - es 716
  - on *near* 197
  trespass 303
  moral trespass 925
  - upon 927
trenchant *energetic* 171
  assertive 535
  concise style 572
  vigorous language 574
  important 642
  emotion 821
  discourteous 895
  censure 932
trencher *plate* 191
  layer 204
trend *tendency* 176
  bend 278
  deviate 279
trennel 45

trepan *opening* 260
  borer 262
  snare 545
trepang 298
trephine 260, 262
trepidation
  agitation 315
  emotion 821
  excitement 825
  fear 860
trespass *go beyond* 303
  vice 945
  guilt 947
tress 256
trestle 215
trews 225
trey 92
triad 92, 193
triadelphous 94
triagonal 244
trial *inquiry* 461
  experiment 463
  essay 675
  difficulty 704
  adversity 735
  suffering 828, 830
  lawsuit 969
  punishment 972
  on - 463
  - of temper 824
triality 92
trialogue 588
triangle *triality* 92, 244
  music 417
  punishment 975
triangular 94
  - duel 720
triarch 92
triarchy 737
tribe *race* 11
  assemblage 72
  class 75
  clan 166
tribulation 828
tribunal 966
tribune *rostrum* 542
  judge 967
tributary *river* 348
  giving 784
tribute *donation* 784
  money paid 809
  reward 973
  pay - to *respect* 928
  approbation 931
tricapsular 94
trice 113
  - up 43
tricennial 138
Trichinopoli cheroot 392
trichogenous 256
trichoid 256
trichosis 226
trichotomy 94
trichroism 440
trick *deception* 545
  indication 550
  habit 613
  contrivance 626
  skill 698
  artifice 702

- *at cards* 775
play -s *bungle* 699
  cunning 702
  amusement 840
  ridicule 856
  - of fortune 509
  - out *adorn* 847
  vulgar 851
  -s of the trade 702
trickery *deceit* 545
  finery 851
trickiness [see tricky]
trickle *ooze* 295
  stream 348
trickster *deceiver* 548
  schemer 702
  rogue 792
tricksy *crafty* 702
  cheery 836
  pretty 845
  ornamented 847
tricky *deceiving* 545
  cunning 702
tricolor *variegated* 440
  flag 550
tricuspid 94
tricycle 272
trident 92, 94, 341
tridental 94
tried *tested* 463
triennial *periodical* 138
  plant 367
  celebration 883
triennium 92
trifid 94
trifle *small* 32
  neglect 460
  folly 499
  unimportant 643
  not stick at -s 604
  not to be -d with 744
  - time away 683
  - with *neglect* 460
  deceive 545
  disrespect 929
trifler 460
  fool 501
trifling 499, 643
  wit 842
trifoliate 94
triforium 1000
triform 92
trifurcate 94
trig 652, 845
trigamy 903
trigger 633
  draw the - 722
trigon 92, 244
trigonal 94
trigonometry 244
trigrammatic 94
trigraph 561
trilateral *triplication* 93
  sides 236
  angles 244
trilogistic *triple* 93
trilogy *drama* 599
trill *stream* 348
  sound 407
  music 413, 415, 416
  thousand -s 402

trillion 98
trilobite 368
trim *state* 7
  adjust 27
  dress 225
  form 240
  garden 367
  lie 544
  waver 605
  change sides 607
  clean 652
  beautify 845
  adorn 847
  scold 932
  flog 972
  (*prepare* 673)
  in - *order* 58
trimmer *fickle* 607
  apostate 941
  timeserver 943
trimming *border* 231
  ornament 847
  dishonesty 940
Trimurti 92, 976
trinal 92
trine 93
trinitrotoluine 727
trinitrotoluol 727
trinity 92
Trinity, Holy - 976
trinket *trifle* 643
  ornament 847
trinkgeld 784
trinomial 92
trio *three* 92
  music 415
trionym 92
trip *jaunt* 266
  run 274
  fall 306
  leap 309
  mistake 495
  bungle 699
  fail 732
  vice 945
  guilt 947
  - up *deceive* 545
  overthrow 731
tripartition 94
tripedal 93
tripetalous 94
triphthong 561
triplane 273
triplasic 93
triple *increase* 35
  triplication 93
  - crown 999
triplet *three* 92
  verse 597
triplication 93
triplicity 92
triplopia 92
tripod *triality* 92
  support 215
  furnace 386
tripodal 94
tripotage 588
tripping [see trip]
  style 578
  nimble 682
  caught - 491

trippingly 584
tripsis 330
Triptolemus 371
triquetral 94
trireme 92, 273
Trisagion 900
triseme 92
trisection **94**
triskelion 92, 993
trismus 655
triste 837
tristful 837
trisula 92
trisulcate *trisected* 94
  furrow 259
trite *known* 490
  conventional 613
  - saying 496
tritheism 984
Triton *sea* 341
  - among the minnows
    superior 33
    huge 192
    important 642
trituration 330
triumph *procession* 69
  success 731
  trophy 733
  exult 838
  celebrate 883
  boast 884
triumvirate 92, 737
triune 93
Triune God 976
triunity 92
trivet *support* 215
  stove 386
  right as a -
    perfect 650
    due 924
trivial *unmeaning* 517
  trifling 643
  useless 645
  ridiculous 853
  (*small* 32)
troat 412
trocar 262
trochaic 597
trochee 597
trochilic 312
trodden down - 749
  well - *habitual* 613
  used 677
troglodyte 893
troll *roll* ,312
  fairy 980
trolley 266, 271, 273
  - car 272
trollibus 273
trollop 59, 962
trombone 417
troop *assemblage* 72
  soldiers 726
  raise -s 722
troopship 726
trope 521
Trophonius, cave of
  - 837

trophoplasm 357
trophy *record* 551
  palm **733**
tropical 382
  metaphorical 521
trot *run* 266, 370
  velocity 274
  translation 539
  - out *manifest* 525
  display 882
troth *belief* 484
  veracity 543
  promise 768
  by my - 535
  plight one's - 902
trothless *false* 544
  dishonorable 940
trotters 266, 298
trottoir 627
troubadour 597
trouble *disorder* 59
  derange 61
  exertion 686
  difficulty 704
  adversity 735
  pain 828
  painful 830
  bring into - 649
  get into - 732
  in - *evil* 619
  adversity 735
  take - 686
  - one for 765
  - oneself 686
  - one's head about
    682
troubled [*see* trouble]
  fish in - waters 704
troublesome
  inexpedient 647
  exertion 686
  difficult 704
  painful 830
troublous 59
  violent 173
  - times 713
trough *hollow* 252
  trench 259
  conduit 350
trounce *censure* 932
  punish 972
troupe 72
trousers 225
  put on long - 131
trousseau 225
trout 298
trouvaille 775
trouvère 597
trover *acquisition* 775
  unlawful 964
trow *think* 451
  believe 484
  know 490
trowel 191
troy weight 319
truant *absent* 187
  runaway 623
  idle 682
  apostate 941
truce *lateness* 133
  cessation 142

deliverance 672
  peace 721
  pacification 723
  flag of - 724
  - of God 142
trucidation 361
truck *summit* 210
  vehicle 272
  barter 794
  - driver 268, 271
  - farm 691
  - garden 371, 691
truckle-bed 215
truckler 886
truckle to *submit* 725
  servile 886
  flatter 933
truckling *servile* 746
truckman 268
truculent 907
trudge *walk* 266
  move slowly 275
true *real* 1
  straight 246
  assent 488
  accurate 494
  veracious 543
  faithful 772
  honorable 939
  orthodox 983a
  see in its - colors 480a
  - bill *vindicate* 937
  accuse 938
  lawsuit 969
  - faith 983a
  - meaning 516
  - to nature 17
  - to oneself 604a
  - saying 496
true-blue 494
true-hearted 543, 939
truelove 897
truelover's knot
  love 897
  endearment 902
trueness [*see* true]
true-penny 939
truffles 298
truism *axiom* 496
  unmeaning 517
trull 962
truly *very* 31
  assent 488
  really 494
  indeed 535
trump *perfect* 650
  cards 840
  honorable 939
  good man 948
  - card *device* 626
  success 731
  - up *falsehood* 544
  accuse 938
  turn up -s 731
trumped up
  counterevidence 468
  deception 545
  untruth 546
trumpery
  unmeaning 517
  trifling 643

,trumpet *music* 417
  war cry 722
  boast 884
  ear - 418
  flourish of -s
    ostentation 882
    celebration 883
    boasting 884
  penny - *skill* 410
  sound of - *alarm* 669
  speaking - 418
  - blast 404
  - call *signal* 550
    command 741
  - forth 531
trumpeter
  musician 416
  messenger 534
  boaster 884
trumpet-toned
  shrill 410
trumpet-tongued
  loud 404
  public 531
truncate *shorten* 201
  formless 241
truncated
  incomplete 53
truncheon *weapon* 727
  staff of office 747
  *instrument of pun-
    ishment* 975
trundle *propel* 284
  roll 312
  - bed 215
trunk *whole* 50
  origin 153
  paternity 166
  box 191
trunk hose 225
trunnion *support* 215
  projection 250
truss *tie* 43
  pack, packet 72
  support 215
trust *belief* 484
  property 780
  credit 805
  hope 858
  - to a broken reed 699
  - to the chapter of
    accidents 621
trusted 484
trustee *consignee* 758
  possessor 779
  treasurer 801
trustful 484
trustless 940
trustworthy
  certain 474
  belief 484
  - *memory* 505
  veracious 543
  reliable 632
  honorable 939
truth *exactness* **494**
  veracity 543
  probity 939
  arrive at the - 480a
  in - *certainly* 474
  love of - 543

of a - *affirmation* 535
  veraciously 543
prove the - of 937
religious - 983*a*
speak the - *disclose*
  529
  veracity 543
Truth, Spirit of - 976
truthless 544
truth-loving 543
truth-telling 543
trutination 319
try *experiment* 463
  adjudge 480
  endeavor 675
  use 677
  lawsuit 969
- a case 967
- a cause 480
- a prisoner 967
- conclusions
  discuss 476
  quarrel 713
  contend 720
- one *difficulty* 704
- one's hand 675
- one's luck 621
- one's temper 824
- one's utmost 686
- the patience 830
trying *fatigue* 688
  difficulty 704
tryst 74, 892
trysting place 74
tsar 745
tub 191, 386
- to a whale
  deception 545
  excuse 617
tuba 417
tubate 260
tubby 201
tube 260
tubercle 250
tubercular 655
tuberculosis 655
tuberosity 250
tubman 968
tubular 260
tubulated 260
tubule 260
tuck *adjunct* 39
  fold 258
  dagger 727
- in *locate* 184
  eat 298
  insert 300
tucker 225
tuft *collection* 72
  rough 256
tufted 256
tufthunter *servile* 886
  selfish 943
tufthunting
  servility 886
  flattery 933
tug *ship* 273
  pull 285
  effort 686
- of war 720
  athletic sport 840

tuition 537
tulip *variegated* 440
  gaudy 882
Tullian 582
tumble *derange* 61
  destruction 162
  fall 306
  agitate 315
  fail 732
  rough and - 59
tumble-down
  weak 160
  tottering 665
tumbler *glass* 191
  actor 599
  buffoon 844
tumbrel 272
tumefaction 194
tumid *expanded* 194
  - *style* 577
  (*big* 192)
tumor *expansion* 194
  prominence 250
tump 206
tumult *disorder* 59
  agitation 315
  revolt 742
  emotion 825
tumultuous
  [*see* tumult]
  violent 173
tumulus 363
tun *receptacle* 191
  large 192
  drunkard 959
tuna 298
tunable 413
tund 972
tundra 344
tune *music* 415, 416
  in - 413
  out of -
    unmusical 414
    imperfect 651
    deteriorated 659
  put in - *prepare* 673
    concord 714
  to the - of *quantity* 25
    payment 807
    price 812
  - up 416
tuneful *music* 413
  poetry 597
  - nine *musician* 416
  poet 597
tuneless 414
tunic 225
tunicle 999
tuning fork 417
tunker 984
tunnage 192
tunnel
  ncave 252
  opening 260
  passage 627
tup *sheep* 366
  male 373
tu quoque 718
- argument
  counterevidence 468
  confutation 479

  accuse 938
turban 225
turbary 367
turbid *opaque* 426
  foul 653
turbinal 248
turbinated
  convoluted 248
  rotation 312
turbine 267, 284, 312,
  633
- steamer 273
turbiniform 245, 248
turbinoid 248
turbulence
  violence 173
  agitation 315
  excitation 825
  (*disorder* 59)
turbulent
  [*see* turbulence]
  disorderly 59
Turcism 984
tureen 191
turf *elasticity* 325
  lawn 344
  grass 367, 371
  fuel 388
  gambling 621
  races 720
  race course 728
  amusement 840
turfman 840
turgid *expanded* 194
  - *style* 577
  redundant 641
  ostentatious 882
  (*exaggerated* 549)
Turk *polygamist* 903
  grand - 745
turkey 298
- trot 840
Turkish bath 386
turlupinade 842
turmeric paper 463
turmoil
  confusion 59
  violence 173
  agitation 315
turn *state* 7
  crisis 134
  period of time 138
  change 140
  tendency 176
  form 240
  curve 245
  blunt 254
  stroll 266
  deviate 279
  recession 287
  circuition 311
  rotate 312
  music 413
  willingness 602
  aptitude 698
  affections 820
  emotion 821
  trepidation 860
  by -s *periodic* 138
  interchange 148

come in its - 138
do a good - *good* 648
  benevolent 906
each in its - 148
give one a - *aid* 707
  excite 824
ill - 907
in - *order* 58
  periodic 138
in his - 148
meet one at every -
  641
one's luck -s 735
serve one's - 644
take a favorable - 658
take a wrong - 732
to a - 494
- about   *interchange*
  148
- a corner *go round* 311
  succeed 731
- a deaf ear to *deaf* 419
  refuse 764
- adrift *disperse* 73
  eject 297
- and turn about
  interchange 148
  changeable 149
- and twist 248
- a penny 775
- aside *change* 140
  deviate 279
  hinder 706
- away *eject* 297
  not look 442
  avoid 623
  dismiss 756
  relinquish 782
- back *reversion* 145
  regression 283
- color 821
- down 258
- end for end 14
- for 698
- from *repent* 950
- in *go to bed* 683
- in an alarm 669
- inside out 529
- into *conversion* 144
  translate 522
  - *money* 796
  - *ridicule* 856
- of expression 566
- off 972
- of mind 820
- of the cards 156
- of the table 156
- of the tide *reverse* 145
  invert 218
- one's attention from
  458
- one's back upon
  oppose 708
  refuse 764
  disrespect 929
  contempt 930
- one's hand to 625
- on one's heel *avoid*
  623
  discourtesy 895
- on the tap 297

letter 561
  printing 591
  - for the blind 442
typescript 21
typesetting 54
typewrite 590
typewriting 590

typhonic 349
typhoon *wind* 349
  (*violent* 173)
typical *special* 79
  conformable 82
  metaphorical 521
  significant 550

typify 511
typist 590
typography 591
tyranny
  authority 737
  severity 739
  illegality 964

tyrant *authority* 737
  severe 739
  ruler 745
  evildoer 913
tyre 230
tyro *ignoramus* 493
  learner 541

U

uberty *luxuriance* 168
  (*sufficiency* 639)
ubiety 186
ubiquitarian 984
ubiquity 186
U-boat 208, 726
udder 191
udometer 348
ugh! 867
uglification 846
ugliness **846**
ugly 846
  call by - names 932
  take an - turn 732
  - customer
    source of danger 667
    evildoer 913
    bad man 949
uhlan 716, 726
ukase 741
ukulele 417
ulcer *disease* 655
  care 830
ulcerate 659
ulema *judge* 967
uliginous 352
ullalulla 839
ulster 225
ulterior *extra* 37
  extraneous 57
  - *in time* 121
  - *in space* 196
ultima ratio 744
  - regum 722
ultimate 67
  - cause 153
ultimately *difference* 15
  future 121
  latest 133
ultima Thule 196
ultimatum *definite* 474
  intention 620
  requirement 630
  terms 770
ultimeter 244
ultimo 122
ultimogeniture 777
ultra *great* 31
  superior 33
ultramarine 438
ultramicroscope 445
ultramontane
  foreign 57
  distant 196
  heterodox 984
  church 995
ultramundane 196
ultra-violet rays 420
ululate 412, 839

ululation 407, **412**
Ulysses 702
umbilicus 222
umbra 421
umbrage *shade* 424
  hatred 898
  take - *anger* 900
umbrageous 421
umbrageousness 421
umbrella *covering* 223
  shade 424
  protection 666
umpire *judgment* 480
  mediator 724
  judge 967
unabashed *bold* 861
  vain 885
  insolent 885
unabated 31
unable 158
  - to say "No" 605
unacceptable 830
unaccommodating
  disagreeing 24
  disagreeable 830
  discourteous 895
  sulky 901a
unaccompanied 87
unaccomplished 730
unaccountable
  exceptional 83
  unintelligible 519
  irresponsible 927a
  arbitrary 964
  (*wonderful* 870)
unaccustomed
  unusual 83
  unused 614
  unskillful 699
unachievable 471
unacknowledged
  ignored 489
  nameless 565
  unrequited 917
unacquainted 491
unacquired 777a
unactuated (616)
unadmonished 665
unadorned *style* 576
  simple 849
  beauty - 845
unadulterated
  simple 42
  genuine 494
  (*good* 648)
unadventurous 864
unadvisable 647
unadvised
  dangerous 665

unskillful 699
unaffected *genuine* 494
  sincere 543
  - *style* 578
  obstinate 606
  artless 703
  insensible 823
  simple 849
  taste 850
  (*physically callous* 376)
unafflicted 831
unaided *weak* 160
  (*unsupported* 706)
unalarmed 861
unalienable 924
unallayed 159
unallied 10
unallowable 923
unallowed 925
unalloyed 42
  - *happiness* 827
  - *truth* 494
unalluring 866
unalterable 150
unaltered *identical* 13
  stable 150
  (*unchanged* 141)
unamazed 871
unambiguous 518
unambitious 866
unamiable 907
unanimated 823
unanimity
  agreement 23
  assent 488
  accord 714
unannexed 44
unanswerable
  demonstrative 478
  irresponsible 927a
  arbitrary 964
  (*certain* 474)
unanswered 478
unanticipated 508
unappalled 861
unappareled 226
unapparent *latent* 526
  (*invisible* 447)
unappeasable 173
unappetizing 867
unapplied 678
unappreciated 483
unapprehended 491
unapprehensive 861
unapprized 491
unapproachable
  great 31
  infinite 105

distant 196
unapproached
  unequal 28
  superior 33
unappropriated 782
unapproved 932
unapt *incongruous* 24
  impotent 158
  unskillful 699
  (*inexpedient* 647)
unarmed 158
unarranged
  disorder 59
  unprepared 674
unarrayed 226, 849
unartificial 849
unascertained
  uncertain 475
  ignorant 491
unasked *voluntary* 602
  not asked 766
unaspiring
  indifferent 866
  modest 881
unassailable 664
unassailed 748
unassembled 73
unassisted *weak* 160
  unaided 706
  - *eye* 441
unassociated 44
unassuming 881
unatoned 951
unattached 44
unattackable 664
unattainable 471
unattained 732
unattempted 623
unattended 87
  - to 460
unattested
  not evidence 468
  (*unrecorded* 552)
unattracted
  indifferent 866 (616)
unattractive 866
unauthenticated
  improved 468
  uncertain 475
  inexact 495
unauthoritative
  uncertain 475
unauthorized
  prohibited 761
  undue 925
  lawless 964
unavailing *useless* 645
  failure 732
unavenged 918

717

unavoidable *certain* 474
  necessary 601
unavowed 489
unawakened 683
unaware *ignorant* 491
  unexpecting 508
unawed 861
unbalanced 28
unbar 750
unbearable 830
unbeaten 123
unbeauteous 846
unbecoming
  incongruous 24
  disreputable 874
  undue 925
  dishonorable 940
  - a gentleman 895
unbefitting *inapt* 24
  undue 925
  improbity 940
  [*see* unbecoming]
unbegotten 2
unbeguile *inform* 527
  disclose 529
unbegun
  unprepared 674
unbeheld (447)
unbelief **485**
  irreligion 989
  (*incredulity* 487)
unbelievable 485
unbeliever *infidel* 989
unbelieving 485
unbeloved 898
unbend *straighten* 246
  repose 687
  - the mind 452
unbending *hard* 323
  resolute 604
unbenevolent 907
unbenign 907
unbent 246
unbeseeming
  vulgar 851
  dishonorable 940
unbesought
  not ask 766
  (*spontaneous* 602)
unbestowed (785)
unbetrayed 939
unbewailed 932
unbiased *wise* 498
  free 748
  (*spontaneous* 602a)
unbidden *willful* 600
  disobedient 742
unbigoted 498
unbind *detach* 44
  release 750
unblamable 946
unblamed 946
unblemished
  perfect 650
  innocent 946
unblenching 861
unblended 42
unblest
  unfortunate 735
  not approved 932
  - with 777a

unblown 674
unblushing *proud* 878
  vain 880
  imprudent 885
unboastful 881
unbodied 317
unboiled 674
unbolt *liberate* 750
  (*unfasten* 44)
unbookish 491
unborn *not existing* 2
  destined 152
  (*future* 121)
unbosom oneself 529
unbought
  not bought 796
  honorary 815
  honorable 939
  unselfish 942
unbound *free* 748
  exempt 927a
unbounded
  infinite 105
  (*great* 31)
  (*large* 192)
  (*space* 180)
unbrace *weaken* 160
  relax 655
unbreathed 526
unbred 895
unbribed
  honorable 939
  disinterested 942
unbridled *violent* 173
  lax 738
  free 748
unbroken *entire* 50
  continuous 69
  preserved 670
  unviolated 939
  - extent 69
unbruised 50
unbuckle 44
unburden
  - one's mind 529
unburdened 705
unburied 362
unbuttoned 748
uncalculating 863
uncalled for
  redundant 641
  useless 645
  not used 678
uncandid *insincere* 544
  morose 907
uncanny *ugly* 846
  spectral 980a
uncanonical 984
uncared for
  neglected 460
  indifferent 866
  disliked 867
  hated 898
uncase (226)
uncate 245
uncaught *free* 748
uncaused 156
unceasing 112, 143
uncensured 931
unceremonious
  vain 880

discourteous 895
uncertain
  irregular 139
  not certain 475
  doubtful 485
  embarrassing 704
  in an - degree 32
uncertainty **475**
unchain *unfasten* 44
  liberate 750
unchained *free* 748
unchallenged *assent* 488
  due 924
unchangeable
  stable 150
  persevering 604a
unchanged 16, 141
unchangingly 136
uncharitable 907
unchartered *undue* 925
  illegal 964
unchaste 961
unchastised 970
unchecked 748
uncheerful 837
unchequered 141
unchivalric 940
unchristian
  heterodox 984
  irreligious 989
uncial 590
unciform 245
uncinated 244
uncircumscribed 180
uncircumspect 460
uncivil *vulgar* 851
  rude 895
uncivilized *low* 876
  uncourteous 895
unclad 226
unclaimed 748
unclassed (59)
unclassical 851
unclassified (59)
uncle *kin* 11
  my -'s *pawnshop* 787
unclean 653
  - spirit 978, 980
uncleanness **653**
Uncle Sam **188**
unclipped 50
unclog *facilitate* 705
  liberate 750
unclose *open* 260
  liberate 750
unclothed 226
unclouded *light* 420
  visible 446
  (*joyful* 827)
unclubbable 893
unclutch 790
uncoif 226
uncoil *evolve* 313
  (*straighten* 246)
uncollected (73)
uncolored
  achromatic 429
  true 494
  (*veracious* 543)
uncombed *dirty* 653

vulgar 851
uncombined
  simple 42
  incoherent 47
uncomeatable 471
uncomely 846
uncomfortable
  annoyed 828
  annoying 830
uncommendable
  blamable 932
  bad 945
  guilt 947
uncommensurable 24
uncommon
  unimitated 20
  exceptional 83
  infrequent 137
uncommonly 31
uncommonness 137
uncommunicated 781
uncommunicative 528
uncompact 322
uncompassionate 914a
uncompelled 748
uncomplaisant 764
  (895)
uncompleted
  incomplete 53
  unfinished 730
  failure 732
uncomplying
  disobedient 742
  refusing 764
uncompounded 42
uncompressed *light* 320
  rare 322
uncompromising
  conformable 82
  severe 739
unconcealable 525
unconceived
  uncreated 12
  unintelligible 519
unconcern
  insensible 823
  indifferent 866
unconcerned *tolerant* 740
  [*see* unconcern]
unconcocted 674
uncondemned 970
unconditional
  complete 52
  free 748
  permission 760
  consent 762
  release 768a
unconducive 175a
unconfined 748
unconfirmed 475
unconformity
  disagreement 24
  irregularity **83**
unconfused
  methodical 58
  clear 518
unconfuted
  demonstrated 478
  true 494
uncongealed 333

uncongenial
 disagreeing 24
 insalubrious 657
unconnected
 irrelative 10
 disjointed 44
 discontinuous 70
 illogical 477
unconquerable
 strong 159
 persevering 604a
 - *will* 604
unconquered 719 ·
unconscientious 940
unconscionable
 excessive 31
 unprincipled 945
unconscious
 ignorant 491
 insensible 823
unconsenting
 unwilling 603
 refusing 764
unconsidered 452
unconsolidated 47
unconsonant 24
unconspicuous
 invisible 447
 (*latent* 526)
unconstitutional
 undue 925
 illegal 964
unconstrained *free* 748
 fashion 852
 unabashed 880
 will 600
unconsumed
 remaining 40
uncontested 474
uncontradicted 488
uncontrite 951
uncontrollable
 violent 173
 necessity 601
 emotion 825
uncontrolled *free* 748
 excitability 825
uncontroverted 488
unconventional 83, 614
unconversable 585
unconversant
 ignorant 491
 unskilled 699
unconverted
 dissenting 489
 irreligious 989
unconvinced 489
uncooked 674
uncopied 20
uncork 750
uncorrupted
 upright 939
 (*innocent* 946)
uncounted 475
uncouple (44)
uncourteous 895
uncourtly *inelegant* 579
 vulgar 851
 rude 895
uncouth - *style* 579
 ugly 846

vulgar 851
 (*ridiculous* 853)
uncouthness
 [*see* uncouth]
 amorphism 241
uncover *denude* 226
 open 260
 disclose 529
 bow 894
uncreated 2
uncritical 931
uncropped 50
uncrown 756
unction
 lubrication 332
 emotion 821, 824
 divine functions 976
 piety 987
 extreme - 998
 lay the flattering - to
  one's soul
 relief 834
 hope 858
unctuous *oily* 355
 bland 894
 flattering 933
 hypocritical 988
unctuousness **355**
unculled *unused* 678
 relinquished 782
unculpable 946
uncultivated
 ignorant 491
 fallow 674
 vulgarity 851
uncurbed 748
uncurl 246
uncustomary
 exceptional 83
 (*desuetude* 614)
uncut 50, 674
undamaged (648)
undamped 340
undated
 without date 115
 waving 248
undaunted 861
undazzled 498
undebauched
 honorable 939
 (*innocent* 946)
undecayed (648)
undeceive
 inform 527
 disclose 529
undeceived
 knowing 490
undecennary 98
undecided
 inquiring 461
 uncertain 475
 irresolute 605
 leave - 609a
undecipherable 519
undecked 849
undecomposed 42
undefaced 845, 847
undefended 725
undefiled *honest* 939
 innocent 946
 chaste 960

undefinable
 uncertain 475
 unmeaning 517
 unintelligible 519
undefined
 invisible 447
 uncertain 475
 (*unintelligible* 519)
undeformed 845, 847
undemolished 50
undemonstrable 485
undemonstrated 475
undemonstrative 826
undeniable 474, 478
undeplored 898
undepraved 939
undeprived 781
under *less* 34
 below 207
 subject to 749
 range - 76
 - *age* 127
 - *agent* 758
 - *breath* 405
 - *cover covered* 223
 hidden 528
 safe 664
 - *foot* [*see below*]
 - full strength 651
 - lock and key 664
 - one's control 743
 - one's eyes 446
 - press of 744
 - protest *dissent* 489
  compulsion 744
 - restraint 751
 - *seal* 467
 - subjection 749
 - the circumstances 8
 - the head of 9
 - the mark 34
 - the sun 1
 - way 282
underbid 794
underbreath 405
underbred 851
underclothing 225
undercurrent
 cause 153
 stream 348, 349
 latent 526
 opposing 709
underdone 298
underestimation **483**
underfed 640
underfoot 207
 tread - 739
undergo 151
 - a change 144
 - pain 828
undergraduate 541
underground *low* 207
 deep 208
 latent 526
 hidden 528
undergrowth 367
underhand *latent* 526
 hidden 528
 - dealing 528
underhung 250
underlay 591

underlessee 779
underlet 787
underlie *low* 207
 latent 526
underline *mark* 550
 emphatic 642
underling *servant* 746
 clown 876
undermine
 impotence 158
 burrow 252
 damage 659
 stratagem 702
 hinder 706
undermost 211
underneath 207
undernourished 640
undern-song 900
underpaid 819
underpin 215
underplot 626
underprop 215
underrate 483, 549
underreckon 483
underscore 550
undersecretary 746
undersell 796
underset 215
undershirt 225
undershot 250
undersign *testify* 467
 (*write* 590)
undersized 193
undersong 104
understand *note* 450
 know 490
 intelligible 518
 latent 526
 be *informed* 527
 give one to - 572
 - by *meaning* 516
 interpret 522
 - one another
 coöperate 709
 concord 714
understanding
 intellect 450
 intelligence 498
 come to an -
 assent 488
 intelligible 518
 agree 714
 pacification 723
 compact 769
 good - *concord* 714
 friendship 888
 with the - 469
understate 555
understood
 meaning 516
 implied 526
 customary 613
 (*metaphorical* 521)
understrapper 746
understudy 634
undertake
 endeavor 676
 promise 768
undertaker 363
undertaking
 business 625

719

unfeminine *manly* 373
  vulgar 851
unfertile 169
unfetter *release* 750
  (*unfasten* 44)
unfettered *free* 748
  (*spontaneous* 600)
unfinished
  incomplete 53
  not completed 730
unfit *inappropriate* 24
  impotence 158
  inexpedient 647
  unskillful 699
  wrong 923
  undue 925
unfitness *inutility* 645
  [see *unfit*]
unfitted
  not prepared 674
unfix 44
unfixed *mutable* 149
  (*irresolute* 605)
unflagging
  persevering 604a
  (*active* 682)
unflammable 385
unflattering *true* 494
  artless 703
  (*sincere* 543)
  unflavored 391)
unfledged
  young 127, 129
  callow 674
unfleshly 317
unflinching *firm* 604
  persevering 604a
  brave 861
unfoiled (731)
unfold *straighten* 246
  evolve 313
  interpret 522
  disclose 529
  - a tale 594
unfoldment [see *unfold*]
  manifestation 525
unforbidden 760
unforced *willing* 602
  free 748
unforeseen
  unexpected 508
  (*wonderful* 870)
unforfeited 781
unforgettable 506
unforgiving 919
unforgotten 505
unformed
  shapeless 241
  unshaped 674
unfortified *pure* 42
  powerless 158
unfortunate
  ill-timed 135
  failure 732
  adversity 735
  unhappy 828
  - woman 962
unfounded *untruth* 546
  (*falsehood* 544)
unfrequent 137
unfrequented 893

unfriended
  powerless 158
  secluded 893
unfriendly *opposed* 708
  hostile 889
  malevolent 907
unfrock *dismiss* 756
  disapprobation 932
  punish 972
unfrozen *warm* 382
  (*liquefied* 335)
unfruitful 169
unfulfilled
  nonobservance 773
  undue 925
unfurl *unfold* 313
  - a flag *manifest* 525
  signal 550
unfurnished
  insufficient 640
  unprepared 674
ungainly *ugly* 846
  rude 895
ungallant 895
ungarmented 226
ungarnished 849
ungathered 678
ungenerous *stingy* 819
  selfish 943
ungenial 657
ungenteel *vulgar* 851
  rude 895
ungentle *violent* 173
  rude 895
ungentlemanly
  vulgar 851
  rude 895
  dishonorable 940
ungifted 32, 499
unglorified 874
unglue *incoherence* 47
  (*disjoin* 44)
ungodly 989
ungovernable
  violent 173
  disobedient 742
  passionate 825
ungoverned 748
ungraceful
  - *language* 579
  ugly 846
  vulgar 851
ungracious
  uncivil 895
  unfriendly 907
ungrammatical 568
ungranted 764
ungrateful 917
ungratified
  discontent 832
  (*pain* 828)
ungrounded
  unsubstantial 4
  erroneous 495
ungrudging 816
unguarded
  neglected 460
  spontaneous 612
  unprepared 674
  (*dangerous* 665)
  in an - moment

unexpectedly 508
unguent 332, 356
unguiculate 245
unguided *ignorant* 491
  impulsive 612
  unskilled 699
unguilty 946
unguinous 355
unguis 781
unhabitable 187
unhabituated 614
unhackneyed 614
unhallowed
  impious 988
  irreligious 989
unhand 750
unhandled 123
unhandseled 123
unhandsome 940
unhandy 699
unhappy *adversity* 735
  pain 828
  dejected 837
  make - 830
unharbored 185
unhardened
  tender 914
  innocent 946
  penitent 950
unharmonious
  incongruous 24
  unmusical 414
unharness
  liberate 750
  (*disjoin* 44)
unhatched
  callow 674
unhazarded 664
unhealthy *ill* 655
  unwholesome 657
unheard of
  exceptional 83
  new 123
  improbable 473
  ignorant 491
  wonderful 870
unheated 383
unheed 460
unheeded 460
unheeding 458
unhelped (708)
unhesitating
  belief 484
  resolved 604
unhewn *formless* 241
  unprepared 674
unhindered 748
unhinge *derange* 61
  make powerless 158
unhinged *impotent* 158
  insane 503
  failure 732
unholy 989
unhonored 874
unhook (44)
unhoped 508
unhorsed 732
unhostile 888
unhouse 297
unhoused 185
unhurt 670

unicorn *monster* 83
  carriage 272
  (*prodigy* 872)
unideal *existing* 1
  no thought 452
  true 494
unidentical 18
unification
  combination 48
  one 87
uniflorous 87
unifoliolate 87
uniform
  homogeneous 16
  simple 42
  orderly 58
  regular 80
  dress 225
  symmetry 242
  livery 550
uniformity 16
unigenital 87
uniglobular 87
unijugate 89
uniliteral 87
unilluminated 421
unilobed 87
unilocular 87
unimaginable
  impossible 471
  improbable 473
  wonderful 870
unimaginative
  plain 576
  dull 843
  expectant 871
unimagined
  existing 1
  true 494
unimitated 20
unimodular 87
unimpaired
  preserved 670
  (*good* 648)
unimpassioned 826
unimpeachable
  certain 474
  true 494
  due 924
  approved 931
  innocent 946
unimpeached 931, **946**
unimpelled (616)
unimportance **643**
unimpressed 838
unimpressible 823
unimproved 659
unincited (616)
unincreased 36
unincumbered *easy* 705
  exempt 927a
uninduced 616
uninfected 652
uninfectious 656
uninflammable 385
uninfluenced
  obstinate 606
  unactuated 616
  unrestricted 748
uninfluential *inert* 172
  no influence 175a

uninformed 491
uningenuous 544
uninhabit *absence* 187
  secluded 893
uninhabitable 187, 893
uninhabited 187, 893
uninitiated
  ignorant 491
  unskillful 699
uninjured *perfect* 650
  healthy 654
  preserved 670
uninjurious 656
uninquisitive 456
uninspired
  unexcited 823
  (*unactuated* 616)
uninstructed 491
unintellectual
  incogitant 452
  imbecile 499
unintellectuality 450a
unintelligent 32, 499
unintelligibility **519,**
  571
unintelligible 519
  - *style* 571
  render - 538
unintended 621
unintentional
  necessary 601
  undesigned 621
uninterested
  incurious 456
  weary 841
  dull 843
uninteresting 643
unintermitting
  unbroken 69
  durable 110
  continuing 143
  persevering 604a
uninterrupted
  continuous 69
  perpetual 112
  unremitting 893
  - *existence* 112
unintroduced 893
uninured
  unaccustomed 614
  (*unprepared* 674)
uninvented 526
uninvestigated 491
uninvited 893
uninviting 830
union *agreement* 23
  junction 43
  combination 48
  concurrence 178
  party 712
  concord 714
  marriage 903
  - down *flag* 550
union jack 550
union pipes 417
unique *dissimilar* 18
  original 20
  unequal 28
  exceptional 83
  alone 87
unirritable 826
722

unirritating 174
unison *agreement* 23
  melody 413
  concord 714
  (*uniform* 16)
  in - *melody* 413
unisulcate 259
unit 87
Unitarian 984
unitary 87
unite *join* 43
  combine 48
  component 56
  assemble 72
  concur 178
  converge 290
  party 712
  (*agree* 23)
  - in pairs 89
  - one's efforts 709
  - with *coöperate* 709
united *coherent* 46
  concord 714
United States courts
  966
unity *identity* 13
  uniformity 16
  whole 50
  complete 52
  single **87**
  concord 714
  - of time 120
Unity, Trinity in - 976
universal 78
  - Church 983a
  - concept 450
  - favorite 899
  - joint 272, 633
  - language 560
  -ly present 186
  - predicament 25
universality 52
universalize 78
universe 318
university 542
  go to the - 539
  - degree 873
  - education 537
unjust *wrong* 923
  impious 988
unjustifiable
  wrong 923
  inexcusable 938
  wicked 945
unjustified 923
  undue 925
unkempt *rough* 256
  unclean 653
  vulgar 851
unkennel *eject* 297
  disclose 529
unkind 907
  -est cut of all 828
unkindness hard - 907
unknightly 940
unknit (44)
unknot 705
unknowable 519
unknowing 491
unknown
  ignorant 491

  latent 526
  - quantities 491
  - to fame
  inglorious 874
  lowborn 876
unlabored
  - *style* 578
  unprepared 674
unlace (44)
unlade 297
unladylike
  vulgar 851
  rude 895
unlamented
  hated 898
  disapproved 932
unlatch 44
unlawful *undue* 925
  illegal 964
unlearn 506
unlearned 491
unleavened 674
unless
  circumstances 8
  except 83
  qualification 469
  (*condition* 770)
unlettered 491
  - Muse 579
unlicensed 761
unlicked
  unprepared 674
  vulgar 851
  clownish 876
  - cub *shapeless* 241
  unmannerly 895
unlike 18
unlikely 471, 473
unlimber 323
unlimited *great* 31
  infinite 105
  free 748
  - space 180
unlink (44)
unliquefied 321
unlively *grave* 837
  dull 843
unload *displace* 185
  eject 297
  disencumber 705
  sell 796
unlock *unfasten* 44
  discover 480a
  (*explain* 462)
unlooked for 508
unloose *unfasten* 44
  liberate 750
unloved 898
unlovely 846
unlucky
  inopportune 135
  bad 649
  unfortunate 735
  in pain 830
unmade 2
unmaimed 654
unmake 145
unman *castrate* 38
  render powerless 158
  madden 837
  frighten 860

unmanageable
  unwieldy 647
  perverse 704
unmanly
  effeminate 374
  dishonorable 940
unmanned
  dejected 837
  cowardly 862
unmannered 895
unmannerly 895
unmarked 460
unmarred *sound* 654
  preserved 670
unmarried 904
unmask *disclose* 529
  (*show* 525)
unmatched
  different 15
  dissimilar 18
  unparalleled 20
  unequal 28
unmeaningness **517**
unmeant 517
unmeasured
  infinite 105
  undistinguished 465a
  abundant 639
unmeditated
  impulsive 612
  (*undesigned* 621)
unmeet 925
unmellowed 674
unmelodious 414, 713
unmelted 321
unmentionable 874
unmentionables 225
unmentioned 526
unmerciful
  pitiless 914a
  (*malevolent* 907)
unmerited 925
unmethodical 59
unmindful
  inattentive 458
  neglectful 460
  ungrateful 917
unmingled 42
unmissed 460
unmistakable
  certain 474
  intelligible 518
  manifest 525
  affirmation 535
  (*visible* 446)
unmitigable 173
unmitigated *great* 31
  complete 52
  violent 173
unmixed 42
unmodified (141)
unmolested *safe* 664
  content 831
unmoneyed 804
unmoral 823
unmourned 898
unmoved *quiescent* 265
  obstinate 606
  insensible 823
  (*resolute* 604)
  (*uninduced* 616)

unmusical 414
- voice 581
unmuzzle 748
unnamed 565
unnatural
  exceptional 83
  affected 855
  spiteful 907
unnecessary
  redundant 641
  useless 645
  inexpedient 647
unneeded 645
unneighborly 895
unnerved *powerless* 158
  weak 160
  dejected 837
unnoted *neglected* 460
  ignoble 874
unnoticed 460, 874
unnumbered 105
unnurtured 674
unobeyed 742
unobjectionable
  good 648
  pretty good 651
  innocent 946
unobnoxious 648
unobscured 420
unobservant 458
unobserved 460
unobstructed *clear* 705
  free 749
  (*unopposed* 709)
unobtainable 471
unobtained 777a
unobtrusive 881
unoccupied *vacant* 187
  unthinking 452
  doing nothing 681
  inactive 683
  leisured 685
  secluded 893
unoffended
  enduring 826
  humble 879
unofficial 964
unoften 137
unopened 261
unopposed 709
unordinary 20, 83
unorganized 358
  unprepared 674
- matter 358
unornamental 846
unornamented
  - *style* 576
  simple 849
unorthodox 984
unostentatious 881
unowed 807
unowned 782
unpacific
  discordant 713
  warfare 722
unpacified 713
unpack *unfasten* 44
  take out 297
unpaid *debt* 806
  honorary 815
- worker *volunteer* 602

unpalatable
  unsavory 395
  disagreeable 830
  (*dislike* 867)
unparagoned
  supreme 33
  best 648
  perfect 650
unparalleled
  unimitated 20
  unequaled 28
  supreme 33
  exceptional 83
  best 648
unpardonable
  inexcusable 938
  wicked 945
unparliamentary
  language
  discourteous 895
  cursing 908
unpassable 261
unpassionate 826
unpatriotic 911
unpatterned 28
unpeaceful
  contention 720
  war 722
unpeered 28
unpeople
  emigration 297
  banishment 893
  (*displace* 185)
unperceived
  neglected 460
  unknown 491
  (*latent* 526)
unperformed 730
unperjured
  truthful 543
  honorable 939
unperplexed 498
unpersuadable
  obstinate 606
unpersuaded 616
unperturbed 826
unphilosophical 499
unpierced 261
unpin (44)
unpitied 932
unpitying *pitiless* 914a
  (*angry* 900)
  (*malevolent* 907)
unplaced 185
unplagued 831
unpleasant 830
unpleasing 830
unplumbed 104
unpoetical *prose* 598
  matter of fact 703
unpointed *blunt* 254
unpolished *rough* 256
  inelegant 579
  unprepared 674
  vulgar 851
  rude 895
unpolite 895
unpolluted *good* 648
  perfect 650
unpopular
  disagreeable 830

  dislike 867
unpopularity
  hatred 898
unportioned 804
unpossessed 777a
unpracticed (699)
unprecedented
  exceptional 83
  rare 137
unprejudiced 498, 748
unpremeditated
  impulsive 612
  undesigned 621
  unprepared 674
unprepared 674
unprepossessed 498
unprepossessing 846
unpresentable 851
unpretending 881
unpretentious 881
unprevented 748
unprincipled 945
unprivileged 925
unprized 483
unproclaimed 526
unproduced
  inexistent 2
unproductive
  useless 645
unproductiveness **169**
unproficiency 699
unprofitable
  unproductive 169
  useless 645
  inexpedient 647
  bad 649
unprogressive 659
unprolific 169
unpromising 859
unprompted 612
unpronounced
  latent 526
unpropitious
  ill-timed 135
  opposed 708
  adverse 735
  hopeless 859
unproportioned
  (*disagreeing* 24)
unprosperous 735
unprotected 665
unproved 477
unprovided
  scanty 640
  unprepared 674
unprovoked (616)
unpublished 526
unpunctual *tardy* 133
  untimely 135
  irregular 139
unpunished 970
unpurchased 796
unpurified 653
unpurposed 621
unpursued 624
unqualified
  incomplete 52
  impotent 158
  certain 474
  unprepared 674
  inexpert 699

  unentitled 925
  - truth 494
unquelled 173
unquenchable
  strong 159
  desire 865
unquenched
  violence 173
  heat 382
unquestionable
  certain 474
unquestionably
  assent 488
unquestioned 474
  agreed upon 488
unquiet *motion* 264
  agitation 315
  excitable 825
unravel *untie* 44
  arrange 60
  straighten 246
  evolve 313
  discover 480a
  interpret 522
  disembarrass 705
  (*solve* 462)
unreached 304
unread *ignorant* 491
unready 674
unreal *not existing* 2
  unsubstantial 4
  erroneous 495
  imaginary 515
unreasonable
  impossible 471
  illogical 477
  misjudging 481
  foolish 499
  capricious 608
  exorbitant 814
  unjust 923
  unreasoning 452
unreclaimed 951
unrecognizable 146
unreconciled 713
unrecorded 552
unrecounted 55
unrecumbent 212
unreduced 31
unrefined 851
unreflecting 458
unreformed 951
unrefreshed 688
unrefuted *proved* 478
  true 494
unregarded
  neglected 460
  unrespected 929
unregenerate 988
unregistered 552
unreined 748
unrelated 10
unrelenting
  pitiless 914a
  revengeful 919
  (*malevolent* 907)
unreliable
  uncertain 475
  vacillating 605
  insecure 665
unrelieved 835

excited 824
all - with
  destruction 162
  failure 732
  adversity 735
  prices looking - 814
  the game is - 735
  time - 111
  - and at them 716
  - and coming 698
  - and doing 682
  - and down 314
  - for discussion 454
  - in 698
  - in arms
    prepared 673
    active 682
    opposition 708
    attack 716
    resistance 719
    warfare 722
  - on end 212
  - to [see below]
Upanishads 986
upas tree 663
upbear support 215
  raise 307
upbraid 932
upcast 305, 307
upgrade 305, 654
upgrow 206
upgrowth
  expansion 194
  ascent 305
upheaval 146, 307
upheave 307
uphill acclivity 217
  ascent 305
  laborious 686
  difficult 704
uphoist 307
uphold continue 143
  support 215
  evidence 467
  aid 707
  praise 931
  preserve 976
upholder 488, 711
upholstery 633
upland 180
uplands 206, 344
uplift elevation 307
  improvement 658
upon - my honor 535
  - oath 535
  - which after 117
  future 121
upper 206
  - case printing 591
  - classes 875
  - hand influence 175
  success 731
  sway 737
  - story summit 210
  intellect 450
  wisdom 498

- ten thousand 875
uppermost summit 210
  say what comes - 612
  - in one's thoughts
  memory 505
  - in the mind
  thought 451
  topic 454
  attention 457
upraise 307
uprear 307
upright vertical 212
  straight 246
  honest 939
  - piano 417
uprise 305
uprising 146, 742
uproar disorder 59
  violence 173
  noise 404
uproarious
  excitable 825
uproariousness 404,
  825
uproot
  extract 301
  (destroy 162)
ups and downs of life
  events 151
  adversity 735
upset destroy 162
  invert 218
  throw down 308
  defeat 731
  excite 824
  disconcert 874
upshot result 154
  judgment 480
  completion 729
  (end 67)
upside down 218
upstairs 206
upstart newness 123
  prosperous 734
  plebeian 876
upstream
  with difficulty 704
up to time 106
  power 157
  knowing 490
  skillful 698
  - one's ears 641
  - one's eyes 641
  - snuff 702
  - the brim 52
  - the mark equal 27
  sufficient 639
  good 648
  due 924
  - the scratch 861
  - this time time 106
  past 122
upturn 210
upturned 305, 307
upward 305
  - flight 305

upwards 206
  - of more 33
  plurality 100
uranic 318
uranography 318
uranolite 318
uranology 318
uranometry 318
urban 189
urbane 894
urceole 998
urceus 191, 998
urchin child 129, 167
  small 193
  wretch 949
urge violence 173
  impel 276
  incite 615
  hasten 684
  beg 765
urgency need 865
  [see urgent]
urgent required 630
  important 642
  haste 684
  request 765
urn vase 191
  funeral 363
  heater 386
  cinerary - 363
Ursa Major 318
Ursa Minor 318
usable 644
usage custom 613
  use 677
  (rule 80)
usance 806
use habit 613
  waste 638
  utility 644
  employ 677
  property 780
  be of - to aid 707
  benevolence 906
  in - 677
  make good - of 658
  - a right 924
  - loosely 465a
  - one's discretion 600
  - one's endeavor 675
  - up 677
used to 613
used up deteriorated 659
  fatigue 688
  weary 841
  satiated 869
useful instrumental 633
  utility 644
  serviceable 746
  render - 677
useless   unproductive
  169
  wasted 638
  inutility 645
user 677
  right of - 780

Ushas 979
usher attendant 263
  receive 296
  teacher 540
  servant 746
  courtesy 894
  marriage 903
  - in precedence 62
  begin 66
  herald 116
  precession 280
  announce 511
  - into the world 161
usine 691
usquebaugh 959
ustulate 384
ustulation 384
usual ordinary 82
  customary 613
usucapion 777
usufruct 677
usurer lender 787
  merchant 797
  credit 805
  miser 819
usurious 819
usurp assume 739
  seize 789
  illegal 925
  - authority 738
usurpation
  [see usurp]
  authority 737
  insolence 885
usurper 706, 737
usury 806
utensil recipient 191
  instrument 633
utilitarian teaching 537
  useful 677
  philanthropy 910
utilitarianism 451
utility 644
  general - actor 599
utilize 677
utmost 33
  do one's - 686
  - height 210
Utopia visionary 515
  hopeful 858
utricle 191
utter extreme 31
  distribute 73
  disclose 529
  publish 531
  speak 580, 582
  money 800
utterance [see utter]
utterly completely 52
uttermost 31
  to the - parts of the
    earth
  space 180
  distance 196
uxoricide 361
uxorious 897

vacancy [*see* vacant]
- of mind 452
vacant *void* 4
  absent 187
  thoughtless 452
  unmeaning 517
  scanty 640
  - hour 685
  - mind *folly* 499
vacate *displace* 185
  absent 187
  depart 293
  resign 757
vacation *repose* 687
  (*leisure* 685)
vacatur 756
vaccine 366
vache 191
vacillate
  changeable 149
  undulate 314
  waver 605
vacuity 187, 452
vacuolar 357
vacuolation 161
vacuolization 161
vacuometer 338, 446
vacuous
  unsubstantial 4
  absent 187
  (*inexistent* 2)
vacuum *absence* 187
  - cleaner 652
vade mecum
  information 527
  schoolbook 542
vadium 771
vagabond *wanderer* 268
  low person 876
  rogue 949
vagabondage 266
vagary *absurdity* 497
  imagination 515
  whim 608
  antic 840
vagas 999
vaginate 223
vagitus 129
vagrant *changeable* 149
  roving 266
  traveler 268
  deviating 279
vague
  unsubstantial 4
  uncertain 475
  unreasoning 477
  unmeaning 517
  obscure 519
  - *language* 571
  - suggestion 514
vails *donation* 784
  reward 973
  (*expenditure* 809)
vain *unreal* 2
  unprofitable 645
  conceited 880
  in - *failure* 732
  labor in -
    come short 304
    useless 645
    fail 732

take a name in - 895
  use - efforts 645
  - attempt 732
  - expectation 509
vainglorious
  haughty 878
  vain 880
  boasting 884
vakas 999
vakil 968
valance 231
vale 252
  - of years 128
valediction *adieu* 293
  courtesy 894
valedictorian 293
valedictory 582
valentine 902
valet 631, 746
  - de chambre 746
  - de place
    interpreter 524
    guide 527
valetudinarian
  invalid 655.
  salubrity 656
valetudinarianism 655
Valhalla 981
valiant 861
valid *confirmed* 150
  powerful 157
  strong 159
  true 494
  sufficient 639
  (*influential* 179)
  - reasoning 476
valise 191
vallation 717
valley 252
  - of the shadow of
    death 360
vallum 717
valor 861
  for - 733
valorization 480
valuable *useful* 644
  good 648
value *color* 428
  measure 466
  estimate 480
  importance 642
  utility 644
  goodness 648
  price 812
  approbation 931
  of priceless - 814
  set a - upon 482
  - received 810
  -s *painting* 556
valueless 646
valve *stop* 263
  conduit 350
  safety - *safety* 664
  refuge 666
  escape 671
vambrace 717
vamose 293
vamp *change* 140
  seduce 615
  improvise 674
  - up *change* 140

improve 658
  restore 660
  prepare 673
vampire *tempter* 615
  taking 789
  evildoer 913
  demon 980
vampirism
  extortion 789
  sorcery 992
van *beginning* 66
  front 234
  wagon 272
  in the - 234
  precession 280
vancourier 64
Vandal *destroyer* 165
  vulgar 851
  commonalty 876
  evildoer 913
Vandalic 241
vandalism 851
vandyke 257
vandyke brown 433
vane
  changeableness 149
  wind 338, 349
  indication 550
vanfoss 717
vanguard 234
vanilla 298
vanish *unsubstantial* 4
  transient 111
  disappear 449
  (*cease to exist* 2)
vanishing *small* 32
  little 193
  disappearing 449
vanity *useless* 645
  conceit 880
Vanity Fair 852
vanquish 731
vantage ground
  superiority 33
  power 157
  influence 175
  height 206
vapid *insipid* 391
  - *style* 575
  (*unattractive* 866)
vaporarium 386
vaporization 336
vapor *gas* 334
  bubbles 353
  fancy 515
  boast 884
  insolence 885
  - bath 386
vaporer 887
vaporific 336
vaporous
  unsubstantial 4
  vaporization 336
  imaginative 515
  (*opaque* 426)
vapors *dejection* 837
vaquero 370
vargueno 191
variable *irregular* 139
  changeable 149
  irresolute 605

variance *difference* 15
  disagreement 24
  discord 713
  at - *enmity* 889
  at - with 489
  at - with the fact 471
variation *difference* 15
  dissimilarity 18
  diverseness 20a
  number 84
  chance 140
  music 415
varicella 655
varicose 655
varied 15
  - assortment 81
variegated 428, 440
variegation 440
variety *difference* 15
  class 75
  multiformity 81
  exception 83
  - the spice of life 81
variform 81
variola 655
variometer 157, 466
variorum 596
various *different* 15
  many 102
  - places 182
  - times 119
varlet 949
varnish *overlay* 223
  resin 352, 356a
  sophistry 477
  falsehood 544
  painting 556
  decorate 847
  excuse 937
Varuna 318, 979
vary *differ* 15
  dissimilar 18
  variation 20a
  change 140
  fluctuate 149
vascular *cells* 191
  holes 260
  pipes 350
vasculum 191
vase 191
vassal 746
vassalage 749
vast *great* 31
  spacious 180
  large 192
  - learning 490
vasty 180, 192
  - deep 341
vat 191
Vatican *churchdom* 995
  temple 1000
  thunders of the - 908
vaticide 361
vaticination 511
vaudeville 599
vault *cellar* 191
  curve 245
  convexity 250
  leap 309
  tomb 363
  - of heaven 318

vaulted *curved* 245
   concave 252
vaulting *superior* 33
   aspiring 865
vaunt 884
vauntmure 717
vaurien 949
vavasour *possessor* 779
   nobleman 875
veal 298
vection 270
Vedanta 451
Vedantism 984
Vedas 986
vedette 668
Vedic 124
veer *change* 140
   deviate 279
   go back 283
   change intention 607
vega 344
vegetability 365
vegetable 298, **367**
   - kingdom 367
   - life 365
   - oil 356
   - physiology 369
vegetality 365
vegetarian 298, 367,
   953
vegetarianism 298
vegetate *exist* 1
   grow 194, 365, 367
   inactive 683
   insensible 823
vegetation 365
   inaction 681
vegetative 365, 367
vegetism 365
vehemence
   violence 173
   feeling 821
   emotion 825
vehement
   - language 574
vehicle *carriage* **272**
   instrument 631
vehicular 272
veil *covering* 225
   shade 424
   conceal 528
   ambush 530
   draw aside the - 529
   take the - seclude 893
   church 995
veiled 475
   (invisible) 447)
vein *intrinsicality* 5
   tendency 176
   thin 203
   thread 205
   conduit 350
   humor 602
   mine 636
   affections 820
   in the - 602
   not in the - 603
veined 440
veinlet 205
veldt 344
veldtschoen 225
728

velitation 720
velleity 600
vellicate 315
vellicating 392
vellicative 315, 392
vellum 590
velo 466
veloce *music* 415
velocimeter 274
velocipede 272
velocity
   rate of motion 264
   swiftness **274**
   angular - 244
velumen 255
velutinous 255
velvet *smooth* 255
   pile 256
   pleasure 377
   fabric 635
   on - easy 705
velveteen 255
vena 350
venal *price* 812
   stingy 819
   dishonest 940
   selfish 943
venation 622
vend 796
vendaval 349
vendee 795
vender 796
vendetta 919
vendible 796
venditation 884
vendor 796
vendue 796
veneer *layer* 204
   covering 223
venenation 659
venerable *old* 124
   aged 128
   sage 500
   respected 928
venerated 500
veneration *respect* 928
   piety 987
venereal disease 655
venery *killing* 361
   hunting 622
   impurity 961
venesection
   ejection 297
   remedy 662
Venetian blinds 351,
   424
vengeance 919
   cry to heaven for -
   923
   with a - greatly 31
   violent 173
vengeful 919
venial 937
venire 969
   - facias 969
venison 298, 394
vennel 627
venom *bane* 663
   malignity 907
venomous *bad* 649
   poisonous 657

   dangerous 666
   rude 895
   maleficent 907
venose 205
vent *opening* 260
   egress 295
   air pipe 351
   disclose 529
   escape 671
   sale 796
   find - egress 295
   passage 302
   publish 531
   escape 671
   give - or emit 297
   disclose 529
   - one's rage 900
   - one's spleen 900
ventage 351
venter 191
venthole 260, 351
ventiduct 351
ventilabrum 349
ventilate *begin* 66
   air 338
   wind 349
   discuss 595
   - a question
   inquiry 461
   reasoning 476
ventilative 349
ventilator *wind* 349
   air pipe 351
ventose 349
ventosity 349
vent peg *stopper* 263
   safety 666
   escape 671
ventricle 191
ventricose 250
ventriloquism 580
ventriloquist 580
venture *experiment* 463
   presume 472
   chance 621
   danger 665
   try 675
   undertaking 676
   invest 787
   courage 861
   I'll - to say 535
venturesome
   undertaking 676
   brave 861
   rash 863
venue 74, 183
venula 205
Venus
   luminary 318, 423
   -'s flytrap 545
   beauty 845
   love 897
veracity 543
veranda 191
verbal 562
   - intercourse
   speech 582
   interlocution 588
   - quibble
   absurdity 497
   wit 842

verbarian 562
verbatim *imitation* 19
   exact 494
   literal 516
   words 562
   - report 551
verbiage
   unmeaning 517
   words 562
   diffuse 573
   (absurdity 497)
verbosity *words* 562
   diffuse 573
   loquacity 584
verdant
   vegetation 367
   green 435
verd antique 435
verdict *opinion* 480
   lawsuit 969
   snatch a - cheat 545
   cunning 702
verdigris 435
verdine 435
verditer 435
verdure *vegetation* 3(7
   green 435
verecundity
   humility 879
   modesty 881
Verein 712
verge *tendency* 176
   near 197
   edge 231
   limit 233
   direction 278
vergent 67
verger 996
veridical 467, 543
   - hallucination 992a
veriest 31
verification *test* 463
   warrant 771
verificative 467
verify 463
   evidence 467
   demonstrate 478
   find out 480a
verily *truly* 494
   (positively 32)
verisimilitude 472
veritable 1, 494
verity 494
verjuice 397
vermeology 368
vermes 368
vermicelli 298
vermicular
   convoluted 248
   worm 366
vermiculation 221
vermiform 248, 249
vermifuge 662
vermilion 434
vermin *animal* 366
   unclean 653
   base 876
vernacular *native* 188
   internal 221
   language 560
   habitual 613

vernal *early* 123
  spring 125
vernier
  minuteness 193
  - scale 466
Vernunft 450
veronica 993
verruca 250
versatile
  changeable 149
  (*irresolute* 605)
  (*fickle* 607)
verse *division* 51
  poetry 597
versed in
  knowledge 490
  (*skill* 698)
versicolor 440
versify 597
version *special* 79
  change 140
  interpretation 522
Verstand 450
versus *towards* 278
  against 708
vert 435
vertebra 215, 222
vertebral 222, 235
  - column 222
vertebrate 368
vertebration 357
vertex 210
vertical 212, 246
  - rays 382
verticality **212**
verticity 312
vertigo *rotation* 312
  delirium 503
verve *imagination* 515
  vigorous language
    574
  activity 682
  feeling 821
very 31
  - best 648
  - image 554
  - many 102
  - minute 113
  - much 31
  - picture 17
  - small 32
  - thing identity 13
  agreement 23
  exact 494
  - true assent 488
  - well content 831
vesicatory 662
vesicle *cell* 191
  covering 223
  globe 249
vesicular *cells* 191
  holes 260
vesper 126
vespers 126, 990
vespertine
  evening 126
vessel *receptacle* 191
  tube 260
  ship 273
vest *place* 184
  dress 225

- in belong to **777**
  give 784
vesta *match* 388
vestal 960
  - virgin 904
vested *fixed* 150
  legal 963
  - in located 184
  - interest given 780
  due 924
vestibule *entrance* 66
  room 191
  hearing 418
vestige 551
vestigial 193
vestment *dress* 225
  canonicals 999
vestry *council* 696
  churchdom 995
  church 1000
vesture 225
vesuvian *match* 388
vet *veterinarian* 370
veteran *old* **130**
  adept 700
  warrior 726
veterinarian 370
veterinary *art* 370
veto 761
vettura 272
vetturino 694
vetust 124
vex 830, 898
vexation *pain* 828, 830
  - of spirit 828
  discontent 832
vexatious 830
vexed question
  difficulty 704
  discord 713
vexillum 550
viâ *direction* 278
  way 627
viable 359
viaduct 627
viagraph 466
vial 191
  -s of hate 898
  -s of wrath 900
via lactea 318
viameter 200
viands 298
viaticum *provision* 637
  rite 998
viatometer 200
vibrate 314
  *- between two ex-
    tremes* 149
vibratile 314
vibration 314, 408
vibratiuncle 314
vibrative 314
vibratory
  changeable 149
vibrograph 314
vibroscope 314
vicar *deputy* 759
  clergyman 996
  - of Bray
  changeableness 149
  tergiversation 607

  servility 886
vicarage 1000
vicarial 147
vicariate 995
vicarious *substitute* 147
vicarship 995
vice *pinion* 752
  deputy 759
  wickedness **945**
vice-admiral 745
vice-chairman 759
Vice-Chancellor 967
  -'s Court 966
vicegerency 755
vicegerent 758, 759
vicenary 98
vice-president 694, 759
vice-regal 759
viceroy *governor* 745
  deputy 759
vicesimal 98
vice versâ
  reciprocal 12
  contrary 14
  interchange 148
vicinage 197, 227
vicinal 197
vicinism 145
vicinity 197, 227
vicious 173, 945
  render - 659
  - reasoning 477
vicissitude
  changeable 149
  (*change* 140)
victim *dupe* 547
  defeated 732
  sufferer 828
  culprit 975
victimize *kill* 361
  deceive 545
  injure 649
  baffle 731
victimized 828
victor 731
victoria *carriage* 272
Victoria Cross 551, 722,
  733
victory 731
victrola 417, 418
victual *provide* 637
victuals 298
videlicet
  specification 79
  namely 522
  (*example* 82)
viduation 905
viduity 905
vie *good* 648
  - with contend 720
  (*oppose* 708)
vielle 417
view *sight* 441
  appearance 448
  attend to 457
  opinion 484
  landscape painting
    556
  intention 520
  bring into - 525
  come into - 446

  commanding - 441
  in - visible 446
  intended 420
  expected 507
  keep in - 457
  on - 448
  present to the - 448
  - as 484
  - halloo 411
  - in a new light 658
  -s tenet 484
  with a - to 620
viewer 444
viewless 447
viewpoint 441, 453
vigesimal 98
vigil *care* 459
vigilance *care* 459
  wisdom 498
  activity 682
vigilant 864
vigils *worship* 990
vigneron 371
vignette *engraving* 558
  sketch 594
  embellishment 847
vigor *strength* 159
  energy 171
  style **574**
  resolution 604
  health 654
  activity 682
viking 792
vile *valueless* 643
  hateful 649
  painful 830
  disgraceful 874
  plebeian 876
  dishonorable 940
  vicious 945
vilification 908
vilify *shame* 874
  censure 932
  detract 934
  (*disrespect* 929)
  (*contempt* 930)
vilipend
  disrespect 929
  censure 932
  detract 934
vilipendency 930
villa 189
village 189
  - talk 588
villager 188
villain *servant* 746
  serf 876
  rascal 949
villainous *evil* 649
  wicked 945
  - saltpeter 727
villainy 940
vellein [*see* villein]
villenage
  subjection 749
  tenure 777
villi 256
villous 256
vim 171, 682
vina 417
vinaceous 434

W

waste *decrease* 36
  decrement 40a
  destroy 162
  unproductive 169
  space 180
  contract 195
  plain 344
  consumption **638**
  useless 645
  spoiled 659
  misuse 679
  loss 776
  prodigality 818
  run to -
   superfluity 641
  deteriorate 659
 - away 655
 - of years 151
 - time *inactive* 683
 watery - 341
wasted *weak* 160
  deteriorated 659
wasteful 818
waste paper
 of no force 158
 - bonds 808
waste pipe 350
waster *neglect* 460
 prodigal 818
wastethrift 818
wasting 638
 wide - 649
wastrel *vagrant* 268
 neglect 460
 outcast 893
watch *company* 72
 clock 114
 observe 441
 attend to 457
 take care of 459
 expect 507
 guardian 664
 warning 668
 keeper 573
 death - *death* 360
 warning 668
 on the - *vigilant* 459
 expectant 507
 - and ward *care* 459
 keeper 573
 - for 507
watchdog *guardian* 664
 warning 668
 keeper 753
watcher 459
watchet 438
watch fire 550
watchful 459
 - waiting
 inaction 681
 caution 864
watchhouse 752
 in the - 938
watchman
 guardian 664
 sentinel 668
 keeper 753
watchman's rattle 417
watchtower *view* 441
 signal 550
 warning 668

watchword *sign* 550
 military 722
water 337
 - animals 370
 transparent 425
 back - 283
 cast one's bread upon
  the -s 638
 depth of - 208
 great -s 341
 hold - *proof* 478
 truth 494
 [keep one's head
  above] - 664
 land covered with -
  343
 of the first - 648
 pour - into a sieve 638
 running - 348
 spend money like -
  818
 throw cold - on 174
 walk the -s 267
water carrier 348
water color 556
water course 350
water cress 298
water cure 662
water dog 269, 361
water drinker 958
watered
 variegated 440
waterfall 348
water gap 350
water glass 556
water gruel 160
watering - cart 348
 - place 189
 - pot 348
waterless 340
water-logged
 powerless 158
 danger 665
 hindrance 706
waterman 269
watermelon 298
water nymph 979
water pipe 350
water polo 840
waterproof *dress* 225
 dry 340
 protection 664
water qualm 655
waters
 on the face of the -
  180
 - of bitterness 830
 - of oblivion 506
watershed 210
water spaniel 366
waterspout 348
water-tight
 closed 261
 dry 340
 protection 664
water wheel 633
waterworks 350
watery *wet* 337
 moist 339
 feeble style 575
 - eyes 839

- grave 360
wattle 219
wattmeter 157
Wat Tyler 742
wave *sinuous* 248
 oscillate 314
 - of water 348
 [see waive]
 - a banner 550
 - a wand 992
waver *changeable* 149
 doubt 485
 irresolute 605
waverer 605
waves 341
 buffet the -
 navigate 267
 difficult 704
 oppose 708
 lash the - 645
 plow the - 267
waveson 73
wavy 248
wax *increase* 35
 become 144
 expand 194
 soft 324
 lubrication 332
 viscid 352
 substance 356
 close as - 528
 - and wane 140
wax candle 423
waxed 356a
waxwork 554
waxy *unctuous* 355
 irate 900
way *degree* 26
 space 180
 habit 613
 road 627
 by the -
 in transitu 270
 accidental 621
 by - of *direction* 278
 method 627
 fall in the - of 186
 fight one's -
 pursue 622
 warfare 722
 find its - 302
 gather - 267
 get into the - of 613
 go one's - 293
 go your - 297
 have one's own -
 will 600
 easy 705
 succeed 731
 authority 737
 freedom 748
 havo - on 267
 in a bad - 655
 in a - *pained* 828
 in the - *near* 197
 in the - of
 hinder 706
 oppose 708
 it must have its - 601
 let it have its - 681
 long - off 196

make one's -
 journey 266
 progression 282
 passage 302
 prosperity 734
make - 302
make - for
 substitution 147
 opening 260
 turn aside 279
 avoid 623
 facilitate 705
 courtesy 894
not know which - to
 turn 475
on the - 282
place in one's -
 offer 763
put in the - of
 enable 470
 teach 537
see one's - 490
show the - 693
under - *move* 264
 sail 267
 progression 282
 depart 293
 - in 294
 - of escape 617
 - of speaking 521
 - of thinking 484
 - out 295
 wing one's - 267
Way, the - 976
wayfarer 268
wayfaring 266
waylay *deception* 545
 cunning 702
wayless 261
ways 692
 inall manner of - 278
 - and means
 means 632
 money 800
wayward
 changeable 149
 obstinate 606
 capricious 608
 sullen 901a
wayworn
 journey 266
 fatigue 688
wayzgoose 840
weak *feeble* 160
 water 337
 insipid 391
 illogical 477
 foolish 499
 - style 575
 irresolute 605
 trifling 643
 lax 738
 compassionate 914
 vicious 945
 (small 32)
 expose one's - point
 confute 479
 - point *illogical* 477
 imperfection 651
 - side *folly* 499
 vice 945

well-founded
existent 1
probable 472
certain 474
- *belief* 484
true 494
well-grounded
existent 1
informed 490
- *hope* 858
well-grouped 845
wellhead 153
well-informed 490
Wellington boots 225
well-intentioned
benevolent 906
virtuous 944
well-knit *strong* 159
well-known
knowledge 490
habitual 613
well-laid 611
well-made *form* 240
beauty 845
well-mannered 894
well-marked 446
well-meaning 906
well-meant 906
well-met 894
well-natured 906
well-nigh *almost* 32
near 197
well-off *prosperous* 734
rich 803
well-proportioned 240,
845
well-provided 639
well-regulated
order 58
conformity 82
circumspect 864
well-set 242
well-spent
successful 731
virtuous 944
wellspring 153, 636
well-timed 134
well-to-do
prosperous 734
rich 803
well-turned periods
578
well-weighed 611
wellwisher 890, 906,
914
Welsh 188
- *rabbit* 298
welsher *swindler* 792
nonpayment 808
welt 321
welter *plunge* 310
roll 311
- *in one's blood* 361
wem 848
wen 250, 848
wench *girl* 129
woman 374
peasant 876
impure 962
wenching 961
wend 266

were, as you - 660
wergild 974
werewolf 980
werowance 745
Wesleyan 984
west *lateral* 236
direction 278
westing 196
Westminster
superior courts of -
966
westward 236
wet *water* 337, 348
moist 339
just enough to - one's
feet 209
- blanket
dissuade 616
hindrance 706
sadden 837
weary 841
dull 843
- one's whistle
drink 298
tipple 959
wether 366
whack 276
whacking *large* 31, 192
whale *large* 192
mammal 366
sprat to catch a - 699
tub to a -
deception 545
excuse 617
whalebone 325
whaler 273
whap 276
wharf *houses* 189
refuge 666
workshop 691
mart 799
wharfage 812
wharf boat 273
what *inquiry* 461
wonder 870
and - not 81
know -'s what
discriminate 465
intelligent 498
skill 698
- d'ye call 'em 563
- in the world
singular 83
wonderful 870
- is the reason? 461
- next 455
- on earth *singular* 83
-'s his name 563
- signifies 643
whatever 78
- may happen 474
wheal 250
wheat 367
winnow the chaff
from the - 609
Wheat Pit *mart* 799
wheedle *coax* 615
endearment 902
flatter 933
wheedler 615
wheel *circle* 247

convexity 250
bicycle 272
deviate 279
turn back 283
circuition 311
rotation 312
rack 975
break on the -
pain 478
punish 972
get the - out of the
rut 672
scotch the - 706
- about 279
- and axle 633
- guard 666
- of Fortune
changeable 149
chance 156
rotation 312
necessity 601
- round *inversion* 218
tergiversation 607
-s within wheels
entangled 59
machinery 633
wheelbarrow 272
wheel chair 272
wheelman 268, 269
wheelwork 633
wheelwright 690
wheeze *blow* 349
hiss 409
wheezy 409
whelk 250, 848
whelm 641
whelp *infant* 129
production 161
dog 366
rogue 949
when *inquiry* 461
(*different time* 119)
in the time - 106
whence
attribution 155
departure 293
inquiry 461
reasoning 476
where
presence 186
inquiry 461
- am I? 870
whereabouts
place 182
situation 183
near 197
whereas *relating to* 9
because 476
whereby 631
wherefore
attribution 155
inquiry 461
reasoning 476
judgment 480
motive 615
wherein 221
whereness 186
whereupon *time* 106
different time 119
after 121
wherever 180, 182

wherewith *means* 632
money 800
wherewithal 639
wherret 830
wherry 273
whet *sharpen* 253
meal 298
incite 615
excite 824
take a - *tipple* 959
- the appetite 865
- the knife 673
whether 514
- or not 609
whetstone 253
which at - time 119
know - is which 465
whiff *wind* 349
excitement 825
whiffet 129, 349
whiffle 349
Whig 274, 712
while *time* 106
(same time 120)
in a - 132
- away time *time* 106
inaction 681
pastime 840
worth - 646
whilom 122
whilst 106
whim *fancy* 515
caprice 608
wet 842
desire 865
whimper 839
whimsical [*see* whim]
ridiculous 853
whimsey *fancy* 515
caprice 608
desire 865
whimwham
imagination 515
caprice 608
unimportance 643
whin 367, 407
whine *cry* 411
complain 839
whinyard 727
whip *coachman* 268
strike 276
stir up 315
- *a horse* 366
indication 550
urge 615
hasten 684
director 694
flog 972
scourge 975
- and spur *swift* 274
- away *depart* 293
- hand *success* 731
authority 737
- in 300 *collect* 72
- on 684
- off 293
- up 789
whipcord 205
whipped cream 298
whipper-in 694
whippersnapper 129

whipping post 975
whipster 129
whir *rotate* 312
  sound 407
whirl *rotate* 312
  flurry 825
whirligig 312
whirlpool *rotate* 312
  agitation 315
  water 348
  danger 667
whirlwind *disorder* 59
  agitation 315
  wind 349
reap the - *product* 154
  fail 732
ride the -
  resolution 604
  authority 737
whisk *rapid* 274
  circuition 311
  agitation 315
  sweep 652
- off 297
whisker 256
whisket 191
whisky 272, 298, 959
whisper
  faint sound 405
  tell 527
  conceal 528
  voice 580
  stammer 583
stage - 580
- about *disclose* 529
  publish 531
- in the ear
  voice 580
whist *hush* 403
  cards 840
whistle *wind* 349
  hiss 409
  stridor 410
  play music 416
  musical instrument 417
clean as a -
  thorough 52
  perfect 650
  neatly 652
pay too dear for one's -
  inexpedient 647
  unskillful 699
  dear 814
wet one's - *drink* 298
  tipple 959
- at 930
- for *request* 765
  desire 865
- for want of thought
  inaction 681
- jigs to a milestone 645
whit *small* 32
  (*part* 51)
white 430
  probity 939
mark with a - stone
  important 642
  approve 931
736

stand in a - sheet 952
- ant 690
- as a sheet 860
- feather 862
- flag 723
- friar 996
- frost 383
- heat 382
- horses 348
- lead 430
- lie *equivocal* 520
  concealment 528
  untruth 546
  plea 617
- liver 862
- man *probity* 939
- metal 430, 545
- of the eye 441
- plague 655
- slave 962
- wings *cleaner* 652
whitechapel
  vehicle 272
whiten 429, 430
whiteness 430
whitening 430
whites 299
whitewash *cover* 223
  whiten 430
  materials 635
  cleanse 652
  ornament 847
  justify 937
  acquit 970
whitewashed
get - 808
whitewasher 935
whitey *brown* 433
whither *tendency* 176
  direction 278
  inquiry 461
whiting *fish* 298
  pigment 430
whitish 430
whitleather *tough* 327
Whitmonday 840
Whitsuntide 998
whittle *cut* 44
  knife 253
whittled *drunk* 959
whiz 409
who 461
- would have thought?
  inexpectation 508
  wonder 870
whole *entire* 50
  healthy 654
go the - hog 729
make - 660
on the - *reasoning* 476
  judgment 480
the - time 106
- truth *truth* 494
  disclosure 529
  veracity 543
wholesale
  large scale 31
  whole 50
  abundant 639
  trade 794
  sell 796

wholesome 502, 656
whole-souled 944
wholly *entirely* 50
  completely 52
whoop 411
-ing cough 655
war - *defiance* 715
  warfare 722
whop *flog* 972
whopper *size* 192
  lie 546
whopping *huge* 192
whore 962
whoredom 961
whoremonger 962
whorl 248
whortleberry 298
who's who 86
why *cause* 153
  attribution 155
  inquiry 461
  indeed 535
  motive 615
wibble-wabble 314
wick *fuel* 388
  luminary 423
wicked 945
the - *bad men* 949
  impious 988
the - one 978
wickedness 945
wicker 219
wicket *entrance* 66
  gateway 260
wide *general* 78
  space 180
  broad 202
in the - world 180
- apart *different* 15
- awake *hat* 225
  intelligent 298
- away 196
- berth 748
- of *distant* 196
- of the mark
  distance 196
  deviation 279
  error 495
- of the truth 495
- open *expanded* 194
  opening 260
- reading 539]
- world 180, 318
widen 194
- the breach
  quarrel 713
  anger 900
widespread *great* 31
  dispersed 73
  space 180
  expanded 194
widow 905
widowhood 905
width 202
wield *brandish* 315
  handle 379
  use 677
- authority 737
- the sword 722
wieldy 705
wife 903

wifeless 904
wig 225
wigging 932
wight 373
wigmaker 599
wigwam 189, 223
wild *unproductive* 169
  violent 173
  space 180
  plain 344
  vegetation 365
  inattentive 458
  mad 503
  shy 623
  unskilled 699
  excited 824, 825
  untamed 851
  rash 863
  angry 900
  licentious 954
run - 825
sow one's - oats
  grow up 131
  improve 658
  amusement 840
  vice 945
  intemperance 954
- animals 366
- beast *fierce* 173
  evildoer 913
- cinnamon 400
- clove 400
- duck 298
- goose chase
  caprice 608
  useless 645
  unskillful 699
- imagination 515
Wild, Jonathan
  thief 792
  bad man 949
wildcat 366, 665
wilderness *disorder* 59
  unproductive 169
  space 180
  solitude 893
- of sweets 827
wildfire 382
spread like -
  violence 173
  influence 175
  expand 194
  publication 531
wilding 893
wildness [see *wild*]
wile *deception* 545
  cunning 702
will *volition* 600
  resolution 604
  testament 771
  gift 784
at - 600
have one's own - 600
  freedom 748
make one's -
  death 360
tenant at - 779
- and will not 605
- be 152
- for the deed
  compromise 774

at one's -'s end
uncertain 475
difficulty 704
mother - 498
soul of - 572
to - 522
witan 696
witch *oracle* 513
ugly 846
sorceress 994
(*proficient* 700)
witchcraft 978, 992
witchery
attraction 615
pleasing 829
sorcery 992
witching time
midnight 126
dark 421
wit-cracker 844
witenagemote 696
with *added* 37
mixed 41
ligature 45
accompanying 88
means 632
(*joined* 43)
go - 178
- all its parts 52
- **a** sting to it 770
- a vengeance
great 31
complete 52
- a witness 31
- regard to 9
withal *in addition* 37
accompanying 88
withdraw *subduct* 38
absent 187
turn back 283
recede 287
depart 293
- from *rexant* 607
relinquish 624
dislike 867
withdrawal
[*see* withdraw]
rejection 610
withe 45
wither *shrink* 195
decay 659
- one's hopes 837
withered *weak* 160
disease 655
withering *harsh* 739
painful 830
contempt 930
censure 932
withers 250
- unwrung *strong* 159
insensible 323
withhold *hide* 528
restrain 751
prohibit 761
retain 781
stint 819
- one's assent 764
within 221
derived from - 5
keep - 221
place - 221
738

- an ace 32
- bounds *small* 32
shortcoming 304
restraint 751
- call 197
- ccmpass
shortcoming 304
temperate 953
- one's memory 505
- reach *near* 197
easy 705
- the mark 304
without *unless* 8
subduction 38
exception 83
absence 187
exterior 220
circumjacent 227
exemption 777a
derived from - 6
not be able to do -
630
- a dissentient voice
488
- a leg to stand on 158
- alloy 827
- a rap 804
- a shadow of turning
141
- ballast *irresolute* 605
unprincipled 945
- ceasing 136
- ceremony 881
- charge 815
- end *infinite* 105
perpetual 112
- exception 16
- excuse 945
- fail *certain* 474
persevering 604a
- fear of contradiction
535
- God 989
- limit 105
- measure 105
- notice 508
- number 105
- parallel 33
- reason 499
- regard to 10
- reluctance 602
- reserve 525
- rime or reason 615a
- stint 639
- warning 508
withstand *oppose* 708
resist 719
(*counteract* 179)
withy 45
witless 491
witling *fool* 501
wag 844
witness *see* 441
spectator 444
evidence 467
voucher 550
call to - 467
witness box 966
wits 450
all one's - about one
care 459

intelligence 498
skin 698
live by one's -
deceive 545
skill 698
cunning 702
steal 791
dishonorable 940
one's - gone a wool-
gathering 458
set one's - to work
think 451
invent 515
plan 626
witsnapper 844
witticism 842
wittingly 620
wittol 962
witty 842, 844
be - 498
wive 903
wivern 83
wizard *sage* 500
deceiver 548
proficient 700
sorcerer 994
- of the air 269
wizen *wither* 195
throat 260
woe *pain* 828
evil 619
- betide
malediction 908
pity 914
- is me 839
- to' 908
woebegone 828
sad 837
woeful *bad* 649
painful 830
woefully *very* 31
wold 344
wolf *ravenous* 865
cry - *false* 544
alarm 669
fear 860
hold the - by the ears
704
keep the - from the
door 359
unable to keep the -
from the door 804
- and the lamb 923
- at the door
source of danger 667
poverty 804
- in sheep's clothing
deceiver 548
knave 941
wolfish 789
woman *adult* 131
human **374**
- of the town 962
- perfected 374
- the lesser man 374
woman hater 911
womanhood 131, 374
womanish 374
womankind 374
womanly
adolescent 131

feminine 374
womb *cause* 153
interior 221
- of time *future* 121
destiny 152
womerah 727
wonder *exception* 83
superexcellence 646
astonishment **870**
prodigy 872
do -s *activity* 682
succeed 731
for a - 870
nine days' - 643
not - 507
-s of the world 872
- whether
uncertain 475
ignorant 491
suppose 514
wonderfully
greatly 31
wonderworking 870
wondrous 870
wont *habitual* 613
(*conformity* 82)
won't do, it -
disapproval 932
woo *desire* 865
courtship 902
wooer 897
wood *trees* 367
material 635
not out of the -
danger 665
difficulty 704
- lot 232
woodbine
gone where the -
twineth 771
woodchuck day 138
woodcut 558
woodcutter 371
wooded, well - 256
wooden 635
- horse 975
- spoon 493
- walls *defense* 717
men-of-war 726
wood engraving 558
woodlands 367
wood-note 412
wood nymph 979
wood pavement 255
wood pigeon 366
woodwind 416
woody 367
woof 329
wool *flocculent* 256
warm 382
wrap 384
fabric 635
much cry and little -
482
woolgathering 458
woolly 255, 256
woolpack *cloud* 353
woolsack *pillow* 215
authority 747
tribunal 966
woon 745

Wop 57
word *maxim* 496
  intelligence 532
  assertion 535
  volable **562**
  phrase 566
  command 741
  promise 768
  give the - 741
  good as one's -
  veracious 543
  complete 729
  probity 939
  in a - 572
  keep one's - 939
  man of his - 939
  not a - to say
  silent 585
  humble 879
  pass - 550
  put in a - 582
  take at one's -
  believe 484
  consent 762
  upon my - 535
  watch - *military* 722
  - and a blow
  hasty 684
  contentious 720
  irascible 901
  - for word
  imitation 19
  truth 494
  - it 566
  - of command
  indication 550
  military 722
  command 741
  - in the ear
  information 527
  allocution 586
  - of honor 768
  - of mouth 582
  - to the wise
  intelligible 518
  advice 695
Word *Deity* 573
  - of God £85
wordbook 86
word-catcher 936
wordiness 562, 573
wording 569
wordless 581
word painter 594
word painting 515
word play
  equivocal 520
  neology 563
  wit 842
words *quarrel* 713
  bandy - 588
  bitter - 932
  choice of - 569
  command of - 574
  express by - 566
  flow of - *eloquence* 582
  loquacity 584
  mere - *sophistry* 477
  unmeaning 517
  no - can paint 872
  play of - 842

put into - 566
war of - *interlocution*
  588
  contest 720
  - that burn 574
  - with *censure* 932
wordy 562, 573
work *product* 154
  operation 170
  pass and repass 302
  ferment 320
  writing 590
  book 593
  business 625
  use 677
  action 680
  exertion 686
  ornament 847
  at - *in operation* 170
  business 625
  doing 680
  active 682
  earth - 717
  field - 717
  hard - *exertion* 686
  difficulty 704
  piece of -
  importance 642
  discord 713
  stick to - 604a
  stitch of - 686
  stroke of - 686
  - a change 140
  - against time 684
  - for 707
  - hard *exertion* 686
  difficult 704
  - ill 732
  - in 228
  - of art *beauty* 845,847
  (*painting* 556)
  (*sculpture* 557)
  (*engraving* 558)
  - of fiction 594
  - of reference 636
  - one's way
  progress 282
  ascent 305
  exertion 686
  succeed 731
  - towards *tend* 176
  - up [*see below*]
  - upon *influence* 175
  incite 615
  excite 824
  - out *conduct* 692
  complete 729
  - out one's salvation
  990
  - well *easy* 705
  successful 731
  - wonders *active* 682
  succeed 731
workability 490
workable 490
workableness 470
workaday *business* 625
  active 682
worker 686, 690, 746
workhouse 691
  prison 752

working *acting* 170
  active 682
  - bee 690
  - man 690
  - order 673
  - towards 176
workman 690
workmanlike 698
workmanship
  production 161
  action 680
works [*see* work]
  board of - 696
  good - 906
  - of the mind 451
workshop **691**
work up
  prepare 673
  use 677
  excite 824
  - into *form* 240
  - into a passion 900
workwoman 690
world *great* 31
  events 151
  space 180
  universe **318**
  mankind 372
  fashion 852
  (*events* 151)
  all the - over 180
  as the - goes 613
  a - of 102
  citizen of the - 910
  come into the - 359
  follow to the -'s end
  743
  for all the - 615
  give to the - 531
  knowledge of the - 698
  man of the -
  proficient 700
  fashion 852
  not for the -
  dissent 489
  refusal 764
  organized - 357
  pendent - 173
  Prince of this - 978
  rise in the - 734
  throughout the - 180
  - and his wife 102
  - beyond the grave
  152
  - forgetting, by the
  world forgot 893
  - of good *good* 618
  do good 648
  - principle 359
  - soul 359
  - spirit 359
  - to come 152
  - wisdom *skill* 698
  caution 864
  selfishness 943
  - without end 112
worldling *selfish* 943
  impious 988
worldly *selfish* 943
  irreligious 989
  - wisdom 864

world-wide *great* 31
  universal 78
  space 180
worm *small* 193
  spiral 248
  animal 366, 368
  bane 663
  food for -s 362
  - in 228
  - oneself *ingress* 294
  love 897
  - one's way *slow* 275
  passage 302
  - out 480a
  - that never dies 982
worm-eaten 659
wormwood
  gall and - 395
worn *weak* 160
  damage 659
  fatigue 688
  well - *used* 677
worn-out 659
  weary 841
worry *vexation* 828
  tease 830
  harass 907
worse
  deteriorated 659
  aggravated 835
  - for wear 160
worship *title* 877
  servility 886
  venerate 987
  religious **990**
  idolize 991
  demon - 991
  idol - 991
  fire - 991
  his - 967
  place of - 1000
  - Mammon 803
  - the rising sun 886
worshiper 990
worshipful 873
worst *defeat* 731
  do one's - *injure* 659
  spite 907
  do your - *defiance* 715
  threat 909
  have the - of it 732
  make the - of 482
  worst come to the -
  certain 474
  bad 649
  hopeless 859
worth *value* 644
  goodness 648
  possession 777
  price 812
  virtue 944
  penny - 812
  what one is - 780
  - a great deal 803
  - one's salt 644
  - the money 815
  - while 646
worthless *trifling* 643
  useless 645
  profligate 945
  - residue 645

X

*y*ach 508
*y*acht 273
*y*achting 267
*y*affie 25
*y*ager 726
Yahoo 702
*y*ak 366
*y*anı 298
Yama 979
*y*ammer 839
*y*ank 285
Yankee 188
*y*ap 406, 411, 412
*y*aıd *abode* 189
 length 200
 inclosure 232
 workshop 691
*y*ardarm to *y*ardarm
 197
*y*ardman 746
*y*are 682
*y*arn *filament* 205
 untruth 546
 exaggeration 549
 ınıngled - 41
 spin a long - 549
 diffuse style 573
*y*arr 412
*y*arrow 662
*y*ataghan 727
*y*aup 411, 412
*y*aw 279
*y*awl *ship* 273
 cry 412
*y*awn *open* 260
 sleepy 683
 tired 688
 weary 841
*y*awning
 gulf 198
 deep 208
y-cleped 564

*y*ea *more* 33
 assent 488
*y*ean 161
*y*ear *time* 106
 period 108
 all the - round 110
 since the - one 124
 tenant from - to year
  779
 - after year 104
*y*ear-book 138
*y*earling 129, 366
*y*early 138
*y*earn *pain* 828
 sad 837
 - for *desire* 865
 pity 914
*y*earning *love* 897
*y*ears 128
 come to - of discre-
  tion 131
 in - 128
 tenant for - 779
 - ago 122
 - old 128
*y*east *leaven* 320
 bubbles 353
*y*ell *cry* 406, 410, 411
 cheer 838
 complain 839
*y*ellow 436
 sensational 824
 - and red 439
 - complexioned 436
 - cover 756
 - fever 655
 - flag 550, 668
 - journalism 824
 - streak 862
*y*ellow-eyed 920
*y*ellowish 436
*y*ellowness **436**

*y*ellows 920
*y*elp *cry* 406, 412
 whine 839
 - at *execrate* 932
*y*eoman *farmer* 371
 man 373
 - of the guard 263, 726
 -'s service 644
*y*eomanry 726
*y*erk *strike* 276
 (*attack* 716)
*y*es *assent* 488
 consent 762
*y*esterday *past* 122
 of - *new* 123
*y*et *in compensation* 30
 exception 83
 time 106
 prior 116
 past 122
 qualification 469
*y*ew 367
*y*ield *soft* 324
 submit 725
 consent 762
 resign 782
 furnish 784
 gain 810
 price 812
 - *assent assent* 488
 consent 762
 - obeisance 725
 - one's breath 360
 - the palm
  inferior 34
  humility 879
 - to despair 859
 - to temptation 615
 - up the ghost 360
*y*ielding *soft* 324
 facile 705
 submissive 725

*y*odel 416
*y*oga 955
*y*ogi *intellect* 450
 adviser 695
 ascetic 955
 priest 996
 - philosophy 992*a*
*y*o-ho 411, 457
*y*oho 457
*y*oick 411
*y*oicks 411, 622
*y*oke *join* 43
 vinculum 45
 couple 89
 - *a horse* 370
 subject 749
 means of restraint
  752
 rivet the - 739
*y*okel *tyro* 701
 rustic 876
*y*okemate 903
*y*olk 436
*y*onder *that* 79
 distant 196
*y*ore 122
Yoshiwara 961
*y*ou - don't say so 870
 -'re another 718
*y*oung 127
 - man *lover* 897
*y*oungling 129
*y*oungster 129
*y*ounker 129
*y*outh *age* **127**
 lad 129
*y*outhful 127
*y*ucca 253
*y*ule 138
 - candle 512
 - log 388, 512
*y*uletide 138

Z

Zadkiel 513
zaffer 438
zambo 41
zambomba 417
zany 501
zarp 664
zeal *willingness* 602
 activity 682
 feeling 821
 desire 865
zealot *dogmatist* 474
 obstinate 606
 active 682
 (*resolute* 604)
zealotry 606
zealous [*see* zeal]
zebra 366, 440
zebrule 41
zebu 366
Zeitgeist 550
zemindar 779
zemindary 780
zemstvo 696
zenana *abode* 189
 woman 374

impurity 961
Zendavesta 986
zendik 487
zenith *climax* 31
 height 206
 summit 210
 in the - *repute* 873
zephyr 349
Zeppelin 273, 726
zero *nothing* 4
 nought **101**
 - hour 716
zest *relish* 394
 enjoyment 827
zetetic 461
Zeus 979
zigzag *oblique* 217
 angle 244
 deviating 279
 oscillating 314
 cicuit 629
 ornament 847
Zimmermann
 disciple of - 893
zincograph 558

zincography 558
zingaro 268
Zion 981
zip 409
zircon 847
zither 417
zocle 215
zodiac *zone* 230
 worlds 318
zodiacal light 423
zoëtic 359
Zoilus 936
Zollverein *compact* 769
 association 712
zone *region* 181
 layer 204
 belt 230
 circle 247
zoo 370
zoöglœa 357
zoögrapher 368
zoögraphist 368
zoögraphy 368
zoöhygiantics 370
zoöid 357

zoölatry 991
zoölogical 366
 - garden 370, 636
zoölogist 357
zoölogy 368
zoönomy 368
zoöphorous 210
zoöphyte 366
zoöspore 357
zoötomy 368
zoril 401
Zoroaster 986
Zoroastrian 382, 984
Zoroastrianism 382,
 976
zouave 726
zounds *wonder* 870
 anger 900
Zulu 876
zygote 357
zyme 320
zymogenic 320
zymologic 320
zymotic *disease* **655**
 unhealthy 657